CW00920424

Mozipedia

For Misery Guts of Bonnyrigg:
Are you still there, or have you moved away?

Mozipedia

The encyclopedia of Morrissey and The Smiths

Simon Goddard

EBURY PRESS

5 7 9 10 8 6

Published in 2009 by Ebury Press, an imprint of Ebury Publishing
A Random House Group Company

Copyright © Simon Goddard 2009

Simon Goddard has asserted his right to be identified as the author of this
Work in accordance with the Copyright, Designs and Patents Act 1988

All rights reserved. No part of this publication may be reproduced,
stored in a retrieval system, or transmitted in any form or by any means,
electronic, mechanical, photocopying, recording or otherwise,
without the prior permission of the copyright owner

The Random House Group Limited Reg. No. 954009

Addresses for companies within the Random House Group can be found at
www.randomhouse.co.uk

A CIP catalogue record for this book is available from the British Library

Designed and set by seagulls.net

Printed and bound in Great Britain by MPG Books Limited, Bodmin, Cornwall

ISBN 9780091927097

To buy books by your favourite authors and register for offers visit
www.randomhouse.co.uk

Contents

Preface
'There is a man, a certain man …'

'I don't mind how I'm remembered so long as they're precious recollections.
I don't want to be remembered for being a silly, prancing, nonsensical village idiot.
But I really do want to be remembered. I want some grain of immortality.
I think it's been deserved. It's been earned.'

So said Morrissey in 1985, just two years into The Smiths' recording career. If he hadn't quite guaranteed his immortality back then, he has now.

Adore him or abhor him, Morrissey has left too big an indentation – upon pop, upon art, upon people's lives – to be erased from history. He's one of those rare artists whose impact upon our culture is as irreversibly dramatic as the asteroid which slammed into the surface of the earth some 65 million years ago, snuffing out all dinosaur life in a flash. The history of art is shaped by such thunderbolts – the Beethovens and Picassos who revolutionise the past conventions of their chosen field, thereby determining its future. The symphony has never been the same since Beethoven, nor the painting since Picasso, nor the pop song since Morrissey, who sometimes in as little as two minutes conveys as much hope, loss, tragedy, comedy, pathos, wit, joy and despair as can be found in the pages of the heftiest Victorian literature. There is Dickens's *David Copperfield* and there is The Smiths' 'Girlfriend In A Coma'. Both are great works of art, and great art such as Dickens, Beethoven, Picasso and Morrissey is forevermore.

Yet Morrissey, the artist and the man, remains an enigma. It is commonly understood that: he's a pop singer; he's a vegetarian; he was celibate in the 1980s (and because of this most people assume he still is); he has a quiff and a prominent chin; he likes Oscar Wilde, James Dean and the New York Dolls; he doesn't like the monarchy, judges or Norfolk poultry farmers; his words are usually heartbreakingly sad, hysterically funny or a combination of both; he's from Manchester, and his Christian names are Steven Patrick.

But the mystery of Morrissey is that the more his surface is scratched, the more puzzlingly contrary he becomes. He likes Jacqueline du Pré but he also likes the Cockney Rejects. His favourite film is *A Taste Of Honey* but it's also *Romper Stomper*. He likes boxing but he also condemns all blood sports. He sings of being 'gentle and kind' but he also likes the Kray twins. He says he's not gay but then he writes a song like 'Dear God Please Help Me', which graphically describes a homosexual encounter. He says reggae is vile but then he revives the 1970s reggae label Attack Records. He sings that England is his but then leaves to live in Los Angeles. And so on.

It is in trying to evaluate all this information simultaneously – a brain-haemorrhaging feat of doublethink to the power of ten – that the riddle of Morrissey is born. But the answer to the riddle might lie in the process of forming the sum. If Morrissey could be deconstructed into as many separate component parts as can be easily defined, if these parts were then scattered on as large a canvas as could accommodate them so they might resemble the stars in the night sky, what would they look like? What shape constellation might Morrissey be? Which of his stars would shine the brightest and which would be

Preface

invisible to the naked eye without the aid of a telescope? Would we, then, have a clearer understanding of Morrissey?

This was the idea in creating *Mozipedia*. To atomise Morrissey, to count the dots and to let those dots be joined in an infinite number of combinations. So that between a favourite 1950s British B-movie, a Smiths sleeve cover star, the recollections of his former bass player, a favourite poet, a forgotten B-side, his choice of record labels and his pathological aversion to garlic and onions the reader might form an independent and unique insight into Morrissey more lucid than that mapped out in a standard narrative biography.

Writing *Mozipedia* was a lot like living in my own version of Orson Welles's *Citizen Kane*, where I was Thompson the reporter and Steven Patrick Morrissey was my equivalent Charles Foster Kane, the subject of investigation. Thompson set out to discover not 'what a man did' but 'who he was' by speaking to those who knew him and examining every available clue. The one difference is that Thompson was trying to form a portrait of the recently deceased. My subject is still very much alive but no less impenetrable or, indeed, inaccessible; there came a point in the research where those contacted still working in the service of Morrissey either refused to speak outright or, equally telling, initially agreed only to then nervously withdraw, seemingly not of their own volition. While frustrating for any writer, such distrust and power of persuasion is in itself another atom, an essential dot to be joined in the outline of Morrissey's psyche.

Thompson's quest is to uncover the identity of 'Rosebud', the final word Kane gasped before dying. He fails to find it but remains philosophical in defeat: 'I don't think any word can explain a man's life.' This is certainly true of Morrissey. Individually, the song 'Maladjusted', his love for the music of Phil Ochs, or Roxy Music, or the films of Margaret Rutherford aren't enough to explain who he is. But collectively, it's a different story. When surveying the mountainous jumble of Kane's worldly goods, one of Thompson's colleagues wonders aloud, 'If you put all this stuff together, palaces, paintings, toys and everything, what would it spell?' Put together 'Maladjusted', Ochs, Roxy and Rutherford and we're already halfway to spelling Morrissey.

True to the spirit of Thompson, I never did find my 'Rosebud' – maybe like Kane's childhood sled it's here hiding within the hotchpotch waiting to be discovered. But better than that, I learned to love Morrissey for the great artist he is. My hope in finishing *Mozipedia* is that the reader will learn something similar.

These are the ways, now yours to assemble.

Simon Goddard

Mozingredients

The entries in *Mozipedia* can be broadly divided into the following categories:

1. The music of Morrissey and The Smiths

Every known song recorded, or attempted, by Morrissey and The Smiths has its own entry. The same goes for every studio album and major compilation.

Songs are annotated by composer and listed by their first release format with the exception of all singles, introduced as such regardless of whether the song first appeared on a studio album. The term 'B-side' is used generally for any track accompanying a single without specifying the exact format, specific details of which can be found in the Mozography appendix.

The song and album entries are written from a personal critical perspective. At the risk of occasionally infuriating or confounding the reader with a conflicting opinion, this has been necessary in order to differentiate between the highs and lows of Morrissey's career. If the reader's estimations differ from my own, this in itself is a healthy catalyst for further debate, discussion and re-evaluation of Morrissey's work in the face of received wisdom and stale critical cliché. Great art such as his defies dispassion and should never suffer the fate of fusty objective analysis.

When discussing the meaning of songs, in most cases I offer an interpretative overview. These should be taken as a guide and by no means a finite reading. Morrissey himself refuses to offer 'pat' explanations to his lyrics and the mystery and beauty of his songs lies in their myriad interpretations from individual to individual. My theories are *a suggestion* informed by whatever supporting evidence is available, and should never be read as an absolute definition.

2. The life of Morrissey

There is no entry in this book for Morrissey himself since he *is* the book. The phases of his life and background history can be found scattered throughout in individual entries, e.g. birthday, family, school, religion, youth, sex, etc.

3. The influences of Morrissey

A large portion of *Mozipedia* concerns the books, authors, films, actors, singers, groups and records which have either had a direct influence upon Morrissey's art or which he's named among his favourites.

The list of potential candidates is so vast that strict(ish) criteria had to be established to avoid needless repetition, double-crossed references and, for reasons of space alone, the potentially superfluous. Because Morrissey once briefly included Benny Hill's 1963 novelty hit 'Harvest Of Love' on his concert interval tapes,[1] does Benny Hill *really* deserve his own entry? Perhaps, but then again (and in this instance) perhaps not.

The rough rule of thumb is this. Those people and works which Morrissey has named in interviews, in published lists of favourite films or records or which have been proven to have incontestably influenced his own work are included. But those people or works to have had purely minor or isolated influence but which he has otherwise never mentioned are not. As an example, there is no entry for the film *Sleuth*, even though it was a lyrical influence on the chorus of 'This Charming Man'. This is because other than admitting the source, Morrissey has never listed *Sleuth* as one of his favourite films. Whereas there *is* an entry for *Long Day's Journey Into Night*, the source of the song title 'This Night Has Opened My Eyes', because beyond its lyrical influence Morrissey has also cited it as a favourite film at least twice.

Where music is concerned, Morrissey is very specific when it comes to individual records and it's sometimes a case of the song, not the singer. For this reason, many of Morrissey's favourites are listed within under song title rather than artist. For example, he's often swooned over 'Heart' by Rita Pavone but since he's never expanded at length about the rest of Pavone's repertoire it is 'Heart' rather than Pavone herself which warrants an entry. Whereas in the case of Vince Eager, Morrissey has named his 'The World's Loneliest Man' as one of his most cherished singles but had previously also toyed with using Eager's name on a run-out-groove message. In the case of such multiple references, it is the singer, not the song, who justifies inclusion.

For Morrissey's heroes, a biographical résumé is applicable only in cases where either their history and background is not widely known (e.g. Angelic Upstarts) or of such importance to Morrissey's character that it deserves reiterating (e.g. the New York Dolls, Oscar Wilde). With popular icons such as Bowie, Elvis and Sinatra, it has only been necessary to discuss their lives and legacies in terms of their relevance to, and influence upon, Morrissey; for example, a potted history of Elvis would, in itself, be an epic digressional indulgence too far.

In discussing films and books, where possible I've tried to describe the basic plot without spoiling it for those who've not seen or read them. There are, however, a handful of rare instances when it's been necessary to reveal endings to make connections between the narrative and Morrissey's art, e.g. the novel *Wuthering Heights*, the film *Billy Liar*.

4. The who's who of Morrissey and The Smiths

Biographical entries for significant people who've worked with, written with or have a connection with Morrissey and The Smiths, from band members and producers to key acquaintances.

5. The world of Morrissey

Specific cities and places of relevance to Morrissey's life and work, e.g. Los Angeles, Rome, Salford Lads Club.

6. The Tao of Morrissey

Everything else. There were some abstract elements which didn't belong to any of the above categories but which still deserved inclusion – Morrissey's thoughts on cats, on football, on love, on tea, on his fondness for swimming. Such wisdoms are scattered within to be discovered at random.

Some textual technicalities. Whenever you see a phrase or name in SMALL CAPITALS that means it/they have their own entry; this only applies to the first mention in any entry. The three exceptions are the names of the other Smiths – Johnny Marr, Andy Rourke and Mike Joyce. All have their own entries – Marr's is the longest in the book, incidentally – but their ubiquity in the text is such that to capitalise their names every time seems unnecessary. Likewise, the cities Dublin, London, Los Angeles, Manchester and Rome, all of which have their own listings within, are also exempt since capitalising their first mention in every entry would be a needless textural encumbrance.

Where hit singles are referenced – e.g. number 22, May 1959 – the listed month is the one in which the record reached that position, not when it was released.

Finally, the numbers in square brackets at the end of each entry – e.g. [5, 22, 59] – refer to the sources listed at the back of the book.

———

1. Throughout *Mozipedia* you will find mention of Morrissey's 'interval tapes' and 'interval video montages': these refer to his ritual compilation of pre-gig music and videos played in the gap between the support act and his stage entrance. These change with every tour, offering a unique insight into his current tastes, inspirations, fads and heroes.

'People fashion their God after their own understanding.
They make their God first and worship him afterwards.'

OSCAR WILDE

a-ha, 80s Norwegian pop trio whom Morrissey liked 'a great deal' during their heyday. Their first major hit, 'Take On Me', was released three times before finally entering the UK top 40 in October 1985 – the same week as The Smiths' 'THE BOY WITH THE THORN IN HIS SIDE' – going on to reach number two in the UK and number one in the US, helped to a large degree by its pioneering semi-animated video. Fronted by the handsomely wolfish Morten Harket, a-ha's success continued for another couple of years, scoring up a lone UK number one with January 1986's baroque block-buster 'The Sun Always Shines On TV' and a James Bond theme with 1988's 'The Living Daylights'. Although Smiths indie purists may have been aghast to hear Morrissey praise such a mainstream synthesiser-driven pop act, he commended a-ha on several occasions during 1987, even confessing he'd been to see them in concert in America but had been put off 'by the squealing fans'. [125, 130, 469]

Accattone, 1961 Italian film referenced in Morrissey's 'YOU HAVE KILLED ME' along with its director, Pier Paolo PASOLINI. The film was Pasolini's directorial debut, loosely based upon his novel *Una Vita Violenta* (*A Violent Life*), and followed the downfall of Vittorio, a Roman pimp nicknamed 'Accattone' (literally 'beggar' or 'scrounger'). The title role was played by Franco Citti, a regular in numerous Pasolini films including Morrissey's personal favourite, 1962's *Mamma Roma* starring Anna MAGNANI, mentioned in the same song. [213, 335, 481]

'Accept Yourself' (Morrissey/Marr), B-side of 'THIS CHARMING MAN' (1983). 'The fundamental request of Smithdom' according to Morrissey, 'Accept Yourself' was his decree to 'be yourself, relax, don't worry about anything as there's no point'.

The first Smiths song where he directly addressed his audience, it reportedly instigated 'floods' of letters from 'totally affected' fans. Certainly, it's among Morrissey's most positive early lyrics. 'I find that so many people have [the song's] dilemma about shoes,' he commented. 'If they have the wrong pair of shoes it can totally destroy their entire life. Similarly, if people think their feet are too big, or that their nose is too big, it can result in a diminished social life for totally false reasons.' Within the song he'd borrow from the dependable Shelagh DELANEY, adapting 'anything's hard to find if you go around looking for it with your eyes shut' from *The Lion In Love*. Further inspiration came from friend Howard DEVOTO's Magazine and their 'A SONG FROM UNDER THE FLOORBOARDS' which Morrissey later covered in 2006. Where Devoto is 'angry', 'ill' and 'ugly as sin', Morrissey becomes 'sick', 'dull' and 'plain'.

Written in the spring of 1983, melodically and rhythmically it betrayed Marr's love of Tamla Motown and in particular his mother's Four Tops singles collection: his sequined guitar riff bounces in the vague direction of their 1965 single 'Something About You', as featured on their first Greatest Hits, named as Marr's favourite album in 1985. 'That was just in the air at the time,' he admits. 'I was listening to and buying a lot of Motown singles.'

Like its accompanying 12-inch B-side 'WONDERFUL WOMAN', 'Accept Yourself' had been earmarked for their debut album with Troy TATE before being re-recorded by producer John PORTER. A different, earlier BBC session version features on HATFUL OF HOLLOW. [17, 18, 27, 168, 270, 299, 419]

acting, In spite of his rarely discussed, if uncanny, resemblance to British screen idol Stanley BAKER, Morrissey himself has no desire to become an actor. 'I don't believe I can act,' he confessed in 1987. He'd soon prove that point the following year when making his cameo in the Channel 4 BROOKSIDE spin-off *South*, in which he valiantly struggled to play himself. His scene, lasting all of 38 seconds, takes place in the foyer of London's Capital Radio, where *Brookside*'s Tracy Corkhill has come in her quest to find a job in the smoke. As she takes a seat, she suddenly notices

the jutting chin and bouncy black quiff of the slender gentleman sat opposite.

> TRACY: I know who you are!
> MORRISSEY: So do I.
> TRACY: You're Morrissey!
> MORRISSEY: I know.
> TRACY: You used to be with The Smiths!
> MORRISSEY: *(nods, says nothing)*
> TRACY: What are you doing 'ere?
> MORRISSEY: I've… *(unnecessary pause)* … come to do an interview.
> TRACY: Great!
> MORRISSEY: *(deathly silence)* What are *you* doing here?
> TRACY: Nothing. Why?
> FEMALE VOICE OFF CAMERA: *(to Morrissey)* We're ready for you now.
> MORRISSEY: Got to go. Nice to meet you.

The singer described his scene as 'compulsive non-viewing … essential kettle-on time'. 'I can't act at all, which is very surprising,' he explained. 'I can't be natural in front of the camera … I can't even be natural when I'm lying in the bath.'

Morrissey has since turned down various offers for similar cameos (including the US sitcom *FRIENDS*) and once claimed he'd declined an invitation to appear in a film directed by Dennis Hopper since it involved him being 'nude and painted turquoise'. [71, 115, 412, 469]

adolescence (of Morrissey), See YOUTH OF MORRISSEY.

ADS speakers, Massachusetts-based home hi-fi manufacturer (Analogue and Digital Systems, Inc.) whose 1980 US press advert for their L730 range provided the original cover for The Smiths' 'WILLIAM, IT WAS REALLY NOTHING' single. The advert, headed 'Will you still respect your speakers in the morning?', was intended as a humorous analogy of a one-night stand, showing a semi-naked man sat in regretful pose with a bulky speaker lying on the bedclothes behind him. 'Sure, they sounded great last night,' began the

'Afternoon Delight', 1976 US number one for the Starland Vocal Band, as purchased by the 17-year-old Morrissey who thereby helped rush it on its way to number 18 in the UK. In total contrast to his more cacophonous punk tastes of the day, 'Afternoon Delight' was a breezy soft-rock ode to daytime sex boiling over with graphic metaphors: 'skyrockets in flight – afternoon delight!' Morrissey found himself 'absolutely loving it despite myself', also acknowledging, 'I was slowly being infiltrated by something terribly devious.' It would be the Starland Vocal Band's only hit. Ironically, when their fame dwindled, founding husband-and-wife duo Bill Danoff and Taffy Nivert soon lost their appetite for 'nibblin' a little afternoon delight' and promptly divorced. [95]

accompanying text, 'but the *real* test of a speaker system is the morning after.' The advert first ran in the winter of 1980 and it's likely that Morrissey would have first encountered it on his trip to visit relatives in New York and Colorado in January 1981. He subsequently confessed he'd 'ripped' it from an issue of American *GQ*, citing it as 'an example of how much of an impact fashion photography and fashion magazines had on me'. Since the image was used without permission, after the release of 'William' the original copyright holders made a claim against The Smiths' record company, ROUGH TRADE, for 'violation of privacy' and 'deceptive trade practices'. Accordingly, the single was reissued in 1987 in a new sleeve featuring Billie WHITELAW from the film *Charlie Bubbles*. (See also DELANEY.) [43, 119, 334, 374]

alcohol, As his earliest lyrical mention of boozy afternoons in The Smiths' 'THESE THINGS TAKE TIME' hinted, Morrissey enjoys a drink. In the early days of The Smiths he confessed to 'spasms of wine' and was famed for avoiding the excesses enjoyed by the other members of the group, claiming 'I can go months and months without a drink'. He later explained it was because 'it was important that I remembered all the words so perhaps I was over-cautious and over-delicate'. In the early 90s he switched to beer. 'I have a great interest in alcohol,' he admitted, 'and as time goes by I find it more comforting, although I'm not by any means an alcoholic.' His preference for 'old men's pubs' saw him frequent various dingy hostelries in north London and the East End, habitually opting for

bottled lager over pints. When moving to America, he raved about its 'fantastic offering of beer', apparently vastly superior to 'those horrible British beers that are made of 95 per cent polyester'. The sleeve of the 2006 single 'THE YOUNGEST WAS THE MOST LOVED' shows him holding a bottle of red label Italian Peroni lager, suitable for vegetarians (not all beers are, depending on the brewing process, some involving animal gelatine or fish-sourced isinglass). In recent years, perhaps fearing the dreaded beer gut, his tastes have shifted to Grey Goose vodka and tonic, though as recently as 2008 Morrissey has still been known to sink as many as nine pints of strong lager in one sitting. [48, 54, 82, 127, 153, 154, 205, 273]

'All The Lazy Dykes' (Morrissey/Whyte), From the album YOU ARE THE QUARRY (2004). A few minutes' drive from Morrissey's former Los Angeles home lay the city's popular lesbian hang-out the Palms Bar on Santa Monica Boulevard. The singer later recalled how he would often pass by admiring its 'absolutely fascinating' clientele of female bikers and other 'very, very strong women'. Taking the Palms Bar as inspiration and name-checking it in the first verse, 'All The Lazy Dykes' was Morrissey's self-styled 'hymn for lesbians who don't know they are', a plea to a married woman in denial about her true sexuality to 'free yourself, be yourself'. 'She needed me to tell her,' he explained, 'because she can't come to that conclusion herself.' Morrissey's altruistic plot to out his friend cleverly allows him the chance to share her liberation, declaring how he has 'never felt so alive in the whole of my life'. For all its celebratory intent, his invitation is lent a disconcertingly tragic atmosphere by Whyte's gloomy, almost funereal tune. Given the surfeit of strong material from the album sessions, in retrospect 'All The Lazy Dykes' may have been better suited to a B-side: Morrissey possibly agreed, dropping the song from his set midway through his 2004 You Are The Quarry tour. [56, 151, 192]

'All You Need Is Me' (Morrissey/Tobias),
Morrissey's 35th solo single (first included on the compilation GREATEST HITS, repeated on the album YEARS OF REFUSAL), released June 2008, highest UK chart position #24. Where THE BEATLES preached love, Morrissey promotes himself as the fundamental reason for the listener's existence, albeit with tongue placed firmly in cheek. Its principal taunt to an exasperated lover recalled 'THE MORE YOU IGNORE ME' with its sketch of a naked Morrissey stalking their dreams as he savours their fevered irritation. The lyrics are rife with gems of self-mockery, not least his youthful flashback of being a chubby boy in a council house (Americanised as 'welfare house') and his droll 'whoopee'. More metaphorically, 'All You Need Is Me' can be read as a cunning jibe at his more critical fans who consistently moan about his work yet can never relinquish him completely. The closing 'you're gonna miss me when I'm gone' would also prove an irresistible quote for reviewers wishing to reiterate his unique place in pop history.

One of Jesse Tobias's best Morrissey offerings, its light punk-pop shudder was the perfect vehicle for its vainglorious humour. Sadly such qualities weren't reflected in its comparatively poor chart position. The second single from his 2008 Greatest Hits album, the following year it was given a deserved second outing on Years Of Refusal. [245]

'Alma Matters' (Morrissey/Whyte), Morrissey's 22nd solo single (from the album MALADJUSTED), released July 1997, highest UK chart position #16. Making wordplay out of the Latin

term for one's former school (alma mater, literally 'fostering mother'), 'Alma Matters' sounded like a homage to a mystery girl of great significance 'to someone, somewhere'. Given his love of CORONATION STREET, it was either uncanny or unfortunate that at the time of the song's release the most famous Alma in Britain was The Street's Alma Baldwin, played by Amanda Barrie who many years previously had starred in 1964's CARRY ON Cleo. More scholarly critics presumed the title to be a nod to 50s/60s British singer Alma Cogan: Morrissey was, at the very least, reputed to be a fan of her 1962 version of Noël COWARD's 'If Love Were All' (itself a lyrical influence on his earlier 'FOUND FOUND FOUND').

At the time, Morrissey professed the song wasn't about a person but a general call for sexual emancipation. 'It means that we should be pleased and proud of the female side of our character, of our nature,' he explained. 'Or if we're female, we should be proud of the male side of our character and give it just as much importance as the other side. Everything's fine. It doesn't matter how you behave.' Over a decade later he'd admit this explanation wasn't strictly honest, merely something he'd 'felt like saying' at the time. Whether intentionally or not, the lyrics also contained the echo of one of his earliest sources, Shelagh DELANEY, specifically the line 'It's your life, ruin it your own way' from A Taste Of Honey.

Recorded at the beginning of the Maladjusted sessions, with its jewel-like guitars and jubilant chorus it was the obvious choice of first single, albeit slightly overdone. Just shy of five minutes, and the longest track on the album, it may have benefited from some trimming for radio purposes, especially during its meandering, key-changing end section. Even so, the alluring 'Alma Matters' was Morrissey's first top 20 hit in over three years and, in terms of chart position, his third most successful single of the 90s – a triumph strangely overlooked by its exclusion from 2008's GREATEST HITS compilation.

The accompanying video, directed by photographer Matthew Rolston, unveiled the short-lived 'quiff-less' Morrissey of 1997, seen wearing a Beck T-shirt (he'd later explain, 'I knew a woman at the time who dared me to wear [it], so I did, and she was thrilled'), toying with a kitten and eating doughnuts and cereal. More surprisingly, it regurgitated the thuggish SKINHEAD imagery from the 'OUR FRANK' video (albeit skinhead girls as well as boys) and appeared to verify Morrissey's love of northern soul music with its dilapidated neon sign spelling out the name of the genre's hallowed early 70s mecca, Wigan Casino. [4, 5, 40, 554, 567, 568]

'Alsatian Cousin' (Morrissey/Street), From the
album VIVA HATE (1988). A fittingly malicious overture for a record christened Viva Hate, 'Alsatian Cousin' cast Morrissey as a betrayed victim, challenging a partner to reveal the details of a previous fling. The mention of notes being left on desks and the school staffroom stereotype of leather elbow patches suggest an illicit affair between teacher and pupil, doubly so that the song's title was taken from a line in Alan BENNETT's play *Forty Years On*, set in an English public school ('I was distantly related to the Woolf family through some Alsatian cousins'). From the graphic metaphor of 'tent flaps open wide' to the description of being taken upon the teacher's desk, Morrissey doesn't so much sing as seethe the words, echoing his vitriol in the backing chorus of canine howls.

A courageous choice of album opener, its venomous guitar and racking rhythm were very much at odds with the indie pigeonhole most fans and critics placed Morrissey within at the time. Street presented the song to Morrissey as a 'rough sketch' for guitarist Vini REILLY to improvise on top, though since his freeform noodlings dominate the arrangement, Reilly himself later contested authorship of the tune. As with Johnny Marr's previous homage to rapper Lovebug Starski on 'HOW SOON IS NOW?', Street also snuck a covert hip hop reference under Morrissey's nose with the song's bass line, consciously modelled on Grandmaster & Melle Mel's 'White Lines (Don't Don't Do It)'. 'I was seeing how far I could push

Morrissey,' says Street, 'and I was impressed at just how far he was willing to go and experiment. He was an incredibly inspiring person to work with.'

A final digression on the song's title: those partial to the opinion that the bulk of Viva Hate was either directed at, or written about, Johnny Marr in the wake of The Smiths' split should consider that at the time Marr was the proud owner of two Alsatians, Rufus and Curtis (as in Thomas and Mayfield). [25, 39, 168, 272, 280]

'Ambitious Outsiders' (Morrissey/Whyte),
From the album MALADJUSTED (1997). Originally planned as the title track for Morrissey's sixth solo album, 'Ambitious Outsiders' was also his favourite from the record duly renamed Maladjusted. Among his most disturbing lyrics, it appeared to voice the unapologetic conscience of a paedophile ring in the face of mounting tabloid hysteria. Teasing society's greatest fears and paranoias about child abusers – that they walk among us unnoticed, monitoring the school-bus run while calculating their opportunity to seize another victim – the song dares to blame their crimes on the children's parents as punishment for 'reproducing'.[1]

Unlike The Smiths' 'SUFFER LITTLE CHILDREN' – his previous treatment of the same theme which highlighted the inexpressible horror and human tragedy of paedophilic murder – his motives on 'Ambitious Outsiders' were unclear. That it managed to slip out unnoticed on a top ten UK album was, in hindsight, quite miraculous. On the few occasions Morrissey was asked to clarify the song's meaning, he skirted the issue other than admitting that it was 'creeping towards' what one interviewer had described as an 'evil child-murdering-incorporated theme song'. 'I'm very proud of it,' he stated. 'I like music to be slightly dangerous. I do. I like to be pushed. There's not really much point making safe music.' His further wishy-washy explanation that it conveyed 'how easy it is to be seen as somebody who doesn't belong and who has strange ideas' similarly failed to satisfy any nagging doubts about its real theme and intentions.

7

For all the power of its lyric, as a recording 'Ambitious Outsiders' failed to achieve its maximum impact, hampered by the decision to embellish Whyte's original demo with synthetic strings rather than attempt a proper orchestral recording. Had his melodramatic score been followed to its logical conclusion with real orchestral accompaniment, the track might have become a showstopping Scott Walker affair. Instead, producer Steve LILLYWHITE did his best to re-create Whyte's elaborate composition with keyboards, resulting in its crooked end-of-the-pier translation which, perhaps deliberately, only made Morrissey's hissed threats of child snatching all the more creepy. [4, 40, 422, 567]

---

1. Since Morrissey has never directly cited the influence of Neil Young, it may only be coincidence that the song contains lyrical similarities with the Charles Manson-inspired 'Revolution Blues' from Young's 1974 album On The Beach, featuring the lines 'you never see us' and 'keep the population down'.

'America Is Not The World' (Morrissey/Whyte),

From the album YOU ARE THE QUARRY (2004). It was apt that Morrissey should choose to open his first album after seven years 'in exile' in Los Angeles with a song which addressed the many criticisms and questions during his absence. 'America Is Not The World' was a poisoned love letter to his adopted home, an explicitly political attack on globalisation, US colonialism and the White House itself. 'I didn't care much for being subtle this time,' explained Morrissey, 'there's just no time for that. And America really isn't the world.'

Lampooning its reputation as 'the land of the free', Morrissey mocks its historically white, male heterosexual presidential lineage, using the term 'gay' for the very first time in his lyrics. Thankfully, the historic election of Barack Obama in 2008 would negate his pessimism over the likelihood of a black president; Morrissey himself pledged his support for Obama throughout the Democrat candidacy contest against Hillary Clinton, even wearing a fan-made T-shirt of his face beside Obama's on stage at London's Roundhouse in January 2008.

The song also contained a soft reminder that meat is murder with its revulsion at the global propagation of hamburger chains.[1] Morrissey elaborated on the subject when explaining his decision to reference the Baltic state of Estonia in the song. 'I imagined the sexy and sharp people of Estonia – which is not considered to be a world leader in anything, as far as I know – looking at the Burger King fast-food hell of the modern American food industry, and actually feeling sorry for Americans.' He went on to condemn America's domestic food industry and its catastrophic effect on the country's obesity and mortality rates. 'It's astonishing that the entire population of America hasn't been killed off by its own food industry,' he claimed. 'The food industry is *certainly trying*, and it is more of a threat to the American people than so-called "terrorism" is.'

Luckily for Morrissey, the majority of his devout American audience embraced the song's political intent. It was unfortunate, however, that such a grand lyrical statement was denied the necessary drama that the first track on Morrissey's eagerly awaited 'comeback album' properly deserved. Whyte's placid theme, agreeable enough and crisply produced, immediately announced that, where his co-writer's musical parameters were concerned, Morrissey hadn't budged a millimetre in the seven years since MALADJUSTED. [119, 231, 241]

---

1. Pedantic food historians would no doubt pull Morrissey up on his crediting America as the nation who 'gave us' the hamburger. Its origins stretch back to mainland Europe and Russia, from the Mongol armies of Genghis Khan who flattened steak under their horse saddles to nineteenth-century Germany where a form of pounded beef was popularised in Hamburg, hence the name. Americans themselves, of course, still insist it was their creation, though as a nation they are incapable of agreeing which state, let alone which restaurant, invented today's familiar hamburger sandwich.

'Ammunition' (Morrissey/Boorer),

From the album MALADJUSTED (1997). It would have been nice to believe, as 'Ammunition' insisted, that immediately after the 1996 COURT CASE the 37-year-old Morrissey had achieved sufficient peace with himself, and his past, to dismiss all thoughts of revenge. Yet in context of the same album's venomous 'SORROW WILL COME IN THE END', its contented sentiment didn't wash. Though Morrissey considered it a strong single contender, in reality Boorer's carefree tune collapsed on the dull side of nice, befitting the singer's metaphorical journey in which he steers his career away from potential hazards with the confidence of a sage 'old hand'. One of many weak links in the latter half of Maladjusted, 'Ammunition' would, at best, have been an adequate B-side. Its one saving grace is Morrissey's admirable use of that rarest of adjectives in pop music, 'salient'. [4, 40]

Angel Inside Went Sour, The, 1970 non-fiction
novel by Esther Rothman, mentioned by Morrissey in a 1983 list of his favourite books. As the jacket describes, it is 'The compassionate story of a very special school by the woman who runs it, and what can be done within the state system by devotion and perseverance.' Rothman was head of New York's Livingston School for predominantly black teenage girls with behavioural problems. The book is Rothman's detailed catalogue of incidents involving drugs, violence, underage sex and pregnancy in context of her own liberal teaching methods and shares common ground with Jim Haskins's *Diary Of A Harlem School Teacher* (1969), a similar memoir which Morrissey read in his late teens. Though both books are positive accounts of teaching and overcoming social prejudices, their respective scenes of classroom confrontation evoke Morrissey's own 'THE TEACHERS ARE AFRAID OF THE PUPILS'. [184, 362, 364]

Angelic Upstarts, Late 70s north-east punk
group whom Morrissey would describe as one of his 'primary influences' during the 90s, even criticising modern Britpop bands of the day for being '[not] actually as good as the Angelic Upstarts'.

Inspired by The Clash, the Upstarts were formed in South Shields, Tyneside in the summer of 1977 by 19-year-old singer and apprentice

'Angel, Angel, Down We Go Together' (Morrissey/Street), From the album VIVA HATE
(1988). Included on the very first cassette of demos Stephen Street sent Morrissey in August 1987 – proposed B-side ideas for the final Smiths singles after Marr's departure – was a sad orchestral tune modelled on the chorus of Kate Bush's 1985 single 'Cloudbusting'. The track so impressed Morrissey that he swiftly abandoned his plans of persevering with the Marr-less Smiths, electing instead to work with Street on a solo career. In his first letter to the producer to break the news, he named 'the orchestral one' as his particular favourite.

The music was subsequently scored for string quartet by John Metcalfe to become Viva Hate's brief baroque interlude, 'Angel, Angel, Down We Go Together'. While the title was borrowed from 1969's *Angel, Angel, Down We Go*, a daft exploitation film about a hippy rock and roll group starring Roddy McDowall, the lyrics were a very sombre declaration of love to a maltreated, beleaguered and potentially suicidal individual with whom Morrissey feels the utmost affinity. Surprisingly, he later named the song's subject as Johnny Marr, detailing what he saw as his ex-partner's manipulation by an uncaring music industry. Though there's no reason to doubt this admission, Morrissey's added claim that it was 'the only song that I have written with [Marr] in mind, post Smiths' is more dubious, especially given the circumstances immediately preceding Viva Hate and their resonance with many of the album's more cutting lyrics.

Though a mere 98 seconds long, as Morrissey's first foray into chamber music, 'Angel, Angel' added a further richness of texture to his solo debut. It also became an unexpected setlist regular on his 1991 KILL UNCLE tour, rearranged as a thumping rock track (as seen on the *LIVE IN DALLAS* video). [25, 39, 272]

miner Thomas 'Mensi' Mensforth. Described by the *NME* as 'a bunch of apparently illiterate and petulant Geordie hooligans', the majority of their songs were furious hymns of working-class frustration, often raging against the police. Their self-released debut single, 'The Murder Of Liddle Towers', set the bar, responding to the recent death in police custody of an amateur boxer, which had been written off by the authorities as 'justifiable homicide'. The accusatory drama of its lyrics was brought to the attention of their local South Shields constabulary, who duly began monitoring Upstarts gigs hoping to arrest them for incitement to violence. The Upstarts, in return, would later thank Northumbria Police 'for inspiration' on their debut album, Teenage Warning.

With the help of Sham 69's Jimmy Pursey, in 1978 they signed to Polydor only to be dropped before they'd recorded a note after Mensi had a fight with a company security guard. Warners picked up the pieces, releasing their major label debut in the spring of '79, 'I'm An Upstart', followed by the boisterous 'Teenage Warning'. Both made the UK charts and later appeared on Morrissey's concert interval tapes in 1995, as would their next single 'Never 'Ad Nothin'', the true story of an 18-year-old tearaway who took a man hostage in an Essex pub only to be gunned down 'in a puff of smoke' by police. The group continued well into the mid-80s, though with the exception of 1981's 'Kids On The Street', judging from his interval tape selections Morrissey seems to prefer their earliest material.

While most of their songs were inspired by social injustice and political anger, the Upstarts were still capable of comedy: when drummer Keith 'Sticks' Warrington left to join COCKNEY REJECTS – because 'they were harder' – the group took revenge by stealing his diary and putting its drippy entries about his girlfriend to music on 1980's shambolic B-side 'Sticks's Diary'. Like the Rejects (with whom they shared a manager, Tony Gordon), the Upstarts were lumped in with the Oi! Movement, attracting a violent SKINHEAD contingent, perhaps exacerbated by the group's

ritual ridicule of the police climaxing in the destruction of a pig's head on stage. As a consequence they faced press accusations of endorsing the far-right politics associated with a minority of their audience. While, to their shame, in the early days of the group they'd been naïve enough to follow London punk fashion and wear swastikas, lyrically the Upstarts' entire ethos was rooted in left-wing ideology. If appearing on the cover of the Socialist Workers Party youth magazine didn't get the message across, then their stage backdrop emblazoned with the slogan 'Smash the [National] Front' left no doubt whatsoever.

That Morrissey's fixation with the Upstarts coincided with his use of skinhead iconography in the early 90s caused some critics to misconstrue his motives, ignoring the group's anti-Nazi politics but instead using their notoriety as Oi! poster boys as further evidence of his 'flirtation' with right-wing youth culture. When Morrissey was photographed 'hanging out' with Mensi in the early 90s, the *NME* chose to ridicule both his 'predilection for Old Pop Stars' and the Upstarts themselves ('pretty horrible 70s fag-end-of-punk skinheads'). In reality, his interest was symptomatic of his fascination with the plight of disappearing English working-class culture as well as a genuine love for the music. As unfashionable as it was to champion Angelic Upstarts during Britpop, Morrissey made a point of doing so in interviews circa 1994's VAUXHALL AND I, also paying homage in the video for 'THE MORE YOU IGNORE ME, THE CLOSER I GET' in which Boz BOORER's daughter, Billie-Rose, is seen wearing a T-shirt featuring the cover of their Greatest Hits Live album. At a concert in Cardiff in February 1995, Morrissey threw a tambourine into the crowd inscribed with the name of Upstarts singer 'MENSI' and would later appear flyposting an advert for their Teenage Warning album in the opening segment of 1996's *INTRODUCING MORRISSEY* video. Only in the late 90s would his love for the Upstarts take a back seat as he instead devoted his attention to their less serious Oi! contemporaries, Cockney Rejects.
[111, 154, 386]

Angels Are Genderless, The proposed name of a group the 21-year-old Morrissey was 'presently forming' in March 1981 according to his correspondence with Scottish pen pal Robert MACKIE. Returning from a trip to visit relatives in America, Morrissey wrote to Mackie that 'Angels Are Genderless … are rehearsing as soon as my jet-lag subsides'. The other members of this 'group', if they existed, are not known. Though it's probable this may have been mere fantasy on Morrissey's part, assuming it *were* true then it's enlightening to know he was considering such an extravagant group name less than 18 months before joining forces with Marr and choosing the very opposite with The Smiths. [334]

Angers, Avril, Liverpool-born comic actress and cover star of the Smiths single 'I STARTED SOMETHING I COULDN'T FINISH'. Morrissey's chosen image was from one of his favourite films, THE FAMILY WAY, picturing Angers's character in church on her daughter's wedding day. Angers was one of the few Smiths cover stars Morrissey met in person, later referring to their encounter when discussing his reactions to meeting famous people he admires. 'I get very nervous when I meet people from the theatre,' he said of Angers. 'I think that's a very hallowed, sacred thing to be in.'

Previously, Angers had cropped up in the 1956 Alastair SIM comedy *The Green Man* and played sweet-shop owner Norah Dawson in CORONATION STREET, often sparring with fellow Smiths cover star Pat PHOENIX as Elsie Tanner. Also of note is her cameo in an episode of Victoria WOOD's 1989 television series alongside CARRY ON (and 'OUIJA BOARD') star Joan Sims. Angers, who insisted she was always 'too busy' for marriage, died of pneumonia in 2005, aged 87. [208, 374, 502]

animal rights, An intrinsic part of Morrissey's character, parallel to his VEGETARIANISM, is his evangelical support of animal rights groups.

During The Smiths he praised the direct action of the Animal Liberation Front who in 1984 claimed they'd contaminated a supermarket shipment of Mars bars with bleach as a protest against the manufacturer's chemical testing on monkeys. The scare was a hoax: Morrissey thoroughly approved.

'I think we have to take these measures now because polite demonstration is pointless,' he argued. 'I find any kind of peaceful demonstration to be useless. You get absolutely no media coverage, millions of people can march but it's pointless when we are discussing a very violent industry. I mean it's murder, it's ritualised slaughter, and you can't simply pass leaflets round and hope that that's going to weigh up the balance.' The video for 1989's 'INTERESTING DRUG' was a humorous homage to the Animal Liberation Front (whom he later listed among his 'Handsome devils'), with Morrissey handing out leaflets to a group of schoolboys who go on to rescue rabbits from a test laboratory. The title of The Smiths' earlier instrumental 'THE DRAIZE TRAIN' was also a reference to a cruel animal toxicology experiment patented by American scientist John Draize.

For the encore of his solo debut concert in WOLVERHAMPTON in December 1988, Morrissey wore a PETA (People for the Ethical Treatment of Animals) T-shirt and has since become one of their most outspoken patrons. The proceeds of his 2003 UNDER THE INFLUENCE compilation were donated to PETA and every Morrissey album since 2004's YOU ARE THE QUARRY has promoted the organisation in its credits. In 2002 he attended PETA's annual vegetarian Thanksgiving dinner hosted by Pamela Anderson where he was photographed with a turkey named Chloe who'd been spared slaughter: Morrissey and the rest of the guests dined instead on the soya-based substitute Tofurkey. In September 2005 PETA honoured Morrissey at their 25th anniversary gala with the Linda MCCARTNEY Memorial Award in recognition 'of all of his hard work for animals'.

In recent years Morrissey has been especially critical of Canada's annual seal cull – 'the largest slaughter of marine animal species found anywhere on the planet' – and has refused to tour the country in protest. Equally controversial, in 2008 he publicly condemned the Budongo Trail, a new chimpanzee enclosure at Edinburgh Zoo. 'If the Budongo Trail at Edinburgh Zoo is such a stimulating highlight, then why don't the zoo staff live in it instead?' he argued. 'How long would they last without cracking up? An hour? Yet they expect the chimps to be delighted and buoyant? Would you be? People just cannot leave animals alone, can they?'

Political campaigning aside, Morrissey's passion for animals (especially CATS) and the welfare of all living creatures bar humans is so deep rooted that – as Mozzerian folklore has it – he once asked his former assistant Jo Slee to rescue a wasp from drowning in a swimming pool.

For more information on the People for the Ethical Treatment of Animals, go to www.peta.org. [71, 123, 175, 211, 221, 228]

anti-depressants, See DRUGS.

Armstrong, Kevin (Morrissey guitarist and co-writer, 1989–90), Session player Kevin Armstrong, who'd previously worked with Thomas Dolby and David BOWIE, first crossed Morrissey's path in the troubled summer of 1987 when approached to replace Marr as guitarist in The Smiths. Contacted through ROUGH TRADE, Armstrong was called for a

meeting with Morrissey, who expressed his plans to continue the group. While flattered in the first instance, Armstrong was honest to a fault in stating his belief that The Smiths minus Marr was 'a mental idea', making a damning comparison between Morrissey's bloody-mindedness to carry on without him and that of the Black Knight in *Monty Python And The Holy Grail* who 'has his arms and legs chopped off, sitting with blood pissing out, wriggling around shouting, "Come back! It's only a flesh wound."'

The following year Armstrong joined Stephen STREET and Andrew PARESI on Sandie SHAW's Hello Angel album, though he was convinced his earlier tactlessness meant he would never get the chance to work with Morrissey again. In all likelihood he probably wouldn't have had it not been for Clive LANGER, who invited him to Hook End Manor in September 1989 to record 'OUIJA BOARD, OUIJA BOARD', thereby becoming Morrissey's studio guitarist for the ensuing BONA DRAG sessions. Upon Langer's recommendation, Armstrong also joined the open submissions for new music following the departure of Street, providing four instrumental demos of which three were developed into finished Morrissey recordings: 'HE KNOWS I'D LOVE TO SEE HIM', 'PICCADILLY PALARE' and the outtake 'OH PHONEY'.

Armstrong's time with Morrissey was brief though he parted on amicable terms and, contrary

Armatrading, Joan, Prominent British black female singer/songwriter, best known for the hits 'Love And Affection' (number ten, November 1976), 'Me Myself I' (number 21, August 1980) and 'Drop The Pilot' (number 11, March 1983). In a 2008 press statement announcing his headline show at that year's Wireless festival in Hyde Park, Morrissey referred to Armatrading as one of the previous 'Hyde Park greats' beside Marc BOLAN's T.Rex and 'someone with insecure teeth'. His public praise for Armatrading confirmed earlier suspicions that her characteristically lovelorn songs had inspired Morrissey's own lyrics. Most obviously 'SUEDEHEAD' appears to owe some debt to 'The Weakness In Me' from her 1982 album Walk Under Ladders with its similar 'Why do you come here? ... and pretend to be just passing by ... when you know I've got troubles enough' and another line about being harassed by telephone. It also seems highly likely that 'BILLY BUDD' was partly inspired by 'Turn Out The Light' from 1980's Me Myself I, featuring the comparable 'Things have looked bad/But now some years later ...' and the identical 'Since I took up with you'. [572]

to other negative allegations about the singer's financial arrangements, describes him as 'very good when it comes to money and songwriting royalties'. [1, 15]

Arthur, Beatrice, American comic actress,

named as one of Morrissey's chosen 'symbolists' in 1983. Sometimes credited as 'Bea' Arthur, she starred in two of the singer's favourite US sitcoms.

Maude (1972–78) was a spin-off of *All In The Family* (the US version of British sitcom *Till Death Us Do Part*) starring Arthur as Maude Findlay, a four-times married, Valium-popping, upper-class liberal feminist living in Tuckahoe, New York. The show was regarded as an extremely radical comedy for its time, dealing with such issues as abortion, alcoholism, racism and the menopause. Maude also crops up in Morrissey's pre-Smiths film essay *EXIT SMILING* during his chapter on Eve Arden, who guest-starred in one episode as Maude's Aunt Lola. '[Arden] sadly wilted next to the modern expertise of Beatrice Arthur,' he wrote, 'who is tough enough competition for anybody.'

In *The Golden Girls* (1985–92), Arthur played no-nonsense divorcee Dorothy, sharing a home in Miami with her widowed Sicilian mother Sophia (Estelle Getty) and two other elderly widows: the sweet-natured Rose (Betty White) and the man-eating Southern belle Blanche (Rue McClanahan, who'd also starred in *Maude* as Arthur's neighbour, Vivian). Morrissey 'enthused about' *The Golden Girls* to at least one reporter during its original run in the mid-80s and later paid tribute to the series on stage at Miami's Gleason Theatre in October 2004 where, between songs, he recited its Andrew Gold signature theme, 'Thank You For Being A Friend'.

Two years earlier, when touring Australia in October 2002 Morrissey found himself playing Melbourne the same night Arthur was opening a short run of her one-woman stage show And Then There's Bea. Walking on stage at The Forum, he thanked his audience, 'for coming around here tonight and choosing me instead of Beatrice Arthur … as you can see there isn't much

difference'. Arthur died in April 2009, aged 86. [52, 175, 184, 341]

Ashkenazi, Lior, Handsome Israeli film star

and Morrissey's named 'favourite actor' circa 2007. Praised by critics for his 'rugged good looks and smooth demeanour' as much as his acting abilities, the swarthy Ashkenazi's first international success was the 2001 Hebrew language film *Late Marriage*. 'It's one of those rare films wherein the entire cast is excellent,' said Morrissey, 'and the film is powerful without one single special effect or any sound trickery.' Ashkenazi stars as a Tel Aviv student whose Georgian-Jewish family are desperate to marry him off. When they learn of his relationship with an older divorcee and single mother (Ronit Elkabetz), they enact a vile campaign of intimidation to end their affair. *Late Marriage* is a funny but ultimately depressing comment on true love in the face of insurmountable religious traditions. As *Time Out New York* observed, it also boasts 'perhaps the most believable sex scene ever filmed'.

Morrissey also praised Ashkenazi's performance in 2004's *Walk On Water* in which he played an Israeli intelligence agent who befriends a homosexual German teacher and his sister in order to trace their Nazi war criminal grandfather. The film is of added interest for its narrative use of Esther and Abi Ofarim's 1968 number one 'Cinderella Rockefella', a song which the eight-year-old Morrissey wrote 'an extravagant critique of' in the weekly homemade pop magazine he compiled as a child.

After raving about Ashkenazi on the TRUE-TO-YOU website (and later mentioning him on stage at a 2006 festival in Istanbul), on 4 July 2008 Morrissey requested a meeting with the actor in London as a precursor to his first concert in Israel later that summer. Ashkenazi and his companion for the day – *Walk On Water* writer Gal Uchovsky – wrote separate accounts of their Morrissey encounter for the Hebrew newspaper *Yedioth Ahronoth* and *Time Out Tel Aviv*. Both were fascinating reports of an exceptionally

a

awkward summit at the Mandarin Oriental hotel on Hyde Park, not far from where Morrissey would headline the 02 Wireless Festival later that day.

The meeting began with the pair being taken to a suite by the singer's personal assistant, 'Sarah', who forewarned them that their interview would last no more than 20 minutes and under no circumstances were they to mention The Smiths. Morrissey arrived – 'very polite but quite suspicious', wrote Ashkenazi – and was presented with some Israeli DVDs to 'break the ice'. But as Uchovsky noted, 'from there the interview quickly deteriorated'. Morrissey was prickly and evasive to the simplest of questions – e.g. Uchovsky: 'Where do you live?', Morrissey: 'Nowhere. Why live somewhere?' – and seemed more interested in talking about the EUROVISION song contest and griping about Kylie Minogue being given an OBE. He did, at least, tell Ashkenazi that he'd like to visit Israel's Dead Sea to re-create the beach scene in *Walk On Water*. The actor told him that could be arranged, though as Uchovsky observed, 'Morrissey works on resistance and hatred. He tends to see the negative in everything.'

Ashkenazi and Uchovsky left the interview in a state of confusion and disappointment, feeling that they and Morrissey 'didn't get each other'. It was especially disheartening for Uchovsky, a passionate Smiths fan who'd enjoyed a brief email correspondence with Morrissey in the run-up to their meeting. They still attended, and enjoyed, Morrissey's Hyde Park concert that evening and afterwards met him backstage where he drank Corona and 'burped without shame' in the company of Chrissie HYNDE, Russell BRAND, his sister Jacqueline and his two nephews. Before leaving, Ashkenazi was given a card with the words 'Don't speak' printed on one side and Morrissey's email address handwritten on the reverse. Three weeks later, Morrissey played Israel's Heatwave Festival. If he ever did visit the Dead Sea during his visit, with or without Ashkenazi, it was never reported. [49, 195, 208, 241, 522, 560]

'Asian Rut' (Morrissey/Nevin), From the album KILL UNCLE (1991). Written by Nevin under the demo title of 'Idiot's Funeral', a dirge of harmonium and the woebegone fiddle of Nawazish Ali Khan is the setting for one of Morrissey's more divisive sketches: a young Asian planning to avenge the racist murder of his friend at the hands of white thugs. Because of the earlier controversy surrounding 'BENGALI IN PLATFORMS', critics were immediately suspicious about the track's subject matter, 'highly unusual' in the wary estimation of one interviewer. 'I disagree,' retorted Morrissey. 'There are a lot of Asian people. Why is it so unusual?'

Ever since, whenever his detractors target what they perceive to be Morrissey's 'racist tendencies', 'Asian Rut' is routinely dragged into their argument beside 'Bengali In Platforms' and 'THE NATIONAL FRONT DISCO'. Which is quite nonsensical. Taking the lyrics at face value, it's hard to imagine how anybody could interpret a song which quite graphically expresses shock, horror and bewilderment at the vicious circle of racially motivated revenge killings as condoning such attacks. Its 'brave Asian boy' is a classic Morrissey third-person sketch in his lyrical armoury of life's outsiders – a figure simultaneously noble yet pathetic, whose only means of retribution is guaranteed to end not only in failure but death. Moreover, Morrissey's own despair over racist violence is made clear in his closing hope of one day finding a 'more civilised' world. [15, 22, 90]

'Ask' (Morrissey/Marr), The Smiths' 12th single, released October 1986, highest UK chart position #14. Cover star: YOOTHA JOYCE.

Released in the wake of THE QUEEN IS DEAD and following 'PANIC', the effervescent 'Ask' was a conscious detour away from controversial agit-pop. 'If the next single [after 'Panic'] had been a slight protest, regardless of the merits of the actual song, people would say, "Here we go again,"' reasoned Morrissey. Intentionally lightweight, 'Ask' was, indeed, The Smiths at their most petty. Beneath its liberating address to the cripplingly shy lay a playful erotic frisson (not least

Morrissey's metaphorical description of sexual desire as the unifying 'bomb that will bring us together'), while its portrait of a timid recluse writing 'frightening verse' to strange foreign pen pals sounded not unlike the adolescent Morrissey. As he'd previously explained, 'I spent every solitary penny on postage stamps. I had this wonderful arrangement with the entire universe without actually meeting anybody, just through the wonderful postal service. The crisis of my teenage life was when postage stamps went up from 12p to 13p. I was outraged.' The lyrics also bore the likely influence of playwright Alan BENNETT, whose 1978 teleplay *Me, I'm Afraid Of Virginia Woolf* contained the line, 'Nature has a language, you see, if only we'd learn to read it.'[1]

Marr's jangling jamboree was among his cheeriest Smiths tunes, though new recruit Craig GANNON would later maintain that he had helped compose its main chord sequence during a previous jam when recording 'Panic'. As a common ascending chord configuration, it's not beyond reason that Gannon may have stumbled across something very close to it. However, without necessarily disputing Gannon's claim, it should be noted that Marr had used the exact same chord sequence within a home demo of what later became 'IS IT REALLY SO STRANGE?' several months earlier and was subconsciously predisposed to those specific chords to use them again as the basis of 'I WON'T SHARE YOU'.

Further controversy surrounded the single's production, which began with John PORTER at the helm. 'Originally, "Ask" was a bit of a tour de force,' says Porter. 'It was pretty complicated with loads of little guitar parts. There was this bit in the middle where they wanted the sound of a waterfall crashing, all done with guitars, and seagull sounds. It was fucking amazing, but it was a jigsaw puzzle.' Due to the technical constraints of the chosen studio (Jam in north London), Porter intended to mix the song 'somewhere else at a later date'. Instead, and apparently unbeknownst to Porter, the tapes were handed to producer Steve LILLYWHITE, the husband of the song's guest

backing singer, Kirsty MACCOLL. Without Porter's 'master plan' of how the track fitted together, Lillywhite was asked to mix what became the finished single. 'I couldn't understand why it was being tampered with because it all came together very simply and with a definite sense of purpose,' comments Marr. '[The final version] wasn't dramatically different, but it felt kind of a little bit muted. Less spirited, absolutely.' Although Porter still insists 'Ask' was a shadow of the 'fantastic single it could have been', it continued The Smiths' siege of the UK top 20 in the aftermath of The Queen Is Dead, instigating a final video collaboration with director Derek JARMAN. [17, 27, 52, 193, 282, 307]

---

1. Bennett aside, the nature-as-a-language simile goes back centuries in English literature. Another of Morrissey's favourite authors, George ELIOT, makes the similar observation in her 1859 novel *Adam Bede*: 'Nature has her language … but we don't know all the intricacies of her syntax just yet, and in a hasty reading we may happen to extract the very opposite of her real meaning.'

'Asleep' (Morrissey/Marr), B-side of 'THE BOY WITH THE THORN IN HIS SIDE' (1985). Morrissey's most explicit advocation of suicide, 'Asleep' was a heart-rending lullaby for the intolerably lonely. Its lyrics anticipated The Smiths' imminent 'I KNOW IT'S OVER' (written shortly afterwards) and their final masterpiece, 'LAST NIGHT I DREAMT THAT SOMEBODY LOVED ME', expressing the agony of a life spent forever waking up alone. In 'Asleep', Morrissey makes specific his wish to end his waking misery by escaping to 'another world'; the sleep he sings of – or rather wishes to be sung *to* – is the sleep of the dead, much like Shakespeare's 'To be or not to be?' soliloquy from *Hamlet*. Yet, for all its implied despondency, 'Asleep' is perversely optimistic in its suicidal resolution. In contrast to the all-consuming hopelessness of 'Last Night I Dreamt', Morrissey is 'glad' to have taken his fate into his own hands, believing, however blindly, that 'there must be' peace on the other side. Even the closing music-box chimes of the traditional New Year's toast

'Auld Lang Syne' seemed to symbolise a new beginning in the hereafter.

The song's heart throbbed more weary for its simplicity: just Morrissey, a deathly squall of wind and the pallbearing jolts of Marr's piano. Melodically, it shared some similarities with an earlier piano piece originally tacked on to the end of The Smiths' earliest demo of 'SUFFER LITTLE CHILDREN'. 'Undoubtedly it is similar,' confirms Marr, 'because that's how I play piano, I can't play it any other way. "Asleep" was worked out on the upright piano I inherited when I moved into my house in Bowdon [at the end of 1984]. The same piano I wrote "Oscillate Wildly" on. It had a pleasingly eerie quality about it.'

As engineer Stephen STREET verifies, 'Asleep' was recorded in 'about two hours' one evening after finishing its accompanying B-side, 'RUBBER RING'; when released together on the 12-inch of 'The Boy With The Thorn In His Side', these two B-sides formed a continuous medley linked by an overlapping segue-way. The Smiths played 'Asleep' in concert just once, on the final date of their mini Scottish tour of autumn 1985 (Inverness Eden Court Theatre, 1 October), a last-minute decision after discovering a piano in the wings of the stage. 'That was a really brilliant gig,' recalls Marr, 'partly because we knew we were gonna do "Asleep" so we had this strange kind of "Is it gonna work?" thing hanging over us.'

When a very small number of isolated cases involving Smiths fans who'd taken their own lives came to light in the year following the song's release, Morrissey found himself answering to press accusations of irresponsibility. 'Asleep' by no means glamorises suicide, but by nature of its courageous honesty on the subject and its empathy with those who arrive at such an extreme mental resolution, it clearly condones it. (See also SUICIDE.) [17, 18, 28, 38, 206]

astrology

astrology, For Morrissey's star sign see GEMINI. The astrological make-up of The Smiths was two Geminis (Morrissey, Joyce), Scorpio (Marr) and Capricorn (Rourke), an elemental mix of air, air, water and earth. The arrival of Craig GANNON in 1986 briefly threw some Leo fire into their equation.

'At Amber'

'At Amber' (Morrissey/Street), B-side of 'PICCADILLY PALARE' (1990). Originally titled 'The Bed Took Fire', this odd vignette on disability finds Morrissey telephoning an 'invalid friend'[1] from the lobby of the Sands Hotel – presumably *the* famous Sands Hotel in Las Vegas synonymous with FRANK SINATRA and since demolished – complaining about the awful time he's having only for them to bitterly remind him that at least he has full use of his limbs. Written and recorded in the winter of 1988 at the 'LAST OF THE FAMOUS INTERNATIONAL PLAYBOYS' sessions at The Wool Hall near Bath, the song was originally slated as a B-side of 'INTERESTING DRUG' before Morrissey decided to shelve it indefinitely. The following year, while recording his intended second album, BONA DRAG, he decided to resurrect it under the new name of 'At Amber' in reference to standard British traffic lights. 'Amber is being in a state of flux,' he explained, 'neither going nor stopping but somewhere in the middle.' None of which shed much light upon the lyrics which, as Morrissey also admitted, were 'not really' referring to a real crippled friend, merely his understanding of 'extreme situations in life'. He'd later revisit the same theme of disability with far greater force on the imminent 'NOVEMBER SPAWNED A MONSTER'.

Morrissey was already recording Bona Drag at Hook End with new producers Clive LANGER and Alan Winstanley when he informed Street, already in litigation with the singer for some months, that he wanted to salvage the song under its new title. Street obligingly visited Hook End to make subtle amendments to his original 'Bed Took Fire' Wool Hall mix; its shiny, sauntering melody and heavy clouting chorus were left largely intact save for some ironing out of Street's original synthetic drum claps, possibly the source of Morrissey's decision not to release it first time around. 'I went down for a day or so,' recalls Street. 'But it felt

'At Last I Am Born' (Morrissey/Farrell), From the album RINGLEADER OF THE TORMENTORS (2006). The sword and sandal finale to Morrissey's 'Roman album' has him mirroring the thoughts of the great German poet, dramatist and philosopher Johann Wolfgang von Goethe who upon arriving in the city in 1788 declared, 'In Rome, I have found myself.'[1] Morrissey proclaims similar symbolic enlightenment, calling historians to mark his 'birth' at the age of 46. Bidding farewell to the introversion and suffering of yore, he maps out his curious life's journey from a troubled childhood to 'spectral hand' and his more recent fascination with French actor Claude BRASSEUR. Its final revelation that he no longer suffered Catholic guilt 'because of the flesh' provided proof positive for those who interpreted Ringleader as a confession that after years of CELIBACY and self-denial Morrissey had come to terms with his sexuality and was now enjoying regular shenanigans. Typically, he refused to elaborate on such wild theorising, commenting only that, 'After a long, long time I am finally born. I mean, it takes some people a long time to finally realise many things about their life. I feel that the last year or so has been better in many, many ways.'

One of only two songs co-written with keyboard player Michael Farrell, 'At Last I Am Born' possessed the distinct echo of the amphitheatre, a proud pageant of military drums, Flamenco frills, Spaghetti Western twangs and gleeful children's choir, together ricocheting around the more neo-realistic touches of revving scooters and Italian street cries. If nothing else, Morrissey at his most resplendently cinematic. [159, 235, 389]

---

1. Other source hunters have been more specific in quoting a line from the second of Goethe's *Roman Elegies* – 'Nun bin ich endlich geborgen!' – as a literal translation of the song title, though its actual meaning is closer to 'Now at last I have found a safe refuge'.

awkward because this legal thing and the money dispute after VIVA HATE was still hanging over us. I didn't stay long.'

By no means one of his best Street collaborations, Morrissey was wise to salvage 'At Amber' as a decent B-side. To date, he has played the song in concert only once in Phoenix, Arizona on 9 August 2002, a flawed performance which seems to have discouraged him from attempting the song ever again. [15, 39, 70, 422]

---

1. The song's 'invalid friend' may have been the subtle influence of Oscar WILDE, whose most famous play *The Importance Of Being Earnest* involves a make-believe 'invalid friend' called Bunbury.

athletics, Contrary to the stereotypical image of Morrissey as an adolescent weed, the singer admitted to being 'quite classically good' when it came to school sports, boasting 'an array of impressive medals'. '[Sport] was the only thing I was good at and I used to love it completely,' he confessed. 'I particularly liked running. But then, I *had* to be a good runner, for reasons I'll leave unstated … The 100 metres was my raison d'être. Yes, I won everything. I was a terrible bore when it came to athletics.' As a consequence of his track and field prowess, Morrissey found himself in a favourable position with the staff of St Mary's Secondary School in Stretford. 'In a working-class school, if you're good at athletics you're the treasured student,' he explained. 'Everything you do is wonderful and you can get away with anything. I was that kind of student.' It was only when he began moving 'in circles where any kind of activity or movement was aesthetically illegal' that he had to choose between sport and 'the other'. Naturally, Morrissey opted for 'the other', later making a humorous reference to that struggle on the run-out-groove message of 1990's BONA DRAG compilation: 'Aesthetics versus athletics'. [100, 258, 448]

Attack Records, Morrissey's record label from 2004–07 under contract to the Sanctuary Music Group. The original label was a reggae imprint founded in the late 60s in Willesden, north London, under the umbrella of Trojan Records whose entire back catalogue was later bought up by Sanctuary. 'They had bought lots of labels and I don't think they realised how many they had,' explained Morrissey. 'So I simply rummaged through their drawers in their desk and out sprang an Attack label. I don't think anything fantastic was on Attack but I liked the jagged imprint. I liked the word.'

As he readily confessed, Attack was never a prestigious label though it was as close as he could get to being on Trojan itself, home to many of his teenage favourites such as Bob And Marcia's 'Young, Gifted And Black' and Dave And Ansel Collins's 'Double Barrel'. Morrissey's only direct reference to an original Attack release was a 2004 photo session where he brandished a copy of the label's 1974 Gregory Isaacs single, 'Love Is Over-due' – a gift from former *NME* writer Len BROWN who'd inherited the record from his brother, Don, who committed suicide in the early 80s.

As part of the deal with Sanctuary, Morrissey was 'given' Attack as his own bespoke label, allowing him to license releases by other artists. 'I'm going to release great records that I want to release,' he announced. 'There's no eye on commercial success. I will not be turning into a record company exec with a sword and steel toe-capped boots. I'm trying to revive something good and true about pop music. I'd like to regenerate and rejuvenate some kind of faith in the pop single. I think people are tired of investing so much of their time and faith in albums that aren't worth it.'

The majority of non-Morrissey Attack records were released during October 2004, beginning with the MELTDOWN concert recording Morrissey Presents: The Return Of The NEW YORK DOLLS Live From Royal Festival Hall 2004 (Attack009), NANCY SINATRA's self-titled album and Irish singer Damien Dempsey's Seize The Day (the latter two under Sanctuary/Attack with no customised

catalogue numbers). Four limited CD singles followed the same month: Nancy Sinatra's 'LET ME KISS YOU' (Attack005), James MAKER & Noko 440's 'Born That Way' (Attack007), JOBRIATH's 'I Love A Good Fight' (Attack012) and 'Worry Young' by Cork indie band Remma (Attack006). Plans for another Attack single by Dolls' singer David Johansen never materialised. The Jobriath compilation Lonely Planet Boy (Attack010, November 2004) would be the last non-Morrissey album on the label.

By 2006's RINGLEADER OF THE TORMENTORS – his third Attack album following YOU ARE THE QUARRY and LIVE AT EARLS COURT – his interest in the label as a concurrent A&R venture beside his own recordings seemed to have fizzled out. The only non-Morrissey releases that year, and the last altogether, were two singles by Kristeen YOUNG, 'Kill The Father' (Attack022, August 2006) and 'London Cry' (Attack024, December 2006). In late 2006, Sanctuary chief executive and Morrissey's current manager Merck Mercuriadis resigned from the company which was by then in financial difficulties. The following June, the entire Sanctuary Music Group was bought out by Universal, where Morrissey would subsequently move under the DECCA label. Attack Records effectively ended with the release of Morrissey's final Ringleader single, 'I JUST WANT TO SEE THE BOY HAPPY'. [55, 156, 290, 436]

Austen, Jane, Popular early-nineteeth-century novelist whose books Morrissey has admitted to 'lapsing into'. Born into a large middle-class family in Hampshire, Austen completed only six novels before her death in 1817 at the age of just 41 after contracting a form of tuberculosis. Her most famous works include *Emma*, *Sense And Sensibility* and the romantic comedy *Pride And Prejudice*, the latter being the novel the 20-year-old Morrissey claimed to have read at home instead of going out and joining in the New Year/new decade festivities on the last night of the 1970s.

Although Morrissey was happy to call Austen 'a genius' as recently as 2006, her influence upon his own work is slight, if nonexistent, when compared to that of other, later, nineteenth-century novelists such as George ELIOT, the Brontë sisters, or even DICKENS. Nor has Morrissey ever cited Austen in any questionnaire about his favourite books or authors. It may be that, while he admires her writing, he agrees with Eliot that Austen's work is emotionally stunted, that she portrays 'too much of the littlenesses and trivialities of life, and [limits herself] so scrupulously to the sayings and doings of dull, ignorant, and disagreeable people that their very truthfulness makes us yawn'. [206, 232, 362, 388]

autobiography, Morrissey has always maintained that he documents his life in his lyrics, yet as early as 1984 he was already being asked whether he'd ever write a memoir. By the late 90s, long after he'd established himself as an iconic figure in the history of British music and in the aftermath of the Smiths COURT CASE, he considered it unlikely. '[I'd] have to mention people I like to avoid,' he mused, 'so I'll have to wait until they've passed away. Because it is not possible to portray an intelligent image of one's life without dragging in these people. So I'll wait.'

It was only during his prolonged absence at the turn of the millennium that he reconsidered. In 2002, he divulged that an autobiography 'has been offered by several [publishers] and I have actually started it. It's to set a multitude of records straight. Whether it reaches the shops, I don't know. There'd be so many injunctions, I'm sure. So many untruths have emerged around my name and my life – maybe we all feel that way, I don't know. But, yes, I've started it and it will be a fascinating thing to finish.'

Thereafter, enquiries on the subject provoked Morrissey's hyperbolic promises that it 'will bring England to its very foundations' and be 'volcanic … you ought to expect names, photos and fingerprints. Everything shall be revealed.' Appetites were further whetted when, in 2004, he told the BBC's Jonathan Ross he only had 'a few chapters left' to finish. Soon rumours of vast advances from major publishing houses began circulating on the

internet, though the singer was quick to nip such speculation in the bud. 'I've agreed *with myself* to do it,' he said in 2006, '[but] I've never had any dialogue with a publisher.' The latter statement, of course, contradicted his previous remarks about being courted 'by several', as well as his admission that Faber & Faber had been in discussions with him to release a compendium of his lyrics ('I thought that was fantastic,' he told Radio 1, 'because they usually just have very established poets').

Looking towards the future, a Morrissey memoir is highly probable, although his doubts about the legal implications of its more candid revelations and character assassinations are likely to be the biggest bone of contention when it comes to inking a deal. Without question, one of the major 'wrongs' his autobiography will hope to 'right' is the 1996 court case and it's safe to predict a scandalously damning portrait of Smiths drummer Mike Joyce. Consequently, it may well be the case that a Morrissey autobiography will be the catalyst for a mini-industry of petty counter-claim memoirs. [48, 159, 192, 231, 410, 424, 425, 451]

awards, To date, the most prestigious music award Morrissey has ever received has been an Ivor Novello for the PRS (Performing Rights Society) Outstanding Contribution To British Music. Morrissey attended the ceremony at London's Grosvenor House Hotel on 28 May 1998, where Anthony NEWLEY presented him with his trophy. His acceptance speech thanked 'John Marr of Wythenshawe for getting me where I am today … which begs the question, "Where am I?"' Asked by an MTV reporter what brought him there that day, the singer replied 'the 138 from Streatham Hill'.

Other awards include 'Best Songwriter' from *Q* magazine in 1994, a Silver Clef 'Inspiration Award' in 2004 and the same year's 'Icon Award' from *Mojo* magazine. He has twice been nominated for a Brit Award for 'Best British Male Solo Artist' in 1995 (for VAUXHALL AND I) and 2005 (for YOU ARE THE QUARRY). He lost on both occasions, though his outspoken comments against the organisers – that 'you'll never see me at the Brits' – have probably forfeited any hope of his ever winning in the future. Morrissey's only US Grammy nomination to date has been 'Best Alternative Album' in 1993 for YOUR ARSENAL.

The humble scattering of music gongs on Morrissey's mantelpiece are probably of less consequence to the singer than the rare honour of the Linda MCCARTNEY Memorial Award he received from PETA on their 25th anniversary in 2005. In December 2006, he also came close to winning BBC2 arts programme *The Culture Show*'s national vote to name Britain's greatest 'Living Icon', beating Paul McCartney but coming second to broadcaster and naturalist Sir David Attenborough. Sadly blinkered to Attenborough's unparalleled contribution to conservationism, natural history and environmental awareness, Morrissey was ungracious in defeat, accusing Sir David of hypocrisy for being a zoologist who ate animal flesh. [68, 444]

'Back To The Old House' (Morrissey/ Marr), B-side of 'WHAT DIFFERENCE DOES IT MAKE?' (1984). Illustrative of the unique creative chemistry between Morrissey and Marr's respective sense of beauty and melancholy, 'Back To The Old House' began as a romantic guitar tune Marr composed with his girlfriend, Angie, in mind. Taking this foundation, Morrissey applied a sad reminiscence about a lost love and an old dwelling he dare not return to for fear of further upset; thematically a rough precursor to his later 'LATE NIGHT, MAUDLIN STREET'. Melodic hope and lyrical heartache bleed together as one in a song both innocent and tragic, a small but sublime entry in the Morrissey/Marr songbook.

Written in September 1983, its first recording for the group's second BBC session for John PEEL, as featured on HATFUL OF HOLLOW, is widely regarded as the definitive version for very obvious reasons. Presenting Morrissey and Marr as a stripped-down folk duo, just voice and humble acoustic squeaking, its simplicity only increased the load upon its already sagging heart-strings. The 19-year-old Marr's picking skills were particularly dazzling, his first explicit nod to covert folk influences such as Pentangle's Bert Jansch.

The studio version issued as a B-side was recorded that winter during THE SMITHS album sessions with producer John PORTER, adding bass and drums but reducing its emotional impact in the process. In concert The Smiths always played the latter band arrangement. With hindsight, Marr agrees that the acoustic Hatful version 'has something special that the other doesn't'. [12, 17, 19]

Baker, Stanley, Brawny Welsh actor and British film star of the 50s and 60s who, in certain films and from certain angles, bears a gobsmacking resemblance to Morrissey: the same prominent chin, the same glowering frown, a hint of a dark quiff and, sometimes, even the same expertly groomed sideboards.

Born into Welsh mining stock, Baker was encouraged by the same local drama teacher who'd previously spotted his future drinking companion, Richard Burton (featured on Morrissey's stage backdrop in 2007). Off camera, Baker was a gregarious drinker and, during the early 60s, socialised with real-life villains from both the RICHARDSON and KRAY gangs. Best known for heading the cast of 1964's *Zulu* (which he also co-produced), Baker famously turned down the role of James Bond, thereby leaving the door open for Sean Connery. Often typecast as working-class criminals – even by himself in the excellent 1967 heist thriller *Robbery* which, again, he co-produced – his performance as a lecherous university don in the same year's Harold Pinter-scripted *Accident* (with Dirk BOGARDE) was evidence enough of a great and versatile dramatic actor. His film career petered out in the early 70s, though he won huge critical acclaim for the 1975 BBC television adaptation of Richard Llewellyn's Welsh mining saga *How Green Was My Valley*. Baker died the following year of lung cancer, aged only 48.

Where that gobsmacking resemblance to Morrissey is concerned, Baker's most striking films are his earlier British B-movies and crime thrillers. In 1954's *The Good Die Young*, he plays an ill-starred boxer coerced into a post-office robbery by the weasely Laurence Harvey; the detail that Baker's character's trainer is called

Band Aid, 'Undiscussable' 80s pop supergroup brought together by Bob Geldof for December 1984's 'Do They Know It's Christmas?', a charity record to provide famine relief in Ethiopia. Morrissey's criticisms of Band Aid, and its 1985 concert spin-off Live Aid, created much controversy in the press and became a popular topic in Smiths interviews of the period.

Band Aid's cast included many of the biggest names in 80s UK pop at that time, including Duran Duran, Spandau Ballet, Paul Young, Boy George, George Michael, Bono, Paul Weller, Sting, Heaven 17, Bananarama, Big Country, Status Quo and the song's co-writer, Midge Ure of Ultravox. The Smiths, who'd had three consecutive top 20 hits at that point (including one top ten) weren't invited, even though they'd been more successful than one-hit-wonder Marilyn, seen skulking shamefaced amid the 'feed the world' finale. Asked, hypothetically, whether or not he'd have accepted an offer, Morrissey said he'd have 'read the letter at least 18 times' first but claimed he would have refused on the grounds of the song itself, 'that foul disgusting thing' which he deemed 'absolutely tuneless'. 'It's one thing to want to save lives in Ethiopia, but it's another thing to inflict so much torture on the British public. So for that reason, I absolutely disapprove.'

Morrissey's repugnance regarding Band Aid knew no bounds, calling the record 'diabolical … the most self-righteous platform ever in the history of popular music', dubbing Geldof 'a nauseating character' and his band, The Boomtown Rats, 'a collection of Brontosaurasi'. Not surprisingly, Geldof hit back at him in a radio interview, a retaliation which Morrissey strangely considered 'totally unfair'. Interviewed shortly after the July 1985 Live Aid concert, Johnny Marr was slightly more gracious. 'I personally think that the cause is admirable and that Bob Geldof has handled it admirably,' said Marr, who nevertheless agreed with Morrissey that 'the record stank, and most of the acts on the day stank but maybe that doesn't matter too much'.

Yet underneath all the petty name calling, Morrissey had a serious political point about 'the guilt of [African famine being] placed upon the shoulders of the British public' at a time of mass unemployment. 'The whole implication was to save these people in Ethiopia,' he argued, 'but who were they asking to save them? Some 13-year-old girl in Wigan! People like THATCHER and the royals could solve the Ethiopian problem within ten seconds. But Band Aid shied away from that.' [105, 123, 167, 206]

'Bunny' bears some consideration as a possible lyrical source of 'NOW MY HEART IS FULL'. More Moz-a-like still is his Irish villain Johnny Bannion in 1960's *The Criminal*, a fantastic prison thriller which saw the screen debut of *A Taste Of Honey*'s Murray Melvin. But the ultimate Baker/Morrissey wonder is *Hell Is A City*, a British film noir set and filmed in and around Manchester in 1959, the year Morrissey was born. For once, Baker is on the other side of the law as Inspector Martineau, out to catch a gang led by an escaped convict who accidentally kill a girl during a robbery. Baker's murder trail takes him out on to Saddleworth Moor (see 'SUFFER LITTLE CHILDREN'), the streets of RUSHOLME and an encounter with future Smiths cover and Morrissey video star Billie WHITELAW. As if that weren't coincidence enough, the premiere of *Hell Is A City* was held in April 1960 at Manchester's Apollo theatre – the very location where, in 1978, Morrissey and Johnny Marr first clapped eyes upon one another at a PATTI SMITH concert and where The Smiths, and Morrissey, would also play many years later.

Surprisingly, the weird Stanley Baker/Morrissey look-a-like phenomenon has seldom been addressed in the media. A rare exception was in November 1995 when the singer appeared on the BBC's *Later With Jools Holland*. During their short interview together, Holland made a passing joke that Morrissey was wearing one of Baker's hand-me-down suits. [457]

'Barbarism Begins At Home' (Morrissey/

Marr), From the album MEAT IS MURDER (1985). The longest recorded Smiths track (just shy of seven minutes), its pronounced funk influence was, at the time, regarded as a bold musical departure. It contains one of Andy Rourke's most celebrated bass lines, his elastic riff providing an anchor for Marr's Chic-inspired guitar improvisations. The overall style of the track also harks back to Marr and Rourke's earlier band, FREAK PARTY, influenced by contemporary post-punk groups including fellow Mancunians A Certain Ratio.

Pre-dating Meat Is Murder by 18 months, Marr composed the tune in the summer of 1983 while jamming in their Manchester rehearsal room prior to their first meeting with prospective debut album producer, Troy TATE. 'It was almost because our first proper producer was about to arrive that I thought we needed a new song,' says Marr. Though its epic length and cyclical structure offered Morrissey space to improvise beyond the three-minute pop norm, he kept the lyrics short and simple, repeating a sinister nursery rhyme threatening 'unruly' children with corporal punishment. There was a faint echo of Shelagh DELANEY in the 'taken in hand' refrain (the phrase appears in Act II of *A Taste Of Honey*), while its live debut in December 1983 included extra lines which Morrissey eventually cut (e.g. 'I've always been such a decent lad'). He'd later describe the words as 'not autobiographical, [just a] recognition that the only channel of communication open to a lot of parents is violence'.

By the time they came to record it for Meat Is Murder, 'Barbarism Begins At Home' had already been in their live set for a whole year. Talk of releasing it as a single in January 1985 resulted in a 12-inch radio promo in a sleeve featuring Viv NICHOLSON, though it was only granted a commercial release in Europe. A live favourite – sometimes lasting as long as 15 minutes and the only song Morrissey performed in concert with friend Pete BURNS – Marr would eventually tire of the tune and today names it among his least favourite Smiths recordings. Nevertheless, it survives as a testament to the group's versatility, as well as a reminder of Rourke's indispensability within their overall sound. [12, 17, 135, 426, 554]

Bardot, Brigitte, French sex goddess, film

star, pop singer and animal rights activist. As France's most famous film export during the 50s and 60s, Bardot's career crossed the paths of many Smiths cover stars and Morrissey favourites, from Alain DELON to Jean MARAIS, Jean COCTEAU and Dirk BOGARDE, though his main interest in Bardot is due to her mid- to late 60s pop recordings, particularly those written by, or performed with, her mentor and lover Serge GAINSBOURG.

Morrissey's love of Bardot's music was probably influenced by his close friend Linder STERLING. In 1982, Sterling's band, Ludus, released a cover of Bardot's 1970 single 'Nue Au Soleil' ('Naked In The Sun'). Two years later, and despite being out of date, Morrissey would name Ludus's version as his favourite single of 1984. Significantly, Morrissey included Bardot's original 'Nue Au Soleil' on his interval music in 1999, though it was when touring YOU ARE THE QUARRY in 2004 that his Bardot fixation was most noticeable: 1968's 'Ce N'est Pas Vrai' ('That's Not True') and the same year's Gainsbourg-penned 'Harley Davidson' and 'Contact' were all included on that tour's interval tapes, as was Gainsbourg's solo tribute anthem, 'Initials B.B.' The promotional video for Bardot's 1966 single 'Bubble Gum', written by Gainsbourg and featuring a smoking, smitten Claude BRASSEUR stalking her every move, was later featured within Morrissey's interval video montages introduced in late 2006.

Bardot's shortcomings as a singer, habitually drifting off in a key (if not a world) of her own, were more than compensated by her radioactive sexiness, even if the end results were usually more camp than erotic. One notable exception was Bardot's prototype of the steamy Gainsbourg duet 'Je T'Aime … Moi Non Plus', later re-recorded with Jane Birkin, which she prevented from being released at the time so as not to offend her husband. Retiring in 1973 at the age of 39, Bardot later established the Brigitte Bardot Foundation for the Welfare and Protection of Animals. Sadly, her commendable efforts in the field of animal rights have been overshadowed, if not entirely negated, by her outspoken comments against Muslims and homosexuals. While many of her objections against the Muslim community are a consequence of her VEGETARIANISM (opposing their particular religious methods of sheep slaughter) her broader comments on immigration and inter-racial marriages have seen her repeatedly fined by the French government for inciting racial hatred.

In view of Morrissey's own controversies regarding similar issues, his respect for Bardot is potentially problematic, as he discovered first hand when playing the Paris Olympia in April 2006. Praising his favourite French singers between songs, his mention of Bardot provoked booing among a large section of the audience. 'Yes, I know,' grimaced Morrissey, 'but she's very good to black widow spiders.' [177, 182, 380, 436]

Barrett, Sean, British actor and cover star of the Smiths single 'HOW SOON IS NOW?', albeit uncredited on the original sleeve. The still in question is taken from the 1958 Ealing film *Dunkirk* starring John MILLS, a dramatisation of the 1940 evacuation of allied troops from French beaches during the Second World War. Barrett plays Frankie, a young lad who insists on accompanying his boss (Richard Attenborough in prime coward-with-a-conscience mode) on one of the rescue ships and ends up briefly stranded at Dunkirk alongside several thousand weary soldiers with no shelter from enemy fire. The cover of 'How Soon Is Now?' shows Barrett kneeling down in prayer during a church service on the beach towards the end of the film. [497]

Barretts Of Wimpole Street, The, 1934 biographical melodrama about the romance between the Victorian poets Elizabeth Barrett and Robert Browning, listed among Morrissey's favourite films. The cast is headed by Charles Laughton as the stern, bewhiskered widower Edward Moulton-Barrett who psychologically terrorises his many grown-up children in the large London townhouse where most of the action takes place. His eldest daughter, Elizabeth (Norma Shearer), is an invalid poet confined to an upstairs room, whom he cruelly forces to drink beer for sustenance. Her chances of recovery seem slim until she receives a visit from a fellow poet, Robert Browning (Fredric March), who claims to have fallen in love with her solely through reading her verse. As their love blossoms Elizabeth's health begins to improve and, upon her doctor's recommendation, the couple make plans for a winter trip to Italy to aid her recuperation. Her incestuously possessive father has other ideas and conspires to move his whole family away from London to avoid what he regards as immoral influences, Browning included.

The film's central themes of poetry, illness and the triumph of love over parental repression were an irresistible formula for the young Morrissey. It's also faintly possible that Laughton's embittered cry against his daughter of 'Self! Self! Self!' was the inspiration for the same slogan written on Morrissey's tambourine during his spring 1995 UK tour. He would later reference Elizabeth Barrett Browning (as she called herself after marriage) in his sleeve note for the 2009 reissue of SOUTHPAW GRAMMAR, quoting her most famous line, 'How do I love thee? Let me count the ways' (*Sonnets From The Portuguese*, No. 43, 1850) which, as some critics have pointed out, also shares some similarity with the opening of 'SHOPLIFTERS OF THE WORLD UNITE'.

Curiously, director Sidney Franklin took the unusual step of remaking *The Barretts Of Wimpole Street* two decades later using the exact same script. This second 1957 colour version featured 'RUBBER RING' star John Gielgud as the oppressive Moulton-Barrett. [184, 484]

Bassey, Shirley, Hurricane-voiced Welsh diva, Dame Commander of the British Empire and one of Morrissey's favourite singers.

Born 8 January 1937 in the Tiger Bay area of Cardiff to a Nigerian sailor father and Yorkshire mother, Bassey shares a birthday with Elvis PRESLEY and David BOWIE. Morrissey was still in the womb when she first topped the UK singles charts in February 1959 with 'As I Love You'. Blessed with a preposterous voice that could buckle scaffolding, Bassey's powerhouse renditions of songs from hit musicals such as *Oliver!* ('As Long As He Needs Me') and *The Sound Of Music* ('Climb Ev'ry Mountain', her second number one in November 1961) kept her high in the charts during the early 60s. She entered her theatrical prime with October 1964's 'Goldfinger', the first

of three James Bond themes which stretched the established rules of pop pronunciation to their elastic extremes. With lyrics by Anthony NEWLEY, 'Goldfinger' became Bassey's signature anthem but was only a moderate chart success in its day, peaking at 21, as did 1967's equally camp and adorably rambunctious 'Big Spender'.

Morrissey's own Bassey favourites are typically more obscure. Among his cherished 'Singles to be cremated with' he listed her 1966 debut for United Artists, the marching 'Don't Take The Lovers From The World', which missed the charts completely. Her 1963 version of 'I (Who Have Nothing)' and 1968's histrionic blubfest 'This Is My Life' have also featured in Morrissey's interval music selections, the latter as a stage exit in 2002.

In Smiths/Morrissey history, the most important Bassey record remains her April 1962 Columbia single 'Ave Maria', which stalled at number 31. A restrained (for Bassey) reading of the Catholic prayer set to music by nineteenth-century French composer Charles Gounod, it became Morrissey's regular concert exit music from 1991 until the end of 1992. The record is doubly significant for its B-side, a version of Rodgers and Hammerstein's 'You'll Never Walk Alone', which had previously been used as The Smiths' stage exit music throughout 1986, and again by Morrissey at his solo WOLVERHAMPTON gig in December 1988.

The subject of Bassey (or 'Burly Chassis' as he and others like to call her) has also cropped up in several interviews. In 1987 Morrissey revealed he was currently listening to a tape of hers in his cassette Walkman despite being appalled by her recent collaboration with Swiss electro duo Yello on 'The Rhythm Divine', a track co-written by The Associates' Billy MACKENZIE. 'I'm really, really distressed,' he confessed, 'because I've written to her so many times and sent her tapes and she's never replied. And now she's made a record with Yello!' The following year he was still raving to the press about her talents the day after seeing her perform in concert. 'She was excellent,' he swooned. 'I'd love to meet her. I'd love to touch the end of her dress.' [120, 175, 203, 304]

b

Bastedo, Alexandra, British actress and cover star of The Smiths' posthumous live album RANK. Bastedo is best remembered for playing prim blonde bombshell Sharron Macready in the 1968 action adventure series *The Champions*. Its premise involved three United Nations agents who after crashing a plane in the Himalayas are rescued by a lost Tibetan civilisation who grant them 'fantastic powers' which they then use to combat neo-Nazis, drug trafficking, mad scientists and the like. While it's possible that, aged nine, Morrissey could have been a fan of *The Champions*, the cover of Rank has nothing to do with the series, culled instead from an earlier Bastedo portrait in *Birds Of Britain*, a 1967 photo collection by John D. Green also featuring Sandie SHAW, Cilla BLACK, Marianne FAITHFULL, LULU, Julie Christie, Hayley Mills and Chrissie (sister of Jean) SHRIMPTON.

By the late 80s Bastedo had all but retired from acting, preferring to focus her time on promoting animal welfare. Like Morrissey, Bastedo is passionate about animal rights and runs her own rescue home in West Sussex, the Alexandra Bastedo Champions Animal Sanctuary (www.abcanimal-sanctuary.co.uk). In 2008 Bastedo was coaxed back before the television cameras for a rare cameo in two episodes of the BBC soap EAST-ENDERS. [374]

'Be Young, Be Foolish, Be Happy', One of Morrissey's favourite records, originally a 1968 single by American vocal group The Tams, which reached the lower reaches of the UK top 40 when re-released in March 1970. During The Smiths, he told journalist Nick Kent that the track specifically reminded him of local social clubs in the early 70s. With its stomping northern-soul rhythm and boundless optimism that 'life is too short to worry about unimportant things', the song embodied the polar opposite of Morrissey's hackneyed 'miserable' media stereotype during the 80s. Yet as he explained, it was because the lyrical sentiment seemed so elusive in his own life that he became so besotted with the record. 'It was [some-thing] I never actually felt,' he told Kent, 'but perhaps that's why it attracted me so much.' Morrissey listed it as one of his favourite records several times during The Smiths, though the earliest recorded evidence of his fixation dates back to December 1980. Writing to pen pal Robert MACKIE, he signed off: 'Be young, be foolish, and be happy, Steven.' [139, 184, 334, 408, 423]

Beatles, The, As the most influential group in the history of pop music, even The Smiths owe some debt to Liverpool's 'Fab Four'. Apart from the obvious similarity of being a conspicuously northern guitar-based quartet, the Morrissey/Marr composer credit has frequently been compared with that of the ordinarily sacrosanct Lennon/McCartney.

Though The Beatles are very far from *the* greatest influence upon Morrissey, in 1984 he admitted to being a fan, something he considered 'dramatically unfashionable' at that time. Significantly, The Smiths had used a Lennon/McCartney song – 'Love Of The Loved' by Cilla BLACK – as their stage entrance music when touring the UK to promote their debut album that spring. Years later, Morrissey would also praise parts of 1967's Sgt Pepper's Lonely Hearts Club Band, specifically 'A Day In The Life' and 'Lovely Rita'.

More obviously it's with Johnny Marr, rather than Morrissey, where The Beatles' influence is most apparent in The Smiths. As several critics have noted, Marr's harmonica on 'HAND IN GLOVE' appeared a symbolic acknowledgement of John Lennon's use of the instrument on The Beatles' equivalent 1962 debut single, 'Love Me Do'. Indeed, Marr's knowledge of, and fondness for, The Beatles' back catalogue was evident early on during The Smiths' career. Studio outtakes of the acoustic version of 'JEANE' by Sandie SHAW catch Marr tuning up with 'In My Life' from Rubber Soul; he'd later incorporate snatches of 1965's 'Day Tripper' into live performances of the same song. Lennon's choice of a Gibson J160 acoustic guitar on early Beatles albums was the reason Marr bought the same model in 1984, using his to write 'PLEASE PLEASE PLEASE LET ME GET WHAT I WANT' and 'WILLIAM, IT WAS REALLY NOTHING'. More prominently, Marr cites The Beatles' eponymous album of 1968, alias The White Album, as one of his main muses when writing and recording STRANGEWAYS, HERE WE COME. Most noticeable are the Lennon-ish 'DEATH OF A DISCO DANCER', evoking both the melody of 'Dear Prudence' and the rhythm of 'I'm So Tired', and the McCartney-ish 'UNHAPPY BIRTHDAY', sharing an acoustic flavour with 'Mother Nature's Son' (a phrase Morrissey himself had used in the lyrics of 'PRETTY GIRLS MAKE GRAVES').

Their songwriting aside, Marr especially admired The Beatles for the musicianship of one of his all-time favourite guitar players, George Harrison. 'The great thing about Harrison,' comments Marr, 'is if you watch early clips of The Beatles and the way he used his Gretsch, sometimes in between verses and choruses he's clicking his switches and using different pick-ups to change the sound; using his guitar like an electric machine, which is what it is. Very few people were doing that at the time. He was amazing, particularly what he did with slide and wah-wah.' As evidence of Harrison's effect on Marr, compare the verse riff for 'THE HEADMASTER RITUAL' with that on 1964's 'I Feel Fine'.

The worlds of Beatledom and SMITHDOM very nearly collided in 1985 when Paul McCartney's wife, Linda, was invited to play piano on THE QUEEN IS DEAD track 'FRANKLY, MR SHANKLY', a task she was sadly unable to fulfil. The bloodlines of both groups have since crossed paths thanks to Marr's solo project, The Healers, whose first line-up featured drummer Zak Starkey, son of Ringo Starr. A purely graphic Beatles/Smiths connection is also offered by the sleeve of 1987's THE WORLD WON'T LISTEN compilation featuring the work of German photographer Jürgen Vollmer, famous for chronicling The Beatles' Hamburg period. (See also Linda MCCARTNEY.) [17, 18, 19, 20, 290, 333, 425]

'Bed Took Fire, The' (Morrissey/Street), See 'AT AMBER'.

Bedford, Mark (Morrissey bass player 1989–91), See MADNESS.

Beethoven Was Deaf, Morrissey's first solo live album, released May 1993, highest UK chart position #13. Tracks: 'YOU'RE THE ONE FOR ME, FATTY', 'CERTAIN PEOPLE I KNOW', 'THE NATIONAL FRONT DISCO', 'NOVEMBER SPAWNED A MONSTER', 'SEASICK, YET STILL DOCKED', 'THE LOOP', 'SISTER I'M A POET', 'JACK THE RIPPER', 'SUCH A LITTLE THING

'Because Of My Poor Education' (Morrissey/Whyte), B-side of 'I'M THROWING MY ARMS AROUND PARIS' (2009). The familiar theme of unrequited love is given a new twist as Morrissey blames his heartache on a lack of formal qualifications. The title raises an interesting truth often overlooked by some critics who mistake his bookish intellect for the product of years in dusty academia. As he's always pointed out, his was a basic, and unpleasant, working-class schooling. After leaving the dreaded St Mary's Secondary, subject of 'THE HEADMASTER RITUAL', in the summer of 1976 he attended Stretford Technical School, gaining just three O Level passes in English Literature, Sociology and the General Paper. He failed a fourth subject, History. When interviewed during The Smiths he would play down even these minor achievements, claiming that he only had one O Level 'in Woodwork'. Sadly, 'Because Of My Poor Education' doesn't really address his 'Poor Education', its brief lyrics instead wallowing in obvious metaphors and rhymes reiterating his emotional solitude. Whyte's tune lurches half-heartedly in the shadows of his earlier 'TROUBLE LOVES ME', embellished by the cocktail-lounge frills of Roger Manning Jr, possibly aiming at a luxurious piano ballad in the vein of early BOWIE, or even JOBRIATH, but missing its mark. [362, 469]

MAKES SUCH A BIG DIFFERENCE', 'I KNOW IT'S GONNA HAPPEN SOMEDAY', 'WE'LL LET YOU KNOW', 'SUEDE-HEAD', 'HE KNOWS I'D LOVE TO SEE HIM', 'YOU'RE GONNA NEED SOMEONE ON YOUR SIDE', 'GLAMOROUS GLUE', 'WE HATE IT WHEN OUR FRIENDS BECOME SUCCESSFUL'.

Marking his first decade as a recording artist (released ten years, to the month, since The Smiths' 'HAND IN GLOVE'), Beethoven Was Deaf was Morrissey's only record of 1993, an otherwise fallow year for the singer. Its main purpose was to celebrate his recent return to the stage and a testament to the visceral energy of his new backing band of BOORER, COBRIN, DAY and WHYTE. Subtitled 'Sixteen songs performed live at The Zenith in Paris on 22 December 1992 before 6,500 people', almost half of the tracks were actually taken from the previous night's show at London's Astoria. Though a fine tour souvenir, as an album it lacked the sense of occasion of its live Smiths predecessor, RANK, with far too much emphasis on YOUR ARSENAL (the whole album, bar 'TOMOR-ROW') and scant stage banter. It did, at least, boast a better version of 'Jack The Ripper' than its B-side counterpart, a stirring rockabilly makeover of 'Sister I'm A Poet' and a wonderfully frantic pelt through 'The Loop'.

The title referred to German composer Ludwig Van Beethoven whose unparalleled genius changed the history of music, despite the cursed hearing loss which first manifested in his late twenties; it's been suggested his deafness came with the onset of syphilis though since his medical records were destroyed at the time of his death this is impossible to corroborate for certain. A portrait of the composer by Ferdinand Schimon circa 1818 was used on press adverts for the album. Painted nine years before his death, Schimon caught the 48-year-old Beethoven at the point where he'd become totally deaf after 16 years' slow deterioration in his hearing. The unusual expression in his eyes is a case of too much caffeine in his bloodstream: Schimon recalled how Beethoven sat for the portrait strung out on the intense '60 bean coffee' he revived

himself with every morning. Placed to the right of Morrissey's daft, lolling-tongue portrait on the press advert, Beethoven's caffeine-distracted gaze gave the impression he was looking at the singer with smouldering disdain.

Other than the curiosity of its title, Beethoven Was Deaf was noteworthy for being the last piece of Morrissey vinyl to contain a handwritten message on the record's matrix. His parting words of run-out-groove wisdom: 'Would you risk it for a biscuit?' [353, 374]

Belloc, Hilaire, French-born, English-bred

poet and writer listed among Morrissey's favourite 'symbolists' in 1983. Belloc is best known for the 1907 collection *Cautionary Tales For Children*, a series of surreal and comically macabre verses in which he details the gory fates of, among others, 'Rebecca, Who slammed Doors for Fun and Perished Miserably', 'Henry King, Who chewed bits of String, and was early cut off in Dreadful Agonies' and 'George, Who played with a Dangerous Toy, and suffered a Catastrophe of considerable Dimensions'. Morrissey would quote from *Cautionary Tales* in his early book on James DEAN, 1983's *James Dean Is Not Dead*: 'There was a Boy whose name was Jim; His Friends were very good to him.' Alas, Jim is no more fortunate than Belloc's other children and is eaten by a lion. [184, 279]

'Bengali In Platforms' (Morrissey/ Street),

From the album VIVA HATE (1988). If only by reputation the most controversial lyric Morrissey has ever written, often used as the crux of his detractors' accusations of 'racism'. Their case hinges on the lyric 'life is hard enough when you belong here', addressed to the title Bengali who, as Morrissey portrays it, has gone out of their way to try and ingratiate themselves into Western culture by adopting ill-suited Western fashions. As a fan of Loudon WAINWRIGHT III it's possible Morrissey may have sought some influence in 'East Indian Princess' from Wainwright's third album of 1972, a similar caricature of an

Asian girl whose newly adopted 'English way of life has got that other life beat'. Morrissey still maintained his own words were 'not being deliberately provocative'.

The title dates back to July 1987 when, as 'The Smiths', Morrissey attempted to carry on minus Marr, hiring ex-Easterhouse guitarist Ivor PERRY for an abortive B-sides session at London's Power Plant studios with Andy Rourke and Mike Joyce. The original 'Bengali In Platforms' featured a furious guitar riff, in keeping with Perry's previous Easterhouse material (specifically their fidgety Clash-inspired 1986 single 'Whistling In The Dark') while Morrissey's first draft took pity on a 'misguided Bengali' in a terrible jumper ('A shame it's an old one/Has anyone told him?'), repeating the call to 'shelve your Western plans'.

The reworked Viva Hate version, the first track recorded for the album, featured a much gentler tune by Stephen Street though the lyrical premise was the same. Yet the only contentious word in the song remains 'Bengali' itself. As Morrissey commented, 'There are many people who are so obsessed with racism that one can't mention the word Bengali. It instantly becomes a racist song, even if you're saying, "Bengali, marry me." But I still can't see any silent racism there.' On closer inspection, the song's main subject isn't race but the more traditional Morrissey theme of outsiderdom, its primary concern being the eponymous Bengali's vain efforts to be accepted by the mainstream. The oft-quoted 'life is hard enough when you belong here' merely reiterates the fact that Morrissey, as a member of Britain's indigenous white majority, doesn't belong himself. His message to the badly dressed Bengali, albeit expressed in a way which could be misconstrued as offensive, is simply to celebrate the beauty of their own culture rather than mimic the worst aspects of Britishness. Rightly or wrongly, the lyrical fuss over 'Bengali In Platforms' has detracted from the duller reality that, as a piece of music, it's probably the weakest offering on Viva Hate, otherwise undeserving of any prolonged scrutiny.

[12, 13, 25, 38, 39, 138, 203, 208, 272]

Bennett, Alan, English playwright whose work Morrissey would liken to that of Shelagh DELANEY, describing it as 'very original, very funny, very northern, very deadpan'. Other than influencing Morrissey's own writing, Bennett would also befriend the singer when the two became London neighbours in the early 1990s.

Born in Leeds, Bennett was educated at both Cambridge and Oxford, first making his mark in the 1960 comedy revue *Beyond The Fringe* with Peter Cook, Dudley Moore and Jonathan Miller. His first major stage success came with 1968's *Forty Years On*, starring John Gielgud as the retiring headmaster of an English public school who finds his archaic values mocked in the end-of-term school play. Morrissey would make various references to *Forty Years On* during 1987: the line 'that's what tradition means' in 'I STARTED SOMETHING I COULDN'T FINISH' was taken from the play, as was the run-out-groove message on the 12-inch single of 'GIRLFRIEND IN A COMA', 'and never more shall be so'. The title of VIVA HATE opener 'ALSATIAN COUSIN', written and recorded that same winter, was also adapted from Bennett's joke in the play: 'I was distantly related to the Woolf family through some Alsatian cousins.'

Bennett followed *Forty Years On* with the plays *Getting On* (1971) and the Orton-esque farce *Habeas Corpus* (1973), the latter featuring the line 'you are my quarry', a possible model for the title of Morrissey's 2004 comeback album. But it was Bennett's television work, rather than theatre, which first 'thunderstruck' the young Morrissey. 'I was the dull, fat kid in spectacles sitting in a Manchester council house who caught the first transmissions of his plays in 1978–79,' he explained. 'It was the first time I'd seen what I pitifully considered to be my sense of humour on screen.' Among these were the 1978 LWT productions *Doris And Doreen* (aka *Green Forms*) with its running gag about NEWPORT PAGNELL, and *Me, I'm Afraid Of Virginia Woolf*, a subtle gay love story which contained the line 'Nature has a language, you see, if only we'd learn to read it', a possible inspiration for the similar lyric in The

Smiths' 'ASK'. '[Bennett's] so terribly funny,' said Morrissey, 'that when he writes a line full of biting sadness it cuts through all the more. I also admire the fact that he doesn't seem to envy or even much care for other writers.'

His 1982 BBC series of plays *Objects Of Affection* included two more Morrissey favourites, *Say Something Happened* (a classic turn from Thora Hird as an 'at risk' pensioner who reduces a patronising social worker to tears) and *A Woman Of No Importance*, the first of Bennett's tragi-comic monologues which set the template for his later *Talking Heads*. Borrowing its title from Oscar WILDE, it told the story of Peggy (Patricia Routledge), a desperately boring woman obsessed with the daily ritual of table groupings in the staff canteen ('To add that bit of excitement, I bring along some of my homemade French dressing'). When a colleague makes her late for lunch, she misses her usual seat and the 'nice little routine' of her anodyne existence begins to unravel, taking its toll on her health. Peggy ends the play terminally ill in hospital, a pitiful figure slowly awakening to her meaningless life. Her dying thoughts concern her luck with catching buses. 'I don't think I've ever had to wait more than two minutes for a bus … even when it's been a really spasmodic service.' Also of note are Bennett's award-winning script for 1987's Joe Orton biopic *Prick Up Your Ears* (see also 'DEATH AT ONE'S ELBOW') and his one Oscar nomination to date for 1994's *The Madness Of King George*, adapted from his earlier stage play *The Madness Of George III*.

Morrissey met Bennett after moving to Regents Park Terrace in Camden in the early 90s. Bennett lived in the next street, Gloucester Crescent, where Morrissey's nearest postbox stood directly opposite the playwright's living-room window. As the singer would explain to the press, thereafter he would usually call on Bennett in the afternoons while Bennett would habitually call on him in the evenings. Over cups of tea, common topics of conversation included the day's obituary columns and Jimmy CLITHEROE. Morrissey presented Bennett with a copy of BONA DRAG (which the singer suspected he never played) and tried, in vain, to lure him to the squalid surroundings of The Good Mixer pub, just around the corner on Inverness Street. To Morrissey's chagrin, Bennett briefly considered quoting 'THE HEADMASTER RITUAL' in his 2004 play *The History Boys* only to replace it with another lyric by the Pet Shop Boys.

Bennett was also the first person Morrissey booked for his June 2004 MELTDOWN festival in London. His one-man show, 'An Evening With Alan Bennett', included an audience question-and-answer session during which he admitted that he'd 'read' (rather than listened to) Morrissey's lyrics, turned down a knighthood from THATCHER and was incapable of using a computer. [175, 212, 257, 280, 281, 282, 414, 453]

Best, George,
In Morrissey's estimation 'absolutely indisputably' the greatest footballer who ever lived. He wasn't alone in his opinions of 'The Belfast Boy'. Bob Bishop, the Manchester United scout who discovered the 15-year-old Best in Northern Ireland in 1963, announced his find to manager Matt Busby with the words: 'I think I've found you a genius.' Off pitch, Best would set the career blueprint for celebrity footballers, pitfalls and all, though it's his antics on the turf as a defender-ridiculing wizard which made his legend. Morrissey's irregular visits to Old Trafford as a childhood Manchester United supporter would have coincided with Best's heyday at the club, which ended in 1974. As a 60s pop-culture icon with specific Manchester ties – Best even opened up a couple of nightclubs in the city at his entrepreneurial playboy peak – he was a logical Smiths cover-star choice. Morrissey hoped to feature him on the sleeve of their 1985 single 'THE BOY WITH THE THORN IN HIS SIDE' but Best declined permission; The Smiths' lost opportunity would be recovered by Leeds indie band The Wedding Present who gained consent for his photo to be used on the cover of their 1987 album titled George Best.

After a notorious lifelong battle with drink, Best died in 2005, aged 59. The following year Morrissey paid tribute by, somewhat surprisingly, naming

'Best Friend On The Payroll' (Morrissey/Whyte), From the album SOUTHPAW GRAMMAR (1995). A pithy observation on the perils of mixing business with pleasure, the sitcom-like 'Best Friend On The Payroll' (Steptoe Grammar?) found Morrissey bowing to the demands of a house guest/employee whose days as both are numbered. Southpaw engineer Danton Supple is among those who speculates that the song 'could well be' about photographer Jake WALTERS, Morrissey's personal assistant who lodged with the singer in Camden circa the previous album, VAUXHALL AND I. Whyte's slowly uncoiling melody and Morrissey's prolonged silences sustained great tension between his sporadic outbursts, his head seemingly so buried in the 'Removals' section of *Yellow Pages* he'd forgotten to supply half the lyrics. [4, 40, 221]

Best as one of his all-time heroes (alongside John BETJEMAN) on BBC2's *The Culture Show*. [374, 444]

Betjeman, John, Quintessentially English

twentieth-century poet whom Morrissey has latterly referred to as both his 'hero' and the only writer other than himself whose 'lyrics' he admires. Although it is generally accepted that Betjeman's bomb-beckoning 1937 poem 'Slough' influenced Morrissey's 1988 single 'EVERYDAY IS LIKE SUNDAY', the singer claimed that the similarity was an unconscious one ('That never really occurred to me').

In any case, it wasn't until 1995 that Morrissey first made an explicit reference to Betjeman, naming his recital of 'A Child Ill' from 1974's *Banana Blush* – the first of three albums of poems set to music by Jim Parker – as the song he wanted to be played at his funeral: in 2002, the same track was used as Morrissey's concert entrance music.

It fitted that his affection for the poet should coincide with his move to Betjeman's native north London in the early 90s. Born near Highgate, many of his most celebrated works are nostalgic snapshots of the local landscape and character, be it tram rides to 'Parliament Hill Fields' or the 'Business Girls' of Morrissey's adopted Camden Town. Yet for all Betjeman's trademark humour, caricature and rich wordplay, the key to Morrissey's empathy lies in what *The Oxford Companion To English Literature* neatly summarises as the poet's 'underlying melancholy, the chill of fear, the religion which dwells more on hope than faith'. This is

certainly true of 'A Child Ill', and equally 'On A Portrait Of A Deaf Man', also heard on Banana Blush, in which he imagines the gruesome decay of a friend's corpse while turning to God in disbelief.

A disciple of Oscar WILDE, whom he referenced in several poems, most famously his 'The Arrest Of Oscar Wilde At The Cadogan Hotel', Betjeman (himself bisexual) also enjoyed a correspondence with Wilde's lover, Lord Alfred 'Bosie' Douglas and, like Morrissey, was besotted with *CORONATION STREET*. Knighted in 1969 and appointed Poet Laureate in 1972, Betjeman died at the age of 77 on 19 May 1984, exactly one week before The Smiths released the unrelated if somehow fitting 'HEAVEN KNOWS I'M MISERABLE NOW'.

'Everyday Is Like Sunday' aside, obvious instances of Betjeman's influence in Morrissey's lyrics are few and far between. Certainly, 'THE NEVER-PLAYED SYMPHONIES' resonates with Betjeman's famous quip in one of his last television interviews that his biggest regret in life was not having 'enough sex'; significantly, a 2003 interview with *Word* magazine disclosed the fact that Morrissey listened to tapes of old Betjeman interviews while driving around Los Angeles. Being more speculative, it's possible that Morrissey's description of 'retroussé nose' in 'THE YOUNGEST WAS THE MOST LOVED' was inspired by Betjeman's use of the same in 'The Olympic Girl'. [115, 283, 208, 242, 444, 569]

Beyond Belief, 1967 dramatised account of

the Moors Murders by Welsh actor and playwright Emlyn Williams, listed among Morrissey's favourite books at the outset of The Smiths and the basis of the song 'SUFFER LITTLE CHILDREN'.

Published one year after Ian Brady and Myra Hindley were sentenced to life imprisonment for the murders of ten-year-old Lesley Ann Downey, 12-year-old John Kilbride and 17-year-old Edward Evans, *Beyond Belief* is a semi-fictionalised account of their crimes, based on interviews and court evidence but colouring in the narrative gaps with literary speculation. Williams attempts to explain how Brady, a Glaswegian former Borstal boy obsessed with Hitler and the Marquis de Sade, found an undemanding office job in Manchester where he lured Hindley, an unsophisticated local girl four years his junior, into aiding his atrocities. The book emphasises the human tragedy of their incomprehensible deeds in context of the social climate of early 60s Manchester, detailing the police investigation leading to the discovery of the bodies of Kilbride and Downey, buried on Saddleworth Moor.

Like 'Suffer Little Children', *Beyond Belief* is only concerned with the three murders Brady and Hindley were convicted of. Only 20 years after their sentencing did they confess to the killing of two other children who went missing during the same period from 1963–65, 16-year-old Pauline Read and 12-year-old Keith Bennett, also buried on the moors. The latter's grave has never been found.

The book's influence upon Morrissey's lyrics is obvious. 'Suffer Little Children' is the title of Chapter 20 while another is called 'Hindley Wakes' (a pun on Stanley Houghton's stage play *Hindle Wakes*). Williams also uses the phrases 'find me, find me', 'the grave is on the moors', 'the two were a team', describes Downey's 'white beads', the 'all-pervading smell' of death and includes the Hindley quote 'wherever he has gone, I have gone'. Its mention of 'the devil found work for idle hands' also may have influenced another early Smiths lyric, 'WHAT DIFFERENCE DOES IT MAKE?'

Just as significant is the book's repeated use of the phrase 'the Smiths' in reference to Hindley's younger sister, Maureen, and her husband David Smith, who shopped the couple to the police after

witnessing the Evans murder. The fact that Morrissey had already written 'Suffer Little Children' prior to his first rehearsal with Marr in the summer of 1982 means it is at the very least feasible that the idea to name themselves The Smiths was planted after seeing it in print in *Beyond Belief*. [184, 395]

'Bigmouth Strikes Again' (Morrissey/Marr), The Smiths' tenth single (from the album THE QUEEN IS DEAD), released May 1986, highest UK chart position #26. Cover star: James DEAN.

Morrissey's tongue-in-cheek bid for sainthood, 'Bigmouth Strikes Again', like its predecessor 'THE BOY WITH THE THORN IN HIS SIDE', satirised the singer's treatment by an unforgiving music industry. It seemed apt that, not two years earlier, Morrissey had expressed his willingness to 'be burned at the stake' in defence of The Smiths' debut album. In 'Bigmouth' he realises that macabre fantasy, likening himself to Catholic martyr JOAN OF ARC as he, too, is burned alive by his enemies. As Morrissey noted to the *NME* just a few months prior to the song's composition, 'The press are still not convinced. We're still at the stage where if I rescued a kitten from drowning they'd say, "Morrissey Mauls Kitten's Body". So what can you do?' 'Bigmouth' was his characteristically arch response, its lyrics revelling in the graphic details of his fiery execution – both his Walkman and trademark HEARING AID melting in the inferno – only to end the song literally laughing in the face of his critics.

'Just the title alone was worthy of a single,' says Marr, who remembers it as one of the many song titles Morrissey first showed him written down rather than telling him verbally. Marr had composed the tune during the MEAT IS MURDER tour in March 1985, using soundchecks with Rourke and Joyce to rehearse a basic arrangement centred around his galloping gypsy guitar riff; though their tunes are unalike, Marr once credited the ROLLING STONES' 'Jumpin' Jack Flash' as his symbolic muse for 'Bigmouth'. Singer Kirsty MACCOLL was invited to its initial recording at London's RAK studios to supply backing vocals, though what Marr calls her 'really *weird* harmonies' would later be replaced by the equally strange tones of Morrissey's pseudonymous Ann COATES.

Chosen as the trailer single from The Queen Is Dead – against stiff opposition from what Marr refers to as 'certain quarters' who'd argued instead for 'THERE IS A LIGHT THAT NEVER GOES OUT' – 'Bigmouth' was The Smiths at their most intrepid: a devil's jig of a pop record which opened with talk of bludgeoning and teeth smashing and furthermore dared to place a guitar solo before the first chorus. It's therefore not that surprising that the single failed to return the group to the top 20, much to Morrissey's customary disappointment. Regardless of its chart performance, 'Bigmouth' became a focal point of The Smiths' final tours, its taut tempo showcasing their seldom acknowledged ferocity, as captured on the outstanding encore closing RANK. '"Bigmouth" was one that I particularly loved playing in the car,' recalls Marr. 'When we were travelling up and down between London and Manchester I must have played that song till the tape wore out. Just one of those moments where, when it was done, I thought *this* is why I'm in a band.' [17, 18, 38, 135, 472]

'Billy Budd' (Morrissey/Whyte), From the album VAUXHALL AND I (1994). Taking its title from the 1960 film *Billy Budd* – based upon the posthumously published novella of *Moby Dick* author Herman Melville and, more pertinently, also the screen debut of Terence STAMP – Morrissey uses the term as a playful nickname for a long-standing and long-suffering companion. As he describes, their relationship provokes public ridicule and discrimination, so much so that Morrissey comically volunteers to have his legs amputated as a sacrifice for Billy's freedom.

The elusive nature of the lyrics offers few clues as to the identity of 'Billy Budd' beyond the mention of '12 years on'. Since the song was released in 1994 (though recorded in 1993) the line was interpreted by many as a reference to Johnny Marr whom he 'took up with' 12 years

earlier in 1982. This theory is somewhat compounded by the outrageously spooky coincidence that in 1888 Melville published a collection of poetry titled *John Marr And Other Sailors*. The song also includes what appears to be another fleeting citation from one of Morrissey's favourite sources, Elizabeth SMART's *By Grand Central Station I Sat Down And Wept* ('[they intercepted our glances because of] what was in our eyes') as well as a few short lines which collectively resonate with 'Turn Out The Light' by Joan ARMATRADING (see entry). The closing audio sample, 'Don't leave us in the dark,' was culled from the 1948 David Lean adaptation of OLIVER TWIST as spoken by a young Anthony NEWLEY.

With its buoyant rhythm and punk-pop hook, Whyte's 'Billy Budd' retained the rocking gusto of YOUR ARSENAL though its production was much more subtle. An early favourite during the rehearsal stages and earmarked as a possible single, according to engineer Chris Dickie it was the first track recorded for Vauxhall prior to the arrival of producer Steve LILLYWHITE before the session properly got underway. The track's full muscle was better flexed in concert, in particular as the mike-cable-lashing set opener of Morrissey's February 1995 UK tour, as seen on the *INTRODUCING MORRISSEY* video. [4, 6, 375, 537]

Billy Liar, 1963 British kitchen-sink comedy drama listed among Morrissey's favourite films and an explicit influence on his lyrics during The Smiths. Based upon the book by Keith Waterhouse (and the play by Waterhouse and Willis Hall), the plot follows 24 hours in the life of young Billy Fisher (the superb Tom Courtenay), a disillusioned undertaker's clerk still living with his parents and grandmother in a grim northern town for whom fibbing and fantasy is a form of Tourette's. With two fiancées on the go (the brassy Rita and the infuriatingly prim Barbara) and his boss awakening to his embezzlement of petty cash, Fisher's lies are fast catching up with him. Rather than face them, he disappears into daydreams of ruling the make-believe military

state of Ambrosia, fooling himself that he'll write a best-selling novel ('*Idle Jack*') and telling everyone he's leaving town to work down south as a scriptwriter for the popular television comedian Danny Boon. A chance to escape arrives in the form of the beautiful and free-spirited Liz (Julie Christie), a recently returned old flame who convinces Billy to flee his miserable life by joining her on the midnight train to London. Pitifully, moments before their train is about to pull away from the station, Billy loses his nerve and disembarks, unable to leave the town that suppresses him and the solitary fantasies of Ambrosia that keep him there.

Directed by John Schlesinger (his second feature film after *A KIND OF LOVING*), although *Billy Liar* is a fantastic comedy, the heart of the story is a much more depressing satire on the fear and resentment towards working-class ambition. The film's reverberations within the songs of The Smiths are numerous. Billy's engagement dilemmas to Rita and Barbara and his hatred of his surroundings are mirrored exactly in the narrative of 'WILLIAM, IT WAS REALLY NOTHING', just as the final train station scene is evoked by that of 'LONDON' while 'FRANKLY, MR SHANKLY' is easily comparable with Billy's resignation speech to Mr Shadrach (the estimable Leonard Rossiter). Stray lines of dialogue also seem conspicuously similar; Billy's ploy to molest Barbara by suggesting they 'go for a walk where it's quiet' ('THE QUEEN IS DEAD') and his fantasy burial speech for his grandmother who 'struggled valiantly to combat ignorance and disease' ('VICAR IN A TUTU'). It's also reasonable to assume that the title of STRANGEWAYS, HERE WE COME was modelled upon the drunken remark by Billy's enemy, Stamp, during the climax in the train station café – 'Borstal, here we come!' [227, 485]

birthday, Morrissey was born in Park Hospital, Davyhulme, Manchester on 22 May 1959. A 'loving and giving' Friday's child, his birth coincided with the local Whit Walks festivities, one of the lead stories in that day's edition of the *Manchester Evening News*. The Apostolic

Bindon, John, London actor and criminal whom Morrissey paid tribute to in the liner of MALADJUSTED ('John Bindon 1943–1993'). Bindon's first screen role was in one of Morrissey's favourite films, 1967's POOR COW directed by Ken Loach. As a known jailbird with an inside knowledge of west London, he was originally hired through writer Nell Dunn as a location scout to find authentic Wandsworth slums before being cast as Tom, the robber husband of Carole White's main character. 'He had a colourful past,' said Loach of Bindon. 'He was a great character and we saw the attractive side of his personality. He was very funny and told us all these tales, so I relied on him for the verisimilitude of some of the scenes.' Typecast by his real-life villainy, Bindon played similar thugs in *Performance* (1970) and *Get Carter* (1971). His greatest claim to fame was working with Stanley Kubrick in a blink-and-miss cameo as a recruiting sergeant in 1975's *Barry Lyndon*. Bindon's last notable role was as a drug dealer in *Quadrophenia*, released in 1979 following his arrest for the murder of south London gangster Johnny Darke. Though he was acquitted, the trial finished Bindon's career as an actor. Years of promiscuity (he was a lover of David BOWIE's wife, Angie) and hardcore drug abuse finally caught up with Bindon in 1993 when he died of AIDS just six days after his 50th birthday.

One of the more bizarre twists to Bindon's life story was his friendship in the early 70s with future Smiths producer John PORTER, then working with ROXY MUSIC. According to Porter, Bindon would use his home as a bolthole to get away from his criminal circles, where he'd smoke pot, play Scrabble, discuss Evelyn Waugh and listen to Hank Williams. [27, 294, 314, 542]

Delegate to Great Britain, Archbishop Gerald Patrick O'Hara, and the Bishop of Salford toured the city centre, during which in all the heat and excitement – temperatures reached a scorching 70 Fahrenheit that weekend – a Polish woman from Stockport had to be restrained by police for rushing the Archbishop, whom she mistook for a famous Polish cardinal. In other local news, the wife of a Salford chauffeur gassed herself while an '"Impulsive" Woman' from Macclesfield was charged with thieving a pint of milk from a neighbour's doorstep. Elsewhere in the world the 'Big Four' foreign ministers were fighting to avoid 'The Big Flop' as talks broke down in Geneva while James DEAN-obsessed American mass murderer Charles Starkweather, sentenced to death, had been granted a temporary reprieve in Nebraska State Prison.

In the previous day's paper, astrologer Carroll Righter had this advice for those such as Mrs Morrissey who'd give birth on the 22nd: 'A lot of discipline will be needed early in life if this child is to be happy and successful. There will be a strong tendency to give up whenever events get too difficult – so parents should try and impart a determination to finish the job in hand. A great deal of personal charm will be in evidence.'

Like strange, coded nativity signals, there were plenty of omens in the city that day that Morrissey had arrived. Currently playing at the Ardwick ABC Apollo cinema – the building where Morrissey and Marr would first meet in 19 years' time – was the John MILLS thriller *Tiger Bay*, as later mentioned in the singer's correspondence with Scottish pen pal Robert MACKIE. The Crescent cinema in Hulme, where Morrissey's family presently lived, was screening a Western titled *The Tall Stranger*. At The Essoldo in Stretford, where he'd spend most of his youth, the bill included *The Lonely House*. And in racing, the winner of that day's 2.30 from Manchester was called – but of course – 'Star Minstrel'.

As a Catholic child, Morrissey may at some point have been alerted to the fact 22 May is the feast day of numerous martyrs: the African Saints Castus and Emilius, burned to death in the third century; Saint Fulk, canonised for his selfless assistance of plague sufferers; the Italian hermits Saint Romanus and Saint Humility; Saint Julia of Corsica who was crucified circa 616 AD after having all her hair yanked out by pagans; the Italian nun Saint Rita whose forehead one day erupted in an inexplicable stigmata wound while praying before a statue of Christ; and the altogether extraordinary French Saint Quiteria who after being beheaded by the Romans stood up, plonked her head back on her shoulders and staggered up a hill to the spot where she wanted to be buried; her equally remarkable sister, Euphemia, jumped off a cliff to avoid capture only to be swallowed by a rock which promptly turned into a hot spring.

Black Box, See 'RIDE ON TIME'.

Black, Cilla, Carrot-topped Scouser, born Priscilla White, who carved a highly lucrative UK pop career during the 1960s before moving into light entertainment television. Although Morrissey's fascination with 60s pop and female singers in particular was a major part of The Smiths' cultural armoury, her reincarnation as the irksome presenter of ITV's *Surprise, Surprise* and *Blind Date* – both primetime ratings winners during the group's existence – made his admiration for Cilla Black more difficult for their audience to swallow. As a consequence, even he referred to his love of her early records as one of his 'uncommon perversions'.

Along with Sandie SHAW and Billy FURY, Morrissey named Cilla as one of the first singers he was ever aware of as a child. She released her debut single, October 1963's brassy 'Love Of The Loved', when he was only four. Written by Lennon and McCartney, who'd helped 'discover' her at Liverpool's Cavern club, thus bringing her to the attention of manager Brian Epstein and landing her a deal with EMI, the song later became The Smiths' stage entrance theme on their spring 1984 UK tour promoting their debut album. Surprisingly, despite its BEATLES connections, 'Love Of The Loved' wasn't a hit, only reaching number 35, though its follow-up offered ample compensation. A screechy take on the Bacharach/David ballad 'Anyone Who Had A Heart', it shamelessly gazumped Dionne Warwick's original in February 1964 to land Cilla her first UK number one. She scored a second with her next warbler, 'You're My World' (May 1964), which even made it on to the hallowed home jukebox of Elvis PRESLEY.

Unhindered by the coarseness of her foghorn delivery, Cilla managed to outsell every other British female singer that decade. 'Black mocked her huge nose so often that the self-abasement was refreshing,' commented Morrissey. 'No, she didn't have the beauty, but so what? She would make it anyway.' Discounting January 1965's hasty, if not heinous, rival version of THE RIGHTEOUS BROTHERS' 'You've Lost That Lovin' Feelin'' (which somehow reached number two before being trounced, quite righteously, by the original) and March 1966's blood-curdling 'Alfie', Cilla recorded some exceptional singles during her first four years on PARLOPHONE; specifically Lennon and McCartney's emotionally bleak jazz-waltz 'It's For You' (number seven, September 1964), Randy Newman's gorgeously glum 'I've Been Wrong Before' (number 17, May 1965), and her plaster-cracking Mozzerian masterpiece, 'Love's Just A Broken Heart' (number five, February 1966).

Morrissey's own Cilla favourite was the forlorn, peculiar pop-waltz 'The Right One Is Left' (B-side of 'Don't Answer Me', number six, June 1966), featured in several lists of his favourite songs during the early days of The Smiths. Notoriously, it was his dogged decision that The Smiths cover another Cilla B-side, 1968's 'WORK IS A FOUR-LETTER WORD', which added to the friction between himself and Marr during the group's final recording session of May 1987, hastening their break-up. [172, 184, 188, 267, 334, 457]

'Black-Eyed Susan' (Morrissey/Whyte), B-side of 'SUNNY' (1995).

An early outtake from the 1993 VAUXHALL AND I sessions, Morrissey's ode to a lazy female took its title from a popular nineteenth-century nautical melodrama, first staged in 1829 by Douglas William Jerrold and later a Victorian 'juvenile drama' (toy theatre) favourite. The lyrics – which have nothing to do with Jerrold's play about a seaman's wife preyed upon by a lecherous uncle during her husband's absence – marked his first citation of Gore Vidal's quote of being a 'born-again atheist', a phrase he'd use again on the later 'NOBODY LOVES US'. Random speculation that the eponymous Susan may be a veiled dig at Siouxsie SIOUX after their 'INTERLUDE' duet is mistaken since it was written and recorded before they met.

Originally, the song also contained an extra verse describing Susan's 'hair like seaweed' and her 'air wear cherry blossom dark tan', though this was lost when Morrissey chose to make dramatic alterations to Whyte's cheerily pleasant

'Black Cloud' (Morrissey/Boorer), From the album YEARS OF REFUSAL (2009).

Perhaps the least engaging track on Refusal, other than the mystery surrounding the identity of Morrissey's figurative 'Black Cloud' this was an undemanding flush of unrequited love nailed to an equally uncomplicated scrap-metal-guitar thump harking back to SOUTHPAW GRAMMAR. Its most intriguing lyric was his admission of favouritism, choosing to 'please' or 'freeze out' his unobtainable love as his mood suited, a trait which certainly tallies with recurring accounts of Morrissey's hot-and-cold behaviour from ex-band members and managers. Yet musically 'Black Cloud' never fulfils the promise of its overcast intro of brooding strings and a child's fragile voice asking 'can you see the black cloud?', the mood obliterated all too soon by its temperate rock din. Stranger still is the presence of guitar legend Jeff Beck on the track: for such an esteemed guest his merry noodling is barely audible.

tune. 'It was much rockier to start off with,' says bassist Jonny BRIDGWOOD, 'more like something from YOUR ARSENAL but then Morrissey decided he didn't like it. He said he wanted "something weird" in the middle so that third verse was cut out and instead we all went in and improvised "something weird" as instructed. I thought it was a bit of a shame because it was fine to begin with.' This new 'Black-Eyed Susan' dominated by its long mid-section of experimental nonsense was shelved indefinitely for two years before finally being rescued as one of Morrissey's stranger B-sides. [4, 6]

Bogarde, Dirk, Dashing and distinguished
British actor whom Morrissey named in 1995 as the person he'd most like to meet. Sadly, Bogarde died four years later before he had the chance, though Morrissey did at least receive a card from his hero circa 1994. 'I almost cried with joy when it arrived,' he confessed, further raving, 'I now feel I *could* live and be Dirk Bogarde.'

Born in London in 1921 as Derek Van den Bogaerde – his father was Dutch – he first considered using the stage name Simon Garde but was talked out of it by his agent who told him Simon was 'a wet name' and that 'there has never been a star called Simon anything' (how depressingly true). As Dirk Bogarde he joined the RANK Organisation in 1947 after serving as an officer in the Second World War where he witnessed the horrors of the holocaust first hand as part of the allied forces who liberated Belsen concentration camp. His breakthrough performance came as the snivelling 'bastard that shot George Dixon' in 1950's *The Blue Lamp*, a film Morrissey sampled on his version of 'MOONRIVER' and which he planned to incorporate into a proposed video for his 1994 single 'HOLD ON TO YOUR FRIENDS' until Bogarde mysteriously refused permission.

The success of *The Blue Lamp* saw Bogarde typecast as similar fugitive types, his favourite being 1952's superior Rank thriller *Hunted*, before securing his matinee idol status with 1954's *Doctor In The House*, the first of four comedies in

which he played the slightly dim Dr Simon Sparrow. By 1960, Bogarde had starred in over 30 films but admitted that he only cared for, at most, half a dozen of them. In a deliberate effort to turn his career around, he accepted the role of the homosexual barrister in the controversial drama *VICTIM*, a part which numerous other leads, including James Mason, had nervously declined. Bogarde later described it as 'the wisest decision I made in my cinematic life'. The critics applauded his courage. 'He risks curdling the adoration of his fans,' wrote the *Evening Standard*'s Alexander Walker, 'but I predict that this brave, sensitive picture of an unhappy, terribly bewildered man will win him and this film a far wider audience.' It was especially brave since Bogarde himself was a closet homosexual and would remain so for the rest of his life.

Victim, one of Morrissey's favourite Bogarde films, was but a taster for far greater art-house roles to come throughout the 60s and 70s, from Joseph Losey's *THE SERVANT* to John Schlesinger's *Darling* and his two films for Italian director LUCHINO VISCONTI, 1969's *The Damned* and 1971's stunning *Death In Venice* in which, according to one critic, he gave 'the performance of his life' as the dying composer Gustav von Aschenbach tormented by desire for an unobtainable teenage boy.

Other than acting, Bogarde was also the author of several novels and many volumes of autobiography, a skilled artist, a keen poet and even dabbled in pop music with his 1960 DECCA album Lyrics For Lovers in which he didn't actually sing but camply recited a dozen standards by the likes of Cole Porter and George Gershwin. His filmography intertwines with that of many other Morrissey favourites: Patric DOONAN (*The Blue Lamp*), Brigitte BARDOT (*Doctor At Sea*), John MILLS (*The Gentle Gunman, The Singer Not The Song, Oh! What A Lovely War*), Stanley BAKER (*Accident*) and even George FORMBY (his first uncredited screen appearance was an extra in 1939's *Come On George!*). Equally coincidentally, he also bought a house in France from the actress YVONNE MITCHELL whom he'd once sent a fan letter.

When Morrissey fantasised about being Bogarde in the mid-90s, he imagined he 'could live in a mansion flat in Chelsea and see nobody, which would be a perfect life'. It was in such a Chelsea flat that Bogarde passed away at the age of 78 on 8 May 1999 having suffered a stroke many years previously. [114, 286, 382, 486, 550, 559, 569]

Bolan, Marc, Bleating, bopping T.Rex main man and the original British glam rock star who had a profound impact on both Morrissey and Marr in the early 1970s. The first record the eight-year-old Marr bought was a copy of T.Rex's November 1971 single 'Jeepster' while the following summer, the just-turned-13-year-old Morrissey witnessed T.Rex in the flesh at Manchester's Belle Vue arena: his first pop concert.

The date was Friday 16 June 1972. Adding to the sense of occasion, that week Bolan was enjoying his fourth week at number one with 'Metal Guru' – T.Rex's fourth and final UK chart topper which would later provide a musical foundation for The Smiths' 'PANIC'. While the newly teenaged Morrissey was deliberating on what to wear to see T.Rex – he'd settle on a purple satin jacket – Marr was still recovering from the shock of seeing Bolan play his latest hit on TOP OF THE POPS a few weeks earlier, an experience which famously caused him to ride his bicycle immediately afterwards in a state of supreme hysteria for several miles before realising he was lost. The next day he and a friend would steal glitter to put on their faces in homage.

Morrissey's life was about to be similarly changed as his father dropped him off outside the venue. 'I think he thought I'd be killed and he waved me off like it was the last time he'd ever see me alive,' Morrissey recalled. 'It must have been like losing your child to a deadly cult and maybe that's exactly how it was … it was the turning of at least eight corners.' That summer Bolan was in the prime of 'T.Rextasy', an equivalent nation-sweeping Beatlemania which the young Morrissey, stood there alone, witnessed first hand. He'd recall not being able to hear a note of music above the screams of fainting Bolan apostles. 'It was incredible, because people literally were breaking their necks against the stage. Really extreme. And a memory to cherish.'[1] By the time his father picked him up afterwards, young Steven was a different son to the one he'd dropped off hours earlier. The metal guru had spoken: his adulatory gospel was now Morrissey's to follow.

For Bolan, still only 24, that adulatory success had been anything but overnight. He was born Mark Feld in Hackney, north-east London, on 30 September 1947: James DEAN died on his eighth birthday. Coming of age during the late 50s rock and roll boom, his career began in the mid-60s, making erratic and faddish moves from Dylanish folk to mod pop and psychedelic R&B with the group John's Children (who would reform decades later with Bolan obsessive Boz BOORER on guitar). In 1968, Bolan teamed up with bongo player Steve Peregrin Took to form the hippy folk-rock duo Tyrannosaurus Rex. Endorsed by DJ John PEEL, they'd be steered to their destiny by producer TONY VISCONTI over four transitional albums between July 1968 and March 1970. By the fourth, A Beard Of Stars, Took had been replaced by Mickey Finn while their early folk-rock axis had now tipped heavily in the latter's favour as Bolan became increasingly electrified in every sense of the word.

In December 1970 an eponymous fifth album announced the new abbreviated name of T.Rex. It was preceded by the single 'Ride A White Swan', the first to establish the defining texture of glam rock, its riff shamelessly stolen by Alain WHYTE as the basis for Morrissey's 'CERTAIN PEOPLE I KNOW'. By January 1971, only the insurmountable geriatric bone rattle of Clive Dunn could stop it from reaching number one. The golden age of T.Rextasy had begun and would last another two and a half years with another ten consecutive top ten hits including the immaculate number one quartet of 'Hot Love' (March 1971), 'Get It On' (July 1971), 'Telegram Sam' (February 1972) and what Morrissey called Bolan's 'moment of complete perfection', 'Metal Guru' (May 1972).

The same era witnessed the number one album Electric Warrior (September 1971), featuring the original 'COSMIC DANCER', as later covered by Morrissey.

Though it was Bolan in all his glitter-cheeked, corkscrew-haired, feather-boaed finery which first snared Morrissey, his favourite records are predominantly those from the pre-T.Rextasy era which he rediscovered thereafter; in particular the first two Tyrannosaurus Rex albums of 1968 – their preposterously titled debut My People Were Fair And Had Sky In Their Hair … But Now They're Content To Wear Stars On Their Brows, and the comparatively subdued Prophets, Seers And Sages, The Angel Of The Ages – along with 1970's T.Rex. That he should specify the latter is especially interesting in view of 'The Visit' with its typical Bolan bleat of 'truly I do love you', highly reminiscent of Morrissey's equivalent holler in 'LATE NIGHT, MAUDLIN STREET'. When selecting a Bolan track for his 2003 UNDER THE INFLUENCE compilation, he also plumped for Tyrannosaurus Rex, choosing the joss-stick fog of 'Great Horse' from A Beard Of Stars.

Bolan's heyday was already behind him when Morrissey approached his idol for an autograph circa 1975. The metal guru refused. This isn't so surprising given the accounts of Bolan, the man, as documented by the likes of Tony Visconti. All evidence paints a vulgar picture of a tyrannical egomaniac whose grip on reality was slackened by booze, cocaine and a unique inability not to recognise how stagnant his art had become. By 1974, Bolan was becoming embarrassingly derivative not only of himself, but of his arch rival David BOWIE. A whole 18 months after Ziggy Stardust And The Spiders From Mars, Bolan delivered the transparent riposte Zinc Alloy And The Hidden Riders Of Tomorrow; except being Bolan he couldn't stop there, adding the futile subtitle A Creamed Cage In August. The same album would be his last produced by the now exasperated Visconti. In his 2007 autobiography Bowie, Bolan And The Brooklyn Boy, Visconti confessed: 'After all these years I am finally able to let go of the

anger I've harboured due to the way [Marc] mistreated his band and myself – which grew worse during the decline of his popularity.'

Morrissey would concur that 'the speed of his decay' still amazed him, though it is too sweeping (and sadly too common) a generalisation to write off everything Bolan recorded post-1973. Rake through the glam compost of Zinc Alloy, Bolan's Zip Gun, Futuristic Dragon and his last, 1977's Dandy In The Underworld, and there are still some diamonds to be found amid the silt of old ideas boiled dry.

Within six months of the latter's release, Bolan was dead in a car crash. He was the passenger in a Mini driven by Gloria Jones which made a fatal collision with a sycamore tree in Barnes, south London, on 16 September 1977, one month to the day after Elvis PRESLEY died. Bolan's death, however tragic, offered him the very thing he'd been chasing for the last four years but was never likely to recover; it's a grim reminder of the extent of his commercial slump that one month before the crash he released the single 'Celebrate Summer' which never even charted. Dancing himself into the tomb aged 29, he now took a permanent place among rock and roll's martyred elite.

When forming The Smiths, their childhood love of Bolan was another reinforcing strut in the foundations of Morrissey's friendship with Marr. The singer would later recount a supernatural Bolan experience after the group's Brixton Academy show in October 1986. As he was being hustled out of the venue, he suddenly noticed a huge Bolan poster in the backstage area. 'His eyes were staring straight at me,' said Morrissey. 'He was looking directly at me, and for me it was a very strange mystical moment. It was like as if he was almost staring at me. It was like a shiver down the spine.'

The glittery ghost of Marc Bolan continues to haunt Morrissey's career, from 'Cosmic Dancer' and 'Certain People I Know' (including its promo single with a tribute 'MOZ' T.Rex sleeve designed by Linder STERLING) to his foreword for the 1992 Bolan biography Wilderness Of The Mind and his

own work with Visconti. 'I can't cleverly theorise about Marc,' gushed Morrissey. 'I just loved him.'
[20, 139, 168, 290, 389, 394, 422, 428, 569]

---

1. Morrissey's recollections of the concert were not as exaggerated as they may sound. Nick Logan reported on the show in the following week's NME, describing how the crowd, 'most of them ordinary enough kids', merged into a human pyramid surging towards the stage 'tumbling forward like a Kop terrace – ribbons of people, wilting, waving – as each twist of Bolan's face or body brings on a further burst of hysteria'. According to Logan one man broke his jaw while afterwards the concert hall 'resembled a battlefield'. The gig also made the lead letter in the following week's edition of *Sounds*. 'I was appalled at the conduct of the people at the T.Rex concert at Belle Vue, Manchester,' complained Gorton's Beverley Smith. 'How can they call themselves fans when all they did was scream and fight to get near the band?'

Bona Drag, Morrissey's first solo compilation album, released October 1990, highest UK chart position #9. Tracks: 'PICCADILLY PALARE', 'INTERESTING DRUG', 'NOVEMBER SPAWNED A MONSTER', 'WILL NEVER MARRY', 'SUCH A LITTLE THING MAKES SUCH A BIG DIFFERENCE', 'THE LAST OF THE FAMOUS INTERNATIONAL PLAYBOYS', 'OUIJA BOARD, OUIJA BOARD', 'HAIRDRESSER ON FIRE', 'EVERYDAY IS LIKE SUNDAY', 'HE KNOWS I'D LOVE TO SEE HIM', 'YES, I AM BLIND', 'LUCKY LISP', 'SUEDEHEAD', 'DISAPPOINTED'.

The first 18 months of Morrissey's solo career had been nothing short of triumphant: four consecutive top ten singles, a number one album and his rapturously received return to the stage in WOLVERHAMPTON. But by the summer of 1989, the honeymoon was over. Stephen STREET, Mike Joyce and Craig GANNON had all deserted him over separate financial disputes. Morrissey now faced the 1990s without a songwriting partner, band or producer. Street's departure left Morrissey especially vulnerable, though in the short term the singer persevered, recording Street's 'Ouija Board, Ouija Board' without him. The relative success of that session, prior to its critical mauling, offered some encouragement as to Morrissey's immediate future. His best, if not only, available option was to simultaneously employ a multitude of co-writers and trusted session musicians, leaving the rest to 'Ouija Board' producers Clive LANGER and Alan Winstanley.

So commenced what Morrissey intended to be his second solo album. The assembled band comprised VIVA HATE drummer Andrew PARESI (back in the fold after briefly being replaced by Joyce), guitarist Kevin ARMSTRONG (who'd proven his worth on the 'Ouija Board' session and was now suggesting musical ideas), and ex-Smiths bassist Andy ROURKE, who unlike Joyce and Gannon had resolved his financial quarrel with Morrissey out of court and was now in the running as potential co-writer. Adding to the song pool, Langer was also invited to submit demos.

Recording commenced in the winter of 1989 at Hook End Manor where Morrissey had already taken to its historic charm during the brief 'Ouija Board' session. 'The environment made him feel more confident,' says Paresi. 'Initially, all the signs were there that it was going to be great.' With scant pre-planning, the album took shape as Morrissey showed little favouritism in choosing almost equal shares from the demos of Langer, Armstrong and Rourke. He'd also settled on a title, Bona Drag, a nod to the Julian and Sandy 60s radio sketches which likewise inspired two of its scheduled tracks, 'Piccadilly Palare' and 'STRIPTEASE WITH A DIFFERENCE'. In palare slang, 'bona drag' literally means 'good clothes'. (See also CARRY ON IV) WILLIAMS.)

It was only with the November release of 'Ouija Board' – his first solo single not to reach the UK top ten, panned by critics – that Morrissey's confidence suffered a hammer blow. 'The "Ouija Board" press wounded him terribly,' confirms Armstrong. 'That's why Bona Drag was never finished. He was extremely depressed. He spent an inordinate amount of time locked away in his room.' As progress ground to a halt while Morrissey consoled himself, his band made do with bowling trips to nearby Reading enlivened by Rourke's supply of amyl nitrate. 'We spent an album's worth of time and money,' says Winstanley, 'but by the end of it we just didn't have an album's worth of material.' Of the seven tracks completed, five were spread across the next two singles and their B-sides ('November Spawned A Monster' and 'Piccadilly Palare') while 'Striptease' and Armstrong's 'OH PHONEY' were shelved indefinitely.

Instead, Bona Drag appeared later than planned as an interim compilation, rounding up Morrissey's first seven solo singles and, more or less, one B-side apiece. 'It was initially for the rest of the world,' claimed Morrissey, 'but EMI were determined to release it here.' It proved to be a shrewd gambit, well received by most critics and an impressive testament to the musical scope and lyrical breadth of Morrissey's first three years as a solo artist. In terms of songwriting, Bona Drag was an even stronger collection than Viva Hate (albeit duplicating 'Suedehead'[1] and 'Everyday Is Like Sunday'), skilfully sequenced and even granting the unfairly derided 'Ouija Board' a fresh context worthy of reassessment. The album also helped rescue quality material such as 'Hairdresser On Fire' and 'Will Never Marry' from mere B-side status, allowing them a more prominent place in Morrissey's discography.

Such was its cumulative impact, Bona Drag augured well for Morrissey as a 90s recording artist, a position he himself regarded as 'one of the most challenging and interesting things that's ever happened to British pop music'. As Bona Drag hit the shelves he was already ploughing ahead, recording his proper second album, KILL UNCLE: the early 90s were, indeed, about to be more 'challenging' than Morrissey could have dared imagine. [1, 15, 25, 29, 70, 138]

---

1. The repetition of 'Suedehead' on Viva Hate and Bona Drag inspired an amusing debate between American singer Ryan Adams and guitarist/backing singer David Rawlings. Their disagreement was caught on tape and used as the opening track of Adams's 2000 solo debut album Heartbreaker, listed as 'Argument With David Rawlings Concerning Morrissey'.

Boorer, Boz (Morrissey guitarist and co-writer, 1990–),
No musician has served Morrissey longer, or more loyally, than Martin James Boorer. Though his co-writing credits are fewer than those of Alain WHYTE, as musical director and technical adviser Boorer is the linchpin of Morrissey's band.

Born in Edgware, Middlesex in 1962, Boorer shared Morrissey's boyhood love of Marc BOLAN, buying T.Rex's 'Get It On' when he was nine. His gift for music was apparent from an early age, already competent on recorder and clarinet before learning guitar from the age of 12. The nickname 'Boz' – nothing to do with the writing pseudonym of the young Charles DICKENS – was coined at school, shortened from 'Bozzy Boy'.[1] He was only 15 when he formed his first group, The Cult Heroes. Heavily influenced by 50s rockabilly but sounding 'too punk', they changed their name to The Polecats, eventually signing with Mercury Records to lead the early 80s British rockabilly revival.

While Morrissey was still clawing at the walls of his Stretford bedroom in 1981, Boorer, three years his junior, was already in the top 40 making records with TONY VISCONTI (producer of The Polecats' cover of Bolan's 'Jeepster'). Boorer's group didn't escape Morrissey's attention, nor his frustrated wrath. Irked by their cover of BOWIE's 'John, I'm Only Dancing' (number 35, April 1981), he told pen pal Robert MACKIE 'if they REALLY had any imagination they'd shoot themselves'. How very differently his own life may have panned out if they had.

Morrissey first met Boorer in the winter of 1990 when planning his aborted 'rockabilly mini-album' having just finished KILL UNCLE. 'I brought Boz and Morrissey together,' explains mutual friend Cathal SMYTH. 'Clive [LANGER] told me Morrissey wanted to put a rockabilly band together so asked me as the only person he knew who was into rockabilly. I told him, "I'm not the man for the job. That man is Boz." Which changed Boz's life.'

Boorer's first session with Morrissey was in December 1990 for 'PREGNANT FOR THE LAST TIME', invited as a guest to add some 50s guitar licks alongside those of writer Mark NEVIN.[2] It was purely by default that Boorer later became Morrissey's permanent guitarist when Nevin proved unavailable to undertake 1991's KILL UNCLE tour. Of the four young rockabilly musicians recruited, Boorer was the oldest and most experienced; not quite 29 but with nearly 14 years of touring and recording under his belt. As Smyth attests, 'Boz is a concerned, hard-working and talented bloke.'

In concert, Boorer's well-practised rockabilly poses, sprints and duck-walks brought a vim and vigour to the Kill Uncle tour, as captured on the LIVE IN DALLAS video. As a co-writer, Boorer was dormant for his first Morrissey album, 1992's YOUR ARSENAL, making his composer debut with the two B-sides to its final single, 'CERTAIN PEOPLE I KNOW', among them the brooding 'JACK THE RIPPER'.

He fully came into his own on VAUXHALL AND I, supplying its pivotal bookends 'NOW MY HEART IS FULL' and 'SPEEDWAY', and the hit single 'THE MORE YOU IGNORE ME, THE CLOSER I GET'.

Stylistically, Boorer's melodies often have an ominous, dramatic quality, exemplified by 'Jack The Ripper' and 'Speedway', though like Whyte he's not averse to sentimentality, be it 'Now My Heart Is Full' or the later 'COME BACK TO CAMDEN'. Morrissey himself distinguishes Boorer's work from Whyte's as being more 'drawn to pulsating rhythms', which is certainly true of the singles 'SATAN REJECTED MY SOUL' and 'THAT'S HOW PEOPLE GROW UP'. In 2006, the singer named 'READER MEET AUTHOR' as 'the best of Boz' to date.

As is standard Morrissey procedure, Boorer's songs are chosen from a wealth of instrumental demos, the tune sometimes modified upon the singer's instruction but often left at the same arrangement. Cathal Smyth speculates that 'Boz writes what he feels is wanted rather than totally original creativity', which may be true but probably also applies to all of Morrissey's co-writers post-Nevin. Boorer himself has described how he tries 'not to stress any strong melodies' in the demos he supplies. Nevertheless, Boorer's designs are sometimes more experimental than his detractors allow. The atmosphere captured on his original 'Now My Heart Is Full' demo was so difficult to re-create, even for an experienced producer like Steve LILLYWHITE, that it had to be sampled on the finished recording. Arguably Boorer's most ambitious submission to date is 'THE TEACHERS ARE AFRAID OF THE PUPILS', built upon a hip hop drum loop and a sample of Shostakovich's Fifth Symphony.

Fellow musicians including bassist Jonny BRIDGWOOD and drummer Spencer COBRIN have admitted that a perhaps inevitable rivalry between Boorer and Whyte has surfaced in the past, though Morrissey vehemently refutes any suggestion of favouritism. As yet, Boorer has never written as much as half of any Morrissey album, though his presence is felt most keenly on Vauxhall And I, YOU ARE THE QUARRY and YEARS OF REFUSAL. Morrissey also explained that even though Boorer contributed nothing to 2006's RINGLEADER OF THE TORMENTORS, it was 'the album on which Boz has been most involved and had such a massive input'.

His writing talents aside, as a musician Boorer has enriched Morrissey's palette with clarinet, saxophone and banjo and has made an invaluable difference as an arranger and occasional engineer, single-handedly producing 1994's 'INTERLUDE'. 'Boz is 24-hour non-stop,' Morrissey has stated, 'and if impetus lulls, Boz steers everyone back on track.'

Between his Morrissey commitments, Boorer has maintained a separate career on the global rockabilly circuit touring with various groups, including his own Boz & The Bozmen, a re-formed Polecats and The Shillelagh Sisters with his wife, Lyn, with whom he has two daughters; the eldest, Billie-Rose, can be seen in the video for 'The More You Ignore Me' wearing an ANGELIC UPSTARTS T-shirt. He has also written and recorded with Kirsty MACCOLL, Adam Ant and had an active role in the re-formed John's Children, the former 60s mod group of his idol, Marc Bolan.

Summing up Boorer in 2007, Morrissey described him as 'perfect company as well as being very funny', calling theirs 'a long and

'Born To Hang' (Morrissey/Nevin), Unfinished studio outtake from December 1990. Recorded at Hook End Manor alongside 'PREGNANT FOR THE LAST TIME' for an intended rockabilly-themed mini album, 'Born To Hang' was Morrissey's spirited eulogy to his own exclusion from everyday life. 'I'll never have to live like you,' he sings, shunning the prospect of children and a loveless marriage and happy to go to the gallows in the belief that 'the noose [will] naturally come loose'. Jonny BRIDGWOOD lent the track the necessary 50s feel with some athletic double-bass scales while Nevin and Boz BOORER supplied its karate-chopping guitars. Sadly, Morrissey's change of heart over the rockabilly project consigned it to the scrap heap. By no means a lost classic, 'Born To Hang' would have made a good B-side and certainly had enough zest to translate well in concert. [4, 22, 25]

precious friendship'. [4, 5, 15, 22, 36, 40, 66, 92, 242, 245, 272, 334]

1. Boorer is listed as 'Boz' on every Morrissey album with the exception of 1997's MALADJUSTED, the only one to credit him as 'Martin Boorer'.
2. His first Morrissey sleeve credit was on 1991's 'SING YOUR LIFE' single as 'Second Guitar' though Boorer never played on the song, or either of its B-sides.

Bowie, David, Morrissey has many personal

heroes who, were they to be removed like a gene from his artistic make-up, would drastically deform whatever remained. Certainly Oscar WILDE and the NEW YORK DOLLS, probably James DEAN, maybe less so NICO. But no gene is more vital to the quintessence of Morrissey than the Jean Genie himself. The leper messiah. The thin white duke. The laughing gnome. The one, the only, Brixton boy David Robert Jones. Or as he once introduced himself at a 1987 press conference, 'I'm David Bowie, and you're not.'

Morrissey would describe Bowie as 'the blueprint for a fantastic career', which in essence is what he gave him: the shocking sexual ambivalence; the messianic fan–star relationship; the cultural magpie, cutting and pasting references from elsewhere; but most of all the model of the literate yet glamorous, aloof yet touchable self-mythologising English pop icon. 'He changed British pop in a very dangerous way,' Morrissey explained, 'because of the way he looked and the things he said.'

It was because of Bowie, Morrissey claimed, that he first had his name published in the music press in 1972 when the UK music weekly *Sounds* ran a competition to win a copy of Bowie's forthcoming album, The Rise And Fall Of Ziggy Stardust And The Spiders From Mars, printing his name among the winners. 'I had bought [April 1972 single] "Starman",' he explained, 'but didn't know anything about David, and hadn't even seen a picture of him.'

Ziggy Stardust was the 25-year-old Bowie's fifth album in as many years. Born 8 January 1947 (same birthday as Shirley BASSEY and Elvis PRESLEY), he'd been playing in groups since he was 15, releasing his first single in 1964, 'Liza Jane', under his real name Davie Jones, with his R&B group The King Bees. He became David Bowie with 1966's mod-pop treasure 'Can't Help Thinking About Me', shortly before entering his 'Anthony NEWLEY period' of quaintly English psychedelic vaudeville, epitomised by 1967's giggly novelty 'The Laughing Gnome', later a Morrissey interval tape fixture when touring KILL UNCLE.

The real, recognisable Bowie didn't emerge until his second eponymous album of 1969 (since renamed Space Oddity after its famous lead track), his first to be produced by his flatmate, TONY VISCONTI. They'd work again on 1970's The Man Who Sold The World, the first to feature Mick RONSON on guitar and Morrissey's favourite Bowie album. 'The first side, especially, is musical literacy delivered,' he'd claim. Like many others,

b

Morrissey discovered the album after its post-Ziggy re-release in November 1972. By then, he'd already seen Bowie in concert at the Hardrock in Stretford on 3 September. The Ziggy show returned to the same venue for two nights in late December, as did the 13-year-old Morrissey. 'Bowie at that time was despised,' he'd recall, 'which made him absolutely loveable to me. I first saw him in '72, and it was an amazing vision, but it was not popular by any means. In retrospect, people consider such artists as Bowie and the early ROXY MUSIC to be much more popular than they actually were at the time.'

Partly inspired by Vince Taylor[1] – a 50s English rock and roller who became obsessed with UFOs and believed himself to be the messiah – the Ziggy Stardust alter-ego was the making, and the saving, of Bowie, who'd soon obliterate his rival, Marc BOLAN, as the undisputed king of UK glam. But his impact upon Morrissey was much more earthly. 'Manchester, then, was full of boot boys and skinheads,' he explained, 'but I saw Bowie's appearance as the ultimate bravery. To me, it took guts to be David Bowie, not to be a shit-kicking skinhead in a pack … He just did not care … He wasn't persecuted by anything. It was the people who objected who were persecuted. I was very grateful, even though it wasn't in my instinct to dress like him or imitate him.'

Morrissey's preferred Bowie period stretches from the Visconti-produced Space Oddity and The Man Who Sold The World, through to 1971's Hunky Dory (including 'Kooks', a likely lyrical influence on The Smiths' 'SHEILA TAKE A BOW'), Ziggy Stardust and peaking with 1973's Aladdin Sane, featuring the original 'DRIVE-IN SATURDAY'. At 14, Morrissey sat transfixed in front of the television in June 1973 as Bowie told BBC Nationwide's Bernard Falk, 'I believe in my part all the way down the line … but I do play it for all it's worth, because that's the way I do my stage thing. That's part of what Bowie's supposedly all about. I'm an actor.'

Bowie promptly 'killed' Ziggy on stage at the Hammersmith Odeon on 3 July 1973, less than a month after Morrissey swooned once more to the live spectacle of 'Rock 'N' Roll Suicide' at Manchester's Free Trade Hall. There followed the covers set Pin Ups and 1974's Orwellian glam opera Diamond Dogs before Bowie's dramatic white soul transformation on 1975's Young Americans – an album Morrissey would blame 'entirely' for what he described as, musically, 'the worst year in social history'.

In fact, there's exceptionally scant evidence that Morrissey continued, as he might say, 'worshipping at the temple of David' for the rest of the 70s. His letters to Scottish pen pal and mutual fan Robert MACKIE boast that Morrissey saw Bowie in concert '14 times',[2] the last being on 3 May 1976 at London's Wembley Empire Pool promoting Station To Station. (To date, this is the only record that Morrissey visited London that week, shortly before his 17th birthday, and could have coincided with his unsuccessful flit to live in the capital as alluded to in The Smiths' 'HALF A PERSON', lasting only one week in a B&B.)

The Mackie letters also reveal his affection for 1979's Lodger (the last of his Visconti and ENO assisted 'Berlin trilogy'), specifically the majestic opener 'Fantastic Voyage', while Morrissey also teased Mackie with the cryptic run-out-groove message of the 'Boys Keep Swinging' single: 'Your bicameral mind … mind your bicameral.' Though his correspondence with Mackie coincided with the release of 1980's Scary Monsters, Morrissey's few comments on Bowie's current material were noncommittal and fairly unenthusiastic, e.g. 'It's a terrible bore that "Up The Hill [Backwards]" is the next single.'

Morrissey didn't meet Bowie until after The Smiths, on 7 August 1990 backstage at Bowie's Manchester Maine Road date on the 'Sound + Vision' tour, promoted as the last chance to hear him play his greatest hits with a setlist partly determined by public phone vote: in one of the NME's more inspired scams, they began a campaign urging people to nominate 'The Laughing Gnome', a request he sadly ignored. Morrissey later described how Bowie offered him some sage career advice at a time when the post-Smiths critical tide was beginning to turn against him: 'You have to jump back and attack.'

The worlds of Suffragette City and SALFORD LADS CLUB would collide again more publicly in Los Angeles the following summer. As the very secret and very special guest of Morrissey's 2 June 1991 show at the Great Western Forum, Bowie appeared to sing the encore cover of Bolan's 'COSMIC DANCER' as a duet. It was a spectacular coup for Morrissey, but equally for Bowie who by then needed all the credibility he could beg for having recently embarked on the near-career suicide of the all-but-undiscussable Tin Machine. Two years later, for his 1993 post-Tin Machine solo comeback Black Tie White Noise, Bowie famously covered Morrissey's 'I KNOW IT'S GONNA HAPPEN SOMEDAY', which itself had paid homage to the coda of Ziggy's 'Rock 'N' Roll Suicide'. 'I do think [Morrissey's] one of the best lyricists in England, and an excellent songwriter,' said Bowie, who called the song 'an affectionate spoof'. His gospelised version of the song made Morrissey 'wail tears of pure happiness'.

The Bowie/Morrissey axis would notoriously be strained to breaking point in November 1995 when they were paired together on a UK arena tour promoting their new albums for RCA: Bowie's 1.Outside and Morrissey's SOUTHPAW GRAMMAR. Naturally placed in the role of support act, Morrissey took to the stage as the cavernous venues were still only half full with half-interested Bowie fans; his own faithful audience packed near the front as best they could but the ambience was doomed from the off.

After ten dates in two weeks, Morrissey had endured enough. On 29 November, the tour arrived at Aberdeen's S.E.C.C. The group soundchecked as normal and all appeared well until 20 minutes before stage time. 'The tour manager came in the dressing room,' says bassist Jonny BRIDGWOOD. 'He called in all the crew, all the personnel. He tells us that we won't be playing tonight and the rest of the tour's off, which is bad enough. Then he says, "Morrissey's gone. And

he's taken the tour bus." Which is what he did. Half an hour before the gig he just walked on the bus and told the driver to drive. I think he went back to his mum's in Manchester. So not only were we not playing that night, we were also stranded in Aberdeen. Everybody just went back to the hotel and got drunk. Then the next day we flew home, paying our own way.'

Morrissey would later blame his sudden exit on Bowie himself. 'He put me under a lot of pressure, and I found it too exhausting,' he claimed. 'He was very odd to me and he asked me to sing a few of his songs in my set which I thought was wrong. Then after a few nights he asked to join me in *my* set which I thought was wrong. I said, "I can't do this." And then he would ask me if he could come on at the end and he would appear and I would disappear so there would be no end, no encore for me. When we played Dublin, I went off and he came on and a lot of the crowd were still calling my name. He was doing his set and he said, "Don't worry, Morrissey will be back later." But I was 100 miles down the road. I thought it was really showbiz and, really, this is David Showie.'

His cancellation of the remaining Bowie support dates resulted in Manchester's MEN Arena issuing an alleged 6,000 compensatory refunds. 'It certainly wasn't the greatest career move that I ever made,' he concluded. 'But then, Bowie is principally a business, and I can't imagine he would have telephoned his own mother without considering the career implications. David surrounded himself with very strong people, and that's the secret of his power: that everything he does will be seen in a certain light.'

In the bitter aftermath, Morrissey likened Bowie to 'a vampire … always searching for fresh blood to suck', even adding the comical snub that by the time he quit the tour, 'I realised that he actually thought I was the singer from Suede – a fate worse than life.' (See 'MY INSATIABLE ONE'.)

Yet, partly through his subsequent work with Tony Visconti, latterly Morrissey has rhapsodised about Bowie's influence with greater passion than ever before. Assessing his impact as 'bigger than punk, because he was a one-man revolution', Morrissey has also remarked how for 'Starman' and 'Drive-In Saturday' alone, he could forgive Bowie 'for anything'. That thin white gene being so crucial to his Morrisseyness, he probably has no choice. [4, 68, 69, 84, 95, 130, 196, 213, 266, 334, 351, 389, 453, 457, 575]

---

1. Morrissey would incorporate a 1961 promo film of Taylor's 'There's A Lot Of Twistin' Going On' on his pre-concert video montages from 2006.
2. The 14 Bowie gigs claim is feasible, but it would have meant that the teenage Morrissey would have had to travel further afield than Manchester. Even if he went to every Bowie gig in the whole of Lancashire during the years specified – including Preston and Blackburn – that's still only eight. Also, he'd have to have been no older than 14 since Bowie never played any UK concerts between November 1973's 'The 1980 Floor Show' fan club gig at London's Marquee and the same London Wembley show in May 1976. Mackie himself remained unconvinced. 'That's YOUR problem,' Morrissey retorted.

boxing, The two-year period from the beginning of 1994, circa the release of VAUXHALL AND I, until the end of 1995, following the end of the SOUTHPAW GRAMMAR campaign, can be loosely termed Morrissey's 'boxing phase'. During this time he'd repeatedly turn to boxing imagery for his record sleeves and videos, discuss the sport in interviews and, eventually, incorporate the theme into his lyrics.

Strange as it seemed that this sensitive, flower-waving vegetarian (or so the media liked to

'Boxers' (Morrissey/Whyte), Morrissey's 18th solo single, released January 1995, highest UK chart position #23. As Morrissey became increasingly passionate about BOXING during the mid-90s, 'Boxers' was the inevitable musical tribute to his new obsession, even going as far as incorporating an audio sample of BBC ringside commentator Reg Gutteridge. Empathising with a fighter being defeated in front of his local crowd, Morrissey highlights the personal humiliation as witnessed by the 'weary wife' and blindly adoring nephew. The battered boxer is merely another of his symbolic tragedians, a romantic loser whose physical and public degradation becomes a perversely heroic form of martyrdom. Nor would it be far fetched to suggest that Morrissey regarded the boxer in the ring as a metaphor for his own artistry. '[It's a] very important song for me,' he admitted. 'I love it. It's very, very close to me.'

For all the blood and tears in its lyrics, 'Boxers' clung to the ropes of a tune which in Morrissey's vocal and Whyte's sensitive strums together emphasised the beauty within the barbarism. The song was one of four recorded in a five-day session at London's Olympic studios in October 1994, all intended for the same EP. 'Morrissey wasn't there for the first couple of days,' says bassist Jonny BRIDGWOOD. 'We did several versions of each song all in different keys and biked them over to him. Then he came in at the end and sung in the key that fitted him best.' Rough mixes of all four were assembled on the final day. 'Morrissey liked them as they were,' says engineer Danton Supple. 'The rough mixes became the final versions.'

The proposed 'Boxers' EP was eventually split as a standard three-track single with the fourth, 'SUNNY', held over for a separate A-side later that year. The video for 'Boxers' still made reference to the latter, using 'Sunny' as the name of the fictitious fighter who receives a battering from Cornelius CARR. Filmed at York Hall in Bethnal Green, Morrissey made only a brief cameo, seen offering Sunny a commiserative handshake towards the end.

The single preceded Morrissey's first UK tour in over two years in February 1995, though it charted only modestly. Introducing 'Boxers' in concert he bitterly lamented its fate by describing it as 'a huge hit nowhere'. [4, 40, 422]

perceive him) should find a new thrill in semi-naked men knocking lumps out of one another, Morrissey's love of boxing was a logical symptom of his longstanding interests both in the tougher elements of working-class culture and an aesthetic appreciation for the male physique. 'For me it's the sense of glamour that's attractive,' he explained. 'The romance – which of course is enormous, as anyone who's attended bouts would know – but mainly it's the aggression that interests me. It has me instantly leaving my seat and heading for the ropes to join in. And it does give me a heightened sense of satisfaction, because in my life obviously there is absolutely no aggression at all. There is very little physical expression at all apart from standing on a stage and singing.'

Morrissey's first explicit visual reference to boxing was in the video for March 1994's 'THE MORE YOU IGNORE ME, THE CLOSER I GET', which featured an image of a young fighter posing with bare fists – actually a 50s snapshot of actor David Baxter, friend of Terence STAMP and sourced from the latter's 1988 autobiography *Coming Attraction*. The set of the video, a narrow corridor with low-hanging lights, also resembled the typical boxing backstage walkways as seen in the 1949 Kirk DOUGLAS film *Champion*. Around the same time, Morrissey was interviewed by *Select* magazine, choosing to do the accompanying photo session in the boxing ring at York Hall in Bethnal Green. The *Select* article marked the first mention of British super-middleweight Cornelius CARR, later featured in the 'BOXERS' video and freeze-framed for the WORLD OF MORRISSEY album cover. Beyond being a keen spectator of the sport in the flesh – allegedly in the front row for the October 1993 Old Trafford bout between Chris Eubank and Nigel Benn – Morrissey also confessed to having gone a few rounds in the ring himself. 'You react instantly,' he explained. 'Your body really obeys this sense of attack within your mind. It's great.'

His boxing phase peaked in 1995 with the 'Boxers' single, the UK cover of which featured a photo of Irish-American late-30s/early-40s

light-heavyweight champion Billy Conn, sourced from an old copy of the US boxing magazine *The Ring*. The same year's Southpaw Grammar album featured another portrait from *The Ring* of 50s American lightweight boxer Kenny Lane (incidentally a southpaw, or left-hander), which became the backdrop for most of his ill-fated tour supporting David BOWIE that winter. Although Morrissey used the Lane image again on press ads for his 1999 UK tour, years later he expressed regret over all of his boxing-themed sleeves from this period by insisting that, even if he provided the images, they weren't 'designed' by him; when Southpaw Grammar was reissued in 2009 the Lane cover was replaced by a self-portrait.

By the end of 1995, he seemed wary of unnecessarily exaggerating his passion for boxing, which was fast turning into a new Morrissey cliché. 'I released a single called "Boxers" and everyone assumes I'm some authority and I'm not,' he stressed. 'I just enjoy the violent aspect of it.' Such statements invited justifiable criticism that his interest in the sport was merely an affectation. 'Well, some people will always say something,' he replied. 'I'm not an expert. I'm just a face in the crowd who enjoys it for maybe a misguided aspect. But I do enjoy the unpleasantness. And the working-class aspect.'

Southpaw Grammar effectively rang the final bell on Morrissey's boxing period, though there have been subsequent flashbacks. Touring the US and South America in 2000, Morrissey played 'Boxers' against a back projection of Kirk Douglas punching his locker from the aforementioned *Champion* while, according to press reports, he's still known to 'hang out' with famous ex-boxers such as Chris Eubank, a fighter he'd once described as 'an astonishing machine'.

There is, however, one painfully ironic footnote to Morrissey's love of boxing. The rules of the sport were properly established in England in the 1860s with the 'Queensberry rules', a code of boxing practice drawn up under the patronage of the ninth Marquess of Queensberry – the same Queensberry who was father to Lord Alfred

b

'Bosie' Douglas and the notorious litigant who instigated the downfall of Morrissey's hero, Oscar WILDE. [40, 54, 114, 153, 217, 378, 490]

'Boy Racer, The' (Morrissey/Whyte), Morrissey's 20th solo single (from the album SOUTHPAW GRAMMAR), released November 1995, highest UK chart position #36. Another of Morrissey's social caricatures in the same vein as 'DAGENHAM DAVE', 'The Boy Racer' described a stereotypical Jack the Lad whose reckless driving and womanising provoked the singer's murderous wrath. Yet behind his hatred lay a peculiar envy – a sentiment Morrissey explored further on the later 'TEENAGE DAD ON HIS ESTATE' – sounding suspiciously resentful that anybody could stand at a urinal believing they hold 'the whole world in [their] hands'. When later asked if he ever felt the same about his own manhood, Morrissey dryly retorted, 'I don't need to walk towards the urinal. I already know.'

Its clanging ironmonger-rock was a vital component asserting Southpaw's intended musical toughness but was to suffer as a single, hampered by a lack of new studio B-sides. It did, at least, prompt an amusing video, a direct sequel to that of 'Dagenham Dave' (where 'The Boy Racer' was first introduced, driving off with Dave's girlfriend at the end), in which Morrissey is collared for speeding and grimacingly frisked by police. [40, 153]

'Boy With The Thorn In His Side, The' (Morrissey/Marr), The Smiths' ninth single, released September 1985, highest UK chart position #23. Cover star: Truman CAPOTE. (A remixed version later appeared on the album THE QUEEN IS DEAD.)

By the summer of 1985 Morrissey had spent roughly two years in the public eye. 'The Boy With The Thorn In His Side' was his first set of lyrics relating his personal experiences of the music industry and, in this instance, his anxieties over his misrepresentation by the media. That this, indeed, thorny issue was foremost in his mind over the summer of 1985 is evident in the batch of songs

written in this period alongside 'The Boy', all of which tackled the same theme from subtly different angles: 'RUBBER RING', 'BIGMOUTH STRIKES AGAIN' and his cutting attack on ROUGH TRADE's Geoff Travis, 'FRANKLY, MR SHANKLY'. Of these, 'The Boy' was the most sincere, missing the others' satirical wit and cynical edginess. Morrissey made it clear that the 'me' and 'us' of the song were he and The Smiths. 'The thorn is the music industry,' he specified. 'All these people who would never believe anything I said, who tried to get rid of me, who wouldn't play the records ... I think we've reached a stage where we feel, "If they don't believe me now, will they ever believe me?"' Cleverly, the song's metaphorical construct ensured most fans interpreted the 'us' as themselves, transforming 'The Boy' into a gentle anthem unifying group and audience against the common enemy of those who doubted the passions of either.

Marr recalls its cheerful melody 'just pouring out on the bus' during the spring '85 MEAT IS MURDER tour. 'It was an effortless piece of music with an effortless spirit. The whole experience of making it was the same as the experience of listening to it. Breezy, and very easy.' Having relocated back to Manchester earlier in the year, 'The Boy' was recorded at the beginning of August in the familiar surroundings of Drone studios, where the final Smiths line-up of Morrissey, Marr, Rourke and Joyce had first played together for an unsuccessful EMI-funded demo in December 1982. 'It was an odd choice,' explains Marr, 'to go back to this bloke's cellar where we did our first demo with Andy, particularly for a band who'd had a few hits and been quite celebrated. But that was my idea because it was us, back in Manchester, away from Rough Trade and all the media. It was the reason we'd moved back there in the first place, to do our own thing, regroup, with no one looking over our shoulder.' It was symptomatic of its relaxed recording that when Marr and Rourke discovered a marimba in the studio, the former used it to add an impromptu harmony part to the song. 'We'd been mucking about playing the riff of THE ROLLING STONES' "Under My Thumb",' says Rourke. 'Johnny decided it would sound good if we used it, so we did.'

Originally intended as a demo, instead the finished recording became the next single, released in late September to coincide with a short tour of Scotland. Under pressure from Rough Trade, the group grudgingly consented to their first official promo video directed by Ken O'Neil: a standard mimed performance filmed the following month at London's RAK studios where they'd begun preliminary work on The Queen Is Dead. 'It was horrible,' says Marr, 'so we just got drunk.'

Later, during the main Queen Is Dead sessions, Morrissey and Marr both decided to include 'The Boy' in the running order, adding extra layers of synthetic strings. 'Some critics since have said it shouldn't have been on the album,' comments Marr, 'but me and Morrissey felt it was a good move because, if you look at the other tracks, we needed a bit of light on there. "The Boy" provides some necessary relief.'

'The Boy With The Thorn In His Side' is exactly that: The Smiths at their most softly flickering and featherlike. Even so, its simple words seem to hold heavier personal significance for Morrissey: in 2003 he named it his joint favourite song of all he'd ever written alongside 'NOW MY HEART IS FULL'. [17, 18, 28, 38, 207, 473]

Bradford, Richard, Texas-born actor[1] and cover star of The Smiths' single 'PANIC'. The latter image was from the late 60s ITC television series *Man In A Suitcase*, one of Morrissey's favourite programmes starring Bradford as McGill (no Christian name), a chain-smoking, slate-grey-haired, American troubleshooter now based in England.

First spotted by British TV mogul Lew Grade in Arthur Penn's 1966 film *The Chase* opposite Marlon Brando, in *Man In A Suitcase* Bradford's 'Method' approach set him apart from the two-dimensional small-screen action heroes of the day such as *The Saint* or *The Avengers*. McGill was an existentialist hero: a Mozzerian loner, more James DEAN than James Bond, framed by his former CIA employers, cursed to eke out a mercenary livelihood as a gun for hire with no girl and no home to call his own. His entire worldly possessions – seemingly a gun, sunglasses, various suits and corduroy leisurewear – are kept in the battered suitcase which gives the programme its name.

'Brando was one of the reasons I became an actor,' says Bradford. 'He warned me, "You gotta fight these guys", meaning the people behind the camera. So that's what I did when I got to England to do *Man In A Suitcase*. I was battling all the time to play it how I wanted. McGill was written as a wise-cracking Mickey Spillane type, but I wanted to do something that hadn't been seen on TV before. More real, more honest. I don't smoke, but I smoked like a fiend on that show because I figured McGill would be the kind of guy who did.'

Another of *Man In A Suitcase*'s distinguishing features was the customary beatings McGill suffered in the line of enquiry. 'I was really intent on showing true pain,' Bradford explains. 'I'd be banging my head off linoleum, off concrete, crawling around in broken glass, but most of the time they wouldn't even move the camera down to film me. I felt as though I was the only one who cared about what we were making. The sad thing is, looking back, now I realise how free I actually was, making that show.'

Only 30 episodes of *Man In A Suitcase* were made, screened on ITV between September 1967 and April 1968 when Morrissey was eight years old. From a Mozzerian perspective, one of the most interesting episodes is 'Web With Four Spiders' where McGill's job takes him to Manchester. Arriving by train in Piccadilly Station, he ventures to a dive bar near Salford called Gulliver's: the owner is a scar-faced gangster played by CORONATION STREET's Fred Elliott (John Savident).

When the series ended, Bradford returned to America. Struggling to find similar lead roles, he drifted into cameo appearances in *The Waltons*, *Kojak* and, much later, CAGNEY & LACEY as Lacey's long-lost father. 'And yes, I remember The Smiths,' says Bradford. 'They wanted to use my picture and I said yeah. I heard they were a great band, but they sent me the finished cover without the record inside. So I've never heard "Panic".' [2, 175, 374]

---

1. Bradford was born in Tyler, Texas which may be the reason Morrissey made reference to the same county during his show at the Palladium Ballroom, Dallas in April 2009.

Bragg, Billy, 'The big-nosed bard of Barking',

Essex-born singer and romantic/political song-writer who befriended The Smiths and has collab-orated regularly with Johnny Marr.

In 1977 Bragg formed his first group, Riff Raff, with his neighbour/best friend Wiggy. Initially inspired by the likes of the Faces and THE ROLLING STONES, after discovering The Clash Bragg changed tack, pushing the group towards an indigenous Essex punk sound. Following one EP for Chiswick Records, 1978's 'I Wanna Be A Cosmonaut', and a handful of singles on their own independent Geezer label, Riff Raff disbanded in 1981. Devoid of purpose, Bragg made the seemingly reckless decision of joining the army only to buy himself out after completing basic training with what he famously termed 'the wisest £175 I ever spent'.

Back in Civvy Street, Bragg bravely relaunched himself as a lone troubadour with an electric guitar. 'In those days it was considered acceptable to be solo, but only on acoustic,' says Bragg. 'I didn't want that – to be a Nick Drake and play folk clubs – because I knew the audience I was looking for wasn't there.' A minimalist novelty to some, the simplicity of Bragg's act successfully highlighted the beauty, wit and brilliance of the repertoire soon to be captured on his 1983 debut mini-album, Life's A Riot With Spy Vs Spy. Bragg's love songs simultaneously touched and amused ('I am the milkman of human kindness, I will leave an extra pint'), often with socio-political overtones as on his momentous 'A New England', later a hit for Kirsty MACCOLL. Smiths patron John PEEL was quick to champion Bragg, who ingratiated himself with the DJ after hearing him crave a mushroom biryani on air and turning up within the hour at BBC Radio 1 with said

piping hot curry and a copy of his album. Luckily, Peel liked Bragg's record even more than the biryani and immediately gave him his first radio session that August; whether Bragg's uncanny resemblance to Peel's skiffle hero Lonnie Donegan had some spooky subliminal influence is also open to debate.

Bragg first crossed paths with The Smiths in February 1984, supporting them at the London Lyceum where backstage, according to Bragg, both Morrissey and Marr congratulated him on his debut. That year's miners' strike profoundly affected Bragg, whose songwriting became more overtly political thereafter, as evinced on his second (and first full-length) album, Brewing Up With Billy Bragg, and 1985's 'Between The Wars' EP (number 15, March 1985). In June 1985, Bragg supported The Smiths again on their first American tour, during which he performed a cover of 'JEANE', a song which the group had already dropped from their set. Encouraged by Bragg's rendition, The Smiths reintroduced it midway through the same tour. Bragg would go on to record two different versions of 'Jeane', a standard 'bash-'em-out Bragg' take for a September 1985 Peel session and a slower arrangement later issued as a B-side.

Bragg's rapport with Marr led to The Smiths' brief involvement with the January 1986 RED WEDGE tour (see separate entry). Marr would also guest on Bragg's third album produced by John PORTER, Talking With The Taxman About Poetry, lending a characteristically Smiths-esque flourish to 'Greetings To The New Brunette' – also featur-ing Kirsty MacColl and issued as a single – and imbuing 'The Passion' with similar silvery magic. During the Taxman session, Bragg overheard Marr casually picking the chords of the Four Tops' 1967 cover of The Left Banke's 'Walk Away Renee', a childhood favourite from his mother's singles collection. Bragg decided to record Marr's arrangement, a simple folk-guitar setting in the manner of the HATFUL OF HOLLOW version of 'BACK TO THE OLD HOUSE', adding his own spoken-word monologue about losing the girl of his dreams to

'Mr Potato Head'. Titled 'Walk Away Renee (Version)', it provided a fitting B-side to Bragg's dramatic 'Levi Stubbs' Tears' single (named after the Four Tops' lead singer). Marr was credited on the single sleeve under the intriguing pseudonym 'Duane Tremelo'.

Burned by the failure of Red Wedge after Thatcher's third consecutive general election victory in 1987, Bragg took a step backwards from politics with 1988's Workers Playtime, a romantically bruised dissection of a recently defunct long-term relationship. It followed an unlikely number one single, by default, after Bragg's version of THE BEATLES' 'She's Leaving Home' was released as a double A-side with Wet Wet Wet's cover of 'With A Little Help From My Friends', both culled from the NME-sponsored ChildLine charity compilation Sgt Pepper Knew My Father, which Morrissey had also been asked to appear on but declined.

After rediscovering his political fire with 1990's The Internationale (including 'I Dreamt I Saw Phil OCHS Last Night'), Bragg reunited with Marr for his 'big pop album', 1991's Don't Try This At Home, also featuring Kirsty MacColl and Michael STIPE. Marr would co-produce and contribute to 'Cindy Of A Thousand Lives' and the first Bragg/Marr composition, 'Sexuality'. 'Originally, "Sexuality" sounded like "Louie, Louie",' says Bragg. 'But then Johnny came along, got hold of it, and started playing these beautiful glistening chords over the top. So he took it back to Manchester and fiddled around with it and sent back this shining pop vehicle. Because Johnny had raised the bar, it was up to us to build an album around that and try and pitch everything on the same level.' 'Sexuality' was a modest hit in the summer of '91, reaching number 27 and dropping out of the charts just as Morrissey's 'PREGNANT FOR THE LAST TIME' was dropping in.

Bragg would team up with Marr again in 1997, recycling a tune the guitarist had given him a few years earlier as the basis of 'The Boy Done Good', released as a single and on the mini-album Bloke On Bloke, also containing Bragg's cover of The

Smiths' 'NEVER HAD NO ONE EVER'. The 90s ended with Bragg's collaboration with American band Wilco and the daughter of legendary American protest singer Woody Guthrie, who commissioned both to write new music to her father's 'lost' lyrics. The project spawned two critically acclaimed albums, Mermaid Avenue volumes one and two.

Still writing and recording, in latter years Bragg has prioritised his political campaigning on challenging notions of Englishness and national identity, the subject of his 2002 album England, Half-English and his 2006 book *The Progressive Patriot*. Bragg's main objective in this field is the promotion of England as a multicultural nation as a means of counter-attacking opportunist far-right propaganda in a decade of marked racial sensitivity. Consequently, Bragg is highly critical of Morrissey's comments on immigration and took a dim view of the 2007 NME racism row. His affection for Morrissey as a lyricist, however, is untainted by any such political discord. Ever the raconteur in concert, among Bragg's favourite anecdotes is the time Morrissey invited him to stay at his house one Christmas. According to Bragg's well-rehearsed patter, he was allocated an upstairs guestroom only to discover his bed had been fitted with a rubber sheet should he accidentally wet himself. Bragg also claims to have gotten up in the middle of the night only to bump into another guest, Bronski Beat/Communards singer Jimmy Somerville. [3, 20, 94, 124, 315]

Brand, Russell, Essex-born comedian, actor, television and radio presenter, writer and devout Morrissey apostle. A former heroin addict who has also received treatment for alcoholism and sex addiction, Brand is renowned for his peculiar appearance, a rakish Struwwelpeter sometimes described as 'Edward Scissorhands without the scissors', and is recognised as one of the most original, intelligent and fearless comic talents of the new millennium. He first met Morrissey in December 2006, interviewing his hero for his BBC Radio 2 programme and inviting him to play a song on his short-lived Channel 4 series *The*

Russell Brand Show. Morrissey immediately returned the tribute, introducing himself as 'Russell Brand' to the audience of his Wembley Arena concert that same month.

Brand has admitted that in stand-up perform-ances he sometimes lashes his microphone cable in homage to the singer, also naming his cat Morrissey. In late 2007 it was rumoured that Brand was to appear in the video for 'THAT'S HOW PEOPLE GROW UP' only for Morrissey to change his mind at the last minute. The same year, Brand published his best-selling autobiography *My Booky Wook* (or as Morrissey later called it, '*My Story Wory*') in which he quoted from The Smiths' 'NOWHERE FAST' and titled a chapter 'Hare Krishna Morrissey' (actually referring to his cat).

In January 2008, Brand along with comedian David Walliams and BBC presenter Jonathan Ross notoriously tried to placate the irate crowd at the fourth night of Morrissey's London Round-house residency when the singer aborted the concert after four songs due to a sore throat. The same week, in his football column for the *Guardian*, Brand shared an amusing story about the time he accidentally compared Morrissey to Hitler in the singer's presence during a discussion about WEST HAM; the same article appears in his 2008 volume of collected columns, *Articles Of Faith*.

Later that year, Morrissey returned as a guest on Brand's Radio 2 show where he evaded all sensible questioning, leaving Brand to fill in the gaps by sharing more anecdotes about going to the pub with the singer where he refused to elab-orate on the *Brighton Rock* reference in 'NOW MY HEART IS FULL', instead steering conversation to 70s ITV sitcom *Man About The House*. The interview ended with Morrissey 'bullying' Brand into singing the West Ham terrace anthem 'I'm Forever Blowing Bubbles'. Brand has since begun a successful film career in Hollywood where he interviewed Morrissey for the 'Wrestle With Russell' segment featured on the special edition bonus DVD with YEARS OF REFUSAL. Their encounter ended with Morrissey once again cajol-ing the besotted Brand into singing the Hammers' anthem for his personal amusement. [287, 288, 414, 415, 478]

'Break Up The Family' (Morrissey/Street),

From the album VIVA HATE (1988). Written and recorded mere weeks after the end of The Smiths had been confirmed in the press, on first impres-sions 'Break Up The Family' seemed a very obvious metaphor for Morrissey's current circum-stances, bidding farewell to his 'old friends' with a tender request that they should wish him luck for his future. Nonetheless, Morrissey denied the

Brasseur, Claude, French film star referenced in 'AT LAST I AM BORN' and subsequently named by Morrissey as one of his favourite actors. The singer explained how during 'a very dark period' he'd found solace in watching Brasseur's films. 'For a few months he was really helping me and lifting me and I'm very grateful.' Morrissey's favourite Brasseur film is 1964's *Bande À Part* (*Band Of Outsiders*) directed by Jean-Luc Godard and revered as a classic of French New Wave cinema; the 'outsiders' of the title are two hapless wannabe gangsters (Brasseur and Sami Frey) and their mutual love interest (Anna Karina).[1] Brasseur also made a cameo in the promotional film for Brigitte BARDOT's 'Bubble Gum', screened amongst the interval video montages Morrissey first introduced on tour in 2006.

---

1. *Bande À Part* is famed for its iconic dancing scene where Brasseur, Frey and Karina perform the Madison in a Paris café. Coincidentally, the scene was later used by Quentin Tarantino as a guide for John Travolta and Uma Thurman's dance-off in 1994's *Pulp Fiction* which takes place in a nightclub modelled upon the diner in SPEEDWAY, Morrissey's favourite Elvis PRESLEY movie co-starring NANCY SINATRA.

song was a Smiths epitaph, instead claiming it to be a nostalgic reflection on his early teens circa 1972 when he hung around with an 'intense' gang who often discussed 'the slim separation between life and death'. 'The family in the song is [that] circle of friends,' he elaborated. 'It almost seemed, because we were so identical, that for anybody to make any progress in life, we'd have to split up. Because there was *no* strength in our unity. And that's what happened, we did all go our separate ways, and quite naturally came to no good. I saw one of them quite recently, and it was a very head-scratching experience.'

Read as autobiography, the lyrics are extremely revealing, alluding to a crush on a 'captain of games' who takes him home in a ramshackle car, yet again revisiting the passenger/driver sexual tension of 'THIS CHARMING MAN', 'THAT JOKE ISN'T FUNNY ANYMORE' and 'THERE IS A LIGHT THAT NEVER GOES OUT'. Even rarer for Morrissey, he makes a positive declaration of being in love as opposed to the more characteristic 'pain and strain' of 'A RUSH AND A PUSH AND THE LAND IS OURS' recorded barely six months earlier.

One of Stephen Street's favourite Viva Hate tracks, and the last completed for the album, he was pleasantly surprised that Morrissey was willing to veer down a musical path which, by his track record, was 'unexpectedly funky'. The tune's languid mood was further enhanced by Morrissey's dreamy harmony vocals floating amid its otherwise sparse instrumentation. [25, 39, 208, 272]

Bridgwood, Jonny (Morrissey bass player
1990, 1993–97), Cursed with a name frequently misspelt on the credits of Morrissey records, Jonny Bridgwood (not 'Johnny' nor 'Bridgewood') had been a member of the rockabilly/ garage revival bands The Stingrays and Fireball XL5. It was guitarist Boz BOORER who first recommended Bridgwood as a potential bassist in December 1990 when producer Clive LANGER was given the task of assembling musicians for Morrissey's proposed 'rockabilly themed' mini-album. Alongside Boorer and Alain WHYTE (on harmonica),

Bridgwood was called to an inaugural session at Hook End Manor. After recording 'PREGNANT FOR THE LAST TIME', the group were curtly dismissed. The following week, Bridgwood was called back to record the unfinished 'BORN TO HANG', though shortly afterwards Morrissey abandoned the mini-album idea.

It would be over two years before Bridgwood worked with Morrissey again. In the meantime, the singer settled on his KILL UNCLE touring band of Boorer plus Whyte's existing rockabilly trio, The Memphis Sinners, featuring Gary DAY on bass and Spencer COBRIN on drums. Confusingly, Bridgwood found himself miscredited on the sleeve of 1991's 'SING YOUR LIFE' single, which he never played on, but absent from the subsequent credits of 'Pregnant For The Last Time', which he had.

After 1992's tour promoting YOUR ARSENAL, Morrissey decided to reshuffle his group personnel and discharge Day and Cobrin. In the spring of 1993, Boorer invited Bridgwood to a rehearsal session at Nomis studios in Shepherds Bush along with fellow new recruit, drummer Woodie TAYLOR. After a few days working on four new songs without the singer, Morrissey made his grand entrance to hear the fruits of their labour. 'He had a listen, didn't say much, and then we went down the pub,' says Bridgwood. 'There was no official "You've got the job!" or "Great! You're going to do the album!" Nothing was really said. Obviously, he must have been happy with what we played but it was all very low key.'

A few weeks later, Bridgwood was back at Hook End Manor for the duration of VAUXHALL AND I. 'When the album was finished, Morrissey said to me, "See you anon,"' recalls Bridgwood. 'I had no idea if I'd ever work with him again. Boz had already told myself and Woodie that we definitely wouldn't be used for touring. That could have been the end of it.' Despite Bridgwood's sterling work on Vauxhall And I, Morrissey decided against using him on his next session to record B-sides for the 'HOLD ON TO YOUR FRIENDS' single. 'He brought back Gary and Spencer instead of myself and Woodie,' explains Bridgwood.

'Apparently, that session didn't work out very well. Morrissey asked Boz why it was so difficult compared to the making of Vauxhall. The answer to that was it wasn't the same band.'

Thereafter, Bridgwood – or 'Jonny Wide Boy' as the singer liked to call him – found himself back in the fold for the 'BOXERS' single, remaining Morrissey's bass player for the next three years including SOUTHPAW GRAMMAR and MALADJUSTED (the only album to spell his name correctly on the credits). Contrary to Boorer's earlier forewarning, Bridgwood would also play on all of Morrissey's tours of 1995 and 1997 before handing in his notice at the end of the latter. 'Myself and Spencer had already decided to leave,' explains Bridgwood. 'There were issues with contracts, some financial stuff, but personally I also felt that musically things were getting very samey, like we were going round in circles. I've never regretted leaving. Looking back, it felt like the right time to go. Plus, with Morrissey, you never knew when you were going to be dropped. It could have been any moment.' Since leaving Morrissey's band, Bridgwood has continued to play electric bass and double bass for various artists, most prominently English singer/songwriter Kathryn Williams. [4, 5, 40]

Bringing Up Baby, 1938 screwball comedy listed among Morrissey's favourite films. Directed by Howard Hawks, its convoluted plot centres around palaeontologist David Huxley (Cary Grant) who is due to receive the missing piece of the brontosaurus skeleton he's been assembling for the past few years on the eve of his wedding to his domineering and frigid secretary. However, his marriage plans go farcically awry when he meets eccentric heiress Susan Vance (Katharine Hepburn), the wealthy niece of a potential patron for his natural history museum. After their comically quarrelsome first encounter, Vance realises she has fallen in love with Huxley and begins to engineer a series of distractions involving her pet leopard (the Baby of the title) to prevent him getting to the church on time.

Now regarded as a Hollywood classic, the film was such a commercial flop upon first release that Hepburn had to buy herself out of her RKO contract after being labelled 'box-office poison'. Some film historians have also credited *Bringing Up Baby* as the first film to use the word 'gay' meaning homosexual. After Hepburn's character hides Grant's clothes, he's forced to wear one of her nightgowns. When her on-screen aunt finds him and demands to know why he's dressed in a woman's nightie, Grant sarcastically remarks 'Because I just went *gay* all of a sudden' while camply leaping in the air. Coincidentally, the set used for Hepburn's country home would be dusted down seven years later for another of Morrissey's favourite comedies, CHRISTMAS IN CONNECTICUT. [184, 488]

Brontë, Charlotte and Emily, See JANE EYRE and WUTHERING HEIGHTS.

Brookside, British television soap opera set in a Liverpool cul-de-sac, launched in 1982 as part of the new UK terrestrial station, Channel 4. Morrissey named it as his favourite soap opera during The Smiths and would later make his first and only acting cameo in a 1988 *Brookside* spin-off called *South*.

'There's some skill in *Brookside*,' Morrissey enthused in 1985. 'They actually make an effort. And the script is quite funny … in a witty way, not a dim way. Most importantly, it's realistic.' In its early years, *Brookside* was a radical and overtly political soap which dealt with some of the most contentious social issues of the day, from unemployment, the Tory destruction of trade unions, the 'Care in the Community' policy towards mental illness, heroin addiction among middle-class professionals, homophobia and the shame and stigma suffered by rape victims. Morrissey was especially impressed by its portrayal of young people, with many of the storylines revolving around Brookside Close's teenagers and students. The original cast featured one of his favourite actresses, Katrin CARTLIDGE, as middle-class rebel

Lucy Collins while another of the show's regulars, Shelagh O'Hara (who played student Karen Grant), appeared with Morrissey and actress Margi Clarke in a comic sketch filmed in a toilet as part of a feature on The Smiths' 1985 Scottish tour on Channel 4's *The Tube*.

Another *Brookside*/Smiths connection was bridged by teenage playwright Shaun Duggan from Liverpool's Norris Green estate. In January 1987, Morrissey returned to *The Tube* to interview Duggan about his play, *William*, inspired by The Smiths' 'WILLIAM, IT WAS REALLY NOTHING'. During their discussion, Duggan enthused about his love for *Brookside*, stating he could 'easily' write for the programme since he knew and loved the characters so well. It was to be a spookily prophetic exchange. By the mid-1990s, Duggan was one of the soap's main scriptwriters, confessing to a women's magazine how he'd often sneak Smiths lyrics into his dialogue as a private joke.

After Morrissey told the press he was 'hopelessly addicted' to *Brookside*, he was offered the chance of a cameo appearance; allegedly, an early script proposal cast the singer as a prospective buyer for the bungalow owned by the curmudgeonly Harry Cross. Instead, he turned up in *South*, a two-part spin-off set in London and broadcast in March 1988 as part of ITV's educational strand, *The English Programme*. Morrissey played himself, appearing in a brief scene in the foyer of Capital Radio opposite Justine Kerrigan,[1] *Brookside*'s Tracy Corkhill (see entry on ACTING).

By the 90s, Morrissey's soap tastes had moved on to EASTENDERS. In the meantime, *Brookside*'s scripts grew ever more sensational with storylines featuring incest, murder and lunatic religious cults. After ratings plummeted, the show was axed with the final episode broadcast on 4 November 2003, 21 years to the very week it first aired. [71, 146, 473, 474, 576]

---

1. Kerrigan would later make headlines in 2007 when it was discovered she was giving acting classes to the inmates of Ashworth high security psychiatric hospital, home to Moors Murderer Ian Brady, subject of The Smiths' 'SUFFER LITTLE CHILDREN'.

Brown, Len

Brown, Len, British journalist, television producer and longtime acquaintance of Morrissey since first interviewing the singer for the *NME* in 1988. Through his combined work in the music press and television, Brown has laid claim to having 'interviewed Morrissey more times than any other journalist'.

His many encounters were the basis of his 2008 Omnibus book *Meetings With Morrissey* which, as its title indicated, collected his interviews with the singer as the basis of a personalised career overview. The book provides a fascinating insight into the private Morrissey away from the spotlight, whether cryptically signing his personal correspondence with the name of obscure CARRY ON bit-part actor Julian Orchard or his telling awkwardness when Brown accidentally bumps into him in a Manchester branch of Waterstone's only to end up discussing the poet A. E. HOUSMAN. Brown also bravely recounts the personal tragedy of his younger brother, Don, a Joy Division obsessive who committed suicide in 1982 and whose copy of a 1974 Gregory Isaacs single on ATTACK RECORDS was given to Morrissey shortly after he revived the label in 2004: Morrissey used the same record as a prop in a photoshoot for the *NME*. Brown has also enjoyed the rare privilege of being namechecked in concert: when Morrissey played Manchester's Opera House in May 2006, he informed his audience, 'Hundreds and hundreds of years ago, as Len Brown will verify, I came here to see Mott The Hoople.' [290]

Brownmiller, Susan

Brownmiller, Susan, See FEMINISM.

Burns, Pete

Burns, Pete, Flamboyant lead singer of 80s pop group Dead Or Alive who became a close friend of Morrissey's during The Smiths. Born in Merseyside in August 1959, Burns's first taste of chart success was a cover of KC & The Sunshine Band's 'That's The Way (I Like It)' (number 22, April 1984). Morrissey immediately declared its accompanying promo video, featuring Burns in latex opera gloves prancing around female bodybuilders in a women's gym, as 'the very first video

I ever liked', further calling Burns 'quite stunning' and 'the only person I want to meet'.

It wasn't long before Morrissey did, introducing himself to Burns backstage at TOP OF THE POPS in early February 1985 when The Smiths were booked to mime 'HOW SOON IS NOW?' the same week as Dead Or Alive's 'You Spin Me Round (Like A Record)' was close to ending its 14-week thrust towards number one. Morrissey and Burns had much in common: both grew up in the northwest during glam and punk rock, both attracted notoriety as a local eccentric (Burns was expelled from school aged 14 for turning up with red hair, no eyebrows and one giant earring), and both were now scrutinised by the press for their respectively atypical 80s pop personas – Morrissey the celibate, vegetarian firebrand, Burns the acid-tongued disco queen. 'He's one of the few people I can feel a great affinity with,' said Morrissey of Burns. 'Namely, because he says exactly what he wants to. Which, of course, is a national sin within music.'

'You Spin Me Round (Like A Record)' was Burns's biggest hit and the first number one for the production team of Stock, Aitken and Waterman. Though he'd later christen the latter 'Stock, Face-ache and Waterbed', Morrissey hailed the record a timeless 'hallmark in British music'. The song was still in the top 20 when Burns joined The Smiths on stage at London's Royal Albert Hall on 6 April 1985 for a 'dramatically under-rehearsed' encore of 'BARBARISM BEGINS AT HOME', making him the only singer other than Sandie SHAW to perform with the group in concert.

Throughout 1985, Morrissey continued to champion Burns in the press, admitting he'd dreamt of them making a record together ('[it] would be great fun') and applauding his feat of 'corrupting a generation' when Dead Or Alive were played on CORONATION STREET ('the height of their career – I told them so and they virtually agreed'). Curiosity over Morrissey's acquaintance with Burns led to them both being interviewed together to discuss their friendship for a *Smash Hits* cover story that October. The feature, titled 'A Friendship Made In Heaven', was a light-hearted dialogue conducted at the home of Burns and his wife, Lynne, in which they discussed their mutual admiration over a packet of coffee creams. Sadly, Morrissey was deeply upset by what he perceived as a stitch-up, the printed interview laced with 'camp symbolism which never occurred'. 'They turned us into Hinge and Bracket,' he seethed. 'It made me out to be a bit poncified. Pete was less annoyed, even though I said to him, "You never said that, you never called me Joan Collins." [*sic – in the article, Burns actually calls Morrissey 'Joan Rivers'*] His attitude was, "Well, forget it." But that's not really my attitude. I think it was absolutely and pathetically stupid.' In truth, other than the inferences to be drawn from the revelation that Burns and Morrissey often sent each other flowers (Burns: 'He's *anybody's* for a lupin'), the article was far more harmless than his wrath suggested.

Burns would remain in Morrissey's circle of friends after the break-up of The Smiths. Through Burns, Morrissey met Pete HOGG, his personal assistant during the BONA DRAG/KILL UNCLE years, while Burns would also borrow the title of The Smiths' 'UNHAPPY BIRTHDAY' for a song on Dead Or Alive's 1990 album Fan The Flame (Part 1). For most of the 90s, Burns and Dead Or Alive were rarely seen or heard outside of Japan, where they'd accrued a fan base large enough to compensate for their obsolescence at home. In the meantime, Burns underwent a drastic physical transformation after multiple cosmetic surgery procedures, not all of which had gone according to plan. By the time he re-emerged in the early 00s, his appearance brought to mind Morrissey's quip in 1989 that 'when Cher and Pete Burns exchange passports, airport officials are none the wiser'.

Promoting a Dead Or Alive greatest hits collection in 2003, Burns told a UK newspaper he was no longer friends with Morrissey because 'I got a fur coat and he blew up'. The following year, Morrissey refuted the story: 'I never fell out with him at all. [Pete] has a very strong personality and you have to be a bit of an athlete to keep up with

Butterworth, Dean (Morrissey drummer 2002–04), Following the departure of Spencer COBRIN, the vacancy for Morrissey's touring drummer was first filled in 1999 by Spike T. Smith, latterly of The Damned. Three years later, for Morrissey's next intermediary tour of 2002 Smith was replaced by 25-year-old Rochdale-born/California-bred musician Dean Butterworth, previously a member of Ben Harper's Innocent Criminals. The singer was sufficiently taken with Butterworth to retain him for the recording of 2004's YOU ARE THE QUARRY and its ensuing world tour. With his aptly Ringo-esque features and ill-suited mohawk, 'Deano' (as he was nicknamed) was frequently serenaded with affectionate chants from the more dedicated pockets of Morrissey's audience. Yet, as a drummer Butterworth's playing was strangely devoid of aggression, 'attacking' his kit the way a Buddhist might shoo away a common housefly through the power of karmic suggestion. Following the end of the Quarry tour, in 2005 Butterworth left Morrissey's band of his own accord to join tattooed dude-rock buffoons Good Charlotte. He was replaced on RINGLEADER OF THE TORMENTORS by Matt CHAMBERLAIN and on tour by Matt WALKER, both of whom found the prospect of hitting a snare drum at full force significantly less terrifying than the timorous 'Deano'.

him … He has a *savage* critique of the people around him, which becomes slightly wearing.'

Burns achieved his greatest infamy to date in 2006 as a contestant on the Channel 4 reality television series *Celebrity Big Brother*, unleashing his 'savage critique' on his fellow housemates and sparking a criminal investigation when he claimed his fur coat was made of gorilla, an endangered species. The coat was removed and subjected to tests which determined it to be made not of gorilla but Colobus monkey, another endangered species; Burns avoided prosecution by proving that the monkey pelts were imported into the UK before their registration as an endangered animal in 1975. After coming fifth in *Celebrity Big Brother*, Burns suffered mental health problems, admitting himself into a London hospital citing 'sleep deprivation and exhaustion'. He's since recovered and continues to appear in various reality television programmes, among them the pulse-weakening one-off special *Pete Burns' Cosmetic Surgery Nightmares*. [52, 87, 129, 145, 175, 192, 200, 204, 206, 475]

Buzzcocks, First and best Manchester punk group and, by proxy, vastly influential upon the next generation of north-west groups to follow in their wake, The Smiths included. Leaving political rabble-rousing to their predominantly southern counterparts, Buzzcocks sang about matters of far greater universal importance – masturbation, self-sufficiency, heartbreak, suicide, life as an illusion and love as a dream. They were at once intense, hilarious, poetic, harmonious, philosophical, sexy and profound. Or as a frothing Morrissey saluted them in a 1977 letter to the NME, 'the best kick-ass rock band in the country'.

Buzzcocks were formed by friends Howard Trafford and Pete McNeish, who'd first met at Bolton Institute of Technology in 1975 and bonded over a love of BOWIE, Brian ENO and The Stooges. In February 1976, they read a live review of an early SEX PISTOLS gig at London's Marquee in the *NME*. Headed 'Don't look over your shoulder but the Sex Pistols are coming', journalist Neil Spencer's description of the Pistols' take on The Stooges' 'No Fun' along with quotes from the band that 'we're not into music … we're into chaos' were enough to inspire Trafford and McNeish to borrow a car and drive south to see the next Pistols show at High Wycombe College of Further Education on 20 February. As the writer Paul Morley would later recount, Trafford and McNeish 'taped the Pistols' High Wycombe show [and then] studied it extremely closely, as if it were a scripture, a series of codes to decipher and turn into their own series of cryptic signals'.

Two monumentally significant acts were to follow their High Wycombe pilgrimage. Firstly, they'd liaise with Pistols manager Malcolm McLaren to arrange the group's two concerts at Manchester's Lesser Free Trade Hall in June and July of 1976 (see Sex Pistols entry). Secondly, they'd form their own group, taking their name from '[it's/that's/get] the buzz, cock!', a catchphrase featured in a new television musical drama, *Rock Follies*, as repeated in a review of the programme in the edition of London listings guide *Time Out* which they'd picked up on their journey south.

Becoming Buzzcocks meant Howard Trafford became Howard DEVOTO while Pete McNeish became Pete Shelley (according to Morley, the name McNeish 'would have had if he'd been born a girl'). Joined by Steve Diggle on bass and just-turned 16-year-old drummer/Stretford schoolboy John Maher – sharing a birth name with Johnny Marr and recruited by Devoto as he was 'about to set off back to school to sit my chemistry O-level' – this first Buzzcocks line-up supported the Pistols at the second Lesser Free Trade Hall show on 20 July, as witnessed by the 17-year-old Morrissey.

The week after Christmas 1976, Buzzcocks recorded the Spiral Scratch EP, the UK's first independent punk record released on their own New Hormones label in January 1977. Yet at this, the precise moment when Buzzcocks were making history, Devoto quit. In February '77, he issued an official leaving statement printed in the *NME*. 'I don't like most of this new-wave music,' he explained. 'I don't like music. I don't like movements. Despite all that, things still have to be said. But I am not confident of the Buzzcocks' intention to get out of the dry land of new waveness to a place from which these things could be said. What was once unhealthily fresh is now a clean old hat.' Devoto returned later that year with Magazine (see main DEVOTO entry).

Meantime, Shelley moved to centre stage as Buzzcocks frontman, with Diggle upgrading to guitar and occasional lead vocals. With the rhythm section of Maher and eventual full-time bassist Steve Garvey, the full beauty of Buzzcocks

came into being. As the young Morrissey enthused in his *NME* letter, 'They possess a spark of originality (that was important once, remember?) and their music gives you the impression they spend longer than the customary ten minutes clutching the quill in preparation to write.'

One of the last groups to be snapped up in that year's major label punk A&R scrum, they finally signed to United Artists on 16 August 1977, the day Elvis PRESLEY died. Their first release for the label that October was offensive enough to its pressing plant workforce to provoke strike action. Announcing Shelley's singing debut – an asphyxiated cluck, at once camp and confrontational – and with lyrics by the recently departed Devoto, 'Orgasm Addict' was an explicit rumination on the perils of onanism set to an appropriate fuzzbox thrash. Just as important was its sleeve, a collage by Linder STERLING of a female nude with mouths for nipples and a steam iron for a head; Morrissey would later use photocopies of the image as writing paper. Another Sterling collage inspired the title of the group's March 1978 debut album, Another Music In A Different Kitchen.

If 'Orgasm Addict' amounted to a roguish cheap thrill, their next, 'What Do I Get?' – a future Morrissey interval-tape favourite apparently inspired by Shelley's affections for Linder – was where the Devoto-less Buzzcocks finally found their winning formula of the great punk love song. Its potential was elastic enough to repeat time and again, from the audaciously succinct 'Love You More' to their heartbroken colossus 'Ever Fallen In Love (With Someone You Shouldn't've)' (number 12, November 1978). By shifting punk's agenda from urban commentary and anarchistic sloganeering to the clumsy mechanics of sexual relationships, Buzzcocks sowed the seeds of what would eventually flower as 80s indie.

Although Shelley's comment to the *Guardian* in 2002 that 'I honestly think Morrissey stole my idea of the non-gender-specific lyric' was somewhat overstaking his claim, it is true that Shelley and Morrissey were kindred spirits when it came to articulating lovelorn angst. Take, for example: 'I only get sleepless nights/Alone here in my half-empty bed' ('What Do I Get?'); 'A fiction romance/I love this love story/That never seems to happen in my life' ('Fiction Romance'); 'I don't know what's gone wrong with my life/But you know I never do seem to win' ('I Don't Know What To Do With My Life'). Even Marr would credit Shelley's simplistic guitar solos as inspiration for his monophonic finale on 'STOP ME IF YOU THINK YOU'VE HEARD THIS ONE BEFORE'. On his part, Morrissey was quick to acknowledge the Buzzcocks' legacy very early on in The Smiths' career. 'They had an endearingly confused quality,' he said in 1984, 'really northern, dim and appealingly camp.'

Singles-wise, Buzzcocks rarely put a foot wrong, as borne out by November 1979's Singles Going Steady, as flawless a collection of A- and B-sides as accrued by any group in pop history. It was only on their third album, 1979's A Different Kind Of Tension – including the single 'YOU SAY YOU DON'T LOVE ME' as covered by Morrissey – that their sparkle slowly started to wane. Though a final triptych of intermediary singles followed in 1980, when sessions for a proposed fourth album fell apart Shelley forged an alliance with Buzzcocks producer Martin Rushent, fresh from sculpting The Human League's Dare! The result was Shelley's 1981 solo debut album Homosapien, its lead single/title track sharing a bass line with Abba's 'Does Your Mother Know?' and clearly alluding to Shelley's bisexuality ('I don't want to classify you like an animal in the zoo'). 'It just got a bit messy,' says Shelley of the break-up. 'I wanted to do this electronic stuff. I really thought Steve and everybody else would carry on as Buzzcocks without me.' Instead, with Shelley now solo, Buzzcocks officially dissolved.

By the time Buzzcocks first re-formed in 1989, The Smiths had been and gone. Shelley had previously supported them at Brixton Academy on 12 December 1986 at what would be their final concert. After Maher left in 1990 to pursue his interest in racing cars (eventually moving to the Isle of Harris), Buzzcocks recruited ex-Smiths drummer Mike Joyce. 'I'd learned to play drums by banging on the back of me mum's sofa listening to the Buzzcocks,' says Joyce, who toured with the group until 1991. 'John Maher was my hero and the Buzzcocks were my favourite band. I was obsessed. Proper berserk about them. To actually *join* the Buzzcocks was, to use a cliché, a dream come true. It was unreal.' Shelley and Diggle would continue making new Buzzcocks albums throughout the 90s and into the twenty-first century between their own solo projects; the most significant to date being the 2002 'ShelleyDevoto' album Buzzkunst – a one-off collaboration from the former Trafford and McNeish marking 25 years since Spiral Scratch. [14, 31, 267, 340, 366]

By Grand Central Station I Sat Down And Wept, See SMART, Elizabeth.

Cagney & Lacey, Popular 80s American police series named by Morrissey as his favourite television programme circa 1986. The show centred on the professional and personal lives of two female New York police detectives, Christine Cagney (Sharon Gless, preceded by Loretta Swit in the 1981 pilot and Meg Foster in 1982's first season) and Mary Beth Lacey (Tyne Daly). Prior to *Cagney & Lacey*, American police dramas had either been exclusively male or served only to portray female cops as novelty sex objects, specifically its 70s forerunner *Police Woman* starring the ever-glamorous Angie Dickinson. By contrast, Cagney and Lacey were strong, intelligent and altogether more credible role models shown having to cope with the domestic challenges of all working women besides the added stresses of fighting crime. During its six-year run between 1982 and 1988 the series also touched on alcoholism, abortion and rape. Its compassionate representation of women and sharp, witty scripts were of obvious appeal to Morrissey, so much so he berated one interviewer for being oblivious to its merits ('You don't watch it? My, you're crumbling before me!'). Coincidentally, Cagney & Lacey featured occasional cameos from 'PANIC' sleeve cover star Richard BRADFORD, who first appeared in 1986's fifth season playing Lacey's long-lost father. [183, 206]

Cajun, Morrissey's love of the indigenous music of Louisiana – defined as a 'syncopated folk', usually sung in Acadian French and heavy on accordion, fiddle, steel guitar and fervent whooping – first came to the fore in 1989 when recording the B-side 'GET OFF THE STAGE', featuring a distinctly Cajun accordion-driven tune by Andy Rourke.

Though the influence of Cajun upon his music has been non-existent ever since, Morrissey has frequently revealed his fondness for the genre, whether on his interval tapes, spelling out to one interviewer that he was 'into Cajun' around the release of 1991's KILL UNCLE or his inclusion of The Sundown Playboys' 'Saturday Nite Special' on his UNDER THE INFLUENCE compilation. His favourite Cajun artist is the accordionist Nathan Abshire, whose 'Hey Mom', an early 60s recording for producer J. D. 'Jay' Miller, Morrissey once named as his 'favourite song of all time'. Two minutes and 14 seconds of breeches-busting squeezebox bliss with a near-evangelical vocal, for clearance reasons it was denied its intended place on Under The Influence. [207, 437]

Caligula, Notorious Roman Emperor and sexual deviant referenced in The Smiths' 'HEAVEN KNOWS I'M MISERABLE NOW' (1984). Born Gaius Julius Caesar Augustus Germanicus in 12 AD, Caligula (a nickname derived from the Latin for 'little boots') ruled from March 37 AD until January 41 AD when he was stabbed to death by his own bodyguards at the age of 28. As his fate indicates, Caligula was a deeply unpopular ruler; cruel, self-absorbed and so insane he famously requested his favourite horse be made an ambassador. Lanky and pallid, he was so paranoid about his thinning hair and caprine features that to look at him from above or mention a goat in his presence carried the death penalty. Many historians attribute his madness to a potent aphrodisiac given to him by his fourth wife (his first committed suicide). His sexual gluttony – the basis of Tinto Brass's lurid 1979 film dramatisation starring Malcolm McDowell and John Gielgud – is a matter of record. If ancient scriptures are to be believed, his appetite was irrepressible; men, women, even blood relatives (his three sisters, whom he also 'pimped out' to friends). Morrissey's citation of Caligula for the sake of comedy – in his case, asked to perform a feat so outrageous that the Emperor 'would have blushed' – wasn't the first. Bette DAVIS made a similar quip in her 1962 autobiography *The Lonely Life*. Praising silent-movie vamp Theda Bara, Davis writes: '[Bara's] monumental wickedness would not have been tolerated by Caligula in his beatnik depths for one moment.' It's also possible that The Smiths' concert entrance music from PROKOFIEV's Romeo And Juliet may have been inspired by its use over the opening credits of the aforementioned 1979 film. [298, 321]

Campbell, Beatrix, See FEMINISM.

Cantona, Eric, Swarthy, metaphysical French footballer and Manchester United forward whom Morrissey was briefly fixated with circa 1995. On 25 January that year, Cantona was sent off the pitch during a United away match against Crystal Palace for kicking one of their defenders. As he walked towards the dressing room past the home supporters, he was subjected to a tirade of verbal abuse from one particular 20-year-old Palace 'fan' near the touchline. Cantona retaliated with a stunning 'kung fu kick' followed by several punches, receiving a nine-month worldwide playing ban, £30,000 in fines from the Football Association and a 120-hour community service sentence after pleading guilty to common assault. Cantona then dumbfounded the media with a surreal press conference in which he arrived, sat down, recited the philosophical proverb 'When seagulls follow the trawler, it is because they think that sardines will be thrown into the sea', then stood up and left. Adding to the drama, the fan was also found guilty of using threatening behaviour and language and disgraced himself by physically attacking his prosecution lawyer in court (it later transpired he had a previous conviction for attempted violent robbery and was known to attend far-right political rallies).

Two weeks later, Morrissey began his UK tour to promote the 'BOXERS' single. By the eighth date at east London's Ilford Island, he was discussing the Cantona incident on stage. 'I thought Eric was completely innocent … however, I could be completely wrong.' By the end of the tour, he'd begun writing 'ERIC', 'CANTONA' or both on the tambourine he routinely threw into the crowd each night. It wasn't until that autumn, when promoting SOUTHPAW GRAMMAR, that he expounded on his admiration for the player, even posing for a *Q* magazine photoshoot wearing a Cantona T-shirt. 'I approved because it was very entertaining and I found the witnesses in the crowd very suspect,' said Morrissey. 'When I saw it on television, I howled. I watched every version

C

of the news. He also happens to be a great player. The negative publicity doesn't matter, as don't the Crystal Palace fans. I think he set a good example. I found it very encouraging and glamorous and exciting. And it wasn't violence as much as self-defence. He is a human being and the abuse hurled at him was incredibly personal and disturbing. How could he have lived with himself if he had not reacted? Everyone secretly agrees with him anyway.'

Following his ban, Cantona returned to United as team captain, scoring the winning goal of the 1996 FA cup final against Liverpool (1-0) and leading them to win the following '96–'97 Premiership season. To the dismay of United fans, 'King Eric' retired from the game at the end of that season, aged 30, handing the team captaincy over to Roy Keane (see 'ROY'S KEEN'). Sadly, Morrissey's admiration for Cantona ended abruptly when, according to the singer, their paths collided and the footballer 'blanked me in a shocking way'. [153, 170]

Capote, Truman, American author, literary celebrity, acid wit and cover star of the Smiths single 'THE BOY WITH THE THORN IN HIS SIDE'. Capote had died just over a year before the single's release, on 25 August 1984, aged 59. On the back of the single, he was credited as simply 'Truman'. The image in question shows Capote caught mid-air leaping in Tangiers in 1949, photographed by Cecil Beaton. (Years later, Morrissey would insinuate that when Mike Joyce first saw the cover he thought it was a picture of comedian Ernie Wise.)

While in his early twenties, with the help of friend/MEMBER OF THE WEDDING author Carson McCullers, Capote found an agent and publisher for his first novel, 1948's semi-autobiographical *Other Voices, Other Rooms*. The story of a fey adolescent boy coming to terms with his mother's death (Capote's mother committed suicide when he was 11) and the acceptance of his homosexuality (about which Capote was notoriously open), it was an instant, if controversial, success. A

decade later came the novella *Breakfast At Tiffany's*, subsequently made into a 1961 Hollywood film with Audrey Hepburn and featuring the original 'MOONRIVER' as later covered by Morrissey. Capote's masterpiece arrived in 1966 with his 'non-fiction novel' *In Cold Blood*, an account of the 1959 murder of a Kansas farmer and his family by two ex-convicts, later turned into a 1967 Hollywood drama. The book's creation also provided the basis for the 2005 biopic *Capote*, starring Philip Seymour Hoffman, another favourite of Morrissey's. His last work prior to his death was the 1980 collection *Music For Chameleons*, the closing chapter of which was a 'self-interview' titled 'Nocturnal Turnings Or How Siamese Twins Have Sex'. It climaxed with Capote declaring, 'I'm an alcoholic. I'm a drug addict. I'm homosexual. I'm a genius.'

Among Morrissey's own favourite Capote books was a collection of interviews with Lawrence Grobel, *Conversations With Capote*. 'I'm not even sure if Truman was a writer at all, or just someone who sneaked around and watched,' the singer concluded, 'but he *was* funny.' [133, 244, 293, 374]

Carry On, British comedy film series created by director Gerald Thomas and producer Peter Rogers which ran for 20 years from 1958 to 1978. Of the 29 original *Carry On* films, Morrissey considered 'at least six of them' to be 'high art'. The first, the National Service farce *Carry On Sergeant*, owed its name to a common British military expression. Subsequent films in the series kept the *Carry On* prefix but substituted 'Sergeant' for the appropriate setting or profession, be it school (*Carry On Teacher*, source of the fictional location lending its name to Morrissey's 'LATE NIGHT, MAUDLIN STREET'), police (*Carry On Constable*) or hospital (*Carry On Nurse/Doctor/Matron*). From the mid-60s they also took turns parodying other contemporary films and/or genres, from James Bond (1964's *Carry On Spying*) to Taylor and Burton's Cleopatra (1964's *Carry On Cleo*) and, one of the best, 1966's Hammer horror spoof *Carry On Screaming!*

Carr, Cornelius, Middlesbrough-born 90s British super-middleweight boxing champion and cover star of the compilation album WORLD OF MORRISSEY. On Friday 11 March 1994, the 24-year-old Carr was fighting at York Hall in Bethnal Green. Morrissey chose the occasion for a photo shoot at the venue for *Select* magazine to accompany an interview promoting VAUXHALL AND I. Carr beat his opponent, James Cook, and was photographed after the bout being congratulated by Morrissey.

Carr next appeared in the video for January 1985's 'BOXERS' single. It was this video which provided the sleeve for World Of Morrissey (used as his UK tour backdrop that February) as well as that of a US CD maxi-single of The Smiths' 'SWEET AND TENDER HOOLIGAN' released the same year. In early November 1995, Morrissey named Carr as his 'favourite boxer' and his 'tip for the top'. There must have been something of the jinx in Morrissey's prediction since two weeks later Carr lost a WBO super-middleweight title challenge against Dublin's Steve Collins. Carr would eventually retire in 2001 having lost only four of his 35 fights. [114, 457]

Produced quickly and cheaply, the *Carry On* scripts revelled in blindingly obvious sexual innuendo, a world of 'crumpet', 'knockers', 'phwoar!', 'cheeky!' and 'Matron!' which became ever cruder as the series staggered into the cul-de-sac of 1970s smut. For that reason, Morrissey declared that 'they finished artistically in '68', though in terms of commercial success the series peaked with 1969's *Carry On Camping*, the highest-grossing film in the UK that year. Chief scriptwriter Talbot Rothwell – whose name, like that of *Carry On* bit-player Julian Orchard, Morrissey later employed as a humorous pseudonym on correspondence – was largely responsible for defining the *Carry On* style since the early 60s but bowed out with nervous exhaustion after 1974's *Carry On Dick*. The already waning quality of scripts plummeted to new lows of vulgarity thereafter, ending with 1978's dire *Carry On Emmannuelle*.

The scripts aside, the *Carry Ons* owe their enduring appeal to their regular stable of British comic actors. As Morrissey enthused, 'When you think of Charles Hawtrey, Kenneth Williams, Hattie Jacques, Barbara Windsor, Joan Sims, Sid James … the wealth of talent!' Four of these have been of greater interest to Morrissey than the others and, perhaps not surprisingly, his preference is for those who were as daft and eccentric on screen as they were tortured and miserable off it:

i) Charles Hawtrey, The effete, impossibly puny, bespectacled mummy's boy of 23 *Carry On* films, beginning with *Carry On Sergeant*. Previously, a young Hawtrey had been seen in a handful of early 40s comedies starring Will Hay (listed among Morrissey's favourite 'Odd fellows', as was Hawtrey himself), also turning up bashing away on a pub piano in the Ealing classic PASSPORT TO PIMLICO. Hawtrey is the only *Carry On* star whose dialogue might – and, admittedly, it's a fairly big might – have inspired a Smiths song title: in 1964's Rothwell-scripted *Carry On Cleo*, during a scene on board a Roman galley, he coyly quips, 'Stop me if you've heard this before.'

Off screen, Hawtrey made no secret of his homosexuality though maintained fierce discretion in his private affairs. A chronic alcoholic, he fell out with the *Carry On* producers after they refused to give him top billing in a 1972 Christmas television special and never worked for them again. The same year's *Carry On Abroad* was his last for the series; scenes of Hawtrey with a lilo in the film were later used in Tim Broad's video for Morrissey's 1988 single 'EVERYDAY IS LIKE SUNDAY'. Months after the latter song reached the UK top ten, Hawtrey died on 27 October 1988, aged 73. Morrissey mourned his passing by calling him 'the very last comic genius … I personally loved him'.

In honour of Hawtrey's death, Morrissey used

C

images of the actor on backstage passes for that December's WOLVERHAMPTON show, paying further homage in the video for the following year's 'INTERESTING DRUG' with its fictitious 'Hawtrey High' school. Morrissey later disclosed that towards the end of The Smiths he'd whittled down several potential sleeve images of Hawtrey to one favourite contender, though the break-up of the group meant it would never be used. Hawtrey finally appeared on Warners' 2001 posthumous compilation The Very Best Of The Smiths, a release concocted without Morrissey's input, nor that of Marr who denounced it as 'the worst cover I've ever seen'.

ii) Hattie Jacques, Another of Morrissey's listed 'Odd fellows' beside *Carry On* co-stars Hawtrey and Kenneth Williams, Jacques (pronounced 'Jakes') was the hulking battleaxe of 14 films in the series, typified by 1972's *Carry On Matron*, in her estimation 'the vulgar with a bit of oo la la … it sort of sums up the *Carry Ons*, doesn't it?' Prior to joining the series in the inaugural *Carry On Sergeant*, Jacques had a minor role in another Morrissey favourite, David Lean's OLIVER TWIST, later becoming a regular of Tony Hancock's 50s radio show *Hancock's Half Hour* alongside Williams and Sid James. Deeply sensitive about her weight and its frequent use as the butt of scriptwriters' jokes, behind the scenes Jacques was a caring Mother Hen figure to the *Carry On* gang's lonelier souls, habitually inviting Hawtrey, Williams and Joan Sims to her house for Christmas dinner. Her affinity with gay men, the former included, was such that according to her biographer 'friend of Hattie' was an equivalent euphemism to 'friend of Dorothy'. Jacques married actor John Le Mesurier with whom she had two sons; one of them, Robin, went on to become guitarist with The Wombles. Her last in the series was 1974's *Carry On Dick*. She died of a heart attack six years later in October 1980, aged 58.

iii) Joan Sims, That Morrissey's *Carry On* fixation peaked in the late 80s following the deaths of Williams and Hawtrey seems obvious, not least because in 1989 he managed to coax Joan Sims,

star of 24 films in the series, into playing the medium in the video for 'OUIJA BOARD, OUIJA BOARD'. He'd later describe it as his highlight of that year, 'mainly because she was so excellent, so enormously gifted, and here was I, a silly sausage from somewhere near Manchester'.

Unlike the majority of the *Carry On* regulars, Sims never played a specific type, alternately prudish, henpecking or lusty as the scripts dictated. Before joining the series with 1959's *Carry On Nurse*, Sims had already appeared in numerous film comedies (including Morrissey's beloved THE NAKED TRUTH) and was one of the few stalwarts to remain to the bitter end of *Carry On Emmannuelle*. Suppressed by a domineering mother, Sims also struggled in vain against alcoholism. Though she regarded Hattie Jacques as both 'a sister and a mother to me', her reliance on booze rendered her incapable of attending Jacques's funeral. Reminiscing about the 'Ouija Board' video shoot, guitarist Kevin ARMSTRONG, who attended the group meal with Sims afterwards, recalls her with succinct gloom as 'a slightly lonely person'. Sims died in June 2001, aged 71, one year after publishing her autobiography, *High Spirits*. The book's only mention of Morrissey is on the penultimate page when Sims discusses the internet, referring to what she considers an 'off-putting' fan's trivia page listing only the fact that she made the 'Ouija Board' video and that she never married.

iv) Kenneth Williams, The true king of *Carry On*, not least by virtue of his appearance in 26 of the original 29 films, absent only from …*Cabby* (1963), …*Up The Jungle* (1970) and …*Girls* (1973). Williams's nasally voice, neck-cricking sneer, camp facial spasms and pantomime outrage combined to make his the most memorable lines: 'Frying tonight!', 'Infamy! Infamy! They've all got it infamy!' or the aghast exhale of 'Ooh! Matron!', which in three simple if inordinately elongated syllables defined not only Williams's screen persona but the entire *Carry On* genre. Ironically, Williams himself was a bitter critic of the films, frequently deploring the 'witless vacuity' of the shooting scripts and usually mortified by the final cut (a rare exception being 1967's *Carry On Again Doctor* which he thought 'very good indeed').

Like Jacques, Williams's comedy career took off with *Hancock's Half Hour* (first on radio, then television) playing a strange Cockney geek whose tease to 'stop messing about' quickly became a popular catchphrase. In contrast, his early *Carry On* roles were more muted until 1964's *...Spying*, the first in which he introduced what he termed his trademark 'snide voice'.

Throughout the 60s *Carry Ons* Williams continued working for radio as a regular on the BBC's *Beyond Our Ken* and *Round The Horne*. The latter show, written by Barry Took and Marty Feldman, paired Hugh Paddick with Williams as the infamous Julian and Sandy, two actors 'between jobs' who tried their hand at everything from gardening to bodybuilding. Each week their latest 'bona' enterprise brought them into contact with host Kenneth Horne, the willing stooge in their outrageous repartee bursting with homosexual double entendre and 'palare' slang. The Julian and Sandy sketches would variously inspire the lyrics of Morrissey's 'PICCADILLY PALARE' and the titles of BONA DRAG and 'STRIPTEASE WITH A DIFFER-ENCE'. The very first Julian and Sandy sketch from March 1965, 'Rentachap', was also used by Morrissey to describe his former personal assistant, Peter HOGG, while a postscript to the March 1966 *Round The Horne* 'Bona Books' sketch provided the run-out-groove message of the 'INTERESTING DRUG' etched 12-inch single, 'The Motorcycle Au-Pair Boy'.

Williams also befriended the playwright Joe Orton (see 'DEATH AT ONE'S ELBOW'), joining him and his lover/eventual killer Kenneth Halliwell on holiday in Tangiers. Unlike Orton, Williams was unable to come to terms with his homosexuality and lived a life of extreme loneliness, reluctant celibacy and intense self-persecution. The extent of his despair was finally laid bare with the posthumous publication of his diaries in 1993. Speaking two years later, Morrissey confessed he'd read them 'a couple of times, and each time it's been like a hammer on the head.

An astonishingly depressing book. It's incredibly witty and well done, but the hollow ring it has throughout is murderous, absolutely murderous. I think he was always depressed, because the diaries spread over a 40-year period and even at the beginning of them he was saying, "Why am I alive? What's the point?" And this was 1952. It's astonishing that he lasted so long.'

Morrissey's morbid fascination with *The Kenneth Williams Diaries* – enough to have read them 'a couple of times' – says much for his own empathy with Williams's profound isolation. At times, it's easy to imagine Williams's words in Morrissey's own voice. 'I wonder if anyone will ever know about the emptiness of my life,' Williams wrote in August 1963. 'I wonder if anyone will ever stand in a room that I have lived in, and touch the things that were once a part of my life, and wonder about me, and ask themselves what manner of man I was. How to ever tell them? How to explain? How to say that I never found Love – how to say that it was all my own fault – that when presented with it, I was afraid and so I spurned it, or laughed at it, or was cruel, and killed it: and knew that in the process I was killing myself.'

Following the death knell of 1978's *Carry On Emmannuelle*, Williams remained a popular face on British television. He died in April 1988 at the age of 62 of an accidental overdose, having mixed medication for a stomach ulcer with regular sleeping pills. The final entry in his diary read: 'Oh – what's the bloody point?' That same month, Morrissey paid the following tribute: 'I loved [Williams's] bomb-shelter Britishness, his touch-me-not wit, his be-ironed figure, stylishly non-sexual; his facial features were as funny as anything he ever said ... The passion absent in his celibate existence appeared to the brim, and past the brim, in his work. Another irreplaceable strip of Britishness falls away.' [12, 70, 175, 206, 290, 337, 371, 374, 397, 532, 540]

cars, Since the early days of The Smiths, motor vehicles and the act of driving have featured heavily in Morrissey's lyrics: tied to the back of a car in 'YOU'VE GOT EVERYTHING NOW', the 'charming' vehicle of 'THIS CHARMING MAN', the roadside parking in 'THAT JOKE ISN'T FUNNY ANYMORE' and, most famously, the unrequited passenger seat romance of 'THERE IS A LIGHT THAT NEVER GOES OUT'. Cars have also been a prominent motif of his solo career: the brake-less journey of 'BREAK UP THE FAMILY', the tale of 'DRIVING YOUR GIRLFRIEND HOME', the speed-obsessed 'BOY RACER' (and 'DAGENHAM DAVE' with his windscreen stickers), the Jensen Interceptor of the 'TEENAGE DAD ON HIS ESTATE' and the spine-breaking melodrama of 'THAT'S HOW PEOPLE GROW UP'.

Morrissey divulged that his fascination with cars began at an early age. 'As a child of the 60s, when the seats of cars were made of leather, to me there was something highly erotic about actually being in a car. I have always found cars highly erotic.' After leaving school, Morrissey took driving lessons but, at 18, failed his test on the Highway Code ('definitely the first major shock I ever had'). Towards the end of The Smiths, in 1986 he purchased a vintage 1961 Ford Consul from a 'widow of a man who died just a couple of weeks after purchasing the car … it had been standing untouched in her garage for 25 years'. Yet without a licence, Morrissey was unable to drive it, at least not legally. 'It's waiting in the garage for the magical day when I learn to drive,' he sighed. 'Which, of course, will never happen because I can't grapple with the Highway Code.'

Cars were equally important to Johnny Marr (the riff for 'HAND IN GLOVE' came together in the passenger seat of his future wife Angie's Volkswagen Beetle). 'My cars and my front rooms were where The Smiths existed when we weren't on stage or in the studio,' says Marr. 'It was where we did all our listening, all our hanging out and all our surviving as it were.' Like Morrissey, Marr also drove without a licence, though in early November 1986 the guitarist received a harsh reality check when he crashed his BMW 528-i under the influence of 'red wine and tequila' just yards from his home in Bowdon. 'I'd dropped Mike Joyce off at about 2.30 in the morning,' he

explains. 'I was listening to what I thought was silence but was actually the blank side of a tape at full volume. As I got to the red light, the tape flipped over to the other side to a demo I'd been working on, possibly "SHOPLIFTERS OF THE WORLD UNITE". So I just went, "Enjoy!", put my foot down, in the rain, and went for a little detour instead of driving to my house. Within seconds, the car went out of control. It bounced off one wall, in the air, hit another wall, and then kind of half turned over then ran into another wall. The steering wheel ended up in the roof. If you see photographs of the wreckage, it's astounding how I made it out of there without being very, very injured. Looking back, it was a very significant moment in my life. I'd taken things to the nth degree. A lot of things had to change after that.'

Morrissey increased his car collection in 1988 with a 'pretty modern' white Golf GTi which he occasionally drove himself, though for the most part he chose to be chauffeured by 'a friend who I'll pay for a certain period when I have to do something, and he'll drive'. Morrissey's driver friends of the 90s would include Pete HOGG and Jake WALTERS. While living in London in the mid-90s, he resumed driving lessons and could occasionally be spotted cruising around Primrose Hill in his Golf GTi with regulation L-plates. According to engineer Danton Supple, Morrissey passed his test circa the making of 1995's SOUTHPAW GRAMMAR. 'We knew he passed because he turned up to the studio one day driving a glass-topped Porsche 911,' says Supple. 'It took us completely by surprise. The most un-Morrissey car you could imagine.' The singer subsequently told the press he found 'the demon car a complete necessity', describing himself as 'a very good driver'.

After moving to Los Angeles in 1998, Morrissey purchased a Jaguar and a 1977 Aston Martin, preferring the former for being 'more silent' since the latter's engine apparently sounded 'a bit like a helicopter'. 'I find driving very liberating,' he confessed. 'It's a shame that it's destroying the planet, but when you are on your own, your mind clears and you drive to relax the brain, even though

Cartlidge, Katrin, Young British actress who died suddenly on 7 September 2002 after contracting pneumonia and blood poisoning. Two weeks later, Morrissey formally dedicated 'LATE NIGHT, MAUDLIN STREET' at his two London Royal Albert Hall concerts to Cartlidge's memory. 'I was absolutely shocked by her death,' he later explained. 'She was 41. I thought she had a great screen presence and was one of the few modern British actors who I thought really had it. Terribly sad. But life is very weird.'

Cartlidge began her career in 1982 on one of Morrissey's favourite soaps, *BROOKSIDE*, where she played Lucy Collins, the rebellious daughter of a stereotypically southern middle-class family often at odds with their Liverpool neighbours. Her most famous roles were in the films of Mike Leigh, who directed her in *Naked* (1993), *Career Girls* (1997) and the period drama *Topsy-Turvy* (1999). Morrissey showed particular interest in *Career Girls* after being told of 'an interesting sex scene [where] one of the people in the film is wearing a T-shirt with my face on it … which is probably the nearest I'll get to a sex scene'. The film tells of two former student flatmates (Cartlidge and Lynda Steadman) who reunite for a weekend in London having not seen one another in six years. The sex scene is during a flashback to their 80s student past where a naked Cartlidge straddles an obnoxious young man in a Smiths T-shirt. By strange cosmic coincidence, the location of the *Career Girls* student flat was Rousden Street, Camden where Morrissey's guitarist Alain WHYTE was living at the time.

Cartlidge was particularly brilliant in Lars Von Triers' harrowing yet remarkable *Breaking The Waves* (1996) and made one of her last screen appearances with Morrissey's LA neighbour, Johnny Depp, in the 2001 JACK THE RIPPER drama, *From Hell*. After her death, an annual arts bursary was set up in her honour, The Katrin Cartlidge Foundation. Tributes to the actress and details of the bursary can be found at www.katrincartlidgefoundation.org.uk. [403, 577, 489]

it is now wholly associated with road rage.' The 2003 Channel 4 documentary *The Importance Of Being Morrissey* revealed that he was equally proficient on two wheels, seen riding an Italian Vespa scooter in the Hollywood hills; as Oasis singer Liam Gallagher put it, 'The Moz has a good bike.' [19, 40, 47, 61, 88, 115, 119, 130, 144, 150, 226, 422]

Catholicism, See RELIGION.

cats, Morrissey's favourite animal. 'I'm mystified by cats,' he admitted. 'I see a cat and I'm in a trance and the union begins.' He also stated that, given the choice of being any animal, he'd choose to be a feline. 'I'm very fond of them and they can lead a relatively luxurious life. They're also very independent beings – not like dogs who need persistent attention. I'd like to be an ordinary scrubber, an alley cat. No, [on second thoughts] a tabby.'

Morrissey has owned 'many, many' pet cats through the years, the most famous being Tibby, who entered his family household when he was barely three years old. Twenty-three years later, Tibby was still going strong. 'He's actually older than the other members of The Smiths, which is remarkable,' said Morrissey in 1985. 'It's quite extraordinary because we have family photographs of me when I was a day old and I'm clutching this cat and there he is today still hobbling around the house.' The singer's only criticism of poor Tibby was that he was 'glued to meat'. 'If I bought a pet today,' he added, 'I'd feed it on non-meat products like Smarties and baked beans.' As well as the ancient Tibby, Morrissey cared for a younger black cat, apparently without a name (referred to only as 'Noname').

The singer may possibly have been referring to the fate of Tibby when he later described the trauma of 'certain situations where I've had to terminate the life for the benefit of the cat and the

C

pain is too much to bear.' '[My cat] was very, very old, and he was arthritic, and he couldn't go to the toilet properly,' he explained. 'I would have to take him to the toilet, I'd have to do everything, but he was very, very happy, and as long as he was with me, he was thrilled to death. So, I held him at the last moment when they inserted the needle and I cried for hours and hours and hours. This sound came out of me, this sound of despair when he went, and I'd never heard it before ... I *howled* ... I still miss him, I really still miss him.' Morrissey's passion for cats is evident in the notable number of photo sessions featuring cats and kittens throughout his career, as well as the 'ALMA MATTERS' video. [123, 176, 232, 573]

celibacy, The most scrutinised and notorious aspect of Morrissey's character when The Smiths first thrust themselves upon the UK media in 1983 was his professed abstinence from sex. Although, since 1997, he has frequently stated he is no longer celibate, it remains a fundamental component of his mythology.

Speaking in 2006, Morrissey protested that, 'I only used the word "celibate" in August 1984 and it's haunted me like a soothsayer walking behind me everywhere I go.' In truth, the singer discussed his celibacy on umpteen occasions throughout The Smiths' career, the earliest recorded mention being their first interview in *Sounds* in June 1983. 'I want a new movement of celibacy,' he declared. 'I want people to abstain.' For the early 80s, a celibate pop star was a revolutionary concept, as shocking, in its way, as BOWIE's famous quip to *Melody Maker* in 1972, 'I am gay and always have been'. Whereas 'queerness' had become acceptable by the age of new romanticism and Boy George (significantly, The Smiths' November 1983 TOP OF THE POPS debut followed a performance by archetypal 'gender bender' Marilyn), celibacy defied the first rule of the hackneyed 'sex, drugs and rock and roll' credo, rendering Morrissey an unfathomable pop creation. 'I think my attitude is quite challenging,' he stated, 'because it's not really happened before,

except with Cliff Richard and he doesn't count. It seems impossible for a public figure in 1984 to be celibate so people find it quite challenging. You know, the whole idea of the pop star bathed in sexuality, yawning at the next round of orgies.'

It was crucial to his public persona that he stressed his celibacy was 'an involuntary decision' and 'something I had no say in'. By doing so, Morrissey set himself up as an empathetic martyr for a whole generation of teenagers coming to terms with their own sexuality and all related fears of rejection and inadequacy. As Marr commented in 1984 when asked what ailments and illnesses a Smiths record could cure, 'It can ease the paranoia of being celibate.' 'For me, [celibacy] was the right decision,' Morrissey said at the time. 'And it's one that I stand by and I'm not ashamed or embarrassed by. It was simply provoked by a series of very blunt and thankfully brief and horrendous experiences that made me decide upon abstaining and it seems quite an easy, natural decision.'

The genius of Morrissey's celibate stance was that, ironically, his abstinence transformed him into a sex symbol. Traditionally, pop stars teased their audiences with the false promise of allowing their loins to be ravaged. Morrissey, on the other hand, presented his audience with a brand-new dilemma: no matter how suggestively he gyrated, there was always the firm understanding his loins weren't for ravaging. By presenting himself as unobtainable, he allowed fans of either sex the unprecedented freedom to fantasise about being *the one* who could break his self-imposed celibacy. Morrissey was quick to realise the benefits of this image he'd established. 'Eventually I realised that [it] was quite interesting,' he acknowledged. 'I thought, "I'll hang on to this."'

It was only towards the end of The Smiths that Morrissey retracted his earlier call for 'a new movement of celibacy', first admitting in early 1986 that he'd recently been 'caught off guard' and 'lapsed slightly'. 'I never wanted to wave a banner for celibate people,' he grumbled in 1987. 'It's accidental that it came out in the first place and now it's become a tatty banner. I've been consistently probed on it, and the statement I make is that I've got nothing to do with it … It's just the way I choose to live and the way I've always lived. I can't even recommend it. It's just right for me and wrong for the rest of the population.' Even so, Morrissey wasn't beyond making light of his abstinence, joking that he was 'inches away from a monastery' and frequently had to resort to eating a cushion 'in frustration'.

Sceptics have reasonably suggested that his gradual aversion to promoting celibacy was a fear of hypocrisy: that, by the demise of The Smiths, he could no longer avow to having had no sexual relations. Nevertheless, at a 1992 press conference in Chicago, he answered the time-honoured query that he was 'unfortunately' still celibate, 'but I don't want to be'. Five years later, however, he was beyond entertaining the topic, dismissing celibacy as 'boring' and claiming he never disliked sex, 'I just didn't have it' – his use of past tense being one of his first public inferences that his self-restraint had now ended. All further enquiries along the same lines were treated with ridicule, telling one radio station he was now only celibate 'on Christmas and bank holidays'. By 2002 the end of Morrissey's celibacy was an open secret, though he refused to divulge any specifics as to when it ended and with whom. 'I don't sob about it,' he stated matter-of-factly. 'It wasn't easy. But it's over now.'

It is impossible to deny his celibacy played a significant part in Morrissey's veneration as a wholly original English pop star, even if he'd belatedly condemn the media for making him an 'icon of celibacy'. 'I was honest about it, briefly, and I spoke about it briefly and I do regret it,' he mourned in 2006. 'If you announce that nothing ever happens to you then you're announcing that you're incapable of roping anybody in – the key phrase being "anybody". Most people do settle for anybody. Certainly, if you're working-class and you're male it's a sin to sleep alone, which is why so many rush into hasty marriages. Working-class males do not ever sleep alone. I was in that environment and I was sleeping alone. So I was an oddity.' (See also HOMOSEXUALITY, SEX.) [54, 58, 63,

69, 120, 128, 130, 132, 144, 152, 165, 166, 191, 196, 204, 206, 404, 411, 448, 453, 567]

'Cemetry Gates' (Morrissey/Marr), From the album THE QUEEN IS DEAD (1986). Morrissey's fondness for stalking around cemeteries dated back to his late adolescence when he and best friend Linder STERLING would idle away afternoons walking around their favourite Manchester graveyard.[1] 'We used to go walking on fine sunny afternoons to Southern Cemetery,' recalled Linder. 'It was very peaceful and very beautiful, but it wasn't done in any sort of morbid sense.' Even after forming The Smiths, Morrissey confessed that he still pursued this 'most gripping pastime', sometimes in the company of singer Howard DEVOTO. In the curiously misspelt 'Cemetry Gates' – curious in that its misspelling has never been explained, dividing opinion as to whether this was deliberate or a genuine mistake – Morrissey uses such encounters as the setting for a playful sketch on literary theft as he and a partner engage in flirtatious, intellectual one-upmanship.

It was extremely ironic, if not deliberately self-parodic, of Morrissey to address the issue of plagiarism in a song which itself brazenly incorporated words which weren't his own. A large part of the first verse (beginning 'all those people' and ending 'I want to cry') is adapted from the screenplay of one of his favourite Bette DAVIS films, THE MAN WHO CAME TO DINNER (see also Sheridan WHITESIDE), while the 'salutation to the dawn' quote stems from Act V of Shakespeare's RICHARD III. It was also the first song where he nailed his colours to the mast by declaring his love of Oscar WILDE, in doing so mocking his partner's inferior poetic armoury of John Keats and W. B. Yeats.

As much as 'Cemetry Gates' was an arch confession of Morrissey's frequent lyrical pilfering, it was also an ingeniously double-edged riposte to the 'big nosed' critics who'd tried to outfox him in exposing his previous sources. 'I love the lyrics on "Cemetry Gates",' enthuses Marr, 'because I, also, was getting a bit tired of people who didn't know us much pulling up

C

Morrissey for doing something that they'd have been more than happy to get anywhere *near*. Smart arses in the press, and around ROUGH TRADE as well. A couple of figures who were a little bit knowing needed a bit of a verbal slap. I think Morrissey delivered that very well.'

Marr also credits Morrissey with 'saving' the song from the dumper. 'It was one of those times when two heads were better than one for The Smiths,' he explains. 'The tune was just something I'd been playing around with. To me I was thinking of The Kinks, almost like "Dandy" or "Days". It was in the key of G, which I tried to avoid writing in because it resonated a certain kind of straightness. I did it with "THE BOY WITH THE THORN IN HIS SIDE", and again with "ASK", but I'd avoid it because it didn't seem to have any dark corners for me to go down. So I might have thrown it in the bin had Morrissey not, by chance, heard me playing it as I was tuning up in my kitchen. He was the one who said, "That's a tune," and suggested we turn it into a song. And he was right.'[2]

Among the later additions to The Queen Is Dead, 'Cemetry Gates' was one of Morrissey and Marr's most blissfully breezy delights, ending the album's predominantly dark and heavy first half with some alleviating wit and delicacy. [17, 18, 57, 190, 206, 333, 468, 485, 529]

---

1. Though the scene was clearly of strong autobiographical origin, it's conspicuous that *BILLY LIAR*, a film which Morrissey sourced on other songs of The Queen Is Dead period, contained a similar cemetery rendezvous between Tom Courtenay and Helen Fraser.

2. Uncanny muso trivia: Marr began writing 'Cemetry Gates' by experimenting with a particular chord change, from the home chord of G to B minor. This same change occurs in THE BEATLES' 'I Want To Hold Your Hand'. As legend has it, when Paul McCartney first played these chords, John Lennon cried 'That's it! Do that again!', thus anticipating Morrissey's similar reaction to Marr's tune. In the interests of milking coincidental spookery for all its worth – for we might as well – it's worth adding that Lennon and McCartney wrote the song in the house belonging to the parents of the latter's girlfriend, Jane Asher, on London's Wimpole Street, scene of one of Morrissey's favourite films, *THE BARRETTS OF WIMPOLE STREET*.

'Certain People I Know' (Morrissey/ Whyte), Morrissey's 14th solo single (from the album YOUR ARSENAL), released December 1992, highest UK chart position #35. Morrissey's playful résumé of his circle of friends, 'Certain People I Know' was a humorous mix of mock sympathy, innuendo ('when I swing it so it catches his eye'), and plain bitchiness. Inevitably, 'certain' acquaintances of the singer speculated whether they were the 'people' in question. Cathal SMYTH, already the dedicatee of the same album's 'YOU'RE THE ONE FOR ME, FATTY', considered himself a likely candidate. 'I always wondered whether that was about me too,' says Smyth. 'The line about, "They look at danger and they laugh their heads off." That really sounds like me and the kind of conversations I had with Morrissey.'

Critics were less concerned about the lyrics than they were its musical plagiarism. Just as Marr borrowed from Marc BOLAN for The Smiths' 'PANIC', so Whyte's tune was an audacious rehash of T.Rex's 'Ride A White Swan' (a record produced by TONY VISCONTI, who himself had been shortlisted to produce Your Arsenal). The singer defended its obvious debt by claiming Bolan's riff was borrowed from early rock and roll in the first place though was honest enough to issue a promotional version of the single in a sleeve mimicking EMI's blue and red 70s T.Rex record bags, the original 'T.REX' logo replaced by 'MOZ'. By the end of the Your Arsenal tour, Morrissey resigned himself to mockingly calling it 'Certain White Swans I Know'.

Unfortunately the success of Bolan's original (number two, January 1971) failed to rub off on Morrissey's 'remake' when released as a single midway through December 1992, its chances hampered by the Christmas chart rush. For the accompanying video, shot on a beach in South Chicago during their summer tour of the US, Morrissey tried, in vain, to coax 'Ringo Whyte' and the rest of the group to don 'real mannish trunks as opposed to the usual huge sexless shorts that you all usually wear'. In the event they kept their jeans on and were barely seen on camera. [5, 36, 94, 374]

Chamberlain, Matt (Morrissey drummer

2005), Standing in for the recently departed Dean BUTTERWORTH, session musician and Tori Amos drummer Matt Chamberlain was hired for the 2005 recording of RINGLEADER OF THE TORMEN-TORS album in Rome. The session was helped by the fact Chamberlain and producer TONY VISCONTI had already worked together on the recent David BOWIE albums Heathen (2002) and Reality (2003). Chamberlain never toured the album with Morrissey (replaced by Matt WALKER), nor did he appear in any of the album's accompanying promo videos where his drums were instead mimed by guitarist Alain WHYTE. [389]

Charlie Bubbles, See DELANEY, Shelagh.

childhood (of Morrissey), See YOUTH OF MORRISSEY.

'Christian Dior' (Morrissey/Boorer), B-side of

'IN THE FUTURE WHEN ALL'S WELL' (2006). A tribute, of sorts, to the legendary French fashion designer who died in 1957 after founding a global clothing and cosmetics empire, the song finds Morrissey pitying Dior for having 'wasted' his life in fashion when he could have better devoted his time to women, drink, drugs or Neapolitan rent boys. As it turns out, he's merely using Dior as a metaphor for himself, confessing to living a similarly ordered life, giving his all to his career, when he would have been happier 'morally bankrupt'. Reiterating the theme of 'THE NEVER-PLAYED SYMPHONIES', 'Christian Dior' is the singer's very honest lament for the wild sex life he never had. Though the lyrics imply that the industrious Dior led a relatively chaste existence, in reality the designer had a succession of gay lovers while one rogue theory about his fatal heart attack at the age of 52 is that it was a severe case of coitus interruptus: the official cause of death was choking on a fishbone.

'Children In Pieces' (Morrissey/Tobias), B-side of 'ALL YOU NEED IS ME' (2008). One of the

most appalling stains upon modern Irish history is the legacy of sexual and physical abuse suffered by orphaned and deprived children in its state-run industrial schools under the care of the Catholic Church's Christian Brothers. The horrifying truth of the institutionalised cruelty only came to light after most had been closed down in the 1970s. The public outcry was such that in March 1998 the Christian Brothers were forced to publish full-page advertisements in Irish newspapers expressing 'deep regret' for the decades of cruelty suffered by their pupils.

'Children In Pieces' is Morrissey's blunt comment on the industrial schools scandal, describing various Catholic authority figures kicking 'the shit' out of their terrified young victims only to mysteriously shy away from sympathy in the final verse as his 'sentimental heart hardens'. It's an appropriate comparison, albeit to Morrissey's detriment, if we contrast his words with those of 'The Magdalene Laundries' from JONI MITCHELL's 1994 album Turbulent Indigo. Mitchell's song deals with a similar subject – the Irish Catholic Church's equally abhorrent 'Magdalene Asylums' for unmarried women – yet manages to highlight the inhumanity and religious hypocrisy with a poetic sensitivity sadly lacking in the crude 'Children In Pieces'. Yet perhaps its biggest drawback is the incongruous musical setting, a clodhopping riff from Jesse Tobias painfully devoid of the sombre drama its subject matter requires, at times making Morrissey sound as if he's mistakenly singing the wrong words over the right melody. First demoed during the earlier RINGLEADER OF THE TORMENTORS sessions, 'Children In Pieces' was recorded in 2007 with Gustavo Santolalla, the award-winning Argentinian composer of the *Brokeback Mountain* soundtrack. (See also 'MY DEAREST LOVE'.)

C

Boorer's atmospheric intro and slow, rolling melody harmonised perfectly with Morrissey's confessional lyrics. It was, therefore, unfortunate that this, Boorer's only song from the RINGLEADER OF THE TORMENTORS sessions, never made the finished album.

Christmas, According to the unrivalled literary demigod Charles DICKENS, 'That man must be a misanthrope indeed in whose breast something like a jovial feeling is not roused – in whose mind some pleasant associations are not awakened – by the recurrence of Christmas.' Alas, Dickens probably wouldn't have been terribly impressed with Morrissey's opposing view that Christmas is 'very annoying'. 'I try to ignore the whole thing,' he said. 'It's a period that just gets in the way and you have to survive it and suffer it, endure it and then you long for January the 6th, 7th, 8th, when life becomes slightly normal again and you don't feel pressurised.' Morrissey's main 'problem' with Christmas is the social obligation to be '[constantly] going out, and you're constantly drunk and insane and so forth … I just endure it, really. When the 6th, 7th, 8th comes around, I think, "Thank God."' In keeping with his 'Bah! Humbug!' outlook, he included SPARKS' 'Thank God It's Not Christmas' on his concert interval tapes in late 2004. However, as the next entry indicates, Morrissey isn't totally immune to a splash of Christmas cheer … [439]

Christmas In Connecticut, 1945 festive comedy listed among Morrissey's favourite films. Recounting his 'miserable' December at home in 1979, the 19-year-old Morrissey wrote to a friend that 'if not for *Christmas In Connecticut* I would have hounded Stretford committing acts of gross indecency'. Its screwball plot centres around the façade of cookery writer Elizabeth Lane (Barbara Stanwyck), whose popular recipe columns portray her as a domestic goddess sharing her kitchen expertise from the idyllic comfort of her Connecticut farm. In reality, and unbeknownst to everybody except her editor and close friends, Lane is

an unmarried hack living in a cramped New York apartment. Not only can she not cook, all her gastronomic hints are borrowed from the friendly chef of her local Hungarian restaurant. The scam is suddenly threatened when her oblivious publisher is moved by a letter from a nurse in love with a wounded sailor asking to visit Lane's 'farm' that Christmas. Facing ruin, she reluctantly agrees to the crackpot scheme of a rich English architect (Reginald Gardiner, also seen in THE MAN WHO CAME TO DINNER), who suggests she hoodwink them by pretending the Connecticut farm he owns is hers: the catch being Lane must marry him. A charming and convoluted romantic farce ensues as Lane struggles to uphold the charade in front of the nurse, the sailor and her publisher. Coincidentally, the set of the Connecticut farm had previously been used in another of Morrissey's favourite films, BRINGING UP BABY. [184, 362, 492]

classical music, Although his lifelong obsession has been with pop music, Morrissey still has time for classical. He once named his favourite piece as Frederic Chopin's Nocturnes – 21 pieces for solo piano, the most popular being his Nocturne No. 6 in G Minor (Opus 15). 'Quite a common choice,' he confessed, recommending a 2003 double CD recording by Canadian pianist Angela Hewitt (Hyperion, CDA67371/2). It was, perhaps, to be expected that he'd gravitate towards a composer who'd led a less than blissful existence; poor Chopin suffered from chronic lung disease most of his adult life and was dead at the age of 39 (he was buried in Paris's Père Lachaise cemetery where Oscar WILDE was later laid to rest).

Morrissey summed up his classical tastes as 'anything that's basically sad'. Not surprisingly, another of his favourites is Henryk Górecki's minimalist choral Symphony No. 3, or the 'Symphony Of Sorrowful Songs'. Composed in 1976, it consists of three movements for orchestra and soprano, all using Polish texts: the first is based on a fifteenth-century prayer known as the 'Holy Cross Lament' in which Mary grieves for Jesus; the second is centred upon a poem scratched upon the wall of a Gestapo cell by an 18-year-old girl shortly before she was murdered; and the third, similar to the first, is a mother's lament for her son killed in the Polish Silesian Uprising around the time of the First World War. A beautiful, grim yet phenomenally popular piece, a special performance by the London Sinfonietta featuring Australian soprano Yvonne Kenny was the closing event of Morrissey's June 2004 MELT-DOWN festival, along with a recital of Arvo Part's equally haunting 1977 minimalist piece Tabula Rasa (the first movement of which, by trivial coincidence, shared its title with Linder STERLING's group, Ludus). Górecki's Symphony No. 3 was also played as exit music on Morrissey's UK tour of February 1995, while future tours would see him play Erik Satie's Gymnopédies and Jacqueline DU PRÉ's famous recital of Edward Elgar's Cello Concerto prior to his support act.

Several of Morrissey's entrance themes have also had classical roots, most famously The Smiths' use of the great Russian composer Sergei PROKOFIEV's 'Dance Of The Knights' from the ballet Romeo And Juliet (as heard on RANK). Among his more popular solo walk-ons is Klaus NOMI's 'Wayward Sisters', based on an excerpt from Act I of Henry Purcell's 1689 opera Dido And Aneas. Nomi's 'The Cold Song', intro music for The Smiths' debut gig in October 1982, was from another Purcell opera, King Arthur, while his 'Der Nussbaum', the entrance for Morrissey's 1988 WOLVERHAMPTON gig, was a lied composed in 1840 by Robert Schumann.

To date, the only overt reference to classical music within a Morrissey recording is Boz BOORER's use of the opening of Shostakovich's Symphony No. 5, sampled throughout 'THE TEACHERS ARE AFRAID OF THE PUPILS'. Other than that, his 1993 live album BEETHOVEN WAS DEAF owes its title to the greatest musical genius of all time (and his affliction) Ludwig van Beethoven, while the sleeve for RINGLEADER OF THE TORMEN-TORS saw Morrissey cast himself as a virtuoso classical violinist complete with tuxedo and bow tie. (See also John GARFIELD.)

As a final note on classical music with regard to The Smiths, it's worth quoting a 1985 television interview between Marr and FACTORY Records founder/Granada reporter Tony Wilson who asked the guitarist where his melodies came from. 'The answer is, I don't know,' replied Marr. 'That's what Mozart used to say, y'know,' Wilson told him. 'Good old Mozart,' grinned Marr. 'Hip guy!' [133, 243, 452, 511]

Clitheroe, Jimmy,

Northern dwarf comedian, best known for his long-running BBC radio series *The Clitheroe Kid* and a pet favourite of Morrissey's. Clitheroe, who was born in the Lancashire town that shared his family name, was 35 when the series began in 1957 but at only four foot and three inches still looked, and sounded, like a pre-pubescent schoolboy, a role he would play on stage, radio, film and television throughout his career.

Morrissey's earliest reference to Clitheroe was in 1989 when discussing his newfound obsession with tapes of vintage BBC radio comedies such as *Round The Horne*, *Beyond Our Ken* and Tommy Handley's *I.T.M.A.* (*It's That Man Again*). 'I've bought a lot of them,' he explained, '[including] *The Clitheroe Kid*.' The latter programme involved 'young' Jimmy getting up to regular mischief underneath the noses of his mother, his Scottish granddad, his big sister Susan and her boyfriend Alfie. *The Clitheroe Kid* ran for 15 years, finishing in 1972 after 290 broadcasts. Though its tame and unsophisticated humour hasn't aged well, there's a notable Mozzerian ring to some of the episode titles: 'History Is A Thing Of The Past', 'New Year, Old Trouble', 'Why Must The Show Go On?' and not least 'Stop The Wedding, I Want To Get Off'.

Morrissey's interest seems to have blossomed during the 90s when, according to his Camden neighbour Alan BENNETT, Clitheroe was a confusingly regular topic of conversation whenever the singer came to visit. Typical of many Morrissey symbolists, Clitheroe's life ended in tragedy. A deeply private and financially prudent man, he lived most of his life with his mother. When she died in 1973, the 51-year-old Clitheroe took an apparently 'accidental' overdose of sleeping pills and was found dead on the day of her funeral. [69, 290, 453]

clothes, As Morrissey's music has changed and evolved over the years, so too has his wardrobe. Significantly, the subject of clothes cropped up in The Smiths' first ever interview for *i-D* magazine in early 1983. 'They don't have the relevance they once had,' said Morrissey. 'Like in the 60s you could look at someone and assess their personality. That's not the case anymore. Clothes are no longer the window of the soul.'

Fashion was to play a major part in the evolution of The Smiths. It was because Johnny Marr worked in X-Clothes, an alternative fashion outlet on Manchester's Chapel Walk, that he befriended the owner of the shop next door, a branch of the Crazy Face clothing emporium run by The Smiths' original manager and benefactor, Joe MOSS. Marr also believes that when he doorstepped Morrissey in the summer of 1982, their shared retro 1950s dress sense (both were 'into' vintage American Levi's) was a contributing factor in establishing a rapport. Dale HIBBERT, The Smiths' first trial bass player, maintains that Marr's fashion-consciousness was paramount in early group discussions, recommending the band all wear identical '50s bowling shirts with different names embroidered on the front'. Certainly, Marr took care, where and when possible, to present a unified image. For their first *TOP OF THE POPS* appearance in November 1983, he took Andy Rourke and Mike Joyce to a local branch of Marks & Spencer to buy matching black roll-neck jumpers, inspired by the look of Stuart Sutcliffe, the doomed 'fifth BEATLE' who died of a brain haemorrhage in 1962. Marr's interest in fashion continued beyond The Smiths, launching his own clothing label, Elk, in 1999 and collaborating with PF Flyer trainers in 2007 to design a collectable 'charity sneaker' limited to 108 pairs.

Morrissey, meantime, would look back upon The Smiths as 'the worst dressed group in the history of cloth', possibly referring to his notorious collection of shirts from Evans, a women's chain store specialising in clothes for the outsized woman. 'They hang very well and show the fact that I have no body whatsoever,' he beamed in 1984. 'They are the kind of shirt I'm fond of for no sensible reason. They are my children.' The singer also admitted he sometimes bought shirts 'from Co-op', wore Marks & Spencer underpants ('white'), and that his favourite jeans were a pair of vintage Levi's purchased on a visit to American relatives in 1979 ('I live in total despair of making a hole in them or something'). His favourite shoes of 1984 were Manuel slip-ons costing an 'extravagant' £55. 'I like them because I can slip in and out of them without having any debate,' he explained. Morrissey also claimed that he washed all his own clothes, by hand, in the bathtub ('every Friday night you'll find [me] immersed in Persil').

By the end of The Smiths, Morrissey had long dispensed of his Evans wardrobe and, as the 90s progressed, developed a taste for classic tailoring and high-end designer brands. 'I'm a Gucci baby,' he declared in 1999. 'These days clothes have a fascination for me – fashion does not. I'm generally 60 per cent Dries Van Noten, 40 per cent Helmut Lang. Marc Jacobs is OK but I think he's a bit of a cruel furrier at times. About five years ago Gucci produced a suit they called the Vegas suit, which I think remains the most beautiful creation ever. I have a few pleather [*plastic leather*] jackets, but people keep pinning notes on the car saying, "How the fuck can you wear leather, you hypocrite?" and, of course, it isn't even leather. So I don't feel quite right in pleather because some very caring and gentle folk think it's the real thing.' Morrissey also revealed he'd long outgrown his taste for Marks & Spencer underwear, preferring to keep his particulars snug in a pair of Swiss Hanro's. [62, 71, 82, 93, 100, 113, 143, 204, 207, 253, 258, 270]

Cobrin, Spencer (Morrissey drummer/co-writer 1991–97), Alongside guitarist Alain WHYTE and bassist Gary DAY, Spencer Cobrin was among

Coates, Ann, Fictitious 'backing voice' on 1986's 'BIGMOUTH STRIKES AGAIN' as credited on the inner sleeve of THE QUEEN IS DEAD. 'Ann Coates' was actually Morrissey's voice, not 'speeded up' as is often misconstrued but filtered through a harmoniser (so it's the same notes at the same speed but transposed to a higher key to produce a comical 'chipmunk' effect). Marr has said that the pseudonym was his suggestion, a play on the Ancoats area north of Manchester city centre. Coincidentally, Anne V. Coates is also the name of an award-winning film editor whose work includes one of Morrissey's favourites, *THE ELEPHANT MAN*. [17, 38, 500]

the three young greenhorns who formed the basis of Morrissey's ideal 'rockabilly band' in the wake of KILL UNCLE, augmented by the more experienced Boz BOORER.

Hailing from the affluent Jewish suburbs of Stanmore in north London, Cobrin began playing drums in his teens. 'I never really considered myself a drummer,' he says. 'I was in love with playing in a band. Had a band I liked needed a banjo player, I'd have taken up banjo. I just happened to choose drums.' In 1988, Cobrin was asked to join north London rockabilly quartet Born Bad, where he first met Whyte and, later, Day. When co-founder/guitarist Guy Bolton quit the group, Cobrin, Whyte and Day continued as a trio, The Memphis Sinners, before producer Clive LANGER intervened in the winter of 1990 with the offer to play with Morrissey (for the full story of the convoluted recruitment process refer to the entry for Whyte).

Initially hired for the 1991 Kill Uncle tour, Cobrin would be Morrissey's main drummer for the rest of the decade and, arguably, the best drummer of his solo career to date. Like Whyte, Cobrin's youthful splendour played a major factor in his recruitment, though he immediately proved his worth in concert as a tough and rhythmically eloquent drummer, infusing the Kill Uncle material with much vim and verve. His playing on 1992's YOUR ARSENAL, Cobrin's first recording session with Morrissey, was equally robust (e.g. 'GLAMOROUS GLUE'). The video for the same album's 'WE HATE IT WHEN OUR FRIENDS BECOME SUCCESSFUL' also played on Cobrin's prettiness, shown teasing the singer by suggestively licking a

Cornetto ice cream: interestingly, Morrissey had originally wanted Cobrin to suck on a more phallic Zoom ice lolly, though none could be found on the day of shooting.

'I was completely green,' says Cobrin. 'When I started playing with Morrissey I was very idealistic, maybe a bit naïve. To begin with it was beyond excitement. I was living on the adrenalin, completely absorbed by the whole thing. There was nothing else in my life, so when we had down time I didn't know how to cope. But things went downhill shortly after Your Arsenal. There was a lot of tension between Boz and Alain about songwriting. I was unaware of the whole publishing aspect and the financial side, but that created incredible tension in the band.'

Cobrin also fell foul of Morrissey's personal assistant at the time, former Smiths sleeve coordinator Jo Slee. 'All communication came through her,' claims Cobrin. 'She was like a teacher, always telling you off for something. There was one night in Chicago where she was screaming at everybody, this blazing row, because she didn't want us to hit the town because she thought we'd miss a video shoot the next day. She was trying to mother me and Gary, begging us not to go out. It was too much.' Cobrin and Day ignored Slee's plea and 'hit the town' regardless, turning up on time for the next day's video shoot for 'CERTAIN PEOPLE I KNOW' looking, in Slee's words, 'puffy-eyed, hungover and defiant'.

In keeping with Morrissey's track record for hiring and firing through third parties, it was Slee who in the spring of 1993 broke the news to Cobrin that he was out of the band. 'It was a

C

phone call,' says the drummer. 'Jo Slee said, "You're no longer required, and neither is Gary." I missed a heartbeat. But that was it.' Cobrin would be replaced by a friend of Boorer's, Woodie TAYLOR, for the recording of VAUXHALL AND I, while Jonny BRIDGWOOD was hired in place of Day. Barely a year later, in early 1994 Cobrin received another phone call out of the blue. 'I was told that they'd been doing stuff with Woodie, but they weren't happy,' says Cobrin, who was called back with Gary Day for a B-sides session. Unfortunately, the recording of 'MOONRIVER' and 'A SWALLOW ON MY NECK' was beset with technical hitches. As a result, Morrissey decided against using Cobrin and Day again, reinstating Taylor and Bridgwood for his next recording, 'BOXERS'.

Cobrin believed he would never work with Morrissey again, only to receive another phone call in January 1995. Once more, Morrissey had expressed his doubts over Taylor after an abortive session at Miraval studios in France (the bones of SOUTHPAW GRAMMAR). After a few days of rehearsal at Abbey Road studios with engineer Danton Supple, Cobrin was back in the band on a permanent basis, first reappearing on the singer's February 1995 UK tour promoting 'Boxers' and the WORLD OF MORRISSEY compilation. As the INTRODUCING MORRISSEY concert video demonstrates, Cobrin brought a harder edge to the Vauxhall material, particularly 'SPEEDWAY' which he attacked with a powerful tribal rhythm. But for Cobrin, the band dynamic already felt strained. 'It was hard for me because Gary wasn't involved,' he says. 'That's nothing against Jonny, but it wasn't the same. The chemistry had changed and it felt strange. For me, it just didn't feel like a band any more.'

1995's Southpaw Grammar would be Cobrin's favourite Morrissey session – the singer would similarly describe Cobrin's work on the album a 'great personal joy' – featuring his solo showpiece on the intro to 'THE OPERATION'. After moving to New York in 1996, Cobrin returned for 1997's MALADJUSTED, by which time he'd sufficiently grown in confidence as a musician to submit homemade keyboard demos for Morrissey's attention.

Of these, three would see the light of day as 'WIDE TO RECEIVE' and the B-sides 'LOST' and 'NOW I AM A WAS', all credited to his full birth name of Spencer James Cobrin. Other Cobrin tunes would also be given lyrics but remain unreleased, among them 'NIGHTMARE', 'HANRATTY' and an early draft of 'IT'S HARD TO WALK TALL WHEN YOU'RE SMALL' (later re-recorded with new music by Whyte).

Sadly, Cobrin's split from Morrissey was over a financial dispute. 'By the end of the Maladjusted tour, it was very depressing,' he explains. 'Things were starting to get weird. There were lawyers and all these contracts being waved under our noses with specific clauses and it was very saddening.' Unhappy with the nature of the short-term contracts they'd been offered as well as a dispute over royalties from the *Introducing Morrissey* video, both Bridgwood and Cobrin decided to leave the band.

Morrissey was angered enough by Cobrin's financial grievances against him to send the drummer an abusive fax message. 'The fax came through and my wife, at the time, picked it up first,' says Cobrin. 'She said, "I don't think you should read this." When I read it, I stayed in bed for a week. I couldn't move. There's no point repeating what it said because it's all water under the bridge now, but at the time it wasn't trivial. That was it, he'd crossed the line. It was the cruellest thing you could say to anyone after working together for so long. It still upsets me, but I realise that I'm one in a long line of people who've been treated like that. If there's anything that gets Morrissey upset more than anything else, it's money.'

A second fax followed. 'A much longer one,' claims Cobrin, 'but there was no apology. It was just more blame, more pointing fingers and being very childish. That was the end of it. I was persona non grata after that.' In 1999, Cobrin would be replaced by former Damned drummer Spike T. Smith before Dean BUTTERWORTH took over in 2002. It was, therefore, very strange that in a 2003 interview Morrissey should discuss his current touring band, saying: 'Boz has his other work, and some of the others like Spencer prefer to work only for me, so they just tend their freesias and wait for the call.'

After parting company with Morrissey, Cobrin tried his luck in a handful of groups before venturing into film music, scoring Angeliki Giannakopoulos's award-winning 2006 documentary about the domestic impact of the war in Iraq, *My Child: Mothers Of War*. 'Looking back, I felt so lucky and fortunate to be playing with Morrissey,' he concludes. 'But my regret is that he was always very distant. I don't think he ever trusted anyone, which shocked me. Once you got into a conversation with him, it was fantastic. You'd have loved to have been really great friends, but you knew if you got too close you'd probably get burnt. It was very sad the way it ended, but that's history now. At the time, Morrissey meant the world to me.' [4, 5, 15, 22, 115, 374]

Cockney Rejects, Self-confessed 'no-nonsense, snot-nosed, brick-wall punk band' from east London whom Morrissey became fixated with during the late 90s. In an age of fake punk posturing, the Rejects prided themselves on being 'the real deal': genuine working-class kids from the notoriously rough Custom House, near Canning Town. They became synonymous with the Oi! movement, a 1980 punk offshoot notorious for attracting a violent SKINHEAD audience, many of whom endorsed right-wing politics and the neo-Nazi British Movement. The Rejects themselves always distanced themselves from the BM and actively spurned their support, but after repeated fighting at their gigs, antagonised by skinhead extremists, they found themselves guilty by association. Such was their reputation for concert violence that the Greater London Council eventually banned them from playing in the capital.

They formed in 1979, fronted by 15-year-old Jeff 'Stinky' Turner (same birthday as Hitler), who'd chosen punk over a promising boxing career: at 13 he was 'Essex Schoolboy Champion'. After a wonderfully raucous indie label debut, 'Flares'N'Slippers' ('slippers' being East End slang for 'trainers'), they signed to EMI, aided by the

support of *Sounds* journalist Garry Bushell who briefly managed the band. Sham 69's Jimmy Pursey produced their major label debut, 'I'm Not A Fool', by which time Bushell had stepped down, replaced by ANGELIC UPSTARTS manager Tony Gordon whom the band would later accuse of embezzling funds. Unlike the more politicised Upstarts, the Rejects were punk music hall, singing about everyday East End characters (their best single, 'Bad Man', was about Turner's in-law who used the gas money to pay off gambling debts) and their beloved WEST HAM United. Sadly, the West Ham connection became their downfall. After covering the Irons' terrace anthem 'I'm Forever Blowing Bubbles' to coincide with the team's victory in the 1980 FA Cup Final (beating Arsenal 1–0), the group became pigeonholed as the club's punk mascots, a reputation exacerbated by tracks like 'War On The Terraces' and 'West Side Boys', which appeared to glamorise football hooliganism. As a result, the violence which followed them around at gigs was more often than not down to rival football factions.

Nevertheless, as Turner later admitted in his autobiography, the Rejects' downfall was largely the fault of their own reckless behaviour, prone to wrecking EMI's studios ('shitting in desks, pissing in filing cabinets, things like that') and refusing to flinch from any aggro that came their way. 'The problem with us was we were too real,' writes Turner. 'We were the genuine article, plus we were white, English and working class – the only group it's permissible to sneer at these days.' It seems for these reasons that Morrissey was drawn to the Rejects. There is no evidence to suggest he ever liked them during their heyday. Certainly if the Robert MACKIE pen pal letters are any indication of his tastes circa 1980, he was the definition of the 'NME pseuds' the group despised and it's difficult to imagine a fan of NICO and THE MONOCHROME SET gaining equal pleasure from typical Rejects' fare like 'Shitter'. Equally significant is a 1987 Smiths article in which Morrissey scornfully accused his interviewer of 'liking Oi! music'. But taking into account his fascination with East End culture (the uncle of Rejects' bassist Vince Riordan was KRAY Twins' victim Jack 'The Hat' McVitie) and the 'forgotten' working-class underdogs eulogised in 'WE'LL LET YOU KNOW', his belated admiration for what he called their 'stories of disorder, and how this country was generally done for' made perfect sense.

Morrissey's Rejects-mania peaked in 1999 on the first of his two in-between tours without a record deal. His interval tape for those shows opened with their biggest UK hit, 'The Greatest Cockney Rip Off' (number 21, May 1980), and also included their B-sides 'East End' and 'I Wanna Be A Star'. Morrissey's stage wear of a West Ham Boys Club T-shirt was another deliberate homage to the Rejects (Turner had worn an identical T-shirt), as were his frequent lyrical changes ('You're gonna need West Ham on your side') and his cry of 'Hello Cockney Rejects!' when addressing the audience of London's Forum. Three years later, he was still paying his respects on stage at London's Royal Albert Hall in September 2002, introducing himself as 'Stinky Turner'.

After inviting them to play in the foyer of London's Royal Festival Hall during his 2004 MELTDOWN festival, Morrissey made the ultimate gesture by providing a foreword for Turner's 2005 memoir, *Cockney Reject*. 'Jeff Turner was obviously singing to avoid murdering someone,' he wrote, 'which was, *I suppose*, diplomatic.' Morrissey likened Turner's voice to 'a kid in Canning Town swimming baths gulping too much chlorinated water … I couldn't detect any S.E.X. in the voice. I imagine he treated all women like buses, or he'd never met one (a woman, not a bus).' It was, however, ironic that Morrissey's foreword should appear in a book co-authored by the Rejects' old manager Garry Bushell, one of The Smiths' first enemies in the press who'd implicated them in the 1983 bogus 'child molesting' scandal surrounding 'REEL AROUND THE FOUNTAIN'. [52, 143, 386]

Cole, Lloyd, Dour, intellectual 80s pop singer/songwriter and frontman of The Commotions who befriended Morrissey in 1984. The Smiths had already established themselves with a couple of hit singles when Lloyd Cole And The Commotions scored their first with 'Perfect Skin' (number 26, July 1984). Their ensuing debut album, Rattlesnakes, met with glowing reviews, some critics likening Cole's glum, sensitive and knowingly intelligent lyrics to those of Morrissey. It was therefore inevitable in the eyes of some sections of the press that the pair should become friends, first meeting backstage at a London Commotions show. 'He was as charming as you'd imagine,' said Cole of Morrissey. 'Lloyd is a tremendously nice person,' said Morrissey of Cole, 'much more fascinating than anything he's ever put on vinyl … which I'm sure will end the relationship straight away. But I think he's a lovely person. We see quite a lot of each other.'

Cocteau, Jean, French surrealist artist, filmmaker, poet, writer and playwright indirectly celebrated on two early Smiths sleeves. The cover of 1983's 'THIS CHARMING MAN' single was sourced from Cocteau's 1950 film *Orphée*, starring his lover, Jean MARAIS. The cover of 1984's HATFUL OF HOLLOW compilation was culled from a 1983 special edition of the French newspaper *Libération* commemorating the 20th anniversary of Cocteau's death: the boy in profile is Cocteau fan Fabrice Collette, showing off his shoulder tattoo copied from Cocteau's anonymously published erotic picture book *Le Livre Blanc* (*The White Book*). Cocteau's distinctive linear drawings, often of faces in profile, might have had some bearing upon the similar graphic sketches of Linder STERLING, which Morrissey himself would copy on his pre-Smiths correspondence with pen pal Robert MACKIE. [334, 374, 538]

There was, it has to be said, an aesthetic similarity between the two – the same black hair (if different styles), dramatic eyebrows, pronounced chin and solemn demeanour. Cole's jangling guitar style also drew comparisons with The Smiths, poising him as a one-man Morrissey/Marr amalgam, though upon closer inspection his means and methods were spectrums apart. When it came to cultural references, Cole was notoriously heavy-handed, peppering his lyrics with the names of Simone de Beauvoir, Grace Kelly and Norman Mailer. Although Morrissey borrowed from literary and cinematic sources, never has he sung anything as crudely referential as 'she looks like Eva Marie Saint in On The Waterfront' ('Rattlesnakes'). The difference between Cole and Morrissey is best illustrated by the fact that the former felt it necessary to namedrop Truman CAPOTE in his lyrics ('Four Flights Up') while the latter thought it more powerful to stick Capote's portrait on a single sleeve ('THE BOY WITH THE THORN IN HIS SIDE').

In 1986, Sandie SHAW bridged the Smiths/Commotions divide with her cover of Cole's 'Are You Ready To Be Heartbroken?' (rumoured to be Morrissey's favourite Commotions track). In 1988 Morrissey was still referring to Cole in interviews as one of the few 'extreme characters' he counted as a friend, though Cole would later play down their acquaintance as lasting only 'a year or two'. 'He changed his phone number pretty much every month,' claimed Cole. 'I would have needed to pester his PR to keep in touch. I wasn't about to do that.'

As a pop group, Lloyd Cole And The Commotions were a moderate success, though by the time Cole disbanded them to go solo in 1990 they could boast only two top 20 hits to The Smiths' eight. Strangely, Morrissey would later crop up in the lyrics of Cole's 1993 album Bad Vibes with 'Seen The Future' and its extremely ambiguous refrain 'Man I need TV/For when I got my Morrissey'. Morrissey has yet to return the favour. When asked about the ex-Smith in 2006, Cole replied that he'd followed his career 'for about the first eight or nine years, but after that point it became apparent that he had a kind of Peter Pan fixation and wasn't interested in growing up. I got to the point where I felt that what he was talking about said nothing to me about my life.' It is therefore assumed that he and Morrissey no longer exchange Christmas cards. [121, 204, 369, 469, 475]

'Come Back To Camden' (Morrissey/Boorer), From the album YOU ARE THE QUARRY (2004). Seven years after leaving London, 'Come Back To Camden' was an apparent kiss-off to the love Morrissey left behind and as such the most titillating slice of autobiography within You Are The Quarry. Camden was the north London borough where he lived throughout the mid-90s, at one time lodging with photographer and personal assistant Jake WALTERS. Inevitably, Walters's name has frequently come up as the song's logical subject matter. 'That song is about a particular person,' admitted Morrissey, though he refused to say who. 'I have a history, yes. And that whole time in my life is a very emotive period for me.' Indeed, 'very emotive' best describes 'Come Back To Camden', a triumph of poetry, speculative soap opera and an impassioned vocal performance over an otherwise indistinct tune swamped in end-of-the-pier synthetic orchestration.

The lyrics were notably BETJEMAN-esque in their descriptiveness of Thames-water tea and chattering taxi drivers – quite apt since Betjeman himself was born in the Camden borough, near the Kentish Town end of Hampstead Heath. Morrissey seemed especially fond of the 'slate-grey Victorian skies' image, slipping a similar phrase in conversation when interviewed around the album's release, pining for Manchester's equivalent 'grey slate of the sky'. Beyond such misty-eyed reminiscences of the city he left behind, 'Come Back To Camden' contained rare affection for its secret flame, foreshadowing the graphic eroticism of 'DEAR GOD PLEASE HELP ME' with its mention of touching legs and upwardly lounging knees. Such gossip-fuelling intrigue and forthright sentimentality made it one of Quarry's obvious highlights though, multiplying that intrigue, it was the only song from the album never played live during the accompanying tour. [119, 207, 212, 458]

Cooke, Sam, See 'THERE I'VE SAID IT AGAIN'.

Coronation Street, The longest-running British television soap opera, which became an obsession of Morrissey's when growing up in the 60s and early 70s. Produced in Manchester by Granada Television and set in the fictitious Mancunian district of Weatherfield, it was first broadcast on 9 December 1960 when Morrissey was barely 18 months old. The brainchild of Lancashire scriptwriter Tony Warren, he'd later boast that 'only a gay man could have created *Coronation Street*'. Warren grew up in the 1940s 'a curiously cissy-ish little boy ... and because I was confused about my sexuality, because I wanted to know what I was, I used to watch very closely what made men and women tick. Out of those very detailed observations, which I'd been making since I was five or six, came the original *Coronation Street* characters. My grandmother, for instance, was the basis for Ena Sharples.'

As a child of the 60s, Morrissey grew up watching the show in its Warren-scripted heyday (what the singer later called the 'venom and spite' years), dominated by matriarchal battleaxe Ena Sharples (played by Violet Carson, whom Morrissey once joked he'd like to see on the cover of *Rolling Stone* magazine) and her constant feuds with the feisty Elsie Tanner (Pat PHOENIX, future cover star of The Smiths' 'SHAKESPEARE'S SISTER'). Such was his fascination with The Street that as a child Morrissey would hang about outside Granada Television studios in central Manchester in the hope of obtaining the autograph of Sharples's timid side-kick Minnie Caldwell, actress Margot Bryant.

Like Warren, Morrissey was also obsessed with 'the way people spoke' from a young age and would often make audio recordings of programmes 'which to most people were of no consequence whatsoever' to study the script. It's fair to assume that *Coronation Street* itself was one such programme, since by the age of 12

Morrissey was sending his own ideas for scripts and storylines for the attention of Granada producer and chief scriptwriter Leslie Duxbury. Among Morrissey's ideas was a plot involving a jukebox being planted in the local pub, the Rovers Return ('much to the obvious horror of the regulars who, for some unknown reason, oppose any kind of change in their lives'), as well as a handful of divorces and 'the odd strangulation'. Though his ideas were rejected, he at least provoked an intrigued response from Duxbury, who began a brief correspondence with the young Morrissey.

As much as the singer reminisced about the glory days of The Street, he was extremely critical about its 'demise', as he saw it, during the mid-80s. 'I think the programme is unsalvageably doomed,' he mourned, blaming the 'plotless' scripts, the lapse into 'caricature', the 'appalling' acting, their absence of any vegetarians ('the very notion of somebody who opposes Betty Turpin's hotpot is a bit too radical') and the loss of strong characters such as Elsie Tanner, who left in January 1984. 'At one time, though, I thought it was full of poetic instinct and it meant a great deal to many people. But those days are certainly gone. I find the thing unbearable now ... There are so many people I'd wish death upon in *Coronation Street* now. I'm still desperately searching for any point to the existence of Deirdre and Ken, who take blandness to a new extreme.'

In spite of these and other misgivings, Morrissey still nominated *Coronation Street* his favourite television programme throughout 1985. Nor was it coincidence that he should choose SALFORD LADS CLUB as the location for the inner sleeve group portrait of THE QUEEN IS DEAD, situated on the corner of the real Coronation Street in Ordsall, Salford (the original set of the programme was based on nearby Archie Street, since demolished). The promo video for his 1988 solo single 'EVERYDAY IS LIKE SUNDAY' would also feature actress Cheryl Murray, who'd left the soap in 1983 after playing Elsie Tanner's wanton young lodger, Suzie Birchall.

Other than Morrissey's love of the programme, another slim degree of separation between *Coronation Street* and The Smiths is provided by the character of Norman 'Curly' Watts played by actor Kevin Kennedy. Prior to joining the soap in 1983, Kennedy played guitar in short-lived local band The Paris Valentinos alongside a young Johnny Marr and Andy Rourke. [87, 139, 146, 168, 175, 211, 268, 362, 425]

'Cosmic Dancer' (Marc Bolan), B-side of
'PREGNANT FOR THE LAST TIME' (1991). Morrissey was drawn to this ghostly space ballad from T.Rex's 1971 album Electric Warrior for the simple reason it was 'a very sad song', one which in its prophetic image of dancing into the grave also offered a poignant analogy of its author's abrupt life. Beyond a mere tribute to one of his teenage heroes, Morrissey brought a chilling personal touch to 'Cosmic Dancer', changing the past tense of the original lyrics so that this same dance 'into the tomb' becomes a fate yet to await him, as if condemning himself to follow Bolan's doomed footsteps.

His decision to tackle the song was a last-minute whim when preparing for his first full solo tour to promote KILL UNCLE in the spring of 1991. According to guitarist and fellow Bolan apostle Boz BOORER, Morrissey had recently bought a VHS copy of the 1972 T.Rex concert film *Born To Boogie*, which they watched during rehearsals. Inspired by its acoustic live version of 'Cosmic Dancer',[1] Morrissey asked Boorer to re-create a similar arrangement, introduced as a regular encore for the early Kill Uncle dates. By far its most historic rendition was that performed as a duet with David BOWIE before 14,000 spontaneously combusting fans at Los Angeles' Great Western Forum on 2 June 1991. The version featured on the 'Pregnant' single was an earlier recording from Utrecht, Holland on 1 May 1991, only the third time Morrissey had played it. A different recording from Costa Mesa on 1 June 1991 can also be heard on the compilation MY EARLY BURGLARY YEARS. [66, 290, 389]

1. It's also been speculated that Morrissey may have covered the track due to its mythical JOBRIATH connection. According to glam rock legend, when Tyrannosaurus Rex played Los Angeles in 1969 Jobriath, then performing in the musical *Hair* with Bolan's future partner Gloria Jones, first introduced the couple and, it's claimed, also inspired the lyrics of 'Cosmic Dancer'. Not that Morrissey needed as indirect a motive: it already had deep nostalgic significance as one of the songs played by T.Rex at Manchester's Belle Vue on 16 June 1972, the 13-year-old Morrissey's first, life-changing pop concert.

County, Wayne/Jayne, Alias 'The Lenny
Bruce of rock and roll'. As a teenage fan of the NEW YORK DOLLS, PATTI SMITH and the RAMONES, Morrissey was inevitably drawn towards Wayne County, one of the most outrageous characters to emerge from the early 70s New York punk scene whom he deemed 'an extraordinary figure'. Born in Georgia as Wayne Rogers, after decamping to New York in the late 60s he befriended Warhol superstars Jackie Curtis and Holly Woodlawn, both immortalised in Lou Reed's 'Walk On The Wild Side' along with Candy DARLING. He made his stage debut as Wayne County playing 'a psychotic lesbian' in Curtis's stage play *Femme Fatale* beside Patti Smith and was subsequently cast in Warhol's play *Pork* before forming his first band, Queen Elizabeth (named not after the English monarch but a 'queen named Elizabeth' he knew back in Atlanta).

On stage, the openly gay County offered an extreme version of the Dolls' gender-bending rock and roll act; donning swastikas, inflated condoms, high heels modelled on male genitalia and 'pretending to sit on the toilet while fucking myself with a dildo'. In 1972, County signed with David BOWIE's management company, MainMan, though proved too controversial to gain a record deal. It was during this period that County regularly performed his song 'Queenage Baby' which he, and others, believe to have inspired Bowie's 1974 hit 'Rebel Rebel'.

The UK punk explosion brought County to London in 1977, encouraged by photographer and friend Lee Childers, then managing Dolls' guitarist Johnny Thunders's new group, The

Heartbreakers, who'd been booked on the SEX PISTOLS' fated Anarchy tour. Forming a new group, The Electric Chairs, County released a handful of UK singles over the next couple of years, the most notorious being 1978's 'Fuck Off' ('If you don't want to fuck me, baby/Fuck off'). By the time he decided to return to New York in 1979, Wayne had changed his name to Jayne County and declared himself a woman, though, technically speaking, he was still a pre-operative transsexual.

It's possible that Morrissey's early lyric written circa 1978 '(I Think) I'm Ready For The Electric Chair' was inspired by the name of County's group (see Billy DUFFY, THE NOSEBLEEDS). Moreover, his interest in County was a logical adjunct to his prevailing Dolls fixation and his admiration for all artists who challenged gender and sexual stereotypes, typified by County's 'Man Enough To Be A Woman' and his cover of 60s garage band The Barbarians' 'Are You A Boy Or Are You A Girl?' Above all else, Morrissey was impressed as much by the look of County as his music – in particular one of his more dramatic wigs which spelt out the name of his favourite British beat group, The Dave Clark Five, in rhinestones. [95, 277]

court case (Joyce v Morrissey and Marr), Casting an indelible blot upon The Smiths' otherwise unblemished legacy is the 1996 High Court case in which drummer Mike Joyce successfully contested his share of group earnings against Morrissey and Johnny Marr. The ruling in Joyce's favour was especially damaging to Morrissey, who would contest the verdict well into the next decade. The singer's refusal to reimburse Joyce according to the judge's decision would also precipitate his decision to leave the United Kingdom for America, beyond the court's jurisdiction. The emotional fallout of the case continues to haunt The Smiths and remains a deeply contentious issue among all concerned, especially Morrissey, who continues to defy the verdict and condemn Joyce whenever interviewed on the subject.

The bare facts of the civil (not criminal) case are as follows. Joyce's objective was to challenge his

share of net profits from SMITHDOM Ltd, a company established in early 1984 where all of the group's income was directed *bar* songwriting and publishing revenue (which Morrissey and Marr alone were exclusively entitled to). His prosecution rested on the premise that, since there were four members of The Smiths, under the 1890 Partnership Act he was entitled to an obligatory equal quarter share of 25 per cent. Morrissey and Marr's defence held that, throughout the entire history of the group, Joyce and Rourke had verbally complied to each take only a 10 per cent share.

The reason the judge awarded in Joyce's favour was because no written contract stipulating this alleged 40-40-10-10 split was ever drawn up. As the court ruled, Morrissey and Marr were unable to '[rebut] the *presumption* of equality contained in section 24 of the Partnership Act' (my italics). That is, Joyce did not have to prove he *was* entitled to 25 per cent but Morrissey and Marr had to prove he *had* agreed to a share lower than 25 per cent. Consequently, without documentary evidence in support of the latter, the law was automatically weighted in the drummer's favour by 'presumption of equality'. Marr would subsequently describe his and Morrissey's failure to formalise a financial contract with all four members as The Smiths' biggest mistake. 'It's the only regret I've got,' he said in 2004. 'That little loophole where we didn't sign *what was agreed*. Someone thought they were being clever by not getting it down, and it ended up blowing up in everyone's faces.'

The legal pursuit of owed band earnings followed their split in 1987; during the trial the official end of the group was named as 31 May 1987, the point where 'the partnership was dissolved'. Within a year of the break-up, Joyce, Rourke and Craig GANNON all began legal proceedings against Morrissey and Marr contesting their share of income (or outstanding payment in Gannon's case). Strangely, all three were still in litigation with Morrissey when they were re-recruited as his solo backing band in the winter of 1988 for the WOLVERHAMPTON gig and the recording of the singles 'THE LAST OF THE FAMOUS

INTERNATIONAL PLAYBOYS' and 'INTERESTING DRUG'. By March 1989, both Joyce and Gannon parted company with Morrissey, each refusing to drop their respective lawsuits which now made their position in his band untenable. Morrissey would later comment, 'What I find particularly abhorrent is that Joyce began legal action in the late 80s [then] worked with me for a while in which time he never mentioned that case. When I told him that I did not want to work with him any longer, that's when he reactivated his case.'

Only the cash-strapped and soon-to-be-married Andy Rourke yielded to Morrissey's offer of an out-of-court settlement in the region of £83,000. His acquiescence ensured he'd stay on as Morrissey's bass player and occasional co-writer for another year until the singer no longer required his services in either field. Gannon successfully won his High Court claim against Morrissey and Marr in 1990 and was awarded £42,000. Joyce, meanwhile, would have to wait seven years before his action finally made it into the courtroom. In the interim, during the early 90s Morrissey's acrimony towards his various plaintiffs (Stephen STREET had also begun a separate lawsuit against the singer) began to bubble over in interviews. Among his more catty remarks regarding The Smiths' rhythm section was his claim in 1992 that they were merely 'lucky', speculating, 'If Andy Rourke and Mike Joyce had had another singer they would never have gotten further than Salford shopping centre.'

Joyce has subsequently recounted a surprising tale in which, not long after the 'Salford shopping centre' comment, he bumped into Morrissey near the singer's home in Altrincham, Greater Manchester, circa early 1993, only to end up taking him 'for a pint'. When the drummer cautiously brought up the subject of the impending court case, apparently Morrissey deliberately changed the subject. Assuming Joyce's version of this story is true, it implies either that Morrissey was able to temporarily set aside his concerns over the lawsuit for old times' sake, or that he had yet to treat the implications of Joyce's grievance with the gravity it deserved. It wasn't until November 1995 that the singer and Marr attempted to avoid taking the case to trial by formally admitting that there had been a partnership agreement between all four members of the group. They paid Joyce £273,000 as a proposed settlement of his share, which they still valued at 10 per cent. 'He wanted more,' Morrissey would later state in court, '[and] I thought the fact he was trying to sue me was extremely unfair.' Unwilling to relinquish his original petition for 25 per cent, Joyce persevered with his claim.

On Monday 2 December 1996, at the High Court in the Royal Courts of Justice on The Strand in central London, the four ex-Smiths found themselves back under the same roof for the first time in over nine years on the opening day of the court hearing. According to Joyce, despite the monies at stake, the atmosphere between the four prior to entering the court was one of surreal bewilderment. 'It was weird,' he says. 'It wasn't like daggers drawn, it was more like nodding "all right?" to one another. Strangely friendly. When we were called into the court, Morrissey walked ahead of me. He did that thing where you hold the door open for someone and then pretend to let it go back in their face as a joke. He had a funny smile. Maybe it was because he didn't honestly believe he was going to lose.' It was during the first day that Joyce's prosecution lawyer, Nigel Davis QC, observed that Morrissey regarded Joyce and Rourke as 'mere session musicians, as readily replaceable as parts of a lawnmower'. In many subsequent reports of the case, the latter statement would be falsely attributed to Morrissey himself. In 2002 the singer added, 'I never said it … but I agree with it.'

It was up to the defence team of Ian Mill QC (for Morrissey) and Robert Englehart QC (for Marr) to convince Judge John Weeks that Joyce had concurred with their specified agreement of 10 per cent of group earnings, excluding songwriting and publishing revenue. Morrissey and Marr's argument consisted of mostly anecdotal evidence, citing various instances when Joyce discussed or contested his 10 per cent share, either way confirming that he understood the financial terms of his employment. Out of their defence came some surprising revelations, among them that in 1986 Joyce had allegedly asked Morrissey if he could make up his group earnings to 25 per cent by taking over as group manager. However, the crux of the 40-40-10-10 agreement centred on an incident during the making of THE SMITHS album at Pluto studios in Manchester in October 1983. After cross-examination, it transpired that Morrissey had threatened to leave the group unless Marr could convince Rourke and Joyce to each accept a 10 per cent share. Marr, allegedly, then informed Rourke and Joyce of the situation, adding that he was also considering leaving the group because of Morrissey's demand. In order to stop Marr from leaving and save the future of The Smiths, Rourke and Joyce complied with Morrissey's stipulated profit split of 10 per cent. Unfortunately, at no point during subsequent meetings with ROUGH TRADE lawyers and accountants did Morrissey or Marr formalise the 40-40-10-10 split in a signed legal document.

Similarly, their defence also relied on another anecdote during the making of STRANGEWAYS, HERE WE COME at The Wool Hall near Bath in the spring of 1987. When the group's new lawyer, Patrick Savage of the firm O. J. Kilkenny & Co., visited The Wool Hall for a business meeting with Morrissey and Marr, he is alleged to have spoken with Rourke and Joyce in the studio kitchen. Savage testified that he'd asked Rourke, in the presence of Joyce, what percentage they were on. Rourke allegedly replied, 'We get ten per cent,' to which Joyce said nothing by way of contradiction. Both Rourke and Joyce would deny this exchange took place and the judge dismissed the credibility of Savage's story.

On the fourth day of the case, Thursday 5 December, Morrissey took the witness stand. His reaction to Joyce's counsel when cross-examined – uncooperative, awkward and frequently insulting (telling his prosecutor '[your questions] are much too time-consuming') – was to cost him dearly. When the verdict was announced, even his own QC admitted the singer had 'betrayed a degree of arrogance'. As the 1998 appeal hearing later ruled, 'Mr Morrissey was a litigant who fell into the common trap of understanding the adversarial process as either obliging him or alternatively presenting him with the opportunity to fight a war of words with his cross-examiner. As many famous trials have demonstrated, however intelligent and gifted the litigant the ground upon which the contest takes place is so uneven that he is inevitably worsted. By misinterpreting his role Mr Morrissey clearly forfeited the judge's sympathy.'

The persecutory similarities between his predicament and that of his hero, Oscar WILDE, wouldn't have been lost on Morrissey and it's reasonable to suggest that like Wilde he regarded his performance in the dock as literally that – a performance of wittier-than-thou psychological jousting to be played to the gallery. After the trial, Andy Rourke offered a surprisingly sympathetic analysis of the singer's behaviour. 'He just sort of came across wrong in court,' said Rourke. 'He just came across as Morrissey, but to a court judge, that probably is truculent. I don't think he did himself any favours. It was a difficult situation to be in, but I think he found it a lot more difficult than the rest of us.'

The case drew to a close on Tuesday 10 December, with a summary from Marr's defence lawyer, stressing that his client 'had come over in his evidence as a very decent, honest person – scrupulously fair – who was not going to cheat his friends. The court has heard that both Michael Joyce and Andy Rourke accepted from an early stage that both Morrissey and Marr would get more than them.' The following day, Wednesday 11 December, Judge John Weeks delivered his lengthy verdict, awarding in favour of Joyce. Morrissey didn't show up to court to hear the damages, estimated at one and a quarter million pounds plus legal costs. Marr did and according to *The Times* left the court looking 'shocked, pale and refusing to comment'.

Weeks found Joyce and Rourke to be 'straightforward and honest, unintellectual and certainly not financially sophisticated or aware'. Marr was considered by Weeks 'a more engaging personality, a more reasonable character and probably the most intelligent of the four, but seemed to me to be willing to embroider his evidence to a point where he became less credible'. Weeks saved his most damning character profile for the absent singer, coining the three adjectives which would dominate all press coverage of the case and become an oft-quoted godsend to his numerous detractors. 'Morrissey was more complicated and didn't find giving evidence easy or a happy experience,' stated Weeks. 'He was *devious, truculent and unreliable* when his own interests were at stake.'

Morrissey immediately issued a statement, expressing his disappointment and surprise at the verdict 'particularly given the weight of evidence against Mike Joyce's claim … I will be considering the terms of the judgment with my solicitors to assess possible grounds for appeal.' He later alleged that 'the following week the word "truculent" was painted across the door of my mother's house'. In January 1997, one month after the hearing, Morrissey returned to the studio to record his MALADJUSTED album, venting some of his indignation upon the controversial track 'SORROW WILL COME IN THE END'. When promoting the album later that year, he unleashed the first of many vicious tirades against Joyce's victory and his own treatment by the British court system. 'It was presided over by a judge who had no knowledge of the music industry,' he claimed. 'He had to have TOP OF THE POPS explained to him. The whole point was, "Get Mozzer. Get him in the witness box and grill him." [Weeks's] words could have ruined my life. But he wanted to do that because he knew the press was writing about it, and all judges want to be famous. It makes me feel that if you ever come up against a judge or have to stand in a witness box, the best thing to do is lie. Don't bother with the truth.'

'The court case was a potted history of the life of The Smiths,' he ruminated. 'Mike, talking constantly and saying nothing. Andy, unable to remember his own name. Johnny, trying to please everyone and consequently pleasing no one. And

Morrissey under the *scorching* spotlight in the *dock*, being *drilled*. "How dare you be successful? How dare you move on?" To me, The Smiths were a beautiful thing and Johnny left it, and Mike has destroyed it … It was like watching a plane crash. And I'd look down at Johnny's face and I would look at Mike and Andy and think, this is probably as sad as life would ever get.'

His despair was exacerbated in November 1998 when his appeal against the verdict – Marr would not contest – was rejected. As well as upholding Weeks's original ruling in favour of Joyce, the appeal refused to accept the plea from Morrissey's new solicitor, Murray Rosen QC, that Weeks's summation of 'devious, truculent and unreliable' was, as he'd protested, 'a gratuitous and unwarranted character assassination'. Morrissey's disappointment fermented into a paranoid conspiracy theory. 'We have to realise that this judge [Weeks] is a Lord of the Hunt [and] I have in the past said things about that,' he declared. '[He'd] obviously been primed on my character, and told that I had written about THATCHER and the Queen. It's likely that Thatcher had appointed [him].' Weeks would become second only to Joyce on Morrissey's most-hated list, describing the judge as '[the] face of human evil' and insisting, 'If I can get somebody to examine his words and the case, I believe he'd have to step down.'

After his appeal was refused by the House of Lords, Morrissey claims he complained to prime minister Tony Blair (who wasn't interested) and, stranger still, the Queen (apparently 'very nice'). In 2002 he announced plans to challenge the case further in the European Court of Human Rights. Although Marr had since paid up his half of the reimbursement to Joyce ('He watched the way my appeals ran and when they were rejected, he settled,' stated Morrissey), seven years after the verdict Morrissey still had not. By moving to America, he ensured that he no longer held any property in his name that could be claimed as capital by Joyce's lawyers still pursuing the funds. According to Morrissey, Joyce retaliated by putting a charge on the house of Morrissey's mother as well as his sister. 'The judge did not explain to Joyce how he could get the money,' he clarified. 'As every contract was always with Morrissey and Marr, no company will recognise Joyce so he's issuing writs left, right and centre. He has been at the stage door of every concert I've played recently, trying to get money. He is a purely evil person and he has persecuted my mother, my nephews and sister, but he presents the public face of a person who's hard done by and has been thrown to the wayside.'

In 2003, Joyce attempted to sue Morrissey under the Insolvency Act but reportedly abandoned the case. At the time of writing, the legal position between Morrissey and Joyce remains in a permanent stalemate. 'Joyce will go on for the rest of his life, a pest to everybody that's in my life,' the singer seethed in 2003. 'That defines him now, that's what his life is. And it allows him to continue and be a part of my story. It has become a complete farce and there is only one victim and the victim is me.'

The fallout from the court case has extinguished whatever shreds of hope existed for a Smiths reunion. Apart from the obvious impossibility of Morrissey and Joyce ever sharing a stage again, the case also put a strain on the relationship between the singer and Marr. Morrissey would accuse his former co-writer of failing to stick up for him in the media concerning Judge Weeks's comments. 'The criticism of me has been so relentless,' he explained, '[but] Johnny has never dispelled it. He didn't stand up and say, "No, Morrissey is not devious, truculent or unreliable." He could have fought Joyce more forcefully. For those reasons, a wedge has occurred.'

Marr's lifelong friendship with Rourke had also been damaged by the case, though happily by 2005 the wounds had healed enough for both to rekindle their bond. Happier still, contrary to Morrissey's biggest fear that Joyce's actions had 'put a slur on the whole thing' and despite Marr's anxieties over 'the industry of negativity' that dogged press reports of the group well into the early 00s, ultimately the court case failed to eclipse their brilliance. As time marches on, though the conflict between Morrissey and Joyce

will surely go to the grave, these ancient business dealings grow increasingly pale, irrelevant and uninteresting to a modern audience for whom the dismal thud of a judge's gavel is but an impotent whimper beside the sublime roar and storm of The Smiths' music. [53, 74, 79, 86, 88, 110, 114, 115, 143, 151, 154, 191, 194, 226, 248, 403, 405, 410, 411]

Coward, Noël, 'I believe that since my life began, the most I've had is just a talent to amuse.' So Morrissey introduced himself on stage at Manchester's Apollo in May 2006, and again that same month at the London Palladium. He was quoting, or rather singing, directly from his greatest forebear of insurmountably English wit, derision and pathos, Noël Coward. Significantly, the line came from 1929's 'If Love Were All', the same Coward song Morrissey previously paraphrased on 1991's 'FOUND FOUND FOUND': 'I believe the more you love a man/the more you give your trust/the more you're bound to lose.'

We know from his letters to pen pal Robert MACKIE that Morrissey was already listening to Coward records in 1981. Twenty-seven years later he was still praising him as a 'fantastic lyricist', singling out 1952's 'There Are Bad Times Just Around The Corner', a humorous state-of-the-nation address almost 'PANIC'-esque in its itinerary of discontent from Humberside to Dublin. Another more oblique Coward reference can be found in the fade-out of 'LIFEGUARD SLEEPING, GIRL DROWNING' featuring a sample of Kay Walsh from 1942's *In Which We Serve*, which Coward wrote, co-directed and starred in. [334, 421]

Cramps, The, On Friday 8 June 1979, the 20-year-old Morrissey witnessed the divinely outrageous godfathers of psychobilly The Cramps support The Police at Manchester's Free Trade Hall. His awestruck enthusiasm was captured in the letters pages of two music weeklies. In the NME, they were 'the kind of group that start revolutionary outrages'. In *Sounds*, he went to great lengths highlighting their superiority to a headline act whom The Smiths would later refuse to support:[1] 'The Cramps are worth their weight in gold for making The Police seem like a great big sloppy bowl of mush. The Police, hardly dabbling in degrees of the unexpected, presented a farcical imitation of their Rock Goes To College thing – several people clapped, but then, I suppose, someone has to. The Cramps were enough to restore faith in the most spiritless. They have it all, and their drummer [Bryan Gregory] is the most compelling in rock history. Back to The Cramps or perish. It is written.'

The following March, Morrissey got to salivate over The Cramps in greater detail when reviewing their Manchester Polytechnic show for *Record Mirror*. 'The Cramps introduced good-natured perversity to a Mancunian crowd of epileptic butterflies. This is a group not to be analysed but to be FELT.' In his conclusion, he hailed them as 'the most important US export since the NEW YORK DOLLS … Manchester will never be the same again. Thank God!' Two months later, he became a founding member of 'The Legion Of The Cramped', a UK fan club co-ordinated by Lindsay Hutton, editor of the Scottish fanzine *The Next Big Thing* which Morrissey had also written for. That autumn, an irate Danny Loker from Bradford complained to *Sounds* that he'd sent £1.50 to a 'Cramps fan club [with] a Manchester address' only for his cheque to be cashed without receiving anything. 'No problem,' *Sounds* informed Loker. 'The Cramps' fan club, originally based at 384 Kings Road, Stretford, Manchester and run by ace supporters Steven Morrissey and Lindsay Hutton has now moved to Scotland … Meanwhile, Steven Morrissey has been waiting, fan club kit at the ready, for some sign of human movement from your direction … your full quota of membership stuff will be with you by the time you read this.'

On 4 February 2009, the tragic news broke that singer Lux Interior, half of the group's core husband-and-wife team with guitarist Ivy Rorschach, was dead at the age of 62. The following day, Morrissey played a short set for the ABC television programme *Jimmy Kimmel Live*, ending 'SOMETHING IS SQUEEZING MY SKULL' with a heartfelt tribute cry of 'Lux Interior!' Evidently, once a Cramped Legionnaire, always a Cramped Legionnaire. [173]

1. As Johnny Marr reasoned at the time, 'We're already more important than The Police will ever be.'

Crazy Face, See MOSS, Joe.

Crystals, The, See 'WHAT A NICE WAY TO TURN SEVENTEEN'.

Cromwell, Oliver, Self-appointed 'Lord Protector' during the English Interregnum of the mid-seventeenth century referenced in 'IRISH BLOOD, ENGLISH HEART'. As some critics pointed out at the time, Morrissey's depiction of Cromwell as a figure whom the present monarchy 'still salute' didn't make a lot of historical sense. As a Parliamentarian military leader in the English Civil War, Cromwell was responsible for abolishing the monarchy after his Roundhead army defeated (and beheaded) Charles I. Refusing to take the royal crown himself, he ruled as Lord Protector from 1653 until his death from malaria in 1658. When the monarchy was eventually restored with the coronation of Charles II in 1660, Cromwell was still considered such an enemy of the crown that his dead body was dug up and symbolically hanged in public. While the context may have been confusing, Morrissey's hatred of Cromwell within the song was symptomatic of its lyrics' Gaelic pride. In Irish history, Cromwell was a genocidal dictator who, as Morrissey noted, 'slaughtered millions of Irishmen just to get them out of the way'. Citations of Cromwell in pop music have been few and far between, though 25 years before 'Irish Blood, English Heart' Elvis Costello preceded Morrissey in scoring a Cromwell-referencing top five hit with 1979's 'Oliver's Army'. [231]

'Dagenham Dave' (Morrissey/Whyte),
Morrissey's 19th solo single (from the album
SOUTHPAW GRAMMAR), released August 1995, highest UK chart position #26. Critically ridiculed as
evidence that Morrissey had finally 'lost it' during
the 90s, 'Dagenham Dave' was a victim of musical fashion. Although he had high hopes for the
single, telling one reporter that in terms of radio
play he'd never received 'a welcome as good', it
had the misfortune to be released just as Britpop
was reaching its zenith: precisely one week after
the famous Oasis vs Blur 'single war' of late
August '95. There was some irony in that Morrissey, and The Smiths in particular, had been a key
influence on both bands, yet the fact 'Dagenham
Dave' failed to crack the top 20 while his Britpop
progeny were battling it out in the top five was
interpreted by the music press as emblematic of
Morrissey's cultural obsolescence.

Ignoring its undue stigma, 'Dagenham Dave' is
a mettlesome pop cartoon featuring, if nothing
else, the greatest utterance of the word 'pie' by any
singer in the entire history of recorded music. Sharing its title with a 1977 album track by The Stran-
glers (a coincidence Morrissey never explained),
and also referencing the birthplace of Sandie SHAW,
'Dagenham Dave' describes an Essex boy grotesquery; gobbling pies, nuzzling women's chests and
advertising the name of his latest girlfriend on his
car windscreen. Yet, just when it seems as if the
song is a mere caricature, Morrissey throws in a
homoerotic punchline. Secretly, Dave desires a very
different physical contact, one he's incapable of
realising for fear 'he might self-combust'.

The shortest track on Southpaw Grammar, it
was the most obvious single contender thanks to
Whyte's bold, stomping chorus and ornate outro.
The sleeve featured an archive mid-60s shot of
Dagenham-born England football manager Terry
VENABLES while its accompanying video starred
former *Grange Hill* actor Mark 'Gripper Stebson'
Savage as the eponymous Dave who tries to
impress his girlfriend with a second-hand gold
disc of VAUXHALL AND I ('For sale – one previous
owner'). [4, 40, 236]

Dallesandro, Joe, American underground film actor, gay sex symbol and cover star of 1984's THE SMITHS album. Dallesandro had an extraordinarily colourful upbringing. His mother gave birth to him when she was 16 and was later sent to prison for car theft. Young Joe ended up in foster care in New York before reuniting with his father in his early teens. Expelled from high school for punching the principal, he then took to stealing cars himself and was eventually wounded by police gunfire after crashing through a toll gate in a stolen vehicle. As punishment he was sent to reform school, but escaped. He then robbed a cinema and fled to Mexico before hitchhiking to Los Angeles, getting arrested in a fight and being ordered to return to his father who was now living in New Jersey. He married the daughter of his father's girlfriend, with whom he had a son, only to leave her for life as a model and male prostitute hanging out in New York's Times Square.

In 1967, he was 'discovered' by Andy Warhol and director Paul Morrissey who later cast him alongside Candy DARLING in 1968's *Flesh*, an underground response to John Schlesinger's *Midnight Cowboy*, with Dallesandro playing the central junkie hustler. The Smiths album cover stems from the same film; the original photo reveals Dallesandro sat on a bed with fellow Warhol regular Louis Waldon, whom he appears to be masturbating out of frame. It's possible Morrissey sourced the image from the 1974 book *A Pictorial History Of Sex In Films* by Parker TYLER, where it appears on page 151 in the chapter on 'The Gay Sexes'.

Considering its original context, the sleeve was a brilliant act of pop subversion on Morrissey's part, even if he'd immediately confess to feeling 'a twinge of sadness' after its release. 'Up till then everything had an icy Britishness to it,' he explained, 'then I succumbed to the whole Warhol thing, like those modernites who crave the Factory thing and everything from late 60s New York which surely was a depressing waste of time.' The Smiths weren't the first group to feature Dallesandro on a record cover, although they were the first to show him from the waist up: his is the ample crotch seen bulging under denim on Warhol's iconic sleeve for THE ROLLING STONES' 1971 album Sticky Fingers. [193, 374, 387]

Dance Hall, 1950 pre-rock and roll Ealing musical drama listed among Morrissey's favourite films and starring one of his favourite actresses, Diana DORS. The flimsy plot follows four west London factory girls who spend most of their spare time jiving in Chiswick Palais to the sound of Ted Heath and his orchestra. The main drama centres on Eve (Natasha Parry) and her possessive lump of a husband (Donald Houston) as well as the Greater London Amateur Dancing Championship hopes of the pleasantly dull Georgie (actress/singer Petula Clark, whose 1964 hit 'Downtown' featured on Morrissey's interval tapes in 1995). Other plot strands involve man-hungry Carole (a permanently puckered-lipped Dors) and the hopelessly dour Mary (Jane Hylton). Much of the film is an unashamed excuse to showcase popular dances of the period and the big bands of Heath and Geraldo. *Dance Hall* is also of interest as one of the more prominent dramatic roles for New York-born actor Bonar Colleano, killed in a car accident in Birkenhead eight years later. After his death it was discovered he owed £8,000 in back taxes, prompting a fundraising all-star football match for his family featuring James Mason and Stanley BAKER. [227, 495]

Darling, Candy, New York transsexual actress/model and cover star of The Smiths' single 'SHEILA TAKE A BOW'. Born James Lawrence Slattery, he grew up fascinated with Hollywood's leading ladies and was often mistaken for a girl. By the age of 17 James was dressing as a woman and hanging out in local gay bars under the alias Hope Slattery, later changed to Candy Darling. As she wrote in her diary, 'The name you choose for yourself is more your own than the name you're born with.'

After meeting Warhol in 1967, Darling starred in the following year's *Flesh* alongside fellow Smiths cover star Joe DALLESANDRO. She followed it with 1971's *Women In Revolt*, another Warhol production satirising the women's lib movement and the source of the 'Sheila' sleeve. Morrissey would later brag that 'to be able to inflict Candy Darling on the record-buying public was a perfect example of my very dangerous sense of humour'. Darling was also immortalised in The Velvet Underground's 'Candy Says' and Lou REED's later homage to Warhol drag queens 'Walk On The Wild Side'; it's Darling who notoriously 'never lost her head even when she was giving head'.

Tragically, the hormone injections she regularly took to maintain her gender were a contributing factor in her death. After contracting leukaemia and pneumonia, Darling died in March 1974, aged only 29. Her last letter from her hospital deathbed ended with '… you know I couldn't last. I always knew it …', a probable source for Morrissey's own 'YOU KNOW I COULDN'T LAST'. Indeed, there's a Mozzerian tone throughout Darling's posthumously published diaries. 'I must honestly say that I believe I am here for a life of suffering, sorrow and longing,' she wrote, 'and not to have it relieved until my death.' Darling was also an avid listmaker, filling her journals with names of favourite actors, actresses and character types under specific subheadings. Doubtless, she would have approved of Morrissey's similar pursuit and her inclusion in his 1989 NME list of 'Handsome devils'. [69, 175, 297]

Davalos, Richard, Minor Hollywood actor

best known for his role in *East Of Eden* opposite James DEAN and cover star of The Smiths' STRANGEWAYS, HERE WE COME. As with Dean, Morrissey's obsession with Davalos pre-dates The Smiths, first mentioning him circa 1980 in his unpublished book EXIT SMILING. 'Davalos was born in 1930 [*sic*] to parents who had little time for him,' wrote Morrissey, concluding that 'despite perennial youthfulness, [Davalos] seems doomed to virtual obscurity. Sad.' Around the same time, Morrissey told his pen pal Robert MACKIE that '*East Of Eden* is a wonderful film. My ambition is to track down Richard Davalos (who played Aron, the angelic brother) and interview him.' It's worth

noting that in both the Mackie letter and *Exit Smiling*, and again in *James Dean Is Not Dead*, Morrissey always used the word 'angelic' to describe Davalos's portrayal of Aron.

Born in 1935, before *East Of Eden* Davalos had been an usher in a New York theatre. He'd later describe the film as 'the singularly most important event in my life'. Director Elia Kazan persuaded Davalos and Dean, brothers Aron and Cal in the film, to intensify their on-screen relationship by rooming together in a flat above a drugstore opposite the Warner Bros lot. 'We were Aron and Cal to the teeth,' said Davalos, 'it crept into our social life.' Sadly for Davalos, his performance in *East Of Eden* was eclipsed by Dean's and the cult arising from his untimely death. Despite some notable bit parts in *Cool Hand Luke* (1967) and *Kelly's Heroes* (1970), Davalos was never given an opportunity to prove his worth as a lead actor.

The cover of Strangeways is a detail of an *East Of Eden* location photo in Salinas Valley, California of Davalos standing above Dean, possibly sourced from 1984's *James Dean: American Icon* by David Dalton and Ron Cayen; the full version can also be seen above Morrissey's bath in the 'SUEDEHEAD' video. The image was Morrissey's hasty replacement for the original Strangeways cover design featuring Harvey KEITEL, who refused to consent to his picture being used. Graphically, the Davalos Strangeways sleeve was the weakest of all the Smiths designs, a factor Morrissey unwittingly highlighted when choosing two infinitely stronger Davalos images for the US versions of the posthumous Smiths compilations Best I and Best II. In late 2006 Morrissey also included silent colour wardrobe tests of Davalos and Dean from the recent *East Of Eden* two-disc special edition DVD among his pre-concert video montage. [295, 296, 334, 341, 342, 374, 498]

Davis, Bette, Feisty Hollywood legend and one

of Morrissey's favourite actresses who, as her tombstone in Forest Lawn Memorial Park attests, 'did it the hard way'.

Morrissey paid tribute to Davis following her death in October 1989, aged 81, by attacking the media's disrespectful response. 'Here was this absolute, total legend, possibly the very last one,' he began, 'and I have the impression that if Joanna Lumley had died it would have gained more space, which foxes me. I'm generally attracted to people who are mildly despised and Bette Davis was. I bought all the newspapers the day after her death, expecting huge, blinding banner headlines. But it was simply "The Bitch Is Dead" on page 15, which I found astonishing. I just assume it's a new generation of journalists who don't really know and don't really care. Perhaps it's too long ago. I think that people do forget. Bette Davis was a very formidable spirit who risked going against audience sympathy to get what she wanted, risked narrowing her audience to convey how she really felt. Which is quite largely how I feel about my career. I'd rather walk away than do anything unnatural. I appreciate that spirit because it's very, very rare.'

Indeed, Davis is a quintessential Morrissey symbolist – an unapologetic rebel equally revered and reviled for refusing to compromise and whose first memoir bore the distinctly Mozzerian title *The Lonely Life*. Davis married four times but never found happiness. 'I knew I would end up this way,' she wrote. 'I have always said I would end up a lonely old woman on a hill.' Even her few brief (and perhaps foolhardy) forays into pop music were profoundly Mozzerian in sentiment, issuing two singles in 1965 called 'Life Is A Lonely Thing' and 'Single'. The latter, on Mercury (home to Morrissey in the 1990s), promoted the joy of living alone: 'Convention, get thee out of my sight!/I'm much too much in love with the single life.'

Though Morrissey's 2002 interval tape would include her equally rare 1962 MGM single with Debbie Burton, 'Whatever Happened To Baby Jane?' (not the theme song to her celebrated gothic horror movie itself but a light-hearted rock and roll cash-in), it was for her acting rather than her nails-down-a-blackboard singing skills that he so admired Davis. Other than *Baby Jane*, which he

mentioned in a 1981 letter to Scottish pen pal Robert MACKIE, Morrissey's favourite Davis films include 1944's MR. SKEFFINGTON and 1942's THE MAN WHO CAME TO DINNER, respective lyrical sources for 'YOU'VE GOT EVERYTHING NOW' and 'CEMETRY GATES'; the latter also provided his short-lived 'Sheridan WHITESIDE' pseudonym. Another of her classic 'woman's pictures', 1943's *Old Acquaintance*, contains the title source of The Smiths' 'GIRL AFRAID'.

Summing up her life and career, Davis once said, 'It has been my experience that one cannot, in any shape or form, depend on human relations for lasting reward. It is only work that truly satisfies.' The same quote could just as easily have come from Morrissey – perhaps too her notorious quip that 'sex is God's joke on human beings'. [226, 298, 334, 360, 361, 529, 531, 535, 562]

Day, Gary (Morrissey bass player and co-writer 1991–93, 1999–2006),

When Morrissey returned to live performance in 1991 flanked by his new band of young rockabillies, none embodied the 50s street-gang aesthetic better than bassist Gary Day. Trim and heavily tattooed from wrist to nape, Day's was the face of a gravedigger on the body of a delinquent dodgems attendant. Where guitarists Boz BOORER and Alain WHYTE swaggered and posed in concert, Day glared from the stage with switchblade-handy menace. In looks as much as talent he was everything Morrissey required in a musician and has yet to be surpassed as the archetypal bass player of his solo career.

Like all the band members Morrissey recruited in the 90s, Day was schooled within the north London rockabilly circuit, spending the mid- to late 80s playing double and electric bass with The Mysterons, The Frantic Flintstones and The Nitros.[1] He was already rehearsing with Whyte and drummer Spencer COBRIN as The Memphis Sinners when all three were chosen to appear in the video for Morrissey's 'SING YOUR LIFE', going on to become his KILL UNCLE touring band. Day's animated double-bass playing made a significant contribution to the live rockabilly makeover of

d

Morrissey's latest material. Sticking with a standard electric model for most of the following year's 1992 YOUR ARSENAL tour, live versions of 'THE LOOP' still provided an excuse for whirling double-bass gymnastics, as captured in the vivacious rendition on BEETHOVEN WAS DEAF. Day also had a hand in one of the first tunes written by Morrissey's new band, claiming co-authorship of 'PASHERNATE LOVE' with Alain Whyte, as he would with 'LET THE RIGHT ONE SLIP IN'; both were issued as B-sides.

Day and Cobrin were abruptly dismissed from Morrissey's band at the beginning of 1993. According to the latter neither was told by the singer himself but through his current assistant, Jo Slee. Cobrin speculates that their exit was the result of tensions on tour over his and Day's perceived 'unruly behaviour'. Replaced by Jonny BRIDGWOOD for the recording of VAUXHALL AND I, Day returned to his rockabilly roots in The Nitros, releasing an album on his own record label, Rockout, as well as joining the newly reformed Sharks. He and Cobrin were temporarily brought back in March 1994 for Morrissey's TOP OF THE POPS performance of 'THE MORE YOU IGNORE ME, THE CLOSER I GET' and a problematic B-sides session resulting in 'MOONRIVER' and 'A SWALLOW ON MY NECK'. Day assumed his return was permanent so was surprised, and upset, when later that year he learned the singer had reinstated Bridgwood for the recording of the 'BOXERS' single. It was during this period that Morrissey awoke one morning to find two words carved into the front door of his Camden home. The first was 'Die', the second rhymed with banker. Whether this had any connection with his recent changes in band personnel is impossible to say.

After Bridgwood quit at the end of 1997, Day was coaxed back into the fold for Morrissey's 1999 tour. Musically, and visually, his was a welcome return; whereas Boorer had ballooned and Whyte had widened, Day remained as sullen and slim as the day he first joined. He would remain Morrissey's touring and studio bass player for the next seven years, resuming a minor role as additional songwriter. With Boorer he'd compose the B-sides 'MEXICO', 'THE SLUM MUMS' and 'NOISE IS THE BEST REVENGE' while he and Whyte would fashion YOU ARE THE QUARRY's finale 'YOU KNOW I COULDN'T LAST'. Day continued to pursue various other projects throughout his latter work with Morrissey, from The Motivators (a trio with Whyte and ex-Morrissey touring drummer Spike T. Smith) to The Caravans and his own rockabilly crew, The Gazmen. His final tour with Morrissey was in support of 2006's RINGLEADER OF THE TORMENTORS before being replaced in 2007 by Solomon WALKER, brother of new Morrissey drummer Matt. [4. 5, 36]

---

1. Morrissey can be seen wearing a Nitros T-shirt in the video for 1991's 'PREGNANT FOR THE LAST TIME'.

Dean, James, Doomed Hollywood actor and one of Morrissey's primary symbolists. Dean starred in only three films before his death in a road accident on 30 September 1955 at the age of just 24, thus living fast, dying young and leaving a corpse good-looking enough to become the ultimate teenage rock and roll icon bar none.

Because of Morrissey's notorious obsession with Dean, it is a common mistake to assume he's a fan of Dean the actor. 'Actually I think he was a bit of a ham,' the singer confessed in 1984. 'I get quite embarrassed when I see those films. But I'm fascinated by the way he seemed to represent his time and his generation.' Twenty years later he reiterated the fact: '[My] interest in James Dean was purely a physical obsession, and certainly nothing to do with his films or the art he may have striven for. I'm not really sure that he had any [acting skills]. He was just a fascinating symbol of self-destruction.'

A succinct précis of Dean's brief life was provided by Morrissey in his second of two pre-Smiths publications by Manchester's Babylon Books, 1983's *James Dean Is Not Dead*. Reading between the lines, it is easy to feel Morrissey's empathetic fascination with Dean, a loner who, like Morrissey, was exceptionally close to his mother but alienated from his father, albeit by much more extreme circumstances; Dean's mother died when he was nine and his father passed him to be raised by his grandparents in Fairmount, Indiana.

Morrissey's portrait of Dean is of a detached, difficult, wilfully disruptive, psychologically damaged and death-fixated outsider, also making sporadic reference to his known homosexual episodes. 'As a person he was immensely valuable,' he later told *Smash Hits*. 'Everything from his birth in a farming town to coming to New York, breaking into film and finding he didn't really want it when he had enormous success … Even though he was making enormous strides with his craft, he was still incredibly miserable and obviously doomed. Which is exactly the quality Oscar WILDE had. That kind of mystical knowledge that there is something incredibly black around the corner. People who feel this are quite special and always end up in quite a mangled mess.'

Mangled mess neatly describes Dean's sticky end, impaled upon the steering wheel of his silver Porsche nicknamed 'Little Bastard' while driving to a racing meet in Salinas, California. Of his three films, his first, Elia Kazan's adaptation of John Steinbeck's *East Of Eden*, is arguably Dean's best performance as the tormented Cal Trask starved of the love of his Bible-thumping father. It would also appear to be Morrissey's favourite Dean film, as much for the performance by future STRANGE-WAYS cover star Richard DAVALOS as Cal's 'angelic brother' Aron. Premiered in March 1955, it would be the only film released in Dean's lifetime.

Four days after his death, *Rebel Without A Cause* opened in October 1955 to become his public epitaph. Nicholas Ray's teenage Greek tragedy about 'the bad boy from a good family', it was the first Dean film Morrissey saw 'quite by accident when I was about six', planting the seed of his adult obsession. 'I was entirely enveloped,' he'd explain. 'I did research about him and it was like unearthing Tutankhamen's tomb. His entire life seemed so magnificently perfect.' Dean's final bow followed in October 1956 with George Stevens's *Giant*, taking third billing below Rock Hudson and Elizabeth Taylor as a surly Texan farmhand who strikes oil only to be morally destroyed by his wealth. The closest Morrissey ever came to complimenting any of Dean's films was a noncommittal aside that he 'quite liked' some though 'was never dramatically obsessive about the plots'.

Morrissey would refer to his boyhood love of Dean as 'an absolute drawback' at school. 'Because nobody really cared about him. If they did, it was only in a synthetic rock and roll way. Nobody had a passion for him as I did, for that constant uneasiness with life.' It's telling that Marr should vividly recall Dean pictures on the walls of Morrissey's bedroom when he made his impromptu house call in the summer of 1982, the period when he must have, presumably, been either writing or planning *James Dean Is Not Dead*, published the following spring. In time, he would grow to be acutely embarrassed by the book, later insisting even the title had been altered against his will from his original pitch of *James Dead Is Not Dean*.

'We must loosely call it a book,' he blushed, calling it the work of an 'incredibly desperate' person. 'There was virtually nothing new that I could add but I thought that by simply thrusting something out on to the market it could regenerate some interest from people who perhaps wouldn't know that much about James Dean. Because at the time that I did it, all the books that had been written on him were out of print. But I had this incredible poetic union with James Dean and that's why I did it. This blending of souls. It's quite mystical and embarrassing. I felt this enormous affinity with almost every aspect of his life.'

While distancing himself from both his book[1] and Dean's celluloid legacy, Morrissey never shied from praising the actor's sartorial flair. 'I was fascinated by the fact that he always looked so good, regardless of what kind of clothes he stumbled into,' he'd enthuse. 'He could wear an old rag and he was still quite stunning, and equally he could clamber into a tuxedo and it would also be incredibly fetching. So for me he is the only person who looked perfect persistently.'

d

In 1986, a young Dean astride a Czech Whizzer motorcycle was chosen as the cover star of The Smiths' 'BIGMOUTH STRIKES AGAIN'; the image, like that of the Davalos Strangeways sleeve, was probably sourced from 1984's *James Dean: American Icon* by David Dalton and Ron Cayen. The following year's 'SHOPLIFTERS OF THE WORLD UNITE' single also featured a cryptic Dean homage in a line sourced from a rare 1953 teleplay, *Life Sentence*, in which he played an escaped psychopath.

The singer's most explicit Dean tribute was the video for 1988's 'SUEDEHEAD', documenting his pilgrimage to Fairmount and based upon a famous series of Dean images taken for *Life* magazine by photographer Dennis Stock. Virtually everything in the video has a Dean connection, from his favourite book, Antoine de Saint Exupéry's *The Little Prince*, to the hat worn by Morrissey's nephew, Sam, identical to that worn by Dean's young cousin Markie in one of Stock's portraits. Many of the shots were deliberate re-creations of famous Dean images, from the 'Bigmouth' motorbike cover re0created on Fairmount's Main Street to the poses with the book of poetry by James Whitcomb Riley, the bongo drums and cows and the grave of great-grandfather Cal Dean. Even Morrissey's school blackboard message, 'you can't go home again', stems from Dean's title for one of Stock's iconic portraits of the actor turning his head away from the farmhouse where he was raised.

'The aura around him always fascinated me,' Morrissey once explained. 'When I mention James Dean to people they seem disappointed because it seems such a standard thing for a young person to be interested in – but I really can't help it.' Age has done little to quell his Dean obsession. In 2007, he used a crop of Stock's Cal Dean graveside image as a tour backdrop. The following year, Morrissey paid in excess of $40,000 for the actor's original 'lucky' gold pocket watch. Evidently, the ties of their 'poetic union' still bind. [47, 119, 135, 149, 165, 204, 209, 267, 270, 295, 296, 342, 424, 425, 448, 475, 498, 505, 545]

---

1. Morrissey's feelings about *James Dean Is Not Dead* were plainly demonstrated when asked by a fan to autograph a copy at a 1994 record store signing for VAUXHALL AND I, whereupon he tossed the offending book into the crowd.

'Dear God Please Help Me' (Morrissey/ Whyte),

From the album RINGLEADER OF THE TORMENTORS (2006). Morrissey's most sexually explicit lyric to date, the words of 'Dear God Please Help Me' were graphic enough for many critics to label it his 'coming out' song. 'Oh my God!' responded Morrissey. 'Coming out? From where? To where? I am myself. End of the story.' He would continually deflect all such interrogation on what many perceived to be an autobiographical account of a recent gay sexual encounter in Rome. 'I don't think homosexuality is mentioned in the song,' he protested. 'It's a matter of having interest from someone who is a he, which one can't help and can't orchestrate, and so turning to God and saying, "Did this happen to you?"'

Taken at face value, the lyrics speak for themselves: Morrissey is walking through Rome, looking to misbehave, his 'explosive kegs' fit to burst when a man gives him the signal. The next thing, he's positioned between their legs in what sounds like a penetrative position; then once the deed is done, he forgets the Catholic guilt which has been torturing him for the entire song, feeling absolved both spiritually as well as physically. Morrissey was right to stress that the song never 'mentioned' homosexuality: it didn't need to. Even so, the presumption of autobiography ignores the possibility that the words could just as easily be read as tortured fantasy – the wishful erotic daydream of a soul too crucified by repression to ever act upon such painful private desires.

As titillating as the lyrics were, 'Dear God Please Help Me' achieved an extraordinary beauty thanks to its much-vaunted musical arrangement, a unique collaboration with Italian soundtrack maestro Ennio MORRICONE. Whyte's aching melody was embellished with a church-like organ, aptly highlighting the theological subtext, and Morricone's sensuous strings which, as Morrissey later swooned, 'enriched the song in an incredible way' without over-egging the pudding in terms of

'Death At One's Elbow' (Morrissey/Marr), From the album STRANGEWAYS, HERE WE COME (1987). Knocked off in the studio 'as a bit of light relief' according to Marr, 'Death At One's Elbow' was another of The Smiths' rockabilly cheap thrills in the same vein as 'VICAR IN A TUTU'. Just under two minutes, a simplistic twanging riff and fuzzy harmonica carries Morrissey's warning to the mysterious 'Glenn' to keep away from his house or risk being bludgeoned out of sexual frustration. It was significant that the song's title was taken from the diaries of 60s playwright Joe Orton, beaten to death with a hammer by his lover Kenneth Halliwell in 1967. Returning to his home in Leicester the day before his mother's funeral on 28 December 1966, Orton wrote: 'As the corpse is downstairs in the main living room it means going out or watching television with death at one's elbow.' In the first draft of the song, Morrissey distanced himself from the lyric by singing in the third person, specifying Glenn's lover as female: 'How the frustration it renders *her* hopeless.'

Co-producer Stephen STREET had his doubts about the track's random use of sound effects, from the opening pneumatic drill to its clanging school bell. 'I think we were struggling a bit with that track to be honest,' says Street. 'We just went a little over the top on the comical side.' Yet as Marr reiterates, that was the point. 'It was good sometimes to just have a track that, for The Smiths anyway, wasn't trying to please everybody. Not trying to win the war like "THERE IS A LIGHT". It was almost like, we have a right to be slight right now, to be slightly less intense. So I was fine with it. I liked the beat, I liked Morrissey's singing and I liked my own weird backing vocal.' The finished track was every bit as 'slight' as intended – certainly not a classic on its own terms but a welcome blast of air amid the asphyxiating gravitas of Strangeways' last lap between 'PAINT A VULGAR PICTURE' and 'I WON'T SHARE YOU'. [17, 19, 38, 348]

crescendo and orchestral melodrama. 'We let [Morricone] do his bit and I edited him in the mix,' said TONY VISCONTI, who described the maestro's uncut score as 'a little baroque and flowery', singling out only 'the most glorious moments'. Morrissey's most moving vocal on Ringleader, for many fans it was the highlight of the album and an equally emotional concert showstopper when introduced towards the end of the accompanying world tour. The song was later given an entirely new sexual spin when Marianne FAITHFULL recorded it for the special two-CD edition of her 2008 album Easy Come Easy Go. 'I have heard Morrissey likes it and I'm terribly glad,' said Faithfull. 'It's a great song, so anarchic and peculiar.' [54, 135, 159, 201, 213, 266, 389, 416, 461]

'Death Of A Disco Dancer' (Morrissey/Marr), From the album STRANGEWAYS, HERE WE COME (1987). The great unsung Smiths masterpiece, 'Death Of A Disco Dancer' perhaps epitomises the group's rare musical chemistry better than any other recording. 'That was a really good performance,' agrees Marr. 'A *proper* performance.'

Written in 1987, Morrissey's lyrics were unnervingly prophetic of the drug-related deaths which soon became common tabloid headlines with the acid house boom, the proliferation of ecstasy and the advent of rave culture. Taking 'disco dancer' as a euphemism, the song could just as easily have been a comment on 'gay-bashing' hate crimes of the period – the victims targeted by sickening lynch mobs as they left gay clubs. Morrissey never specifies the details of the death, commenting only on its regularity and his refusal to 'get involved' before philosophising on the unrealistic hippy myth of 'love, peace and harmony'.

'I think I made some connection between the subject of "RUSHOLME RUFFIANS" and the title "Death Of A Disco Dancer", which I was told in advance,' says Marr, who consciously wrote a 'circular' melody. 'It was almost like a hangover from something we did in 1983,' he elaborates. 'Things like "MISERABLE LIE" which was a cyclical song, and "MEAT IS MURDER" as well. My agenda was to create something similar.' For inspiration, Marr drew from THE BEATLES' The White Album, his main Strangeways muse. Although, as Rourke notes, its woozy, descending riff is 'really just "Dear Prudence" slowed down', in terms of rhythm and psychedelic ambience the song's most obvious debt to The White Album is Lennon's 'I'm So Tired'.

The song would also be unique as the only Smiths track where Morrissey played a musical instrument, adding its irregular and discordant piano part reminiscent of that in the title track of David BOWIE's 1973 album Aladdin Sane. The singer claimed he 'just fell on to a piano and began to bang away'. For Marr, Morrissey's erratic Joanna-bashing was a rare joy eclipsed only by his own uncomforting keyboard drone. 'That's one of the best things about it, that drone. It really captures the band. Like "Goldfinger" on bad acid. Which is kind of The Smiths in a nutshell.'

At the end of the final take, Marr was caught on mike exclaiming, 'Some bits of that were incredible!' – you can just about hear the beginning of this if you turn the volume up at around 5.23 on the CD counter. Between his own hypnotic guitar groove, Rourke's bedrock bass, Joyce's cascading drums and a wild and elevating Morrissey vocal, 'Death Of A Disco Dancer' was, indeed, an incredible Smiths moment. If lacking the obvious anthemic qualities of more popular tracks such as 'HOW SOON IS NOW?' or 'THERE IS A LIGHT THAT NEVER GOES OUT', its strange joyful glitter is every inch as grand a testament to The Smiths' inimitability. [17, 19, 29, 38, 143, 194, 203]

Decca, Morrissey's record label as of December 2007 under the umbrella of the Universal Music Company. It followed Universal's takeover of the Sanctuary Music Group, home to his previous ATTACK RECORDS imprint. A press statement boldly announced that 'with [Morrissey's] signing, Decca re-enter the credible pop market as a label historically associated with artists such as THE ROLLING STONES, Small Faces, Marianne FAITHFULL and Them'.

Morrissey's arrival on Decca was a symbolic dream fulfilled. The first pop record he ever bought in 1965 was a Decca single, Marianne Faithfull's 'Come And Stay With Me' while Johnny Marr has referred to his and Morrissey's main objective in forming The Smiths as a desire to see their names on a navy blue label 'like The Stones or Marianne Faithfull [on Decca]'. Not surprisingly, Morrissey's relaunch of the label employed the very same navy and silver 60s designs.

The full list of Morrissey favourites in the Decca vaults extends to Anthony NEWLEY, Kathleen FERRIER, CARRY ON's Kenneth Williams, TWINKLE, early David BOWIE and, probably most significant of all, the 'totally treasurable' Billy FURY. Decca's popular budget 'World Of ...' compilation series had also inspired the title of Morrissey's own 1995 WORLD OF MORRISSEY collection. 'I am delighted to be part of the Decca and Polydor family,' he declared, 'and am very excited about the new singles and albums we are going to do together in 2008.'

Originally licensed to Decca worldwide, Morrissey renegotiated his US deal following the poor Stateside performance of 2008's GREATEST HITS compilation. The American release of 2009's YEARS OF REFUSAL was licensed to Universal's affiliated country music imprint Lost Highway. Though technically still part of the Decca Music Group, as of 2009 Morrissey's UK releases have borne the red Polydor label. [59, 69, 113]

Delaney, Shelagh, Salford playwright and Smiths cover star, best known for her 1958 play and 1961 film A Taste Of Honey, whom Morrissey has openly acknowledged as a 'massive influence'.

Speaking in 1986, he confessed, 'I've never made any secret of the fact that at least 50 per cent of my reason for writing can be blamed on Shelagh Delaney.' Recalling a rare Ken Russell documentary on Delaney from 1961, Morrissey also spoke of the 'strange sexiness about her, even with her overcoat on'. A strangely sexy and overcoated Delaney was featured on the cover of 1987's LOUDER THAN BOMBS (Morrissey's favourite Smiths sleeve) and, minus overcoat, the same year's 'GIRLFRIEND IN A COMA' single.

Born in 1939, Delaney left school at 16 and ended up in an engineering factory; her later success despite any educational qualifications was most likely the catalyst for the homework-burning heroine of The Smiths' 'SHEILA TAKE A BOW' (which altered the Irish spelling of her name). Aged 17, Delaney began writing *A Taste Of Honey*, first as a novel until, as legend has it, she witnessed a touring production of Terence Rattigan's *Variation On A Theme* and decided she could write a better, more realistic drama which properly represented her own surroundings. Her original draft of *A Taste Of Honey* was adapted and brought to the stage by Joan Littlewood's Theatre Workshop, who first performed it in Stratford, east London in May 1958. It would be the first of only a handful of dramatic/literary works over the next decade, of varying significance to Morrissey:

i) A Taste Of Honey (1958), Delaney's masterpiece, a funny, poignant and fairly simple story yet courageous in its day for tackling the taboo subjects of unwanted pregnancy, interracial sex and homosexuality. The play is 'set in Salford, Lancashire, today' and begins with a teenage girl, Jo, and her mother Helen (described as a 'semi-whore') moving into their new, shabby lodgings. When Helen tells her she's going to marry her latest fancy man, Peter, Jo finds comfort and affection in a brief fling with a black sailor on shore leave (known only as 'The Boy'). The second act begins with Jo, now pregnant by the departed sailor, in her new lodgings with a homosexual art student called Geof who acts as her substitute mother. Their domestic bliss is shattered by the return of Helen, deserted by Peter, who eventually ousts Geof to assume responsibility for the pregnant daughter she's so sorely neglected.

The extraordinary critical and commercial success of the play, famously praised by Graham Greene as possessing 'greater maturity' than John Osborne's *Look Back In Anger*, led to the 1961 film adaptation, scripted by Delaney with the assistance of director Tony Richardson. Starring Rita Tushingham as Jo (seen on the sleeve of the original Sandie SHAW single of 'HAND IN GLOVE'), the film fills in background story details absent in the original play (e.g. Jo and Geof's first meeting), also making extensive use of Salford and Manchester locations to lend the story an at times documentary-style authenticity, most vividly during Jo's miserable day out to Blackpool with Helen and Peter.

Morrissey's love of *A Taste Of Honey* began with the film version, which he deemed 'virtually the only important thing in British film in the 1960s as far as I'm concerned', also boasting that he could recite the script 'word-for-word'. The latter would account for its reputation as Morrissey's single most quoted source, nearly all of which can be found in the early Smiths repertoire: 'REEL AROUND THE FOUNTAIN' – 'I dreamt about you last night. Fell out of bed twice'; 'YOU'VE GOT EVERYTHING NOW' – 'merry as the day is long' (after Shakespeare's *Much Ado About Nothing*); and 'Hand In Glove' – 'I'll probably never see you again' (the same line also features in *The Lion In Love*).

His most explicit citations occur in 'THIS NIGHT HAS OPENED MY EYES' which he'd even refer to as 'a *Taste Of Honey* song – putting the entire play into words', specifically: 'That river, it's the colour of lead', 'GEOF: You can't just wrap it up in a bundle of newspaper./JO: And dump it on a doorstep', 'Oh well, the dream's gone, but the baby's real enough' and 'I'm not sorry and I'm not glad'. The title of 'I DON'T OWE YOU ANYTHING' could, plausibly, be inspired by either 'I don't owe you a thing' in *A Taste Of Honey* and/or the similar 'Do I owe you anything?' in *The Lion In Love*. Also of note is a scene exclusive to the film version; during the prologue, Jo tells her classmates in the changing rooms she can't go out that night since 'I haven't got any clothes to wear for one thing' ('THIS CHARMING MAN').

Other phrases also bear minor consideration: 'It's a long time, six months' ('SHOPLIFTERS OF THE

WORLD UNITE'), 'You want taking in hand' ('BARBARISM BEGINS AT HOME'), 'Sing me to sleep' ('ASLEEP') and, most tenuous of all, 'What would you say if I started something?' ('I STARTED SOMETHING'). Those of the belief that Delaney still influences Morrissey's later solo lyrics (and this author's not entirely convinced that's the case) would also point out 'Put your arms around me' ('TOMORROW') and 'Anyway, it's your life, ruin it your own way' ('ALMA MATTERS'; a very similar line also appears in *The Lion In Love*).[1]

ii) The Lion In Love (1960), Delaney's second play was, commercially, something of a flop, leading to the suggestion by cynical critics that *A Taste Of Honey* had been 'a freak success'. Taking its name from one of Aesop's fables and set 'in a town in the north of England' (presumably Manchester), its multiple narrative follows the various private dramas of a typical working-class family; the drunken mother Kit, the father Frank and his fancy woman Nora, and their grown-up children Peg and Banner. Summed up by the critic John Russell Taylor, its action 'counts for virtually nothing; rather do the fragments of plot serve as an excuse for us to examine these people, to see how they live together and to try and understand why they are as they are as we follow them through a few inconclusive weeks of their life'.

In 1983 Morrissey listed *The Lion In Love* as one of his favourite books and, as with *A Taste Of Honey*, its impact is felt most keenly on early Smiths songs. The play's most conspicuous lyrical sources are as follows: 'JEANE' – 'Paid cash on the nail'; 'ACCEPT YOURSELF' – 'Anything's hard to find if you go around looking for it with your eyes shut'; 'THE HAND THAT ROCKS THE CRADLE' – 'That's it – that's right – rattle her bones over the stones, she's only a beggar whom nobody owns ...'; 'YOU'VE GOT EVERYTHING NOW' – 'Shall I tell you something? I don't like your face.'; 'STILL ILL' – 'KIT: I'll go out and get a job tomorrow./JESSE: You needn't bother,' and 'I'd sooner spit in everybody's eye'; 'Reel Around The Fountain' –'It's time our tale were told'; and the titles of both 'NOWHERE FAST' and 'THESE THINGS TAKE TIME' which appear as sequential dialogue.

Other phrases also bear lesser consideration, be it the mention of a 'ten-ton truck' ('THERE IS A LIGHT') or 'tied to his mother's apron strings' ('THE QUEEN IS DEAD'). Again, those convinced that Delaney still influences Morrissey's more recent lyrics will note the (surely coincidental?) parallel between the play's 'Pagliacci – that's me' and the opening of 'YOU HAVE KILLED ME'.

iii) Sweetly Sings The Donkey (1964), Delaney's first (and only to date) collection of prose featuring eight short stories, many seemingly autobiographical. The title story concerns a young girl in a convalescence home run by nuns; 'Tom Riley' is the Mozzerian tragedy of a strange and delicate boy who comes to a cruel and sad end; 'The Teacher' tells of the sinister Mr Slovve's unhealthy affection for one of his pupils; 'My Uncle, The Spy' is a two-page vignette about literally that; 'Pavan For A Dead Prince' is a touching account of a friend with a heart condition who chooses to dance himself into the grave to escape mollycoddling misery; 'All About And To A Female Artist' satirises the press reviews and lunatic fan mail which Delaney's fame have brought her; 'Vodka And Small Pieces Of Gold' documents her visit to Poland; and 'The White Bus' involves a surreal sightseeing trip round Manchester used as the basis for a short film of the same name made by Lindsay Anderson in 1967.

Morrissey has never directly referred to *Sweetly Sings The Donkey*, but his admission in 1984 that 'I've only got three books of [Delaney's]' tells us he must have owned it; beside the two previous plays, it was the only other title she'd published. Its only conspicuous Smiths lyric is the title story's 'The Devil finds work for idle hands' ('WHAT DIFFERENCE DOES IT MAKE?') though as a common proverb it would be wrong to assume that Morrissey sourced it from Delaney alone.

iv) Charlie Bubbles (1967), Delaney's first bespoke screenplay, listed among Morrissey's favourite films and directed by/starring fellow Salfordian Albert FINNEY. Unlike her previous theatre work, *Charlie Bubbles* is much less dialogue-driven – tellingly, there are no conspicuous Morrissey steals to be found – and with a subtly surreal undercurrent. Bubbles (Finney) is a northerner now living a successful and swanky life as a famous writer in London. The film follows him over a 48-hour period as he drives back home from London to Manchester to visit ex-wife Billie WHITELAW (as seen on the revised cover of The Smiths' 'WILLIAM, IT WAS REALLY NOTHING'). On the way he's accompanied by his American secretary (Liza Minnelli in her first starring role), meets old flame YOOTHA JOYCE in NEWPORT PAGNELL services and takes his estranged son to see Manchester United play at Old Trafford. The film's dreamlike conclusion is purely symbolic and, in essence, *Charlie Bubbles* is a darkly comic satire about one man's identity crisis; bored with his wealth and fame yet just as much an alien among the London jet-set as he is back in the redbrick northern streets where he was born. As such it was a pertinent parable to both Finney and Delaney as northerners who'd 'made good' down south and was of equal relevance to Morrissey's position in the mid-1980s.

Since the end of the 60s, Delaney's writing has been even more sporadic, limited to occasional television and radio plays. Her most prominent post-60s work to date has been the screenplay for Mike Newell's 1985 dramatisation of the life of Ruth Ellis, *Dance With A Stranger* (see also *YIELD TO THE NIGHT*), and her 1992 adaptation of Jennifer Johnston's *The Railway Station Man* starring Julie Christie and Donald Sutherland. Speaking in 2003, Morrissey believed Delaney had 'ended up in Islington'. At the time of writing Delaney is working on her memoir. [46, 168, 176, 184, 206, 207, 299, 300, 301, 374, 383, 425, 491, 496, 554]

---

1. An age-old Smiths myth credits Delaney's A *Taste Of Honey* as the source of 'you're the bee's knees but so am I' in 'Reel Around The Fountain'. The line appears in neither the play nor the film.

Devoto, Howard, Original singer with

BUZZCOCKS (1976–77), then Magazine (1977–81), and a friend of, and hero to, Morrissey before, during and after The Smiths. Such is Devoto's importance that his story is covered in three interconnected entries in this book: see SEX PISTOLS for the background on how Devoto first brought the Pistols to Manchester, thus changing the city's cultural climate (and Morrissey) for ever; how Devoto then formed the first and best Manchester punk group only to then quit them in January 1977 is covered in the separate entry on Buzzcocks; chronologically, this entry deals with his work thereafter.

Born in Scunthorpe as Howard Trafford, he became Devoto in early '76 when forming Buzzcocks with Pete Shelley. According to Paul Morley, he chose Devoto because it's 'Latin for

Delon, Alain, The 'French James DEAN', actor and cover star of The Smiths' album THE QUEEN IS DEAD. The latter image and another featured on the same album's inner record bag were taken from 1964's *L'Insoumis* (*The Unvanquished*) directed by Alain Cavalier in which Delon plays a deserter legionnaire hired by the secret service to kidnap a female lawyer whom he eventually falls in love with. Many years after the break-up of The Smiths, Morrissey would admit that he'd thrown away all personal memorabilia connected with the group with the exception of a letter from Delon about the Queen Is Dead sleeve.

Delon is also the star of one of Morrissey's favourite LUCHINO VISCONTI films, *Rocco And His Brothers*, though his film career is not without its blemishes: 1968's dreadful *Girl On A Motorcycle* springs to mind in which Delon serenades a leather-clad Marianne FAITHFULL with the sweet nothing that her 'body is like a violin in a velvet case'. Delon is also the father of NICO's son, Ari, heard singing 'Le Petit Chevalier' on 1970's Desertshore. [207, 213, 374, 546]

"bewitching"': Devoto told Jon Savage it was acually borrowed from a distant relative. Of all Devoto's many musical incarnations, it was Magazine, his second group formed in the months following his departure from Buzzcocks, who had the greatest impact on Morrissey. Magazine ran in a very different direction to their punk contemporaries, one that entailed covering Shirley BASSEY and Sly Stone with no fear of ever crossing purposes. Their invincible January 1978 debut single would be post-punk's starting pistol, appropriately enough titled 'Shot By Both Sides'. The chorus riff was actually Shelley's, who later that year recorded his own version of the same tune called 'Lipstick', B-side of Buzzcocks' 'Promises' single. The difference between Devoto and Shelley, Buzzcocks and Magazine, punk and post-punk is easily defined by comparing both. Where Shelley sings of dreams, romance and cosmetics, Devoto sings of 'what's real', existentialism and ballistics. Where 'Lipstick' is (quite obviously) the sound of the end of a love affair, 'Shot By Both Sides' is (less definably) the sound of the end of humanity itself.

A re-recording of 'Shot By Both Sides' featured on April 1978's debut album, Real Life, sleeved in a monoprint of floating heads designed by Devoto's then-girlfriend Linder STERLING. A few weeks after its release, on 8 May Magazine headlined Manchester's Ritz where Morrissey, fronting THE NOSEBLEEDS, supported. It was around this time that, through Linder, Morrissey was introduced to Devoto although their subsequent testimonies differ greatly as to when they met and the extent of their friendship. Speaking in 1988, Devoto stated that although Linder had told him about 'this guy [who's] very interesting' he never met Morrissey properly until 1985. Conflictingly, Morrissey wrote about his friendship with Devoto in two of his 1981 letters to pen pal Robert MACKIE. 'Isn't Howard a riot?' he quipped in the first. 'To think we used to drink together – more name-dropping, I'm such a bore. He once told me how he'd love to sleep with skinny Iggy Flop. Such ambition! And I'm sure it's been fulfilled by now.' The second was more straightforward. 'Howard

Devoto is staying with my friend Linder this week,' he told Mackie, 'so I'm going over tomorrow to chew the fat, as they say.' While it's possible Morrissey may have exaggerated the truth to impress Mackie, in one of the first Smiths interviews conducted for Sounds in May 1983 he still claimed that, 'Devoto I know quite well and I know he formed a group in order to make friends … I can only say I'm the same.'

The Mackie letters also attest to Morrissey's fanaticism for Devoto's art, referring to Magazine's second album, 1979's Secondhand Daylight, as well as their 1980 single 'Sweetheart Contract' from third album The Correct Use Of Soap. The latter also included 'A SONG FROM UNDER THE FLOORBOARDS' which Morrissey quoted in his final letter to Mackie – 'I am angry, I am ill and I'm as ugly as sin' (see also 'ACCEPT YOURSELF') – and which he later covered in 2006. Yet Devoto's influence upon Morrissey went beyond such articulate and unnervingly self-deprecating lyrics. In his second letter to Mackie, he writes, 'Besides BOWIE, I dribble over the NEW YORK DOLLS, JOBRIATH, NICO and Magazine.' Out of that list, Magazine were unique in being the only act fronted by somebody not just on his doorstep but, through Linder, on the peripheries of his small social circle. Bowie, the Dolls and Jobriath were fantasy figures, several galaxies away from the stark reality of Manchester. So was the music of Nico, even if, ironically, she actually was living on his doorstep at the time having moved to Hulme. Devoto, on the other hand, was a recognisable local hero offering Morrissey realistic hope that a deeply intelligent if unconventional northern singer could succeed in forming a band, signing a major record deal (Magazine were on Virgin) and earning the admiration of the serious music press. If as queer and clever a fellow as Devoto could do it, so, feasibly, might Morrissey.

By the time The Smiths took shape in 1982, Devoto had already disbanded Magazine after four albums. The first three had been an almost immaculate trilogy, not just in terms of Devoto's lyrics – profound ('The Light Pours Out Of Me'), exhilarating ('Believe That I Understand') and tragic ('You Never Knew Me') – but equally in the glistening soundscapes of keyboard player Dave Formula, bassist Barry Adamson and particularly guitarist John McGeoch who left the group in 1980, throwing his lot in with Siouxsie And The Banshees (see SIOUX). They'd make a fourth without McGeoch, 1981's Magic, Murder And The Weather, though by the time it was released Devoto had already announced he was leaving. 'I really feel that a change for me had been long overdue,' he explained. 'I didn't want to tour to promote [it], and even if the album was hugely successful I'd still want to leave. So what was the point in waiting?' The rest of Magazine sensibly split up without him.

Devoto's first and only solo album, Jerky Versions Of The Dream, came out in 1983. On 7 August that year The Smiths supported his show at London's Lyceum. The roles were reversed three years later when, in July 1986, Devoto and Liverpool multi-instrumentalist Noko (Norman Fisher-Jones, whom he'd met via Shelley) played a short set under the name Adultery as one of many supports to The Smiths at the Manchester G-Mex 'Festival Of The Tenth Summer'. It followed Morrissey's confession to the press that, away from the limelight – and in what read like a re-enactment of 'CEMETRY GATES' – he and Devoto spent their spare time touring London graveyards together. 'Cheerful little buggers that we are,' he joked. 'You know, "Get the Guinness and cheese butties out and head down to Brompton Cemetery."'[1]

Immediately following The Smiths' split, in October 1987 an extremely giggly Morrissey and ghoulishly deadpan Devoto appeared together on Radio 1's Singled Out, passing acid verdicts on the latest waxings from Bob Dylan and Samantha Fox (Morrissey: 'If I was Samantha Fox's manager I'd put her in a large box and send her to the Shetland Islands'). They'd reunite six months later when Devoto and Noko's Adultery project, now renamed Luxuria, played London's Town & Country Club on 13 March 1988. Morrissey made his first, brief, post-Smiths live appearance

that night reading an excerpt from Marcel PROUST's Remembrance Of Things Past at the opening of Luxuria's 'Mlle'.

Luxuria released two albums, Unanswerable Lust (1988) and Beast Box (1990), before a disillusioned Devoto once again called time on his own group. Whereas Noko would continue working in music, later collaborating with James MAKER, Devoto deliberately slid into obscurity and took a job as a librarian at a London photographers agency. In his absence, Morrissey continued to praise his mentor whenever the opportunity arose, even citing Devoto as one of the real life 'LAST OF THE FAMOUS INTERNATIONAL PLAYBOYS' beside Bowie, BOLAN and himself. 'In assessments of Manchester, they never mention Magazine,' he later complained. 'I don't know why. [They were] an excellent group. Very strong [and with] great lyrics.' Morrissey also included Magazine's 1980 B-side 'The Book', a Devoto monologue about a man who walks all too willingly into Hell, on his interval tapes when touring 1997's MALADJUSTED. Devoto has resurfaced only occasionally since the demise of Luxuria: most notably his 2002 Buzzkunst album with Pete Shelley, a surprise cameo in the same year's FACTORY Records biopic 24 Hour Party People, and, more surprising still, his re-formation of Magazine for a series of concerts in early 2009 where the late McGeoch was replaced by Noko. [69, 166, 220, 334, 340, 366, 409, 567]

—————
1. On one such jaunt Devoto told Morrissey '[about] some old corporal dying, smothered in blood, having a very artistic coronary arrest and his right-hand man was saying, "Don't be silly, Charles. Cheer up, cheer up, we're going to Bognor [Regis] this weekend." And he turned round to his friend and said, "Bugger Bognor!" and "Bugger Bognor!" actually appeared on his tombstone as his famous last words. I think that should be an LP title. "Bugger Bognor!"' According to apocryphal myth and The Oxford Dictionary Of Quotations, the 'old corporal' of the story was actually King George V.

'Dial-A-Cliché' (Morrissey/Street), From the album VIVA HATE (1988). A gentle reflection on the social pressure to conform to emotionally impervious male stereotypes, 'Dial-A-Cliché' was among

d

the earliest tracks written and recorded for Morrissey's solo debut album. Frank and unfussy, it still contained flashes of elegance in its opening alliteration ('Further into the fog I fall') and prompted a lovely vocal performance. Stephen Street's soft acoustic tune, augmented by synthetic French horn, was his homage to the 'major to minor chord changes' favoured by Lennon and McCartney and owed a conscious debt to THE BEATLES' 'Norwegian Wood'. Studio outtakes since circulated on the internet reveal that the song was originally tried in a higher key which Morrissey found 'a bit uncomfortable'. [25, 39]

Dickens, Charles, It wasn't until the early

1990s that Morrissey finally succumbed to the irresistible lure of Dickens, arguably the greatest writer in the history of English literature and inarguably the most popular. 'Charles Dickens is very exciting to me,' he enthused, 'because he was a terribly gloomy character, terribly embittered, and quite depressed.'

Indeed, the life of Dickens is a Dickensian, if not Mozzerian, soap opera unto itself. His childhood was entirely miserable: his father was sent to a debtor's prison and the young Charles was forced to work, aged 12, in a blacking warehouse, an experience which scarred him for life. Using the pseudonym 'Boz', his literary success began with *The Pickwick Papers* in 1836 though only after a very shaky start when the book's original illustrator, Robert Seymour, committed suicide after a disagreement over one of the plates. The same year the 24-year-old Dickens married 20-year-old Catherine Hogarth only to develop an intense bond with her 17-year-old sister, Mary, who mysteriously fell ill and died 24 hours later. His grief over Mary inspired him to create the mawkish Little Nell of *The Old Curiosity Shop* whose death caused a public outcry among his besotted Victorian readership (bar Dickens cynic Oscar WILDE who'd wickedly comment, 'One must have a heart of stone to read the death of Little Nell without laughing').

Dickens fathered ten children, one of whom died of an aneurysm aged 22 while another died in infancy aged eight months. After starting an affair with the actress Ellen Ternan, he eventually separated from his wife. In 1865, Dickens and Ternan were involved in a train crash which killed ten people and for the final few years of his life he suffered recurring nightmares about the incident. Halfway through completing his 15th novel, *The Mystery Of Edwin Drood*, Dickens died on 9 June 1870, aged 58. Already the most famous and successful novelist in the world, against his wishes for a low-key burial his body was interred in London's Westminster Abbey with full ceremony.

In 1992, Morrissey revealed he was currently engrossed by one of Dickens's most popular novels, OLIVER TWIST, also the source of one of his favourite films as sampled at the end of 'BILLY BUDD'. 'I love the grim, dim description of the East End,' he explained, 'all those murky, winding passages, full of desperate characters like our friend Fagin.' The same year another interviewer noted how he was 'deep into Dickens' and searching for what they misleadingly described as his 'obscure novel' *Our Mutual Friend* while two years later another journalist spotted him reading *Bleak House*. He'd refer to Dickens again in 1997 when quizzed on the hypothetical prospect of fatherhood, joking how his brood would be 'Oliver Twist-like, no food, no bed, no water', though his tease that he'd call his kids 'Morrissey one, Morrissey two, Morrissey three' sounded more like the poor charges of schoolmaster Wackford Squeers in Chapter Five of *Nicholas Nickleby*.

Dickens was also a resident of Camden some 170 years before Morrissey, though the house on Bayham Street where he lived as a child has since been demolished; today a plaque marks the spot. His only surviving London residence is at 48 Doughty Street off Gray's Inn Road, the house where Dickens wrote Morrissey's beloved *Oliver Twist* and where Mary Hogarth died. It's now The Charles Dickens Museum, a fascinating attraction for those in, near, or visiting London keen to imbibe the spirits of Morrissey's literary heroes. [133, 197, 217, 237, 302, 537, 567]

Didion, Joan, See FEMINISM.

'Disappointed' (**Morrissey/Street**), B-side of 'EVERYDAY IS LIKE SUNDAY' (1988). A brilliant feat of self-satire, here Morrissey playfully bemoans his loneliness, drowning his sorrows in alcohol and cursing the 'nice' people who've become the bane of his existence. Most intriguing is his final declaration of love for a 'young girl' before its wonderfully comic finale, vowing never to sing again only to immediately change his mind. The accompanying hoorays and disgruntled sighs came courtesy of Stephen Street, guitarist Vini REILLY, drummer Andrew PARESI and engineer Steve Williams.

The tune was among the first Street had sent him in January 1988 as the first batch of post-VIVA HATE songs to be used as B-sides. Morrissey made radical adjustments to Street's original arrangement until it resembled something like a brighter cousin of The Smiths' 'HOW SOON IS NOW?' 'There was a bit of that in there,' admits Street, 'but I was just trying to write a dark, brooding guitar track.' Recorded at The Wool Hall in March 1988 along with the other 'Everyday Is Like Sunday' B-sides 'SISTER I'M A POET' and 'WILL NEVER MARRY', Morrissey would hail all three tracks as 'quite magical', marking 'a progression from Viva Hate'. Possibly he was referring to 'Disappointed' itself when he told the press he felt cheered by the session's 'pulverised manic sound'. Although Street shared the singer's enthusiasm for the recordings, their creation had been an unpleasant experience, tainted by his worsening relationship with Reilly and, to a lesser extent, Paresi, both of whom were now vying for Morrissey's attention to replace Street as co-writer.

Among the eight songs played at his solo debut WOLVERHAMPTON gig in December 1988, 'Disappointed' has remained a live favourite ever since; Morrissey concert ritual dictates that the audience assume an interactive role for the closing cheers and boos. A chaotic version sabotaged by stage-invading fans recorded in Holland in May 1991 was later featured as a B-side of 'PREGNANT FOR THE LAST TIME'. [25, 39, 203]

Distel, Sacha, Eminently handsome French pop singer, best known in the UK for his 1970 hit version of Bacharach and David's 'Raindrops Keep Falling On My Head'. Morrissey's admiration of Distel first came to light in 2004 when named as one of the acts he hoped to include in that June's MELTDOWN festival. Tragically, Distel was too ill to comply and died of cancer a few weeks later on 22 July, aged 71. When Morrissey next played Paris in November that year, he paid tribute to the singer on stage, also introducing himself as 'Sacha Distel'. Thereafter, Morrissey used a portrait of a young Distel as a stage backdrop when touring RINGLEADER OF THE TORMENTORS in early 2006, also posing with various items of Distel ephemera during magazine photoshoots around the same period. An early Scopitones reel of Distel performing 'Où ça, Où ça' ('Where, Where') was included in Morrissey's pre-gig video montage introduced in November 2006. The clip captures Distel in all his Gallic gorgeousness, hamming it up as he acts out the song's globe-trotting tour of Puerto Rico, Russia, Germany, Hawaii and Spain before arriving back where he began in Paris. 'Où ça, Où ça' was first released on a 1963 four-track EP on the RCA VICTOR label alongside what was to become Distel's signature tune, 'La Belle Vie', later popularised by Tony Bennett under its English translation, 'The Good Life', and also covered by FRANK SINATRA.

Curiously, the first recorded mention of Distel in Smiths history belongs to Johnny Marr. Asked by *Smash Hits* in 1984 to name his favourite character from history, Marr chose Napoleon, describing him as 'the only French superstar apart from Charles Aznavour and Sacha Distel, of course'. [85, 93, 119, 160]

'Do Your Best And Don't Worry' (**Morrissey/Whyte**), From the album SOUTHPAW GRAMMAR (1995). As a last-minute addition to the album, the sentiment of 'Do Your Best And Don't Worry' with its talk of 'high standards' meeting with 'low spirits' seemed a self-referential analysis of the making of Southpaw, the echo of Morrissey attempting to comfort his own uncertainty in the task at hand if not life itself. Its otherwise slurry rock tune was whisked into a vigorous froth climaxing in a helter-skelter finale where Spencer COBRIN appeared to swap snare drum for sub-machine gun. Since Jonny BRIDGWOOD had already been told he was no longer needed at the session, Boz BOORER stood in on bass. Evidently Morrissey was cock-a-hoop with the result, choosing the song as set opener for the accompanying Southpaw tour, and again for the latter half of 1997's MALADJUSTED shows. [4, 40]

'Don't Blow Your Own Horn' (Morrissey/Marr),

The exact chronology of Morrissey and Marr's earliest collaborations is foggy, but what we do know is that alongside 'SUFFER LITTLE CHILDREN' and 'THE HAND THAT ROCKS THE CRADLE', during their first week of writing together in the summer of 1982 they composed at least one other song. In 1985, Marr told journalist Nick Kent there'd actually been a couple of non-starters: one 'country-esque' song and another in the same mould as 'JEANE'. The latter was most probably 'Don't Blow Your Own Horn', a title all but forgotten had it not been for original Smiths bassist Dale HIBBERT, who retained Marr's handwritten chord sheet; its three major chords are, indeed, suggestive of a 'Jeane'-type riff. Marr has since confirmed the song's

existence. 'We lived with it for a week then decided not to bother with it,' he says. 'It didn't cut it and I don't think Morrissey really liked it either.' Although it's feasible that they recorded the song in some basic bedroom demo form on Marr's TEAC three-track cassette machine (as they did with 'Suffer Little Children' and 'The Hand That Rocks The Cradle'), 'Don't Blow Your Own Horn' is probably lost to history. The other 'country-esque' song is still a mystery. [10, 17, 362, 423]

Doonan, Patric,

Minor 50s British film actor referenced in 'NOW MY HEART IS FULL'. Born in Derby of Irish heritage, Doonan made his screen debut in the 1949 SPEEDWAY racing drama *Once A Jolly Swagman* starring Dirk BOGARDE. He'd act alongside Bogarde again in Ealing's 1950 crime drama *The Blue Lamp* (see also 'MOONRIVER'), playing the conscientious Spud to Bogarde's 'bastard that shot George Dixon', his performance '[touching] at times the nerve of reality' according to one reviewer. Supporting roles in other Ealing films followed, most prominently as Frank the shop steward alarmed by the financial consequences of Alec GUINNESS's scientific breakthrough in the 1951 comedy *The Man In The White Suit*. Yet despite one lead role in the 1953 B-movie *Wheel Of Fate*, Doonan found himself typecast as bit-part thugs or military types. His last feature

'Don't Make Fun Of Daddy's Voice' (Morrissey/Whyte),

B-side of 'LET ME KISS YOU' (2004). Certainly one of Morrissey's most original works, if also one of his most ridiculous, it is difficult to imagine anyone else even contemplating a pop song about a child mocking their afflicted father now suffering for the follies of adolescence when 'something' – dare our minds boggle to guess – lodged itself in his oesophagus. With a premise this absurd there's nothing worth losing by translating the title in Spanish, which is precisely what Morrissey attempts with his closing quaver of 'No te divertes con Pappy!'

Its billowing grunge chug dates back to Alain Whyte's band Johnny Panic And The Bible Of Dreams who recorded it in 1998 with different lyrics as 'Paranoia'. When Whyte submitted the melody to Morrissey, the singer kept the exact same arrangement but lowered the key for its chorus as if to deliberately serrate its edges. Bewildered festival audiences patiently endured the song as Morrissey's irregular set opener during the summer of 2004, but less so when he deemed it a worthy last encore for his European arena tour in late 2006 when it emptied venues with all the swift stampede of a bomb scare.

film was 1955's *The Cockleshell Heroes*, playing the sailor whose bar brawl prompts Anthony NEWLEY's 'splendid defeat' speech sampled at the beginning of 'MALADJUSTED'.

Morrissey's fascination with Doonan, beyond his aesthetic appeal – ruggedly handsome with a Kirk DOUGLAS cleft chin and frequently sporting some variation on a quiff – had much to do with his tragic biography. On 10 March 1958, just over a month before his 33rd birthday, he gassed himself in the basement kitchen of his Chelsea home in Margareta Terrace, as referenced in the video for 'SUEDEHEAD'. Morrissey later admitted that he'd tried to contact the actor's relatives but to no avail. Coincidentally, Doonan's elder brother, Tony, was also an actor and played the blackmailer Alfred Wood in the 1960 biopic of Oscar WILDE starring Robert Morley. Also of note, their comedian father, George, had a minor part in the same year's *The Entertainer*, the film debut of Albert FINNEY. [159, 171, 382, 486, 493, 501, 528]

Dors, Diana, 'A real cheap-looking tomato

with a tremendous bust, platinumised hair, big lips and a hard trashy face.' So Candy DARLING described 'England's answer to Jayne Mansfield', 1950s sex bomb Diana Dors, a recurring icon throughout Morrissey's career. 'A fantastic British figure,' he claimed, 'and because she was so overtly sexual she was always underrated as an actress. She was decades before her time in standing up and saying, "Yes, I enjoy sex."'

The singer's interest was doubtless aided by the NEW YORK DOLLS, who name-checked her on 1974's 'It's Too Late' ('you spend most [of] your time in the powder room where you chit-chat with Diana Dors'). He'd write a brief summary of Dors's career within his recollection of 'screen also-rans', *EXIT SMILING*, emphasising her failed attempt to crack Hollywood in the wake of fellow 'blonde and buxom' Marilyn Monroe clones. Cursed with the birth name Diana Fluck, at the age of nine she wrote in a school essay: 'I am going to be a film star with a cream telephone and a swimming pool.' Ditching Fluck for her grandmother's maiden

name of Dors, by 17 she was on a £10-a-week contract with the RANK Organisation. Her first notable performance was in one of Morrissey's favourite films, David Lean's 1948 version of DICKENS'S *OLIVER TWIST*, playing the undertaker's 'slutty maid'. Before long she was romantically embroiled with co-star Anthony NEWLEY.

Dors's Rank contract ended with another Morrissey favourite, 1950's *DANCE HALL*. Her best dramatic role came six years later as the condemned murderess in *YIELD TO THE NIGHT*, images from which provided Morrissey with a stage backdrop for his YOUR ARSENAL tour and the sleeve of The Smiths' posthumous Singles compilation. The same year 'adorable Dors' headed for America, in Morrissey's words '[looking] all set to dig the heels of her size fives into welcoming Hollywoodland'. Instead, she stumbled into some dreadful B-movies while her wanton off-set behaviour filled Tinseltown's gossip magazines, as it would the UK tabloids in the 60s. As Morrissey noted, 'Dors, it seemed, achieved her highest ambitions in the Sunday newspapers, who ransacked her private life once a week in search of scandalous claptrap. They always found it.'

She dabbled in music, releasing an album of light standards, Swingin' Dors, in 1960. Morrissey dismissed it in *Exit Smiling* as the work of a 'zombified voice', though he was considerably more flattering when discovering a now rare 1964 follow-up single on Fontana, 'So Little Time'; bizarrely, the other side was called 'It's Too Late', pre-empting the Dolls' song which paid her homage. Played on interval tapes in the early 90s, Morrissey later included 'So Little Time' on his UNDER THE INFLUENCE compilation. 'The voice teeters with a knowing smile,' he wrote in the liner notes, 'but the heart is on the gravel as she tells us so much more than what she literally says.'

Outside of the redtop tales of sex parties and voyeurism, Dors's private life was pretty miserable. Her first husband died of tertiary syphilis aged 27. Her second ended in divorce. Her third husband, actor Alan Lake (who had a walk-on role in the Shelagh DELANEY-scripted *Charlie*

Bubbles) was an alcoholic who spent 18 months in prison after a pub brawl involving late-60s one-hit-wonder Leapy Lee. To celebrate his release, Dors bought Lake a horse. It threw him, breaking his back and shoulder and exacerbating his dependence on drink as a painkiller. Five months after Dors died of cancer in 1984 at the age of only 52, Lake shot himself: it transpired he'd been secretly suffering from a brain tumour. Following her death, Morrissey paid tribute in the video for 1989's 'INTERESTING DRUG' where one of the schoolboys is seen reading a mock-up *NME* with a classic Dors glamour pose on the cover. By the time he moved to Los Angeles in the late 90s Morrissey was the proud owner of an autographed Dors print which he hung – pride of place – in his toilet. [159, 171, 382, 486, 493, 501, 528]

Douglas, Kirk,

Cleft-chinned Hollywood legend whom Morrissey once referred to as his favourite actor. His obsession with Douglas seems to have developed during the mid-1990s, exemplified by his handwritten introduction to the 'SUNNY' video included on the multimedia CD release of MY EARLY BURGLARY YEARS: 'I can't stop thinking about Kirk Douglas. Do you know him?' He'd later quote Douglas in 1999 when discussing his 'nervous' attitude towards money. 'It's like Kirk Douglas saying that he *always* expects his money to be taken away from him, even now, because he was born in extreme poverty.'

To date Morrissey's only direct reference to the actor in his work has been on his spring 2000 concerts in California and Latin America; performances of 'BOXERS' were accompanied by a back projection showing Douglas punching a locker in the 1949 boxing drama *Champion*, the film which established his incorrigibly tough screen persona. Other than *Champion*, Morrissey has also mentioned 1947's *Build My Gallows High* (aka *Out Of The Past*) in which he co-starred with Robert Mitchum and, more generally, that he enjoys 'anything' vintage with Douglas. His high regard for the actor was only soured after reading Douglas's 1988 autobiography *The Ragman's*

Son in which he shared what Morrissey glumly described as a 'candid passion for killing animals'. [179, 405, 490, 568]

'Draize Train, The' (Johnny Marr),

B-side of 'PANIC' (1986). The last of The Smiths' three instrumentals, as with the preceding 'OSCILLATE WILDLY' and 'MONEY CHANGES EVERYTHING', Marr wrote it – as always – in the hope that Morrissey would provide lyrics. According to the singer, ROUGH TRADE's Geoff Travis had tried to pressurise him into providing words for the tune, insisting that the result could be The Smiths' first number one. '[But] I thought it was the weakest thing Johnny had ever done,' explained Morrissey. 'I said, "No, Geoff, it's not right."' Producer John PORTER also regretted Morrissey's vetoing of the tune ('It could have made a great song') though agreed that as an instrumental it was 'a bit of a throwaway'. While its spacious riff sometimes yearned for an absent vocal, musically 'The Draize Train' was full of classic Marr-isms, whether in its pale-faced Wythenshawe reflection of Chic's Nile Rodgers or the fact that for all its funk ambition its feet forever clank with the chains of melancholy. 'To me, the music was so romantic,' states Marr.

In keeping with Morrissey's animal rights rhetoric, the title was a reference to the 'Draize test' (patented by American scientist John Draize) in which commercial and cosmetic chemicals are tested on the skin, eyeballs and genitals of rabbits. Marr has refuted the suggestion that the 'Train' in the title is a homage to The Doobie Brothers' 'Long Train Running', based around a comparable funky riff. 'It honestly wasn't,' he says, 'but I can see how people could make that comparison because of that little guitar figure.' The similarity was even more pronounced in concert, where Marr and Craig GANNON's dual rhythm guitars made a formidable double act. Despite his earlier comments, that 'The Draize Train' should become an encore fixture of The Smiths' final UK tour of October 1986 suggests that Morrissey not only approved of the tune but was happy for Marr and the other members to enjoy their five minutes in the spotlight without him, as emphasised by its inclusion on RANK, compiled by Morrissey alone. [17, 27, 71]

drink, See ALCOHOL.

'Drive-In Saturday' (David Bowie), B-side of

'ALL YOU NEED IS ME' (2008). Although Bowie's influence upon Morrissey made him a likely cover version contender, his decision to first tackle 'Drive-In Saturday' in 2000 was mildly surprising given that five years earlier he'd notoriously walked out of his support slot on Bowie's winter 1995 UK tour after an apparent fall-out. Yet as Morrissey confessed, 'I simply have to play "Starman" or "Drive-In Saturday" and I will forgive him for anything.'

The second single from Bowie's 1973 album Aladdin Sane, 'Drive-In Saturday' reached number three in the UK that May and was still in the top ten the week of Morrissey's 14th birthday. 'It was a strong song in its time, and a very clever song too,' he recalled, 'a fascinating piece of art infiltrating a very, very drab top 30.' A musical homage to 50s doo-wop, Bowie's lyrics were inspired by an overnight train journey between Seattle and Phoenix in November 1972 when he spied '17 or 18 enormous silver domes' amid the moonlit desert landscape. The vision was the catalyst for the song's post-apocalyptic world where nuclear fallout has affected dome-dwelling mankind's ability to 'make love'. Their only hope, Bowie explained, is to watch old films 'of how it used to be done'. 'Drive-In Saturday' was first offered to Mott The Hoople (who'd already had a top three hit with his 'All The Young Dudes') before Bowie changed his mind. More dubiously, Morrissey has also referred to a supposed cover by JOBRIATH which has yet to surface.

Morrissey's first attempt at this sci-fi sex-education fantasy was a one-off encore at New York's Beacon Theatre on 29 February 2000. The audience's reaction was sufficiently muted and bemused for him to sing 'You don't like this song, do you?' halfway through. Seven years later, he reintroduced it on his US tour of May 2007 when the

officially released B-side version was recorded at Omaha's Orpheum Theatre. An assured cover, brilliantly sung, Morrissey made a few significant lyrical amendments. Other than substituting Bowie's nod to THE ROLLING STONES' '[Mick] Jagger' for his own to the NEW YORK DOLLS' 'David Johansen', he also changed 'Twig the wonder kid' – a reference to the model Twiggy, who appeared on the cover of Bowie's Pin Ups album – to the mysterious 'Chris the wonder kid'. Sadly, audiences were no more receptive to the song than they had been seven years earlier. Exhausted by their apathy, Morrissey dropped it after just six performances. [68, 195, 351]

'Driving Your Girlfriend Home' (Morrissey/Nevin), From the album KILL UNCLE (1991).

Revisiting the unrealised driver/passenger romance of 'THERE IS A LIGHT THAT NEVER GOES OUT', Morrissey would boldly describe 'Driving Your Girlfriend Home' as 'more powerful' than that Smiths epic. Typically, he refused to be drawn on the love triangle described in the song, adding only that, 'Yes, there is a loss for the driver.' Speculation was amplified by a cameo from old friend Linder STERLING on harmony vocals. Mark Nevin, who scored its cruising melody, believes her presence to have been very pointed. 'Linder was there a lot,' says Nevin, 'but I think that's about her, that song. How do I know that? Morrissey might have told me. I was sure it was about their situation and that's why she's singing on it. But I might be wrong.' Whether autobiographical or not (and perhaps not since at the time of its recording in 1990 the singer had yet to pass his driving test), 'Driving Your Girlfriend Home' is a beautiful Morrissey vignette: certainly not 'more powerful' than 'There Is A Light', but still Kill Uncle's hidden treasure. [15, 22, 437]

drugs, The subject of drugs was a thorny one

for The Smiths. In public, Morrissey stated he had 'no interest whatsoever in drugs', distancing the group from the usual rock and roll cliché. Yet, in private, Marr, Rourke and Joyce were all recreational drug users while even Morrissey was prone to prescription anti-depressants. Rourke's

d

well-documented heroin problem aside, Marr makes no secret of the fact that his creativity was often aided by marijuana, also admitting that by their final American tour of 1986 cocaine was in plentiful supply. Protected by Marr, Morrissey remained oblivious to what was going on under his nose and up those of his bandmates. 'I went back to the hotel every night with a tangerine,' he quipped, later stating that he never once saw drugs backstage during The Smiths. 'Which is quite annoying for me,' he joked. 'They could have offered it to me, it could have been good for me to join the club.' More notoriously, it was Morrissey's belated discovery of Rourke's addiction problems which led to the bassist's temporary sacking in the spring of 1986.

Although Morrissey was famously naïve when it came to drugs – an ignorance he'd self-mockingly allude to in the lyrics of 'THE QUEEN IS DEAD' – his history of prescription barbiturates such as Valium stretched back to his teens and the first symptoms of clinical depression. 'I used to make my weekly trip to the GP and come away laden,' he admitted in 1989 and has since spoken frankly about his trials with lithium, Prozac and similar anti-depressants. 'A lot of extreme things happen to you on them, which sometimes cannot seem to be worth it,' he explained, 'because I don't want something that's going to affect me in any way other than to perhaps cure me.' Andy Rourke, who tempered his heroin habit when touring by stocking up on 'valiums, temazepams and mogadons' from a crooked Harley Street physician, also recalls Morrissey, among others, sometimes knocking on the door of his hotel room door asking if he had 'any sweeties' to share.

In 1992, Morrissey made the more surprising confession that he'd tried ecstasy 'a couple of times'. 'The first time I took it was the most astonishing moment of my life,' he recalled. 'Because – and I don't want to sound truly pathetic – I looked in the mirror and saw somebody very, very attractive. Now, of course, this was the delusion of the drug, and it wears off. But it was astonishing for that hour, or for however long it was, to look into

the mirror and really, really like what came back at me.' Yet, in the same breath he reiterated, 'I'm not actually interested in drugs of any kind. I'm not prudish, I don't mind if other people take them, but it's not for me.'

Drugs have repeatedly cropped up in Morrissey's lyrics, from the 'strange pills' of 'LATE NIGHT, MAUDLIN STREET' and the heroin reference in 'SUNNY' to, more obviously, 'INTERESTING DRUG' and 'SOMETHING IS SQUEEZING MY SKULL'. Discussing the latter in 2008, Morrissey revealed a more mellowed and liberal outlook on drugs which, while he still avoided, he nevertheless regarded as an inevitable escape from 'pathetic' human existence: 'If it helps you, then take it.' [14, 17, 18, 29, 32, 33, 56, 58, 61, 69, 93, 94, 128, 133, 137, 138, 204, 217, 226, 236, 568, 453]

drums, Morrissey's favourite musical instrument. He revealed that he owned 'a reasonably impressive drum kit' at the age of 14, inspired by Jerry Nolan of the NEW YORK DOLLS. 'I thought, "That's me! Off I go!"' he confessed, 'but it wasn't me, and I didn't go anywhere.' His fondness for the drums is evident in his handful of pre-Smiths live reviews for *Record Mirror* between 1980–81, singling out the drummers of The Photos, Linder STERLING's Ludus and THE CRAMPS for special praise. When showing a television crew around his Hollywood home for 2003's *The Importance Of Being Morrissey* documentary, the cameras picked up a snare drum and some bongos while he later divulged that Dean BUTTERWORTH presented him with a full kit 'to bash around on' at home. Morrissey's love of the drums is all the more curious bearing in mind their obvious connotations with his nemesis, Mike Joyce. [241, 453]

Dublin, Morrissey's effective 'second home', also of great significance to his family's ancestry: his father, Peter, and mother, Elizabeth, were born and first met in the city before emigrating to Manchester in the 1950s. Just as relevant is the Irish capital's rich cultural heritage as the proud birthplace of his hero, Oscar WILDE.

du Pré, Jacqueline, English cellist whom Morrissey once named as his joint favourite musician along with the NEW YORK DOLLS. Among his 1989 list of 'election promises' printed in the *NME* was his vow to have 'Jacqueline du Pré dug up', referring to her death two years earlier at the age of 42 due to multiple sclerosis, the condition which put an end to her career in 1973 before she'd yet turned 30.

Like that of so many other Morrissey idols, hers was a tragic and troubled life, a factor which doubtless attracted him to her music in the first place. Following du Pré's death, her sister Hilary published the controversial memoir *A Genius In The Family* in which she claimed she consensually let Jacqueline have an affair with her own husband as a means of helping her overcome a mental breakdown. Friends of du Pré, and other members of the family, have strongly challenged Hilary's account, which was later dramatised in the 1998 film *Hilary And Jackie* starring Emily Watson as the doomed cellist and Rachel Griffiths as her compliant cuckolded sister.

Such private scandals are nevertheless irrelevant in the face of her musical legacy as the greatest cellist ever to have raised a bow. Her most famous recording remains her benchmark 1965 recital of Edward Elgar's brooding Cello Concerto in E Major, deemed by the majority of classical scholars to be its definitive recording; that du Pré was only 20 at the time made her achievement all the more remarkable. It was this version of the Elgar concerto which Morrissey played as pre-support band interval music on his 2006 RINGLEADER OF THE TORMENTORS tour. [141, 175, 509]

Before settling in Los Angeles in the late 1990s, Morrissey briefly moved to Dublin where he'd purchased property a few years earlier. A photo of his 'tax-sheltered' Dublin home with outdoor swimming pool was printed in *Q* magazine in 1998 at a time when his fortune was estimated at £8 million, making him, by their calculations, the 68th 'richest star in rock 'n' roll'. He decided to leave Dublin as a permanent base because 'it just wasn't exciting enough' though is still a frequent visitor, often stopping there during his transatlantic hops between America and England. Immortalised in the lyrics of 'PANIC', Morrissey also chose Dublin to launch his first post-Smiths solo tour at the National Stadium on 27 April 1991. Dublin audiences usually bring out the best in Morrissey and his concerts there are, by tradition, exceptionally jubilant occasions. [362]

Duffy, Billy, Manchester guitarist who played a significant role in bringing together Morrissey and Johnny Marr. A fan of the NEW YORK DOLLS, Duffy was introduced to Morrissey in the autumn of 1977 through mutual friend Phil Fletcher. As detailed in *THE SEVERED ALLIANCE*, Fletcher had approached Morrissey in the Manchester branch of Virgin Records having seen him at various gigs and kept abreast of his letters to the music press. Fletcher told Morrissey about a contingent of Dolls fans living in the Wythenshawe area and offered to arrange a meet-up. That September, Morrissey finally met Fletcher's gang, who included 16-year-old Duffy and another aspiring guitar player, Steven POMFRET. A few weeks later Morrissey, Duffy and Pomfret were rehearsing together, first as Sulky Young, then The Tee-Shirts (both Morrissey's names) though by the time The Tee-Shirts played their first gig Duffy and Morrissey had already left.

In early 1978, Duffy teamed up with two other Wythenshawe musicians, bassist Peter Crookes and drummer Philip Tomanov, formerly of punk band Ed Banger And The Nosebleeds. Now calling themselves simply THE NOSEBLEEDS, they were still in need of a new singer. Duffy persuaded them to audition Morrissey, who successfully joined the group for a three-month period in the spring of 1978. During that time, Duffy became Morrissey's first 'serious' co-writer, collaborating on several

Morrissey/Duffy originals including 'I Get Nervous', 'The Living Jukebox', 'Peppermint Heaven' and '(I Think) I'm Ready For The Electric Chair'.

The Nosebleeds disbanded after just two gigs. 'I tried with Billy, and I was just too shy,' said Morrissey. 'I was too closed up. I'm glad that I didn't record in those years because it would have been absolutely appalling.' In the summer of '78 Duffy went on to join the remnants of another fragmented Wythenshawe punk group, SLAUGHTER AND THE DOGS, whom it's alleged Morrissey also auditioned for (a myth the singer strongly refutes). It was in this post-Nosebleeds period, on the night of 31 August 1978, that Duffy went to see the PATTI SMITH Group at Manchester's Apollo with a local Wythenshawe crew including Slaughter bassist Howard Bates and Johnny Marr. Seeing Morrissey in the crowd, he introduced him to his friends. Thanks to Duffy, the 19-year-old Morrissey and the 14-year-old Marr first said hello to one another. His part in the formation of The Smiths unknowingly fulfilled, within the year Duffy would relocate to London, making his first record with his ex-Slaughter And The Dogs friends as The Studio Sweethearts before reverting to their original name.

Both Morrissey and Marr have since paid tribute to Duffy's role as their musical matchmaker. 'Billy Duffy was the first person I wrote songs with,' confirmed Morrissey, 'and in fact he pushed Johnny Marr in my direction which was very decent of him.' Marr, similarly, cites Duffy as 'one of the people who led me to Morrissey – he was the one who told me that he was good with words and wrote interesting lyrics'. Andy Rourke also notes Duffy's influence in alerting himself and Marr to the Morrissey enigma. 'Johnny and I had hung around at school together with Billy, who was a bit older than us,' says Rourke. 'He'd crossed Morrissey's path a few times and had told us all about being in The Nosebleeds and the time he'd tried to dye his hair green or something [see 'I KNOW VERY WELL HOW I GOT MY NAME']. So myself and Johnny were being told that Morrissey was a

bit of a crazy character years before we ever met him. I can definitely remember Billy saying that Morrissey was this guy who'd spent years in his bedroom at his typewriter. I think that was the thing that really must have stuck in Johnny's head. Billy had given him this idea that Morrissey had all these ready-made lyrics, so with Johnny's ready-made tunes it made perfect sense that they should try working together.'

Duffy, meanwhile, was cast adrift when Slaughter And The Dogs broke up in 1980. The following year he joined Theatre Of Hate, fresh from recording their debut album, Westworld. Though Duffy never played on the record, he'd make his TOP OF THE POPS debut in February 1982 miming with a Gretsch White Falcon to the semi-title track 'Do You Believe In The Westworld?' after it just scraped into the top 40.

By the time The Smiths released their debut single 'HAND IN GLOVE' in May 1983, Duffy had joined forces with Bradford's Ian Astbury of goth scaremongers Southern Death Cult. After one EP and one single as Death Cult, by 1984 they'd become simply The Cult, the band in which Duffy properly made his name as a writer and player, scoring hits with, among others, the contagious shamanistic riff of 'She Sells Sanctuary' (number 15, August 1985) and the steely retro-rock of 'Lil Devil' (number 11, May 1987). Marr also remembers a key moment when both The Smiths and The Cult found themselves on the same episode of Top Of The Pops in October 1985, respectively promoting the singles 'THE BOY WITH THE THORN IN HIS SIDE' and 'Rain'. 'That was very significant for me,' says Marr, 'because I hadn't seen Billy for a while. We'd both grown up on the same estate, plus he was the connection between me and Morrissey, so I remember us looking at each other in the BBC dressing rooms and shrugging, like, "Wow. Who'd have thought it? Here we are." It was kind of symbolic, from where we'd come from and what we'd both been through. Billy had really put the work in to get where he got, same as I had.' [18, 29, 139, 206, 226, 338, 362]

Eager, Vince, British rock and roll also-ran whose name Morrissey came close to immortalising on the run-out-groove message of the final Smiths single, 'LAST NIGHT I DREAMT THAT SOME-BODY LOVED ME'. After considering the cryptic invitation 'Vince Eager, come and get me', he opted for 'Eaten by Vince Eager' only to abandon the joke altogether. His reference to Eager was in keeping with the single's cover star, Billy FURY. 'Mr Eager was made from the same mould as Fury,' he explained, referring to 50s British rock and roll svengali Larry Parnes who discovered both. 'Mr Parnes, Shillings and Pence' (as he was known) made his wealth by offering naïve Elvis wannabes a stab at stardom in exchange for a Faustian recording contract and a ridiculous pseudonym. Thus Greenwich's Reg Smith became Marty Wilde, Croydon's Richard Knellar became Dickie Pride and Roy Taylor from Grantham was christened Vince Eager. Between 1958 and 1963, Eager released 11 singles – none charted – which Morrissey rightly described as 'completely impossible to listen to'. The one exception was his 1960 Top Rank disc, 'The World's Loneliest Man', another of Morrissey's 'Singles to be cremated with'. By his own admission, the title alone was 'pretty Morrissey-esque'. On this occasion not even Eager's overstretched gizzard could ruin the tune's pathos and drama, in places weirdly evocative of BOWIE's later 'Rock 'N' Roll Suicide'. Sadly for Eager, he had neither the larynx nor the luck to survive in pop, finding himself better suited to the cut and thrust of cabaret, Elvis tributes and pantomime. [150, 175, 374]

'East West' (Graham Gouldman), B-side of 'OUIJA BOARD, OUIJA BOARD' (1989). Originally a lower top 40 hit for Manchester's Herman's Hermits during Christmas 1966, like TWINKLE's 'GOLDEN LIGHTS' (as previously covered by The Smiths), 'East West' touched on the downside of musical fame in the homesick lament of a globe-trotting pop star. 'I feel homesickness very strongly,' Morrissey admitted. 'When I travel, which I rarely do, I feel very queasy and very lost.

I can't adapt to new cities and that's why I liked "East West" because to me it was the kind of song you would listen to when you were away from home and you would want to be home.'

Morrissey made a subtle change to the lyrics, addressing them to a specific loved one back home as opposed to the more general yearning of the original. He also ditched its final Christmas-themed verse and replaced it with his own, reinforcing this same narrative – so shackled by fame that he's 'unable to see' the person he desires. His backing band of session musicians Kevin ARMSTRONG, Matthew Seligman and drummer Andrew PARESI learned the tune from the singer's copy of the original Columbia seven-inch single, jangling up its basic melody and attacking its soft waltz-time beat with a clunkier rock treatment. Upon its release, Morrissey referred to 'East West' as both a reaffirmation of his roots in 60s Manchester and a 'way of saying goodbye to certain things, a certain period in my life'.

It came as no surprise that Morrissey should finally get round to covering Herman's Hermits, a band he'd championed in private throughout The Smiths (Rourke recalls him 'sometimes putting on a Herman's Hermits tape' in the tour bus) and whom he'd later feature on his concert interval music tapes in 1991. Like Morrissey, singer Peter Noone was born in Park Hospital, Davyhulme, and prior to joining the group starred in CORONATION STREET as Len Fairclough's teenage son, Stanley. The group's only UK number one, 1964's 'I'm Into Something Good', was first recorded by Earl-Jean McCree, formerly of The Cookies (whose 'I WANT A BOY FOR MY BIRTHDAY' was covered by The Smiths in 1982).

Though less prolific at home than their greater Manchester rivals The Hollies, in America Herman's Hermits' squeaky-clean image made them, after THE BEATLES, the most successful group of the British Invasion, scoring two US number ones in 1965 with 'Mrs Brown, You've Got A Lovely Daughter' and the inane 'I'm Henry VIII, I Am'. The latter's aside from Noone, 'second verse, same as the first', was later borrowed by the

RAMONES for 'Judy Is A Punk', as heard on Morrissey's UNDER THE INFLUENCE. In the sleeve notes of the same compilation Morrissey also refers to a quote from David Johansen, likening his NEW YORK DOLLS to Herman's Hermits.

Perhaps more significant than the group who recorded 'East West' is its author, Graham Gouldman. Born in Salford, Gouldman spent the 60s also writing hits for the Yardbirds ('For Your Love', 'Heart Full Of Soul') and fellow Salfordians The Hollies ('Bus Stop', 'Look Through Any Window') before his 70s prime as a member of 10cc. Gouldman was also instrumental in setting up the group's home-recording facility in Stockport, Strawberry studios, where 10cc created their ingenious, ethereal 1975 number one 'I'm Not In Love' and where The Smiths later recorded their debut single, 'HAND IN GLOVE'. [1, 25, 83, 226]

EastEnders, BBC television soap opera which Morrissey became 'affixed to' during the 1990s. Set in the fictitious east London borough of Walford, *EastEnders* was launched in February 1985 as a southern rival to CORONATION STREET. Morrissey's initial verdict was that 'it can be witty, but I find it a little bit "how's your father" and "stone the crows" … a bit "cor, blimey!"' In August 1991, Morrissey visited the *EastEnders* set when recording his TOP OF THE POPS performance of 'PREGNANT FOR THE LAST TIME' (both shows were filmed next door to one another at the BBC's Elstree Studios). Photos of the singer with band members Alain WHYTE and Gary DAY posing in and around Albert Square, the Bridge Street Café and the Queen Vic pub were later featured in the autumn '91 KILL UNCLE tour programme.

Morrissey maintained a love/hate relationship with *EastEnders*. On the one hand he 'despaired' of the writers ('I argue back at it'). On the other, he admired its fantasy portrayal of an idealistic English community. 'I think people wish that life really was like that,' he confessed. 'That we couldn't avoid seeing 40 people every day that we spoke to, that knew everything about us, and that we couldn't avoid being caught up in these

Ecover, Brand name of ecologically friendly ('100% bio-degradable') washing-up liquid which became something of an obsession with Morrissey shortly after the release of VIVA HATE. Guitarist Vini REILLY claims the singer used to turn up at his flat 'clutching bottles of [Ecover]'. He later appeared inside the *NME* pretending to drink the liquid and on its front cover glowering from behind a row of Ecover bottles beside the headline 'Morrissey comes clean'. Along the same lines, and during the same period, he once sent a consignment of Ecover to an *NME* journalist with the instruction to 'clean up your act'. [69, 221]

relationships all the time, and that there was somebody standing on the doorstep throughout the day. I think that's how we'd all secretly like to live. Within *EastEnders* there are no age barriers. Senior citizens, young children, they all blend, and they all like one another and they all have a great deal to say, which isn't how life is.'

Morrissey's *EastEnders* obsession seems to have peaked circa 1995's SOUTHPAW GRAMMAR. The videos for both its singles contained references to the soap. In 'DAGENHAM DAVE', Morrissey walks through a suburban house, its walls adorned with two framed portraits of the characters Frank Butcher (Mike Reid) and his wife Pat (Pam St Clement). 'THE BOY RACER' video featured cameos from actresses Nicola Stapleton (who'd just left the soap as Mandy) and Martine McCutcheon (who'd just joined the soap as Tiffany). Three years later, and in a neat but odd little coincidence in the Southpaw Grammar/*EastEnders* axis, McCutcheon's Tiffany was accidentally run over and killed by Frank Butcher. Morrissey was less than impressed by his former video co-star's on-screen death. 'I just thought it was the worst television ever,' he groaned. 'I just thought, never again can I watch this programme.' [146, 154, 215, 405]

'Edges Are No Longer Parallel, The'
(Morrissey/Whyte), B-side of 'ROY'S KEEN' (1997). Behind the mathematical metaphor of its title, 'The Edges Are No Longer Parallel' appeared a straightforward lyric about a once-meaningful relationship 'now suddenly meaningless'. Analysing his own depression, Morrissey concludes his 'only

mistake' is a false optimism that his solitude and suffering will end, inspiring an astonishingly emotional vocal. Whyte's tune – among the guitarist's favourites, and not unlike The La's' 'Looking Glass' – complemented the singer's thunder and lightning delivery; a longing, acoustic melody brewing towards a devastating tempest of artery-popping drums and wah-wah. Only ever played twice in concert, 'The Edges Are No Longer Parallel' is a slow scalpel across the heart-strings, among the absolute best of Morrissey. [4, 40]

El Vez, Asked in 1999 why he'd suddenly taken an interest in Mexican culture, Morrissey quipped, 'Because I saw El Vez recently and I'd like to have a go at stealing all his ideas.' Sometimes referred to as 'The Mexican Elvis', El Vez is the stage name of Robert Lopez, formerly of Chula Vista punks The Zeros and LA's Catholic Discipline (who also featured future Morrissey tour support, Phranc). Though Lopez's act is primarily based upon the music and iconography of Elvis PRESLEY, he often incorporates homages to David BOWIE (who shares The King's birthday, 8 January), simultaneously parodying both artists while adding the Latino influence of his Mexican heritage. Morrissey had wanted El Vez to support him in England and Europe in 1999, though he opened for him only once in Santa Barbara in October that year. The effect of El Vez upon Morrissey was most conspicuous when he toured Latin America for the first time in March and April 2000 employing similar visual homages to Elvis in keeping with Lopez's stage show. 'He's influenced me greatly,' Morrissey admitted. [143, 191]

e

Elephant Man, The, 1980 film by David Lynch based upon the life of severely deformed Victorian sideshow 'freak' Joseph Merrick (or 'John Merrick' in the film). 'The first time I saw *The Elephant Man*, just the introduction made me cry,' said Morrissey. 'It was so powerful and what followed was equally powerful, but I was really taken aback by the introduction.' The scene Morrissey spoke of was Lynch's dreamlike montage of Merrick's mother being attacked by a wild elephant during pregnancy, a codswallop story invented by his sideshow 'owner' in the film to explain his nickname.

Originally, Merrick was thought to have suffered from elephantiasis, though in recent times his condition has been identified as an even rarer hereditary disorder known as 'Proteus Syndrome'. Although the film takes many liberties with historical fact – for example, the villainous Bytes (Freddie Jones) is entirely fictitious – it's a largely faithful and extremely moving account of Merrick's rehabilitation from social outcast to distinguished gentleman with the help of a leading physician, Dr Frederick Treves (played by Anthony Hopkins). John Hurt received an Oscar nomination for his heart-rending portrayal of Merrick, buried under heavy make-up based upon body casts preserved at the London Hospital which took seven hours to apply. Morrissey's empathy with Merrick's story is understandable given its parallels with his own lyrical references to his perceived repulsiveness, be it the 'world's ugliest man' of 'LATE NIGHT, MAUDLIN STREET' or his physically despicable form in 'LET ME KISS YOU'. Thematically the film also resonates loudly with 'NOVEMBER SPAWNED A MONSTER'. [83, 500]

Eliot, George, Following the death of Charles DICKENS in 1870, for the last ten years of her life George Eliot was revered as the greatest living Victorian novelist and has been frequently cited by Morrissey as one of his favourite writers.

She was born Mary Ann Evans, later morphing into Marian Evans but chose a male pen name in order to be taken seriously by the male-dominated nineteenth-century literary establishment. Eliot's own proto-feminist traits were often reflected in her rebellious, strong-willed heroines such as the semi-autobiographical figures of Maggie Tulliver in *The Mill On The Floss* (1860) and Dorothea Brooke in *Middlemarch* (1871–72).

The majority of her seven completed novels were set in rural England, their plots often Mozzerian in their breadth of human tragedy, be it the shocking infanticide of *Adam Bede*, the opium-assisted death from hypothermia in *Silas Marner* or the devastatingly bleak conclusion of *The Mill On The Floss* as warring brother and sister rekindle their love for one another mere milliseconds before drowning. In the words of 'SHAKESPEARE'S SISTER' muse Virginia Woolf, '[Eliot] gathers in her large grasp a great bunch of the main elements of human nature and groups them loosely together with a tolerant and wholesome understanding which, as one finds upon rereading, has not only kept her figures fresh and free, but has given them an unexpected hold upon our laughter and tears.'

Morrissey has never specified a favourite Eliot novel, although he famously quoted from *Middlemarch*, her most celebrated masterpiece, in 'HOW SOON IS NOW?': its opening line is adapted from Chapter 12's description of Fred Vincy, 'born the son of a Middlemarch manufacturer, and inevitable heir to nothing in particular'. The vinyl run-out-groove of his 1990 single 'PICCADILLY PALARE' also contained the cryptic message that 'George Eliot knew'.

Eliot spent much of her adult life in a then-scandalous relationship with critic and philosopher George Henry Lewes who, technically, was still married to another woman. Two years after Lewes's death, in May 1880 Eliot remarried an American banker 20 years her junior, John Walter Cross. Already stricken with liver failure, she contracted a fatal throat infection and died seven months later, aged 61. Under the name of Mary Ann Cross, Eliot was buried in London's Highgate Cemetery: her grave, next to that of Lewes, is very near Karl Marx's monument and a short walk form the resting place of actor Sir Ralph Richardson, star of one of Morrissey's favourite films, *LONG DAY'S JOURNEY INTO NIGHT.* Another of the singer's favourite writers, *WELL OF LONELINESS* author Radclyffe Hall, is buried across the road in Highgate West Cemetery. [141, 175, 307, 308, 309, 388]

EMI, In early 1986, The Smiths' grievances with ROUGH TRADE had erupted in a complex contractual dispute delaying the release of THE QUEEN IS DEAD and furthering Morrissey and Marr's resolve to find an alternative label. In October that year, it was announced that they'd signed to EMI, causing minor controversy among indie purists who accused the group of selling out. 'I really can't tolerate the trite attitude that's surrounded The Smiths signing to EMI,' Morrissey retaliated. 'The concept that it's like getting into bed with Hitler is pathetic. The indie scene in England is very negative.' Ironically, long before signing with Rough Trade, in the winter of 1982 it was EMI who paid for The Smiths' second demo recording at Drone studios in Manchester thanks to a vague acquaintance of Marr now working for the company who managed to wangle funding.

As fate had it, The Smiths split in the summer of 1987 before they recorded a note for EMI. In a statement to the *NME,* the label's A&R spokesman Nick Gatfield explained that since 'every contract has a clause which gives the label the rights to any work they do whether the band splits up or not, essentially we now have two acts [Morrissey and Marr] for the price of one'. Years later Morrissey claimed he'd never actually wanted to sign to the label and felt unduly pressured into a solo career as a legal obligation to honour his contract, which he did, recording for their HMV and PARLOPHONE imprints until leaving in 1995. [18, 19, 134, 144, 153, 236, 433]

'End Of The Family Line, (I'm) The'

(Morrissey/Nevin), From the album KILL UNCLE (1991). On The Smiths' 'STRETCH OUT AND WAIT', Morrissey still seemed unsure of his thoughts about 'ever having children'. 'Sometimes I sit down and I quite like the idea,' he told one interviewer, 'but I realise now over the years I've become uncommonly selfish.' By the time of '(I'm) The End Of The Family Line', his most explicit musical statement on the subject, all hopes of fatherhood had been eradicated (likewise on 'BORN TO HANG', written soon afterwards). 'I can't imagine anything as terrible as little Morrisseys running around below the plum tree in my kitchen garden,' he joked. While the title was purely symbolic – he isn't actually the last branch on the Morrissey family tree – its message was solemn nonetheless.

Based on Mark Nevin's original demo featuring murky samples of an unidentified jazz record, the song also wove in a throwback to The Smiths with its false fade-out similar to 'THAT JOKE ISN'T FUNNY ANYMORE'. Its positioning in Kill Uncle's running order after the lethargic 'THE HARSH TRUTH OF THE CAMERA EYE' was unfortunate, but in isolation '(I'm) The End Of The Family Line' is both an admirable and thematically quintessential Morrissey ballad. [15, 22, 150, 192, 448]

Eno, Brian,

Aged 13, Morrissey first witnessed Brian Eno tweaking a synthesiser on stage with

Enchanted Desna, The, 1964 Ukrainian film which provided the cover image of The Smiths' 'THAT JOKE ISN'T FUNNY ANYMORE' single, also used as a backdrop for Morrissey's 1988 WOLVERHAMPTON gig. The image was a detail from a larger still of the dark-haired child, Sashko, being held by his mother. Morrissey sourced the picture from the February 1965 edition of *Film And Filmmaking* magazine. Beyond his fondness for the visual power of that specific image, it's safe to assume *The Enchanted Desna* has no great significance to Morrissey who, in all probability, had never seen this relatively obscure piece of world cinema. [374]

ROXY MUSIC at Manchester's Hardrock in November 1972 having stalked the venue earlier in the day thrilled by the sight of his 'psychedelic ostrich feather cape' hanging up in their tour bus. The following summer, Eno left Roxy due to differences with singer Bryan Ferry and threw himself into a solo career. Interviewed at the time for the *NME* by a young Chrissie HYNDE, she'd describe his voice as 'not unlike the shriek of a hare that's just caught an air gun pellet up the ass', though his first two albums of 1974, Here Come The Warm Jets and Taking Tiger Mountain (By Strategy) were acutely influential, anticipating the rhythms, textures and lyrical tantrums of post-punk, not least Howard DEVOTO's Magazine. Morrissey would praise both records in his correspondence with Scottish pen pal Robert MACKIE circa 1980–81, calling the former 'fab' and the latter 'one of the best albums ever'. The passing of time clearly did nothing to erode his affection since he included tracks from both among his interval music when touring in 2004: Eno's wicked Ferry pisstake 'Dead Finks Don't Talk', the fuzzy assault of 'Here Come The Warm Jets' and the blissful, drowsy 'Taking Tiger Mountain'.

Eno spent the latter half of the 70s furthering experiments in ambient music and helping BOWIE sculpt his groundbreaking 'Berlin trilogy' of Low, "Heroes" and Lodger (see also TONY VISCONTI). In between he recorded 1977's Before And After Science, the sleeve of which Morrissey photocopied and sent to Mackie in October 1980, in the same letter praising the tuneful thump of 'Backwater', another future interval tape favourite. Eno would also be Morrissey's first choice of producer for 1995's SOUTHPAW GRAMMAR, a collaboration which sadly never materialised. [126, 334]

Eurovision Song Contest, With the release
of his 2006 album RINGLEADER OF THE TORMEN-TORS, Morrissey chose to disclose his hitherto-unknown fascination with the Eurovision Song Contest and its 60s and 70s 'golden years' in particular. 'As a child I was almost religiously fascinated with it,' he confessed. 'I was one of those boys who'd watch every [year] with a pen and paper on their lap.'

Other than dazzling interviewers with his knowledge of contest trivia, Morrissey made an explicit homage with the video for 'YOU HAVE KILLED ME', made to look like a 70s Eurovision performance and intercut with original archive audience footage (the promo for 'IN THE FUTURE WHEN ALL'S WELL' was also in a similar 70s retro vein). When touring the album that May, on stage at the second of three London Palladium shows he mocked Britain's disastrous performance in that year's competition. 'I was horrified, yet not really surprised, to see the United Kingdom fail again,' he told his audience. 'The question that kept running through my mind was why didn't they ask me?'

Possibly prompted by this very outburst, Morrissey would later reveal that the BBC approached him soon afterwards to discuss representing the UK in the 2007 Eurovision. 'I said, "Yes, as long as I don't have to compete against anyone else." Cliff Richard didn't, so why should I? They agreed, but a few weeks later changed their minds and said they'd rather have a competition phone-in thing with me pitted against people called Splooch from SIDCUP. I said no thanks.'

Further Eurovision tributes were to come in his choice of 2006 interval video montages, featuring archive clips of 1969's ninth place, Sweden's Tommy Körberg with 'Judy Min Vän [Judy, My Friend]', and 1974's second place, Italy's Gigliola Cinquetti with 'Si [Yes]'. Previously his interval music also included what he named his 'all-time favourite' Eurovision track, Monique Melsen's 'Pomme, Pomme, Pomme [Apple, Apple, Apple]' which came an unlucky thirteenth for Luxembourg in 1971.

While Morrissey's 'Eurovision phase' seemed a logical consequence of Ringleader's Roman subtext and his newfound European awareness (name-checking the likes of Claude BRASSEUR and Serge GAINSBOURG), it also correlated with his long-established love of 60s UK pop. Two of his childhood favourites, Sandie SHAW and LULU, had both won the contest with 1967's 'Puppet On A String' and 1969's 'Boom Bang-A-Bang' respectively. Doubtless it was the prospect of following in either footsteps and recapturing some sense of national pride in a music competition where Britain has failed dismally of late which first kindled Morrissey's short-lived dreams of Eurovision glory. 'I think they'll ask me again,' he concluded sarcastically, 'and allow me to sing "LIFE IS A PIGSTY" – that should do it.' [49, 266, 568]

'Everyday Is Like Sunday' (Morrissey/Street), Morrissey's second solo single (from the album VIVA HATE), released June 1988, highest UK chart position #9. One of Morrissey's best-known and best-loved songs, behind the title's downcast resignation 'Everyday Is Like Sunday' seemed an anthemic roar against Britain's social malaise during the final years of the THATCHER government. Though the action is restricted to a depressed coastal town, the 'silent and grey' landscape he sings of may as well have been any inner-city council estate the length and breadth of the country.

Its central call for a nuclear apocalypse bore very obvious comparisons with John BETJEMAN's famous 1937 poem on the Berkshire town of 'Slough': 'Come, friendly bombs, and fall on Slough/It isn't fit for humans now.' But the root of the song's power, the secret to its eminence among the most exhilarating Morrissey moments of his entire career, is its ingenious inverted patriotism. While Morrissey begs for his surroundings to be obliterated in a mushroom cloud, his descriptions of wet sandy beaches, the ritual of writing postcards home and drinking greasy tea in a seaside café betray an aching nostalgia for a fast-disappearing English existence. At heart, 'Everyday Is Like Sunday' is a call for preservation in the language of annihilation – an ironic 'White Cliffs Of Dover' for the post-atomic age.

Included on the first cassette of demos Stephen Street sent Morrissey in August 1987, the tune hinged on a bass line inspired by Echo & The Bunnymen's 1984 single 'Seven Seas'. Guitarist Vini REILLY helped Street develop its mock

orchestration – all played on a keyboard – resulting in a richly romantic score propelled by the distant shunt of steam trains carrying passengers bound for brief encounters.

The single was aided by three very strong B-sides – 'DISAPPOINTED', 'SISTER I'M A POET' and 'WILL NEVER MARRY' – though the accompanying video was hindered by Morrissey's decision not to turn up at the designated location shoot in Southend-on-Sea, forcing frantic last-minute script changes. The final version starred Smiths fan Lucette Henderson (previously one of the cyclists in 'I STARTED SOMETHING I COULDN'T FINISH') acting a day in the life of a typical Morrissey apostle: repulsed by butcher's shop windows and fur coats, going for a solitary walk on the promenade and returning home to sit sulkily in front of the telly watching CARRY ON *Abroad*. Billie WHITELAW and ex-*CORONATION STREET* star Cheryl Murray co-starred, along with Nuneaton pensioners Lil Holmes and Joyce Armshaw. The closing scene where Morrissey is spied through a telescope wearing a T-shirt of Henderson's face was filmed in London and tacked on afterwards.

Strangely, Morrissey would describe the single's UK chart peak at number nine as something of a failure. 'I thought it was going to be a really big hit and it wasn't,' he grumbled. 'In England, it reached number nine and it had no airplay whatsoever.' Whatever his fears at the time, 'Everyday Is Like Sunday' has rightly become as celebrated a Morrissey song as any other, and with it one of his most instantly defining. [25, 39, 208, 272, 283, 374, 437, 564]

Exit Smiling, Film essay 'by Steven Morrissey', subtitled 'An affectionate recollection of some of the screen's also-rans', which he submitted to local Manchester publisher Babylon Books circa 1980. While Babylon published two other similar-length booklets of his in the early 80s, *The New York Dolls* and *James Dean Is Not Dead*, they passed on *Exit Smiling* until belatedly cashing in on his fame in 1998. Much to Morrissey's annoyance, the owner of Babylon Books, John Muir, printed a facsimile edition of Morrissey's original typed

e

manuscript with handwritten corrections in an alleged limited edition of 1,000 copies. This 'publication' of *Exit Smiling* provoked a stinging disclaimer from Morrissey. 'Please do not think that this book is in any way sanctioned by me,' he raged, claiming he was powerless to stop Muir since he had accepted a £50 advance 'in 1978' and that Babylon were 'exploiting my name in the shabbiest manner'.

The book is, nevertheless, a valuable insight into understanding Morrissey's artistic development and general outlook in the years immediately preceding The Smiths. As with many of his early lyrics, *Exit Smiling* is heavily influenced by 70s feminist film criticism and reads like a humble attempt to emulate Marjorie Rosen's POPCORN VENUS or Molly Haskell's FROM REVERENCE TO RAPE; even its title is taken from a 1926 silent comedy starring Bea Lillie mentioned in the latter. Divided into 14 very short chapters, it's a strange feat of camp style and dry wit over detailed content, meandering from one subject to another and lacking any unity or coherence as a 'book'. Even so, in his choice of subjects the 20-year-old Morrissey (or thereabouts – even he vaguely recalls it being 'written (I think) around 1979') shows himself to be consistent with his later armoury of Smiths cover stars and symbolists, from Diana DORS to Richard DAVALOS, Terence STAMP and Rita Tushingham. Among the films discussed are Shelagh DELANEY's *A Taste Of Honey*, THE LEATHER BOYS and THE MAN WHO CAME TO DINNER, while he also borrows Haskell's 'pinned and mounted' metaphor when examining Stamp's role in *The Collector*, a phrase he later reused in 'REEL AROUND THE FOUNTAIN'. As with the Robert MACKIE letters, the voice rising from the pages of *Exit Smiling* is immediately recognisable as that which soon emerged in The Smiths: 'Her arm is in a sling,' he writes of Thelma Ritter in 1961's *The Misfits*, 'and if it be known, so too is her world.' [186, 326, 341, 363]

Factory, Legendary Manchester independent record label, founded in 1978 by Granada television reporter Tony Wilson and partners Alan Erasmus, Rob Gretton and designer Peter Saville. Home to Joy Division, New Order and later Happy Mondays, Factory 'failed' to sign The Smiths in 1982.

Wilson already knew Morrissey, or 'Steven', the kid from Stretford who used to write to him via Granada, sending a copy of the NEW YORK DOLLS' first album cover with the message 'Why can't we have groups like this on television?' On another occasion, he received one of Morrissey's earliest attempts at drama, a DELANEY-esque teleplay 'about young people in a bedsit in central Manchester', which Wilson famously summarised as a play 'about eating toast in Hulme'.

'I always thought Steven was going to be our novelist, our Dostoyevsky,' Wilson later explained. 'But I got a phone call one day asking me to come over because he had something to tell me. I went to his mum's house and he took me into his bedroom with a poster of James DEAN on the wall, and he told me that he was going to be a pop star. I had to stifle my laughter because I thought this was the last person in the world about to become a pop star. I had a conversation with Richard Boon, BUZZCOCKS' manager and a mutual friend, saying, "Can you believe he'd ever be a pop star?" Four months later I went to their [second] gig at the Manhattan club … I remember walking out and Richard saying, "Now do you believe me?" Obviously I did, it was stunning.'

Marr confirms that Morrissey alone met Wilson in the winter of 1982 to try and interest him in his new group with their first demo. 'He physically brought the tape to Wilson to play him,' says Marr. 'I can remember I was working in X-Clothes the day when he rang me up and told me the news that Tony wasn't into it.'

'I didn't know what it was we'd lost,' said Wilson. '[New Order manager] Rob Gretton, who was more significant within the company than me, was wandering around Manchester telling everyone that The Smiths were the new BEATLES, but he was telling The Smiths that their demo was shit, and "I'm not signing you until you've got a good demo". But whatever, The Smiths have their own version of the story.'

After signing with ROUGH TRADE, The Smiths were quick to distance themselves from the Factory-dominated Manchester music scene in early interviews. 'Factory aren't really interested in new groups,' claimed Morrissey. 'Factory have been good, but they now belong to a time that is past. Look, we had a great social life, Factory has been great, but let's leave all that behind us now.'

With hindsight Marr would also state it was 'absolutely crucial' that The Smiths didn't sign with Wilson, even though he was much closer to the extended Factory family than Morrissey through his friendship with Andrew Berry, DJ and in-house hairdresser at the label's newly launched Haçienda nightclub. It therefore wasn't so much ironic as inevitable that Marr would later appear on Factory, first making a cameo on the label's 1984 single 'Atom Rock' by Quando Quango, the group of another Haçienda DJ friend, Mike Pickering (later of M People). The record was produced by New Order's Bernard Sumner, Marr's future partner in Electronic who themselves released their first three singles and debut album on Factory.

By stark and depressing contrast, Morrissey's relationship with Tony Wilson grew increasingly frosty, noticeably so when he was interviewed by Wilson for a *Granada Reports* feature about The Smiths' escalating success in February 1985. When Wilson later commented that Morrissey was 'a woman trapped in a man's body', he retaliated by likening Wilson to 'a pig trapped in a man's body'. When asked to justify the latter insult, Morrissey claimed he'd been misquoted. 'What I actually said was that he is a *man* trapped in a *pig's* body.' In the latter years of his life, Wilson was always painfully honest in sharing his hatred of Morrissey, 'with a venom that is only matched by the same venom that the arsehole feels for me'.

Factory enjoyed a second flush of success in the late 80s and early 90s with Happy Mondays (who

once tried to 'kidnap' Marr) only to go spectacularly bankrupt in 1991 after years of absurd business practices which have become British pop folklore. Wilson, and Factory's, story was dramatised in Michael Winterbottom's 2002 biopic *24 Hour Party People*. Morrissey refused to have any dealings with the film or allow any Smiths music be used on its soundtrack as a result of the shooting script's alleged 'humiliation' of his friend Linder STERLING, whose 1978 sketch for a 'menstrual egg timer' was given its own Factory catalogue number (Fac 8).

Tony Wilson died of cancer in August 2007, aged 57. As a mark of respect for all he'd done for the city, Manchester Town Hall flew its Union Jack at half mast. Wilson's coffin was given its own Factory catalogue number, Fac 501. The following November, Johnny Marr paid personal tribute to Wilson in his Salford University lecture on mavericks and outsiders.

'Tony Wilson was against quite a few things,' said Marr, 'but as everyone from the north knows, the main thing he was against was London. He practically led a 30-year movement against the perceived cultural superiority of London over Manchester. A fantastic outsider. And he totally championed the outside, not slick, naff music that was going to make him a lot of money really quickly. He championed rough, dangerous, messy outsiders, such as Happy Mondays from Salford. They had great poetry, great confrontation and took what was happening into the suburbs and on to television screens. They were proper outsiders. I can't really imagine that we would have known about them without Wilson but no one else could have related to them. God bless him.' [19, 47, 63, 79, 94, 398, 452, 468, 467]

Faithfull, Marianne, Forlorn-voiced ex-convent girl and 60s English pop icon among Morrissey's first music loves. The proverbial posh-girl-gone-bad, Faithfull's mother was an Austro-Hungarian aristocrat; her great-great-uncle was Leopold von Sacher-Masoch, author of the nine-teenth-century erotic novella *Venus In Furs* (inspiring The Velvet Underground song) and whose surname coined the term 'masochism'. Aged 17, she was 'discovered' in 1964 by ROLLING STONES manager Andrew Loog Oldham at a party for singer/actress Adrienne Posta (who'd later star in TO SIR, WITH LOVE). Oldham signed Faithfull to the Stones' label, DECCA, launching her career with a new Jagger/Richards song, 'As Tears Go By'. The apocryphal story behind its origins is that Oldham locked Mick and Keith in a kitchen for two hours, ordering them to write 'a song with brick walls all around it, high windows and no sex'. Faithfull would liken 'As Tears Go By' to Tennyson's 'The Lady Of Shalott' to the tune of 'These Foolish Things'. Released in August 1964, the song climbed to number nine.

Exploiting Faithfull's privileged upbringing, Oldham defined her image by presenting her to the music industry as a ballet-loving, Woodbine-smoking baroness's daughter with 'a waif-like beauty all of her own'. After her second single flopped – a standard folk cover of Dylan's 'Blowin' In The Wind' – Faithfull manoeuvred herself away from Oldham. Her third single, the tender, twittering 'Come And Stay With Me', would be the biggest hit of her career, reaching number four in late March 1965. Among those who helped it get there was a young Morrissey, just two months shy of his sixth birthday, buying his copy in Manchester record store Paul Marsh on Alexandra Road, Moss Side. 'I remember it had a profound effect on me,' he'd explain. 'I didn't understand what she was singing, but I lost myself to it.'[1]

In spite of such auspicious beginnings, Faithfull's 60s chart heyday was short-lived, with only two more singles reaching the UK top ten: 'This Little Bird' (number six, June 1965) and 'Summer Nights' (number ten, August 1965). The latter was a favourite of Morrissey and Marr during the formation of The Smiths in 1982, more so for its B-side, 'The Sha La La Song'. 'I can remember when Morrissey gave me [a tape with] Marianne Faithfull's "The Sha La La Song",' confirms Marr. 'It was like, "Wow!" That really hit the jackpot

for about two weeks.' Written by Faithfull producer Mike Leander under his birth name of Michael Farr, 'The Sha La La Song' mourned the end of a romance while optimistically anticipating 'a brand-new love that waits for me'. Morrissey and Marr briefly considered covering it.

In early 1967, Faithfull's public image was drastically altered by her shenanigans with various members of The Rolling Stones and her notoriety as the tabloids' 'Miss X' in the Redlands drugs bust at Keith Richards's Sussex home. That August, she displayed her loyalty to the group by appearing in the promo film for their 'We Love You' single, a homage to Oscar WILDE in which she played the poet's lover, Lord Alfred Douglas. Faithfull's escalating nymphet status was cemented by 1968's Girl On A Motorcycle (aka Naked Under Leather), a wonky attempt at psychedelic erotica co-starring Alain DELON.

By the early 70s she was acting out the lyrics of her own 'Sister Morphine', the 1969 single she'd co-written with the Stones: when her relationship with Jagger ended, Faithfull spent over a year as a homeless junkie living 'on a wall' in St Anne's Court, Soho, home to Trident studios where The Smiths would later record 'SHOPLIFTERS OF THE WORLD UNITE'. After a spell in rehab, she was invited by David BOWIE to be special guest on his October 1973 US TV special, The 1980 Floor Show, singing a duet of Sonny and Cher's 'I've Got You Babe' dressed in a nun's habit (Bowie's idea) and with Mick RONSON on guitar. She'd later claim that during this period she tried to engage Bowie in an oral sex act but, scared of her current boyfriend, he couldn't comply.

Faithfull made a comeback in 1979 with the acclaimed Broken English album, closing with the controversial 'Why D'Ya Do It?', a violent diatribe against an unfaithful lover written by Heathcoate WILLIAMS. Years of abuse had transformed Faithfull's once light and tremulous voice into a husky, cancer-dodging croak, making her delivery of its expletive-ridden lyrics all the more potent and earning a ban in Australia where it was removed from the running order.

In 1985, Morrissey made the surprising disclosure that The Smiths hoped to record a single with Faithfull. 'I'm quite nervous,' he explained, 'because we worked with Sandie SHAW and to work with Marianne – even though we all earnestly want to – might be construed by many, many people as careerism and just grabbing as many things as possible to keep The Smiths in the spotlight. So I'm sure it will happen but we're going to go about it very delicately and in a way that I could never be suspicious to anybody for whatever reasons.'

The Faithfull/Smiths collaboration sadly never materialised. Faithfull would later recall how Morrissey tried to contact her again during the 90s when she was living in Dublin. 'This wonderful sort of tortured voice came on the telephone and asked if he could meet me,' she described. 'And I was afraid. I just said "no". With no explanation. I didn't really mean it. I just didn't know what to do. I can't believe I did that to him. He didn't say anything, he just put the phone down. What could he say? I think I was also frightened of meeting people who just wanted to meet "The Legend". I was terrified of disappointing them. Or not being interesting enough. All that shit, y'know? I'm deeply, *deeply* sorry I did that. I think it was an *awful* thing to do.'

Faithfull would belatedly make amends by covering the RINGLEADER OF THE TORMENTORS ballad 'DEAR GOD PLEASE HELP ME' on her 2008 covers album, Easy Come, Easy Go. 'I wanted to do something great for him,' Faithfull explained. 'So I did that song because I didn't know what else to do!' [74, 139, 201, 275, 311, 351]

---

1. According to Faithfull's 1994 autobiography, 'Come And Stay With Me' was written on tour by US singer/songwriter Jackie DeShannon in the midst of her affair with guitarist Jimmy Page. The two lovers would also write the exceedingly Mozzerian 'In My Time Of Sorrow', one of the highlights of Faithfull's eponymous 1965 debut album.

family (of Morrissey), Irish defiance. Northern humility. Implacable benevolence. And not bad looks. These are the characteristics which, according to Morrissey, he's inherited from his parents.

The Morrissey clan is vast, though his own branch of the family tree is comparatively small. His father, Peter, and his mother, Elizabeth, had only two children: Jacqueline Mary, born 10 September 1957, and Steven Patrick, born 22 May 1959. Less than two years apart, the young Morrissey was close to his sister, also a pop fan, though he would claim that Jackie never 'experienced the kind of isolation' he suffered as an adolescent. 'She always had quite a spirited social life. She was never without the odd clump of friends. She felt alive at least.' Jackie married in 1983, taking the surname Rayner, and had two sons. The eldest, Sam Rayner, is the little boy in the video for 'SUEDEHEAD'. In May 2006, Morrissey introduced the grown-up Sam on stage at his Birmingham Symphony Hall Concert, calling his nephew his 'pride and joy'. Morrissey's other nephew, Sam's younger brother Johnny, has followed in his uncle's footsteps with his own group named after the Morrissey B-side 'NOISE IS THE BEST REVENGE'; Johnny has adopted his grandmother's maiden name of Dwyer.

Morrissey's parents separated when he was 17, his father moving out of the family home in Stretford just before Christmas 1976. For the next seven years, give or take the odd unsuccessful flit to 'foul, decrepit bedsits' in London or round the corner in Whalley Range, Morrissey remained there with his mother and sister. During The Smiths, detailed interrogation on the subject of his dad (to whom he bears a strong facial resemblance) was fiercely deflected, though there was enough insinuation to suggest an understandably emotionally complex relationship. 'He works in a hospital,' Morrissey explained in 1987, 'but he isn't a brain surgeon. He's a porter, which isn't quite the same scale.' Peter Morrissey would still be immensely proud of his son ('he has T-shirts and cassettes') and his presence at Morrissey's September 2002 Albert Hall shows alone would suggest that theirs isn't quite the dramatic 'estrangement' of *East Of Eden* proportions often inferred by some biographers.

Nevertheless, the breakdown in his parents'

marriage has had a lifelong effect on Morrissey; he often refers to it as instrumental in his notoriously pessimistic view of loving human relationships. 'My parents got divorced when I was 17 though they were working towards it for many years,' he'd claim. 'Realising that your parents aren't compatible, I think, gives you a premature sense of wisdom that life isn't easy and it isn't simple to be happy. Happiness is something you're very lucky to find. So I grew up with a serious attitude.'

When asked how his parents felt about such comments in the press, Morrissey calmly argued that they agreed with him. 'They don't leap back in horror or pin me against the wall and scream, "What have you been saying?" They don't have that kind of attitude. They're quite realistic and intellectual people. I did voice it to them some years ago. They weren't shocked to see it in blazing print.'

'I love them both very much,' he stressed, 'but I didn't raise them, and I can't really alter the past. It's nothing unique. Millions upon millions of people come from "damaged backgrounds", shall we say. Mine wasn't so much damaged as merely *nothing at all*.'

Of all his family, Morrissey's closest relationship is with his mother. Nobody has exerted greater influence upon his life, and his career, than Elizabeth Dwyer, a former assistant librarian. Born 13 November 1937, she was only 21 when her only son was born. 'She's not an old mum,' Morrissey boasted. 'She's only 20 years older than I am. My parents were very young when they had kids so they're not old, dotty, doting parents.'

Morrissey is very much a chip off his mother's block, to a profound degree. 'She really steered me in most of the directions which later were to become valuable for me,' he'd admit. Those directions included vegetarianism and animal rights (she'd often attend anti-hunt protests), early musical influences including Timi YURO, and, most fundamental of all, Oscar WILDE whom she 'thrust into' her son 'at a very early age'.

'Frankly, she always let me do what I wanted,' said Morrissey. 'If I didn't want to work, she said fine. If I wanted to go somewhere, she said here's the money, go. If I wanted a new typewriter, she'd provide it. She always supported me in an artistic sense, when many people around her said she was entirely insane for allowing me to stay in and write. It's this working-class idea that one is born simply to work, so if you don't you must be of no value to the human race. Because I didn't work, it was a cardinal sin. But everything has worked out well. It's all proved to have some value and she feels as great a sense of achievement as I do. It's nice to have the last laugh.'

Herein lies the crux of Morrissey's motherly bond, the vengeful and vindicating 'last laugh' against a cruel, unbelieving outside world. As he later paid tribute, 'It was entirely because of her that I survived to be in The Smiths.' It also goes some way to explaining Ms Dwyer's notorious 'hands-on' approach to her son's career. 'When The Smiths began, she was very strong-willed and business-minded,' he admitted. Known to keep tabs on ROUGH TRADE boss Geoff Travis, allegedly making frequent phone calls to ensure they weren't exploiting her boy, after retiring from her library job she assumed a managerial role in his business affairs, fending off accountants, lawyers and various dissatisfied collaborators.

'It was quite strange,' recalls engineer Danton Supple, who after chasing up an outstanding payment for a Morrissey session found himself on the phone to the hyper-protective Ms Dwyer. 'Because I'd be saying, "I'm owed this money," and she'd be saying, "Why do you need as much as that?" I thought, "Hang on! I'm chasing money Morrissey owes me and I end up having to justify what I do for a living to his mum?" It was mad.' Stephen STREET encountered similar problems. 'I ended up speaking to his mum because she'd started looking after his business,' says Street. 'I was trying to explain that there was money owed. She said, "Haven't you been paid enough by now?" Which really wasn't the point. But that was her attitude and maybe that says a lot about Morrissey's attitude to money as well.'

Morrissey would confess that his mum's is the only opinion he truly values. 'She takes it very seriously and reads my interviews religiously,' he'd elaborate. 'She dissects them, she completely dissects everything that happens ... She produces long monologues. She's very, very much involved in what I do.' Such is his mum's influence upon Morrissey that in February 2009 he appeared on BBC television's primetime *The One Show* to promote YEARS OF REFUSAL purely because it was one of her favourite programmes. When the presenters mistakenly referred to her as 'Mrs Morrissey' he was quick to put them right. 'It's Ms,' he corrected, 'and it's Ms Dwyer.'

The extended Morrissey family include Ms Dwyer's sisters Mary and Patti, both of whom emigrated to America. It was thanks to his Aunt Mary and Aunt Patti that Morrissey first visited the US as a teenager in the late 70s, briefly entertaining thoughts of starting a new life there as an escape from the depression and tedium of his Stretford existence. That he didn't may also have been the influence of his mum. As he'd later confess, 'She doesn't like Americans.' [39, 40, 95, 108, 115, 120, 128, 129, 139, 152, 211, 217, 267, 408, 411, 448, 453, 573]

fans, Morrissey has repeatedly expressed his distaste for the word 'fans' ever since The Smiths. Instead, he'd refer to the group's followers as 'Smiths apostles'. Similarly, in his solo career he rarely recognises the term, choosing to call them simply 'the audience'.

Family Way, The, 1966 British northern drama listed among Morrissey's favourite films and source of The Smiths' single sleeve for 'I STARTED SOMETHING I COULDN'T FINISH' with Avril ANGERS. Based on Bill Naughton's play *All In Good Time*, the action takes place in a provincial northern working-class town (shot on location in Bolton) and revolves around newly-weds Hywel Bennett and Hayley Mills, swindled out of their honeymoon and forced to lodge with the groom's parents played by Morrissey screen favourites John MILLS and Marjorie RHODES. The couple's subsequent delay in consummating their marriage creates a local scandal, the basis of the film's comic drama.

The Family Way touches on several key themes in Morrissey's lyrics, from the hopelessness of marriage to sexual anxiety and a strained father-and-son relationship. There's also an underlying subplot of repressed homosexuality in John Mills's role. His is a brilliant performance, outwardly a flat-cap-wearing northern stereotype until he begins reminiscing about his long-lost 'best mate, Billy' whom he was evidently in love with. Some of the film's dialogue also has coincidental reverberations with Morrissey's lyrics: in its most famous scene where Bennett's teenage brother, Murray Head, disturbs a naked Hayley Mills in the bathtub, he tells her 'let me know if you need a back scrubber' ('HALF A PERSON'); later in the film, Angers's concern over her daughter finds her pre-empting the title of a RINGLEADER OF THE TORMENTORS track in her weary sigh, 'I just want to see the girl happy.'

Another production still from the film featuring Murray Head was used on The Smiths' European import single of 'STOP ME IF YOU THINK YOU'VE HEARD THIS ONE BEFORE'. Head was originally cast to sing the intended theme song, 'Someday Soon', though his efforts were overshadowed when Paul McCartney agreed to write the film's soundtrack at the height of THE BEATLES' fame. Head confesses that he 'fell absolutely in love' with Hayley Mills on set though, to his dismay, she in turn developed a crush on director Roy Boulting. During filming, the majority of the cast stayed in Manchester where, according to Head, he and Bennett once made the mistake of wandering around Moss Side only to find themselves at knifepoint from a couple of real-life Rusholme ruffians. Drawing on their very best acting skills, they managed to talk their way out of being stabbed by pretending that Bennett, who was wearing dark glasses, did so because he was blind. [9, 168, 175, 502]

As much as Morrissey craved recognition during The Smiths, publicly he expressed embarrassment at the level of adoration he regularly aroused among his 'apostles'. 'They seem to expect so much of me,' he fretted. 'Many of them see me as some kind of religious character who can solve all their problems with a wave of a syllable. It's daunting … I don't always have the answers for everybody else's lives. It's quite sad to study the letters I receive, and I receive a huge amount of mail every day, vast volumes on people's lives [saying], "Only you can help me and if you don't reply to this letter I'll drown."' This wasn't exaggeration on Morrissey's part. A former EMI employee informed this author that during the early to mid-1990s, incidents involving hysterical phone calls or disturbed visitors in reception threatening to do themselves harm unless they spoke to Morrissey were not necessarily isolated. 'It didn't happen too often,' they recalled, 'but when it did, it was very scary. We'd have to get the police to remove them. Of course, we'd have to inform Morrissey whenever it happened and he was always deeply upset.'

One of the most extreme cases to have taken place was at Colorado radio station KRXY in autumn 1987 where crazed Smiths fan James Charles Kiss planned to hold a DJ at gunpoint, demanding they only play Smiths records from then on. Losing his nerve, Kiss instead surrendered his rifle to staff and was later arrested and sent to Jefferson County jail for attempted extortion and kidnapping. Tellingly, Morrissey was piqued that the story never gained greater media coverage at the time. 'Any other artist, it would have been world news,' he grumbled. 'Because it was the poor old tatty Smiths it was of no consequence whatsoever.'

Analysing his unique appeal, Morrissey put it down to the fact that 'a lot of young people are very lonely and maybe hearing my records will make them feel less lonely. And there may be many people who are like I was, desperate, incapable, but needing so much to do something. I would like to think a record of mine will make them feel if *he* can do it, et cetera, then so can I.'

He'd also admit that in his audience's zealous fanaticism, with queues of front-row 'irregular regulars' forming outside his concerts anything up to ten hours before the doors open, he recognised something of his younger self. 'I was one of those people who would actually turn up at noon,' he confessed. 'I would be pressed against the door if it wasn't a seated venue, so you'd have to run straight to the front and you'd just stare for 15 hours and by the time the group came on you were so exhausted and you left ten minutes later. You saw nothing. It was great.'

The concert ritual of 'apostles' leaping on stage to hug, touch, kiss or shake the hand of Morrissey dates back to the beginnings of The Smiths when the stage invasion was encouraged as a means of breaking down the barrier between the group and their audience. Yet, as demonstrated by the group's appearance on BBC2's *Oxford Road Show* on 10 February 1984 – the first time on television that an audience member jumped on stage and clung to Morrissey like a limpet – within that communal celebration the singer provoked individual acts of worship unique to him alone. These would become more intense, and more bizarre, as his career progressed. While living in Los Angeles, one young man tracked down his Hollywood address, covered the singer's car in Morrissey pictures, removed his clothes and danced naked outside his house. 'I think he was trying to tell me something,' pondered Morrissey. 'Somebody called the police, oddly enough, and they carted him off. I believe they charged him with being too happy and enjoying his body far too much.'

Morrissey has the highest regard for his fans, the core of whom are notoriously obsessive and ruthlessly dedicated. It's the latter virtue, an unyielding faith in his every move, which the singer seems to prize above all others. 'I seem to have a very loyal audience,' he surmised, 'a reasonably serious audience who think very deeply about the things that I do. They criticise me a great deal, and most of the time they're wrong. Sometimes they're right [but] they're so staunchly loyal.' [171, 204, 207, 208, 226, 374, 414, 422, 441]

125

f

'Fantastic Bird' (Morrissey/Whyte), Studio outtake from 1992, officially released on the 2009 redux edition of the unrelated album SOUTHPAW GRAMMAR. Among Morrissey's strangest love songs, the bird he sings of is neither the feathered nor colloquial female variety but some form of rocket ship belonging to his lover who plans to become 'the first stand-up comedian in space'. His lyrical sci-fi fantasy ends when his beloved funny-man comes, literally, crashing back down to earth where Morrissey is waiting to shower him with affection. Recorded as a possible B-side for the YOUR ARSENAL single 'CERTAIN PEOPLE I KNOW', Morrissey would attempt only one vocal take, writing off the result as an 'unmixed throwaway'. Though mildly entertaining, the decision not to release it at the time was by no means a bad one. Still, its inclusion on the revamped Southpaw Grammar, while bizarre in terms of chronology – 'Fantastic Bird' was recorded over two years before that album – made some sense purely in terms of Whyte's complementary vigorous guitar riff. [5]

Far From The Madding Crowd, 1874 novel by Thomas Hardy which Morrissey has cited on several occasions. The story is quintessentially Hardy in its defeatist narrative involving farm owner Bathsheba Everdene and her three suitors – the shepherd Gabriel Oak, the ageing farmer William Boldwood and the dashing yet dreadful army sergeant Frank Troy – ending in murder, betrayal, insanity and the ruination of several lives by sheer accident of fate. Morrissey stipulated that he was a fan of the novel rather than of Hardy himself. 'I'm moved by certain books rather than people,' he elaborated. '*Far From The Madding Crowd* set me alight, but [Hardy's] *The Mayor Of Casterbridge* didn't. I feel that way about so many [authors].' Asked in 1985 if he'd ever 'stolen' any lyrics from *Madding Crowd*, Morrissey joked, 'There's nothing worth stealing from that. Don't worry, if there was, I'd have it.' However, five years later he referred to the book, likening his own resilience with that of its female protagonist. 'There's a famous quote in *Far From The Madding*

Crowd by Thomas Hardy, where Bathsheba Everdene says, "I shall be breakfasted before you have risen and, in short, I shall astonish you all." It has no relevance of course but I honestly do believe that, once they've raked away all the nonsense, I'll still be here.' Other critics, including his friend Michael Bracewell (partner of Linder STERLING) have since repeated the quote in their own evaluations of Morrissey. His interest in Hardy's novel was doubtless encouraged by its 1967 film adaptation, directed by BILLY LIAR's John Schlesinger and starring Julie Christie (Bathsheba), Alan Bates (Gabriel) and Terence STAMP as, in Morrissey's words, the 'seamy and hateful' Sgt Troy. [70, 124, 221, 341, 435, 503]

Farrell, Michael (Morrissey keyboard player and co-writer 2004–07), Morrissey's first full-time touring keyboard player, Cleveland's Michael Farrell – sometimes 'Mikey Farrell' or 'Mike V. Farrell' (perplexingly the 'V' stands for 'Kevin') – joined his group in 2004 to tour YOU ARE THE QUARRY having previously worked with Macy Gray. It was a logical addition to Morrissey's live set-up, particularly as keyboards featured prominently on the album itself, as played by session musician Roger Manning Jr.

Farrell made a major difference to Morrissey's live group dynamic, lending a richness of texture to the sound be it mimicking the original 'flute' part of 'THERE IS A LIGHT THAT NEVER GOES OUT' or re-creating the atmospheric piano intro to 'LAST NIGHT I DREAMT THAT SOMEBODY LOVED ME'. His skills as a multi-instrumentalist were best demonstrated on Morrissey's next album, 2006's RING-LEADER OF THE TORMENTORS, playing trumpet and trombone as well as keys. Farrell also co-wrote its showstopping finale 'AT LAST I AM BORN' and another track, 'SWEETIE-PIE', which to his understandable befuddlement was mixed beyond recognition before being issued as a B-side. His presence was more keenly felt on the ensuing Ringleader tour where regular performances of 'TROUBLE LOVES ME' were preceded by a different piano intro every night determined by the location, from

Gracie Fields' 'Sally' in Manchester to the traditional 'Molly Malone' in Dublin. Equally distinctive was his live 'Auld Lang Syne' coda to 'LIFE IS A PIGSTY', itself a nod to the same tune's use on The Smiths' 'ASLEEP'.

Farrell's last session for Morrissey in 2007 was one of his best, the piano-driven B-side 'MY DEAREST LOVE' with producer Gustavo Santolalla. Due to family commitments Farrell left on amicable terms after the singer's epic US tour of 2007. While Manning returned for the recording of YEARS OF REFUSAL, Farrell was replaced on stage in 2008 by Kristopher Pooley, former touring keyboard player with Gwen Stefani and Smashing Pumpkins. [389]

father (of Morrissey), See FAMILY.

'Father Who Must Be Killed, The'
(Morrissey/Whyte), From the album RINGLEADER OF THE TORMENTORS (2006). Pop as only Edgar Allan Poe might have imagined it, Morrissey's gothic melodrama about a girl compelled to stab her stepfather only to then slit her own throat was a thrilling departure from his (seemingly) autobiographical norm. Surprisingly, it was one of the least-performed Ringleader tracks in concert despite being one of its most distinct and expressive tunes; Whyte's sinister arrangement was the perfect backdrop to its macabre tale of steppatricide, punctuated by a contrasting jumpstart-punk chorus with the frolicsome touch of an Italian children's choir. In its final throes, Morrissey so convincingly serenades the young murderess to her fate it's as if his own life is ebbing away between each increasingly shrill syllable. [389, 543]

feminism and the women's movement
As he has freely admitted on numerous occasions, many of Morrissey's philosophies and beliefs were shaped by women writers, particularly those in the 1970s whose work challenged accepted stereotypes of sex and gender. Not all would happily describe themselves 'feminists', though each contributed to the debate in the women's movement and, at the risk of ghettoising,

can be loosely grouped together as Morrissey's feminist icons.

A key early influence was New York's Susan Brownmiller, whom he referred to several times during The Smiths, also naming *Against Our Will*, her 1975 study on 'Men, Women and Rape', one of his favourite books. A detailed catalogue of rape crimes throughout American history, wartime and up until the early 70s, it's an astoundingly powerful, unflinching work. Though it obviously had a great effect on Morrissey, unlike other books he named during the same period such as Marjorie Rosen's *POPCORN VENUS* and Molly Haskell's *FROM REVERENCE TO RAPE*, *Against Our Will* contains no obvious lyrical sources.

The American journalist Joan Didion was deeply critical of the early 70s women's movement, accusing its believers of being romantics rather than true revolutionaries less concerned with 'the oppression of women [than] their own chances for a new life in exactly the mould of their old life'. Didion would no doubt balk at being labelled one of Morrissey's 'favourite feminists', though as a revered political essayist in the 60s and 70s her work is, at the very least, indicative of his interest in the sharp, provocative and intelligent female voice.

Another of his 'abiding passions', Nancy Friday first caused a sensation with 1973's *My Secret Garden*, a groundbreaking collection of interviews with women about their sexual fantasies, though it was her later *My Mother, My Self* (1977) and, especially, 1985's *Jealousy* which had Morrissey in a lather of admiration. 'It's remarkable,' he raved in 1987. 'I'm just underlining everything … I don't know how to describe it, let's just say that I'm learning so much from it … I think everyone has their particular traits, and I don't think jealousy is particularly negative. But I only learned that through reading Nancy Friday.'

Of the British feminist movement, Morrissey has previously cited Beatrix Campbell, author of 1984's *Wigan Pier Revisited*, among his 'bedside material', though his ultimate feminist icon is, inarguably, *the* great feminist icon, the Australian-born Germaine Greer. Speaking about his adolescence in 1985,

f

Morrissey described how he'd kept Greer's 1970 feminist bible *The Female Eunuch* 'strapped to my waist night and day', also telling another interviewer how he'd 'like to eventually turn into Germaine Greer'.

His praise for Greer was duly reciprocated in her 2008 *Guardian* blog attacking bad lyricists. Dismissing Bob Dylan as a 'creep', Greer ended the piece with a glowing tribute to her famous disciple. 'When Morrissey sings a Morrissey song, he knows exactly what colour every part of every word is meant to be, and whether it crosses the rhythm to build up tension, or cannons into it to gain emphasis. If Morrissey repeats a line, he may vary it in a new context, or he may keep it exactly the same, as he does with "EVERYDAY IS LIKE SUNDAY", because part of the point of the song is the anguish of monotony as perceived by hapless youth – but the music catapults the repetition towards us like a javelin.' [91, 95, 133, 175, 184, 196, 291, 345, 425]

Ferry, Bryan, See ROXY MUSIC.

Finn, Jerry (Morrissey producer 2003–08),
The architect of Morrissey's 2004 comeback album YOU ARE THE QUARRY, Finn was regarded by most UK critics as a 'surprise' choice of producer in view of his history with American punk groups such as Blink 182, Green Day and Rancid. Morrissey's interest in Finn stems from his work on the 1997 album Destination Failure by Chicago's Smoking Popes, one of his favourite contemporary bands who supported him in the US during that year's MALADJUSTED tour.

He first met Finn through 'a mutual friend' and was immediately impressed. 'I had met so many producers and I thought they were all monsters,' explained Morrissey. 'I just knew instinctively that Jerry was the one and I knew that he had a bright sound that I wanted because I felt some of the albums I'd done in the past had been a bit dull overall, their sound had been a bit muffly. So I thought if I could combine bits of Jerry, bits of me and bits of the musicians then we'd have a fantastic mix.'

The 34-year-old Finn brought a vigour and vitality to the Quarry material, encouraging Morrissey and his band to go hell for leather when the need arose but just as capable of creating delicate and subdued atmospheres on its more reflective moments. He'd later explain he also coaxed Morrissey into breaking his traditional habit of recording music and vocals separately, instead creating 'a much more listenable album because everyone was in the same room at the same time and it made the album much tighter'. Finn also brought in his regular session collaborator, keyboard player Roger Manning Jr, to add to Quarry's richness of texture.

Although Morrissey decided on TONY VISCONTI for 2006's RINGLEADER OF THE TORMENTORS, he returned to Finn when commencing YEARS OF REFUSAL in late 2007. 'I wanted to try Jerry again,'

Ferrier, Kathleen, Blackburn-born classical contralto whom Morrissey once listed among his favourite singers. In the post-war/pre-pop era, Ferrier was a household name in Britain and an international star abroad, recording for DECCA from 1946 until her death from breast cancer in 1953 at the age of 41. The combination of her earthy Lancashire roots (despite her prim appearance and vocal refinement, she apparently drank pints, smoked unfiltered cigarettes and enjoyed bawdy humour), her tragic life and the grief-stricken nature of her most popular arias makes Ferrier a prime Morrissey icon. Her choice of material has an eerily Mozzerian ring to it: Malcolm Sargent's 'What Is Life?', Mendelssohn's 'Woe Unto Them', Handel's 'He Was Despised' and Bach's 'Have Mercy, Lord On Me' – in title not so very far away from the second track on RINGLEADER OF THE TORMENTORS. [175]

he explained, refuting allegations of favouritism by referring to both Finn and Visconti as his 'two ideal producers … fantastic in equal measure'. Refusal was to be Morrissey's strongest album of the decade, thanks again to Finn's gift for presenting clamour with clarity. 'He liked very loud music and nothing too complicated,' said Morrissey, 'but he was very fastidious also. He had everything, really.'

Shortly after completing the album, in July 2008 the 39-year-old Finn suffered a heart attack followed by a brain haemorrhage. Placed in Los Angeles' Cedars-Sinai Medical Center, he never regained consciousness. His family decided to take him off life support and Finn died on 21 August. 'We had the [album] playback at his house, and a couple of weeks later he was in [hospital],' Morrissey recalled. 'It was absolutely dreadful. Completely unbelievable. It's astonishing that one minute you can be making an album with somebody and looking forward to the future, and he isn't around to see the release … it was horribly, horribly sad.'

Finn's untimely death cast a tragic shadow over the release of Refusal, his fate cropping up in many interviews of the period, prompting warm if philosophical tributes from Morrissey. 'It's a lesson for everybody. There's no such thing as safety. It can happen to anyone at any time.' Like the death of Mick RONSON 15 years earlier, Finn's passing put an end to a uniquely prosperous Morrissey/producer partnership that still had much to offer. Horribly sad, indeed. [60, 202, 420, 480]

Finney, Albert, One of Morrissey's favourite
actors, mainly due to his role as 'fighting pit prop of a man' Arthur Seaton in 1960's SATURDAY NIGHT AND SUNDAY MORNING. An obvious choice of Smiths cover star, Finney would decline permission for a Seaton portrait to be used on the sleeve of 1984's 'HEAVEN KNOWS I'M MISERABLE NOW'. 'He's always been immensely dear to me,' Morrissey mourned, 'and he refused, wouldn't have anything to do with it.' By the time Finney's children cajoled him into changing his mind, The Smiths had split.

Born and raised in Salford, it was Finney's childhood membership of SALFORD LADS CLUB which probably inspired Morrissey to choose the building as a photo backdrop. The derelict shopfront of the Salford bookmaker's shop owned by his father who shared the name Albert Finney was also used for a Smiths photoshoot in early 1987 and later featured in the video for 'I STARTED SOMETHING I COULDN'T FINISH'.

'Finney was the northern boy made good,' explained Morrissey, 'which is why I can relate to him even more.' After moving to London to study at RADA, in 1960 Finney made his big screen debut playing the ill-fated soldier son of Laurence Olivier in The Entertainer prior to the same year's Saturday Night And Sunday Morning. He maintained his commitment to theatre, playing BILLY LIAR in the original London stage production, before the surprise international success of 1963's Tom Jones, Tony Richardson's bawdy interpretation of Henry Fielding's eighteenth-century novel which earned Finney his first Oscar nomination.

Morrissey would proclaim that 'the beauty of Finney was his natural quality as an actor', though nothing among his subsequent 60s work would surpass the early promise of Saturday Night And Sunday Morning. At his worst, he made a dreadful Welsh psychopath with a disconcertingly sculpted quiff in 1964's Night Must Fall, adapted from the stage play by BEYOND BELIEF author Emlyn Williams. His best post-Seaton roles were opposite Audrey Hepburn in Stanley Donen's tragicomic romance Two For The Road (1967) and the same year's Shelagh DELANEY-scripted Morrissey favourite Charlie Bubbles, which Finney also directed.

For reasons which the end result failed to make logical sense of, in 1977 Finney also recorded an album for Motown. Simply titled Albert Finney's Album, it featured a dozen tracks of orchestrated easy listening scored by Denis King with original lyrics by the actor. Finney's singing was brave if sadly no better than his McGonagall-esque rhyming couplets: 'The bird of paradise is very rare/Of a kind beyond compare.' [57, 275, 374, 491, 501, 548]

Finsbury Park, See *NME.*

'First Of The Gang To Die' (Morrissey/ Whyte),

Morrissey's 26th solo single (from the album YOU ARE THE QUARRY), released July 2004, highest UK chart position #6.

Written after moving to Los Angeles, 'First Of The Gang To Die' was Morrissey's joyful requiem to a local young Latino criminal whose wayward lifestyle led him inevitably to an early grave. 'Hector' may be a scarce name in Britain – synonymous with Scottish gentry and the upper classes – but commonplace in Mexican communities. As a case in point, Hector 'Weasel' Marroquin was the notorious leader of LA's 18th Street Latino gang before trying to reform by founding an anti-gang violence organisation called 'NO GUNS'. Marroquin was later re-arrested in 2006 for – absurdly enough – possession of an illegal firearm. Even so, there's something tangibly perverse about any pop song that dares to christen its hero 'Hector', an audacious joke magnified by its supreme popularity in Morrissey's repertoire as, to date, the track he's sung in concert more than any other since first introducing it in August 2002, nearly two years before its official release.

In the song, 'Hector' himself is but a vehicle – Morrissey's Hitchcockian MacGuffin if you like – to contrast the extremities of life and death within a romantic world view where love is reserved only for those able to marvel at the irony of watching sunrise behind a care home for the blind. Fitting neatly into his existing canon of crime songs such as 'THE LAST OF THE FAMOUS INTERNATIONAL PLAY-BOYS', it also provided him with a chance to wallow in his own gang fantasies of life among the 'pretty petty thieves'. If anything, 'First Of The Gang To Die' is Morrissey's most shameless glamorisation of villainy, smitten by the memory of the lost lad who 'stole all hearts away'.

The song's mass appeal owes a great, *great* deal to Whyte's languid but loveable rosy-cheeked guitar riff, its milkman-friendly melody anchoring a lyric which otherwise lacks any obvious anthemic qualities, certainly paling in significance beside the human gravitas of, say, 'THERE IS A LIGHT'. Yet if it seems outrageous that several thousand people at a time bounce up and down at Morrissey gigs in beery chants of 'Hector-was-the …', then perhaps that's the whole point. Its victory of preposterous pop spirit over rational common sense is reason enough.

Flame In The Streets, 1961 British drama listed

among Morrissey's favourite films. Based on Ted Willis's play *Hot Summer Night*, written in response to the 1959 Notting Hill race riots, it examines the conflicting prejudices and racial tensions in post-war Britain. John MILLS stars as Jacko Palmer, a devoutly socialist union leader trying to overcome factory-floor racism by supporting the promotion of a black co-worker. However, Mills's own bigotry is called into question when his deeply racist wife breaks the news that their only daughter (Sylvia Syms) plans to marry a Jamaican teacher. The action takes place over 24 hours on 5 November, culminating in a mini race riot around a community bonfire (hence the double-edged literal/metaphorical title). Directed by Roy Ward Baker (see also THE OCTOBER MAN, A NIGHT TO REMEMBER), *Flame In The Streets* is a clever and unflinching exposé of attitudes to immigration, even if its representation of the black community as randy calypso addicts seems condescending by modern standards. Beyond his fascination with John Mills, it makes sense that Morrissey should show interest in a film sharing similar themes to those explored within his own 'ASIAN RUT' and 'THE NATIONAL FRONT DISCO'. [227, 504]

flowers, Morrissey introduced flowers to The

Smiths' visual aesthetic for the group's third concert at Manchester's Haçienda on 4 February 1983 (the same gig where their debut B-side 'HANDSOME DEVIL' was recorded). As he'd explain, his original intentions were a specific local response to what he regarded as the 'sterile and inhuman' surroundings of the Manchester music community and the Haçienda itself. 'Everybody was anti-human and it was so very cold,' he elaborated. 'The flowers were a very human gesture. They integrated harmony with nature, something people seemed so terribly afraid of. It had got to the point in music where people were really afraid to show how they felt. To show their emotions. I thought that was a shame and very boring. The flowers offered hope.'

He later admitted The Smiths' symbolic use of flowers had 'a faint link to WILDE-ism', being the direct influence of his literary hero. 'As I became a Smith, I used flowers because Oscar Wilde always used flowers. He once went to the Colorado salt mines and addressed a mass of miners there. He started the speech with, "Let me tell you why we worship the daffodil." … I really admired his bravery and the idea of being constantly attached to some form of plant.'

Whereas Wilde favoured the Malmaison carnation, dyed green and worn in his buttonhole, Morrissey opted for the gladiolus, or 'sword lily', for 'no specific reason [other than] they just simply leapt out at me [and] seemed really powerful'. The size of gladioli depended on the season, though Morrissey favoured the larger variety, as wielded above his head on their debut TOP OF THE POPS appearance in November 1983. A few months earlier, the first Smiths photo session with flowers – daffodils on this occasion – took place on 16 May 1983 for their first major interview in *Sounds* magazine, published the following month. Photographer Paul Slattery captured the first truly iconic images of the group, and the rapport between the young Morrissey and Marr especially, as they prowled the ruins of Manchester's dilapidated central railway station, later transformed into the Greater Manchester Exhibition Centre, or G-Mex. In the same article, Morrissey told journalist Dave McCullough that 'in six months' time [our audience will] be bringing flowers to our gigs'. His seemingly absurd prediction was proved accurate; to this day, audience members at Morrissey concerts still turn up clutching sprays of varying sizes.

'I think flowers are very beautiful things,' stated Morrissey. 'Very nice and innocent things. They don't harm anybody.' On the contrary, flowers would present The Smiths with hazards which they and they alone had to contend with. The biggest, and most lethal, was the threat of falling over on stage. After a while, the amount of flowers thrown around by the front rows and trodden on by Morrissey, Marr and Rourke would form a slippy stage carpet of crushed petals, sap and stems. Almost as dangerous was the well-meaning but badly aimed flower from a fan. Those who weren't careful risked blinding the group if it made contact stalk-end first. Which is precisely what happened to Morrissey when they were filmed in concert by the BBC's *Whistle Test On The Road* series at Derby Assembly Rooms on 7 December 1983: during 'MISERABLE LIE', the singer received a direct hit to the cornea and had to temporarily leave the stage.

The Smiths' 'flower period' peaked in early 1984 with their first major UK tour to promote the debut album. Their rider specified 'flowers to the approximate value of £50 sterling, including gladioli, no roses or flowers with thorns' and later 'a live tree with a minimum height of 3ft and a maximum height of 5ft'. As legend has it, the group's tour manager carried a saw in a briefcase lest the tree was too tall. Morrissey would joke that the amount of money The Smiths spent on flowers could have 'kept the DHSS afloat'. 'I don't buy them myself,' he added, 'I have a flower aide. Now the flowers are written into the contract for each venue and they're provided. They're virtually more important than the PA system.'

Tired of carrying flowers on stage ('it was quite clumsy'), by the late spring of '84 Morrissey moved his shrubbery to his back jeans pocket so he could free his hands. 'It just seemed perfectly natural,' he reasoned, adding, 'I suppose it really has to end.' By the close of 1984, the group had completely ceased using flowers as stage decoration, even if their bouquet-hurling audience ensured they remained an integral component of Smiths gigs until the very last. 'It was the end of a stage for us,' Morrissey explained, '[but] I did think it was quite artistic. For one thing, it had never been done before.'

In 2004 Morrissey briefly reintroduced foliage to his concert attire, appearing on stage with a distinctly phallic plant drooping from the top of his trousers just in front of his crotch, most probably inspired by a sequence in Jean Genet's 1950 short film *Un Chant d'Amour*. [53, 59, 166, 193, 270, 274, 275, 373, 419, 420, 446]

food, Though Morrissey's eating habits are predicated on his devout VEGETARIANISM, his own idiosyncratic and selective attitude to food goes far beyond those ethics. 'I don't eat anything that has burped or ran or swam so it has to be something really quite dry and lifeless and exotic,' he once explained, 'rather like me.'

Johnny Marr once joked that The Smiths subsisted on a diet of biscuits and yoghurt, which seems to have been literally the case. 'I like yoghurt with orange in it and almonds on the orange,' Morrissey admitted in 1984, adding how he'd also 'developed an absurd passion for Farley's rusks'. Toast with 'plum preserve' was also a dietary staple. 'When the sky is overcast,' he explained, 'and there's thunder and there's rain and you're watching the Monday matinee and you've got a nice big solid piece of toast in front of you, that to me is life lived to its fullest.' During The Smiths, interviewers monitored his intake of everything from 'Marks & Spencer's Apricot and Guava Thick & Creamy Yoghurt' to cheese sandwiches, fruit shortcake biscuits and 'an ornate silver samovar filled with hot chocolate'.

In 1992, the singer summarised his core foodstuffs as 'potatoes, bread, scrambled eggs and the odd orange'. Yet perhaps the biggest irony is that, for a vegetarian, Morrissey is not especially fond of vegetables. 'I thought being a veggie, he'd be really healthy,' recalls guitarist Kevin ARMSTRONG. 'But when we were making BONA DRAG I just remember getting fat. All the recipes he asked the cook for were all dairy based, full of cream and very rich. But he had this caterer who must have cost a fortune and yet Morrissey seemed to live on toast.'

Engineer Danton Supple backs up Armstrong's stories of Morrissey's artery-clogging dairy diet, as does Andy Rourke. 'Everything was egg based,' says Rourke. 'Especially in the early days of The Smiths. I remember once working out that each of us had 30 or 40 eggs a week. It was like *Cool Hand Luke*. Egg and chips. That's all we ate.'

'The only way you could get Morrissey to eat vegetables was to puree them like baby food,' comments producer Clive LANGER. 'He'd like mushy peas deep fried in filo pastry. Pea parcels, they were called. But everything else had to be mashed up.'

'I remember it being something to do with when he was younger,' says VIVA HATE drummer Andrew PARESI. 'I think he was ill as a child and the upshot of it was that he had a digestive system that was incredibly choosy about what he could eat. He couldn't eat anything that required his stomach to do a lot of work. So often studio meals were made up of the kind of stuff you'd find in baby jars in Boots. It was very strange. We had this lovely, talented cook at The Wool Hall, Jane Sen, who spent the whole time trying to make this pureed lifestyle more interesting that could pass for a meal everyone could eat.' As Danton Supple adds, it was considered a major breakthrough when, by the making of 1997's MALADJUSTED, the caterer managed to coax Morrissey into eating pureed courgettes.

Notoriously, the singer also has a strong aversion to spicy food. 'Could anything be more horrifying than garlic and onions?' he quipped in 1984. 'I have this pathetic phobia about them. Everything, especially the smell, frightens me to death.' Twenty years later he still confessed, 'I'd cry if I had to eat curry, or what's commonly referred to as "a Chinese".'

More recent confirmation of Morrissey's dietary requirements is provided by the rider for his 2008 concert in Israel, since published on the internet, including 'quality vegetarian cheddar cheese from Ireland or New Zealand', 'wholewheat bread only', 'Kerrygold salted butter', 'organic marmalade with no gelatin', 'fries made from organic potatoes with no salt, plus one pack of Cheez-It crackers, red or white cheese flavour',

Lonely planet boy: Steven Patrick Morrissey, born 22 May 1959.

Above: A pause for thought on stage at the University of Sheffield, January 1984.

Left: Mourning glory – Morrissey drives his point home at Manchester's G-Mex, July 1986.

Opposite – Clockwise from top left: Morrissey (Voice), Johnny Marr (Guitar), Mike Joyce (The Drums) and Andy Rourke (The Bass Guitar).

Overleaf: Mind-readers of the world unite, January 1987.

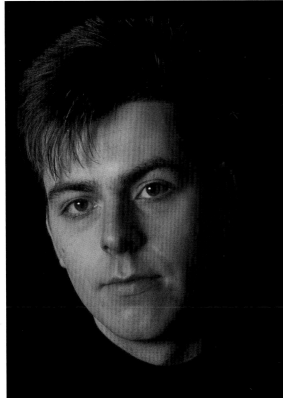

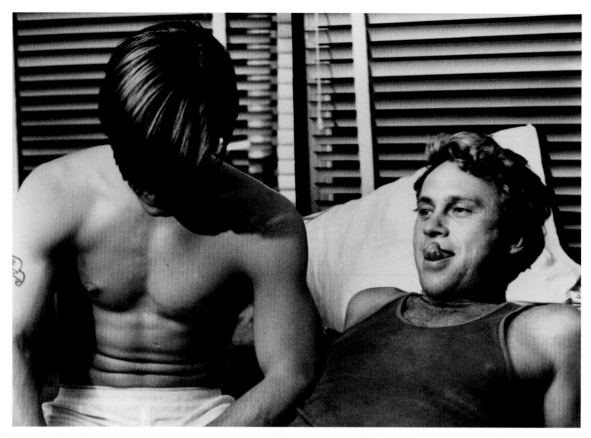

Top: 1984's The Smiths album cover uncut – Joe Dallesandro (left) with Louis Waldon in *Flesh*.

Left: This charming homme, Jean Marais in Cocteau's *Orphée*.

Below: Original soldier prior to his Meat Is Murder makeover.

Above: Laurence Olivier canes Terence Stamp in *Term Of Trial*. Morrissey's original cover choice for a European single of 'The Headmaster Ritual' – Olivier refused permission.

Right: 'Strangeways, Here I Don't Come.' Morrissey's original cover choice for The Smiths' final album was Harvey Keitel in *Who's That Knocking At My Door*. Keitel vetoed the sleeve but later agreed to its use as a Kill Uncle tour backdrop.

Jet boy: John Martin Maher, born 31 October 1963.

'Fool Such As I, A' (Bill Trader), Unreleased Smiths recording from their final session at the Streatham studio of soundman Grant Showbiz in May 1987. Originally recorded by country singer Hank Snow in 1952 (as heard on the soundtrack to one of Morrissey's favourite films, THE LAST PICTURE SHOW), 'A Fool Such As I' was later a UK number one hit for Elvis PRESLEY in May 1959. Significantly, it topped the chart the week Morrissey was born.

During their fateful last stand recording B-sides for the 'GIRLFRIEND IN A COMA' single, besides 'WORK IS A FOUR-LETTER WORD', 'I KEEP MINE HIDDEN' and two unfinished, untitled instrumentals (presumably awaiting lyrics), The Smiths also attempted a cover of 'A Fool Such As I'. Although its coincidence with his birth must have influenced Morrissey's decision to tackle the song, it may be that, like 'Work Is A Four-Letter Word', he saw its lyrics as an opportunity to express his feelings towards Marr at a point when their relationship was rapidly disintegrating beyond repair: 'Now you say that we are through/I'm a fool, but I'll love you dear until the day I die.'

The other Smiths all verify that the Elvis song made it to tape, though according to Showbiz it was not only 'dreadful' but deemed unusable after the first verse was allegedly 'wiped' by accident. Showbiz later gave Marr the masters for safekeeping: what's left of The Smiths' 'A Fool Such As I' has remained under lock and key ever since. [13, 19, 29, 32, 33]

'a small variety of fresh fruits, including apples and bananas', 'a small pack of rich, organic muesli' and 'a small bag of cashew nuts, roasted, not salted'. The organisers were also instructed that their kitchen 'should be stocked with the following for the artist: peas, spinach, carrots – all steamed. Roasted potatoes and grilled asparagus. Pasta – only with simple tomato sauce. Morrissey does not eat any kind of chilli or spices.'

Prior to his Israel concert, Morrissey had informed actor Lior ASHKENAZI that he only eats 'light-coloured food', a fact confirmed by *Happy Days* actor Henry 'The Fonz' Winkler, whose son Jed Weitzman worked with the singer. Speaking to the BBC as a guest during the 2008 Wimbledon tennis championships, Winkler remarked that most of what the singer ate 'is white', recalling the time he visited their house for dinner and was 'so precise' about how he liked his mashed potato that he insisted The Fonz telephone Morrissey's mum to get the specific recipe.

Beyond his bland savoury palate, Morrissey has a sweet tooth with a weakness for ice cream and Cadbury's chocolate. Both James MAKER and NANCY SINATRA also insist that Morrissey is a 'good cook', especially, says Nancy, when it comes to pasta. [5, 6, 15, 19, 22, 34, 39, 40, 52, 71, 93, 115, 120, 135, 237, 267, 357]

football, Though by his own admission 'not an expert on the subject', Morrissey does have an interest in the beautiful game. Raised in Stretford, near Old Trafford, his official local team are Manchester United (Johnny Marr, incidentally, is a Manchester City fan). As a boy he went to several home games, only to be traumatised when a complete stranger once whipped the Man Utd hat costing '12 shillings' off his young head and ran away with it. 'I thought, "It's a very cruel world, I'm not prepared for this." And I decided to get my revenge on society.'

Contrary to the press stereotype of Morrissey as a sport-weary bookworm, he'd explain how football offered him a form of mental escape: 'It's light entertainment. I can just put on the television, watch a game of football, get the cans out and drift.' Living in London in the 1990s, he revealed how he'd go to live matches 'whenever I can and whenever seems decent … and whenever I can get in for free'. Morrissey usually expressed strong opinions about particular players. He once deemed Bryan Robson 'impressive' while in 1994 he bragged how he could kick a ball better than Dennis Wise, Ian Rush and Neil Ruddock after watching a Chelsea game. He was far more enthusiastic about Eric CANTONA and in recent years has named the late George BEST as one of his all-time heroes.

Morrissey's Man. Utd roots aside, he has no strong allegiance to any team and usually chooses his side for reasons which have nothing to do with athletic ability. In the early 90s he took an interest in Tranmere Rovers, merely because they had a midfielder called John Morrissey, while his WEST HAM United 'phase' in the late 90s was entirely prompted by his love for East End punk group COCKNEY REJECTS. In 2005 he'd start pinning his colours to Queens Park Rangers after meeting striker Kevin Gallen and becoming 'email friends'. Gallen later presented him with a specially made number ten QPR top embroidered with 'Mozalini', which he wore during the making of RINGLEADER OF THE TORMENTORS.

Two years on, Morrissey was spotted in Los Angeles watching Mexican team Club Deportivo Guadalajara, nicknamed Chivas. Touring Mexico and America in the autumn of 2007, he regularly appeared on stage in a Chivas top, sometimes making his whole band wear the full team strip. Even before Chivas, Morrissey has a history of wearing football tops on stage, whether slipping into the national Irish strip in 1999 for performances of 'ROY'S KEEN' (his awful pun on former Man. Utd/Ireland international midfielder Roy Keane), or his February 1995 UK tour where he often appeared for the encore wearing a vintage football jersey of that city's local team.

The closest Morrissey has come to writing a 'football song' is the terrace hooligan's charter 'WE'LL LET YOU KNOW' and the hymn to the Man. Utd squad killed in the 'MUNICH AIR DISASTER 1958'. Football iconography has also cropped up very occasionally in his sleeve art (the Terry VENABLES cover of 'DAGENHAM DAVE') and stage backdrops, specifically his Los Angeles and Central and South America dates in early 2000. Among the images projected during the latter tour was a 1960s black-and-white portrait of former England captain

Bobby Moore practising keepie-ups during his career at West Ham. A giant framed print of the same also adorned the living room of his Hollywood home. His friend and writer Michael Bracewell (partner of Linder STERLING) astutely pointed out that Morrissey's fixation with the photo probably had less to do with Moore than it did the little row of semi-detached houses in the background on the horizon. The same could be said of Morrissey's attitude to football in general – never an abiding passion but merely a symptom of his nostalgia for, and romanticising of, English working-class culture. [44, 54, 71, 114, 148, 154, 411, 453]

Formby, George, Wigan-born comedian, film star, singer and ukulele man, best known for 'When I'm Cleaning Windows' and hailed by Morrissey as 'one of the greatest lyricists of all time'. Son of music-hall star George Formby Sr (who turned the bronchial cough which eventually killed him into a stage gimmick), Formby Jr owed much of his success to the business savvy of his wife Beryl, a former champion clog dancer. As Formby biographer John Fisher notes, 'Under Beryl's svengali-like guidance the air of good-natured, gormless naivety that had informed his father's characterisation was burnished free of any traces of melancholy and mock despair. His son developed a lighter, fresher approach, typified in his films not so much by the resilience with which he met the blows dealt out by fate but by the smile of everlasting wonder that appeared as he met them.'

Formby's big screen heyday lasted from the mid-1930s until the early 40s in a series of formulaic Ealing comedy musicals. Forever the lovable ukulele-strumming buffoon whose good heart was sufficient compensation for his milk-curdling face, however implausibly, Formby always got the girl, whether as a TT races driver (*No Limit*, 1936), an ice-hockey player (*I See Ice*, 1938), a jockey (*Come On, George*, 1939), a policeman (*Spare A Copper*, 1941) or a Nazi-battling sailor who fantasises about belting Hitler in the face (*Let George Do It!*, 1940). Such films made Formby the highest-paid British entertainer of the day, albeit in private a 'frustrated Casanova' forever under Beryl's vigilant guard lest he become too close to leading ladies such as Kay Walsh (see also 'LIFEGUARD SLEEPING, GIRL DROWNING').

As Morrissey specified, it was for his music rather than his films that he thought Formby 'a tremendous figure'. From his letters to pen pal Robert MACKIE we know that Morrissey was scrutinising Formby's records in the early 80s before forming The Smiths. 'His more obscure songs are so hilarious,' he explained in 1984. 'The language was so flat and Lancastrian and always focused on domestic things. Not academically funny, not witty, just morosely humorous and that really appeals to me.' Among his personal favourites was the self-deprecating tour de force 'Why Don't Women Like Me?', a song he'd include on The Smiths' later interval music tapes: 'Now I know I'm not handsome, no good looks or wealth/But the girls I chase say my plain face will compromise their health ...' Morrissey also admired Formby's mastery of 'total innuendo', never more outrageous than on 'With My Little Stick Of Blackpool Rock' ('It may be sticky but I never complain'). Any similarities between Formby's lyrics and Morrissey's own are purely thematic – e.g. 'When I'm Cleaning Windows' and 'ROY'S KEEN' – though it's arguable that the rhyming of 'smother' and 'mother' in Formby's 'Our Sergeant Major' had already imbedded itself in Morrissey's subconscious before he repeated it on The Smiths' 'RUBBER RING'.

As well as nominating Formby as the best male singer of 1985 in the following spring's annual NME polls (even though Formby died in 1961), Morrissey would make an obscure reference to the singer with the back cover of 1988's VIVA HATE: the clouds are a tiny detail from a specially commissioned photograph of his father George Formby Sr's grave in Warrington cemetery, taken by Stephen Wright. [100, 142, 183, 196, 312, 334]

'Found Found Found' (Morrissey/Langer),

From the album KILL UNCLE (1991). Co-writer Clive Langer insists he came up with this heel-dragging lumber in response to a vague request by Morrissey to 'write me a punk song'. On a purely musical level, punk or otherwise, 'Found Found Found' was among the album's least memorable offerings, one which the producer admits was merely 'chucked together in five minutes'. By contrast, the lyrics were among Kill Uncle's most profound, based on Morrissey's belief that 'you are either somebody who is chosen by others or somebody who chooses others. I was never a person who chose other people. They always chose me to be their friend and I always found that I could not choose other people because it didn't work.' The song also shows the discernible influence of Noël COWARD's 'If Love Were All', both in its echo of the line 'I believe the more you love a man/The more you give your trust/The more you're bound to lose' and its equivalent ricochet of Coward's 'somebody splendid ... someone affectionate and dear'. A daft rumour that its real subject is Michael STIPE stems from a 1991 interview with *Select* magazine: Morrissey discussed 'Found Found Found' in one breath before next answering a different (unrelated) question about his friendship with the R.E.M. singer. [15, 83, 136]

'Frankly, Mr Shankly' (Morrissey/Marr),

From the album THE QUEEN IS DEAD (1986). Written when relations between The Smiths and their record company, ROUGH TRADE, were so strained that they'd already begun plotting an exit strategy from their original contract, 'Frankly, Mr Shankly' was Morrissey's thinly veiled resignation letter to his current employer, Rough Trade's Geoff Travis. The lyrics contained a deliberate dig at Travis with its mention of Shankly's 'bloody awful poetry', in reference to an apocryphal incident where Travis tried to impress Morrissey with his own attempt at verse. 'That story is true,' confirms Marr, 'or at least I believe so. It was told to me at the time by someone at Rough Trade.'

Transcending whatever personal gripes inspired it, 'Frankly, Mr Shankly' was a fantastically witty tirade empathising with all those whose dreams of pop or film stardom are squashed by the curse of menial employment. In particular, Morrissey's address to the fictitious Shankly evoked the scene in *BILLY LIAR* where Tom Courtenay rehearses giving his notice to his undertaker boss Mr Shadrach; significantly, the same film clip was used to accompany the song during ITV's post-humous *South Bank Show* Smiths documentary in 1987. 'It really is odd,' said Morrissey of the song's deliberation upon 'fatal fame', 'when one reaches so painfully for something and suddenly it's flooding over one's body, there is pain in the pleasure. Don't get me wrong, I still want [fame], and I still need it but … doing something remarkably simple like making a candle can seem more intriguing in a perverted sense than writing another song. But what is anything without pain?' Morrissey also seems to have adapted the 'Christmas cards' line from another by comedienne Victoria WOOD, whose 1983 song 'Funny How Things Turn Out' contained a similar gag about '[singing] Lerner and Lowe to the mentally ill'.

According to Marr, the song's basis was an attempt to re-create 'the vibe' of 'Yesterday Man', a 1965 solo hit for Sandie SHAW's main songwriter, Chris Andrews, though as he states, 'It didn't *quite* work out that way.' Created in a near-mythical 'eyeball-to-eyeball' marathon writing session with Morrissey at Marr's home in Bowdon, which also produced 'THERE IS A LIGHT THAT NEVER GOES OUT' and 'I KNOW IT'S OVER', Marr's jerky chords did, indeed, owe something to the Jamaican rhythm of 'Yesterday Man', although the end result was more music hall than Andrews's 60s reggae-pop. One of the few Queen Is Dead songs previewed in concert on the group's autumn '85 Scottish tour prior to its studio recording, a first take included an additional jaunty trumpet part courtesy of a BBC session player which was eventually scrapped for being too comedic (see also 'NEVER HAD NO ONE EVER'). Morrissey and Marr had also tried in vain to coerce Linda MCCARTNEY into coming to the studio to play piano on the song.

Due to an alleged technical problem with the master tapes from the main album sessions – according to engineer Stephen STREET, they'd been ruined by an accidental half second's 'dropout', or silence – 'Frankly, Mr Shankly' ended up being re-recorded with the help of producer John PORTER in a final fix-it session at Wessex studios in north London, making it the last track completed for The Queen Is Dead. 'Johnny was a bit burned out by the whole thing,' recalls Porter. 'He'd reached a point when he just had enough.'

'I just couldn't face it,' explains Marr. 'I couldn't face mixing it on my own so I had to get John in to do it. By that stage, I couldn't stand to hear the song again and with good reason. It's not really one of our best. There was a place for that kind of song in our repertoire but I never really dug vaudeville music, which is what it was.' Vaudeville it may be, but 'Frankly, Mr Shankly' still stands as arguably Morrissey's best, and funniest, lyrics on the theme of work, offering untold solace to all those trapped in life's seemingly inescapable treadmill of soul-destroying labour. [13, 17, 19, 27, 38, 206, 468, 485]

Freak Party, Short-lived Manchester funk-influenced instrumental trio formed by Johnny Marr and Andy Rourke in 1981 with drummer Simon WOLSTENCROFT. They disbanded the same year having played no concerts. Freak Party's importance in pre-Smiths history is restricted to one rare demo recording of the early Marr tune 'Crak Therapy'. (See main MARR entry.)

'Friday Mourning' (Morrissey/Whyte), B-side of 'LET ME KISS YOU' (2004). A flashback in more ways than one to the VIVA HATE period, 'Friday Mourning' revisited the themes of departure, loss and Morrissey's own nudity from 'LATE NIGHT, MAUDLIN STREET' while Whyte's sweeping arrangement borrowed from Stephen STREET's similarly grand orchestration on the B-side 'WILL NEVER MARRY'. In the context of his wider repertoire the lyrics are timeworn in their over-familiarity – bidding a loved one farewell only to be dragged away kicking and screaming, haunted by the voices of his family, old teachers and employers calling him 'a loser'. Microwave Morrissey it may be, but somehow its lush melody and mock-epic

Friends, According to Morrissey, the producers of this phenomenally popular 90s American sitcom tried to coax him into making a guest-star cameo as himself. He told *Word* magazine that they envisaged a scene where the 'kooky' Phoebe Buffay (played by Lisa Kudrow, herself a big Morrissey fan) would throw her arms around him and say, 'Oh, Morrissey. You're just so miserable!' His response? 'As you could imagine, I turned on my heels and ran.' [115]

qualities have made 'Friday Mourning' a favourite among his more militant apostles.

Friday, Nancy, See FEMINISM.

From Reverence To Rape, 1974 book by

American film critic Molly Haskell, a favourite of Morrissey's when forming The Smiths and an influence upon some of his earliest lyrics. Subtitled 'The treatment of women in the movies', Haskell's book chronicles the changes in female representation on the big screen from the 'reverence' of the 20s and 30s to the symbolic, and sometimes literal, 'rape' as portrayed in modern cinema from the 60s onwards. Alongside Marjorie Rosen's earlier *POPCORN VENUS* – devoured by Morrissey with similar enthusiasm during the same period – *From Reverence To Rape* was a key work in the development of feminist film theory.

Morrissey's citations from Haskell are numerous. It's likely that the title of his own unpublished film study *EXIT SMILING* was taken from that of the 1926 Bea Lillie silent mentioned in Haskell's chapter on 'The Twenties'. Yet the book's impact upon Morrissey is felt most keenly on 'MISERABLE LIE' in which he borrows from Haskell's description of the 1940s femme fatale: 'she kept going – down, down like Eurydice, to the depths of the criminal world', and later when describing Ava Gardner in *The Killers*: '[she] double-crossed him, not once but twice'. 'THESE THINGS TAKE TIME' also incorporated a line adapted from the same chapter: 'But even then she knew where she had come from and where she belonged.'

Other distinct Smiths 'Haskell-isms' include: 'REEL AROUND THE FOUNTAIN' which used her description of 1965's *The Collector* ('Samantha Eggar who, as Terence STAMP's captive, is pinned and mounted like one of his butterflies …'); the titles of 'OSCILLATE WILDLY' ('Films like *MR SKEFFINGTON* oscillate wildly in mood …') and 'HALF A PERSON' ('each woman will be half a person'); and a handful of words and phrases which may have entered Morrissey's lyrical vocabulary through Haskell's writing, be it 'flowerlike' ('Miserable Lie'), 'tremulous' ('RUSHOLME RUFFIANS') or her repeated use of 'self-validation' ('I WANT THE ONE I CAN'T HAVE'). [166, 184, 326, 425]

Fury, Billy, Early British rock and roll star

featured on the cover of the final Smiths single, 'LAST NIGHT I DREAMT THAT SOMEBODY LOVED ME'. Though, chronologically speaking, not the first English response to Elvis PRESLEY – Cliff Richard, Marty Wilde, Vince Taylor and even Vince EAGER had already released their debut singles long before Fury first appeared with February 1959's 'Maybe Tomorrow' – for many, Fury *was* 'the English Elvis', exuding a visual cool and a vocal vulnerability that none of his peers could match. His status as the UK's biggest male pop idol prior to the arrival of THE BEATLES was rivalled only by Cliff: a telling pop statistic is that Fury had more top 40 hit singles in the 60s than The Beatles did.

At the outset of The Smiths, Morrissey was vociferous in his admiration for Fury, placing him alongside Oscar WILDE and James DEAN as one of his main symbolic influences. 'He was entirely doomed and I find that quite affectionate,' Morrissey explained, summing Fury's life story thus: 'He was discovered working on the docks in Liverpool, was dragged to London, styled and forced to make records. He always wanted to make very emotional overblown ballads but

137

f

found himself in the midst of the popular arena. He despised almost every aspect of the music industry and was very, very ill from an early age.'

Which was all true. Fury was born Ronald Wycherley in Liverpool's Smithdown Hospital on 17 April 1940. Aged six, he suffered his first attack of the rheumatic fever which would plague his entire life. He was 18 when, in October 1958, he hustled his way backstage with a guitar at a package concert in Birkenhead organised by British rock and roll svengali Larry Parnes and headlined by Marty Wilde. After auditioning his own songs for Wilde and Parnes, Wycherley was shoved on stage that same evening and invited to join the rest of the tour. It was Parnes who christened him Billy Fury, securing him a deal with DECCA. Uniquely for UK pop stars of the period, Fury wrote his own material: 1960's debut ten-inch album, The Sound Of Fury, was the first entirely self-penned LP by a British rock and roll artist, its ten tracks credited either to Fury or his writing pseudonym, 'Wilbur Wilberforce'. The same album was Morrissey's probable muse for the title of 2008's posthumous compilation The Sound Of The Smiths.

Despite the success of early singles such as his Everly Brothers-esque 'Colette' (number nine, March 1960), from 1961 onwards Fury's writing would be restricted to occasional B-sides and album tracks as Parnes moulded him into a pop balladeer forced to interpret the works of others. This transition from rocker to crooner marked the beginning of Fury's chart heyday and his biggest single successes: 'Halfway To Paradise' (number three, August 1961), 'Jealousy' (number two, October 1961) and another eight top ten hits up to and including July 1965's 'In Thoughts Of You'. Such records would have a great impact on the young Morrissey who'd later admit being 'exposed to [Fury] at a very early age'.

'Billy's singles are totally treasurable,' he enthused. 'I get quite passionate about the vocal melodies and the orchestration always sweeps me away. He always had such profound passion.' Morrissey's own Fury favourites include April 1964's 'I Will' and his gloomy 1966 masterpiece

'I'll Never Quite Get Over You'. The latter's chart peak of 35 was indicative of Fury's slump in popularity, which never recovered. In 1967 he left Decca for PARLOPHONE, trying to broaden his appeal with more contemporary material including a grand arrangement of David BOWIE's 'Silly Boy Blue' which, like everything else for his new label, failed to chart. With his health also failing, as the 60s closed he retreated to a farm in Wales to live with his wife and their many animals, leaving the pop world behind for horse breeding and ornithology. Like Morrissey, Fury was passionate about animals, as commemorated in his earlier 1965 pop musical I've Gotta Horse – an admittedly awful film co-starring future CORONATION STREET regular Amanda Barrie and fellow Morrissey screen favourite Marjorie RHODES.

In 1973, Fury was coaxed out of retirement to play Stormy Tempest in the film That'll Be The Day, though recurring heart operations put paid to a full-scale comeback. Declared bankrupt in 1978, he managed to sign a new deal in the early 80s, recording an album for Polydor, The One And Only. By the time of its release in March 1983, Fury was dead, his heart finally packing in two months earlier on 28 January. Morrissey later claimed that when he heard the news he cried 'persistently [and] loudly', berating the media's response to Fury's passing which failed to fully recognise the extent of his contribution to UK pop music. 'He had something of his own,' stressed Morrissey, 'and was quite absolutely British.'

Fury's influence upon Morrissey's own music is subtle yet tangible. The fact that he'd grace the sleeve of 'Last Night I Dreamt That Somebody Loved Me' would provoke rational comparison with the title of Fury's 1962 hit 'Last Night Was Made For Love'. More substantial is the similarity between the lyrics of 'SHAKESPEARE'S SISTER' and 'Don't Jump' from the 1962 EP Billy Fury No. 2, while 1966's ethereal 'I Belong To The Wind' (B-side to Morrissey's beloved 'I'll Never Quite Get Over You') pre-empts 'SING YOUR LIFE' with its declaration, 'My life wasn't meant to be lived/It was meant to be sung.' [59, 184, 188, 267, 408]

Gainsbourg, Serge, Gallic pop colossus best known for 'Je T'Aime Moi Non Plus', his breathless duet with lover Jane Birkin which defied a BBC ban by reaching UK number one in October 1969. One of the greatest singers and songwriters in the history of French popular music, Gainsbourg wrote for and recorded with Morrissey favourites Françoise HARDY, NICO, Sacha DISTEL and, most significantly, Brigitte BARDOT, who first recorded 'Je T'Aime …' in 1968 but begged him not to release it lest her husband get wind of their affair. It's primarily Gainsbourg's work with and for Bardot which attracted Morrissey, specifically their 1968 duet 'Bonnie And Clyde' inspired by Arthur Penn's recent biopic and 'Initials B.B.', Gainsbourg's tribute to Bardot recorded the same year. Both songs would be included in Morrissey's interval music tapes on 2004's YOU ARE THE QUARRY tour. Indeed, the majority of Bardot songs featured on Morrissey's interval tapes and later video montages since 2004 are those written by Gainsbourg, including 'Harley Davidson', 'Contact' and 'Bubble Gum'.

Gainsbourg himself was, as Morrissey rightly observed, a 'fascinatingly strange character' who never shied away from controversy: recording a whole album on the subject of Nazis (1975's Rock Around The Bunker), provoking death threats from right-wing war veterans after rewriting the French national anthem as a reggae song (1978's 'Aux Armes Et Caetera') or releasing his scandalous 1984 duet with his and Birkin's daughter, Charlotte, brazenly titled 'Lemon Incest'. Yet beneath such divisive sensationalism, Gainsbourg's songs were poetic, satirical, witty, macabre and exceptional, be it 'L'Homme À Tête De Chou' ('The Man With The Cabbage Head'), 'Meurtre À L'Extincteur' (a fantasy about beating his lover to death with a fire extinguisher) or one of his earliest successes, 1958's 'Le Poinçonneur Des Lilas' about a ticket puncher on the Paris underground driven to suicide by the monotony of his job. Gainsbourg was also responsible for 1965's 'Poupée De Cire, Poupée De Son', France Gall's winning entry for Luxembourg in the 1965

EUROVISION song content, subsequently recorded in English by TWINKLE as 'A Lonely Singing Doll'. Following his death of a heart attack in March 1991 at the age of 62 – not altogether surprising given Gainsbourg's appetite for fags and booze – French president François Mitterrand paid tribute by saying '[Gainsbourg] elevated the song to the level of art', a noble pursuit Morrissey would surely identify with. [436]

Gannon, Craig (Smiths second guitarist 1986, Morrissey guitarist 1988–89), For a six-month period in 1986 from the beginning of May until the end of October The Smiths were a quintet. The short-lived official 'Fifth Smith' was 19-year-old Craig Gannon, a Salford guitarist who despite his youth had already toured with Aztec Camera, recorded with Glasgow's The Bluebells (whom he left twice) and had just joined The Colourfield, the latest project from ex-Specials/Fun Boy Three singer Terry Hall. It was the latter group's Simon WOLSTENCROFT, the one-time Smiths demo drummer, who provided Gannon's bridge to the group during the spring of 1986 after the private dismissal of Andy Rourke.

'Simon was still friends with The Smiths,' explains Gannon. 'One day he said, "Johnny Marr wants to get in touch with you." I didn't have a clue what it was about so I just gave him my number. Eventually Johnny rang us and said, "Do you want to get together?" Before that I didn't even realise that they were looking for another guitarist.'

Gannon's account of how and why he was brought into The Smiths contradicts the accepted version of events that Marr wanted to find a bassist to fill the void left by Rourke's sacking. 'I'm not a bass player, especially on the lines of what Andy Rourke could play. I couldn't imagine anyone filling his shoes easily. What happened was, I went up to Johnny's house and we had a big meeting there for a couple of hours. He was saying that they had to get rid of Andy because of his problems and that they'd love me to be in the band as an extra guitar player, but if I fancied playing the bass then I could join right away. So that was the only time it was ever mentioned and I never once picked up a bass with The Smiths.'

'Craig was *always* brought in to play bass,' refutes Marr. 'The very short, honest and truthful version of it is that he came in to play bass, which was quite an exciting prospect for him as you can imagine. And then because Andy, quite rightly, came back and we got his hopes up, it

'Ganglord' (Morrissey/Whyte), B-side of 'THE YOUNGEST WAS THE MOST LOVED' (2006). Returning to the streets, or rather Latino ghettos, of Los Angeles first visited on 'FIRST OF THE GANG TO DIE', Morrissey casts himself as a petty felon to whom crime is the inevitable life choice in a neighbourhood oppressed by the city's police force. With the law on his back, he turns to the title 'Ganglord' for salvation, hoping that bribery will spare him from the clutches of the LAPD, whose motto, 'To protect and to serve', seems laughable in the face of their innate prejudice against his creed. The narrative is lent an existential edge with the contemplation of his own mortality, noting how each passing second of the clock mocks the brevity of life. 'Ganglord' swayed to an exotic Whyte riff, comparable with the same era's 'TO ME YOU ARE A WORK OF ART' and, in some corners, the hook of Oasis's 2002 number one 'The Hindu Times'. Morrissey's delivery was altogether mesmerising, making wild religious ceremony out of its pivotal 'save me' refrain. When producer TONY VISCONTI bemoaned the fact that some of his favourite songs from the RINGLEADER OF THE TORMENTORS sessions ended up as B-sides, he may well have been referring to 'Ganglord', a track superior to a good portion of that album. It was some consolation that it became a live favourite, sometimes introduced under its alternative working title, 'Get Back To The Ghetto'. [259]

just felt really cruel to fire Craig before he'd even had a chance to be in the band, so we let him stay. We just saw it as a way to turn that to our advantage. It wasn't that I was trying to turn the group into a big rock sound. He'd had a few weeks of getting excited about the idea of being the new Smith and I just didn't have the heart to take it away from him.'

Rourke's exit was brief, already back in the group by the time of Gannon's first rehearsal in late April. 'Straight away, I thought it sounded fantastic,' he recalls. 'Right from that first rehearsal. I'd never felt that before, maybe a little bit in Aztec Camera, but nothing like The Smiths. It was real chemistry, you could just feel it in the room.' With his boyish features and Brylcreemed quiff, Gannon looked like a member of The Smiths' audience who'd somehow managed to creep through security, shyly skulking his way into their midst. But it was his sonic, rather than aesthetic, qualities which made the greater difference. Given the safety net of Gannon's solid rhythm guitar, Marr no longer had to worry about holes in the group's sound, freeing him to adorn the music with whatever six-stringed spookery he saw fit. Morrissey agreed, describing Rourke's retracted sacking and their accidental expansion into a five-piece as divine serendipity. 'Now Craig Gannon has also joined we sound more formidable as you'll hear on the next single,' he declared, 'so perhaps Andy's brief departure was a benefit.'

The 'next single' was 'PANIC', Gannon's first, listed as 'Second Guitar' as he would be again on 'ASK', a song which he'd later controversially claim was based on a chord progression he'd played during a previous group rehearsal (this alleged authorship remains unproven). After two television appearances and four UK concerts in mid-July – including their momentous Salford University gig of 20 July, among the best they ever played – the five-strong Smiths commenced what would be their final tour of North America. The opening date in London, Canada on 30 July was Gannon's 20th birthday where, after the show, he was encouraged to drink a shot of brandy for each of his 20 years.

Not surprisingly, the next morning Gannon awoke to find his hotel room caked in vomit – feeling, and looking, like a freshly dredged corpse.

Sadly, the American tour was the undoing of Gannon as far as his long-term future in The Smiths was concerned. Though he enjoyed the gigs, and the occasional hotel-trashing excesses, he failed to gain acceptance into the group's insular gang mentality for a variety of reasons. Scared of flying, on the occasions when he had the choice to go by plane with his bandmates, Gannon's decision to travel from city to city by bus with the crew inadvertently alienated him further. Just as damaging, his naïveté towards the gravity of Morrissey's anti-meat policy resulted in an incident where Marr publicly chastised him for foolishly bringing a bacon sandwich on to their tour bus. By the time the US tour ended in early September, his fate had already been decided. As Morrissey later commented: 'When we toured America, which was a very long time, you get to know people very well and it all came forth as it were.'

Returning to the UK, Gannon took part in one final recording session for the proposed single 'YOU JUST HAVEN'T EARNED IT YET, BABY' and its B-sides 'HALF A PERSON' and 'LONDON'. He played his final gig with The Smiths at Manchester's Free Trade Hall on 30 October 1986, the last date of a two-week tour of England and Wales to promote THE QUEEN IS DEAD. For all his offstage unease, Gannon proved himself a treasured asset in concert to the very last, as captured for posterity on the posthumous live album RANK where his complementary buttressing of Marr can be plainly heard, especially on the instrumental 'THE DRAIZE TRAIN'.

Bitterly, Gannon never learned he'd been dismissed from The Smiths from Morrissey or Marr but through his friend Gary Rostock, the drummer from ROUGH TRADE signings Easterhouse who'd later join him and guitarist Ivor PERRY in The Cradle. 'I think Geoff Travis had let it slip to him,' says Gannon. 'It was a horrible way to find out but, really, by then I didn't even want to be in the band any more.'

After one single with The Cradle, 1987's 'It's Too High', Gannon reunited with Andy Rourke and Mike Joyce in the aftermath of The Smiths' split to play with The Adult Net, the solo side project for The Fall's Brix Smith. In the meantime he'd begun legal proceedings against Morrissey and Marr to claim unpaid earnings from his six months in The Smiths. Being asked to play guitar on Morrissey's next batch of solo recordings in November 1988 was the last thing he expected. 'Despite being booted out of The Smiths, I had always gotten on with Morrissey,' says Gannon. 'Even after I was kicked out, he wrote me a nice letter wishing me luck for the future. Later he sent me a copy of STRANGEWAYS, HERE WE COME before it came out. So I was happy to record with him again. It was only weird because I'd started my court case. We were talking in the studio once and I started bringing it up but he said, "It's OK, we don't need to talk about that." So it was never discussed.'

Along with Rourke and Joyce, Gannon completed a phantom 'Smiths reunion' line-up on the session for the singles 'THE LAST OF THE FAMOUS INTERNATIONAL PLAYBOYS' and 'INTERESTING DRUG' prior to Morrissey's momentous WOLVERHAMPTON solo live debut on 22 December 1988. His final appearance with Morrissey was miming to 'Playboys' on TOP OF THE POPS in February 1989, by which time Gannon was already submitting original music to the singer in the hope of being accepted as a new co-writer. 'Morrissey started asking me for song ideas so I started doing bits of writing,' he explains. 'He really liked them and said that he wanted to start recording so I was hoping it was gonna be a continuous thing. In my mind things were going really well, he seemed really into it. Until I got a letter from him which said something along the lines of, "Things are looking good and I'm looking forward to working with you. The only thing is if you want to keep on doing this with me then you've got to drop your court case." I wanted to work with him but I wasn't going to drop the case out of principle. As far as I'm aware, Andy and Mike were told the

same thing about their court cases. I think he knew I was going to win the case and that he didn't have a leg to stand on. But he had to say that really.' Gannon did, indeed, win his case and was awarded £42,000, a verdict Morrissey described as 'an outrage of public justice'.

After Morrissey, Gannon would join Manchester's Blue Orchids (led by ex-Fall guitarist Martin Bramah), later reuniting with Terry Hall for his 1994 solo album Home. Still playing guitar, he's since established a new career scoring soundtracks for various television documentaries. [7, 12, 13, 17, 18, 28, 33, 38, 57, 261, 433]

Garfield, John, One of Morrissey's favourite Hollywood actors and the inspiration for the cover of the RINGLEADER OF THE TORMENTORS album. The portrait was a homage to the 1946 film *Humoresque* in which Garfield plays a virtuoso violinist tormented by his love for Joan Crawford. Several times during the film we see Garfield on concert posters and magazine covers adopting a similar pose in tuxedo with violin. 'I thought the Garfield picture was so touching,' said Morrissey, 'so I tried to copy it.'

Typical of many Morrissey favourites, Garfield's life was clouded by tragedy: losing his mother during childhood, he was sent to a problem school where he began acting and boxing only to be diagnosed with a debilitating heart complaint. Best remembered for the classic noir thriller *The Postman Always Rings Twice* (1946) and the boxing drama *Body And Soul* (1947), he was blacklisted during McCarthyism as an un-American 'Communist' in spite of his patriotic efforts with Bette DAVIS setting up the Hollywood Canteen for US servicemen. The experience took its toll on his health and he died in 1952, aged only 39.

Morrissey first mentioned Garfield in an overview of Hollywood rebels in the opening chapter of his 1983 book *James Dean Is Not Dead*. Other than the Ringleader/*Humoresque* homage, he'd also refer to the actor's 'far-away gaze' in the 1940 depression melodrama *Saturday's Children* in the sleeve notes of his UNDER THE

INFLUENCE compilation to provide a descriptive comparison with 'TRASH' by the NEW YORK DOLLS. [245, 298, 342, 511, 549, 568]

Gemini, Morrissey's astrological birth sign, the third phase in the Zodiac from 21 May to 21 June: born 22 May, Morrissey just misses the cusp with Taurus. Gemini is an 'air sign', represented by 'the twins'. Consequently, it is a common trait of astrologers to analyse Geminis as being, at best inconsistent, at worst duplicitous in their supposed dual personality. Morrissey has agreed that being Gemini means 'I AM TWO PEOPLE', hence the song of that name.

According to the oracle of all things astrological, the late, great Linda Goodman, a Gemini man can be characterised as: usually pale in complexion with beautiful eyes which have 'that twinkle dart here and there'; 'sharply satirical … disconcerting slower minds with their lightning-fast mental processes'; knowing 'instinctively just where the skeletons are buried in your closet and using his fast mind and clever tongue to rattle those bones dangerously'; and a master of words who 'cut his teeth on the Oxford dictionary'. In summarising, Goodman states: 'He has a brilliant humour, tact, diplomacy and adroitness – yet he lacks persistence and patience … In spite of all the people around him, he shares his deepest emotions only with his one constant companion – his other twin self. The air is his element and his real home. He's a stranger to earth.' Which may be true of Morrissey, but taking Goodman at her word it would also apply to fellow Geminis Paul Weller (25 May), Siouxsie SIOUX (27 May), Kylie Minogue (28 May), Noel Gallagher (29 May), Prince (7 June), Paul McCartney (18 June), and The Smiths' other Zodiacal twin, Mike Joyce (1 June).

Most interesting is the perceived astrological relationship between Gemini and Scorpio, Johnny Marr's 'water sign'. Almost every horoscope compatibility test concludes that whether in business or pleasure, although there is initial intrigue on both sides, they don't mix well for long and the chances of a lasting friendship are extremely slim.

Which may well be irrelevant hoopla, in which case the reader may wish to excuse the author on the grounds of Linda Goodman's evidently astute observation that 'Sagittarians have a tendency to go off on tangents'. [119, 319]

'Get Off The Stage' (Morrissey/Rourke), B-side of 'PICCADILLY PALARE' (1990). Morrissey's comic critique of ageing rock stars dated back to the spring of 1988 when he first wrote the lyrics for a tune by Stephen STREET in the aftermath of VIVA HATE. The Street version never materialised though the following year he'd remodel the song for a chipper accordion-led melody by Andy Rourke with a distinct CAJUN influence. Recorded at Hook End in the winter of 1989 during the BONA DRAG sessions, at the time its mockery was aimed at THE ROLLING STONES' Mick Jagger, then 46. 'I just feel immense anger that they don't just *get out of the way*,' seethed Morrissey. 'You open papers in this country, and every day there's the obligatory picture of, y'know, Mick-with-bags-at-the-airport, or Keith [Richards] saying he's completely normal now. They just won't *move away*!' Perhaps inevitably, by the time Morrissey himself turned 46 in 2005, he felt very differently about 'Get Off The Stage', naming it as one of the few songs which '[now] make me shudder' and ridiculing its lyrics: 'Pathetically, I once tried to rhyme mascara with Fender guitar.' Like its A-side, the track also featured the additional voice of Suggs from MADNESS. [39, 93, 138, 241]

ghosts, Morrissey has a strong belief in the afterlife and has claimed to have seen ghosts on several occasions. The month before his 21st birthday, on 18 April 1980, he documented a strange presence in his family home, 384 Kings Road in Stretford. That afternoon he spied an apparition in the kitchen, then later heard it walk up the stairs and turn the bathroom light on: other than himself, the house was completely empty at the time. Four years later, after moving to London during The Smiths, he discovered that his rented flat on Campden Park Road in Kensington was

g

haunted by the spirit of a previous occupant who had died there. 'There was definitely a presence,' he explained. 'A friend of mine who is a medium came to the flat, and I didn't tell her that I'd had vibrations. When she came in she immediately went into a semi-trance, walked around every corner of the flat and stood outside the bathroom door and said, "It's here". It's coincidental that each time I'd stepped outside the bathroom, even though I'd always keep the heating on really high, I'd felt a great chill.'

One January evening in 1989, Morrissey received a terrible fright while driving with friends through Saddleworth Moor, near Manchester, where the Moors Murderers buried their victims. 'As we turned on to [Wessenden Road], from the side of the road, from the heather, somebody pleaded to the car,' he claimed. 'A boy of maybe 18 years, and he was totally grey, and he had long hair in a sort of 1970s style, one of those strange feather cuts, and he wore a very small anorak and nothing else – he was completely naked. He just emerged from the heather and pleaded to the lights, and we drove past because we all instinctively knew that this was a spirit … He seemed like something from beyond.' The party drove to the next village and telephoned the police who told Morrissey and his companions '[to] keep an open mind'.

The singer also experienced multiple hauntings in his favourite studio, Hook End Manor near Reading. According to engineer Danton Supple, Morrissey's favourite bedroom – 'The Brown Room' – had a history of ghostly activity. 'He seemed genuinely upset about the ghosts,' adds BONA DRAG-era guitarist/co-writer Kevin ARMSTRONG. 'He came down to breakfast one day saying he couldn't sleep and all he could feel was freezing wind. At the time I was a practising Buddhist so I took my Buddhist accoutrements into his room and chanted for the ghost to be laid to rest. I don't know if it worked.' In 1990, Morrissey spoke to the press about the Hook End hauntings, convinced that the spirits were those of monks who'd run a monastery on the site several centuries earlier. 'Several people have had certain visitations at night time, including me,' he revealed. 'It happened for each person at ten past four in the morning. It felt like a hand on your chest, as if you were being woken or stirred. The conclusion I've come to is that it's the ghost of some misguided monk going round waking people up for prayers.'

His fascination with the spirit world is reflected in many of his lyrics, notably 'RUBBER RING', 'A RUSH AND A PUSH AND THE LAND IS OURS' and most explicitly 'OUIJA BOARD, OUIJA BOARD'. Other than experiments with Ouija boards, Morrissey's practical knowledge of the occult stretched to the superstitious ritual known as '12 o'clock candle'. As he elaborated, it involves staring into a mirror with a candle below your face in an otherwise pitch black room, just before the stroke of midnight. 'Your face supposedly changes into the face of either somebody who has died and wants to reach you or somebody who has died and doesn't particularly want to reach you but is there anyway,' he explained. 'It's extremely frightening because most people's faces do change automatically and totally. It's not just a matter of a dark shadow and moustache … so I do believe in that and I have a very open mind.' [1, 70, 226, 232, 362, 437]

Gide, André, French writer, friend of Oscar WILDE and pioneering gay activist listed among Morrissey's favourite 'symbolists' in 1983. Most likely it is Gide's connection with Wilde which stirred Morrissey's interest.

André first met Oscar in Paris in 1891 and was thoroughly bedevilled by him. At the time Gide, 22, had just published his first novel, *The Notebooks Of André Walter*, while Wilde, 36, had several works to his name and was currently basking in the furore over *The Picture Of Dorian Gray*. The extent of Gide's mental corruption was documented in a letter to the poet Paul Valéry: 'Wilde is piously setting about killing what remained of my soul …'

They would meet again, in Florence three years later, then Algeria in 1895 where Wilde and his lover Lord Alfred 'Bosie' Douglas would introduce

Gilbert and George, Though Morrissey has cited Hannah GLUCKSTEIN as his favourite artist, he's also expressed a love for the work of besuited, deadpan conceptual/performance art duo Gilbert Proesch (the short one) and George Passmore (the tall thin one with glasses). Best known for their distinctive photo montages using symmetrical designs reminiscent of stained glass windows and usually featuring images of themselves, Gilbert and George's work has often attracted controversy, not least their 1996 series of 'Naked Shit Pictures'. Other than bodily fluids, recurring themes in their art include religion, swearing, death, mental illness, sex and national identity. Despite Gilbert's Italian origins, the couple are archetypal English eccentrics. Always immaculately dressed in smart suits and ties, for 30 years they breakfasted every day in the same east London café. Doubtless Morrissey's fascination with Gilbert and George is as much to do with their day-to-day existence as living works of art in the true Wildean sense than it is with any of their creations, though one suspects their famous dance routine to Dave Dee, Dozy, Beaky, Mick & Tich's 1966 hit 'Bend It!' tickles his fancy for the absurd. [111, 175]

Gide to the personal services of local Arab boys. By now, the storm over Wilde and Bosie's relationship was already gathering in England. Gide was as awed by Wilde's indiscretion as he was fearful of the inevitable consequence. He wrote to his mother from Algiers: 'Wilde! Wilde!! What more tragic life is there than his! If only he were more careful – if he were capable of being careful – he would be a genius, a great genius.'

Wilde would provide inspiration for the decadent Menalque in Gide's 1897 novel *Les Nourritures Terrestres* (*Earthly Nourishment*), written while Oscar was in prison. In the meantime, Gide had similarly tried to find salvation in normal family life, taking a wife but unable to consummate the marriage. The next time the writers met in Berneval, France, Gide was embarrassed by the extent of Wilde's decline. Their last communication was in Paris when Oscar wrote to André begging for money, which he felt obliged to send.

In 1902, two years after Wilde's death, Gide revived the pseudonymous Menalque for *L'Immoraliste* (*The Immoralist*).[1] He'd later write a slim, highly personal biography of Oscar, still the subject of debate among some Wilde scholars who doubt the reliability of Gide's testimonies. In 1909 he privately distributed a brave yet potentially self-ruinous text called *Corydon*, fiercely defending homosexuality. When published publicly in

1920, his friends still feared it would do him 'the greatest harm', yet by the time of his death in 1951, aged 82, Gide had been awarded the Nobel Prize for Literature and was revered as one of the most influential voices in modern French literature. [184, 313, 318]

———

1. It was James DEAN's role as an Arab boy in the February 1954 Broadway adaptation of Gide's *The Immoralist* which caught the attention of *East Of Eden* director Elia Kazan, earning him his ticket to Hollywood.

'Girl Afraid' (Morrissey/Marr), B-side of 'HEAVEN KNOWS I'M MISERABLE NOW' (1984). Another of Morrissey's pessimistic musings on conventional heterosexual relationships, 'Girl Afraid' played like a pithy one-act drama in which boy and girl alternately soliloquise their reservations about one another. As the singer later explained to the press, '"Girl Afraid" simply implied that even within relationships, there's no real certainty and nobody knows how anybody feels. People feel that just simply because they're having this cemented communion with another person that the two of you will become whole, which is something I detested.'

The title was taken from the 1943 Bette DAVIS film *Old Acquaintance*, about two friends who unwittingly become rival authors: near the beginning of the film, *Girl Afraid* appears in a montage of trashy potboilers from Davis's on-screen nemesis played by Miriam Hopkins. Marr's sabre-toothed twang, written the day after returning from their illness-stricken New Year's trip to New York, was inspired by his current obsession with Little Richard. 'I just kept thinking, "What'd sound like a Little Richard piano figure on guitar?"' he explains. 'Which is how I came up with it.' The finished track was a classic example of The Smiths' thrifty brilliance, being largely instrumental with just two pithy verses. Marr's brief prologue mocked the God that only gave him ten fingers, a plectrum hummingbird blur almost ditched in favour of an alternate vocal intro. [17, 167, 535]

'Girl Least Likely To' (Morrissey/Rourke),

B-side of 'NOVEMBER SPAWNED A MONSTER' (1990). Returning to the theme of frustrated ambition previously touched upon in 'FRANKLY, MR SHANKLY' and 'YOU JUST HAVEN'T EARNED IT YET, BABY', this time Morrissey takes a more comically condescending attitude to, as he put it, 'that friend you have who really believes in the imminence of her success yet secretly you know it's never going to happen for her'. Years later he also confessed that its real-life subject 'immediately' recognised themselves in his lyrics, instigating a 'terrible fight' with the singer. 'I wish I'd been a bit more secretive,' he confessed, 'but what the hell!' The most peculiar aspect of the song is its music: written by Andy Rourke but blatantly borrowing the chord pattern of 'Only To Other People', a 1962 track by New York girl group The Cookies whose 'I WANT A BOY FOR MY BIRTHDAY' was briefly covered by The Smiths before he joined them in the autumn of 1982. Recorded at Hook End in the winter of 1989, in theory 'Girl Least Likely To' would have made the tracklisting of the original BONA DRAG album, instead becoming an above-average B-side. [28, 138, 422]

'Girlfriend In A Coma' (Morrissey/Marr),

The Smiths' 15th single (from the album STRANGEWAYS, HERE WE COME), released August 1987, highest UK chart position #13. The shortest Smiths single of all, the audacious 'Girlfriend In A Coma' concentrated the pop genius of Morrissey and Marr in just two minutes and two seconds. Within this briefest of time scales, the singer delivers a rich melodrama of hospital waiting-room grief, fretting over an unconscious lover nearing death's door after an unspecified accident. The scene was very much that of an early 60s death disc, when the likes of Ricky Valance's 'Tell Laura I Love Her' found a mutilated racing driver pledging undying love to his fiancée with his final breath. What makes 'Girlfriend In A Coma' so effective is the sheer honesty of Morrissey's angst; tormented by guilty memories of past arguments when he 'could have strangled her', nervously quizzing the doctors about her chances of recovery and unable to bring himself to see her until he realises 'it's serious'. Amid his distress he also manages to murmur what sounds like a vague imitation of The 4 Seasons' 1965 US hit 'Bye Bye Baby' (later a 1975 UK number one for The Bay City Rollers).

This desperate narrative was countered by Marr's dainty oscilloscopic guitar. Marking another Smiths first, the tune was consciously inspired by a reggae track, 1970's hit version of Nina Simone's 'Young, Gifted And Black' by Bob (Andy) & Marcia (Griffiths). 'Myself and Morrissey both absolutely adored it,' says Marr, 'so "Girlfriend In A Coma" was trying to capture the spirit of that. If you listen to the string parts on both you can maybe see it.' Marr's string parts, which do indeed sound similar, were created synthetically and credited to the fictitious ORCHESTRAZIA ARDWICK.

As Morrissey serenaded his comatose girlfriend, Michael Jackson was at number one with 'I Just Can't Stop Loving You': therein lies The Smiths' fiendish brilliance in a nutshell. Alas, by the time it was released, The Smiths were already over. With Marr gone and Rourke and Joyce in limbo, Morrissey carried the can single-handedly in a hastily filmed video by Tim Broad, blending a mimed performance with footage of the 1963 film THE LEATHER BOYS. To his evident consternation, it missed the UK top ten: in a letter to

146

Stephen STREET, he bemoaned the fact that in the midweek charts it had been number seven. Not that this disappointment, nor the fraught circumstances in the Smiths camp at the time of its release, tarnished his affection for the song. Five years later Morrissey named 'Girlfriend In A Coma' one of his all-time favourite Smiths tracks. [17, 19, 38, 404, 524]

gladioli, The flower most commonly associated with The Smiths, as chosen by Morrissey for their early concerts, television appearances and photoshoots. See main entry on FLOWERS.

'Glamorous Glue' (Morrissey/Whyte), From the album YOUR ARSENAL (1992). Returning to the devastated post-THATCHER urban landscape of 'THE QUEEN IS DEAD', Morrissey laments a desensitised British working class rapidly losing its identity in the face of Americanisation. For some, the only means of mental escape from this dismal, unfeeling environment is solvent abuse – the 'Glamorous Glue' of the title. The sentiment wasn't so very far away from the RAMONES' immortal limbic grunt 'Now I Wanna Sniff Some Glue', albeit riddled with political irony. Speaking about its climactic refrain where he suggests that in England, Los Angeles has now taken cultural precedence over London, Morrissey blamed the media. 'British broadcasting is obsessed with LA,' he mourned. 'It's really upsetting and I think it's sad as well.'

Musically, its riff was a throwback to the rumbustious glam thump of The Smiths' 'PANIC', complete with slide guitar break. Mick RONSON's production assured it a fittingly pronounced 70s sheen, bumping and grinding after BOWIE's 'The Jean Genie' while the middle eight cruised towards BOLAN's 'The Slider'. Although a promo video for the song was shot on location in Chicago, 'Glamorous Glue' was never released as a single despite being among Your Arsenal's more outstanding rock rumpuses. [45]

glasses, Morrissey's need for optical assistance was diagnosed as a child though it wasn't until the age of 13 that he was 'forced' to wear glasses. 'I needed to wear them much sooner,' he divulged, 'but glasses had this awful thing attached to them that if you wore them you were a horrible green monster and you'd be shot in the middle of the street.' At the outset of The Smiths, though he alternated them with contact lenses, National Health glasses became an essential accessory to Morrissey's self-styled 'tongue-in-cheek chicdom' pop wardrobe. 'It was a complete accident,' he explained. 'I wore NHS spectacles, which I still do, so it wasn't a mantle or a badge. And suddenly I saw all these people who didn't need to wear spectacles doing so in imitation of The Smiths and bumping into an awful lot of walls.' To date, Morrissey has only ever appeared twice wearing glasses upon, or within, one of his records: the first in the Glastonbury backstage portrait inside 1984's HATFUL OF HOLLOW, the second upon the cover of his 1992 single 'WE HATE IT WHEN OUR FRIENDS BECOME SUCCESSFUL'. Except when off stage and out of the public eye, Morrissey mostly wears contact lenses. 'Without [them], I'm paralysed,' he admits. [82, 144, 203, 206, 453, 573]

Gluckstein, Hannah, Morrissey's favourite painter, more commonly known by her abbreviated signature, Gluck. Born into the wealthy north London Jewish dynasty who established the J. Lyons & Co. catering empire, Gluckstein rebelled against such privileged roots in spectacular fashion. An obvious and uninhibited lesbian, after running away from home to become a painter, she returned to London in her early twenties, now wearing men's suits, sporting cropped hair, smoking a pipe and calling herself 'Peter': bear in mind this was 1918. Her first cousin once removed, the actress YVONNE MITCHELL, summed up her black-sheep status in her veiled autobiographical novel *The Family* in which Gluckstein was pseudonymously cast as 'Frances', '… who had run away from home to put on trousers, and paint. She had always been a difficult daughter … she had even gone further in her rebellion by signing her paintings, Frank.'

Initially torn between singing and painting, Gluckstein later reminisced how a chance sight of John Singer Sargent's portrait of the violinist Joseph Joachim 'hit me plumb in the solar plexus', convincing her to choose the latter career. A prodigiously gifted painter, her own portraits possessed an extraordinarily warm, near-photographic realism. Others, such as that of the stage actor Ernest Thesiger (see THE OLD DARK HOUSE) were more stylised. Her most famous work, 'Medallion', depicts herself and her married lover Nesta Obermer in joint profile. Gluckstein herself called it the 'YouWe' picture, a commemoration of her own private lesbian 'marriage' ceremony to Obermer in 1935 in which they exchanged rings. She was also an accomplished landscape and still-life artist, creating a series of flower paintings, many suggestively erotic in their gynaecological arrangements of blossoming petals and aroused stamens. Her muse was the floral designer and writer Constance Spry, another of her lovers.

Among Gluckstein's other achievements was the invention of the 'Gluck frame' used to exhibit all her works; the painting sits at the centre of three equiangular panels of decreasing size placed atop one another, giving the effect of the picture being 'projected' from the wall. She also played a part in the scandal over the disinterment of Yeats's bones but fought her biggest war against British paint manufacturers. Infuriated by the poor quality of post-war oil paints which lost colour after application and created a dull 'suede effect' on canvas, Gluckstein spent over a decade campaigning for a new British Standard for oil paints. She eventually won, but at the expense of her own art: the 'paint war' had so consumed her that she'd forsaken years of creativity in the process.

Gluckstein died in 1978 at the ripe old age of 82, leaving behind only a hundred paintings. Many others had been burned in 1936 when she deliberately destroyed artworks and other personal effects at her Hampstead studio in an attempt to purge herself of the 'clinging unrealities' of her past. Her final canvas was completed in 1973, a sombre still life of a dead fish head she'd discovered on Worthing beach four years earlier, titled 'Rage, rage against the dying of the light' after a line from 'Do Not Go Gentle Into That Good Night', Dylan Thomas's poem to his dying father. Reflecting on its symbolism, she wrote: 'I am living daily with death and decay and it is beautiful and calming.' A rebel, a sexual free spirit and a great artist conveying the emotional intensities of both love and death with rare lucidity, it's easy to see why Gluckstein should appeal to Morrissey. Sadly, the majority of her work remains in private hands though two paintings, including a 1942 self-portrait, hang in the primary collection of London's National Portrait Gallery. Gluckstein is the subject of a solitary biography, Diana Souhami's superb *Gluck*, which Morrissey posed with on the cover of *Record Mirror* in early 1989. [141, 148, 175, 339, 377]

Golden Girls, The, See ARTHUR, Beatrice.

'Golden Lights' (Lynn Ripley), B-side of 'ASK' (1986). Originally a minor hit for TWINKLE in 1965, The Smiths' version of 'Golden Lights' (their first recorded cover) is, beyond question, the worst thing they ever committed to vinyl. It's not the fault of the song itself. Written by Twinkle and inspired by her relationship with Dec Cluskey of The Bachelors, 'Golden Lights' was a tender pop parable about a young girl sidelined by her fickle boyfriend when he suddenly becomes a famous singer: 'You made a record, they liked your singing/All of a sudden my phone stops ringing.' Thematically, its critical perspective on fame perfectly complemented The Smiths' existing repertoire (e.g. 'FRANKLY, MR SHANKLY') while its simple tune offered ample scope for reinvention. 'I remember thinking it could have been great,' says producer John PORTER. 'We did a brilliant monitor mix and it was starting to sound really lovely. But I could see Mozzer stood there, not liking it at all. He just wanted it to be weirded out, which it was in the end. It was fucked up deliberately and I didn't understand why.'

'Good Looking Man About Town' (Morrissey/Whyte), B-side of 'YOU HAVE KILLED ME' (2006). A likeable light-hearted skip through the familiar terrain of repressed lust, Morrissey wickedly ribs a lonely brainbox whose academic success is no compensation for an unfulfilled desire to bed the eponymous dreamboat. Yet for all his teasing, the singer is soon left to mourn his own nocturnal loneliness, his hopes of ever finding love slipping between his fingers like grains of sand. Among the better off-cuts from the RINGLEADER OF THE TORMENTORS sessions, Whyte's snaking melody was heavily perfumed with a Middle Eastern incense similar to that found in 'I WILL SEE YOU IN FAR-OFF PLACES'.

Porter's original mix lent the song a subtle South American feel, featuring acoustic guitar, mandolin and harmony vocals courtesy of Kirsty MACCOLL. Unhappy with the result, Morrissey took it to Stephen STREET, who was instructed to adapt it to the singer's inscrutable specifications. What later appeared on the 12-inch single of 'Ask' was altogether heinous. 'It ended up like [THE BEATLES'] "Octopus's Garden" gone wrong,' notes Rourke who, like Joyce, never actually played on the track: Porter provided bass while a simple drum machine loop kept rhythm. The finished mix buried any instrumental subtleties amid a smog of needless effects, Morrissey now sounding as if he were trying to sing while scoffing vast quantities of blancmange. Many years later, he defended his decision to tackle the tune as a frivolous act 'of playful perversity'. Perverse it may have been, but The Smiths' 'Golden Lights' remains an intolerable horror – that it was subsequently given the honour of a place on the LOUDER THAN BOMBS compilation still beggars all human reasoning. [7, 13, 17, 27, 29, 245]

grave, Morrissey would like to be buried rather than cremated and has expressed a preference to be interred in the final resting place of many a Tinseltown legend, Hollywood Forever cemetery on Los Angeles' Santa Monica Boulevard. His ideal burial plot would be beside the grave/statue of Johnny RAMONE – as seen on the sleeve of the 2009 single 'SOMETHING IS SQUEEZING MY SKULL' – situated directly opposite the reflecting pool in front of the impressive mausoleum holding the remains of Douglas Fairbanks Sr. 'I thought [Johnny Ramone's] stone was very nicely placed,' he enthused. 'I sat there for a very long time, and I felt quite good about it. I felt it was a nice position, and it was nice that his bones were under the soil that I was sitting on. So, yeah. That's my spot. And I have considered putting [reservation] money down.'

He has, in the past, spoken on various occasions about his desired epitaph. 'I think I'd have a jam jar, not a gravestone,' he quipped during The Smiths, 'saying, "He lived, he died." That says enough, really.' By 1987 he was deliberating on the alternative of 'Well at least he tried', though two decades later he'd settled on an altogether simpler inscription. 'I always felt that I wanted nothing other than name, birth date, death date, nothing else,' he admitted. 'All three names. Steven Patrick Morrissey.' [50, 144, 232]

Greatest Hits, Morrissey best-of compilation album released February 2008, highest UK chart position #5. Tracks: 'FIRST OF THE GANG TO DIE', 'IN THE FUTURE WHEN ALL'S WELL', 'I JUST WANT TO SEE THE BOY HAPPY', 'IRISH BLOOD, ENGLISH HEART', 'YOU HAVE KILLED ME', 'THAT'S HOW PEOPLE GROW UP', 'EVERYDAY IS LIKE SUNDAY', 'REDONDO BEACH', 'SUEDEHEAD', 'THE YOUNGEST WAS THE MOST LOVED', 'THE LAST OF THE FAMOUS INTERNATIONAL PLAYBOYS', 'THE MORE YOU IGNORE ME, THE CLOSER I GET', 'ALL YOU NEED IS ME', 'LET ME KISS YOU', 'I HAVE FORGIVEN JESUS'.

His first major release for the specially revived DECCA label, the plainly named Greatest Hits celebrated Morrissey's 20th year as a solo artist

g

and, surprisingly, was his first fully authorised UK best of (excluding 1997's Suedehead – The Best Of Morrissey, a singles anthology issued by EMI circa the ISLAND release of MALADJUSTED). Coming four years after his jubilant comeback of 2004, it offered a timely opportunity to celebrate recent top ten victories from the YOU ARE THE QUARRY and RINGLEADER OF THE TORMENTORS albums beside his most successful post-Smiths hits of the 80s and 90s and the added draw of two new tracks – current single 'That's How People Grow Up' and its follow-up 'All You Need Is Me'.

The tracklisting was roundly criticised in the press as drawing too heavily on Quarry and Ringleader with only a smattering of earlier singles. Yet technically, of its 15 tracks, and excluding the two new additions, in terms of chart position 11 of the remaining 13 were, indeed, Morrissey's literal greatest UK hits to date. The two anomalies were 'In The Future When All's Well' (#17) and 'I Just Want To See The Boy Happy' (#16) which should, by rights,

have been replaced by 'INTERESTING DRUG' (#9) and 'NOVEMBER SPAWNED A MONSTER' (#12), while 'ALMA MATTERS' (#16) and 'WE HATE IT WHEN OUR FRIENDS BECOME SUCCESSFUL' (#17) also hovered on the fringes of inclusion. Even stranger, its two exclusive new songs would resurface again over a year later on YEARS OF REFUSAL; a bizarre, possibly even unique, circumstance whereby two singles appear on a best-of compilation before their parent studio album.

In the end, Greatest Hits wasn't the glorious lap of honour it ought to have been and its poor performance in America (a grim #178) was cause enough for Morrissey to change his US label in the year prior to Years Of Refusal. Its admittedly uneven running order was at least compensated by its sumptuous gatefold packaging, including an archive photo of 'Morrissey's arse' by Jake WALTERS, as well as a limited edition double CD version featuring a bonus disc, Live At The Hollywood Bowl.

Greer, Germaine, See FEMINISM.

'Groovin' With Mr Bloe', Harmonica-driven soul instrumental by the mysterious Mr Bloe, named by Morrissey as one of his favourite singles and a UK number two hit in June 1970. 'I bought it when I was 11 and there was no picture of Mr Bloe on the sleeve and no one ever found out his real identity,' he explained. 'It was believed that Mr Bloe was Dutch and that he never recorded anything after "Groovin'". But it is an astonishing record. I recall being fascinated by Mr Bloe when I watched TOP OF THE POPS. During the chart countdown they used to illustrate every song with a picture of the band or the artist but when they got to Mr Bloe there was nothing. There weren't any pictures of him.'

At the risk of shattering the mystery, Mr Bloe was a short-lived project for British pianist Zack Laurence with harmonica by Harry Pitch, who'd later provide the maudlin theme tune warble of the BBC sitcom Last Of The Summer Wine. The Mr Bloe pseudonym came from the instrumental itself, originally the B-side of 'Make Believe', a 1969 single by psychedelic pop group Wind, the brainchild of American producer and songwriter Bo Gentry (the Wind original is actually a better record than the Mr Bloe remake). Strangely, for such a Top Of The Pops obsessive Morrissey failed to mention – or possibly never saw – Mr Bloe's one appearance on the programme featuring a harmonica player in full American-Indian headdress and a court jester on bass. Johnny Marr has also referred to 'Groovin' With Mr Bloe' as a favourite of his and Morrissey's around the recording of STRANGEWAYS, HERE WE COME, possibly even accounting for the not-so-dissimilar mournful harmonica parp at the end of 'I WON'T SHARE YOU'. [19, 48]

Guinness, Alec, Chameleonic British actor whose role in the 1955 Ealing Studios comedy THE LADYKILLERS was named by Morrissey as one of his favourite screen performances. Born in Maida Vale, London, Guinness received his first break from director David Lean who cast him in 1947's adaptation of DICKENS's *Great Expectations* with John MILLS, and again as Fagin in the following year's OLIVER TWIST, another Morrissey favourite. 1949's *Kind Hearts And Coronets*, the first of four Ealing comedies, fully showed off his mercurial brilliance by taking on all eight roles of the doomed D'Ascoyne dynasty. *The Lavender Hill Mob* and *The Man In The White Suit*, both 1951, confirmed his genius for underplayed comedy, just as his sinister Alistair SIM homage in *The Ladykillers* was overplayed for maximum ghastliness. He moved to heavier dramatic roles thereafter in Lean's Oscar-hoarding blockbusters *The Bridge On The River Kwai*, *Lawrence Of Arabia* and *Doctor Zhivago*, though is still perhaps best remembered as croaky Jedi recluse Obi Wan Kenobi, the universe's 'only hope' in the original *Star Wars* trilogy.

One of the more curious aspects about Guinness's life was his alleged supernatural encounter with James DEAN. The story goes that one night Guinness was having problems trying to find a free restaurant table in Hollywood when he was spotted by Dean who asked him to share his. Before they sat down, Dean insisted on showing him his new silver Porsche parked in the courtyard. 'Some strange thing came over me,' Guinness later recalled. He told Dean never to drive it because if he did he'd be dead within a week. This was 23 September 1955. Exactly one week later, Dean's corpse was corkscrewed around the car's steering mechanism. 'It was a very, very odd, spooky experience,' said Guinness, who died in August 2000, aged 86. [168, 520, 528, 537]

H-Bomb (hydrogen bomb), Asked in the 1991 KILL UNCLE tour programme how he'd like to be remembered, Morrissey answered 'Manchester's answer to the H-Bomb'. This remark was possibly adapted from Nell Dunn's *Up The Junction* where the phrase 'Britain's answer to the H-Bomb' appears in Chapter Two. [141, 306]

'Hairdresser On Fire' (Morrissey/Street), B-side of 'SUEDEHEAD' (1988). 'A very simple song about trying to get hold of a hairdresser' is how Morrissey described this frivolous autobiographical sketch: during the period the song was written the singer lived in a flat just off 'Sloane Square' in Chelsea. The lyrics betray an erotic fascination with 'the power' the hairdresser wields at their fingertips – capable of destroying or saving his physical appearance with a casual snip – tempered only by his exasperation at being unable to book an appointment in their hectic schedule.[1]

'To me, it was just one of his typical camp character songs,' says Stephen Street. 'At the time, Morrissey felt the same way too. That's why it never made Viva Hate.' Many would mourn the decision not to include the glossy, gambolling 'Hairdresser On Fire' on the album, especially in view of its strong tune, John Metcalfe's sumptuous strings and its memorable wedding-bell chorus. Days before the first Viva Hate test pressings, EMI pushed hard to persuade Morrissey and Street to amend the tracklisting but to no avail. Only with 1990's BONA DRAG compilation would this ever-popular B-side be granted a more deserving plinth. [25, 39, 71]

---

1. Evidence of the high esteem with which Morrissey regarded hairdressing can be seen on the credits of his early solo records, most of which list his current coiffeur: Robert Stanley ('Suedehead', VIVA HATE and 'EVERYDAY IS LIKE SUNDAY'), Stephen Powner ('INTERESTING DRUG') and Dave Gerrard ('OUIJA BOARD, OUIJA BOARD' and BONA DRAG).

'Half A Person' (Morrissey/Marr), B-side of 'SHOPLIFTERS OF THE WORLD UNITE' (1987). The best of the three north-to-south travelogue lyrics written by Morrissey during 1986 (after 'IS IT REALLY SO

STRANGE?' and 'LONDON'), 'Half A Person' remains among the most beautiful songs The Smiths ever recorded. 'Absolutely, one of the best things we ever wrote,' agrees Marr. 'It was entirely improvised on the stairway of Mayfair studios in Primrose Hill when we were doing "YOU JUST HAVEN'T EARNED IT YET, BABY". I already had the chords and Morrissey had gotten his part together overnight so we sat on the stairs and it came into being. An amazing moment, and probably the best songwriting moment me and Morrissey ever had. We were so close, practically touching. I could see him kind of willing me on, waiting to see what I was going to play. Then I could see him thinking, "That's exactly where I was hoping you'd go." It was a fantastic, shared moment.'

Unusually, Morrissey was candid enough to reveal that the song's first person account of a shy, retiring teenager who pursues a woman for six years only to be continually rejected was 'absolutely true' and that his female love interest 'does exist'. The flit to London specified in the chorus was also rooted in autobiography. 'I moved to London when I was 17,' Morrissey confessed. 'I lasted seven or eight days. I brought everything that I possessed [in] these huge cases and it was a really awful experience.'

Due to Morrissey's previous citations from Molly Haskell's FROM REVERENCE TO RAPE, it's likely that 'Half A Person' also owes its title to a sentence in the same book even if, by strange coincidence, the phrase also appears in the novel of John Fowles's The Collector, as filmed with Terence STAMP and featured on the sleeve of 'WHAT DIFFERENCE DOES IT MAKE?'; unlike Haskell, Morrissey has never referred to Fowles as a favourite author and there is no evidence to suggest he read the novel of a film he'd publicly dismiss as 'quite sexist [and] objectionable'.

The spectre of Stamp may, however, still have inspired the reference to the YWCA (Young Women's Christian Association). In the 1962 film Term Of Trial, Stamp plays a young thug taken on a school trip to Paris. When the party return to London and find themselves stuck for a hotel,

Stamp teases his teacher (Laurence Olivier) that they should 'all go to the YWCA'.[1] Equally conceivable, Morrissey's closing lyric may have been a deliberate nod to The Velvet Underground's plaintive 'That's The Story Of My Life' from their eponymous third album of 1969.

'Half A Person' also offers a prime example of Morrissey's unconventional sense of phrasing. Rather than follow the same ebb and flow of Marr's soft acoustic tide, he disregards where chorus and verses begin and end. If you imagine the song without lyrics, the chorus section is actually quite short, ending at the point where Morrissey sings 'YWCA'. A conventional singer would stop the chorus there and return to the melody they'd established in the opening verse. Morrissey does the exact opposite, continuing his chorus (the 'I like it here/Can I stay?' bit) even though Marr has already reverted back to playing the chords of the first verse. Such inherently unorthodox impulses were integral to The Smiths' magic and the fragile splendour of 'Half A Person' in particular. [17, 19, 58, 138, 430, 469, 555]

―――――――

1. Morrissey was certainly familiar with Term Of Trial, having earlier chosen a still of Stamp being caned by Olivier as a proposed sleeve for a 1985 European single release of 'THE HEADMASTER RITUAL'.

Hall, Radclyffe, See WELL OF LONELINESS, THE.

'Hand In Glove' (Morrissey/Marr), The Smiths' debut single, released May 1983, highest UK chart position #126. Cover star: George O'MARA. A remixed version later appeared on the album THE SMITHS (1984).

A pledge of self-sacrificial devotion to an idealised love shaded only by the pessimistic belief that the union will be brief, 'Hand In Glove' was the soundtrack to Morrissey's blossoming partnership with Marr. Written in January 1983, approximately six months after they'd started collaborating, it was as romantic a mission statement of The Smiths' beginning as it was prophetic of their end, destined to part within the next five years. Of the dozens of Morrissey lyrics believed

h

to be about Marr, 'Hand In Glove' is as blatant as they come. 'Even I assumed that it was about the two of us when we did it,' Marr admits, 'purely because we were the only people hanging out with each other at the time.'

As befits a song of such magnitude, the writing of 'Hand In Glove' is a Greek myth unto itself. One dank, drizzly January Sunday evening, Marr and his girlfriend, Angie, were visiting his parents in Wythenshawe. 'I went round to visit me little brother,' recalls Marr. 'There was a crappy old acoustic that I'd left there and I started to play these chords. I was playing it quite clipped, almost funky. I thought, "I'm really on to something here." Angie said to me, "That sounds pretty good." So I looked round for something to record it on, but there wasn't anything.'

The nearest tape recorder Marr knew he could lay his hands on for certain was six miles away: 384 Kings Road, Stretford to be precise. 'I had to get to a tape recorder,' says Marr, 'so I needed to get to Morrissey's, even though I didn't know if he was going to be home or not.'

Luckily for Marr, Angie had the loan of her parents' Volkswagen Beetle. 'We used to drive around in it when we had nowhere to go. More often than not it was where I used to practise me harmonica playing as she was driving which, looking back on it now, was probably really irritating!' As Angie drove him towards Stretford, Marr continued jamming his new tune. 'I was trying not to change or forget it, when Angie suddenly says to me, "Make it sound more like Iggy." So because of the car journey, and her screaming, I started to bring it more in line with something off [Iggy & The Stooges'] Raw Power. Finally, we get to Morrissey's. And he's like, "Oh ... hullo?" He wasn't expecting me. It was a bit, y'know, "On a Sunday night! Without an appointment!" But anyway, we made a cassette of the riff. So the genesis of "Hand In Glove" metamorphosised somewhere down the M56.'

Morrissey claimed he wrote the lyrics the same night in just two hours. Describing its theme of 'complete loneliness', he explained, 'it was

important to me that there'd be something searingly poetic in it, in a lyrical sense, and yet jubilant at the same time. Being searingly poetic and jubilant was, I always thought, quite difficult because they're two extreme emotions and I wanted to blend them together.'

Alone in his Stretford bedroom 'surrounded by lots of words', within the jigsaw of 'Hand In Glove' are recognisable pieces of Morrissey's bookshelf and record collection. The closing 'I'll probably never see you again' occurs in the two published plays of his lyrical mentor, Shelagh DELANEY, A Taste Of Honey and The Lion In Love. It's also likely that Buffy SAINTE-MARIE's 1971 album track 'Bells', written by Leonard Cohen (who'd later record his own version as 'Take This Longing'), provided another source in its line: 'Everything depends upon how near you sleep to me.' Taking into account his obsession with Sandie SHAW's 1967 hit 'You've Not Changed', it's not beyond reason that Morrissey's line about rags owed a little to that song's 'If you wore rags, you'd still look good to me'.

Morrissey later referred to his own 'hidden by rags' line as his 'favourite lyric', explaining '[it's] how I felt when I couldn't afford to buy clothes and used to dress in rags but I didn't really feel mentally impoverished. The inspiration? Just the very idea of people putting enormous importance on what they had and how they dressed and this very materialistic sense of value which is completely redundant. It goes back to the old cliché of what one has inside is really what one is.'

Five days after Marr's impromptu Sunday night visit, Morrissey unveiled the song during a group rehearsal. As Marr recalls, 'When we heard the vocals, we were all like "Wow!" From then on, it was always going to be the first single.' Even before its live debut at Manchester's Haçienda in early February, opinion that 'Hand In Glove' was their strongest track to date was unanimous within the group. 'It was as if these four people had to play that song,' Morrissey later reflected. 'It was so essential. Those words had to be sung.'

Funded by manger Joe MOSS at a cost of £250,

'Hand In Glove' was recorded in the last weekend of February at Stockport's Strawberry studios where previous Mancunian music legends BUZZCOCKS, Joy Division and studio owners 10cc had previously trodden. The 'Iggy-ness' of Marr's tune, a chip off James Williamson's riff from Raw Power's 'Gimme Danger', was never glaringly obvious in its execution, his sad yet aggressive chords broken up by Rourke's granite bass and Joyce's violent cymbal smashes. After the stony baritone of The Smiths' early demos, on 'Hand In Glove' Morrissey finally found his true voice: raw in passion, precise in diction, a flicker of hope emanating from an ash heap of despair. Further melancholic ambience was offered by Marr's ghostly harmonica, whether intentionally or not offering a textural parallel with the debut single of their esteemed northern forebears THE BEATLES, 1962's 'Love Me Do'.

This same Strawberry studios recording of 'Hand In Glove' was used to woo ROUGH TRADE, who released it as The Smiths' debut single that May. 'It must be heard by everybody,' Morrissey declared. 'It must be translated into all languages. I feel so strongly about the song. It seems to be the soundtrack of my entire life. It seemed that everything I did before "Hand In Glove" was simply working towards it. I think the record is so absolutely perfect in every respect that if it just dribbles away I shall be ill, probably for ever.'

As the first release by a new band on an independent record label yet to boast a single inside the UK top 40, 'Hand In Glove' failed to bring The Smiths into the pop mainstream; for that they'd have to wait until its follow-up, 'THIS CHARMING MAN'. Morrissey never fully recovered from its commercial disappointment, mourning its fate as the group's 'only tragedy'. They'd re-record it with producer Troy TATE for the abandoned first album, then again with John PORTER in an unsettlingly cheerful arrangement pre-empting its future cover by Sandie Shaw. Unhappy with the result, they decided to return to the Strawberry original, remixed by Porter for 1984's The Smiths, replacing its fade-in and fade-out with an abrupt start and finish. A clearer mix, it lost something of the tangible northern grit of the single version, as Morrissey belatedly agreed.

Speaking in 1984, the singer nominated 'Hand In Glove' as 'the most special' song he and Marr had written so far, a record of 'great romantic' personal value which he hoped would 'become somewhat of an anthem'. Though denied the hit status he desperately craved, over time the song has more than achieved his anthemic ambitions and remains one of Morrissey and Marr's most treasured and essential works. With spooky poignancy, their debut single would also be the last song The Smiths ever played live, the final encore of their unbeknown farewell concert at London's Brixton Academy on 12 December 1986. [12, 17, 19, 65, 258, 270, 275, 301, 424, 406]

'Hand That Rocks The Cradle, The'

(**Morrissey/Marr**), From the album THE SMITHS (1984). The exact order of their early writing is hazy but Marr's main recollection is that the first proper song he and Morrissey completed was 'The Hand That Rocks The Cradle'. As with those of 'SUFFER LITTLE CHILDREN', Morrissey had already written the lyrics before collaborating with Marr. Friend and BUZZCOCKS manager Richard Boon would later recall hearing Morrissey's a cappella bedroom demo of the song to a different vocal melody circa 1980.

While a common phrase, the most likely title source is a 1917 silent film mentioned in Marjorie Rosen's POPCORN VENUS, one of his key references in early Smiths lyrics. Structurally, the words are not typical of Morrissey and, indeed, it reads more like a poem put to music than a bespoke pop song. His only cryptic explanation that it 'comes from a relationship I had that didn't really involve romance' further clouds the mystery of what autobiography, if any, its first-person expression of a parent's protective love for their child may contain. Amid its strange collage of similes and alliterative images he also weaves in a snatch of Al Jolson's 'Sonny Boy' and his first Shelagh DELANEY reference, repeating her citation of

Thomas Noel's 'rattle my bones' from *The Lion In Love*.

Written during their first rehearsal in Marr's attic lodgings in Bowdon in the summer of 1982, after seeing Morrissey's typed lyrics, the guitarist suggested a melody directly modelled upon PATTI SMITH's 'Kimberly' from Horses. 'I just thought it scanned over the tempo of "Kimberly",' says Marr. 'Also it was terra firma. Patti Smith was a really big touchstone for us. We didn't know each other then, so it was really important to the two of us that it worked.' Marr's decision to base the tune on that specific Smith track seems a subconscious recognition that 'Kimberly' was also about a baby (Patti's younger sister) and contained the line 'so with one hand I rocked you'.

As the first Morrissey/Marr original, the song would also be the first they recorded in the studio – cutting a basic demo at Manchester's Decibel in August 1982 with Dale HIBBERT on bass and Simon WOLSTENCROFT on drums – and the first they played live as the opening number of their October 1982 debut concert at Manchester's Ritz with Hibbert and Joyce. While noticeably the same chord configuration as 'Kimberly', both its main guitar riff and bass line were distinctly different. By the time they recorded it again in the summer of 1983 with Troy TATE as the proposed title track of their debut album, the tune had assumed a more individual melodic character.

Of all the tracks on their first album re-recorded with producer John PORTER, 'The Hand That Rocks The Cradle'

was altered more radically than most. Marr's original riff was replaced by a more complex layering of feathery guitar arpeggios interlocking as one, creating a hypnotic foundation for Morrissey's serenade to newborn innocence. As page one in the Morrissey/Marr songbook, it represents not so much a blueprint for future glories as a tentative experiment in their creative compatibility; an odd, if absorbing, anomaly within The Smiths' repertoire. [10, 13, 17, 27, 129, 139, 376]

'Handsome Devil' (Morrissey/Marr), B-side of 'HAND IN GLOVE' (1983). The catalyst for Morrissey's first taste of media controversy, false allegations and negative publicity, 'Handsome Devil' voiced the wicked thoughts of a ravenous sexual predator targeting their inexperienced and bookish prey. Its references to 'exams' and 'scholarly room' would be twisted by critics as implying underage sex between teacher and pupil: these isolated words aside, there is nothing else in the context of the song to contradict Morrissey's assertion that it 'has nothing to do with children'.

His full explanation further hinted at a theme he'd reiterate on the later 'Still Ill'. 'The message of the song is to forget the cultivation of the brain and to concentrate on the cultivation of the body,' he clarified. '"A boy in the bush" is addressed to a scholar. "There's more to life than books you know, but not much more" is the essence of the song. So you can just take it and stick it in an article about child molesting and it will make

Handbook Of Non-Sexist Writing, The, 1980 manual by American journalists Casey Miller and Kate Swift aimed at freeing writers, editors and speakers of 'unconscious semantic bias'. Morrissey listed the book among his favourites in 1983, two years after its UK publication. The crux of Miller and Swift's mission was to change the way society discriminates against women through use of language and to promote a new non-gender-specific vocabulary which avoids 'man' as a noun, verb, suffix or prefix. Thus, 'mankind' becomes 'humankind', 'to man the ship' becomes 'to operate the ship', 'fireman' becomes 'fire fighter' and even 'Scotsman' becomes simply 'Scot'. Morrissey's interest in the book was logical considering his own lyrics which often avoided interpretation from specifically male or female perspectives, a quality integral to his genius as a wordsmith. [184]

absolutely perfect sense. But you can do that with anybody. You can do it with Abba.'

'Handsome Devil' was unusual nonetheless and nowhere else in The Smiths' repertoire does Morrissey assume so rapacious an attitude towards sex. That it was among the first four songs he and Marr ever wrote together suggests that as a lyricist he may still have been finding his voice; this would at least explain its uncharacteristic sexual aggression compared with subsequent songs like 'MISERABLE LIE' and 'THESE THINGS TAKE TIME' which found him, by contrast, on the sexual defensive.

Nor does it contain any of the obvious second-hand sources traditionally found in other lyrics of the period. Only the pivotal 'books' line has been proposed as possibly lifted from Kurt Vonnegut's 1969 sci-fi novel *Slaughterhouse-Five*, featuring the almost identical, 'There's more to life than what you read in books.' More tenuously, a photo caption in Parker TYLER's *A Pictorial History Of Sex In Films* ('it seems only a question of who is going to swallow whom') might also have had a subtle influence.

Morrissey and Marr's first outright post-punk rocker, the guitarist describes the tune as a vague 'Mancunian anaemic' homage to the PATTI SMITH Group's 'Ask The Angels', lead track on 1976's Radio Ethiopia. In keeping with the lyrics, Marr's fierce riff set the bar for future Smiths savageries such as 'WHAT SHE SAID' and 'LONDON', the first to unleash the full force of the Rourke/Joyce rhythm section. Written prior to their debut gig at Manchester's Ritz on 4 October 1982, 'Handsome Devil' was the second of three tracks recorded for an EMI-funded demo that December, notable for its odd addition of guest saxophone in a not-entirely-successful attempt to re-create a 'Memphis horn sound'. Remarkably, the version released as the B-side of 'Hand In Glove' was that taped through a mixing desk at only the third Smiths concert at Manchester's Haçienda on 4 February 1983: introducing the song that night, Morrissey declared 'the only thing to be, in 1983, is handsome'.

They'd record an equally thrilling studio version for their debut John PEEL BBC radio session in May 1983 (as heard on HATFUL OF HOLLOW) and again with producer Troy TATE for their intended debut album. When the Tate LP was scrapped, 'Handsome Devil' would also be dropped from the re-recorded album schedule with John PORTER, possibly on account of the unfortunate tabloid allegations which ran in the *Sun* in the first week of September 1983. The story, such as it was, claimed that the group had recorded a 'child-sex song' which the BBC planned to broadcast, though 'after the *Sun* drew the attention of Radio 1 to its sleazy lyrics, it could be taken off the air for good'. Although the paper quoted lyrics from 'Handsome Devil', the song the BBC *were* planning to broadcast was the equally misconstrued 'REEL AROUND THE FOUNTAIN' which, as a result, was indeed censored from being aired as part of their second session for David Jensen. The implications were grave enough for Morrissey to make an unambiguous public defence. 'Quite obviously we don't condone child molesting or anything that vaguely resembles it,' he stressed. 'What more can be said?' [12, 17, 98, 249, 387, 390]

'Hanratty' (Morrissey/Cobrin), Unreleased 1997 studio recording from B-side sessions following the MALADJUSTED album. According to bassist Jonny BRIDGWOOD, 'Hanratty' was a title 'floating around' in the aftermath of Maladjusted, which he believes to have been earmarked for one of drummer Spencer Cobrin's demos.

Presumably, the lyrics would in some way have addressed the fate of James Hanratty, the 'A6 murderer' whose crime is detailed in one of Morrissey's favourite books, Gaute and Odell's *THE MURDERERS' WHO'S WHO*. Hanratty was identified as the gunman who, in August 1961, took a married man and his mistress hostage in their car, later killing him, raping her and leaving the woman for dead. She survived, paralysed, to give the police a description, leading to the 25-year-old Hanratty's eventual arrest and trial. Though a known petty thief, at first there were grave doubts whether he was capable of such a gruesome crime. Only when Hanratty changed his alibi in court did his defence weaken, leading to his conviction and execution. He was hanged on 4 April 1962, still pleading his innocence.

While his story neatly slotted into Morrissey's existing canon of songs dealing with British criminal history (e.g. 'SUFFER LITTLE CHILDREN', 'JACK THE RIPPER') it may also have been that following the 1996 COURT CASE the singer empathised with Hanratty as a (potentially) innocent man framed by the legal system. Nevertheless, subsequent appeals and forensic DNA tests on behalf of Hanratty's relatives have all reached the same conclusion as Gaute and Odell, that 'there is little doubt that the verdict was the correct one'. [4, 5, 317]

Happiest Days Of Your Life, The, 1950 British comedy listed among Morrissey's favourite films. A precursor to the St Trinian's series, *The Happiest Days Of Your Life* is a similarly riotous boarding-school farce featuring the same core cast of Alastair SIM, Joyce Grenfell and Richard Wattis, with even a brief George Cole cameo. Sim plays Wetherby Pond, headmaster of Nutbourne College for boys, who due to 'an appalling sexual aberration' by the Ministry of Education is forced to share his premises with the staff and pupils of St Swithin's Girls School run by the formidable Miss Whitchurch (Margaret RUTHERFORD). The film also provides a distant, yet possible, lyrical source for Morrissey's 'HOLD ON TO YOUR FRIENDS' when an indignant Sim tells Rutherford: 'We have a bond of trust here at Nutbourne, the boys and I, which is never abused.' [168, 175, 508]

'Happy Lovers At Last United' (Morrissey/ Street), Studio outtake from the 1988 B-sides session for 'EVERYDAY IS LIKE SUNDAY'. Committed to doing 'something good for once', Morrissey plays matchmaker to a couple of friends who've recently broken up. Thanks to his intervention, they reunite, only to cast him out of their lives as a now-superfluous gooseberry. All of which is an extremely clever, and touching, vehicle for him to reiterate his solitude by contrasting it with their rekindled romantic bliss. The real power of 'Happy Lovers' lies in Morrissey's superbly glum delivery: the gladder he pretends to be to see them 'hand in hand', the sadder his voice becomes. Street's tune shared some of the grand pathos of its intended A-side, complete with string harmonies, while its basic chord pattern was not unlike 'Build', a recent top 20 hit for The Housemartins. Though it would have made a strong B-side, Morrissey soon had a change of heart and regrettably consigned it to the scrapheap. Evidently the tune still remained in his vocal subconscious: a specific melody line in 'Happy Lovers' where he sings 'he is so kind' later reappeared as the 'she has now gone' refrain on the later 'OUIJA BOARD, OUIJA BOARD'. [25, 39]

Hardy, Françoise, Gobsmackingly beautiful and perpetually stylish 60s French pop singer and songwriter. Her biggest UK hit, 'All Over The World', reached number 16 in late May 1965, just as Morrissey was turning six. He'd later list the song among his favourite singles during the early years of The Smiths. 'It's the record [itself] more than her,' he explained, adding, 'She made lots of blunders, this was her prima moment.' The song was an English translation of her own 'Dans Le Monde Entier', a heartbroken ballad in which Françoise serenades her own loneliness, watching 'the sun's fading light' while reminiscing over a lost love. Hardy's model looks, sartorial elegance and sullen sex appeal established her as an international icon of 60s Parisian chic. Morrissey probably regretted being so dismissive of her other supposed 'blunders', since he later included 1966's 'You Just Have To Say The Word' (the English version of her 'Tu N'as Qu'un Mot À Dire') on his interval tape when touring 1997's MALADJUSTED and would make a point of praising her between songs on stage at the Paris Olympia in April 2006. [188, 408]

'Harry Rag' (Ray Davies), In the summer of 1991, during the planning stages of the album

'Harsh Truth Of The Camera Eye, The' (Morrissey/Nevin), From the album KILL UNCLE (1991). The horror that comes with being photographed in vivid, unflattering detail is the basis of Kill Uncle's longest song, lurching past the five-minute mark to a deathly organ stutter. Producers LANGER and Winstanley threw every available sound effect at their disposal to try and breathe life into the track, including some camp horror screams and camera shutter noises courtesy of Steve Nieve's infinite keyboard samples, though nothing about 'The Harsh Truth Of The Camera Eye'– not the music nor the lyrics – justified its disproportionately epic length. In its favour, it does at least contain one of Morrissey's most impressively original opening lines – 'Churchillian legs' – as well as the confession, much quoted by some critics, that he'd 'sooner be blindly loved' than judged. [15, 22]

YOUR ARSENAL, Morrissey sent Mark NEVIN a cassette of the 13 instrumental demos he'd chosen to work on – '11 Squire Nevin, 2 Alain White' – along with an extra 'Ray Kink schoolboy prank' he was 'toying with'. The latter was The Kinks' 'Harry Rag', a tongue-in-cheek ode to the British working classes' fatal romance with cigarettes ('Harry rag' being cockney rhyming slang for 'fag') from their 1967 album Something Else By The Kinks. The prospect of Morrissey singing Ray Davies – the greatest English pop lyricist of one era interpreting the work of his equally brilliant forerunner – was extremely tantalising. It was also fascinating to speculate that after covering Paul Weller's 'THAT'S ENTERTAINMENT', Morrissey was tracing the lineage of the 'British mod sophisticate' (as he'd taken to calling himself on a recent press advert for the single 'SING YOUR LIFE') back further to Davies. Though his band did learn and rehearse 'Harry Rag', Morrissey swiftly abandoned the idea. [22]

Haskell, Molly, See FROM REVERENCE TO RAPE.

Hated Salford Ensemble, The, Fictitious
'orchestration' on The Smiths' album THE QUEEN IS DEAD. Tying in with its iconic band portrait outside SALFORD LADS CLUB, the 'Ensemble' joke was Morrissey's playful means of disguising the fact that the album's strings were all synthetic; played by Marr on an Emulator keyboard, hence the accompanying credit 'string arrangements by Johnny Marr'. (See also ORCHESTRAZIA ARDWICK.) [17, 38]

Hatful Of Hollow, The Smiths' first compilation album, released November 1984, highest UK chart position #7. Cover star: Fabrice Colette (see COCTEAU). Tracks: 'WILLIAM, IT WAS REALLY NOTHING', 'WHAT DIFFERENCE DOES IT MAKE?', 'THESE THINGS TAKE TIME', 'THIS CHARMING MAN', 'HOW SOON IS NOW?', 'HANDSOME DEVIL', 'HAND IN GLOVE', 'STILL ILL', 'HEAVEN KNOWS I'M MISERABLE NOW', 'THIS NIGHT HAS OPENED MY EYES', 'YOU'VE GOT EVERYTHING NOW', 'ACCEPT YOURSELF', 'GIRL AFRAID', 'BACK TO THE OLD HOUSE', 'REEL AROUND THE FOUNTAIN', 'PLEASE PLEASE PLEASE LET ME GET WHAT I WANT'.

Though not a 'proper' studio work, Hatful Of Hollow is considered by many to be The Smiths' best album, and it's easy to hear why. Judged purely in terms of songwriting, its 16 tracks – most culled from early BBC radio sessions mixed in with select non-album singles and B-sides – are as flawless a collection of Morrissey/Marr originals as any of the group's four main studio albums. 'We wanted it released on purely selfish terms,' Morrissey explained, 'because we liked all those tracks and those versions. I wanted to present those songs again in the most flattering form. Those [BBC] sessions almost caught the very heart of what we did. There was something positively messy about them, which was very positive. People are so nervous and desperate when they do those sessions, so it seems to bring out the best of them.'

As Morrissey intimated, Hatful Of Hollow was, in part, prompted by belated misgivings over the production quality of their recent debut

159

album, as well as a response to 'imploring demands' from fans to make their early radio sessions available. '[We] suddenly realised that we hadn't even proper sounding tapes of them ourselves,' he added, 'except for a few dire bootlegs that we bought at our concerts. As far as we're concerned, those were the sessions that got us excited in the first place, and apparently it was how a lot of other people discovered us also.' Marr admits to being pleasantly surprised by the compilation's reverence from fans and critics, having originally considered it a simple budget best-of; crucially, Hatful Of Hollow was a 16-track album in an impressive gatefold vinyl sleeve retailing at a very affordable £3.99. 'I realise now what an important record that was for us,' he says. 'People still ask me about Hatful like it's one of our proper albums which probably says a lot about the effect it had on our audience back then.'

Where The Smiths' debut album was a final draft after a whole year's recording and exhaustive re-recording, Hatful Of Hollow properly documented the group's musical development from May 1983's 'Hand In Glove', here in its original single version, to the polished pop splendour of August 1984's 'William, It Was Really Nothing' via the learning curve of those raw, formative BBC radio sessions: from their first, for John PEEL, in May 1983 – 'Handsome Devil', 'Reel Around The Fountain' and, in Morrissey's view, the definitive version of 'What Difference Does It Make?'; from their second, for David Jensen, in July 1983 – 'These Things Take Time' and 'You've Got Everything Now'; from their third, again for Jensen, in September 1983 – 'Accept Yourself'; from their fourth, and second for Peel, also that September – 'Still Ill', a nimble first stab at 'This Charming Man', the exclusive 'This Night Has Opened My Eyes' and the superior acoustic version of 'Back To The Old House'. The running order was completed by 'Heaven Knows' and its 12-inch B-side 'Girl Afraid' plus all three tracks from the recent 'William' single, thereby bringing the latter's 12-inch B-side 'How Soon Is Now?' to deservedly wider public attention.

Anybody who insists on calling it their 'favourite Smiths album' should always be on guard to have their heads snapped off by pedantic sticklers telling them it's 'only' a compilation. But those who do rate it their best work have a valid point. As a ready-to-hand primer for the uninitiated or uninformed yet to understand The Smiths' uniqueness or why Morrissey and Marr were the greatest songwriters of their age, Hatful Of Hollow is evidence enough. [18, 38, 275, 425]

'Have-A-Go Merchant' (Morrissey/Whyte),

B-side of 'BOXERS' (1995). As much as Morrissey can often be accused of glamorising working-class thuggery, in 'Have-A-Go Merchant' he reveals a genuine distaste for the title bully, a tiresome drunken hard man always on the lookout for a ruckus who in the process, it seems, has neglected all affection for his young daughter. Among Morrissey's lesser character sketches, Whyte's bletherin', blusterin' riff made for a fine B-side and a surprisingly rousing concert staple of his February 1995 UK tour. The popular rumour that the title was secretly directed at Natalie Merchant – singer with 10,000 Maniacs who'd 'had a go' at covering 'EVERYDAY IS LIKE SUNDAY' on the B-side of her group's 1993 single 'Candy Everybody Wants' – has never been verified but certainly isn't beyond the realms of Morrissey's notoriously wicked sense of humour. [4]

Hawtrey, Charles, See CARRY ON.

Hayward, Susan, Hollywood star of the 40s and 50s whom Morrissey mentioned when discussing his favourite films showing 'old' Los Angeles. The two Hayward films he specified were both Oscar-nominated performances. In 1946's Smash-Up: The Story Of A Woman, based on an original story by Dorothy Parker, Hayward played a nightclub singer with a disastrous Jekyll and Hyde alcohol dependence. Equally dramatic is 1958's I Want To Live! (for which she'd win the Oscar), a 'factual drama' about the execution of Barbara Graham, arrested by the LAPD for her

part in a murder and sentenced to die in the gas chamber at San Quentin. The Hollywood equivalent of YIELD TO THE NIGHT, Hayward's Graham is a classic Mozzerian martyr; a strong, fearless woman with a love of music and poetry, persecuted by a merciless authority and condemned to die, fighting for her dignity until her final breath. [513, 552, 568]

'He Cried' (Morrissey/Whyte), From the album MALADJUSTED (1997). Sharing a title with one of the lesser hits by 60s girl group The Shangri-Las (itself a rewrite of Jay & The Americans' 'She Cried'), whereas in their 'He Cried' the tears are that of a boy who's just been dumped, in Morrissey's song they're caused by the shock of never having being told 'I need you'. Though he uses third person, the loveless weeping male in question, presumably, is Morrissey; emotionally 'stoned to death' while rebelling against the shackles of his repressed roots. Although Whyte's tepid tune was mid-tempo business as usual, Morrissey's impassioned delivery pushed the song into Maladjusted's slender handful of highlights. [40, 152]

'He Knows I'd Love To See Him' (Morrissey/Armstrong), B-side of 'NOVEMBER SPAWNED A MONSTER' (1990). A bloodshot-eyed acoustic yawn from guitarist Kevin Armstrong stirs Morrissey into a quietly eldritch croon to an old acquaintance. Recorded only two years after the break-up of The Smiths, the 'He' was interpreted by some critics to be Johnny Marr. More obviously, his former life in 'the arse of the world' refers to his depressed existence in early 80s Manchester. The police interrogation detailed in its second half was inspired by a genuine Special Branch investigation in the wake of 'MARGARET ON THE GUILLOTINE'. As Morrissey later told the press, he was grilled for an hour about his political views while they searched his house, after which he was asked to sign autographs. Mary Margaret O'HARA added backing vocals while double bass was provided by revered session player Danny Thompson, formerly

of Pentangle, though never credited on the accompanying single sleeve or any subsequent compilations. [1, 153, 224]

'Headmaster Ritual, The' (Morrissey/Marr), From the album MEAT IS MURDER (1985). Where on 1984's THE SMITHS, Morrissey's lyrics were mostly concerned with the romantic failures and social isolation of his late teens and early twenties, the opening track on its follow-up saw him delve further into his past. 'The Headmaster Ritual' picked over the still-scabbing psychological wounds of his education, a personal and very specific attack on the staff of St Mary's Secondary Modern in Stretford, where he was, in his words, 'emotionally sodomised' from the age of 11 to 16. 'I remember it all in great detail,' he explained. 'The horror of it cannot be over-emphasised. Every single day was a human nightmare.'

As Morrissey melodramatically put it, St Mary's 'ultimately got global attention for being the most brutal school in the country', referring to a government report condemning its excessive use of corporal punishment. When it came to answering questions about his own experiences with caning at St Mary's, Morrissey was prone to inconsistency. 'For some obscure reason, I always avoided it,' he said in 1984. 'I always felt they considered me far too delicate.' A year later, after 'The Headmaster Ritual' had been released, Morrissey instead declared he had indeed been 'hit and beaten for totally pointless reasons'. Nevertheless, taking into account such anecdotal discrepancies, the song's minor borrowing from Elizabeth SMART (the phrase 'grabs and devours') and images of a PE teacher bullying a pupil in the showers identical to a scene in Ken Loach's 1969 film *Kes*, the lucidity of its spleen-venting lyrics were very obviously the result of his own tormented youth.

Predictably, the Manchester Education Committee weren't impressed by his gratuitous criticism. According to Morrissey, they tried, in vain, to 'ban' it within the Greater Manchester area while the demonised headmaster of the title, Mr Morgan, tried to defend himself on local radio. '[He] said,

"[Morrissey] was such a good boy and he was never hit,"' the singer explained. 'Of course, which does the image no good whatsoever.' Unrepentant, Morrissey decreed that any school which fails to serve its pupils 'is there to be attacked,' though ten years later, 1995's 'THE TEACHERS ARE AFRAID OF THE PUPILS' saw him return to the same source but deliberating on classroom violence as experienced from the other side of the desk.

Musically, the roots of 'The Headmaster Ritual' were much more convoluted. Marr had written the basic chord sequence with its 'shades of JONI MITCHELL' during the 1983 Troy TATE sessions. It took him another 12 months of intensive development, adding its George Harrison-inspired verses treading softly in the shadows of THE BEAT-LES' 'I Feel Fine', before it was ready to give to Morrissey. Driving back together to Manchester from the Meat Is Murder sessions in Liverpool, Marr would make a very rare lyrical suggestion, telling Morrissey that 'bruises bigger than dinner plates' might sound better if phrased 'as big as dinner plates'. Though he quietly ignored the guitarist's advice at the time, when Morrissey revived the track in concert in 2004, strangely, he sang Marr's version.

In its finished form, 'The Headmaster Ritual' was a dynamic opener to The Smiths' second album. For all the horror of Morrissey's painful school flashbacks, thanks to Marr's vivacious guitar assembly (and Rourke's equally energetic bass figure), the song instead became a triumphant score-settler against his adolescent oppressors. A 1985 single in Holland (instead of 'THAT JOKE ISN'T FUNNY ANYMORE'), ROUGH TRADE also issued it as a posthumous CD single in 1988 in another Viv NICHOLSON sleeve. To the label's surprise, Nicholson objected. Having become a Jehovah's Witness, she disapproved of its 'spineless bastards' lyric, forcing the majority of the 5,000 copies pressed to be withdrawn. [17, 129, 168, 171, 180, 219, 362, 374, 426, 448, 452]

hearing aid, One of Morrissey's most famous stage props in the early years of The Smiths. 'It was purely sexual,' he wryly explained, 'part of the disability-chic movement that I created in 1983.' The hearing aid was a non-functioning display model borrowed from a central London store and first appeared on their second TOP OF THE POPS appearance on 26 January 1984 performing 'WHAT DIFFERENCE DOES IT MAKE?'

Although Morrissey would later account for his use of the prop as being a signal of solidarity to a deaf girl who'd written him a fan letter, many commentators noted its possible homage to hearing-impaired crooner Johnnie Ray whose 1951 hit 'Cry' earned him the nicknames 'Nabob Of Sob' and 'Prince Of Wails'. Ray lost hearing in his left ear aged 13 during a blanket-tossing game with some scout friends. When they dropped the blanket instead of bouncing him, Ray hit the ground, falling on a hard, dry straw stem which pierced his eardrum. It was the first of many tragedies in a life as tear-strewn as the songs which made him a pre-rock and roll bobbysoxer icon, attracting the kind of frenzied audience hysteria later provoked by Elvis PRESLEY. When he later risked surgery to fix his hearing, the operation failed, wrecking both ears: thereafter, Ray was forced to wear hearing aids on stage, the only popular singer to do so before Morrissey. Ray eventually became a chronic alcoholic and died of liver failure in 1990.

Morrissey's hearing aid became a mandatory accessory for the majority of Smiths television appearances in 1984, as well as on stage and in photoshoots as late as 1986. The following year, Morrissey commented how, although he'd never needed a hearing aid, he'd 'caught a serious ear infection and literally went deaf for about four weeks. Naturally I took this as retribution for wearing a hearing aid. It was hellish – four weeks of "pardon" jokes at my expense.' When working with the singer in the 1990s, engineer Danton Supple discovered Morrissey actually did suffer from 'perforated eardrums' and recurring hearing problems. 'I only know this because I was about to throw him in a swimming pool once,' says Supple. 'Morrissey started screaming not to do it because of his eardrum.' [40, 78, 133, 144, 362, 392]

'Heart', 1966 single by Italian pop singer Rita Pavone which Morrissey has listed as one of his favourite singles on numerous occasions. Written by Brill Building duo Barry Mann and Cynthia Weil, in 1963 Pavone first took a translated version of the song to number one in Italy ('Cuore'). Her re-recorded 'Heart' was the first of two UK hits, reaching number 27 in January 1967. Morrissey stated that he bought it 'when I was six [*sic; he must have been seven*]', also hailing it as 'the most incredible vocal performance that I've ever heard'. It is, indeed, a genius pop record, a two-minute bolero crescendo in which Pavone serenades her vital organ, vainly trying to stop it palpitating over another boy destined to break it, whipping herself up into a state of lung-busting hysteria in the process ('Don't make such a fuss!/There's no hope for us!'). Though probably just coincidence, it's worth speculating whether Morrissey's endorsement of 'Heart' in the early years of The Smiths may have had some strange subliminal influence upon an instrumental demo of 'I KNOW IT'S OVER' from September 1985, notable for Rourke's experiment with a very similar staccato bass line. [175, 184, 188, 213, 408]

'Heaven Knows I'm Miserable Now'

(**Morrissey/Marr**), The Smiths' fourth single, released May 1984, highest UK chart position #10. Cover star: Viv NICHOLSON.

If The Smiths discography has its albatross, then this – the joint biggest hit single during their lifespan alongside 'SHEILA TAKE A BOW' – is it. No other song is more responsible for their detractors' misconstrued clichés and lazy criticisms of the group's music as being literally 'miserable'.

In truth, 'Heaven Knows I'm Miserable Now' was unadulterated pop comedy, right down to its title: Morrissey's knowing pun on an obscure Sandie SHAW single from 1969, 'Heaven Knows I'm Missing Him Now'. That it became their first top ten hit owes much to Marr's denture-threateningly sweet tune, itself a powerful counterpoint to Morrissey's tragicomic lyrics. As it is, his woeful verse is entirely whimsical; wishing he were still drunk enough to forget his misery, plunged into despair by the mere sight of 'two lovers entwined' reminding him of his own solitude and idly reminiscing about a previous sexual proposition so outrageous that the notoriously degenerate Roman Emperor CALIGULA 'would have blushed'.

In the context of its release in 1984, a time of high unemployment in Britain during THATCHER's second term in office, its most powerful lyric was the repeated moan about looking for work, finding it, yet still being miserable. This, effectively, was Morrissey's first real political statement as a lyricist and, as he later explained, 'the absolute basis of [the song]' informed by his own 'brief spasms of employment' in the past. 'It always seemed to me there were moments of the day when I would realise that I was here working with these people that I despised,' he elaborated. 'I had to talk to these horrible people and ask them what they did yesterday. And I would have to report to a boss that I couldn't stand. When you're in that position [you] realise that you're actually spending your entire life living with people that you do not like … I mean, "Kick in the eye"? Yes, literally. Let's be perfectly honest, sometimes we do get so angry with people that we're not averse to violence.'

Nevertheless, for all its lightness of humour and astute social commentary – even if Morrissey himself referred to the 'looking for a job' line as relatively 'ineffectual' – the song was written as a catharsis for genuine unhappiness as experienced on The Smiths' first fleeting visit to America at the end of December 1983. Booked to play a New Year's Eve gig at New York's Danceteria, the group arrived jetlagged, largely malnourished and with drummer Mike Joyce coming down with chickenpox. During the opening number, Morrissey fell off the venue's stage. The following day,

h

1 January 1984, he and Marr sought comfort in writing 'Heaven Knows' together in a bedroom of the Iroquois Hotel (where James DEAN once lodged), before flying home.

The single's release instigated the most prominent television media blitz of The Smiths' career, with Morrissey appearing on the BBC panel shows *Eight Days A Week* and *Pop Quiz* and the whole group finding themselves visiting Kew Gardens with a double-decker's worth of children aboard Charlie's Bus (part of TV-am's Saturday morning *S.P.L.A.T.* programme). It was regrettable that the record would later provoke controversy over its B-side, the Moors Murders elegy 'SUFFER LITTLE CHILDREN' and confusion over its peroxide-beehived cover star Viv Nicholson's resemblance to Myra Hindley.

Arguably more damaging was the song's unforeseen gift to those wishing to mock The Smiths, or more particularly Morrissey, by way of a cheapshot impression; a pantomime wail of 'Heaven Knows' accompanied by frantic flower waving and much exaggerated lolling of tongues is enough to crack the ribs of most village idiots. A shrewd exception was ITV's satirical puppet show *Spitting Image*, who used the song in 1992 as the basis of a sketch about the breakdown in the marriage of Prince Charles and Princess Diana, the latter flailing on a bed in beads and flowers singing, 'Heaven knows one's miserable now.' [17, 27, 38, 275, 448]

'Heir Apparent' (Morrissey/Whyte), B-side of 'ALMA MATTERS' (1997). Another absorbing Morrissey lyric about fame and ambition, on 'Heir Apparent' he returns home to Manchester only to spot an idealistic younger version of himself about to follow his footsteps to London with 'wide-eyed' dreams of success. The singer is unnerved by his heir's seeming naïveté, warning him of the perils of an industry destined to 'seduce your heart then smack your arse'. Yet beneath his sage cautioning, there's the implicit jealousy of a corrupted veteran longing to relive his own lost youth, as if irritated by his handsome young successor's 'winning smile'. Ordinarily, this conventional Alain Whyte

tune with a wallopingly woeful chorus would have been a fair choice of B-side. However, in context of the erratic fruits of the MALADJUSTED sessions, it seems odd that 'Heir Apparent' wasn't saved for the album itself – a wrong belatedly righted by 2009's Maladjusted redux re-release. Morrissey played the song in concert only once, at Spokane, Washington on 1 February 2000.

Herman's Hermits, See 'EAST WEST'.

Hibbert, Dale, Before Morrissey and Marr finalised their group's line-up with the addition of Andy Rourke in December 1982, The Smiths' first bass player was local sound engineer Dale Hibbert, an employee of Manchester's Decibel studios where they'd record their first demo.

A year earlier, Hibbert had recorded the 'Crak Therapy' demo by Marr's short-lived instrumental post-punk trio Freak Party featuring Rourke and drummer Simon WOLSTENCROFT. It would seem that Hibbert's access to free studio time, rather than his capabilities on bass, was the deciding factor when Marr involved him in the early stages of The Smiths. However, Hibbert argues that 'as a friend of Johnny's I would've given them that anyway, whether I was in the band or not'.

In the late summer/autumn of '82 Hibbert attended a handful of practices with Morrissey and Marr at the latter's attic room in Bowdon, under strict warning only to call Morrissey 'Steven' and not 'Steve'. 'Me and Johnny both had semi-acoustic guitars,' remembers Hibbert. 'I had a Hofner and he had a Gretsch, so we didn't even need amplifiers. I used to have to pick Steven up from his mum's house on Kings Road in Stretford and take him to band practices on my motorbike, with him clinging on to the back of me. I got to know him quite well. He certainly didn't appear shy or retiring. I was told he had a history of journalism and had a lot of contacts in the music business which is why they were gonna take a shortcut to getting signed.'

Among the songs Hibbert either rehearsed with Morrissey and Marr or was given on a cassette to learn were the lost 'DON'T BLOW YOUR OWN HORN' and the Cookies cover 'I WANT A BOY FOR MY BIRTHDAY'. Hibbert refers to the latter song to support a contentious claim that Morrissey and Marr were deliberately choreographing The Smiths towards a 'gay' image. 'They actually came out and said it,' Hibbert insists. 'It was Steven's idea. It wasn't something that was mentioned and then dropped, it was something they wanted to follow through. Obviously a song like "I Want A Boy For My Birthday" would go hand in hand with that image. Steven said, "We're going to be a gay band, but not in a Tom Robinson [*70s singer/songwriter of '(Sing If You're) Glad To Be Gay*'] effeminate kind of way but more in an underlying kind of macho type way." It was a very strongly manufactured image that was being prepared.' For the record, Marr dismisses Hibbert's recollections as a crude misinterpretation, laughing off any suggestion that he and Morrissey ever sat down with Dale and told him to 'get with the programme!'

It was still thanks to Hibbert that a prototype Smiths line-up (with Wolstencroft on drums) made their first demo at Decibel in August 1982 of 'THE HAND THAT ROCKS THE CRADLE' and 'SUFFER LITTLE CHILDREN'. Hibbert only played on the first track as Marr chose to overdub bass on the second. With the group's scheduled live debut at Manchester's Ritz pending in early October, Hibbert also recalls being given an image makeover by the more fashion savvy Morrissey and Marr, 'told' to get a flat-top haircut and wear a 1950s bowling shirt from the local Army & Navy Store.

The Ritz would be Hibbert's first and last Smiths gig. A few weeks later, at a group rehearsal in Manchester's Spirit studios, Marr told him he was no longer required. 'I can remember it well,' says Hibbert. 'It was on the stairs as I was going out. Johnny said something like "We need a parting of the waves" and I thought they meant they wanted to rehearse somewhere else. So I said, "Yeah, all right. So where d'you wanna rehearse then?" Johnny went, "Er, no. I mean we don't need you!" It fell to him to tell me because he was

the one that introduced me to the band. But there was no way I would have made it with them. There was no way I'd have gone on tour and done all that stuff because I was married with kids. I just didn't suit the image that was being prepared.'

His incongruity within the group was perfectly illustrated the month after he left with the publication of their first press interview in *i-D* magazine in which, to Marr's embarrassment, Hibbert stuck up for Edinburgh punk band The Exploited. After The Smiths Hibbert eventually left the recording business but retained the studio masters of their historic Decibel demo. He later sold them to a private collector along with a very rare cassette of Morrissey and Marr rehearsing 'I Want A Boy For My Birthday'. [10, 12, 17, 253, 362]

Hindley, Myra, See *BEYOND BELIEF*, 'SUFFER LITTLE CHILDREN'.

HMV (His Master's Voice), Morrissey's record label for the first five years of his solo career from 1988 to 1993 under the umbrella of EMI. His decision to revive the HMV imprint was illustrative of his discerning label fetishism, setting a precedent for the rest of his solo career whereby he'd ally himself with similarly 'defunct' or vintage imprints under contract to major parent companies; PARLOPHONE (also under EMI), RCA VICTOR (under BMG), ISLAND (Mercury), ATTACK RECORDS (Sanctuary) and DECCA (Universal). 'His Master's Voice, I thought, had a certain perverted grandiosity and thus spoke to me very directly,' he beamed, proud to be 'the only artist on it'.

Resurrecting HMV's trademark 'Nipper the dog' logo, EMI also recommenced its original 'POP' singles catalogue number system. Morrissey's 'SUEDEHEAD' – POP 1618 – became the first in the label's history since Joyce Grenfell's 'Nursery School' – POP 1617 – released 20 years earlier (see also *THE HAPPIEST DAYS OF YOUR LIFE*). It helped that many of Morrissey's favourite records bore the original HMV label, including Paul Jones' 'I'VE BEEN A BAD, BAD BOY' and Sam Cooke's 'THERE I'VE SAID IT AGAIN'. Smiths cover star Pat

PHOENIX had also graced the label with 1962's 'The Rovers Chorus' while among the 'hundreds of HMV records in my collection' he also referred to a near miss by 'JOHNNY REMEMBER ME' singer John Leyton, 1963's 'I'll Cut Your Tail Off'. The 1993 live album BEETHOVEN WAS DEAF was Morrissey's last on HMV before joining EMI's non-exclusive Parlophone roster. [208, 226]

Hogg, Peter,

Morrissey's friend and aide circa 1989 to 1992 during the making of BONA DRAG, KILL UNCLE and YOUR ARSENAL. Hogg met Morrissey in the late 80s through fellow Scouser, Dead Or Alive singer Pete BURNS. His official listed job title on the 1991 Kill Uncle tour was 'Rentachap', a reference to the first Julian and Sandy radio sketch with CARRY ON star Kenneth Williams.

Opinions differ among eyewitnesses during that period as to what Hogg's role exactly entailed. Guitarist Kevin ARMSTRONG describes him as Morrissey's 'minder and confidant'. Drummer Andrew PARESI refers to him as the singer's 'driver'. 'Peter Hogg was kind of a "personal assistant", if you want to be nice about it,' offers co-writer Mark NEVIN. 'He was a very bitchy Scouse queen, a friend of Pete Burns and Frankie Goes To Hollywood, part of the whole gay Liverpool crowd. A bit of a sycophant, really.' Hogg was certainly all these things – minder, driver, confidant, assistant but, above all else, a close friend. 'He absolutely loved Morrissey,' says Paresi. 'Just adored him. Hoggy used to drive him absolutely everywhere. But he was also fantastically mischievous.'

'He was hysterical,' remembers Cathal SMYTH. 'I remember one time it was myself, Morrissey, Pete Burns, Hoggy and [Frankie Goes To Hollywood's] Paul Rutherford, all in this car driving to a gay disco. Hoggy goes, "I'm going out with a postman." Somebody says, "You're scraping the barrel," to which Hoggy replies, "Well, at least he's got a big sack". It was hilarious to listen to. But when we got to the club, we get in and they're all happy as Larry having a hop, a skip and a jump, except Morrissey who says, "Shall we go now?" We're in, then next thing we're out.'

'I did hear some funny stories about what they used to get up to,' adds Armstrong. 'There were weekends when they did get rambunctious and go out picking up boys. Well, Hogg would, I have no idea about Morrissey. It just seemed to me that Hogg was there on hand whenever Morrissey

Hobson's Choice, 1954 British comedy drama listed among Morrissey's favourite films. Directed by David Lean (see also OLIVER TWIST) and based upon the play by Harold Brighouse, the story takes place in late-nineteenth-century Salford towards the end of the Industrial Revolution. Domineering widower Henry Hobson (Charles Laughton) owns a bootmaker's shop, staffed by his three daughters while he spends most of his time in the tavern across the road. In his drunken complacency, he is unaware that the success of his business is solely down to the craftsmanship of his simple-minded boot maker, Willie Mossop (John MILLS), and his eldest daughter Maggie's sales expertise. When Hobson ridicules Maggie for being too old to take a husband she plots a brazen and brilliant rebellion, marrying the bewildered Mossop and together setting up a rival business to her father's. As they begin to steal the indignant Hobson's trade, he descends further into alcoholism and potential bankruptcy until Maggie and her new husband offer him a bittersweet solution. Smiths fans should pay close attention to the scene where Maggie takes Mossop to break off his engagement to poor Ada Figgins: the temperance band marching outside the Figginses' slum was sampled on the intro of 'SHEILA TAKE A BOW' while the banner they carry – 'Beware the wrath to come' – was the source of Morrissey's run-out-groove message on the original vinyl release of 'BIGMOUTH STRIKES AGAIN'. [168, 175, 176, 184, 510]

chose to let his hair down.' Others, such as bassist Gary DAY, would accuse Hogg of being 'a real troublemaker, always sticking the knife in other people's backs'. Although Hogg was dedicated to Morrissey, producers Clive LANGER and Alan Winstanley remember one incident at Hook End Manor studios during the making of Kill Uncle which created a serious rift. 'There was one time when Morrissey must have pissed Hogg off or something,' says Langer. 'Morrissey went to bed so Peter was like, "Right! Bacon!" He fried up a load of meat and started wafting the fumes up the stairs to Morrissey's bedroom.'

'It wasn't just bacon,' adds Winstanley. 'It was every piece of meat he could find. The whole studio was under instructions that there was to be no meat on site during the session. Obviously, there was meat still in the freezer in the outhouse from the previous session, so Peter went and got everything he could lay his hands on. Steak, sausages, the lot. He fried it all up on the Aga in the middle of the night so the whole place stank of meat. Morrissey had stiff words with Peter after that. Well, he left him a little note and didn't speak to him for six months.'

Hogg's tenure with Morrissey ended circa 1992. By 1994, his role as personal assistant and designated driver had been taken by Morrissey's lodger, photographer Jake WALTERS. [1, 15, 22, 25, 36, 221]

'Hold On To Your Friends' (Morrissey/Whyte), Morrissey's 16th solo single (from the album VAUXHALL AND I), released June 1994, highest UK chart position #47. An aggrieved reprimand which Morrissey admitted was written 'about somebody I know in relation to their treatment toward me', behind the cautionary advice of its title lay a bitter criticism of a fickle friend who'd betrayed the singer's confidence. 'It is a lack of trust,' said Morrissey of his problems in forming close friendships. 'I'm simply waiting for people to do something damaging. And they inevitably do.' Critical speculation about the friend in question threw up the usual suspects including the ex-Smiths, though according to

Morrissey the song's real target 'never understood it'. Ironically, for all the emotional gravitas of the song, the opening line seems to have been inspired by a quote from Alastair SIM in one of Morrissey's favourite British comedies, THE HAPPIEST DAYS OF YOUR LIFE (see entry).

Musically, it stands as Whyte's most audacious theft from The Smiths' catalogue: compare its despondent cascade with Marr's sleight of hand at the close of 'PRETTY GIRLS MAKE GRAVES'. The song's recording process proved extremely laborious as, according to engineer Chris Dickie, each note of Whyte's arpeggiated melody was recorded on a separate track. 'It was so painstaking,' says Dickie. 'Every note had its own track to create this delicate gossamer guitar effect that Steve [LILLYWHITE] was after. Alain did the whole thing over and over, one note at a time. It took *forever*. Finally, we finished it and played it to Morrissey. He said, "That's nice, but it's in the wrong key." I nearly died. We had to do the entire thing all over again.'

As one of the more commercial ballads on the album, 'Hold On To Your Friends' was a fair choice for Vauxhall's second single but fared extremely badly, missing the top 40 altogether. Morrissey would later describe its failure as 'a terrible shock'. In truth, the record was poorly marketed with only one B-side on all formats ('MOONRIVER') and no accompanying video. Morrissey blamed the latter on Dirk BOGARDE's refusal to allow a proposed promo featuring clips from the 1950 Ealing drama *The Blue Lamp* co-starring Patric DOONAN. [4, 6, 217, 236, 290, 508]

Hollywood Bowl, Morrissey is particularly proud of the fact that on 8 August 1992, the 35,000 tickets for his two nights at Los Angeles' Hollywood Bowl on 10 and 11 October that year sold out in 23 minutes, smashing the previous record held by THE BEATLES. Fifteen years later, Morrissey returned to the venue on 8 June 2007. Eight tracks from the latter gig were compiled as the Live At The Hollywood Bowl CD, part of a UK limited edition of 2008's GREATEST HITS (a US edition featured nine tracks). A full concert DVD

of the same name was planned for October 2008 only to be withdrawn after Morrissey issued a statement on TRUE-TO-YOU.net, claiming he'd never been consulted and dismissing it as 'slapdash'. [92, 237]

Holmes, Sherlock, 'Very cosy, very English,

very drizzly and rainy and safe.' So Morrissey described the stories of Sir Arthur Conan Doyle's immortal fictional detective. 'I find them fascinating, really fascinating,' he added. Morrissey had a vested interest in the 80s Granada Television series *The Adventures Of Sherlock Holmes* starring Jeremy Brett since one episode had been filmed in 'Beechmount', the Victorian house he bought outside Manchester in the late 80s. The property can be seen in the episode The Norwood Builder, in which a young lawyer is accused of murdering a client. When Holmes investigates, he finds the real culprit (who's murdered a tramp as part of his cover-up), living in a secret room at the top of the house and proceeds to smoke him out: hence Morrissey's exaggerated and inaccurate description that, 'It was the episode where there's a tramp who is at the top of the house [and] for some reason he causes a fire in this attic loft and he goes on fire.' However, fans hoping for a sneaky glimpse of Morrissey's fixtures and fittings should be warned that, its period setting aside, the Holmes episode was filmed in 1984, several years before the singer took residence. Still, The Norwood Builder gives an indication of the sheer size of the house and its garden, the latter used for a 1989 NME photo session in which Morrissey posed with framed portraits of the NEW YORK DOLLS and Terence STAMP. [442, 567]

'Home Is A Question Mark' (Morrissey/

Whyte), Studio outtake from the YOU ARE THE QUARRY sessions, recorded in the autumn of 2003. Morrissey had previously used the title when interviewed in 2002 by Radio 2's Janice Long, who welcomed the singer 'home' to England. 'Home is a question mark,' was Morrissey's immediate reply, suggesting the phrase was already fully formed in his vocabulary. The song's only official mention was in January 2004 when TRUE-TO-YOU.NET announced it as one of 16 tracks recorded during the Quarry sessions (the other 15 have all surfaced). Being purely speculative, it's plausible the lyrics may have addressed his sense of identity as an Englishman displaced in Los Angeles, perhaps reiterating the 'cannot find a safety haven' conundrum expressed on the same album's 'LET ME KISS YOU'. [411]

homosexuality, It is a common mistake to

refer to Morrissey as being 'gay'. At no point in his career has he ever made such a statement which, in itself, is a violent contradiction of his strong personal beliefs against sexual stereotyping and the need to label his orientation as either hetero-, bi- or homosexual. 'Because it's limiting and restrictive,' he insisted.

In 1984, a journalist from America's *Rolling Stone* magazine wrote that Morrissey 'calls himself a "prophet for the fourth gender", admits that he's gay but adds that he's also celibate'. Morrissey was outraged, as much over the suggestion that he *admitted* to being gay as the accusation itself. In numerous follow-up interviews he denied that he'd ever said it ('absolute crap') but still refused to be drawn on clarifying his sexuality either way. 'I don't want to be slotted into any category like that in any way. Because it's pointless. I mean, all these terms and all these categories, they've not really proved to be of any value within music.'

His refusal to be pigeonholed by his sex is fundamental to the enigma of Morrissey (see also CELIBACY, SEX). But the issue of homosexuality is altogether more thorny and has, in the past, roused the depressing voice of latent homophobia among his critics in the press, also becoming the primary concern of some writers (including at least one alarming biographer) whose main agenda appears a futile attempt to 'out' Morrissey as if his entire career has been some form of mincing hoodwink on the general populace. On this, the specific 'gay issue', his determination not to be classified by his sexuality has, if only by accident, acted as an ingenious barometer of his audience and critics' own tolerance or prejudice, entirely unique within pop.

The majority of his audience, by now, care little whether Morrissey may or may not be homosexual. Some assume he is – perhaps wrongly – based on some of his less ambiguous lyrics (e.g. 'DEAR GOD PLEASE HELP ME') and what could be construed as a predilection for 'gay icons' – Oscar WILDE, James DEAN, Bette DAVIS, Shirley BASSEY, Radclyffe Hall, A. E. HOUSMAN, JOBRIATH, Parker TYLER et cetera, et cetera, et cetera. Others are content to leave the age-old mystery integral to his art and their adoration unsolved. Those who still persist in trying to pin down Morrissey's sexuality as being exclusively gay do so either purely for personal titillation (or as Morrissey himself has said, 'wish fulfilment') or, worse still, for vile motives as twisted and injurious as those of the Marquess of Queensberry himself.

By the same token, it would be equally wrong to remove Morrissey from gay culture. Like many teenagers who came of age during punk, he sometimes frequented gay pubs in Manchester though later confessed he found the local gay scene 'always atrocious'. The polysexual nature of his lyrics was also quite deliberate and, in print, he has always welcomed multiple interpretations from male, female, gay and straight perspectives. There is also much to be said not only for that same aforementioned gallery of gay heroes but also his long-running, often humorous, homoerotic symbolism on record sleeves, stage backdrops, in videos and in his physical live performance. From the naked male cover of 1983's 'HAND IN GLOVE' to his own marker-penned 'Your arse'n'all' backside inside 2008's GREATEST HITS, a quarter century later it should be blaringly obvious that Morrissey is not, as he might say, your average Tetley Bitter man. Without ever having to declare himself a fully-paid-up, card-carrying member, Morrissey has been warmly embraced by the homosexual community as a modern gay icon.

Those still confused, or perhaps obsessed, as to whether Morrissey really is 'gay' in the conventional sense would do well to bear in mind his answer to that direct question when asked in 1985. 'I'm not embarrassed about the word "gay" but it's not in the least bit relevant. I'm beyond that frankly.' [52, 73, 96, 119, 137, 138, 139, 196]

'Honey, You Know Where To Find Me'

(Morrissey/Boorer), Studio outtake from the 1995 SOUTHPAW GRAMMAR sessions, officially released on the 2009 redux reissue of the same album. As the title indicates, the lyrics are Morrissey's come-hither epistle to a lost love. 'I'm not gonna cry for the things that never occurred,' he sings, inviting his 'Honey' to find him in his usual place 'kicking away from the mundane' – Morrissey's sleeve notes for the album's 2009 re-release hinted that place was in fact The Good Mixer, his local Camden pub in the early 90s.

The song's genesis can be traced back to VAUXHALL AND I when the word 'Honey' was evidently at the forefront of Morrissey's vocabulary: a photo by Jake WALTERS on the inner sleeve of the 'HOLD ON TO YOUR FRIENDS' single shows a naked Morrissey with 'HONEY' written in ink around his left nipple. Originally, the lyrics had been assigned to a faster, lighter tune by Alain WHYTE for possible inclusion on Vauxhall itself. Any tensions between Whyte and Boorer over co-writer favouritism must surely have been brought to the surface when Morrissey decided to scrap Whyte's song only to exhume the title and lyrics the following year for Boorer's blissful acoustic canter which, with hindsight, definitely deserved a proper release at the time. [4, 40]

Housman, A. E. (Alfred Edward), English

Victorian poet whom Morrissey named as his favourite circa the release of MALADJUSTED in 1997. '[He is] the poet who means the most to me,' he explained. 'He had a 30-year gap between his poetry books, which is very interesting … they're really, really sad and really powerful but beautiful poems.' Housman's most famous work,

h

the 63-poem cycle *A Shropshire Lad*, also crops up in one of Morrissey's favourite films, YIELD TO THE NIGHT. During Morrissey's 1992 American tour promoting YOUR ARSENAL, a fan threw a copy of *A Shropshire Lad* on stage which guitarist Boz BOORER sometimes read from during the chaotic finale of 'THE NATIONAL FRONT DISCO'.

Housman himself was a deeply unhappy and fundamentally Mozzerian soul whose simple verses on death, lost loves and happiness doomed to end in tragedy resonated with Morrissey's own lyrics. Born a Worcestershire lad in 1859, his life was permanently scarred by the death of his mother when he was only 12. Winning a scholarship to Oxford to study Latin and Greek, he was said to have been 'arrogantly brilliant' only to mysteriously sabotage his final exam by handing in 'blank, or nearly blank, papers' and failing completely. It's possible his behaviour was affected by his unrequited love for a fellow student, Moses Jackson, a relationship which would dominate not only the rest of his life but also some of his most profound poetry.

After a period in the civil service, Housman managed to return to academia as a Cambridge lecturer, described as 'jealous of his privacy, a man of few friends … proud, taciturn and chilly'. He was 35 when he collected his first volume of poetry, originally titled *Poems By Terence Hearsay* but self-published (after several rejections) in 1896 as *A Shropshire Lad*. The cycle offered a nostalgic portrait of English rural life as enjoyed by young men fated to die overseas fighting for their country. With the outbreak of the Second Boer War in 1899, it became a bestseller.

Housman waited 26 years before he published a follow-up, 1922's *Last Poems*, so called because he believed his creative faculties were exhausted. After his death in 1936 his brother, the writer and dramatist Laurence Housman, released *More Poems* followed by *Additional Poems*. The latter collections contained verses directly relating to his homosexuality, including an impassioned critique of the persecution of Oscar WILDE (in which Housman euphemistically damned Victorian society for 'taking him to prison for the colour of his hair') and his own painful farewell to Jackson: 'Because I liked you better/Than suits a man to say/It irked you, and I promised/To throw the thought away.' [92, 111, 328, 422, 566]

'How Soon Is Now?' (Morrissey/Marr), First

released as the 12-inch B-side of 'WILLIAM, IT WAS REALLY NOTHING' (1984). Subsequently released as The Smiths' sixth single, February 1985, highest UK chart position #24. Cover star: Sean BARRETT.

The most famous Smiths recording, 'How Soon Is Now?' has achieved a popularity unique among their repertoire, the one track most likely to be embraced by those otherwise hostile to the group. The universal appeal of 'How Soon Is Now?' isn't so much to do with songwriting – Morrissey and Marr have written far greater *songs* – as sonic atmosphere. It's the actual *sound* of 'How Soon Is Now?' – that intoxicating,

'How Can Anybody Possibly Know How I Feel?' (Morrissey/Whyte), From the

album YOU ARE THE QUARRY (2004). Not so much a song as a belching rock tantrum, rarely has Morrissey expressed himself so bluntly, or so crudely. It says much that the line 'I am I' appears in the script of one of his favourite films, THE MEMBER OF THE WEDDING, within the confused and rambling outburst of a hysterical 12-year-old. 'How Can Anybody Possibly Know How I Feel?' is similarly adolescent in its emotional aggression, dismissing those who 'love' and 'respect' him as being 'insane', complaining of authority figures in 'smelly' uniforms and griping about the '15 miles of shit' he's been metaphorically dragged through. Another of Quarry's cathartic post-COURT CASE rages, it was by far the ugliest, over-labouring its point and lacking the saving grace of a memorable tune. [530]

voodoo shudder punctuated by those sliding miaows echoing into infinity – which has driven listeners gaga since it first appeared in 1984.

Seymour Stein, the head of their American label, Sire, famously hailed it 'the "Stairway To Heaven" of the 80s', an analogy which, while flattering to a degree in terms of epic comparison, is completely wrong. 'Stairway To Heaven' is a clumpy and pernickety folk-rock ballad. 'How Soon Is Now?' is, in essence, a club record. If anything, it's the 'I Feel Love' of the 80s. Or, more literally, 'I (Want To) Feel Love'.

Taking its title from a question in Marjorie Rosen's feminist film study POPCORN VENUS ('How soon is "now"?'), it sees Morrissey switch between self-pity and self-defensive anger as he describes his own sense of social isolation, majestically adapting a line from Chapter 12 of George ELIOT's masterpiece *Middlemarch*: 'To be born the son of a Middlemarch manufacturer, and inevitable heir to nothing in particular.' The lyrics amount to a dialogue between a withdrawn loner convinced they'll never find physical love and a friend, whose patronising optimism (that 'it' will happen 'now') and useless advice only serves to amplify their loneliness. The key passage – in many ways *the* passage which encapsulates Morrissey's entire lyrical agenda and the reason for The Smiths' existence – is the excruciatingly familiar description of going to a club in the futile hope of finding 'somebody' only to stand and leave 'on your own'.

Because of its unusual texture, markedly different to the jangly guitar backdrops Marr had provided so far, 'How Soon Is Now?' was the first Smiths record where the power of Morrissey's voice really stood out. His delivery is magnificent (whistling included), showing a confidence and control vastly superior to that heard on THE SMITHS album recorded less than a year earlier. But while Morrissey's lyrics were quintessentially Smiths in tone, the music set 'How Soon Is Now?' apart from everything else in their canon.

The genesis of Marr's 'groove' was an idea to imbibe the spirit of 60s swamp-rockers Creedence

Clearwater Revival, though his first source wasn't Creedence themselves but a 1982 cover of their 'Run Through The Jungle' by The Gun Club. Hoping to 'capture the same vibe', Marr recorded a demo at his Earls Court flat in the summer of 1984 which he nicknamed 'Swamp' before giving Morrissey a copy to work with. A week later at Jam studios in north London, after recording its original A-side, 'William, It Was Really Nothing', and accompanying B-side, 'PLEASE PLEASE PLEASE LET ME GET WHAT I WANT', Morrissey returned to his Kensington flat, leaving Marr, Rourke and Joyce to work on 'Swamp' with producer John PORTER.

'I remember us playing it for a while and really hoping we could make it sound like a Smiths track,' says Marr, 'because it might not have.' As an atmospheric encouragement, they replaced the studio's standard light bulbs with red ones to mellow the mood already softened by the producer's supply of 'vast quantities of weed'. 'I told them to play it as long as they needed,' says Porter. 'They did a good four or five minutes. I got two good takes and cut out the bits which weren't so good then chopped them together. That's why it ended up as long as it did.'

Marr was satisfied that, for all its weirdness, 'it did feel like The Smiths' but sensed it still needed something. 'So, I saw my opportunity to throw the tremolo part down,' he says. 'Something that I'd been looking to use for quite a while.' Marr's inspiration for the tremolo effect – the signature judder of 'How Soon Is Now?' – came from several different sources. Its earliest pioneer was Bo Diddley who patented the sound in 1955, thereafter making it his calling card. Marr also cites 'I Want More', a rare chart hit for Krautrock experimentalists Can (number 26, October 1976) and a favourite from his youth, Hamilton Bohannon's Diddley-esque 'Disco Stomp' (number six, July 1975). 'I was obsessed with that track,' he admits. 'I remember hearing it in the back of the car with my parents, driving back from Wales on a hot day. The sound of it really turned my head. So the tremolo on "How Soon Is Now?", altogether, was my boyhood love of "Disco Stomp", Can's "I

Want More" and then tying the whole thing together with the Bo Diddley bow, as it were.'

Those unconcerned with the technicalities of *how* the sound of 'How Soon Is Now?' was created can skip this paragraph. For the rest, I'll try and describe it in as jargon-free an explanation as possible. What you hear isn't the sound of the guitar as Marr played it at the time. To begin with, he recorded a normal rhythm guitar part with no effects whatsoever. Once that was done, he and Porter each took control of two guitar amplifiers (Fender Twin Reverbs) which had their own tremolo control knobs. Marr's effect-free guitar track was then played back through the four amplifiers while he and Porter twiddled their respective tremolo controls back and forth to create its hallucinogenic magma: a laborious manual process which meant that whenever their tremolos went out of sync they had to stop the tape and start again. So what you hear on 'How Soon Is Now?' is actually two very patient men – possibly stoned men at that – twiddling amplifiers under red light bulbs. Modern sampling methods would've achieved the same effect in half the time but, doubtless, a fraction of the fun.

Marr's sense of adventurism on 'How Soon Is Now?' is highlighted by his inclusion of a private homage to a genre his writing partner would later describe as 'a great musical stench'. The high-pitched harmonic riff Marr drops in occasionally (you first hear it after the 'you want to die' chorus at around 3.11) is lifted from the keyboard hook of 'You've Gotta Believe', a 1982 single by rap pioneer Lovebug Starski, one of the claimants to inventing the term 'hip hop' (Morrissey's aforementioned 'stench'). Seven months before recording 'How Soon Is Now?', Marr met Starski when The Smiths played a mildly disastrous show at New York's Danceteria on New Year's Eve, 1983. 'Afterwards we were all a bit bugged out,' he explains. 'He came over and was very nice and took care of me. I was really excited by that music. I'd heard his records in Manchester but he was still this pretty obscure hip hop guy. So to suddenly be there in New York and meet him, at

the time, I was like, "Whoa! There he is! Lovebug Starski!" So that bit in "How Soon Is Now?" is a motif he'd used that I thought was unusual and appropriate, so long as it worked. Which it did.'

Once the backing track was completed, Porter posted a cassette through Morrissey's letterbox on his way home from the studio. The next day, the singer laid down his vocal, finalising its transition from 'Swamp' to 'How Soon Is Now?' As Porter likes to recount, during the first run he thought Morrissey was singing about the elements (hearing 'I am the *sun*, and the *air*'). The producer was so enthused with the track, rightly convinced that they'd 'broken new ground', that he called ROUGH TRADE boss Geoff Travis to the studio that night to hear it. 'I could tell Geoff didn't like it very much,' Porter claims. 'He kept looking at me constantly and I could sense him thinking, "What the fuck is this?" I was very disappointed by Geoff. I got the vibe that he thought I was pushing them in a direction which he didn't want them to go in. So, in the end, they threw it away. Rough Trade shot themselves in the foot.'

The fact that 'How Soon Is Now?' was originally issued as a 12-inch bonus does, now, seem ludicrous. However, in Rough Trade's defence it ought to be noted that the high standard of The Smiths' B-sides was such that, at the time, it wasn't regarded as the absurd oversight history has since recorded. The label's real mistake was to backtrack too late. Five months after appearing on the 'William' 12-inch, and two months after its second outing on the HATFUL OF HOLLOW compilation, Rough Trade pressured the group to belatedly re-release 'How Soon Is Now?' as their sixth single in February 1985. They defended the move by referring to a European issue of the single, released as an A-side in Holland instead of 'William', which they claimed fans were being forced to pay 'extortionate prices' for: a UK release was, by their reckoning, a charitable substitution.

Unfortunately, on its own terms 'How Soon Is Now?' wasn't a great chart success, peaking at a disappointing number 24. Equally confusing was its release the same month as MEAT IS MURDER. As Morrissey later explained, their desire to precede their second album with a spin-off single (contenders included 'I WANT THE ONE I CAN'T HAVE', 'NOWHERE FAST' and 'BARBARISM BEGINS AT HOME', the latter already issued as a radio-only promo) was overruled by Rough Trade's dogged insistence to compensate for their previous indecision by reissuing 'How Soon Is Now?' The singer was equally unhappy when the track was added to the US version of Meat Is Murder, an amendment carried forth by all CD reissues of the album to this day, while its apparently 'unauthorised' US video caused him further grief.

For all Rough Trade's original bungling, 'How Soon Is Now?' would transcend the confusion of its release history to become The Smiths' populist 'rock anthem': used to sell Pepe Jeans on a 1988 television commercial ('Which nobody remembers,' sighed Morrissey in 2007); sampled as the basis of 'Hippy Chick', the one hit by UK pop/dance collective Soho (number eight, February 1991); and a posthumous, and respectable, number 16 hit for The Smiths themselves when reissued by Warners in September 1992 to promote the Best I compilation (the single sleeve, not designed by Morrissey, featured a still of Vanessa Redgrave and David Hemmings from the 1966 film *Blow-Up*).

Among the song's most notable cover versions was that by The Psychedelic Furs' offshoot Love Spit Love, recorded for the soundtrack of the 1996 witchcraft drama *The Craft* and subsequently used as the theme tune to the far fluffier teen witchcraft series *Charmed*. A 2000 version by Snake River Conspiracy was allegedly endorsed by Morrissey as 'better than the original' though after seeing the group play live in LA he'd admit to being less certain. He was also less impressed than amused by the 2003 cover by 'fake Russian lesbian' duo t.A.T.u. 'I love the way they sing, "I am a yeoman and I need to be loved",' joked Morrissey. 'A yeoman is a small farmer from the 1700s, isn't it? I had no idea that song was all about small farmers.'

A final important footnote to 'How Soon Is Now?', and the great irony of its popularity, was The Smiths' inability to convincingly pull it off in concert. For their last two years as a touring group, Marr tried repeatedly with various tremolo and delay pedals to re-create the original sound but rarely succeeded, even when assisted by Craig GANNON. As Rourke notes, seconded by Marr, the song became 'the bane of our live career … we never got it right'. After The Smiths, Marr was first to perform 'How Soon Is Now?' in concert with Crowded House singer Neil Finn when touring America in 2002. Two years later, Morrissey added it to his setlist, his band's heavy, stuttering guitars strangely reminiscent of the Love Spit Love/*Charmed* version (as heard on LIVE AT EARLS COURT). Its most historic post-Smiths performance to date was at the January 2006 Manchester v. Cancer charity concert at Manchester's MEN Arena, organised by Andy Rourke, which saw Marr play (and sing) 'How Soon Is Now?' joined by Rourke on bass – a 50 per cent Smiths reunion.
[12, 13, 17, 27, 71, 207, 232, 308, 363]

Hulmerist, Morrissey's first solo video compilation, released June 1990. See Mozography appendix for full tracklisting.

The basis for *Hulmerist* – a reference to the Manchester district Hulme where Morrissey lived as a child before moving to Stretford and pronounced 'hume' as in 'humorist', hence the pun – was his December 1988 WOLVERHAMPTON gig, filmed by friend and video director Tim Broad with the intention of releasing it in its entirety as a live concert film. Due to the chaotic nature of the event, which greatly affected the quality of Morrissey's vocal performance, *Hulmerist* was reconfigured as a more straightforward compilation of Morrissey's first six single promos, also by Broad, using the best Wolverhampton footage as linking material and with the added bonus of one full track from the concert, 'SISTER I'M A POET'. The scenes of Morrissey/Smiths apostles queuing up outside Wolverhampton Civic Hall before the gig are a priceless time capsule of the hysterical fandom he attracted at that time and the near-biblical expectations of the show itself. More than the actual promos, it's this documentary element which makes *Hulmerist* such enjoyable and essential viewing.

Hynde, Chrissie, Ohio-born singer/song-writer with The Pretenders, female rock icon and prolific animal rights campaigner who would befriend, and record with, both Morrissey and Johnny Marr after The Smiths.

Hynde moved to London from Ohio in 1973 hoping to start a band. Already in her early twenties, she feared she'd already missed her chance and, with the help of journalist Nick Kent, became a writer for the NME. The teenage Morrissey would most likely have read Hynde's interview with ROXY MUSIC's Andy Mackay (promoting his In Search Of Eddie Riff album, later the source of a Morrissey hotel check-in pseudonym) and her steamy encounter with a porn-fixated Brian ENO and his shaved pubis. 'I never meant to be a writer,' says Hynde. 'I was offered the job and it wasn't my thing. I ended up doing some interviews and I didn't know what I was talking about. I felt very self-conscious. I knew I was crap.'

By the time punk arrived in 1976, the 25-year-old Hynde had given up on journalism, briefly working as an assistant in Malcolm McLaren and Vivienne Westwood's King's Road clothing store SEX but mostly walking around town with her guitar, approaching total strangers at bus stops and asking if they wanted to be in a band. 'I felt like a total fucking loser,' explains Hynde. 'It was awful. I can remember getting on the Underground with a bottle of wine and just going from one end of the station to the other and just crying because I had nothing to do. But I had a philosophy that maybe I didn't know *what* I wanted to do, but I knew what I *didn't* want to do. And then I focused on what I really did want to do and tried to get a band together. At that point I became pretty unstoppable because I didn't have anything and I didn't want anything, so nothing was holding me back. It was just a matter of finding the right guys.'

After many false starts – from Masters Of The Backside (an early incarnation of The Damned) to

'Human Being' (Johnny Thunders/David Johansen), B-side of 'YOU HAVE KILLED ME' (2006). Although previously Morrissey had covered the NEW YORK DOLLS' 'TRASH' and an excerpt from 'SUBWAY TRAIN' in concert, 'Human Being' marked his first studio recording of one of their songs. The original closed the Dolls' second album, 1974's Too Much, Too Soon, with singer David Johansen declaring himself to be 'a riff-raff human being' over a gloriously scuzzy Johnny Thunders riff. In his 1981 book on the Dolls, Morrissey praised Johansen's '[plea] for acceptance' as saying 'more for psycho-sexual misunderstandings than [*child psychologist*] Bruno Bettelheim ever could'. As Johansen told the press at the time, the song was his address to those who'd branded the group as social outcasts, adding, 'We don't want our fans to think we're weird or anything.'

Twenty-two years after he'd declared himself human and in need of love on 'HOW SOON IS NOW?', 'Human Being' allowed Morrissey to reiterate the point with slight amendments to both Johansen's lyrics and the original vocal melody. As with the Dolls' version, there was knowing irony in Morrissey's delivery, especially taking into account his comments to the press only two years earlier that, 'I'm not really that hot on the human race to be honest. Very few people have anything to offer.' Though the opening verse featured a more hesitant tempo, the bulk of Morrissey's interpretation was a straight copy of the original (right down to the saxophone part at the end) albeit lacking the Dolls' feverish energy. As such, 'Human Being' was pure fannish indulgence on Morrissey's part as he'd more or less admit on stage when playing it during the RINGLEADER OF THE TORMENTORS tour. [151, 277, 343]

Steve Strange's appalling anonymous shock-punks The Moors Murderers – the right guys eventually turned up in the shape of three gifted and eager musicians from Hereford: bassist Pete Farndon, guitarist James Honeyman Scott and drummer Martin Chambers. With the formidable Hynde out front – a tomboyish siren blinded by eyeliner with a cat-call voice caught between purr and miaow – they became The Pretenders. Their February 1979 debut single, a cover of The Kinks' 'Stop Your Sobbing' written by Hynde's future partner Ray Davies, reached the lower 30s, as did Hynde's original follow-up, 'Kid'. The latter became a favourite of the then 15-year-old Johnny Marr who'd first admire, then mimic, the spangling skills of Honeyman Scott in his Wythenshawe bedroom.

With their third single, the stunningly sultry 'Brass In Pocket' – the first new UK number one of the 1980s – The Pretenders positioned themselves as chart rivals to the likes of Blondie and The Police at the forefront of mainstream newwave pop. Other hits followed throughout '80 and '81 until the group was dramatically blown apart by the consecutive fatal overdoses of Honeyman Scott in June 1982, then Farndon in April 1983. Thereafter, Hynde and Chambers kept The Pretenders going with a rotating cast of guitarists and bassists, scoring equal hits and misses.

In the meantime, Hynde remained blissfully oblivious to The Smiths – despite vain attempts by her then-husband, Simple Minds' Jim Kerr, to get her to listen to THE QUEEN IS DEAD – until after they'd split up in 1987. In need of a new Pretenders guitarist following the departure of Robbie McIntosh, Hynde's manager recommended Marr. 'I said "Johnny Who? OK, whatever,"' laughs Hynde. 'So a couple of days later my doorbell goes. I didn't know if Johnny Marr was six foot tall, blond or anything. I didn't even know what he looked like. So I opened the door and there was me and Johnny and as soon as we looked at each other we felt as if we were in a band together. It was just amazing.' As Hynde describes it, the pair spent the afternoon rolling

spliffs before deciding to go to the Marquee club in Soho. 'We were watching this band and we both looked at each other at the same time and said, "This sucks! Let's go smoke some dope." So we left the Marquee and went down an alley and rolled some more spiffs, went back to my house and he played me a demo of his which sounded just like an early Pretenders song. It was just like we were absolutely smitten with each other right from the start. It was fantastic and we were really into this thing of being in a band together. It didn't last long but it was fucking great while it lasted.'

Bearing in mind Marr's teenage love of the group (not to mention the uncanny Smithsian jangle to Hynde's 1983 Christmas single '2000 Miles'), it was by no means unusual that he should join The Pretenders, regardless of their mainstream pedigree which upset only the most narrowminded indie purists. Unfortunately, in his postSmiths independence, Marr oversubscribed himself by committing to Hynde at the same time as he'd committed to Matt Johnson's The The. 'We did a bit of touring and stuff,' explains Hynde, 'but Johnny had his own thing going on and I felt like he started jerking me about a little bit. I was totally burnt out from touring and he was raring to go. The chemistry was already a bit wonky. And he was also playing on the side with [The The] so he'd come in off his face from the night before, pretending that he'd just arrived and was bright-eyed and bushy-tailed. So the whole thing went down fast.' Marr's recorded output with The Pretenders amounted to just one single in November 1988, a cover of the Bacharach/David song 'Windows Of The World' from the soundtrack to the film *1969*. It failed to chart.

Three years passed before Hynde's next exSmith encounter in early 1991. 'I'd never met Morrissey but out of the blue he sent me a note,' she explains. 'It said, "I'm staying in London in this hotel under the name of so and so." Eddie Riff? It could have been. So anyway I went and met him and, again, there was a weird fascination and some kind of a bond. I never quite knew what it was, but I just loved taking him out and going around

London, trawling all these old pubs and working men's clubs. I don't know what he saw in me.'

Whatever Morrissey did see in Hynde – at the very least a hardcore ally in the fight against animal cruelty – was sufficient to earn her a backing vocalist spot on 'MY LOVE LIFE' and guest appearance as one of the 50s rock and roll dancers in the video for 'SING YOUR LIFE'. Hynde returned the compliment by recording a cover of 'EVERYDAY IS LIKE SUNDAY'. Prior to its belated release on the soundtrack to 1995 film *Boys On The Side*, Morrissey told the press it was 'astonishingly good'. 'Oh, he fucking loved it, man,' confirms Hynde. 'He had it in his car and he played it nonstop. It was a good version. Fuck, it was a *great* version.' Spookily, the recording of The Pretenders' 'Everyday Is Like Sunday' also saw Hynde's third ex-Smith encounter. 'Andy Rourke played on that. We got him in to do some session work and he was a great bass player. I told him, "Andy, you're as underrated as Johnny is overrated." He loved me for that.'

In April 1999, following the death of Linda MCCARTNEY, Hynde persuaded Marr to sing 'MEAT IS MURDER' with The Pretenders at an all-star memorial concert at London's Royal Albert Hall. A close friend of McCartney's daughter, Stella (they've been spotted at Morrissey concerts together), Hynde continues to promote veganism and, like Morrissey, is an active member of PETA. 'Morrissey pretty much keeps himself to himself,' says Hynde. 'I can still drag him out of his hole for an animal rights thing now and again but he tends to come in and out of my life at the oddest times.'

One such odd time was 2004 when Morrissey tentatively suggested Hynde as a guitarist for the NEW YORK DOLLS prior to their re-formation for his MELTDOWN festival. Had she agreed, he'd already decided she'd be called 'Chrissie Thunders'. Four years later, Morrissey asked her to sing backing vocals on his 2009 B-side 'SHAME IS THE NAME', recorded the previous year in Los Angeles. 'Driving around with Morrissey, what a fucking *riot* it is,' says Hynde. 'The last thing you expect is to be in a sports car in LA with him driving. With his bedsit image of this lonely creature, surrounded by thousands of cars and they're "beep-beep!" with all these Man. United fans. They all see him and know him and come out with scarves and stuff. Astonishing. We've had some moments.' [11, 17, 19, 40, 74, 217]

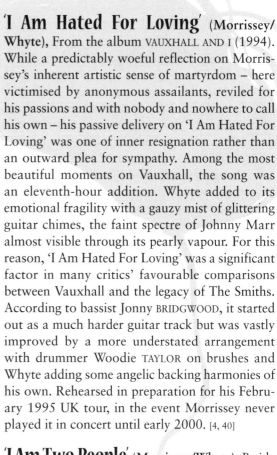

'I Am Hated For Loving' (Morrissey/ Whyte), From the album VAUXHALL AND I (1994). While a predictably woeful reflection on Morrissey's inherent artistic sense of martyrdom – here victimised by anonymous assailants, reviled for his passions and with nobody and nowhere to call his own – his passive delivery on 'I Am Hated For Loving' was one of inner resignation rather than an outward plea for sympathy. Among the most beautiful moments on Vauxhall, the song was an eleventh-hour addition. Whyte added to its emotional fragility with a gauzy mist of glittering guitar chimes, the faint spectre of Johnny Marr almost visible through its pearly vapour. For this reason, 'I Am Hated For Loving' was a significant factor in many critics' favourable comparisons between Vauxhall and the legacy of The Smiths. According to bassist Jonny BRIDGWOOD, it started out as a much harder guitar track but was vastly improved by a more understated arrangement with drummer Woodie TAYLOR on brushes and Whyte adding some angelic backing harmonies of his own. Rehearsed in preparation for his February 1995 UK tour, in the event Morrissey never played it in concert until early 2000. [4, 40]

'I Am Two People' (Morrissey/Whyte), B-side of 'LET ME KISS YOU' (2004). Shortly before this track's release, Morrissey was asked about his astrological birth sign of GEMINI, symbolised by twins. 'I am two people,' he replied. 'One gregarious and one impossibly shy.' A few months later came this, an ostensible theme song to that duality. Tortured by self-loathing and unable to reconcile his 'two faces', Morrissey spurns the object of his love, wishing that 'one or the other of us' would die. Sadly, such lyrical hysteria fell flat on the back of a duff, assembly-line Alain Whyte tune and the singer's unusually horrible yodelling delivery. [119]

I Believe In You, 1952 Ealing Studios drama which Morrissey once named as his joint favourite film alongside David Lean's OLIVER TWIST. Made in response to the success of Ealing's previous police drama *The Blue Lamp* (starring

Dirk BOGARDE and Patric DOONAN), *I Believe In You* is a similar study in post-war crime and the court system. The plot centres around an oafish middle-aged probation officer, Phipps (Cecil Parker), and his more experienced colleague played by Celia Johnson, who between them attempt to keep various young offenders on the straight and narrow. The supporting cast of tearaways includes a young Laurence Harvey and an even younger Joan Collins. The film is typical of Morrissey's taste in the more obscure examples of vintage British cinema as well as his fascination with juvenile crime, a recurring theme in many of his lyrics. [207, 512]

'I Can Have Both' (Morrissey/Boorer), B-side of 'ALMA MATTERS' (1997).

Perusing the 'treats' on display in a shop window, Morrissey tries to convince himself he can choose more than one of his desires while haunted by flashbacks of a 'small shy boy' brainwashed into believing he could only decide either or. Ostensibly, 'I Can Have Both' was a liberated admission of bisexuality, and a deliberately frolicsome one at that; not least the camp innuendo, 'I've not been feeling myself tonight.' Originally selected for inclusion on MALADJUSTED, in the final stages Morrissey removed it from the running order in favour of the Spencer COBRIN co-penned 'WIDE TO RECEIVE', much to the dismay of Boz Boorer whose Smithsesque sun-drenched jingle was among his best of the period. Released, instead, as an excellent B-side, 'I Can Have Both' thereby avoided the scrutiny of album reviewers who doubtless would have boldly highlighted its implied sexual symbolism. The 2009 redux reissue of Maladjusted made amends for its original exclusion with Morrissey going as far as to hail it one of his 'favourite songs' in the accompanying sleeve note. [4]

'I Don't Mind If You Forget Me' (Morrissey/Street), From the album VIVA HATE (1988).

Another of the more transparent allusions to the break-up of The Smiths featured on Morrissey's solo debut, it was nigh but impossible to hear this barbed farewell to a partner who felt 'the pressure to change, to move on' and not apply it to Johnny Marr. Far from not minding if he's been forgotten, Morrissey ends the song confused and annoyed to have been rejected by somebody he now considers a 'fool'. Though one of the album's weaker tracks, it still contained one of Morrissey's more wittily original rhyming couplets: 'Your mild "best wishes"/They make me suspicious.' Street's perky design was conceived as 'Motown meets the BUZZCOCKS' and plainly bore such origins with its Supremes-style rhythm and its minimal two-note guitar break – so minimal Street played it himself as Vini REILLY refused. [25, 39]

'I Don't Owe You Anything' (Morrissey/Marr), From the album THE SMITHS (1984).

Supposedly written with Sandie SHAW in mind, 'I Don't Owe You Anything' would later be used to successfully entice Shaw into working with The Smiths, releasing her own version as the B-side of her 1984 cover of 'HAND IN GLOVE'. Nevertheless, the lyrics seemed typical of Morrissey's early autobiographical vignettes, a coy demand for sexual gratification from a reluctant partner 'bought on stolen wine'.

Written in April 1983, early rehearsals were extraordinarily long, ending with an additional verse where Morrissey vows to 'forget tonight, and I will, as will you'. The narrative enticement to 'go out tonight' presaged the later 'THIS CHARMING MAN' while it may also be the case that the title was another of Morrissey's Shelagh DELANEY steals after 'I don't owe you a thing' from *A Taste Of Honey*.

Marr's unanxious tune emitted a distinct 60s aroma, if not *explicitly* Sandie Shaw then in mood and melody not so terribly far from some of her more soulful ballads by Chris Andrews. By the time The Smiths recorded it for their second attempt at their debut album, Morrissey had added a subtle but vital inflexion in his vocal melody. Producer John PORTER added organ to the arrangement, courtesy of Paul Carrack, in an attempt to 'bring colour' to a song he otherwise considered too linear and lacking in variety. Such

'I Don't Want Us To Finish' (Morrissey/ Street), 1987 demo recording by Morrissey and Stephen Street and an early candidate for VIVA HATE. The lyrics are not known, but since it was written in August/September 1987 just as The Smiths broke up it would be logical to assume that the 'Us' of the title is Morrissey and Marr. According to Street, it belonged to a whole batch of songs written at the beginning of his partnership with Morrissey in the autumn of 1987, soon jettisoned as they came up with superior contenders. These other early sketches include 'LIFEGUARD ON DUTY', 'SAFE WARM LANCASHIRE HOME', 'TREAT ME LIKE A HUMAN BEING' and 'PLEASE HELP THE CAUSE AGAINST LONELINESS'. If nothing else, the existence of 'I Don't Want Us To Finish' confirms Morrissey's preoccupation with, and grief over, the end of The Smiths while creating Viva Hate, still evident in more subtle lyrics and song titles on the finished album. [39]

perhaps sentimental contrivances seemed apt in view of its contagious romanticism and clear torch song objectives.

As is minor Smiths legend, the song *almost* reduced Mike Joyce to tears on stage at London's Dingwalls in August 1983. This detail may have some bearing on Morrissey's subsequent revelation in 2005 that 'I Don't Owe You Anything' was one of the few he'd written which now made him 'shudder' and, to date, is the only Smiths song he's officially disowned. [12, 17, 27, 124, 241, 369, 544]

'I Have Forgiven Jesus' (Morrissey/Whyte),

Morrissey's 28th solo single (from the album YOU ARE THE QUARRY), released December 2004, highest UK chart position #10. As early as 1984, during The Smiths' first flush of success, Morrissey spoke of the 'detrimental influence' of his Catholic schooling. 'It always seemed to me entirely wrong to inflict all these foul, ugly images on to children,' he complained. 'Serpents being trampled underfoot with fire coming out of their nostrils and things like that. This constant fear of whatever you do you're wrong, guilty. I despised that.'

Twenty years later, 'I Have Forgiven Jesus' was Morrissey's revenge, of sorts, against the religion which inflicted that damage, though instead of attacking those who implemented such repressive teachings he speaks directly to Jesus himself. Contrasting his innocent boyhood 'with a nice paper round' – Morrissey had previously admitted he had indeed been a paper boy – against his

'self-deprecating' adult self, he dares to forgive Christ for instilling him with physical needs and desires which his Catholic guilt prevents him from realising. As a calculated piece of pop blasphemy, it was an ingenious lyric, not without humour in its diary rundown of the week where 'Thursday is pathetic'.

It helped that 'I Have Forgiven Jesus' boasted a near-Biblical arrangement, a pious Mellotron murmur summoning strength to shake its fist up to heaven. Morrissey's delivery was also his best overall vocal performance on Quarry, veering from saintly remorse ('Oh, pretty one') to mental anguish ('Do you hate me?'). Though a potentially controversial single choice – especially with its accompanying video of Morrissey in full Catholic priest garb, a uniform he also wore during concerts of the period – 'I Have Forgiven Jesus' rewarded him with a defiant top ten hit during Christmas week 2004. [408, 448]

'I Just Want To See The Boy Happy'

(Morrissey/Tobias), Morrissey's 33rd solo single (from the album RINGLEADER OF THE TORMENTORS), released December 2006, highest UK chart position #16. The last of three tracks on Ringleader in which Morrissey directly addressed the Almighty (after 'DEAR GOD PLEASE HELP ME' and 'ON THE STREETS I RAN'), there was an intriguingly paternal sentiment to the song's dying plea that the boy of the title be granted eternal happiness. Typically, this becomes a grand gesture of self-martyrdom, the singer surrendering the life he considers worthless in order that his altruistic 'final dream' be realised. A cloggy if tolerable Tobias rocker, 'I Just Want To See The Boy Happy' was among the more superfluous tracks on the album, sounding like a refried 'THE YOUNGEST WAS THE MOST LOVED' and distinguished only by its Mariachi trumpet finish.

'I Keep Mine Hidden' (Morrissey/Marr), B-side of 'GIRLFRIEND IN A COMA' (1987). The last song Morrissey and Marr wrote and recorded together, 'I Keep Mine Hidden' therefore marks the official end of The Smiths.

After five years of poetry, grandeur, melodrama and sublimity, their final bow wasn't some profoundly melancholic torch song but a jaunty one minute 57 second music-hall knees-up: 'SHEILA TAKE A BOW' in miniature with added whistling. Yet given the autobiographical nature of Morrissey's lyrics, it's impossible not to scrutinise 'I Keep Mine Hidden' for insight into his state of mind at a time when – surely – he knew his relationship with Marr had run its course. Written on the first day of their final session at the Streatham studio of soundman Grant Showbiz, it finds Morrissey simultaneously excusing an inability to convey his emotions while envying the freedom of another who allows theirs to 'flail into public view'. Mike Joyce speculates that the 'yellow and green stumbling block' may be a reference to the singer's medication at the time (yellow and green are the colour of temazepam capsules, a prescription antidepressant), while Morrissey also hints at the scars of a repressed upbringing. His final groan is even more cryptic: 'use your loaf' (i.e. 'use your head').

As its producer, Showbiz was particularly struck by the song and what he perceived as a candid confession of psychological unbalance. 'I thought "I Keep Mine Hidden" was extraordinary,' enthuses Showbiz. 'He was going somewhere with that, somewhere really confessional. There are very few songs where Morrissey says "This is me", but I think that was a very personal song. A very direct song from Morrissey to Johnny.'

'Did I take notice of the lyrics? Well, through one ear,' says Marr. 'But if anybody was trying to keep me around at the time, a redraft might have been advisable.' The session itself was a regrettable finale to The Smiths' career, also resulting in the much-reviled Cilla BLACK cover 'WORK IS A FOUR-LETTER WORD', another abortive cover of Elvis PRESLEY's 'A FOOL SUCH AS I' which never saw the light of day and a couple of incomplete instrumental tracks. While Marr dismisses the entire fruits of the session as 'sounding like the work of impostors', as the last song he and Morrissey collaborated on he reserves some tiny grain of affection for 'I Keep Mine Hidden'. 'The chord change and the solo had some beauty in it,' he admits, 'but I wouldn't say I like it.'

Morrissey finished his vocal for 'I Keep Mine Hidden' on 19 May 1987, three days before his 28th birthday: the last time he and Marr saw one another for many years. The singer later confessed that in the aftermath of their break-up he still listened to The Smiths often and 'I Keep Mine Hidden' in particular. '[It] was the last song Johnny and I wrote together and the last song The Smiths recorded together,' he explained. 'And it's the one that makes me feel the happiest.' [13, 17, 19, 32, 33, 138]

'I Knew I Was Next' (Morrissey/Tobias), B-side of 'YOU HAVE KILLED ME' (2006). Morrissey cruises on auto-pilot in this predictably defeatist lament: he is nothing but 'a decent skin' staggering through life; everybody hates him; when he's dead they'll realise he wasn't all bad; and he's had so many bruisings that another one (he knows it's coming next) won't make a blind bit of difference. Producer TONY VISCONTI did his best to enliven Jesse Tobias's cold-semolina tune with brass and organ flourishes but, at best, 'I Knew I Was Next' is a strictly mediocre B-side.

'I Know It's Gonna Happen Someday' (Morrissey/Nevin), From the album YOUR ARSENAL (1992). Shortly after the release of KILL UNCLE,

Mark Nevin sent Morrissey a fresh batch of demos in the hope of co-writing the bulk of its follow-up, jokingly codenamed 'Kill Auntie'. None impressed the singer more than a slow ballad he'd provisionally titled 'French Epic'. 'Today, "French Epic" introduced a new joy to my life,' wrote Morrissey in an enthusiastic letter of reply. 'I've listened to it so much that I've actually lost my eyesight. Three rubber bed sheets later I conclude that you have written your best ever. Please bear in mind I was certified insane during flower power.'

By the time the recording of Your Arsenal began, Nevin had been usurped by Alain WHYTE as Morrissey's main collaborator, though 'French Epic' would survive to take its place on the album as the golden glimmering 'I Know It's Gonna Happen Someday'. Notwithstanding the equally emotive 'I'VE CHANGED MY PLEA TO GUILTY', it probably *was* Nevin's 'best ever' Morrissey song. His original 'French Epic' demo featuring random short-wave radio interference became the basis of the final recording which Nevin still took part in, borrowing a 12-string guitar for the occasion from Louise Goffin (daughter of Brill Building songwriters Carole King and Gerry Goffin).

Such was its irrepressible chest-heaving passion that Morrissey needed only supply the simplest of words, beseeching an unknown love not to lose faith in the impossible. Amid his habitually pessimistic tracts on the likelihood of finding true love, it remains a rare instance of romantic optimism. As Morrissey reaches out to the listener with a reassuring grasp, it's apt that in searching for an appropriate climax the tune should slip through space and time to crash-land on stage at the Hammersmith Apollo in 1973 just as BOWIE screams 'Give me your hands!' in 'Rock 'N' Roll Suicide'. The presence of producer and ex-Spiders guitarist Mick RONSON probably helped, even if Nevin insists that his revival of Bowie's 'won-der-ful' crest and fall was entirely unconscious. 'Mick was in hospital the day we did that bit,' explains Nevin, 'but when he came back he was listening to it and he looked over at me right at that bit. I

could feel him thinking, "Hang on. Isn't this 'Rock 'N' Roll Suicide'?" But he was far too nice and polite to say it.'

Morrissey concurred that the same Bowie homage was 'an absolute accident' and would later insist 'it was Mick who added the "Rock 'N' Roll Suicide" tag'. Events took an even stranger twist when Bowie himself decided to cover the track on his 1993 album Black Tie, White Noise. 'It occurred to me [that he] was possibly spoofing one of my earlier songs,' explained Bowie, 'and I thought, I'm not going to let him get away with that.' Rather than 'spoof' Morrissey's version of himself, Bowie decided it would be better to 'do it the way I would have done it in 1974-ish', omitting the 'Rock 'N' Roll Suicide' coda and lending it a gospel treatment more in keeping with Young Americans than the track's original Ziggy Stardust influence. Bowie invited him to hear the finished article at The Hit Factory studio in New York. Morrissey arrived with best friend Linder STERLING and was played the track at deafening volume. 'Linder and I just sat there sobbing with joy,' recalled Morrissey, 'because she knew me when I was a pitiful 17-year-old when I could live for a fortnight on 75p.'

It's easy to understand just how profound a moment that must have been for Morrissey: to hear one of his main musical inspirations sing one of his songs back at him, the words 'I know it's gonna happen someday' a poignant reminder of the desperate dreams of his own bleak youth. 'David was a bit nasty to me later on,' added Morrissey, referring to the fall-out from their abortive 1995 tour together, 'but I was very grateful for that moment in New York.' [22, 45, 84, 217, 221, 568]

'I Know It's Over' (Morrissey/Marr), From the album THE QUEEN IS DEAD (1986). 'This was something that The Smiths were always threatening to do,' recalls Marr. 'A big melancholic torch ballad, but still DIY, still post-punk. Not an overblown production but still heavily loaded with emotion. "I Know It's Over" is something only *we* could have done.'

Among the indisputable leviathans of the Morrissey/Marr songbook, for a great many fans 'I Know It's Over' is second only to 'THERE IS A LIGHT THAT NEVER GOES OUT' as the perfect Smiths ballad. More accurately, as Marr believes, the song was 'the precursor' to what *would* be the ultimate Smiths ballad, 'LAST NIGHT I DREAMT THAT SOMEBODY LOVED ME'. Lyrically, 'I Know It's Over' shares elements with both the aforementioned: the former's suicidal overtones, the latter's agonising diary of one too many mornings waking up alone (a theme also tackled in the earlier 'ASLEEP'). Still, it would be wrong, as some have, to call it The Smiths' 'bleakest' song. The sincerity of Morrissey's emotional anguish is unquestionable, but even its opening line – calling for his mother as he hears the first shovel of earth drumming upon his coffin lid – while astonishingly dismal still contains a crumb of black comedy, especially if considered in the same context as 'Mother, What'll I Do Now?' by George FORMBY (a favourite lyricist of Morrissey's during this period).

Between its author's obvious depression, 'I Know It's Over' retains some hope in its message, that being 'gentle and kind' is a noble trait requiring rare courage, and that love is 'natural and real', even if not for Morrissey whose unfulfilled heart's desire is further tormented by the sight of 'loutish lovers' taking their partners for granted. Even so, the song does contain a disabling emotional hammer blow in its final verse as the love he's chasing taunts Morrissey with some home truths, a dialogue which forces the listener to undergo the same interrogation as to 'Why are you on your own tonight?' By addressing his audience so precisely, it's one of the most intimate passages Morrissey's ever written and it's for this reason so many have taken 'I Know It's Over' to their hearts with such reverential awe.

Though Marr states the song was 'written' together with Morrissey at his house in Bowdon one late summer's evening in 1985 – the same night as 'There Is A Light That Never Goes Out' and 'FRANKLY, MR SHANKLY' – Marr never heard Morrissey's full lyrics until the moment of recording for The Queen Is Dead; as was Smiths custom, the backing track was recorded first before adding vocals. When he did, Marr was floored by his partner's brilliance. 'It was a definite moment in time,' he recalls. 'That song was something that could only have been done then.' Morrissey wrung his emotions out over a couple of takes, in the process making the slightest lyrical change to 'empty bed' from the original 'icy bed'.

When touring The Queen Is Dead, 'I Know It's Over' became a grand set piece, usually played as the last number before the encore; as evidence, refer to the intense version on RANK. An intentionally

'I Know Very Well How I Got My Name' (Morrissey/Street), B-side of 'SUEDEHEAD' (1988). An explicitly autobiographical tale of a 'curious' child who grew into a 'sullen' man, this was one of Morrissey's most candid lyrics of the VIVA HATE period. Written in the months directly after the end of The Smiths, it's reasonable to assume that, like much of that album, the words were a cathartic post mortem on the end of his partnership with Marr ('the only one who's come and gone'?). The song also contained a humorous anecdote about the time in 1972 when the 13-year-old Morrissey attempted to dye his hair in homage to David BOWIE's Ziggy Stardust. 'I did experiment with bottles of bleach and so forth,' he confessed. 'I tried to dye it yellow and it came out gold, then I tried to get rid of it and it came out purple. I was sent home from school.' Among Stephen Street's simpler tunes, Vini REILLY's delicate guitar picking and its subtle orchestration imbued the track with an appropriately wistful air. Reilly later released a live alternate take ruined by a hilarious duff note – 'I Know Very Well How I Got My Note Wrong' by 'Vincent Gerard and Steven Patrick' – as a free single with The Durutti Column's 1989 album, Vini Reilly. [25, 39, 71]

epic Smiths song, it was later covered with stunning tenderness by doomed American singer Jeff Buckley, both on its own and as an inspired medley with his celebrated version of Leonard Cohen's 'Hallelujah'. If it's true that most Smiths covers are doomed to fall far short of the original, Buckley's 'I Know It's Over' is a rare exception. [17, 18, 38, 362]

'I Know Who I Love' (Morrissey/Boorer),
Studio outtake from the 1997 MALADJUSTED album sessions. In context of Maladjusted's weaker crop, it's baffling that Morrissey should have consigned one of its strongest contenders to the bin. With its starry-eyed melody and blood-rushing chorus the charming 'I Know Who I Love' was even worthy of consideration for a single. To the chagrin of co-writer Boz Boorer, it was bumped off the album, relegated as a potential B-side and then scrapped outright. It may be that, by the time of the album's completion, Morrissey no longer empathised with its affectionate sentiment: 'These words I scribble down/Observe the way that you work/You see it, you want it, you take it/And then it's yours … I know who I love.' The song also contained a reference to medication – 'these pills that I'm prescribed' – while his 'Having had the worst of times/Now I want the best of times' evoked Charles DICKENS's famous opening to *A Tale Of Two Cities*. Whatever the reasons for its exclusion from Maladjusted, the loss of 'I Know Who I Love' was a major oversight. [4, 5, 40]

'I Like You' (Morrissey/Boorer), From the album
YOU ARE THE QUARRY (2004). It's a common enough knee-jerk reaction among fans and full-time Morrissey theorists to interpret any song about a deep or unusual friendship as being a covert ode to Johnny Marr. By You Are The Quarry, such instances had become fewer and further between though 'I Like You' stood out as that album's token contender: meditating on his love, or rather like, of a critical friend unlike anybody else Morrissey's ever met who between them incur the envy of court magistrates 'hiding their mistakes'. Certainly there were elements in its lyrics that seemed directly applicable to the COURT CASE he and Marr had undergone, an experience Morrissey himself had 'just about scraped through'. Nevertheless, the closing diagnosis that his 'like' interest is as psychologically unbalanced as he – his second plea of mental instability on the album after the earlier 'I'M NOT SORRY' – was much less flattering. By no means the strongest offering on You Are The Quarry, 'I Like You' is a shining example of the invaluable contribution of producer Jerry FINN even if, ironically, he wasn't especially keen on the song. Compared with its lumpy live arrangement previewed in concert in 2002, Finn brought Boorer's rocking dirge to life with a sharper rhythm and the unusual textural addition of squelching 'acid house' keyboards. The result was strong enough to be considered for a US single release, though it never materialised. Rumours that Robbie Williams had asked to perform a duet of the track at the 2005 Brit Awards were later confirmed by Morrissey. 'I saw the list of people nominated,' he said, 'and thought, "I don't think so."' [93, 580]

'I Misses You' (Morrissey/Marr), One of very
few abandoned Smiths songs which fell by the wayside, written as they were putting the finishing touches to MEAT IS MURDER. The group cut a working instrumental demo in December 1984. Marr confirms that Morrissey had named the song 'I Misses You', although his accompanying lyrics were never recorded. The main melody was plaintive and mid-tempo, in the same vein as 'HEAVEN KNOWS I'M MISERABLE KNOW', while some passages were also prescient of 'UNLOVEABLE', written the following year. Without Morrissey's vocal, the surviving demo is only a rough sketch which Marr readily admits is 'not exactly the Smiths Holy Grail on closer inspection'. [17, 19]

'I Started Something I Couldn't Finish'
(Morrissey/Marr), The Smiths' 16th single (taken from the album STRANGEWAYS, HERE WE COME), released November 1987, highest UK chart position #23.

Morrissey's shamefaced recollection of a brazen

sexual proposal gone horribly wrong, its opening description of deserted lanes suggested action took place in a parked car, thus revisiting the erotic passenger/driver intimacy of 'THIS CHARMING MAN', 'THAT JOKE ISN'T FUNNY ANYMORE' and 'THERE IS A LIGHT THAT NEVER GOES OUT'. Riddled with remorse, Morrissey gladly accepts his punishment, akin to that suffered by Oscar WILDE, sentenced to two years' 'hard labour' when convicted of sodomy in 1895. The phrase 'that's what tradition means' was culled from Alan BENNETT's play *Forty Years On* which Morrissey would source again on 'ALSATIAN COUSIN' written later that year. The closing remark, 'OK, Stephen? Shall we do that again?', was simply a piece of studio chat directed at co-producer Stephen STREET left on the finished mix.

Less than a year after its release, Morrissey dismissed this jovial glam rock imitation as representative of The Smiths' more 'bumptious' moments which he wasn't so keen on. According to Street, the singer expressed his misgivings at the time, criticising the backing track Marr had been working on and creating a rare moment of tension between the normally harmonious songwriting partnership. 'I played it to Morrissey and he started complaining. "Oh no, I don't like this bit,"' says Street. 'So I took the tape back to Johnny and said, "Mozzer doesn't like these things." And Johnny flipped. He snapped back, "Well, fuck him! Let him think of something." I think Johnny was getting exhausted always having to be the one to come up with musical ideas.'

While Marr doesn't deny the now semi-mythical 'tape incident', he refuses to sensationalise its importance. 'I remember it,' he says, 'and whatever anyone else has said about that is true. But it didn't happen very often. Sometimes, when you're getting ideas down you can be vulnerable. It's hard enough without people throwing stones in the pathway. But there was unity there and there always was with me and Morrissey. We weren't sitting around like THE BEATLES in Let It Be, scowling at each other and falling apart. Too much has been made of that story.'

Regardless of this and other possible hindrances – previously Marr has commented that Rourke and Joyce had also shown a lack of enthusiasm towards the song, though he's subsequently attributed their apathy to 'STOP ME IF YOU THINK YOU'VE HEARD THIS ONE BEFORE' – 'I Started Something' turned out a glam-pop treat, its cocksure guitar riff sashaying around David BOWIE's 'The Jean Genie' (a source Marr readily admits, citing 1973's Aladdin Sane album as another influence on Strangeways). The song only became the penultimate Smiths single by default. When ROUGH TRADE decided against releasing 'Stop Me' due to lyrical sensitivity after the Hungerford massacre, it seemed the most radio-friendly Strangeways alternative. Although the group had already broken up, Morrissey hoped to keep their profile alive and aid the single's chances by agreeing to a promotional video.

With the help of the Bristol-based fanzine *Smiths Indeed*, a dozen 'Morrissey look-a-likes' were recruited to star alongside the singer in a cycling tour of Manchester. Filmed on 18 October 1987, a typically grey and drizzly Mancunian Sunday, Morrissey led his twelve disciples around some of the city's iconic Smiths landmarks including Strangeways prison and SALFORD LADS CLUB.[1] 'That's an example of something Johnny would never have agreed to,' states Rourke. 'A bunch of Morrissey clones following Morrissey? Well, it's not a Smiths video, is it? It's a Morrissey video. You could already see where he was going to go next.' [17, 19, 38, 29, 208, 280]

---

1. The same video was later re-edited to the soundtrack of 'Stop Me If You Think You've Heard This One Before'.

'I Take It Back', 1967 single by American pop/country singer Sandy Posey, mentioned by Morrissey as one of his favourite singles. Rarely photographed cracking a smile and forever grimacing beneath a coal-black beehive, Posey cut a striking – and strikingly miserable – figure, an image enhanced by the tragic hillbilly twang in her voice betraying her Memphis upbringing. Signing with MGM, she enjoyed a handful of hits during the mid-60s, most famously the painfully masochistic 'Born A Woman' and the lonesome 'Single Girl', both of which made the UK top 30, unlike the rhythmically punchier 'I Take It Back'. Sharing a lyrical scenario with The Shangri-Las' 'Train From Kansas City' and Sandie SHAW's 'Tomorrow', Posey must meet her boyfriend to tell him it's over but finds herself thoroughly unprepared for his grief-stricken blubbing. Unable to play the merciless jilter, she pretends 'she didn't mean it' and agrees to continue as they were, leaving the listener with the wretched moral that 'sometimes it's better to be loved than it is to love'. Posey went on to sing backing vocals for Elvis PRESLEY. [175, 408]

'I Want A Boy For My Birthday' (Sylvester Bradford), Early Smiths cover of a 1963 single by The Cookies, played in concert though never professionally recorded. Morrissey also named the original as one of his favourite records in a couple of magazine lists during the early days of The Smiths.

As he began writing songs with Marr in the summer of 1982, Morrissey proposed they should interpret a 60s girl group track, itself an indirect homage to his beloved NEW YORK DOLLS who'd set the precedent with their cover of The Shangri-Las' 'Give Him A Great Big Kiss', also borrowing its opening lyric for their own 'Looking For A Kiss'. Morrissey nominated the reasonably obscure 'I Want A Boy For My Birthday' by The Cookies, a black New York vocal trio best known for 1962's 'Chains', later covered by THE BEATLES. As its title suggested, the song was a simple lovelorn plea for 'the present that I need the most', namely 'a boy to love'. Marr had never heard the record before but immediately agreed with Morrissey, keenly aware that the lyrics would assume a different sexual connotation if sung from a male perspective. 'I thought, "Great, this'll really freak 'em out!"' admits Marr. 'But us doing that Cookies song was absolutely echoing the New York Dolls, who everyone had forgotten about at the time but Morrissey hadn't and I hadn't. We wanted to bring something to our audience that the Dolls had brought to us. That was it.'

Sometime around August 1982 or thereabouts, Morrissey and Marr recorded a basic bedroom demo of 'I Want A Boy For My Birthday' featuring just vocal and guitar. The tape was given to early Smiths bassist Dale HIBBERT, who claims he was told to learn it in preparation for the group's first demo at Manchester's Decibel studios that autumn. In the event, this prototype Smiths line-up never got round to recording the Cookies track at Decibel and the bedroom demo, which Hibbert later sold to a private collector, is all that survives. A rare sample clip posted on the internet gives us an idea of how they tackled the song; Marr's thickly strummed chords followed the original ascending melody while Morrissey applied a gentle vocal carefully avoiding camp or irony.

'I Want A Boy For My Birthday' was unveiled as the last of four songs played at The Smiths' first gig at Manchester's Ritz on 4 October 1982, with Hibbert on bass and dancer James MAKER also present. It was probably played again at their second, and first with Rourke, at Manchester's Manhattan club on 25 January 1983 – recollections vary and no tape or setlist seems to have survived – though by the following month Morrissey and Marr had sufficient original material to dispense with the song. (See also 'GIRL LEAST LIKELY TO'.) [10, 17, 184, 188]

'I Want The One I Can't Have' (Morrissey/ Marr), From the album MEAT IS MURDER (1985). One of many Smiths-singles-that-almost-were, when first introduced on stage in November 1984 Morrissey prematurely announced it as their next release. Instead it became an integral component of Meat Is Murder's flawless first half and a perennial Smiths live favourite.

Between its governing yelp of sexual frustration, the lyrics contained several familiar Morrissey motifs, from the sexual fumblings behind a railway yard already referenced in 'THESE THINGS TAKE TIME' to the juvenile toughs of 'THE QUEEN IS DEAD' (an early draft had Morrissey's young thug killing not 'a policeman' but 'his mother'). Also of interest was his piteous description of the working-class

185

marital bed among 'the riches of the poor', a term he'd previously used in interviews (possibly sourced from Edith SITWELL). 'When people get married and are getting their flat,' explained Morrissey, 'the most important thing was getting the double bed. It was like the prized exhibit; the cooker, the fire, everything else came later.'

Though Marr would later assert that its fabulously frisky tune emerged accidentally during a group jam, it does loosely recall an earlier abandoned Smiths track recorded with John PORTER in July 1984, never given lyrics but nicknamed 'Fast One'. Though not identical they share a similar exhilarating melody, structure and briskness of tempo. Years later, Morrissey would nominate 'I Want The One I Can't Have' as his worst vocal performance on a Smiths record. 'I'm singing rather abrasively [and] off-key,' he confessed, 'and rather wished that I hadn't because it's a great song and it was slightly ruined because of me.' It was probably because of this same self-criticism that Morrissey removed the song from Warners' dummy running order of the 2008 compilation The Sound Of The Smiths in favour of 'NOWHERE FAST'. [17, 142, 267, 372, 426, 434, 535]

'I Will See You In Far-Off Places' (Morrissey/Whyte), From the album RINGLEADER OF THE TORMENTORS (2006). Beneath its ostensible pessimism about the inevitability of death, the impossibility of finding true love and the murder of innocent people as a result of US foreign policy, the core of 'I Will See You In Far-Off Places' is Morrissey's optimistic hope of some form of happy afterlife. As he explained, the song is – quite literally – his equivalent of Vera Lynn's Second World War standard 'We'll Meet Again': 'Within the song I feel there's a certain spiritual sensation whereby, although we know that life will end we all have a feeling that we will meet again. Now why should we have that feeling? If we realise that everything is temporary, why do we all have this innate feeling that we will be together in the same place?' Positioned at the beginning of Ringleader, Morrissey admitted that

its first line was deliberately designed as a statement of intent for the whole album. 'It's absolutely [meant to be] the first line,' he stressed. 'I thought at the time, why write anything else, why not just leave it at that: "Nobody knows what human life is." That says it all.'

Written two years after the beginning of the American-led invasion of Iraq in 2003, its reference to being bombed by the US military was one of the most explicitly political lyrics Morrissey had written yet, widely interpreted as a hymn to the victims of the wars in both Iraq and Afghanistan, prompting obligatory diatribes against George Bush and Tony Blair in most interviews of the period. 'Blair and Bush are not terrorism. They're *worse* than terrorism,' raged Morrissey. 'Bush views Iraq and thinks, "Well, we will control this country eventually anyway so it doesn't matter how many innocent people we kill."'

The lyrical allusions to war in the Middle East were amplified by Whyte's powerful and exotic score, driven by a snake-charmer guitar riff and wailing harmonies sensuously evocative of Arabic prayer. Even its chorus bass-drum rumbles seemed to suggest the deathly reverberations of an American air strike. The mighty 'I Will See You In Far-Off Places' was as dynamic an opening to any Morrissey album thus far, destined to become a live highlight of the Ringleader tour. [54, 170, 389]

'I Won't Share You' (Morrissey/Marr), From the album STRANGEWAYS, HERE WE COME (1987). Though not actually the last track The Smiths ever recorded – that was 'I KEEP MINE HIDDEN' – as the last song on the last album 'I Won't Share You' would come to be regarded as the epitaph for the Morrissey/Marr composer credit, widely believed to be the singer's frank admission of his possessive feelings towards his writing partner.

From original Smiths benefactor Joe MOSS to producers Troy TATE, John PORTER and manager Matthew Stzumpf, those who posed a threat to Morrissey's intimate working relationship with Marr found themselves inevitably jettisoned from the Smiths entourage. Even as 'I Won't

Share You' was being recorded, their latest manager, Ken Friedman, found himself excommunicated by Morrissey for the same reason. Against this backdrop of interminable management crisis, the song's heartfelt lyrics seemed an all-too-obvious autobiographical confession. When co-producer Stephen STREET first heard it, he burst into tears.

'The lyrics were brought to my attention by somebody even before we got out of the studio,' says Marr. 'There were raised eyebrows and, "Whaddya think of that then?" If I was bothered about it, I'd say, "Well, I ain't anyone's to share." But if that sentiment was directed towards me then, quite rightly, I feel good about it. It's nice.' The closing line was particularly interesting since Morrissey had already used it two years earlier in a proposed sleeve note for a 1985 compilation by Ludus, the band of his best friend Linder STERLING. 'Oh Linder, Oh Linder,' wrote Morrissey, 'I will see you sometime, somewhere.' But regardless of the singer's specific muse in writing 'I Won't Share You' (and the Marr theory is highly likely), it stands, or rather floats heavenward, as one of The Smiths' greatest love songs – the love of a man who, as he always knew and always vowed, would fight to the last breath.

Remarkably, considering its hallowed place within The Smiths' repertoire,

according to Marr it was 'probably all done in about 20 minutes'. Stephen Street remembers Marr finding an autoharp in a windowsill in the studio staircase, dusting it down and tinkering around. 'It sounded absolutely beautiful,' says Street, 'so we recorded it there and then.' Marr confirms its spontaneous origins. 'I was just playing the chords and I think it was Stephen Street's enthusiasm as much as anyone else that he got me to record it. I put it down, then put the acoustic on it, then Morrissey sang on it and I put harmonica on at the very end of it.'

What neither Marr nor Street realised was that the main chords were actually the same as 'ASK'. 'I'm glad I didn't realise it was the same as "Ask",' says Marr, 'because I might not have done it. I was just making a tune that resonated with the day.' The divine simplicity and otherworldly echo of its arrangement only served to amplify the poignancy of Morrissey's lyrics. As fate decreed, The Smiths' last goodbye ended with the remote wail of a lonesome harmonica, symbolically returning them full circle to the melancholic mouth organ ushering in their debut, 'HAND IN GLOVE'. For its sheer romance as much as its circumstantial gravitas, 'I Won't Share You' will forever be one of The Smiths' most precious recordings. Or, as Marr describes it, 'another unusual little star in our galaxy'. [17, 19, 38, 178]

'I'd Love To' (Morrissey/Boorer), B-side of 'THE MORE YOU IGNORE ME, THE CLOSER I GET' (1994). An agonised but ultimately more hopeful return to the nocturnal torture of 'LAST NIGHT I DREAMT THAT SOMEBODY LOVED ME', 'I'd Love To' finds Morrissey once more alone and crying in the darkness but at least reconciled to his true feelings for the one person he craves to share his bed linen. While catalysed by misery, his amorous confession casts a romantic rather than melancholic mood, serenaded by Boorer's velvety, dreamlike chords.[1] Morrissey himself agreed 'it's quite a nice romantic song' (even if he comically retracted the statement in the same breath). At nearly five minutes long, 'I'd Love To' had the potential to be an epic ballad with a similarly sentimental melody to Boorer's 'NOW MY HEART IS FULL' from the same session. Instead, it ended up something of a three-quarters-finished sketch with Morrissey's delicate vocal vanishing prematurely before a long instrumental crescendo. [4, 422]

1. Two delicately different mixes of the song were released in the UK and the US. The latter, as included on MY EARLY BURGLARY YEARS, is noticeably more ethereal, featuring less guitar.

'I'll Never Be Anybody's Hero Now'

(Morrissey/Whyte), From the album RINGLEADER OF THE TORMENTORS (2006). A languid shuffle through the deck of Morrissey's most familiar playing cards – loneliness, social isolation, romantic loss and, with the confession that his true love is 'under the ground', death – 'I'll Never Be Anybody's Hero Now' offered a classic example of his playful irony: mourning his hopes of ever being idolised when he is, of course, a hero to thousands. An archetypal outsider ballad, its self-caressing melody and scarf-waving chorus aroused one of his more sensational vocal lines, by the end staggering stage left in a dying nightingale falsetto. While none of Whyte's contributions to Ringleader was issued as a single, this seemed the most obvious contender and, with hindsight, was an opportunity missed.

'I'm Not Sorry' (Morrissey/Boorer), From the

album YOU ARE THE QUARRY (2004). In its defiant lack of remorse this was very nearly Morrissey's equivalent of Edith Piaf's 'Non, Je Ne Regrette Rien', albeit purely in sentiment rather than musical melodrama. Yet whereas Piaf finds love at the end of her song, Morrissey is left half drowning in his loneliness, too proud to be rescued by the helping hand of 'just anyone'. Boorer's fluidly forlorn melody serves only to wash him further away from shore, a wistful flute beckoning in vain on some faraway beach while, beneath the waves, a sonar pulse ripples hopelessly through the infinite gloom. Among the album's subtler moments, 'I'm Not Sorry' was also one of its most beautiful thanks to Jerry FINN's onomatopoeic lost-at-sea production.

'I'm OK By Myself' (Morrissey/Tobias), From

the album YEARS OF REFUSAL (2009). The resplendently raucous punchline not only to Years Of Refusal, the album, but literally years of refusal, the life of Morrissey. After bleeding his heart on record for the last quarter century, crucified by loneliness, self-disgust and wounded by an endless succession of rebuffed romances, he arrives at the bitterly simple conclusion, 'I'm OK By Myself'. The words

are an unapologetic justification of his paranoia and misanthropy, a record of survival in a world of smiling assassins where every caressing arm is a potential stab in the back. There's no regret in his resolution, only a manic, battle-scarred pride inspiring one of his wildest vocals, not least its psychotic goatherd's yodel of 'Noooooooo!'

To Morrissey's dismay, after two run-throughs producer Jerry FINN told him he didn't like it – by the third and final take, Finn had his hands over his ears. As a performance, its execution hauled extraordinary drama out of Tobias's typically harsh and otherwise undistinguished racket. Special credit must go to the formidable rhythm section of brothers Matt and Solomon WALKER whose respective drum rattle and fuzzing bass carry the song to its nerve-wracking fade-out. 'I'm OK By Myself' was destined to become a dead-wakening highlight of the Refusal tour in all its phone-the-ambulance lunacy. [580]

'I'm Playing Easy To Get' (Morrissey/

Boorer), Rare song broadcast as part of a December 2004 Janice Long BBC radio session but never officially released. Morrissey later explained 'it was recorded, but not very well, so we hid it – although my experience is that nothing can ever be hidden'. Over a breezy guitar and organ backdrop, the lyrics are extremely flirtatious, detailing his blatant attempts to be picked up in his Hollywood neighbourhood. Judging from the location details 'between Cole [Place] and Cahuenga [Boulevard]', Morrissey is being 'just plain desperate' on Sunset Boulevard, possibly loitering around the cavernous Amoeba Music record shop, enjoying a coffee in Groundworks or dawdling on his way to his local 'English pub' the Cat & Fiddle a few blocks down the road. An unusually candid love song for Morrissey, 'I'm Playing Easy To Get' was a revealing glimpse into how he may have bided his time in Los Angeles during his dry spell without a record deal. [243]

'I'm Throwing My Arms Around Paris'

(Morrissey/Boorer), Morrissey's 36th solo single

(taken from the album YEARS OF REFUSAL), released February 2009, highest UK chart position #21. A triumphant cry of liberation from the gutter of loneliness, Morrissey offers rare insight into his nomadic existence as of the late 00s. Spurned by the one he loves, he's driven to roam with no fixed abode, directing his affections towards the 'stone and steel' of the French capital.

The title concept, a metaphysical romance with Paris, had already been touched upon in literature, poetry and the biographies of Morrissey's own heroes, not least Oscar WILDE who was buried in the city's Père Lachaise cemetery. Also of note, in Radclyffe Hall's *THE WELL OF LONE-LINESS*, the playwright Brockett encourages the heroine Stephen to stay in Paris: 'I'm going to make you simply adore her … There's nothing so stimulating as love – you've got to have an affair with Paris!'

Matching the succinct beauty of the lyrics, its arrangement and production were classic pop: the opening sound of a motorbike throttle recalling the gravel and car intro of ROXY MUSIC's 'Love Is The Drug', Boorer's pensively plucked baroque melody and the euphoric swell of the chorus, all condensed in barely two and a half minutes. In its dignified defiance in the face of despair, 'I'm Throwing My Arms Around Paris' is one of the best Morrissey songs, and certainly one of his best singles, of its decade.

The Parisian theme was echoed in the single's packaging, incorporating the Paris Metro font and inner bags reproducing Parisian scenes by the impressionist Jules Herve and nineteenth-century painter/photography pioneer Louis Daguerre. More eyebrow-raising were the series of group portraits inside each of the three formats: Morrissey in Al Jolson pose while behind him his band curdle their faces at copies of his recent GREATEST HITS; the band minus Morrissey posing with four different Herb Alpert albums; and Morrissey plus full band stark naked, their modesties hidden by five vintage seven-inch singles on the labels DECCA, Top Rank, Philips, Pye and HMV. [322]

'I've Been A Bad, Bad Boy',

1967 top five hit by former Manfred Mann singer Paul Jones, listed by Morrissey as one of his 'Singles to be cremated with'. The song was taken from the film *Privilege*, a swinging 60s take on *Nineteen Eighty-Four* set in a dystopian future in which the state uses pop star Steve Shorter (Jones) to control and exploit the masses. Based on a story by Alf Garnett creator Johnny Speight, it boasted the tagline 'a film so bizarre, so controversial, it shall crucify your mind to the tree of conscience', possibly referring to the acting skills of Jones's co-star, Jean SHRIMPTON. The richly orchestrated pop ballad 'I've Been A Bad, Bad Boy' was written by Mike Leander, who'd previously worked with Marianne FAITHFULL, and offers a likely source for the Morrissey line 'I'm not the man you think I am' from The Smiths' 'PRETTY GIRLS MAKE GRAVES'. An alternate version of the song appeared on the Privilege soundtrack album, which also featured the track 'Free Me', later covered by PATTI SMITH on her 1978 album Easter under the title 'Privilege (Set Me Free)'. [175]

'I've Changed My Plea To Guilty'

(Morrissey/Nevin), B-side of 'MY LOVE LIFE' (1991). Perhaps his finest collaboration with Mark Nevin, 'I've Changed My Plea To Guilty' is, furthermore, one of the greatest tracks in Morrissey's entire catalogue. At the time, he seemed to agree, telling one interviewer in all sincerity it was 'the best song, in my mind, that I have recorded'.

'Sometimes there's no point pretending that you're innocent and so forth,' he explained. 'You may as well just jump off the cliff and say, "I'm guilty."' Standing in the shadow, if not the shackles, of Oscar WILDE, Morrissey throws his loveless heart to the lions, a willing martyr to an agonising loneliness trembling through his every soul-torn syllable. While in one sense eerily prophetic of the 1996 Smiths COURT CASE (bar the obvious difference in plea), the 'emotional air-raid' metaphor harked back to his earlier sleeve note for a never-released 1985 compilation by Ludus, the band of his best friend Linder STERLING. Reminiscing about his and Linder's walks through Manchester, Morrissey wrote of their 'hearts damaged by too many air-raids'.

The song's power and beauty owed much to its simplicity, developing the stark piano and vocal template of Nevin's earlier 'THERE'S A PLACE IN HELL FOR ME AND MY FRIENDS'. Modelled on his home demo, Nevin constructed the opening and closing sound collage using samples of country singer Skeeter Davis's 1963 hit 'The End Of The World' alongside Dictaphone recordings of a waitress friend from Minneapolis called Suzy Solan. The delicate mood cast was perfect for Morrissey's condemned cell surrender, which is why the song inevitably lost some of its grace in concert when rearranged as a guitar track. But in its original form, 'I've Changed My Plea To Guilty' still hits the bullseye of heartache with a poetry and poise few Morrissey songs have matched since. [22, 83, 178, 422]

'If You Don't Like Me, Don't Look At Me'

(Morrissey/Tobias), B-side of 'THE YOUNGEST WAS THE MOST LOVED' (2006). Beyond the title sentiment – a direct message to his detractors to find 'somebody else to take your gaze away' – there was little substance to this inconsequential leftover from the RINGLEADER OF THE TORMENTORS sessions. The only lyrical curiosity was its barmy reference to young men running 'through the glen' which, unavoidably, brought to mind the feisty theme song to the 50s UK television serial *The Adventures Of Robin Hood*. Despite a strong vocal from Morrissey, Tobias's rice-pudding rock tune predestined the track as obvious B-side filler.

'In The Future When All's Well' (Morrissey/Tobias), Morrissey's 32nd solo single (from RINGLEADER OF THE TORMENTORS), released August 2006, highest UK chart position #17. Sharing the basic philosophy of the same album's 'I WILL SEE YOU IN FAR-OFF PLACES' – that death and the hereafter is preferable to the miserable reality of human existence – the chorus of 'In The Future When All's Well' calls to be defended by the mysterious 'Lee', Morrissey yet again cleverly choosing a genderless name open to interpretation as either sex. The song's finale finds him typically yearning for the grave and, one suspects, doffing his cap to Emily Dickinson's poem 'A Long Long Sleep, A Famous Sleep'.

Tobias's most appealing tune on the album, its retro-glam swagger inspired some novel touches from TONY VISCONTI, from its sweet xylophone underscore to its admittedly hammy nod to the producer's past with Marc BOLAN: Gary DAY's opening bass scale-down is identical to that at around 2.23 on T.Rex's 1971 number one, 'Get It On'. The single's sleeve recalled the ice-cream eroticism of the 'WE HATE IT WHEN OUR FRIENDS BECOME SUCCESSFUL' promo showing Morrissey lapping a vanilla cone, while its accompanying video was another semi-pastiche of a 70s Italian television broadcast

Ian, Janis, New York-born folk singer/songwriter, best known for her 1975 US hit 'At Seventeen', a perceptive acoustic ballad about adolescent loneliness. Morrissey mentioned Ian very briefly when he was given the chance to interview JONI MITCHELL in 1996, asking her if she'd heard the title track of Ian's 1974 album Stars, an equally insightful analysis of fame and the music industry which appears to have been an influence on Morrissey's own lyrics. Ian's line 'You never saw the eyes of grown men of 25 that followed as you walked and asked for autographs' has echoes in both 'THIS NIGHT HAS OPENED MY EYES' and 'PAINT A VULGAR PICTURE'. Other than 'Stars', Ian's most interesting recordings are her earliest with Shangri-Las and future NEW YORK DOLLS producer Shadow Morton, particularly 1965's 'Society's Child', an impassioned anti-racism protest written when she was 15 years old. [179]

similar to the EUROVISION homage of the 'YOU HAVE KILLED ME' promo. [93, 389]

Inspector Calls, An, 1954 British big-screen adaptation of J. B. Priestley's celebrated play, listed among Morrissey's favourite films. Set in 1912, it stars Alastair SIM as the mysterious Inspector Poole (Goole in the original play) who disrupts the dinner party of the wealthy Birling family to question them about the death of a young girl, Eva Smith, who committed suicide that afternoon by drinking poison. As Poole interrogates each member of the Birling household, it transpires that, unbeknownst to one another, they all contributed to the poor girl's social downfall: Mr Birling fired her from his factory after she asked for a wage increase; his daughter, Sheila, then got her fired from her next job in a clothes shop after making a spiteful complaint; Sheila's fiancé, Gerald, made her his mistress before abandoning her; the young alcoholic Eric Birling then got the girl pregnant before stealing money to fend for her, which she proudly refused; and finally Mrs Birling denied Smith any help when she begged for assistance from her charity fund. The drama ends with the entire Birling clan forced to deal with the moral consequences of their individually selfish actions only to then question the legitimacy of Poole's credentials, culminating in its famous twist ending. Sim is perfectly cast as the central inquisitor, amplifying the play's darkly comic qualities. Also worthy of note is the role of the doomed Eva Smith, played in flashback sequences by Jane Wenham, later to become the first wife of another Morrissey screen favourite, Albert FINNEY. [227, 514]

'Interesting Drug' (Morrissey/Street), Morrissey's fourth solo single, released April 1989, highest UK chart position #9. A blatantly political comment on the vicious circle of working-class poverty and narcotic abuse, Morrissey empathises with those driven to take the 'Interesting Drug' of the title as a means of blocking out the misery of their breadline existence. Instead, he lays the blame on the predatory dealers and, more obliquely, the oppressive policies of the ruling THATCHER administration. 'In the video [for the single] we wrote the words on the wall, "Bad people on the right", which would apply to the Conservative government,' he explained. 'Or it could be, if you like, people who push drugs who are saving their own skins by ruining people's lives.' The song's absence of any moral judgement on drug use caused minor controversy, as Morrissey acknowledged some years later. 'I have a very clear idea what I want to say lyrically and the approach I have is just far too direct for most people … If you say, "Interesting drug, the one that you took, God it really *helped* you" … That line was just far too direct.'

While the title applied generally to all drugs, it was widely interpreted to be a specific comment on growing ecstasy use in the wake of 1988's 'Second Summer Of Love' and the recently reinvigorated Manchester club scene. It was therefore a fitting coincidence that Street's tune should bounce to a bright, funk-lite rhythm in keeping with those of the new wave of 'Madchester' bands such as The Stone Roses and Inspiral Carpets who, ironically, would contribute to Morrissey's fall from fashion in the year ahead. Recorded at the same session as the preceding 'LAST OF THE FAMOUS INTERNATIONAL PLAYBOYS' single at The Wool Hall near Bath in late November/December 1988, 'Interesting Drug' was an adorably provocative pop thrill, the guest harmonies of Kirsty MACCOLL adding to its rare effervescence.

The song's promo video directed by Tim Broad reiterated its political targets by lampooning the 'government schemes' of the Prince's Trust advertisement campaign (also seen in the 'Playboys' promo). Starring the buxom Diane Alton, the 'Interesting Drug' video is rife with symbolism, from the fictitious Hawtrey High School (after CARRY ON star Charles Hawtrey) to carefully placed references to Heathcoate WILLIAMS's *Whale Nation*, Diana DORS, schoolboys in court shoes (a likely NEW YORK DOLLS homage) and even old Smiths lyrics (Alton's badge quoting a line from

'YOU'VE GOT EVERYTHING NOW'). Disregarding the song's main theme, Morrissey instead used the video to promote animal rights, appearing only briefly handing out anti-vivisection leaflets to Alton and her schoolboy accomplices who then go on to liberate rabbits from the laboratory of 'Clever Brothers' (a euphemism for Lever Brothers, a frequent target of animal welfare groups due to their chemical testing processes).

'Interesting Drug' marked Morrissey's fourth consecutive solo top ten hit, but also his last for the next five years and the bitter end of his partnership with Stephen Street. Aggrieved that he had yet to resolve his financial concerns over VIVA HATE, Street placed a temporary injunction on the release of 'Interesting Drug', 'out of desperation' he says. Though Morrissey would still record a couple of Street's tunes, also asking him to remix an abandoned track from the same session, 'The Bed Took Fire' (released as 'AT AMBER'), they would never write, or work, together again. It was poignant to say the least that during their dispute Morrissey reverted to quoting 'Interesting Drug' in their correspondence – sending Street a torn strip from a lawyer's letter upon which he'd written just four words: 'Enough is too much.' [29, 39, 94, 437]

'Interlude' (Georges Delerue/Hal Shaper),

Morrissey's duet with Siouxsie SIOUX, technically his 17th solo single, released as 'Morrissey & Siouxsie' in August 1994, highest UK chart position #25.

The song was first recorded by Timi YURO as the title theme to the 1968 film *Interlude* starring Oskar Werner as a married conductor who begins an affair with a young reporter played by Barbara Ferris. As the original Colgems soundtrack album trumpeted, the song's composer Georges Delerue 'has penned a wistfully romantic score. At times his plaintive melodies and gossamer scoring suggests a mood of immediate heartbreak. At other times, as the story demands, the music projects passionate rapture.' With lyrics by Hal Shaper, 'Interlude' blended both elements in an epic orchestral ballad in which two lovers celebrate their transitory romance ever conscious that it may end imminently. As such, in sentiment the song shared something of the knowingly doomed euphoria of 'HAND IN GLOVE'.

Other than the film soundtrack album, Yuro released her original as a US single in August 1968 and on the following month's Something Bad On My Mind album. It's likely Morrissey first heard the track on the latter since his reasons for covering 'Interlude' had everything to do with his love of Yuro and nothing to do with the film itself. It was an inspired choice, and a courageous one. Not only did Morrissey have to do justice to Yuro's breathtaking original, he complicated matters by turning a solo lyric into a duet. Possibly unsure as to how this would work, both Morrissey and Siouxsie Sioux each sang a separate solo version of the entire song which was later fabricated into a duet in the final mix. The illusion was successful. Like a baroque pop Gilbert and Garbo, Morrissey and Siouxsie collapsed into one another with the same fated sensuality, echoing the other's tacit understanding that the love they share is already damned.

The song was recorded towards the end of the VAUXHALL AND I sessions in the summer of 1993. Siouxsie, accompanied by her husband/Banshees drummer Budgie, came to the studio at Hook End Manor to record her vocal one quiet weekend while the rest of the Vauxhall recording team were away. The production was overseen by Boz BOORER, who also recruited the string section from London indie band My Life Story. As well as a standard single arrangement, Boorer concocted two longer mixes, the '(Extended)' and '(Instrumental)' versions used as B-sides.

It would be a whole year before 'Interlude' was finally released. Previously, Morrissey had fretted to the press that because of 'legal wrangles' between his and Sioux's respective record companies 'it will never see the light of day'. In the end it was released with minimum fanfare as a postscript marking the end of the Vauxhall campaign in August '94. Neither Morrissey nor Siouxsie promoted the record, having fallen out in the interim over discussions for an accompanying video (for the full story see SIOUX entry). Sadly, if not criminally, this historic collaboration between the most iconic alternative British male and female singers of their respective generations dipped in and out of the charts virtually unnoticed. [4, 35, 40, 217]

Introducing Morrissey, Official concert video filmed at Sheffield City Hall and Blackpool Winter Gardens on 7 and 8 February 1995, released October 1996. See Mozography appendix for full tracklisting.

Directed by his friend James O'Brien, *Introducing Morrissey* is a vivid document of the singer's February 1995 UK tour in the wake of VAUXHALL AND I, featuring the regular setlist in its entirety minus the routine encore of The Smiths' 'SHOPLIFTERS OF THE WORLD UNITE'. The concert entrance music (the hymn 'Jerusalem' as featured in 1962's *The Loneliness Of The Long Distance Runner*) was accompanied by a short black-and-white film following an Eric CANTONA-loving boot boy's tour of key London Morrissey landmarks, from Vauxhall and Arsenal tube stations to Tench Street (as seen in the film *TO SIR, WITH LOVE*) and the famous Southwark boxing pub, the Thomas A'Becket. Blink and you'll miss Morrissey's fleeting cameo pasting up some fly posters for the ANGELIC UPSTARTS' 1979 debut album Teenage Warning.

Among the best performances are the tribal live arrangement of 'SPEEDWAY' and the serene, stripped-down 'MOONRIVER', though arguably the highlight of the video isn't the concert itself but the closing slow-motion montage of fans clambering on stage to manhandle the singer to the soundtrack of 1988 B-side 'WILL NEVER MARRY', a visually stunning and supremely moving testament to the quasi-religious nature of the Morrissey concert experience.

'Irish Blood, English Heart' (Morrissey/ Whyte), Morrissey's 25th solo single (from the album YOU ARE THE QUARRY), released May 2004, highest UK chart position #3.

Morrissey's dramatic 'comeback' single and his joint biggest UK hit to date (alongside 'YOU HAVE KILLED ME'), 'Irish Blood, English Heart' was a jackboot in the faces of all who'd ever opposed him. Simultaneously asserting his Anglo-Irish roots and his patriotism to his mother country, it appeared a long overdue response to the specific accusations levelled against him after the 1992 NME Madstock incident, sharing his dream to stand beside the Union Jack 'not feeling shameful, racist or partial'.

Among the oldest tracks on Quarry, Morrissey had been sitting on 'Irish Blood, English Heart' since at least 1999 when he first revealed its existence to *The Irish Times*, also expressing a wish to make it the title track of his next album. Whyte's tune was even older, written during his stint in Johnny Panic And The Bible Of Dreams, who recorded it in 1998 as 'Not Bitter But Bored'.

First introduced in concert in 2002, Morrissey referred to the title as 'the components that make up my tubby little body'. Taken as a whole, the lyrics were the most unambiguously political of his career to date, drooling with anarchistic contempt for the British constitution. '[They] touch upon the disgust I feel for the British political system,' he explained. 'The Tories, the Labour government, this circle that goes round and round and doesn't make anybody happy. I can't believe there isn't somebody in the universe who can come forward with a better way of being politically.' The song also contained a potted history lesson with its mention of seventeenth-century 'Lord Protector' Oliver CROMWELL, still 'saluted' by today's monarchy despite his attempts to end the royal succession after the English Civil War.

The most thrilling track on Quarry, Whyte's tune was a slow-brewing riot of tense, shifty guitar, its chorus havoc heralded by his string-bending sneer whistling above enemy lines like a precision-thrown Molotov cocktail. Morrissey would liken the latter to 'a Nordic retch', instructing producer Jerry FINN to make Whyte's guitar sound as if it were 'rising from the ocean bed'.

Finn obliged, awakening the full might of Morrissey's parliament-storming Kraken.

The single's video of Morrissey and his band performing before an approving young audience was to be accurately prophetic. Such was the media hype surrounding his comeback, it was predicted 'Irish Blood' may even reach number one; Morrissey possibly believed it himself since the week it entered at number three he chastised Radio 1 on air for not playing it enough, despite being 'the only British single in the top five'. As Morrissey's genetic DNA squeezed into two and a half minutes of baton-charging rock and roll, 'Irish Blood, English Heart' remains one of his greatest and most important works to date – not so much *essential* Morrissey as the literal *essence* of Morrissey. [67, 231, 410, 411, 420, 580]

'Is It Really So Strange?' (Morrissey/

Marr), B-side of 'SHEILA TAKE A BOW' (1987). The first of three Smiths lyrics written during 1986 on the subject of north-to-south migration (see also 'LONDON' and 'HALF A PERSON'), 'Is It Really So Strange?' took the form of a blackly comic love song in which Morrissey pursues a hostile love interest up and down the country, killing both a horse and a nun in his confusion, only to lose his bag at NEWPORT PAGNELL services on the M1.

The singer explained how he found 'that mood of a northern person going to London and then returning home very poignant. You can't describe how you feel when you go from south to north, stopping at the service stations. It hits a deafening note.' According to Marr, the journey from north to south was of fundamental significance to the history and trajectory of The Smiths. 'Road trips were a big part of the group,' he says. 'We opted to live in Manchester most of the time but were always travelling back and forth to London. It was in cars on the motorway where myself and Morrissey did a lot of our profound talking and thinking and listening. We loved it, because we'd take off at half three in the morning back to Manchester or down to London, just razzing about. That came out in "Is It Really So Strange?"'

Both the song's title and Marr's rock and roll flashback resonated with the ghost of Elvis PRESLEY. It may have been coincidence that 'Is It So Strange?' was the title of a lesser-known track recorded by Presley in 1957, though the textural influence of his 1954 debut Sun single, 'That's All Right' was deliberate. Hearing Marr's basic framework, producer John PORTER encouraged Marr to embellish his riff with 50s rockabilly twangs in the manner of Presley's pioneering lead guitarist, Scotty Moore. The result was The Smiths-go-Memphis, albeit via Newport Pagnell.

The song was first recorded alongside 'ASK' in June 1986 and intended as that single's B-side, though the take proved unsatisfactory; the version finally released was a re-recording from their last John PEEL session that December. [17, 19, 27, 57, 191]

Island Records, Morrissey's record label for

the duration of 1997 under the umbrella of Mercury Records. Though Mercury was the former label of his all-time music heroes, the NEW YORK DOLLS, for his domestic UK releases circa the album MALADJUSTED he chose the affiliated Island Records. First established in Jamaica by Englishman Chris Blackwell, in the 70s Island brought reggae into the mainstream via its first superstar, Bob Marley. For Morrissey, Island represented his early teenage glam obsessions with SPARKS, ROXY MUSIC and Brian ENO, borrowing their original early 70s paper label designs for his own Maladjusted album and singles. Equally relevant was NICO's solitary Island album, 1974's The End, featuring Morrissey's concert tape perennial 'Innocent And Vain'; he'd dip further into the label's back catalogue when touring Maladjusted, including Traffic's 1967 Island hit 'Hole In My Shoe' on his pre-gig interval tapes. Although leased to Island in the UK, Mercury still exercised full control over his deal, so when their parent company, PolyGram, was taken over in 1998, Morrissey found himself out of contract. His final Island release was the December 1997 single 'SATAN REJECTED MY SOUL', his last for seven years until his 2004 comeback on ATTACK RECORDS.

It Always Rains On Sunday, 1947 Ealing drama listed among Morrissey's favourite films. Set in a post-war London of bombsites, ration books and black market racketeers, it stars the exquisitely named Googie Withers as an East End housewife who wakes up one Sunday morning to discover her former lover and convicted robber Tommy Swann (Australian actor John McCallum, who later married Withers) has broken out of Dartmoor prison and is now hiding in her Anderson shelter. She instinctively agrees to harbour Swann, carefully shielding him from her troubled stepdaughters and her docile husband, who disappears to the pub to plays darts utterly oblivious to the fact his wife is rekindling her passions with Britain's Most Wanted upon their marital bed. The film climaxes with Swann being discovered, Withers attempting to gas herself and a thrilling police chase in a railway yard. Its combination of East End working-class drudgery, a tough heroine, a swarthy criminal and attempted suicide made it prime Morrissey fodder (not to mention its quintessentially Mozzerian title). Coincidentally, although the action is set in Bethnal Green, the actual street with the railway bridge where Withers and her family live was Hartland Road in Camden, home to Mark NEVIN at the time of recording KILL UNCLE and where he first 'bumped into' Morrissey on the corner with Chalk Farm Road. [227, 515]

'It's Hard To Walk Tall When You're Small'

(Morrissey/Whyte), B-side of 'IRISH BLOOD, ENGLISH HEART' (2004). First attempted in very different form during the 1997 MALADJUSTED B-side sessions, the original 'It's Hard To Walk Tall', while less detailed, expressed the same threats of gawping his foes to death as its more explicitly dwarf-mocking YOU ARE THE QUARRY-era remake. The main difference was its score, set to a slow ballad written by Spencer COBRIN in a similar vein to his 'WIDE TO RECEIVE' and 'LOST'. Morrissey got as far as a guide vocal and the track was muted as a B-side for 'SATAN REJECTED MY SOUL' but never finished. In stark contrast, the song's second incarnation was a doleful metal bash, in places reminiscent of The Ruts' 'Babylon's Burning' with Morrissey now yodelling about 'Ringo' and 'Gringo' but, alas, not making much in the way of sense. [4, 5]

'It's Not Your Birthday Anymore'

(Morrissey/Whyte), From the album YEARS OF REFUSAL (2009). The rousing highlight of Morrissey's ninth album was this sexually charged statement of intent towards a partner who's not long blown out the candles on their cake. Unlike the malice of his earlier 'UNHAPPY BIRTHDAY', here there is an irrepressible desire for his subject, albeit barbed with verbal cruelty and culminating in an act of sexual aggression tantamount to rape. Elsewhere, its comparison of friends' birthday gifts with physical love was very faintly suggestive of a verse in one of his favourite Phil Spector records, The Crystals' 'WHAT A NICE WAY TO TURN SEVENTEEN'. Yet the knee-weakening force of 'It's Not Your Birthday Anymore' lay entirely in the performance and Morrissey's vocal in particular, gliding over Whyte's simple, spacious melody from tender sensitivity to rapacious hysteria, hitting spine-tingling falsetto highs not touched since the early days of The Smiths; Morrissey himself agreed that he 'moved up several notches' on the song. Stunning in its emotional and musical volatility, 'Birthday' was a heartening indication that for all his weakness for the clamorous rock dominating the bulk of Refusal, Morrissey could still write such epic and affecting balladry. [580]

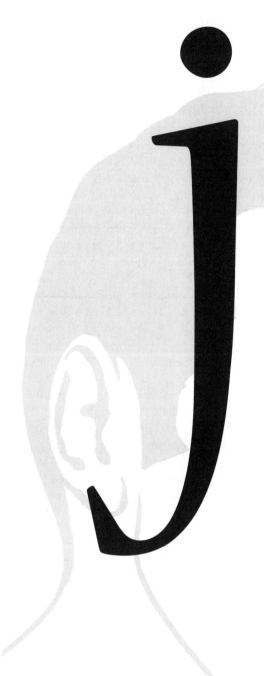

Jablonska, Annalisa, Female voice heard on The Smiths' 'SUFFER LITTLE CHILDREN' and 'PRETTY GIRLS MAKE GRAVES'. Little is known about Jablonska other than that she was 'a friend of Morrissey's' according to Smiths trial bassist Dale HIBBERT. It is, therefore, logical to assume that she is the same 'Annalisa' whom Morrissey referred to in a December 1981 letter to Scottish pen pal Robert MACKIE: 'I have a girlfriend called Annalisa. We're both bisexual. Real hip, huh? I hate sex.'

Even Johnny Marr insists he never saw, or knew of, Jablonska other than when she was called in to do the Hindley laughter on 'Suffer Little Children' and the 'Oh, really?' on 'Pretty Girls Make Graves'. 'She was nice,' recalls Marr. 'Very kind of studenty. From what I remember she had an archetypal 60s vibe. A bob haircut and a duffel coat – Morrissey never being one to miss a sartorial angle.'

Among the many mysteries surrounding Jablonska (whose name suggests Polish roots) is the number of times she was actually present in the studio with The Smiths. Assuming that it *is* her voice on all recorded versions of 'Suffer Little Children' and 'Pretty Girls Make Graves' then, unless her parts were resampled from earlier versions, she must have attended three different sessions – the first demo in the autumn of 1982, the aborted Troy TATE album session and the final sessions for what became THE SMITHS album. Sadly, recollections among those in attendance are either uselessly fuzzy or unforthcoming, leaving Jablonska a shadowy enigma in the footnotes of Smiths history. [10, 12, 17, 27, 334]

'Jack The Ripper' (Morrissey/Boorer), B-side of 'CERTAIN PEOPLE I KNOW' (1992). A longstanding live favourite, Morrissey has often introduced the song as being directly related to the Victorian serial killer of its title. 'Imagine it's 1888,' he said at London's Royal Albert Hall in 2002, 'you're in Whitechapel and someone touches your knee – or at least he thinks it's your knee – and you turn and are faced with the thoughts of Jack The Ripper.' On other occasions he'd describe it as 'a song about the most famous person who ever came from London' and 'a song about the 80s … the 1880s'.

To quote from Morrissey's own bookshelf, Gaute and Odell's THE MURDERERS' WHO'S WHO, 'Probably more has been written about Jack The Ripper than about any other murderer; theories of identity are legion.' The Ripper, so named because of the 'unparalleled ferocity of his crimes', killed and mutilated five prostitutes (and possibly others) in and around the poor Whitechapel district of London's East End between August and November 1888. The killer was never caught, leading to a host of conspiracy theories, one of the most common involving a Masonic plot to cover up the existence of the royal 'bastard child' of Queen Victoria's grandson, the Duke of Clarence.

Morrissey wasn't the first to immortalise the Ripper in pop music. In 1961, pioneering rock and roll guitarist Link Wray had used the title 'Jack The Ripper' for one of his most celebrated instrumentals. In 1963, Screaming Lord Sutch earned himself a BBC radio ban for his 'Jack The Ripper', a sick comedy rocker produced by Joe Meek (of 'JOHNNY REMEMBER ME' fame) made unnecessarily explicit by the sound of running footsteps on cobblestones, screaming women and naming victim Marie Kelly. Just months before Morrissey's song, in April 1992 Nick Cave also released his own grisly 'Jack The Ripper', though nothing in Cave's lyrics directly relates to the murders of 1888.

Despite the levity of its concert introductions and Morrissey's other comical allusions to the Ripper in interviews ('I just hang around the East End in a long black cape'), his lyrics were entirely sombre. While ambiguous enough to stand on their own as a dark and disturbed love song ('Crash into my arms/I want you'), they portray the Ripper as a calculating predator, sickened by his victims' appearance and their apathetic surrender. The original studio recording also contained a more obvious association with the unidentified killer in its haunting jeer: 'No one knows a thing about my life … nobody knows me.'

'Jack The Ripper' is also significant as the first Morrissey song written with Boz Boorer: its withered, wrinkled and appropriately loathsome minor-key visage cracking in a creepily serene smile. An awe-inspiring entry in the singer's repertoire, it still ranks among Boorer's best Morrissey tunes, even if its recording didn't quite meet expectations. Mick RONSON's last session for Morrissey, 'Jack The Ripper' and its accompanying B-side 'YOU'VE HAD HER' were rushed in a few days at Abbey Road in October 1992 before resuming American commitments to promote YOUR ARSENAL. During a four-day break in New Orleans the following month another attempt was made, without Ronson, at the Sea-Saint studios of local R&B hero Allen Touissant. According to drummer Spencer COBRIN, this session 'didn't work out at all'. Ronson's mix was kept as a B-side, though a more dramatic version was caught live for BEETHOVEN WAS DEAF and has taken precedence over the original on all subsequent compilation appearances. [5, 153, 317, 358, 422]

Jacques, Hattie, See CARRY ON.

Jagger, Mick, See ROLLING STONES, THE.

Jake, See WALTERS, Jake.

James, See 'WE HATE IT WHEN OUR FRIENDS BECOME SUCCESSFUL', 'WHAT'S THE WORLD'.

Jane Eyre, 1944 Hollywood adaptation of Charlotte Brontë's famous novel of 1847, listed among Morrissey's favourite films. Condensing Brontë's semi-autobiographical gothic melodrama into a pithy 97 minutes, it follows the plight of ten-year-old orphan Jane Eyre, plucked from the custody of her rich abusive aunt only to suffer even harsher maltreatment at the Lowood Institute, a charity school on the Yorkshire moors. Her only friend is young Helen Burns (played by an uncredited Elizabeth Taylor), who soon dies of consumption after she and Jane are forced by their arch-bastard of a headmaster to march around the

j

schoolyard holding flat irons during a rainstorm. Traumatised by Helen's avoidable death, she channels her hatred of Lowood into bettering her education there so she can eventually escape by finding work as a governess. Ten years later, the older Jane (Joan Fontaine) does just that after a job offer from Thornfield Manor, run by the cranky, neurotic but strangely charismatic Mr Rochester (Orson Welles). Inevitably they fall in love and decide to marry, though moments before they exchange 'I do's the ceremony is interrupted by an irate gentleman named Mr Mason. 'Parson, close your book,' groans Rochester, 'there'll be no wedding today.' It turns out that Rochester is still married and keeps his wife – Mason's sister, Bertha – locked up in a tower at Thornfield because she's a deranged arsonist descended from a family of similar lunatics. This, at least, explains the distant witchy cackling and mysterious freak fires around the manor which have plagued Jane since she arrived there. Heartbroken by the revelation, Jane runs away but is finally lured back after learning that Thornfield has been destroyed by fire: in a supreme act of madness, batty Bertha set the house ablaze before throwing herself off the roof. She rushes to the smoking ruins to find Rochester, now blind, stumbling among the charcoal. They embrace. The End. Interviewed in 1994, Morrissey confessed that he'd recently seen the film by accident 'and was shocked that the floodgates opened'. (See also WUTHERING HEIGHTS.) [154, 175, 516]

Jarman, Derek,
English avant-garde artist and filmmaker who directed four promos for The Smiths. Jarman had previously made videos for Marianne FAITHFULL, Orange Juice and Bryan Ferry but was best known for his controversial cinema work: notably *Sebastiane* (1976), an explicit homoerotic account of the martyrdom of Saint Sebastian scripted in Latin; and *Jubilee* (1977), a fantasy about Queen Elizabeth I magically transported to a punk-rock London wasteland with a cast including Wayne COUNTY and music by Brian ENO.

His main Smiths commission was 1986's *The Queen Is Dead: A Film By Derek Jarman*, a compilation of three erratic and expressionistic super 8mm interpretations of 'THE QUEEN IS DEAD', 'THERE IS A LIGHT THAT NEVER GOES OUT' and, Morrissey's personal favourite, 'PANIC'. The latter, partly filmed around London's Victoria Embankment and featuring an outstretched palm leading the camera down graffiti-splattered back alleys, was also used as the single's official promo in a bastardised version superimposing footage of a group soundcheck in Canada. 'He did them privately while we were [touring] in America,' Morrissey later explained, 'which was absolutely the only way we'd agree to it.' The singer added that 'when Derek Jarman made three films for The Smiths, I don't think anyone expected them to be popular – how could they be? Jarman was far too talented.' First televised on BBC2 in September 1986, Jarman's *The Queen Is Dead* was also shown theatrically in select UK cinemas before screenings of Alex Cox's *Sid And Nancy*.

Jarman made a similar video for their next single, 'ASK', also fiddled with by the record company to include more soundcheck clips of the group themselves. After The Smiths, Jarman worked more extensively with the Pet Shop Boys and continued directing ever more challenging and experimental films up until his AIDS-related death in February 1994, aged 52. [46, 65, 125, 144]

'Jeane'
(Morrissey/Marr), B-side of 'THIS CHARMING MAN' (1983). One of the more intriguing scraps of (assumed) autobiography in the early Smiths repertoire was Morrissey's account of the squalid dwelling he shared with the pseudonymous, and androgynous, 'Jeane'. Since Morrissey spent most of his late adolescence living at home save for his brief 'rented room' with Linder STERLING in Whalley Range (as documented in 'MISERABLE LIE' written shortly before), journalist Nick Kent was the first to posit the theory that Sterling is the real 'Jeane'.

While a feasible muse, more broadly the song is an obvious by-product of Morrissey's fascination

Joan of Arc, The 'Maid of Orleans', fifteenth-century Catholic martyr referenced in The Smiths' 'BIGMOUTH STRIKES AGAIN'. A teenage she-warrior who claimed to be acting on divine orders, Saint Joan (as she'd be canonised) led French troops to victory against the invading English in several battles before her eventual capture and execution in 1431. The 19-year-old Joan was tied to a stake and ceremoniously burned alive. It's likely that in employing Joan of Arc as a lyrical allegory Morrissey took inspiration from PATTI SMITH. In 1975's 'Kimberly', also Marr's musical blueprint for 'THE HAND THAT ROCKS THE CRADLE', Smith sings of the sea rushing 'up my knees like flame and I feel like just some misplaced Joan of Arc'. Coincidentally, when Sandie SHAW first collaborated with The Smiths in 1984, she'd describe her version of 'HAND IN GLOVE' to the press as 'real Joan of Arc stuff'. [251, 376]

with Shelagh DELANEY, including the duplication of the phrase 'cash on the nail' from *The Lion In Love*. Like his earlier attempts at writing Delaney-esque dramas such as that read by FACTORY Records boss Tony Wilson about a couple struggling to survive in a flat in Hulme, it wouldn't be so difficult for a kitchen-sink scholar such as Morrissey to invent or embellish a narrative such as 'Jeane', though its pathos and observational poetry are still convincingly first-hand.

Written and rehearsed in the winter of 1982, Marr's original riff was 'a slow Drifters-type thing' until Morrissey suggested he should speed it up. The result was a clamorous Smiths stomp veering towards the football terrace in its Kinks-esque hiccupping chords. 'I was just trying to get away from the other jangly riffs I was playing at the time,' says Marr, 'just to get a bit of variety. I always thought "Jeane" was quite original.' In finding beauteous pop in the dampest of bedsit rot, 'Jeane' was a uniquely Smithsian hubbub, made more glorious by Morrissey's yelping harmonies. Recorded with producer Troy TATE during the original debut album sessions, it became the only Tate track officially released during the group's existence. An obvious A-side for lesser groups, being neither obvious nor lesser The Smiths issued it as a seven-inch-only B-side.

The effervescent 'Jeane' has enjoyed a special cult reputation among Smiths fans ever since, largely due to its rarity; never issued on a CD compilation until 2008's deluxe version of The Sound Of The Smiths. First covered by Sandie SHAW, who cut a beautiful acoustic version with Marr as a B-side to her 1984 'HAND IN GLOVE', it was also adapted by Billy BRAGG, both versions together serving to highlight Morrissey's uniquely genderless lyrics. [17, 139, 299, 423]

Jobriath, 1970s American glam rock singer whom Morrissey has championed zealously, obsessively, and almost exclusively. 'He was a singer who released two glam rock albums in '73 and '74,' he explained. 'At the time, the press either ridiculed him or didn't bother to write about him at all.'

In the UK, Jobriath was dismissed outright as a transparent, and bad, imitation of David BOWIE. In the US, his openness about his homosexuality – telling the press 'I'm a true fairy' – negated any chance of success at home. Vanishing into obscurity in 1975, it was only when Morrissey made vague efforts to trace him as a potential support act on his 1992 YOUR ARSENAL tour that he discovered Jobriath had died of AIDS nine years earlier in July 1983.

A detailed overview of Jobriath's life is provided by Manchester poet and writer Robert Cochrane in the sleeve notes of the Morrissey-compiled 2004 best-of Lonely Planet Boy (named after a NEW YORK DOLLS song). He was born Bruce Campbell in Pennsylvania, becoming Jobriath Salisbury after deserting the army in the mid-60s. He took a role in the New York production of the

j

musical *Hair*, and again in Los Angeles where, as legend has it, in 1969 he introduced the cast's Gloria Jones to visiting English rock singer Marc BOLAN. Accordingly, rumours persist that Jobriath is the subject of Bolan's later 'COSMIC DANCER', as covered by Morrissey.

After one album for DECCA with hippy rock band Pidgeon, Jobriath was caught by the military, spending six months in a Pennsylvania mental hospital. Upon his release, now calling himself Jobriath Boone, he was discovered by Carly Simon manager Jerry Brandt, who brokered a deal with Elektra Records.

His first album was 1973's eponymous *Jobriath*, hyped by ubiquitous press ads and a giant billboard in New York's Times Square. The Jobriath publicity machine soon crossed the Atlantic, as Morrissey vividly recalled. 'In the early 70s there were four weekly music papers – the NME, *Melody Maker*, *Disc* and *Record*. I used to buy all of them every single week, without fail. Jobriath got dreadful reviews. Then I saw his first album cover – he's lying down with his legs morphed into a broken statue. It was the most fantastic picture, so I bought the album.' Eight of its 11 tracks were later compiled on Lonely Planet Boy, including Morrissey's favourite Jobriath song, 'Morning Starship' and the sublime proto-Mozzerian piano ballad 'Inside'; his least favourite, 'Rock Of Ages', was among the three that weren't.

The Bowie-clone slurs against Jobriath were not without foundation and his best tunes sound as if pickaxed from a neighbouring coal face to Aladdin Sane's 'Time' or 'Lady Grinning Soul'; chest-heaving torch songs from a cabaret somewhere in Alpha Centauri, delivered in a strange honky-tonk twang more cowhand than extra-terrestrial superstar. Or as Morrissey put it, 'Cinematic themes of desperate dramas in paranoid shadows were presented as choppy and carnivalesque melodies.'

The *Jobriath* album was followed six months later by a comparatively sloppy sequel, 1974's *Creatures Of The Street* (seen flicked into the

camera lens in the 'PREGNANT FOR THE LAST TIME' video). Its shortcomings are illustrated by the fact that only half of its dozen tracks were rounded up by Morrissey on Lonely Planet Boy, among them the arresting opener 'Heartbeat' and the unnerving 'What A Pretty' (Morrissey's concert entrance music in 2006). The Creatures cover showed him looking, as Cochrane notes, like 'an alien Liberace', though this time there'd be no media blitz and the album sank even lower than its predecessor.

Sessions for a third album were never completed, though they'd result in the superb vamping funk of 'I Love A Good Fight', a song destined never to see the light of day until rescued by Morrissey in 2004 for Lonely Planet Boy, also releasing it as a single on his ATTACK label. Charting at 102 it remains Jobriath's biggest hit. Succumbing to the time-honoured 70s rock temptresses of drink and drugs, Jobriath was dropped by Elektra. Severely embarrassed by the failure of their investment, they continued as if their 'true fairy' had never fluttered into their midst. As Morrissey noted in 2004, 'In a recent, detailed book on the history of Elektra Records, Jobriath was not even mentioned.'

Changing his name to Cole Berlin, Campbell spent the rest of his life as a lounge singer. When interviewed about Jobriath, he always used the third person, claiming 'Jobriath committed suicide in a drug, alcohol and publicity overdose'. In the last years of his life he submitted songs to FRANK SINATRA, living in a pyramid-shaped apartment at the top of New York's Chelsea Hotel. It was there, in July 1983, that his decomposing body was discovered, having been lying several days undisturbed by visitors (a scenario eerily reminiscent of that in Morrissey's first, unreleased, draft of 'PAINT A VULGAR PICTURE').

Morrissey would trumpet Jobriath in a handful of letters to the music press during the mid- to late 70s, later telling pen pal Robert MACKIE in 1980 that he still 'dribbled' over Jobriath. Johnny Marr also remembers Morrissey referring to Jobriath when forming The Smiths in the summer of 1982. 'There was stuff he liked that I didn't,' says Marr, 'like Jobriath, for example. I didn't have any violent objection to it. I thought it was kind of intriguing.'

His Jobriath mania renewed momentum after The Smiths. Captioning some 1991 Japanese tour photos for the *NME*, Morrissey labelled a picture of him signing an autograph for a fan in Tokyo with the words 'Mistaken for Jobriath yet again.' After using the Creatures album in the 'Pregnant' video, a photo by Morrissey of bassist Gary DAY and guitarist Alain WHYTE perusing the gatefold lyrics of Jobriath's debut album was used for the cover of the Japanese 'MY LOVE LIFE' single.

Originally planned for release on Rhino's specialist subsidiary Handmade, in 2004 Morrissey achieved his ambition of seeing Jobriath on CD for the first time with his own Lonely Planet Boy, a 15-track best of both albums plus the previously unheard 'I Love A Good Fight' issued in a deluxe package through his own ATTACK label. 'Thirty years on [Jobriath] is no less an insoluble mystery,' wrote Morrissey in his sleeve note introduction, 'and the songs remain hugely enjoyable.'

Second only to his terminal devotion to the Dolls, Morrissey's rampant Jobriath fixation knows no bounds, from interval music to stage wear (making his band don Jobriath T-shirts in 2004) and even his wild hopes of coaxing Elton John into performing a set of Jobriath covers at his 2004 MELTDOWN festival. That Morrissey had previously requested Elton's head on a plate – 'one instance in which meat would not be murder' – may explain why his John-sings-Jobriath pipedream never came to fruition.

Beyond his obvious affection for the music, Jobriath represents the ultimate Morrissey pop martyr: a doomed outsider, shunned, ridiculed and discriminated against as much for his Wildean honesty in admitting who and what he really was as for his flamboyancy in creating an otherwise absurd alter-ego. And while Jobriath's fate is the stuff of Morrissey's nightmares – ignominious in life, obscure in death – then his art, in all its weird finesse and epic aspiration, is the stuff of Morrissey's sweetest dreams. [17, 55, 80, 108, 156, 174, 175, 231, 241]

jobs, For Morrissey's employment history see WORK.

Johansen, David, See NEW YORK DOLLS.

'Johnny Remember Me', 1961 UK number one by John Leyton, frequently included in Morrissey's lists of his favourite records during the early years of The Smiths.

Written by spiritualist/composer Geoff Goddard, the record was the first of three number ones to hail from the home studio of British recording wizard Joe Meek, situated above a leather goods shop on London's bustling Holloway Road. Legend has it Leyton recorded his vocals in Meek's bathroom (hence press criticisms at the time that he sounded as if he was 'singing at the bottom of an empty well'). With its devil's-gallop rhythm and morbid lyrics reminiscent of Heathcliff's torment by Cathy's ghost in *WUTHERING HEIGHTS*, 'Johnny Remember Me' was a masterclass in the art of the death disc genre prevalent in UK pop in the late 50s and early 60s (e.g. Marty Wilde's 'Endless Sleep', Ricky Valance's 'Tell Laura I Love Her'). It's also one of the earliest examples of pop's exploitation of television audiences, originally written to order for an episode of *Harpers West One*, an ATV soap opera set in a central London department store. Leyton, an actor first and foremost, was due to make a cameo as fictitious rocker Johnny St Cyr and needed a song. His primetime performance of 'Johnny Remember Me' offered his label, Top Rank, the kind of publicity money couldn't buy, making the real single an effortless hit. Goddard, meantime, controversially informed the press that he'd been assured of success by the ghost of Buddy Holly during a séance.

Leyton became a minor UK pop star thereafter, reaching number two with a rushed, sound-a-like sequel, 'Wild Wind' (another blustery, if slightly cheerier, Geoff Goddard creation),before struggling, as Morrissey termed it, '[with] a ragbag of semi-failures like "I'll Cut Your Tail Off" which, for some unknown reason, staggered and died in

j

the lower forties'. Though he enjoyed prestigious supporting roles in big-screen war dramas *The Great Escape* and *Von-Ryan's Express*, musically Leyton would never surpass 'Johnny Remember Me', in Morrissey's opinion 'the best two minutes 45 seconds he ever contributed to the world'. Morrissey has repeatedly echoed the song's theme of voices from beyond the grave in his own lyrics, i.e. 'RUBBER RING', 'A RUSH AND A PUSH AND THE LAND IS OURS' and 'OUIJA BOARD, OUIJA BOARD'. Nor would it be beyond reason to speculate that, in title alone, 'Johnny Remember Me' possesses some degree of poignancy for Morrissey in view of The Smiths' demise.

Offering a tragic, if suitably ghoulish, footnote is the fate of its producer, Joe Meek. Despite subsequent UK number ones with The Tornados' 'Telstar' (which he wrote) and The Honeycombs' 'Have I The Right?', he quickly fell behind the 60s' rapidly changing fashions. Arrested for cottaging in 1963, Meek was subsequently targeted by blackmailers (homosexuality still being an imprisonable offence in the UK at that time) and slowly drove himself mad through pills and his own crippling paranoia. On 3 February 1967, Meek shot his landlady after an argument about rent, then turned the gun on himself.

Today a plaque high in the brickwork of 304 Holloway Road marks the spot where Meek 'lived, worked and died' and where 'Johnny Remember Me' was recorded. [184, 188, 208, 358, 408]

Jones, Paul, See 'I'VE BEEN A BAD, BAD BOY'.

journalism, From 1974, having just turned 15, Morrissey's voice became an infrequent if noticeable spectral echo in the letter pages of the UK music weeklies. As his efforts to form and front various punk-related groups between 1977 and '78 repeatedly ended in disappointment, out of boredom and desperation as much as ambition his thoughts hesitatingly turned to a career in music journalism.

The move seemed logical, given that he'd been compiling his own homemade pop magazine from the age of six, was by his later admission 'dangerously obsessed' by the music press and was already finding his critical voice between his many pro-NEW YORK DOLLS rants in the *NME*'s 'Gasbag' and sporadic articles for punk fanzines such as fellow CRAMPS devotee Lindsay Hutton's *The Next Big Thing*.

'I tried to be a journalist but failed miserably,' Morrissey confessed in 1984, presumably defining

Jones, Jimmy, American R&B/soul singer, famed for his octave-leaping falsetto voice, whose 1960 hit 'Handy Man' has been cited by Marr as a musical influence on 'REEL AROUND THE FOUNTAIN'. The guitarist recalls listening to it during a 'marathon R&B record session' at Crazy Face, the shop of early Smiths manager Joe MOSS. Marr already knew Jones's song from his childhood, possibly from the version by his parents' favourite, Del Shannon. 'I remembered the melody of "Handy Man" but then when I tried to play it myself I got it all wrong,' says Marr, whose incorrect 'Handy Man' formed the basis of the Smiths ballad.

Morrissey would also applaud Jones's follow-up hit, 'Good Timin'',which reached number one in the UK in July 1960. Interviewed in 1991, he revealed he was currently infatuated with the track. 'It's just simple, straight, boring, dull, floppy old pop music,' said Morrissey, 'but to me it's … [*he lowers his voice to a whisper*) it's like skin against skin. It's better than fine cuisine. It's better than sex! There, now, that's how I feel.' Morrissey may well have felt a very personal connection with the song's final verse: 'What would've happened if you and I hadn't just happened to meet?/We might've spent the rest of our lives walkin' down Misery Street.' As a reflection on his partnership with Marr, 'Good Timin'' offers a perfect analogy. [17, 136]

failure by his rejection from the leading weeklies such as *Sounds*, *Melody Maker* and the then-mighty *NME*; when he summoned the courage to ring the latter's offices they blithely hung up on him, an attitude by no means uncommon in the industry's hothouse of ego and arrogance.

Instead, his freelance writing career would be restricted to some half-dozen live reviews for another rival weekly elbowing for fourth position, *Record Mirror*. As with the other London-based papers, it was the custom to employ willing and able writers out in the sticks to cover gigs of interest in their area: the money was poor but the reward of a printed by-line was lure enough to instigate vicious competition. Thus Morrissey briefly became *Record Mirror*'s 'Man in Manchester'. Joining his full name of 'STEVEN MORRISSEY' in the paper's 'Roadshows' section (later changed to the simpler 'Gigs') were those of Scotland's Billy Sloan, future Manic Street Preachers manager and PR Philip Hall and Mark Cooper who, as fate would have it, found himself interviewing Morrissey for *No 1* magazine at the outset of The Smiths, crossing paths again many years later when Cooper became producer of the BBC's *Later With Jools Holland*, booking the singer for numerous appearances.

Whether down to editorial favouritism or his own purely sporadic interest, Morrissey's reviews appeared in two short bursts: the first between March and May of 1980, the second in the late summer of 1981. That first burst begins in the 29 March 1980 edition with his account of The Photos supported by Mark Andrews & The Gents at Manchester Polytechnic. The following week's issue he was back at the same venue to lavish praise upon The Cramps. The 10 May edition witnessed his bosom heave to Linder STERLING's Ludus at The Beach Club only for it to sag three weeks later when witnessing Wasted Youth and Lonesome No More at Manchester University. The second shorter burst begins on the 18 July 1981 issue with his drubbing of Iggy Pop, TV Smith's Explorers and Telephone at the Apollo, and ends in the 22 August edition with his withering dismissal of Depeche

Mode at Rafters, thrown into sharp relief by more plaudits for support act Ludus.

Spinning abstract sentences such as 'But no songs are suicide. I miss the old days', it is perhaps easy to see why Morrissey's journalistic career never took off. The reviews are permeated by a sarcastic humour ('Shocksville, eh kids?') and his critical bite is severe. Of Iggy Pop's band: 'A notably faceless crop of Egyptian mummies.' Of glam punks Wasted Youth: 'The fab guitarist offers furtive sneers, and so would you if you had to apply your foundation with a shovel.' Of Depeche Mode: '[They] may not be the most remarkably boring group ever to walk the face of the earth, but they're certainly in the running.' His admiration was streaked with equal hysteria, declaring The Cramps 'the most beautiful – yes, BEAUTIFUL group I've ever seen' and theatrically insisting 'that Ludus are valuable and special is impossible to deny'.

It is interesting, or rather terrifying, to speculate on what might have happened had Morrissey's journalistic ventures been more plentiful and successful during those two years before his 'unearthing' by Johnny Marr in the summer of 1982. The possibility of his singing destiny being diverted by the lesser glory of becoming the critic rather than the subject must have entertained his thoughts, if only fleetingly. Some perverse gratitude must therefore be directed to those in positions of editorial power who ignored, refused, ridiculed or hung up on Steven Morrissey the journalist. Each and every one of those knockbacks would chisel their mark, however small, upon the ultimate creation of Morrissey the pop star. [155, 173]

'Journalists Who Lie' (Morrissey/Street), B-side of 'OUR FRANK' (1991). Written in the aftermath of his first press backlash since going solo (specifically the negative critical reaction to 'OUIJA BOARD, OUIJA BOARD'), 'Journalists Who Lie' was Morrissey's blunt counter-attack on the hacks he believed were deliberately 'stick[ing] in the knife' to further their fame. Once an aspiring journalist

j

himself (see previous entry), after six years of dealing with the press he came to the conclusion that 'a lot of them aren't massively equipped upstairs. I don't want to be rude but it's the case, it's a cast-iron fact. Some journalists do astound me, they get the spade out and try to dig but can't quite manage it.'

It was also Morrissey's final joint composer credit with Stephen Street, based on a demo left over from before their partnership turned sour. Without Street's studio presence to oversee the tune, it became an amorphous rush of dampened rockabilly guitars and stray sound effects, somewhat devoid of focus. The second track recorded during the KILL UNCLE sessions, according to co-producer Clive LANGER it was 'definitely going on the album' until Morrissey decided otherwise. Years later, the singer would disown it as one of his worst. [15, 22, 25, 39, 69, 241]

Joyce, Mike (Smiths drummer 1982–87, Morrissey drummer 1988–89),

Throughout the history of The Smiths, Morrissey and Marr would frequently praise the group's rhythm section in the media. To Morrissey, they were 'the most capable musicians that I've ever come across in Manchester and it's a perfect little family', while Marr stated the outrageous hyperbole that 'if Elvis PRESLEY had had Mike Joyce and Andy Rourke in his band he would have been an even bigger name'.

Where Mike Joyce is concerned, such statements now resonate with a hollow and bitter sadness. The scorn with which Morrissey, in particular, regards Joyce since the drummer's victory in the 1996 Smiths COURT CASE is unequivocal. He has accused Joyce of 'destroying' The Smiths, having 'no career, so he just lives off me' and, on national television, has wished 'the very, very worst for Joyce for the rest of his life'. It's a hatred that is deep seated and explicitly personal, far beyond the animosity of a defendant towards their plaintiff. If Morrissey has such a thing as a life's nemesis then judging from the singer's diatribes in the press and the venom dripping through 1997's post-court case riposte

'SORROW WILL COME IN THE END', unquestionably Joyce is that person.

Michael Joyce was born in Fallowfield, Manchester, on 1 June 1963 as THE BEATLES were enjoying their first UK number one with 'From Me To You'. The youngest of five children, Joyce's family, like those of Morrissey and Marr, had emigrated from Ireland. He began playing drums in his early teens and immediately became besotted with local punk heroes BUZZCOCKS.

Joyce was still only 15 when he joined his first group, The Hoax, an unsophisticated din of regressive punk buffoonery. After two singles, he left in 1980 for another punk group, Victim. Originally from Belfast, they moved to Manchester after being offered a deal with local punk label TJM Records. Joyce joined them in the wake of their third single, though by September 1982 Victim were lost in a musical cul-de-sac from which they would never return, one where Joyce may also have remained had it not been for his flatmate, Pete Hope, an acquaintance of Marr's.

Hearing that Marr was looking for a drummer, Hope recommended Joyce, who himself had brushed coat-rails with the guitarist as a regular customer in X-Clothes; sizing up mohair jumpers while behind the counter Marr daydreamed of escape. Joyce had nothing to lose by agreeing to audition, yet very nearly risked what would be a life-changing opportunity by consuming some magic mushrooms beforehand. By the time he arrived at Spirit studios on Tariff Street where Marr, Morrissey and provisional bassist Dale HIBBERT were waiting to assess him, Joyce was 'out of it'. Marr was impressed, as much by his nerve in showing up 'tripping his head off' as his aggressive playing. Musically, The Smiths were unknown territory to Joyce, who could only equate them as potentially 'the next Psychedelic Furs'. Marr asked him to join. Joyce had reservations, mainly guilt over deserting Victim. But as his only escape out of their punk cul-de-sac, he accepted.

Joyce's full history within The Smiths would be scrutinised in detail during the court case when it came to light that in his first year with the group

Morrissey and Marr doubted his proficiency, briefly entertaining thoughts of replacing him with old friend Simon WOLSTENCROFT. But scything through the fog of tainted hindsight, history cannot be rewritten and Joyce's drums – 'The Drums' – are there for posterity on every record The Smiths ever made.

By his own admission, Joyce was never a technically skilled drummer, but what he lacked in mathematical precision he compensated for in instinct, belief and an eager rhythmic fervour. It's in his drumming that we can hear the stepping stones of The Smiths' evolution: the blissful naïveté of the early BBC sessions; the nervous suppression under John PORTER on 1984's THE SMITHS; the sense of liberation on the self-produced MEAT IS MURDER; the imperial push for the summit on THE QUEEN IS DEAD; and the accomplished grace of STRANGEWAYS, HERE WE COME. The Smiths made Joyce the drummer he is and he, in turn, faithfully provided Marr's music with the necessary scaffolding whatever the brief. His greatest testimonials are: for vigour, 'THE QUEEN IS DEAD'; for passion and flair, 'LAST NIGHT I DREAMT THAT SOMEBODY LOVED ME'; for sheer hardiness and spirit, the whole of the live album RANK.

It is another consequence of the court case that history has obscured Joyce's special relationship with Morrissey. Even after the court case, Joyce has never shied away from expressing the intense devotion he once felt for the singer. 'It is amazing when you're in that situation, the bond that comes between people,' says Joyce. 'The more intense the subject then the more intense the situation, and The Smiths *was* intense, sometimes so intense that you could shift from the reality of a relationship and then it kind of goes into an obsession. It did with me. A kind of unhealthy obsession. Wanting to make sure everybody was happy. I would have done anything for Morrissey. Absolutely anything. As the song goes, I'd have leapt in front of a flying bullet if he'd asked me.'

In the dying days of The Smiths, Morrissey turned to Joyce as his second-in-command during their doomed final session with replacement guitarist Ivor PERRY. 'I felt as though I'd taken Johnny's mantle,' he admits. 'I'd become the interpreter of what Morrissey wanted, the one having to give orders to the rest. Being pulled aside and whispered conversations, having to tell people they weren't allowed to eat with us. Silly stuff, really. Because he didn't have Johnny to sound off or grieve to, he decided to go for me. I only had it for a few days, but I just couldn't cope with it.'

Following the collapse of the group, Joyce paired off with Andy Rourke, briefly playing for The Adult Net, the solo project of Fall guitarist Brix Smith also featuring Craig GANNON, before touring with Sinead O'Connor. He'd join Rourke and Gannon again when reunited with Morrissey in November 1988 for the recording of the singles 'THE LAST OF THE FAMOUS INTERNATIONAL PLAYBOYS' and 'INTERESTING DRUG'. Joyce's legal proceedings contesting his share of Smiths performance royalties had already begun when he appeared on stage at Morrissey's historic solo live debut in WOLVERHAMPTON the following month. Only his refusal to drop the case made Joyce's severance from Morrissey inevitable.

It would be another seven years before Joyce had his day in court. In that time he'd tour with his childhood heroes, Buzzcocks, as well as Public Image Ltd and Julian Cope. At his loosest end, Joyce once responded to a musicians wanted ad in the music press from a group seeking a drummer who liked The Smiths: the group turned out to be a young Suede (see 'MY INSATIABLE ONE'). Since his 1996 court victory, though Joyce continues to play his projects have been sporadic, restricting himself to various Manchester-based groups, many of them with Andy Rourke.

But the irresolvable financial feud continues. Joyce has attempted to present his side of the story in an official documentary, 2007's *Inside The Smiths*, also featuring Rourke. Alas, nothing can pacify Morrissey's unforgiving wrath. In November 2005, Joyce appeared as a guest on the BBC's digital radio channel 6Music, broadcasting a one-minute clip of a Smiths studio outtake which he referred to as 'The Click Track' (the real working title was actually 'Fast One', an instrumental demo recorded in July 1984 with producer John Porter). In doing so, he provoked a brutal retribution from Morrissey who issued a statement on the TRUE-TO-YOU.NET website, detailing the full personal cost of Joyce's court proceedings and furiously highlighting the illegality of his action in sharing unreleased Smiths material which he didn't technically 'own'. Though he made no similar public statement, privately Marr was equally upset by Joyce's broadcast.

While the 6Music incident was only a minor storm in a teacup, it neatly illustrates the tundra of eggshells surrounding Joyce's every move when it comes to asserting his place within The Smiths' legacy. Yet although the more extremist Morrissey apostles have since typecast him as a traitorous Judas figure – selling out their messiah for his proverbial 30 pieces of silver, as it were – to the legion of Smiths fans, then and now, Mike Joyce will always be the one, the only 'The Drums'. [7, 12, 13, 14, 17, 18, 19, 28, 29, 38, 39, 53, 167, 233, 403, 406, 453]

Joyce, Yootha, English actress and cover star of the Smiths single 'ASK'. Joyce became a household name in the early 1970s as Mildred Roper, the domineering, sexually frustrated wife of George (Brian Murphy), landlords to Robin O'Sullivan and friends in the popular ITV sitcom *Man About The House* (1973–76), and later stars of their own spin-off series, *George & Mildred* (1976–80). Joyce died in August 1980 of liver failure just days after her 53rd birthday. Trained as a serious dramatic actress with Joan Littlewood's Theatre Workshop (it was through Littlewood that Joyce was friends with Kirsty MACCOLL's parents), the inescapable fame of the frivolous Mildred Roper exacerbated her struggle with alcoholism: an inquest revealed that for the last ten years of her life, and throughout the making of *George & Mildred*, Joyce had been averaging a bottle of brandy a day.

As both a tortured celebrity, iconic battleaxe and uniquely British character actress, Joyce was classic Morrissey material, an obsession he'd share with his friend James MAKER. In choosing her for the cover of 'Ask', he highlighted her pre-sitcom roots as a bit player in 60s British cinema with a still from 1965's *Catch Us If You Can*, The Dave Clark Five's brazen attempt to follow THE BEATLES on to the big screen. Joyce plays Nan, half of a posh married couple who pick up Clark and his girlfriend and try to seduce them in their Bath townhouse before taking the whole group to a fancy dress party.

In Morrissey terms, Joyce's most significant film is Shelagh DELANEY and Albert FINNEY's *Charlie Bubbles* (1967) in which she appears in a scene at NEWPORT PAGNELL services (see also 'IS IT REALLY SO STRANGE?'). Also of interest are 1963's *Sparrows Can't Sing*, Joyce's film debut as an East End barmaid, shot on the KRAYS' manor and featuring a cameo from the brothers themselves; 1965's utterly strange *Die! Die! My Darling!* (aka *Fanatic*), a novel British attempt at gothic horror in which she plays the panicky maid helping vegetarian Bible-basher Tallulah Bankhead imprison Stefanie Powers in the attic; and 1967's *Our Mother's House*, an even more macabre melodrama in which Joyce plays the concerned schoolteacher of Dirk BOGARDE's murderous brood. [332, 357, 374, 382, 491]

Julian and Sandy, See under Kenneth Williams in the *CARRY ON* entry.

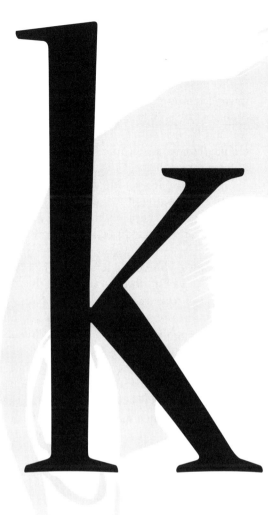

Kane, Arthur, See NEW YORK DOLLS.

karaoke, 'There are easier ways to embarrass yourself' is Morrissey's verdict on karaoke, largely based on a 'shocking' experience having his senses assaulted by the local clientele of the Little Driver pub in Bow, east London during the early 90s. 'I like simple pleasures and uncomplicated people but that takes the biscuit,' he added. 'I can't understand why anybody would want to do it.' [153]

Keitel, Harvey, American actor and almost-cover star of The Smiths' last album, STRANGE-WAYS, HERE WE COME. The image Morrissey had wanted to use was from 1967's *Who's That Knocking At My Door*, Keitel's first feature film and the directorial debut of his friend Martin Scorsese. Showing a young Keitel sat at a bar with a shot glass and a cigarette, his eyes closed with maniacal laughter, it would have perfectly complemented the album title. Keitel was on location in Scotland filming the BBC drama *Down Where The Buffalo Go* when he was approached for permission. Unfortunately, not having heard of The Smiths, he declined, instigating the much less effective substitute sleeve of Richard DAVALOS. Four years later, Morrissey asked to use the same image a second time as a backdrop and programme cover for his 1991 KILL UNCLE tour. Though still apparently 'bemused by the request' Keitel liberally gave his consent. [141, 374]

Kill Uncle, Morrissey's second solo album, released March 1991, highest UK chart position #8. Tracks: 'OUR FRANK', 'ASIAN RUT', 'SING YOUR LIFE', 'MUTE WITNESS', 'KING LEER', 'FOUND FOUND FOUND', 'DRIVING YOUR GIRLFRIEND HOME', 'THE HARSH TRUTH OF THE CAMERA EYE', '(I'M) THE END OF THE FAMILY LINE', 'THERE'S A PLACE IN HELL FOR ME AND MY FRIENDS'. Produced by Clive LANGER and Alan Winstanley. (US version also includes 'TONY THE PONY'.)

The three-year gap between the release of Morrissey's first and second solo albums says much about the difficult genesis of the latter. The original plan had been to follow up 1988's VIVA HATE in the spring of 1990 with BONA DRAG, his intended second album which was eventually scrapped and substituted for its compilation namesake. It was only when Morrissey recruited Mark Nevin as co-writer that enough new material presented itself to take a second stab at his second album proper. (For a detailed development of their friendship and the songwriting process in the run-up to the album, refer to the separate NEVIN entry.)

Recorded at Hook End Manor in the autumn of 1990, Kill Uncle introduced further personnel changes in Morrissey's studio band. The ever-faithful Andrew PARESI remained on drums, joined by new faces Mark Bedford of MADNESS (bass) and Nevin on guitar. Keyboards were shared between another Madness associate, session pianist Seamus Beaghen, and Steve Nieve of Elvis Costello's Attractions (real name Steve Nason, renamed 'Steve Heart' by Morrissey on Kill Uncle's inner sleeve). Continuing from where previous single 'PICCADILLY PALARE' had left off, producers Langer and Winstanley once again imprinted the recordings with their inimitable Madness-lite flourishes.

The session was largely uneventful and its critics would probably argue so too is the record itself. Texturally, Kill Uncle sounds unlike any other Morrissey album. Musically, it's his most subtle, the backing melodies rarely forcing themselves forward but hidden within some very refined production full of even subtler sonic frolics. This lightness of touch is echoed in some of Morrissey's frothiest rhyming couplets: 'photographer' with 'had it in for yer' ('The Harsh Truth Of The Camera Eye'); 'surprise ya' with 'Tizer' ('King Leer'). It's also an album of two very distinct halves, the first noticeably frivolous (bar 'Asian Rut'), the second much gloomier and sluggish.

On his part, Nevin would later criticise its production for 'lacking middle', claiming that they'd been self-consciously trying 'not to copy The Smiths' to the point of deliberately stripping back guitars in favour of piano. Langer argues that the tracks weren't perhaps as strong as the earlier Bona Drag material he and Winstanley had worked on,

not so much songs as 'a bunch of poems stuck to music'. It's interesting that in making the latter observation, Langer should further compare the feel of Kill Uncle with that of John BETJEMAN's 1974 album Banana Blush, the source of Morrissey's 2002 entrance theme, 'A Child Ill'.

Upon its release, Morrissey promoted the album with routine pride, calling it 'more listenable' and 'much happier' than Viva Hate and 'a much better record, particularly in terms of lyrics'. His opinions weren't shared by the press, nor those critics who continue to vilify Kill Uncle as one of the worst albums ever to be thrust upon humanity, a reputation it ill deserves. Nonetheless, three years after its release Morrissey himself joined the public drubbing, labelling it 'substandard' and describing it as 'a great shock to me to actually make a few records which I didn't really think were exceptional'. By way of excuse, he explained Kill Uncle had been 'a very bad time for me privately', which itself cast fresh light upon its more obviously autobiographical moments (e.g. 'FOUND FOUND FOUND').

In the event, Kill Uncle was of less importance as a record than it was a catalyst for Morrissey's permanent return to the stage as a solo artist. Just seven weeks after its release, on 27 April 1991 he began his first tour in five years at Dublin National Stadium. His live band of Boz BOORER, Spencer COBRIN, Gary DAY and Alain WHYTE infused the Kill Uncle material with a refreshing rockabilly slant, even rising to the live challenge of 'Asian Rut'. Whatever its shortcomings as an album, Kill Uncle gave Morrissey his long-awaited excuse to acquire the one thing he'd been sorely missing since The Smiths: his own gang.

As time marches on, few have rushed to Kill Uncle's defence and it's unlikely its reputation as the nadir of Morrissey's recording career will ever be easily expunged. Even its brevity is targeted by some as a weakness when, at 33 minutes, it's only three minutes shy of STRANGEWAYS, HERE WE COME, and would have clocked in several minutes longer had its proposed title track not been excised (see next entry). Yet because of its peculiarity when

'**Kill Uncle**' (Morrissey/Nevin), Morrissey's second album owes its name to an abandoned title track inspired by a low-budget 1966 American horror comedy, *Let's Kill Uncle*. The film's plot is very similar to the basic premise of Lemony Snicket's later *A Series Of Unfortunate Events* books: a young orphan who is bequeathed a fortune finds himself stranded on an island with a mad uncle who concocts various evil schemes in order to kill him and steal the inheritance. The boy and his friend, a resourceful girl the same age, must therefore 'kill uncle before uncle kills us'.

According to Andrew PARESI, Morrissey's lyric reversed the scenario. 'The spine of the song was that uncle's got money and he's not giving it to us,' recalls Paresi, 'but if we kill him, then we'll have the cash.' Morrissey's song had a repeated chorus hook ('Kill un-cle! Kill un-cle!') and even made it as far as a finished vocal take before he abandoned it. According to Paresi, the singer asked 'the tapes to be trashed' but kept the title for the album in any case. [22, 25]

contrasted against every other Morrissey album (not to mention every other album of 1991, an especially dreadful year in British music), there's something uniquely fascinating about it. Asked to summarise its central theme at the time, Morrissey simply described it as 'Just me [and] my views of life as I live it'. It's in this same laissez faire spirit that the runt-like Kill Uncle is best appreciated. [15, 22, 25, 83, 90, 96, 437]

Killing Of Sister George, The, 1968 British

drama listed among Morrissey's favourite films. Adapted from the play by Frank Marcus, Beryl Reid stars as the eponymous 'Sister George', the district nurse in a BBC television soap opera set in the rural village of Applehurst (loosely based on the real BBC radio soap, *The Archers*). Off camera, 'George' is a sour, cantankerous, alcoholic lesbian, June Bainbridge, who takes out her frustration on her younger live-in lover, an aspiring poet nick-named Childie (Susannah York). After drunkenly assaulting two nuns in a taxi, Bainbridge becomes paranoid that the Applehurst producers are plan-ning to get rid of her by killing off Sister George. Adding to her misery are fears that a BBC execu-tive, Miss Croft (Coral Browne), is conspiring to snatch the beautiful Childie away from her.

The Killing Of Sister George was markedly courageous for its day in its overt discussion of lesbianism, featuring scenes shot in Chelsea's legendary Gateway club on the King's Road using regulars as extras. Director Robert Aldrich, respon-sible for other Morrissey favourites such as *Kiss Me Deadly* and *Whatever Happened To Baby Jane?*, first considered the latter's star, Bette DAVIS, for the lead role, only to give it to Reid who'd already played the part on stage in London and on Broad-way. It's faintly possible that a scene in the film where Sister George's screen death is discussed – 'Bang! Collision with a ten-ton truck!' – may have had some bearing upon the chorus of 'THERE IS A LIGHT THAT NEVER GOES OUT'. More probable is that another line in the script coined the title of Morris-sey's 1992 B-side, 'THERE SPEAKS A TRUE FRIEND'.

Of purely trivial interest, the opening credit sequence was filmed in Hampstead, in the area circling the Holly Bush pub (the Marquis Of Granby in the film), round the corner from the former home of Morrissey's favourite artist, Hannah GLUCKSTEIN, and opposite the lane where Terence STAMP abducts Samantha Eggar in *The Collector*; Beryl Reid is seen passing the same spot, Mount Vernon Terrace. [184, 227, 517, 561]

Kind Of Loving, A, 1962 British kitchen-sink

drama listed among Morrissey's favourite films. Adapted from Stan Barstow's novel – the first in his 'Vic Brown trilogy' – it was the feature direc-torial debut of John Schlesinger, who'd go on to make *BILLY LIAR* the following year with the same scriptwriters (Keith Waterhouse and Willis Hall) and some of the same support cast (Leonard

Rossiter and Helen Fraser). The story is an ordinary but honest account of the domestic problems and social pressures thrust upon young working-class couples in the early 60s. Draughtsman Vic (played by Alan Bates after Albert FINNEY turned down the role) falls in love with 19-year-old Ingrid (June Ritchie) whom he passes every day in the works canteen. They start courting and eventually he persuades her to sleep with him. Both are virgins and find the experience so awkward and upsetting it ruins their relationship. Unfortunately, Ingrid becomes pregnant and they are forced into marriage. Unable to afford a place of their own, they lodge with Ingrid's mother (Thora Hird), an insufferable, opinionated busybody who immediately drives Vic to the brink of insanity. Exasperated, he walks out on Ingrid shortly after she suffers a miscarriage. They eventually reunite to make a second go at it, only upon Vic's condition that they live in whatever grimy hovel they can afford to get away from her mother.

A Kind Of Loving is quintessential Smiths viewing, tackling many of the themes Morrissey would address in his early lyrics: the unhappy, obligatory marriage ('WILLIAM, IT WAS REALLY NOTHING'), newlywed poverty ('I WANT THE ONE I CAN'T HAVE') and the fear, expectation and humiliation of sex ('MISERABLE LIE', 'PRETTY GIRLS MAKE GRAVES'). [184, 227, 518]

'King Leer' (Morrissey/Nevin), From the album KILL UNCLE (1991). One vowel away from one of Shakespeare's greatest tragedies, 'King Leer' was, by contrast, one of Morrissey's most superficial offerings. Its lyrics are regarded by some critics as among his poorest, particularly its opening stanza's much ridiculed 'one knee' rhyme. Alternatively, it could be argued that 'King Leer' is an intentionally whimsical situation comedy played strictly for laughs as the singer falls over himself trying to impress the indifferent object of his desire with everything from fizzy pop (Tizer) to a homeless dog. 'We just thought it was funny,' agrees producer Clive LANGER. Morrissey even named 'King Leer' his 'favourite track' from Kill Uncle,

describing Nevin's score as having 'a very English tea room feel'. It fared even better live, translating easily to a rockabilly arrangement complete with slapback stand-up bass solo from Gary DAY and effective vocal interjection from Alain WHYTE who routinely sang the last line. [15, 22, 437]

'Kit' (Morrissey/Boorer), Studio outtake from the 1997 MALADJUSTED album sessions. Never specifying whether his subject is male (Kit as in Christopher) or female (Kit as in Kathleen, like the character in Shelagh DELANEY's *The Lion In Love*), Morrissey's 'Kit' tells of an emotionally damaged 28-year-old; unwilling to take down the pictures or throw away the cigarette butts of their former male lover, and seemingly deaf to the offers of comfort from concerned friends. The narrative was granted unusual melodrama thanks to Boorer's ambitious arrangement, its gothic intro and lurching verses (vaguely reminiscent of 'THE HARSH TRUTH OF THE CAMERA EYE') building to a chorus of marching snare drums and a histrionic finale which had Morrissey wailing 'make your mind up soon' in falsetto. Much time and effort was spent on recording 'Kit' though it was eventually binned despite protestations from producer Steve LILLYWHITE who, according to bassist Jonny BRIDGWOOD, 'did his best to save it'. Asked about the song two years later, Morrissey explained that 'it was never released [because] it's a little irrelevant'. Boorer possibly disagreed, going on to perform an acoustic version at a solo concert in Los Angeles in April 2001. [4, 5, 40, 143]

Kray, Ronnie and Reggie, Notorious twin brother ganglords who ruled London's East End during the 1960s, as referenced in 'THE LAST OF THE FAMOUS INTERNATIONAL PLAYBOYS'. Morrissey admitted he was fascinated by 'the level of notoriety that surrounded them – the level of fame they gained from being unreachably notorious'. In 1991, he also referred to the criminally insane Ronnie Kray, then serving a life sentence in Broadmoor, as the living person he most admired alongside actor John MILLS. He'd deny this eight years later: 'I don't think I ever said I admired the Kray twins. Did I?'

As Britain's first 'celebrity gangsters' – hanging out with film stars, pop singers, interviewed on television and photographed by David Bailey – the Krays were the ultimate emblem of Morrissey's 'International Playboys' thesis on criminality and media stardom. Rather than reject this phenomenon, Morrissey would embrace the cult of the Krays, using key locations for photoshoots – Vallance Road in Bethnal Green where the twins were raised and the Grave Maurice pub in Whitechapel where they extorted protection money – and even joining in the campaign to repeal their life sentences with the message 'FREE REG, FREE RON' carved into the run-out-groove of 1991's 'OUR FRANK' single.

Born and bred in the East End, as teenagers the twins both took up lightweight boxing: Reggie, the better fighter, ended his career in the ring undefeated after seven bouts. Called up for national service, they absconded from basic training and were sent to Shepton Mallet military prison where they first crossed paths with future gangland rival Charlie RICHARDSON (seen on the inner sleeve of YOUR ARSENAL). Upon release, the twins began building their East End empire, though it wasn't long before Ronnie's mental instability, aggravated by paranoia over his homosexuality (he'd later kill Richardson associate George Cornell for calling him a 'fat poof') saw him back inside after assaulting a man with a bayonet. While in prison the full extent of his psychotic nature came to light when he was transferred to a mental hospital suffering delusions that Reggie had been replaced by a doppelganger Russian spy.

It wasn't until 1968 that the Krays were finally arrested and brought to trial in January 1969 after a concerted effort by Detective Leonard 'Nipper' Read of Scotland Yard to gather witness testimonies against them. Enough came forward to convict them of the murders of Cornell and drug dealer Jack 'The Hat' McVitie, uncle of future COCKNEY REJECTS bassist Vince Riordan, so named because he always covered his baldness with a

trilby. McVitie had been paid by the Krays to kill a suspected grass but failed to carry out the murder. Stupidly, he kept the dosh. He was subsequently lured to a flat in Stoke Newington in October 1967 where the twins were waiting. Reggie attempted to shoot him but the gun jammed. McVitie tried escaping through a window but was restrained by Ronnie while his twin brother stabbed him to death with a carving knife.

Found guilty of the deaths of Cornell and McVitie, few doubt that the twins probably murdered others. At the age of 35, Ronnie and Reggie both received life sentences with a minimum tariff of 30 years. 'The Krays weren't really as horrendous as people think they were,' argued Morrissey, 'but they mocked the police and mocked British law and that's really quite unforgivable … For the most part they won so therefore they had to be brought to their knees at some point, which obviously they were.'

Certified insane, Ronnie would end his life in Broadmoor, where he died in March 1995: Morrissey sent a wreath to his funeral. Born-again Christian Reggie was released on compassionate grounds in August 2000 after being diagnosed with cancer. He died the following month. 'Like Ron, I was a product of my environment,' Reggie stated in his 1993 book *Villains We Have Known*, adding, 'I hope that my writings show that it is better to read such stories from the comfort of an armchair than to participate in such criminal activities.'

The Krays remain the patron saints of London villainy, icons in their own lifetime long before their imprisonment: a prime example is the 1967 *Man In A Suitcase* episode 'The Sitting Pigeon', starring George Sewell (who actually knew the Krays) as a cowardly hoodlum turned grass on his Kray-esque brothers (see also Richard BRADFORD). Their own story was later brought to the big screen in Peter Medak's 1990 film, *The Krays*, starring Spandau Ballet brothers Gary and Martin Kemp as Ronnie and Reggie and former Smiths cover star Billie WHITELAW as their mum, Violet.
[141, 148, 191, 330, 331, 359, 384, 437]

L-Shaped Room, The, 1962 British kitchen-sink drama listed among Morrissey's favourite films and the source of the sample used at the beginning of The Smiths' 'THE QUEEN IS DEAD'. Adapted from Lynne Reid Banks's novel by director Bryan Forbes (who also scripted *The Cockleshell Heroes*, as sampled on 'MALADJUSTED'), it follows the plight of Jane (Leslie Caron), a 27-year-old French woman who takes the bug-infested lodgings of the title in a dingy Notting Hill boarding house. Friendless and alone, Jane has come there to have her illegitimate child in secret, but soon develops a romance with fellow lodger Toby (Tom Bell), a struggling writer making ends meet in a cracker factory. The main drama revolves around the early 60s social stigma of Jane's unmarried pregnancy and how that affects her affair with Toby when he eventually finds out.

There are numerous Smiths connections among the principal cast. 'SHAKESPEARE'S SISTER' cover star Pat PHOENIX plays a blonde prostitute living in the basement flat while the self-absorbed Dr Weaver whose private clinic Jane visits early on is played by Emlyn Williams, actor and author of the Moors Murders book *BEYOND BELIEF* which inspired 'SUFFER LITTLE CHILDREN'.

The scene sampled on 'The Queen Is Dead' is near the end of the film when most of the lodgers gather for a party in Doris the landlady's front room on Christmas Day. Cicely Courtneidge plays the old lesbian Mavis, a sweet but batty former actress who's coerced into performing an old music hall turn, choosing 'TAKE ME BACK TO DEAR OLD BLIGHTY'. Look out also for the lecherous yob loitering on the street corner who harasses Caron just after the opening credits. That's Anthony Booth, later to become Mr Pat Phoenix and father-in-law to a man who would make Morrissey 'very depressed': prime minister Tony Blair. [56, 227, 267, 519]

Ladykillers, The, 1955 Ealing comedy listed among Morrissey's favourite films and featuring one of his favourite acting performances by Alec GUINNESS. Mrs Wilberforce, a batty old widow who lives alone with her parrots in a lopsided boarding house on a railway embankment near London's King's Cross, has been advertising rooms to let with little success. Her fortunes change when the ghoulish-looking Professor Marcus (Guinness) inquires if he and his fellow 'musicians' in a travelling string quintet can take the rooms. Mrs Wilberforce is thrilled, oblivious to the truth that Marcus and his cronies are actually criminals planning a cunning heist at King's Cross station. The robbery is a success, aided by the ignorant old lady who unknowingly helps them 'carry the lolly' back to the boarding house. As the crooks pack up and leave, she rumbles them when they carelessly spill a cello case stuffed with banknotes. Marcus tries, but fails, to persuade her that if she shops them to the police she'll be implicated as an accomplice. The gang draw straws to determine which of them is to murder Mrs Wilberforce, all the while plotting to double-cross one another and escape with the loot single-handed. Morrissey's admiration of Guinness's performance in *The Ladykillers* was in keeping with his love of fellow Ealing player Alastair SIM: the role of Professor Marcus had originally been considered for Sim, which Guinness duly honoured in an affectionate homage complete with false overbite. [168, 227, 520]

Langer, Clive (Morrissey producer and co-writer, 1989–91),

When Morrissey's initial post-Smiths honeymoon period with Stephen STREET turned sour, the key figure who oversaw the next phase of his solo career was Clive Langer.

Half of an esteemed production team with Alan Winstanley, the duo were best known for their work with MADNESS, as well as Dexys Midnight Runners (second album Too-Rye-Aye featuring UK number one, 'Come On, Eileen'), David BOWIE ('Absolute Beginners' and the Mick Jagger duet 'Dancing In The Street') and Elvis Costello. Besides producing, Langer had also achieved notable success as a composer, writing the melody of Costello's celebrated Falklands War protest ballad, 'Shipbuilding'. Prior to working with Morrissey, Langer and Winstanley had been on the periphery

of his world since 1986 when they produced Sandie SHAW's cover of Lloyd COLE's 'Are You Ready To Be Heartbroken?' Langer also co-wrote its Morrissey-tribute B-side, 'Steven, You Don't Eat Meat', and later another Shaw track, 'Comrade In Arms', one of two Langer/Winstanley productions from her 1988 album, Hello Angel.

By 1989, the pair had taken ownership of Hook End, a converted Tudor monastery in 22 acres of Berkshire countryside near Reading, which they'd renamed Outside studios. That September, EMI booked a fortnight's session at Outside where Morrissey was supposed to record his fifth single with Street, 'OUIJA BOARD, OUIJA BOARD'. Unable to resolve his ongoing financial dispute with Morrissey, Street vetoed the session, leaving the record without a producer and EMI with two weeks' studio time which they were duty bound to pay for. As the studio owners, Langer and Winstanley were the label's obvious choice for an emergency replacement.

When the session resumed with new musicians hired by Langer (including guitarist Kevin ARMSTRONG), omens were far from encouraging. After one day trying to rebuild 'Ouija Board' from scratch, Langer sensed Morrissey's unhappiness and invited him for a walk around Hook End's vast grounds to discuss their predicament. Agreeing that it was 'nice to have met' but that the session wasn't working, they returned to the studio only to hear a rough take of B-side 'YES, I AM BLIND', which Winstanley had developed during their absence. Morrissey was sufficiently impressed to instantly cast aside any previous reservations. Langer and Winstanley were now firmly back on board, completing 'Ouija Board, Ouija Board' and remaining Morrissey's producers for the next two years – by far the most creatively uncertain and commercially unrewarding of the singer's career.

Whereas Winstanley's relationship with Morrissey was purely professional, Langer developed a much closer friendship. Between late '89 and the summer of '91, Langer became the next in a growing line of deputies, subject to similar extra-curricular social demands as experienced by Marr, Joyce and Street before him, from personal chauffeur to mealtime Führer whose job it was to banish whichever studio personnel the singer disliked from the dining table. Though both producers were committed family men, Langer's willingness to entertain Morrissey contrasted sharply with Winstanley's protective distance. 'Alan put up a barrier,' confirms Langer. 'It wasn't part of his life whereas I was doing whatever Morrissey wanted. So it caused a bit of friction between Alan and myself.'

The bond between singer and producer was fortified when, following Street's exit, Langer threw his hat into the ring of prospective co-writers for BONA DRAG alongside Armstrong, Andy Rourke and the routinely unsuccessful Andrew PARESI. 'Everyone was allowed to submit,' recalls Langer. 'Probably because of "Shipbuilding", he knew I could write a tune. As well as that, I used to be in a band before called Deaf School. Morrissey used to go on about how good the name was but how shit our music was. So I gave him around eight demos and he picked out the ones I thought he'd never go for.' Four Morrissey/Langer tunes emerged in total: 'NOVEMBER SPAWNED A MONSTER', 'STRIPTEASE WITH A DIFFERENCE' and KILL UNCLE's 'MUTE WITNESS' and 'FOUND FOUND FOUND'.

Beyond the enduring 'November Spawned A Monster', Langer's most significant contribution to Morrissey's career was his bridge to the Madness camp and the Camden rockabilly scene. Through Langer, Morrissey befriended Cathal SMYTH, who in turn introduced him to Boz BOORER. Alongside Mark NEVIN, Langer also took an active part in the audition process of Alain WHYTE, Gary DAY and Spencer COBRIN until choosing to relinquish his work for Morrissey due to the strain their involvement placed upon his family.

'There came a point when I had to pull back,' says Langer. 'I was losing touch with my wife because I was getting more and more into Morrissey World. I don't think he really liked the fact I had a family. Morrissey was very lonely. You give your life to him, and he's your best friend for ever,

but if you've got other things going on in your life, it's hard for him to deal with that. Morrissey's sense of reality has nothing to do with anyone else's. I loved working with him, it was a great experience. But he's not your normal Joe.' As a fellow Camden resident, Langer would remain on the fringes of 'Morrissey World' until the singer left London in the late 1990s. [1, 15, 22, 25, 36, 39]

'Last Night I Dreamt That Somebody Loved Me' (Morrissey/Marr), The Smiths' 17th and final single (taken from the album STRANGEWAYS, HERE WE COME), released December 1987, highest UK chart position #30.

Speaking in November 1986, Morrissey expressed his desire for The Smiths 'to do some very searing ballads … very soft, heavily orchestrated ballads'. His wish would soon be realised with what was to become the *ultimate* Smiths record, 'Last Night I Dreamt That Somebody Loved Me'. For Johnny Marr, it's the one track that sums up the spirit of the group over all others. 'It has drama, poetry and an almost gothic intensity,' he says. 'The emotions it gives off, and that went into writing it, pretty much personified what it was like being in The Smiths and forming The Smiths. "Last Night I Dreamt" seems to come from the heart of all of us without having any influences or agenda. It's an outpouring. Like a little movie. It's beyond four people playing rock and roll, which sounds grandiose but I do feel that it has a certain classicism to it. Almost operatic.'

If, as Marr suggests, it really is the signature theme to life in The Smiths and forming The Smiths then it speaks volumes for the psychological intensity at the heart of his creative partnership with Morrissey. As a piece of music, it stands as the supreme example of their search to find 'the beauty in melancholy' and their understanding of pop music as a sublime art form. If pop officially 'began' in 1956 with Elvis PRESLEY's 'Heartbreak Hotel' – a song inspired by the newspaper report of a man who committed suicide leaving a note which read 'I walk a lonely street' – then 'Last

Night I Dreamt' is its respondent death knell, Morrissey checking in to the same dwelling vacated by Elvis 31 years earlier, closing the curtains, locking the door and slowly perishing in the still-stale gloom of undisturbed grief and isolation. His is the loneliest street of all: baby hasn't left him because baby doesn't exist. In the icy vacuum of human solitude, love has become an impossibility tortured by futile romantic fantasies (the phrase 'another false alarm' is probably borrowed from JONI MITCHELL's 'Amelia'). There is no hope, only an awaiting eternity of fathomless pain and suffering. With its closing surrender, 'This story is old, I know, but it goes on' – once named by Morrissey as his favourite lyric – he finally yields his grip, plummeting into the abyss of infinite sorrow. At the time *Smash Hits* described it with appropriate melodrama as 'the saddest, most woefully heart-sizzling Smiths song ever'. Beyond question, as an articulation of loneliness in all its soul-corroding agony, 'Last Night I Dreamt' is without equal in pop music.

'I remember when I came up with the riff,' says Marr. 'Me and Morrissey were sitting in the back lounge of a tour bus on the way back from a gig in Carlisle [13 October 1986]. I had my guitar, unplugged, and came up with it but I was scared of losing it. I couldn't work out how my fingers were playing it so I was holding my breath in case I lost it. I heard the whole thing in my head there and then as I came up with those chords.' Marr's orchestral requiem mass would be prefixed by a complementary piano prologue which he'd originally sketched out as a separate song; the lonesome echo of the pianist refusing to leave the sinking ship, rattled by the additional sound effects of whale song and a jeering crowd.

The symphonic body of the track inspired some of if not *the* finest performances on any Smiths record, be it Joyce's gallows-bound drums, Rourke's brooding bass or Marr's Beethovenian tidal wave created using only an Emulator keyboard – Strangeways' fictitious 'ORCHESTRAZIA ARDWICK'. As Marr affirms, 'it's an amazing ensemble piece'. But the greatest performance of all is Morrissey's. According to co-producer Stephen STREET, he nailed it in one take. 'The reason he was that intense was because he used to really build himself up for it, almost like an actor. On "Last Night I Dreamt" he just gave his all first time round. It was one of those where he came in, did it and everybody watching just went, "Whoa!"' In 1989, Morrissey would refer to his singing as being 'at its best around *Strangeways* which was due to extensive touring and really pushing your voice beyond the boundaries'. 'Last Night I Dreamt That Somebody Loved Me' more than bears out his self-assessment, his every pining syllable a panic-stricken assault on the listener's senses.

Morrissey and Marr's last masterpiece, in December 1987 it became their final official Rough Trade single, less a credible chart contender than a symbolic obituary. The seven-inch single chopped off the intro for radio purposes, making it a pithy and intense three minutes. But the majesty of 'Last Night I Dreamt That Somebody Loved Me' has to be appreciated in its full five-minute Strangeways entirety. Beyond rock and roll, beyond pop, it's also beyond everything else The Smiths ever recorded. Though Marr has said that, had they continued, this song represented another 'more orchestral route' the group could have feasibly gone down, it's difficult to imagine them ever surpassing it. Morrissey hasn't. Nor has Marr. It's unlikely they, or anybody else, ever will. [17, 19, 38, 69, 143, 428]

'Last Of The Famous International Playboys, The' (Morrissey/Street), Morrissey's third solo single, released January 1989, highest UK chart position #6. Following on from his earlier B-side 'SISTER I'M A POET' and its admission of loving the 'romance of crime', 'The Last Of The Famous International Playboys' was a more explicit examination of the same theme: a besotted fan letter to notorious imprisoned 60s London gangsters Reggie and Ronnie KRAY from a young criminal wannabe intent on achieving public fame through similarly villainous means.

'The Krays became celebrities in England for being notorious and for being powerful,' Morrissey explained. 'Within the song, the quest to be an international playboy is a myth. Just simply by being notorious and wanting to be extreme and a part of the criminal underworld, desperate to be so. A lot of people, in order to be famous, and in order to be acknowledged do something destructive. Or commit murder.' The title suggested various amalgamated sources, from NANCY SINATRA's 'The Last Of The Secret Agents' (B-side to Morrissey's 1966 favourite 'How Does That Grab Ya Darlin'?') to Irish playwright J. M. Synge's *The Playboy Of The Western World*. More cryptic, if not outright flippant, was Morrissey's own explanation that 'the last of the famous international playboys are BOWIE, BOLAN, DEVOTO and me'.

An early version of the song with a different Street tune (and possibly different lyrics) was trialled in autumn 1987 during the demo stages of VIVA HATE. For its second draft, Street came up with its bootboy power-riff by attempting to write what he describes as 'a simple song like The Fall, really basic and punky'. In its thumping drums and, indeed, Fall-esque chugging guitars, 'Playboys' was a brutish, knuckle-cracking pop Cyclops, crowned by Morrissey's thrilling vocal, from the baritone dip as he sings 'failed' to the quintessential example of the 'Morrissey quaver': those pre-chorus yelps echoing somewhere between Tarzan and Jimmy Savile.

The 'Playboys' session took place at The Wool Hall near Bath in late November and throughout December of 1988 in the run-up to the WOLVER-HAMPTON gig, also resulting in the next single, 'INTERESTING DRUG', and their relevant B-sides. Prior to recording, Morrissey had decided to dispense with his VIVA HATE band of Vini REILLY and Andrew PARESI, instead recruiting ex-Smiths Andy Rourke and Mike Joyce, as well as Craig GANNON. Street also hired a second guitarist, local session player Neil Taylor. Though initially pleased to be reunited with the ex-Smiths contingent, Street found the 'Playboys' session unusually stressful in terms of the group dynamic. 'Much as I enjoyed working with Mike, Andy and Craig, I found it frustrating,' he explains. 'Because I'm sure they felt as if it really was The Smiths all over again. Without Johnny, obviously. That's how it seemed to me because I couldn't get the same drive or respect out of them. I think they still saw me as "Streety the engineer" like in the Smiths days when, in fact, I was there as producer and co-writer. I definitely felt pushed aside.'

Street still managed to put his own stamp on 'Playboys' with its atmospheric keyboard squeals, even earning himself a fleeting cameo in the accompanying video performance filmed in Bath two days prior to the Wolverhampton gig. The finished video by Tim Broad incorporated a literal narrative with young actor Jason Rush wearing a Krays T-shirt (comically labelled 'EASTENDERS' after the BBC soap which Rush himself later appeared in), while later running for his life on Bermondsey Street; a possible link with Krays south London rival Charlie RICHARDSON, whose gang controlled that area.

'Playboys' marked an auspicious start to 1989, issued in an amusing sleeve showing the singer as a six-year-old seemingly caught in a tree trunk and rewarding Morrissey with his third consecutive top ten hit. He'd proudly hail the song as the first solo record he felt 'hysterical about', likening the thrill of hearing it on the radio with that of hearing The Smiths' earlier 'SHOPLIFTERS OF THE WORLD UNITE' being broadcast. Undoubtedly, in its confident musical swagger and audacious lyrical proclamation, 'Playboys' remains one of the most exhilarating singles of Morrissey's entire career. The song even won the cautious approval of the Krays themselves. In *Our Story*, their autobiography with Fred Dineage published later that year, Reggie admitted that he 'liked the tune' though thought the lyrics were 'lacking a little'. Morrissey may well have had this passage in mind when he changed the lyrics in later live performances, stating that the brothers '*always* knew my name'.

[7, 13, 39, 69, 90, 148, 191, 437]

Last Picture Show, The, Among Morrissey's earliest cinematic influences, he described the experience of watching this 1971 coming-of-age drama as 'my first real sexual relationship'. Filmed in black-and-white by Peter Bogdanovich and based upon the novel by Larry McMurtry (who'd later win a screenwriting Oscar for *Brokeback Mountain*), the story is set in a desolate backwater Texas town in the early 50s and follows the sexual rites of passage of a group of high-school friends. The main plot focuses on the sensitive Sonny (Timothy Bottoms), who begins an affair with the neglected wife of the school sports coach only to be tempted away by the beautiful Jacy (Cybill Shepherd), the promiscuous ex-girlfriend of his best friend Duane (Jeff Bridges). The film's soundtrack was comprised of period country and western, dominated by Hank Williams but also including Hank Snow's original of 'A FOOL SUCH AS I', later covered by Elvis PRESLEY and attempted by The Smiths in 1987. *The Last Picture Show* spawned a sequel McMurtry novel and 1990 Bogdanovich film, *Texasville*, which updated the story to the early 80s. [334, 521]

'Late Night, Maudlin Street' (Morrissey/

Street), From the album VIVA HATE (1988). An epic meditation on youth and loss, 'Late Night, Maudlin Street' was the outstanding centrepiece of Morrissey's solo debut. Though located in the fictional Maudlin Street (probably named after the school in 1959's CARRY ON *Teacher*), the song was, he admitted, an autobiographical review of his relatively bleak adolescence in 70s Manchester. The year is specified as 1972, when lack of fuel due to a miners' strike caused nationwide power cuts (as mentioned) and the advent of Ted Heath's 'three-day week'. Above and beyond the raw recollections of anti-depressants, unexplained injuries, family deaths and bodily insecurity, whether intentional or not the prevailing themes of bidding goodbye to a lost love had heavy metaphorical resonance with the very recent break-up of The Smiths, adding much to its emotional impact upon fans at the time.

It's been speculated that the title could have been modelled upon *Late Night On Watling Street*, a collection of short stories by the playwright Bill Naughton (a logical presumption given that Naughton wrote two of Morrissey's favourite films, THE FAMILY WAY and SPRING AND PORT WINE). The lyrics also include yet more echoes of one of Morrissey's staple sources, Elizabeth SMART's *By Grand Central Station I Sat Down And Wept*, which contains the parallel phrases: 'They are

taking me away in a police car', '... Inspector? Do you not believe in love?', and the faint but still pertinent 'Every yellow or scarlet leaf hangs like a flag waving me on'. Equally fascinating is the significance of the lyric about sleeping with a framed portrait beside his bed. During the making of Viva Hate, Morrissey prepared the artwork for the final Smiths single, 'LAST NIGHT I DREAMT THAT SOMEBODY LOVED ME', which was originally going to include a very similar inscription on the back sleeve: 'When I sleep with that picture beside me ... I really think it's you.' The single's inner sleeve was also going to feature a lyric from 'WELL I WONDER', 'please keep me in mind'. If, for sake of argument, these were overt messages to Marr, it adds weight to the popular theory that 'Late Night, Maudlin Street' is also another of his post-Smiths 'Johnny songs' shrouded in a fog of teenage nostalgia.

Like all the best Morrissey lyrics, the power and passion of his performance transcends whatever specific events inspired him to write it in the first place. The consistency of his delivery (a full seven minutes with very few interludes) and the range of his vocal inflexions – from his 'truly I do love you' refrain possibly modelled on an identical Marc BOLAN passage in T.Rex's 'The Visit' to the spectacular yodel he gives 'clothes line' – have a hypnotic effect, dragging the listener with him back into his murky past with all its regret and heartache, forcing them to relive and reassess their own. Tellingly, Sandie SHAW remembers first hearing the track during the making of the album when Morrissey turned and caught her eye 'with such a pained expression ... I cried, he cried. I sensed his fear and I felt so frightened for him.' Yet even at his most soul-searching, 'Late Night, Maudlin Street' still manages a shred of humour in the concept of the whole country throwing up at the sight of a naked Morrissey. This bodily self-abhorrence had been alluded to before in 'MISERABLE LIE' and would resurface again many years later on 'FRIDAY MOURNING'.

Since the strength of the song was entirely in the lyric and Morrissey's vocal melody, there was little need for overpowering musical dramatics. Stephen Street wrote the basic chords during the break between the two Viva Hate recording sessions in November 1987 after Morrissey had told him he wanted 'a long, rambling track like JONI MITCHELL'. By strange coincidence, Mitchell had been in the same studio, The Wool Hall, earlier in the year recording part of her 1988 album Chalk Mark In A Rain Storm: Morrissey was keen to discover which of the guest bedrooms she'd slept in and later offered it to Sandie SHAW when she visited. Both Street and drummer Andrew PARESI have a loose recollection of Mitchell's 1975 album The Hissing Of Summer Lawns being Morrissey's blueprint for the track. It's possible, though in mood, length and lyrical introspection 'Late Night, Maudlin Street' has much more in common with the contents of 1976's Hejira (featuring 'Amelia' which had already left its mark upon the lyrics of 'Last Night I Dreamt That Somebody Loved Me').

Street nominates Vini REILLY's added piano flourishes as 'making it even more special', also admitting the sharp drum beat underpinning the track was sampled from 'Housequake' off Prince's recent Sign O' The Times album (rather apt since Prince, like Morrissey, was a similarly besotted Joni fan). 'Late Night, Maudlin Street' was finally played in concert in 2002, with Morrissey dedicating its rendition at London's Royal Albert Hall

that September to the late actress Katrin CARTLIDGE. [25, 33, 38, 39, 208, 344, 369, 375]

Latino fans,

A sizeable and significant throng among Morrissey's global audience is his staunch Hispanic fan base. From the Mexican communities of East and South Central Los Angeles down through Central and South America, the number of black-pompadoured Latino Morrissey apostles is vast.

It was after Morrissey moved to Los Angeles in the late 1990s that the Latino fan phenomenon first stirred the puzzled interest of the UK media, at odds to understand how lyrics about rented rooms in Whalley Range could resonate with those in similar accommodation over 5,000 miles away in the predominantly Hispanic Lincoln Heights.

'I don't know what the connection is, to be honest, but it is there,' pondered Morrissey. 'It might be the emotional outpouring, which Mexicans also do very well. The high pitch and the stretching out of songs. The songs are reaching out towards people and asking for some form of communication, they're not mumbled or sung into the chest. Their music is very out and there is a great sense of building rhythm. It could be that.'

Various magazine articles investigating Morrissey's 'Latino appeal' and even a documentary film (William E. Jones's Is It Really So Strange?) have all arrived at the same demographic conclusions: Latinos, and especially Los Angeles Mexicans as an ethnic minority subject to prejudice and exclusion, immediately identify with his gospel of outsiderdom; their love of his music is a conscious rebellion against the prevalent hip hop culture as a means of asserting their own identity; and, aesthetically, his rock and roll trappings of black quiff, sideburns and jeans sit very comfortably with the 'greaser' tradition endemic in Hispanic youth culture since the 50s.

Morrissey has also speculated that Latin America's love of 'crooners' may also be a contributing factor. 'Because I'm a crooner.' There's certainly something in this, especially if, for example, we place Morrissey in context of the great

Argentinian Tango singers who captivated a national audience with their passionate yet pained ballads of love, torment and death.

In response to his growing popularity in Central and South America, in the spring of 2000 Morrissey played his first concerts in Mexico, Chile, Argentina and Brazil. He'd later pay his respects in the 2004 B-side 'MEXICO' also making a Latino martyr in 'FIRST OF THE GANG TO DIE' and returning to a similar crime scene with 'GANGLORD'. [68, 115, 459]

'Laughing Anne' (Morrissey/Whyte), One of several working titles demoed in instrumental form only by Morrissey's band during the first abortive sessions for SOUTHPAW GRAMMAR at Miraval studios, France in December 1994. There are two possible title sources: the 1953 Hollywood film starring Margaret Lockwood as a Parisian singer who runs away to the South Seas with her ex-prizefighter boyfriend; or, slightly more obscure, *Punch* humorist A. P. Herbert's 1920s comedic poem 'Laughing Ann' about an alluring banker's wife who 'With two bright eyes/Can kill a man/Of any size' (probably mere coincidence, but reminiscent of Morrissey's own threats of staring his opponent to death in 'IT'S HARD TO WALK TALL WHEN YOU'RE SMALL'). Devoid of vocals, the surviving instrumental is long, lumbering and lacks form, nor does it appear to have ever been salvaged under an alternate title. [4]

'Lazy Sunbathers, The' (Morrissey/Whyte), From the album VAUXHALL AND I (1994). A sarcastic reproach of selfish indifference to war forms the basis of this caricature study of sun-worshipping bourgeois sloth. Morrissey's anger manifests itself in absurd satire with the final image of the tanned, idle rich complaining about the noise of children being blown to smithereens within earshot. As a general comment on the ignorance of the privileged few, 'The Lazy Sunbathers' marked Vauxhall's one foray into broadly political territory.[1] Whyte's pleasing melody was suitably languid though its initial arrangement proved

problematic, so much so that Morrissey made the rare gesture of singing a live guide vocal while his band rehearsed – the only instance during the making of Vauxhall where he and his musicians played simultaneously. [4, 6, 40]

———

1. On the subject of 'The Lazy Sunbathers', it is necessary to end a persistent but wholly inaccurate rumour that the title has a connection with George FORMBY. This bizarre Chinese whisper begins and ends with the author David Bret. In his 1994 book *Morrissey: Landscapes Of The Mind*, Bret suggested the song was reminiscent of Marlene Dietrich's feelings about entertainers who failed to support the Second World War. Five years later, Bret wrote *George Formby: A Troubled Genius* in which he likened Formby's attitude towards war-shy performers as being similar to Dietrich's. Confusingly, this time he now cited 'lazy sunbathers' as a direct quote from Dietrich, something he hadn't done in his earlier Morrissey book. To muddy the waters even further, both the *Guardian* and the *Daily Telegraph* reviewed *A Troubled Genius* misquoting 'lazy sunbathers' as being from Formby. If Formby ever did use the term 'lazy sunbathers' then neither Bret, nor anyone else, has ever presented written, visual or audio documentary evidence of such a quotation. Even assuming such evidence could yet be found to support this theory then it still doesn't explain how Morrissey, in the summer of 1993, would record a song inspired by a George Formby quote so obscure that it had yet to appear in print. Sadly, this hasn't stopped others repeating parrot-fashion Bret's idiosyncratic belief that Morrissey's 'The Lazy Sunbathers' is some cunning Formby homage. It isn't.

Leather Boys, The, 1964 British kitchen-sink drama, listed among Morrissey's favourite films and featured in the video for 'GIRLFRIEND IN A COMA'. Written by Gillian Freeman (based on her pulp paperback first published in 1961 under the knowing pseudonym Eliot George), the story follows Reggie (Colin Campbell), a naïve south London ton-up boy who weds his even dimmer teenage girlfriend, Dot (Rita Tushingham). Their married domesticity proves far from blissful and they soon separate. While Dot cries on the shoulder of rival biker Brian (played by Johnny Briggs, *CORONATION STREET*'s Mike Baldwin), Reggie takes refuge with his new friend, Pete, whom he slowly suspects of being 'queer'.

Morrissey's interest in the film can be traced back to his pre-Smiths film essay EXIT SMILING written circa 1979. Referring to Tushingham's character, he comments: 'Such is Rita's negative sex appeal that her husband will not make love to her, and in search of something better he discovers the homosexual underworld.' Thematically, *The Leather Boys* chimes loudest with Morrissey's lyrical observations on the hopelessness of young working-class marriages: when Reggie confides in Dot prior to their wedding that 'all I want is a double bed' he could almost be singing Morrissey's 'riches of the poor' inventory in 'I WANT THE ONE I CAN'T HAVE'.

Other than the extensive use of footage in Tim Broad's video for 'Girlfriend In A Coma', a publicity shot of Colin Campbell also graced the cover of the 1986 German single release of 'ASK'. Although his agent approved the sleeve, Campbell attempted to have it withdrawn. Consequently, it was the only original Smiths cover absent from Jo Slee's *Peepholism* anthology. Morrissey next mentioned the film during a February 1988 NME interview with Len BROWN at London's Cadogan Hotel, scene of Oscar WILDE's arrest. 'To be sitting here staring at Oscar's television,' he joked, 'and the very video that Oscar watched *The Leather Boys* on.' A less obvious allusion cropped up in a 1995 *Q* interview. In the film, Reggie and Dot spend their honeymoon in the exotic surroundings of Butlins holiday camp, Bognor Regis. When asked where he went on holiday, Morrissey replied, 'I don't go on holiday. Not since

they shut down Butlins at Bognor.' For the record, Butlins at Bognor is still very much open for business. [51, 71, 153, 175, 227, 341, 524]

Leiber and Stoller, Rock and roll songwriters Jerry Leiber and Mike Stoller whose story inspired Marr to seek out Morrissey and form a writing partnership, thereby creating The Smiths. Their most famous songs include the Elvis PRESLEY hits 'Hound Dog' and 'Jailhouse Rock'; The Coasters' 'Yakety Yak', 'Poison Ivy' and 'Charlie Brown'; The Clovers' 'Love Potion No. 9'; and the Ben E. King co-written 'Stand By Me'.

The duo were the subject of an ITV *South Bank Show* documentary broadcast on Sunday 21 February 1982. Future Smiths manager Joe MOSS videotaped the programme and later played it to the young Marr. The documentary recounted the story of how they first met in 1950: Leiber, a Los Angeles teenager obsessed with blues and jazz, was told about another local kid, Stoller, who played boogie-woogie piano; after finding his address, Leiber decided to call unannounced, suggesting they should try writing songs together. In the words of Stoller's wife, when they first clapped eyes on one another, 'It was like, "Wow! Where did you come from, soul mate?"'

The Leiber and Stoller meeting story was a 'eureka!' moment for the 18-year-old Marr, setting him towards his destiny when he re-enacted a similar encounter on the doorstep of 384 Kings Road in Stretford a few months later. During The Smiths' very first NME interview

'Leeches Go On Removing, The' (Morrissey/Whyte), A working title for a song from the tail end of the MALADJUSTED sessions. No vocal was recorded, only its instrumental backing which bears a strong resemblance to the soaring melody of David BOWIE's '"Heroes"'. The title phrase would eventually reappear seven years later as 'The Northern leeches go on removing' within the lyrics of YOU ARE THE QUARRY's closing track, 'YOU KNOW I COULDN'T LAST'. Given that the term had first entered his lyrical vocabulary in 1997, directly following the 1996 COURT CASE, it was widely interpreted as a blatant metaphorical reference to Mike Joyce. Asked in 2004 whether Joyce was indeed the bloodsucker in question, Morrissey coyly responded, 'He would certainly fit the bill, wouldn't he?' [4, 5, 74]

published in May 1983, Marr would also make a point of referring to Leiber and Stoller when calling for a revival of classic songwriting partnerships. In 1987, The Smiths followed Leiber and Stoller to become the focus of their own *South Bank Show* documentary, though by the time it was broadcast on 18 October they'd already broken up. [17, 75, 310, 468]

'Let Me Kiss You' (Morrissey/Whyte), Morrissey's 27th solo single (from the album YOU ARE THE QUARRY), released October 2004, highest UK chart position #8. Referencing the 1951 Montgomery Clift film *A Place In The Sun* in its first line, 'Let Me Kiss You' is Morrissey's respective American tragedy – the plea of a lovesick wanderer meandering in search of their 'safety haven' in the so-called land of the free, his passionate appeal for affection numbed by the truth that his heart's desire finds him repulsive. As on the earlier 'LATE NIGHT, MAUDLIN STREET', Morrissey casts himself as the world's ugliest man, his feeble dreams of love growing ever crueller in their impossibility.

Originally written for his friend NANCY SINATRA, details of 'Let Me Kiss You' began circulating in May 2003 when she told the press about her new album featuring tracks written by contemporary artists. 'The first song we cut last week in Hoboken was a song by Morrissey,' said Sinatra, who described it as 'a very difficult song for me, a real challenge'. Morrissey had apparently sent her the tune with the promise that 'if you sing it and we release it as a single, you'll be in the charts for the first time since 1972'.

His own version preceded Sinatra's as the best of Quarry's ballads and its third top ten hit. Whyte's tune rolled down its own lonely highway, fuelled by an eerie engine hum reminiscent of the thematically similar 'SEASICK, YET STILL DOCKED'. The same applied to Sinatra's which, essentially, was the same track with different vocals; the same key, the same tempo and with almost identical instrumentation, Morrissey's harmony lines included. Adding to the sense of occasion, both

his and Sinatra's version were released as singles on his ATTACK label on the same day. 'It was amusing to see what would happen,' said Morrissey. 'She entered at 46. I entered at eight.' [34, 106, 413]

'Let The Right One Slip In' (Morrissey/Whyte/Day), B-side of the US single 'TOMORROW' (1992). Morrissey's ambiguous stew about relinquishing 'wrong ones', 'old dreams' and 'old days', in title alone 'Let The Right One Slip In' trembled with obvious sexual innuendo, as emphasised when it became the packaging slogan on official Morrissey condoms sold on his 1999 UK and 2000 US dates. Less plausible, but still worth pondering, is its debt to the name of his favourite Cilla BLACK record, 'The Right One Is Left'. Whyte's satin-jacketed riff was stolen from the same clothes rail as 'YOU'RE THE ONE FOR ME, FATTY', even repeating its middle eight of frantic power chords. Arguably the best off-cut from the YOUR ARSENAL sessions, Morrissey would perform the song live just once as the encore at New York's Roseland Ballroom, 25 November 1992. Swedish Morrissey fan and author John Ajvide Lindqvist would use the song's title for his 2004 vampire novel *Låt Den Rätte Komma In* (*Let The Right One In*), later a 2008 film by director Tomas Alfredson.

Leyton, John, See 'JOHNNY REMEMBER ME'.

'Life Is A Pigsty' (Morrissey/Whyte), From the album RINGLEADER OF THE TORMENTORS (2006). Named by Morrissey as the song which most sums up his life and, by proxy, his personal favourite, in its epic dirge of lovelorn wretchedness 'Life Is A Pigsty' is also his most self-indulgent. The old story of The Smiths' 'LAST NIGHT I DREAMT THAT SOMEBODY LOVED ME' drags on, wearily acknowledged as the 'same old S.O.S.' echoing in the darkness of an inhuman world only fit for swine. 'I think life for many people *is* a pigsty,' Morrissey explained. 'I don't think the world is a particularly fantastic place. But once again, we're not supposed to say these things, are

we? It's supposed to be rock 'n' roll, and wild, and beer, and madness. I'm just being realistic.' Yet, even amid life's mucky squalor he finds himself inexorably 'falling in love again', the song's one positive admission that, as he explained, 'within the quagmire you can find time to – not rejoice, God forbid – but to feel some contentment'.

Given his recent discovery of the films of PASOLINI (as referenced on 'YOU HAVE KILLED ME'), its title and nihilistic sentiment were possibly inspired by the director's challenging, and some might say unwatchable, 1969 offering *Porcile* (*Pigsty*): a strange and horrific story about medieval cannibals who embark on a spree of rape and murder, inexplicably interwoven with the contemporary tale of a family of bourgeois ex-Nazis whose son ends up falling into a pigsty containing a rare breed of flesh-eating hogs and is promptly scoffed alive. It's tempting to speculate also whether the opening part of the film's tag line, 'I killed my father …', had some bearing on the same album's 'THE FATHER WHO MUST BE KILLED'.

Prior to the album's release, TONY VISCONTI described 'Life Is A Pigsty' as not so much a song as 'a suite'. Morrissey himself hailed it as 'the best' work of his longest serving co-writer Alain Whyte, though in execution the song was more a triumph of overblown production and lyrical hysteria over an otherwise muddy melancholic score, staggering awkwardly from its cunningly grim piano preamble to its central trudging death march. If only coincidence, Whyte's dreary crossover strums recalled Visconti's past with David BOWIE, sharing something with the gloomy intro ushering in 1969's 'Space Oddity' (a track which, ironically, Visconti passed on the opportunity to produce).

The focal track on Ringleader by virtue of its size, many apostles share his high estimation of the song, all too willing to accept his gospel that it's one of *the* great Morrissey masterpieces. But for all its grandiose pomp there's a weakness of pulse throughout, a cadaverous, waxy hollowness which never convinces no matter how violently he gnashes his teeth, no matter how deafening its cymbal-smashing din. Whatever his own preference, beside the matchless swoons of 'Last Night I Dreamt', 'I'VE CHANGED MY PLEA TO GUILTY' and 'NOW MY HEART IS FULL' to name but a few, such claims to isolate 'Life Is A Pigsty' as the summation of Morrissey's art and life appear – excuse the pun – laughable hogwash. [54, 235, 242, 259, 389, 471, 543, 568, 579]

'Lifeguard On Duty' (Morrissey/Street),

Studio outtake from the 1987 VIVA HATE sessions. An amusing play on the concept of a lifeguard, Morrissey calls for a poolside attendant to literally guard him from life itself. He supports his plea by listing his many 'ails' and 'ills', from being spat upon by strangers to the threat of a 'baseball bat across the collarbone'. The song also boasts what must be one of the few, if only, uses of 'vestibule' in the history of pop.

One of his first collaborations with Stephen Street, its casually skipping melody was in a similar vein to 'BENGALI IN PLATFORMS'. 'It wasn't particularly strong,' recalls Street, 'so as we came up with better material for Viva Hate I wasn't surprised that it fell by the wayside.' Drummer Andrew PARESI concurs that the song 'never really worked', though six years later Morrissey revived the lifeguard concept from a very different perspective on 'LIFEGUARD SLEEPING, GIRL DROWNING' (see next entry). Other 'lost' Viva Hate tracks which fell at the same hurdle included 'I DON'T WANT US TO FINISH', 'SAFE WARM LANCASHIRE HOME' and 'TREAT ME LIKE A HUMAN BEING'. [25, 39]

'Lifeguard Sleeping, Girl Drowning'

(Morrissey/Boorer), From the album VAUXHALL AND I (1994). 'Inspired by real facts', or so Morrissey teased, this sinister if blackly comic vignette was strongly reminiscent of Stevie Smith's famous 1957 poem 'Not Waving, But Drowning'. Whereas in Smith's tale a man drowns out at sea watched by oblivious bystanders who mistake his flailing arms for playful 'larking', in Morrissey's version an exhausted lifeguard calmly and maliciously allows a girl in similar peril to drown so he can sleep in peace.

'I can be as cruel with women as with men,' Morrissey later explained, adding that the real girl who'd given him the idea for the song 'sank a long time ago'. It's therefore worth considering the suspicion of his personal assistant of the period, Jo Slee, who told ex-NME journalist Len BROWN she believed the song referred to her earlier 'pleas for help' while being 'frozen out' by his new manager Nigel Thomas prior to the latter's death in early 1993.

The lyrical juxtaposition between the girl's violent death and the lifeguard's callousness is superbly measured, rendered all the more chilling by Morrissey's uncharacteristic delivery in a high, theatrical hiss. Both engineer Chris Dickie and bassist Jonny BRIDGWOOD note the singer's problems in perfecting his vocal on the song. 'We spent a long time trying to get that right,' says Dickie while Bridgwood also recalls the studio being cleared so Morrissey and producer Steve LILLY-WHITE were left alone to find the appropriate 'mood' between them.

Boorer's score of maudlin clarinet offered a perfectly eerie accompaniment, in places suggestive of the gothic signature tune to the late 70s ITV series *Armchair Thriller* by ROXY MUSIC's Andy Mackay. At the end of 'Lifeguard Sleeping, Girl Drowning' is an audio sample from the 1942 British war film *In Which We Serve*, written/co-directed by and starring Noël COWARD alongside John MILLS. The clip in question is when Mills, clinging to a life raft at sea, starts reminiscing about the first time he met his wife in a train compartment. The repeated voice heard is actress Kay Walsh asking, 'What's your name?' [4, 6, 40, 290]

Lillywhite, Steve (Morrissey producer 1993–97), 'An astonishingly gifted person', in Morrissey's estimation, Egham-born Lillywhite gained his first co-production credit beside Brian ENO on the 1977 eponymous debut album by Ultravox! (who'd drop the exclamation mark prior to their career-defining 1981 hit 'Vienna', a song the young Morrissey deemed 'hogwash'). The following year he oversaw So Alone by ex-NEW YORK DOLL Johnny Thunders

and The Scream, the debut album by Siouxsie And The Banshees which included future Morrissey interval tape favourites 'Mirage' and 'Jigsaw Feeling' (see SIOUX). In 1979 Lillywhite also helped his brother Adrian's group, The Members, score a top 20 hit with the much-loved punk-pop thumper 'The Sound Of The Suburbs'.

The 80s were to be Lillywhite's glory years, beginning with the third self-titled solo album by Peter Gabriel and its 'Games Without Frontiers' single. His success continued with the first two albums by The Psychedelic Furs, Big Country's The Crossing and Steeltown, Simple Minds' Sparkle In The Rain, and, most prominently, the U2 albums Boy, October and War. All of these records, to varying degrees, patented a stadium-sized power-pop clamour that was to dominate 80s guitar music, sometimes referred to by name as 'The Lillywhite Sound'.

After Lillywhite married singer Kirsty MACCOLL in August 1984, he befriended Johnny Marr, a frequent lodger at the couple's west London home during the latter years of The Smiths. When MacColl was invited to supply backing vocals on 1986's 'ASK', Lillywhite also became involved when Morrissey asked him to remix John PORTER's production. After 1987's triumphant Pogues album If I Should Fall From Grace With God, Lillywhite next produced Talking Heads' Naked, inviting Marr to provide some guest guitar work. He and Marr would continue working together on MacColl's Kite (1989) and Electric Landlady (1991). The predominantly Mark NEVIN co-written Titanic Days (1993) would be Lillywhite's last for MacColl prior to their amicable divorce.

In May 1993, Lillywhite was approached to take over Morrissey's fourth album after the death of Mick RONSON. The resulting VAUXHALL AND I was a major success for both parties, encouraging an artist–producer relationship that was to last the next four years. Force of habit ensured that the three albums they made together all took place at the same studio (Hook End Manor near Reading) and, bar a change of drummer after Vauxhall, the same band.

'[Morrissey is] one of the strangest people I've ever worked with,' recalled Lillywhite. 'I've made three albums with him [so] I must have spent a total of five or six months with him and I can't say I know him. He's a wonderful, wonderful man. He's gentle. He's beautiful. He wears Morrissey T-shirts. He comes down for breakfast completely done up. You never see him not looking his best. Very few words, but when he says what he says you absolutely get it.'

Though Morrissey had no regrets over 1995's SOUTHPAW GRAMMAR, he'd later refer to his decision 'to work with Steve Lillywhite for the third time' on 1997's MALADJUSTED as one of that album's 'many mistakes'. In the sleeve notes for the latter's 2009 reissue, Morrissey recalled the producer was at that time 'slipping into his own mental agonies, and a mild heart attack was only months away'.

Lillywhite remains one of the most respected and commercially successful British record producers of all time. Asked to contribute to this book, he politely declined with the intriguing tease that he was 'saving all my Morrissey gossip for my own book'. [6, 40, 56, 96, 334, 427]

Linder, See STERLING, Linder.

Lion In Love, The, See DELANEY, Shelagh.

'Little Man, What Now?' (Morrissey/
Street), From the album VIVA HATE (1988). Taking its name from a 1934 film (based upon the German novel by Hans Fallada and, significantly, mentioned in Marjorie Rosen's POPCORN VENUS), 'Little Man, What Now?' stands among Morrissey's best lyrics on the nature of fame, lamenting a late 60s juvenile television star who soon slips into obscurity. During the 80s, they reappear on an 'afternoon nostalgia television show'; most probably ITV's *Looks Familiar* presented by Denis Norden in which a panel had to guess the identity of a star of yesteryear obscured in silhouette. The panel fail to recognise him, but Morrissey does, causing him to shudder at the prospect of being dealt a similar fate.

The identity of the unsmiling juvenile actor has prompted various rogue theories. The most common error is to cite Jack Wild, briefly seen in POOR COW but best known as the Artful Dodger in 1968's *Oliver!* and star of the 1969 children's television series *H. R. Pufnstuf* in which he sang and smiled his head off. Consequently, Morrissey's description of the glum 'nervous juvenile' doesn't tally with Wild, even though he failed to make the transition to adult star and became an alcoholic, dying from cancer in 2006, aged 53. Equally wide of the mark is the suggestion that the song is about Roger Tonge, who starred as the wheelchair-bound Sandy Richardson in the long-running Midlands soap *Crossroads* from 1964 until 1981. Again, the specifics of being axed after four seasons don't add up in Tonge's case, plus the fact that the tragedy of Tonge's life wasn't his loss of fame but his early death, aged 35, of glandular cancer.

The most sensible, and likely, 'Little Man, What Now?' theory to have surfaced concerns Malcolm McFee, who played wide boy Peter Craven in the popular late 60s school sitcom *Please Sir!* There are still some discrepancies: *Please Sir!* was screened on Saturday, not Friday, nights and McFee was axed after three, not four, seasons along with the rest of his on-screen classmates, plus he returned for the second and third seasons of its early 70s spin-off series, *The Fenn Street Gang*. But, in terms of the character he played, his subsequent plummet from fame to crummy bit parts and taking into account the kind of programme the young Morrissey would have watched (*Please Sir!* being a sitcom TO SIR, WITH LOVE minus the racial tension), McFee is otherwise the most logical candidate. Sadly, like Wild and Tonge, McFee also died of cancer in 2001, aged 52.

Seguing out of 'ALSATIAN COUSIN', 'Little Man, What Now?' was one of the more experimental, and best, tracks on Viva Hate. Street's disjointed flamenco-style arrangement was inspired by David BOWIE's 'Andy Warhol' from 1971's Hunky Dory. Vini REILLY added some wonderfully atmospheric twangy guitar while its bashing rhythm was a looped varispeed sample of Andrew PARESI simultaneously thwacking a drum and cymbal. The song later became a fixture of Morrissey's 2002 tour where the mention of the faded teenage annual was changed to 'the mean melancholy streets that you came from'. [25, 39, 272, 363]

Live At Earls Court, Morrissey's second solo

live album, released April 2005, highest UK chart position #18. Tracks: 'HOW SOON IS NOW?', 'FIRST OF THE GANG TO DIE', 'NOVEMBER SPAWNED A MONSTER', 'DON'T MAKE FUN OF DADDY'S VOICE', 'BIGMOUTH STRIKES AGAIN', 'I LIKE YOU', 'REDONDO BEACH', 'LET ME KISS YOU', 'SUBWAY TRAIN/MUNICH AIR DISASTER 1958', 'THERE IS A LIGHT THAT NEVER GOES OUT', 'THE MORE YOU IGNORE ME, THE CLOSER I GET', 'FRIDAY MOURNING', 'I HAVE FORGIVEN JESUS', 'THE WORLD IS FULL OF CRASHING BORES', 'SHOPLIFTERS OF THE WORLD UNITE', 'IRISH BLOOD, ENGLISH HEART', 'YOU KNOW I COULDN'T LAST', 'LAST NIGHT I DREAMT THAT SOMEBODY LOVED ME'.

Released in tandem with the WHO PUT THE 'M' IN MANCHESTER? DVD of his May 2004 Manchester MEN Arena show, Live At Earls Court was a similar fan souvenir of the YOU ARE THE QUARRY tour, recorded in London 'on the 18th of December 2004 in front of 17,183 people'. Its tracklisting was much more varied than his previous live album, BEETHOVEN WAS DEAF, featuring three non-album B-sides, a handful of Smiths favourites (all included with Marr's publishing consent) and two rare covers. Its liner notes stipulated that everything had been recorded live with nothing 'added or replaced in the studio' while listeners also had the chance to contrast and compare the fretboard skills of Boz BOORER (in the left channel) and new recruit Jesse TOBIAS (right channel). As such, it was an honest and mostly impressive account of Morrissey's current band, even if their handling of such sacred Smiths fare as 'There Is A Light That Never Goes Out' and 'Last Night I Dreamt That Somebody Loved Me' was somewhat arthritic in nature. More disappointing was the perfunctory album title itself, also a misnomer in that, as with Beethoven Was Deaf, some of its tracks were sourced from other concerts of the period.

The Earls Court show itself was the penultimate gig of the nine-month Quarry tour. With no dates planned for 2005, his closing farewell of 'Please don't forget me … I love you' and his emotions on stage two nights later at Dublin's The Point (where he played 'There Is A Light' twice) prompted rumours that Morrissey may be about to retire. As if.

Live In Dallas, Official video of Morrissey's

concert at the Starplex Amphitheatre in Dallas, Texas on 17 June 1991 'before an audience of 11,000 people' during his first solo US tour to promote KILL UNCLE, released in the UK in April 1993. See Mozography appendix for full tracklisting.

A very basic video recording using the venue's two security cameras, *Live In Dallas* was never intended for commercial release. It was only when Morrissey reviewed the footage that he was taken with its 'no frills' honesty and decided to put it out as cheaply as possible, at a cost of only $3,000. This low budget was reflected in its original VHS packaging, which didn't even feature a tracklisting.

Rough and ready it may be, but *Dallas* is unique in capturing for posterity the thrill of Morrissey's early solo gigs when his new band of Boz BOORER, Spencer COBRIN, Gary DAY and Alain WHYTE were as irrepressibly animate as Gene Vincent's Blue Caps. It's especially interesting to compare the showmanship of Boorer, running back and forth across the stage, even lapsing into a Chuck Berry duck walk, with that of Morrissey's gigs from 1995 onwards when such exhibitionism among his band members was quite obviously prohibited. As Cathal SMYTH verifies, 'Morrissey once asked me to tell Boz that his turn-ups were too big and to stop moving around on stage so much.'

Indeed, the dynamism of his young musicians is one of the main highlights of the video, also conveying the kind of crowd pandemonium soon to become par for the course at Morrissey gigs – unforgettable scenes of front-row hysteria, bemused security guards and a riotous final stage invasion sabotaging 'EVERYDAY IS LIKE SUNDAY'. Their frenzy is understandable given Morrissey's latest incarnation as a rubber-limbed rockabilly Jesus, quiff and sideboards sculpted to perfection.

The set list was typical for the period, mixing BONA DRAG with some entertainingly boisterous arrangements of the new Kill Uncle material. *Live In Dallas* is also, to date, the only official means of hearing Morrissey's cover of the NEW YORK DOLLS' 'TRASH' as well as the export-strength versions of 'ANGEL, ANGEL, DOWN WE GO TOGETHER' and The Jam's 'THAT'S ENTERTAINMENT', both significantly different to their studio counterparts. The full inclusion of Klaus NOMI's entrance theme, 'Wayward Sisters', and Shirley BASSEY's exit music, 'Ave Maria', neatly completes its intimate virtual concert experience. [438]

London, The once-biggest, still-greatest city in the world and Morrissey's second home from 1984 until moving to Los Angeles in the late 1990s. Throughout this period the singer also owned properties outside his native Manchester and later Dublin, though by the early 90s London was his main place of residence.

Morrissey first moved to the capital aged 17, lasting barely a week. 'I brought everything I possessed in these huge cases,' he explained. 'It was a really awful experience.' During his late teens and early twenties he occasionally visited London to see his friend James MAKER, who lived south of the river in Peckham. When The Smiths moved to London at the beginning of 1984, both Morrissey and Marr chose accommodation in west London to be near the Notting Hill offices of their label, ROUGH TRADE (who, ironically, relocated near King's Cross in north central London soon after). Marr lived in Earls Court while Morrissey took a flat on Campden Park Road between Kensington High Street and Notting Hill. Its previous owner was former Skids singer Richard Jobson. Morrissey later claimed the flat was haunted.

Relocating back to Manchester at the end of 1984, he'd eventually take the lease on a second home on Cadogan Square in Chelsea where he remained until the late 80s. The location seems to have been influenced by his love of Oscar WILDE who was famously arrested in the Cadogan Hotel in the next road, Sloane Street; nearby Sloane Square was also mentioned in the lyrics of 1988 B-side 'HAIRDRESSER ON FIRE'. 'It was a bizarre building he lived in,' recalls Smiths soundman Grant Showbiz, 'his flat felt like a big, old lonely place.' Morrissey himself described it as 'very dark … the flat is at the back [of the building] and it has no natural daylight. That was the deciding factor. It's very closed, very away from the world. Nobody can get to me and if there was a fire I would probably die. It's full of books and pictures and records and old furniture. A very musty place.'

In the early 90s, he'd move to north London, eventually settling in Regents Park Terrace in the Camden/Primrose Hill borders, subject of 2004's 'COME BACK TO CAMDEN'. The house was suggested to him by producer Clive LANGER who was friends with the seller, fashion and music photographer Tony McGee. Its previous occupants included a high court judge, the actress Tallulah Bankhead and fashion designer Jasper Conran, while its interior was designed by William Haines, a former silent Hollywood star whose career was cut short due to controversy over his homosexuality (coincidentally, Haines also designed Morrissey's later Los Angeles home commissioned by Clark Gable for his wife Carole Lombard). It was there, in Regents Park Terrace, where Morrissey befriended next-street-neighbour Alan BENNETT and also briefly lodged with friend and photographer Jake WALTERS.

Despite his comments in early Smiths interviews that he considered London 'an impersonal place' which he wanted to avoid moving to 'if scientifically possible', Morrissey quickly fell in love with the city. 'London is really quite perfect,' he swooned. 'I regret to say it really is as exciting living here as some people who are always considered to be misguided say that it is. I think when you visit London and you only stay for a few days you get a completely obscure vision of the place and it seems impersonal and hateful and

'London' (Morrissey/Marr), B-side of 'SHOPLIFTERS OF THE WORLD UNITE' (1987). Alongside 'IS IT REALLY SO STRANGE?' and 'HALF A PERSON', 'London' formed part of a triptych of songs written between the spring and autumn of 1986, each taking a different perspective on the exodus from north to south. Of the three, 'London' was Morrissey's most removed (written in the second person), juxtaposing the uncertainty of the nervous traveller boarding a train to Euston with the resentment of those still stuck in the dull northern province they're escaping. The latter image was another example of the influence of Elizabeth SMART upon Morrissey's work: the comparable line 'because you notice the jealousy of those that stay at home' appears in *By Grand Central Station I Sat Down And Wept*. The scenario also bore some similarity with the film *BILLY LIAR*, specifically the finale in which Tom Courtenay hesitatingly boards the London train with Julie Christie.

Appropriately enough, Marr first rehearsed the bones of the song at the soundcheck for the opening night of their summer '86 North American tour in London, Ontario, Canada. Among The Smiths' most forceful tunes, Joyce's express-train rhythm and Marr's telegraphic feedback provided a brilliant onomatopoeic foil for Morrissey's train-carriage drama. Marr also praises Craig GANNON for his work on its powerful end section. 'The high picking part on the end is all Craig,' admits Marr. 'He did a good job on that.' An even better version of 'London' was later taped for their final John PEEL session of 1986. [17, 19, 38, 375]

synthetic. But when you stay here for a long time, you realise the enormous advantages. It's really quite simple – there are just endless things to do here, and mobility is so easy. In Manchester the entire place closed at 8 p.m. and you were just totally paralysed, but here you can go wherever you want to, whenever you want to, and do whatever you want to.' Even after selling his Camden home in 1997, he confessed, 'even when I hate London I love it. I love the good and the bad, the barren and the plush.'

Morrissey also spent a lot of time in east London, spiritual home of the KRAY twins and JACK THE RIPPER where his best friend Linder STERLING also lived in the early 1990s. Other than those already listed there have been numerous references to London and specific locales in his lyrics and titles, most blatantly 'LONDON' itself but also 'PANIC', 'HALF A PERSON', 'PICCADILLY PALARE' (Piccadilly Circus, Earls Court), 'MUTE WITNESS' (Clapham Common), YOUR ARSENAL, 'GLAMOROUS GLUE', 'YOU'RE THE ONE FOR ME, FATTY' (Battersea), VAUXHALL AND I, 'DAGENHAM DAVE', 'MALADJUSTED' (Fulham Road and Parkside by Wimbledon Common) and 'TROUBLE LOVES ME' (Soho).

Speaking to this author in 2003, Clive Langer mentioned Morrissey 'was looking to buy in north London again' with the help of his friend Cathal SMYTH though he hasn't as yet. Since then, on visits to London it is customary for Morrissey to take a suite at a five-star hotel such as The Dorchester on Park Lane or the Mandarin Oriental in Knightsbridge. [15, 18, 33, 88, 145, 165, 205, 212, 419, 475]

'Loneliness Remembers What Happiness Forgets', 1970 Dionne Warwick B-side

(of 'Let Me Go To Him') listed among Morrissey's favourite records. Composed by prolific American songwriting duo Burt Bacharach and Hal David, Morrissey would also name it as the song he wished he'd written. Against Bacharach's contrasting up-tempo samba, its words, like its title, are wholly Mozzerian in sentiment, lamenting the end of a short-lived and doomed romance, not unlike that in 'HAND IN GLOVE', and ending in Warwick's long, deliberate murmur of 'pain'.

As with Morrissey and Marr's role models LEIBER AND STOLLER, Bacharach and David began their partnership in New York's Brill Building during the late 1950s. Their importance in the history of popular music, especially during the 60s, cannot be overstated. Many of Morrissey's favourite singers owe either their biggest or breakthrough UK hits to Bacharach/David, among them Sandie SHAW ('(There's) Always Something There To Remind Me'), Cilla BLACK ('Anyone Who Had A Heart', 'Alfie') and Sacha DISTEL ('Raindrops Keep Falling On My Head'). Bacharach's were immediate pop melodies imbued with a sophisticated melancholic undercurrent and arranged with the orchestrated melodrama of a classical symphony. David's lyrics complemented Bacharach's tunes with the requisite emotional depth, a perfect illustration being 'I Just Don't Know What To Do With Myself' as wrenched from the gut of Dusty Springfield in 1963. Equally sublime and sorrowful is 1962's '(There Goes) The Forgotten Man', a rare single by soul singer Jimmy Radcliffe which appeared on Morrissey's 2003 various artists compilation UNDER THE INFLUENCE. Johnny Marr has also cited the influence of Burt Bacharach, naming his 1963 Del Shannon song 'The Answer To Everything' (lyrics by Bob Hilliard) as a melodic inspiration for The Smiths' 'PLEASE PLEASE PLEASE LET ME GET WHAT I WANT'. [175, 310, 569]

Long Day's Journey Into Night, 1962 drama

based upon Eugene O'Neill's stage play listed among Morrissey's favourite films and featuring one of his favourite acting performances from Ralph Richardson. Its screenplay also provided the source for the title of The Smiths' 'THIS NIGHT HAS OPENED MY EYES', spoken by Jason Robards towards the end of the film: 'This night has opened my eyes to a great career in store for me, my boy!'

The story is O'Neill's veiled autobiography of his early family life, originally written in 1941 as a present to his third wife on their twelfth wedding anniversary. 'A sadly inappropriate gift, it would seem, for a day celebrating happiness,' wrote O'Neill. He wasn't joking. *Long Day's Journey Into Night* is psychologically draining from start to finish. O'Neill was so sensitive about

its content, detailing his dysfunctional upbringing in a house riddled with addictions, illness and misery, that he decreed it not be published until 25 years after his death. His wife, however, waited only three years after his funeral before publishing the play in 1956. Six years later, Sidney Lumet directed the faithful film version, just shy of an exhausting three hours long. Set in Connecticut in 1912, it follows a day in the desperate lives of the Tyrone family: James (Richardson), a failed actor and heavy drinker; his wife, Mary (Katharine Hepburn), a pitiful morphine addict dependent on their housemaid to help her pick up her prescriptions; their eldest son Jamie (Robards), a failed actor like his father and an even more chronic alcoholic frittering his money away on local prostitutes; and Edmund (Dean Stockwell), the sensitive younger son, psychologically scarred by his family and further stricken with tuberculosis. The fact that Morrissey could repeatedly watch this bleak and dismal film itself says much about the darkest recesses of his own troubled mind. [168, 176, 227, 347, 526]

'Loop, The' (Morrissey/Nevin), B-side of 'SING

YOUR LIFE' (1991). Morrissey's gradual slide towards rockabilly was evident on this twangy Nevin tune recorded at the end of the KILL UNCLE sessions. Like The Smiths' 'GIRL AFRAID', it's predominantly a guitar instrumental with minimal words; the singer's short message to an old friend telling them 'by all means call me' and inevitably interpreted by Smiths romantics as being directed towards Marr. 'It's called "The Loop" because I called it "The Loop" on the tape I sent him,' reveals Nevin, 'so it's not some deep and meaningful title.' Although producers LANGER and Winstanley deemed it 'a bit throwaway, sort of rockabilly going down dance 12-inch territory', Morrissey was especially proud of it, even telling Nevin in a letter that '"The Loop" is my favourite'. Speeded up in concert, it became a knee-knocking rockabilly showcase for his new solo touring band, as captured on BEETHOVEN WAS DEAF. [4, 15, 22]

I am a living V-sign: Morrissey goes solo.

This page – Top: Morrissey reaches to the converted in Atlanta, October 2004. Above and right: His Master's Scrawl – setlist (signed on rear) handed to front row fan at London's Forum, November 1999.

Opposite page – Mozmania. Top: Wolverhampton, December 1988. Bottom: Hanley, October 1991.

Overleaf: Rebel without a care on the balcony of Los Angeles' Griffith Observatory, 1994.

LONDON 4

YOU'RE GONNA NEED

BOY RACER

BILLY BUDD

READER MEET AUTHOR

SUNNY

IS IT REALLY SO STRANGE

HAIRDRESSER ON FIRE

TROUBLE LOVES ME

LOST

ALMA MATTERS

TOMORROW

SPEEDWAY

NOW MY HEART IS FULL

NOVEMBER

BREAK UP THE FAMILY

MEAT IS MURDER

********** *****

LAST NIGHT I DREAMT

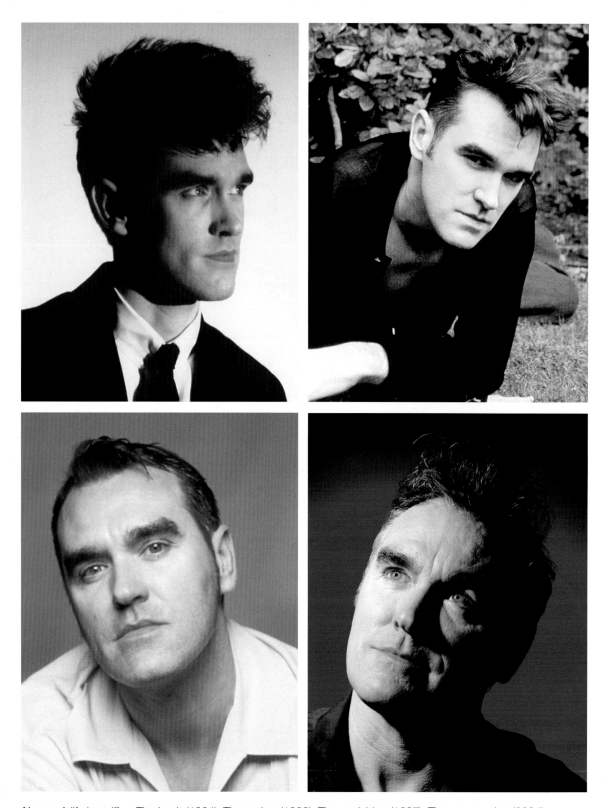

Above: A life in quiffs – The bush (1984). The rocker (1989). The vanishing (1997). The resurrection (2004).

Opposite: 'Why meddle with a masterpiece?' Perfection, 1991.

Tomb it may concern: A good lay in Hollywood Forever Cemetery, 2004.

Los Angeles, Morrissey's main city of residence from 1998 to 2005 where he still spends much of his time living and working.

When he first left the UK for permanent residence in 'Loose Angela' (as he called it) his critics were utterly bemused. His friend, the writer Michael Bracewell, perfectly summarised the cultural conundrum when interviewing Morrissey for *The Times* in 1999. 'To the original generation of Smiths fans, back in the middle of the 80s,' wrote Bracewell, 'ecstatic boys and girls, all mimicking Morrissey's kitchen-sink cinema-style of quiff and National Health glasses as they mobbed the stage at the Dundee Caird Hall or the Liverpool Empire, the idea of their idol moving to California would have seemed heretical. The whole point about Morrissey, back in those days, was his romantic nostalgia for an archaic notion of Englishness.'

Morrissey's move to Los Angeles in 1998 is commonly referred to as a period of 'exile'; turning his back on the UK after the disaster of the 1996 Smiths COURT CASE and the poor critical reception to the following year's MALADJUSTED album.

'The England that I have loved, and I have sung about, and whose death I had sung about, I felt had just finally slipped away,' he told Bracewell. 'And so I was no longer saying, "England is dying." I was beginning to say, "Well, yes, it has died and here's the carcass" – so why hang around? Los Angeles offered brightness, and so I packed up my troubles in my old kit bag, and I didn't smile, smile, smile, but I went anyway.'

Although years earlier he'd commented how he could never live in LA since 'we all need rain and good old depression ... life can't be all beer and skittles', his relocation wasn't quite the 'heretical' anomaly most critics portrayed given his childhood love of classic Hollywood films. As a fan of the likes of Bette DAVIS and John GARFIELD, not to mention James DEAN, it made perfect sense that Morrissey, like they, should seek refuge amid the Hollywood hills.

The four-bedroom Hispanic villa he 'stumbled across' on North Sweetzer Avenue off Sunset Boulevard was designed by William Haines, a former silent screen star whose career was cut short due to controversy over his homosexuality and who, coincidentally, had also designed the interior of Morrissey's previous home on London's Regents Park Terrace in Camden. The build was commissioned by actor Clark Gable for his wife, actress Carole Lombard. 'But she was killed in a plane crash before she'd had time to pick out the curtains,' the singer explained. 'Since then, I'm told F. Scott Fitzgerald lived here, and [BILLY LIAR director] John Schlesinger. But not together. Also, [producer] Robert Stigwood threw the *Saturday Night Fever* party here on the night of its premiere. So, all those people have sat on my toilet. Incredible, isn't it?' Morrissey's next-door neighbour was actor Johnny Depp, living in a replica gothic castle falsely rumoured to have been home to *Dracula* star Bela Lugosi. 'I like the light,' Morrissey said of Los Angeles life. 'It's astonishing to wake up in the morning and see that light and say, yes, you can do things today. That really doesn't happen in Manchester.'

Key Morrissey Hollywood landmarks include: his favourite local book shop, Book Soup near the Whisky a Go Go end of Sunset Strip ('where I can smell that nice smell of culture'); his local 'English pub' the Cat & Fiddle on West Sunset Blvd; the nearby Amoeba Music record warehouse a few blocks east on Sunset where he's sometimes been spotted by fans; the Sunset Marquis Hotel and Villas on North La Cienega Blvd where he regularly stayed in the years before settling in the city; and the Hollywood Forever Cemetery on Santa Monica Blvd, final resting place of Johnny and Dee Dee RAMONE where Morrissey also wishes to be buried. Further afield but also of note are the Griffith Observatory, seen in the 1955 James DEAN film *Rebel Without A Cause* and used in homage for a 1994 Morrissey photoshoot, and the HOLLYWOOD BOWL where Morrissey broke the box-office record in 1992.

Away from Hollywood, the singer also spent his free time in the city cruising the Mexican districts of East and South Central LA where the local gang culture would inspire 'FIRST OF THE

GANG TO DIE' and 'GANGLORD' (see also LATINO FANS). Morrissey had previously mentioned LA in song on 1992's 'GLAMOROUS GLUE' though more specific references can be found much later in 2004's 'ALL THE LAZY DYKES' (naming local lesbian bar the Palms on Santa Monica Blvd) and 'I'M PLAYING EASY TO GET' (naming the stretch of Sunset Blvd between Cole Place and Cahuenga Blvd near Amoeba and the Cat & Fiddle).

Although Morrissey officially sold his North Sweetzer villa in 2005, putting it on the market for just under $2m, he returned to the city for 2009's YEARS OF REFUSAL. 'I like the film history of Los Angeles,' he confessed during the album's recording, 'and I'm constantly searching for the smogginess and dim-light of those old films ... I also like the Herb Alpertness of it all, and the Burt Bacharachness and the Wayne Manor bit. You know, Bruce Wayne and his youthful ward Dick Grayson? No? Oh. Well, then.' [56, 68, 88, 93, 115, 120, 153, 191, 223, 453, 568]

Louder Than Bombs, The Smiths' third
compilation album, released in the US on Sire Records in March 1987, highest UK chart position #38. Cover star: Shelagh DELANEY. Tracks: 'IS IT REALLY SO STRANGE?', 'SHEILA TAKE A BOW', 'SHOPLIFTERS OF THE WORLD UNITE', 'SWEET AND TENDER HOOLIGAN', 'HALF A PERSON', 'LONDON', 'PANIC', 'GIRL AFRAID', 'SHAKESPEARE'S SISTER', 'WILLIAM, IT WAS REALLY NOTHING', 'YOU JUST HAVEN'T EARNED IT YET, BABY', 'HEAVEN KNOWS I'M MISERABLE NOW', 'ASK', 'GOLDEN LIGHTS', 'OSCILLATE WILDLY', 'THESE THINGS TAKE TIME', 'RUBBER RING', 'BACK TO THE OLD HOUSE', 'HAND IN GLOVE', 'STRETCH OUT AND WAIT', 'PLEASE PLEASE PLEASE LET ME GET WHAT I WANT', 'THIS NIGHT HAS OPENED MY EYES', 'UNLOVEABLE', 'ASLEEP'.

Taking its name from a passage in Elizabeth SMART's *By Grand Central Station I Sat Down And Wept*, Louder Than Bombs was intended strictly for US audiences who had been denied a release of HATFUL OF HOLLOW and swathes of Smiths material only available as UK or European import singles. Its two dozen tracks mopped up the bulk of their non-album material from 1983 to 1987, offering American fans the ultimate catch-up exercise from the original seven-inch version of 'Hand In Glove' and the BBC session rarity 'This Night Has Opened My Eyes' to previously unavailable B-sides and singles up to and including 'Sheila Take A Bow'.

It was, therefore, unfortunate that the album proved so popular on import sales that ROUGH TRADE decided to distribute it in the UK barely months after its domestic equivalent, THE WORLD WON'T LISTEN. As a result, the rapid appearance of two similar compilations unintentionally muddied the waters of The Smiths' discography, provoking minor outcries of opportunist exploitation. Confusing the issue further, Louder Than Bombs

'Lost' (Morrissey/Cobrin), B-side of 'ROY'S KEEN' (1997). Morrissey's favourite among the few tracks he co-wrote with drummer Spencer Cobrin, 'Lost' was greater than the sum of its parts: its lyrics were a poetic, if vague, reflection on a world where 'everybody's lost, but they're pretending they're not', ending in the singer's nervous advance towards a love interest while the tune was a fairly simple, lingering indie ballad. Yet the combination of the two was an alchemical bombshell, a fitting metaphor for the relationship between Morrissey and his audience – the 'lost' singer calling out to be found by his equally dispossessed followers. Cobrin was similarly touched when he heard the finished track. 'It was an incredible feeling,' he says, 'hearing my music with Morrissey's words. I thought "Lost" was beautiful. I was beyond happy.' An immediate fan favourite, the song was played regularly on Morrissey's tours of 1999 and 2000, once jokingly introduced by the singer as 'Why Don't Women Like Me?', the title of one of his favourite George FORMBY tunes. [5, 40]

boasted a handful of tracks as yet unavailable on any UK album: 'Sheila Take A Bow' and its B-sides 'Is It Really So Strange?' and 'Sweet And Tender Hooligan'; the studio versions of 'These Things Take Time' and 'Back To The Old House'; the TWINKLE cover 'Golden Lights'; and the original 12-inch take of 'Stretch Out And Wait' (as opposed to The World Won't Listen alternate mix). Those with keen hearing would also have detected a slightly different mix of 'You Just Haven't Earned It Yet, Baby'.

'There was some confusion with the two compilations,' admits Marr, 'but I'm really glad about Louder Than Bombs because it was really significant to American fans. That was the point of it, really. In that respect, it was a great release and an important one for us as a group.' Although Morrissey condemned Rough Trade's remarketing of the album in the UK (even expressing his regret that he hadn't 'given it a better title'), it didn't stop him later nominating Louder Than Bombs' cover portrait of playwright Shelagh Delaney as his favourite Smiths sleeve. 'That said it all, really,' he gushed. 'Salford, struggle, cigs, squalid back-to-backs, mental anguish, knots of houses, battered roofs, old roads, scant resources, overcoats, untreated sewage … lovely.' [17, 19, 207]

love, A miserable lie. Or so Morrissey has always maintained. 'Being in love is something I would never claim to fully understand,' he once admitted. 'I do think it's actually possible to go through life and never fall in love or find someone who loves you.'

As made excruciatingly obvious in virtually everything he's ever said or sung, Morrissey's faith in loving human relationships is worse than bleak, fashioned by dire first-hand experience; whether witnessing the collapse of his parents' marriage or the notoriously disastrous attempts to find love in adolescence which informed many of his early Smiths lyrics. 'The few times when I tried to build relationships – when I was younger – they never worked out for very long,' he confessed. 'So I gave up.'

Speaking in 1985, he explained how he associated 'love' with 'pain': 'Because it's never been reciprocated. Desire is extremely excruciating to me, and as far as I know, that's all there is. I can't imagine response, and I can't imagine being loved by somebody whom one loves … A lot of people don't want you to say, "I love you," because it's almost the final moment, the death knell of intimacy. A lot of people don't want to carry around with them the notion that you care that much.'

A decade later, his hopes of ever finding reciprocal romantic bliss remained just as glum. 'It's the same, whether it's an attraction to a man or a woman. Nothing seems to go well with me. The concept of attraction doesn't work for me. Human relations don't work. If I see someone I find attractive, then I flee in the other direction. I'd be absolutely unable to go and talk to this person. What's the use of going and saying that I find this person attractive? It could never go well between us … So I put up with it. I'm resigned to it.'

Only once, in 1997, did Morrissey admit in an interview with the *Guardian* that he'd recently been in a relationship which, compounding his misery, had been terminated by the other person. 'I'm delightful in love,' he's alleged to have said, adding that he was 'excellent at everything … cooking, conversation, planning'. Otherwise Morrissey has always told us far more about his love life in song than in print. Be that the case, then between the despair of the 1982-penned 'MISERABLE LIE' and 'I'M OK BY MYSELF', recorded 26 years later, little seems to have changed. Shakespeare famously coined the analogy of music being the food of love. Inverting the same, if love be the food of music, clearly Morrissey has forever been in a constant state of starvation. [61, 133, 135, 152, 236, 237]

'Lucky Lisp' (Morrissey/Street), B-side of 'THE LAST OF THE FAMOUS INTERNATIONAL PLAYBOYS' (1989). More evidence that Morrissey can't resist a good (or perhaps bad) pun, 'Lucky Lisp' makes consonant-swapping mirth of the LEIBER AND STOLLER tune 'Lucky Lips', a top five UK hit for

Cliff Richard in May 1963. Serenading a friend, Morrissey enthusiastically predicts that their speech impediment will bring them fame, fortune and mass adulation, even picturing himself one day 'gurgling' with the fans in the upper circles. A slight, if supremely catchy, Morrissey morsel, its prominent pulsing synthesiser couldn't disguise the fact Street's sugary melody was one of his more Smiths-conscious offerings, granted a suitably jangly guitar gloss by Craig GANNON. [39]

Ludus, See STERLING, Linder.

Lulu, 'That pint-sized bundle of energy from Scotland' (according to the sleeve of her 1971 compilation The Most Of Lulu), some of whose 60s hits Morrissey confessed to loving. 'Do I need therapy?' he asked.

Born Marie McDonald McLaughlin Lawrie, Lulu became an overnight success at the age of 15 with her guttural cover of The Isley Brothers' 'Shout' (number seven, June 1964). Originally teamed with R&B backing band The Luvvers, Lulu was soon shunted off into more mainstream pop territory with producer Mickie Most. Among Morrissey's favourites were: 1967's 'The Boat That I Row' ('[Lulu] saying to the world, "You're not going to change me. This is me. Take me as I am"'); its B-side, 'Dreary Days And Nights'; 1968's 'I'm A Tiger' ('genius gibberish') and her 1969 EUROVISION entry 'Boom Bang-A-Bang' which he'd include on his 1991 concert interval tapes despite deeming it 'a record which we might not even be bothered to burn, but there's a cleverness, there is a craft'. In a 1980 letter to pen pal Robert MACKIE, Morrissey also confessed he was 'presently gaga' over Lulu's theme song to 1967's

TO SIR, WITH LOVE which he'd later name as one of his favourite films. In 1991 Morrissey put in a request to the producers of ITV's Amnesty International 30th Anniversary Special to have Lulu introduce his performance of 'WE HATE IT WHEN OUR FRIENDS BECOME SUCCESSFUL'; when she proved unavailable, fellow 60s icon/former Ready Steady Go! presenter Cathy McGowan took her place. Of coincidental note, Lulu's younger sister, Edwina Lawrie, was the presenter of the children's television show Datarun which The Smiths appeared on in April 1984 being 'interviewed' by pupils of Morrissey's old primary school, St Wilfred's. [227, 290, 334, 443, 556]

Lypsinka, Performance pseudonym of American drag artist and actor John Epperson whom Morrissey has described as 'an absolute genius'. Epperson unveiled Lypsinka in 1988, transforming himself into a glamorous starlet (modelled upon the 'fantabulous' Dolores Gray) and lip-synching to old show tune recordings between cleverly edited film dialogue from the likes of Joan Crawford and Gloria Swanson. Morrissey invited Epperson to perform his Lypsinka! The Boxed Set show during his 2004 MELTDOWN festival and later included a clip of him miming to Vegas cabaret singer Fay McKay's 'The Twelve Daze Of Christmas' among his first concert interval video montage introduced in late 2006. Off stage, Epperson shares Morrissey's love of Hollywood trivia and provided an excellent commentary to the 2006 special edition DVD of another of Morrissey's favourite Bette DAVIS films, Whatever Happened To Baby Jane? [190, 436, 562]

lyrics, See WRITING PROCESS.

m

MacColl, Kirsty, Much loved and much missed Croydon singer/songwriter and friend of The Smiths. MacColl sang backing vocals on 1986's 'ASK' and its B-side 'GOLDEN LIGHTS'. After The Smiths she worked extensively with Johnny Marr, also singing backing vocals on Morrissey's 1989 solo hit 'INTERESTING DRUG'. Morrissey would famously describe her as 'a supreme original, although not – as far as I know – one of the original Supremes'. While holidaying in Mexico in December 2000, MacColl was killed by a reckless speedboat driver: the campaign to bring the culprit to justice continues.

The daughter of Salford-born folk singer/playwright Ewan MacColl – who, with his first wife Joan Littlewood, helped found Theatre Workshop, the company which later staged the first production of Shelagh DELANEY's *A Taste Of Honey* – she was raised in Croydon with her mother, Jean, and elder brother, Hamish. Using the punk pseudonym 'Mandy Doubt', MacColl made her vinyl debut in 1978 as backing singer in The Drug Addix, who released just one EP on Chiswick (lead track: 'Gay Boys In Bondage'). Her first as Kirsty MacColl followed in June 1979 with the Stiff Records' single 'They Don't Know', a tender pledge of idealistic love recalling vintage Shangri-Las. Though it failed to trouble the charts, four years later comedian-turned-singer Tracey Ullman would take the song to number two in October 1983, offering a significant boost to MacColl's own career which by then rested on the lone success of her novelty country rocker, 'There's A Guy Works Down The Chip Shop Swears He's Elvis' (number 14, July 1981).

A glistening pop transformation of Billy BRAGG's 'A New England' produced by husband Steve LILLYWHITE took her to number seven in February 1985 and would be her biggest solo hit. Bragg extended his song for MacColl with two extra verses (performing the song after her death, Bragg now ritually includes these extra 'Kirsty verses' as a tribute). MacColl and Bragg would later work together on his albums Talking With The Taxman About Poetry (1986) and Don't Try

m

This At Home (1991), both of which also featured Johnny Marr.

MacColl first collaborated with The Smiths in 1985, invited to sing backing vocals on an early draft of 'BIGMOUTH STRIKES AGAIN', though her performance would eventually be replaced by Morrissey's 'Ann COATES' vocal. The following year she was called back to harmonise on 'Ask' and 'Golden Lights'. Marr, especially, would form a close friendship with MacColl and became a frequent lodger at her London home near Shepherds Bush during the last years of The Smiths. Consequently, it was Marr who christened her 'Electric Landlady' – a pun on Jimi Hendrix's Electric Ladyland, later used for the title of her third solo album. MacColl and Marr would also work together on Talking Heads' 1988 album Naked, produced by Lillywhite.

If for nothing else, MacColl's immortality is assured by 'Fairytale Of New York', her 1987 duet with The Pogues in which she sparred with 'scumbag maggot' Shane MacGowan to create a festive perennial ingeniously seesawing between pie-eyed sentiment and poetic grit; only the Pet Shop Boys prevented it from becoming that year's hallowed Christmas number one. Spurred on by the success of 'Fairytale', MacColl resumed her solo career, releasing her second solo album, Kite, in April 1989. As well as playing on its hit cover of The Kinks' 'Days' (number 12, August 1989), Marr co-wrote two tracks, 'The End Of A Perfect Day' and 'You And Me Baby'. The first single from the album, 'Free World', also carried a cover of The Smiths' 'YOU JUST HAVEN'T EARNED IT YET, BABY' on the B-side. It's worth noting that in the initial post-Smiths vacuum and all its attendant gossip of acrimony between Morrissey and Marr, MacColl was unique in being the only person to work with both at the same time: the Marr-assisted Kite and Morrissey's 'Interesting Drug' were released the same month.

1991's Electric Landlady featured two more MacColl/Marr songs, the single 'Walking Down Madison' and 'Children Of The Revolution' while another, 'Can't Stop Killing You' (which Marr

also produced), featured on 1994's Titanic Days. The bulk of the latter album was co-written with long-time MacColl collaborator Mark NEVIN using music he'd originally prepared with Morrissey in mind during the demo stages of YOUR ARSENAL. One of these, 'Soho Square', would later inspire fans to dedicate a bench to Kirsty's memory in the song's location. Titanic Days itself coincided with, and lyrically documented, the end of MacColl's marriage to Lillywhite who by the time of its release was Morrissey's new producer.

MacColl's discovery of Cuban music led to 2000's Latin-influenced Tropical Brainstorm including 'Treachery' co-written with ex-10cc Graham Gouldman, author of Herman's Hermits 'EAST WEST'. A critical success, it was to be her last album. The second week of December 2000, MacColl, her new partner, musician James Knight, and her two sons by Lillywhite, Louis and Jamie, arrived in Cozumel, Mexico for a winter holiday. On 18 December, Kirsty and her boys were scuba diving in an area which restricted watercraft from entering, a rule which the millionaire Guillermo Gonzalez Nova and his family ignored. It was Gonzalez Nova's speedboat which killed Kirsty. She died saving the life of her son, Jamie, who had originally been in the boat's path. 'She is irreplaceable to me,' grieved Morrissey who by his own guilty admission allegedly encouraged her to visit Mexico after touring there in early 2000. In September 2002, a tribute concert at London's Royal Festival Hall celebrated MacColl's life and work resulting in a chance union of three Morrissey co-writers – Marr, Nevin and MacColl's friend Boz BOORER – all of whom shared the same stage during the final ensemble encore of 'There's A Guy Works Down The Chip Shop'.

The tragedy of Kirsty's death and the failure of the Mexican authorities to bring those responsible to justice are conveyed with great dignity by her mother, Jean MacColl, in 2008's Sun On The Water, an in-places harrowing book which no parent should ever have to write. Though the millionaire Gonzalez Nova captained the speedboat, it was his poor and inexperienced deckhand,

José Cen Yam, who was convicted in his place. Unbelievably, Cen Yam avoided prison after paying a fine equivalent to £61.

When questioned about the accident, Gonzalez Nova insisted the speedboat hadn't even been travelling in the restricted zone. Even after his boat had killed Kirsty MacColl, Gonzalez Nova offered her sons no assistance as they swam in their mother's blood. It is for these reasons that the Justice For Kirsty campaign was set up with the aims of raising funds and public awareness so that the memory of Kirsty MacColl will be honoured by the conviction of those whose selfish negligence caused her death at the age of just 41. For details of the campaign history and information on how to pledge support, please visit www.justiceforkirsty.org. [18, 22, 115, 332]

MacKenzie, Billy,

Flamboyant, whippet-rearing leader of 80s pop group The Associates whom Morrissey befriended circa 1984 and a likely muse for The Smiths' 'WILLIAM, IT WAS REALLY NOTHING' written during that period.

A fitting, and touching, introduction to MacKenzie was given by Bono in the foreword to Tom Doyle's authoritative biography *The Glamour Chase*: 'Disco ball of nerves that he was, Billy was an aesthete … Caruso on a balloon of oxygen … When the world was brown or black or khaki and the raincoat was that year's duffel, Billy was ultra violet, ultra bright, ultra everything except ultra cool.'

Born in Dundee in 1957, MacKenzie formed The Associates in the late 70s with keyboard/guitar player Alan Rankine, bonded by a love of film soundtracks, 60s baroque pop, classic crooners and, first and foremost, David BOWIE. The duo's 1979 independent debut single was a cover of Bowie's most recent hit, 'Boys Keep Swinging', recorded without clearing publishing approval.

By 1980, The Associates found themselves loosely grouped alongside other Edinburgh-based post-punk bands of the time though as their 1980 debut album, The Affectionate Punch, clearly demonstrated, there was an arch elegance about

their sound – and MacKenzie's histrionic vocals in particular – anomalous within the British new wave. They persevered with a series of increasingly uncompromising singles – some magnificent ('White Car In Germany'), others merely magnificent titles ('Tell Me Easter's On Friday') – before striking pop gold with the rhapsodic 'Party Fears Two'. MacKenzie's biggest hit (peaking at number nine, March 1982), its diamante score propelled his vocal theatrics to new peaks of crockery-smashing, alcohol-drenched hysteria. That he'd promote the song on national television dressed like an airline pilot or shimmying in a beret and raincoat on TOP OF THE POPS lent his performances an extra, albeit unfathomable, star quality. The Associates enjoyed two further hits, 'Club Country' (number 13, June 1982) and '18 Carat Love Affair' (a double A-side with a cover of Diana Ross's 'Love Hangover', number 21, August 1982). Sadly, the outwardly debonair yet secretly self-doubting MacKenzie was ill equipped for success. Unsure of their future, and the perils of what MacKenzie later referred to as their 'cocaine frenzy', Rankine left the group.

When MacKenzie contacted Morrissey in the spring of 1984, he was working on Perhaps, the 1985 album released as The Associates, a name he was now carrying single-handedly; it's possible that their contact bridge was mutual friend and journalist Jim Shelley who'd interviewed both men for *Blitz* magazine that same spring. '[Billy] sent me a tape of his new recordings the other day,' Morrissey told a fanzine. 'Apparently he's very fond of [The Smiths].' A rendezvous was swiftly arranged at his Kensington flat where the pair apparently 'spent hours searching for some common ground … but ultimately there wasn't any'. Morrissey described MacKenzie as, 'Very erratic. Quite indescribable. He was like a whirlwind. He simply swept into the place and he seemed to be instantly all over the room. It was a fascinating study but one, I think, that would make me dizzy if it happened too often.'

Because MacKenzie's homosexuality was no secret among the press, many were quick to misconstrue the exact nature of their brief dalliance, adding fuel to the popular theory that 'William, It Was Really Nothing' may be a coded message to The Associates' singer. If the title has any connection with MacKenzie, it probably refers to his casual theft of one of Morrissey's James DEAN books during that fabled meeting. 'He walked off with [it], which is a persistent cause of anxiety,' he claimed. 'I was quite speechless. I watched him walk out the door. It wasn't my favourite book but these things are sacrosanct. Billy has got this sense of uncontrollable mischief, though. I think that's exactly how he wants to be seen.'

It wasn't until 1993, having reunited with Rankine, that MacKenzie addressed the rumour with their misspelt 'Stephen, You're Really Something', an uncharacteristic glam rock homage.[1] Unfortunately, the song wasn't released until 2000, three years after MacKenzie committed suicide at the age of 39. For the last few years of his life, the singer had battled with clinical depression as his career became an increasingly irregular sequence of collaborations, cameos and contractual disappointments. The death of his mother in 1996 appeared to have been the final trigger. On 22 January 1997, he took a fatal overdose of antidepressants in his father's garden shed just outside his native Dundee. [204, 263, 267, 304]

---

1. Some have disputed the relevance of 'Stephen, You're Really Something' by falsely claiming MacKenzie never wrote the song. The credits on 2000's posthumous Associates rarities compilation Double Hipness clearly state it was, indeed, 'written by Rankine/MacKenzie' while even the sleeve note by biographer Tom Doyle, an expert in such matters, spells out that it was 'Billy's riposte to Morrissey's skewed tribute "William, It Was Really Nothing".'

Mackie, Robert, Glasgow BOWIE fan who became Morrissey's pen pal for just over a year between the autumn of 1980 and the winter of 1981. Although Morrissey corresponded with many pen pals, Mackie is unique in being the only one to fully share his letters with the outside world. In 1992, Mackie reproduced his correspondence

from Morrissey in a 44-page A5-sized photocopied fanzine, *Words By Morrissey*. The Mackie letters have since become semi-mythological documents of tremendous interest to fans and biographers, offering a fascinating insight into the murky years before Marr knocked upon his door to form The Smiths.

Words By Morrissey comprises nine letters in total; unfortunately Mackie's own replies, which it's unlikely he'd have ever copied, are not included. The first, undated but presumably late September/early October 1980, is Morrissey's short response to a personal ad Mackie placed in *Sounds*.[1] It came on the reverse of a photocopied picture of James DEAN, with Morrissey making wordplay of Bowie's recent hit 'Ashes To Ashes' in his sign-off, 'I'm unhappy, hope you're unhappy too.' Two longer letters follow dated 13 October (opening 'Dear Paganini', signed 'Natalie Wood') and 22 October ('Dear Sir Laurence', signed 'Oscar WILDE'). A fourth is undated but presumably November 1980 ('Dear Tugboat Annie' – a name taken from a film mentioned in Marjorie Rosen's *POPCORN VENUS* – and signed 'Ronald Reagan'). Letters five and six are 4 December and 10 December (both sincerely addressed 'Dear Robert/Rab' and signed 'Steven'). The final three are spread over 1981 – 15 March, one undated and the last 10 December accompanied by a Clark Gable postcard inscribed with a verse from THE MONOCHROME SET's 'Ici Les Enfants'. The final letter is especially interesting when bearing in mind it was written approximately six months before Marr properly entered his life. The writing, both in calligraphy and content, is that of a desperate soul fast giving up hope, ending with his grim conclusion, borrowed from Wilde, that 'life is a terrible, terrible thing , Robert'.

Although they've since been transcribed on the internet, Mackie's original fanzine is much more satisfying due to its faithful reproduction of Morrissey's handwriting, developing from simple non-cursive text to the more familiar deranged-child scrawl he'd settle upon in The Smiths, and his various COCTEAU-esque doodles, the likely influence of his friend Linder STERLING. The fanzine also replicates the photocopied record sleeves Morrissey used as writing paper, including Brian ENO's Before And After Science, Ludus' 'My Cherry Is In Sherry', The Monochrome Set's Love Zombies, NICO's Desertshore and BUZZCOCKS' 'Orgasm Addict' (designed by Linder), as well as a Hershey's Milk Chocolate wrapper (possibly a souvenir from his visit to family in America) and two rare photo-booth snapshots.

A very small minority of disbelievers have questioned the authenticity of Mackie's letters but they are quite obviously genuine. The references to his current listening and viewing are astonishingly consistent with his later interval music selections and sleeve artwork, citing, among others, the NEW YORK DOLLS, JOBRIATH, Sandie SHAW, Cilla BLACK, George FORMBY and future STRANGEWAYS cover star Richard DAVALOS. More tellingly, the wit and withering putdowns of the 21-year-old Morrissey are immediately comparable with those of his elder self. One of the funniest aspects of the Mackie letters is the near-sadistic glee Morrissey takes in ridiculing his correspondent: 'Thank you for your letter which had nothing remotely to do with the English language as we know it'; 'Thank you for your photo, it came in handy until the plumber arrived'; and, 'I suppose [you] masturbate to pictures of Anna Ford. So typical.' Such taunts didn't deter Mackie from travelling by coach to visit Morrissey in the spring of 1981. After an afternoon's stationery and clothes shopping, Mackie was taken to a local bar with a transvestite host where Morrissey declared how he'd 'rather look fascinating than have a permanent income.'

Morrissey has never commented on the Mackie letters, distributed without his consent, though it's safe to assume he was less than delighted that they should enter the public domain. Yet other than the revelation, in his own handwriting, that in December 1980 he has a girlfriend (see Annalisa JABLONSKA) and that she and he were 'both bisexual', the deeply engrossing and hugely entertaining Mackie letters are otherwise devoid of any great myth-

deflating scandal. Quite the opposite, they merely confirm that even as a 21-year-old in his bedroom – writing 'I'm sure there are worse groups than Duran Duran but I'll be damned if I can think of any' – Morrissey was already perfecting the art of being Morrissey. [334]

———

1. Scouring through *Sounds* classified pages of the period, Mackie's original ad was most likely that of 'Male Bowie wants female Bowie for friendship. Glasgow area.' Presumably Morrissey wasn't quite the 'female Bowie' Mackie amorously anticipated.

Madness, Following Morrissey's severance from co-writer and producer Stephen STREET, in August 1989 he began working with producers Clive LANGER and Alan Winstanley, most famously associated with the English ska/pop group Madness. Over the next couple of years, the hitherto exclusive worlds of Morrissey and Madness would collide as the singer began praising the group in the press, also collaborating with various members on his solo recordings.

'I was a serious Madness fan years ago,' Morrissey admitted at the time. 'It was largely their sense of perverse fun I quite liked. I never considered the records to be standard pop fare. I quite liked the peculiarity. People say music hall, which I suppose is quite true.'

Formed in Camden Town as The North London Invaders, they later chose the name Madness after a 1963 ska tune by Jamaica's Prince Buster, subject of their 1979 2 Tone debut single and first top 20 hit 'The Prince'. Over the next four years all but one of their ensuing 16 UK singles made the top ten, from the SKINHEAD rampage 'nutty sound' of the Buster cover 'One Step Beyond'[1] to their socio-political pop satires of education ('Baggy Trousers'), interracial sex ('Embarrassment') and contraception (their sole UK number one, May 1982's 'House Of Fun'). Their imaginative videos and cartoonish 'nutty boys' image helped establish Madness as one of the most successful UK pop acts of the decade, though their heyday ended by the time The Smiths arrived at the end of 1983, eventually splitting up in 1987.[2]

m

Madness were currently non-operational when Morrissey began working with Langer and Winstanley, whose production on his 1990 single 'PICCADILLY PALARE' would provoke critical comparisons with their former charges. The latter also featured the first Madness cameo on a Morrissey record, with guest vocals from lead singer Suggs (born Graham McPherson), also heard on its B-side 'GET OFF THE STAGE'. By the time of its release, Morrissey had begun recording KILL UNCLE with Madness bass player Mark Bedford, aka 'Bedders', who'd play on all of his recordings up to and including 1991's 'MY LOVE LIFE' single.

Morrissey's closest Madness acquaintance would be backing singer/dancer Cathal SMYTH whom he courted as a potential manager, also inviting him to add harmonies on his cover of The Jam's 'THAT'S ENTERTAINMENT'. A screen grab of Smyth from the video for Madness's 1982 single 'Cardiac Arrest' can be seen in the promo for 'WE HATE IT WHEN OUR FRIENDS BECOME SUCCESSFUL'. Smyth has also confessed to be the dedicatee of 'YOU'RE THE ONE FOR ME, FATTY'.

Morrissey's association with the group would wane in the aftermath of August 1992's Madstock festival, a two-day weekend event in London's Finsbury Park to celebrate Madness's re-formation where, notoriously, Morrissey aborted his support set on the first day due to missiles from a hostile minority of the audience. The incident became a catalyst for the false press allegations of racism which haunted him for the next decade (see NME and RACISM). The following year, Suggs demonstrated his allegiance to Morrissey by performing a cover of 'SUEDEHEAD' on the BBC's *The Danny Baker Show*, also ad-libbing some lyrics from 'OUR FRANK'. [1, 15, 22, 36, 226, 445]

———

1. Madness's 1979 debut album, also called One Step Beyond, included a cover of Tchaikovsky's 'Swan Lake' based upon the 1968 ska version by The Cats as featured on Morrissey's UNDER THE INFLUENCE compilation.
2. In several interviews, Madness singer Suggs has gone into great detail describing how his group performed on the same November 1983 episode of the BBC's TOP OF THE POPS that The Smiths made their debut with 'THIS CHARMING MAN'. Sadly, Suggs is very much mistaken. Madness didn't appear on the show. Even stranger is his repeated anecdotal inaccuracy that Madness were there to play 'Night Boat To Cairo', a single which charted over three years earlier in April 1980, before The Smiths existed.

Magazine, See DEVOTO, Howard.

Maker, James, London singer, writer and a friend of Morrissey since the late 1970s. Maker also danced on stage with The Smiths for their first two concerts and later formed his own group, Raymonde, whose 'NO ONE CAN HOLD A CANDLE TO YOU' was covered by Morrissey in 2004.

Magnani, Anna, Italian film star referenced in 'YOU HAVE KILLED ME'. Magnani came to prominence in Roberto Rossellini's *Rome, Open City* (1945), the first internationally successful Italian neo-realist film. She later went to Hollywood, winning an Oscar for 1955's *The Rose Tattoo* and gaining the admiration of leading Tinseltown actresses such as Bette DAVIS, whom she once visited in hospital. 'I couldn't have been more thrilled,' said Davis, describing Magnani as being 'as vivid as her beautiful country, as explosive as a happy child', also observing 'her eyes have known the tragic'.

Twenty years before 'You Have Killed Me', in 1985 Magnani was brought up in conversation by Pat PHOENIX when Morrissey interviewed her for *Blitz* magazine. 'Anna Magnani had what I would call sexuality in the very force of her passion, and I mean passion about *life*,' said Phoenix. 'She was alive and she was living and you felt you could rush into her bosom and she would embrace you.' Morrissey's own interest in Magnani primarily stems from 1962's *Mamma Roma*, his favourite film by director Pier Paolo PASOLINI, mentioned in the same song. [181, 213, 298, 527]

As a fellow NEW YORK DOLLS obsessive (who by his own admission bore 'more than a passing resemblance to James DEAN') the 17-year-old Maker first contacted the 18-year-old Morrissey in September 1977 after reading his ravings about the Dolls in the NME's letters pages, noting his address, then asking directory enquiries for his number. After that first phone call, Maker took the train from London to Manchester the following weekend to meet him in person. The trip proved memorable for all the wrong reasons as Morrissey (looking like 'an intellectual RAMONE') and Maker (in bowler hat) were chased out of the city centre by a gang of 'beer monsters'. Their respective accounts of what Morrissey called 'the worst night of my life' and Maker his 'Manchester Chainsaw Mascara' tally in every detail. The new friends were chased after leaving a restaurant and ended up seeking refuge on a bus where Maker somewhat foolishly decided to throw coins at their pursuers through the window. 'Suddenly the emergency doors swing open and these tattooed arms fly in,' Morrissey recalled. 'It was like *A Clockwork Orange*.' Refusing to leave the bus for their own safety, they ended up alone near the Moors, calling at a manor house where a 'decrepit Teddy Boy' informed them he didn't have a telephone. 'We had to walk back to Manchester,' said Morrissey. 'It took us seven days. We came back home to my place, finally, at something like 5 a.m. and listened to Horses by PATTI SMITH and wept on the bed. That's my youth for you in a nutshell.'

Despite the drama and misery of that first encounter, Morrissey and Maker's friendship intensified over the next few years. Morrissey would visit Maker (whom he always referred to as 'Jimmy') at his flat in Peckham where, among other things, they sat looking out for flying saucers. Maker was also given a special dedication in Morrissey's 1981 book *The New York Dolls*: 'For Jimmy, who lives it.' When Morrissey met Marr and formed The Smiths in the summer of 1982, he kept Maker informed of their progress, sending him cassettes and inviting him

up to Manchester to watch a couple of early rehearsals.

Upon Morrissey's invitation, Maker was asked to join them for their live debut at Manchester's Ritz on 4 October 1982 as part of a student/music fashion show titled 'An Evening Of Pure Pleasure', headlined by pop/jazz ensemble Blue Rondo A La Turk. Maker also introduced the group in French: 'J'ai l'honneur de vous introduire The Smiths. Je crois qu'ils vont faire BOUM ici – et je suis certain que leur musique vous sera fascinant.' ('I'm honoured to introduce you to The Smiths. I believe they are going to make a BANG here – and I know that you'll find their music fascinating.')

'I think it was generally accepted that I would *improvise*,' says Maker who danced beside The Smiths in women's black court shoes while shaking maracas and making 'extraneous' hand gestures. 'There was no discussion on how I would fit into the stage show. My involvement was not part of any long-term plan. Morrissey had wanted me to appear at the early concerts and I had agreed to it. Johnny was always affable towards me. Rourke rarely spoke and Joyce, I sensed, was strongly opposed. I never [canvassed] anyone's opinion, and neither was opinion offered.'

Maker appeared only once more with The Smiths at their next gig at Manchester's Manhattan in January 1983. Shortly afterwards, Morrissey phoned Maker in London. '[He] related a conversation that Joe [MOSS], their manager at the time, had had with the group,' explains Maker. 'It went along the lines of: "There can't be two lead singers in one band." Which, retrospectively, was true. My guest appearances with them was quite superfluous, really. And I would have been the first to agree with that sentiment. It was not a problem. It was a good decision. I never belonged with The Smiths. And I didn't wish for it. I was 21. The maracas-shaking, go-go dancing was just a silly and enjoyable temporary diversion. I very much had my own plans – and went on to formulate them.'

Those plans came to fruition with Raymonde, the group he formed with guitarist Phil Huish naming themselves after Dusty Springfield arranger

m

Ivor Raymonde. Their frantic 1986 debut single, also 'Raymonde', was a taster for greater histrionics to come and demonstrated Maker's distinctive vibrato trembling between those of Pete BURNS and The Cult's Ian Astbury. Backed with an idle cover of NANCY SINATRA's 'These Boots Are Made For Walking', Maker's message on the record sleeve provided further evidence of his and Morrissey's earlier UFO fixation. 'I believe in Rock, in Excitement, in Sex, I also believe in Speed, Madness and Flying Saucers.'

Raymonde supported The Smiths for their final UK tour in October 1986, with Maker drunkenly joining them for their encore on the fourth night in St Austell, Cornwall. 'I was backstage that night when I heard the chords of "BIGMOUTH STRIKES AGAIN",' explains Maker. 'Spontaneity, instinct, and Remy Martin drove me out on to the stage – just briefly – to join them. It seemed fitting and ironic. Johnny was beaming. Afterwards, Morrissey dispatched me an Agatha Christie book titled, *Murder Is Easy*. To which I sent him the Sandie SHAW single, "Message Understood".'

Signing with an imprint of Chrysalis, in 1987 Raymonde released their only album, Babelogue, named after a Patti Smith track and opening with the anthemic 'No One Can Hold A Candle To You'. While Maker's old associations with The Smiths were initially useful in arousing the interest of the music press, they quickly became an albatross as Raymonde found themselves critically constrained by constant comparison. Their 1988 swansong single 'Destination Breakdown' marked a shift towards a heavier quasi-Dolls hard rock sound as Maker's hair grew further past his shoulders. Musically, it pre-empted his next group, RPLA, who signed with EMI and were touted in the early 90s as the world's first 'openly gay heavy metal band'.

Looking back, Maker admitted that 'Morrissey has certainly influenced me in terms of our exchange of ideas and the fact that, at one time, we had an awful lot in common', even if their contrasting career trajectories meant that, by 2001, he and Morrissey were 'no longer close'.

Three years later, the tide must have turned for Morrissey to not only cover the Raymonde song on record and in concert but also to sign Maker to his own Sanctuary imprint, ATTACK RECORDS. Teamed with Noko 440 (Howard DEVOTO's ex-partner in Luxuria), Maker released one single, 'Born That Way', an unapologetic confession of shoving Mother Theresa off cliffs and annihilating Sylvia Plath to a captivating Stooges/drum and bass hybrid. Maker has since announced the completion of his autobiography. Titled *Autofellatio*, it promises more insightful anecdotes about his friendship with Morrissey, including that beer-monster-bus incident in all its horror. [16, 163, 175, 196, 357]

Maladjusted, Morrissey's sixth solo album, released August 1997, highest UK chart position #8. Tracks: 'MALADJUSTED', 'ALMA MATTERS', 'AMBITIOUS OUTSIDERS', 'TROUBLE LOVES ME', 'PAPA JACK', 'AMMUNITION', 'WIDE TO RECEIVE', 'ROY'S KEEN', 'HE CRIED', 'SORROW WILL COME IN THE END',* 'SATAN REJECTED MY SOUL'. Produced by Steve LILLYWHITE. [*Included on non-UK editions only.]

Where 1994 had been a great year for Morrissey due to the vindicating success of VAUXHALL AND I, 1995 was one in which his career started to veer irreversibly off the rails. It began with his first UK tour after a two-year lay-off to promote the WORLD OF MORRISSEY compilation album; a tour which, arguably, he should have taken nine months earlier to capitalise on the welcome reception granted Vauxhall And I. Ominously, its accompanying 'BOXERS' single never made the top 20, a fate shared by the three other singles Morrissey released in 1995. The SOUTHPAW GRAMMAR album augured a potential fresh start on a new label (RCA VICTOR), yet its critical reception was mixed while its failure to follow Vauxhall And I to number one presented further cause for concern. Most damaging of all was his doomed winter UK arena tour supporting David BOWIE which Morrissey abandoned halfway through.

The cumulative effect of these various follies and failures would take its heavy toll in 1996 – the

240

first year since 1982 that Morrissey never set foot in a recording studio. Beyond behind-the-scenes contractual issues, the singer's main hindrance was his own lack of confidence. In January 1996, a session had been booked to record a new EP. The designated producer was former Clash frontman Joe Strummer, who'd attended one of the opening Wembley Arena shows on the Southpaw/Bowie tour and popped backstage to meet Morrissey's band. As respective legendary figureheads of two different eras of British music, the combination of Morrissey and Strummer was a fascinating prospect, especially for guitarist Alain WHYTE, a besotted Clash fan. Unfortunately, with barely a day's notice, the session was cancelled. Morrissey would never have another opportunity to work with Strummer, who died of a heart attack in 2002 at the age of 50.[1]

There'd be other cancellations throughout 1996, including an extensive North American tour and muted promises of a proper album session that summer which never materialised. Eventually, Morrissey admitted to his band members patiently waiting on permanent standby that there would be no album. However frustrating, his indecisiveness seemed fully excusable in view of the far more troublesome bugbear dominating his life at the time. Former Smiths drummer Mike Joyce's claim against Morrissey and Marr over unpaid performance royalties was about to reach the High Court in December 1996. The year ended with Morrissey losing the case, having his character denigrated in the judge's summation and being further humiliated in the press.

It was in this, indeed, maladjusted frame of mind (or, as he put it, 'despair bordering on elation') that the singer returned to his preferred studio of Hook End Manor in January 1997, less than a month after the verdict was passed, to record his long-delayed sixth album originally christened Ambitious Outsiders. That the end result was the least focused, least satisfying and most artistically dithering of his career perhaps isn't surprising. 'I made many mistakes on Maladjusted,' he later confessed. 'To work with [producer] Steve Lillywhite for the

third time, and to sign with a label [Mercury] that showed no interest to me. In front of this, I lowered my arms. The press was killing me, radio were not playing my records. I began doubting. I could not give the best of me any more.'

Nevertheless, the session itself was far from miserable. 'Of course we all knew about the court case,' says engineer Danton Supple. 'But it wasn't this big taboo. I can remember Steve laughing about the judge's comments and having a joke with him. In the studio, certainly, Morrissey seemed in good spirits.' Although the COURT CASE was still at the forefront of his mind, the cathartic rage which could have very easily swamped Maladjusted was confined to just one track, the theatrical monologue 'Sorrow Will Come In The End', deemed contentious enough to be removed from UK versions of the album for fear of provoking libel action. Another lyric of the period, 'THE LEECHES GO ON REMOVING', had also addressed Joyce's legal victory but would remain unreleased: the phrase later reappeared on 'YOU KNOW I COULDN'T LAST' from 2004's YOU ARE THE QUARRY, an album which dealt with Morrissey's feelings about the court case far more lucidly than Maladjusted.

The album itself was otherwise business as usual, the over-familiarity of studio, producer, musicians and co-writers perhaps another contributory factor to its creative malaise. The one significant difference was drummer Spencer COBRIN's entry into the latter category. Having taken up piano lessons the previous year, Cobrin was now submitting demos for Morrissey's consideration, a factor which added further strain to the existing rivalry between Whyte and BOORER. 'Morrissey was aware of that, and I think he quite enjoyed it,' reasons bassist Jonny BRIDGWOOD. 'They were competing with each other to get the most songs on the album. Morrissey liked the fact they were desperately trying to please him and be the one with the lion's share.'

To begin with, Whyte and Boorer's contributions were evenly matched while Cobrin's efforts were first only considered worthy enough for B-sides. But Maladjusted proved a bitter experience for Boorer, who saw his quota halved on the eventual running order. His three casualties were eventual B-side 'I CAN HAVE BOTH' (replaced by Cobrin's 'Wide To Receive' at the last minute) along with the strange and complex 'KIT' and the cheery 'I KNOW WHO I LOVE', both of which were shelved indefinitely. Whyte, as usual, took his 'lion's share' with seven songs to Boorer's three and Cobrin's one.

With the material to hand – a mixed bag of ballads, ambitious faux-orchestral set-pieces and routine indie guitar rock – though Maladjusted was never going to be a *great* Morrissey album it could easily have been improved had his final tracklisting not excluded some of the aforementioned Boorer tunes. Equally, had Morrissey waited another six months and considered some of the excellent songs he recorded at a later B-side session for its latter two singles, it *could* have been a great album (as its radically reshuffled 2009 version made manifest).

As it was, Maladjusted was a flawed affair desperately lacking any sense of cohesion. While, on an individual basis, some of its tracks were much stronger than those on the previous Southpaw Grammar, as a whole it felt an inferior work. The main problem was the disparity between its highs and lows, each annulling one another to create a homogeneous mediocrity. If the beautiful 'Trouble Loves Me', the endearing 'Alma Matters' and the formidable title track were Morrissey at his best, then the spiritless 'Ammunition', the ludicrous 'Papa Jack' and the unforgivable 'Roy's Keen' were Morrissey at his worst. Beside such nadirs, ordinarily laudable efforts such as 'Wide To Receive' and 'He Cried' drifted past the listener virtually unnoticed. Even the upbeat finale of Boorer's rocking 'Satan Rejected My Soul' felt anticlimactic after such unremitting patchiness.

Only so much liability can be apportioned to Morrissey's co-writers. Lyrically, Maladjusted is also the singer's worst album: sporadically touching and clever but all too frequently vague and lazy. It was, therefore, telling to hear him discuss the record and admit, 'What's always been most important to me are the vocal melodies, even more so than the lyrical content. That's really the key to the songs surviving.'

By the time the album appeared in August 1997 amid the dying days of Britpop (a bad month for Manchester music, released just ten days before the Hindenburg disaster of Oasis's Be Here Now), Morrissey had signed with Mercury Records, once home to the NEW YORK DOLLS. In the UK, it was released on the subsidiary ISLAND imprint, reviving the early 70s label design of his beloved SPARKS and ROXY MUSIC singles. Sadly, the retro vinyl labelling was the only impressive aspect of the album artwork. The sleeve of Maladjusted was horrendous. Isolated against a silver background, the singer squats on his haunches in jeans and a striped jumper. Most disturbing is his face, which barely registers as that of Morrissey, such is its lack of charisma or expression. Many years later, the singer curdled with embarrassment over the portrait, likening his hairline to that of Tony Blair while comparing his pose to 'a mushroom or a leprechaun', adding 'I look as if I'm sat on the lavatory crying my eyes out. Nothing new there, then …'

Upon its release Morrissey bravely trumpeted Maladjusted as 'a perfect album that reflects exactly what I am today'. But although he also bragged to the press about it being his best album vocally ('I'm sure it has something to do with the oesophagus'), the majority of promotional interviews exposed his severe pessimism and paranoia over his current position in British music, at times seemingly willing Maladjusted to fail. 'It will probably sink without trace,' he mourned. 'I won't have any hit single with [this] album. I won't sell millions … There are too many people who can't see beyond Morrissey. It's "No!" all the time. "We won't play your single! We won't sell your record!" … Once the tide turns, it turns, and unless you have the wind in your sails there's very little you can do.'

It was typical of Morrissey that he should accurately forecast Maladjusted's modest sales and the poor performance of its three singles bar 'Alma

Matters' (his first top 20 hit in three years) yet blame conspiratorial media rather than take personal responsibility for the album's inadequacies. 'I don't really seem to ever fit in,' he reasoned when explaining the main 'theme' of Maladjusted. 'In the 80s, when independent/alternative music was not played or listened to, that's obviously the kind of music I was making. And then when it was listened to, certainly in England, I was "box-office poison", if you like. So, Maladjusted really means constantly not fitting in.'

Critically, Maladjusted was given a surprisingly soft ride by the majority of the British music press. Only in hindsight has it become shorthand for Morrissey's 90s decline, particularly circa the release of 2004's You Are The Quarry when some reviewers felt it necessary to praise the 'new' Morrissey by criticising the 'old'. In truth, the outstanding moments on Maladjusted, though they may be few, are as good as anything he's done subsequently, just as Morrissey's musical evolution has progressed little since in terms of style. Even so, Maladjusted is an album that's easy to tolerate but difficult to truly love. It's revealing enough that when touring to promote it in the US and Europe in the winter of 1997 there were nights when Morrissey's setlist included only two tracks from the album.

The following year, Morrissey moved to Los Angeles. When his label, Mercury, were taken over by the multi-national Seagram corporation, the singer spent 'a long time trying to get disentangled' from his contract. He did, but it would be five difficult years in exile before he signed another. Without planning to, with Maladjusted Morrissey had made his final album of the 90s, closing the lid on his life as a recording artist in the twentieth-century.

However, the story of Maladjusted doesn't end there. Over a decade later, Morrissey returned to its crime scene along with that of Southpaw Grammar, reissuing both albums in early 2009 in repackaged, reconfigured formats in a concerted attempt to correct the mistakes of the past. The redux Maladjusted was the most radical of the

two: the embarrassments of 'Roy's Keen' and 'Papa Jack' were removed altogether while the six B-sides of its three singles were added along with the contentious 'Sorrow Will Come In The End'.[2] Gone too was the loathsome 'leprechaun' cover, replaced by a more tasteful period photo of the singer near the Alone In London charity headquarters near King's Cross. In doing so, Morrissey vastly improved what was always his most inconsistent work, though time will tell if the new bionic Maladjusted is capable of fully eradicating all memories of its sickly predecessor from history.
[4, 5, 40, 56, 67, 74, 88, 161, 194, 197, 228, 567]

---

1. Morrissey later claimed that his inability to withstand Strummer's need to smoke in the studio was the reason the collaboration fell through.
2. The tracklisting for the 2009 version is: 'Maladjusted', 'Ambitious Outsiders', 'Trouble Loves Me', 'LOST', 'He Cried', 'Alma Matters', 'HEIR APPARENT', 'Ammunition', 'THE EDGES ARE NO LONGER PARALLEL', 'THIS IS NOT YOUR COUNTRY', 'Wide To Receive', 'I Can Have Both', 'NOW I AM A WAS', 'Satan Rejected My Soul', 'Sorrow Will Come In The End'.

'Maladjusted' (Morrissey/Boorer), From the album MALADJUSTED (1997). An impressively forceful opener to an album which sadly failed to sustain the same momentum, its title track was salvaged from a much 'riskier' Boorer tune which had only impressed Morrissey in its ascending three-chord outro; a slow ogreish 'Purple Haze' which repeated ad infinitum duly became 'Maladjusted'.

The first words heard are those of Anthony NEWLEY, sampled from the 1955 British war film *The Cockleshell Heroes*, the true story of a Royal Marines mission to blow up a blockade of German ships in Bordeaux using a crack team of specially trained canoeists armed with explosives. The original line was Newley's comic speech to his fellow marines following a bar brawl with a group of sailors lcd by Patric DOONAN: 'On this glorious occasion, of the splendid defeat [*and complete victory over the Royal Navy …*]' 'It's just a masculine war movie,' explained Morrissey, 'where everyone's a marine soldier and everybody's happy all the time and every officer has a stiff upper lip

m

... one of those old films that gives us wonderful insight to merry old England.'

Newley's words usher in Morrissey's admission of a youth led astray, rejecting polite society for the twilight world of petty criminals and ne'er-do-wells. The description of peering in 'stable homes' and speculating on their occupants' happiness resonated with Linder STERLING's recollections of walking for hours with the young Morrissey around the streets of Manchester and 'looking in people's windows' (a similar lyrical scene would also open the later 'I'LL NEVER BE ANYBODY'S HERO NOW'). Yet any autobiographical reading was quickly muddied by the specific references to west London and the gradual revelation that Morrissey's narrator appears to be a young prostitute corrupted from the age of 15 onwards. It's also possible Morrissey was inspired by JONI MITCHELL's 'The Jungle Line' from 1975's The Hissing Of Summer Lawns with its similar lyrical motifs of a 'working girl' in a 'low-cut blouse'. An awesome overture for an album dominated by themes of outsiderdom, within its self-condemning hiss 'never to be trusted', 'Maladjusted' perhaps also exposed Morrissey's bitter sense of persecution following the verdict of the 1996 COURT CASE. [4, 5, 40, 48, 468, 493, 542]

Malady Lingers On, The, Morrissey's second solo video compilation, released November 1992. See Mozography appendix for full tracklisting.

A sequel volume to the previous HULMERIST, its title repeated a pun on Irving Berlin's 'The Song Is Ended (But The Melody Lingers On)' previously squeezed by comedian Les Dawson for his 1982 book The Malady Lingers On And Other Great Groaners. The collection featured all his official promos of the previous two years bar 'OUR FRANK', in all likelihood omitted due to its SKIN-HEAD imagery which may have exacerbated controversy over the recent NME Madstock furore.

Malone, Amanda, 18-year-old plump '1960s freak' who recorded an unsuccessful session with The Smiths in April 1984. Morrissey's intention was for Malone to follow in the footsteps of Sandie SHAW as the next female singer to interpret their music, specifically 'THIS CHARMING MAN' to be released as a single on ROUGH TRADE backed with 'GIRL AFRAID'. In the event, the recordings were deemed unusable and the project was hastily forgotten.

In December 1983 Malone was working in New York alongside promoter Ruth Polsky who'd help secure The Smiths their debut US gig at the city's Danceteria that New Year's Eve. Malone and Polsky were to be the group's welcoming committee, taking them to dinner when they arrived. Morrissey was immediately taken with Malone, who shared the same birthday of 22 May and, by her own confession, 'was a very freaky-looking kid – enormously fat with a big bouffant hairdo, all done up in 60s clothes. I looked a lot like Ricki Lake in Hairspray.' Though her singing experience was limited to the odd impromptu club performance, Morrissey offered her a wild proposition. 'He said, "Why don't you come over to England and make a record with us." I was just a kid, I wanted to be a pop star, so I thought, "Wow! This is brilliant!" So a few months later I went to England to do just that.'

Morrissey was demonstrably serious enough about Malone's career to forewarn the press. 'We're also intending to record some songs with a woman called Amanda,' he trumpeted in February 1984. 'We met her in America, though she's from Brighton. She's going to be the next "singing sensation". She's got an English accent like Lady Penelope and she won't wear a stitch of clothing unless it's pre-1962. She seems to have sprung straight out of Liverpool's Cavern. We'll begin as soon as we can ship her over ... she's quite large.'

Malone was shipped to London soon afterwards and spent a couple of weeks signing on the dole, waiting in anticipation for Morrissey to fulfil his promise. In early April, with one day's notice, he rang Malone with the news that they'd be recording the next day at the Power Plant studio in Willesden. According to Marr, the rest of the band were bemused by the whole concept.

'Mama Lay Softly On The Riverbed' (Morrissey/Whyte), From the album YEARS OF REFUSAL (2009). The story of a son grieving over his mother's suicide is the catalyst for another of Morrissey's impassioned attacks on authority figures and money men in particular. The scenario immediately brought to mind 'SHAKESPEARE'S SISTER' muse Virginia Woolf who in March 1941 weighted her coat pockets with stones then drowned herself on the bed of the River Ouse in Sussex.[1] Though Morrissey vows to bring murderous retribution to those who drove Mama to kill herself, ultimately the narrative was a symbolic vehicle to reiterate his nihilistic doctrine that 'life is nothing much to lose', finding perverse victory in a suicidal vow to join her in the grave. Such morbid triumphalism was underscored by its vigorous rhythm; a euphoric death march complete with church organ and other adorably deranged synthesiser seizures from 'the great' Roger Manning Jr. Introduced in concert in early 2008, live versions routinely climaxed in a mini-military tattoo with guitarist Boz BOORER and keyboardist Kristopher Pooley joining in its snare drum assault.

---

1. The Woolf connection shouldn't be taken literally since she had no children, though it is interesting that 'Mama Lay Softly On The Riverbed' should follow 'SOMETHING IS SQUEEZING MY SKULL' on the album's running order: Woolf was driven to suicide after a prolonged period of mental illness.

'Morrissey knew more about her than we did, even though we had to endure playing behind her,' he says. 'But it was comical. She sang like Cicely Courtneidge in a 16-year-old Barbara Windsor's body.'

Rough Trade's Geoff Travis was on hand as executive producer, though as Malone notes, 'I have a feeling that maybe he wasn't really into the idea.' Unfortunately, Malone was so nervous about the session that she'd stayed up the previous night in a state of panic. By the time she entered the vocal booth, Malone was delirious and exhausted. Morrissey vainly tried to coax her through 'This Charming Man' after she struggled to find her key. 'He came into the recording booth and sang along with me,' she recalls. 'He was trying to get my nerves at bay and give me my starting note. But it was terrible.' The intended B-side, 'Girl Afraid', was 'a little better', says Malone, 'but after we'd finished it I kind of knew it wasn't going to happen because I sounded dreadful'. As she suspected, Rough Trade, and most probably Morrissey himself, vetoed the release of the single. Malone's transatlantic trip to become 'the next "singing sensation"' had been in vain, though she maintains 'secretly, I was a bit relieved'.

Ruth Polsky, meanwhile, had also travelled over to London and would briefly throw her hat into the ring as The Smiths' caretaker manager around the same period. Two years later, on 7 September 1986, Polsky was killed outside New York's Limelight club when a taxi span out of control and pinned her against a wall. The Smiths paid tribute with a dedication on the back cover of February 1987's 'SHOPLIFTERS OF THE WORLD UNITE' single. As for Amanda Malone, she would shift a considerable amount of weight and is better known today as writer and vintage clothing guru Amanda Hallay. 'Somewhere, in some box', Hallay still has a cassette of that hapless Smiths session, very possibly one of the few, perhaps only, in existence. [8, 17, 32, 82]

Man In A Suitcase, See BRADFORD, Richard.

Man Who Came To Dinner, The, 1942
comedy starring Bette DAVIS listed among Morrissey's favourite films. His early occasional pseudonym of Sheridan WHITESIDE was borrowed from the main character while dialogue from the screenplay was also incorporated into the lyrics of 'CEMETRY GATES'.

m

Based upon the Broadway play by George S. Kaufman and Moss Hart, it stars Monty Woolley as the obnoxious radio host and critic Sheridan Whiteside who, accompanied by his long-suffering secretary Maggie Cutler (Davis), is obliged to have dinner at the Ohio home of the Stanley family prior to a lecture the week before Christmas. On entering the Stanleys' home, Whiteside slips on an icy step and appears to injure himself. Confined to a wheelchair 'for an indefinite period', he is forced to recuperate at their home but quickly tyrannises the entire household with his offensive remarks, impossible demands and promises of legal action to the tune of $150,000. In the meantime, he learns that his loyal Maggie has fallen in love with a local newshound and aspiring playwright and may soon leave his service to get married. When Whiteside is then diagnosed by the local doctor who tells him that he's fully recovered, he conspires a wicked plot to continue faking his injury in order to scupper Maggie's romance and keep her in his employment.

The narrative becomes ever more complex with the arrival of English actor Beverly Carlton (played by Reginald Gardiner and apparently modelled upon Noël COWARD), the lunatic comedian 'Banjo' (Jimmy Durante) and Hollywood vamp Lorraine Sheldon (Ann Sheridan). The latter is responsible for the 'Cemetry Gates' speech when, towards the end of the film, she reminisces about a visit to the Roman ruins of Pompeii while perusing an Egyptian mummy which Whiteside has been sent as a Christmas gift: 'All those people. All those lives. Where are they now? Here was a woman like myself, a woman who once lived and loved, full of the same passions, fears, jealousies, hates. What remains of it now? … I want to cry.' [184, 529]

managers, If the world of pop music has such a thing as a poisoned chalice, then the role of managing Morrissey is probably it. 'I'm not easy to manage,' he confessed in 2009, an understatement which the small army of administrative walking wounded dumped along the roadside of his long career would no doubt consider criminal.

'Nobody can look after me,' he explained in 1996. 'It's too difficult. Managers always end up bypassing me. They don't know how to represent me faithfully. They speak for me but don't know what they say … As soon as people get to work with a group they have the impression they possess full power. Guided by money and covetousness, they start doing anything. It's one of my biggest regrets in life. I've never found any person clever enough to represent me. This person doesn't exist.'

It is well documented that The Smiths' managerial problems were a major factor in the group's eventual demise. After their original backer Joe MOSS stepped down at the end of 1983, the group never found a satisfactory replacement and for much of their career the administrative burden was borne by Marr alone; an unnecessary pressure which, by May 1987, ultimately proved unbearable.

'Johnny put forward at least two managers who seemed fine to me,' says Andy Rourke. 'Matthew Stzumpf, who managed MADNESS, was doing a great job. And Ken Friedman, the American guy who came in on STRANGEWAYS. Both competent managers. But I think it was because Morrissey didn't know them so he had a suspicion that they were working more for Johnny than for him. So he wouldn't communicate with them as managers. I think Morrissey's idea of a manager is a mouthpiece for himself, really, just to do what he said rather than a manager who advises you what to do. Morrissey wasn't prepared to do that.'

Friedman, a Californian promoter in his late twenties who'd previously worked with Simple Minds and UB40, was to be The Smiths' last manager. He lasted just five and a half weeks, in which time Morrissey notoriously vetoed a video shoot for the single 'SHEILA TAKE A BOW' by not turning up. When Friedman called at the singer's flat to demand an answer, so the story goes, Morrissey refused to answer the door, leaving Friedman shouting in vain through his letterbox.

'[We] never found a potential manager who

could deal with the whole situation without wanting creative input,' Morrissey later mourned. 'We just wanted to be helped along with our own ideas. And managers are never capable of doing that. They can't resist meddling, believing they too are making the new album, designing the cover. You must understand that The Smiths was an absolutely closed society. It really, really was.'

Morrissey's notorious passive-aggressive behaviour towards managers is best illustrated by a semi-legendary incident in the mid-90s, as recounted, and possibly a little embellished, by friend Cathal SMYTH. 'We were at Hook End studios,' explains Smyth, 'and Morrissey had invited four of the top managers from America. Each one came into the room having flown from America, gotten off at Heathrow, driven into London, booked a hotel, then booked a car to go out to Reading to Hook End. So they arrive at the studio, Morrissey shakes their hand and then says, "I'm just popping out to get some tea." And he doesn't come back. Two minutes with each geezer. Morrissey isn't coming back. Each one of them went back to America fucking livid. Michael Jackson's manager was one of them. These were the top managers who beat a path to his door, he fucked them off within half a minute on the pretence of going out for a cuppa. But the legend grew. It was a brilliant move.'

In spite of his troublesome reputation, not all of Morrissey's management relations have been disastrous. He was especially fond of Nigel Thomas, his manager circa YOUR ARSENAL who died in 1993 shortly before the making of VAUXHALL AND I. Similarly, former Sanctuary Records CEO Merck Mercuriadis 'at the helm' of Morrissey's 00s comeback with YOU ARE THE QUARRY and RINGLEADER OF THE TORMENTORS. Not forgetting his own mother, who according to both Stephen STREET and engineer Danton Supple took control of her son's purse strings during one of his managerial lulls in the 90s.

Nevertheless, Morrissey continues to go through managers like a rambler through corn plasters. In the course of 2008 alone, the baton was passed between three managers in the run-up to the release of YEARS OF REFUSAL. It seems that his ideal manager, like that of his ideal partner, is an ever elusive if not impossible quest, one which in its perpetually chaotic soap opera somehow reaffirms Morrissey's fundamental Morrisseyness. 'I always feel,' he once said, 'that I stand alone, in every sense.'

'The mistake that people make with Morrissey is they try to manage him efficiently,' concludes Cathal Smyth, who himself turned down the job so as not to damage his friendship with the singer. 'That's unnecessary. What you need to do with Morrissey is just do his bidding.' [17, 19, 29, 36, 39, 40, 99, 115, 137, 138, 198, 236, 480]

Manchester, Morrissey's native city, The
Smiths' spiritual home and the cultural heart of the north-west of England. *CORONATION STREET*, BUZZCOCKS, Howard DEVOTO, FACTORY ... *so much* to answer for.

Morrissey was born and bred in south Manchester where most of his lyrical references to the city can be found, including the areas of Whalley Range ('MISERABLE LIE'), RUSHOLME (as in 'Ruffians') and Southern Cemetery in Chorlton-cum-Hardy, the inspiration for 'CEMETRY GATES' and burial place of both Moors Murder victim Lesley Ann Downey ('SUFFER LITTLE CHILDREN') and Sir Matt Busby, manager of the fated Manchester United 'Busby Babes' involved in the 'MUNICH AIR DISASTER 1958'.

Steven Patrick Morrissey was delivered in Davyhulme Park Hospital on 22 May 1959. At the time, his parents and older sister Jacqueline were living in Harper Street, Hulme (as in *HULMERIST*). Three years later they moved to Queen's Square near Moss Side. Both houses have since been demolished.

By 1964, when Morrissey was five years old, the family settled in Stretford at 384 Kings Road where the singer would spend his formative years and where, in the summer of 1982, Johnny Marr eventually 'unearthed' him to start The Smiths. The house is still a private residence no longer connected to the Morrissey family yet remains a Mecca for Smiths and Morrissey pilgrims from around the world.[1]

Other key Smiths landmarks in the city are the Holy Name Church on Wilmslow Road, as immortalised in 'VICAR IN A TUTU' (where Smiths cover star Pat PHOENIX also had her funeral service in 1986) and the Victorian prison on Southall Street which gave its name to the group's final album, STRANGEWAYS, HERE WE COME. The building that used to house The Smiths' original HQ above Joe MOSS's Crazy Face clothing business still stands on the corner of 70 Portland Street near Manchester's Chinatown, as does the Apollo Theatre on Stockport Road in Ardwick, Johnny Marr's heartland where he first spoke to Morrissey at a PATTI SMITH concert in August 1978. Marr's family later moved further south to Wythenshawe.

Neighbouring (but not technically *in*) Manchester is the separate city of Salford, home to the most famous Smiths landmark of all, SALFORD LADS CLUB. Though geographically part of the same Greater Manchester urban spread, Salford fiercely maintains a separate identity to Manchester itself. Famous Salfordians include Morrissey heroes Shelagh DELANEY, Albert FINNEY and the creator of CORONATION STREET, Tony Warren.

In the early days of The Smiths, Morrissey often spoke unfavourably of Manchester as a place of entrapment. 'I don't really feel any kinship with the place,' he claimed in 1983. 'It's just somewhere that I happen to live. It doesn't mean a great deal to me and I'm sure I'll leave very soon. When I'm rich.' Yet, despite briefly relocating to London once the group took off, The Smiths returned in early 1985. Their insular group HQ for the rest of their career would be Marr's home in the Cheshire green belt near Altrincham Grammar School in Bowdon. Though Morrissey would maintain properties in London, he bought a house in nearby Hale before moving into a bigger mansion property in Altrincham, later home to his mother. Johnny Marr, Andy Rourke and Mike Joyce still live in Greater Manchester.

Since the turn of the millennium, Morrissey has shown great affection for his hometown, witness to his historic 45th and 50th birthday concerts of 2004 and 2009 respectively. That affection has been fully reciprocated, Morrissey voted the 'Greatest Living Mancunian' by the readers of local listings magazine *CityLife* in 2002 in a landslide victory. Even after relocating to Los Angeles, he admitted that Manchester still felt 'indelibly' like home. 'It really does,' he enthused. 'I was born and raised there, and for better or worse, it made me. You can rally against the negative things

Marais, Jean, French actor and cover star of the Smiths single 'THIS CHARMING MAN'. The image of Marais sleeping against his own reflection was a production still from the 1950 film *Orphée* directed by Marais's former lover, Jean COCTEAU. Loosely based upon the Greek myth of Orpheus in the Underworld, Cocteau's is an allegorical fantasy with symbolic allusions to the recent Nazi occupation of France. The 'This Charming Man' scene appears roughly 17 minutes in. Having been taken to the threshold of the film's equivalent Underworld by the deathly princess, Marais, as the poet Orphée, tries to follow her through a mirror but is unable to pass. He eventually collapses against the glass only to awake lying over a pool in a deserted landscape (as it looks, the pool was filmed using a mirror surrounded by sand). Although the image's inherent narcissism seemed perfectly suited to the title of 'This Charming Man', the fact that the same picture was employed on a premature press ad for the group's original choice of second single, 'REEL AROUND THE FOUNTAIN', suggests Morrissey was intent on using it for the next Smiths release irrespective of the song in question. [374, 538]

that you don't particularly like about yourself and you can easily blame Manchester for that. The only thing I blame Manchester for was my terrible education, not because of anything else. I find it a fantastic place now. It's nothing like the city I grew up in. It's a lot cleaner and more cosmopolitan. The shops are fantastic and the people look great. The people there look so sexy. It is less of the Manchester that I used to know.' [14, 17, 18, 28, 165, 316, 362, 406, 436, 463]

---

1. Those wishing to visit Manchester specifically to follow in Morrissey's footsteps and undertake a Smiths-centric sightseeing tour should arm themselves with a copy of the only essential guide book, *Morrissey's Manchester* by Phill Gatenby (Empire Publications).

'Margaret On The Guillotine' (Morrissey/Street), From the album VIVA HATE (1988). An old Morrissey title dating back to the winter of 1985 when it was briefly considered as an alternative for THE QUEEN IS DEAD, 'Margaret On The Guillotine' was an unapologetically blunt expression of his feelings for Britain's reigning prime minister, Margaret THATCHER, who at the time of recording had just entered her third term in office. Mentioned only once in the song by her Christian name (Morrissey, perhaps deliberately, actually mumbles the song title), the lyrics fantasise about the day 'the kind people' of the United Kingdom stage their own equivalent French Revolution and publicly behead Thatcher for the damage she's wreaked. His message to Maggie: 'When will you die?' His message to the nation: 'Make the dream real.'

Since the whole point of 'Margaret On The Guillotine' was the title *cause célèbre,* the song itself was immaterial. Indeed, Street's simple acoustic tune was fine if forgettable, though the embellishment of some backwards guitar and Vini REILLY's improvised picking radiated its share of beauty. The final guillotine slice was the sound effect of a door being slammed, filtered to sound like a plummeting blade.

Morrissey told the press the track wasn't meant to be controversial for controversy's sake, merely a sincere declaration that he wished Thatcher to

die 'instantly'. By 1988, he wasn't alone, though by documenting his feelings on a number one album he'd earn the unwelcome attention of Special Branch who, as he recounted, paid him a visit and 'searched the house for a guillotine'. Morrissey alluded to this incident the following year when recording the B-side 'HE KNOWS I'D LOVE TO SEE HIM'. [25, 39, 153, 203, 208, 272]

'(Marie's The Name) His Latest Flame' (Doc Pomus/Mort Shuman), 1961 UK number one for Elvis PRESLEY covered in concert by The Smiths in acknowledgement of its influence upon Marr's melody for 'RUSHOLME RUFFIANS'; it's also possible that while growing up Marr would have been familiar with the cover by his parents' favourite, Del Shannon. Brill Building team Pomus and Shuman originally wrote the song for Bobby Vee, then passing it to Bobby Darin before offering Presley third refusal. Elvis adored its thumping Bo Diddley rhythm while its lyrics about an ex-girlfriend's overnight betrayal inspired a magnificent vocal shaking with pain and pathos. When touring Scotland in autumn 1985, The Smiths modified 'Rusholme Ruffians' to incorporate the first two verses of '(Marie's The Name) His Latest Flame' as a special medley. All future performances of 'Rusholme Ruffians' throughout their final tours of 1986 would contain this same Elvis tribute, as captured for posterity on RANK. [17, 310]

Marr, Johnny (Smiths founder, guitar hero, co-writer and producer 1982–87), It would not be over-sensationalising fact to describe Johnny Marr as, musically speaking, the love of Morrissey's life. In its mystery, sublimity, romance and intrigue, the Morrissey/Marr composer credit dwarfs not only every other writing partnership the singer's entered since but every other pop writing partnership of the latter quarter of the twentieth-century bar none. There is Lennon/McCartney, there is Jagger/Richards, and there is Morrissey/Marr.

While there are many narrative threads to the group's history involving a large extended cast, ultimately the story of The Smiths is the story of

Morrissey and Marr – a Mancunian Estragon and Vladimir in a two-man drama that is theirs alone. It has often been told as a love story, one that ended in tragedy, perhaps even betrayal. But while there is certainly much drama and upset within its plot twists, the story of Morrissey and Marr is one of epic heroism, of escape and salvation, of courage and conviction, of battles won, of destinies seized, and of the absolute triumph of art and beauty over all else.

i) Marr before The Smiths, Like Morrissey, Marr's family – the Mahers – were Irish immigrants, moving to Manchester from Kildare at the beginning of the 60s. He was born John Martin Maher on Everton Road, Chorlton-on-Medlock, a Halloween baby on 31 October 1963: the number one record that week was Gerry And The Pacemakers' version of 'You'll Never Walk Alone', destined to become The Smiths' ceremonial stage exit theme as sung by Shirley BASSEY.

The eldest of three, he was nicknamed Johnny partly as a means of avoiding confusion with his father, also John Maher. Twenty years later he'd adapt the spelling of his surname to Marr, both emphasising the correct pronunciation (as opposed to 'Mah-her') and asserting his own identity in the face of potential mix-up with the *other* John Maher, drummer with local punk heroes BUZZCOCKS.

Marr spent his early childhood in Ardwick, south of Manchester city centre. His parents, like Morrissey's, were still young when he was born: father John was 20, mother Frances 17. Crucially, both were fans of pop music, ensuring Marr was exposed to the heartbroken moods and melodies of The Everly Brothers, Del Shannon, Johnny Cash and Motown at a very young age. Equally decisive was the social life governed by his extended Irish family: weddings, birthdays, christenings, wakes and all other excuses for a traditional Irish singsong. It was at such events that Johnny first became spellbound by the red Stratocaster belonging to the house band's guitarist, his young nostrils savouring the alluring exotic smell of the guitar case, an aroma which would haunt, and determine, the rest of his life.

It was at these same family gatherings that Marr first recognised music as an echo of human sadness, an emotion already filtering into his senses amid the economic repression of 60s inner-city Manchester. 'I was sad when I was a little kid because the area where I grew up was very heavy,' he explains. 'Ardwick in the 60s was *actually* grim. It did always seem to be very rainy and there was a lot of traffic. Women in beehives bringing up large families on not a lot of money, wearing coats on HP. It was a young Irish community, a lot of music and a lot of drinking. There were always parties, and weddings, and a lot of melancholy in the music that was around me at that age. Old Irish ballads like "Black Velvet Band" which I really used to love. A lot of minor keys and minor scales. Even the stuff my folks were listening to, like Del Shannon, there was a dark, gothic sadness about it. That really hooked me and seemed to resonate with my surroundings.'

By the age of ten, as part of a housing clearance Marr's family had moved from Ardwick out to the grey concrete sprawl of Wythenshawe, a council estate much further south. 'It's amazing because it was one of the most notorious housing estates in the country but it was only there that I was able to feel artistic and creative,' says Marr. 'It was only then, when I got to about 12 or 13, that I started to feel a bit more outgoing. Wythenshawe allowed me to feel all right about being a guitar player.'

The seeds of Marr's musical obsession had already been sown, thanks to his parents' record collection, his early fascination with the electric guitar and his discovery, aged eight, of Marc BOLAN. But it was the move to Wythenshawe that gave Marr his first footing on his destined trail to Smithdom. A pupil of St Augustine's Grammar School (later renamed St John Plessington after a merger in 1977), in his second year he noticed a boy newly moved into his class wearing a button badge of the recent Neil Young album, Tonight's The Night.

'It was because I was wearing that badge that Johnny first came up to me and we started talking,' says Andy Rourke. 'Originally, we'd been in different classes. I was in the bad lads' class and basically I got a bit too bad. So they switched me and another kid, Phil Powell – who later became Johnny's guitar roadie in The Smiths – into Johnny's class, the good lads' class, to sort us out.'

Ironically, it was the future Smiths bassist who was more competent on guitar to begin with. 'Johnny was dead keen,' Rourke elaborates. 'Our form room was also the music class so there was a piano in the corner which we used to muck around on and we'd both bring our guitars in. I'd show him something and a week later he could play it better than me. That's how keen he was.'

Marr and Rourke befriended another pupil two years older, Billy DUFFY, who proved just as important in the foundations of The Smiths. As they began mucking around with their first shambolic after-school groups – including the near mythical Paris Valentinos featuring future CORONATION STREET actor Kevin 'Curly Watts' Kennedy – Duffy was rehearsing and writing with Morrissey in THE NOSEBLEEDS. The first Marr ever heard of Morrissey was through Duffy, also responsible for first introducing the 19-year-old Morrissey to the 14-year-old Marr when PATTI SMITH played the Manchester Apollo on 31 August 1978. It was, Marr hazily recalls, 'just a quick hello'.

By the time Marr left school the following summer he'd already met his soul mate and future wife, Angie. Two years younger than Marr, Angie Brown not only shared his birthday but the same dark colouring and petite physique; as Smiths soundman Grant Showbiz would later comment, 'they were like twins'.

Angie would be Johnny's rock during his next three years of trial and frustration as music, guitar playing and the need to form a group became his raison d'être. Not even an ambition-conflicting talent for football – trialled for Manchester City and approached by a scout for Nottingham Forest – could sway Marr's commitment.

His first semi-serious group was the American rock-influenced White Dice, formed in 1980 with Rourke (now on bass) and fronted by another older Wythenshawe guitarist and singer, Rob Allman. His dreams of rock and roll glory would be teased when they sent a tape to F-Beat Records, run by ex-Stiff founder and Elvis Costello manager Jake Riviera, who invited them to London to record a demo. Beyond the temporary excitement of a trip down south and their first visit to a proper recording studio, nothing came of it. In the wake of their rejection, White Dice broke up.

Marr and Rourke persevered as Freak Party, an instrumental punk-funk trio featuring drummer Simon WOLSTENCROFT. 'We got a rehearsal room at this place in Ancoats, Decibel,' says Rourke. 'We'd be there about three nights a week, every week, but we never did any gigs. We made one demo, this instrumental "Crak Therapy", but it wasn't going anywhere. The problem was finding a singer. We auditioned a couple and it was just disastrous. There was one girl who just wailed like a banshee. And this other guy who went on to become a male model, whose catchphrase was "They call me Donkey". So he was never going to work. In the end, Johnny just got bored and disillusioned with the stuff we were playing. He was more hungry for it so he quit. That must have been about the end of '81. So I never heard from him after that for another year.'

Marr freely admits cutting himself off from his past in a conscious effort to change his social and musical circles. 'I decided to get a whole new life, one away from the suburbs that Andy and I were stuck in. I finally came into my own when I got *out* of the suburbs and *into* Manchester. I was a townie. A definite line was drawn from when I'd stopped playing with Andy. I just dived into a load of new influences.'

His 'whole new life' involved a new job at X-Clothes, an alternative fashion boutique in the city centre, and a new home, now one of several lodgers in a house belonging to journalist and Granada television presenter Shelley Rohde. Still inseparable from Angie, new friendships would further open his eyes and ears. There was record shop manager Pete Hunt, who asked Marr to babysit his vinyl collection while he travelled around Europe and who first introduced Marr to Matt Johnson, then in the process of forming The The in London. Johnson was impressed with Marr's obvious guitar talent and invited him to join the group: unwilling to move down south, Marr declined.

There was also Andrew Berry,[1] the hairdresser and DJ who stayed on Palatine Road, home to FACTORY Records, where Marr would also briefly lodge. Berry would turn Marr on to the new rhythms of early electro and hip hop, also keeping tabs on the current crop of alternative guitar bands from LA's The Gun Club to Edinburgh's Josef K. But neither Hunt, nor Johnson, nor Berry represented The One he was searching for.

At this point, it is worth pausing to picture Johnny Marr at the close of 1981. Just turned 18, time is ticking away. He leads a mercurial life, bouncing from Rohde's home in Bowdon to Berry's in Didsbury, surrounded by local musicians and DJs, a charismatic young man with a gift of the gab desperate to prove himself. But he is also emotionally volatile, intensely frustrated and highly eccentric – an eccentricity that sometimes gets lost in conventional histories of The Smiths which too easily pigeonhole Marr as the outgoing boy about town to Morrissey's suicidal back-bedroom hermit. For it is now that Marr befriends the owner of the shop next to X-Clothes, Crazy Face, a clothing entrepreneur 16 years his senior called Joe MOSS who opens his ears further to the sounds of vintage R&B, blues and early rock and roll.

By the start of 1982, when his peers are still approaching music with a post-punk mentality, their eyes on the NME and their ears on whatever John PEEL happens to be playing that week, Marr's mind is already hurtling down avenues of nostalgic fantasy that others would consider cranky and perverse. In his maverick madness, he becomes convinced that it is possible, in Manchester in 1982, to re-create a classic songwriting partnership similar to those of New York's Brill Building in the late 50s and early 60s. His brain is now revolving at a constant 45 rotations per minute to the sounds of the Red Bird label, and when Moss shows him a documentary on Brill Building legends LEIBER AND STOLLER, it shoves Marr over the edge into a mental distraction from which there are only two outcomes: success or insanity.

So picture him again. The 18-year-old Johnny Marr who, in his head, thinks he's Jerry Leiber. He just needs to find his Mike Stoller and all will be right with the universe. But this is Manchester, this is 1982, and the chances of there being anybody out there as desperate, as committed and as gifted as him are a billion to one. For all his exterior charm and sociability, inside Johnny Marr feels very alone. As alone as the strange boy from Stretford whom he met just fleetingly not four years earlier at a Patti Smith concert, who, as fate would have it, he has never fully forgotten. Which is where the greatest love story in the history of pop finally unfolds.

ii) The 'unearthing' of Morrissey and creation of The Smiths,

No individual person can rightfully claim credit for being 'the one' who led Marr to Morrissey, but several, all of whom have their own entries in this book.

First, Billy Duffy, who'd played and written with Morrissey and who, most importantly, imparted the vital information that he wrote unique and interesting lyrics.

Secondly, the mutual obsessions of the NEW YORK DOLLS and Patti Smith; as Marr states, 'It was because of the Dolls that I was first told about Morrissey, which was really what brought me to him.'

Thirdly, the influence of Joe Moss, not least in showing Marr the Leiber and Stoller documentary which gave him the idea of cold-calling Morrissey, just as Leiber had done to Stoller.

And lastly, the person who physically took Marr to Morrissey's front door in the summer of 1982, Wythenshawe guitarist Steven POMFRET who, like Duffy, had rehearsed with Morrissey many years previous. From Duffy to Moss to Pomfret via the Dolls and Leiber and Stoller: this was the domino effect which brought Marr to 384 Kings Road, Stretford.

'It's still really clear,' recalls Marr. 'It was a sunny day. About one o'clock in the afternoon.

There was no advance phone call or anything. I just knocked, and he opened the door.'

The exact details of this, the first proper meeting of Morrissey and Marr have, inevitably, been exaggerated into rock and roll mythology as much through their own accounts as those of anybody else. Pomfret's presence – superfluous from the moment Marr began talking '300 words a second' – is usually ignored for reasons of narrative simplicity. In an early 1984 *Smash Hits* interview, Morrissey joked that Marr had first pressed his nose against his living-room window, describing how 'it left a terrible smudge. I think he'd been eating chocolate or something.' The fabled chocolate smudge would be repeated as fact in several summaries of the group's formation thereafter.

In other accounts, Morrissey placed himself in his front garden when 'this creature' appeared at the garden gate. Other versions of the tale have his sister, Jacqueline, first answering the door. But the precise stage directions are no longer relevant, only the outcome which Morrissey would always describe as an act of fate. 'It was an event I'd always looked forward to and unconsciously been waiting for since my childhood,' he recalled. 'Time was passing. I was 22 and Johnny was much younger, but it seemed that I'd hung around for a very long time waiting for this magical mystical event, which definitely occurred. I had a slight tremulous feeling a long time before then, that something very unusual would happen to me and I interpreted it as fame of some magnitude.'

'I was pretty confident that he'd like me,' Marr disclosed in 1984, 'but I was a bit worried in case he thought I looked too outrageous … I had this really silly haircut at the time, this quiff. It looked like I had a French loaf sticking out of me head. I was afraid he'd think I was some kind of Gene Vincent freak.'

Invited up into Morrissey's bedroom, they discussed, among other things, the Dolls, girl groups, Patti Smith and Leiber and Stoller. 'When I came across Morrissey, in terms of influences it was pretty phenomenal that we were so in sync,' says Marr. 'Because the influences that we had individually were pretty obscure. So it was absolutely like fucking lightning bolts to the two of us. This wasn't stuff we liked. This was stuff we lived for really.'

That first visit was enough for Morrissey to agree to Marr's proposition that they begin working together as respective wordsmith and composer. Marr left elated, if somewhat cautious. 'My feeling, as I left him, was, "Well, yeah, OK. But I'll wait to see if he calls me tomorrow."'

The next day, Marr was back at work in X-Clothes when he received the phone call from Morrissey he'd been hoping for. 'And that was it,' says Marr. 'I thought, "Right. OK. We're on."'

The crucial compatibility test came a few days later in Marr's attic room in Bowdon where the first Morrissey/Marr originals took shape: the quickly abandoned 'DON'T BLOW YOUR OWN HORN', the Patti Smith-influenced 'THE HAND THAT ROCKS THE CRADLE' and 'SUFFER LITTLE CHILDREN'. 'After that first meeting we really couldn't get together often enough,' says Marr. 'It was a few times a week. We got a hell of a lot done in that first month.'

They were, Marr admits, in awe of one another's potential. 'He and I almost had this unspoken relationship where we were both able to be ourselves but we both knew how important we were to each other. What shouldn't be forgotten is that we really, *really* liked each other. It wasn't some business arrangement or relationship of convenience. There was intrigue and understanding because as different as we were, the thing that was paramount inside each of us was pop records and that absolute promise of escape. And he understood that without us ever having to talk about it.'

The period from late summer to early autumn saw Morrissey and Marr intensify their shared ambition. Morrissey chose the name, The Smiths, while Marr set about turning their songwriting partnership into an actual group.

'I was inspired by Andrew Loog Oldham and his example,' explains Marr. 'I thought that was really noble, someone who was able to make things happen. In my head I thought I was running around the Brill Building. But that's how I was. I wore hyperactivity as a badge of honour. With Morrissey, he didn't actually need to physically get involved in that side. I was happy finding group members, places to rehearse, places to record, clothes, haircuts, managers and record companies. All he had to do was be brilliant and be with me, for us to be next to each other. That's what it was about. However, he was by no means sat in his front room with the telly on. What connections he was able to draw on, he could. There was a guy in Stretford he'd known for a number of years who was a drummer. He got us all together one evening. This guy was really amiable and chatty but he just didn't seem like a living breathing musician to me, just a nice guy with a drum kit, so obviously he wasn't in. But whatever could be done we both did.'

It would be several months of trial and error before they found Mike Joyce and Marr decided to re-establish contact with Andy Rourke, completing the final Smiths line-up in December 1982. Henceforth, the group would prove unstoppable as the full wonder and magic of both Johnny Marr the guitar player and Morrissey/Marr the composer credit was about to be unleashed upon an unsuspecting world.

iii) Marr's guitar style, By the time The Smiths recorded 'HAND IN GLOVE' in early 1983, Marr's playing was already recognisably 'Marr-esque' if unrecognisable from anything preceding it in nearly three decades of pop history. Just as there is no single influence upon Morrissey's lyrics, stylistically Marr wove together many different disciplines and techniques to create a signature wizardry that was uniquely his.

He once admitted his ambition was 'to be Phil Spector with a guitar', a statement which says much for his arranger's approach to the instrument. It's telling that Joe Moss's earliest memories of hearing Marr play are being mesmerised by his one-man renditions of Motown tunes, hearing him pick out the chords, the brass part and the vocal melody simultaneously.

The same methodology was applied throughout The Smiths. What is usually described as Marr's 'jingly jangly' sound is his use of arpeggiated chords; playing a guitar chord by the rapid picking of its individual constituent notes rather than the standard simultaneous ke-rrang, pirouetting across the strings where others might simply trudge. This aspect of Marr's style shows the clear influence of folk guitar, in particular Pentangle, the late 60s English folk baroque super group formed by guitarist Bert Jansch.

Other than Jansch and his boyhood love of Marc Bolan, many of Marr's formative teenage guitar heroes can be found in US punk of the mid-to late 70s: James Williamson of Iggy & The Stooges, Lenny Kaye and Ivan Kral of The Patti Smith Group, Tom Verlaine and Richard Lloyd of Television and the Dolls' Johnny Thunders and Sylvain Sylvain. Equally, his carpal witchcraft sometimes conjures colours and shapes plucked from more traditional rock models: Neil Young and Crazy Horse's Nils Lofgren, THE ROLLING STONES' Keith Richards, Ireland's Rory Gallagher and THE BEATLES' George Harrison. All of the above sparkle and flicker amid the 'Marrchestra' but none takes precedence as his sole puppet master.

There are other more technical factors to the Marr sound: variant guitar tunings, capos, specific guitar–amp combos, novel chord fingerings and other dark arts which only he seems capable of mastering. But, try as we might to decode and deconstruct the Johnny Marr guitar style, it is an equation impossible to quantify. Like Beethoven said, 'Music is the one incorporeal entrance into the higher world of knowledge which comprehends mankind but which mankind cannot comprehend.' Johnny Marr's fingers are living proof.

iv) The genius of the Morrissey/Marr partnership, Future stereotype would miscast Morrissey and Marr as pop's odd couple, an unlikely meeting of bookish loner and flash tearaway. In truth, they recognised in one another the same solemn ambition and an alarmingly similar inner sadness.

'I thought his music combined sorrow and happiness,' said Morrissey. 'I thought it was very, very sad music. Even the jovial tunes that he produced I thought had a tinge of terrible sadness … that really drew me to his music.'

'We both recognised the beauty in melancholia,' agrees Marr. 'We both understood that. We talked about it, and often, about the difference between depression and melancholia. About how depression was just useless but melancholia was a real emotion, a real place; a creative place that dealt in images and music and creative aspects of the self. I would often simplify it by saying, "It's that feeling where you've got your head leaning against the bus window on a November Wednesday morning with the rain coming down, driving through Manchester." That's what a lot of my songs sounded like because I spent a lot of time doing exactly that. In that respect, mine and Morrissey's concept of melancholia was absolutely the same.'

Beauty and melancholy would be their primary song colours, albeit with added shades of humour, absurdity, profanity, profundity and an irrepressible northern archness. Morrissey was a lyrical one-off, but The Smiths could never have taken flight had he not met his musical equal in Marr. As the former once explained, 'I often feel that whereas I can lay eggs, Johnny can make omelettes.'

The ever-suspicious outside world was bewildered by the bond between Morrissey and Marr, but then so were they. Their writing methods were strangely furtive, silently flirtatious, as if each recognised the value in maintaining a sense of intrigue and inscrutability, of forever keeping some cards close to their chest. Marr would record his tunes on a cassette, skulk over to Morrissey's house, post it through his letterbox, then scarper. Morrissey would forewarn Marr of album and song titles, avoiding verbal communication by showing him a postcard with the names written down. Such coy behaviour allowed them to maintain a magic and mystery inherent in only the greatest pop music. When Morrissey paid private homage to George ELIOT with the opening verse of 'HOW SOON IS NOW?' – adapted from a line in Chapter 12 of Eliot's 1871 novel *Middlemarch* – Marr would have been none the wiser. And

when Marr paid private homage to New York rapper Lovebug Starski with the harmonic pings on 'How Soon Is Now?' – adapted from the keyboard riff of Starski's 1982 single 'You've Gotta Believe' – Morrissey would have been equally oblivious. In perfect ignorance of their impossible achievement, The Smiths created a pop masterpiece which beneath its Martian vapours secretly bridged the divide between Victorian literature and hip hop. (And being The Smiths, being prolific to the point of foolishness, they first stuck it on a 12-inch B-side.)

From their first record in May 1983 until their last in December 1987, over four albums, 17 singles and some 70 or so Morrissey/Marr originals, The Smiths covered every conceivable pop genre, often reconfiguring it into their own unfathomable offspring. 'SHAKESPEARE'S SISTER' was rockabilly, but what sort of rockabilly – Johnny Cash to the nose, the Brontë sisters on the tongue – it was impossible to say. If 'PANIC' was glam rock then it was a new kind of glam, possibly a Gordon-Riots-glam or a Storm-The-Bastille-glam, a glam that wore gunpowder on its face in place of glitter. 'THERE IS A LIGHT THAT NEVER GOES OUT' was a love song, but one which dared to replace tender caresses with jugulars severed through a car windscreen. They tried writing a reggae single but ended up writing 'GIRLFRIEND IN A COMA' which wasn't actually reggae, or if it was then it was the first, and last, reggae single about a life support machine.

'The Smiths were our success, mine and Johnny's, completely,' Morrissey would argue. The nuances of their history and the intricacy of their songbook can be found scattered throughout this book, but in summing up the uniqueness of Morrissey/Marr, and The Smiths, it need only be said that no group before or since have nailed so many shocking colours to so tall a mast. None have had the courage to call an album anything so divisive as MEAT IS MURDER or THE QUEEN IS DEAD, or a single 'SHOPLIFTERS OF THE WORLD UNITE', or write a chorus as inciting as 'hang the DJ!' and record it, literally, out of the mouths of babes. None has summed up work with the same comic despair as 'FRANKLY, MR SHANKLY', or school with the same scarred vengeance as 'THE HEADMASTER RITUAL'. None has proved that less is more with the same thrifty brilliance as 'PLEASE PLEASE PLEASE LET ME GET WHAT I WANT'. None has shown so much beauty in so much melancholy with the same terrifying tenderness as 'ASLEEP'. None has dredged the well of loneliness to the same depths as 'LAST NIGHT I DREAMT THAT SOME-BODY LOVED ME'.

No, none has.

v) The separation of Morrissey and Marr, The Smiths lasted only five years, the time it took for the blissful friction between Marr's unstoppable force and Morrissey's immovable object to implode for reasons which have been scrutinised, debated and sensationalised ever since. Though a simple enough question – Why did The Smiths break up? – there is no short, simple answer.

In the first instance, it is important to remember what is often obscured by the conspiracy theories of jealousy and hatred usually attributed to the end of the group: that Morrissey and Marr genuinely cared for one another. Their friendship is perhaps summed up by the story of how sometime in the spring of 1986 or thereabouts the two of them drove 250 miles by car from Manchester to Brighton for the sole purpose of buying a second-hand copy of Chicory Tip's 1973 single 'Good Grief Christina'. When it came to pop music in all its dizzy ecstasy and daft minutiae, theirs was a unifying love without measure.

Nevertheless, by the end of 1986 the sanctity of the writing partnership was being seriously and irrevocably threatened by the pressures of the group's success. One of the main reasons for the split was the lack of managerial guidance and Marr's refusal to continue shouldering the administrative burdens of the group's already complex contractual and legal machinery. Early warning signs of their imminent collapse could be detected in an interview Marr gave to the *NME* in early 1987. Though he was eager to reiterate 'Morrissey's my best friend', for the first time he confessed

to his alcoholic excess on their last US tour, his need to distinguish his personal life as separate from The Smiths and the 'unbelievable' pressure he'd been under.

The management nightmare aside, there were also aesthetic concerns. After five years, Morrissey and Marr were finally starting to deviate over The Smiths' future direction. 'My agenda didn't include repeating everything we'd done since 1982,' says Marr. 'I was tired of SATURDAY NIGHT AND SUNDAY MORNING and all those influences. We had to move on.'

Following the completion of STRANGEWAYS, HERE WE COME in April 1987, Marr suggested a recuperative group holiday. 'I still think mine was a good plan,' he says. 'We'd made a great record so let's get some sun for two weeks and then think about the future. If we'd have followed my idea The Smiths could still be going.'

Morrissey, by contrast, was intent on returning to the studio at the earliest opportunity to record B-sides for the album's first single, even though nothing was scheduled for release for another four months. In early May, Marr had a private summit with Morrissey at his flat in Chelsea to discuss the undiscussable. 'One night we had a conversation about it,' Morrissey later recalled, 'and he said, "I think it's about time and I've had enough." I was saying, "Well, yes, I understand." But I didn't really mean it. I didn't really think that he'd completely pull the plug.'

Within the week, Marr summoned a second 'emergency meeting' with Morrissey, this time with Rourke and Joyce in attendance, at Geales fish restaurant in Notting Hill. 'When we sat down, Johnny pulled this face,' recalls Joyce. 'It was like, uh-oh. Something was up.' Over the next hour picking at chips and peas, Marr tried to argue his need for a break and his trepidation over their future direction. Unfortunately, Marr's attempts to convince his bandmates that, among other things, 'the quiffs have got to go', backfired horribly. 'I can remember all our chins hitting the table,' says Rourke, 'apart from Morrissey's, which hit the floor.'

Marr maintains they misunderstood him: 'Splitting the band wasn't my intention.' Joyce's memories are different, claiming Marr clearly expressed his resignation. Whatever was or wasn't said, by the end of the meal the writing was on the wall as far as Rourke was concerned. 'All I remember is leaving Geales thinking, "Fucking hell. We're splitting up."'

The Smiths' final stand took place the following week when Marr surrendered to Morrissey's demands for a B-sides session at the studio of soundman Grant Showbiz. The producer describes a tangible 'atmosphere', that Morrissey and Marr weren't speaking. 'It was fraught,' says Showbiz. 'Johnny said to me, "This is the last thing that I should be doing."' (See 'I KEEP MINE HIDDEN', 'WORK IS A FOUR-LETTER WORD'.)

Immediately afterwards, Marr flew to Los Angeles where his friend David Palmer, drummer with The The, was the first to be told that he'd left The Smiths. 'But I could have changed my mind,' he adds, 'had the band not proceeded in the way that they did.' Meanwhile, back in London Morrissey's respondent anguish became so worrying that Showbiz spent a night at the singer's Chelsea flat to monitor his depression. 'I'd never seen him so upset,' says Showbiz. 'Morrissey wasn't so much crying as physically swooning.'

After two months' silence, in early August rumours in the *NME* prompted a statement from ROUGH TRADE: 'The Smiths announce that Johnny Marr has left the group.' Marr says he never authorised it. Showbiz doesn't believe it came from Morrissey either. Regardless of its source, it forced Marr's hand to confirm his departure. 'Johnny was pissed off that it had come from somebody else,' speculates Rourke. 'It implied that he'd left and we were carrying on. Which, as it turned out, was what Morrissey wanted to do.'

Morrissey responded with comic belligerence: 'Whoever says The Smiths have split shall be severely spanked by me with a wet plimsoll.' Only after an abortive day's session with replacement guitarist Ivor PERRY did the futility of pursuing the

band minus Marr strike home; the official end of the group was announced just before the release of the now-posthumous Strangeways in September. Marr, then aged a mere 22, has never regretted his decision. Nor has Morrissey ever entirely forgiven him for closing the door which he opened five years earlier.

vi) Marr after The Smiths, The fallout from The Smiths and how it affected relations between Morrissey and Marr remains an ongoing public soap opera. Both have been baited by the press through the years into saying things which have been used for the sensational benefit of the media alone, whether it be offhand remarks about each other's post-Smiths careers fuelling the industry of negativity or the disclosure of a sustained friendship which inevitably breeds gossip of an imminent reunion.

The truth is that in the initial aftermath vibes were horrifically bad between Morrissey and Marr, a situation which never righted itself until the early 90s when they first regained proper contact. Due to the phenomenal scrutiny surrounding their friendship, since then they keep their sporadic get-togethers as private as possible. Otherwise, their relationship is sustained by business and the management of The Smiths' back catalogue through Warners, as well as legal issues concerning the outcome of the 1996 COURT CASE. Speaking in 2007, Morrissey described how 20 years after the end of The Smiths he and Marr 'have an understanding these days'.

'There'll always be a connection,' confirms Marr. 'Simply because he'll always be Morrissey, and I'll always be Johnny Marr.'

The full history of Marr's post-Smiths career is enough to warrant its own equivalent *Marripedia* (now there's a thought). Since 1987 he's been an active member of The Pretenders with Chrissie HYNDE, The The with Matt Johnson, Electronic with New Order's Bernard Sumner, his own group The Healers, Modest Mouse and latterly The Cribs. He's also guested as writer, producer and guitarist on albums by Billy BRAGG, Kirsty MACCOLL, ROXY MUSIC's Bryan Ferry, Talking

m

Heads, Pet Shop Boys, his Pentangle hero Bert Jansch, Black Grape, Beth Orton, Neil Finn, Beck, Jane Birkin and Oasis, whom he famously helped nurture.

In 2007, Marr was appointed visiting professor of music at Salford University and an honorary fellow of Trinity College Dublin. Today, his status as the most influential guitar player in British pop music of the last 30 years is unchallenged. But, it is as half of the greatest composer credit in that same time period that his greater reputation still rests. As a co-writer, as a musician, as a foil of equal genius, Morrissey has never found another like Marr. We can hypothesise a hundred and one 'what ifs' as to what they could still have achieved had they stayed together, but history tells us they already achieved enough. As a group, The Smiths had everything. In pop, The Smiths changed everything. And at their best, which was most of the time, The Smiths *were* everything.

As Morrissey once surmised, 'It was a special musical relationship. And those are few and far between. For Johnny and I, it won't come again. I think he knows that and I know it. The Smiths had the best of Johnny, and me. Those were definitely *the* days.' [7, 10, 12, 13, 14, 16, 17, 18, 19, 20, 21, 28, 29, 32, 33, 52, 53, 56, 71, 90, 93, 96, 97, 114, 115, 118, 120, 130, 134, 136, 137, 138, 139, 144, 147, 148, 152, 154, 160, 165, 185, 208, 211, 235, 247, 255, 403, 453, 468]

---

1. Berry would remain a significant support player during The Smiths, responsible for Marr's many haircuts, promoter of their first gig at Manchester's Ritz in October 1982 and also cited by Marr as the only person 'allowed to sit between' himself and Morrissey while they were writing songs in the early days. Berry would later form his own group, The Weeds, who featured Simon Wolstencroft on drums and released one single on Marc Riley's In Tape Records, 1986's 'China Doll'. The B-side was named after Joe Moss's clothing business, 'Crazy Face'. Berry later persevered with a solo career, releasing two more singles, 1988's 'Unsatisfied' on Mark E. Smith's Cog-Sinister label (worth tracking down if only for Fallish B-side, 'Sly Jelly Jim') and 1990's 'Kiss Me I'm Cold' featuring a cameo from Marr. Berry now runs a major central London hair salon.

Martha & The Vandellas, See 'THIRD FINGER, LEFT HAND'.

Marvelettes, The, 1960s Tamla Motown girl group whom Morrissey has repeatedly cited as one of his favourite artists ever since his earliest Smiths interviews. It's possible his interest may have been encouraged by NEW YORK DOLLS' singer David Johansen who paid homage on 'Frenchette', the closing track of his self-titled 1978 solo debut album: 'We were marvellous/Yeah, we were marvelling at The Marvelettes.'

Originally a quintet called The Marvels, they were brought to the attention of Motown boss Berry Gordy after a talent scout spotted them at a high school 'record hop' in Inkster, Michigan. Renamed The Marvelettes, their doo-wop-ish 1961 debut 'Please Mr Postman' (later covered by THE BEATLES) rewarded Motown with their first US number one single. Ironically, the girl group formula they established would see them usurped by subsequent Motown signings The Supremes and Martha & The Vandellas, both of whom enjoyed greater success in the long run.

After a handful of minor follow-ups (including 1963's 'Strange I Know', another of Morrissey's 'Singles to be cremated with') they returned to the US top ten with 1966's 'Don't Mess With Bill', now reduced to the trio of founder Gladys Horton (named by Morrissey as one of his favourite singers), Wanda Young and Katherine Anderson. It was followed by 'You're The One' (not to be confused with their 1971 B-side 'You're The One For Me, Bobby', a likely inspiration for the title of 'YOU'RE THE ONE FOR ME, FATTY'), backed by one of Morrissey's most prized Marvelettes offerings, 'Paper Boy'. Co-written by Smokey Robinson, who oversaw the bulk of their output, it typified their gentler version of the more rigorous Motown sound then being bashed out by The Supremes, heralded by the news vendor intro: 'Extra! Extra! Read all about it! Lost love needs affection! Can't live without it!' While they continued to enjoy moderate success in America with 1967's divine 'The Hunter Gets Captured By

'Matter Of Opinion, A' (Morrissey/Marr), Rare early Smiths song, never played in concert nor professionally recorded. All that's survived is a rough demo taped on a domestic cassette recorder during a band rehearsal above Joe MOSS's Crazy Face warehouse on Portland Street, Manchester, circa December 1982. Judging from the other songs on the same tape, Morrissey and Marr wrote 'A Matter Of Opinion' in the same 'batch' as 'THESE THINGS TAKE TIME', the 'WONDERFUL WOMAN'-prototype 'What Do You See In Him?' and 'JEANE'.

Though the quality of the tape isn't bad, Morrissey's vocals are sadly muffled, which hinders a fully coherent lyrical reading. However, the thrust of 'A Matter Of Opinion' is one of bitter sarcasm, from the opening couplet which appears to be 'Oh, sit by the fire with your book and pretend that you're active/But the very last stage of a nuclear age is not attractive'. There's something equally biting about his later 'God bless the boys on the factory floor …', 'This is just something that happens to other people' and 'When will you stand up and say what you really want to?' Each verse ends on an elongated chorus groan of 'oh, it's aaaaaaall a matter of opinion'.

It seems none of the lyrics was ever recycled for later Smiths songs, nor the tune which, as Marr confirms, was the main reason it was scrapped shortly after the tape was made. Its thumping rhythm and bluesy guitar riff were directly lifted from one of his favourite Neil Young tracks, Buffalo Springfield's 'Mr Soul'. So close are the two that Smiths fans desperate for a taster of 'A Matter Of Opinion' need only play 'Mr Soul' – opening track of 1967's Buffalo Springfield Again – and imagine Morrissey singing over the top for a 90 per cent approximation of what they're actually missing. In this respect Marr's tune was actually a third-hand steal: ironically Young admitted that to begin with he'd based his riff on THE ROLLING STONES' '(I Can't Get No) Satisfaction'.

'We weren't bothered about copying a tune,' Marr insists, 'but it was too blatant, almost so blatant that if it had worked I wouldn't have had a problem with it. For me, at that time, it was such a cool association to do a Buffalo Springfield tune, but it just didn't have our heart or spirit in it. It didn't sound like us, which is why we got rid of it.' Indeed, 'A Matter Of Opinion' is by no means a lost Morrissey/Marr classic. From a purely musical perspective it stands as a poor musical cousin of 'HANDSOME DEVIL' and 'WHAT DIFFERENCE DOES IT MAKE?', complete with un-Smiths-like guitar solo. Yet its very existence and the knowledge that they chose to bin it at so early a stage in their career is of enough historical value, saying much for Morrissey and Marr's rigid sense of purpose, self-belief and not least quality control. [12, 17]

The Game' and 'My Baby Must Be A Magician', Britain remained embarrassingly deaf to The Marvelettes. Their only UK hit was the sappy 'When You're Young And In Love' (number 13, July 1967), a record even a devout fan like Morrissey couldn't help but dismiss as among their 'weaker moments'. [96, 103, 175, 184, 199, 408]

Maude, See ARTHUR, Beatrice.

Mayne, Roger, British photographer best known for documenting the young working-class community around Southam Street in North Kensington, London during the late 1950s and early 60s. The 1986 collection *The Street Photography Of Roger Mayne*, reprinted in 1993, included several images subsequently used by Morrissey. 'Girl Jiving In Southam Street, 1957' was featured on the sleeve of the 1994 Morrissey and Siouxsie SIOUX single 'INTERLUDE' while a photo of two boys holding a bicycle was featured on 1997's 'ROY'S KEEN'. Three other images from the same book were also used as backdrops in the early stages of the MALADJUSTED tour.

m

Mayne's portraits of impish street urchins playing in the road and surly teddy boys loitering on corners with nowhere to go fitted neatly into Morrissey's existing British post-war iconography (e.g. the 1958 documentary WE ARE THE LAMBETH BOYS as sampled on 'SPRING-HEELED JIM'). The critic Martin Harrison summed up the power of Mayne's work in his 1998 study of British photojournalism, *Young Meteors*: 'The phenomenon of people at play in the city streets had been popular with photographers throughout the century, but in Mayne's photographs it appears to function as something more – a cypher for profounder changes in society, the release from post-war austerity, a defiance of authority and an awareness of the freely moving body as a form of uninhibited self-expression.' [324]

McCartney, Linda, Late wife of Morrissey's 'favourite BEATLE', Paul McCartney, whom the singer tried to coax into playing piano on The Smiths' 'FRANKLY, MR SHANKLY'. McCartney declined, though she and Morrissey would later become pen pals.

Born Linda Eastman in New York, before marrying a Beatle she made her name as a photographer, documenting the major rock and roll stars of the 60s and becoming the first woman to shoot the cover of *Rolling Stone* magazine (Eric Clapton, May 1968). She became Mrs McCartney in March 1969, learning to play keyboards and later joining her husband in Wings, whose most successful album, 1973's Band On The Run, would feature string arrangements by BOWIE, BOLAN and future Morrissey producer TONY VISCONTI. Her biggest achievements, and lasting legacy, were her promotion of VEGETARIANISM (she converted Paul in 1975) and her work as an animal rights activist, traits which Morrissey greatly admired.

Diagnosed with breast cancer in 1995, Linda died three years later at the age of only 56. Paul McCartney told the media that the best tribute mourners could pay her memory was to 'go veggie'. On 10 April 1999, Paul headed an all-star memorial concert at London's Royal Albert Hall. Among the acts were Chrissie HYNDE and The Pretenders, joined by Johnny Marr who, for the first time in public, sang lead vocals on a rendition of The Smiths' 'MEAT IS MURDER'. 'Chrissie Hynde bullied me, I'm glad to say, into singing [it],' recalled Marr. 'Before I was about to sing, I realised a truism about singing: that if you don't believe in what you're singing, then it isn't right. I've been vegetarian for 18 years now, but some of the lyrics I didn't agree with because I believe each to their own. I had a bit of a dilemma about it, but then I just changed some of the lyrics.' In the event, Marr's lyrical changes were barely noticeable. During the performance, Morrissey's original lyrics were projected on screens behind the stage. Afterwards Hynde told the crowd, 'That's really what this show is all about. Linda's motto – Go veggie.'

In 2005, Morrissey was honoured with a Linda McCartney Memorial Award at the 25th anniversary gala of PETA. Unable to attend the ceremony, he sent a video acceptance speech in which he regretted the fact he never actually met Linda though maintained 'she was a wonderful person'. Linda and Paul's daughter, fashion designer Stella McCartney, has also been spotted in attendance at Morrissey gigs. For reasons known only to Morrissey, he's since referred to her in the press as 'Stellar McCartload'. [11, 18, 170, 254, 444, 466]

Meat Is Murder, The Smiths' second album, released February 1985, highest UK chart position #1. Cover star: unknown US soldier from the Vietnam documentary *In The Year Of The Pig*. Tracks: 'THE HEADMASTER RITUAL', 'RUSHOLME RUFFIANS', 'I WANT THE ONE I CAN'T HAVE', 'WHAT SHE SAID', 'THAT JOKE ISN'T FUNNY ANYMORE', 'NOWHERE FAST', 'WELL I WONDER', 'BARBARISM BEGINS AT HOME', 'MEAT IS MURDER'. Produced by The Smiths. (US version also includes 'HOW SOON IS NOW?' produced by John PORTER.)

It is rock and roll tradition, if not cliché, for most groups to follow a critically lauded debut with a 'difficult' second album. Defying such traditions, and intrinsically allergic to cliché, The Smiths encountered no such problems when they came to record the follow-up to February 1984's THE SMITHS. 'We never had those hang-ups,' states Marr, who instead describes the creation of what became Meat Is Murder as one of 'youthful pioneering'.

The buoyant spirit with which they approached their second album was cemented by their continued chart success in the six months following their debut's release with the interim singles 'HEAVEN KNOWS I'M MISERABLE NOW' (their first top ten hit) and 'WILLIAM, IT WAS REALLY NOTHING'. These two singles were themselves illustrative both of Morrissey and Marr's creative confidence and their shared sense of urgency – that they dispatched such first-rate songs on stand-alone 45s (not to mention their B-sides, the epic 'How Soon Is Now?' included) rather than stockpile for album number two.

By the early summer of 1984 they were already accruing a sizeable new repertoire to choose from. The oldest contender, 'Barbarism Begins At Home', was a longstanding live staple first introduced the previous December (this probably explains Marr's disclosure at the time that their second album would include 'old songs we wrote a really long time ago [which] have resurfaced'). Some elements of 'The Headmaster Ritual' dated back even further, to the summer of 1983 when recording their debut's first draft with producer Troy TATE, though it, like the bulk of Meat Is Murder, would take its main shape over the summer of 1984 while The Smiths were living in London. Most of its tunes were written and demoed by Marr at his flat in Earls Court before being passed on to Morrissey, living up the road in Kensington. Consequently, Meat Is Murder is unique as the only Smiths album to have been largely (but not wholly) written down south.

In the meantime, the July 1984 'William' session at Jam studios in north London with producer John Porter witnessed their first attempts at 'Nowhere Fast' (intended for a future single) and 'Rusholme Ruffians'. Both would be re-recorded with Porter again for a John PEEL

session the following month, though by the autumn the single had been abandoned while Porter, too, was to learn that The Smiths intended to record their second album without him. Having worked with the producer for almost a year, Marr had now accrued the necessary technical skills to steer the group in their own autonomous direction. Morrissey agreed that their best solution was to produce the next record themselves.

Added to this new spirit of wilful independence, the group deliberately chose a northern studio – Amazon, on an industrial estate on the outskirts of Liverpool – as a means of escaping London and the distractions of their label, ROUGH TRADE. By the time recording began that October, The Smiths were already plotting a permanent exodus back to Manchester, taking temporary hotel lodgings there and commuting back and forth to their Liverpool studio en masse in a white 1970s Mercedes limousine ('always inconspicuous', notes Marr).

The next vital component was the recruitment of engineer Stephen STREET, whom they'd first met seven months earlier when recording 'Heaven Knows I'm Miserable Now'. Though Street's initial impression of their chosen studio was 'a bit of a dump' beset with technical difficulties, his youthful energy and enthusiasm synchronised perfectly with that of The Smiths. 'Stephen was absolutely crucial,' stresses Marr. 'He was exactly the right person for us at that time because he was so talented and, crucially, round about the same age as us. He was also fledgling, if you like, and not too experienced so his trajectory was similar to us. He had his own agendas that he wanted to bring in that were really in sync with ours, so he was a very sympathetic guy to be around. We couldn't have made the album we did without him.'

The freshness of the material to hand – only a third of its nine tracks had been previously tested in concert – combined with the studio atmosphere of spontaneity and experimentation would show itself in the sonic vibrancy of the finished album. Other than the customary dark shadows cast by the title track and its pivotal ballad 'That Joke Isn't

Funny Anymore' (a foretaste of the grander gothic dramas of albums to come), Meat Is Murder would be The Smiths' most playful album. Its contents showcased not only Morrissey and Marr's versatility as writers but their improving musicianship as a four-piece guitar group; an eclectic mix of styles from BEATLES-esque pop ('The Headmaster Ritual', 'I Want The One I Can't Have') to acoustic melancholy ('Well I Wonder'), rockabilly ('Nowhere Fast', 'Rusholme Ruffians'), garage rock ('What She Said') and Mancunian punk-funk ('Barbarism Begins At Home').

The album also marked a major leap in Morrissey's confidence and ingenuity as a lyricist. Where The Smiths' debut was for the most part an autobiographical catharsis of his emotional upsets in the years immediately prior to forming the group, Meat Is Murder was the first time he utilised his position as a newly established pop star to create a soapbox to spew forth his political beliefs. Other than the explicit vegetarian propagandising of the title track, he made his first jeer at the monarchy with 'Nowhere Fast' and lambasted the state education system which had brutalised him in 'The Headmaster Ritual'. The earlier 'GIRL AFRAID' and 'William' had introduced a seemingly less subjective, character-orientated thread to his work which he expanded with the third-person account of 'What She Said' and the fairground tableau 'Rusholme Ruffians'. Even so, its most potent passages were those where Morrissey was clearly singing from his own heart and if, as he insists, his records are his diary then 'That Joke Isn't Funny Anymore' and 'Well I Wonder' tell us enough about his private sorrows of 1984.

Meat Is Murder was completed by mid-December after a further session at Ridge Farm studios in Surrey. Perhaps the most telling example of Morrissey and Marr's prolific partnership is that, even while putting the final touches to their second album in London's Fallout Shelter studio, they were already writing and rehearsing new material for its intended follow-up – the unfinished 'I MISSES YOU' and a rough instrumental sketch later to become 'NEVER HAD NO ONE EVER'.

Strangely, and perhaps foolishly, Rough Trade's determination to reissue former B-side 'How Soon Is Now?' as a single in January 1985 meant that Meat Is Murder was released without a trailer single. Despite this anomaly it still entered the UK album charts at number one, knocking off Bruce Springsteen's Born In The USA and making it the greatest commercial achievement during The Smiths' lifetime, albeit short-lived: Morrissey would subsequently mourn its 'embarrassingly short' chart success, dropping from the top 100 'after 13 weeks'. At least there was still consolation to be had that an album with such an aggressive and divisive pro-vegetarian title had gotten to number one. Morrissey proudly stated it had been his intention to 'cause great discomfort' in the charts, hailing Meat Is Murder as 'obviously a title that shouldn't be there'. The cover art was also a premeditated declaration of war, repeating a modified image from Emile de Antonio's 1969 Vietnam documentary *In The Year Of The Pig* of an unknown soldier whose helmet is emblazoned with the album title (changed from the original hippy-inverting inscription, 'Make war not love'). 'As [that] image hopefully illustrates,' Morrissey added, 'the only way that we can get rid of such things as the meat industry, and other things like nuclear weapons, is by really giving people a taste of their own medicine.'

Although the chart-topping victory of Meat Is Murder augured well for the remainder of 1985, it turned out to be an unexpectedly difficult year for The Smiths as relations between the group and their label took a turn for the worse, exacerbated by a succession of poorly performing singles. But away from home, in North America, where they'd tour that June, the group finally began to make headway thanks to the US version of Meat Is Murder which added 'How Soon Is Now?' 'Ask a lot of American fans, and they'll tell you that was the record that got them into The Smiths,' says Marr, 'so I'm proud of it for that alone.'

Though critically overshadowed by THE QUEEN IS DEAD, and lacking the mature gravitas of STRANGEWAYS, HERE WE COME, Meat Is Murder remains the most accessible and most dynamically sequenced of The Smiths' four studio albums. At the time, Rough Trade giddily trumpeted it to the press as the group's equivalent of 'Sgt Pepper'. If a Beatles comparison *has* to be made, it would be more accurate to dub it their Rubber Soul – not *the* all-time masterpiece but a valiant leap in its general direction not so very far off the mark. [17, 38, 129, 145, 168, 426, 432, 477]

'Meat Is Murder' (Morrissey/Marr), From

The Smiths' album MEAT IS MURDER (1985). Among Morrissey's most powerful pop statements, the title track of The Smiths' second album expressed the solemnity of his views on ANIMAL RIGHTS and VEGETARIANISM. During his first 18 months in the media spotlight, Morrissey's outspokenness on the subject had often been trivialised by the press, many of whom regarded his vegetarianism as another affected eccentricity. 'Meat Is Murder' was the singer's bold retaliation, a deliberately graphic and poetically gruesome argument that animal slaughter for human consumption was akin to a criminal act.

Before The Smiths, American singer-songwriter Melanie Safka had taken a comic approach to the same issue, first on 1968's extremely daft 'Animal Crackers' and again on 1970's wittier 'I Don't Eat Animals' ('I'll live on life, I want nothing dead in me'). By contrast, Morrissey's lyrics intentionally avoided any trace of humour or irony, directly imploring carnivores to contemplate the moral consequences of their lifestyle. 'If they eat meat I'd like them just to think about it and take it from there,' he explained. 'Many people are still under the assumption that meat has absolutely nothing whatsoever to do with animals. Animals play in fields et cetera and meat is something that just appears on the plate.'

Morrissey first mentioned the title during a 1984 radio phone-in when quizzed by a fan about his beliefs ('Meat is murder as far as I can see'). He later admitted that the song had been 'influenced' by the adverts for the products of Norfolk poultry farmer Bernard Matthews and other 'TV ads

which show chickens laughing as if they can't wait to get in the oven'. The finished lyrics pulled no punches. 'Beautiful creatures' cry like humans. The abattoir's instruments of death 'scream' in horror. A domestic grotesquery of smiling families carve up carcasses at the dinner table, gorging themselves on the 'unholy stench' of 'sizzling blood' and 'death'. 'Meat Is Murder' is an unremitting bloodbath of images carefully chosen to provoke and alert the unenlightened to the uncomfortable truth that the meat industry *is* a murder industry.

Marr had been forewarned of the song's title, presenting Morrissey with a 'really nasty' waltz-time riff he'd been playing around with for a few days beforehand. It provided the perfect monochrome hue to Morrissey's bovine Guernica, made yet more dramatic by its explicit sound collage of slaughterhouse apparatus and distressed cows, one of the more ingenious studio feats of engineer Stephen STREET.

Whatever its shortcomings as a piece of music – arguably a triumph of mood over melody – 'Meat Is Murder' was fundamental to the group's ideology. Morrissey would later claim, with good grounds, that the song was instrumental in turning hundreds, if not thousands, of people into becoming vegetarian. At the time, The Smiths' audience responded positively to the track, if at times over-enthusiastically. On stage at Hanley's Victoria Hall in March 1985, a fan threw a string of sausages inscribed with the words 'Meat Is Murder' on to the stage as the song began, hitting Morrissey in the mouth. 'They hurled it so accurately,' he recalled, 'that I actually bit into it in the action of singing the word "murder".' (See also Linda MCCARTNEY.) [17, 135, 211, 425, 426, 477]

Meltdown, Established in 1993, Meltdown is

an annual summer arts festival at London's South Bank Centre curated by a different artist each year. Past curators include Elvis Costello (1995), John PEEL (1998), Scott Walker (2000) and David BOWIE (2002). In 2004, to coincide with the comeback release of YOU ARE THE QUARRY, the festival was handed over to Morrissey. He later disclosed that he was second choice to Yoko Ono ('a smallish Japanese woman whose name I can't mention, but she has atrocious taste in eye furniture [and] a Red Setter called John'). In the accompanying programme, the singer declared: 'Curating Meltdown is a great opportunity for me to acknowledge some of the music and words that have excited me over the years. Some of you have iPods. I have Meltdown.'

Morrissey's Meltdown ran from 11–27 June, opening with his first London show in over 18 months, minus guitarist Alain WHYTE who'd dropped out of the band after the previous concert in Dublin due to 'illness', temporarily replaced by Barrie Cadogan of Little Barrie. The singer played the Royal Festival Hall three times during the Meltdown fortnight, with different support each night from Irish singer Damien Dempsey, best friend Linder STERLING and indie band The Ordinary Boys. The most significant event, and major coup, of his Meltdown was the unexpected re-formation of the NEW YORK DOLLS who played twice, with highlights from the second concert released later that year as the ATTACK RECORDS album Morrissey Presents The Return Of The New York Dolls Live From Royal Festival Hall 2004.

Also appearing at Morrissey's Meltdown were: SPARKS, who gave a special performance of their current album, L'il Beethoven, plus Morrissey's favourite, 1974's Kimono My House; iconic singer/songwriter Loudon WAINWRIGHT III; an audience with playwright Alan BENNETT (Morrissey himself sat among said audience); LA friend, daughter of Frank and 60s pop legend NANCY SINATRA (supported by Linder); Serge GAINS-BOURG's former muse, Anglo-French singer Jane Birkin (supported by Morrissey's old friend, James MAKER); American performance/drag artists Ennio Marchetto and LYPSINKA; an 'acoustic evening' with Smiths-lite 90s indie band Gene; a free performance in the Royal Festival Hall foyer from Morrissey's favourite East End punks, COCK-NEY REJECTS; and a closing classical recital of Henryk Górecki's Symphony No. 3 (Symphony

Of Sorrowful Songs) and Arvo Part's Tabula Rasa by the London Sinfonietta featuring soprano Yvonne Kenny. (See also CLASSICAL MUSIC.)

Those booked to play his Meltdown who never appeared included The Libertines, due to support Morrissey's opening concert but unable due to internal problems, and Ari Up from The Slits, stranded in Jamaica due to adverse weather conditions. Among the acts Morrissey hoped to book but never managed to secure were French singing icons Françoise HARDY, Brigitte BARDOT and Sacha DISTEL (the latter was seriously ill and died the month after the festival) as well as Buffy SAINTE-MARIE and the Afro-American poet, writer and actress Maya Angelou.

The following year's Meltdown was curated by PATTI SMITH, including a couple of events featuring Johnny Marr. [119, 190, 436]

Member Of The Wedding, The, 1952 big-screen adaptation of Carson McCullers's book and play listed among Morrissey's favourite films. Set in the Deep South, the plot revolves around Frankie, a friendless and confused 12-year-old tomboy (played with admirable conviction by 27-year-old Julie Harris) whose mother died giving birth to her. Ignored by her father, she has only the family's black maid, Berenice, and her young cousin, John Henry, for company. With adolescence approaching, Frankie becomes unnaturally obsessed with the imminent wedding of her older brother, Jarvis, to the point where she invents a fantasy that she will be leaving town with the bride and groom after the ceremony. The main thrust of the drama is Frankie's rude awakening to these immature delusions created by her overwhelming sense of isolation from all those around her. As an essay on youthful loneliness, *The Member Of The Wedding* is profoundly Mozzerian in theme, though any similarities between its dialogue and sporadic phrases in the singer's lyrics are most likely harmless coincidences rather than conscious steals, be it 'That only shows how little you know' ('DEATH OF A DISCO DANCER') or 'I am I' ('HOW CAN ANYBODY POSSIBLY KNOW HOW I FEEL?').

Julie Harris was nominated for an Oscar for her performance, going on to star in *East Of Eden* opposite James DEAN. Ten-year-old Brandon De Wilde won a Golden Globe as John Henry, though his would be a career cut tragically short, killed in a car crash at the age of 30. Author Carson McCullers, a friend of Truman CAPOTE, also endured an astonishingly desperate life of depression, alcoholism, attempted suicides, bisexual marital infidelities, paralysing strokes and a brain haemorrhage, dying at the age of 50. [175, 184, 530]

Men's Liberation, Pioneering 1975 book by American gay activist Jack Nichols, subtitled 'A New Definition of Masculinity', which had a profound impact upon the teenage Morrissey. 'When I was 14 I became totally immersed in feminism,' he explained. 'I read this book called *Men's Liberation* and it seemed like the Bible to me. I realised how terrible it was that people were rigidly divided, that men could only like "men's things" and women "women's things".' Nichols's book challenges such rigid stereotypes, with whole chapters devoted to topics such as fatherhood, sexuality, penis insecurity and the workplace. Much of *Men's Liberation* analyses the conflict between the mind and the body, a key theme in Morrissey's early lyrics.

'The quote that best sums up The Smiths is from Jack Nichols's book

Men's Liberation,' he told *Sounds* in the summer of 1983. '"We are here and it is now." I feel really strongly about NOW. I don't want to wait around, I don't care about two years' time, things have got to happen RIGHT NOW for The Smiths. And I think they will.' The same quote would later be used in the lyrics of 'STRETCH OUT AND WAIT' and is actually sourced from the 1968 film *Planet Of The Apes*, as spoken by Charlton Heston. Nichols first quotes it in his chapter on 'Instincts', and again in his main chapter on 'Sexuality': 'The psychology of play demands an end to arrangement and speculation about what might be, what was, and what is. It asks for the realisation that *we are here and it is now*. Instead of thinking about doing – pondering, deliberating, considering and brooding – a man must simply do.'

The book contains another more minor Smiths reference, citing the heading of a Hemingway book review in the US porn magazine *Screw*, 'The Impotence Of Being Ernest', a pun on the WILDE play which, minus the 'Being', appeared as the vinyl run-out-groove message on the single 'WILLIAM, IT WAS REALLY NOTHING' and the album HATFUL OF HOLLOW. [91, 139, 166, 184, 345]

'**Michael's Bones**' (Morrissey/ Street), B-side of 'THE LAST OF THE FAMOUS INTERNATIONAL PLAYBOYS' (1989). An especially gloomy elegy describing the dead body of a loveless young man, on the

'**Mexico**' (Morrissey/Boorer/Day), B-side of 'FIRST OF THE GANG TO DIE' (2004). Not long after settling in Los Angeles and discovering its local Latino community, Morrissey spoke of his growing affection for Mexico. 'I think it's so, so glamorous,' he enthused. Written during his millennium-straddling wilderness years without a record deal, 'Mexico' was a sincere tribute to the country and its culture, one tinged with sadness and political anger about its exploitation by the US as a dumping ground for chemical waste and the hostility of its Texas border controls. Coming after so many false allegations of racism against Morrissey, it was particularly enlightening to hear him defend an ethnic minority against the 'rich ... white' bullies of the world's superpower. Of the five new songs Morrissey previewed live in 2002, 'Mexico' was the only one not to make the final running order of YOU ARE THE QUARRY. Though its subtleties weren't so easily conveyed in concert, on record its mellow jet-trail melody and indignant sorrow were given due magnification – an excellent B-side arguably deserving of inclusion on the album. [422]

rare occasion Morrissey was asked to explain the sullen and mysterious 'Michael's Bones' he failed to clarify the song's basis. 'It's probably too sad for me to tell you what it's really about,' he shirked, 'but there he lay.'

Such ambiguity only adds to the popular belief that the song's 'Michael' is in fact the mass-murderer Michael Ryan responsible for the 'Hungerford Massacre'. On 19 August 1987, Ryan – a 27-year-old loner and firearms collector who lived with his doting mother – went on a killing spree in the Berkshire market town of Hungerford. In total he murdered 16 people, his mother included, before shooting himself in a school besieged by armed police. Other than the discrepancy of his body's location – Ryan died in a classroom, not on a 'sports ground' – 'Michael's Bones' is easily applicable to the tragedy of Hungerford, not least the obvious horror of 'look what he's done'. Just as relevant is the existing Hungerford/Morrissey axis with regard to 'STOP ME IF YOU THINK YOU'VE HEARD THIS ONE BEFORE', intended as the penultimate Smiths single in the autumn of '87 but abandoned due to the 'mass-murder' line which the BBC deemed insensitive in the wake of the Hungerford killings. Hypothetically, it would be typically controversial, and original, of Morrissey to write a song which dared to pity Ryan for being an unloved loser driven mad by loneliness rather than an evil slaughterer of the innocent. For the time being, the Hungerford reading is a reasonable, if by no means definite, interpretation of a song which otherwise offers few clues to its morbid muse.

Stephen Street was 'especially proud' of his tune, a funereal ballad which betrays a debt to Marr's slower, melancholic Smiths creations, in particular the opening bars of 'THAT JOKE ISN'T FUNNY ANYMORE'. The first song recorded at the winter 1988 'Playboys'/'INTERESTING DRUG' sessions at The Wool Hall near Bath, Street recalls building the song on a drum-machine loop with Mike Joyce overdubbing live percussion at the end of its recording. [39, 422]

Mills, John, Legendary British film star, named by Morrissey as one of his favourite actors and, in 1991, as one of the two living people he most admired: the other was incarcerated gangland villain Ronnie KRAY. By contrast, Mills was the archetypal British hero; a chap among chaps driven by ration-book decency and an almost debilitating respect for fair play who in uniform boasted the stiffest upper lip behind allied lines (what Morrissey himself referred to as 'John Mills stiff-upperness'). Whether extraordinarily jolly ordinary seaman Shorty Blake in Noël COWARD's *In Which We Serve* (see also 'LIFEGUARD SLEEPING, GIRL DROWNING'), or charred alcoholic Captain Anson trying to contend with desert heat, a Nazi spy and an insatiable lust for the wholesome Sylvia Syms in *Ice-Cold In Alex*, Mills single-handedly defined the classic British war movie.

While Morrissey clearly loved Mills's war output – enough, at least, to use a still of 1958's *Dunkirk* featuring co-star Sean BARRETT on the sleeve of 'HOW SOON IS NOW?' – his listed favourite Mills films highlight the actor's wider repertoire as a versatile character actor. 1947's THE OCTOBER MAN typified his many innocent-man-on-the-run melodramas while 1959's *Tiger Bay* – a film Morrissey mentioned in a letter to pen pal Robert MACKIE – placed him on the other side of the law as a detective trying to trace passion-criminal Horst Buchholz and the 12-year-old runaway tomboy played by his own daughter, Hayley. More morally complex was his role in 1961's FLAME IN THE STREETS, no longer the straightforward hero but a stalwart socialist who soon forgets his anti-racist beliefs when his own daughter takes a black boyfriend.

Perhaps not surprisingly, the two Mills films most significant to Morrissey are those set in the north. In 1954's HOBSON'S CHOICE, source of the brass fanfare heralding The Smiths' 'SHEILA TAKE A BOW', Mills is the naïve cobbler prodigy Willie Mossop who takes on his former boss Charles Laughton, while in 1966's THE FAMILY WAY he invests all his 'stiff-upperness' in his Lancashire flat cap as the beer-suppin' but sadly deluded father of the bride.

It's easy to appreciate Morrissey's love for Mills, not merely as a screen star but as an icon of Englishness, or rather what Morrissey himself might call a 'lost' Englishness: of beer and skittles, tea and jam buns, bread and dripping, bunting on VE Day, pub Joanna sing-songs, bobbies-on-the-beat, penny arcades and polite conversation with strangers in train compartments. The much-loved Sir John Mills (as he became in 1976) died in April 2005 at the grand old age of 97. [141, 175, 497, 502, 504, 510, 534, 572]

'Miserable Lie' (Morrissey/Marr), From the album THE SMITHS (1984). One of the earliest Smiths songs, 'Miserable Lie' is Morrissey's tortured farewell to a corrupting femme fatale. The specific mention of rented lodgings in Manchester's Whalley Range where he briefly lived with friend and Ludus singer Linder STERLING has given rise to the popular (if purely speculative) theory first put forward by journalist Nick Kent that the song was, indeed, about 'Morrissey's relationship with Linder'. Morrissey would only confirm that the room in Whalley Range was real, though he lived there a 'miraculously short time'.

In its title pronouncement that 'love is just a miserable lie', it was Morrissey's first lyric to lay bare his inborn romantic pessimism, also introducing the theme of bodily embarrassment and self-disgust ('you laugh at mine') which would recur again in the likes of 'LATE NIGHT, MAUDLIN STREET' and 'FRIDAY MOURNING'. There was a hint of WILDE in the use of 'flower-like life', a phrase Oscar employed in *De Profundis*, though it also crops up in Morrissey's main source for 'Miserable Lie', Molly Haskell's *FROM REVERENCE TO RAPE*. Describing the femme fatale of Whalley Range, he borrows from Haskell's descriptions of the femme fatale of Hollywood film noir who went 'down like Eurydice, to the depths of the criminal world', double-crossing her prey 'not once but twice'.

Musically, it was one of Marr's most original if erratic designs, as he freely admits. Written in the guitarist's attic room in Bowdon in the early winter of 1982, he recalls giving Morrissey his 'bananas idea' of a gentle prologue suddenly switching gear into a fast, aggressive improvised freak-out. 'It was an odd, quirky little thing,' says Marr. 'Used to confuse the hell out of people at early gigs.' A strange first punk-funk draft was demoed in December 1982 for an EMI-funded Smiths demo at Manchester's Drone studios, their first with Rourke on bass. With practice the tempo change became much more dramatic, the end section an arm-flailing chaos of twanging guitar and splashing drums. Of all the studio versions they recorded, its manic majesty was best captured somewhere between their debut John PEEL session and the aborted Troy TATE album.

Sadly the 'Miserable Lie' which finally appeared on their debut proper was a little too clinical, producer John PORTER separating each group member in the mix instead of letting the combined might of The Smiths merge as one in the stage-invading anarchy of its live translation. Marr concurs that the main culprit was Porter's inappropriately thin guitar sound: 'It just wasn't rocky enough to pull that song off properly.' [17, 27, 139, 204, 326, 393]

Mitchell, Joni, 'The greatest lyricist that has ever lived' according to Morrissey, who believes Mitchell to be 'very underrated'. Customarily labelled the most important '*female* singer/songwriter' of the 1970s, her genius transcends any such gender ghettoising.

Born in Canada as Roberta Joan Anderson (Mitchell was the surname of her first husband whom she married in 1965 and divorced in 1967), before making her 1968 debut album Song To A Seagull her work was already being recorded by other folk singers such as Buffy SAINTE-MARIE. Her second, 1969's Clouds, established her as a prolific musical talent, albeit one immediately stereotyped as the acoustic-strumming 'daughter who never left home', an image cemented by 1970's Ladies

Of The Canyon featuring her career albatross, 'Big Yellow Taxi'. Morrissey 'came in on' her fourth album, 1971's Blue, a deeply confessional set partly inspired by the end of her recent relationship with Salford lad Graham Nash.

Mitchell's biggest influence upon Morrissey is what he refers to as her 'second period' in the mid-70s and a specific trio of lyrically epic, musically ambitious albums marked by her growing interest in complex guitar tunings and modern jazz: 1975's The Hissing Of Summer Lawns (the first to 'completely captivate' Morrissey), 1976's brooding, introspective Hejira and especially the 1977 double Don Juan's Reckless Daughter. 'Everything about that record completely mesmerises me,' said Morrissey, 'and when I first saw the lyric sheet and the vastness of these words I actually had to close the record. I thought, "I have to leave this for another day, this is just … a monster!"'

All three albums contain either lyrical motifs or whole stanzas which have evidently shaped Morrissey's own. Summer Lawns' 'The Jungle Line', with its 'working girl' in 'a low-cut blouse' is echoed in 'MALADJUSTED'. Similarly, Hejira's 'Amelia' with its repeated 'false alarm' was raw clay to be moulded into 'LAST NIGHT I DREAMT THAT SOMEBODY LOVED ME'. But it's the 'monster' of Don Juan's Reckless Daughter which has provided Morrissey with the richest ore. His first noticeable 'Mitchell-isms' crop up towards the end of The Smiths. 'SHOPLIFTERS OF THE WORLD UNITE' contains a conspicuously comparable line with the album's title track: 'Last night the ghost of my old ideals reran on channel five.' Given the circumstances, it could also be argued that its corresponding B-side, 'HALF A PERSON', was just as mindful of Mitchell's opening verse in which she records 'I came out two days on your tail'. The impact of 'Don Juan's Reckless Daughter' on Morrissey was compounded by 1988's 'SISTER I'M A POET', mirroring Mitchell's phrase 'They love the romance of the crime'. More obvious still is the album's closing track, 'The Silky Veils Of Ardor', an apparent model for 'SEASICK, YET STILL DOCKED' with more lyrical repercussions than can be freely quoted.

In October 1996, Mitchell released two simultaneous best-of compilations, Hits and Misses, her first career retrospective after 15 albums in 18 years. To mark its release, Reprise Records, also Morrissey's US label at the time, invited him to interview Mitchell about her work for a promotional CD. The same interview was later used as the basis of a 1997 Rolling Stone feature. An informal 'chat over tea and cigarettes' (presumably Morrissey only indulging in the former), it stands as an enlightening discussion on the part of both artists. Morrissey spoke of how he was a fan of Mitchell around the emergence of the SEX PISTOLS – an unfashionable stance at the time – and his refusal to accept the demeaning label of 'female songwriter'. Equally revealing were his concerns over Mitchell's relationship with her fans, that her audience felt 'the better if you walk off the stage and take the sadness with you' and his personal belief that 'songs can't ever be depressing because the act of writing a song is so positive'. Titled Words + Music, the Mitchell/ Morrissey CD is a collector's gem, worth seeking if only to hear him pose the immortal if otherwise preposterous question: 'Is Mingus your ugly duckling?' [179, 571]

Mitchell, **Yvonne**, British actress popular during the 1950s who Morrissey named as one of his chosen 'Thespians of the world', also nominating several of her films among his favourites. Her porcelain beauty was best captured in TURN THE KEY SOFTLY (1953) where she attempts to go straight after 12 months in HMP Holloway only to be hoodwinked by her super-caddish ex. She switched from jailed to jailer in YIELD TO THE NIGHT (1956) as guard to murderess Diana DORS, her coolness amplifying the script's subtle lesbian undertones. Her most celebrated role was in 1957's WOMAN IN A DRESSING GOWN as the dizzy but devoted London housewife who goes into meltdown when her husband announces he's leaving her for his prissy young secretary. Also worth seeing are: 1954's BBC Sunday Night Theatre production of Orwell's Nineteen Eighty-Four as Julia to Peter Cushing's Winston Smith; 1959's

monarchy, That Morrissey 'despises' royalty is surely obvious to anyone with even the dimmest understanding of the man. After first expressing his desire to drop his trousers to Her Majesty in 1985's 'NOWHERE FAST' he'd later cause greater controversy with the release of 1986's THE QUEEN IS DEAD, using interviews to denounce the Windsors as 'fascist' and 'cruel'.

'To me there's something dramatically ugly about a person who can wear a dress for £6,000 when at the same time there are people who can't afford to eat,' he fumed. 'When [the Queen] puts on that dress for £6,000 the statement she is making to the nation is, "I am the fantastically gifted royalty, and you are the snivelling peasants." The very idea that people would be interested in the facts about this dress is massively insulting to the human race.' Similar tirades were aimed at Princess Diana ('has [she] ever uttered a sentence of any vague interest or use to the world?') while in 1987 he promised that the day the Queen Mother died he'd be 'hammering the nails in the coffin to make sure she was in there'. Suffice to say that the chances of Morrissey's name ever cropping up on a future Honours List are somewhat slim. [57, 120, 105, 477]

Tiger Bay (a film Morrissey referred to in his Robert MACKIE correspondence) where Mitchell quickly comes a cropper as Horst Buchholz's Polish girlfriend; the same year's *Sapphire*, a whodunit about the killing of a mixed-race girl with Mitchell providing the final shock when exposed as the racist culprit; and 1960's *The Trial Of Oscar* WILDE where she portrayed the poet's stoical wife, Constance. Mitchell was also first cousin once removed of Morrissey's favourite painter, Hannah GLUCKSTEIN, and tried in vain to buy her final and most cherished canvas, 'Rage, rage against the dying of the light'. In her later years, Mitchell became a successful author of fiction, non-fiction and children's books. Most notable is 1969's *The Family*, a thinly veiled autobiography of the large north London Jewish dynasty to which she and Gluckstein belonged. Mitchell died of cancer in 1979, aged 53. [175, 339, 377, 558, 563, 566]

'Money Changes Everything' (Johnny Marr), B-side of 'BIGMOUTH STRIKES AGAIN' (1986).

Marr's second Smiths instrumental, unlike the previous 'OSCILLATE WILDLY', 'Money Changes Everything' wasn't so much a bespoke piece of music as a riff without words. Recorded at the very end of the sessions for THE QUEEN IS DEAD in the winter of 1985 when contractual relations

between The Smiths and their label, ROUGH TRADE, were at an all-time low, the title was clearly pointed. Interviewed in 1984, less than midway through The Smiths' career, Morrissey claimed 'money doesn't change anything'. Yet, within a year he'd arrived at the complete opposite conclusion that money 'makes the absolute difference between everything'. Though it was Marr's track, the title sentiment was almost certainly the direct influence of his writing partner.

Its main twangy blues riff was an accidental discovery: Marr had been toying with another tune on a four-track recorder which, when he heard backwards after flipping over the tape, he liked enough to 'learn in reverse'. Even without Morrissey, the finished track possessed a sullenness – a *darkness* even – which was unmistakably the sound of The Smiths. With the addition of Craig GANNON in the summer of 1986, 'Money Changes Everything' became the first instrumental The Smiths played live, introduced in July 1986 for their epic tour of North America; on return to the UK its place in the setlist would be taken by 'THE DRAIZE TRAIN'.

Morrissey's decision not to write lyrics for the track was later thrown into sharp relief when ROXY MUSIC's Bryan Ferry invited Marr to rework the tune for his 1987 solo album, Bête Noire. The result, credited to Ferry/Marr, was 'The Right

Stuff', a glossy (if otherwise faithful) re-recording of 'Money Changes Everything' with a new dimension of snaky drivel about being sent 'a woman on a bended knee'. Those around the group such as soundman Grant Showbiz maintain Morrissey had grave misgivings about Marr's collaboration with Ferry, though the guitarist insists 'nobody told me they were unhappy at the time'. Recorded in June 1986, long before The Smiths disbanded, it was unfortunate timing that 'The Right Stuff' should end up being released over a year later in October 1987 in the very midst of the split aftermath, thereby casting Marr as some sort of 'indie turncoat' in the eyes of some inconsolably grief-stricken apostles. In the event, Ferry's single performed poorly, charting at 37 and dropping out the following week. [17, 18, 27, 71, 267]

Monochrome Set, The, Arty and artful

London post-punk group and one of Morrissey's favourite bands in the years directly before forming The Smiths. Significantly, The Monochrome Set released three singles on ROUGH TRADE in 1979 which, as Johnny Marr has speculated, may have been a factor in Morrissey's preference for the same label as a suitable home for The Smiths. Concrete evidence of his obsession with the group can be found in his correspondence with pen pal Robert MACKIE circa 1980–81. Morrissey sent Mackie a postcard of Clark Gable – in itself extremely weird bearing in mind that 20 years later he'd be living in a Hollywood home built by Gable – on the reverse of which he transcribed a verse from 'Ici Les Enfants', a track from their 1980 debut album Strange Boutique. In November 1980 he'd write to Mackie on the day he spent £3.99 on their follow-up album, Love Zombies, also sending him a photocopy of the album sleeve. 'It's a lovely record,' wrote Morrissey, 'but I feel I would enjoy it much more if I had a long mac. Actually, I have three.' He'd later chide Mackie in another letter for not having heard the group: 'How can anyone go through life without the dear, cuddly Monochrome Set?'

The Monochrome Set formed out of Hornsey art school punks The B-Sides, an early vehicle for Stuart Goddard, soon to become Adam Ant. (In March 1981 Morrissey would also tell Mackie that 'Adam Ant bores the shit out of me'.) Led by enigmatic Anglo-Indian frontman Ganesh Seshadri, who wrote and performed under the pseudonym of Bid, The Monochrome Set's songs were witty, sexually provocative, intellectually playful and peppered with learned cinematic references from Mae West to Fritz Lang. Bid's lyrics, and the music of guitarist Lester Square, were comparable with Howard DEVOTO's Magazine in their respective archness and intricacy and as such were of obvious fascination to Morrissey. Consider the morbid affection of 1979's Rough Trade single 'Eine Symphonie Des Grauens': 'I'm dead and dank and rotten/My arms are wrapped in cotton/My corpse loves you, let's marry.' Or the similar black humour of Love Zombies' 'Apocalypso': 'All I desire is a Swiss bank account/Given an OBE and made a Count/Country estate with a resident staff/Acute angina and an epitaph.' It's also worth pointing out the sombre poise to Bid's vocals which may well have influenced Morrissey's early phrasing at the outset of The Smiths.

The Monochrome Set underwent various lineup and label changes during the early 80s, coming dangerously close to the UK singles chart with the crazed indie-gospel of 1985's 'Jacob's Ladder', but – peaking at number 81 – not close enough. They disbanded soon after only to re-form for a handful of albums in the 1990s. Those interested in assessing for themselves the group's stylistic influence upon Morrissey should refer to both the aforementioned Strange Boutique and Love Zombies as well as Volume, Contrast, Brilliance ..., an anthology of early singles and radio sessions. [17, 334]

'Moonriver' (Henry Mancini/Johnny Mercer), B-

side of 'HOLD ON TO YOUR FRIENDS' (1994). Forever associated with the divine vision of Audrey Hepburn, hair wrapped in a towel, strumming her guitar while sat on a window sill, Morrissey bravely attempted to add his own lachrymose spin on this popular standard. 'It does mean a great deal to me,' he explained. 'I always found it a very passionate song and very lonely … I never really understood it, but [it seemed] always a very lonely sound.'

Composed by Henry Mancini with lyrics by Johnny Mercer, the song was commissioned for *Breakfast At Tiffany's*, the 1961 film version of Truman CAPOTE's novel starring Hepburn and George Peppard; strangely, Morrissey neglected to mention it in his derisive overview of Peppard's career in his film essay EXIT SMILING. It immediately become a crooner classic, tackled by FRANK SINATRA, Andy Williams and a UK number one for South Africa's Danny Williams. While it was surprising to hear Morrissey undertake such a cabaret perennial, on closer inspection its lyrics celebrating love, eternal friendship and youthful ambition are analogous with 'HAND IN GLOVE'. Condensing the original title of 'Moon River' to a single word,[1] Morrissey also discarded the mawkish 'my huckleberry friend' referring to Mercer's childhood picking berries near the Georgia inlet which gave the song its name. There's a softly heaving sadness in his delivery, inverting its original optimism with a sense of loss and impending tragedy, that the dream 'just around the bend' will never arrive. The sombre air is reinforced by its tear-dabbing arrangement of guitar and omnichord, while the 12-inch version added the disturbing sobs of a girl in distress. The cries belonged to actress Peggy Evans, bawling in agony having been slapped in the face by the weasely Dirk BOGARDE in the 1950 Ealing drama *The Blue Lamp*, co-starring Patric DOONAN.

Haunting as Morrissey's rendition was, it still didn't justify the excessive length of the nine-and-a-half-minute 'Moonriver (extended version)' as it also appeared on WORLD OF MORRISSEY. The song was more effective in concert, played on his February 1995 UK tour in a simple, shorter acoustic arrangement with Morrissey bathed in a spotlight accompanied by Evans's ghostly moans on a backing tape, as captured on the *INTRODUCING MORRISSEY* video. [40, 486, 577]

1. The condensing of 'Moon River' into one word seems to have been natural instinct for Morrissey: in his March 1980 live review of Mark Andrews & The Gents for *Record Mirror* he also referred to the song as 'Moonriver'.

Moors Murders, See BEYOND BELIEF, 'SUFFER LITTLE CHILDREN'.

'More You Ignore Me, The Closer I Get, The' (Morrissey/Boorer), Morrissey's 15th solo single (from the album VAUXHALL AND I), released February 1994, highest UK chart position #8. Among Morrissey's most brilliantly unorthodox love songs, this funny, smart and vastly intriguing tale of psychological stalking rewarded him with his first top ten hit after a gap of nearly five years. Like some omnipresent Beelzebub, Morrissey boasts how he haunts his piteous prey's every conscious and unconscious move, rendering any resistance futile. Recorded three years before the 1996 Smiths COURT CASE, the final declaration of war and the uncanny references to 'a bad debt' and 'high court judges' have led to the not unreasonable assumption that the song's target was Mike Joyce, then preparing his legal case against the singer and Marr. Even if Joyce wasn't the subject, years after the 1996 verdict its lyrics provided Morrissey with an opportunity to vent his fury over the case, changing the words in concert to 'stupid British judges'. While the song also seemed as much a cry of imminent sexual conquest as a celebration of revenge, as Morrissey later pointed out, 'As the song ends, I don't necessarily succeed. Though I am quite determined.'

The first Morrissey single co-written with Boz Boorer, its commercial potential only came to light midway through the Vauxhall sessions. Boorer's original demo was much heavier, noticeably slower and failed to emphasise the winking barrow-boy guitar hook highlighted by producer Steve LILLYWHITE who duly transformed the tune into one of Morrissey's biggest, and catchiest, hits. An accompanying video directed by Mark Romanek also witnessed the beginnings of Morrissey's use of BOXING imagery as well as a sneaky reference to his new obsession with UK punk group ANGELIC UPSTARTS. [4, 6, 40, 217]

Morricone, Ennio,

Legendary Italian film composer who provided string arrangements on Morrissey's 'DEAR GOD PLEASE HELP ME' from the album RINGLEADER OF THE TORMENTORS. Surprisingly, the singer confessed that prior to their collaboration he knew very little of Morricone's work other than his haunting harmonica theme to 1968's *Once Upon A Time In The West*. Surprising since he must, surely, have been familiar with the composer's most famous soundtrack to 1966's *The Good, The Bad And The Ugly*: a version of the title theme by Hugo Montenegro spent four weeks at number one in November 1968 when the nine-year-old Morrissey was already monitoring and commenting on the singles charts in his home-made pop magazine.

Best known for his 60s Spaghetti Western themes, Morricone's 400-plus film scores include several works by PASOLINI and his Oscar-nominated soundtracks to *Days Of Heaven*, *The Mission* and *The Untouchables*. Before working in cinema, he began his career in pop, co-writing Mina's 1966 hit 'Se Telefonado', later covered by Françoise HARDY as 'Je Changerais D'Avis'. In 1981 he enjoyed a surprise UK hit when his 1978 piece 'Chi Mai' was used as the theme to the BBC series *The Life And Times Of David Lloyd George*, reaching number two and still riding in the top ten when Morrissey turned 22 that May.

Morricone's involvement on 'Dear God Please Help Me' was pure serendipity since he and Morrissey both happened to be recording in Rome's Forum Music Village at the same time in the autumn of 2005. 'We were hopeless because he is very shy and tends to keep people away from him,' Morrissey explained. 'But he accepted. He didn't talk that much. He is a legend and he doesn't care about human beings. He does his job and then goes home.' The singer was especially thrilled, almost to the point of smugness, that Morricone had previously turned down offers to work with David BOWIE and U2, though neglected to mention that Morricone had co-written a song with the Pet Shop Boys back in 1987 ('It Couldn't Happen Here'). According to producer TONY VISCONTI, the 77-year-old Morricone was completely oblivious to the song's risqué lyrical content, having little grasp of English. Morrissey also admitted that, though involved in the track's arrangement, there was little fraternisation. 'He was heavily surrounded and shielded. There was no way that he and I would end up at the local pub playing darts.'

In September 2006, Morrissey announced that Morricone had asked him 'to sing and supply words for one of his musical pieces with a view to presenting this song at Carnegie Hall. Joy, joy, joy.' Sadly, the concert which eventually took place at New York's Radio City Music Hall on 3 February 2007 came and went without Morrissey, clashing with his concert in Pasadena the same night. [213, 240, 266, 389, 461]

Morrissey-Solo.com,

Not Morrissey's official website but still the main hub of Morrissey and Smiths-related news and activity on the internet. The site was launched in February 1997 by David

'Morr-iss-ey! Morr-iss-ey! Morr-iss-ey!', The traditional Morrissey concert chant, mimicking the common football anthem 'Here we go! Here we go! Here we go!', sung to the melody of the patriotic American march 'Stars And Stripes Forever'. His British fans alone can take credit for introducing the 'Morr-iss-ey!' ritual which actually pre-dates his solo career. As early as The Smiths' spring 1984 UK tour, pockets of the crowd would launch into the chant between songs, as bootleg tapes attest. Nor was it restricted to Morrissey: many a Smiths gig echoed to similar choruses of 'Johnn-y-Marr! Johnn-y-Marr! Johnn-y-Marr!'

Tseng, a Santa Monica-based web developer and former editor of the Morrissey fanzine *Sing Your Life*. Its first year coincided with the release of MALADJUSTED, though, significantly, it was during Morrissey's 'wilderness' years and especially surrounding his tours of 1999–2000 and 2002 that it blossomed. The importance of Morrissey-Solo during this period is all too easily overlooked: surviving purely on donations at a time when Morrissey was unsigned with no record company-funded web presence, Tseng's site sustained a growing internet community of fans otherwise uncatered for. In 2002, Morrissey himself acknowledged the site's existence, commenting, somewhat confusingly, that though he'd 'never actually logged on' he considered it 'a great site'.

Since then, Morrissey has grown more critical of the domain name he has sometimes smeared as 'Morrissey SoLow'. His main issue with Morrissey-Solo is that, unlike the unfalteringly loyal Julia Riley's TRUE-TO-YOU.NET which he's officially endorsed, Tseng's site operates a more objective news policy resulting in the posting of stories, leaked correspondence and sometimes gossip which casts the singer in a less than flattering light. The worst incident, in May 2003, ended in Tseng being served with a 'cease and desist' document from Morrissey's solicitors after running a story which questioned whether rumours the singer had failed to pay members of his tour personnel the previous year were true: the claims were never proven.

These infrequent storms aside, Morrissey-Solo still attracts the majority of Morrissey internet traffic. Admittedly, its egalitarian interactive portals of user comments have a habit of drawing in the lunatic fringe minority, but as Tseng argues, 'I believe keeping it as open as possible makes for an active and interesting site and keeps everyone in check … People looking for something sane and sanitised can find that type of atmosphere on the official sites.' [242, 411]

Moss, Joe, The Smiths' first manager whose mentoring of the young Johnny Marr played a

significant role in the formation of the group. Though Moss modestly plays down the extent of his influence, his financial and personal support was fundamental to the group's rapid rise from a Manchester rehearsal room in the winter of 1982 to their first top 30 hit barely 12 months later. Marr has since stated, 'Without him, there's no question The Smiths would never have formed at all.'

His success with the group was all the more extraordinary given that Moss's business background was clothing, not music. In the early 70s, he and a partner began manufacturing sandals, shammy skirts and other Indian-influenced items to be sold through a local Manchester hippy cooperative called On The Eighth Day. As a brand name, Moss chose Crazy Face after a song on Van Morrison's recent fourth solo album of 1970, His Band And The Street Choir.

They soon struck sartorial gold with loon pants, in such demand that Moss eventually gave up his day job as a 'Technical Officer In Charge' at Bramhall telephone exchange to expand the Crazy Face line into a full-scale commercial enterprise with factory production. After years building up the business, trading predominantly with shops in London, Moss decided to open his own Crazy Face boutiques back home, first in Stockport, then in Manchester in the basement of 70 Portland Street, a corner office building where Moss's machinists worked on the second floor: the floor above would, in due course, become The Smiths' private rehearsal space.

By 1981, Moss had opened a second Manchester branch of Crazy Face nearer the centre of town on Chapel Walks. The shop's walls were covered with rare vintage pop photographs collected from a Paris flea market including some obscure portraits of THE ROLLING STONES. They immediately attracted the attention of an unfulfilled 18-year-old sales assistant working in the contemporary fashion outlet next door, X-Clothes, who began asking the girls behind the counter about their boss. 'They kept telling me there was this lad who wanted to meet me to talk about my photographs,' says Moss. 'I wasn't in the shop that often because I was more on the wholesale and manufacturing side rather than retail. But the next time I was in, one of the girls went and told him. So he came upstairs and introduced himself. This lad walks in and sticks out his hand. He says, "Hi, I'm Johnny Marr. I'm a frustrated musician." And that's how it all began.'

Marr was 16 years younger than Moss but they immediately recognised kindred spirits with much to learn from one another. For Marr, Moss was a walking rock and roll masterclass, ruling his shops with a 'tyrannical' music policy restricted to his own meticulously compiled cassettes from his vast vinyl collection. 'Quite a lot of Van Morrison,' says Moss, 'but also John Lee Hooker, some R&B. It was quite mixed, only the poor people who worked in the shop didn't think it was mixed. But I just wanted a different vibe in Crazy Face to other places.'

Moss, meantime, was just as excited by Marr's enthusiasm, not to mention his guitar skills. Soon, Marr was spending most of his X-Clothes lunch hours in Moss's offices on Portland Street, hanging out, listening to records and giving masterclasses of his own. 'I had a guitar in my office,' Moss elaborates. 'I wasn't what you called a guitarist but I played around on it. So Johnny used to come in and teach me stuff. By the time he'd finished showing me things I was ten times better than before he started, but I still couldn't really play guitar. But to see him play was incredible. He'd play Motown covers, things like Smokey Robinson's "The Tracks Of My Tears", but he'd perform the whole arrangement, including the vocal melody, all at the same time, just on guitar.'

To begin with, Marr's friendship with Moss was based purely on mutual interests in music, guitars and dope. It was only when they began socialising more after hours, spending evenings round Moss's house with Marr's girlfriend, Angie, that regular conversation slowly turned to the dream of putting a band together. 'We began to talk more and more about it,' says Moss. 'The big thing for Johnny was finding a frontman. He

knew he could sort a bass player and a drummer no problem, but he needed a frontman.'

In the spring of 1982, Moss showed Marr a documentary he'd taped off ITV's *South Bank Show* about rock and roll songwriting legends LEIBER AND STOLLER, who mythically formed their partnership when the former acted on curious rumours about the latter, turning up unannounced on his doorstep. 'That had a massive impact on Johnny,' says Moss. 'He kept talking about that. And then one day, he told me he thought that there *was* someone he'd heard about who would be a really good frontman, but he didn't know how to approach it. So I told him to go and knock on his door and ask him.'

Though Moss still had doubts as to whether he could wholly commit to giving Marr's group 'management', he'd already guaranteed him a rehearsal space at Crazy Face on Portland Street and basic financial support. 'So when he went to call on Morrissey, I wouldn't say I was a big part of it, but in Johnny's mind I was,' says Moss. 'Because he wasn't just some kid saying, "Do you wanna be in my band?" There were already things in place which I'd promised him so straight away they had some foundation.'

Moss's first impressions of Morrissey were 'a very shy, dead nice bloke'. 'But it was clear at the same time that he had an agenda,' he adds, 'in terms of his lyrics and what he wanted to say. My role, once I became manager, was helping him to facilitate that. Which I think I did. I put a massive amount of time into Morrissey, a lot more time looking after him and his situation than I did Johnny's situation.'

Once Moss assumed full managerial responsibility, he concentrated his efforts on Morrissey and Marr's resolution to target ROUGH TRADE as their ideal label. It was Moss who negotiated and funded the recording of 'HAND IN GLOVE' at Stockport's Strawberry studios in February 1983. Local 'legend' Demetrius Christopholus, formerly of 60s Merseybeat group Four Just Men and prog-rockers Wimple Witch, charged The Smiths the 'special rate' of £250. 'It seemed cheap in those days,' reflects Moss, 'but probably not now.' Moss and his wife, Janet, were later thanked on the back of the single sleeve, the first pressing of which carried the Crazy Face Portland Street contact address.

The reasons for Moss's decision to relinquish his post as Smiths manager at the end of 1983 were both personal and professional. By getting the group signed, fostering them through their make-or-break first year and watching them enter the pantheon of British pop history on TOP OF THE POPS with 'THIS CHARMING MAN', Moss had already achieved his objective in a phenomenally short space of time.

'People sometimes say to me that I was wrong to have stepped down,' says Moss, 'but I had my reasons. I had an amazing time with The Smiths but it was completely the right move for everyone concerned to leave when I did. I would have loved to have been able to carry on, but who's to say that it wouldn't have turned sour had I stayed? It was an emotional decision, and a big part of it was to do with the fact that I'd just had a baby daughter. The Smiths went home for Christmas break in 1983. I can remember being with my family that Boxing Day and I just decided there and then. That was the end of it. I never went back to The Smiths.'

For the rest of their career, The Smiths would never have as stable or secure a manager as Moss, who returned to the clothing business. Over a decade later he was coerced back into management by a young group from Macclesfield, Marion, who in February 1995 found themselves supporting Morrissey.[1] 'I saw quite a lot of him on that tour,' says Moss. 'The thing is, whatever anybody's said or written about why I walked away from The Smiths, I always got on well with Morrissey. Cos there's no question, he's a bloody interesting bloke to talk to. And a fun bloke to talk to as well.' Events have since come full circle and today – nearly three decades after a 'frustrated musician' was first intrigued by unusual photos of The Rolling Stones from a Parisian flea market stuck on the walls of his

shop – Moss is back managing Johnny Marr. [12, 13, 17, 18, 19, 21, 113]

---

1. At the time of the Morrissey tour, Marion were promoting the single 'Sleep', produced by Stephen STREET, which was later used on a television car advert. Their second album, 1998's The Program, was produced by Johnny Marr who also co-wrote its only single, 'Miyako Hideaway'.

mother (of Morrissey), See FAMILY.

Moz, or Mozzer, It was Johnny Marr who, circa 1983, coined the common abbreviation of Morrissey's name to the two-syllable 'Mozzer', subsequently shortened to the one-syllable 'Moz'.

Neither became common currency in the music press until 1984. The NME would later boast that they'd coined the term in their 'T-Zers' back-page gossip column, though this is untrue. One of the first printed mentions was by his friend, the journalist Jim Shelley. Interviewing Morrissey for the May 1984 edition of Blitz, Shelley comments how '[people] slap you on the back and call you "Mozzer"'.

Morrissey has expressed something of a love/hate relationship with both nicknames. In a 1990 interview, he refused to be addressed as 'Moz' claiming 'it makes me sound like a racehorse'. He was still squirming at the phrase 13 years later, revealing he'd asked people to stop calling him 'Moz' because 'it doesn't suit me and it sounds like something you'd squirt on a kitchen floor'. Even so, Morrissey has embraced, and used, his abbreviation at various points during his career. A promotional single of 1992's 'CERTAIN PEOPLE I KNOW' was issued in a mock vintage T.Rex design bag with 'MOZ' printed in a facsimile of the original T.Rex logo. The back cover of 1994's 'THE MORE YOU IGNORE ME, THE CLOSER I GET' also featured a photo of his friend Jake WALTERS's torso with 'MOZ' written around his bellybutton. He's also referred to himself in interviews using 'Moz', 'Mozzer' (telling the BBC's Jonathan Ross the latter was his official passport name) and even the cat-like 'Mogsy'. The latter, strangely, never caught on.

m

As in The Smiths, his backing band also commonly refer to him by both nicknames: watch closely at the end of the video for 'TOMORROW' and you'll see Boz BOORER mouth 'All right, Moz' as he shakes his hand; and, again, in the 2003 Channel 4 documentary *The Importance Of Being Morrissey* his whole band wish him 'Good luck, Moz' backstage at London's Royal Albert Hall. Doubtless, such usage of the undeniably laddish and over-familiar 'Moz' or 'Mozzer' while in his company is strictly the reserve of those permitted to do so. Where the rest of the human race is concerned, as he says himself, 'I prefer to be called Morrissey.' [17, 27, 87, 138, 153, 207, 218, 451, 453]

Mozzerian, By definition, an adjective 'relating to, or characteristic of, the popular English singer Morrissey, especially regarding his principal lyrical themes of human loneliness, romantic pessimism and gallows humour'. It is pronounced 'moss-*air*-ee-an' with the emphasis on the second syllable and should rhyme with caesarean. Mozzerian was coined as a means of eradicating the cumbersome and ugly hyphenated likes of 'Morrissey-esque' and 'Morrissey-ish' which journalists previously struggled with.

Mr. Skeffington, 1944 Hollywood melodrama listed among Morrissey's favourite films. The story begins in New York at the outbreak of the First World War. Fanny Trellis (Bette DAVIS) is a beautiful yet outrageously conceited New York socialite who cares only for her own reflection and her wastrel brother, Trippy. When it comes to light that Trippy has been embezzling money from his bank-manager boss, Mr Skeffington (Claude Rains), Fanny decides to help her brother avoid prison by marrying the besotted Skeffington. Her altruism backfires when Trippy, disgusted by their marriage, joins the war and gets himself killed. Fanny, now Mrs Skeffington, blames her new husband for Trippy's death and makes a mockery of their wedding vows with her constant infidelity. Described by one critic of the day as a 'super soap opera', the plot ends during the Second World War, by which time Fanny has lost her looks and realises, all too late, the moral that 'a woman is only beautiful when she is loved'. Most Davis fans, Morrissey included, rate it among her finest performances. The film writer Jeffrey Robinson also cites *Mr. Skeffington* as pivotal in her canonisation as a gay icon: '[It] immediately gave birth to a characterisation of Bette Davis that is so often mimicked by male actors in drag. It was probably right here that the gay community discovered the Bette Davis character that is so often impersonated.' Since Morrissey referred to the film in 1983, at the outset of The Smiths' career, it seems likely that Davis's remark to Rains after their wedding – 'Although I've never really seen you smile I always have the feeling you're laughing at me … besides the fact you're very rich' – was paraphrased within the lyrics of 'YOU'VE GOT EVERYTHING NOW'. [184, 298, 360, 361, 531]

'Munich Air Disaster 1958' (Morrissey/Whyte), B-side of 'IRISH BLOOD, ENGLISH HEART' (2004). Once asked when he was happiest, Morrissey answered 'May 21, 1959' – the day before he was born. Using the tragic events of 6 February 1958 as an analogy, 'Munich Air Disaster 1958' was a continuation of the same theme as Morrissey wishes he'd 'gone down' in that year's Manchester United plane crash some 15 months before he came into the world.

On the aforesaid date, a charter flight carrying the squad, staff and journalists back home after a European Cup away game against Red Star Belgrade stopped to refuel in Munich. The aircraft crashed on the third attempt to take off, killing 23 people including eight of manager Matt Busby's star players, the 'Busby Babes'. Among the most promising was Duncan Edwards, who died in hospital 15 days later aged only 21. According to team-mate, survivor and future World Cup winner Bobby Charlton, Edwards was 'the best footballer I've ever seen'. Morrissey salutes Busby's 'unlucky boys of red' but his words betray a morbid envy of their premature death. Cut down in their prime, their youth, talent and 'style'

Murderers' Who's Who, The, 1979 encyclopedia of killers by J. H. H. Gaute and Robin Odell, listed among Morrissey's favourite books. 'I'm never interested in those murders where the wife poisons the husband and the husband suffocates the wife,' he explained in 1984. 'Very extreme cases of murder have to be a constant source of bewilderment – where the police burst into a flat and find seven bodies in the fridge. It's not amusing, though you titter. It's a magnificent study of human nature although I wouldn't want to be so close to the actual study that I'm squashed in the fridge.' Among the crimes collated by Gaute and Odell – over 150 years of stranglings, stabbings, matricide, arsenic poisonings and even a lone instance of death-by-karate – are those of JACK THE RIPPER, James HANRATTY, the KRAY twins and Moors Murderers Hindley and Brady (see BEYOND BELIEF, 'SUFFER LITTLE CHILDREN'). Morrissey's personal 'favourites' included the case of the Chalkpit Murder and the alarming history of Albert Fish, described by Gaute and Odell as 'a sex murderer with extraordinary perversions, including sado-masochism and cannibalism'. Fish's catalogue of criminal perversity included the abduction of a 12-year-old girl whom he strangled, dismembered then 'cooked with vegetables' (thus keeping him 'in a state of continuous sexual fervour') and the habit of inserting needles – 29 to be precise – in his genital area. 'I am not insane,' Fish protested, 'I am just queer. I don't understand myself.' He was electrocuted in New York's Sing Sing Prison in 1936; a first attempt short-circuited due to those needles in his pelvis. [57, 184, 267, 317]

are preserved for ever – unlike his own. Highlighting its lyrical drama, the roar of plane propellers ushered Whyte's crash-diving melody to an appropriately solemn end.

A timely reminder of Morrissey's roots – himself a Man. Utd fan who lived near their Old Trafford ground in Stretford – for its sense of history and subject matter (commemorating modern Mancunian folklore much like 'SUFFER LITTLE CHILDREN'), the song was of greater significance within Morrissey's catalogue than its B-side status implied. In concert, it was often played as part of an admittedly stilted medley with the NEW YORK DOLLS' 'SUBWAY TRAIN', as captured on LIVE AT EARLS COURT. [141]

Murcia, Billy, See NEW YORK DOLLS.

'Mute Witness' (Morrissey/Langer), From the album KILL UNCLE (1991). Another Morrissey character study about disability, its protagonist brought to mind the 1952 Ealing drama *Mandy* about a deaf-mute girl 'testing the strength' of her parents' straining marriage. Despite the inference of some dreadful event which the girl's handicap

prevents her from describing to her assembled audience, the tone is lighter than that of the thematically related 'NOVEMBER SPAWNED A MONSTER'. There's even potential mischief in its choice of crime scene: 'Northside, Clapham Common' is a notorious cottaging hotspot.

Among the strongest tracks on Kill Uncle, Clive Langer's tuneful cavort was a conscious appeal to Morrissey's love of early 70s glam, particularly SPARKS and ROXY MUSIC; its intro is suspiciously similar to the latter's 1972 hit 'Virginia Plain'. Langer also played the guitar solo, earning praise from co-producer Alan Winstanley for 'sounding like Ariel Bender from Mott The Hoople'. 'Mute Witness' later became the title of a 1996 slasher movie, though whether its writer/director Anthony Waller was inspired by the Kill Uncle song has never been established. Morrissey, at least, 'hoped so'. [15, 22, 25, 243]

'My Dearest Love' (Morrissey/Whyte), B-side of 'ALL YOU NEED IS ME' (2008). A prototypical Morrissey ballad, within its void of century-old human misery glimmered a dim light of romantic optimism, albeit the phantasmic reverie

m

of reciprocal love between 'the grotesquely lonely'. Such relatively simple lyrics were intensified by the boom and gloom of Whyte's pulsing bass and piano pattern, only just guided clear of a wrong turn into EMF's 'Unbelievable' by Morrissey's distracted scatting. Originally issued on vinyl only, 'My Dearest Love' was a superior B-side, one of two produced by Gustavo Santolalla, the award-winning Argentinian composer of the *Brokeback Mountain* soundtrack. (See also 'CHILDREN IN PIECES'.)

My Early Burglary Years, Morrissey

compilation album, released on the American label Reprise in September 1998. Tracks: 'SUNNY', 'AT AMBER', 'COSMIC DANCER', 'NOBODY LOVES US', 'A SWALLOW ON MY NECK', 'SISTER I'M A POET', 'BLACK-EYED SUSAN', 'MICHAEL'S BONES', 'I'D LOVE TO', 'READER MEET AUTHOR', 'PASHERNATE LOVE', 'GIRL LEAST LIKELY TO', 'JACK THE RIPPER', 'I'VE CHANGED MY PLEA TO GUILTY', 'THE BOY RACER', 'BOXERS'.

A worthwhile round-up of non-album singles and B-sides for American audiences, the wryly named My Early Burglary Years was of similar value to UK fans as the first album to mop up collectable tracks missing from the previous collections BONA DRAG and WORLD OF MORRISSEY. 'There's no great concept,' Morrissey explained, 'it's just gathering certain things that have strayed away over the years. It's a very, very nice package.' While some critics interpreted the title as a coy double entendre ('burglary' as in 'buggery'), its literal criminal element was nevertheless the perfect umbrella for the enclosed tales of lowlife misadventure, social rejects and mysterious rogues, enforced by the accompanying booklet which revisited a past Smiths reference with the inclusion of 'HMP [Her Majesty's Prison] M60 9AH' – the Manchester postcode for STRANGEWAYS. The CD also contained a multimedia extra of the 'Sunny' video preceded by a handwritten introduction which, again, echoed the suggested prison theme with Morrissey's scribbled avowal, 'I'm singing from Sing Sing.' [422]

'My Insatiable One' (Brett Anderson/

Bernard Butler), Song by London indie band Suede covered live by Morrissey on 1992's YOUR ARSENAL tour. First released as the B-side of Suede's May 1992 debut single, 'The Drowners', the track was relatively unknown when Morrissey introduced it into his set in early July. One press report alleged that he'd been seen in the audience at Suede's Camden Palace gig a few weeks earlier on 15 June with a notebook 'jotting down lyrics'. Its yearning for a lost love ('Oh, he is gone') and jaded view of 'the ridiculous world' were certainly in keeping with Morrissey's oeuvre, though less so its graphic description of 'shitting paracetamol'.

Suede were oblivious to Morrissey's cover until singer Brett Anderson was alerted by a Camden Market trader dealing in live bootlegs. 'I took it home and there was Morrissey singing it,' Anderson recalled. 'That was a headfuck, to say the least.' The Smiths had been a key influence on Anderson and co-writer/guitarist Bernard Butler, so much so that in 1990 they'd placed a musicians wanted classified ad specifying their need for a Smiths-loving drummer. To their amazement, Mike Joyce replied, joining them for a couple of gigs and a limited edition single which was never released.

At the time, Morrissey praised Suede as 'probably the most exciting thing to happen to pop music since a long time', an opinion shared by most of the British music press, though his admiration for the group barely lasted as long as his cover's concert shelf life, performing 'My Insatiable One' just 17 times (16 of those as a medley with 'SUCH A LITTLE THING MAKES SUCH A BIG DIFFERENCE'). In March 1993, as Suede's debut album entered the charts at number one, Anderson gave an interview in which he described an alleged meeting with Morrissey. 'I didn't really like him,' said Anderson. 'He's like some kind of useless teenager.' Such impertinence inevitably provoked a stinging retort. 'I have never met Brett and wouldn't wish to,' claimed Morrissey, likening the Suede singer to 'a deeply boring young man with Mr Kipling crumbs in his bed'.

Morrissey's closing cat's miaow referred to Anderson's recent *NME* summit meeting with David BOWIE. 'He'll never forgive God for not making him Angie Bowie.'

In contrast, after Bernard Butler acrimoniously quit Suede in 1994, he sought the advice of, and became good friends with, Johnny Marr. Both would play on Bert Jansch's 2000 album Crimson Moon, while Marr also presented Butler with the gift of the 12-string Gibson guitar he played on the majority OF STRANGEWAYS, HERE WE COME. More intriguingly, when Alain WHYTE dropped out of Morrissey's live band in June 2004, Butler was among the first considered as an emergency replacement. Contacted through a third party, he declined the offer. [48, 150, 323]

'My Life Is A Succession Of People Saying Goodbye' (Morrissey/ Whyte), B-side of 'FIRST OF THE GANG TO DIE' (2004). A woeful meditation on his own mortality and the catalogue of loved ones who've deserted him, Morrissey reaches the conclusion that life has nothing better to offer beyond 'money, jewellery and flesh'. The song's rhetorical sigh, 'What's left for me?', brought to mind an interview conducted nearly 20 years earlier when he was asked about his plans to visit James DEAN's birthplace. 'They've taken away the monument,' he complained in 1985, 'they've taken away the stone and they've taken away the grass … What's left for me?' Whyte's soft, swaying air, harp showering like confetti, offered a strikingly exotic accompaniment to Morrissey's fate-surrendering sigh, stretching 'be-hiiiind' in a voice mere inches from the gas oven. [135]

'My Love Life' (Morrissey/Nevin), Morrissey's 11th solo single, released October 1991, highest UK chart position #29. Modelled on a Mark Nevin demo nicknamed 'Smooth Track', Morrissey originally conceived 'My Love Life' as a potential B-side for 'SING YOUR LIFE' (or as he wrote to Nevin, 'Sling Your Wife') along with 'SKIN STORM'.

He also jokingly asked the guitarist to knock up a 'Noël COWARD type one minute 32 rocker or plink plonker' as a third reserve.

After the residential comfort of Hook End, Morrissey found the B-side session at LANGER and Winstanley's Westside studios in Notting Hill much less inviting. 'He hated it there,' says Langer, 'there were days when he didn't even turn up.' Even the support of friend Chrissie HYNDE, invited as backing vocalist, failed to improve his mood. When engineer Danton Supple innocently offered her a digestive biscuit – oblivious to the animal fats they contained and the offence she'd take as a strident vegan – Hynde lobbed the packet back at his head in disgust and unleashed a tirade of abuse. For all its friction and theatrics, the session exceeded expectations with the gently beguiling 'My Love Life' – complete with Hynde's skyscraping 'additional harmonies' – saved from its intended B-side fate and commandeered as a stand-alone single. Nevin's one concession to the 'jangly Smiths sound' he'd deliberately avoided on KILL UNCLE, its lyrics read like 'I WON'T SHARE YOU' in reverse: a needy appeal to become the third party in an existing relationship. It also contained a, perhaps accidental, SPARKS reference: the opening 'Come on to my house' mirrored Rosemary Clooney's 50s hit 'Come-On-A My House', the pun source for the Mael brothers' 1974 album Kimono My House.

Although the back sleeve credited the track to his new band of BOORER, COBRIN, DAY and WHYTE (who also starred in the accompanying video where Morrissey drives them through Phoenix, Arizona in a Rolls-Royce convertible), 'My Love Life' was actually the last recording by the Kill Uncle trio of MADNESS bassist Mark Bedford, Nevin and PARESI. Disappointingly, it barely scraped inside the UK top 30. Morrissey was doubly depressed by EMI's shoddy manufacturing of the single – issued in a cheap paper sleeve instead of a card one and with injection-moulded labels breeching his contractual specification of paper ones. [15, 22, 25, 40, 374]

n

Naked Truth, The, 1957 British comedy listed among Morrissey's favourite films. It stars Dennis Price as the caddish and cunning Nigel Dennis, editor of the scandal magazine of the title ('vulgar, but terribly apt'). Using an incriminating draft copy as bait, Dennis makes his money by blackmailing the people whose closet skeletons he plans to expose, offering them a chance to 'donate' £10,000 to his 'distressed journalists association' in exchange for the issue not going to press. Dennis's four victims are a judge (Terry-Thomas), a young model (Shirley Eaton), a television celebrity (Peter Sellers) and a crime writer (Peggy Mount). Unbeknownst to one another, all four are separately plotting to bump him off in order to put an end to his extortion. When they finally realise they're not alone, the blackmailed quartet pool their resources to finish him once and for all. Or so they hope.

Though not an Ealing film, *The Naked Truth* is markedly Ealing-esque in its uniquely British black humour which – like another Morrissey favourite, THE LADYKILLERS – makes high farce out of murder and assassination. Significantly, Morrissey referred to the film in his September 1989 list extravaganza printed in the NME, which also included one of its stars, Peggy Mount, in a separate round-up of his favourite 'Odd fellows'. Mount all but steals the film as brash crime writer Flora Ransom, bumbling around East End pubs looking to buy some 'Mickey Finns' and doing her best to ignore the hysterics of daughter Joan Sims (see CARRY ON). [175, 532]

'National Front Disco, The' (Morrissey/ Whyte), From the album YOUR ARSENAL (1992). The germ of one of Morrissey's most controversial songs can be found in *Among The Thugs*, Bill Buford's 1991 investigation into English football hooliganism. Buford devotes a whole chapter of the book to an account of a Saturday night in Bury St Edmunds spent observing 'a National Front disco'. The event at a local pub is mostly attended by drunken skinheads, though as the night progresses Buford realises that the deafening 'White Power music' and its brainwashing effect on the crowd is being carefully orchestrated by well-dressed 'visitors from London' including future BNP leader Nick Griffin. 'There was a menacing feeling in the air,' notes Buford, 'sexual and dangerous … Some of the lads appeared to be in a trance.'

'The National Front Disco' is Morrissey's elegy to the entranced, centring on a pathetic boy called David now 'lost' to the NF much to the despair of his friends and family. Rather than berate his naïve bigotry, Morrissey pities David; his humanity slowly blown away bit by bit, filling the loveless void with 'England for the English' and other brainwashed mantras. It was this sympathetic condescension towards an NF follower as opposed to the righteous finger-wagging which had been the norm of left-wing British pop during the 1980s which angered Morrissey's critics. Since the album carried no lyric sheet, the 'England for the English' lyric, intended as a quotation, was misconstrued as an endorsement of NF sloganeering. Combined with the perceived ambiguities surrounding his use of SKINHEAD imagery and the ensuing NME Madstock fiasco, the song's absence of any explicit denunciation of the National Front was prone to wild misinterpretation by those deaf to its subtle sorrow.

Morrissey was acutely aware of its potential controversy before the recording was finished, warning composer Alain Whyte 'you're not going to like the title'. Cleverly, the singer seems to have deliberately selected a tune which skipped merrily through the daisies towards the indie-disco dance-floor, thus accentuating its title provocation. Less a pop song than a pop disturbance, early concert performances routinely ended in a hooligan stampede of white noise and detuned guitars (as heard on BEETHOVEN WAS DEAF and seen on *INTRODUCING MORRISSEY*). It was a mark of proud defiance on Morrissey's part that neither the original Madstock controversy nor the 2007 *NME* immigration row dissuaded him from playing 'The National Front Disco' live for fear of misinterpretation, even including it on the Live At Hollywood Bowl bonus disc of 2008's GREATEST HITS. [5, 292, 453]

'Never Had No One Ever' (Morrissey/Marr),

From the album THE QUEEN IS DEAD (1986). Seldom celebrated as one of their best, 'Never Had No One Ever' is nevertheless the defining – as opposed to *definitive* – Smiths song, a stark expression of the silent inner sadness which bonded Morrissey and Marr to begin with.

In just two concise verses Morrissey articulates his isolation with devastating intensity. The first, he explained, relayed 'the frustration that I felt at the age of 20 when I still didn't feel easy walking around the streets on which I'd been born, where all my family had lived. They're originally from Ireland but had been here since the 50s. It was a constant confusion to me why I never really felt, "This is my patch. This is my home. I know these people. I can do what I like, because this is mine." It never was. I could never walk easily.' The second, unprinted in the accompanying album lyric sheet, saw him forlornly stalking his unrequited love, unable to bring himself to make contact. An early rehearsal tape reveals that this second verse was the germ of Morrissey's lyrics, continually repeating the 'I'm outside your house' line before ad-libbing a series of slow, tortured groans. Both Morrissey and Marr would regret erasing his vocal improvisations from the final version. 'It was a really great two-part harmony,' recalls Marr. 'It wasn't any words, just a sort of lilt. Years later Morrissey finally agreed with me that we should have kept it on.'

Of all the Queen Is Dead songs, 'Never Had No One Ever' had the longest gestation period, dating back to December 1984 as the group were completing the previous album, MEAT IS MURDER. Alongside the soon-to-be-abandoned 'I MISSES YOU', Marr recorded an instrumental demo of a very similar melody which he'd adapt over the course of the following year. It was apt, if uncanny, that the lyrics Morrissey later applied to the tune of 'Never Had No One Ever' resonated with Marr's musical inspiration: 'I Need Somebody' from Iggy & The Stooges' 1973 album Raw Power. 'I can never divorce "Never Had No One Ever" from the emotion which inspired it,' explains Marr. 'It's

n

totally subjective and personal, but it's me in my teenage bedroom on my estate on dark nights, surrounded by concrete and trying to find some beauty in Raw Power through James Williamson's guitar playing. There's a certain kind of gothic beauty in "I Need Somebody". I wasn't looking to cop a riff to get a tune out of it, I was looking to cop a feeling out of it. It's an odd thing, but it occurred to me that in spite of where I was in my life – Johnny Marr, guitarist with The Smiths and everything – that music could have come out of my bedroom when I was 16. It was weird.'

As with Marr's previous Raw Power homage, 'HAND IN GLOVE' (shaped by Williamson's riff on the same album's 'Gimme Danger'), there was a subtle but clear resemblance between the hungry prowl of 'I Need Somebody' and Marr's missed-the-last-bus rain-sodden trudge on 'Never Had No One Ever'. The night before its recording, Marr even forewarned engineer Stephen STREET that the next day they were 'gonna do this one that sounds like The Stooges'. To ensure 'the right vibe', Marr stayed up through the night, working on the song until he was confident he'd found its true character. During the early mixing stages, it was given an experimental trumpet overdub by a session player who reacted to Morrissey's improvised vocal shrieks towards the end with a bluesy solo evocative of a New Orleans 'jazz funeral'. As with

the parallel 'trumpet version' of 'FRANKLY, MR SHANKLY', this mix was binned.

The finished version, replacing trumpet with Marr's lonesome twanging and Morrissey's echoing ethereal sobs, was The Queen Is Dead's secret centrepiece: not obviously anthemic but in many ways the fulcrum of the nine tracks on either side of it. 'The atmosphere of that track pretty much sums up the whole album and what it was like recording it,' confirms Marr. Though they'd record better songs, in its naked despair, in its deafening peal of loneliness, 'Never Had No One Ever' was the pure and true sound of The Smiths. [17, 18, 38, 196]

Nevin, Mark (Morrissey guitarist and co-writer, 1990–92), Morrissey began the 90s without a steady writing partner for the first time in his professional career. The deficit of enough decent material from the 1989 BONA DRAG sessions to create a proper second album dramatically highlighted his need to find a permanent replacement for the recently departed Stephen STREET, his former 'rock' who'd helped establish Morrissey as a solo artist in the two years directly following the break-up of The Smiths. For Bona Drag he'd tried, but failed, to patch an album out of multiple contributions from producer Clive LANGER, guitarist Kevin ARMSTRONG and Andy Rourke. Dispensing with the services of the latter two, in early 1990 Morrissey now turned in hope to

'Never-Played Symphonies, The' (Morrissey/ Whyte), B-side of 'IRISH BLOOD, ENGLISH HEART' (2004). By far the most stunning track from the YOU ARE THE QUARRY sessions, its prevailing sentiment echoed that of John BETJEMAN's notorious quip shortly before his death in 1984 that his biggest regret in life was 'not having more sex'. Morrissey croons from his deathbed, bypassing the memories of all those who've loved or even 'patiently put up with me', instead contemplating the metaphorical human symphonies of those he 'never laid'. Like Bette DAVIS in *Dark Victory*, blackening skies announce the final curtain and it's with all of Davis's dignified resignation that Morrissey stumbles blindly but willingly towards the inevitable. Whyte's tune provides a full military burial, lowering his sexless body into the earth before a mock-orchestral Technicolor sunset, a last smash of the gong spelling 'THE END' in widescreen capitals. Among his most thrilling pop arias, not since 1991's 'I'VE CHANGED MY PLEA TO GUILTY' had such a champion contender been denied its due place on a Morrissey album.

Mark Nevin – guitarist and songwriter with Fairground Attraction, whose debut single, 'Perfect', spent one week at number one in May 1988.

By strange coincidence – the first of many – Fairground Attraction had been the previous booking at Hook End studio in the autumn of 1989 prior to the Bona Drag session. Due to irresolvable differences between Nevin and singer Eddi Reader, the session was abandoned and Fairground Attraction subsequently split. Cast adrift from Reader (who would continue as a solo artist and, weirdly enough, later record her own version of The Smiths' 'LAST NIGHT I DREAMT THAT SOMEBODY LOVED ME'), the downhearted Nevin was as much in need of a new muse as Morrissey.

It was an equally odd twist of fate that when Nevin was first approached to work with Morrissey he was in the midst of contributing to Kirsty MACCOLL's Electric Landlady album, also featuring Johnny Marr (though he and Nevin recorded separately and never met at the time). A devoted Smiths fan, Nevin was dumbstruck and delighted when drummer Andrew PARESI, acting as mediator, contacted him asking to send Morrissey 'some music'. Nevin rose to the challenge somewhat self-consciously. 'I knew I couldn't copy The Smiths and I wanted it to be different,' he says, 'but not so different that Morrissey wouldn't like it. There was no direction. It was left very vague.'

Shortly after sending Morrissey his first cassette of music – under Paresi's instructions, addressed to the pseudonym 'Burt Reynolds' – Nevin received a postcard containing just one word scrawled in crayon: 'PERFECT!' When Paresi next asked Nevin to send more music, he duly compiled another tape, packaged it up in an envelope addressed to 'Burt Reynolds' and walked to the postbox near his house on the corner of Hartland Road in Camden. Just as Nevin was about to drop the envelope in the postbox, his attention was diverted by a strangely familiar figure stalking along Chalk Farm Road. It was Morrissey. A highly bamboozled Nevin recovered his faculties enough to introduce himself and hand Morrissey the 'Burt Reynolds' package. 'It was bizarre,' says

Nevin. 'I gave him the tape. He went bright red. Then he walked away.'

Morrissey's sense of timing continued to haunt Nevin. The night before commencing the sessions for what became KILL UNCLE, Nevin was at home holding an informal wake for a friend who'd recently died. The guitarist was drunk, maudlin and in similar company when his phone rang. 'Of course, it was Morrissey,' he says. 'I was pissed, trying to talk to him in the middle of this wake. I was slurring, telling him my friend had died. I think he just said, "Oh, dear." He couldn't have picked a worse time to call.' The next day, Nevin made his return to Hook End where less than a year earlier Fairground Attraction fell to pieces. As he approached the studio, driving through the winding rural lanes of the Berkshire countryside, a gaunt, quiffed figure cycled towards him in the opposite direction. 'That was my first memory of making Kill Uncle,' says Nevin. 'Driving to the studio and seeing Morrissey go past on a pushbike. He looked just like he did in that Smiths video ['I STARTED SOMETHING I COULDN'T FINISH']. It was like somebody up there was taking the piss.'

Kill Uncle was the beginning of a period lasting a little under a year in which Nevin became Morrissey's main co-writer, composing eight of its ten tracks and in doing so marking himself out as the obvious culprit (after the singer himself) for Morrissey's most critically derided album to date. In his defence, Nevin regrets that Morrissey's unorthodox writing methods – keeping words and music separate, with no eye-to-eye collaboration – prevented him from developing his tunes beyond their original rough sketches. 'I'd give him a demo thinking it was a base on which to build upwards,' explains Nevin, 'but we never did. He just used the bones of what I gave him. There was no discussion about how we might improve the music. It took me a while to get my head around that.'

Once Kill Uncle was finished, Nevin continued to submit material for future Morrissey records. Having accompanied the singer to the Camden Workers Social Club's regular rockabilly nights, his next commission was to write a batch of songs for a proposed mini album with a strong 50s rock and roll flavour. Out of that directive came 'THE LOOP', 'PREGNANT FOR THE LAST TIME', 'BORN TO HANG' and 'YOU'RE GONNA NEED SOMEONE ON YOUR SIDE'. Nevin would also join Langer on a reconnaissance mission to assess a young rocka-billy trio hoping to play on the sessions: Spencer COBRIN, Gary DAY and Alain WHYTE. The mini album never materialised, though 'Pregnant For The Last Time' was rescued as a stopgap single, followed by another Nevin song, 'MY LOVE LIFE'.

In the interim, Morrissey began planning his overdue return to the concert stage. The promo video for 'SING YOUR LIFE' offers a glimpse at the band line-up he originally envisaged, backed by the Cobrin, Day and Whyte trio but with Nevin as right-hand man and musical director. Nevin was more than willing to tour with Morrissey but was shackled by a clause in his original Fairground Attraction contract. Although the band had split, he still owed RCA one more album. Following Kill Uncle, he set about fulfilling that obligation, recording and touring unfinished Fairground Attraction songs with Irish singer Brian Kennedy under the name Sweetmouth. According to Nevin, he was contacted by acting manager Jo Slee to begin Morrissey tour rehearsals with only two days' notice. The Sweetmouth project made it impossible for him to commit. Further coercion was to follow from Morrissey's personal assistant Peter HOGG. 'I'd just come off stage in Glasgow with Sweetmouth,' says Nevin, 'and there was a phone call for me at the bar. It was Hogg. He was saying to me, "What the fuck are you doing up there? You could be playing Madison Square Gardens with Morrissey." I assumed Morrissey was there with him in the background.'

Bound by his RCA contract, Nevin's inability to join the tour resulted in Boz BOORER being recruited instead. Morrissey wrote to Nevin the following week: 'I'll press on then laddie, before Kill Uncle is all but buried like a dead cat. If I fall flat on my fat arse then at least the record shows I took the blows and did it my way, etc.' Nevin continued to submit music for the next album,

which Morrissey temporarily code-named 'Kill Auntie', and was also active in hiring its producer, Mick RONSON, after being assured that 11 of his new tunes were to be recorded. His suspicions were only aroused to the contrary when Boz Boorer rang Nevin asking to be taught the chords of one of the proposed tracks. An appointment was arranged at Nevin's house. When Boorer turned up, he brought with him a cassette of Morrissey's final track selection. Bar two of Nevin's demos, the rest were new instrumentals by Alain Whyte. 'I was furious,' says Nevin. 'I couldn't understand why he hadn't told me. So I rang Morrissey. Normally his phone went straight to a fax machine, but very unusually he picked up the receiver. I said, "Boz has been round. What the hell are all these songs? Why didn't you tell me?" It was the worst thing I could've done, because he just doesn't do confrontation. He could hardly speak. He just hung up.'

A week later, Nevin received a letter from Morrissey which offered something of an apology but no explanation. 'Kill Auntie', which became YOUR ARSENAL, continued without him, though relations between singer and guitarist were cordial enough for Nevin to visit the session for the recording of 'I KNOW IT'S GONNA HAPPEN SOMEDAY' (later covered by David BOWIE). The majority of Nevin's unused 'Kill Auntie' demos were subse-quently adapted for Kirsty MacColl's Titanic Days album and a handful of tracks with ex-Specials singer Terry Hall.

Nevin's contribution to the Morrissey canon is all too often underplayed by critics blinkered by the stigma surrounding Kill Uncle. In truth, his input, though slim, was significant. One look at the composer credits of 'Pregnant For The Last Time', 'The Loop' and 'You're Gonna Need Someone On Your Side' is evidence enough that Nevin was the one who developed the rockabilly template which relaunched Morrissey's live career, not Whyte or Boorer. Two of Morrissey's greatest ballads – 'I Know It's Gonna Happen Someday' and the sublime 'I'VE CHANGED MY PLEA TO GUILTY' – are also Nevin's handiwork. For these alone, his brief tenure during an intensely unstable period in Morrissey's career should be given its due recognition. [5, 15, 22, 25]

New York Dolls, The greatest single musical influence upon Morrissey, who over the years has named them his 'favourite musicians'; his 'primary influence'; the 'best group ever to come out of America'; 'the mafia of rock and roll', 'the official end of the 60s'; 'the real beginning for me'; 'the single most important group to me as an adolescent'; 'the world's most perfect pop group' and the band 'who completely destroyed and changed my life'.

As he'd elaborate, 'the New York Dolls were my private "Heartbreak Hotel" in the sense that they were as important to me as Elvis PRESLEY was important to the entire language of rock and roll. They were my only friends. I firmly believed that. I knew those people intimately. I knew everything about their lives. Of course, I really didn't, but in my own sheltered way I certainly thought I did.'

i) The original New York Dolls and the death of Billy Murcia, Five young, straight, shaggy-maned Bowery bucks in lipstick, chiffon and stack heels, the New York Dolls applied the savagery of The Stooges to the bubblegum melodrama of The Shangri-Las. In doing so they created a new pop language, one of mystery girls, jet boys, hanging in powder rooms with Diana DORS and sexual intimacy with Frankenstein's monster.

'I was drawn to them because the songs were fantastic and at that point they were like a bolt out of hell,' explained Morrissey. 'They were the most peculiar thing that anybody had ever seen. They were very tough but they had this almost gender-less appearance and they absolutely did not care. They were very, very funny. The humour was in the interviews. They almost didn't care if they were successful. The name of the group alone just sounded so incredibly important.'

'We were a totally revolutionary way to play rock and roll,' says Dolls frontman David Johansen. 'The real deal, not manufactured. We played rock and roll music and made it look like rock and roll music as well. With the clothes, it wasn't really considered drag. We were kind of lost souls. We took male and female and made this kind of third choice. It wasn't like we were trying to be girls. We were trying to mix and match, y'know? It was, "Look at me, I'm masculine, and I'm feminine."'

'We were stealing our girlfriends' make-up to get more girlfriends,' adds Sylvain Mizrahi, alias Sylvain Sylvain, the guitarist who christened the group after a local toy repair centre, the New York Dolls Hospital. Sylvain laid the foundations of the band at the tail end of 1970 after early rehearsals with his childhood best friend Billy Murcia (drums) and a Keith Richards wannabe guitarist from Queens named Johnny Genzale. Twelve months later, after various personnel shuffles including the recruitment of bassist Arthur 'Killer' Kane, then Johansen, and following Genzale's rebirth as Johnny Thunders, the Dolls were ready.

Come the summer of 1972, they'd already attracted a local following – 'freaks and weirdos the same as us,' said Kane – after landing a regular Tuesday-night spot at the Mercer Arts Centre, a recently converted disused hotel on lower Broadway. It was there, in the Mercer's Oscar WILDE Room, that the Dolls first caught the attention of A&R man Marty Thau. 'I've said this before, but that first night I saw them I couldn't decide if they were the best band I'd ever seen or the worst band I'd ever seen,' says Thau. Deciding they were the former, a few weeks later he became their manager.

Thau wasn't the only influential witness at the Oscar Wilde Room. Roy Hollingworth, the New York correspondent for *Melody Maker*, could barely contain his enthusiasm for what he'd describe as 'the best new young band I've ever seen' in a full-page feature which appeared in the paper's 22 July edition. This blessing from the UK couldn't have come soon enough for the Dolls, already beginning to despair at the hostile conservatism of the US music industry.

'It was very much a homophobic reaction in the US,' says Thau. 'They took one look at them, the way they were dressed, and they were scared. The

n

record company chief executives, the head honchos, they all thought the Dolls were gonna corrupt the whole industry.'

Among such hostility, the Dolls still managed to attract the esteemed admiration of David BOWIE when his Ziggy Stardust tour hit New York in late September 1972. The week after the Dolls saw him play Carnegie Hall, Bowie came to see them in the Oscar Wilde Room. It was Johansen's performance that night which, allegedly, inspired the lyrics of 'Watch That Man' from 1973's Aladdin Sane. Legend has it that after the show, Billy Murcia and Cyrinda Foxe (Johansen's wife-to-be, also rumoured to be the muse of Bowie's 'The Jean Genie') were lured back to the luxury hotel suite Bowie shared with his wife, Angie, only to emerge 48 hours later somewhat the worse for wear. The Dolls also granted their thin white guest a neighbourhood tour of their native Bowery district until a passing truck driver leered 'I want to eat your cunt!' At which point Bowie, not unreasonably, demanded their limo retreat to safety forthwith.

Propelled by the *Melody Maker* article, Thau arranged a UK tour with the ulterior motive of securing a record deal through British A&R representatives. And so, in October 1972, the Dolls crash-landed on to an unsuspecting British music scene then preoccupied with the glam of Bowie, BOLAN and Slade. 'England absolutely hated the New York Dolls,' commented Morrissey. 'They thought they were the most absurd rock creation ever. They considered them to be clamorous transsexuals, which of course was not acceptable, and which of course they weren't anyway.'

Fate decreed the Dolls would play only five shows that visit, including the biggest of their career on 29 October at London's 8,000-capacity Wembley Empire Pool as part of the Wembley Festival of Music. The following week, on the evening of 4 November, they were due to open for fellow New Yorker Lou REED at the Liverpool Stadium. Unfortunately, the Dolls never got the chance. For reasons he never explained, Reed dispatched a lackey to deliver the bombshell that if the Dolls went on, he wouldn't. The devastated

Dolls consoled themselves with a steak dinner and the prospect of their next gig supporting ROXY MUSIC at the Hardrock theatre in Stretford, Manchester the following week.

In the meantime, with five days to kill, they returned to London and the temporary home of their South Kensington hotel. On the evening of 7 November, Billy Murcia went to a party by himself; the other Dolls were too exhausted to join him. They'd later be awoken with the news that Murcia was dead. 'It was purely accidental and poor judgement on the part of the people whose party he attended,' muses Thau. 'It seemed that he had mixed drugs with alcohol and he'd passed out so they put him in a cold bath and tried to pour hot coffee down his throat. Billy choked on his own regurgitations.'

Unaware of Murcia's death, two days later the 13-year-old Morrissey was hoping to catch his first glimpse of the Dolls opening for Roxy Music at the Hardrock. 'I was at the front, waiting for them to come on stage,' he'd recall, 'but instead I was faced with somebody who announced that the gig was cancelled due to the death of the drummer. That was a terrible experience. Everybody wept. I still have the ticket.'

ii) The New York Dolls album: 'The most perfect piece of pop presentation',

Returning to New York, the Dolls hired experienced club drummer Jerry Nolan. Though still grieving for Murcia, the Dolls sought solace in Nolan's superior musicianship, tethering their furious trashabilly to a leaner, tighter backbeat. The elusive record contract followed when Thau brokered a deal with Mercury in March 1973.

The next hurdle was finding a producer. Among their first choices were Bowie and Wizzard's Roy Wood. Both proved unavailable though Bowie, at least, went on to pay further homage to the Dolls on another Aladdin Sane track, 'Time', with its mention of 'Billy dolls' in reference to the recently deceased Murcia.

Instead, they settled on singer/songwriter Todd Rundgren. 'Their references were very local,' says Rundgren. 'Like on "SUBWAY TRAIN", they wanted it to *sound* like the subway. They were very much true to their environment and what they sang about. They were authentic in that sense, but the problem was they were really green. I don't think anybody at their label knew how to even talk to them, despite the fact they got signed. I always felt there was always a germ of volatility about the New York Dolls that prevented them from getting very far.'

New York Dolls (1973), a never-to-be-repeated collision of 50s rock and roll, 60s bubblegum and 70s urban sleaze, ranks among the greatest debuts ever. In Morrissey's estimation, it's *the* greatest album ever. 'I think it still has no competition as the most perfect piece of pop presentation,' he surmised. From the opening mad dog howl of 'Personality Crisis' to their Manhattan-gothic masterpiece 'Frankenstein', the divine 'TRASH' and the jackhammer riff of 'Jet Boy', Rundgren managed to illuminate their brilliance without neutering their adorable disorder.

The Dolls returned to Europe in November 1973, almost exactly one year on from that doomed first visit. The tour began in London, playing two nights at Biba's department store on Kensington High Street (where Arthur Kane would be arrested for switching price tags on a jacket) before making a historic UK TV appearance on BBC2's *Old Grey Whistle Test*. Among those at home watching them perform 'Looking For A Kiss' and 'Jet Boy' was a 14-year-old Morrissey who'd been denied the chance to see them in the flesh 12 months earlier. 'I was 13 [*sic*],' he'd reminisce, 'and it was my first real emotional experience. The next day I was 29.' Dare we imagine the clunking depths to which the teenage Morrissey's jaw would have plummeted had he foreseen that, 30 years later, he'd be given the very white Vox Teardrop guitar Johnny Thunders played on that programme. In 2003 his new record company, Sanctuary, did just that: the guitar, signed by Sylvain Sylvain, can be seen on the sleeve of the live 'REDONDO BEACH' single.

'Being devoted to the Dolls ruined my education,' said Morrissey. 'I was thrown off the track and football teams at school for turning up to games in desperately self-designed Dolls T-shirts. The teachers were very worried and expected me to turn up for Maths in drag.'

After buying a copy of their debut album, Morrissey immediately began '[backing] my schoolbooks with pictures of the Dolls' and would later bring their records into art lessons in a vain attempt to convert his classmates. 'I made my teacher play a song so the whole class would listen,' he explained. 'Everyone got to say how they felt afterwards … and they didn't feel too well, I'm afraid. But that was my fault, I shouldn't have done it. That was 1974 in Manchester. I went to a rough school so it shouldn't have surprised anyone that there was an appalling silence afterwards during the break.' He'd also refer to a similar incident where he created 'a montage of Dolls photos' which so appalled the teacher 'that she burst into tears and passed it around to each boy in the class denouncing the sickness and depravity of the Dolls'.

While the young Morrissey was fruitlessly spreading their gospel in the corridors of St Mary's Secondary Modern, the Dolls were already on the road to inevitable ruin. On 23 November 1973 they played Leeds University. Morrissey wouldn't attend but some older friends did, spending the night with the band at the city's Dragonara Hotel and returning to taunt him with 'tales that witness madness'. Five days later, the Dolls left England for France where, at a routine press conference at Paris's Orly airport, Thunders vomited in full view of the media. According to Kane, the French were not amused. 'It created a lot of negativity in the papers. They just wrote us off as a bunch of transsexual junkies. But I don't think the world was ready for us. We weren't designed for the world. We just did what we wanted to do because we were like a teenage gang. To us it was Benny Hill in drag, y'know? It was a joke but no one got the joke. So it was the five of us against the world.'

'We didn't know what we were inventing,' agrees Sylvain. 'It all took natural form. It was so pure, so naïve. The New York Dolls were first in the horse race and running as fast as we could, man. Everyone was behind us. That's Blondie, Talking Heads, Kiss, Aerosmith, Lou Reed, all of 'em. But we were running so fast and living our lives in such a wild, trashy way that we fell and broke our legs. The others made it to the finishing line and collected their prize. We ended up losing the race.'

iii) Too Much, Too Soon and the end of the New York Dolls,
They returned to New York from their European campaign battle-fatigued from its excesses and more reviled by the mainstream media than ever before. The damage became painfully obvious when they returned to the studio in January 1974 to record a hastily assembled second album, named Too Much, Too Soon after the salacious biography of actress Diana Barrymore to whom the album was formally dedicated.[1]

With only a handful of new songs prepared, it was a pale shadow of its predecessor padded out with cover versions, including Morrissey's favourite '(There's Gonna Be A) Showdown', originally by Archie Bell & The Drells. When its intended producers, the legendary Brill Building writers LEIBER AND STOLLER, pulled out at the eleventh hour, Johansen's chosen substitute was former Shangri-Las producer Shadow Morton. Sadly, Johansen remains alone in thinking that the collaboration with Morton was 'a beautiful experience'. Aside from a few inspired moments – Thunders' sneering 'Chatterbox', old stage favourites 'Babylon' and 'HUMAN BEING' – Too Much, Too Soon was the sound of a group treading water on the brink of exhaustion, guided by an eccentric producer long past his prime who, as Sylvain notes, 'hadn't a fucking clue who we were'.

Forced back on the road by their record company, the Dolls' combined substance abuse was worsening daily. 'It really came down to drugs and alcohol,' says Thau. 'Out of five members of the group, two were very serious drug addicts – Johnny and Jerry. Arthur was an alcoholic. So that's 60 per cent of your group which you can't count on. It was bound to fail.'

Fail it did. When an exasperated Thau quit, in their desperate search for a managerial saviour they chose Malcolm McLaren. The future SEX PISTOLS svengali could do little to stop the inevitable plane crash, hopelessly steering them through their final 'Red Patent Leather' phase of scarlet PVC clothing and a Soviet hammer and sickle stage backdrop.[2] 'Now, first of all America didn't accept the Dolls for being gay or whatever they thought they were,' explains Sylvain. 'They didn't accept us for our music, they didn't accept us for their wildness. Now they're gonna accept us for *this* and the Vietnam War's still going on? If they didn't accept us as we were they were not gonna accept us being Communist.'

In May 1975 the Dolls finally fell apart on a disastrous trip to Florida. 'Johnny and Jerry were being supplied heroin by some kids down there,' explained Arthur Kane. 'One night these kids didn't show. So John and Jerry hit the ceiling and wanted to get on the plane back to New York to go get some fuckin' heroin. But by then I don't think they ever wanted to play with David again. So they left and formed The Heartbreakers, who were basically a band of junkies.'

There was nothing McLaren could do to prevent the premature departure of Thunders and Nolan, who upped and left with three gig commitments outstanding. Whatever their reason for quitting the band, their exit was the decree absolute and the bitter end of the New York Dolls.

iv) Morrissey, president of the New York Dolls fan club,
That the Dolls no longer existed was immaterial back in Manchester where the teenage Morrissey's crusade on their behalf had driven him to set up a UK fan club.

'They lived in New York, I lived in Manchester,' he'd explain. 'They hardly ever came to England so we never met and they never sent me any communications. I communicated with the secretary which wasn't quite the same thing but I didn't mind. It was just a great honour to do what I did in those days. It was the first real adventure that I ever had.'

Through personal ads in the music weeklies Morrissey began corresponding with other like-minded Dolls fans, among them London guitarist Mick Jones, yet to form The Clash, and friend/singer James MAKER. 'It was a very threadbare affair,' Morrissey would add, 'very rudimentary. I merely stuck a few stamps on an envelope one day. It wasn't very dramatic.'

The subject of the Dolls also dominated Morrissey's letters to the music press in the mid- to late 70s, praising their superiority to the emerging UK punk groups such as the Sex Pistols and denouncing pale American imitators such as Aerosmith for having 'as much to offer 70s rock as [CORONATION STREET's] Ena Sharples'. His passion for the Dolls could be surprisingly persuasive. On 20 November '76 the NME printed his letter demanding that the paper run a feature on the Dolls ('You know it makes sense'). A fortnight later, they obliged with a two-page retrospective in Roy Carr's 'Junkyard Angels' section. Carr began his sincere tribute declaring: 'The New York Dolls were the right band in the wrong place at the wrong time. It was as simple as that.'

Morrissey's later reminiscence that he 'was so fanatical about the Dolls to an almost unhealthy obsession' wasn't an exaggeration. Eyewitnesses remember him attending the second Pistols' Manchester Lesser Free Trade Hall concert on 20 July 1976 brandishing a copy of the Dolls' debut album under his arm. FACTORY Records founder and Granada television presenter Tony Wilson also received a 'battered copy of a New York Dolls album [from] a kid called Steve Morrissey' in early 1976 with a letter asking, 'Why can't we have more music like this, Mr Wilson?' At the time, Mr Wilson had never heard of the New York Dolls.

Although years later Morrissey claimed the ex-Dolls' 'solo permutations simply crushed whatever image I had of them as individuals', his letters to Sounds and the NME circa '77–'78 reveal an initial enthusiasm for both David Johansen's first eponymous solo album and Thunders and Nolan's new group, The Heartbreakers. Around the same period, his first musical dabblings with friends Steven POMFRET and Billy DUFFY as The Tee-Shirts, and later with Duffy in THE NOSEBLEEDS, also

betrayed his Dolls obsession, covering their unreleased 'Teenage News' (later featured on Sylvain Sylvain's eponymous 1979 solo album) and The Foundations' hit 'Build Me Up Buttercup' which had since become a Johansen live favourite.

Johansen's return as a solo artist, initially backed by Sylvain, also resulted in a couple of magazine features which had a notable impact upon the young Johnny Marr, specifically an April '78 Melody Maker interview by Stanley Mieses, 'The Last Doll Comes In From The Cold', and another from the NME in September '78 by Tony Parsons, 'Whatever Happened To Davie Doll?'. The latter is especially interesting in that it reiterates Johansen's love of THE MARVELETTES and Sandie SHAW, which may possibly have had some bearing upon Morrissey's fondness for both as later expressed in early Smiths interviews. 'David certainly changed my life,' he later admitted. 'Johnny Thunders did as well, but David was the one for me because he was so witty, really taking control of everything, and had a complete disregard for the American music industry.'

His obsession peaked with the 1981 book, The New York Dolls. 'It wasn't really a book,' he'd demurely explain. 'It was an extensive essay that was fortunately published by this small company in Manchester. But that was just motivated by the basic zest I felt personally for the Dolls.'

At a little over 6,000 words, Morrissey's essay was an impassioned résumé of the group's career. 'The Dolls became a derelict monument to devastated teenage America,' wrote Morrissey. 'They were directly representative of their generation's frustrations. They dressed ambisexually not as a political statement but simply to show that they at least had the ability to laugh at themselves.'

The book also included quotations culled from the vast archive of interviews he'd assembled over the years, among the most interesting being Johansen's discussion of blurring sexual stereotypes which Morrissey would dutifully honour in his own work. 'Kids are finding out that there isn't much difference between them sexually,' said Johansen. 'They're finding out that the sexual terms homosexual, bisexual, heterosexual, all those are just words in front of "sexual". People are just "sexual".' Morrissey dedicated the book to his friend 'Jimmy' (James Maker) who, in homage to Johansen, would later wear women's court shoes on stage during his brief appearances dancing with The Smiths. Morrissey would also mention his book in his pre-Smiths correspondence to Glasgow pen pal Robert MACKIE. 'I'd love to send you a copy,' he apologised, 'but I only have two myself.'

One of the most curious aspects of Morrissey's lifelong love of the Dolls was his uncharacteristic, Peter-like denial of their brilliance during early Smiths interviews. Perhaps in an effort to cut any ties with his pre-Smiths self, Morrissey dismissed his teenage obsession on a number of occasions in 1984. 'That was a horrible period and I hate the Dolls now,' he snapped. 'Five years ago I would have lain on the tracks for them. Now I could never *possibly* listen to one of their records.' He'd blame his over-enthusiasm on being 'laughably young', writing it off as 'just a phase' and 'not terribly important to me'. 'One day I just simply woke up and suddenly [the Dolls] didn't mean a thing to me,' he tried to explain. 'Which was quite frightening.'

Time would expose such renunciations as pure flannel. The Dolls would have a greater influence on The Smiths than Morrissey would care to admit at the time. Most significantly, it was because of Morrissey's reputation as a local Dolls fanatic that Marr was first alerted to his presence. 'We came together because of the New York Dolls,' concurs Marr. As The Smiths progressed, the Dolls would infiltrate both Morrissey's lyrics – 'THERE IS A LIGHT THAT NEVER GOES OUT' with its citation from 'Lonely Planet Boy' – and Marr's music; the closing guitar riff of 'SWEET AND TENDER HOOLIGAN' was a loose homage to 'Jet Boy'.

Morrissey's subsequent descriptions of the Dolls as pop's ultimate outsiders would echo his own estimation of The Smiths. 'I wanted them to become the biggest band in the world,' he confessed. 'I simply couldn't understand why they weren't. All their songs sounded like hit singles and they were incredibly funny. Plus they looked incredibly good. What could possibly have stopped them? But times were heavy in England at that time, more or less since 1967. Today of course we are used to the spandex of heavy metal and big fluffy hair, but at that time is was basically illegal for a man to walk down a street dressed like a woman, and because of that the New York Dolls were very revolutionary.'

Morrissey fully re-embraced the Dolls after the break-up of The Smiths, slowly integrating their mythology into his solo career. The cryptic message etched into the run-out-groove of 1988's one-sided etched 'INTERESTING DRUG' 12 inch – 'What kind of man reads *Denim Delinquent?*' – was an obscure Dolls reference. The phrase had originally appeared on the back cover of issue three of cult 70s US fanzine *Denim Delinquent*, accompanying a shot of Johansen in a dressing room with an arrow pointing to a discarded copy of issue one on the table behind him.

When touring KILL UNCLE in 1991, Morrissey performed his first Dolls cover, 'Trash'. On 4 November that year he played the song before honoured guests Sylvain Sylvain and Arthur Kane at Santa Monica Civic Auditorium. 'We met him backstage afterwards and he was really sweet,' says Sylvain. Morrissey had previously met Thunders and Nolan ('completely unfriendly') prior to their separate deaths after years of drug damage. Thunders died in suspicious circumstances in New Orleans on 23 April 1991, aged 38. Nolan died 14 January 1992, aged 45, after suffering a stroke which put him into a coma from which he never recovered.

It wasn't until the late 90s that Morrissey finally crossed paths with Johansen – 'the final Doll I hadn't met' – though he found him surprisingly cagey on the subject of his old group. 'He was very pleasant to me,' said Morrissey, '[but] he seemed weary of talking about that time and those two albums. And of course, because I'd had all these questions burning inside of me for the past 40 years, they all just splurged out. He kept saying, "Well, it was so long ago."'

v) The 2004 reunion and the death of Arthur Kane,

By the beginning of the millennium, the likelihood of the Dolls ever re-forming seemed incredibly slim. Thunders and Nolan were dead. Sylvain had played in various groups since the Dolls, from The Criminals to The Ugly Americans (with Nolan) but was now touring with his own Sylvain Sylvain band. Johansen had reinvented himself many times: as pseudonymous lounge act Buster Poindexter; a character actor in films such as *Scrooged* and *Married To The Mob*; and finally a backwater bluesman with The Harry Smiths. But most dramatic of all was the fate of Arthur Kane. When the Dolls broke up in 1975, his problems with alcohol intensified. In 1989 he fell out of a window, shattering his kneecaps. Three years later he was beaten with a baseball bat during the LA riots and hospitalised for 12 months. Now working in a Los Angeles library, he was sober but, by his own admission, still 'far from over the Dolls.'

These were their circumstances in the winter of 2003 when this author first contacted the ex-Dolls for a magazine article. Johansen's attitude to the Dolls' legacy tallied with Morrissey's previous comments about his uncomfortable wariness. 'I don't want my grave to say, "Here lies the singer with the New York Dolls,"' he told me.

I later repeated his comment to Sylvain. 'Well, that does hurt me if Johansen said that,' Sylvain reacted, 'because, don't forget, that's what it says on Billy Murcia's grave. "The drummer with the New York Dolls." But Johansen's got things to work out, I don't know. As far as Arthur is concerned, he should not shed one more tear of bitterness over Johansen and just get out there and fucking work.'

Arthur Kane was a gentle soul but, as Sylvain hinted, one who harboured profound pain over the break-up of the Dolls and was unforgiving in his scorn towards Johansen. Even so, he still insisted, 'the final chapter is yet to come'.

At the time, I genuinely didn't believe such a chapter was possible. Nor, perhaps, did Morrissey, but when asked to curate a bill for his June 2004 MELTDOWN festival in London, he achieved the extraordinary. Having already asked Johansen to open for his five-day residency at New York's Harlem Apollo Theatre in early May 2004, he went one further by persuading Johansen to reunite with Sylvain and Kane and resurrect the Dolls. 'People had told me they'd tried to get the surviving Dolls back together for years and they'd never ever, ever do it,' he modestly explained. 'I made one call to David Johansen at his home in upstate New York and he immediately said yes.'

The fragile bridge-building process, especially that between Kane and Johansen, would be documented in Greg Whiteley's 2005 film *New York Doll* which followed the bassist's life during the months leading up to their Meltdown reunion with added commentary from Morrissey, Chrissie HYNDE, Iggy Pop and Mick Jones. '[That] film, I think, greatly helped the Dolls' status because everyone who has seen the film loves it even if they hadn't much cared for the Dolls,' enthused Morrissey. 'I'm no good in the film because I felt too emotional and I could barely speak. But, me aside, it's so well done, and must be the best ever rock docu-film.'

With session player Steve Conte filling in for Johnny Thunders (after Morrissey failed to persuade Chrissie Hynde to join as 'Chrissie Thunders') and Gary Powell from The Libertines on drums, the New York Dolls played their first concert on Wednesday 16 June 2004 at London's Royal Festival Hall. 'As for Meltdown,' said Morrissey, 'that moment when David, Sylvain and Arthur trooped on – I was standing up in the balcony, frozen, unable to hold back the tears.' It was, indeed, an extraordinarily emotional night, not least when Johansen embraced Kane on stage and the bassist's mouth curled in a childlike smile. Morrissey's weren't the only tears of joy.

Two days later, on Friday 18 June, they played the same venue, Johansen now struggling without his hefty lyric book which had 'gone missing' after Wednesday's show. This second gig would form the ATTACK RECORDS live CD and DVD Morrissey Presents The Return Of The New York Dolls – Live From Royal Festival Hall 2004.

n

The following week, I emailed Arthur Kane to tell him how much I'd enjoyed that first Meltdown show. This is his unedited reply, received on Friday 25 June 2004: 'Dear Simon. If you had some fun watching us New York Dolls have fun also, then the equation is complete! Rock band plus audience = FUN! Please keep in touch for any reason. I hope to meet up with you some time in the future. I did meet up with Nina Antonia, which was great! Cheers, LUV, ak.'

Nina Antonia was the author of the first, and best, in-depth biography of the group, *Too Much Too Soon*, who'd kindly put me in touch with Kane in the first place. And it was Nina who, less than a fortnight later, texted me with the news that Kane was dead. In the interim he'd returned to Los Angeles where, on 13 July, he checked himself into hospital believing he had flu. He was diagnosed with leukaemia and died two hours later. But what at first seemed a cruel twist of fate was, for Kane, a Hollywood ending. He lived to see out his final chapter, completing his life's equation. Thanks to Morrissey.

Johansen and Sylvain would continue the Dolls, replacing the irreplaceable Kane with ex-Hanoi Rocks bassist Sami Yaffa. In 2006, the New York Dolls released their first album in 32 years, One Day It Will Please Us To Remember Even This, featuring cameos from Michael STIPE and Iggy Pop. Morrissey was also asked to contribute but refused because 'I'm not from New York and I'm not a Doll and I know my place … if nothing else'.

Following 1991's 'Trash' and his 2004 live excerpt from 'Subway Train', in 2006 Morrissey released his first studio recording of a Dolls cover with the B-side 'Human Being', subsequently played on the RINGLEADER OF THE TORMENTORS tour. Performing the song in Greenock, he'd tell his audience, 'I realise over the years I've New York Dolled people to death. But I can't actually help it. I can't help it!'

The older Morrissey gets, the more his love of the Dolls seems to intensify. As he admits, the boy can't help it. [17, 19, 23, 47, 56, 69, 95, 97, 104, 111, 136, 139, 141, 169, 199, 204, 231, 245, 247, 267, 277, 334, 343, 357, 408, 414, 423, 436, 448, 457, 463]

---

1. Morrissey was later photographed with a copy of the original *Too Much, Too Soon* book for *Spin* magazine in 2004.
2. It was Johansen's girlfriend Cyrinda Foxe, not McLaren, who persuaded the group to adopt the Soviet flag which she made herself. 'She was really into the Red motif,' explained Johansen. 'We had Chairman Mao posters hanging around the pad and she showed me what great productions the Communists create and suggested we apply it to the Dolls.'

Newley, Anthony, Cockney actor, singer and songwriter whom Morrissey has repeatedly referenced since the mid-1990s, most prominently with the opening 'glorious defeat' sample on 'MALADJUSTED', originally spoken by Newley in the 1955 film *The Cockleshell Heroes*. A younger Newley can also be heard at the end of 'BILLY BUDD' as sampled from one of Morrissey's favourite films, David Lean's OLIVER TWIST.

Beginning his film career in the late 40s, Hackney-born Newley was a contract player with the RANK Organisation until making a successful stab at pop stardom in 1959 with 'I've Waited So Long', the first of seven top ten hits on DECCA including the number ones 'Why' and 'Do You Mind'. The latter's B-side, 'Girls Were Made To Love And Kiss', was featured on Morrissey's concert interval tapes in 1997. Newley's comic rendition of the English folk standard 'Strawberry Fair' (with extra 'oojahs') was also featured on his 1999 tour interval tape while, in 2007, a rare clip of Newley singing 'I'm The Boy You Should Say "Yes" To' was added to Morrissey's interval video montage.

Newley's distinctive gizzard-wobbling vocal style – exaggerating his Jewish Cockney twang and lapsing into spoken asides – was also a huge influence on the young David BOWIE, in particular Bowie's eponymous 1967 debut album. His last major chart success was another novelty disc, 1961's 'Pop Goes The Weasel' backed with 'Bee-Bom', a vocal version of the theme tune from his short-lived surrealist ATV television series *The*

Newport Pagnell, A popular service station on the M1 close to Milton Keynes where Morrissey loses his bag in The Smiths' 'IS IT REALLY SO STRANGE?' While it's very likely he'd have stopped there during his many travels between London and Manchester, it may also be a reference to the Shelagh DELANEY-scripted 1967 film *Charlie Bubbles* in which Albert FINNEY meets YOOTHA JOYCE in Newport Pagnell services' café. Morrissey's fondness for service stations greatly amused the late John PEEL, who remembered bumping into the singer at another motorway café just south of Newcastle. 'I saw him and I was like, "Oh! Hello!"' said Peel. 'And Morrissey said, "This is my favourite motorway service station." I thought it extraordinary that *anybody*, particularly Morrissey, could have a favourite motorway service station.' [26, 491]

Strange World Of Gurney Slade (also 'valued' by Morrissey according to journalist acquaintance Len BROWN).

Though synonymous with comedy pop, at heart Newley was a serious crooner. A case in point is his 1964 album of lonesome ballads *In My Solitude*, later reissued as *The Lonely World Of Anthony Newley* in a sleeve depicting the dejected singer in Mozzerian pose clutching a drooping posy of flowers. Arguably his greatest successes were as a writer rather than performer; the lyricist of several hits by Shirley BASSEY (including 'Goldfinger') and Nina Simone ('Feeling Good'). The year after his cameo on 'Maladjusted', in May 1998 Newley presented Morrissey with his Ivor Novello award for Outstanding Contribution To British Music and was duly thanked in the singer's acceptance speech. Already ill with cancer, Newley died less than 12 months later in April 1999, aged 67. [68, 290, 493, 537]

Nicholson, Viv, Notoriously ill-fated 1961

pools winner, cover star of The Smiths' 'HEAVEN KNOWS I'M MISERABLE NOW' single and the promotional/import single 'BARBARISM BEGINS AT HOME'. Both sleeve images appeared in Nicholson's 1977 autobiography *Spend, Spend, Spend*, a favourite of Morrissey's. The same book also offers a possible source for a lyric from 'STILL ILL'. At the beginning of Chapter Eight, Nicholson writes about her courtship with her second husband, Keith: 'We walked for miles ... right over the iron bridge and down underneath it on to the tow path. We were

kissing away and touching and getting really sore lips from biting one another.'

In 1961, Nicholson was a 21-year-old, twice-married mother-of-three making ends meet on her husband's £7-a-week trainee miner's wage in a poor terrace house in Castleford, West Yorkshire. A chance win on the football pools suddenly transformed her and husband Keith into millionaires. Asked by a reporter what she intended to do with her winnings, Nicholson remarked, 'I'm going to spend, spend, spend, that's what I'm going to do.' True to her word, she squandered her fortune as her fairy tale slowly became a tragedy. After Keith died in a car crash – the cover of 'Heaven Knows' shows her outside her childhood home after his death – she went from one disastrous relationship to another, remarrying another four times while struggling with alcoholism, bankruptcy and a brief spell in a mental home.

'I have always admired Viv Nicholson,' explained Morrissey, 'because of her background and the way she fought against her background of total poverty and practical destitution – her whole story of winning the pools and her husband dying and the disasters that followed and the way that the newspaper tabloids haunted her and tried to drag her down and decry her as an individual. But constantly through the face of this disaster she had a remarkable resilience, fortitude, humour and a great sense of living which I think is quite rare.'

Prior to using her image on a Smiths sleeve, Morrissey first referred to Nicholson in his 1983 *NME* list of 'symbolists'. After she gave her permission for the 'Heaven Knows' sleeve, Morrissey thanked Nicholson on the credits of MEAT IS MURDER, also listing her as one of his heroes in the accompanying 1985 UK tour programme, the cover of which featured the same 'Barbarism' still of Nicholson stood with her suitcase outside a pithead before going to Malta on a late spending spree. According to Nicholson, she and Morrissey first met on Blackpool seafront where they joked about getting married and the singer declared, 'We're too much for this world at the moment. They're not ready for us, Viv.' Morrissey was much less complimentary about their subsequent meeting filmed for 1987's *South Bank Show* Smiths documentary, describing Nicholson as 'a beautiful woman' but regretting the encounter as 'very awkward' and 'like some curious Polish play'.

In 1988, ROUGH TRADE issued a CD single of 'THE HEADMASTER RITUAL' featuring another still of Nicholson sat in front of a painting easel. To the label's surprise, Nicholson – now a Jehovah's Witness – objected to the 'spineless bastards' lyric in the song and requested the sleeve be withdrawn. By the mid-90s, whatever friendship Morrissey and Nicholson had cultivated was firmly in the past. 'He does excommunicate people,' Nicholson later reflected, 'but you've got to learn to be forgiving and I don't think he wants to.' In 1999, Morrissey was asked if he was tempted by the musical of Nicholson's life, also called *Spend, Spend, Spend*. 'Yes,' he replied. 'I'm tempted to avoid it.' [71, 168, 184, 191, 221, 346, 374, 468]

Nico, Beautiful, distant, doom-voiced Valkyrie and one of Morrissey's main musical influences. 'Her voice equalled the sound of a body being thrown out of a window,' stated Morrissey, 'entirely without hope, of this world, or the next, or the previous.' Though commonly mentioned in the same breath as The Velvet Underground, it's Nico's post-Velvets work that Morrissey most admires, specifically the albums Chelsea Girl (1967), Desertshore (1970) and The End (1974), which he's named either individually or collectively

on several occasions as his favourite album(s) of all time.

She was born Christa Paffgen in Cologne, Germany, on 16 October 1938: Nico was a nickname later given to her by gay fashion photographer Herbert Tobias after his ex-boyfriend, Nico Papatakis. Her father was a Nazi conscript who was brain damaged in active service then sent to a concentration camp, where he was 'terminated' when she was only four years old. Her mother, too, would eventually die in similarly tragic circumstances, sectioned to a mental asylum, riddled with cancer. More distressing still, after the war, while living with her grandfather in Berlin, Nico was raped by a US Air Force sergeant who was subsequently tried and executed: future lover Lou REED later referred to this event in 'The Kids' on 1973's Berlin.

At 15, she escaped Germany, embarking on a successful career as a fashion model, turning up in Federico Fellini's *La Dolce Vita* (1960) and briefly entertaining ambitions as a professional actress. Moving to Paris, in 1962 she had a son, Ari, by actor Alain DELON, also starring in Jacques Poitrenaud's *Strip-Tease* (1963). One of her first recordings was a version of the latter's title theme written by Serge GAINSBOURG but unreleased until after her death. Another dalliance with THE ROLLING STONES' Brian Jones brought her to the attention of the group's manager, Andrew Loog Oldham, who paired her with guitarist Jimmy Page for a single on his Immediate label. Although 1965's 'I'm Not Sayin''/'The Last Mile' wasn't a hit, it began her accidental stagger towards a singing career. Further encouragement came from Bob Dylan, whom she met after moving to New York. Providing her with the song 'I'll Keep It With Mine' (featured on Chelsea Girl), Dylan also introduced her to the city's bohemian social elite, among them Andy Warhol.

It was Warhol's idea to 'add' Nico to his existing group, The Velvet Underground. After much initial protestation, both principal singer/songwriter Lou Reed and co-founder John Cale were convinced that her raw, Dietrich-esque vocals and icy Aryan beauty would be an asset to the band both musically and visually. Reed showed willingness by composing a handful of tailor-made songs such as 'Femme Fatale' as he and Nico became embroiled in a brief yet doomed affair marked by physical and psychological cruelty: when recording 'I'll Be Your Mirror' for 1966's debut album The Velvet Underground And Nico, Reed bullied Nico to tears in the studio prior to taping her finished vocal. John Cale would also have a short and torrid fling with Nico though, unlike Reed, their working relationship would outlast the Velvets' brief lifespan. 'She was much more ready to adopt new ideas,' said Cale. 'She had a thirst for it. I don't think particularly that she and I got along any better than anybody else in the band. They all thought that she was a little bit of a fly in the ointment.'

In 1967, with tension in the Velvet Underground camp increasing, Nico took up a solo residency downstairs at New York's Dom club. She asked Reed if he'd provide backing. He refused, instead recommending she sing along to a cassette of him playing guitar. After struggling with this proto-karaoke set-up for the first few nights, she eventually sought help from Cale and Velvets guitarist Sterling Morrison, as well as Tim Buckley and Jackson Browne. Nico was technically still 'in' The Velvet Underground when she began recording her second album and solo debut, Chelsea Girl. Half of its tracks were written by the group, including the Reed/Morrison title song and its improvised centrepiece, 'It Was A Pleasure Then', the first to credit Nico as co-composer. 'Everybody in the band was really involved in contributing to Chelsea Girl,' explained Cale, 'but the record label didn't really want The Velvet Underground. They wanted Nico. They thought they had a better chance of selling records with Nico as a blonde bombshell than they did with four irascible individuals trying to make noisy, cacophonous music.'

Nico's label, MGM, may have thought they had a new star in the making but Chelsea Girl sold poorly and the label dropped her. The album itself was a great personal disappointment, not because of the songs – almost entirely authored by ex-lovers – so much as the Greenwich Village folk gloss administered by Dylan producer Tom Wilson. As Reed would later comment with characteristic brusqueness, 'It was a pity about the idiot who produced the album and put all those strings in.' Morrissey would disagree, later including 'Somewhere There's A Feather', one of three Jackson Browne songs on the album, on his concert interval tapes in 2006.

Her dissatisfaction with Chelsea Girl followed her exit from The Velvet Underground and coincided both with her transition from platinum-blonde ice maiden to brunette banshee and the discovery of the harmonium which radically altered the course of her career. According to Cale, the pedal-powered reed instrument was the influence of another of her famous lovers, Leonard Cohen, as well as her 'interest in the exotic'. In the harmonium's atonal drones Nico found an odd but comfortable platform for musical self-expression which she'd been denied by the bitter experience of Chelsea Girl. It was on her third album and first for Elektra, 1968's The Marble Index, that this, the real sound of Nico, was unleashed: a bleak pumping misery which would define her music for the last two decades of her life. (Regarded by most critics as her defining avant-garde masterpiece, strangely Morrissey has yet to specify The Marble Index as a favourite Nico album, though he has included its stand-out track, 'Frozen Borderline', on concert interval tapes.)

While the heart of The Marble Index was all Nico's, the presence of Cale as arranger and uncredited co-producer was critical. Having also recently left the Velvets following a protracted spat with Reed, Cale and Nico shared a common bond, despite fighting at every opportunity. 'On every record we did, you could count on that happening,' Cale lamented. 'But you've got to remember that on those solo albums she was really in pain. Then afterwards she'd burst into tears of gratitude. It's that whole thing of self-loathing and the discovery of your personality.' Cale graduated to producer for her next record, 1970's Desertshore, an album Morrissey loved enough to send a photocopy of its cover to pen pal Robert MACKIE circa 1980, frequently quoting it in his correspondence. 'Such a refined record,' he enthused to Mackie, naming his favourite track as 'All That Is My Own' which over 20 years later he'd include on his 2003 UNDER THE INFLUENCE compilation. Even heavier on harmonium gloom than The Marble Index, Desertshore nevertheless contained as much light as shadow on 'My Only Child' and the vulnerable piano ballad 'Afraid': picturing the late-adolescent Morrissey in his Stretford bedroom listening to the latter's 'You are beautiful and you are alone' is enough to explain his profound connection to Nico. As he'd explain, 'I was enormously comforted by her isolation and depression.'

1974's The End completed her loose post-Chelsea Girl trilogy, once again produced by Cale and featuring contributions from Brian ENO and ROXY MUSIC guitarist Phil Manzanera. The former provided the electronic seagull massacre book-ending 'Innocent And Vain', a song Morrissey once described as 'my youth in one piece of music'. From the mid-90s until 2002, 'Innocent And Vain' was also the last song on Morrissey's concert interval tapes prior to his stage entrance music. The album's title track was an especially sombre cover of The Doors' song in tribute to Jim Morrison, another former lover and also the subject of The End's 'You Forget To Answer', the last song Nico would ever play live, also included on Morrissey's interval tapes in 2000.

The End was itself an end of sorts: Nico's last album for another seven years and certainly the last classic Nico record. By the late 70s, the heroin habit which had snowballed since the mid-60s had become the be-all and end-all of her increasingly pitiful existence. Booked to support SIOUXSIE And The Banshees on a UK tour in the winter of 1978, she dropped out after two shows due to hostile audience reception. The year 1981 witnessed a tentative foray into post-punk, Drama Of Exile, though unhappy with the finished mix she immediately re-recorded a second version issued on a rival label. Both were flawed, save for the mesmeric 'Sixty Four' and a version of BOWIE's '"Heroes"' which, though painful, is worthy of note since it was Nico's idiosyncratic belief that the song was written with her in mind.

By now Nico had relocated to Manchester, at one point living in the downstairs flat from Linder STERLING in Whalley Range. According to Sterling, Nico would wake up in the early afternoon and 'began her day with a tumbler half-filled with brandy'. The close proximity of Nico was an obvious thrill for the young Morrissey. 'I experienced Nico too,' he told Mackie. 'She's living nearby and can often be seen whirling about glamorous Manchester in a long black cape humming [Desertshore's] "Le Petit Chevalier".' Nico vacated the flat below Sterling still owing rent, though not before she gave Linder some sage musical advice: 'When you sing a high note you should imagine it falling to the floor and all low notes rising up.' Nico subsequently became involved with Salford punk poet and fellow addict, John Cooper Clarke.

The full junkie squalor of her twilight Manchester years and the recording of her final album, 1985's Camera Obscura, would be documented in Songs They Never Play On The Radio, a compulsive memoir by her keyboard player James Young. Despite being reunited with Cale as producer, Camera Obscura was little better than its predecessor save a rumbling, smoky take on Rodgers and Hart's 'My Funny Valentine' and the closing 'Koenig', a return to the austere harmonium distress of her early 70s creative peak.

Having dodged death by overdose for two decades or more, it was bitterly ironic that after weaning herself off heroin and moving to Ibiza to live with her son, Ari, Nico died in July 1988 from falling off a bicycle on her way to score some hashish. Though the fall wasn't fatal, it was hours before she received medical attention and she later died of a cerebral haemorrhage, alone in hospital aged 49. None of The Velvet Underground attended her funeral in Berlin's Grunewald Forest Cemetery that August, where her ashes were buried

'**Nightmare**' (**Morrissey/Cobrin**), Unreleased song from the 1997 B-side sessions following the MALADJUSTED album. According to its co-writer, Spencer Cobrin, 'Nightmare' was a 'great, rocking track' which never got beyond the rough demo stages. Its existence is verified by an ISLAND studio tape log (numbered #H36677). The lyrics are unknown.

On the subject of nightmares, Morrissey recalled his first, aged six, after watching an episode of ITV horror series *Mystery And Imagination* about lepers which haunted him 'for a very long time'. He also confessed that he suffered both nightmares and 'daymares'. 'I think it's a very neglected state of being,' he explained. 'I remember being on buses and having these horrible, dreadful thoughts during the day so they have to override nightmares at any rate. At least with nightmares you're in bed and you're relatively safe!' [4, 5, 217, 419]

next to those of her mother as Ari played a cassette of 'Mutterlein' from Desertshore. Translated from the original German, its lyrics offered the epitaph, 'Longing and loneliness/Are redeemed by inner peace.' [24, 111, 114, 168, 182, 217, 334, 380, 385, 401]

Night To Remember, A, 1958 British dramatisation of the *Titanic* disaster listed among Morrissey's favourite films. Kenneth More heads an ensemble cast as the ship's Second Officer Charles Lightoller who tries his best to suppress pandemonium as the crew and passengers of RMS *Titanic* come a cropper on its maiden transatlantic voyage of 14 April 1912. Cries of 'Iceberg! Dead ahead!' soon become 'Women and children first!' and eventually 'Abandon ship! Every man for himself!', though such are the number of stiff upper lips on board it's a wonder it sank at all. The mood is perfectly summed up during a scene in the turbine room not long after the crew have been told of the irreparable damage. 'If any of you feel like praying, you'd better go ahead,' says a chief engineer, 'the rest of you can join me for a cup of tea.' As in the real disaster, the story also paints a shameful portrait of class prejudice as the aristocratic elite save their skins while the poor and predominantly Irish steerage passengers are left to die. Adapted from the 1955 book by Walter Lord, *A Night To Remember* was based upon interviews with survivors, many of whom visited the set during the making of the film as well as offering technical advice. Directed by Roy Ward

Baker (responsible for other Morrissey favourites *THE OCTOBER MAN* and *FLAME IN THE STREETS*), its epic cast included Geoffrey Bayldon (star of early 70s children's show *Catweazle* who also makes a cameo in Marc BOLAN's *Born To Boogie* film) and Honor Blackman (*The Avengers*' Cathy Gale whose 1964 duet with Patrick Macnee, 'Kinky Boots', was later featured among Morrissey's concert interval music in 1991). [175]

NME (*New Musical Express*), Morrissey's relationship with what was once the most important music magazine in Britain began shortly after his 15th birthday in June 1974 when they printed the first of his many letters to the paper, praising SPARKS. His subsequent history with the *NME* is a tragicomedy unto itself. In the 1970s, they shunned his attempts to join their exclusive club as a freelance writer, barring him at the threshold of their letters page and the classified columns. Exacting the ultimate revenge, in the 1980s they lauded him as their pop saviour, the would-be critic having transformed himself into the object of their stupefied desire. In the 1990s, as if suddenly humiliated by their sycophancy, they would try to 'destroy' him. And in the 2000s they would beg him back on bended knee only to end their affair once and for all with an act of monumental dull-wittedness.

The *NME* that Morrissey first fell in love with during the 1970s was, as he'd describe, 'A propelling force that answered to no one. It led the way by the quality of its writers – Paul Morley, Julie Burchill, Paul Du Noyer, Charles Shaar Murray, Nick Kent, Ian Penman, Miles – who would write more words than the articles demanded, and whose views saved some of us, and who pulled us all away from the electrifying boredom of everything and anything that represented the industry. As a consequence the chanting believers of the *NME* could not bear to miss a single issue; the torrential fluency of its writers left almost no space between words, and the *NME* became a culture in itself, whereas *Melody Maker* or *Sounds* just didn't.'

NME writer and friend Cath Carroll, former 'manager' of Linder STERLING's group Ludus (who herself went on to record for FACTORY), conducted the paper's first interview with The Smiths, printed in May 1983 under the excruciating title 'Crisp tunes and salted lyrics'. Yet, to their shame, the *NME* were the last of the three main UK music weeklies to put the group on their cover (not until February 1984). Quick to compensate for their dilly-dallying thereafter, judging from The Smiths' dominance of their annual readers' polls they had little choice.

Undoubtedly, some of the best pieces of Smiths journalism were Morrissey's interviews with the *NME*, none more iconic than their edition circa THE QUEEN IS DEAD dated 7 June 1986 when its cover displayed only the paper's logo and a black-and-white photo of Morrissey, his eyes tinted blue; as legend has it, the rest of the intended cover type had 'fallen off' by accident. Although Morrissey accused the *NME* of having a hand in the end of The Smiths for being the first paper to print rumours of Marr's departure in the summer of 1987, he forgave them when his embryonic solo career resulted in coverage ubiquitous enough to coin the sarcastic nickname 'New Morrissey Express'. The honeymoon wasn't to last.

'The *NME* had become so obsessed with me that they then were embarrassed by it,' he later reflected. 'They decided to get rid of me … From being the New Morrissey Express, with me in it every other week, it had gone to the point when

they actively wanted to drive me out of their world. They had a board meeting and decided "Morrissey must go".'

i) The *NME* and the 1992 Madstock/Union Jack controversy, On Saturday 8 August 1992, Morrissey played Madstock, a two-day event in London's Finsbury Park organised by MADNESS to celebrate their reunion. The concert was only his third of that year in support of his new album, YOUR ARSENAL, and his first UK date in over 18 months.

The previous month he played two festivals in Europe, on both occasions waving a Union Jack on stage. He'd do the same at Madstock during the second song, 'GLAMOROUS GLUE', at the end of which he threw the flag into the audience. Within the crowd was a small faction who didn't take kindly to Morrissey, especially his chanted lyric 'London is dead'; bear in mind that the proud London Madness crowd were a notoriously irascible and expressive bunch who'd later score 4.5 on the Richter Scale that weekend moonstomping to 'One Step Beyond'.

As Morrissey's set progressed, they began throwing coins and beer at irregular intervals. Upset by this, he made the impromptu decision to cut his setlist, leading his band off stage after nine songs. Subsequent accounts of the event have been vastly sensationalised and it's a common mistake to believe Morrissey was bottled off stage as a direct consequence of parading the national flag around. In truth, after launching it into the crowd he continued for another seven songs. As amateur video footage shows, neither the flag, nor his backdrop of two SKINHEAD girls, nor even his setlist including 'THE NATIONAL FRONT DISCO' had anything to do with their hostile reaction.

'The main problem was there weren't that many Morrissey fans there,' explains Clive LANGER. 'Originally Madstock was just the Sunday, 9 August. When it sold out, they added the Saturday as an extra date. Morrissey was only advertised for the Sunday, but he agreed to do both dates. The irony was that Morrissey refused to do the second night, which was stupid of him because his fans turned up and he would have had a great time. Looking back, I'd say out of 30,000 Madness fans who were there, 29,000 of them were soft skinheads with their girlfriends and it was the other 1,000 hard skins who decided to let him have it. They just didn't want him.'

'It was just a few yobbos at the front,' recalls Spencer Cobrin. 'I was lucky that I could duck behind the cymbals. Quite a few coins were pinging off. Morrissey was very brave up there but it did feel very nervous. That's why it was cut short. I was still disappointed we never had the chance to do the second day.'

Langer, Madness singer Suggs and Cathal 'Chas Smash' SMYTH all tried in vain to talk Morrissey back for the second night to no avail. This, his cancellation of the Sunday night which the majority of his fans travelling to Madstock had bought tickets for, was the real 'drama'. It was only when the *NME* began to investigate the reasons *why* he cancelled that second-hand stories of that first night with its skinhead backdrops, Union Jacks and crowd aggro snowballed into Morrissey's equivalent Nuremberg Rally depicted two weeks later.[1]

Under the editorship of Danny Kelly, ironically a huge Smiths fan who'd conducted one of the *NME*'s best Morrissey interviews back in 1985, the 22 August edition cover pictured the singer on stage at Madstock holding a Union Jack. Headline: 'Flying the flag or flirting with disaster?' Inside, Kelly and writers Andrew Collins, Gavin Martin and Dele Fadele assessed the 'recent worrying developments' in Morrissey's career under the pun banners 'Caucasian Rut' and 'This Alarming Man'. Their concerns were not without some validity, particularly Fadele (significantly the *NME*'s only black writer) who concluded 'I don't think Morrissey is a racist' but still denounced his use of skinhead iconography as dangerously irresponsible. But, in doing so, the paper placed itself on a lofty moral high horse. 'In Europe in 1992, with "Ethnic Cleansing" a reality and the new Nazis on the rise across the continent, the need for clear thinking and clear statements is more acute than ever.' So trumpeted the politically passionate

NME, who until Madstock had the clear thought of putting Kylie Minogue on that week's cover.

'If the *NME* thought I really was racist, they wouldn't stick me on the cover,' Morrissey later argued, 'because groups who really are racist don't receive any attention in the media. I think it would be really irresponsible of the *NME*, or anybody who believed I was racist, to stick me all over the place and say he's racist because then I could capitalise upon it and get all these people to do all these fascinating things. I've never felt remotely racist and I don't think people ever believed I was. But the editor of the *NME* at that time wanted to get rid of me and they found something. I never responded to them so it went on and on and on.'

Morrissey's resilience not to be press-ganged into a response only added to the *NME*'s misplaced sense of justification. During the ensuing stalemate – a staggering 12 years before Morrissey spoke to them again – they went to desperate lengths to include him in their paper by any means necessary. By far the most farcical was in March 1994. Denied an interview to coincide with his number one victory of VAUXHALL AND I, they concocted a Morrissey cover story out of his two record signings at HMV stores in London and Manchester, sending undercover journalists to queue in line with fans in the hope of asking him a question. The first bottled it at the vital moment. The second was recognised by Morrissey who had security remove them.

Such shenanigans only emulsified the grudge match. For evidence of the paper's institutionalised prejudice against Morrissey, we need only look at the following year's *NME* review of his 'BOXERS' single. 'However much you try to be objective,' wrote that week's line-towing hack, 'any enjoyment of his records nowadays is tainted by the fact that a nasty taste from all those obnoxious, apologist, quasi-libertarian quotes still lingers. We will not forget, *mate*.'

With hindsight, the cruellest irony was that much of their post-Madstock witch hunt centred on his specific use of the Union Jack as an emblem of British nationalism. Only a few years later, the same flag was on Noel Gallagher's guitar and Geri Halliwell's dress: questions about 'flirting with disaster' in the *NME* were conspicuously unforthcoming. 'It has really got nothing to do with racism,' reasoned Morrissey, 'it is to do with *me*.'

Inevitably, Morrissey's late 90s creative slump was manna to the *NME*. When he fled to Los Angeles without a record contract at the end of the decade it was to the sound of popping champagne corks in King's Reach Tower toasting a battle won. The war, however, was far from over.

ii) The *NME* and the 2007 'immigration controversy',

In 2002, ten years after the Madstock affair, the *NME* celebrated its 50th anniversary with a poll ranking the artists who'd had the most influence *upon the paper's history*. The Smiths and solo Morrissey were joint number one. THE BEATLES came second.

It was the first of many olive branches which eventually coaxed Morrissey back on to their pages in 2004. No longer an 'alarming man', they christened him 'The Mozfather' for his first *NME* interview in over 12 years. The Union Jack incident was mentioned, but the 'grilling' was polite, the tone one of gracious excitement at the historic symbolism of the interview rather than any momentous exchanges in the conversation itself. Morrissey explained he'd agreed to speak to them because the paper was populated by 'a different breed' to 'the smelly old *NME*' who'd harangued him for most of the 90s. They, in turn, commemorated his return with a Morrissey-curated free cover-mount CD compilation, Songs To Save Your Life. It was as if Madstock had never happened. Until, three years later, it happened again.

In November 2007, Morrissey was interviewed in New York by an *NME* journalist for a forthcoming cover story. Originally, the intention was for the paper to give away a free vinyl single featuring his live cover of David BOWIE's 'DRIVE-IN SATURDAY'. Between the interview taking place and appearing in print, plans for the single fell through. Morrissey later claimed that during this period he'd also declined an offer to attend the

following year's hair-gel-sponsored *NME* awards show to receive a 'Godlike Genius' trophy.

During his interview, Morrissey brought up the ever contentious issue of UK immigration and the loss of 'British identity'. A second interview by phone was conducted a week or so later to clarify any misunderstanding. In the first (New York) interview, Morrissey commented, 'Other countries have held on to their basic identity, yet it seems to me that England was thrown away.' In the second (phone) interview, he referred to the UK's lax immigration controls as he perceived them: 'Because the gates are flooded. And anybody can have access to England and join in.' Both quotes were fudged together on the cover of the *NME*'s 1 December 2007 edition to read: 'The gates of England are flooded. The country's been thrown away.' Morrissey never said such a statement.

The article itself, headed 'Has the world changed or has he changed?' was altogether bizarre. In a first for the magazine, its by-line credited the original journalist with 'interview' but confusingly attributed 'words' to the faceless being of '*NME*' itself. Those 'words' spliced 'pertinent extracts' from the interviews with a kangaroo court prosecution adding together quotes from 'BENGALI IN PLATFORMS' (which they misdated as 1998) and 'The National Front Disco' to reach the predetermined conclusion that Morrissey spoke in the language 'of the crypto-fascist BNP'.

There were those who agreed, and still agree, that Morrissey's views on immigration are archaic and narrow-minded. But, regardless of anything he may or may not have said in the interview, the bias in its presentation was indisputable.

Morrissey's response was as swift as it was severe. The Monday following the magazine's publication, he issued an electrifying on-line riposte which began: 'On Friday of last week I issued writs against the *NME (New Musical Express)* and its editor … as I believe they have deliberately tried to characterise me as a racist in a recent interview I gave them in order to boost their dwindling circulation.'

Leaving no scope for ambiguity, Morrissey spelt out his abhorrence of racism ('beyond common sense and I believe it has no place in our society') before striking an authoritative body blow against 'the "new" *NME*' with a pithy summary of its cerebral erosion over the past three decades. His own hugely amusing account of the interview which took place was especially humiliating for the journalist, now a mere pawn in an ancient feud. 'When I first caught sight of him I assumed that someone had brought their child along to the interview,' Morrissey recounted. 'The runny nose told the whole story.'

At the time of writing, those 'writs' have yet to be resolved. Suffice to say, whatever the outcome, the chances of Morrissey ever granting the *NME* an interview in the near future seem marginally less than those of his endorsing face ever gracing packets of Mr Porky pork scratchings. Nor did it help the *NME*'s position when in April 2008 *The Word* magazine were forced to apologise to the singer in the High Court for making similar accusations in their review of his GREATEST HITS album. 'I am obviously delighted with this victory and the clearing of my name in public, where it is loud and clear for all to hear,' he told the press. 'The *NME* have calculatedly tried to damage my integrity and to label me as a racist in order to boost their diminishing circulation. *Word* magazine made the mistake of repeating those allegations, which they now accept are false and, as a result, have apologised in open court. I will now continue to pursue my legal action against the *NME* and its editor until they do the same.' [54, 55, 69, 71, 75, 98, 101, 114, 115, 124, 135, 142, 149, 153, 155, 170, 187, 192, 195, 206, 214, 403, 453]

----

1. The *NME* has long considered itself something of a fascist-finder general. Even PATTI SMITH found herself accused of 'Nazi Chic' by the paper in December 1976 for wearing a T-shirt of ROLLING STONE Brian Jones dressed in a German SS uniform.

'Nobody Loves Us' (Morrissey/Whyte), B-side

of 'DAGENHAM DAVE' (1995). Morrissey once called this 'a beautiful song [and] one of my best', an opinion shared by many who believe it should have been included on its parent album SOUTHPAW GRAMMAR rather than consigned to a B-side. Such is its stirring chorus of the disapproved that 'Nobody Loves Us' would have made a strong single in its own right (a hypothesis borne out by its melodic similarity to Whyte's later top 20 hit 'ALMA MATTERS'). Morrissey nominates himself group spokesman for a gaggle of social misfits, 'dab hands at trouble with four days of stubble', who wish only to be mollycoddled with cake, jam

'No One Can Hold A Candle To You' (James Maker/Phil Huish), B-side of 'I HAVE

FORGIVEN JESUS' (2004). It was magnanimous of Morrissey, to say the least, that when returning with YOU ARE THE QUARRY in 2004 he should choose to make this cover of a song by his old friend James MAKER an integral fixture of his setlists. The original was recorded in 1987 by Maker's band Raymonde, then being hyped as 'the new Smiths', and was the lead track on their only album, Babelogue (named after a track on PATTI SMITH's Easter). Morrissey had originally wanted to cover the song circa 1997 but 'something silly and messy [to do] with publishing and so forth' prevented him. Its liberating lyrics about cutting loose from a 'life among ruins' were ideal Morrissey material, likewise its uplifting chorus and the passing reference to 'Frankenstein', a knowing homage to his and Maker's bonding obsession with the NEW YORK DOLLS. He also changed the final line from Maker's 'Hiroshima? No, thanks' to 'Hiroshima? Yes, yes, yes!' As a soul-mate serenade, Morrissey's was a faithful copy of Raymonde's version if lacking its admittedly sparklier production. Fans were given a chance to compare for themselves when he included the original on the Songs To Save Your Life CD he compiled as an *NME* giveaway in June 2004. [16, 245, 422]

n

and motherly hugs. Reviving Gore Vidal's 'born-again atheist' concept previously used in 'BLACK-EYED SUSAN', the lyrics amounted to an anthem for his apostles: a romantic metaphor for their unswerving devotion – 'useless and shiftless … but we're all yours' – finding ironic unity through a shared belief in outsiderdom. [4, 40, 422]

'Noise Is The Best Revenge' (Morrissey/Boorer/Day), B-side of the live 'THERE IS A LIGHT THAT NEVER GOES OUT'/'REDONDO BEACH' double A-side single (2005). A twist on the maxim of seventeenth-century metaphysical poet George Herbert that 'living well is the best revenge' (with, maybe, just a sliver of BUZZCOCKS' 'Noise Annoys'), an exceptionally jaded Morrissey addresses a younger fan who insists on repeating the title slogan. There's a subtle throwback to 'LAST NIGHT I DREAMT THAT SOMEBODY LOVED ME' in his confession 'I've been hawking this song for too long', though more worrying was its mention of 'a Victorian legal system', evidence that even after the spleen-venting of YOU ARE THE QUARRY his preoccupation with the Smiths COURT CASE was now becoming a form of lyrical Tourettes. Recorded live for a Janice Long radio session in December 2004, 'Noise Is The Best Revenge' is hard to love on account of its damp BBC production which does nothing to enhance its belching ugliness and Morrissey's brake-screeching vocal hiccups, among his worst recorded singing performances. His nephew, Johnny Dwyer, clearly disagreed, borrowing the song title for the name of his own uncle-inspired indie group.

Nolan, Jerry, See NEW YORK DOLLS.

Nomi, Klaus, Opera singer from Outer Space (or so he appeared) whom Morrissey has hailed as one of his 'primary influences'.

He was born Klaus Sperber in Essen, Germany towards the end of the Second World War. As a child, Klaus was torn between his love of opera and rock and roll: after stealing money from his mother to buy a copy of Elvis PRESLEY's King Creole album, she took it back to the shop and exchanged it for a Maria Callas record instead. In the late 60s, he studied music in Berlin, earning his keep as an usher at the Deutsche Oper. By the age of 30 he was living in New York and working as a pastry chef, his operatic ambitions still unrealised.

It took the mid-70s punk explosion to create an unlikely opening for his extraordinary vocal talents. In October 1978, a new science fiction magazine was launched, *Omni*. Shuffling the letters around, Sperber created his new alias, Klaus Nomi, making his debut the following month at the 'New Wave Vaudeville' punk variety show at New York's Irving Plaza where he performed an aria from Saint-Saëns's *Samson And Delilah*. His marrow-rattling falsetto combined with his androgynous alien stage costume were an immediate hit with the hip young arts crowd. Before long, Nomi had his own band, performing a mix of arias, pop covers and new-wave originals within a stage show as much performance art as rock and roll.

His big break came in December 1979 after he and fellow performance artist Joey Arias were spotted by David BOWIE playing live mannequins in the window of Fiorucci's, the super chic New York fashion boutique with the atmosphere of a 'daytime disco' whose clientele included Jackie Onassis, Truman CAPOTE and Andy Warhol. Both would be hired by Bowie to join him as backing singers on NBC's *Saturday Night Live*, broadcast 5 January 1980. 'The Man Who Sold The World' began with Bowie encased in a triangular plastic tuxedo costume being carried by Nomi and Arias towards his microphone. During the song's finale, Nomi's high-pitched harmonies very nearly overshadowed those of Bowie himself. For 'TVC15', Bowie sang in a blue air hostess uniform, complete with pencil skirt, while behind him the geometric-haired Nomi pulled a toy poodle on wheels. If it was typical of Bowie's magpie guile that he should exploit Nomi as a visual accessory to accentuate his own art, it was equally magnanimous in exposing the as-yet-unsigned singer to a national audience.

'Nobody Loves Us'—Nosebleeds, The

The Bowie broadcast inspired Nomi to commission his own plastic tux as well as further developing his image as an other-worldly visitor, itself derivative of Bowie's Ziggy Stardust model. After being continually rejected by American record companies, Nomi settled for a European deal with RCA France. Controversially, his management dismissed his long-serving New York backing band led by his chief songwriter Kristian Hoffman, instead pairing Nomi with professional session musicians. He'd record just two albums, 1981's Klaus Nomi and 1982's Simple Man. By the latter, his health was already failing due to the onset of AIDS. In private, Nomi had led a desperately lonely life, 'a freak among freaks' according to one friend, forever failing to find love within New York's gay community. He died in August 1983, aged 39. Because of ignorance and fear over AIDS, a relatively new disease sensationalised in the media at the time as 'the gay cancer', few if any of his friends visited him on his deathbed.

Nomi has been one of the few artists whom Morrissey has consistently championed throughout his career. Intriguingly, his preferred Nomi recordings are all classical interpretations rather than his pop output. Nomi's haunting rendition of 'The Cold Song' from Henry Purcell's opera *King Arthur* was played as entrance music at The Smiths' debut concert at Mancheser's Ritz on 4 October 1982. 'Wayward Sisters', another Purcell piece from the opera *Dido And Aeneas*, was used as entrance music on his 1991 KILL UNCLE and 1992 YOUR ARSENAL tours and revived again in 2007. Robert Schumann's 'Der Nussbaum' ('The Nut Tree') heralded Morrissey's entrance on stage at his WOLVERHAMPTON gig in December 1988 and was included on subsequent interval tapes.

Morrissey's favourite Nomi record, and one of his favourite records of all time, is yet another Purcell aria, 'Death', first featured on 1982's Simple Man. In its original context 'Death' is the final scene in *Dido And Aeneas*: Dido, the Queen of Carthage, is heartbroken that her Trojan lover, Aeneas, has been tricked by the evil witches (the same 'Wayward Sisters') into leaving her to sail to Rome. As he departs, the inconsolable Dido kills herself, singing 'remember me, but forget my fate'.

Morrissey would praise Nomi's version of 'Death' on numerous occasions, including it as the final track on 2003's UNDER THE INFLUENCE compilation. 'Nomi sang like a man trapped in the body of a dead girl,' he wrote in the accompanying sleeve notes. '"Death" is his dying speech, after which he was – quite literally – led away to die, an early bull's eye for the AIDS machine gun. The words have a dreadful ring because they came true, and so soon: "remember me, remember me, but ah, forget my fate".' He may have found the song 'incredibly moving', but Morrissey wasn't beyond making mischief of 'Death'. Closing a concert in Seattle in February 2000, he bid farewell to the crowd by saying, 'In the words of the great Klaus Nomi, "Remember me, but forget my feet."' [74, 111, 168, 175, 267, 408, 533]

Nosebleeds, The, Manchester punk group, formerly Ed Banger And The Nosebleeds, whom Morrissey joined in early 1978. Although Morrissey has since disputed that he was ever in a group called 'The Nosebleeds', it was under that name that they performed two local gigs, one of which was reviewed by Paul Morley in the NME, the first time Morrissey was mentioned in print as a singer.

Hailing from Johnny Marr's Wythenshawe, the group started out under the name of Wild Ram only to transform themselves after singer Ed Garrity watched fellow Wythenshawe punks SLAUGHTER AND THE DOGS support the SEX PISTOLS at Manchester's Lesser Free Trade Hall on 20 June 1976. Garrity duly became Ed Banger and Wild Ram became The Nosebleeds. With a young Vini REILLY on guitar they released their first and only single in the summer of '77, 'Ain't Bin To No Music School', on the local Rabid Records label. After a handful of gigs down south, the group disbanded. Reilly went on to create The Durutti Column and become the first signing to FACTORY while Garrity persevered as Ed Banger before joining a later incarnation of his old pals Slaughter And The Dogs.

n

Meanwhile, in the summer of '77 Morrissey befriended Billy DUFFY, a young Wythenshawe guitarist and NEW YORK DOLLS fan. They'd briefly rehearsed with another guitarist, Steven POMFRET, calling themselves The Tee-Shirts, though never played any gigs. In early 1978, Duffy teamed up with Nosebleeds bassist Peter Crookes and drummer Philip Tomanov. In need of a singer, Duffy suggested Morrissey, based on his brief experience rehearsing together with Pomfret. Morrissey, currently sporting long dark hair in a vague approximation of Dolls singer David Johansen, duly joined The Nosebleeds circa February 1978 and would play two concerts with the group, both promoted using the Nosebleeds name. The first, supporting Slaughter And The Dogs and Jilted John at Manchester Polytechnic on 15 April 1978, marked Morrissey's stage debut. The second, supporting Howard DEVOTO's Magazine and John Cooper Clarke at Manchester's New Ritz on 8 May 1978 and billed as 'The Nose Bleeds', would be their final performance.

No recorded documentary evidence appears to have survived other than Morley's *NME* review of the latter gig in which Morrissey's all-important surname was sadly fudged. 'The Nosebleeds resurface boasting A Front Man With Charisma, always an advantage,' wrote Morley. 'Lead singer is now minor local legend Steve Morrisson, who, in his own way, is at least aware that rock and roll is about magic and inspiration. So The Nosebleeds are now a more obvious rock and roll group than they've ever been. Only their name can prevent them being this year's surprise.'

Ever the protector of his own mystique, Morrissey was reluctant to discuss his venture with The Nosebleeds when it later came to light during The Smiths. He'd describe his term with them as 'two weeks in 1979' as opposed to approximately three months in 1978 and later denied that he was ever a member. 'I wasn't in The Nosebleeds,' he explained, ignoring all printed evidence to the contrary with regard to their two concerts. 'Most people will say I was … I wrote songs with [Billy Duffy] and we tried these songs out with the rhythm section that had once belonged to The Nosebleeds. Because of that it seems that I was a member of The Nosebleeds.'

Morrissey would, however, divulge that he persuaded the group to cover The Velvelettes' Motown hit 'Needle In A Haystack'. 'These were four individuals who seemed in tune with this mode of thinking,' he recalled. 'It wasn't "camp

'Nothing Rhymed' (O'Sullivan), Cover of 70s Anglo-Irish singer-songwriter Gilbert O'Sullivan, played live by Morrissey during his two shows at Dublin's Ambassador Theatre on 2 and 3 October 2002. Born Raymond O'Sullivan (changing his forename as a crass pun on Victorian opera composers Gilbert *and* Sullivan), 'Nothing Rhymed' was his first UK hit, reaching number eight in December 1970. Dressed in cloth cap, waistcoat, braces and half-mast trousers, O'Sullivan looked as if he'd just fallen on to the piano out of a Lowry painting. Yet, beneath his gimmicky name and dress was a sharp and severely gifted lyricist. The melancholic if abstruse wordplay of 'Nothing Rhymed' was perfectly suited to Morrissey, although in choosing to cover the song whether by accident or design his rendition exposed its melodic similarity to his own Andy Rourke-penned B-side, 'YES, I AM BLIND'. Played exclusively on those two nights in Dublin and yet to be performed since, it's likely Morrissey was acknowledging O'Sullivan's Irish roots, even introducing himself onstage with the words 'I'm Gilbert O'Sullivan'. Nor is 'Nothing Rhymed' the only Mozzerian entry in O'Sullivan's catalogue. Perhaps not 'Ooh-Wakka-Doo-Wakka-Day' or the superbly titled 'January Git', but most definitely his 1972 top three hit and sole US number one 'Alone Again (Naturally)' which compresses suicidal intent, heartbreak, atheism and death into a contrastingly gentle and ingenious piano pop ballad.

surrealism" or "wackiness". It was pure intellectual devotion that made me want to do a song like that.' Thankfully, testimonies in THE SEVERED ALLIANCE give us a more detailed picture of Morrissey's earliest group. As well as covering 'Teenage News', an unrecorded Dolls song by guitarist Sylvain Sylvain which Morrissey could only have known at the time from a bootleg, and The Shangri-Las' 'Give Him A Great Big Kiss' (another Dolls favourite), there were at least four Morrissey/Duffy originals – 'I Get Nervous', 'The Living Jukebox', 'Peppermint Heaven' (during which Morrissey handed out peppermints to the audience) and '(I Think) I'm Ready For The Electric Chair'.

By the time Morley's review appeared in the NME, The Nosebleeds had disbanded. Duffy went on to join Slaughter And The Dogs whom Morrissey would allegedly consider joining in the latter half of 1978. [47, 139, 226, 340, 362, 423]

'November Spawned A Monster'

(**Morrissey/Langer**), Morrissey's sixth solo single released April 1990, highest UK chart position #12. A work of pop genius limping out of the leprous shadows of THE ELEPHANT MAN, Morrissey would cite this as 'a turning point' in his career, marking the first time since the end of The Smiths that he no longer 'missed' Marr with the realisation that, as a solo artist, he was finally 'in a better position'.

Examining society's condescension towards a severely disabled girl whose one ambition is to choose her own clothes, the lyrics owed a vague debt (which Morrissey openly admitted) to the NEW YORK DOLLS' 'Frankenstein' in which David Johansen asked 'is it a crime?' to fall in love with the title monster. Morrissey is similarly direct, asking if the listener dare kiss his wheelchair-bound subject 'full on the mouth, or anywhere'. In being so forthright the song was certain to divide opinion as to whether it was socially challenging or grossly insensitive; all but a couple of critics applauded his intentions as the former.

'It's a matter of understanding many extreme situations in life,' explained Morrissey. 'And if you

see someone in what we oddly refer to as an unfortunate situation, someone who's wheelchair bound, if you're very perceptive and sensitive you can fully imagine the lifelong frustrations of constantly being discussed by other people, and constantly having people being irritatingly kind to you.'

Built around Langer's nerve-jangling piano, its expressionistic mid-section was added later when the producer convinced Morrissey to expand the track, turning it into a five-minute Hammer Horror pop epic. It fell to Mary Margaret O'HARA – invited to the session at Hook End to perform on a separate track, 'HE KNOWS I'D LOVE TO SEE HIM' – to re-create the monster's actual spawning. Morrissey told O'Hara to 'just simply give birth' in the darkened recording booth. 'When she came out I think she felt bad that she'd done it,' says Langer, 'almost like it was a therapeutic release of something. She was emotionally drained but it helped the whole movie of that song fall into place. It was incredibly visual.' The resulting whinnies of umbilical agony were deemed so disturbing by daytime radio DJs and TOP OF THE POPS that both prematurely faded the single prior to the O'Hara sequence.

Regardless, Morrissey was so ecstatic about the finished track that he sent Langer a thank you postcard inscribed 'I am the happiest I could possibly be'. His pride is further demonstrated by its continued status as one of the longest surviving songs in his live career, as marked by the versions on LIVE IN DALLAS, BEETHOVEN WAS DEAF, WHO PUT THE 'M' IN MANCHESTER? and LIVE AT EARLS COURT. Also worthy of note is an alternate mix, still unreleased, titled 'November The 2nd' (coincidentally the birthday of co-producer Alan Winstanley) and its video by Tim Broad. The latter was shot in Death Valley, Nevada and witnesses an especially lean Morrissey humping various desert cacti and mistaking a bar of chocolate for a mouth organ. A re-coloured still from the 'November' video was later used for the cover of BONA DRAG. [15, 25, 70, 83, 138]

'Now I Am A Was' (**Morrissey/Cobrin**), B-side
of 'SATAN REJECTED MY SOUL' (1997). With a chorus

which incorporated Orson Welles's famous summary of his fall from grace in Hollywood – 'I started at the top and worked down' – 'Now I Am A Was' sounded like a self-conscious admission of defeat at a time when Morrissey's career seemed to have hit rocky ground towards the end of the 90s. The lyrics actually referred to his sorrowful status as an ex following the collapse of a recent relationship, blaming himself for his impossible behaviour which habitually made his partner unhappy. The song's subject was most probably the same partner referred to in a newspaper interview conducted around the same time. According to the *Guardian*'s Suzie Mackenzie, 'The relationship ended recently without his wanting it to. The other person stopped loving him, "as they do", and broke his heart. But he has got used to consoling himself, he says.'

The wispiest of Cobrin's Morrissey tunes, its rattling bass intro was very similar to the opening of 'Harley Davidson', a 1967 Brigitte BARDOT single written by Serge GAINSBOURG which Morrissey later included on his concert interval tapes. [5, 40, 152]

'Now My Heart Is Full' (Morrissey/ Boorer),

From the album VAUXHALL AND I (1994). 'This song was the definitive expression of my change to adulthood, of my maturity,' explained Morrissey. 'And, to be honest, I was very happy to be able to sing this text, to have reached this state. After this song I could perfectly retire.'

In its public declaration of private bliss, 'Now My Heart Is Full' implied that Morrissey had found, if not necessarily love, then an equally soul-nourishing inner happiness. The 'text', as he calls it, is poetry in its purest sense, a collage of oblique metaphors and disconnected cinematic references which he expressively weaves together to convey this spiritual rebirth. As he'd elaborate, '[it] has a sense of jubilant exhaustion with looking over one's shoulder all the time and draining one's reference points. I have perhaps overtapped my sources and now all that is over, basically. I have a vast record and video and tape collection, but I look at it now in a different light. It's no

longer something I feel I need to be embroiled in night and day. I have realised that the past is actually over, and it is a great relief to me.'

In bidding farewell to Morrissey's past, 'Now My Heart Is Full' offers a gracious salute to some of his British big-screen favourites, from Dallow, Spicer, Pinkie and Cubitt – characters from the 1947 film version of Graham Greene's *Brighton Rock* – to doomed actor Patric DOONAN, co-star of *The Blue Lamp* who later committed suicide. More obviously, the 'Stressford poet' is Morrissey himself, often reiterated in live performances with the more direct lyrical switch to 'Stretford poet' or 'Manchester poet'. There were echoes of other poets elsewhere in the song: the title had a ring of Stevie Smith's 'My Heart Was Full' while the phrase 'rush to danger' resonated with Australian poet Henry Lawson's 'At The Beating Of A Drum' from 1910; 'The glorious words and music from a lonely heart shall come/When our sons shall rush to danger at the beating of the drum.'[1]

Yet for all its lyrical mystery, the sheer torrent of joy he brings to his vocal needs no deciphering. In 'Now My Heart Is Full' we hear Morrissey alone in the cinema, the Saturday matinee all to himself, dancing naked down the aisles silhouetted in silver beam, becoming ever drunker on the screen's pure neon glow and deafened by the echo of his own Hallelujah chorus. The perfect opening overture to the predominantly introspective Vauxhall And I, its sentiment was matched by a tune which blinded with similar light. Such was the uncluttered simplicity of Boorer's original demo that when producer Steve LILLYWHITE came to re-record it in the studio the result fell far short of Morrissey's expectations. It therefore made sense to go back and build the track around the same demo, adding only minimal overdubs and some percussive passion from drummer Woodie TAYLOR. Even Boorer's demo bass line was left as it was.

Released as a single in America, the song was denied the same honour in the UK in favour of 'HOLD ON TO YOUR FRIENDS'. Due to its anthemic spirit and its popularity in concert as a reciprocal celebration of love between the singer and his audience, like its Vauxhall opposite, 'SPEEDWAY', 'Now My Heart Is Full' towers above much of his solo discography as one of Morrissey's most sacred creations. [4, 5, 6, 114, 159, 236, 487, 506]

———

1. Whatever its source, the latter term had been in Morrissey's vocabulary since the end of The Smiths when photographed by ROUGH TRADE press officer Pat Bellis holding up a torn page of Oscar WILDE's poem 'Requiescat' with 'rush to danger' written across the bottom.

'Nowhere Fast' (Morrissey/Marr), From the album MEAT IS MURDER (1985). Another likely Shelagh DELANEY reference – though a common enough phrase, the title appears in *The Lion In Love* – as with 'WILLIAM, IT WAS REALLY NOTHING', written during the same period, the subtly political 'Nowhere Fast' finds Morrissey shackled by a humdrum provincial environment; symbolically as confined by his surroundings as Johnny Cash in 'Folsom Prison Blues' and similarly tortured by the echo of nearby railway tracks and the dream of escape. The scenario also invites close comparison with The Jam's 'Town Called Malice'. Just as Paul Weller's is a decaying suburbia where '[peering] at

the kids' new gear' is a major event, Morrissey's townsfolk treat the most basic domestic gadgets 'like a new science'.

More significant is Morrissey's first lyrical attack on the royal family. Though his fantasy of dropping his trousers to the Queen was only a comical diversion from the main theme of small-town entrapment, 'Nowhere Fast' still became a catalyst to promote his views on the monarchy in interviews of the period, whetting appetites for his later masterpiece, 'THE QUEEN IS DEAD'.

A national anthem for the provincially shipwrecked, its pointed lyrics combined with Marr's equally forceful rockabilly twang (he'd later use the riff as an example of the influence of Elvis PRESLEY's original 50s mentor Sam Phillips) earmarked it as the intended follow-up single to 'William'. Though John PORTER produced an early version during the same session in July 1984, the result proved unsatisfactory. Admittedly, its eventual Meat Is Murder re-recording was a far craftier production, Morrissey's 'sad sound' of a passing train re-enacted in its middle eight of ricocheting drums clattering like a distant locomotive. [17, 27, 299, 425, 426, 477]

O'Hara, Mary Margaret, Canadian harpy and 'additional voice' on 1990's 'NOVEMBER SPAWNED A MONSTER' and 'HE KNOWS I'D LOVE TO SEE HIM'. Morrissey became a fan after hearing O'Hara's 1988 debut album Miss America, likening its impact to that of PATTI SMITH's Horses: 'I hadn't in a decade heard someone singing because of deep-set personal neurosis, absolute need and desperation. You'd think she might fall apart at any second and become a pile of rags and bones on stage.' O'Hara's woozy vocals and loose, semi-jazz arrangements were also loosely reminiscent of late 70s JONI MITCHELL.

Invited to the BONA DRAG sessions at Hook End, studio eyewitnesses variously describe O'Hara as 'like a trembling butterfly', 'pretty potty' and 'a nutcase'. Her own, equally odd, self-analysis was that of 'an ancient baby whose cranium never quite fused together'. Morrissey himself called her 'the oddest, most eccentric person I've ever met' and encouraged her to provide the notorious birth section (or 'scatty bits') on 'November Spawned A Monster', later joking that he'd stood behind her the whole time with 'a mop and bucket'. Prior to the single's release, he'd also confessed his fantasy to 'daydream off to Llandudno with Mary Margaret O'Hara' under 'Hopes' in a 1989 NME list. [1, 15, 25, 70, 138, 175]

O'Mara, George, Likely identity of the uncredited nude cover star of The Smiths' debut single 'HAND IN GLOVE'. The photo, initially thought to be by Jim French, was sourced from Margaret Walters's 1978 book *The Nude Male: A New Perspective* where it was captioned simply 'Nude study, 1970s'. In the book, Walters describes French's nude photography as 'a protest, and an important and valid one, against the unthinking assumption that beauty belongs only to women'. Unfortunately, subsequent research has revealed that the photo wasn't actually French's but that of his ex-partner, Lou Thomas of Target studios. Bodybuilder George O'Mara, a regular Thomas subject, is believed to be the model in the picture. As has also been noted, what appears on the record sleeve to be a large mole or birthmark on the right shoulder blade is actually a stain since it's absent from the original photograph as reproduced in Walters's book. [374, 391]

Ochs, Phil, Doomed, Texas-born protest singer,
first cited by Morrissey in a letter to the NME in 1977. Ochs's early work followed the guitar-and-harmonica Bob Dylan tradition until 1968 when he suffered first-hand police brutality during an anti-Vietnam war rally. His ensuing depression and disillusionment forced his writing into more bleakly introspective and politically cynical territory. Those unfamiliar with Ochs's sweet yet haunting voice should refer to the extraordinarily sad title track of 1969's Rehearsals For Retirement, the sleeve of which showed a facsimile of the singer's gravestone (a concept Morrissey himself adapted for a 1986 NME photoshoot). His next studio album in 1970, facetiously titled GREATEST HITS (though an unlikely stimulus for Morrissey's 2008 compilation), saw Ochs ditch his folk troubadour garbs for a gold lamé suit similar to that worn by Elvis PRESLEY. The same album included Ochs's heartfelt James DEAN tribute, 'Jim Dean Of Indiana'. To the horror of his early fans Ochs then took his gold Elvis suit on tour, further subjecting audiences to sets of classic rock and roll covers (including 'A FOOL SUCH AS I'). It proved career suicide and Ochs fell deeper into depression and drunkenness. His health worsened after being mugged on a trip to Africa in 1973 where his attackers permanently damaged his vocal cords, ensuring he would never sing again. Returning to New York, Ochs began showing signs of schizophrenia, assuming the alter-ego 'John Butler Train', before hanging himself in April 1976. His death, aged just 35, provoked a renewed interest in Ochs, and we can gather from his NME letter that Morrissey was listening to him within 18 months of his suicide. To date, Morrissey's only other direct nod to Ochs has been the inclusion of 'City Boy' (issued posthumously on the 1986 Rhino compilation A Toast To Those Who Are Gone) during the interval tape on his February 1995 UK tour. [206]

October Man, The, 1947 British thriller listed
among Morrissey's favourite films. John MILLS stars as a chemist mentally scarred by a bus crash which kills the child of a friend he was looking after on a daytrip. After a year recuperating in hospital with a fractured skull and its attendant psychological side-effects, he attempts to rebuild his life, taking lodgings in a hotel where he befriends and lends money to an impoverished, horoscope-obsessed lingerie model (Kay Walsh, as heard on Morrissey's 'LIFEGUARD SLEEPING, GIRL DROWNING'). When she's later found strangled on a nearby common with his crumpled cheque beside the body, Mills's medical history as 'a mental case' singles him out as prime suspect. The Hitchcockian plot sees him struggle to prove his innocence and finger the real killer while fighting his own post-traumatic suicidal tendencies. The film's title refers to Mills's character's birth sign of Libra: prior to her murder, Walsh tells him he's 'an October man' whereas she is 'June' (so probably GEMINI, the same as Morrissey). A great stiff-upper-lipped romp, The October Man was the directorial debut of Roy Ward Baker who'd go on to make two other Morrissey favourites, FLAME IN THE STREETS and A NIGHT TO REMEMBER. [227, 534]

'Oh Phoney' (Morrissey/Armstrong), Studio
outtake from the 1989 BONA DRAG album sessions. A poisonous missive to a 'phoney' fellow singer whose 'words spell out my name', Morrissey offers them the damning character comparison of making 'Hitler seem like a bus conductor' (a line which inadvertently brought to mind Führer-moustached Inspector Blakey from 70s sitcom On The Buses, a favourite of Morrissey's). As with 'PICCADILLY PALARE', Armstrong's tuneful gambol was given the piano-heavy 'MADNESS stamp' of producers LANGER and Winstanley. 'Oh Phoney' eventually fell by the wayside when the original Bona Drag album was cancelled and restructured as a stopgap singles compilation. [1, 15, 25]

'Oh Well, I'll Never Learn' (Morrissey/
Street), B-side of 'SUEDEHEAD' (1988). Composed

by Stephen Street as a deliberate pastiche of an early Lou REED/Velvet Underground ballad, its airy strumming and mock-Velvets tambourine shakes were complemented by Morrissey's similarly uncomplicated lyric, highlighting the title's self-critical resignation but concluding 'Why should I care?' An insignificant work, yet still worth savouring if only for the treacly warmth of Morrissey's vocal.

Old Dark House, The, 1932 Universal horror comedy listed by Morrissey as one of his favourite films. Based on a novel by J. B. Priestley (see AN INSPECTOR CALLS), the story is set in an unwelcoming mansion in the Welsh countryside, home to the extremely bizarre Femm dynasty. A violent rainstorm drives a group of travellers to seek emergency shelter under their roof (among them HOBSON'S CHOICE star Charles Laughton in his first Hollywood role) only for the Femms' full lunacy to unfold in the course of one short but sensational evening. Reuniting the director and star of the previous year's *Frankenstein* – James Whale and Boris Karloff as a psychopathic mute – *The Old Dark House* was only a moderate box-office success in its day but has since gained cult status.

Significantly, Morrissey named the film in his 1989 list extravaganza for the NME which also included Ernest Thesiger, who plays the especially ghoulish Horace Femm, among his favourite 'Odd fellows'. The term doesn't quite do justice to the marvellously peculiar Thesiger, a skeletal, sprite-like English stage actor, painter,[1] friend of Noël COWARD and master sewer who celebrated his needlecraft skills in a book, *Adventures In Embroidery*. Thesiger would work once more with Whale on 1935's *Bride Of Frankenstein*, cast as the preposterously queer, preposterously mad Doctor Pretorius, before returning to England. Among his later films was the 1951 Ealing comedy *The Man In The White Suit* with Alec GUINNESS and Patric DOONAN. [175, 377, 528, 536]

---

1. Besides being a painter himself, Thesiger was the subject of an early portrait by Morrissey's favourite artist Hannah GLUCKSTEIN.

Oliver Twist, 1948 David Lean adaptation of Charles DICKENS's famous novel which Morrissey once named as his joint favourite film alongside the Ealing drama I BELIEVE IN YOU. It also contains the 'Don't leave us in the dark' sample heard at the end of 1994's 'BILLY BUDD'. Morrissey's use of the *Oliver Twist* clip coincided with his rediscovery of Dickens in the early 90s; he'd read the original novel the year prior to recording VAUXHALL AND I. Though Lean's film isn't a wholly accurate interpretation, merging some sub-plots and characters to save time, it's still one of the best cinematic translations of one of Dickens's most popular stories, following an orphan boy's adventure from misery and starvation in the parish workhouse to the grimy Victorian London underworld of petty thieves and kind-hearted prostitutes. The film starred several Morrissey favourites including Anthony NEWLEY (The Artful Dodger), Alec GUINNESS (Fagin) and an early cameo from Diana DORS as, in her words, 'the slutty little maid in the coffin maker's shop'. When asked in 2006 which director he preferred, 'David Lean or David Lynch?', Morrissey answered 'Lean', quoting Guinness's cry at the climax of the film when Fagin is apprehended by the vigilante mob: 'What right have you to butcher me?' [170, 207, 237, 302, 303,537]

'On The Streets I Ran' (Morrissey/Tobias), From the album RINGLEADER OF THE TORMENTORS (2006). A harsh look into the mirror of his past, Morrissey contemplates his northern working-class roots and his own mortality, strangely begging forgiveness for having made a career out of 'turning sickness into popular song' and haunted by the vivid memories of the streets he left behind laying claim to the 'real' him; an effective jab perhaps aimed at certain factions within the Manchester media who frequently maligned the singer for having left the city for London, then Los Angeles. Things then become more hysterical after a fortune teller predicts he'll die on a particular Thursday, instigating a frantic and selfish prayer to God to take 'anyone ... people from

'One Day Goodbye Will Be Farewell' (Morrissey/Boorer), From the album YEARS OF REFUSAL (2009). A brilliantly Byronic bluster about the constant threat of sudden death, 'One Day Goodbye Will Be Farewell' was Morrissey's equivalent 'carpe diem'; a humanitarian plea to love now, die later. Gleefully looking forward to his due place in hell, his closing demand to be grabbed 'while we still have the time' though clearly a very literal request aimed at one particular individual, was an equally symbolic appeal to his audience to embrace rather than criticise him while he's still in the land of the living. Among the first Refusal tracks to be previewed in concert (as early as September 2007, nearly 18 months before its release), Boorer's swashbuckling tune and the galloping-horseman drums of Matt WALKER were the perfect staging for Morrissey's grimly great soothsaying.

Pittsburgh, Pennsylvania' rather than himself. Asked if the song meant he often thought about death, Morrissey admitted it did. 'It's going to happen,' he said. 'That particular second on a Thursday like many others.' Despite flashes of humour and a fine histrionic finish, the tune was another typically glutinous dollop of Tobias macaroni, his only contribution to Ringleader not to be released as a single. [159, 213]

'Operation, The' (Morrissey/Whyte), From the album SOUTHPAW GRAMMAR (1995). Sharing its title with an unrelated poem by Anne SEXTON, 'The Operation' read like an exasperated memo to a former love now in a permanently altered state, its words carrying the strong scent of autobiography in its tattoo-sick embarrassment. Lyrical coherence mattered little within its epic structure, a seven-minute triptych of rhythmic thunder, hiccupping punk pop and screaming blue murder (its closing bawls of chaos not Morrissey but Whyte, recorded shouting through his guitar pick-up). There was a palpable sense of musicianly joy in its manic finale, while Spencer COBRIN's drum prologue allowed him a rare opportunity to hog the limelight. 'They wanted a Keith Moon type solo,' says Cobrin, though the result, spliced together from various takes, was more Sandy Nelson in passion and patter. His tom tom seizure was imbedded with overdubs of the whole band and studio team running back and forth in the studio car park, as well as the sound of assistant engineer Tom Elmhirst doing handbrake turns in

a Range Rover. Cobrin never had the chance to perform his solo in concert since 'The Operation' was always played minus its opening as part of a medley with 'DAGENHAM DAVE'. Morrissey would, however, use Cobrin's same two-minute drum intro as his stage entrance music for his 1997 concerts promoting MALADJUSTED, and again when touring in 1999. [4, 5, 40, 368]

Orchestrazia Ardwick, Fictitious 'string and saxophone' players on the album credits of STRANGEWAYS, HERE WE COME. Repeating a gag first established with the HATED SALFORD ENSEMBLE of THE QUEEN IS DEAD, Orchestrazia Ardwick is Morrissey's spoof pseudonym for Johnny Marr who played the relevant synthetic sounds using an Emulator keyboard. The word 'Orchestrazia' doesn't exist in any language (its closest root is 'Orchestrazione', Italian for orchestration). Ardwick is the area south of Manchester city centre where Marr spent his childhood. [17, 38]

'Ordinary Boys, The' (Morrissey/Street), From the album VIVA HATE (1988). Morrissey's serenade to those, like himself, unafraid to stand apart from the rest of shepherded society. Originally titled 'Ordinary Boys, Ordinary Girls', as much as it lauded courageous individualism, the overall lyrical sentiment betrayed a streak of arrogance in its résumé of 'empty fools' in 'supermarket clothes'. In 1979, Paul Weller had tackled the same subject on The Jam's 'Saturday Kids' from a much more sympathetic but no less indignant

311

perspective, blaming not the ordinary boys themselves but 'the system' that contained them. By comparison, Morrissey's stance was much more condescending towards those who thought themselves 'lucky' for having their lives 'mapped out before them'. 'I envy their sense of freedom,' he explained by way of recompense. 'They don't need to use their imagination all that much, they act upon impulse, and that's very enviable.'

Stephen Street intended the tune as a 'big piano ballad' and came close to succeeding, adding some pizzicato string samples and using his trademark 'infinite reverb' effect to resurrect something of the spirit of The Smiths' 'THAT JOKE ISN'T FUNNY ANYMORE' towards the climax. The dramatic ending with an irregular change of key would also be repeated on 'WILL NEVER MARRY'. Prior to its inclusion on Viva Hate, the song was 'accidentally' leaked on mispressings of the 'SUEDEHEAD' 12-inch and cassette. 'The Ordinary Boys' would later christen a flash-in-the-pan indie mod group who supported Morrissey during his 2004 MELTDOWN festival. Their lead singer, Samuel Preston, mimicked Morrissey by referring to himself only by his surname and later appeared in the 2006 series of Channel 4's *Celebrity Big Brother* with Pete BURNS. [25, 39, 272]

'Oscillate Wildly' (Morrissey/Marr), B-side of 'HOW SOON IS NOW?' (1985). The first, and best, of three Smiths instrumentals. Though written by Marr, the song's publishing is officially registered to the group's usual joint composer credit, presumably because the title was coined by Morrissey: not, as commonly suspected, a pun on the name of Oscar WILDE but taken from Molly Haskell's *FROM REVERENCE TO RAPE* where she uses the term to describe 'films like MR SKEFFINGTON [which] oscillate wildly in mood'.

Surprisingly, the concept of a vocal-free Smiths track came from Morrissey rather than Marr. 'I suggested that "Oscillate Wildly" should be an instrumental,' the singer revealed. 'Up until that point Johnny had very little interest in non-vocal tracks ... I totally approved but, obviously, I

didn't physically contribute.' As Marr verifies, 'There was never any plan for it to have lyrics. It was always going to be an instrumental and Morrissey encouraged me all the way.'

The tune was 'the first thing' Marr wrote on an old upright piano which he had recently inherited with the purchase of his new home in Bowdon, outside Manchester, at the end of 1984. Although he had previously experimented with piano on early versions of 'SUFFER LITTLE CHILDREN', 'Oscillate Wildly' was the first Smiths track to use it as a lead instrument. Recorded in one evening, it marked a major progression in Marr's sense of arrangement. Hinting at the grander, semi-orchestral Smiths epics to come (specifically 'THERE IS A LIGHT THAT NEVER GOES OUT' written approximately eight months later), its central piano theme was enhanced by cello (played by Rourke), synthetic woodwind (created on an Emulator keyboard) and atmospheric guitar surges achieved via clever reverb trickery courtesy of engineer Stephen STREET.

The fact that 'Oscillate Wildly' managed to epitomise the distinctive spirit of the group through melody alone says much for Marr's contribution to their core 'melancholic aesthetic' commonly attributed to Morrissey's lyrics. Even without his partner's words it still conveyed a wintry walk home under blackening skies, the distant moan of thunder and the onset of twilight drizzle; a theme tune for everyday life in SMITHDOM. Unlike the later guitar-driven instrumentals 'MONEY CHANGES EVERYTHING' and 'THE DRAIZE TRAIN', The Smiths would never perform 'Oscillate Wildly' in concert. [17, 38, 71, 326]

'Ouija Board, Ouija Board' (Morrissey/Street), Morrissey's fifth solo single, released November 1989, highest UK chart position #18. His much maligned paranormal pop novelty, 'Ouija Board, Ouija Board' was possessed by the spirits of early 60s death discs; perhaps even a distant echo of John Leyton's 'JOHNNY REMEMBER ME' with its voices from beyond the grave (and whose author, Geoff Goddard, and producer, Joe

Meek, were, coincidentally, both ouija board practitioners).

Morrissey's séance on a wet afternoon took his lovelorn isolation to comically absurd extremes. Trying to contact a deceased female friend via a ouija board, her spirit abruptly tells him to 'P-U-S-H O-F-F': not even the dead, it seems, have time for the perennially lonely singer. Despite its farcical punchline, the lyrics may have been more autobiographical than their levity disguised. In particular, it's worth speculating if the 'dear friend' Morrissey yearns to contact is the same friend, a girl of 21, who killed herself when the singer was in his teens (see SUICIDE). Also of note is his use of the word 'carnivores' when describing those who comprise 'this unhappy planet', a subtle but lucid reiteration of his vegetarian ethics.

The tune followed on from Street's earlier 'SUCH A LITTLE THING MAKES SUCH A BIG DIFFERENCE', based on a similar arpeggiated piano riff reminiscent of early 70s SPARKS. Interestingly, both Street and the single's eventual producer Clive LANGER would refer to it as being in the same vein as early Brian ENO circa 1973's Here Come The Warm Jets, suggesting that Morrissey, as an Eno fan, may have briefed both accordingly as to the mood he wanted to create.

The song's recording was altogether fraught. Since the ongoing post-VIVA HATE financial wrangle between Morrissey and Street had yet to be resolved to the latter's satisfaction, the producer refused to commit to the session, already booked at Hook End Manor, the residential Berkshire studio then owned by Langer and his partner, Alan Winstanley. The latter duo stepped in as emergency replacements, trying to piece 'Ouija Board' together from Street's original piano demo, in the process lending the tune something of their own trademark 'MADNESS stamp'. Dissatisfied with their first attempts, Morrissey very nearly cancelled the session and, according to Langer, would have done had it not been for his and Winstanley's work on its B-side, 'YES, I AM BLIND', which impressed Morrissey enough to persevere and finish 'Ouija Board' with them.

More intriguing is the recollection of guitarist Kevin ARMSTRONG that during the session Morrissey organised a proper ouija board séance. 'Hook End was meant to be haunted so it was a spooky place anyway,' says Armstrong. 'There was one time Morrissey played ouija board and things did happen. Just like in the song. The glass moved, the table rumbled. He was genuinely interested in all that spiritualism stuff.'

For all its ingenuity, 'Ouija Board' was savaged by the press. By only reaching number 18 it broke the post-Smiths honeymoon spell of his previous four solo top ten hits and was generally regarded as a flop. With hindsight, it's very obvious that 'Ouija Board' was the victim of musical fashion. Significantly, it charted the same week as The Stone Roses' 'Fools Gold' and Happy Mondays' 'Hallelujah', the definitive sounds of the new Manchester. Immediately, and for the first time in his career, Morrissey now represented the old Manchester, and with 'Ouija Board' he couldn't have chosen a more unapologetically archaic pop vehicle had he tried. Ironically, had 'INTERESTING DRUG' been released that same week instead, its infectious dance beat and Ecstasy-alluding title would doubtless have been embraced within the spirit of baggy 'Madchester'. Doubly ironic, 'Ouija Board' session pianist Steve Hopkins had previously played with Happy Mondays.

Nevertheless, the single's bad reviews deeply wounded Morrissey. 'I do think the backlash has been slightly overdone,' he mourned. According to those involved such as Langer and Armstrong, the perceived public hanging of 'Ouija Board' had a lasting and detrimental effect on Morrissey's confidence, so much so he eventually abandoned plans for the original BONA DRAG studio album. 'I still think "Ouija Board" is a great song,' laments Langer. 'We tried to make it as simple as possible but it was the Happy Mondays days. Everything had a dance beat. It was slammed everywhere. But, a funny thing, many years later I saw Johnny Marr and he told me how much he liked "Ouija Board". That was really nice.'

O

No doubt as a consequence of its poor press reception, Morrissey shied away from playing 'Ouija Board' in concert until 2002; prior to that, he'd only incorporated a teasing snippet of its signature riff as an intro to 'NOVEMBER SPAWNED A MONSTER' (as heard on BEETHOVEN WAS DEAF).

Brushing aside its critical drubbing, 'Ouija Board' can at least boast having the best Morrissey promo video in terms of plot, his attempts at 'acting' and not least his exquisitely groomed quiff and sideboards. Directed by his friend Tim Broad, it was filmed at Hook End itself and featured cameos from CARRY ON star Joan Sims as a medium and a young Kathy Burke as the impish spirit she conjures forth. Burke, a huge Morrissey fan, would later win multiple awards, including Best Actress at the 1997 Cannes Film Festival, for her stunning performance in Gary Oldman's brutal south London drama *Nil By Mouth*, a film Morrissey claimed to have spent 'two weeks watching non-stop'. [1, 15, 25, 39, 70, 138, 152, 191]

'Our Frank' (Morrissey/Nevin), Morrissey's eighth solo single (from the album KILL UNCLE), released February 1991, highest UK chart position #26. Acknowledging its title wordplay where 'Frank' is an adjective not a name, Morrissey noted how 'most people would initially think that it would be about a person, a member of the family, which obviously it isn't'. Such a phrase crops up in the script of THE FAMILY WAY: 'Our Frank could hardly face his dad next morning.'

The first track recorded for the Kill Uncle sessions, 'Our Frank' was also the first time Mark Nevin heard Morrissey's lyrics with his music. During its initial live run-through, its comical chorus about vomiting on knitwear reduced the guitarist to tears of laughter as he was playing.

'Myself and Bedders [bassist Mark Bedford] were cracking up,' says Nevin. 'But afterwards we were a bit nervous in case Morrissey thought we were laughing *at* him, not with him.' Typically, the singer never identified the song's addressee by name, explaining the nucleus of the song as his exhaustion with 'wearing' friends intent on deep and meaningful chats about human existence. 'The conclusion that I finally come to about the state of the world [is] that the world *is* ending,' said Morrissey. 'We are in the debris [but] you just have to get on with it.'

In the hands of producers LANGER and Winstanley, Nevin's stylish 'Our Frank' assumed a piano-driven briskness not unlike their previous (and similarly titled) 1982 MADNESS hit, 'Our House'. Sadly, Morrissey's song wasn't nearly as successful, becoming his first solo single not to make the UK top 20 and setting a precedent for a rarely broken run of near misses charting in the lower twenties and thirties for the rest of the decade. More controversial was its rarely seen video directed by John Maybury, who'd previously worked on Derek Jarman's Smiths promos, featuring the singer miming in chiaroscuro intercut with scenes of a SKINHEAD gang running amok near London's King's Cross. 'So awful,' according to Morrissey, 'that we tried to hide it.' [15, 22, 25, 243, 437, 502]

Oye Esteban!, Mexican for 'Hey Steven!', the title of an American DVD compilation of Morrissey promos released through Reprise in October 2000. 'Oye Esteban!' had previously been used as the name of his world tour from October 1999 to April 2000. The DVD features most (but not all) of his official videos from 1988's 'SUEDEHEAD' to 1995's 'SUNNY', including the rare 'SEASICK, YET STILL DOCKED' promo.

'Paint A Vulgar Picture' (Morrissey/Marr),
From the album STRANGEWAYS, HERE WE COME
(1987). A Smithdom state burial for pop murdered
by big business, its vulgar picture was that of a
soulless Pottersville where corpses set cash registers ringing and fans are mere suckers, duped by
the marketing of 'tacky badges' and the endless
repackaging of old rope sold as new.

Originally, the song placed greater emphasis on
the dead star with an extra verse later scrubbed in
favour of Marr's guitar solo: 'Anecdotes and
stories/"Oh yes, we were so close, you know"/So
why did the body lie for seven days/Before someone passed his way?' The same first draft also
contained a nod to TWINKLE's 1964 death disc
'Terry' ('It's too late to tell him how great he really
was') as well as the signature line 'and so they
paint a vulgar picture of the way they say that
you were'. The lyrics also drew from Janis IAN's
1973 ode to the music business, 'Stars', with its
portrayal of fans 'that followed as you walked
and asked for autographs' as well as Morrissey's
previous writing on the NEW YORK DOLLS. In his
1981 book on the group, he described a fan
throwing themselves at singer David Johansen
after a gig in LA's Whisky a Go Go: 'A very young
girl clutched David's arm and pleaded, "Take me
with you pl-eeaasse, wherever you're going …"'

Given The Smiths' recent troubles with ROUGH
TRADE at the time of recording and their imminent
move to EMI, it was reasonable to assume its inci-
sive critique of the music industry was Morrissey's
thinly veiled attack on the former. 'It wasn't about
Rough Trade at all,' he retorted. 'So I was a bit
confused when Geoff Travis, the Rough Trade big
boy, despised it and stamped on it. It was about
the music industry in general, about practically
anybody who's died and left behind that frenetic
fanatical legacy which sends people scrambling,
[like] Billy FURY, Marc BOLAN.'

As much as Morrissey refuted accusations,
'Paint A Vulgar Picture' contained obvious autobiographical parallels with The Smiths' career: the
lyrical repetition of a previous song title, 'YOU JUST
HAVEN'T EARNED IT YET, BABY', famously attributed

to Geoff Travis; the pressure to 'please' institutions such as the BBC (whom Morrissey had once shunned by not turning up for a performance on *Wogan* in July 1985), MTV (taking into account his vocal criticism of pop videos) and the BPI (later 'Brit') Awards which he repeatedly insulted in the press; and the religious devotion of the children from 'the ugly new houses' who constituted their audience. Even the track's closing group applause was subliminally self-referential. Five years earlier, The Smiths had tried the same effect on their first demo of 'WHAT DIFFERENCE DOES IT MAKE?' in December 1982.

Marr's summit-pushing score was the culmination of months experimenting with a rotating key change, trying it 'on keyboards and anything I could' before finalising its reeling guitar gracefully dipping and cresting in time with Morrissey's grand pop obituary. Epic in size (Strangeways' longest track at five and a half minutes), its self-martyring scars unavoidably added to the album's reception as The Smiths' knowing epitaph. Morrissey would return to its themes of fame, fortune and the singer–fan relationship on 2004's 'YOU KNOW I COULDN'T LAST'. [17, 19, 38, 71]

'Panic' (Morrissey/Marr), The Smiths' 11th single, released August 1986, highest UK chart position #11. Cover star: Richard BRADFORD. The Smiths' pop knockout punch, 'Panic' was an explicit declaration of war on the 80s music establishment. Morrissey's lyrics offered a violent fantasy of Smiths fans rampaging throughout the British Isles, burning discotheques and lynching disc jockeys like some demented indie restaging of the Gordon Riots; a quiffed and bespectacled Barnaby Rudge with a noose in one hand and gladioli in the other. In its rejection of the music that 'says nothing to me about my life', 'Panic' also contained one of the most profound truisms of SMITHDOM, simultaneously reminding the listener of the soul-nourishing force of the group's own glorious din.

The title may have been the subliminal influence of a popular northern soul track, 1968's 'Panic' by Reparata And The Delrons (whose leader went on to score a minor solo hit with the Morrissey and Marr favourite 'SHOES'). Marr first remembers Morrissey 'showing' him the title on the group's tour bus prior to a gig at Belfast's Queens University in February 1986. Marvelling at the amount of Smiths fly posters on show in the town centre, Morrissey asked Marr to imagine what would happen if the rest of the British Isles suddenly found itself similarly plastered in images of the group before revealing a pre-prepared postcard bearing one word in his child-like scrawl: 'PANIC!'

Two months later, on 26 April 1986 Morrissey and Marr were listening to Radio 1 in the latter's home kitchen and heard a news report about the Chernobyl nuclear power plant accident in the former USSR. 'The story about this shocking disaster comes to an end,' recalled Marr, 'and then immediately we're off into Wham!'s "I'm Your Man". I remember actually saying, "What the fuck has this got to do with people's lives?" We hear about Chernobyl, then, seconds later, we're expected to be jumping around to "I'm Your Man". And so, "hang the blessed DJ". I think it was a great lyric. Important and applicable to anyone who lives in England.'

The DJ responsible for the crass Chernobyl/Wham! juxtaposition was Steve Wright. Despite having his portrait vilified on a fan-made 'Hang the DJ!' T-shirt which Morrissey wore onstage (routinely swirling a hangman's noose above his head at the same time), Wright allegedly asked to join The Smiths for a performance of the song at the London Palladium in October 1986. He was refused, but for all his subsequent on-air lampooning of Morrissey at the time, in due course Wright revealed himself to be a genuine fan, inviting the singer on to his Radio 2 programme in 2004 where they even joked about the sentiment of 'Panic'.

Clearly aimed at the inanity of mainstream pop of the time, 'Panic' was still misread by a minority of detractors in the music press as an attack on black music culture, principally because of the

'**Papa Jack**' **(Morrissey/Whyte),** From the album MALADJUSTED (1997). It's tempting to think Morrissey may have written 'Papa Jack' as a pessimistic prophecy of his own possible fate: that of a faded star now grieving over old memories of the adoring young fans he somehow 'pushed away'. Otherwise, it's a lame character study devoid of his usually astute observations of the fickle nature of fame (e.g. 'PAINT A VULGAR PICTURE') and with a title which may have been a hangover from his boxing obsession on the previous SOUTHPAW GRAMMAR: 'Papa Jack' was a nickname of Jack Johnson, the first black heavyweight world boxing champion, also used as the title of his 1983 biography by Randy Roberts.

Whyte's sickly cream puff score veered from soft acoustic balladry to a thundering pomp-rock Who pastiche and is *probably* the track which producer Steve LILLYWHITE was referring to when sharing an anecdote about Morrissey's unique briefing methods for the sound he wished to create: 'We were working on a song and he came up to me and said, "Steve ... The Who. Shepherds Bush. 1965." And I said, "Yes, I get it!"' The tune was more of a showcase for the musical ambition of Whyte, who carries it to the end with his high-pitched harmony vocals, than it is for Morrissey, who exits stage left just after the halfway mark. One of the album's lowest ebbs, 'Papa Jack' was fussy but meaningless filler – so meaningless that it was erased from the 2009 redux Maladjusted altogether along with 'ROY'S KEEN'. [40, 427]

word 'disco'. While Morrissey's comments in a September 1986 *Melody Maker* interview about a 'black pop conspiracy' certainly didn't help matters, Marr immediately rushed to his defence, refuting all such allegations as idiotic. 'You can't just interchange the words "black" and "disco", or the phrases "black music" and "disco music",' he argued. 'It makes no earthly sense.'

For Morrissey, the song was simply 'extremely funny ... a tiny revolution in its own sweet way', though he'd also confess to being secretly 'intensely envious' of DJs such as Wright who inspired its malice. 'To simply sit on this cushion at the BBC day after day and flip on anything they thought was moving – well, I thought that was the most sacred and powerful position in the universe. To me, it was more important than politics. At a tender age, I craved that power – to impose one's record collection on people in launderettes and on scaffolding.'

Musically, 'Panic' was Marr's most explicit theft within The Smiths, hoicking Marc BOLAN's riff from T.Rex's 1972 number one 'Metal Guru'. Producer John PORTER vividly recalls Marr ringing him up prior to the session with the brief of 'making a T.Rex record'. 'Of course it was deliberate,' says Marr, 'but "Panic" doesn't sound like T.Rex. It still sounds like us. It still sounds like The Smiths.' His simple glam foundations were given an unexpected twist when Morrissey requested a children's choir for its 'Hang the DJ' finale. Porter duly assembled some volunteers from a primary school near to the studio in Wood Green, north London ('I must have gone round with a bag of lollipops,' he jokes). The press were also alerted to The Smiths' presence in the area when Morrissey was spotted in Wood Green's local branch of WH Smiths, allegedly buying a computer magazine and a Now That's What I Call Music compilation album. 'For a relative.'

The first Smiths single featuring the new five-man line-up augmented by Craig GANNON, 'Panic' was released while overseas on a North American tour; aided only by Derek JARMAN's video in their absence, it took them within inches of the UK top ten. Years later Morrissey would name it 'the [song] I like the most from The Smiths'. [12, 17, 19, 27, 52, 134, 196, 208, 413, 422]

parents (of Morrissey), See FAMILY.

Paresi, Andrew (Morrissey drummer 1987–91), With a past drumming for Jim Diamond, Sal Solo and Bucks Fizz, Andrew Paresi wasn't the most obvious candidate to work with Morrissey. Nor would he have done had it not been for Stephen STREET, who in 1987 was called in to mix a single for a new CBS signing taking their name from the Thomas Hardy novel *A Pair Of Blue Eyes*. Listening to the playback of their 'You Used To Go To My Head', Street was surprised and impressed to discover that the group's drummer had recorded his part without the familiar crutch of a click track. 'I was enormously flattered,' says Paresi. 'Stephen took my details and I never heard anything for about three months. Then out of the blue he rang me up and asked if I'd like to drum on some tracks with Morrissey. I'd read that The Smiths had split up but I was very surprised. And ecstatic. From doing odds and sods with various bands, suddenly this was a big deal.'

It was also a gamble on Street's part. Handed the task of assembling a suitable team to create VIVA HATE, he could only hope that his choice of guitarist Vini REILLY and Paresi somehow gelled with Morrissey in the studio. After 'passing' his informal first meeting with the singer at Street's flat in Mortlake, Paresi was in.

Technically slick yet willing to experiment, Paresi's style was clean and precise, forceful yet unobtrusive, whether lending a crisp rhythmic punch to 'SUEDEHEAD' or building up delicate percussive textures on 'LATE NIGHT, MAUDLIN STREET'. 'I definitely became much more confident as the session progressed,' says Paresi. 'I think everyone did. Initially Morrissey kept himself to himself but as it went on he opened up more. We were a new group of people to him and anxious to make everything work so we weren't threatening. And we were all sensitive to him as a person. We played charades a lot, in teams. Morrissey would always pick increasingly obscure films all the time like THE L-SHAPED ROOM. Sometimes we'd go out together in Bath, but we must have looked like the Addams Family – Morrissey, then Vini, then Stephen, a normal lad, then me in this ludicrous jumper which looked like a broken-down television set.'

By his own admission, Paresi became intensely devoted to Morrissey. Sandie SHAW, who visited the Viva Hate sessions, made the following observation of the drummer in her 1991 autobiography *The World At My Feet*: 'Andrew was the most profoundly affected, being an intensely emotional young man with enough unresolved hang-ups to fill a man-sized wardrobe – the stuff that Morrissey worshippers are made of. When this was channelled positively into his drumming, the result was a uniquely quirky style. When it was not, it was excruciating for him and everyone else.'

In an effort to strengthen their working relationship, Paresi began submitting musical ideas to Morrissey, much to Street's surprise and annoyance. He'd continue throughout the three years or more they'd work together, always unsuccessfully. Only one tune, he says, got as far as a working title circa KILL UNCLE. 'It was going to be called "Angie". He started a vocal to it: "Oh, Angie, oh, Angie." But it didn't go anywhere. There was another one we started, but he didn't like that either.' Nothing more is known of the lost Morrissey/Paresi chestnut 'Angie', though the title is certainly intriguing, being the name of Johnny Marr's wife who'd been a key player in the day-to-day administration of The Smiths.

After his sterling work on Viva Hate, Paresi was understandably upset when, at the end of 1988, he was ousted in favour of Mike Joyce for the recording of 'THE LAST OF THE FAMOUS INTERNATIONAL PLAYBOYS' and 'INTERESTING DRUG'. 'When he brought Mike back I thought that was it,' says Paresi. 'But then I used to get the odd postcard. I helped him out with something and he sent one which read, "Andrew, you're one of the loveliest people I know (please note – I don't know many people)." They were often very oblique and rather cryptic.'

As with his first chance encounter with Street, Paresi's re-entry into Morrissey's studio band was a similar stroke of luck. In the summer of 1989 Clive LANGER was the next producer lumbered with the mission of finding musicians for the recording of 'OUIJA BOARD, OUIJA BOARD'. Langer put the offer to guitarist Kevin ARMSTRONG, currently working with Paresi on Sandie Shaw's Hello Angel album. When it came to light Langer was also scouting for a drummer, Paresi found himself back in the fold, remaining there for the next two years for the aborted BONA DRAG album and Kill Uncle.

Echoing Shaw's comments about Viva Hate, his fellow musicians recall a certain covetousness towards Morrissey. 'He was clearly enamoured with Morrissey,' says Armstrong. 'Sometimes he could be very protective and competitive. He was always pitching song ideas that weren't used and I think the fact that other people's ideas *were* being used probably upset him.' Mark NEVIN concurs: 'He definitely saw himself as Morrissey's second-in-command.'

Regardless of any tensions his loyalty to Morrissey may have unintentionally created, Paresi proved himself as equally versatile a musician on the latter recordings, injecting requisite thunder beneath 'NOVEMBER SPAWNED A MONSTER', rattling rockabilly rhythms on an upturned bin for 'PREGNANT FOR THE LAST TIME' and even joining Suggs from MADNESS on backing vocals for 'SING YOUR LIFE'. Paresi's final Morrissey session was 1991's 'MY LOVE LIFE', but by then he'd already read the omens of his imminent departure.

'I can remember it very clearly,' he explains. 'Myself, Mark Nevin and a few others were at the Camden Workers Social Club. We'd gone there because it was a rockabilly night. I remember following Morrissey in, there was loud rockabilly music, young men with quiffs jiving, and he was transformed. He leant back against a wall and said, "My God! This is heaven!" At that moment, I knew I'd been fired! Because that was it. The image of how things were presented was much more important to him, and I think he was getting sick of making records and everything feeling like "a session band". It's funny, Morrissey once said to me, "Andrew, I would've taken you live but every time you do a drum fill, you open your mouth." I'd

never been that self-conscious before, but I had a look in the mirror next time and it's true.'

Morrissey went on to recruit his new Kill Uncle touring band with drummer Spencer COBRIN. Paresi continued session drumming before reverting to his birth name, Andrew McGibbon, and pursuing a successful career in radio comedy. He'd use his experiences with Morrissey as the basis of a 2005 Radio 4 programme, *I Was Morrissey's Drummer*. [1, 15, 22, 25, 39, 369]

Parlophone, Morrissey's record label from 1994 to 1995, his second under the umbrella of EMI. Synonymous with THE BEATLES' chart reign from 1962 until the formation of their own Apple label in '68, Morrissey had first shied away from Parlophone back in 1987 as the 'obvious mod suggestion which I didn't really want', choosing instead to resurrect EMI's defunct HMV imprint for his first five years as a solo artist. His later shunt to Parlophone coincided with the last years of his EMI contract, chiefly the release of VAUXHALL AND I, the WORLD OF MORRISSEY compilation and five singles. Whereas he'd enjoyed the privilege of having HMV to himself, Parlophone lumped him beside such disparate labelmates as Pet Shop Boys, Radiohead and the still-bellowing corpse of Freddie Mercury. Yet in spite of his apparent reticence, Parlophone was a spiritually perfect home for Morrissey as the former label of Cilla BLACK, original SALFORD LADS The Hollies, a young David BOWIE (when still David Jones) and a couple of novelty singles by CARRY ON star Joan Sims. Morrissey's last record for Parlophone was the 'SUNNY' single, released in December 1995 when he'd already left EMI for a brief spell on RCA VICTOR. [208]

'Pashernate Love' (Morrissey/Whyte/Day), B-side of 'YOU'RE THE ONE FOR ME, FATTY' (1992). By the autumn of 1991 new recruit Alain Whyte had begun submitting demos to Morrissey in the hope of becoming his co-writer. The tune of 'Pashernate Love', the result of a jam with bassist Gary Day, would be among the first tracks Morrissey accepted and the first new song from his KILL UNCLE touring band to be played live. The words offered a conventional Morrissey meditation on his immunity from the phonetically spelt title emotion; a passionate love which has the power to make 'your grandmother zoom roller-skating back from the grave' but which fails to stir his senses. Its heavy footing and 70s fuzz hinted at the shinier glam rock designs which would dominate YOUR ARSENAL. A minor B-side, Morrissey himself admitted it was nothing more than 'a very simple pop song'. [422]

Pasolini, Pier Paolo, Italian neo-realist film

director referenced in 'YOU HAVE KILLED ME' along with the title of his debut feature film, 1961's ACCATONE. Morrissey likened his unearthing of Pasolini's work to 'discovering poetry', hailing him 'an extreme genius'. 'He was a genuine talent with many skills,' he noted. 'Films, novels, essays. In interviews he was wonderful, never unprepared or nervous.'

Born in Bologna in 1922, Pasolini would become one of the most controversial figures in the history of Italian cinema as a vociferous Communist who made no secret of his homosexuality. His films were shocking, deliberately so, while he spent much of his life and career fighting – sometimes literally – with Italy's far right and Catholic orthodoxy. Before directing Accatone at the age of 38, Pasolini had already established himself as a poet, novelist, political activist, critic and scriptwriter. The film's graphic portrayal of the life and death of a pimp in the slums of contemporary Rome was deemed scandalous. His next, 1962's Mamma Roma starring Anna MAGNANI, brought further charges of immorality and remains Morrissey's favourite. 'A masterpiece,' he raved. 'It's still so modern. I don't think [Pasolini] reached those levels again.' It tells the tragic story of an ageing Roman prostitute trying to make a clean start in life as a market trader. Her pride and joy is her withdrawn teenage son, Ettore (Ettore Garofolo who, weirdly enough, bears an unnerving facial resemblance to adolescent

pictures of Morrissey). He eventually discovers the truth of her former profession and, in protest, joins a gang of petty thieves, leading to its harrowing conclusion.

Pasolini's work became increasingly controversial thereafter. His contribution to 1963's portmanteau piece RoGoPaG (named after its four directors Rossellini, Godard, Pasolini and Gregoretti) starred Orson Welles as a pompous Hollywood director filming the life of Christ and earned Pasolini a four-month suspended sentence for blasphemy. His ingenious reaction to that arrest was to make one of the most revered Christian biopics in cinema history, 1964's The Gospel According To St Matthew, though his days of upsetting the church were far from over. 1968's Theorem, starring Terence STAMP, was a symbolic parable about the corruption of a bourgeois family household by a stranger who sexually seduces every one of its male and female inhabitants. After winning the Jury prize at the Venice Film Festival, it was seized by the public prosecutor by order of the Vatican.

His later works were in equal parts baffling – such as 1969's Porcile (Pigsty, as in 'LIFE IS A …'), an allegorical yarn about medieval cannibalism and modern-day Nazis – and sexually explicit, none more so than his final and most litigious bequest, 1975's Salò, a stomach-churning adaptation of the Marquis de Sade's The 120 Days Of Sodom featuring horrific re-enactments of rape, torture and the eating of human faeces. After one screening in a Soho film club, Scotland Yard confiscated Salò on grounds of indecency, only releasing it on condition it be re-edited beyond comprehension and prefixed with a lengthy, cautionary prologue.

Unfortunately, Pasolini never lived to answer Salò's obscenity charges. On 2 November 1975, his mutilated body, bruised beyond recognition after being run over several times by his own car, was discovered lying near the beach at Ostia just outside Rome. A young hustler, Pino 'The Frog' Pelosi, confessed to the crime and was sentenced to nine years. Two decades after his release, in

Passport To Pimlico, 1949 Ealing comedy listed among Morrissey's favourite films. Sarcastically dedicated to the memory of wartime rationing, the deeply satirical plot focuses on a working-class community in Pimlico, London, where an unexploded bomb has been discovered. When a group of mischievous children set it off, the explosion reveals the existence of a cellar full of treasure belonging to a fifteenth-century French duke. Among the valuables is a royal charter signed by Edward IV which declares the surrounding district to be under the jurisdiction of Burgundy. As nobody has known of the charter's existence for nearly 500 years, its decree has yet to be overturned by the crown, meaning Pimlico is its own Burgundian state separate from the rest of England. The residents seize this as an opportunity for economic anarchy, hoarding their new wealth, tearing up their ration books and keeping the local pub open past closing time because, as they insist, 'This is Burgundy!'

An affectionate spoof of the English national character, the film's spirit is encapsulated by the line, 'We always *were* English, and we'll always *be* English, and it's just because we *are* English that we're sticking up for our rights to be Burgundians!' Morrissey mentioned *Passport To Pimlico* in his correspondence with pen pal Robert MACKIE and would praise it again when interviewed in 1989, calling it 'a triumphant film littered with outstanding faces'. Those faces include Ealing stalwart Stanley Holloway, Morrissey favourite Margaret RUTHERFORD and another of his preferred 'Odd fellows', a pre-*CARRY ON* Charles Hawtrey. Contrary to its title, the film wasn't actually filmed in Pimlico but just across the river Thames in Lambeth, north of VAUXHALL. [69, 168, 334, 540]

2005 Pelosi retracted his confession, claiming that he'd taken the rap for three anti-Communist, homophobic thugs who threatened to terrorise his family. Even the original trial judge publicly admitted that Pasolini's murder was most likely political, motivated by his aggressively outspoken comments against Italy's ruling classes.

Morrissey's interest in Pasolini may have been stirred by PATTI SMITH, who mentioned him on the liner notes of 1978's Easter (Smith would later cite his *The Gospel According To St Matthew* as a major influence in her own reassessment of Jesus as 'a revolutionary figure ... a teacher, a fighter, a guerrilla'). Other than namechecking the director in 'You Have Killed Me', Morrissey chose a striking portrait of Pasolini as a stage backdrop towards the end of the RINGLEADER OF THE TORMENTORS tour. 'I understand [Pasolini] and I appreciate his art,' he explained. 'He also looked great and he didn't seem to be impressed by other people. He didn't have to be anybody else. He was being himself in his own world.' [54, 159, 213, 335, 376, 461, 481, 527, 543]

Pavone, Rita, See 'HEART'.

Peel, John, To the oblivious viewers of TOP OF THE POPS John Peel was, in his own words, 'The one who comes on Radio 1 late at night and plays records made by sulky Belgian art students in basements dying of TB.' To the rest of us he was an immeasurably influential DJ and broadcaster whose early patronage and constant support of The Smiths played a significant part in their success, as it had in the past for innumerable others from Marc BOLAN to The Fall and Joy Division. 'I was impressed,' recalled Peel, 'because unlike most bands – and I've said this before because it remains true – you couldn't immediately tell what records they'd been listening to. That's fairly unusual, very rare indeed. It made you think, "How have they got to where they are?" And "Where have they come from?" It was that aspect of The Smiths that I found most impressive.'

The Smiths recorded the first of four sessions for his weekday Radio 1 programme in May 1983: three of its tracks were later included on

HATFUL OF HOLLOW as well as all four of their second. Speaking to this author in 2003, Peel modestly credited his producer, John Walters, for first booking the group after seeing them play their second London gig at ULU a few weeks earlier. Tellingly, Morrissey named Walters his 'most wonderful human being' in his 1984 NME poll. The Smiths would also come to dominate Peel's annual listeners' poll, the Festive 50, topping it in 1984 with 'HOW SOON IS NOW?', and in 1986 with 'THERE IS A LIGHT THAT NEVER GOES OUT', also scoring a record 11 entries in 1987.

For many fans, Peel's night-time Radio 1 show provided the first preview of new Smiths material, whether in session or on record weeks in advance of official release. On air, his warmth for the group was rarely less than rapturous: following their debut session's first broadcast on 31 May 1983, as Morrissey's high-pitched wails faded at the end of 'WHAT DIFFERENCE DOES IT MAKE?', Peel sighed, 'Ah! The distant cry of the herring gull.' Marr also recalls the night he previewed six tracks from MEAT IS MURDER as a major boost to his confidence. 'I didn't take it for granted that he was gonna rave about it,' says Marr, 'and I certainly didn't expect that he was going to play six or seven tracks. But I remember him raving about "NOWHERE FAST" and saying "Hats off to The Smiths" after playing it. His excitement about the record was palpable. That meant a lot to us at the time.'

Writing about the group for *The Observer* in 1987, Peel commented: 'More than one Morrissey lyric has caused my laughter to tinkle among the teacups. His ability to indicate a whole way of life by briefly highlighting a darkened corner of that life is matched only by his skill at delivering his lyrics in a manner that leaves the listener with no choice but to consider seriously what is being sung. These are rare gifts in popular music.'

Peel once, allegedly, compiled a cassette for Morrissey of 'rare skiffle tunes', though his cordial relationship with the singer waned in the wake of The Smiths' split. A solo Morrissey session recorded in late 1987 as a precursor to VIVA HATE was never broadcast due to the singer's

unease with the studio technicians who, as he put it, treated him and his musicians 'like [we] were some insignificant, unsigned group from Poole'. Peel died in October 2004, aged only 65, leaving an irreplaceable void in the world of broadcasting and the championing of new music in particular. His death followed that of John Walters three years earlier, aged 62. [26, 182, 203, 350, 468]

Perry, Ivor, Manchester guitarist and songwriter whom Morrissey invited to join The Smiths in July 1987 as a replacement for the recently departed Johnny Marr.

Perry and Morrissey had known each other since their teens, both growing up on Kings Road in Stretford although they were never close friends. When The Smiths were forming in the autumn of 1982, Perry, also in the process of forming his own local group, heard their first demo of 'THE HAND THAT ROCKS THE CRADLE' and 'SUFFER LITTLE CHILDREN', but thought Morrissey's singing was 'flat' and the music was 'weird'.

By the summer of 1983, Perry's scepticism towards Morrissey's musical endeavours gave way to admiration after watching The Smiths blossom with the release of their Rough Trade debut single, 'HAND IN GLOVE'. In the interim, Perry's group had finalised a line-up including his highly politicised younger brother, Andy, and decided upon the name of Easterhouse after a notoriously deprived and violent Glasgow housing estate. With nothing to lose, Perry was bold enough to doorstep Morrissey, still living with his mother at 384 Kings Road, and ask if there was any chance of Easterhouse being given a Smiths support slot. Morrissey very graciously agreed, arranging for them to play their first London gig opening for The Smiths at Dingwalls in early August.

Compared with The Smiths' life-affirming guitar pop, Easterhouse's music was harsher and frequently melancholic as befitted their stern lyrics shaped by Andy Perry's Communist ideology. Beyond merely condemning the current THATCHER administration, Perry espoused hardline socialism which equally demonised the

Labour Party. The mid-80s being an extremely politicised climate in British music, the group soon found an attentive audience and eventually followed The Smiths to a deal with ROUGH TRADE in 1985. Their debut EP, In Our Own Hands, was released shortly before another invitation to support The Smiths on a seven-date tour of Scotland that September. It was followed in January 1986 by the Perry brothers' best moment, 'Whistling In The Dark', which set Andy's soulful preaching about the plight of the trade unions above Ivor's stiff guitar jabbing in the wounds of The Clash's 'London Calling'. The single's sleeve featured an image of striking miners fighting with the police while the reverse carried Andy Perry's written decree to 'smash the influence of the Labour Party' beside a photo of Arthur Scargill.

Their debut album, Contenders, was buckling under the weight of similar political discourse (opening line: 'Here comes a union leader with a brand new deal'). It reached number three in the independent charts though before 1986 was through the Perry brothers' sibling rivalry came to a head. After one volatile conflict too many, Ivor quit, taking drummer Gary Rostock with him to form The Cradle with recently sacked 'fifth Smith' Craig GANNON. Andy Perry would persevere alone as Easterhouse, recording a second and final album with an entirely new line-up (1989's Waiting For The Red Bird).

In the meantime, The Cradle released their Rough Trade debut single, 'It's Too High', in May 1987, just as The Smiths were splitting. The same month, Perry told the press he considered himself and Morrissey to be kindred spirits. 'I'm not a happy person,' he admitted. 'Life's a trial, I've got the band but if I was working I'd top meself. Morrissey's right, there's no point in living a shitty life. I used to work as a trainee accountant. God, it was terrible.'

Perry heard about the fate of The Smiths on the local Manchester music grapevine but was still surprised when, in July 1987, the offer came to fill Johnny Marr's shoes as guitarist and co-writer, not least because The Cradle were still a going concern.

His view that Marr was irreplaceable was shared by other candidates such as Kevin ARMSTRONG, though upon the label's request for ideas for new Smiths B-sides, Perry obligingly sent Morrissey a cassette of rough guitar sketches. Possibly in desperation, Morrissey decided they were good enough to arrange a recording session with producer Stephen STREET that same month at the Power Plant studio in Willesden, north London.

To Morrissey, at least, the group were still 'The Smiths', being himself, Perry, Andy Rourke and Mike Joyce. Legally, however, had the session even been a success Marr would never have allowed them to use the group name.

'I'm really sorry that I ever agreed to go along with it,' says Rourke. 'I was in shock and clutching at straws. No slur on Ivor. It wasn't his fault, it could have been anybody, but it wasn't Johnny so it was never going to work. It was more upsetting doing that session than it was splitting up in the first place because we were just rubbing our own noses in it. I felt stupid for even attempting it.'

Perry's tenure with 'The Smiths' lasted all of 24 hours, long enough to record two tracks. The first was a slow, lolloping instrumental driven by Rourke's bass (roughly the same tempo as 'I KNOW IT'S OVER', but a much jollier tune) which remained untitled since Morrissey never got round to doing a vocal.

The second was an early draft of 'BENGALI IN PLATFORMS' featuring similar lyrics to the later VIVA HATE version over a typical Perry riff not far removed from Easterhouse's 'Whistling In The Dark'. As if the weirdness over Marr's void wasn't bad enough to contend with, tensions between Street and Perry compounded the atmosphere of misery and futility. Though both had crossed paths before during Easterhouse, there was scant mutual admiration. 'I just didn't like Ivor,' admits Street. 'We just didn't get on as people and I thought he was completely the wrong person as far as working with Morrissey was concerned. No way was he going to replace Johnny Marr.'

Sensing the session was doomed, Morrissey pulled the plug after the end of the first day.

P

Taking a characteristically non-confrontational tack, the singer asked Mike Joyce to inform Perry on his behalf back at their hotel. 'Ivor was getting really defensive and began shouting, "Why can't he tell me himself?"' claims Joyce. 'He lost it. He was threatening to go round Morrissey's flat that night. I had to calm him down.'

It was a bitter experience for all concerned, not least Perry who would thereafter gain minor infamy as The Smiths' 'nearly man'. In truth, as Rourke highlighted, his was the impossible task of a predestined scapegoat whose skills as a musician and writer (as Easterhouse's Contenders album bears witness) were irrelevant to the fate of the Power Plant session. If Morrissey had secretly feared The Smiths minus Marr was an impossible cause, the Perry trial forced him to face those fears head on and concede defeat. Ironically, it was the hellish experience of that session which prompted Stephen Street to send Morrissey his own musical ideas. With that in mind, Perry should be remembered not as the man who nailed the coffin in The Smiths but, by proxy, the unwitting catalyst for Morrissey's rebirth as a solo artist. [13, 17, 19, 29, 38, 39, 72, 362]

PETA (People for the Ethical Treatment of Animals), See ANIMAL RIGHTS.

'Piccadilly Palare' (Morrissey/Armstrong),

Morrissey's seventh solo single, released October 1990, highest UK chart position #18. A song partly inspired by the Julian and Sandy sketches from the 60s BBC radio series *Round The Horne*, Palare (or Polari) was a gay slang which acted as a secret code at a time when homosexuality was still a criminal offence in Britain. Morrissey coyly described it as 'a private language between people … in order to discuss who is approaching them, who they should avoid so therefore nobody eavesdropping can understand what they're saying'.

Palare has fairly complex roots, incorporating Italian, Yiddish and backwards English (e.g. 'hair' becomes 'riah') and was especially prevalent among those working in the theatre business. The characters of Julian and Sandy were themselves actors whose use of the slang formed the basis of their hysterical sketches rife with camp innuendo. The song's lyrics even paraphrase Sandy's customary palare catchphrase to host Kenneth Horne – 'lovely to vada your jolly old eek', the basis of Morrissey's 'so *bona* to *vada* … your lovely *eek* and your lovely *riah*' (in English, 'so *good* to *see* your lovely *face* and your lovely *hair*').

But despite its comic inspiration, 'Piccadilly Palare' cracked few smiles, telling the story of a young runaway lured into London's underworld of male prostitution in fearlessly graphic detail. Morrissey admitted he had first-hand experience of hearing palare among male prostitutes in the 70s, also citing the influence of *Johnny Go Home*, a two-part ITV documentary about the dangers faced by northern teenage runaways in London first broadcast in 1975. 'In the north, among most people I know, there was something oddly romantic about the whole thing,' he explained. 'It spelt freedom. Catching a coach and spending a day in Piccadilly was extraordinary.'

'Piccadilly Palare' would be the only Morrissey single co-written with guitarist Kevin Armstrong. 'I grew up listening to Julian and Sandy,' comments Armstrong, 'so it was great to find somebody in pop music doing that.' Recorded at Hook End during the original BONA DRAG sessions, Armstrong's initial guitar riff was refashioned by producer Clive LANGER into a trampling piano stomp strongly evocative of his previous work with MADNESS. Amplifying the connection, Langer roped in Madness lead singer Suggs to add backing vocals and snatches of spoken dialogue. 'Everybody knew it sounded like Madness,' confesses Langer, 'but Morrissey didn't mind that.' Prior to release, its four-minute master would be edited down to remove a third verse describing the protagonist's 'cold water room' lodgings and sections of its outro where Morrissey sobs 'No Dad, I won't be home tomorrow'.

Reeking with the late-night coach station despair of piss, diesel and watery tea, 'Piccadilly Palare' was a convincingly grim popumentary,

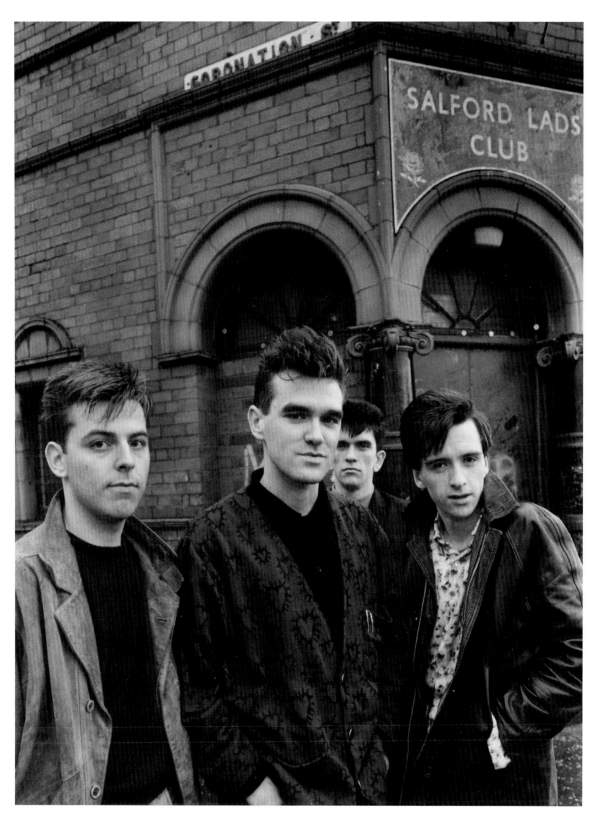

Manchester, so much to answer for: The pretend Salford lads, December 1985.

Above: The original 'Smiths', David and Maureen, arrive to give evidence in the 1966 Moors Murders trial. **Right:** The sign seen on the reverse of 1987's Strangeways, Here We Come.

Opposite – Top: The wreckage of the 'Munich Air Disaster, 1958'. **Bottom:** The Sex Pistols play the Lesser Free Trade Hall, 4 June 1976 – Manchester life is never sane again.

Home is where the art is: The Smiths begin to blossom at Manchester's derelict Central Station, May 1983 – within three years the same venue would reopen as G-Mex.

Left: The 'strangely sexy' Shelagh Delaney. Above: Rita Tushingham sparkles in *A Taste Of Honey*. Below left: The 'indisputably' great George Best. Below right: Salford lad Albert Finney, who, like Best, declined the offer to appear on a Smiths sleeve.

Pat Phoenix (left) daydreams of Smiths cover stardom in *Coronation Street*.

Outside odds: The Smiths at the Salford bookmakers shop of Albert Finney's father, January 1987.

Phoenix, Pat, Manchester-born actress best known for her role as Elsie Tanner in CORONATION STREET and cover star of the Smiths single 'SHAKESPEARE'S SISTER'. Around the time of the latter's release in early 1985 Morrissey interviewed Phoenix, then 61, for *Blitz* magazine. 'Elsie [Tanner] was the screen's first "angry young woman",' wrote Morrissey in his introduction, 'a wised-up, tongue-lashing cylindrical tempest, sewn into cheap and overstuffed dresses, harnessed by severe poverty, staunchly defending her fatherless children, devouring a blizzard of temporary husbands in dour Salford council dwellings. It was the skill of Pat's acting that earned Elsie great distinction as mother, sister and lover to millions.'

During the interview, Morrissey and Phoenix discussed her role as a prostitute in THE L-SHAPED ROOM, her Irish heritage, the 'rape' of Manchester, Bette DAVIS, Anna MAGNANI, James DEAN (Phoenix briefly worked under the pseudonym Patricia Dean) and life beyond *Coronation Street* now that she'd left the soap. Morrissey later revealed that at the end of their interview Phoenix told him, 'You're a very unhappy person.'

'I was momentarily frozen,' he explained. 'It seems that throughout the day she had been analysing the way I am. It was a very solemn half hour for me to listen to because she was so accurate. It seemed at that instant that there was even more to her than I had ever imagined – her skill and her ability as an observant person was quite awesome.'

Tragically, the year after their interview, in September 1986 Phoenix died of lung cancer at the age of 62. The week before her death she married actor Anthony Booth, who himself had had a small cameo in *The L-Shaped Room*. Morrissey attended her funeral service at Manchester's Holy Name Church. Also in the congregation was Booth's son-in-law and future prime minister, Tony Blair. [146, 181, 290, 374]

even if Morrissey himself showed a surprising lack of confidence, telling the press it was 'not a particularly strong record … not overwhelming [and] the subject is even slightly dated'. Lacking an accompanying video and with little promotion, that it still charted inside the UK top 20 was itself a triumph. [1, 15, 70, 138, 437]

plagiarism, As many of the entries in this book make plain, Morrissey is renowned for sourcing lyrics and titles from favourite books, films and records, as humorously alluded to in 'CEMETRY GATES'. Consequently, some critics have chastised Morrissey for, as they see it, 'plagiarism', more of a discerning cultural magpie than an original artist. But such detractors are being crude, both in their ignorance of the history of the creative arts, and in their misuse of the term plagiarism.

By definition, a plagiarist is somebody who passes off another's work as their own. Were Morrissey to copy Shelagh DELANEY's *A Taste Of Honey*, word for word, and pass it off as a play he'd written himself, that would, indeed, be plagiarism. But for Morrissey to copy some dialogue from *A Taste Of Honey*, place it in a new artistic context – in a pop song, as opposed to a stage play – then call it 'THIS NIGHT HAS OPENED MY EYES' (a title taken from a completely different theatrical source, Eugene O'Neill's LONG DAY'S JOURNEY INTO NIGHT) is, strictly speaking, not plagiarism but appropriation and bricolage. He might still warrant being called a plagiarist if he were to *deny* that the song was inspired by *A Taste Of Honey*, but, as with many of his other references, he freely admitted the fact: 'I've always been quite honest when I've been light-fingered about the words I use.'

Similarly, walk into any decent bookshop, go to the classics section and in most modern paperback editions of the great novelists such as

DICKENS or ELIOT you will find an appendix of chapter notes, detailing particular phrases in the text taken from Shakespeare, the Bible and the classical poets. The story of art, of all the arts, is of influence, words and images handed down through the centuries, adapted, refashioned and reinvented by each generation. In this respect Morrissey is the consummate artist, approaching pop music no differently to how Eliot approached the novel. As he asserted in 2006, 'I always considered the great mesh of all of my influences had emerged in me as something that was *unique enough*.'

Alas, one of the inevitable consequences of Morrissey's habit of appropriation is that his lyrics are frequently over-scrutinised to the point where some fans and critics use the most tenuous similarities between his words and those of others as a means of attributing thoroughly bogus sources as an influence. Intriguing and amusing as it may be to ponder whether 'HAIRDRESSER ON FIRE' has any connection with playwright Joe Orton's early novel *The Boy Hairdresser* (it hasn't, by the way), using the same two-plus-two-equals-five approach hinging on a single word it would be as well to assume the same song also owes its title to The Crazy World Of Arthur Brown's 'Fire' or, perhaps, some veiled homage to CORONATION STREET salon owner Audrey Roberts. Lack of common sense and chronological awareness has already resulted in dozens of such red herrings too numerous (too silly) to mention. While there is no harm in speculating – and this book is full of many *speculations* – care should be taken in all such assessments so as not to further cloud the already polluted waters of Mozological study. [159, 206, 435]

'Please Help The Cause Against Loneliness' (Morrissey/Street), studio outtake from the 1987 VIVA HATE sessions, subsequently covered by Sandie SHAW. A basic yell for affection buried beneath the placards of a mock-protest anthem and the spatter of a Motown-lite tune (not unlike 'I DON'T MIND IF YOU FORGET ME'), 'Please Help The Cause' was free and easy pop vaudeville.

Morrissey had invited Shaw to the Viva Hate session specifically to sing harmony vocals on the track only to then discard it among a clutch of early album contenders which fell at the first hurdle. As consolation he suggested Shaw take it for herself, which she did, recording it for her 1988 album Hello Angel. 'There wasn't enough space [for it on Viva Hate] and it was frozen,' Morrissey explained. 'Sandie picked it up and put it in the microwave.'

Modified to a higher key, Shaw's version was otherwise identical to Morrissey's prototype, produced by Street and with Andrew PARESI on drums and Kevin ARMSTRONG on guitar. Despite being released as a single in September 1988, right at the height of Mozmania in Viva Hate's slipstream, Shaw's recording failed to chart, vindicating Morrissey's decision to deep freeze it in the first place. The accompanying video featured Shaw dancing around a series of celebrity cardboard cut-outs, including a kneeling Morrissey with added angel wings. By coincidence, the B-side of Shaw's single was 'Lover Of The Century', a track co-written with future Morrissey co-writer Mark NEVIN. [25, 39, 203, 369]

'Please Please Please Let Me Get What I Want' (Morrissey/Marr), B-side of 'WILLIAM, IT WAS REALLY NOTHING' (1984). 'Like a very brief punch in the face' is how Morrissey described this, the shortest Smiths track which compacted the full range of their melancholic majesty into one minute and 50 seconds; a fragile ember of hope softly fading amid a snowstorm of hopelessness. Considering that in interviews of the period Morrissey had spoken of the group's current chart success as 'good times', in a personal sense 'Please Please Please' appeared his simple prayer that they never end, even if the desperation in his appeal betrayed the fear of his inborn pessimism.

Marr had first sketched its folky melody with his girlfriend and future wife Angie in mind, also seeking inspiration in childhood memories of his parents' favourite 'The Answer To Everything', a 1962 Del Shannon B-side. 'I tried to capture the essence of the Del Shannon tune,' he says, 'in terms of its spookiness and sense of yearning.' Its final arrangement radiated a unique sensual doom, Morrissey's desirous whispers blowing away in a trembling squall of mandolin – the uncredited minstrelship of producer John PORTER. Its distinguishing cliffhanger ending would cause minor concern within the corridors of their label, ROUGH TRADE. 'They kept asking, "Where's the rest of the song?"' explained Morrissey, who insisted that 'lengthening [it] would, to my mind, have been explaining the blindingly obvious'.

Morrissey's initial regret that 'hiding it away on a B-side was sinful' no longer holds sway in the light of its enduring esteem among fans and critics who frequently rank it high among The Smiths' most sacred recordings. Discounting their own Sandie SHAW collaboration, the song was also the first Morrissey/Marr track to be covered by another artist, released in elongated three-minute form as an A-side by The Dream Academy in 1985. 'Everyone despised it and it got to number 81, which is nearly a hit,' mourned Morrissey, who liked their version enough to later include it in Smiths concert interval tapes. 'Please Please Please' has since become one of the most frequently featured Smiths songs on film soundtracks, first appearing in John Hughes's *Pretty In Pink* in 1986.

For such a simple song, The Smiths never quite mastered it in concert until the addition of Craig GANNON in 1986, whose presence finally freed Marr to re-create its mandolin outro on guitar. Since then, both Morrissey and Marr have performed 'Please Please Please' in solo concerts. In June 2005 Marr played it fronting The Healers at PATTI SMITH's Meltdown festival at London's Royal Festival Hall, introducing it as 'a northern folk song'. Morrissey took a premature pop at it on the opening date of his 2002 US tour but didn't bring it back as a setlist regular until 2006. The latter version found Morrissey making the sexually suggestive lyrical amendment of 'let me *have who* I want', strangling much of its original beauty in the process. [17, 19, 27, 144, 203]

Pomfret, Steven, Aspiring Manchester guitar player who befriended Morrissey in 1977 and would later act as chaperon when Marr made his historic impromptu house call on Morrissey in the summer of 1982. As first detailed in THE SEVERED ALLIANCE, Pomfret had rehearsed with fellow Wythenshawe guitarist Billy DUFFY and the 18-year-old Morrissey in the autumn of 1977, tentatively calling themselves Sulky Young, then The Tee-Shirts. Although Pomfret tried writing with Morrissey, the rehearsals came to nothing. Duffy and Morrissey both moved on to play with THE NOSEBLEEDS the following spring. The young Marr would also get to know Pomfret, or 'Pommy' as he called him, as part of Duffy's older gang of Wythenshawe mates into The Stooges and the NEW YORK DOLLS.

In 1982, when Marr decided he'd heard enough about Morrissey to make his move, he asked Pomfret (the only available mutual friend now that Duffy had moved to London) if he would take him round to the singer's house. The fact that Marr wasn't alone when he turned up on Morrissey's doorstep is frequently written out of the mythology of The Smiths, largely due to both Morrissey and Marr's convenient neglect to mention Pomfret when asked to recount how they met. However, Marr doesn't deny Pomfret's presence. 'Pommy was there,' he confirms, 'but as soon as Morrissey came to the door Pommy took two very firm steps back which is one of the things that got me to talk so fast. It was just plain exuberance.'

Although Pomfret was under the impression that he too would be joining Morrissey and Marr in whatever group they formed, after a couple of rehearsals he sensed his rhythm guitar playing was superfluous and very graciously bowed out. In the creation of The Smiths, Pomfret's role was the last small but essential link in Marr's chain to Morrissey, one which had begun with the stories he'd heard from Billy Duffy and developed under the tutorage of Joe MOSS and his obsession with LEIBER AND STOLLER. Hypothetically, had Pomfret not been around to make that introduction, Marr's steely determination would have certainly driven him to find some other way – *any* way – to get to Morrissey. Luckily, the dependable 'Pommy' made the inevitable that bit easier. [17, 362]

Poor Cow, 1967 British kitchen-sink drama listed among Morrissey's favourite films. The directorial debut of Ken Loach (based on the novel by Nell Dunn) it followed the struggles of Joy (Carol White), a young west London working-class wife with a newborn son and a criminal husband, Tom (played by John BINDON, the dedicatee of Morrissey's MALADJUSTED album). When Tom is sent to prison for a botched robbery, Joy begins an affair with another burglar, Dave (Terence STAMP). They spend six months of happiness together until he, too, is caught and sent to prison. The rest of the story sees Joy trying to earn her way first as a barmaid, then as a 'model' for a dirty old men's photography club, taking various casual lovers along the way. The film also starred another of Morrissey's minor favourites, character actress Queenie Watts, included in the singer's 1989 NME list of 'Odd fellows'.

Shot in semi-documentary style, *Poor Cow* was Loach's attempt to re-create the tone of his gritty 60s television dramas *Up The Junction* and *Cathy Come Home* on the big screen. He later criticised his efforts as 'immature', regretting his use of 'post-synching' over-dubbed dialogue which robbed many of the scenes of their intended authenticity. From a purely Mozzerian perspective, *Poor Cow* is most interesting as a feminist character study of a working-class girl who, for all the misery and squalor in her life, exercises her sexual freedom. Like the protagonist of 'PREGNANT FOR THE LAST TIME', Joy 'sees someone new and has someone new' as she pleases. The film's Fulham locale would also be referenced in Maladjusted's title track. [227, 305, 314, 542]

Popcorn Venus, 1973 feminist film study by Marjorie Rosen, listed among Morrissey's favourite books at the outset of The Smiths and an influence upon some of his earliest lyrics.

Subtitled 'Women, Movies & The American Dream', Rosen's exhaustively researched and wittily written history of women in film traces their representation on screen and its sociological impact from the late 1800s up until the early 1970s. Alongside Molly Haskell's FROM REVERENCE TO RAPE published a year later, *Popcorn Venus* set the blueprint for feminist film theory. Significantly, Morrissey would cite both authors and both books as influences.

Rosen's text refers to several films which he'd later use for song titles – 'THE HAND THAT ROCKS THE CRADLE', 'LITTLE MAN, WHAT NOW?', 'ANGEL, ANGEL, DOWN WE GO' – though its most notable bequest to The Smiths occurs in Chapter 21, 'Flower Children'. Discussing the 60s 'beach-party' genre, Rosen writes: 'At a glance these precious beach-party innocents seemed worlds apart from the hip, aggressive teenyboppers or alienated swingers who would people pop movies. Actually, the difference would be in degrees of impatience as unformulated questions were tested: *How immediately can we be gratified? How soon is "now"?*'

Rosen also describes actress Anita Ekberg 'reeling around the fountain' in Fellini's *La Dolce Vita*, though other possible lyrical sources in the book are more subtle, be it the dim echo of 'HANDSOME DEVIL' in 'Who would subjugate whom? Who would crack the whip?' or Rosen's quotation from 1973's *The Year Of The Women*, 'Mine eyes have seen the glory of the flame of women's rage' which may have had some bearing upon 'THESE THINGS TAKE TIME'. It's worth noting that all of these citations, bar 'HOW SOON IS NOW?', relate to Morrissey's first Smiths lyrics written in the period between autumn 1982 and spring 1983, adding to the probability that *Popcorn Venus* was a favourite source of inspiration at that time. Elsewhere, Rosen analyses many of Morrissey's favourite films and film stars, from THE LEATHER BOYS and THE KILLING OF SISTER GEORGE (which Rosen hates) to James DEAN, Bette DAVIS and Smiths cover star Joe DALLESANDRO. To cap it all, there's even a very brief mention of the NEW YORK DOLLS. [166, 184, 363]

'Poppycocteau', Short verse by Morrissey (written in 'August/Winter Eighty-hate') describing a comical scene in which he's forced to hand his trousers to a couple of sailors who accost him outside a Liverpool nightclub. First printed in Morrissey's handwriting on the reverse of a flexi-disc of 'LONDON' from RANK (free with the September 1988 issue of *The Catalogue* magazine), it was later included in Jo Slee's *Peepholism*. [374]

Porter, John (Smiths producer 1983–87), The

sonic Midas responsible for first taking The Smiths into the national singles charts was producer and musician John Porter.

Born in Leeds, as a student in late 60s Newcastle he first met Bryan Ferry, briefly playing guitar in his R&B band The Gas Board. Porter moved to London in the early 70s, living in the hippy community around Portobello Road where he began an unlikely friendship with actor and criminal John BINDON. Meantime, Ferry had also travelled south to form ROXY MUSIC. After firing their original bass player, fellow Gas Board veteran Graham Simpson, Ferry brought in Porter to play on the group's second album, 1973's For Your Pleasure. It was the beginning of a long association with the Roxy camp that would see him work on various solo projects over the next few years, from Ferry's first four solo albums to Andy Mackay's In Search Of Eddie Riff; the latter, named after an obscure 50s R&B singer, would also provide Morrissey's sleeve art and hotel check-in pseudonym in the early 1990s.

Prior to The Smiths, Porter had recently worked with Killing Joke and had already established himself as a regular radio session producer for the BBC. It was in the latter capacity that he first met The Smiths in late August 1983 for a David Jensen session, just as the group were finishing their intended debut album with producer Troy TATE. Over the next couple of weeks, doubts over the quality of the Tate tapes led to Porter being asked by ROUGH TRADE's Geoff Travis if he could remix them. Porter's verdict sealed Tate's fate, informing Travis that it would be easier to start again, thereby landing himself the job of Smiths producer for the next 12 months.

'I actually felt like we were kindred spirits,' Porter says of The Smiths. 'I'd originally come down to London from the north. I was pretty green, I didn't have much of a clue when I was younger. I recognised them as being very similar. Just down from the north and they hadn't got a fucking clue. But I was immediately impressed with Johnny's playing. He became like a younger brother to me.'

The importance of Porter's brotherly nurturing and technical instruction of Marr to the musical development of The Smiths cannot be overstated. 'I always felt as though John was there for Johnny,' comments Mike Joyce. 'They worked together like a dream and when Johnny was happy that contentment and inspiration filtered through to the rest of us. Johnny learnt so much which he stored up for later years. There were loads of tiny, subtle things we'd have never have done without John Porter's guidance.'

Among Porter's main bequests was the layering of overdubs to create the 'Marrchestra'. 'Early on they made it clear they didn't want any other instruments on their records,' says Porter. 'They wouldn't allow backing vocals or whatever. Mozzer was clear about that so it was a case of, "OK, any sound we need we'll do it with guitars." So me and Johnny would be dropping spanners on them, taping bits up, just having fun smoking a lot of dope while staying up all night and making silly noises.'

While his production on 1984's THE SMITHS has often been criticised, Porter is first to admit the album's shortcomings, in part due to desperate time and budgetary constraints. To his chagrin, he would never have the chance to make another album with the group, though Porter would still make a sizeable contribution by crafting some of their finest moments at 45 rpm.

'We eventually came up with a formula for singles,' he explains, 'We had this thing of putting signature guitar intros on because I was crazy about them. As a kid I'd buy a record on the strength of a guitar intro. People had stopped doing that so this was another idea I suggested to Johnny. We had a lot of other musical conventions, for instance we wouldn't allow any musical note to be higher than the voice during the verses so there was some kind of payback in the choruses by bringing in all these high jangly things. By "WILLIAM, IT WAS REALLY NOTHING", we'd gotten really good at this formula, putting in all these backwards guitar bits, backwards cymbals, all these things that we'd use in every record at some point which became trademarks. Sometimes they were almost peripheral, you could barely hear them.'

Despite Morrissey's assertion to a radio interviewer in January 1984 that they intended to stick with Porter for the next album, it wasn't long before the producer realised his close relationship with Marr placed his long-term future with the group in jeopardy. During the recording of 'HEAVEN KNOWS I'M MISERABLE NOW' at Island Records' Fallout Shelter studio that March, Morrissey began paying close attention to the in-house engineer, Stephen STREET. 'I saw the writing on the wall then,' says Porter. 'I think Mozzer was starting to resent that me and Johnny had become good pals … I don't think he liked it. I could also see that in Stephen Street he saw somebody that could be, like, "his guy". Which was fair enough.' Street himself concurs, 'I think Johnny formed a stronger relationship with John Porter than he did with me. They definitely had a great understanding and a real bond. Morrissey was probably envious of that.'

The special chemistry between Marr and Porter hit its creative zenith on 'HOW SOON IS NOW?' By then, Marr's studio apprenticeship was complete and henceforth The Smiths would mainly produce themselves with Street's assistance bar a couple of late Porter singles, 'PANIC' and 'ASK'. To Porter's well-documented dismay, the latter was remixed by Steve LILLYWHITE without his foreknowledge. Worse fates befell his final two Smiths A-sides. 'YOU JUST HAVEN'T EARNED IT YET, BABY' would be replaced as a single by 'SHOPLIFTERS OF THE WORLD UNITE' while his version of 1987's 'SHEILA TAKE A BOW' was rejected in favour of a re-recording with Stephen Street which sampled a small portion of his blueprint.

'Looking back I would say that I was disappointed more than anything,' Porter concludes. 'I felt that I never really got to make a proper album with The Smiths because that first one was so rushed. They were getting better all the time, but I don't think we'd got it as good as we could. It all felt like a rehearsal for the great album we never made. That's my only regret. But all the bullshit I understood. I mean it's the music industry – shit happens! As soon as a band becomes successful, well, money changes everything as somebody once said.' [12, 17, 18, 27, 28, 294, 431]

Posey, Sandy, See 'I TAKE IT BACK'.

Pratt, Guy, Session bass player who, for a brief period in June and July 1986, rehearsed with The Smiths as a potential replacement for Andy Rourke for their North American tour later that summer. Although Rourke was still in the group, his recent arrest in an Oldham drugs bust put his chances of acquiring a US work visa at risk. Pratt was brought in, by Marr, as a contingency plan to ensure the tour would go ahead even if Rourke failed to acquire a visa.

The son of former Tommy Steele songwriter and actor Mike Pratt, star of the late 60s cult television series *Randall And Hopkirk (Deceased)*, Pratt met Marr when the guitarist was hired by ROXY MUSIC singer Bryan Ferry to play on 'The Right Stuff', a reworking of The Smiths' 'MONEY CHANGES EVERYTHING'. Pratt, already a member of Ferry's band, quickly developed a friendship with Marr. Shortly after that session, with the indecision hanging over Rourke's visa, Marr invited Pratt to Smiths residential rehearsals at

Stanbridge Farm in the Sussex countryside near Gatwick Airport.

In his 2007 autobiography *My Bass And Other Animals*, Pratt paints an extremely candid picture of the rock and roll excesses he and Marr got up to during that period, recounting how Marr's guitar tech and lodger, Phil Powell, would drive to London and back to score cocaine and acid, also claiming The Smiths' drink of choice was 'a champagne cocktail, consisting of cognac and champagne with a lump of sugar in it'. Rourke was there to teach Pratt the necessary bass parts while Marr's old Manchester friend, Andrew Berry, transformed his long bob into a 'post-modern Billy FURY' cut to complement The Smiths' image. As it turned out, Rourke's visa was successful and the newly shorn Pratt wasn't required, perhaps just as well since Morrissey took an instant dislike to him. 'I don't think he liked the look of me from the start,' mused Pratt, who admits he permanently marked his card at Stanbridge when he mistakenly hammered on the singer's door early one morning, thinking it was Marr's bedroom, having stayed up all night in a coked-up stupor. Morrissey was on the next train to London within the hour.

It was unfortunate that Morrissey and Pratt never hit it off since they shared some common ground. Because of his dad's television career, as a child Pratt used to visit the sets of *Man In A Suitcase* and *The Champions* (respectively starring Smiths cover stars Richard BRADFORD and Alexandra BASTEDO). He also, very briefly, played bass for ex-NEW YORK DOLL Sylvain Sylvain. Following his non-appearance in The Smiths, Pratt would work with Marr again on Kirsty MACCOLL's 1989 album Kite and Electronic's 1996 album Raise The Pressure before becoming touring bassist with Pink Floyd. [18, 28, 112, 352]

'Pregnant For The Last Time' (Morrissey/ Nevin),

Morrissey's tenth solo single, released July 1991, highest UK chart position #25. His most explicit attempt at a full-on rockabilly record ('not extremist rockabilly', he argued, 'just flavouring'),

'Pregnant For The Last Time' is to Morrissey's solo discography what 'SHAKESPEARE'S SISTER' was to The Smiths': a non-album single tipping its turn-ups to the earliest tremors of rock and roll, completely at odds with everything else in the charts of its day.

An archetypal example of Morrissey's uniqueness as a pop lyricist, it empathised with the mundane aspects of pregnancy as experienced by a several-times single mum whose constant need for having 'someone new' has gotten her in the family way yet again. At a time when single mothers were repeatedly targeted by the right-wing media for being Social Security scroungers, 'Pregnant For The Last Time' was a marvellously comic redress: the mention of doctor's waiting room staple *The People's Friend*, the irrational dietary urges for 'chips with cream' and the ingeniously original opening, 'Phlegm lapels'.

When Mark Nevin sent Morrissey a rough demo of the tune, he immediately received an enthusiastic letter of reply. 'The twang strikes again!' wrote Morrissey. 'I'm whistling, drumming fingers and doing the stroll.' Its recording was more of a tribulation for the singer and the only track salvaged from a whimsical attempt in December 1990 to cut a rockabilly-themed mini album with new musicians Boz BOORER, Jonny BRIDGWOOD and Alain WHYTE. The latter tagged along to the session not as guitarist but as 'harmonica player', though his part was eventually wiped from the 'Pregnant For The Last Time' master. Nevin and Andrew PARESI also played on the track, though by the time of its release they'd be out of Morrissey's band. Always bananas in concert, a frenetic live version later appeared on the 12-inch of 'WE HATE IT WHEN OUR FRIENDS BECOME SUCCESSFUL'.

Though the *NME* enthusiastically awarded it with 'Single of the week', the song tends to be overlooked in critical reassessments of Morrissey's solo output and, regrettably, even he later referred to it as 'pretty ropey'. On the contrary, 'Pregnant For The Last Time' is Morrissey at his most gloriously arcane: Nell Dunn's *Up The*

Junction to the tune of Gene Vincent's 'Be Bop A Lula', a blink-and-miss flinch of Brylcreemed pop genius. [4, 15, 22, 25, 194, 437]

Presley, Elvis, The undisputed King of Rock and Roll, cover star of the Smiths single 'SHOPLIFTERS OF THE WORLD UNITE' and one of Morrissey's main musical influences.

During the late 50s British rock and roll explosion, various singers nominated themselves 'the English Elvis', from Cliff Richard to Billy FURY. It could be argued, perhaps shakily, that the true heir to the title of 'English Elvis' never emerged until the 1980s with the arrival of Morrissey. There are many similarities with Presley: the shared working-class roots, the close mother–son relationship and, of course, the resplendent quiff and sideboards combo. More fundamentally, Presley's 1956 debut for RCA VICTOR, 'Heartbreak Hotel', can be seen as a Mozzerian holy scripture which in its simple parable of romantic rejection and suicidal loneliness set a template for the future Smith's entire lyrical oeuvre.

In contrast to the subtle, sometimes obscure, nods to some of his other heroes, Morrissey's Elvis homages have almost always been fairly explicit, beginning in 1985 with The Smiths' cover of '(MARIE'S THE NAME) HIS LATEST FLAME' as part of a live medley with their own Elvis-influenced 'RUSHOLME RUFFIANS'. Marr has also cited Presley's early rockabilly recordings on Sun Records as a conscious guide for his guitar pickings on 'IS IT REALLY SO STRANGE?', itself one word away from Elvis's 1957 cover of Faron Young's 'Is It So Strange?'

The 'Shoplifters' sleeve (1987) featured Presley's first official press photograph taken shortly after he signed with Sun in the mid-50s. Speculation that Morrissey had deliberately chosen the image to highlight his own passing resemblance to the young Elvis was heightened by a photo session for *Record Mirror* magazine where he tried to recreate the same pose with heavy eye make-up only to end up looking, as he put it, 'like a ponce'. A subtler Elvis reference had also featured on the previous Smiths single, 'ASK', where the pun 'Are you loathsome tonight?' was etched into the vinyl run-out-groove.

For what became the final Smiths recording session in May 1987, the group attempted another Elvis cover, 'A FOOL SUCH AS I', the UK number one the week Morrissey was born in May 1959. A few months earlier he discussed his love of Elvis with the *NME*. 'Has a greater voice ever been heard?' enthused Morrissey, also admitting he worshipped 'his leatherised look, although personally I could never wear anything that had run in a field'. He named one of his favourite records as 1956's 'Don't', written by LEIBER AND STOLLER ('The upsurging passion is so powerful that surely no one can listen to it without marrying their own mother') though dismissed 1970's 'Polk Salad Annie' ('all the graceful spirit of a dropped prayer book'). That Morrissey referred to 1968's *Speedway* as his favourite Elvis film also merits some consideration as an influence on the 1994 VAUXHALL AND I song of the same name.

The spectre of Elvis still hovers over Morrissey's post-Smiths career, especially in concert. Other than the occasional Elvis tune on his interval tapes – from 'I Need Your Love Tonight' (the B-side of 'A Fool Such As I') to the furious 'Tiger Man' – another early Presley portrait was used as a backdrop on 1992's YOUR ARSENAL tour. When touring Latin America in 2000 Morrissey adopted a pleather facsimile of the aforementioned 'leatherised look' worn on Presley's career-reviving 1968 television *Comeback Special*. The illuminated 'MORRISSEY' stage lettering of 2004's YOU ARE THE QUARRY tour was another palpable tribute to the iconic 'ELVIS' logo from the same programme.

As time goes by, Morrissey's admiration for Presley seems to have intensified. Visual aesthetics aside, it is the enduring *voice* of Elvis which continues to bedazzle him, almost certainly the greatest in the entire history of popular music and the reason Morrissey ranks Elvis among his sacred 'royal three' beside FRANK SINATRA and the NEW YORK DOLLS. [52, 69, 150, 225, 240]

'Pretty Girls Make Graves' (Morrissey/ Marr),

From the album THE SMITHS (1984). Morrissey's bitter tale of losing his 'faith in womanhood', 'Pretty Girls Make Graves' was one of his more graphic recollections of sexual failure. The scene: an unspecified coastal location. The subject: a sexually voracious female who repeatedly pressurises him to succumb to her carnal urges. The tragedy: his crippling sense of inadequacy which eventually drives her into the arms of another more ready and willing lover. The moral: a miserable realisation that nature has dealt him a losing hand.

The latter lyric may, possibly, have been inspired by a line in the Dirk BOGARDE film VICTIM ('nature played me a dirty trick') while the pivotal 'I'm not the man you think I am' stems from one of Morrissey's favourite 60s singles, Paul Jones's 'I'VE BEEN A BAD, BAD BOY'. The title itself crops up in Jack Kerouac's 1958 autobiographical novel *The Dharma Bums* where the author's pseudonymous alter-ego, Ray Smith, discusses his celibacy, describing how every time a beautiful woman caught his eye he'd remind himself 'pretty girls make graves'.

One of the last songs written for their debut album, a strangely medieval prototype was recorded with producer Troy TATE in the summer of 1983, distinguished by a clip-clop rhythm and guest cellist Audrey Riley further darkening Marr's pastoral gloom; this version was eventually released in 1987 as the B-side of the penultimate Smiths single, 'I STARTED SOMETHING I COULDN'T FINISH'. In its final form, 'Pretty Girls Make Graves' assumed a more even tempo if still disrupted by Morrissey's sporadic choruses of baying agony. As on the Tate version, guest Annalisa JABLONSKA provided the derisive 'Oh, really?' Its ambient finale where Morrissey repeats the opening lines of 'HAND IN GLOVE' was made more distinct thanks to producer John PORTER who wove Marr's improvised pluckings into a more orderly sonic tapestry.

According to Smiths sleeve designer Jo Slee, Morrissey wanted the song to be the group's third single instead of 'WHAT DIFFERENCE DOES IT MAKE?' – a bold if commercially disastrous concept which luckily never came to pass. Along with 'THESE THINGS TAKE TIME' and the same album's 'MISERABLE LIE', 'Pretty Girls Make Graves' still gained prominence in cementing his early media image of a young man scarred by his few calamitous fumblings and now seeking refuge in CELIBACY. [17, 27, 329, 559]

Prokofiev, Sergei,

Twentieth-century Russian composer whose dramatic 'Dance Of The Knights' from the 1935 ballet *Romeo And Juliet* was used as The Smiths' entrance music for the majority of their concert career.

In the original ballet, based upon Shakespeare's play, the music accompanies the masked ball in the Capulets' home where Romeo and Juliet first fall in love: the same piece is sometimes referred to as 'Montagues And Capulets' or 'March Of The Capulets'. The Smiths first used Prokofiev as entrance music at Gloucester Leisure Centre on 24 September 1984, replacing their previous walk-on theme of 'Love Of The Loved' by Cilla BLACK. 'Dance Of The Knights' was used as the introduction at every concert thereafter up to and including the last date of their autumn 1986 UK tour at Manchester's Free Trade Hall on 30 October. For their final Brixton Academy concert of 12 December 1986, they entered the stage to THE L-SHAPED ROOM sample of 'TAKE ME BACK TO DEAR OLD BLIGHTY' instead.

Morrissey has never explained his reasons for choosing the Prokofiev piece, though it may be that he was inspired by its use over the opening credits of the 1979 film CALIGULA (as referenced in 'HEAVEN KNOWS I'M MISERABLE NOW'). The specific version used by The Smiths, as heard briefly at the beginning of RANK, was a 1982 recording by The Philadelphia Orchestra conducted by Riccardo Muti.

p

Proust, Marcel, Early twentieth-century French author best known for his seven-volume work *Remembrance Of Things Past* (aka *In Search Of Lost Time*), about a man who eats a tea cake and suffers 3,000 pages' worth of flash-backs as a result. On 13 March 1988, Morrissey joined his friend Howard DEVOTO's band Luxuria on stage at London's Kentish Town And Country Club (later renamed The Forum) and read an extract from the English translation of Proust's second instalment, *Within A Budding Grove*, at the beginning of their song 'Mlle'. His unan-nounced one-minute cameo – introduced by Devoto as 'Ladies and gentlemen, Marcel Proust!' – marked his first public concert appear-ance since The Smiths' final Brixton Academy concert 15 months earlier. Morrissey read the following passage from Chapter Four, as trans-lated by C. K. Scott-Moncrieff: 'Those few steps from the landing to Albertine's door, those few steps which no one now could prevent my taking, I took with delight, with prudence, as though plunged into a new and strange element, as if in going forward I had been gently displac-ing the liquid stream of happiness, and at the same time with a strange feeling of absolute POWER! – POWER! – and of entering at length into an inheritance which had belonged to me from all time.' [220]

'Public Image, The' (Morrissey/Boorer), B-side of 'I HAVE FORGIVEN JESUS' (2004). Salvaged from the autumn 2003 Hook End session for YOU ARE THE QUARRY as an extra track on the album's final single, 'The Public Image' seemed to concur with Cathal SMYTH's comment to this author that, 'Morrissey does not exist as a person outside of his career.' Confessing to being 5 per cent human to 95 per cent 'image', Morrissey warns his critics that his thin-skinned sort don't take disapproval easily. Particularly intriguing was his reference to a female old flame and his frank admission that one of his biggest mistakes had been trying to 'pass myself off as a human being', itself a profound inversion of his famous declaration in 'HOW SOON IS NOW?' The accompanying tune – a gentle inhalation of harp and piano, exhaling in a boisterous crescendo – contained just enough slow-boiling drama to engage for its full five minutes. [36]

Queen Is Dead, The, The Smiths' third album, released June 1986, highest UK chart position #2. Cover star: Alain DELON. Tracks: 'THE QUEEN IS DEAD', 'FRANKLY, MR SHANKLY', 'I KNOW IT'S OVER', 'NEVER HAD NO ONE EVER', 'CEMETRY GATES', 'BIGMOUTH STRIKES AGAIN', 'THE BOY WITH THE THORN IN HIS SIDE', 'VICAR IN A TUTU', 'THERE IS A LIGHT THAT NEVER GOES OUT', 'SOME GIRLS ARE BIGGER THAN OTHERS'. Produced by Morrissey and Marr.

Conventionally regarded as The Smiths' best album, The Queen Is Dead has, thanks to a banal media age of endless top 100s and all-time classic album polls, been lauded to a dangerously tokenistic degree at the expense of the group's other work. Significantly, neither Morrissey nor Marr considers it to be their masterpiece, as the former stated very clearly in 1994: 'The Queen Is Dead is not our masterpiece. I should know. I was there. I supplied the sandwiches.' Marr is just as cautious in his appraisal. 'When The Smiths split, it wasn't my favourite record,' he says. 'Not that it was my *least* favourite, but I felt that we'd made better albums.' In fact, all four ex-Smiths agree that their fourth and final album, STRANGEWAYS, HERE WE COME, is their finest.

That said, The Queen Is Dead was the album where The Smiths impacted upon their rapidly increasing audience, their peers and the media with an authoritative force greater than ever before. Reviewing the album for *Melody Maker*, journalist Nick Kent made the most accurate prophecy when he praised it as 'the album which history will in due course denote as being the key work in forcing the group's philistine opposition to down chisels and embrace the concept of The Smiths as the only truly vital voice of the 80s'. The Queen Is Dead would also be the last album The Smiths toured, the nostalgic memories of which have played some part in its canonisation. If not their best overall, for convenience's sake it is the record which best represents The Smiths in context of their cultural times and the general social climate of Britain in the 1980s. For these reasons, The Queen Is Dead has become more emblem than album.

The making of The Queen Is Dead, from its earliest musical sketch to its eventual release, covers a period of over 18 months. The Smiths were only just finishing their second album MEAT IS MURDER in December 1984 when Marr began demoing new ideas, one of which blossomed many months later into 'Never Had No One Ever'. But the real seeds of The Queen Is Dead were sown when, after spending the past year based in London, Marr instigated a group return back to Greater Manchester that same winter. Morrissey settled in the village of Hale while Marr bought a house in neighbouring Bowdon. The latter was destined to become The Smiths' HQ for the remainder of their career. It was there – in what Mike Joyce, renting a cottage round the corner, refers to as 'Johnny's Brill Building' – that much of The Queen Is Dead would be written.

'I think we knew, subconsciously, that we had to shut the outside world out,' says Marr. 'In London, when we weren't in the studio or on the road, it was all getting a bit NME-centric. We were surrounded by the record company all the time, people who were nice but clucking round us, holding us up. We were all isolated in flats, with no good hang-out, so I bought a hang-out back up here and everything fell into place creatively. It was all very insular. We just shut up shop, moved back and became incredibly Mancunian again. Even more Mancunian, if that's possible.'

In the spring of 1985 The Smiths embarked on an extensive UK tour to promote Meat Is Murder. The ever-economical Marr regularly used sound-checks to rehearse the riffs and melodies he'd written on the road: surviving tapes show that the singles 'The Boy With The Thorn In His Side', 'Bigmouth Strikes Again' and other less recognisable instrumental sketches (possible precursors to 'Some Girls Are Bigger Than Others' and the B-side 'RUBBER RING') were formed during this period. Following the group's first American tour in June, The Smiths returned to Manchester where, throughout the summer, Morrissey and Marr continued writing in earnest. As the latter

has famously recounted, the bones of three of the album's ten tracks – 'Frankly, Mr Shankly', 'I Know It's Over' and 'There Is A Light That Never Goes Out' – were composed by the duo together in a single evening.

While the intuitive creative dynamic between Morrissey and Marr continued to prosper and intensify, the same could not be said for The Smiths' commercial trajectory. Although Meat Is Murder had rewarded them with their first (and only) number one album, in the singles chart – the frontline of pop – they were rapidly losing presence. That spring's re-released 'HOW SOON IS NOW?' and the idiosyncratic non-album surprise of 'SHAKESPEARE'S SISTER' had both missed the top 20. Morrissey held ROUGH TRADE responsible, accusing them of inadequate promotion. When July's belated Meat Is Murder single 'THAT JOKE ISN'T FUNNY ANYMORE' didn't even make the top 40, his worst suspicions were confirmed. 'Morrissey did draw my attention to several problems with Rough Trade and us not getting in the charts,' recalls Marr. 'It wasn't sinister, but it was a fair bit of incompetence. Mundane elementary things like distribution, not pressing up enough records, not putting up posters. They'd definitely taken their eye off the ball a few times. But behind the scenes there were more significant issues. It was bad business, which is why we tried to do something about it.'

Without a manager, it was the 21-year-old Marr who bore most of the brunt of their complex financial and legal administration at this critical period in their career. Throughout the recording of The Queen Is Dead, these responsibilities, coupled with that of composer, arranger and co-producer, would take their toll on Marr's physical and mental well-being. The die was cast when Morrissey and Marr were persuaded by, in the latter's words, 'an absolute shark of a lawyer' that they were in a position to leave Rough Trade. 'He was not good news,' shivers Marr. 'He caused a lot of bad feeling between us and the label. Basically, he convinced us that we were out of contract and that they'd either have to re-sign us or we could go and sign with somebody else. Which proved to be wrong.'

Morrissey's intentions towards Rough Trade were made abundantly clear on 'Frankly, Mr Shankly', a thinly veiled resignation letter to label boss Geoff Travis among a handful of tracks The Smiths tackled in a preliminary album session at London's RAK studios in September 1985. Along with 'Bigmouth Strikes Again', the RAK session made serious headway on The Queen Is Dead, laying down the bare bones of 'There Is A Light', an instrumental 'I Know It's Over' and a spectral first vocal take of 'Never Had No One Ever'. As the knives sharpened in preparation for their imminent legal battle, a temporary halt in recording was called for a short tour of Scotland to promote their fourth single that year, 'The Boy With The Thorn In His Side'. The Smiths' Caledonian crusade stretched from Ayrshire to the Shetland Isles where, as Rourke speculates, 'I think we were the first live event there since the Wicker Man.' 'It was such an event that the island gazette was dispatched to take a photo of us,' adds Marr. 'All I remember is this guy who'd probably been photographing a prize lettuce the week before asking if he could take a photo with all of us in a highland fling pose. The four of us scattered to the four winds.'

Despite, in Marr's estimation, 'the celebratory mood' of the Scottish tour, when The Smiths recommenced recording that winter at Jacobs, a residential studio near Farnham, the stresses of their rash attempt to leave Rough Trade and their ongoing management vacuum became an ineradicable burden, one which subconsciously drip-fed the ambient gloom of the record itself

'It was a heavy atmosphere, a weird atmosphere,' explains Marr. 'The music, and the writing of the music between me and Morrissey, that was always a buzz. I can't stress that enough. Not just some of the greatest times I've ever had, but some of the greatest times that have *been* had. It was everything else. Outside influences, all the business stuff. Me having to take phone calls about van hire because we didn't have a manager, same as me

having to meet this lawyer, sometimes on my own in the control room where I'd have to vacate everybody. That happened a couple of times and would really cut the flow of the day's music, which was all I cared about in the world. To suddenly be dragged away from that to talk to lawyers was a fucking joke. That kind of shit was just too much.'

Isolated at Jacobs from October through November, the main pieces of The Queen Is Dead fell into place between uninvited visits from their wily solicitor, as well as other interruptions of a more farcical nature. 'We came in the studio one day and saw this huge crate of wine,' recalls Joyce. 'We thought "Great!", but then we were told, "Keep yer hands off. It's for Status Quo, they're in the other studio next door." It was obvious they were on a bit of a mission.'

'I remember one Friday afternoon,' adds Marr, 'and [Quo guitarist] Rick Parfitt was walking towards me with Ray-Bans falling off his face, a bottle of champagne in one hand and a broken cig hanging out the corner of his mouth. We went away for the weekend but the first thing I saw when we got back on Sunday night was Rick Parfitt with his sunglasses on at the same angle, presumably a different bottle of champagne in his hand but still with a broken cigarette in his mouth. He must have been walking into walls the whole time.'

Completed shortly before Christmas 1985, ordinarily The Queen Is Dead would have been released the following February, exactly one year after Meat Is Murder. Instead, having angered Rough Trade with their ill-advised legal subterfuge, the label refused to schedule it until an agreement could be settled. In desperation, Marr even tried to 'steal back' the studio tapes from Jacobs, driving overnight from Manchester to Farnham but unable to convince the owners to surrender the masters without payment. Having painstakingly sculpted their most demanding record to date, The Smiths found themselves in the insane situation of being unable to release it.

The months that followed would be the most dramatic in the group's career prior to the split itself. In February 1986, with nothing to promote and their contractual fiasco still in deadlock, The Smiths undertook a mini tour of Ireland where Rourke's hitherto private drug problem began to manifest itself on stage. Upon returning to Manchester, Rourke hit rock bottom after being arrested in a drugs raid and, for a brief period, was officially dismissed from The Smiths (see the ROURKE entry for full details). In the interim, Marr recruited ex-Bluebells/Aztec Camera guitarist Craig GANNON, not to replace Rourke but to flesh out the group's live sound as 'Second Guitar'. The rehabilitated Rourke was readmitted in late April. A few weeks later, on 20 May 1986, the public got their first glimpse of the revitalised five-man Smiths on BBC2's *Whistle Test*. Looking, and sounding, sharper than ever, they premiered 'Bigmouth Strikes Again', the 'comeback' teaser single marking the merciful resolution of their quarrel with Rough Trade.

The Queen Is Dead followed on 16 June. As was to be expected, the mainstream loyalist press immediately took umbrage. Conservative MP Teddy Taylor typified those outraged by the title's implicit treason, calling for its ban in the *Sun* newspaper. 'It didn't really occur to me ever that people would consider the title offensive,' Morrissey coyly responded. Fans and their critics, on the other hand, received its contents with mutual fervour (sadly, it was kept from reaching number one by Peter Gabriel's So). In spite of, or perhaps *because* of, the psychological strains handicapping its recording, the finished album exceeded all existing Smiths precedents as their boldest, saddest, funniest, prettiest, toughest and most dramatic work yet, distilling every facet of Morrissey and Marr's combined musical and ideological genius into a pithy 37 minutes. 'I can see how it encompasses pretty much all aspects of the band,' concurs Marr. 'I'm pleased about that because we *were* multi-faceted, even though we still get tarred with the one-dimensional miserablism brush. The Queen Is Dead is representative of the progressive side of us. It definitely captures that "night time" side of The Smiths. But even

though it was acclaimed at the time, I always felt that was dangerous to wallow in. My compulsion, always, was to move on.'

If The Smiths were already the most *important* group in Britain, in the aftermath of The Queen Is Dead they now looked set to become, potentially, the biggest. In the months that followed, they'd make a fresh assault on the singles charts with the top 20 hits 'PANIC' and 'ASK' while provoking hitherto unwitnessed scenes of crowd hysteria on their final tours of North America and England. When it was announced in late autumn that The Smiths would soon be leaving Rough Trade for a new deal with EMI, their position among the big league on the global pop stage seemed more feasible than ever. But, just as The Queen Is Dead was a new beginning thrusting the group into uncharted territories of commercial success and recognition, so too it marked the beginning of the end of The Smiths. Over the next year, the same business anxieties which had coloured the making of the album would multiply in ratio with their increasing popularity, straining Morrissey and Marr's relationship to breaking point.

As for the record itself, disregarding any comparative evaluation, on its own merit The Queen Is Dead is a phenomenal album by any measure: the fearsome power and anarchic sentiment of the title track; the legs-in-the-air comedy of 'Frankly, Mr Shankly' and 'Vicar In A Tutu'; the ache of 'I Know It's Over', cubed by 'Never Had No One Ever'; the Wildean madrigal of 'Cemetry Gates'; the supremely arch 'Bigmouth Strikes Again'; the honest charm of 'The Boy With The Thorn In His Side'; the romantic death wish of 'There Is A Light That Never Goes Out'; and the bewildering punchline that 'Some Girls Are Bigger Than Others'. Among these shine more than a few of Morrissey and Marr's most glittering prizes. The weight of critical consensus notwithstanding, those of their own opinion that The Queen Is Dead really *is* the greatest Smiths album have ample ammunition at their disposal to prove so. [12, 14, 17, 18, 27, 28, 38, 50, 112, 154, 206, 374]

'Queen Is Dead, The' (Morrissey/Marr),

From the album THE QUEEN IS DEAD (1986). Every truly great rock and roll group has their no-holds-barred showstopper, the one epic in which they strive to venture beyond the norm and in doing so manage to encapsulate all their audacity and individuality in one unique moment. For THE BEATLES, it was 'A Day In The Life'. For THE ROLLING STONES, 'Sympathy For The Devil'. For The Who, 'Won't Get Fooled Again'.

For The Smiths, it was 'The Queen Is Dead'. While it would be wrong to call it the *quintessential* Smiths track – an honour reserved for the later ballad 'LAST NIGHT I DREAMT THAT SOMEBODY LOVED ME', which is more representative of their repertoire as a whole – it *is* the Smiths track where they conclusively proved themselves the greatest and most original group of their day. Not only did its musical ferocity obliterate the stale cliché of The Smiths as a fey, jangling 'indie band', lyrically it hit new peaks of insurgency, humour and poignancy. Morrissey's magnificent 'state of the nation' public broadcast, 'The Queen Is Dead' was, in political terms, the timeliest song The Smiths ever recorded.

The ghostly echo of an idyllic England of yore – the First World War song 'TAKE ME BACK TO DEAR OLD BLIGHTY' as sung by Cicely Courtneidge in the 1962 film *THE L-SHAPED ROOM* – acts as an ironic prelude to Morrissey's farewell speech to the 'dear old Blighty' that no longer exists. In its place he describes a desecrated husk of its former imperial stature: THATCHER's mid-80s wasteland of half-dead scavengers whose only solace is alcohol, the corrupt clergy or hard drugs peddled by pre-pubescent hooligans. Though barely decipherable, Morrissey's opening moan of 'by land, by sea' highlights his desperation to flee such surroundings by any means necessary.

At the heart of this damning critique of Britain is a comic, but vicious, attack on the monarchy. Having previously mooned at Her Majesty in 'NOWHERE FAST', in 'The Queen Is Dead' Morrissey first reveals his treasonable fantasies of her swinging from the gallows, then places himself in the

shoes of real-life Buckingham Palace intruder Michael Fagan. In July 1982, the unemployed Irishman managed to evade ineffectual security and break into the Queen's bedroom: she and Fagan spoke for ten minutes before he was arrested by armed police. Highlighting Fagan's wasted opportunity as potential royal assassin, Morrissey pictures himself in the same scene, armed with a rusty tool to bash her brains in (and 'a sponge' to clean the mess) only to engage in an absurd conversation about his singing abilities. These lines alone offer a shining example of Morrissey's unrivalled genius as a lyricist, mixing contemptuous political diatribe with uproarious farce.

'I didn't want to attack the monarchy in a sort of beer monster way,' explained Morrissey, 'but I find as time goes by this happiness we had slowly slips away and is replaced by something that is wholly grey and wholly saddening. The very idea of the monarchy and the Queen of England is being reinforced and made to seem more useful than it really is … When you consider what minimal contribution they make in helping people. They never under any circumstances make a useful statement about the world or people's lives. The whole thing seems like a joke, a hideous joke. We don't believe in leprechauns so why should we believe in the Queen?'

The most intriguing of what Marr calls the song's 'many different levels' is its esoteric camp subtext: the scandalous image of a transvestite Prince Charles, Morrissey's mock horror upon tracing 'some old queen' in his genealogy and the hidden lyric – unprinted in the album liner – acknowledging that ancient 'lies about make-up and long hair' are still prevalent. There's also the title itself, from a chapter in Hubert Selby Jr's 1964 novel *Last Exit To Brooklyn*, the cause of several obscenity trials upon first publication due to its explicit subject matter. Significantly, Selby Jr's 'The Queen Is Dead' concerns a transsexual named Georgette. Even when Morrissey first sent the album artwork to ROUGH TRADE, he joked that the title referred to 'the death of a panto queen … yes, it's autobiographical'.

The brilliance of 'The Queen Is Dead' is that it's all these things: an impassioned requiem for a nation gone to ruin; a barefaced rejection of the monarchy; perhaps even a secretive ode to transsexualism. It could even be argued that the song's unforgettable final line summed up Morrissey's entire lyrical agenda in seven words. 'Life is very long, when you're lonely.'

For Marr, it was his partner's best lyric. 'All the aspects of everything Morrissey was doing in The Smiths are in there,' he states. 'It was also the first time it seemed he wasn't just singing a song but layering his voice with all these ghostly effects. It gave the whole album a strange haunted quality.' Undoubtedly it ranks high among the singer's most flamboyantly original works, the only discernible lyrical source being one very vague link with the film BILLY LIAR: a noticeable influence on Morrissey during the making of the album, it shares the similar line 'let's go for a walk, where it's quiet'.

Forewarned only of the song title in advance, Marr saw 'The Queen Is Dead' as an opportunity to 'shut up' their critics and write 'a track that rocks as good as any rock and roll band I've ever heard'. Thinking, in purely broad terms, about late 60s counter-culture rockers MC5, Marr drew more specific rhythmic influence from The Velvet Underground's 'I Can't Stand It', a 1969 outtake featured on the newly released compilation album VU. 'That Velvets comp was a big record for me at the time,' he confirms, 'but the whole idea for "The Queen Is Dead" was a tricky one. I'd had it hanging around my mind for a while for us to do this big romping MC5 track, but I felt that if we played it at the wrong time it would go horribly wrong. It could very easily not have worked, so I had to be really sure that the moment to try it had come.'

Marr's intuition resulted in arguably the best group performance on any Smiths record. Within his own wah-wah inferno, Joyce's firing-squad drums and Rourke's debris-clearing bass line added to its wild halloo of brutal noise. The Midas touch was its eerie feedback gluing all the elements together, a spontaneous addition which Marr stumbled upon by chance. After recording the backing track, he took off his guitar, still plugged in to his wah-wah pedal, and placed it on its stand. As he did so, it hit an odd harmonic which began to feedback while the group were listening to a playback in the control room. Realising it sounded good, Marr quickly returned to the recording booth and began playing about with the pedal, changing the pitch in time to the music to create its familiar ghostly whistle. 'It was just one of those inspired performances,' observes engineer Stephen STREET. 'Johnny did it pretty much live, in one take.' The rabble-rousing drum intro – Joyce's most celebrated Smiths moment – was added last using a looped sample of his playing.

Originally just over seven and a half minutes in length, Stephen Street voiced his concern that the track might be overlong. 'Johnny didn't agree at first,' recalls Street, 'but then after we'd mixed it we all finally agreed it was just slightly too much.' This decision to shorten it with four small cuts in the instrumental finale was a judicious move, ensuring, if only by a fraction, that its dramatic momentum wasn't lost in unnecessary repetition.

An explosive overture to their third album, with 'The Queen Is Dead' The Smiths finally went stratospheric, out of reach of their nearest rivals and above and beyond even their audience's preconceptions to prove themselves not just a *pop* group but one of *the* great rock and roll groups. Its magnitude was proven in concert, normally placed as the ecstatic opener – as heard on RANK – during which Morrissey wielded a protester's placard bearing the title; for their last ever concert at Brixton Academy in December 1986 this sign was substituted for the droll alternative 'Two light ales please'.

Although Morrissey would later add it to his solo setlist in 2007 (excluding a one-off ramshackle attempt ten years earlier), 'The Queen Is Dead' is one track all but impossible to successfully recapture. As a piece of music, as a piece of art, its full glory belongs to the never-to-be-repeated combined chemistry of Morrissey, Marr, Rourke and Joyce, all for one and one for all – the group masterpiece from the masterpiece of groups. [14, 17, 18, 28, 38, 206, 367, 485, 519]

racism, In December 2007 Morrissey began court proceedings against the *NME* for, as he put it, conspiring to characterise him as a racist in their publication of a recent interview he'd given them. His unprecedented legal action accompanied by a press release clearly stating 'I abhor racism' was the final act in a long-running battle with the British media dating back over 20 years. During that time, Morrissey suffered repeated accusations of racism, based upon his outspoken views on race relations, immigration and aspects of black music, as well as a handful of lyrics which made explicit reference to racial conflict. As he sadly noted in 1999, 'If the press continue to say, "Morrissey is racist", then somewhere along the line people begin to associate you with the word and it becomes a part of your biography.'

During The Smiths he was famously criticised for his 'reggae is vile' quip in 1985 while some critics idiotically misconstrued 'PANIC' as an attack on black music purely due to the associations with the word 'disco'. After going solo, 1988's much misunderstood 'BENGALI IN PLATFORMS' aroused further concern, as did 1991's 'ASIAN RUT'. Yet it wasn't until 1992, with the release of YOUR ARSE-NAL including 'THE NATIONAL FRONT DISCO' and his aborted performance at that year's Madstock weekend in London's Finsbury Park that the *NME* dedicated an entire cover story to challenging his stance on race and calling his lyrics on the subject into question (see *NME* entry for full story). Ironically, much of their argument centred on his use of the Union Jack, synonymous with the extreme right British National Party, yet within a couple of years the same flag would be embraced by the UK music industry in celebration of Brit-pop. Neither Noel Gallagher of Oasis, who made iconic use of a Union Jack guitar, nor THATCHER-supporting Spice Girl Geri Halliwell, who performed at the 1997 Brit Awards in an equally iconic Union Jack dress, suffered the racist smear campaign levelled at Morrissey alone.

In the wake of his Madstock appearance, as sensationalised by the *NME*, Morrissey would spend the next decade or more wasting an inordinate amount of interview time defending himself against increasingly tired and inaccurate charges of racism. Discussing the specific fuss over 'The National Front Disco', he recalled, 'I was stopped by many, many journalists who obviously raised the topic in an accusatory way. And I would say to them, "Please, *now*, list the lines in the song which you feel are racist and dangerous and hateful." And they couldn't. Nobody ever ever could, and that irked me. Even though, simply in the voice on all of those songs, on "Asian Rut" or "Bengali In Platforms" or "The National Front Disco", one can plainly hear that there is no hate at all. But you soon realise that they are just out for you, and that it doesn't matter what you say or do.'

Morrissey's comments on racism are unambiguous. In 1994: 'I think that if the National Front were to hate anyone, it would be me. I would be top of the list.' In 1997: 'I can't imagine why anybody would want to be racist. It's so beyond me I feel unqualified to talk about it.' In 1999: 'I have never in my life been racist.' In 2004, he even told the *NME* itself, 'I don't have any racist feelings, so it's ludicrous.' It was therefore entirely regrettable, and avoidable, that three years later the paper should still choose to use his outspoken views on the ever contentious subject of immigration – a concern which Morrissey discussed purely in terms of cultural rather than racial impact – as a means of regurgitating further false suggestions of racist tendencies.

In April 2008 *The Word* magazine were forced to make a public apology in open court after running a review of his GREATEST HITS album which, as his solicitor summarised, could be construed as suggesting 'that Mr Morrissey was a racist, held racist opinions or that (as the child of migrant parents) he was a hypocrite'. Morrissey has since pledged support for the Love Music Hate Racism campaign, who were invited to set up a stall in the foyer of London's Roundhouse during his residency there in January 2008. At the time of finishing this edition of *Mozipedia*, his court action against the *NME* is ongoing.

There will always be those who take issue with the lyrical implications of songs like 'Bengali In Platforms', or who choose to interpret Morrissey's comments that Whitney Houston is 'vile in the extreme' as being more sinister than a purely artistic viewpoint. Yet, there is much truth in the writer Tony Parsons's old joke that 'Morrissey could invade Poland and I still wouldn't believe he is a Nazi'. His recent determination to clear his name in court aside, it has surely been dumbfoundingly obvious for quite some time that Morrissey, the outsider's outsider, is by his very Morrisseyness entirely incapable of racism. [68, 79, 88, 94, 101, 114, 180, 192, 194, 195, 196, 198]

Rank, The Smiths' posthumous live album, released September 1988, highest UK chart position #2. Cover star: Alexandra BASTEDO. Tracks:

Ramones, When Johnny Marr once remarked that during The Smiths he remembered Morrissey listening to the Ramones 'as much as he listened to Sandie SHAW' he highlighted the folly of many critics who, to this day, pigeonhole the singer by his 50s and 60s music tastes alone. Although he'd describe the Ramones' 1975 debut album as 'awful to listen to on first play', Morrissey's affection for the noise, simplicity and celebratory dysfunction of the heroic New York punk pioneers is so acute that he's since expressed a wish to be buried in the vicinity of guitarist Johnny Ramone's grave in Hollywood Forever Cemetery in Los Angeles, as shown on the cover of his 2009 single 'SOMETHING IS SQUEEZING MY SKULL'. Several early Ramones tracks have cropped up on his interval tapes, including 'Judy Is A Punk', later featured on his 2003 compilation UNDER THE INFLUENCE. 'The Ramones do nothing to conceal their disabilities,' wrote Morrissey in the sleeve notes, 'and I am once again in love.' [60, 210]

'THE QUEEN IS DEAD', 'PANIC', 'VICAR IN A TUTU', 'ASK', 'RUSHOLME RUFFIANS', 'THE BOY WITH THE THORN IN HIS SIDE', 'WHAT SHE SAID', 'IS IT REALLY SO STRANGE?', 'CEMETRY GATES', 'LONDON', 'I KNOW IT'S OVER', 'THE DRAIZE TRAIN', 'STILL ILL', 'BIGMOUTH STRIKES AGAIN'. Produced by Grant Showbiz and Peter Dauncey.

Compiled by Morrissey one year after the end of The Smiths, and approved by Marr, Rank was adapted from a BBC Radio 1 In Concert recording of their gig at the National Ballroom, Kilburn in London on 23 October 1986 towards the end of their final UK tour. 'There is surprisingly little of The Smiths' performances captured on film or on tape,' explained Morrissey. '[The Kilburn gig] is used because it is available and good … very good, although there were brighter moments.'[1]

As a live document, Rank is a fair indication of their combined power and passion at the premature end of their stage career, lent extra solidity by the additional guitar of Craig GANNON and stressing the rhythmic vigour of Mike Joyce as their indispensable live anchor.

While there were, as Morrissey says, 'brighter moments' (and better bootlegs), Rank is proof enough that Smiths gigs could be raucous, wild affairs, as Marr says, 'like a football match where the home side keeps winning'. Its highlights included the frenzied wah-wah overture of 'The Queen Is Dead', a giddy 'Rusholme Ruffians' (incorporating a playful flash of the tune that inspired it, Elvis PRESLEY's '(MARIE'S THE NAME) HIS LATEST FLAME'), a ferocious 'What She Said' (bookended by the uncredited 'RUBBER RING'), a rampaging 'London' and an epic and intense 'I Know It's Over'. Best of all were its closing triptych: the mesmerising instrumental 'The Draize Train', a euphoric 'Still Ill' and a growling 'Bigmouth Strikes Again'. Brief snippets of their 'Entrance' and 'Exitus' music, respectively PROKOFIEV's 'Dance Of The Knights' from *Romeo And Juliet* and Shirley BASSEY's 'You'll Never Walk Alone', were also included.

Originally titled The Smiths In Heat, Morrissey chose Rank 'as in J. Arthur', a reference to the Hull-born British cinema mogul who set up the Rank Organisation though, typical of the singer's self-confessed 'very dangerous sense of humour', more commonly a euphemistic rhyming slang for masturbation. Issued six months after Morrissey's solo debut VIVA HATE, Rank was a remarkable testament to The Smiths' continued popularity, only blocked from reaching number one by the diminutive yet immoveable Kylie Minogue.

At the time, Morrissey spoke about Rank as a means of closure on The Smiths, stating that 'none of those songs will ever be heard again'; since then he's performed at least half of its tracks in his solo concerts. Though he joked upon its release that 'it's impossible for me to hear it without eating the pillow', in 2004 Morrissey named it his favourite Smiths album. [17, 65, 69, 71, 203, 410]

---

1. Of the 20 songs played, the BBC originally broadcast 15 including 'THERE IS A LIGHT THAT NEVER GOES OUT', 'FRANKLY, MR SHANKLY' and 'HOW SOON IS NOW?' Morrissey's own selection for Rank whittled it down to 14, removing these three but adding 'Is It Really So Strange?' and 'Still Ill' while remaining faithful to the set's chronological order. The remaining candidates were 'I WANT THE ONE I CAN'T HAVE', 'NEVER HAD NO ONE EVER' and 'MEAT IS MURDER'.

The album's gatefold photo of front row fans desecrating one of Morrissey's shirts was taken from a different gig, the 'Festival Of The Tenth Summer' at Manchester's G-Mex on 19 July 1986. The original album's inner sleeve also featured a much earlier snapshot of Morrissey and Marr on stage at the GLC's 'Jobs For A Change' open-air concert at London's Jubilee Gardens on 10 June 1984.

After the Kilburn Rank gig, The Smiths played only five more shows, one of which (Preston Guildhall, 27 October 1986) would be aborted after the opening number.

Raymonde, See MAKER, James, 'NO ONE CAN HOLD A CANDLE TO YOU'.

RCA Victor, Morrissey's record label for the duration of 1995 under the umbrella of BMG Records. Further evidence of his fastidious label fetishism, as with his previous resurrection of HMV through EMI, RCA Victor was no longer in operation when he signed to BMG. With the help of his friend and video director James O'Brien, Morrissey presented his new company officials

with 'the idea of RCA' for the release of SOUTH-PAW GRAMMAR and its two accompanying singles. 'Modern record labels don't sound good,' he confessed. 'Morrissey and RCA sounds good, don't you agree?'

The revival of RCA Victor was a blatant act of wish fulfilment, aligning him with its most famous sons and his own heroes Elvis PRESLEY and David BOWIE, who by sheer coincidence had also 'come home' to the label that year for his album 1.Outside. The reproduction of its chunky 70s logo was actually copied from a Lou REED album which Morrissey loaned to BMG's graphics department.

Sadly, his fleeting stint on RCA was an uneasy period for Morrissey. 'I was presented with lots of media hoops and I couldn't do it,' he said of their proposed Southpaw campaign. 'I didn't want to be exposed and I didn't want people to know too much about me. They took the view that, "If that's your attitude then we will back off." So overnight it sort of deflated itself.' Morrissey's last RCA Victor release was the November 1995 single 'THE BOY RACER' prior to his next deal with Mercury/ISLAND. [74, 153, 236, 455]

'Reader Meet Author' (Morrissey/ Boorer),
From the album SOUTHPAW GRAMMAR (1995). Morrissey's personal favourite from his fifth solo album, he's since named 'Reader Meet Author' as the song he most enjoys singing and his best composition by Boorer; a tough yet twinkling punk swagger distracted by the symphonic echoes of an all-girls conservatory. '[It's] about a lot of middle-class journalists I know who think they have an understanding of the working classes and their fascinations, which they patently do not,' Morrissey explained. 'Middle-class writers are fascinated by those who struggle. They find it righteous and amusing.'

'I'm pretty sure that song's to do with him meeting Julie Burchill,' speculates its engineer, Danton Supple. 'She was always a fan but then they met and she wrote this article. I think it was always meant as some kind of response to that.'

The meeting between Morrissey and Burchill took place in early 1994 circa the release of VAUXHALL AND I. The resulting *Sunday Times* article was an extremely odd non-interview in which Burchill unashamedly portrays herself as a neurotic fan whose only means of communicating with the singer was a self-loathing compulsion to antagonise him. She begins by reminiscing how during her time as an NME writer during the late 70s, Morrissey would send her fan mail with suggestive remarks about 'the breakfast he would make me on The Morning After'. When Morrissey arrives at her home for the designated interview, Burchill is deliberately rude to his press officer, then proceeds to sabotage the rest of their meeting, calling him a 'girl' when he asks for jasmine tea, teasing him about a 'boyfriend' in San Diego and bluntly asking, 'So, you're gay?' ('I haven't made up my mind yet,' answers Morrissey.) The article ended with Burchill brooding over their disastrous rendezvous: 'Do not meet your hero, do not look at him, do not touch him, do not respond to him in any way, shape or form whatsoever. For he will break your heart, even as you seal his fate.'

Burchill's piece caused uproar in Morrissey's camp; the morning it was published, his assistant/bodyguard Jake WALTERS claimed he had to 'work off the aggression' with a ten-mile run. It's more than plausible that the Burchill 'stitch-up' was a catalyst for 'Reader Meet Author', even if a few years later he found himself agreeing with her article's conclusion: 'As the great Julie Burchill says, maybe it's best not to have tea with the one you love.' [4, 40, 73, 84, 114, 143, 153, 194, 422]

Red Wedge, A collective of British left-wing
pop musicians who formed in 1985 to promote the policies of the Labour Party and support leader Neil Kinnock's bid to oust THATCHER as prime minister in the run-up to the 1987 general election. The Smiths were very briefly involved with Red Wedge, whose leading protagonists were Billy BRAGG, The Style Council, The Communards, Junior Giscombe and ex-Special Jerry

Dammers. Their main means of raising youth awareness was through a series of concerts, often involving cameos from other acts who, while not necessarily diehard Kinnock supporters, still shared their core political aim to displace the current Conservative government.

The Smiths may never have engaged with Red Wedge had its tour of January 1986 not coincided with the group's imposed hiatus while the legal dispute with ROUGH TRADE over the release of THE QUEEN IS DEAD was being thrashed out. As a friend of Bragg, Johnny Marr was quick to lend his support as a means of occupying an otherwise bleak January. On the tenth of that month, Marr visited Bragg in his Chiswick flat to rehearse for the opening night in Manchester. Together they contrived a short set featuring a cover of THE ROLLING STONES' 'The Last Time' (with Marr on backing vocals), 'BACK TO THE OLD HOUSE' (Bragg's favourite Smiths song) and Bragg's 'A Lover Sings' into which Marr craftily managed to incorporate the signature riff of 'THIS CHARMING MAN'.[1] Andy Rourke would join Marr and Bragg on stage at the Manchester Apollo on 25 January, and again two days later when the Red Wedge tour moved to Birmingham.

'It was fun hanging out with Billy and we enjoyed playing with him,' says Marr, 'but the atmosphere around the other bands on that tour was really shitty. They treated me and Andy pretty scrappily. Anyway, I was telling Morrissey about it and he was fairly up for just doing an impromptu show.'

The following week, for the final night of the tour at Newcastle City Hall on 31 January, Marr turned up, unannounced, joined by Morrissey, Rourke and Joyce.

'I walked into the soundcheck, having already been a bit of a feature the week before, but this time with *the gang*. The other bands were a little bit perplexed as to what we were doing there. We had no instruments, so we borrowed The Style Council's equipment and just tore the roof off the place. In the middle of the set we just walked on to this announcement and the place went

bananas. I was so proud of the band. It was like *my* mates showed up and shut everybody up. I always felt very proud of us when there were other bands knocking about because I felt that we were the best. And that was one of the best things we ever did.'

The Smiths played just four songs – 'SHAKE-SPEARE'S SISTER', 'I WANT THE ONE I CAN'T HAVE', 'THE BOY WITH THE THORN IN HIS SIDE' and the yet to be released 'BIGMOUTH STRIKES AGAIN'. Even The Style Council's Paul Weller would later concede that, having never previously 'got' The Smiths, seeing the audience's hysterical reaction at that Newcastle gig was a minor personal epiphany. 'When we took to the stage the audience reeled back in horror,' recalled Morrissey. 'They took their Walkmans off and threw down their cardigans. Suddenly the place was aflame with passion!' Though proud of their 'brief but stormy appearance', Morrissey was altogether more critical of Red Wedge itself, calling its presentation 'middle-aged' and admitting that, while preferable to Thatcher, 'I can't really see anything especially useful in Neil Kinnock.'

Sadly, nor could the voting public. Red Wedge fizzled out after Thatcher goose-stepped to victory for a third consecutive term in June 1987. Their mission had failed though, as Bragg proudly reflects, 'You can say what you like about the politics but the gigs were exemplary, that night in Newcastle especially.' [3, 17, 28, 206]

---

1. Demos of all three were issued as bonus tracks on the 2006 Cooking Vinyl reissue of 1984's Brewing Up With Billy Bragg.

'Redondo Beach' (Patti Smith/Richard Sohl/Lenny Kaye), Morrissey's 29th solo single (double A-side with a live version of 'THERE IS A LIGHT THAT NEVER GOES OUT', both taken from the album LIVE AT EARLS COURT), released March 2005, highest UK chart position #11.

Morrissey's decision to cover a song from Patti Smith's Horses – in his words '[the] album [that] changed my life' – returned him full circle to the origins of The Smiths: it was at a Smith concert in 1978 that he first met Marr while another Horses track, 'Kimberly', provided a foundation for one of the very first Morrissey/Marr originals, 'THE HAND THAT ROCKS THE CRADLE'. Smith wrote the words as a poem in 1971 when sharing an apartment near New York's Chelsea Hotel with photographer Robert Mapplethorpe and her sister, Linda. After 'a rare argument', her sister left and didn't return for the rest of the evening. Smith took a train to Coney Island and spent the night on the beach before going home and writing the song's morbid daydream of what would have happened had her sister killed herself and been found washed up on the shore of Redondo Beach in California. Thankfully, Linda returned home safe and, according to Patti, the sisters 'never quarrelled again'.

Stripped of all such autobiographical resonance, Morrissey's version – played live just seven times towards the end of 2004's YOU ARE THE QUARRY tour – fitted snugly into his existing canon of SUICIDE songs. If the backing was a nervously faithful reggae-lite copy of the original, at least his vocals offered a pleasingly enunciated contrast to Smith's New York garble. As a case in point, even Morrissey misheard – and mis-sang – the opening line as 'Let it be known': it should be 'Late afternoon'. When he informed Smith he was releasing it as a single, she pessimistically warned him it wouldn't chart on account of 'the Patti Smith curse'. Aided by a much-loved Smiths anthem on the reverse, Morrissey would later state it 'only missed the top ten by a few copies, even though, as usual, zero airplay'. [245, 376]

'Reel Around The Fountain' (Morrissey/Marr),

From the album THE SMITHS (1984). Opening the curtains on an album largely informed by Morrissey's chequered history of failed relationships, past infatuations and sexual failures, 'Reel Around The Fountain' was a bittersweet flashback to his transition from child to man and the loss of virginity. 'Until one has a physical commitment with another person, there's something childlike about the soul,' he explained.

The title's origin throws out an uncanny link with Morrissey's much later Roman period circa RINGLEADER OF THE TORMENTORS. In an iconic moment from Federico Fellini's *La Dolce Vita*, Anita Ekberg dances around Rome's Trevi Fountain. The scene is mentioned in one of Morrissey's main early Smiths sources, *POPCORN VENUS* by Marjorie Rosen, who describes Ekberg 'reeling

Reed, Lou, Legendary Velvet Underground frontman and New York rock and roll icon whom the 13-year-old Morrissey first saw in concert at Stretford's Hardrock theatre in Manchester in October 1972.

In the UK Reed's popularity was aided by David BOWIE, who'd cover the Velvets in concert and would later co-produce his 1973 solo masterpiece Transformer with Mick RONSON. Morrissey referred to discovering The Velvet Underground a year or so earlier and spending his 'entire twelfth year' locked in his bedroom transfixed by the woozy splendour of 1967's 'All Tomorrow's Parties'. Johnny Marr would also cite The Velvet Underground as a key Smiths influence, telling *Creem* magazine in 1984 that 'they were art' and naming their Reed-penned 'I Can't Stand It' as a conscious model for 'THE QUEEN IS DEAD'.

Writing to pen pal Robert MACKIE in 1980, Morrissey bragged how he'd seen Reed four times in concert and owned 'most of his stuff', naming his most recent album, 1979's The Bells, as his 'meisterwork'. When touring the UK in February 1995, Morrissey included the Velvets' hissing, violin-chafing oddity 'The Black Angel's Death Song' on his interval tape. Ten years later he was still swooning, 'I loved, and still love, The Velvet Underground.' (See also NICO.) [107, 108, 239, 334, 385]

around the fountain'; the book's influence on early Smiths lyrics is too great for this to be coincidence. Another feminist film critic, Molly Haskell, provides the 'pin and mount' metaphor, adapted from her description of Terence STAMP's *The Collector* in FROM REVERENCE TO RAPE. More obviously, the song contains one of Morrissey's most glaring debts to Shelagh DELANEY, quoting from *A Taste Of Honey*: 'I dreamed about you last night. Fell out of bed twice.' Similarly, the opening lyric was probably inspired by the closing line of Delaney's *The Lion In Love*. As Morrissey was keen to stress to critics who accused him of lazy plagiarism, 'The rest of it almost certainly comes from my brain.'

Marr's muse was equally specific, its seed planted by a morning spent listening to old R&B records at Crazy Face, the shop of his mentor and the group's first manager Joe MOSS. 'We went from listening to The Platters, who I wasn't really getting behind, to "Handy Man" by Jimmy JONES,' he recalls. 'I remembered hearing the track from when I was a kid, cos one of me aunties or somebody used to play it. So I remembered the melody of "Handy Man" but then when I tried to play it myself on the guitar I got it all wrong, which was useful really.'

His resplendent 'Handy Man'-gone-wrong was the basis of the first epic Smiths ballad, a candlelit vigil for the corruption of innocence originally scheduled as the group's second single. Recorded with producer Troy TATE in the summer of 1983, around 50 white labels were pressed prior to its reluctant cancellation. In the first week of September, the *Sun* ran a sensationalist story involving false allegations that their earlier 'HANDSOME DEVIL' was a 'child-sex song', mistakenly claiming that the BBC intended to broadcast it as part of a new radio session for David Jensen. Though neither was true, the very mention of the word 'child' in 'Reel Around The Fountain', which they *had* recorded for Jensen, led to it being dropped by the BBC. While entirely without substance, the story forced the group's label to reconsider their single plans. Yet even after the substitution of

'THIS CHARMING MAN', Morrissey still voiced his belief that 'Reel Around The Fountain' would be a single, even naming his chosen cover star as Albert FINNEY in SATURDAY NIGHT AND SUNDAY MORNING. It wasn't to be.

Both the Tate version and that recorded for their earlier debut John PEEL session in May 1983 (as heard on HATFUL OF HOLLOW) captured an alarmed passion which the final album version never quite regained; producer John PORTER tried to enhance its arrangement by sprinkling some piano from Paul Carrack only to inadvertently dull its potential lustre, its pulse too steady, its central cry too far away from its rightful tether's end. Marr later expressed regret that Carrack's piano 'didn't work', agreeing that the end result failed to deliver. Yet, even in its final subdued form, the wild, patio-slapping romanticism of 'Reel Around The Fountain' still awes in its strength of emotion, enough to be cherished in the hearts of many as a cornerstone of the Morrissey/Marr songbook. [17, 27, 98, 104, 205, 206, 249, 326, 363, 423, 554]

Reeves, Vic,
Surreal British comedian who briefly befriended Morrissey circa 1990 only to become something of a minor nemesis after the singer took offence at one of his television sketches.

Reeves and his comedy partner Bob Mortimer came to prominence with their preposterously daft 1990 Channel 4 show *Vic Reeves Big Night Out*. Morrissey enjoyed the first series and, while making KILL UNCLE that autumn, invited Reeves and Mortimer down to the studio at Hook End Manor near Reading. Cathal SMYTH remembers 'having a laugh with them at the piano, singing some bollocks about biscuits', though according to producer Clive LANGER, Morrissey entertained the pair only very briefly before retiring to bed.

'He could be a bit odd like that,' says Langer. 'He'd invite people down to the studio but then go off to bed as soon as they'd arrived so we'd be stuck with them. All I remember of Vic and Bob is that we recorded them trying to be funny. We were all pissed and I think they suddenly got studio fever so we just chucked them in the

r

recording booth. So we taped about half an hour's worth of routines and it wasn't funny at all, which was a shock.' None of Reeves and Mortimer's clowning around would be salvaged for Kill Uncle – had it even been the intention – though Morrissey would still recognise their presence on the sleeve of the 'Sing Your Life' single with its thanks to 'Jim Moir', Reeves's birth name. Shortly after its release the singer described Reeves as a kindred spirit, or rather kindred lunatic: 'If he'd been born 30 years previous, his mother and auntie would have locked him away in a very dark room.'

Reeves would immediately fall out of Morrissey's favour with the second series of *Big Night Out* featuring 'Morrissey The Consumer Monkey' – a puppet monkey with a crude plastic approximation of the singer's face (glasses, bushy eyebrows, high quiff, hearing aid) who would test out goods and offer warnings on suspect brands. 'I saw it for a split second and instantly loathed its creator,' seethed Morrissey. 'It was meant to be hurtful. I've met Vic Reeves a few times and it hasn't gone too well. He is a person who cannot close his mouth for three seconds because he feels he'll disintegrate into a bowl of dust ... completely loathsome [but] Bob Mortimer I liked. I think he should make a hasty exit from that duo.' Morrissey was still smarting over Reeves three years later, stating, 'If I met Vic Reeves, I'd have no desire other than to smack him in the face.'

Such comments did nothing to deter Reeves's incorporation of Smiths and Morrissey songs into his various television shows and sketches throughout the 90s, often making absurd lyrical changes. Reeves's 1999 book *Sun Boiled Onions* also included a humorous portrait of Morrissey in which, according to the accompanying text, he's supposedly deliberating on how best to replace his loose kitchen tiles. [22, 36, 94, 154, 155, 355, 356]

reggae, One of the more infamous quotes ever attributed to Morrissey was his flippant quip – for that's exactly what it was – that 'reggae is vile'. It was prompted by the *NME*'s question to name the 'Best Reggae Act' of 1984 in their annual end-of-year poll published in February 1985. Morrissey wasn't alone in offering a facetious answer, with U2's Bono naming BAND AID's Bob Geldof and Midge Ure as his reggae stars of the year. But, to Morrissey's critics, the inference of 'reggae is vile' was too broad and dismissive a brushstroke, one which suggested racist undertones. More troubling still were his seemingly sincere comments in 1986 that 'reggae is to me the most racist music in the entire world ... it's an absolute total glorification of black supremacy'.

Twenty years later, Morrissey conceded that he only said 'reggae is vile' to tease the *NME*. 'And God knows it [worked]. Let's not underestimate our power to wind up.' As dumb or debatable as his 'black supremacy' theory goes – a comment the singer almost certainly must regret with hindsight – as he's made abundantly clear himself, Morrissey is a discriminating reggae fan with a nostalgic fondness for early 70s ska and rocksteady. Among his favourite records of that era evoking memories of 'the grime' of Manchester youth clubs he'd attended in his early teens were the Dave And Ansel Collins instrumental 'Double Barrel' (number one, May 1971), The Pioneers' 'Let Your Yeah Be Yeah' (number five, September 1971) and Bob And Marcia's 'Young, Gifted And Black' (number five, April 1970). All three would feature on Morrissey's interval music selections during the late 90s while the latter, also a favourite of Johnny Marr, would have a melodic influence upon The Smiths' 'GIRLFRIEND IN A COMA'.

By way of eradicating all doubt as to how unvile he considered certain reggae, Morrissey included the 1968 ska version of Tchaikovsky's 'Swan Lake' by The Cats on his UNDER THE INFLUENCE various artists compilation; it too had previously featured among his interval playlist circa 1999. In the sleeve notes to the same album he also made reference to watching 70s youth club dancefloors move to other ska tunes including Jimmy Cliff's 'Vietnam' and another called 'Stop Enoch Powell' (perhaps meaning Millie Small's 'Enoch Power'). The biggest irony of all over the overblown 'reggae is vile' furore is that in 2004

Morrissey resurrected the defunct Trojan reggae imprint ATTACK RECORDS when signing with Sanctuary. [71, 151, 182, 196]

Reilly, Vini (Morrissey guitarist 1987–88),

Twenty years before their paths crossed on VIVA HATE, Morrissey and Manchester guitar phenomenon Vini Reilly had shared diverging branches of the same rock family tree. Reilly began his career playing guitar with Wythenshawe punks Ed Banger and THE NOSEBLEEDS, featuring on their only single of 1977, 'Ain't Bin To No Music School'. The following year, after losing Banger and Reilly, Morrissey would briefly join the remaining Nosebleeds as lead singer for two local gigs in early 1978.

In the interim, Reilly became the first artist to be signed to Tony Wilson's FACTORY Records. It was Wilson who christened Reilly's 'group' (though essentially a solo project) The Durutti Column, named after an anarchist resistance movement during the Spanish Civil War (the proper spelling is actually 'Durruti' after founder Buenaventura Durruti). Predominantly instrumental, The Durutti Column's delicate but complex music was shaped by Reilly's classical training and his interest in jazz.

One of four acts on the label's January 1979 debut EP, A Factory Sampler, Reilly's first album, 1980's The Return Of The Durutti Column, was famously issued in a sandpaper sleeve, another of Wilson's ruses borrowed from the French situationist Guy Debord; the idea being that every time the listener removed the record from their shelf, the abrasive sandpaper would scratch and, in time, destroy the record sleeves filed on either side. The sleeves were assembled by hand with Joy Division's Ian Curtis apparently responsible for 500 copies. Wilson would subsequently hail Reilly as 'an invalid genius' referring to his lifelong battle with a rare eating disorder which meant he'd be 'OK for one day and then ill for two weeks'. Frequently misrepresented as an anorexic, Reilly suffers from extreme digestion problems limiting the amount of food he can eat, aggravated by the psychological symptoms of stress and depression.

Despite the Manchester connection, Morrissey had never met Reilly or even seen him perform prior to recording VIVA HATE. It was Stephen Street, who'd recently produced The Durutti Column's album The Guitar And Other Machines, who first brought them together at his Mortlake flat in September 1987. 'Before we went into the studio, myself and Morrissey discussed what musicians we wanted to work with,' explains Street. 'I suggested Vini because I'd just done an album with him. He was a much better guitar player than myself so I knew if I showed him what the chords were then he'd be able to take it to the next level. I arranged for them to meet round mine, but I was quite nervous. Neither Morrissey nor Vini make friends that easily so there was no guarantee they were going to get on. But they did, very well in fact. They shared the same very droll northern humour.'

As Morrissey confirmed, 'Stephen suggested [Vini] and it was perfect. What I liked was the extremity of his beauty, and the erratic quality. He's also extremely humorous … But Vini's not terribly interested in pop music, whereas Johnny [Marr] was absolutely steeped in every manifestation of pop.' Reilly would describe his relationship with the singer as 'very happy … Morrissey made fun of me in a very affectionate way'.[1]

Sadly, Reilly's contribution to Morrissey's career and the creation of Viva Hate has been clouded by his highly controversial claims to the album's authorship. Undoubtedly Reilly's playing was a major contribution to the sonic texture of Morrissey's solo debut, but his allegations that he wrote most of the music are unconvincing. First and foremost, none of the tunes on Viva Hate resembles the inherent musical style of The Durutti Column; as Morrissey reiterated, Reilly had no regard for 'pop' whereas Street did. Drummer Andrew PARESI backs up Street's claims that Reilly would occasionally throw wobblers for the very reason that Street's music was 'too obvious'. Reilly's assertion that he was asked to contribute to Morrissey's 'next album' but turned the offer

r

down also contradicts Street's documentary evidence that as early as January 1988 the singer had prematurely decided 'not to use [Vini] in the future' and was uncertain whether their respective vocal and playing styles were compatible.

On his part, Street forcefully contests Reilly's claims. Though he still praises Reilly for his playing on Viva Hate, his admiration is obscured by bitter memories of studio friction. 'There was a definite change in Vini,' he says. 'After Viva Hate we went back to record the B-sides for "EVERYDAY IS LIKE SUNDAY", which was a bad session in terms of atmosphere. I was starting to struggle with Vini. He was constantly complaining about the music I'd written and refusing to play on stuff. I later found out that he'd started submitting music to Morrissey himself but of course none of it was used. Maybe that had something to do with it. I definitely felt like Vini was trying to get closer to Morrissey and undermine me. Because they had the Manchester connection, they'd sometimes drive back up north together. So if I was paranoid about being pushed aside, then I had good reason to be.'

In Reilly's defence, Street's 1988 diary reveals that after that fractious B-sides session the guitarist telephoned him to apologise for his behaviour. Nor did the experience prevent Street from producing the next Durutti Column album, 1989's eponymous Vini Reilly, widely considered to be among his best and most accessible works to date.

Reilly remains, indisputably, a supremely talented musician, one often and deservedly cited among the greatest guitar players of the post-punk era. For this reason alone, his spurious and petty claims upon Viva Hate are entirely unnecessary. [25, 39, 175, 208, 221, 265 467]

---

1. In his 1989 list of 'Hopes' printed in the NME, Morrissey joked, 'That somebody spells Vini Really's name correctly.'

religion, Born into a 'monstrously large [and] quite absurdly Catholic' family, Morrissey maintains a dim view of organised religion. At the age of six, the sudden death of his grandfather, Patrick

Dwyer, at the age of only 52 and that of his alcoholic uncle Ernie Dwyer at the age of just 24 had a dramatic impact upon the Morrissey household's hitherto devout Catholicism. '[Those] two very serious tragedies within the family caused everybody to turn away from the church, and quite rightly so,' he explained. 'From that period onwards there was just a total disregard for something that was really quite sacrosanct previous to the tragedies.'

Morrissey's strict Catholic schooling had a similarly negative effect. 'I could never really make the connection between Christian and Catholic,' he stated. 'I always imagined that Christ would look down upon the Catholic church and totally disassociate himself from it. I went to severe schools, working-class schools, where they would almost chop your fingers off for your own good, and if you missed church on Sunday and went to school on a Monday and they quizzed you on it, you'd be sent to the gallows … I remember all these religious figures, statues, which used to petrify every living child. All these snakes trodden underfoot and blood everywhere. I thought it was so morbid.'

Despite the psychological wounds of Catholic guilt (as eloquently expressed in 'I HAVE FORGIVEN JESUS') and his constant criticism of the Roman Catholic church – describing Ireland as 'the most repressed country in the world', accusing the Pope of hypocrisy and misogyny – Morrissey maintains a fondness for Catholic symbolism. Photos of his Hollywood home in the late 90s revealed an ornamental Gucci crucifix above his fireplace while in recent years he's worn a pendant of Saint Anthony, the patron saint of 'lost things'. Similarly, in 1985 he appeared on the cover of the NME with a mock halo and stigmata wound (the concept was his idea, not the paper's) and has frequently played with religious imagery since, be it appearing in concert in 2004 in full priest regalia or posing for a 2006 Uncut magazine shoot mimicking the martyrdom of Saint Sebastian.

Asked in 1995 if he believed in God, Morrissey answered 'I try to'. While many of his lyrics acknowledge the existence of heaven, hell, God and Jesus, invariably they veer towards what many

reunion rumours (Smiths), If the old cliché rings true that following the nuclear holocaust only cockroaches will be left to scuttle upon the earth's scorched surface, should radiation grant them the power of speech their first post-apocalyptic conversation will probably begin, 'So, when do you think The Smiths will get back together?'

The 'Smiths reunion' rumour mill has become a tiresome media industry unto itself. Barely a year now passes when some thoroughly unsubstantiated 'story' suggesting an imminent reformation doesn't spread across internet and tabloid gossip columns like nits in a crèche. Such stories are, by their nature, the invention of those whose amassed ignorance of the post-split history between the four ex-members and the outcome of the 1996 COURT CASE could dwarf a continent. Had these gossip-mongers bothered to keep track of Morrissey's many comments since 1987 – that 'The Smiths is dead boys', 'We are not friends … Why on earth would we be on a stage together?', 'The only way we'd ever get back together in the same studio is if we were all shot and somebody dragged the bodies in' and, not least, 'I would rather eat my own testicles than re-form The Smiths, and that's saying something for a vegetarian' – the realisation may have dawned that they'd get better odds down Ladbrokes for a full Beatles reunion complete with Stuart Sutcliffe.

Admittedly, in the immediate post-split confusion circa 1988's VIVA HATE Morrissey lowered his guard by stating 'I would be totally in favour of a reunion', but such wishful thinking had dissipated by the early 1990s. The court case buried any last vestiges of hope that Morrissey, Marr, Rourke and Joyce could share the same stage ever again. Yet still the daftest of rumours persist.

Sadly, it's a by-product of an age when so many other groups *have* re-formed that such a lack of understanding has arisen. Being, as Marr once put it, 'hypothetical, with the emphasis on pathetic', a Smiths reunion would be a purely nostalgic exercise to satisfy the curiosity of youth, the aching regret of those who never saw or appreciated the group at the time, and misty-eyed old romantics with more pristinely preserved ROUGH TRADE vinyl than common sense.

Nostalgia be damned, much of The Smiths' beauty and character lay in their timing as the thorn in the side of 80s pop culture. Theirs was a war already fought and won in the 1980s and no twenty-first-century cenotaph parades will make their victory any greater or sweeter than it already is. The Smiths' omnipresent legacy, both their own music and that of all since who've aspired to reach as high as their turn-ups, is itself the light that never goes out. And while the financial offers would be, and allegedly *have* been, ludicrous (reports ranging from $5 million to $75 million), the risk of snuffing that flame is too great to ever tamper with. Believe 'Smiths reunion' tittle-tattle at your peril. They won't re-form, nor do they need to. [58, 71, 88, 143, 154, 170, 192]

Christians would consider blasphemy, whether demanding God show himself in 'YES, I AM BLIND' or the audacity of 'I Have Forgiven Jesus' itself. Even 'DEAR GOD PLEASE HELP ME' could be deemed profane in its questioning of whether God ever struggled with sexual guilt similar to his own.

When once describing himself as 'a seriously lapsed Catholic' he added, 'I can only have faith in things I see.' Indeed, assessing his lyrics, and life, as a whole, it is hard not to arrive at the conclusion that Morrissey's pessimistic view of human existence is that of a confirmed – or perhaps even 'born again' – atheist. [68, 135, 165, 226, 448, 569]

Reparata, See 'SHOES'.

Rendezvous In Black, 1948 crime novel by Cornell Woolrich which boasts an uncanny Smiths coincidence in featuring a central character called Johnny Marr and another called Morrissey.

r

Woolrich's Johnny Marr is a calculating serial killer scheming a callous psychological revenge on the five men he suspects responsible for his fiancée's accidental death. Marr's fourth murder plot involves hustling in on the girlfriend of Bill Morrissey resulting in a scene where the jilted Morrissey confronts and punches Marr. Contacted by this author, the real Johnny Marr professed no prior knowledge of Woolrich's book, describing the coincidence as 'too weird'. It had, however, been previously mentioned in a 1985 Smiths feature in *Time Out* where journalist Simon Garfield rhetorically speculated, 'Where did the names Morrissey and Johnny Marr come from anyway? Was it just coincidence that they were respectively a murder victim and the hero [*sic*] of Cornell Woolrich's novel *Rendezvous In Black*?'

Woolrich himself is an intriguingly Mozzerian character and, until recent times, something of an unsung hero of American crime fiction. His was a bitterly sad life of failed romances and, in the words of fan and novelist Richard Dooling, 'self-loathing over his promiscuous, clandestine homosexual activity'. Woolrich spent most of his adulthood lodging with his mother in shabby hotel rooms, eventually succumbing to alcoholism, losing a leg to gangrene and dying alone of a stroke in 1968, aged 64. He did at least enjoy great commercial success, writing the novels and short stories which inspired Alfred Hitchcock's *Rear Window*, François Truffaut's *The Bride Wore Black* and the Edward G. Robinson thriller *Night Has A Thousand Eyes*. Despite Woolrich's self-deprecating remarks to his agent before his death that he 'wasn't that good, you know', the tense, page-turning drama of *Rendezvous In Black* attests otherwise. [105, 400]

Rhodes, Marjorie, Hull-born actress who
Morrissey once named as his favourite, specifically for her role as the long-suffering wife of John MILLS in THE FAMILY WAY. Rhodes also appeared in minor roles in other Morrissey favourites, THE NAKED TRUTH, YIELD TO THE NIGHT and SPRING AND PORT WINE, as well as a brief cameo in the dire Billy FURY musical, *I've Gotta Horse*. Rhodes died in 1979, aged 76. [168, 175, 502, 532, 566]

Richard III, Alongside fictitious Italian puppet
boy and chronic fibber Pinocchio, the 'historical figure' Morrissey most identifies himself with, or so he claimed in 1991. Doubtless the Richard III Morrissey had in mind was that famously dramatised in the play by William Shakespeare – a royal villain so deformed, so 'lamely and unfashionable that dogs bark at me as I halt by them' who proceeds to murder and connive his way to the throne via infanticide and the spiteful seduction of his brother's widow. Historians have since challenged Shakespeare's portrayal of the real Richard III who ruled England for just over two years from June 1483 until his death at the Battle of Bosworth in August 1485 and who, in actuality, probably wasn't quite the hunchbacked, power-hungry killer of 'the princes in the tower' of legend. That said, he's still the prime historical suspect in the unsolved mystery of the disappearance of his two nephew princes, the 12-year-old Edward V and his brother Richard, whom he imprisoned in the Tower of London after seizing the crown. Contemporary portraits of Richard also hint that, while not necessarily a hunchback, he did have one shoulder higher than the other.

Morrissey's fondness for Shakespeare's Richard III would also account for the citation from the play in The Smiths' 'CEMETRY GATES': 'The early village cock hath twice done salutation to the morn' (Act V, Scene III). [141]

Richards, Keith, See ROLLING STONES, THE.

Richardson, Charlie, 1960s south London
gangland boss featured on the inner sleeve of YOUR ARSENAL. The image, culled from Richardson's 1991 autobiography *My Manor*, shows him with his daughter on Dymchurch beach in the early 60s: its original caption read: 'I wasn't a conventional father, but I was a good one.' The same photo was used as a backdrop during Morrissey's 1992 tour to promote the album.

While the KRAY twins controlled London's East End during the early to mid-60s, across the river Charlie, his brother Eddie and a team of villains including 'Mad' Frankie Frazer known as the Richardson Gang ruled south London. Charlie had first crossed paths with Reggie and Ronnie Kray at Shepton Mallet military prison in the 50s where the three of them had been sent to finish their national service after absconding. 'We were all friends at the time,' said Richardson, though their rival firms would later clash in 1965 after a Richardson associate, George Cornell, made the fatal mistake of calling the overweight homosexual Ronnie Kray 'a fat poof'. A gang war ensued, coming to a head with a notorious shootout in March 1966 at Mr Smith's, a Catford nightclub recently opened by Diana DORS, where Kray associate Dickie Hart was murdered. Two days later, Richardson man Cornell had the audacity to go for a drink at the Blind Beggar pub on the Krays' turf where Ronnie shot him at point-blank range. As Richardson later philosophised, 'No matter how hard and fearless you are, if the other man has got a gun the odds are very uneven.'

Morrissey's interest in Richardson was symptomatic of his romanticised view of English villainy and his particular fascination with the Krays. Throughout *My Manor*, Richardson presents himself as a heroic, anti-authoritarian working-class rebel, victimised by the upper classes and the repressed British legal system and aching with a nostalgia for 'the good old days, when a fiver fed a family for a fortnight, dog shit stuck to the nails in your boots and fraud was simple'.

But the details of the Richardson Gang's practices which emerged during their 1966 trial after being 'grassed up' by a former business associate summon little sympathy or admiration. Richardson would deny the headline-making graphic descriptions of torture – electrocution, nailing feet to the floor, beating a naked man unconscious and then making them mop up their own blood with their underpants as he ate scampi and chips – but the weight of evidence against him was enough to warrant a 25-year sentence. During his stretch,

Richardson was reunited with Reggie Kray in Parkhurst prison. Kray later commented that '[Charlie's] sense of humour, which always appealed to me, had not been lost'. After serving 14 years, Richardson soon ceased to see the funny side of 'eating dog's vomit with three white slices and a tot of margarine' and escaped from HMP Spring Hill, an open prison near Aylesbury. Spending two years on the run, he gave himself up and was finally released in 1984, 18 years after his conviction. A film of his life, *Charlie*, was released in 2004 starring former Bros drummer Luke Goss in the title role for reasons which make mockery of all common sense. [330, 331, 359, 374, 384]

'Ride On Time', 1989 UK number one single

by Italian house DJ collective Black Box and a big favourite of Morrissey's during the BONA DRAG sessions. 'I can remember him buying the 12-inch,' says Kevin ARMSTRONG. 'He absolutely loved it.' Clive LANGER concurs that Morrissey 'would sometimes be dancing to Black Box all night, full blast on the giant studio speakers'. As he later told the press, 'It's odd for me because it's not my world at all and there's no reason on earth why I should enjoy that record, but when I first saw them on *TOP OF THE POPS* I thought it was pretty extreme. She also looked brilliant, and I still love the record after nine weeks.' The 'she' was Amazonian Black Box frontwoman Katrin, alias model Catherine Quinol, who never sang a note but mimed to the band's samples from old disco records. The voice on 'Ride On Time' was that of Loleatta Holloway, ripped from 1980's 'Love Sensation'. Holloway successfully took Black Box to court and was awarded a settlement, as did The Weather Girls' Martha Walsh who found herself sampled on a number of their follow-up singles. Morrissey was less concerned about Katrin being a fake singer than more scurrilous rumours suggesting that she'd once been a man. 'I'm hoping that it's true because it makes it more interesting,' he enthused. 'If you look at her from a certain angle, you could possibly see her playing for Wigan.' [1, 15, 226]

Righteous Brothers, The, 60s American 'blue-eyed soul' duo whom Morrissey has credited as inspiring him to become a singer. 'When I was two years old [*sic*] I saw [them] on television,' he recalled. 'Bill and Bobby. I thought fantastic. That's me ... I wanted to be Bobby out of The Righteous Brothers.'

In fact, Morrissey would have been five when fictitious siblings Bill Medley and Bobby Hatfield topped the UK charts in February 1965 with their humungous Phil Spector production, 'You've Lost That Lovin' Feelin''. 'I was obsessed with [that song],' he raved. 'The way the two voices are jumping around and when I saw it on *TOP OF THE POPS*, the way they would not look at each other and sing those parts was extraordinary.' The 'Brothers' enjoyed other hits though only August 1965's 'Unchained Melody' (technically a solo record by Hatfield) would follow 'Lovin' Feelin'' to number one when re-released in 1990 after its use in the film *Ghost*. Morrissey's dreams of wanting to become Hatfield probably ended upon hearing the news in early November 2003 that he'd been found dead in his Kalamazoo hotel room of a cocaine-induced heart attack, aged 63. [159, 170]

Ringleader Of The Tormentors, Morrissey's eighth solo album, released April 2006, highest UK chart position #1. Tracks: 'I WILL SEE YOU IN FAR-OFF PLACES', 'DEAR GOD PLEASE HELP ME', 'YOU HAVE KILLED ME', 'THE YOUNGEST WAS THE MOST LOVED', 'IN THE FUTURE WHEN ALL'S WELL', 'THE FATHER WHO MUST BE KILLED', 'LIFE IS A PIGSTY', 'I'LL NEVER BE ANYBODY'S HERO NOW', 'ON THE STREETS I RAN', 'TO ME YOU ARE A WORK OF ART', 'I JUST WANT TO SEE THE BOY HAPPY', 'AT LAST I AM BORN'. Produced by TONY VISCONTI.

Even while Morrissey's triumphant comeback of 2004 was in full flow, idle rumours were already circulating that YOU ARE THE QUARRY was nothing more than a carefully planned last hurrah before retirement. As unlikely as that sounded – that after seven years out of the game Morrissey would even *think* of relinquishing the recovered glory he'd fought tooth and nail for – the final UK arena shows of the Quarry tour in December 2004 were marked by an eerie sense of closure. On the penultimate night at London's Earls Court the singer began the encore by announcing, 'There are goodbyes and there are farewells. This is farewell.' His final words before leaving the stage were more ominous still: 'Please don't forget me. I love you.'

Although You Are The Quarry had been a resounding victory, not least in spawning four top ten singles, the real challenge now facing Morrissey

was to sustain that momentum. Bearing in mind his track record for following a hit album with a 'difficult' sequel – VIVA HATE with KILL UNCLE, VAUXHALL AND I with SOUTHPAW GRAMMAR – there was no guarantee that Quarry wasn't a freak success which he'd never be able to repeat. The retirement gossip notwithstanding, by the end of 2004 there were serious questions regarding the future stability of Morrissey's band. First and foremost was the ambiguity surrounding long-term co-writer, Alain WHYTE, who'd dropped out of the Quarry tour after 14 shows amid unsubstantiated rumours of a nervous collapse. Morrissey still had Boz BOORER and new boy Jesse TOBIAS, though whether either or both could comfortably fill Whyte's shoes between them was another uncertainty.

In the meantime, at the beginning of 2005, after selling his Los Angeles home, the singer relocated to Europe, finding himself 'by accident' living in the Italian capital, Rome. The city had an immediate and profound impact upon his writing, becoming his primary muse for Ringleader Of The Tormentors: in essence, Morrissey's 'Roman album'. Its eventual producer, Tony Visconti, would observe, 'He's totally in love with the city. He must have been walking around Rome writing the songs in his head.' As well as making lyrical references to his new home, Morrissey sought further inspiration in Italian cinema and the films of Pier Paolo PASOLINI and LUCHINO VISCONTI, both namechecked on the album's 'You Have Killed Me'. As he'd tell the press, 'I've become an Italianophile.'

As it also transpired, despite being out of Morrissey's touring band, Whyte's longstanding writing relationship with Morrissey remained unchanged. On Ringleader Whyte would, once again, become an indispensable contributor responsible for all of its main highlights. Boorer also submitted ideas but was largely unsuccessful bar one B-side, 'CHRISTIAN DIOR'. In a concerted effort to invalidate any accusations of favouritism, Morrissey made a point of praising Boorer after the album's completion. 'There are no Boz songs on this album,' he confirmed, 'but strangely it is the album on which Boz has been most involved and had such a massive input.'

As it was, Boorer had since been usurped by two new challengers: Jesse Tobias and, to a lesser extent, keyboard player Michael FARRELL. Tobias, especially, would make what the singer called 'a marked difference in sound' upon Ringleader. Of his five songs, four would be released as singles. 'Personally and musically, Jesse has made a big impact,' stated Morrissey, also citing Tobias as the album's other 'muse' besides Rome; even Visconti would remark, 'it sounds like Morrissey has found a new muse', possibly meaning Tobias.

By late August 2005 Morrissey was ready to record, choosing to stay in Rome and make the album at Forum Music Village, a converted church and the studio of choice for the Italian film industry. Alongside Boorer and the three co-writers Whyte, Tobias and Farrell, the session saw Gary DAY back on bass but a new drummer, Matt CHAMBERLAIN, hired in place of the recently departed Dean BUTTERWORTH. Morrissey's first choice of producer was Jeff Saltzman, currently in big demand after the quadruple platinum success of The Killers' Hot Fuss album. When Saltzman proved 'unable to undertake the project' (in another interview Morrissey referred to hiring 'a producer [that] just didn't work out'), the singer decided that, with Boorer's technical experience, they'd be able to oversee it themselves. After three

weeks of trial and much error, further hampered by interruptions from carpenters and electricians carrying out studio renovations, it became painfully obvious they needed outside help. '[It was] an enormous self-overestimation,' Morrissey confessed.

The chosen cavalry was Visconti, the legendary BOWIE and BOLAN producer whom Morrissey 'always knew' he'd one day work with. Approached in New York by Morrissey's manager, Merck Mercuriadis, Visconti was played two of the works in progress. Immediately impressed by the singer's 'new, more powerful voice', Visconti considered it 'an offer I couldn't refuse'. Within 48 hours he'd cancelled another album he was due to record in France to board a plane for Rome. After meeting Morrissey and assuring him he *really* loved' the new songs, Visconti worked solidly from late September until early November rebuilding the album. 'They had already recorded their drum tracks and some guitars which we ended up using,' he later commented. 'It wasn't in bad shape. It just wasn't organised.'

For Morrissey, weaned on and inspired by Visconti's work with Bowie and Bolan since the age of 11, working with the producer was 'a mad dream' come true. Discussing the album's unifying Italian influence, the singer proudly acknowledged that Visconti, too, was of Italian descent, commenting 'the fact he became involved is also a fascinating part of the whole jigsaw', also singling out engineer Marco Martin, 'a dazzling talent and very much a crucial part of the final picture'. Luck also intervened when soundtrack maestro Ennio MORRICONE, a regular at Forum Music Village, agreed to score and arrange strings for the confessional ballad, 'Dear God Please Help Me' after studio MD Marco Patrignani put in a friendly word. As a final twist of local colour, a seven-strong Italian children's choir was roped in to provide backing on three of the tracks.

Early reports hinted that Ringleader would be Morrissey's 'most beautiful' and 'most gentle' so far. 'I imagined it would be,' he said. 'That's the way I was feeling … very wistful and slightly wearisome. But when all the Italian components fell together and the new songs came together, mostly in [Rome], then it developed itself as strong and confrontational. We used more instrumentation, so there seems to be a lot more happening in the songs.' Visconti also remarked how the singer had wanted 'a band sound' and 'paid attention to everyone's part ... Morrissey was great for championing the individual players'.

With the exception of 'Dear God Please Help Me', Ringleader was anything but the genteel album Morrissey had first announced. In context of its seven predecessors, its predominance of chugging rock guitars and mighty rhythms made it his toughest-sounding record since SOUTHPAW GRAMMAR. The 'guttural' (as Morrissey called them) songs of Jesse Tobias were largely responsible, offering a stodgy contrast to the subtleties of Whyte's melodies and the cinematic pomp of Farrell's one contribution, 'At Last I Am Born'. Of the 20 tracks recorded during the session, a dozen were chosen for the final tracklisting. 'Some of my favourites have ended up as B-sides,' mourned Visconti. 'To turn this into a 12-track CD was a heartbreaker for me. It deserved to be a double.' Among the casualties were Boorer's 'Christian Dior', Farrell's 'SWEETIE-PIE' and two strong Whyte contenders, 'GOOD LOOKING MAN ABOUT TOWN' and the excellent 'GANGLORD'.

Quizzed by the press about the album title, Morrissey declared that he was the eponymous ringleader. 'For many years, I was accused in England of being very negative and the way I sang was very depressing but suddenly in recent years in British music many younger groups were singing in a similar style to me and giving credit to me so I felt like I was leading something.' Elsewhere, he'd refer to it as meaning 'disturber of the peace'. 'It doesn't come naturally to me to endear myself to the public,' he quipped. 'In fact, if that was 1773, I probably would have been hanged and burned by now, which gives even more credence to the album title.'

The sleeve was a superbly self-aggrandising classical pastiche with Morrissey in tux and bow-tie playing a violin and looking like some world-renowned virtuoso on an old Deutsche Grammophon LP sleeve. As he later revealed on TRUE-TO-YOU.NET, the image was actually inspired by the 1946 John GARFIELD film *Humoresque*. An inner gatefold portrait of Morrissey resting on a Piaggio Vespa scooter reiterated the album's Italian themes, as did the cover subtitle 'Registrato e Mescolato a Roma in Autunno' ('Recorded and Mixed in Rome in Autumn').

Heralded in March 2006 by the 'You Have Killed Me' single which equalled the career-high number-three success of Quarry's 'IRISH BLOOD, ENGLISH HEART', the reaction to Ringleader was everything Morrissey could have wished for. Despite some middling reviews from cooler critics, possibly burned by the exaggerated giddiness they lavished upon Quarry, there were enough pre-release plaudits declaring it 'genius' and 'the Morrissey masterpiece' to warrant a sticker on the CD cover. More significantly, it entered the charts at number one; his third solo number one album and his first since Vauxhall And I 12 years earlier. 'Ringleader Of The Tormentors stands as a joy greater than pleasure to me,' he concluded, noting how 'in several countries across Europe ... it zaps to #1'. Only in private would he grumble that it subsequently bombed out of the charts becoming, as he melodramatically likened it, the quickest downward plunge in pop history.

Within the media, Ringleader created a minor sensation in terms of its lyrical insinuations about Morrissey's private life, largely down to the explicit content of 'Dear God Please Help Me', a frank account of a liberating sexual experience in Rome, written in the first person and with vivid homosexual overtones. The closing 'At Last I Am Born' also outlined some form of sexual rejuvenation and the overcoming of lifelong repression and guilt, a subject echoed in Morrissey's teasing yet ultimately cryptic quotes to the press that 'the past year has been an eye-opener in many, many ways'. There was also the question of why the singer had moved to Rome in the first place, prompting assumptions that he'd relocated there to be close to a partner. Assessing his new circumstances in context of the album's lyrics, it was a very reasonable hypothesis. The hostility with which Morrissey reacted to this supposition was, in itself, quite revealing. On stage at London's Alexandra Palace on May Day 2006, he told his audience, 'Recently the press, the *glorious* press, say I'm in love. Which, of course, is complete shit.' A year later, he was still picking over the bones of the Ringleader conspiracy theories. 'In a few interviews, the quotes were chopped up so it seemed I was deeply in love and having some wild, mysterious affair in foreign lands,' he foamed. 'Which was absolute cobblers.'

The album itself was a superior work to Quarry in many respects and certainly more cohesive. While it lacked Quarry's ratio of strong hit singles (as their chart positions, bar 'You Have Killed Me', would systematically demonstrate), there was a consistency of sound gluing its dozen tracks together into a unified whole. Yet in terms of songwriting, with hindsight those early critical estimations of 'the Morrissey masterpiece' seem rather reckless. There were some absorbing character sketches ('The Youngest Was The Most Loved', 'The Father Who Must Be Killed'), much titillating autobiography ('Dear God Please Help Me', 'You Have Killed Me', 'To Me You Are A Work Of Art') and a frisson of political anger ('I Will See You In Far-Off Places'), but nothing truly extraordinary by Morrissey's standards. Musically, too, although governed by a discernibly harder sound than Quarry, Ringleader was unchallenging in terms of Whyte's typically wistful ballads and Tobias's lumpy guitar mash. Even its much vaunted centrepiece, 'Life Is A Pigsty', was glorified bluster at times lapsing into sluggishness.

Not that Visconti, let alone Morrissey, would possibly agree. 'The scope of the melodies and the depths of the lyrics are brilliant,' the producer frothed. 'I couldn't believe he'd written the songs on this record. They were really high in his register. They were melodies that Bowie would write, using a whole range of notes.'

Indeed, it's as a vocal performance that Ringleader is best appreciated. While it may not contain his greatest songs, it does feature some of his greatest singing, especially during its first half. Whatever its flaws, in cementing Morrissey's twenty-first-century comeback Ringleader Of The Tormentors was an incontestable triumph. [54, 116, 259, 266, 269, 235, 195, 242, 245, 389, 441, 456, 461, 471, 511]

rockabilly, One of the biggest myths about Morrissey's solo career is that he has 'a rockabilly band'. This is only true in the sense that his original 1991 KILL UNCLE touring group of Boz BOORER, Spencer COBRIN, Gary DAY and Alain WHYTE were all recruited from the north London rockabilly circuit, all looked and dressed in a 50s rockabilly style (quiffed hair, turned-up jeans, the odd tattoo) and, on that tour at least, lent a rockabilly flavouring to Morrissey's existing repertoire. 'People always overstate the case,' he grumbled at the time. 'If I mention one rockabilly artist, it doesn't follow that I'm running around in drainpipes and a huge DA. I simply find a lot of rockabilly exciting in a way that modern pop songs aren't.'

Indeed, while Morrissey is a fan of the genre, he has only recorded a handful of songs that could be accurately termed rockabilly: by definition a hybrid of 50s rock and roll and hillbilly country music, mixing the syncopated rhythms of the former with the melodic elements and guitar pickings of the latter. Rockabilly is a very specific, and unmistakeable sound, applicable only to music which fulfils strict stylistic criteria; for the classic model refer to Charlie Feathers's 'One Hand Loose' and Nat Couty's 'Woodpecker Rock' on Morrissey's UNDER THE INFLUENCE compilation.

The Smiths never recorded outright rockabilly, though an obvious 50s rock and roll influence trembles through 'RUSHOLME RUFFIANS', 'NOWHERE FAST', 'SHAKESPEARE'S SISTER', 'VICAR IN A TUTU' and 'DEATH AT ONE'S ELBOW'. As a solo artist, the few rockabilly songs Morrissey *has* made have all been written by Mark NEVIN. There's a subtle influence on 'SING YOUR LIFE' (made more explicit in live performance) while both 'THE LOOP' and 'PREG-NANT FOR THE LAST TIME' were conscious rocka-billy creations, written in response to the singer's short-lived plans to record 'a rockabilly-themed mini album' in the winter of 1990. Similarly, Nevin's 'YOU'RE GONNA NEED SOMEONE ON YOUR SIDE' was also a deliberate appeal to Morrissey's love of 50s music.

By contrast, Boorer and Whyte have never written anything for Morrissey that could be remotely described as rockabilly, bar Whyte's 'CERTAIN PEOPLE I KNOW', itself a pastiche of T.Rex's 'Ride A White Swan'. 'All I seem to hear these days is that I'm "working with a young rockabilly band",' Morrissey fumed in 1992. 'They're not "young" and they're not "rocka-billy", but everything gets expanded until it becomes a cliché.' Sadly, the cliché still hovers. As recent as 2009's YEARS OF REFUSAL, some critics still made bafflingly daft references to Morrissey's 'rockabilly sound', a sound which exists only in the empty heads of those who'd crack under pres-sure to differentiate between Hasil Adkins and Hazell Dean. [4, 5, 17, 94, 155]

Rogan, Johnny, See SEVERED ALLIANCE, THE.

Rolling Stones, The, The most influential
group in the history of pop music remain THE BEATLES, but it's their rubber-hipped and bigger-lipped southern rivals, The Rolling Stones, who exerted the greater impact upon The Smiths, or specifically Johnny Marr. Whereas Morrissey has only ever discussed the Stones in a negative sense – naming singer Mick Jagger as the catalyst for his 1990 B-side ridiculing rock and roll geriatrics, 'GET OFF THE STAGE' – Marr lists guitarist Keith Richards and their early manager, hustler extraordinaire Andrew Oldham, as two of his biggest heroes.

Marr's love of the Stones came forcefully to the fore in early 1985. As The Smiths' TV appear-ances of February and March that year bear witness, Marr's haircut and stage poses were easily mistaken for those of Keith Richards two decades earlier. It followed that their current

single, 'SHAKESPEARE'S SISTER', would also be The Smiths' 'Stones-iest' moment, bringing to mind the satanic boogie of 1966's 'Have You Seen Your Mother Baby, Standing In The Shadow?' Whether true or not, the NME's report in May '85 that The Smiths had recently approached Andrew Oldham to become their manager seemed entirely logical.

The cassette archive of Mike Joyce also testifies to Marr's love of the Stones' earlier R&B period; among these tapes are Marr's tour-bus compila-tions featuring rare album tracks such as 1964's 'Confessin' The Blues'. 'Shakespeare's Sister' notwithstanding, their influence on Marr was more one of mood and a tangible melodic dark-ness than any specific mimicry. As Andy Rourke notes: 'Around the time of THE QUEEN IS DEAD I can remember myself and Johnny listening to [the Stones' 1967 album] Their Satanic Majesties' Request. There was a certain heaviness that seemed to fit how we were feeling as a group around that time which must have rubbed off on our own music.'

Marr names his favourite Stones track as 'Gimme Shelter' from 1969's Let It Bleed. 'That's it for me,' he enthuses, 'my desert island disc. That's where you hear the voodoo Keith Richards found. That period from Beggar's Banquet through to Let It Bleed, though it wasn't the stuff that necessarily influenced me during The Smiths, as I've gotten older I've realised just what it took for a young man to follow that ideal instead of swanning around and buying cars. What you hear in what he uncovered was the pursuit of a lifestyle to be creative as opposed to just recreative. To me, he's almost like an alchemist.'

Marr first met Richards circa 1986 thanks to Kirsty MACCOLL, who sang backing vocals on the Stones' Dirty Work album produced by husband Steve LILLYWHITE. The idol and the fan ended up jamming through the night on acoustic guitars while MacColl berated Richards for getting the chords wrong to an Everly Brothers tune.

When The Smiths broke up, Marr received a second invitation to 'hang' with Richards in Los Angeles. 'The atmosphere between us was one of two guitar players licking our wounds,' recalled Marr, 'because we had both recently gone through serious shit with our [musical] partners. It took me a while to realise that, because I would never assume that he would ever relate to me in any way. So I had the honour of being given some incredibly philosophical and personal advice, reassurance and encouragement. At one stage, there was just me and him, and he said, "Come on, then, 'fess up. What did you want to be when you were a kid?" And I sat there thinking, "How do I answer this question?" So I said, "You." And he said, "Well, I'm telling you that you're all right as you are. You're a good player and a good person, so don't go killing yourself for rock 'n' roll because it ain't worth it." It was an incredible experience for a shitkicker from Wythenshawe.' [17, 18, 19, 89, 332]

Rome, Capital city of Italy, Morrissey's 'home' from early 2005 until 2006 and a major lyrical influence on the RINGLEADER OF THE TORMENTORS album.

According to the singer's version of events, he ended up in Rome by accident. Following the end of 2004's YOU ARE THE QUARRY tour, he'd planned to return to Los Angeles via Dublin. The flight to Dublin had been 'a terrible journey' and for whatever reason Morrissey wasn't able to board the next transatlantic long-haul flight to the US. Instead of waiting, he decided to take the next available short flight, which happened to be Rome. Upon arrival, he immediately 'sank into the place'.

The press became extremely suspicious about his ulterior motives for moving to Rome. Coupled with the more revealing lyrical content on Ringleader (particularly 'DEAR GOD PLEASE HELP ME'), many journalists suspected that he'd gone to the city because of a newfound love interest and tried to probe him for details accordingly. 'It isn't true,' Morrissey protested, condemning *Mojo* magazine for having quoted him as saying 'Yes, I'm in love' when he'd actually said, 'Yes, I'm in love … with the city of Rome.'

'Everybody else followed,' he grumbled. 'But no, it isn't true. Everything remains the same. I am an island.'

Regardless of why he settled in Rome, Morrissey's adoption of a European base seemed a surprisingly contrary move considering his comments of two decades earlier. 'When you go to Rome, you're bored and you want to come straight back home to Scunthorpe,' he quipped back in 1984. 'Italy is a very passionate country,' he admitted in 1989, 'but the smoke and the meat, no, not really. The heat is quite nice, occasionally, but generally I'm perfectly, perfectly happy to live in England till the day I choke of boredom.'

The new 'Roman Morrissey' of 2005 was acutely aware of his track record for droll xenophobia. 'I thought that England was the best place on the planet,' he confessed. 'I would travel around Europe and I would never be interested. I was very closed and now very embarrassed that I was so blinkered.' Referring to his previous visits to Rome – including just once with The Smiths in May 1985 – Morrissey stated that his arrival there in 2005 felt like 'my first real experience of the city'. Its appeal, he explained was, 'its splendour, humour and beauty … Rome is very idle and spontaneous. There's something within the people that is very modern.'

For the duration of his stay in Rome, Morrissey lived in a suite at the Hotel de Russie near the Piazza del Popolo in the city's historical centre. Other key Morrissey Roman landmarks are his favourite restaurant, La Montecarlo pizzeria on Vicolo Savelli (Morrissey usually plumped for basic spaghetti 'al pomodoro'/'with tomatoes'), the old historic Caffe Greco on Via Condotti, Via del Babuino and the nearby Spanish Steps on the Piazza di Spagna (where the English poet Keats died), and Piazza Cavour as referenced in the song 'YOU HAVE KILLED ME'. With the release of Ringleader Of The Tormentors, Morrissey embarked on an extensive world tour lasting more than a year, during which time he ended his occupancy of the Hotel de Russie, and with it his extended Roman holiday. [54, 58, 69, 159, 235, 275, 461]

Romper Stomper, 1992 Australian film named as Morrissey's favourite on the press release for 1997's MALADJUSTED album. The same press release was written by the singer under the pseudonym 'Stoney Hando'. The 'Stoney' is unrelated but 'Hando' is also the name of Romper Stomper's central character played by Russell Crowe.

The film focuses on a Nazi SKINHEAD gang in the Footscray suburb of Melbourne and features graphic scenes of racial violence. Beyond the presiding theme of the futility and ugliness of racism, its central drama revolves around the love triangle between the ruthless Hando, his best friend Davey (Daniel Pollock), and a middle-class dropout, Gabe (Jacqueline McKenzie). Pollock and McKenzie continued their relationship off-screen until the former's suicide in April 1992. Pollock had been struggling with heroin addiction and threw himself in front of a train in Sydney shortly after filming was completed; Crowe would later write a tribute song with his band 30 Odd Foot Of Grunts called 'The Night That Davey Hit The Train'. The opening of *Romper Stomper* also offers a source for the title of Morrissey's 1997 B-side 'THIS IS NOT YOUR COUNTRY'. [111, 547]

Ronson, Mick (Morrissey producer 1991–92),

'One of the most astonishingly human and attractive people that I've ever met,' is how Morrissey remembered YOUR ARSENAL producer Mick Ronson, who died within a year of the album's release after a battle with cancer.

Born in Hull, Ronson was a classically trained pianist who took up guitar in his teens having also tried violin and recorder. After playing with various local bands and on one album with singer-songwriter Michael Chapman, by November 1969 Ronson had given up hope of a career in music and was back in Hull working for the city council. As apocryphal myth has it, he was marking out the lines on a local rugby pitch the day an ex-band mate, drummer John Cambridge, tracked him down with the news that he'd been successfully recommended to join David BOWIE's new band, The Hype.

Ronson stayed with Bowie for the next four years, the most critical in the latter's career as he transformed himself from a folk-rock failure to a glam rock messiah. Ronson's part in that transformation was vital. As a guitar player and backing vocalist, he immediately made his presence felt on the heavy thunder of 1970's The Man Who Sold The World, produced by TONY VISCONTI. By 1971's Hunky Dory, Ronson had become Bowie's arranger, crafting such ornate orchestrations as 'Life On Mars' and 'Changes'. The Bowie/Ronson axis hit its creative peak on 1972's The Rise And Fall Of Ziggy Stardust And The Spiders From Mars and 1973's Aladdin Sane, with Ronson as much in vogue as a pianist (the former's 'Five Years', the latter's 'Lady Grinning Soul') as a guitar hero. So integral was Ronson to Bowie's legacy that the defining images of UK glam are those of both men together: Mick Rock's iconic photo of David clambering between Mick's knees and biting his guitar in mock fellatio, and the generational watershed moment in July 1972's TOP OF THE POPS broadcast of 'Starman' when Bowie tenderly threw his left arm around Ronson's neck.

After Bowie's 1973 covers album, Pin Ups, Ronson was coerced by manager Tony DeFries into launching himself as a solo artist. Bowie contributed to the writing of Ronson's 1974 debut album Slaughter On 10th Avenue, but had no role in its recording. At the same time Ronson was ousted from Bowie's band. Various rumours suggest Bowie was 'very, very upset' by Ronson's decision to go solo, though the proper rift didn't occur until 1975 when Ronson told *Melody Maker* that he wanted to 'kick some sense' into Bowie, then a cocaine addict living in Los Angeles. It would be eight years before they repaired their friendship when Ronson made a surprise appearance on stage with Bowie in Toronto in September 1983.

Though his manager believed Ronson had the potential to become 'the new David Cassidy', his solo career was short-lived. Of his two albums, both 'partly brilliant' in Morrissey's view, only Slaughter On 10th Avenue made the UK top ten while its single, a cover of Elvis PRESLEY's 'Love Me Tender', failed to chart. The album revealed Ronson to be a more-than-capable vocalist and is, indeed, 'brilliant' in parts, particularly the strangely JOBRIATH-esque 'Growing Up And I'm Fine' (written by Bowie) and the histrionic drama of 'Music Is Lethal'. 1975's Play Don't Worry wasn't quite as impressive, though it contained a noteworthy cover of The Velvet Underground's 'White Light/White Heat' salvaged from Bowie's earlier Pin Ups session. By the time of the latter's release, Ronson had since joined Mott The Hoople for their 'Saturday Gigs' single and would continue to work with lead singer Ian Hunter after the band split. In 1975 he also came close to joining SPARKS, even demoing a handful of songs for their Big Beat album until accepting an offer from Bob Dylan to join his Rolling Thunder Revue.

As a producer, Ronson was best known for Lou REED's 1972 Transformer, co-produced with Bowie though the lush string arrangements on 'Perfect Day' and 'Satellite Of Love' were entirely his own. He'd also work with Manchester punks SLAUGHTER AND THE DOGS (whose name was, in part, a homage to his 10th Avenue album) as well as ex-NEW YORK DOLLS singer David Johansen, producing his second solo album, In Style.

When Morrissey first decided to approach Ronson for Your Arsenal, it was left to current co-writer Mark NEVIN to make initial contact. Nevin discovered that Ronson was back in Hull and, to his surprise, had never heard or even heard *of* Morrissey or The Smiths. 'He was asking me, "So what does Morrissey sound like?",' says Nevin. 'Then I asked him if he could come down for a meeting with Morrissey. He says, "I'm not sure, I'm supposed to be babysitting for my sister." He honestly had no idea who he was.'

Fortunately, Ronson's sister Maggi made alternative childcare arrangements. A few days later, the Spiders From Mars legend turned up at Nevin's north London home for the arranged rendezvous. He'd been diagnosed with liver cancer the previous year and, as Nevin notes, 'looked slightly frail', not that it stopped him accepting a hospitable glass of red wine. Morrissey duly arrived with his current personal assistant, Peter HOGG.

'It was a pretty mental moment in my life,' says Nevin. 'Being a massive Bowie fan and a Smiths fan, suddenly I've got Mick Ronson and Morrissey, together, in my house, sat across from one another on my two sofas.' According to Nevin, it took the extrovert Hogg to break the ice. 'So, Mick, did David ever try to shag you?' asked Hogg. 'Well, he tried a few times,' Ronson dryly retorted, 'but he never succeeded.'

In spite of his ailing health, Ronson agreed to produce the album. 'He refuses to let that affect his working pace,' explained Morrissey. 'He's not confined to his bed or disabled in any way. Neither has he showed any signs of bitterness. On the contrary, he's been, to say the least, entertaining, uplifting company.' Shortly after Your Arsenal's completion, Ronson reunited with Bowie on stage at Wembley Stadium for the Freddie Mercury Tribute Concert on 20 April 1992. In a nice twist, Ronson next made a cameo on Bowie's 1993 album Black Tie White Noise (playing guitar on a version of Cream's 'I Feel Free'), the same record which saw Bowie cover Morrissey's 'I KNOW IT'S GONNA HAPPEN SOMEDAY'. Tragically, three weeks after the album's release, Ronson finally lost his fight against cancer. He died on 29 April 1993, aged just 46.

His death followed that of Morrissey's manager Nigel Thomas and his friend and video director Tim Broad. 'The three deaths were quite literally on top of each other,' said Morrissey. 'It was so painful and so sad for me, because I had become so attached to [Ronson] that I couldn't actually attend the funeral.' Only days before he received the dreadful news from Ronson's wife, Morrissey had last spoken with him about the prospect of collaborating again on what would become VAUX-HALL AND I. 'He was very happy, very enthusiastic about writing songs with me and getting back into the studio. He was very positive about his health, and positive about his future.'

It's sad to speculate on how much Morrissey and Ronson might have achieved in the long term, especially if, as the singer indicates, a Morrissey/Ronson composer credit was in the offing. While Vauxhall And I was still a success in the hands of Steve LILLYWHITE, it would have been equally thrilling to hear its songs given the same touch Ronson applied to Your Arsenal. Morrissey's career survived without him but the devastating impact of his death shouldn't be underestimated. Asked in 1995 when and why he last cried, Morrissey replied, '[The] death of Michael R.' [5, 22, 36, 45, 96, 150, 235, 351, 569]

Rosen, Marjorie, See POPCORN VENUS.

Rough Trade, The Smiths' independent UK record label from their 1983 debut single, 'HAND IN GLOVE', to their 1988 posthumous live album, RANK. As their career progressed, Morrissey became increasingly vocal in his public criticisms of the label, also expressing his concerns in song. It is commonly believed that 'FRANKLY, MR SHANKLY', 'YOU JUST HAVEN'T EARNED IT YET, BABY' and 'PAINT A VULGAR PICTURE' contain veiled references to Rough Trade, and in particular its founder, Cambridge graduate Geoff Travis.

Rough Trade began as a record shop in London's Notting Hill in 1976, specialising in punk, reggae and import vinyl. Two years later, Travis launched the independent Rough Trade Records which soon flowered into Rough Trade Distribution. The label's early roster included Stiff Little Fingers, Subway Sect, Cabaret Voltaire, The Raincoats, THE MONOCHROME SET and The Fall. According to Marr, though The Smiths had approached Manchester's FACTORY and also courted EMI, by the end of 1982 he and Morrissey were already warming to the prospect

of Rough Trade as their ideal home. 'Because of The Monochrome Set,' says Marr, 'and certainly The Fall.'

While the label had credibility as a haven for post-punk's arty outsiders, commercially Rough Trade had yet to demonstrate to a keen chart statistician such as Morrissey that they were capable of achieving a top ten single. Significantly, in the two years directly before signing The Smiths, Travis had 'lost' a succession of acts to major labels, including Aztec Camera, Scritti Politti, The Go-Betweens and Orange Juice (who recorded their debut album with Rough Trade money only to release it on Polydor). All, bar The Go-Betweens, were to have UK top ten hits only after leaving Rough Trade.

'With The Smiths it was a different time,' says Travis. 'After those groups went to majors it was absolutely a case of lessons learned in the sense that we'd started to understand what we needed to do to be a competitive, fully rounded record company. Certainly The Smiths was the first long-term contract we signed and so I must have realised that I didn't want that to happen again, that we were in a position where we felt we could do justice to people. That was the key.'

Even before signing, The Smiths were fortunate to have what Marr refers to as their 'inside man' at Rough Trade in the shape of Richard Boon, the former BUZZCOCKS manager and founder of Manchester's independent New Hormones label, home to Linder STERLING's Ludus. 'Morrissey was closer to Richard than I was,' notes Marr, 'but he was an interesting character. Everyone else at Rough Trade was a stranger to us so that connection with him was really important.'

But Boon alone couldn't guarantee The Smiths a Rough Trade contract. After their early demo tapes had failed to elicit any response, on Friday 4 March 1983 Marr and Rourke made a pilgrimage down south armed with a cassette containing their newly recorded, self-funded 'Hand In Glove' and the live recording of 'HANDSOME DEVIL' which would become its B-side. Blagging their way inside Rough Trade's Blenheim Crescent offices, they cornered Travis in the kitchen while he was making a mug of coffee. 'Listen to this,' said Marr, handing him the cassette, 'it's not just another tape.' Impressed by their gall, Travis promised he would. Over the weekend, The Smiths stewed in Manchester awaiting his response. Monday morning, Travis rang Marr with the offer to release 'Hand In Glove' as a seven-inch single.

It was several months before Rough Trade technically 'signed' The Smiths in a contract which, by specifying Morrissey and Marr as sole signatories, irreversibly cast the die for the future percentage claims of Rourke and Joyce culminating in the 1996 COURT CASE.

At the time, Morrissey told the press they'd chosen Rough Trade because 'there seemed to be less talk about money and more talk about artistic integrity'.

'We had lots of company interest,' he elaborated, 'and it just seemed that Rough Trade were the most human. I liked that idea. They were down to earth, and they were very forthright. They said, "This is what we can do for you, and this is what we cannot do for you, but ultimately we'll do our best." … Rough Trade just seemed to suit us more than anybody else. And that's why we chose them.'

Such honeymoon talk was short-lived. The label's 12-inch remix of November 1983's 'THIS CHARMING MAN' by New York DJ François Kevorkian – issued, according to Morrissey, against his or Marr's better wishes – was the first breech of trust. As he and Marr would later phrase it, the group's temporary move from Manchester to London in 1984 was in order 'to keep an eye on the record company' and prevent similar reoccurrences.

By 1985, when The Smiths returned to Manchester as a base, the relationship between group and label had worsened. In numerous interviews at the time, and when later assessing the group's career in hindsight, Morrissey would blame Rough Trade's promotional resources for The Smiths' singles slump and lack of media presence. The crunch came during the making of THE QUEEN IS DEAD when, as detailed in that album's entry in this book, Morrissey and Marr acted on bad advice and plotted to leave the label, a decision which was to have far-reaching consequences not only for the record's release but the long-term stability of The Smiths as a group.

In Travis and Rough Trade's defence, where The Smiths are concerned their David-like victory over the major Goliaths speaks for itself. That a UK indie label who released fewer than 12 albums in 1985 could knock Columbia's Bruce Springsteen off the top of the UK album charts (with MEAT IS MURDER) was nothing short of heroic. And while there is much validity in Morrissey's accusations of poor advertising and scant airplay, consider that between January 1984 and August 1987 The Smiths had eight top 20 hits while their Factory counterparts New Order and their major-affiliated peers Echo & The Bunnymen and The Jesus And Mary Chain scored just two apiece. In this respect, tribute should be paid to their publicist, the late Scott Piering, for his part in their success, and the devotion of press officers Gill Smith and Pat Bellis, also both since passed away.

Nevertheless, in 1986 The Smiths broke free, signing a new deal with EMI but agreeing to work out their Rough Trade contract with one more studio album (1987's STRANGEWAYS, HERE WE COME). Interviewed for Rob Young's 2006 *Rough Trade* biography, Travis admitted to a 'sense of betrayal' though found 'a certain poetry' in the fact they split up before recording a note for EMI. 'I think we did a good job with The Smiths,' he said proudly, 'and I don't have any regrets about that.'

Beset with financial difficulties and commercial failures in the wake of The Smiths' demise, Rough Trade itself broke up in 1991. Prior to its bankruptcy, Morrissey and Marr purchased the rights to the Smiths back catalogue, which they sold on to Warners. Travis would resume Rough Trade in 2000, enjoying a clean sheet of new successes with The Strokes and The Libertines. He still speaks to Morrissey, who apparently rings him 'every once in a while for advice'. [12, 13, 17, 18, 19, 27, 28, 29, 41, 46, 71, 105, 135, 138, 274, 402, 406, 419, 431]

r

Rourke, Andy (Smiths bass player 1982–87, Morrissey bass player and co-writer 1988–90), Although Johnny Marr acknowledges that the relationship between himself and Morrissey was the creative core of The Smiths, the oldest and strongest bond in the group was that between himself and school friend Andy Rourke. 'That took a less prominent place in the mythology and story of The Smiths,' says Marr, 'but it was the feet-on-the-ground reality. There was *absolute* synchronicity between myself and Andy because we were best mates. We had that thing that friends have where you can sit around and not talk and it makes no difference. And you can hear it in the music. Some of the stuff going on in The Smiths between the guitar and the bass is unique, something no other group has ever done.'

The youngest Smith, Andrew Michael Rourke was born in Manchester on 17 January 1964 as The Dave Clark Five's 'Glad All Over' topped the UK singles chart. The third of four brothers, he was raised by his dad in Ashton upon Mersey after his parents divorced. In the autumn of 1974, he started his secondary education at St Augustine's Grammar School in nearby Wythenshawe. It would be another year of 'general naughtiness' before he properly befriended Marr after teachers moved Rourke into his class in a bid to improve his behaviour. As Smiths legend has it, their first conversation was over Rourke's Neil Young badge. Both played guitar and would practise together often, either in school or at the house of another school friend, Mark Johnson. 'It wasn't really a band,' says Rourke, 'just the three of us sat round with guitars trying to harmonise, singing Neil Young covers.'

Marr and Rourke's first 'real' band was the almost mythical Paris Valentinos alongside *CORONATION STREET* actor Kevin 'Curly Watts' Kennedy. They disbanded at the end of their final school year, but not before Marr made the life-changing suggestion that Rourke may be better off switching from guitar to bass. It was as bassist that Rourke followed Marr into their next group, the country rock-influenced White Dice, who

unsuccessfully auditioned in London for Elvis Costello's label, F-Beat Records, in the spring of 1980. Their shared musical apprenticeship ended the following year with the short-lived Freak Party, a trio with drummer Simon WOLSTENCROFT following the punk-funk model of local FACTORY Records signings A Certain Ratio. Exasperated by their failure to find the right singer, Marr left Rourke and Wolstencroft to it, vanishing from his friend's life for the best part of a year.

Rourke continued playing bass but in the short term his prospects while stuck in a dead-end day job in a timber yard looked grim. His fate was decided for him when Marr re-established contact at the end of 1982. The Smiths were already in existence with one demo and one gig to their name but provisionally lumbered with an incongruous bassist in studio engineer Dale HIBBERT. When Marr gave Hibbert his marching orders, he called Rourke out of the blue. 'I probably always knew it was going to be Andy on bass,' says Marr. 'It seemed the right time, then, to bring him in. So I called him round to my house, but I think he was a bit confused at first. A year ago we'd been listening to A Certain Ratio, and BOWIE's Low, and now here I was banging on about The Drifters. "And, by the way, I'm vegetarian." But it was really good to see him again.'

Rourke's inauguration into The Smiths was at Drone studios in Manchester in early December 1982 for the group's second demo tape, funded by Marr's contact in EMI. It was the first time Rourke met either Morrissey or Joyce. 'Because Johnny was at ease with Morrissey, it immediately put me at ease,' says Rourke. 'I never used to socialise with Morrissey, it was purely a working relationship. We used to have a laugh, but I would never dream of phoning Morrissey up and saying, "Fancy going out for a pint?" Whereas Johnny could do that, or go out for drives with him. Johnny put in the time and effort to get to know Morrissey and got the rewards out of him.'

Stylistically, Rourke's influences were no more obvious to pin down than Marr's. Though besotted with the music of Neil Young, as a bass player

Rourke has cited Bowie's Low, THE ROLLING STONES' Bill Wyman and Japan's Mick Karn among his main inspirations. The magic of The Smiths may have been the songs of Morrissey and Marr but the *sound* of The Smiths was to rely heavily on Rourke's lyrical bass lines; solidly snaking between the spaces in Marr's trebly decorations, each a distinct pop sonata unto itself. Rarely satisfied with standard root-note responsibilities, Rourke often crammed in more melody than seemed feasible, yet never once threatened to over-egg the pudding. Where other bassists drew straight lines, Rourke's signature was positively Picasso-esque. From 'THIS CHARMING MAN' and 'BARBARISM BEGINS AT HOME' to 'THE HEADMASTER RITUAL', 'THE QUEEN IS DEAD' and 'DEATH OF A DISCO DANCER', without Rourke's feet of clay Marr's house of cards would otherwise collapse.

His indispensability within The Smiths is not a matter for debate, but regrettably Rourke's story has frequently been overshadowed by his well-documented drug problems. 'Since my early teens I'd been messing about with all sorts,' Rourke explains. 'Mushrooms, dope. Then, because of where I was raised, Ashton upon Mersey, there was heroin everywhere. All me mates were on smack. A couple of my brothers got into it, so even before The Smiths started I was dabbling in that stuff. Then, of course, all of a sudden you're in a band getting loads of money. That's when I kind of went nuts on it.'

Initially, Rourke kept his addiction as private as possible. Marr had always known. Joyce only discovered 'about a year' after joining the band. Which left only Morrissey, vociferously anti-drugs in the press, and none the wiser on account of Marr's constant shielding.

Rourke was smart enough not to smoke heroin on the road ('I didn't want to jeopardise the band'), instead supplementing his habit with valiums, temazepams and mogadons, all courtesy of a crooked Harley Street GP who'd 'give you a bag of whatever you wanted for 50 quid'.

'Unfortunately,' he continues, 'the thing about valium is you take a couple and then you forget.

Well, I used to anyway. Then before you know it you're in a kind of a stupor, being really clumsy, really embarrassing. Eventually it all came to a head in Ireland.'

In February 1986, while The Smiths were still embroiled in a legal dispute with ROUGH TRADE over the delayed release of THE QUEEN IS DEAD, the group played three concerts in Ireland. By his own admission, Rourke was screwing up his medication backstage and his bass lines out front. As Marr confesses, 'People were starting to make comments about our live shows. We rarely made howling errors but there were a few big mistakes which made for a very, very bad atmosphere on the bus. I know Andy felt really awful about it, but he just wasn't able to keep it together any more.'

Following a group discussion, Rourke was 'asked to leave so I could go and get my head together'. Sadly, the intended wake-up call backfired. Rourke plummeted into depression, tempering his misery by driving to a dealer's house in Oldham. He reasoned it would be 'safer' than scoring in Manchester, only to find himself walking into the climactic raid of a six-month police surveillance operation on an international drug cartel. Locked in a cell over the weekend, his family learned of his arrest on local TV news. So did Morrissey. 'I knew as soon as he found out it was gonna be the nail in the coffin, really,' says Rourke, 'and it was. The drug had me by the balls at that point. You're quite powerless. To coin the cliché, you've got this monkey on your back and it's giving you a nudge all the time. I was kind of using it as a crutch, I suppose. For what, I don't know.'

As has since become part and parcel of Smiths legend, Rourke's dismissal from the group came in the form of a note left under his car windscreen wiper: 'Andy. You have left The Smiths. Good luck and goodbye. Morrissey.'

'That situation with Andy was something which I'd been dreading since day one,' says Marr. 'I didn't feel let down. My overriding feeling was, "This is a fucking disaster." When he'd been told he was fired and he came over to my house, it was a moment for me and him that was *way* beyond the band. We'd been best friends at school, y'know. I mean he was only out of the band for like three weeks but it seemed like three years in our world.'

Those three weeks saw Rourke recuperate at his mum's house in Majorca before being read-mitted into The Smiths, now clean and vowing to behave himself. Mercifully, he avoided prison with a £1,000 fine and a two-year suspended sentence, though it was concerns over his future which origi-nally led to Craig GANNON being drafted in to the group in April 1986. Even after his return, doubts over Rourke's eligibility for a work visa for their upcoming tour of Canada and North America resulted in another auxiliary member, Bryan Ferry bassist Guy PRATT, brought in as understudy until his visa came through at the eleventh hour.

The end of The Smiths in 1987 shocked Rourke as much as anybody. 'I just felt helpless because I didn't have a clue what I was gonna do next,' he admits. In the initial aftermath, he joined Joyce and Gannon in The Adult Net, the solo project of Fall guitarist Brix Smith. With Joyce he went on to tour with Sinead O'Connor; Rourke alone played on O'Connor's 1990 album I Do Not Want What I Haven't Got.

In November 1988, Rourke formed part of the virtual Smiths reunion with Joyce and Gannon for the recording of Morrissey's post-VIVA HATE singles 'THE LAST OF THE FAMOUS INTERNATIONAL PLAY-BOYS' and 'INTERESTING DRUG'. All three would back Morrissey the following month for his solo live debut in WOLVERHAMPTON in spite of their separate legal proceedings against the singer, each contesting various financial grievances after the dissolution of The Smiths. Morrissey asked them all to drop their cases: Rourke was the only one who obliged, accepting a settlement in the region of £83,000. 'I was broke,' he later explained. 'I'd just got married. I had no money and I was dangled a carrot.'

Rourke's acquiescence coincided with Morris-sey's separation from Stephen STREET, who'd also joined the singer's growing queue of litigants. Invited to step forward as potential co-writer,

Rourke eagerly obliged, submitting a handful of demos featuring guitar, bass and drum machine. Morrissey would record only three. The first, 1989's 'YES, I AM BLIND', was recorded without Rourke. The remaining two, 'GIRL LEAST LIKELY TO' and 'GET OFF THE STAGE', were taped during the autumn 1989 BONA DRAG sessions at Hook End studios. All three were issued as B-sides. By the summer of 1989 Rourke found himself super-fluous to Morrissey's requirements, replaced on KILL UNCLE by MADNESS bassist Mark Bedford.

The next time Rourke saw Morrissey was during the December 1996 Smiths COURT CASE, a bittersweet experience in view of his earlier settle-ment. Three years later, Rourke was forced to declare himself bankrupt. The late 90s and early 00s saw Rourke join Joyce in various Manches-ter-based groups, though he has always enjoyed his greatest post-Smiths successes on his own, whether as bassist with Chrissie HYNDE and The Pretenders (playing, ironically enough, on their 1995 cover of 'EVERYDAY IS LIKE SUNDAY'), Badly Drawn Boy or Ian Brown.

The Smiths' legal miseries put paid to Rourke's relationship with Marr for many years until he decided to mend their friendship in 2005. 'It was important to me,' says Rourke, 'and luckily it was important to Johnny. That thing of time being a great healer, it's certainly very true.' On 28 Janu-ary 2006, Rourke and Marr shared the stage of Manchester's MEN Arena as part of the Manches-ter Versus Cancer charity event, organised by the bassist and his manager Nova Rehman after the latter's father and sister were diagnosed with the disease. Rourke joined Marr's group, The Heal-ers, for a recital of 'HOW SOON IS NOW?', making it their first concert together since The Smiths' final gig at Brixton Academy over 19 years earlier.

Unlike Joyce, Rourke has avoided the full vitriol of Morrissey in the bitter aftermath of the court case. Though, initially, he'd be stigmatised with the same 'disposable parts of a lawnmower' slur as the drummer, with the passing of time Morrissey has let slip a rare sign of affection for the bassist. Reminiscing about The Smiths in a

2007 Q&A with the TRUE-TO-YOU.NET website, Morrissey rhapsodised, 'I thought Johnny was the greatest … and also … those masterful bass lines.' It is, indeed, as a masterful bass player that Andy Rourke will always be remembered. [7, 10, 11, 12, 13, 14, 17, 18, 19, 27, 28, 29, 245, 352, 362]

Roxy Music, Hugely influential British glam/art pop band formed by Tyneside ex-pottery teacher Bryan Ferry in 1970. Intelligent, arty, glamorous and eccentrically sexy, they were also frighteningly prolific, releasing their first three groundbreaking albums in an 18-month period between June 1972 and November 1973: Roxy Music, For Your Pleasure and Stranded.

Like BOWIE and BOLAN, Roxy had a dramatic musical and aesthetic impact upon those who later came of age during punk, Morrissey included. He caught them numerous times in concert, including 9 November 1972 at Manchester's Hardrock in his native Stretford where he also hoped to see their support act, the NEW YORK DOLLS. It wasn't until the show itself that he learned they wouldn't be playing: Dolls drummer Billy Murcia had died in London two days earlier. 'Everyone wept,' he recalled. The fact that earlier in the day he'd caught a glimpse of Roxy synth-wizard Brian ENO's 'psychedelic ostrich feather cape' hanging from their tour bus was some consolation.

During the mid- to late 70s, Roxy's music shifted towards elegant disco-rock, pioneering a generic style which would prove just as influential on the post-punk generation of 80s new romantics. By that time, however, Morrissey's attitude towards them, and Ferry in particular, had cooled considerably. Writing to pen pal Robert MACKIE in 1981, he dismissed Roxy as 'still looking for something they've always wanted but was never theirs'. Even reminiscences about his past infatuation became an excuse to slate Ferry. 'I received letters from brainy Bryan because I tugged at his sleeve and begged him to write. He did so. What a jerk!'

As fate would have it, less than three years later Morrissey was working with former Roxy bassist John PORTER, producer of THE SMITHS. Yet when it came to their respectively unorthodox recording methods, Morrissey and Ferry were very much kindred spirits. In his 1976 biography The Bryan Ferry Story, Rex Balfour (nom de plume of Ferry's publicist Simon Puxley) describes his practice of finishing the backing track first before adding vocals: 'Eventually [Bryan] would arrive at the studio after being up most of the night perfecting the lyrics, and would add them in one or two takes. Until that moment, nobody had any idea what the song they had been working on was about, or even what the melody line might be.' Morrissey employed precisely the same practice from the July 1984 recording of 'HOW SOON IS NOW?' onwards, sticking to it for the bulk of Smiths and later solo recordings; keeping his musicians, engineers and producers in the dark about lyrics and song titles until the last moment.

Of more adverse influence was Roxy's distinctive artwork featuring highly stylised and often scantily clad supermodels, epitomising a 70s trend of, as Morrissey put it, 'using naked female images [which were] never held into question', something he'd consciously react against with his own male-dominated sleeve art.

Marr has also cited The Smiths' debt to Roxy's 'instantly recognisable song intros' such as the gravel footsteps and car ignition opening 1975's 'Love Is The Drug', a trend he and producer John Porter aspired to incorporate into the group's own singles.

In May 1986, The Smiths and Ferry finally crossed paths when the group were recording 'PANIC'. 'I didn't bother asking him for his autograph,' sneered Morrissey. 'I'd had it since I was 14.' His love/hate relationship with the Roxy singer was to intensify when Marr took time out from the group to record Ferry's 'The Right Stuff', a vocal version of the Smiths instrumental 'MONEY CHANGES EVERYTHING'. Some commentators, soundman Grant Showbiz included, cite this as a contributing factor to the gradual breakdown of Morrissey and Marr's working relationship.

Regardless, Morrissey's fascination with Roxy continued well into the 1990s. Aside from 'MUTE

WITNESS', a Clive LANGER tune from KILL UNCLE loosely inspired by 1972's 'Virginia Plain', in 1992 Morrissey adopted the name 'Eddie Riff' for sleeve design credits. This alias, also his frequent hotel check-in pseudonym, was a homage to In Search Of Eddie Riff, a 1974 instrumental album by Roxy saxophonist Andy Mackay.

Ferry himself has acknowledged his influence upon Morrissey, 'a progeny of mine', describing him in 2001 as 'a sad sort of chap … though I don't think he's nearly as virile'. Five years later, Morrissey must have either forgiven or forgotten such condescension enough to tackle a foolhardy live cover of Roxy's 1973 single 'STREET LIFE'. Alas, the gods must have been on Ferry's side, ensuring Morrissey's shaky effort bombed so badly that after two performances he vowed never to sing it again. It would be especially interesting to know what Morrissey's mother thought of his attempt. According to her son Roxy Music are her joint favourite artists alongside Johnny Mathis. [17, 32, 57, 108, 278, 334, 460, 463]

royalty, See MONARCHY, 'NOWHERE FAST', 'THE QUEEN IS DEAD'.

'Roy's Keen' (**Morrissey/Whyte**), Morrissey's 23rd solo single (from the album MALADJUSTED), released October 1997, highest UK chart position #42. There are only grim things to say about what is, by some distance, one of the worst records of Morrissey's career, an appalling pun on quarrelsome Irish footballer and former Manchester United captain Roy Keane.

A straightforward tribute to Keane may well have been preferable to this excruciating tale of obsessive love for a window cleaner. Though its subject brought to mind George FORMBY's famous comic song 'When I'm Cleaning Windows', there was nothing nearly so amusing about Morrissey's ode to a man repeatedly dunking his chamois leather.

This embarrassed fascination with window cleaners was by no means new. A decade earlier, he'd confessed to the press, 'When the window cleaner calls, I have to go in another room than the one he is cleaning. It's very silly.' But in its rhyming of 'satellite' with 'set alight' and 'bucket' with 'wreck it', 'Roy's Keen' was Morrissey at his lyrically groggiest. Whyte's thumping tune was a brave face collapsing into a defeated grin, too flimsy a scrap to paper over such a gaping chasm of manure.

Chosen as the album's second single, nobody ought to have been surprised when it missed the top 40, only the third time that had ever happened in Morrissey's solo career. Its poor performance meant that a live rendition recorded in advance for TOP OF THE POPS was never broadcast. 'Roy's Keen' was also one of his very few solo singles not to feature the singer on its sleeve, instead using an archive 50s photograph of two boys on a terraced London street (one throwing a ball, the other raising a bicycle) taken by Roger MAYNE. In concert, Morrissey often made the title pun painfully obvious by substituting the words 'window cleaner' for 'midfielder' (Keane's position). When touring Ireland in 1999, before playing the song he undertook the added homage of ritually changing into the country's national football shirt.

As Morrissey's bottom-of-the-barrel Arthur Mullard moment, it came as some relief when 11 years later he offered an almost Nixon-esque public apology. 'Over a 25-year recording stretch there's bound to be a few stinkers,' he told Hot Press in 2008. 'There are a few older songs that confuse me – I have no idea what I was thinking. "Roy's Keen" for example.' His shame was writ large by its absence from the 2009 redux version of Maladjusted. Like the same album's 'PAPA JACK', 'Roy's Keen' has become Morrissey's Syme, the 'unperson' of Orwell's Nineteen Eighty-Four – an 'unsong' vaporised with equivalent Stalinist zeal. [4, 40, 171, 568]

'**Rubber Ring**' (Morrissey/Marr), B-side of
'THE BOY WITH THE THORN IN HIS SIDE' (1985). A
masterful analysis of the intense relationship
between The Smiths and their audience, 'Rubber
Ring' was Morrissey's metaphor for 'the songs
that saved your life' as valued by their emotionally
neediest fans, yet clouded by his suspicion that
one day they will outgrow that dependency.
Sympathetic yet subtly mocking, at its core is a
fear for the singer's own hope of achieving immortality through song. While warning the older,
wiser listener (now 'finally living') not to forget
the psychological support he offered during their
youth, his final taunt – 'do you love me like you
used to?' – is less a reproach than a desperate plea
to avoid the abyss of musical obscurity.

The bedroom martyr described in 'Rubber
Ring' was very obviously Morrissey's younger self.
Asked about the obsessive dedication of certain
Smiths fans, he admitted he understood 'that form
of drama' only too well. 'I get a lot of letters from
people who don't have jobs, and from back
bedroom casualties, if you like, who are very
worried because they can't focus on anything in
human life that makes them feel comfortable. And
I get letters from people who say, "When The
Smiths break up I will die, I will make a reserva-
tion for the next world." But to me that's not
extreme … I think it primarily stems from feeling
quite isolated and believing that the people who
make the records you buy are your personal
friends, they understand you, and the more
records that you buy and pictures you collect the
closer you get to these people. And if you *are* quite
isolated and you hear this voice that you identify
with, it's really quite immensely important.'

Marr's danse macabre was a parallel nightmare,
propelled by Rourke's creeping funk and haunted
by stray sound effects. Morrissey overdubbed
what he described as 'a lift shaft noise' at the end
of the third verse. 'He cupped his hand over the
microphone,' explains Marr. 'I put a load of reverb
on it and he made this whooshing sound. It was
fantastic.' The singer also imbedded a couple
of samples. The first was from a 1953 audio

recording of Oscar WILDE's *The Importance Of
Being Earnest*, splicing together two separate lines
spoken by John Gielgud in Act I: 'Is that clever?'
and 'Everybody's clever nowadays' (a purely coincidental nod towards the BUZZCOCKS' 1979 single
'Everybody's Happy Nowadays'). The second
intensified its otherworldly squall, taken from a
seven-inch single originally distributed with Dr
Konstantin Raudive's 1971 book *Breakthrough:
An Amazing Experiment In Electronic Communication With The Dead*. Raudive was a Latvian
parapsychologist who dedicated himself to the
study of Electronic Voice Phenomena: the belief
that spirits could communicate from beyond the
grave by leaving static noises on tape which could
then be deciphered. The voice on 'Rubber Ring'
belongs to Nadia Fowler, offering an English translation of a message Raudive has 'received' from a
deceased colleague in a mixture of Swedish and
German: 'Du sovas/willst nicht glaube!' – 'You are
sleeping/You do not want to believe'.

When 'Rubber Ring' first appeared on the 12-
inch of 'The Boy With The Thorn In His Side', it
formed part of a continuous medley with 'ASLEEP',
repeating the Raudive sample while fading in the
latter's howling wind effect to segue the two songs
together. Sadly, when included on THE WORLD
WON'T LISTEN and subsequent compilation
albums, the two were separated. The Smiths never
played the full 'Rubber Ring' in concert, though
they would incorporate its intro and outro in a
medley with 'WHAT SHE SAID', as heard on RANK.

Their sternest gospel, it was also The Smiths at
their most eloquently self-aware, a song which
quickly fulfilled its own prophecy as a lifebelt for
the listener in distress. While there are songs
which better illustrate what The Smiths *were*,
'Rubber Ring' alone best encapsulates what The
Smiths *meant*. [17, 18, 99, 354, 453]

'**Rush And A Push And The Land Is
Ours, A**' (Morrissey/Marr), From the album
STRANGEWAYS, HERE WE COME (1987). As the
overture for the final Smiths album, 'A Rush
And A Push And The Land Is Ours' read like a

self-spurring pledge to make one last leap towards immortality in their dying moments. Indeed, its title was lifted from a traditional Irish rallying call, the result of Morrissey's expert scholarship of Oscar WILDE. In Chapter One of Hesketh Pearson's 1946 biography *The Life Of Oscar Wilde,*[1] the author refers to Wilde's mother, Lady Jane Wilde, who wrote Irish nationalist prose and poetry for the political newspaper *The Nation* under the pseudonym 'Speranza' (Italian for 'hope'). In 1848, 'Speranza' wrote an editorial titled 'Jacta Alea Est' ('The die is cast'), urging the Irish to rise up against the British army: 'One bold, one decisive move. One instant to take breath, and then a rising; a rush, a charge from north, south, east and west upon the English garrison, and *the land is ours.*'

Beyond its chorus call to arms, the lyrics offered a surreal brew of time travel, parental reprimands and weird ghostly voices (Morrissey's entrance as the mysterious spectre of the hanged 'Troubled Joe'). All of which is fancy smoke and mirrors diverting from the crux of the song, Morrissey's realisation that, much to his horror, he has fallen in love, leaving him no choice but to ride once more into its valley of insufferable pain and inevitable heartache.

Marr's military two-step was a crafty homage to a favourite single from his youth, its main piano vamp based on the riff of 1975's 'SHOES' by former Delrons' leader Reparata. 'I was determined to have a track starting the album with no guitars on it,' says Marr. 'I really had a bee in my bonnet. I was so adamant about getting away from this jingle-jangle thing.' As co-producer Stephen STREET concurs, 'Johnny really wanted to announce that this would be a new chapter in The Smiths' recording career.' Though piano had featured on previous recordings (e.g. 'OSCILLATE WILDLY', 'ASLEEP'), as a full band performance with no guitars 'A Rush And A Push' was a Smiths first and a brilliantly bold album opener, one which Mike Joyce would later hail as incontestable evidence that on Strangeways Morrissey and Marr hit their songwriting peak. [17, 19, 38, 349]

---

1. Morrissey had previously been photographed with a copy of the 60s Penguin paperback edition of Pearson's book for *Smash Hits* in 1984.

'Rusholme Ruffians' (Morrissey/Marr),

From the album MEAT IS MURDER (1985). Following the same album's 'THE HEADMASTER RITUAL', 'Rusholme Ruffians' continued Morrissey's youthful reminiscences, moving from the violence of the schoolroom to that of the Manchester fairground (Rusholme is an area south of the city centre).

'As a child I was literally educated at fairgrounds,' he explained. 'It was a [place] of tremendous violence and hate and stress and high romance and all the true vital things in life. It was really the patch of ground where you learned about everything simultaneously whether you wanted to or not.'

The lyrics mixed Morrissey's own gory memories ('Somebody always ends up being stabbed,' he said, 'which of course adds to the excitement') and rash contemplations of suicide (leaping from the top of the parachute) with the more romantic teenage fairground flashbacks of Victoria WOOD. One of his most explicit instances of theft in the Smiths songbook, 'Rusholme Ruffians' owes a great deal to Wood's comic verse 'Fourteen Again' with its parallel phrases 'the last night of the fair', 'behind the generators', 'when I was funny I was famous' and 'the Brylcreem in his hair'. The last line is also borrowed from a different Wood song, 'Funny How Things Turn Out', with its 'my faith in myself is still devout'.

First recorded with John PORTER in July 1984 during the 'WILLIAM, IT WAS REALLY NOTHING' session, the original 'Rusholme Ruffians' lasted seven minutes, its vocal much more spontaneous in its spacing, Morrissey hollering how 'the pulses being beat are mine'. Halved in length for Meat Is Murder, it kept the same chord gyration looted from Elvis PRESLEY's 1961 hit '(MARIE'S THE NAME) HIS LATEST FLAME'. 'That was blatantly done,' says Marr. 'Morrissey said to me, "Let's do a song about the fair," and for some reason my association with the fair was to pull out that Elvis riff.

We tried, but we couldn't get away from it.' The tune's debt was later acknowledged in concert, introducing a medley of the Elvis original and their idiosyncratic rewrite, as heard on RANK.

Regardless of its many second-hand elements, 'Rusholme Ruffians' perfectly captured the 'violence, hate, stress and high romance' Morrissey intended, aided by its bookends of fairground sound effects. The end result was a record pungent with the aroma of sugar, chip fat, cheap perfume and cigarettes, spinning its head to the muffled cries of Ringo Starr's living daylights being kicked from his body in *That'll Be The Day*. An exhilarating Smiths ride in every sense. [17, 79, 168, 426, 477]

Rutherford, Margaret, Bulldog-jowled English comic actress, listed among Morrissey's favourites; especially for her role as girls' school headmistress Miss Whitchurch in 1950's THE HAPPIEST DAYS OF YOUR LIFE, aggrieving boys' school headmaster Alastair SIM with the pressing enquiry, 'Have you digestive?'

Her first major, and perhaps defining, role was as the batty clairvoyant Madame Arcati in David Lean's 1945 film adaptation of Noël COWARD's

Blithe Spirit. Her other notable Morrissey favourites are 1949's PASSPORT TO PIMLICO and the series of early 60s Miss Marple films inspired by the novels of Agatha Christie (herself one of Morrissey's listed 'Odd fellows'). In December 1980, he told his Scottish pen pal Robert MACKIE to watch her second Marple film, *Murder She Said*, being screened on BBC1 the following weekend. 'A fab film,' said Morrissey, 'with Margaret Rutherford as the groovy Miss Marple as created by the un-groovy Agatha Christie. Watch it you cretin.'

Four years later, he was still referring to Rutherford's Marple films when telling the NME how he regarded himself as a 'sympathetic figure', likening his role to that of Marple's assistant, Mr Stringer, played by Rutherford's husband Stringer Davis. 'Do you know Stringer Davis?' he asked. 'He's in a lot of Miss Marple films. He's her good friend. Very sympathetically he'd listen to all her japes and problems. Well, [I see myself] like him.'

Rutherford was made a Dame in 1967. She died on Morrissey's 13th birthday in 1972, aged 80. Stringer Davis died the following year. Both are buried together in St James's Church, Gerrards Cross in Buckinghamshire. [142, 168, 334, 508]

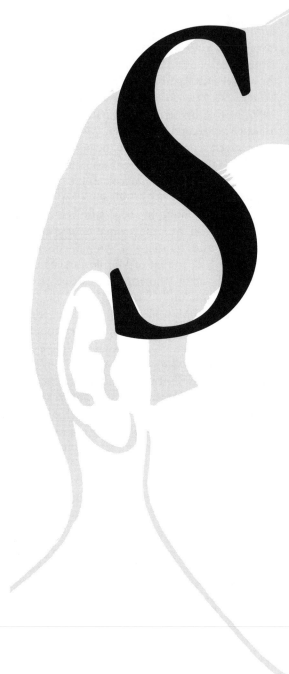

'Safe Warm Lancashire Home' (Morrissey/Street),

Studio outtake from the 1987 VIVA HATE sessions. One of Morrissey's earliest collaborations with Stephen Street, 'Safe Warm Lancashire Home' was, says Street, another 'Lou REED type mellow guitar ballad' in the same vein as 'OH WELL, I'LL NEVER LEARN' written during the same period. The title seems to have been a conscious pun on The Clash's 1978 track 'Safe European Home'. Recorded during the initial Viva Hate session at The Wool Hall near Bath in October 1987, according to drummer Andrew PARESI Morrissey was far from satisfied with the end result and consigned it to the scrapheap since 'he said it reminded him of an Arran sweater'. [25, 39]

Sainte-Marie, Buffy, Canadian/Native

American singer and songwriter whose 60s recordings Morrissey particularly admired. 'I thought she had a great voice and great passion,' he explained. 'In 1964 she was singing about drugs in a very exciting way. "My mother, my father, said whisky's a curse, but the fate of their baby's a million times worse." This was 1964. THE BEATLES were singing "She loves you, yeah, yeah". It didn't catch on and I can't imagine why. A very underrated artist.'

Born on a Saskatchewan Cree reserve, Sainte-Marie came to prominence in the early 60s folk club circuit around New York's Greenwich Village, releasing her debut album, It's My Way, in 1964. Its dozen tracks included the one Morrissey quoted above, 'Cod'ine', written about her experiences with codeine addiction after being prescribed the drug for a throat infection.

Like so many of Morrissey's favourite singers, Sainte-Marie's voice was highly unusual, marked by a shrill witchy vibrato. Her first three albums were all acoustic, mixing folk standards with her own material (including 'Until It's Time For You To Go' later covered by Elvis PRESLEY). On 1967's Fire & Fleet & Candlelight she introduced orchestral pop arrangements, including two songs by her Canadian contemporary JONI MITCHELL. More radical still was 1969's Illuminations, an experimental work mixing psychedelic rock with haunting choral pieces using prototype synthesiser techniques. 1971's She Used To Wanna Be A Ballerina teamed her with her future husband, Phil Spector protégé Jack Nitzsche, and included Leonard Cohen's 'The Bells', a lyrical source for 'HAND IN GLOVE'.

Other than naming her as one of his favourite singers, a handful of Morrissey song titles also bear similarity with those of Sainte-Marie's, specifically 'You're Gonna Need Somebody On Your Bond' (1964), 'Better To Find Out For Yourself' (1969) and 'Suffer The Little Children' (1969). His regard for her was high enough to earn a place on his dream shortlist for his 2004 MELTDOWN festival. Sainte-Marie declined, citing her commitments as a working art teacher which made her attendance impossible. Two years later, Morrissey gave a very different version of events, claiming she had 'shunned' him altogether.

His distress was brief since in March 2008 he announced he'd accepted the 'honour' of taking part in a television special commemorating Sainte-Marie's 50 years in music organised by the Montreal Symphony. 'I first bought a Buffy Sainte-Marie record when I was 12,' he revealed, 'and her music has always remained with me. In the 1960s, as a political activist, Buffy's lyrics were fearless, and I'm very grateful for all the risks that she took.' For whatever reason, the proposed television special never materialised. [119, 170, 175, 226]

Salford Lads Club, The Smiths' adopted

spiritual Mecca after its exterior was used as the location for the group photograph on the inner-gatefold sleeve of 1986's THE QUEEN IS DEAD. This iconic portrait aside, Salford Lads Club has no personal significance to any member of The Smiths, none of whom attended the club since none was born, nor raised, in the city of Salford. Nevertheless, for devout Smiths and Morrissey apostles across the globe, the building has achieved near holy land status as a place of cultural pilgrimage. If, like Johnnie Ray before him, Morrissey really is the 'Pope of mope' then,

to his followers, Salford Lads Club is his designated Vatican.

Situated on the corner of the real-life CORONATION STREET in the Ordsall district, the club was founded in 1903 and officially opened the following year by scout movement creator Robert Baden-Powell. Typical of other boys' clubs up and down the country, its objective was 'to brighten young minds' and 'make good citizens' out of the local community through sports such as boxing and annual camping trips. Famous ex-members include Salfordians Allan Clark and Graham Nash of The Hollies, Joy Division/New Order's Peter Hook and, the primary reason Morrissey chose it as a backdrop, Albert FINNEY.

Yet The Smiths weren't the first pop group to reference the club. The exterior was featured very briefly in a second (remade) video of 'Life In A Northern Town', a top 20 hit for The Dream Academy in April 1985. The coincidence that they also covered 'PLEASE PLEASE PLEASE LET ME GET WHAT I WANT' for a follow-up single is certainly a strange one, doubly so that Morrissey included their version on interval tapes when The Smiths toured Scotland in September '85, three months before the Queen Is Dead photoshoot.

The Smiths' now-historic Salford Lads Club portrait was taken on a cold, grey morning in December 1985 by Stephen Wright, a local postgrad student and aspiring photographer who'd impressed Morrissey with some live Smiths shots he'd sent to ROUGH TRADE. Press officer Pat Bellis also took photos that day under her 'BIGMOUTH'-inspired pseudonym 'Jo Novark'. Morrissey later recounted the shoot with embellished melodrama: 'While we were setting up a gang of ten-year-old girls came and terrorised us. Everyone in the street had a club foot and a vicious dog.' Such tribulations clearly weren't in vain since Morrissey would scribble a warm-hearted thank-you postcard to Wright, dated Boxing Day 1985: 'A sweeter set of pictures were never taken. I smiled for a full minute (phone Roy Castle, that's a record). I quite fancy Southport's wet sands next, or the tropical shores of Belle Vue. It must be done. Fatal regret: I should have worn my mud-coloured cardigan.'

'I remember going down in the car,' says Marr of the shoot, 'and it being freezing cold and a bit drizzly and getting out there and being paraded round and not being very happy. Then sometime when the album was being finished, Morrissey showed me a bunch of pictures from the session and asked me what I thought of them. I said, "Yeah. They're pretty good. As long as you don't use *that* one." Guess what happened next? So when the remastered CD came out I changed the photo in the booklet to another one. There were times when I thought the whole thing was a bit corny, but I didn't mind. It was still a good move on Morrissey's part.'

Rourke's main recollections are also those of 'freezing cold' and grubby children. 'There were these kids on bikes throwing stones at us, telling us to fuck off. It was quite a dodgy area back then; you could see Morrissey was fretting a bit. We all were, because even 12-year-old kids can be pretty threatening when there's a gang of them. By the time we stood outside the club there was quite a crowd so we took a few shots then ran away quick as we could.'

Joyce has an equally vivid memory of seeing a man 'with a quiff and a white vest' sat on a dining chair on the pavement outside his house. 'It was still 1958 in his head.' As Joyce also notes, the photo would provoke the wrath of proud Salfordians who regarded the group as 'slumming' Mancunian tourists. 'We got a lot of stick, because none of us were from Salford. People like Hooky from New Order slagged us off for, as he put it, jumping out of a taxi, taking a photo, then fucking off back to [*Manchester suburb*] Hale. But to me it wasn't Morrissey trying to say, "Look, we're from Salford!" It was more, "This is *our* lads club. This is the *Smiths* Lads Club." We look like a gang in that photo and that was the whole idea. A northern gang.'

The Salford Lads Club committee initially objected to the use of their frontage on the inner of The Queen Is Dead, claiming, somewhat absurdly, that listeners would confuse Morrissey's anti-monarchist beliefs as being those of the club and its members. Yet in time they'd embrace the Smiths connection, even if constant vandalism from souvenir hunters stealing pieces of the sign and bits of brickwork necessitated an extra set of railings erected around the front entrance.[1]

Today, Salford Lads Club is now Salford Lads *and* Girls Club, still a fully operational youth facility for the surrounding area. Morrissey pilgrims continue to flock there from hemispheres

'Satan Rejected My Soul' (Morrissey/Boorer), Morrissey's 24th solo single (from the album MALADJUSTED), released December 1997, highest UK chart position #39. Taking his outsider ideal to its comical extremes, Morrissey overruled his previous conviction that 'THERE'S A PLACE IN HELL FOR ME AND MY FRIENDS', finding himself now spurned by Beelzebub. God, too, seems equally uninterested, with the singer borrowing a phrase from one of his favourite novels, Emily Brontë's WUTHERING HEIGHTS: 'Heaven did not seem to be my home.' With his 'sly' soul lost in permanent purgatory, Morrissey beseeches the listener to claim him for eternity instead.

An enjoyably frolicsome piece of pop theologising, 'Satan Rejected My Soul' opened with a chord ascent similar to that of The Tornados' 'Telstar' (a 1962 number one written by 'JOHNNY REMEMBER ME' producer Joe Meek) before turning up the heat with its devilishly catchy glam signature riff. A logical choice for the final Maladjusted single, though introduced in his December 1997 concerts as his 'Christmas single' it only scraped into the top 40 in the first week of January. As it turned out, 'Satan Rejected My Soul' would be Morrissey's last record of the decade, marking the end of his tenure on ISLAND and the beginning of his label-less wilderness years in Los Angeles exile. [4, 289]

far and wide, just to park their behinds on a bollard for the obligatory Queen Is Dead photo homage (for which Rourke strongly discourages repeating his mistake of wearing inordinately tight jeans) and to peruse its designated 'Smiths Room'. Those who do should be pleasantly surprised to find that, Smiths connections aside, the club is far more impressive for its own unique story. A living, breathing museum of twentieth-century British social history, its every nook and cranny is worthy of investigation as much as preservation. For this reason, Morrissey donated £20,000 to its restoration fund in December 2007, a 'private gesture' which he eventually made public 'at the request of the club directors as they felt very strongly that it would encourage further contributions and guarantee the success of the campaign and the club's survival'. Those wishing to visit, or donate to, the good people of Salford Lads Club should check the latest information at www.salford ladsclub.org.uk. [14, 18, 28, 57, 374]

---

1. The Smiths returned to Salford Lads Club in the snowy January of 1987 with photographer Lawrence Watson to re-create the same portrait. Morrissey returned again that October for the video shoot of 'I STARTED SOMETHING I COULDN'T FINISH'.

Saturday Night And Sunday Morning, 1960

British kitchen-sink drama starring Albert FINNEY, listed among Morrissey's favourite films. Speaking in 1984, he confessed to being 'completely handcuffed to *Saturday Night And Sunday Morning*, which I will never tire of. I find it disturbing that I can watch particular scenes for the 112th time and I'm still caught unawares by a line which I have said repeatedly throughout the day. I can't describe the poetry that film has for me.'

Adapted by Alan Sillitoe from his original novel set in working-class Nottingham and directed by Karel Reisz (see also WE ARE THE LAMBETH BOYS), it tells the story of young factory worker Arthur Seaton (Finney), a 'fighting pit prop of a man' determined not to let the bastards grind him down. 'What I'm out for is a good time,' he declares, 'all the rest is propaganda.' In Seaton's

head, 'a good time' involves everything from drinking contests with sailors, voting Communist for a laugh, firing air rifles at the neighbourhood gossip and having an affair with a co-worker's wife, Brenda (Rachel Roberts in a role allegedly turned down by Diana DORS). In the meantime, he begins courting Doreen (Shirley Anne Field), though the fun soon stops when Brenda becomes pregnant and Arthur is forced to suffer the literally bloody consequences of his actions. The film remains one of the finest examples of the British kitchen-sink drama, a credible depiction of northern working-class life and a grim reminder of the days before legalised abortion; Brenda is forced to 'sit in a hot bath and drink a pint of gin' in a vain effort to end her pregnancy.

Morrissey wanted to use a still of Finney as Seaton for the sleeve of 1984's 'HEAVEN KNOWS I'M MISERABLE NOW' but, to his dismay, the actor refused permission. *Saturday Night And Sunday Morning* would later make its mark on the vinyl run-out-groove of THE QUEEN IS DEAD: the phrase 'Them was rotten days', spoken by actress Hylda Baker in a pub scene in the first half of the film. Given Morrissey's admission of being 'caught unawares' by its dialogue, it also seems likely that Shirley Anne Field's question to Finney 'Why don't you ever take me where it's lively and there's plenty of people?' inspired a similar lyric on the same album's 'THERE IS A LIGHT THAT NEVER GOES OUT'. [124, 168, 548]

Schoeffling, Michael, 'Hunky' American model and actor, best known for his role in the 1984 'Brat pack' film *Sixteen Candles*. In the early 80s, Morrissey developed an obsession with Schoeffling after seeing him on the cover of *GQ* magazine. 'He was this astonishingly good-looking model,' he enthused. 'He tried to become an actor, made about three films in Hollywood, then went off and had loads of children. He was an absolute hero to me.' Schoeffling and the young Morrissey shared similar features; dark hair, thick eyebrows, chiselled bone structure and a prominent chin. The singer even hinted that his

attraction to Schoeffling may have been a form of narcissistic fantasy. 'I used to write to this magazine claiming I would be the next Michael Schoeffling. That kind of glamour completely fascinated me.' [119]

school, Morrissey began his formal education in 1964 at St Wilfred's RC Primary School in Hulme, Manchester. He'd speak fondly of St Wilfred's, describing it as a school 'full of character', albeit allegedly haunted. The original building was demolished in 1969. Pupils from St Wilfred's were later invited to 'interview' Morrissey and Marr for the Saturday morning kids' television programme *Datarun* in early 1984. The singer returned there later in the year to meet his old teachers for another television feature about his Manchester childhood.

In the autumn of 1970, he moved to his nightmarish alma mater, the all-boys St Mary's Secondary School in Stretford. 'A very sadistic school,' he'd recall, 'very barbaric and by some strange miscalculation of nature or whatever I ended up there.' His experiences of, and anger towards, the violent regime of St Mary's famously provided the inspiration for 1985's 'THE HEADMASTER RITUAL'. 'It was a very deprived school,' claimed Morrissey. 'Total disinterest thrust on the pupils, the absolute belief that when you left you would just go down and down and down. It was horrible. A secondary modern school with no facilities, no books, the type of school where one book has to be shared by 79 pupils – that kind of arrangement. If you dropped a pencil you'd be beaten to death. It was very aggressive. It seemed that the only activity of the teachers was whipping the pupils – which they managed expertly.'

In Smiths interviews, he'd describe St Mary's with a gory melodrama veering on the absurd. 'I really did think I'd get a purple heart when I left,' he declared, recalling how he'd made the fatal mistake of telling the careers officer his ambitions of becoming a pop singer. 'He virtually beat me up and I ended up leaving with leaflets for the civil service. So a lesson to be learned there somewhere.'

Morrissey's saving grace at school was ATHLETICS. Otherwise, he likened himself to an 'intellectual idiot', describing how he 'never was kissed behind the bicycle shed' as 'people were convinced that if they talked to me I'd quote Genesis and bolts of lightning would descend from the sky'.

For someone whose own experience of school was so horrendous, perversely Morrissey showed a keen interest in the theme of problem schooling, be it the film *TO SIR, WITH LOVE*, the popular late 60s television comedy *Please Sir!* (starring Malcolm McFee, the likely subject of 'LITTLE MAN, WHAT NOW?') or books such as Jim Haskins's *Diary Of A Harlem Schoolteacher* or Esther Rothman's *THE ANGEL INSIDE WENT SOUR*. He'd revisit the subject of classroom tensions many years later in 1995's 'THE TEACHERS ARE AFRAID OF THE PUPILS'.

Morrissey left St Mary's in 1975, finishing his education at Stretford Technical School where he'd graduate the following summer with three O Levels in English Literature, Sociology and the General Paper, failing a fourth, History. 'I learned that if I ever wanted to be educated I'd have to leave school,' he affirmed, 'so anything I learned was from outside of the education system.' Nor would the psychological scars of his five years at St Mary's ever fully heal. 'I didn't survive school,' Morrissey confessed in 2004. 'It still gives me nightmares.' (See also 'BECAUSE OF MY POOR EDUCATION'.) [142, 204, 267, 408, 446, 448, 463, 464]

Searle, Ronald, English cartoonist and creator of St Trinian's, the fictitious boarding school for unruly girls which spawned a series of popular British film comedies. Cited by Morrissey as one of his favourite 'symbolists' in 1983, Searle's drawings appear in the opening credits of one of his favourite films, *THE HAPPIEST DAYS OF YOUR LIFE*, an ostensible blueprint for 1954's *The Belles Of St Trinian's* and its many sequels. [184]

'Seasick, Yet Still Docked' (Morrissey/ Whyte), From the album YOUR ARSENAL (1992). Harking back to the isolation and agony of 'LAST

NIGHT I DREAMT THAT SOMEBODY LOVED ME', the metaphorical 'Seasick, Yet Still Docked' was a guttural, self-loathing sob echoing in the infinite cavity of Morrissey's loneliness. Alain Whyte's languid waltz was similarly Smiths-like in spirit, benefiting from the sleek ripples of producer Mick RONSON adding to its acoustic foam. Its lyrics were loosely based upon JONI MITCHELL's 'The Silky Veils Of Ardor', a comparable self-pitying folk ballad from 1977's Don Juan's Reckless Daughter; of the many parallels between the two, Morrissey introduces himself as a 'poor freezingly cold soul' much like Mitchell's 'poor wayfaring stranger'. His solitude is further confined by the lonesome ticking clock at the song's finish, seamlessly merging into the equally moving but more hopeful alarm call of 'I KNOW IT'S GONNA HAPPEN SOMEDAY'. [5]

Servant, The, 1963 British psychological drama

starring Dirk BOGARDE listed among Morrissey's favourite films. Based on Robin Maugham's novella and scripted by Harold Pinter, it concerns a young, ineffectual aristocrat, Tony (James Fox), who decides to hire a manservant for his new Chelsea townhouse. The successful applicant is Barrett (Bogarde), a softly spoken if slightly spooky 'gentleman's gentleman' from the north with a meticulous eye for detail. Tony's girlfriend, Susan (Wendy Craig), is the first to sense Barrett's indefinable creepiness and his passive-aggressive influence upon her boyfriend. When Barrett persuades Tony to allow his sister Vera (Sarah Miles) to join them as a live-in maid, his ulterior motives gradually become apparent as Tony's world is steadily inverted.

A symbolic parable about the British class divide, *The Servant* was a simultaneously sinister yet darkly comic film owing its unnerving tension to Pinter's pristine script. Among Bogarde's best roles, he thought it 'one of the funniest pictures ever made', an opinion Morrissey may well have shared in view of the exquisite wickedness and camp Lancastrian twang he brings to the character of Barrett. It's also tempting to picture

Morrissey making a local pilgrimage to its main location, 30 Royal Avenue, just off Chelsea's King's Road and a short walk from Cadogan Square where he lived in the late 80s. [175, 286, 382, 550]

Severed Alliance, The, 1992 Smiths biography

by Johnny Rogan, published by Omnibus Press, or to give it its full title *Morrissey & Marr: The Severed Alliance*. Though not the first book on the group (that honour goes to Mick Middles's slight and not altogether accurate *The Smiths* in 1985), it remains the most famous, largely due to the controversy surrounding its first publication when Morrissey went to great lengths to denounce its contents and curse the author. 'Personally, I hope Johnny Rogan ends his days very soon in an M3 pile-up,' he fumed, later changing his fatwa to death 'in a hotel fire'.

When asked to elaborate on his irritation over what he renamed '*The Sausage Appliance*', Morrissey explained '[The book is] just filled with lies. I was very sad when I realised that many will buy it and make the author enormously rich. It's got dazzling reviews in the British music press, who should know better. And it's introduced as the definitive history. And it isn't! The definitive biography of The Smiths won't be written before I do it myself. Or choose to tell it to someone.' He was especially irked by the suggestion that he'd collaborated with the author. 'This Rogan person called me up one night and managed to say just one sentence before I hung up. Still he claimed in the book that he'd had "deep conversations" with me.'

Marr was equally critical. 'I didn't think it was very good,' he said in 1993. 'Johnny Rodent pestered people who were close to me and to the group and they were too sussed to talk to somebody like him. He's not a very good writer, he over-researches little things and misses the overall picture. And because he couldn't get to the people in the know he got responses from people who knew me, and not very well, when I was 13 and 14 … I talked to him because he pestered people who then pestered my parents. I went there to defend myself but his opinions were already formed and he hung me with my own quotes.'

What most upset Morrissey, and what in turn delighted the press, was its unprecedented depth of gumshoe research into the singer's pre-Smiths past; a bedrock foundation for every subsequent investigation into the group, this one included. Though not without its flaws – Rogan's hairy-rock perspective of Marr's musical influences is often off the mark while his sudden digression to describe to the reader his own 'ascetically sparse' kitchen borders on the insane – its critical and commercial success is a matter of record and no Smiths or Morrissey book since *The Severed Alliance* has escaped either the shadow of its influence or an inevitable comparative evaluation.

The great irony of Rogan's notoriety as Morrissey's 'bête noire' was the singer's use of the book's full title in the 1996 COURT CASE as part of his defence against Joyce's percentage claims. More curious was an earlier incident where Rogan was in Los Angeles for a book signing at West Hollywood's Book Soup when Morrissey turned up with his assistant Jake WALTERS. Pandemonium ensued. Morrissey later claimed, somewhat coyly, that it was sheer coincidence.

Rogan revised *The Severed Alliance* in 1993 and has written various related sequels either adding to or reconfiguring its material in different formats. According to his official author biog, Rogan is something of a technophobe, resisting such newfangled cumbrances as bank cards, the internet and fridge-freezers and claims to subsist on 'out-of-date food at bargain prices' foraged from his local supermarket. Since this author prefers his comestibles garden-fresh, our paths have yet to cross. [12, 17, 94, 150, 157, 231, 362]

sex, No subject has dominated the public history of Morrissey, especially in interviews, quite so much as sex: his views with regard to sex in society in general, his own sex life (or lack of one) and the specifics of his sexual preferences. To this day, there exists great confusion, error, myth and contradiction when it comes to the discussion of sex and Morrissey, which itself says much for his deft handling of the media and the ingenious enigma he has created for himself.

The fascination with Morrissey's sex life is twofold. Firstly, when he began giving interviews in 1983, he instantly aroused suspicion and amazement by declaring that he abstained from sex; this is dealt with in greater detail in the separate entry in this book on CELIBACY. Secondly, he has continually refused to be pigeonholed in terms of his private sexual orientation and refuses to publicly declare himself as 'straight', 'bisexual' or 'gay'; the debate over, and his comments on, the latter are, again, dealt with in greater detail in the separate entry in this book on HOMOSEXUALITY. And yet, in context of the wealth of songs he's written graphically detailing first-hand sexual experience, his professed asexuality and refusal to be labelled raise some very obvious questions about the correlation between those lyrics and the life of the man who wrote them.

To start with, and to immediately shove aside archaic myths so as to concentrate on fact, it is worth recounting Morrissey's most candid on-record confessions on his sexual history. He says he lost his virginity circa 1971–72 when aged '12 or 13 … an isolated incident, an accident … I've got no pleasant memories from it whatsoever'. His letters to pen pal Robert MACKIE tell us that in the winter of 1980, aged 21, he had a girlfriend, Annalisa JABLONSKA, describing themselves as a 'bisexual' couple, but adding 'I hate sex'. Sometime around 1982 (as he admitted ten years later), 'one of my physical encounters was with a man … It was just a very brief, absurd and amusing moment.' In 1987, around the time of the end of The Smiths, he'd recall his 'first sexual urge' at the age of 28, bashfully admitting that he 'responded to it'. In 1988 he claimed he had, in the past, made tentative advances 'once or twice' to 'girls and boys' but with little success. Two years later he added, 'I was always attracted to men or women who were never attracted to me. And I was never attracted to women or men who *were* attracted to me.' In 1992, he answered 'Yes' to the question of whether he had ever slept with women. In 1996, he spoke of how he genuinely wanted 'to have a sex life' having recently been in love, albeit 'an impossible romance'.

Using the restrictive terminology Morrissey despises, his statements tell us that at various moments in his adult life he could be broadly categorised as 'bisexual' (as he told Mackie). Yet, to do so would be to ignore one of the fundamental purposes of Morrissey's art, and life, which is to challenge and explore (if only by questioning) the unfathomable absurdity of human sexuality and sexual segregation. As detailed elsewhere in this book, many of his core sexual beliefs were largely informed by his teenage reading of FEMINISM and gender politics, in particular Jack Nichols's MEN'S LIBERATION.

'Obviously I'm interested in sex and *every* song is about sex,' he explained in 1983, '[but] I'm very interested in GENDER. I feel I'm a kind of prophet for the fourth sex … I just want something different. I want to make it easier for people. I'm bored with men and I'm bored with women. All this sexual segregation that goes on, even in rock and roll, I really despise it.' In many of his early Smiths interviews he spoke about 'cleansing the world of sexual stereotypes'. 'I don't know anybody who is absolutely, exclusively heterosexual,' he insisted. 'I refuse to recognise the terms heterosexual, bisexual and homosexual. Everybody has exactly the same sexual needs. People are just sexual, the prefix is immaterial.'

Regardless of the few 'lapses' or 'impossible romances' in his life, it is precisely because Morrissey has, both sometimes physically and metaphorically, taken a step back from sex that he's been able to document it in his art with such affecting truth; much like a hot-air balloonist alone in the sky has a grand perspective on any given landscape that those physically among it, stood on the ground, could only imagine. He literally said so himself: 'I've always felt *above* sex and love … I believe that all those things like love, sex, sharing a life with somebody, are actually quite

vague. Being only with yourself can be much more intense. I personally have always felt trapped within the feeling of being constantly disappointed with people. In a way I do feel things that are conceivably better and more important than sexual situations. I mean, sex is presumably the final point one reaches, I don't know. It doesn't matter to me. All the emotions I need to express come from within me. They don't really come from other people. I seem to feel things far more intensely and precisely than people who express a rag-bag of emotions and survive, just, loads of relationships. I see all situations, even when I'm not involved and it's nothing to do with me, in a very dramatic way.'

The magnificent Mozzerian punchline is that by famously not having, or professing not to have, a sex life, he has created the *ultimate* sex life. It was his hero, Oscar WILDE, who argued that it was only worth talking about things that do not exist in the physical world. Morrissey's 'sex life' is the ultimate example. The more it is discussed, the more interviewers who are fooled into still quizzing him about the where, when and with whom, the more he reiterates that 'there are some people on this earth who aren't obsessed with sex and I'm one of them', the more he teases that when he feels sexual urges he sits down and has 'a chip butty', the more he fuels the fires of scrutiny with the explicit detail of a lyric such as 'DEAR GOD PLEASE HELP ME', the deeper it is carved in stone the myth that Morrissey doesn't have and doesn't like sex, the wilder the quoted contradictions, the foggier the public mystery, the more inscrute-ish the inscrutability, then the more epic and omnipresent Morrissey's sex life becomes. It is a breathless, earthquaking, deafening sex life quite unlike that of anybody else on the planet because it belongs to everyone and to no one, not even Morrissey himself. It is his art. It is his fame. It is who he is. 'I think I must be, absolutely, a total sex object,' he once confessed. 'In every sense of the word.'

[53, 61, 69, 79, 97, 122, 128, 130, 132, 138, 139, 142, 152, 166, 171, 204, 216, 217, 223, 234, 236, 275, 448, 567, 573]

Sex Pistols, The original UK punk band, formed in London in 1975 and of immeasurable influence upon the future of rock and roll thereafter. Morrissey's ambivalent attitude to the Pistols at the time – briefly appreciative but mostly critical – was due to his staunch commitment to the NEW YORK DOLLS, a group who'd not only influenced the Pistols but also played a part in their formation.

In early 1975, future Pistols manager and King's Road SEX clothing boutique co-owner Malcolm McLaren had stepped in to try and manage the Dolls when they were on the brink of disbanding. McLaren failed, watching helplessly as they broke up before his eyes in Tampa, Florida that March. Before returning to London, where Vivienne Westwood had been keeping an eye on SEX during his absence, McLaren made a solemn promise that he would find Sylvain a replacement band in London and wire him a plane ticket to come and join them. Sylvain trusted McLaren enough to loan him an electric piano and his cherished white Les Paul guitar. A few weeks later McLaren wrote to Sylvain telling him about the group he'd been assembling which he was thinking of christening the Sex Pistols. 'It's funny,' laughs Sylvain, 'but the Pistols were supposed to be my band. And you know what? I'm still waiting for my fuckin' plane ticket!'

'The New York Dolls were an early version of the Sex Pistols,' Morrissey reiterated many years later, 'and if Americans and the American music industry had only been alert enough in 1972 and 1973, the New York Dolls could have changed so much. But, not to be.' It was this injustice which limited Morrissey's capability to recognise the Pistols as an original group in their own right. Admittedly, the Dolls' guitar sound patented by Sylvain and Johnny Thunders set a precedent for that of the Pistols' Steve Jones. But in terms of lyrics, style and stage theatrics, the skill, sneer and Gorgon stare of John 'Johnny Rotten' Lydon owed little to David Johansen. (The one notable exception was the Pistols' scornful 'New York' including Lydon's mocking parody of the Dolls' 'Looking For A Kiss'.)

Nevertheless, there was much truth in Morrissey's conclusion to his 1981 book on the Dolls that 'their influence upon what would happen in 1976 with the Sex Pistols cannot be emphasised enough. That the Pistols took their approach directly from the Dolls is undebatable, and often admitted by the group and their manager Malcolm McLaren, who confessed that the Dolls were the only group of the 70s that interested him.'

On 4 June 1976, the Pistols played the first of two concerts at Manchester's Lesser Free Trade Hall organised by BUZZCOCKS' Howard DEVOTO and Pete Shelley. 'Malcolm McLaren asked us if we could help organise a gig in Manchester,' says Shelley. 'I think he was just anxious to get a gig somewhere north of Watford. There wasn't a master plan. But that's how we came to organise the show at Manchester Lesser Free Trade Hall which sort of started everything. Joy Division, Morrissey, Paul Morley, Tony Wilson … they were all there.'

That first Manchester Pistols gig was so significant that over the course of time more people would claim to have been in the audience than the venue was ever capable of holding. Perhaps sensing the need to document his attendance for history's sake, in the days that followed Morrissey wrote about the event in a letter to the *NME*. 'I pen this epistle after witnessing the infamous Sex Pistols in concert at the Manchester Lesser Free Trade Hall,' he began. 'The bumptious Pistols in jumble sale attire had those few that attended dancing in the aisles despite their discordant music and barely audible lyrics.' Even here, Morrissey couldn't resist making Dolls comparisons, likening Lydon to Johansen and concluding 'it's nice to see that the British have produced a band capable of producing atmosphere created by the New York Dolls and their many imitators, even though it may be too late. I'd love to see the Pistols make it. Maybe they will be able to afford some clothes which don't look as though they've been slept in.'

Many years later, Morrissey would recount the experience in Jon Savage's definitive chronicle of the rise of the Pistols and UK punk, *England's Dreaming*. 'That first appearance was quite difficult,' he told Savage. 'There weren't any instructions. Being northern, we didn't know how to react: people were very rigid … I liked them, but they seemed like a clued-in singer and three patched musicians.'

On 20 July 1976 the Pistols returned to the same venue, supported by Buzzcocks and SLAUGHTER AND THE DOGS. So did Morrissey, this time reportedly brandishing a copy of the Dolls' 1973 debut album under his arm, perhaps as a show of punk solidarity, perhaps as a cryptic, private protest. Indeed, although he'd see them a third time at Manchester's Electric Circus on 9 December, his support for the Pistols was fleeting. By the end of the year he'd authored numerous letters printed in the music press, denouncing them as 'no-talents', 'lesser mortals' than the Dolls and predicting that 'their audacious lyrics and discordant music will not hold their heads above water when their followers tire of jumpers and safety pins'.

As it turned out, the Pistols didn't hold their heads above water for so very long. In early 1977, a few months after the release of their November '76 debut single 'Anarchy In The UK', original bassist Glen Matlock quit. According to apocryphal punk legend he was sacked for, among other things, listening to JONI MITCHELL; Morrissey would relish sharing this anecdote with Mitchell when interviewing her in 1996. Matlock was replaced by Sid Vicious prior to the Pistols' masterpiece, 'God Save The Queen' (number two, June 1977), British pop's most brazen slur on the monarchy until The Smiths' 'THE QUEEN IS DEAD' nearly a decade later. 'Pretty Vacant' followed (number six, July 1977) prior to their only studio album, Never Mind The Bollocks, Here's The Sex Pistols, less a bright new beginning than a last gasp for glory. Bollocks producer Chris Thomas would later be approached by Morrissey in 1995 to produce SOUTHPAW GRAMMAR, but declined.

History was to repeat itself when, like the Dolls before them, the Pistols became the second band under McLaren's auspices to break up on the road in America, playing their final concert on 14 January 1978 at San Francisco's Winterland. The last

song of the night was 'No Fun', the same Stooges cover which stirred Devoto and Shelley to travel to London two years earlier, thus sowing the seeds for the two Lesser Free Trade Hall gigs, the Manchester punk scene's Big Bang. Lydon would re-emerge later that year with Public Image Ltd, though the remaining Pistols would plod on under the band's banner in (sometimes literal) cartoon form for The Great Rock'N'Roll Swindle film and accompanying soundtrack album.

By the time of the latter's release, Sid Vicious was dead, having spent the last two years of his life succumbing to heroin addiction with his American junkie girlfriend Nancy Spungen. This was the final ironic, and fatal, twist in the Dolls–Pistols connection: Spungen, a New York groupie who'd claim to have slept with all the Dolls, came to London on a mission to bed ex-Dolls drummer Jerry Nolan, now with Johnny Thunders and The Heartbreakers. When Spungen failed to ensnare Nolan, she settled for Sid. The relationship cost both their lives. In October '78, Spungen was found dead in their room at New York's Chelsea Hotel (where JOBRIATH would also have been living at the time). She'd been stabbed with Sid's knife. The pitiful Sid had no recollection of what had happened and was arrested on suspicion of murder. Released on bail, after a failed suicide attempt he landed himself back in jail for smashing a glass in the face of PATTI SMITH's brother, Todd. Bailed again, he died of a heroin overdose on 12 February 1979.

The original Pistols line-up of Lydon, Jones, Matlock and drummer Paul Cook re-formed for a series of concerts in 1996, the first of many reunions. Momentarily setting aside his Dolls bias, in 2006 Morrissey was gracious enough to honour the Pistols' seismic impact upon the history of popular music. 'I think they changed the world and I'm very grateful for that,' he told the NME. 'I saw them three times at the very beginning and they were breathtaking and very necessary and I simply feel gratitude. Everybody on the planet has shortcomings, and most people can't see it through, but it doesn't matter because most people give nothing and they gave so much and they've sustained.' [23, 31, 136, 340, 362, 366, 571]

'Shakespeare's Sister' (Morrissey/Marr),

The Smiths' seventh single, released March 1985, highest UK chart position #26. Cover star: Pat PHOENIX. The ultimate example of the disorienting speed and blinding ambition of The Smiths' trajectory, 'Shakespeare's Sister' bolted out of the blue just one month after MEAT IS MURDER. A Brontë-force torrent of satanic ragtime, it finds Morrissey possessed with thoughts of suicide, struggling against maternal constraints and mocking his ludicrous early attempts to become an acoustic protest singer: he'd later describe it as 'the song of my life'.

The title was inspired by Virginia Woolf's 1928 essay *A Room Of One's Own*, in which she argues that chauvinism in Elizabethan society would have made it impossible for a woman with the same genius as Shakespeare to become a successful playwright. 'What would have happened had Shakespeare had a wonderfully gifted sister?' asks Woolf, before imagining a grim fate of destitution, unwanted pregnancy and eventually suicide. Morrissey reiterated Woolf's thesis when explaining the song. 'In the history of literature Shakespeare, of course, never had a sister and in almost every aspect of art there is no female voice whatsoever. So really by "Shakespeare's Sister" it's merely the voice of the downtrodden. The song is really about shrugging off the shackles of depression and shedding the skins of one's parent and getting out and living and doing what one wants to do.'

The lyrics also drew heavily from one of Morrissey's most popular sources of the period, Elizabeth SMART's *By Grand Central Station I Sat Down And Wept*: specifically 'the rocks below could promise certain death', 'our bones groaned' and 'I am going to meet my lover'. Further inspiration may have been provided by 'Don't Jump', a 1962 EP track by Billy FURY in which he finds himself 'standing at the edge of a clifftop high above', staring down at 'the rugged rocks' and trying to resist the deathly voice beckoning him forth from beyond the grave.

Marr, too, threw a mishmash of influences into its whirlwind, from what he describes as 'the ghost of Johnny Cash' to a favourite R&B riff from Bo Diddley's 'Diddley Daddy', repeated in Chuck Berry's 'You Can't Catch Me'. As he also freely acknowledged, its piano boogie trembled with the aftershock of THE ROLLING STONES' 1966 hit 'Have You Seen Your Mother, Baby, Standing In The Shadow?'.

The finished song came together at the very last minute when Marr played Morrissey his riff the

Sexton, Anne, Twentieth-century American poet whose art and fame, like that of her more famous friend and contemporary Sylvia Plath, is embroiled with her suicide. Morrissey has referred to Sexton in passing as one of his favourite poets, once telling a 2007 audience in Boston (where she killed herself) that she 'died for you, and me'. She suffered her first breakdown aged 25 and made her first suicide attempt on her 28th birthday. It was while in therapy that she was encouraged by her psychiatrist to express herself through poetry, publishing her first collection – 1960's *To Bedlam And Part Way Back* – at the age of 32. Morrissey's interest in Sexton is logical since the majority of her confessional poetry is preoccupied with themes of death, sex, misery and the graphic functions of the female body: 'Wanting To Die', 'The Ballad Of The Lonely Masturbator', 'In Celebration Of My Uterus' and the prophetic 'Suicide Note'. Another of her more famous poems shares a title with Morrissey's 1995 song 'THE OPERATION'. Plagued by mental illness her whole adult life, after many failed suicide attempts she finally succeeded in October 1974, aged 45, dying of carbon monoxide poisoning in her Boston garage. [60, 133, 368]

morning they were heading to the studio. His decision to make piano the melodic lead was motivated by his recent acquisition of an old upright model which came with the new house he'd bought in Bowdon, outside Manchester, at the end of 1984. Along with 'OSCILLATE WILDLY', 'Shakespeare's Sister' was one of the first tunes Marr wrote on the instrument. The two tracks were recorded together at the same session, with Andy Rourke nervously trying his hand at cello on both.

'Shakespeare's Sister' would be one of The Smiths' most courageous if strangely underrated endeavours, its rockabilly simplicity confounding those who'd hitherto pigeonholed them as a jingly-jangly pop group. Three weeks before its release, they unveiled it with a mimed performance on BBC2's *Oxford Road Show*, upsetting the programme's producers who'd expected them to play their current single, 'HOW SOON IS NOW?' 'We were so buzzed about "Shakespeare's Sister" that we said, "Well, we're not going to do it unless we can play this new one,"' says Marr. 'It caused much drama, but we stuck to our guns.'

Sadly, their enthusiasm wasn't shared by everyone. Engineer Stephen STREET believes the finished version 'could have been much better', an opinion seconded by journalist Nick Kent who witnessed its mixing process only to criticise the result as 'an abomination of the song's potential'. Peaking at 26 and the first Smiths single to chart to be denied a *TOP OF THE POPS* appearance, Morrissey would lay all blame for its failure not on the song, but upon ROUGH TRADE. Released during their UK Meat Is Murder tour, Morrissey would make sarcastic remarks about 'Rough Trade promotion' when introducing it on stage. 'The height of suspicion surrounds the fate of that record,' he brooded. 'Rough Trade released [it] with a monstrous amount of defeatism. They had no faith in it whatsoever. They liked it, but they allowed it to dribble, to stall. They didn't service it or market it in any way.'

While Marr shared Morrissey's concerns about its 'lack of presence', with hindsight he remains more philosophical about the fate of a record he praised at the time for containing 'one of the best rhythm patterns and grooves I've ever heard'. 'To be honest, it didn't surprise me that a song like "Shakespeare's Sister" didn't get in the charts,' he admits. 'It was a very arch record to release at that time. Quite audacious, a bit mad. And that's why I loved it.'

Arch, audacious and more than just *a bit* mad, 'Shakespeare's Sister' is a damsel too busy enjoying her distress to care that the train has already sliced her in half. One of the ten greatest records in the history of rock and roll. [17, 18, 28, 38, 135, 137, 145, 167, 426, 399]

'Shame Is The Name' (Morrissey/Whyte), B-side of 'I'M THROWING MY ARMS AROUND PARIS' (2009).

Berating 'dim-ass' teenagers who spend their time drinking and vomiting, then politicians who send kids to war while penny-pinching from the elderly, Morrissey grimly concludes that 'shame makes the world go round'. If hardly his most poetic soapbox rant, Whyte's wrecking-ball riff was rendered with convincing ferocity, bolstered by the atmospheric embellishments of piano, harmonica and the elevating harmonies of Chrissie HYNDE. 'He was giving me directions,' Hynde later explained. 'He said, "Imagine you're on an estate in Made Available [*Maida Vale, Hynde's London residence*]," and I'm saying, "What do you mean, on an estate?" I was supposed to be going [*in Cockney accent*] "Shyme is the nyme!" So I said, "Well, y'know, you don't want my hillbilly roots to come out!"'

Further substance was provided by the opening sample from François Truffaut's nouvelle vague masterpiece *Les Quatre Cents Coups*,[1] offering a smartly subtle complement to the song's Francophilian A-side. Interestingly, Shame actually *is* the name of Morrissey's dog, or so he revealed in 2005. [93, 544]

---

1. The clip from 1959's *Les Quatre Cents Coups* (*The 400 Blows*) occurs roughly ten minutes into the film. Twelve-year-old schoolboy Antoine Doinel (Jean-Pierre Léaud) insults the class swot, a boy called Mauricet whose name is pronounced very similar to 'Morrissey'. Roughly

translated Léaud shouts, 'You bastard, Mauricet ... you'll get yours, Mauricet!'

'Sharp Bend, Fast Car, Goodbye' (Morrissey/Whyte),

Studio outtake from the 1993 VAUXHALL AND I sessions. Among the dozen tunes selected prior to recording the album was Whyte's heavy-handed homage to the classic Phil Spector sound of The Ronettes. Its inherent retro girl group vibe inspired Morrissey to furnish it with a working title which, in its humorous equation of a road traffic accident, brought to mind the death discs of The Shangri-Las, in particular 1965's 'Give Us Your Blessings' in which eloping couple Mary and Jimmy come a cropper after failing to see 'the sign that read detour'. Sadly, since Morrissey abandoned the song in the early stages of the album before supplying a vocal we'll never know whether 'Sharp Bend, Fast Car, Goodbye' was strictly black comedy or, potentially, some more meaningful return to the fatalistic four-wheeled romance of 'THERE IS A LIGHT THAT NEVER GOES OUT'. [4, 40]

Shaw, Sandie, 'The most prolific figure in the

entire history of British popular music.' Or so said Morrissey in 1983 prior to her first collaboration with The Smiths. If not *the* most successful British female pop star of the 1960s, Shaw was by far the most consistent, and the most radical. As Morrissey surmised, 'Without supernatural beauty, Sandie Shaw cut an unusual figure, and would herald a new abandoned casualness for female singers.' Such casualness extended to her trademark of performing barefooted; her means of being able to move on stage without her glasses and not trip over, instead using her toes to locate any obstacles.

Born Sandra Goodgrich in Dagenham, Essex, at the age of 17 she was discovered by Adam Faith manager Eve Taylor who lumbered her with the pun pseudonym Sandie Shaw and paired her with Faith songwriter Chris Andrews. Their first collaboration for Pye, July 1964's 'As Long As You're Happy', sunk without trace. Andrews stood down

for her second, Shaw's uniquely Essex back-alley knee-tremble through Bacharach/David's '(There's) Always Something There To Remind Me', her first UK number one in October 1964. Morrissey, then aged five, later referred to his 'first musical experience' as watching Shaw on television.

The majority of her hits thereafter were Andrews originals orchestrated by Ken Woodman. Morrissey correctly noted that 'it would only be when Shaw, in a fit of mental abstraction, disposed of either Andrews or Woodman, that an artistic slump would arise'. Her next four all went top ten in 1965 including the sultry drama of 'Girl Don't Come' (later covered by ex-NEW YORK DOLL David Johansen as 'Boy Don't Come') and her second number one, the irresistibly bouncy 'Long Live Love'. Morrissey would frequently include Shaw singles when asked to compile lists of his favourite records during The Smiths, usually nominating 'Stop Before You Start' (B-side of 1966's 'Nothing Comes Easy'), 1968's 'Today' and, more frequently, 1967's bold, brassy 'You've Not Changed'. 'It sums up everything she ever had,' he said of the latter, 'youth, vitality and a certain coyness.' The song also merits consideration as a possible lyrical influence upon 'HAND IN GLOVE': 'If you wore rags you'd still look good to me.'

Sadly, the quality of Shaw's later 60s output was rarely reflected in worthy chart positions. September 1966's brilliant 'Run', a torrent of Del Shannon dread and Joe Meek thunder claps, failed to make the top 30 despite Andrews's equally powerful B-side, 'Long Walk Home'. More often than not, Shaw's Bs outshone her increasingly stilted As, including other Morrissey favourites 'Keep In Touch' and 'Voice In The Crowd'; the latter title he'd use as his signature name on early fan letters to Sandie. Such triumphs were overshadowed by the two barely discussable sore thumbs which became her final 60s successes. 1967's EUROVISION winner 'Puppet On A String' provided her third UK number one: Shaw would later denounce it as 'sexist drivel to a cuckoo clock tune'; Morrissey deemed it merely 'disturbingly pleasant'. The ghastly 'Monsieur Dupont' (number six, April

1969) was even worse. When the 60s ended, Shaw's limelight evaporated.

Prior to her Smiths-driven renaissance, her most prominent comeback bid had been a 1982 cover of 'Anyone Who Had A Heart' with the Heaven 17-affiliated B.E.F. (British Electric Foundation). In early August 1983, when The Smiths only had one single to their name, Morrissey made his first tentative contact with Shaw through ROUGH TRADE's Geoff Travis, who passed a letter and cassette on to her husband, Virgin Records' Nik Powell.

'We could never begin to emphasise the endless joy we would feel if you would care to listen to our song with a view to possibly covering it,' he wrote. 'Obviously the song was written with you in mind. It is an absolute fact that your influence more than any other permeates all our music. Without doubt we are incurable Sandie Shaw fans … the Sandie Shaw legend cannot be over yet – there is more to be done!' The letter was signed 'Morrissey (wordsmith/voice), Johnny (multi-instrumentalist/composer) – The Smiths'.

The song in question was their admittedly Andrews-esque 'I DON'T OWE YOU ANYTHING'. Shaw was initially sceptical, concerned by the current tabloid smear over their supposedly 'paedophilic' lyrics and the sleeve of 'HAND IN GLOVE' which alarmed her enough to tell her husband 'he's started sending me pictures of naked men with their bums showing'. Eventually she was persuaded, but strictly 'on the proviso that if I didn't like the result we'd scrap it'.

The result was April 1984's Rough Trade single 'Hand In Glove', her vivacious take on The Smiths' debut backed by 'I Don't Owe You Anything', plus an acoustic version of Morrissey and Marr's 'JEANE' on the 12-inch; all tracks were produced by John PORTER. Riding the wave of The Smiths' recent chart successes and their debut album, the Shaw single reached number 27 in the first week of May. Her first hit in 15 years, it also returned her to TOP OF THE POPS where she writhed on the studio floor in a pleather Macintosh beside a barefooted Marr and Rourke. 'To prove to my teenage

daughter that there's some life in the old bat yet.' The month before its release, Shaw twice joined The Smiths on their March 1984 UK tour, singing lead vocal on 'I Don't Owe You Anything' in London and Manchester.

For Morrissey, it was a childhood dream come true. 'I've worshipped her for so long,' he admitted, 'and then to work with her is just the highest thrill that I can possibly think of.' For Marr, it was a chance to confound their critics' expectations. 'I loved the fact that the group's identity had expanded. It was a thing that couldn't be pigeonholed. People like Smash Hits and Radio 1 suddenly had to view us in a slightly different way.' Only in the aftermath would Morrissey share his private concerns over the fate of the single and its reception. While he considered their endeavour 'the absolute envy of the entire industry', Shaw's thornier press comments about the singer reduced him to 'a quivering jelly'.

Whatever the record's flaws, it was a daring achievement which set an oft-repeated template for future modern pop group/60s icon collaborations beginning with the Pet Shop Boys' 1987 makeover of Dusty Springfield. Writing for other artists had always been part of Morrissey and Marr's initial modus operandi and, certainly, the Shaw single alerted their more insolent critics to reconsider their importance as classic songwriters outwith the confines of The Smiths' group dynamic. Yet other than the failed Amanda MALONE project that same year and various pipedreams reported in the music press – a Marianne FAITHFULL single, a Kirsty MACCOLL version of 'I WANT THE ONE I CAN'T HAVE' and even 'an unrecorded Smiths song to be covered by Kim Wilde' – Shaw's was their only such exercise.

The spectre of Shaw also had a hand in The Smiths' next single, 'HEAVEN KNOWS I'M MISERABLE NOW', a pun on her September 1969 chart miss 'Heaven Knows I'm Missing Him Now'. Shaw remembers that Morrissey 'was so naïve in those days' that he wrote to her for permission to change the title rather than ask songwriters Tony Macaulay and John MacLeod.[1]

Plans for a Rough Trade album to capitalise on the 'Hand In Glove' single were put on hold when Shaw became pregnant. She returned in 1986 with two singles on Polydor produced by Clive LANGER and Alan Winstanley. The first, a cover of Lloyd COLE's 'Are You Ready To Be Heartbroken?' was backed by her Langer co-penned Morrissey tribute, 'Steven (You Don't Eat Meat)' which inspired its subject to send Shaw a bouquet of white roses, also autographing a skirt she wore for a performance of the song on BBC2's *Whistle Test*: 'I've heard it. Thank you XXX. Love for a lifetime, Steven.' The second was a cover of PATTI SMITH's 'Frederick', this time coupled with the Marr homage 'Go Johnny Go!' co-written with Mark NEVIN. Neither single charted.

In December 1986, Morrissey invited Shaw to sing backing vocals on a first stab at 'SHEILA TAKE A BOW'. The session was something of a fiasco, hindered by one of Morrissey's sporadic no-shows, and her vocals were eventually discarded. Shaw's friendship with Morrissey survived the end of The Smiths and in October 1987 he made a repeat offer to sing backing vocals on a proposed VIVA HATE track, 'PLEASE HELP THE CAUSE AGAINST LONELINESS'. When he ditched his version, Morrissey passed the song to Shaw who took it for the lead single of her 1988 Rough Trade album titled Hello Angel after a postcard he'd sent her. That album's support cast almost reads like some fantasy roll call were Morrissey ever to be tricked (or possibly sedated) into appearing on *This Is Your Life*: producers and co-writers Stephen STREET, Kevin ARMSTRONG and Clive Langer; harmonica by Chrissie HYNDE; drums by Andrew PARESI and even castanets by DJ and friend Janice Long on 'Take Him', Shaw's song about dragging Morrissey to a disco in Bath. Mark Nevin only just missed out with 'Lover Of The Century', commandeered as a B-side, though the album's inclusion of a remixed 'Hand In Glove' ensured all three Smiths were also present and correct, along with producer John Porter.

In the sleeve notes of Hello Angel, Shaw thanked 'Steven, for incessant inspiration'. Yet, for whatever reason, their friendship wouldn't survive long into the 1990s. On her part, Shaw respectfully insists 'in my heart I feel I'm always in contact with Morrissey. I genuinely believe he's a really lovely man.' Morrissey hasn't been quite so gracious. 'We were never really great friends to be honest,' he stated in 1992. 'She's a very, very strong character. And a bit mad actually.' Five years later he was even more dismissive, claiming Shaw 'has lost the ability to feel' due to having had 'too much success when she was young, and no success after that'.

'Sandie kind of fell in love with Morrissey in a way,' speculates Mike Joyce. 'I think it happened to a lot of people who got near Morrissey. That enigmatic side of him. And the mystery. It was easily done, I did it myself. I think Sandie just went in a little bit too deep.'

'I completely support Morrissey for ever,' Shaw told this author, 'even when he's behaving badly. I think The Smiths have had more impact than any other band apart from THE BEATLES, so for me to be associated with that is just fantastic.'

If the closeness they shared in the 80s has long since dissipated, nothing can rewrite the ineradicable history of Shaw's profound influence upon Morrissey, who once described the moment he first heard her sing 'Hand In Glove' as the happiest day in his life. '[Her songs] are part of my life,' he affirmed. 'They're not just songs. They really are a part of me.' [13, 15, 17, 22, 25, 30, 100, 103, 124, 131, 161, 162, 172, 176, 184, 188, 204, 238, 251, 260, 267, 290, 334, 369, 404, 419, 447, 448, 468]

---

1. Whether the Shaw song titles 'LONDON' and 'TOMORROW' had similar influence on those of Morrissey is debatable, if not simply coincidence.

'Sheila Take A Bow' (Morrissey/Marr), The Smiths' 14th single, released April 1987, highest UK chart position #10. Cover star: Candy DARLING. Despite the difference in spelling, 'Sheila Take A Bow' appeared to be another of Morrissey's homages to Shelagh DELANEY, depicting a similar adolescent girl whose sad words provoke

concern from her elders. Inciting Sheila and her ilk to kick life's miseries 'in the crotch' and throw their homework on to the fire (the latter line adapted from an identical passage in David BOWIE's 'Kooks'), as a celebratory anthem for the group's younger audience it was The Smiths' equivalent of 'School's Out'.

Following on from 'PANIC', the tune was another of Marr's bumpier glam rock fantasies. 'In my mind, I was going for a Mott The Hoople sound,' says Marr. 'But it ended up like Mott The Hoople as performed by The Salvation Army Band. Which is very Smiths. So I suppose it was a success in our own weird way, but it's not one of my favourites.'

For a relatively straightforward pop song, the recording of 'Sheila Take A Bow' proved disconcertingly complex. It had been Morrissey's original idea to bring Sandie SHAW back into the fray as an additional vocalist. Whereas Shaw punctually arrived for the first day of recording on 13 December 1986, Morrissey didn't turn up, claiming he was 'desperately unwell'. 'Sandie was getting a bit frantic,' says Mike Joyce. 'In the end, she phoned up Morrissey and managed to get hold of him. She was saying, "Just hum me the tune down the phone that you want me to do!" I think she took it all personally.' Shaw finally added her vocal at a rescheduled session, though as Marr comments, 'I was as confused by the whole thing as she was. She gamely gave it a go, but it didn't really work.'

'I thought it was a *horrid* song,' explains Shaw. 'The atmosphere within the group was really bad at that time, so I'm glad they scrubbed that version. Anyway, I ain't somebody's backing singer.' The same prototype, produced by John PORTER, also featured a different Indian-flavoured intro based around a mystical, sitar-style riff. 'It didn't really work,' says Marr, 'so we went and finished it with Stephen STREET which was when it finally came together.' Porter, who would never work with The Smiths thereafter, claims he was never told about Street's intervention. As a consequence, he was narked to hear the finished

re-recording and spot a specific guitar part Street had sampled from his original in order to save time. Yet in all other respects, Street's punchier remake was a vast improvement, right down to the new intro which replaced Porter's sitar melody with a marching temperance band sampled from one of Morrissey's favourite films, HOBSON'S CHOICE.

By the time of the single's release, the group were in the studio completing STRANGEWAYS, HERE WE COME. When their current manager, Ken Friedman, arranged a video shoot for the song in early April, Morrissey vetoed it by not turning up on set. 'It was meant to be done at Brixton Academy,' recalls Marr, 'so it wasn't like we was being asked to abseil down the Post Office Tower.' Though of minor significance in the group's history, the costly cancellation of the 'Sheila' video added to the already escalating drama resulting in the break-up of The Smiths that summer.

As a record, 'Sheila Take A Bow' became an eleventh-hour testament to their mounting popularity, matching 'HEAVEN KNOWS I'M MISERABLE NOW' by becoming the second (and last) Smiths single to make the UK top ten during their existence. Sadly, it would also be the last they promoted together as a group, playing it on Channel 4's *The Tube* – its only live performance before an audience – and miming to it on TOP OF THE POPS in what would be The Smiths' final television appearance of 23 April 1987. [13, 19, 27, 29, 30, 38, 510]

Shine On Harvey Moon, Listing his favourite actors to the NME in 1989, Morrissey included Kenneth Cranham, Maggie Steed and Elizabeth Spriggs. Since these three were best known at the time for collectively heading the cast of the 80s ITV comedy drama series *Shine On Harvey Moon*, it's logical to assume that Morrissey was an avid viewer. Written by Laurence Marks and Maurice Gran, it starred Cranham as RAF clerk Harvey Moon, returning to London from India at the end of the Second World War where he tries to resume normality. His rose-tinted dreams of family bliss are immediately shattered when he discovers his home's been flattened by a gas explosion while his

S

wife (Steed) has been carrying on with a succession of American servicemen. When she refuses to let him back into her Tottenham prefab, Harvey is forced to lodge with his elderly mum (Spriggs). An affectionate yet sharp satire of post-war Britain, Moon's involvement with trade unions and the Labour Party would also strike a political chord in the contemporary climate of the THATCHER government. The show ran for four series from 1982 to 1985, with a fifth minus Cranham in 1995. The estimable Spriggs had previously appeared as a manic personnel officer in 1968's awful WORK IS A FOUR-LETTER WORD with its Smiths-wrecking theme tune by Cilla Black. [175]

'Shoplifters Of The World Unite'

(Morrissey/Marr), The Smiths' 13th single, released February 1987, highest UK chart position #12. Cover star: Elvis PRESLEY.

One of Morrissey's all-time favourites ('a great song that means so much to me'), 'Shoplifters Of The World Unite' was as lyrically bold and musically ambitious a record as The Smiths ever released. Superficially a celebration of petty theft, the song's ambiguity suggests 'shoplifter' is actually a metaphor for all those repressed and marginalised by society. Morrissey was very particular never to clarify its real meaning other than it being about 'spiritual shoplifting … taking things and using them

to your own advantage', as well as a means of highlighting the triviality of minor crimes in context of much greater dangers to the public. 'I often wonder why shoplifting can be such a serious crime when making nuclear weapons isn't,' he argued. 'That should really be a crime, I think, but it isn't. We live in a very twisted world, with a very twisted morality.'

Fittingly, its lyrics were rife with figures and phrases shoplifted from elsewhere: so many that, like 'CEMETRY GATES' before it, 'Shoplifters' becomes a double-edged admission of Morrissey's scavenging from other sources. The title, based upon Karl Marx's entreaty at the end of The Communist Manifesto ('WORKING MEN OF ALL COUNTRIES, UNITE!'), recalled that of 'Lovers Of The World Unite', a 1966 UK top ten hit for songwriters Roger Greenaway and Roger Cook under their singing pseudonym of David And Jonathan. His description of watching a news report on Channel 4 seems to have been based on a JONI MITCHELL lyric from 1977's 'Don Juan's Reckless Daughter'. Similarly, another passage was borrowed from Rickie Lee Jones's 1979 track 'The Last Chance Texaco' ('He tried living in a world/And in a shell'), a favourite song of Morrissey's which drummer Andrew PARESI recalls him enthusing over while making the later VIVA HATE. More obscure is a snatch of dialogue from a 1953 television drama starring James DEAN. In

'Shoes', 1975 solo single by Reparata (Mary Aiese, formerly of 60s Brooklyn girl group Reparata And The Delrons), which influenced the tune of The Smiths' 'A RUSH AND A PUSH AND THE LAND IS OURS' and was later listed among Morrissey's favourite singles. The song is a detailed description of a traditional wedding between 'Johnny' and his bride, 'Louise' (who is careful not to 'forget her shoes'). What ought to be a joyous celebration is lent an unsettling edge by its foreboding minor key melody evoking the specific ceremonial drama of a Greek wedding: the main riff is played on a bouzouki.

'Shoes' was very nearly a UK hit in October 1975 but was stalled by a legal dispute over use of the name Reparata by another former Delron, Lorraine Mazzola, which prevented Aiese from promoting her single. According to Marr, it was a record he and Morrissey 'both loved and listened to' in the run-up to making STRANGEWAYS, HERE WE COME, which would explain the very obvious influence upon its opening track. [18, 19, 175]

Life Sentence, an episode of *Campbell Playhouse*, Dean plays an escaped convict who tells Georgann Johnson, 'Before I was a convict I was an intern. A good intern with a bad temper. My only weakness was … never mind.'[1] Lastly, there's even a tenuous link with Shelagh DELANEY's *A Taste Of Honey* which features the similar, 'It's a long time, six months'.

For Marr, the writing and recording of the single coincided with a potentially fatal car crash in early November 1986 (see entry on CARS). The accident left him with severe whiplash, necessitating the wearing of a neck brace. 'Morrissey always used to claim he was jealous,' says Marr. 'He thought it was my best fashion statement.' In spite of the brace, Marr still managed to single-handedly oversee the recording of 'Shoplifters' less than a fortnight later in what would be his first and only solo Smiths production. 'We nailed it very quickly,' he says. 'There was a sense of occasion because I was very specifically given the job of being the sole producer, so I wanted to do a good job. I was very proud of it, sonically.'

Ostensibly another of Marr's self-professed 'groove tracks', 'Shoplifters' was a spirited single choice, its voodoo smog conjuring new colours and shapes within the rare rhythmic chemistry between Marr, Rourke and Joyce. 'It was us being slightly confounding,' agrees Marr. 'I really liked the words. "Alabaster crashes down." I thought that was brilliant. But it wasn't us doing another "ASK", or "THERE IS A LIGHT". It caught people off-guard, I think.' Even Smiths producer John PORTER gave Marr's handiwork his seal of approval; an especially magnanimous gesture since 'Shoplifters' would replace their previous choice of A-side, the Porter-produced 'YOU JUST HAVEN'T EARNED IT YET, BABY'.

Its release instigated a minor flutter of moral panic, with Tory MP Geoffrey Dickens denouncing the song in the tabloids and the Tesco supermarket chain threatening to take action against *Smash Hits* magazine after they printed the lyrics over a photo of one of their shopping bags. Rough Trade added to the hype by marketing special 'Shoplifter' carrier bags sent to participating record shops on the day of release. Charting at number 12 (and staying there a second week), Morrissey later recalled how hearing it on a radio chart rundown made him 'laugh hysterically as I listened to it'.

The last 'new song' The Smiths ever played live (just once at their final Brixton Academy show of 12 December 1986), discounting his one-off WOLVERHAMPTON gig, 'Shoplifters' would also be the first Smiths tune to become a regular fixture of Morrissey solo concerts. '[It was a] very witty single and a great moment for The Smiths,' he reminisced. 'I think it was probably the best days of our career … a time of very sparky rebellion and [that] song, more than any, I think, exemplifies that.' [17, 19, 25, 52, 69, 84, 474, 567]

---

1. It is doubtful that, in November 1986 when he recorded the song, Morrissey would have seen such a rare early Dean broadcast in its entirety. More likely, he could have quoted the scene as featured in a 1974 television documentary, *James Dean Remembered*, hosted by Peter Lawford.

Shrimpton, Jean, Alias 'The Shrimp', lanky, doe-eyed fashion model who became an emblem of the 'swinging 60s'. When Morrissey was asked in 1991's KILL UNCLE tour programme 'How would you like to die?', he answered, 'With Jean Shrimpton.' His quip was the follow-up gag to an earlier response in the same interview that his idea of happiness was 'Being Terence STAMP': Stamp and The Shrimp were one of the most famous media couples of the 60s. Whether coincidence or cunning, Morrissey also stated that his 'biggest regret' was 'not being born in 1942' – the very year The Shrimp was born in High Wycombe, home of Fuzzy Felt.

No sooner had The Shrimp met Stamp at the start of 1964 than she immediately traded in her old boyfriend, photographer David Bailey: ironically, they first crossed paths at a Bailey photo-shoot for *Vogue*. The actor and the model were a frighteningly handsome pair, though theirs was a tempestuous relationship. According to The

S

Shrimp, Stamp was cold and controlling, adding that 'for him, lovemaking was never a great priority'. He was also far from encouraging when The Shrimp was given her acting debut in 1967's *Privilege* (which spawned one of Morrissey's most cherished singles, Paul Jones's 'I'VE BEEN A BAD, BAD BOY'). Her role of Vanessa the artist was originally intended for Maggie Smith. Stamp told the press that her decision to act was akin to him announcing that he was 'going to perform complicated brain surgery the next morning' and warned her to her face, 'You won't be any good.' She wasn't. According to one critic, on screen The Shrimp looked as if she was being 'directed by an anaesthetist'.

Shortly afterwards, she broke up with Stamp. 'I suppose Terry did love me,' she'd summarise, 'in the working-class way, in which the men love their women as long as the women aren't any trouble.' Convinced that they'd marry, Stamp was emotionally banjaxed by her rejection and ran off to India to de-scramble his brain.

At least Stamp got off lightly when compared with The Shrimp's later conquest (and another Morrissey favourite), Heathcoate WILLIAMS. Instead of psychological damage, their 'strange relationship' ended with Williams wincing in hospital with second-degree burns after turning up on her doorstep and setting himself alight. [141, 370, 379]

Sidcup, Suburb of south-east London which became a running gag of Morrissey's in the early months of 2008. On stage at London's Roundhouse that January he introduced himself as the *CORONATION STREET* character 'Stanley Ogden', adding, 'I come from Sidcup.' Morrissey made further mention of Sidcup in a statement announcing his Hyde Park Wireless Festival show on the fourth of July ('the day America celebrated its independence from Sidcup'), while a farcical radio interview with Russell BRAND in April 2008 was littered with comic references to the town. His Sidcup 'fixation' was probably inspired by Harold Pinter's *The Caretaker* since Morrissey had recently included a clip from Clive Donner's 1963

film version starring Alan Bates, Robert Shaw and Donald Pleasence in his concert interval video montage. In *The Caretaker*, Sidcup is also a running gag of sorts as the fabled location where the tramp Davies (Pleasence) keeps vowing to go and retrieve 'the papers' he needs to start work. [415, 568, 572, 578]

Sim, Alastair, Spirited British actor and one of Morrissey's favourite 'thespians of the world'. During The Smiths, he once referred to Sim as his all-time hero.

Born in Edinburgh, among Sim's earliest roles was a genie in the 1938 Crazy Gang farce *Alf's Button Afloat*: in 1991 Morrissey used the pseudonym 'Alf Button' when captioning his Japanese tour photos for an *NME* feature. Sim's ever-collapsing basset-hound face and inappropriately solemn timbre were used only sparingly in 1947's *Hue And Cry*, his first and, surprisingly, only Ealing Studios comedy. Morrissey's personal Sim favourite remains 1950's boarding-school romp THE HAPPIEST DAYS OF YOUR LIFE, a precursor to his more celebrated role in drag as gambling headmistress Miss Fritton in 1954's *The Belles Of St Trinian's*. The same year saw him head the cast of the first film adaptation of J. B. Priestley's AN INSPECTOR CALLS, another favourite of Morrissey's. So too was 1955's THE LADYKILLERS in which Alec GUINNESS impersonated Sim's screen mannerisms in a role originally written with Sim in mind. Notoriously ambivalent towards fame, Sim seldom signed autographs. Of his film career, he once said, 'I stand or fall in my profession by the public's judgement of my performances. No amount of publicity can dampen a good one or gloss over a bad one.' Sim died in August 1976, aged 75. [168, 175, 508, 514, 520]

Sims, Joan, See CARRY ON.

Sinatra, Frank, As much as Morrissey has accrued a reputation as a champion of music's obscure or doomed underdogs – e.g. JOBRIATH, NICO, Klaus NOMI – in latter years when asked to

390

name his favourite singers it's rare that he doesn't follow majority opinion by nominating Frank Sinatra, widely regarded as the greatest male vocalist of the twentieth-century.

'He had patches of brilliance and I thought he gave a great deal to people,' said Morrissey shortly after Sinatra's death in May 1988. 'Lots of people didn't like him as a person, I gather, and the eulogies in England were very, very bad but I think he was one of the greatest.'

Sinatra's epic life would spawn numerous biographies, most famously Kitty Kelley's scandalous 1986 bestseller *His Way* dwelling on his many marital infidelities and his alleged links with Italian-American organised crime. But his legacy as a singer is without equal. Sinatra's phrasing – extending breath from the end of one line into the next bar – revolutionised popular music in the 1940s over a decade before the advent of rock and roll. Though his posthumous reputation is often cheapened by the cliché of 'Ol' Blue Eyes' – the wisecracking Rat Packer crooning 'Fly Me To The Moon' on autopilot – on record Sinatra could infuse a song with the same emotion, pain and psychological gravitas as Olivier's *Hamlet*.

Even if Morrissey normally opts for the high camp end of Sinatra for his stage exit music – using his signature anthem 'My Way' from 1999 to 2004 and 'That's Life' from 2006 – it's telling that when asked to name his favourite Frank song, Morrissey nominated 'Where Do You Go?' (Wilder/Sundgaard). A sombre ballad from 1959's No One Cares, the album cover shows Frank cradling a drink at a bar while smiling lovers dance behind him ignorant of his loneliness: pictorially, it's Sinatra living out the lyrics of 'HOW SOON IS NOW?' The original liner notes to No One Cares by jazz journalist Ralph J. Gleason neatly account for Sinatra's obvious appeal to Morrissey: 'The Italians and the Irish, the Jews and yes, even the English, have a melancholy side to their nature and thus we have a great appetite for the song of unrequited love, the lament of love grown cold or hopeless. This underlying note of tragedy is imbedded in most American art, as it is

in American life. It is one of the reasons Frank Sinatra can sing the sad songs in this album so well. Those bittersweet, late night, sad songs of days that used to be require an interpreter who can be sad without being maudlin, who can, in short, be man enough to cry a little and with the tears gain dignity.'

Morrissey's admiration for Sinatra was strengthened by his friendship with daughter Nancy (see next entry). 'Morrissey reminds me of my dad,' Nancy told this author. 'They would've hit it off. They have the same body language, the same magnetic attraction to the crowd. And the same blue eyes.' Morrissey has since referred to Frank Sinatra as being among his holy triumvirate of main musical influences – 'the royal three' – beside Elvis PRESLEY and the NEW YORK DOLLS. [34, 240, 422, 436]

Sinatra, Nancy, Daughter of Frank, singer, actress and friend of Morrissey. According to him, it was Nancy who instigated their friendship when visiting the UK in 1995. 'She actually asked if she could meet me,' he explained, 'and I went to [her] hotel in London and we just became fantastic friends.' According to her, it was the other way round: Morrissey, she claims, contacted her hotel asking if she wouldn't mind signing some records for him.

Nancy's pop career got off to a slow start, releasing a succession of unsuccessful singles on her father's Reprise label in the early 60s and making some fairly bad film choices, not least the dire *The Ghost In The Invisible Bikini*. Salvation finally arrived in the shape of guitarist/arranger Billy Strange and songwriter/producer Lee Hazlewood who between them would transform Nancy from the twee daddy's girl of her early Reprise flops to the sexy, go-go-booted she-wolf of 'These Boots Are Made For Walkin', her signature hit which reached UK number one in February 1966. Morrissey was one of the few who preferred its sound-a-like follow-up, 'How Does That Grab You, Darlin'?', naming it one of his favourite records in 1983. Its B-side was the theme tune to

S

Nancy's spoof James Bond film, 'The Last Of The Secret Agents' which, as some shakily suggest, may have inspired the wording of Morrissey's own 'THE LAST OF THE FAMOUS INTERNATIONAL PLAYBOYS'.

Within a year Nancy progressed from mock-Bond themes to the real thing with the elegant sway of 'You Only Live Twice' (number 11, July 1967). Yet in total her UK hits were relatively few with many of her best Hazlewood-penned singles failing to chart, among them her personal favourite, the icy gloom of 'Friday's Child', and the devoutly romantic '100 Years'. Her second UK number one came in April 1967 with 'Somethin' Stupid', a duet with her father. 1971's country-leaning 'Did You Ever', another duet, this time with Hazlewood, came close at number two but remains her last UK hit to date. Her film career proved equally erratic: after co-starring in 1968's *Speedway*, Morrissey's favourite Elvis PRESLEY film, she never acted again.

Morrissey's friendship with Nancy fully blossomed after he relocated to Los Angeles and the two became Hollywood 'neighbours' (in truth 'a seven-minute drive from one another' says Sinatra). Speaking in 2003, he recalled how she'd recently visited his home. 'I served tea, which she wisely did not drink. We talked about her, her music and her life – she knows absolutely everything about my music, which is extraordinary.' A similar encounter (possibly even the same?) was filmed for the Channel 4 documentary *The Importance Of Being Morrissey* in which Nancy raved about his hugging skills. On the same subject, she'd later tell this author Morrissey was 'a better hugger than Elvis' and also refutes the myth that his cooking abilities stretch only as far as toasting bread and opening a packet of biscuits. 'He makes good pasta,' Nancy insists.

Morrissey has since referred to Nancy as his 'Lili St. Cyr' while Nancy refers to him as her 'mentor', mainly for encouraging her return to

---

'Sing Your Life' (Morrissey/Nevin), Morrissey's ninth solo single (taken from the album KILL UNCLE), released April 1991, highest UK chart position #33. In title and sentiment, the carefree 'Sing Your Life' resonated with Billy FURY's vow from his 1967 B-side 'I Belong To The Wind': 'My life wasn't meant to be lived/It was meant to be sung.' Morrissey called it 'a small message to anybody who might be in the audience', explaining how as a teenager he 'reached a point where I could no longer be a member of the audience. I had to be on the stage and I think a lot of people do feel that.'

Between Nevin's dampened guitar prangs and LANGER and Winstanley's slapback production, 'Sing Your Life' was the first Morrissey record to distantly gyrate in the general direction of 50s rockabilly, a texture he'd amplify to greater degrees on its follow-up single, 'PREGNANT FOR THE LAST TIME'. As a result, it became a gift for his new touring band of young rockabilly recruits spearheaded by Boz BOORER and Alain WHYTE; a great version of their souped-up arrangement can be found on an American EP of a 1991 Los Angeles radio session, Morrissey Live At KROQ.

Prior to the Kill Uncle tour, a video for the single filmed by Tim Broad at Camden Workers Social Club pre-empted Morrissey's imminent live renaissance, albeit featuring Nevin instead of Boorer. Replicating the club's 50s nights where the singer had first succumbed to rockabilly during the making of the album, its dancing extras included friend and singer Chrissie HYNDE in period dress. 'Morrissey insisted I come down,' says Hynde. 'Then somebody else said, "Can you drive?" I said, "Yes, I can drive." And the next thing I know I'm in this working men's club surrounded by these 15-year-old rockabilly kids. The guy had actually said, "Can you *jive*?" I didn't know what I was doing there.' [5, 11, 15, 22, 437]

music at the age of 64 with her eponymous 2004 album on his ATTACK label. Alongside contributions from U2 and Sonic Youth, its standout track was her excellent version of 'LET ME KISS YOU'. 'I've told him,' she says, 'now he's responsible for saving my life, he has to take care of me for ever.'

[34, 115, 184, 225, 230, 453, 568, 413]

Sioux, Siouxsie, The first lady of British punk
and iconic frontwoman of The Banshees who duetted with Morrissey on the 1994 single 'INTERLUDE'.

Born Susan Ballion in Chislehurst, aged 19 Siouxsie first found infamy as a tabloid 'punk shocker' for her part in the SEX PISTOLS' historic Bill Grundy television broadcast in December 1976. Within two years, she'd be in the UK top ten with 'Hong Kong Garden', the debut single by her own group, The Banshees. Debut album The Scream followed in November 1978. Produced by Steve LILLYWHITE, it arrived between Magazine's Real Life (see DEVOTO) and Public Image Ltd's Public Image as the second in that year's triptych of albums laying the foundations of post-punk. Within its claustrophobic abyss of angst and angularity was 'Mirage', the first of many Banshees tracks to be included on Morrissey's interval music tapes in the early to mid-90s.

1979's second album, Join Hands, was darker still, featuring another Morrissey interval tape favourite, the disturbing lullaby 'Mother/Oh Mein Papa'. When guitarist John McKay and drummer Kenny Morris walked out midway through the UK tour to promote the album, Sioux reconfigured the group adding ex-Slits drummer (and future husband) Pete 'Budgie' Clarke and ex-Magazine guitarist John McGeoch. This Banshees Mk II – musically 'almost a different band' says Siouxsie – would become one of the biggest alternative pop groups of the 80s, securing her status as a style icon for a generation of teenage Siouxsie copycats, much like the epidemic of quiffed, bespectacled mimicry among Morrissey's own audience.

The Banshees would go through further line-up changes prior to disbanding in 1994, though their creative heyday was the McGeoch era as captured

on 1980's Kaleidoscope (featuring the hits 'Happy House' and 'Christine', the latter single backed by another Morrissey interval pick, 'Eve White/Eve Black'), 1981's Juju and 1982's woozy, exotic A Kiss In The Dreamhouse. Johnny Marr would later praise the McGeoch-era Banshees as a significant inspiration. 'When I was in my teens, there weren't many new guitar players who were interesting and of their time,' he elaborates. 'Bernard Sumner was doing good stuff in Joy Division but the only other consistently good player was John McGeoch. His was really innovative guitar music which was pretty hard to find back then. To a young player like myself, those early Banshees singles were just class.' Sadly, McGeoch's problems with alcohol saw him dismissed from The Banshees after two disastrous concerts in Madrid in October 1982. In March 2004, McGeoch passed away in his sleep, aged 48.

During the mid-80s The Smiths and The Banshees ducked and dived around one another in the singles and albums charts without ever colliding. It was only after The Smiths broke up that Morrissey began acknowledging Siouxsie's group, first on interval tapes and later namedropping them in interviews as being 'very underrated', further stating that modern 90s groups could never be 'as good as Siouxsie And The Banshees at full pelt'. Siouxsie became aware of his admiration when she started to receive 'letters in that mad childish handwriting' proposing they should work together. 'As an idea it was really fun,' she says. 'I was flattered, I suppose. I've always liked him, not particularly for his material but just because he was a personality that didn't fit into a pigeonhole.'

Eventually, in the summer of 1993 Morrissey persuaded Siouxsie to sing with him on a duet arrangement of the Timi YURO ballad 'Interlude', though their vocals were recorded separately and spliced together. Prior to the single's belated release almost a year later, Morrissey and Siouxsie fell out over discussions for the accompanying video. The original idea, claims Siouxsie, was to base the video around 'footage of Ruth Ellis', the last woman to be hanged in Britain, being led to the gallows. When they failed to gain the rights to the 'Ellis footage',[1] Siouxsie contends that Morrissey's alternative suggestion was to use a bulldog, an animal with symbolically problematic connotations. It was a highly sensitive issue for Siouxsie, once photographed wearing a Nazi armband purely for shock purposes in the punk summer of 1976 and harangued by some unforgiving critics ever since.

'I'd been living in France,' she explains, 'so I never read or saw the music press. I knew nothing of Morrissey's history with the whole Union Jack business until a few people warned me that he had this "British movement" type vibe about him. So when we had this meeting about the video, my first reaction was, "Why a bulldog?" I asked him about the whole nationalism thing and he didn't deny it. He kind of defended it. My attitude was that I didn't want anything to do with using a bulldog. If he wanted to use a dog then use a Chihuahua, use a bloody monkey, anything but a bulldog. His principle was that I didn't want to go with that imagery and I don't know why he wanted to stick to his guns so much. But he took real offence and I can't understand why he'd be surprised if I was aggressive if something was happening that I didn't like. I was surprised that *he* was surprised that's how I reacted.'

Judging from his continued praise of the Banshees thereafter, the 'Interlude' video fall-out didn't dampen Morrissey's admiration for her music. 'Well, that's big of him,' glints Siouxsie. 'But we haven't crossed paths since but we've come close. We were in Japan together and he was protected all the time so I couldn't see him. Another time we were supposed to play a KROQ show just outside LA. He was supposed to be headlining and we were on the spot before. He didn't show up. Apparently he had laryngitis.'

Siouxsie would, however, join the line-up of Morrissey's July 2008 Wireless Fetival in London's Hyde Park and was also due to appear on the same bill again later that month at the Heatwave festival in Tel Aviv. Ironically, this time it was Siouxsie who cancelled. Morrissey marked the occasion by opening his set with a brief a cappella blast of the Banshees' 1980 single 'Israel' and later telling the crowd, 'Our friend Siouxsie was supposed to be with us here tonight. But she isn't. I don't know why. She doesn't know why.' [20, 35, 154, 567]

---

1. Since no known footage of Ellis being taken to the gallows exists, it seems far more likely that Morrissey proposed using clips of Diana DORS in *YIELD TO THE NIGHT*, a film frequently (but erroneously) referred to as a dramatisation of the Ellis story.

sister (of Morrissey), See FAMILY.

'Sister I'm A Poet' (Morrissey/Street), B-side

of 'EVERYDAY IS LIKE SUNDAY' (1988). A self-congratulatory ode to his own eccentricity, the catapulting pop punch of 'Sister I'm A Poet' was worthy of a single release in its own right. Whether it was actually addressed to his own sister (Jacqueline) or not, it was clearly autobiographical in its recollections of being the local weirdo in a hostile town rife with meths-drinking thugs, cataloguing his many quirks from his love of literature to his fascination with crime. The latter seemed another lyrical debt to JONI MITCHELL who wrote of 'the romance of the crime' in 1977's 'Don Juan's Reckless Daughter', a song which had previously inspired a passage in 'SHOPLIFTERS OF THE WORLD UNITE'. Curiously, the word 'poet' is never mentioned in the lyrics, hence its alternative working title 'Sisterama' (as in ROXY MUSIC's 1973 single 'Pyjamarama').

Stephen Street freely admits his tune was one of the more overt 'Smiths-influenced' demos he presented Morrissey, employing a deliberate Andy Rourke-style bass line and strong guitar accents in homage to Johnny Marr. Recorded in March 1988, three months after the completion of VIVA HATE, both Morrissey and Street agreed the song was one of their finest collaborations. Only guitarist Vini REILLY differed, throwing what Street describes as 'a wobbler' during the song's recording because he considered the tune unworthy of his talents.

One of the eight songs played at Morrissey's December 1988 WOLVERHAMPTON gig (as featured on the *HULMERIST* video), 'Sister I'm A Poet' would remain a live favourite throughout his career, initially revamped rockabilly style in the early 90s (as heard on BEETHOVEN WAS DEAF) and still in his setlists as recently as 2008. [25, 39, 272]

Sitwell, Edith, English poet, critic and controversial aristocrat whose portrait by Cecil Beaton was featured as a stage backdrop on Morrissey's 1991 KILL UNCLE tour. The same photo originally appeared on the front of the 70s Penguin paperback edition of her 1933 study of fellow *English Eccentrics*. Though Morrissey never referred to Sitwell during The Smiths, it's been speculated that the book's inclusion of the phrase 'the Riches of the Poor' may have inspired the same in 'I WANT THE ONE I CAN'T HAVE'. Regardless of any possible lyrical influence, Sitwell was a model Morrissey symbolist; odd in appearance, unreservedly opinionated and with an arch wit akin to WILDE. 'I have often wished I had time to cultivate modesty,' she wrote, 'but I am too busy thinking about myself.' The eldest of three children, her younger brothers Osbert and Sacheverell also wrote poetry, prose and criticism. Their father, Sir George Sitwell, so disliked Edith that he tried to coax the great society painter John Singer Sargent into exaggerating her crooked nose on a 1900 family portrait. Sargent resisted, instead straightening the 12-year-old Edith's nose and mischievously putting a bend in Sir George's own hooter. Dirk BOGARDE chose this portrait as his 'luxury object' on the BBC's *Desert Island Discs* in 1964, the year Dame Edith died. [141, 372, 374]

'Skin Storm' (Ian Michael Hodgson), B-side of 'PREGNANT FOR THE LAST TIME' (1991). An unusually (for Morrissey) positive account of sexual intimacy, 'Skin Storm' was a cover of the 1988 debut single by Bradford, a Smiths-inspired band from Blackburn, Lancashire. Other than the flattery of their musical deference, Morrissey no doubt admired Bradford's visual aesthetic, sporting cropped suedehead haircuts which set them apart from their floppier indie peers. Previously, he'd invited the group to open for his December 1988 live debut in WOLVERHAMPTON. The following year, Bradford signed to Foundation, a new label set up by Stephen STREET who produced their only album, 1990's Shouting Quietly. Morrissey's 'Skin Storm' closely follows Bradford's lissom original apart from a handful of idiosyncratic lyrical changes. Where Bradford's Ian Hodgson sang 'love is a wonderful emotion', Morrissey is characteristically more dubious: 'love *could be* a wonderful emotion'. [15, 25, 39]

skinheads, One of the contributing factors to Morrissey's media harassment on the topic of racism was his prolific use of 70s skinhead imagery in the early 90s. Though the title of 1988's 'SUEDEHEAD' referred to an associated youth cult (skinheads who'd let their hair grow a few extra millimetres), the first explicit visual reference cropped up in the video for 1991's 'OUR FRANK' in which a gang of skins are shown larking around London's King's Cross.

Shortly afterwards, in a May 1991 interview with the *NME*, he made his much-quoted pronouncement that his 'perfect audience' would be 'skinheads in nail varnish'. 'The sight of streams of skinheads in nail varnish, it somehow represents the Britain I love,' he cooed. 'Wouldn't it be awful to find yourself followed by people you didn't want? Correct me if I'm wrong, but I thought the skinhead was an entirely British invention.'

The great irony over skinheads' unshakably distorted reputation as racist thugs is that, as Morrissey explained, the original British skinhead movement was united by a love of Jamaican ska and reggae. 'That the rest of the world around us looks upon skinheads as people who tattoo swastikas in their foreheads and throw fruit at innocent football supporters is a shame,' he mourned. 'Of course I'm aware of the fact that there exist such "skinheads". But the original idea of skinheads was just about clothes and music. And in England it still is to a pretty great extent.

Style and everything it involves for me have their roots in the British working class. That's where all culture I appreciate passes on and in some degree is updated. The British working class and its youth cultures are never vulgar or excessive. Whereas the middle class never has created a bit.'

Though Morrissey's intentions were clear, his decision to use a photograph of two skinhead girls as a backdrop when touring 1992's YOUR ARSENAL offered grist to the mill of the *NME*'s racist allegations following that year's Madstock fiasco, especially in context of the similarly misconstrued 'THE NATIONAL FRONT DISCO' and the eulogy to football violence 'WE'LL LET YOU KNOW'. It was only in 1995, after the dust had settled, that he admitted there'd been 'a certain flippancy' to the skinheads in nail varnish remark and that his use of skinhead iconography was a premeditated rebranding exercise. 'I really did get tired of being considered the flat-footed wallflower,' he explained. 'I listen to other people's music and it never strikes me as anything like as hard or confrontational as mine. But I'm still considered this weakling.'

Other critics have offered various cod-psychoanalytical explanations of Morrissey's love of skinhead culture: that his is the eternal loner's envy of the gang mentality; that as a teenager who, as he admitted, had been chased by such thugs maybe his was the victim's strange masochistic desire for their former oppressor; or that he's simply a bootboy fetishist. Whatever the reason, Morrissey's 'skinhead period' effectively ended in 1992 though there've been occasional relapses since, most notably the 1997 video for 'ALMA MATTERS'. (See also *ROMPER STOMPER*.) [101, 150, 153, 155]

Slaughter And The Dogs, Manchester punk group whose name would be linked with Morrissey circa 1978 although whether he was ever 'in' the band is questionable.

After Morrissey's first real group, THE NOSE-BLEEDS, disbanded in the summer of 1978, their guitarist Billy DUFFY joined ex-members of Slaughter And The Dogs, a band from Duffy and Johnny Marr's native Wythenshawe who'd formed two

years earlier. Taking their name from the album titles of Mick RONSON's Slaughter On 10th Avenue and David BOWIE's Diamond Dogs, they famously supported the SEX PISTOLS at their second Manchester Lesser Free Trade Hall show of 20 July 1976. Following a debut single on local indie label Rabid Records, May 1977's cement-chewing 'Cranked Up Really High', they signed with DECCA. After one album and three more singles, including February 1978's 'Quick Joey Small' featuring a guitar cameo from Mick Ronson himself, disillusioned singer Wayne Barrett – a man prone to covering himself with talcum powder on stage – decided to quit.

It was at this point that Duffy entered the fray, joining forces with ex-Slaughter guitarist Mick Rossi and bassist Howard Bates who were looking to form a new group. Because of his history with Duffy in The Nosebleeds, according to testimonies in *THE SEVERED ALLIANCE* sometime in the late summer/autumn of '78 Morrissey attended one 'audition' as a potential vocalist, wherein he apparently suggested they cover The Velvelettes' Motown hit 'Needle In A Haystack', a song he'd previously persuaded The Nosebleeds to tackle. That October he also joined them for an unsuccessful record company audition in London. This was the extent of Morrissey's involvement in this phantom group who played no gigs, made no recordings and were only loosely clinging to the name of Slaughter And The Dogs. Duffy, Rossi and Bates moved to London soon afterwards and formed a new group with ex-Eater drummer Phil Rowland, The Studio Sweethearts. After one single, June 1979's 'I Believe', they reverted back to the name of Slaughter And The Dogs before shortening it to Slaughter in 1980.

'I have no understanding why my name has been linked with Slaughter And The Dogs,' Morrissey later protested, 'about whom I know absolutely nothing. But I've read several times that I was either *in* Slaughter And The Dogs or I *auditioned* for them and was rejected ... which is news to me.' While this may be selective memory on his part – especially since in the same 2004 interview

'Slum Mums, The' (Morrissey/Boorer/Day), B-side of 'I HAVE FORGIVEN JESUS' (2004). Among the last dregs scraped from the barrel of the YOU ARE THE QUARRY sessions, 'The Slum Mums' was a bleak sequel to 'PREGNANT FOR THE LAST TIME' yet with none of the wit and not much in the way of a tune either. Morrissey is simultaneously vicious and sympathetic to the single mothers on welfare with 'six filthy children from six absent fathers'. Anybody who's ever signed on will recognise his astute description of the Social Security office 'strategically placed' in the grimmest part of town, but the rest of the lyrics are thin gruel, from its appalling rhyme of 'succour' with 'sucker' to its sloppy chorus rant about 'the Labour government' and the thoroughly miserable conclusion advising the title slum mums to kill themselves along with their 'rat pack brood'. While Boorer's sustained squealing guitar notes were reminiscent of his earlier 'SPRING-HEELED JIM', its marshy plod was otherwise forgettable. The song's only point of interest is the opening sound effect of screaming children, a possible homage to those featured in 'The Kids' on Lou REED's Berlin.

he denied being a member of The Nosebleeds, which he certainly was, and the fact that he knew enough about Slaughter to mention them in his 1978 feature on punk printed in the fanzine *Kids Stuff* – it does seem that the Morrissey–Slaughter connection has been hugely exaggerated, more for the mythological benefit of the latter. As Paul Morley would speculate, 'Some of us have spent many sleepless nights wondering what the world would now be like if Morrissey had started his singing career performing "Cranked Up Really High".' [47, 340, 362]

Smart, Elizabeth, Canadian author and poet whose 1945 novella *By Grand Central Station I Sat Down And Wept* would provide a source for many Morrissey lyrics both during and after The Smiths.

Smart's book was an autobiographical account of her affair with the English poet George Barker. After first discovering and falling in love with his poetry in the late 1930s, Smart became obsessed with Barker, eventually paying for him and his wife to come and stay with her in California in 1941. Their torrid, alcohol-soaked affair spawned four illegitimate children (the eldest of whom, Rose, later died of drug addiction). The Catholic Barker's unfulfilled promises to leave his wife were the root of Smart's anguish expressed so forcefully in *By Grand Central* itself. Like its title, a wordplay on

Byron's 1815 poem 'By The Rivers Of Babylon We Sat Down And Wept', the book was steeped in literary analogy and inspired metaphors. Only 2,000 copies were originally published though its cult reputation led to a paperback reissue in 1966. 'This is a profoundly honest, open wound of a book,' claimed *Cosmopolitan* magazine, 'and if you can take a searing experience you will be rewarded by the sheer poetic power of the writing.' Barker later gave his version of their romance in his 1950 novel, *The Dead Seagull*.

Morrissey first cited Smart among his favourite writers in the autumn of 1984, the period when the influence of *By Grand Central* upon his lyrics was at its most pronounced. These, his most explicit 'Smart songs', would emerge the following spring, including the MEAT IS MURDER tracks 'WHAT SHE SAID' ('I have learned to smoke because I need something to hold on to'; 'I wonder why no one had noticed I am dead and taken the trouble to bury me') and 'WELL I WONDER' ('gasping, but still living'; 'the fierce last stand of all I have'; 'cries out hoarsely'; 'do you hear me where you sleep?'), as well as 'SHAKESPEARE'S SISTER' ('the rocks below could promise certain death'; 'our bones groaned'; 'I am going to meet my lover') while minor phrases from *By Grand Central* could be heard in 'THE HEADMASTER RITUAL' ('grabs and devours') and the later 'RUBBER RING' ('the passing of time'). Towards the end of The Smiths,

S

'LONDON' would also borrow from Smart's book ('because you notice the jealousy of those that stay at home'), so too the title of 1987's LOUDER THAN BOMBS compilation.

After The Smiths, 'LATE NIGHT MAUDLIN STREET' would cull yet more passages while 'BILLY BUDD' also contains a likely reference. Other instances in Morrissey's solo career are more indefinite and, in most cases, probably coincidence: 'YES, I AM BLIND' ('God, come down'), 'DO YOUR BEST AND DON'T WORRY' ('drab dress') and the title of 'MY DEAREST LOVE' included.

Following *By Grand Central*, Smart worked in advertising and journalism before retiring to a cottage in Suffolk in the late 60s. There she wrote her belated follow-up novel, *The Assumption Of The Rogues And Rascals*, and the poetry collection, *A Bonus*. Smart died in March 1986, aged 72. George Barker died five years later in October 1991, aged 78. [375, 425]

Smith, Patti, If Morrissey and Marr have a
mutual patron saint, a guardian angel even, then it's New York punk poet Patti Smith. Not only did she physically bring them together for the first time in 1978, Smith was also a unifying musical touchstone when they began writing songs in the summer of 1982. Such is her influence upon Morrissey and Marr that it's likely her surname was a contributing factor in the christening of The Smiths. Early bassist Dale HIBBERT insists this was actually the case: 'I seem to remember them saying it was to do with Patti Smith because they were fans of hers.'

Smith's most influential album, arguably one of *the* most influential albums of all time, remains her 1975 debut, Horses. 'After hearing Horses I was never the same again,' stated Morrissey, 'and I don't say that lightly.' Recorded when she was 28, Smith had already spent years writing and performing poetry, making the first steps towards an alternative rock and roll career with her 1974 single 'Piss Factory'. A true account of a miserable summer job on a baby-buggy assembly line with only a shoplifted copy of Arthur Rimbaud's

Illuminations for comfort, the young Morrissey was known to type out its lyrics and send them to friends. Its B-side was a cover of Jimi Hendrix's 'Hey Joe', referencing kidnapped heiress-turned-terrorist Patty Hearst, and was released on CD for the first time on Morrissey's 2003 UNDER THE INFLUENCE compilation. 'Smith was, of course, punished for knowing too much,' he claimed in the sleeve notes, 'but she provided a world and a journey to those who cared to listen.'

On Horses Smith bridged the divide between punk rock and beat poetry, both with her own songs and by mutating R&B covers with provocative, wordy improvisation; most famously her opening spin on Van Morrison's 'Gloria' with its defiantly sacrilegious avowal 'Jesus died for somebody's sins but not mine'. Writing to *Sounds* in September 1976, the 17-year-old Morrissey described it as 'the most exciting rock album of the year … Patti is intriguing without being boring and every track is laced with her own brand of sardonic humour.' Produced by John Cale, its eight tracks included the softly skanking 'REDONDO BEACH', which he later covered, and 'Kimberly', Smith's ode to her baby sister which Marr used as a melodic guide for 'THE HAND THAT ROCKS THE CRADLE' and which also, possibly, inspired the JOAN OF ARC lyric in 'BIGMOUTH STRIKES AGAIN'.

Smith followed Horses with 1976's Radio Ethiopia, her first attributed to The Patti Smith Group. An admittedly inferior sequel, poorly received by most critics, its harder sound inspired the aspiring Marr who has cited guitarists Ivan Kral and Lenny Kaye as early role models. The opening track, 'Ask The Angels', was also, Marr admits, 'a subconscious influence' upon his chords for 'HANDSOME DEVIL'.

Touring Radio Ethiopia in January 1977, Smith fell off stage in Florida, fracturing several vertebrae in her neck and spine. While recuperating, she became fixated with the films of Pier Paolo PASOLINI whom she'd reference on the sleeve notes of her next album, Easter, also posing for photographer Lynn Goldsmith beside her own graffitied slogan 'Pasolini et vie' ('Pasolini and life'). To

398

promote Easter's release in late February 1978, Smith staged a 'fanzine press conference' in London. Morrissey attended the event only to be repulsed by her vulgar remark to a young boy of 17 and would describe it as 'hugely disappointing'.

Later that year, on 31 August Morrissey and his friend Steven POMFRET stalked Smith around Manchester prior to her performance at the Apollo. Following her to a music shop on Oxford Road, they were finally rewarded with a couple of plectrums inscribed with the title of Easter's controversial 'Rock N Roll Nigger'. At the concert itself, Morrissey met up with his friend and recent NOSEBLEEDS collaborator Billy DUFFY who introduced the 19-year-old singer to a young kid from his estate in Wythenshawe, the 14-year-old Johnny Maher. Though Duffy did the honours, as the catalyst for them both being under the same roof, it was Smith herself who became their symbolic matchmaker.

Though dominated by the twin themes of religion and revolution, Easter also contained Smith's biggest commercial hit, the Bruce Springsteen co-written 'Because The Night' (number five, May 1978). In the wake of its success, Smith became increasingly disenchanted with the music industry and exhausted by touring. Wave (1979) was intended as her 'farewell album'. Overseen by former NEW YORK DOLLS producer Todd Rundgren, it featured a pointed cover of The Byrds' 'So You Want To Be (A Rock'N'Roll Star)' and the single 'Frederick', dedicated to her husband-to-be, former MC5 guitarist Fred 'Sonic' Smith. The latter's UK B-side was a recording of her early death poem 'Fire Of Unknown Origin' which Morrissey once referred to as his 'favourite single'.

After a long hiatus, Smith returned to music in the late 80s with the album Dream Of Life. It took a succession of family and friends' deaths, among them her brother Todd and husband Fred, to prompt a permanent comeback with 1996's Gone Again. Yet for Morrissey, it's those first four albums – Horses, Radio Ethiopia, Easter and Wave – which 'changed everything … they changed me'.

Smith and Morrissey have since become 'email friends'. Marr would also meet Smith in 2005 when invited to play her MELTDOWN festival in London, also attending her momentous live performance of Horses in its entirety. The extent of Patti Smith's influence – as a wordsmith, as a rock and roll performer, as a woman, as a face, as an attitude – remains seismic. [17, 168, 171, 213, 285, 362, 376]

Smithdom,
A word coined by Morrissey when forming The Smiths (it was on his original shortlist of group names along with 'Smiths Family') referring to a symbolic world separate to the rest of society inhabited by the group and their fans. Morrissey began using the phrase in interviews circa October 1983, the first recorded mention being in Melody Maker the following month. 'We don't have to be cool any more,' he said. 'That is really the most basic thing about Smithdom.' Shortly afterwards he'd also refer to the song 'ACCEPT YOURSELF' as 'the fundamental request of Smithdom'. Journalists soon began buying into the concept, with The Face's Nick Kent referring to 'the precincts of Smithdom' in early 1985. Prior to Morrissey's use of 'Smithdom', in June 1983 Sounds writer Dave McCullough had already pre-empted the phrase with his own concept of a 'Smithsland'.

Beyond the Utopian fantasy of Smithdom as an almost BILLY LIAR-esque 'Ambrosia' dream state, it would also be used to christen a limited company established in early 1984, Smithdom Ltd, where the group's non-songwriting and publishing revenue was directed for the duration of their career. Debate and disagreement over the division of profits from Smithdom Ltd would eventually lead to the 1996 COURT CASE instigated by Mike Joyce against Morrissey and Marr. [17, 139, 166, 205, 362, 419]

Smiths, The,
The Smiths' debut album released February 1984, highest UK chart position #2. Cover star: Joe DALLESANDRO. Tracks: 'REEL AROUND THE FOUNTAIN', 'YOU'VE GOT EVERYTHING NOW', 'MISERABLE LIE', 'PRETTY GIRLS MAKE GRAVES', 'THE HAND THAT ROCKS THE CRADLE',[1] 'STILL ILL',

'HAND IN GLOVE', 'WHAT DIFFERENCE DOES IT MAKE?', 'I DON'T OWE YOU ANYTHING', 'SUFFER LITTLE CHILDREN'. Produced by John PORTER.

The Smiths' eponymous debut album was the most difficult of their career, the result of an arduous process of trial, error, frustration, haste and, ultimately, disappointment. Though still a great debut, and one of *the* great debuts for that matter, it failed to fulfil Morrissey and Marr's exacting perfectionism. They would be as quick to acknowledge their regret as they would to learn from its mistakes. In this sense, their debut's flaws proved a necessary catalyst for the more assured triumphs that followed and, in more ways than one, The Smiths (the album) marked the end of a long opening chapter in their history rather than the glorious beginning of another.

By June 1983, having signed with ROUGH TRADE, the group were evidently prepared to record their debut with just over a dozen Morrissey/Marr originals. Label boss Geoff Travis didn't venture far to find a producer, choosing recent Rough Trade signing Troy TATE as the man for the job. The Smiths spent over a month with Tate in London over July and August recording their entire 14-song repertoire only for the sessions to be scrapped.

Neither Morrissey nor Marr was certain that the Tate album, provisionally titled The Hand That Rocks The Cradle, did the group's sound adequate justice though the final decision rested with Travis. Conscious of budget restraints, Travis tried to salvage the Tate tapes by asking producer John Porter, by his own admission a reputable 'clean-up-guy', if he could fix them. After a playback at Regent Sound on London's Denmark St, Porter told Travis the album was already beyond fixing. 'Geoff wanted an honest opinion of what could make it good,' says Porter, 'and sadly my opinion was that it would be easier, cheaper and quicker to do it again rather than try and fix it. That's no slight against Troy Tate, that was just the state of the game at that time.'

The decision to start the album from scratch only exacerbated the intense pressure already upon the group. After their four BBC radio sessions recorded between May and September and escalating press hype in the wake of the 'Hand In Glove' single, expectations were high. Rough Trade were just as nervous, but equally skint. 'We had very little money,' confirms Porter. 'Seriously, I think there was something like £500 left.' Unable to afford another lengthy session similar to that with Tate, The Smiths' debut-number-two was recorded at speed, piecemeal fashion, beginning in September at Matrix in London, continuing in mid-October at Pluto studios in Manchester and finished back in London at Eden studios.

As if the sense of urgency and economising wasn't constraint enough, there were even greater background dramas gnawing at the stability of The Smiths at such a crucial moment in their career. Ever since signing with Rough Trade, Morrissey had been stewing over the group's financial arrangements, yet to be finalised to his satisfaction. Events came to a head during the Pluto session when the singer left the studio during the recording of 'What Difference Does It Make?' Presuming he'd merely 'popped out for a bag of chips', Porter and the rest of the group hung around awaiting his imminent return. When one hour became five it was obvious Morrissey wasn't coming back.

Finally, a phone call came from Geoff Travis at Rough Trade's London offices. Morrissey had walked out of Pluto, caught the next train south and gone straight to Travis expressing his concerns over the split of band earnings later contested during the 1996 COURT CASE. As Marr later testified during the trial, he reacted by threatening to quit the group unless Rourke and Joyce accepted Morrissey's stipulation that they should each receive only a 10 per cent share of earnings. Both verbally acquiesced for Marr's sake, not wishing to split the group on the cusp of success.

With the matter 'sorted', albeit not in writing, Morrissey returned to finish the album which was already proving difficult for all concerned. Porter's influence upon the music was greater than anybody had anticipated. Guitar melodies were changed, drum and bass patterns altered and piano and organ added courtesy of Paul Carrack, a session musician whose past included Ace, Squeeze and ROXY MUSIC and who found future fame with Mike + The Mechanics. Rourke recalls his confidence taking a knock, feeling 'a bit belittled' by Porter's instruction. Joyce claims Morrissey privately voiced his concerns at the time. Even Porter admits he 'actively butchered' some of their arrangements.

'Poor old John gets so much criticism for that first album,' says Marr, 'but I always took the view that a few of those songs we'd tried to get right for the third time so it wasn't a case of John putting a gun to our heads and saying, "Now you must change your arrangements, fellas." By that time we were desperate to get the record finished, so I think having done those Peel sessions, the amount of times we'd played them live and having gone through that very intensive recording that we did with Troy, we took our hands off the wheel. John came in and steered it as best he could. He was put up in some really crummy little place in Manchester, having to remake a record with now famously strange vibes. Technically, obviously, it didn't suit what the band was about but the experience of working with John was amazing for us and quite difficult for him.'

'I think the band were realistic,' reflects Porter. 'I mean, yeah, at first they probably thought, "Who is this guy and what the fuck is this?" But then I think they got used to trying new ideas out to see if they worked, and after a while they *did* work. As for Morrissey, I wouldn't say he was the easiest of people to work with; in fact he didn't seem very interested in the studio process particularly. I remember trying to get him interested in recording, like Johnny was interested and learned very quickly. But not Mozzer. I can remember showing him the mixing desk one time with all the faders explaining what everything did, showing him reverb and asking him, "Would you like your voice to sound like this?" He just wouldn't touch it, he wasn't bothered.'

Many years later, Morrissey would describe Porter's handiwork as 'a complete disaster', likening the album's production to that of a technical 'wet blanket'. 'I thought it was badly produced,' he said frankly. 'I remember a drive from Brixton to Derby where I listened on a Walkman to The Smiths' first album which we'd recorded for the second time. I turned to Geoff Travis on my right and John Porter on my left and said, "This is not good enough." They both squashed me in the seat and said that it cost £60,000, it has to be released and there's no going back. I had two very moist cheeks and there's an anger there that has never subsided because The Smiths' first album should have been so much better than it was.'

Marr would also belatedly confess to the press that on their debut 'the fire was missing', a regret in some way redressed by the same year's HATFUL OF HOLLOW containing what many still consider the definitive BBC session versions of the same songs. Undoubtedly, there's a coldness about much of Porter's production. For all its myriad guitar overdubs there's a thinness of sound; Marr apportions some blame on his choice of amplifier, the Roland Jazz Chorus. Rourke's vivacious bass lines are often lost while the drums, though loud, are much too rigid.

But while these are valid criticisms, they apply only to the album's presentation, not its content. As a collection of songs, The Smiths is astonishing in its melodic originality and emotional depth, defying obvious comparison with anything from the previous 30 years of pop history. Even with Porter's inconsistent sonic cinematography, its tales of sexual insecurity, past regrets, love rebuked and human suffering are conveyed with vivid force. It is, by his own admission, Morrissey's most personal album containing none of the third person portraits, political protests or vaudevillian sketches of its successors: even the Moors Murders elegy 'Suffer Little Children' is, at heart, an autobiographical remembrance of the 60s Manchester of his childhood.

Poetic licence notwithstanding, we should assume that everything Morrissey sings on The

Smiths comes from personal experience. As he'd admit, it was 'like launching your own diary to music'. Inspired by the few brief, failed relationships and early sexual experiences of his late teens and early twenties, he'd reveal how its words were written over a five- to six-year period between (roughly) 1977 and 1983, a collage of 'lines and interesting quotes' which he'd kept 'shoved in books'. Put simply, The Smiths was Morrissey's exorcism of an unhappy youth with all its rude awakenings ('Reel Around The Fountain'), jealousy ('You've Got Everything Now'), humiliation ('Miserable Lie', 'Pretty Girls Make Graves'), hopes ('The Hand That Rocks The Cradle'), desperation ('Still Ill', 'Hand In Glove'), pain ('What Difference Does It Make?'), injustice ('I Don't Owe You Anything') and fear ('Suffer Little Children').

For Marr, equally, the album was a transitional coming of age, as a writer and as a musician. Regardless of how it sounded, the experience of working with Porter taught him new studio skills to further fuel his limitless creativity which, in time, would allow him and Morrissey to take complete control of the production process. Now that they'd emptied their backlog of material composed in their first 18 months together, the completion of The Smiths posed a new and untested writing challenge for Morrissey and Marr, one which they'd rise to with extraordinary speed and confidence for the remainder of their career.

At the time of its release, Morrissey disguised his private anxiety, boldly declaring The Smiths 'a signal post in the history of popular music' and that he expected 'the highest critical praise'. Predominantly, this proved to be the case while only Simple Minds' Steve LILLYWHITE-produced Sparkle In The Rain stopped it from entering the charts at number one. To the loyal apostles who'd followed them through their formative BBC sessions and first few singles it was the long-awaited holy gospel, a chance to finally savour and scrutinise the group's extended repertoire in all its profound and provocative glory. Hindsight alone has bestowed The Smiths with its reputation as a potentially sublime first

footing handicapped by poor production: at the time, it was a resounding victory.

'I'm really ready to be burned at the stake in total defence of the record,' Morrissey told *Melody Maker*. 'It means so much to me that I could never explain, however long you gave me. It becomes almost difficult and one is just simply swamped in emotion about the whole thing. It's getting to the point where I almost can't even talk about it, which many people will see as an absolute blessing. It just seems absolutely perfect to me. From my own personal standpoint, it seems to convey exactly what I wanted to.'

His opinion would of course change in the years that followed but even if its textures have dated, even if many of its songs *are* better rendered on Hatful Of Hollow, in light of its historical significance, not to mention influence, any and all criticisms are immaterial. As an album The Smiths tells us as much, if not more, about who Morrissey is and how he became so than any other record he's made since. It shows us not only the heart of the artist but the hurt of the man beneath. It may not be a perfect album, but it is inarguably priceless. [12, 13, 17, 19, 27, 83, 102, 119, 128, 154, 167, 229, 408, 423, 453, 472, 479]

---

1. 'THIS CHARMING MAN' was never part of the debut Morrissey and Marr originally envisaged. However, its appearance as an extra track on the first UK cassette and US vinyl versions set a precedent for its modern CD equivalent where it appears between 'The Hand That Rocks The Cradle' and 'Still Ill'.

Smyth, Cathal, Aka 'Chas Smash', MADNESS backing singer, dancer and co-writer of their 1982 hit 'Our House'. Smyth befriended Morrissey circa 1990 and sang backing vocals on his cover of The Jam's 'THAT'S ENTERTAINMENT'. By his own admission, Smyth is also the alleged subject of 'YOU'RE THE ONE FOR ME, FATTY'.

Smyth entered the singer's life through producer Clive LANGER during the making of KILL UNCLE. A late convert to The Smiths, he only began taking real notice of Morrissey with the release of 'SUEDEHEAD'. 'Being an ex-skinhead, that

Smiths songs performed solo by Morrissey,

Before resuming his concert career as a solo artist with the December 1988 WOLVERHAMPTON gig, Morrissey expressed his intention to continue playing Smiths songs live. 'I was there when those songs were recorded,' he protested, 'I wrote the words. Just because the group ended didn't mean that suddenly all those feelings dissolve. It's still very much a part of me in 1988.' For the Wolverhampton show itself, Morrissey chose three songs which The Smiths never had the chance to play live prior to their split, as he'd later explain 'so that people won't make tedious comparisons and say, "Well, it wasn't as good or blah blah blah"'.

Three years later, when his solo live career properly began with the 1991 KILL UNCLE tour, he deliberately avoided playing Smiths songs. The same applied to the following year's tours in support of YOUR ARSENAL. 'I think that if I had begun as a solo performer and immediately played The Smiths' songs, people would accuse me of trying to latch on to The Smiths completely,' he reasoned. 'It was important for me to establish a solo identity, which I think I've done. So, that's the only reason. I still love all those old songs, most of them, and listen to them every day.'

It wasn't until 1995, eight years after he and Marr parted company, that Morrissey slowly began introducing select Smiths tracks into his live repertoire with the emphasis still on those songs which the group never had a chance to play in concert. Only in 2002 did Morrissey delve much deeper into the group's earlier repertoire and, as of 2004, it has become the norm for him to dust down a different selection of old Smiths songs for every tour.

Below is a complete list of the Smiths songs Morrissey has performed solo, in chronological order in the year they were first introduced into his set; those Smiths songs played only once but reintroduced at a later date as a set regular have been listed twice.

1988: The setlist of Morrissey's solo live debut gig in Wolverhampton included 'STOP ME IF YOU THINK YOU'VE HEARD THIS ONE BEFORE', 'DEATH AT ONE'S ELBOW' and 'SWEET AND TENDER HOOLIGAN'.

1995: 'SHOPLIFTERS OF THE WORLD UNITE', 'LONDON'.

1997: 'PAINT A VULGAR PICTURE', 'THE QUEEN IS DEAD' (played once at Claremont 26/10/97).

1999: 'IS IT REALLY SO STRANGE?', 'MEAT IS MURDER', 'LAST NIGHT I DREAMT THAT SOMEBODY LOVED ME', 'HALF A PERSON'.

2002: 'PLEASE PLEASE PLEASE LET ME GET WHAT I WANT' (played once at Phoenix 9/8/02), 'I WANT THE ONE I CAN'T HAVE', 'THERE IS A LIGHT THAT NEVER GOES OUT', 'HAND IN GLOVE'.

2004: 'THE HEADMASTER RITUAL', 'A RUSH AND A PUSH AND THE LAND IS OURS', 'RUBBER RING', 'HOW SOON IS NOW?', 'SHAKESPEARE'S SISTER', 'BIGMOUTH STRIKES AGAIN'.

2006: 'STILL ILL', 'GIRLFRIEND IN A COMA', 'Stop Me If You Think You've Heard This One Before' (as set regular), 'PANIC', 'WILLIAM, IT WAS REALLY NOTHING', 'Please Please Please Let Me Get What I Want' (as set regular).

2007: 'The Queen Is Dead' (as set regular), 'THE BOY WITH THE THORN IN HIS SIDE', 'STRETCH OUT AND WAIT', 'DEATH OF A DISCO DANCER'.

2008: 'ASK', 'VICAR IN A TUTU', 'WHAT SHE SAID'.

2009: 'THIS CHARMING MAN', 'I KEEP MINE HIDDEN', 'SOME GIRLS ARE BIGGER THAN OTHERS'. [203, 422]

meant a lot to me,' he says. Smyth's brother, Brendan, was also a renowned skinhead during the early 80s and crops up in the memoir of Jeff 'Stinky' Turner, lead singer of COCKNEY REJECTS.

According to Turner, Brendan Smyth eventually ran away to join the French Foreign Legion. '[Cathal] had to go out and get him back,' says Turner, who also claims Brendan subsequently took his own life.

Langer invited Smyth to meet Morrissey at Julie's restaurant in Notting Hill. Being a keen masseuse, during that first meeting Smyth offered to give Morrissey a back rub. 'I clicked his neck, loosened him up a bit. That first massage, I think it proper shivered his timbers because I don't think many people touch him.'

Whether for their shared Irish ancestry, his witty conversation or, indeed, his rub-down skills, Morrissey was sufficiently taken with Smyth to welcome him into his private circle of close friends for the next few years. 'He collects people like objects,' explains Smyth. 'People are like Fabergé eggs to him. I think he's amazing, but I feel sorry for him that he doesn't know love. He's manipulative, in a positive way, but that's his art. People may think he has affection for them. They may think that. They're probably wrong. I've seen lots of people who think they're close to him. In my opinion, they're only close because they have a use to benefit his career. But, don't misunderstand me, I love the man.'

Originally invited by Langer to assist Morrissey's quest to form a rockabilly band, Smyth declined, but proved of even greater assistance by passing the task on to his friend, Boz BOORER. He'd similarly decline Morrissey's offer to become his manager, even though there were times when he found himself already being treated like one. Backstage at Morrissey's Wembley Arena show in July 1991, Smyth claims the singer asked him to tell Boorer 'that he's moving around on stage too much and I don't like the size of his turn-ups'.

Morrissey used little discretion in exhibiting his fondness for Smyth, developing what even Langer describes as 'an infatuation'. Other than the tribute of 'You're The One For Me, Fatty', he snuck in a coy reference in the video for 'WE HATE IT WHEN OUR FRIENDS BECOME SUCCESSFUL': a still of Smyth feigning a heart attack from the video for Madness's 1982 single, 'Cardiac Arrest'. Smyth is also in possession of personal letters 'in safe-keeping' which he jokingly describes as 'a bit homoerotic', while in 1992 Morrissey duly presented him with a copy of YOUR ARSENAL, signed in gold pen: 'To Cathal – Be bold, be brave, be a man. It's a great game. Love, Morrissey.'

Smyth maintained sporadic contact with the singer after he left London in the late 90s and still retains great affection for him. 'Morrissey is a total samurai,' he concludes. 'There's no confusion for him. He lives on instinct and the truthful recognition of how he feels. He's got that amazing ability to create a vacuum around himself that people are frightened to enter. His depth and his stillness is frightening to most people. He's got the skill of a martial artist, to be visible or invisible. If you want to understand Morrissey, just read the Bushido, the code of the samurai. A brilliant geezer.' [15, 36, 386]

'Some Girls Are Bigger Than Others'

(Morrissey/Marr), From the album THE QUEEN IS DEAD (1986). The Smiths' ironic ode to the female form, Morrissey makes ingenious mockery of mammary-fixated male sexism as a late developer finally awakening to the varying sizes of women's busts. 'The whole idea of womanhood is something that, to me, is largely unexplored,' he coyly explained. 'I'm realising things about women that I never realised before and "Some Girls ..." is just taking it down to the basic absurdity of recognising the contours to one's body.'

Tapping into the grand British tradition of saucy seaside postcard humour as exemplified in his beloved CARRY ON films (even if the frisson between his ale-popping Antony and Cleopatra is more Burton and Taylor than Carry On Cleo's respective Sid James and Amanda Barrie), Morrissey's comedy is the veneer over a more meaningful agenda. Its principal satire of sexual stereotypes and the building-site mindset was made more explicit on an extra verse about a page-three calendar added for its one and only live performance during The Smiths' final concert at London's Brixton Academy in December 1986; a recording of the same was later issued as a B-side of 'I STARTED SOMETHING I COULDN'T FINISH'. Also of note are its closing lines, a puzzling paraphrase of Johnny Tillotson's 1962 ballad, 'Send Me The Pillow You Dream On'.

Marr had been soundchecking a similar spidery tune with Rourke and Joyce during the spring '85 MEAT IS MURDER tour, though it would be a few months before its full starry beauty finally revealed itself when noodling at home watching television with the sound turned down. That same summer's night he also wrote 'UNLOVEABLE', later driving over to Morrissey's house and posting a cassette of both tunes through the singer's letterbox.

'It is true that I preferred the music to the lyrics,' admits Marr. 'It's a beautiful piece of music. Sometimes things would evolve from my original demo as we were recording them, but "Some Girls" was one where Morrissey had already worked it out over my cassette so we had to play it exactly as I'd given it to him. Just this daft, really nice tune.'

Its trademark false intro was suggested by engineer Stephen STREET as a deliberate inversion of the false fade-out previously used on 'THAT JOKE ISN'T FUNNY ANYMORE'. 'The effect was supposed to be like the music's in a hall somewhere, it goes away, then it comes back,' says Street. 'A bit like opening a door, closing it, then opening it again and walking in.' As the final track on The Queen Is Dead, 'Some Girls' was an unusual choice, lacking the obvious epic qualities of previous Smiths album closers, in itself confirmation of Morrissey and Marr's maverick methodology and invincible self-confidence. [17, 18, 28, 38, 206]

'Something Is Squeezing My Skull'

(Morrissey/Whyte), Morrissey's 37th solo single (from the album YEARS OF REFUSAL), released April 2009, highest UK chart position #46. A hysterical (in every sense of the word) satire on what Morrissey described as the 'immobilisation' of modern medicated society. 'Whatever gets you through,' he explained. 'I'm not judgemental

about these things. Booze, drugs, if it helps you, then take it. Life is a difficult business, and most people find it acutely impossible ... even Jesus only made it to 33.'

Given Morrissey's previous confessions on his use of anti-depressants, including lithium, there was an obvious autobiographical undercurrent. Yet for all the seriousness of its subject – why people are forced to scrape through life mentally deadened by anti-depressants or even hormone replacement therapy – 'Something Is Squeezing My Skull' was pop at its most uproarious. Morrissey hollers 'skuuuuuulllll' in a straitjacketed fit as if being literally administered ECT during the recording process, possibly by Whyte's punk sucker punch climaxing in a bedlam of rhythmic epilepsy and his own cuckoo-nest gibbering. Even on paper, the words hyperventilate with humour: listing 'diazepam' then adding the informative 'that's valium' in brackets. The crisp echo from a ping-pong match between Eddie Cochran's 'Nervous Breakdown' and the RAMONES' 'I Wanna Be Sedated', 'Skull' finds and takes full occupancy of a square centimetre of virgin territory in rock and roll's otherwise finite wasteland. Morrissey at his most brilliantly, and literally, bonkers. [217, 480, 568]

'Song From Under The Floorboards, A'

(Howard Devoto/David Tomlinson/Barry Adamson/John Doyle/John McGeoch), B-side of 'THE YOUNGEST WAS THE MOST LOVED' (2006). By covering this 1980 single by Magazine (from their third album, The Correct Use Of Soap), Morrissey was belatedly confirming the influence of singer, and friend, Howard Devoto upon his earliest writing with The Smiths: specifically 'ACCEPT YOURSELF', which loosely paraphrased its opening line, 'I am angry, I am ill and I'm as ugly as sin.'

Devoto's lyrics were inspired by Fyodor Dostoevsky's existentialist novel of 1864 Notes From Underground (the original Russian can also be translated as 'Notes From Under The Floorboards'). 'I think that story is one of the most amazing pieces of writing,' said Devoto. 'The whole idea of man rejecting paradise – if he finds

S

that he's programmed for paradise and lust, he'll fuck it up.' The song's striking combination of self-deprecation and arrogance – being a mere 'insect' but 'proud as hell of that fact' – was a perfect vehicle for Morrissey, even if his delivery lacked Devoto's spiky neurosis while his band's faithful arrangement didn't quite scale the icy peaks of Magazine's original. 'A Song From Under The Floorboards' was still a worthwhile exercise, pointing younger Morrissey fans in the direction of Magazine and played regularly during the early stages of the 2006 RINGLEADER OF THE TORMEN-TORS tour.

songwriting, See WRITING PROCESS.

'Sorrow Will Come In The End' (Morrissey/Whyte), From the album MALADJUSTED (1997).
For 'legal reasons' the song was omitted from the original UK version on ISLAND and was originally only available on the Mercury edition issued overseas; the 2009 redux Maladjusted marked its first official UK release.

Such unusual censorship was due to its lyrics, being the singer's overt response to the 1996 COURT CASE in which he attacked both the judicial system that found him guilty and ex-Smiths drummer Mike Joyce, who won his claim for back payment of performance royalties against Morrissey and Marr.

Morrissey chose to recite rather than sing his spleen-venting monologue about 'legalised theft' and senile judges, barbed with a direct character assassination of Joyce whom he accused of lying in court. As hammy as his throat-slitting threats and bogeyman taunts of 'I'm gonna get you' might have sounded, his feelings were made perfectly clear. By his reckoning, Joyce may have won the court case but by doing so, and crossing Morrissey, had cursed himself for the rest of his life. Or so the singer hoped.

According to engineer Danton Supple, for all its severity, Morrissey recorded the track in good humour. 'There was almost a smile on his face as he was doing it,' recalls Supple. 'The way we saw it, recording that song was cheaper for him to deal with his feelings about the court case than the psychiatrist's couch. We were all laughing our heads off when we listened back. It's just theatre, isn't it?'

Such theatrics extended to the score itself, a demented carnival freakshow flinching to the whip-crack ricochets of a gavel. One of the oddest things Morrissey's ever recorded, it turned out to be the first of many embittered lyrics provoked by the court case, with more following seven years later on YOU ARE THE QUARRY. When touring Maladjusted in December 1997, Morrissey teasingly introduced the song as the final encore of his London Battersea Power Station gig only to play 'SHOPLIFTERS OF THE WORLD UNITE' instead. To date, he has never attempted the pure pantomime of 'Sorrow Will Come In The End' in concert for real. [4, 13, 14, 40]

'**Sorry Doesn't Help**' (Morrissey/Tobias), From the album YEARS OF REFUSAL (2009). A bitter declaration of unforgiveness, Morrissey rejects all apologies from an old acquaintance who has wreaked irreparable havoc in his life. Smiths-centric theorists immediately interpreted 'Sorry Doesn't Help' as directed at a former bandmate, compounded by what seemed a deliberate allusion to the 1996 COURT CASE in its scorn towards a two-faced QC. Yet by specifying the loss of his pre-Smiths 'teen years' and the denial of his true 'love', taken as a whole the lyrics appeared a general reproof to all who've ever wronged him, also serving as an abstract thesis on the futility of language as adequate compensation for personal harm. Morrissey's histrionic vocal graffitied vivid colours across Tobias's typically gritty cement surface, further enlivened by its staccato keyboards subtly suggestive of SPARKS' 'This Town Ain't Big Enough For Both Of Us'.

South, See ACTING, *BROOKSIDE*.

Southpaw Grammar, Morrissey's fifth solo
album, released August 1995, highest UK chart
position #4. Tracks: 'THE TEACHERS ARE AFRAID OF
THE PUPILS', 'READER MEET AUTHOR', 'THE BOY
RACER', 'THE OPERATION', 'DAGENHAM DAVE', 'DO
YOUR BEST AND DON'T WORRY', 'BEST FRIEND ON
THE PAYROLL', 'SOUTHPAW'. Produced by Steve
LILLYWHITE.

While the number one success and critical
huzzah surrounding VAUXHALL AND I returned
Morrissey to the forefront of British music, it
placed new pressure on the singer to maintain his
position with its follow-up. Conscious of such
high expectations, he later insisted that he deliberately shied away from writing Vauxhall And I:
Part Two. 'I was delighted by the original version,'
he explained. 'What's the use of trying to invent a
sequel to it? So I asked Steve Lillywhite, the
producer, to work with me, explaining to him that
I wanted to record a hard and solid album without any slow songs. I wanted to create for myself
a new universe, more twisted, rougher.'

Out of that 'hard and solid' brief came Morrissey's most unusual album, Southpaw Grammar,
his first (and only) as part of a £250,000 deal for
new label, RCA VICTOR. Keeping the same Vauxhall band of BOORER, BRIDGWOOD, TAYLOR and
WHYTE, work commenced in December 1994, two
months after the same line-up had recorded
the 'BOXERS' single. Since his favoured studio,
Hook End, was unavailable, Steve Lillywhite –
back in the producer's chair after Morrissey's first
and second choices Brian ENO and Chris Thomas
declined – suggested Miraval, a converted
mansion in the south of France. Surprisingly,
Morrissey agreed to the first non-UK recording
session of his career.

'We got there a few days before,' recalls engineer Danton Supple. 'I could see there was no way
Morrissey was going to last there. It was a dilapidated manor with no central heating in winter-
time. This is Provence, and we had to give these
French chefs instructions to cook no meat, no

herbs, no garlic and no onions. It was a bit of a
disaster.' Sure enough, within 24 hours of Morrissey's arrival, his bags were back in reception,
packed and ready for the first flight back to
England. 'I seem to remember he arrived, we had
dinner, all went to bed and the next day he was
gone,' concurs Bridgwood. 'But the studio was all
booked so we decided to stay on and get some
work done on the backing tracks, thinking he
could add vocals at a later date.'

Over December '94 and early January '95, the
band managed to record the instrumental foundations for approximately ten tracks: 'The Teachers Are Afraid Of The Pupils', 'Reader Meet
Author', 'The Boy Racer', 'Dagenham Dave' and
'Best Friend On The Payroll', plus future B-sides
'NOBODY LOVES US' and 'YOU MUST PLEASE REMEM-
BER' and three other working titles, 'LAUGHING
ANNE', 'YOU SHOULD HAVE BEEN NICE TO ME' and
'HONEY, YOU KNOW WHERE TO FIND ME'. 'It had a
very acoustic feel,' says Supple, 'very different to
how Southpaw turned out in the end. But there'd
been a massive mistake. Morrissey's tape player
had been playing Boz and Alain's demos at the
wrong speed so the instructions he gave them
about what musical key to use on the Miraval
tracks didn't correlate. Everything was in the
wrong key so it was irrelevant. The entire session
had to be scrapped.'

The Miraval sessions also marked the end of
Woodie Taylor's tenure with Morrissey. By early
'95, Spencer COBRIN had been reinstated as drummer for the singer's first UK tour in over two years
that February. His performance on that tour, as
well as a trial session at Abbey Road playing
along to the Miraval demos, convinced Morrissey
to retain him for Southpaw. 'He suddenly decided
he wanted it rockier,' says Supple, 'and Spencer
was a harder drummer.'

Fresh from touring, in March '95 the band
reconvened in the familiar surroundings of Hook
End. 'The whole session was very full-on,' says
Cobrin. 'We'd just come off the road, so there was
a real energy about Southpaw.' Morrissey would
later describe the experience as the 'first fruit' of

a reinvigorated muse, 'which has appeared as if by magic. Everything's happened so quickly and so easily. I'm very surprised at having been able to give birth so quickly to an album.'

In keeping with its new, heavier sound, many of the tracks rehearsed at Miraval were discarded for being either incongruously slow (the ballads 'Laughing Anne' and 'You Should Have Been Nice To Me') or light pop ('Honey, You Know Where To Find Me') while others including 'The Boy Racer' and 'Dagenham Dave' were sufficiently fortified by harder arrangements.

What separates Southpaw from every other Morrissey album is its uncharacteristic emphasis on music and mood over lyrics. In a rare and extremely magnanimous gesture towards his musicians, over half of its running time would be instrumental, featuring swathes of clanging guitars and improvised percussion. Despite containing just eight songs, it would be Morrissey's longest album, largely thanks to its book-ending leviathans 'The Teachers Are Afraid Of The Pupils' and 'Southpaw', which both broke the ten-minute barrier.

That Morrissey's voice wasn't at its finest during the recording may have had some bearing on its use of long, vocal-free interludes. Many tracks suffer from an audibly 'blocked' delivery, as Danton Supple elaborates. 'One of the constant problems with Morrissey was that he often got colds. I used to think it might be something to do with his diet. It's very dairy laden, everything was egg and milk based which can play havoc with people's sinuses and breathing and he used to get bunged up a lot. You can hear it on a couple of tracks on Southpaw, where his voice is quite stuffy.' Even Morrissey would later recount accidentally overhearing Lillywhite and Supple criticise his performance on 'The Teachers Are Afraid Of The Pupils' at the time.

By his own admission, whereas on Vauxhall And I he 'gave a lot' in terms of introspective writing, on much of Southpaw Morrissey stood back. 'Best Friend On The Payroll' seemed suspiciously autobiographical, as did elements of 'Southpaw',

'The Operation' and 'Do Your Best And Don't Worry', but the remaining half consisted of objective character portraits: working-class Jack the Lads ('Dagenham Dave', 'The Boy Racer'), phoney writers ('Reader Meet Author') and suicidal white-collar professionals ('The Teachers Are Afraid Of The Pupils'). Its instrumental majority notwithstanding, by Morrissey's standards its lyrical content was still decidedly slim, a shortcoming partly masked by the absence of a customary lyric sheet on the inner sleeve.

Prior to its release, Morrissey announced Southpaw as 'the return of chaos in my life, like a new start. Unless it's the final strait before death … who knows? [It] may well be a bitter failure.' Continuing his recent use of BOXING iconography – southpaw referred to a left-handed fighter – he explained the title as his concept of 'the school of hard knocks'. The sleeve featured a portrait of American lightweight champion, and southpaw, Kenny Lane, taken from a 1963 issue of boxing magazine The Ring. As such, it was his first (and to date only) studio album not to feature himself on the cover. 'I liked the artwork for about three days when everything was going to press,' Morrissey would later recall. 'But then a few weeks later I looked at it and went, "What the hell have you done?" The sleeve was terrible and that's my fault. All the artwork was atrocious, and unfortunately there's no one else I can blame.' Limited vinyl copies also contained an eight-page booklet of photographs by Rankin, showing Morrissey posing with mock scars and bruises in a concerted bid to subvert his fey media stereotype. 'It was make-up,' he confessed. 'I was very satisfied with those photos at the time. I found them very nice.'

Released in late August '95, Southpaw Grammar arrived as Britpop was reaching its critical mass, preceding Blur's The Great Escape and Oasis's (What's The Story) Morning Glory? by a matter of weeks. Unlike the romantic Smiths comparisons instigated by Vauxhall And I, Southpaw polarised critical opinion. For every reviewer who applauded its experimental indulgences there were others who persecuted its musical 'flab'.

Though it charted at number four, the failure of either of its boisterous singles to impact upon the top 20 was an unforeseen setback. Worse still, the album's promotional UK and European arena tour with David BOWIE ended prematurely when Morrissey cancelled after nine shows. By the end of '95, after four final consolatory concerts in Japan, Southpaw was laid to rest. It would be over a year before Morrissey recorded again.

The album was not a commercial success. Consequently, in subsequent overviews of his work it's been a common fault among critics to lump Southpaw together with its follow-up MALAD-JUSTED, blaming both for derailing his career in the late 90s by failing to live up to the standards of Vauxhall And I. But while Morrissey has since admitted the latter's shortfalls, he remains 'very, very proud' of Southpaw Grammar, even naming it his favourite solo album in 2004 (bar his current release, YOU ARE THE QUARRY). Beyond his own high regard, it remains generally underrated by those incapable of divorcing its content from its original context when it was deemed cloggy and cumbersome beside Britpop's nimble young pretenders. In truth, the coughing thunder of 'The Teachers Are Afraid Of The Pupils' and 'The Operation' demonstrated a gutsiness somewhat lacking in the peeps and squeaks of skinny-trousered fly-by-nights Menswear, Sleeper and even Morrissey's Britpop favourites Echobelly.

While it could never brag to be his finest collection of songs, there's something undeniably impressive about its scale and swagger. From an artist often accused, perhaps with good reason, of musical conservatism, Southpaw was a genuine attempt to make music outside his comfort zone. Even if on their individual merits, some of its tracks may seem incidental footnotes, as a whole there's a dynamic if sooty consistency which negates its weaknesses. Southpaw Grammar plays like an *album*, a humungous, sulphur-spewing, behemoth-sized *rock* album at that.

The original Southpaw Grammar has since been swallowed up by history and swept under the rug of Morrissey's keen revisionism. In April 2009, a remastered, expanded, repackaged and radically reconfigured Southpaw Grammar was reissued through Sony BMG. This redux version featured 12 tracks and a new, improved cover: a mid-90s black and white Morrissey portrait by Linder STERLING under type seemingly based upon that of David Bowie's 1976 compilation ChangesOneBowie. The original running order was dramatically reshuffled and cut with four additions: the B-side 'Nobody Loves Us', the outtakes 'Honey, You Know Where To Find Me' and 'You Should Have Been Nice To Me', and the altogether unrelated 1992 studio outtake 'FANTASTIC BIRD'.

The full tracklisting for the redux Southpaw 'Director's Cut' is: 'The Boy Racer', 'Do Your Best And Don't Worry', 'Reader Meet Author', 'Honey, You Know Where To Find Me', 'Dagenham Dave', 'Southpaw', 'Best Friend On The Payroll', 'Fantastic Bird', 'The Operation', 'The Teachers Are Afraid Of The Pupils', 'You Should Have Been Nice To Me', 'Nobody Loves Us'. [4, 5, 40, 74, 115, 153, 236, 410, 455]

'Southpaw' (Morrissey/Whyte), From the album SOUTHPAW GRAMMAR (1995). The almost-title track of his fifth album, 'Southpaw' was a victory of colour over composition, of sound over song and of aura over lyrical awe. Reduced to its nuts and bolts, its pensive tune and steady tempo are typical Whyte fare while its lyrical themes of childhood longing and adult loneliness were equally par for the course. But as a *recording*, 'Southpaw' stands out as, potentially, the most experimental track of Morrissey's career: five minutes of pop melancholy, sprinting in search of escape but tumbling helplessly into a trance-like abyss of sedated misery. 'It would have been longer,' says bassist Jonny BRIDGWOOD. 'The reason it ends abruptly at ten minutes is because that's when the tape ran out.'

For Morrissey, it was an extremely courageous piece – his 'Radio Ethiopia' perhaps – even if some critics saw its length as unnecessary blubber on a song which otherwise had no noticeably epic qualities. Nor did the title, referring to a left-handed fighter, have any obvious bearing on Morrissey's tale of 'a sick boy' whose happy days of playing with friends ended all too quickly. Though directed to another person, 'Southpaw' contains profound autobiographical undercurrents – the boy who runs 'back to Ma' which 'set the pace for the rest of your days' could just as easily refer to his close relationship with his own mother and her influence on his career. Inevitably, the narrative ends bleakly, with mother's boy and the girl of his dreams both 'sad and all alone', their paths destined never to cross. As his voice finds its horizon and fades away, the instrumental coda's trembling heart-strings and hollow, hopeless rhythms serve only to reiterate the never-to-be-lovers' unalterable sorrow. Explaining why he never played it live, Morrissey insisted that the beguiling 'Southpaw' belonged 'only to that moment in 1995, and none other'. [4, 40]

Sparks,

Witty and invariably parodic American pop group centred around brothers Russell and Ron Mael, both heroes, friends and fans of Morrissey.

Formed in 1968 under the name Halfnelson, among Sparks' earliest recordings was the odd 'Arts & Crafts Spectacular' later included on Morrissey's UNDER THE INFLUENCE compilation. 'There is no category for this madness,' wrote Morrissey in the accompanying sleeve notes, 'except the category of madness and Sparks are only let down by their name.' After two albums, the Mael brothers relocated to London, recruiting a new Sparks line-up and recording 1974's arch glam masterwork Kimono My House. Hooked by the panicky pop ricochet of its lead single 'This Town Ain't Big Enough For Both Of Us' (number two, June 1974), we can gather that Morrissey bought the album shortly after his 15th birthday from his first letter printed in the NME in mid-June. Describing it as 'the album of the year', he praised four tracks including their next single, 'Amateur Hour' (number seven, August 1974). Just as Marr has cited the latter as a vague muse for some of the more glam orientated moments on STRANGE-

WAYS, HERE WE COME, so it's possible that Morrissey's opening lines of 'WILLIAM, IT WAS REALLY NOTHING' may owe something to Sparks' 'This Town': 'The rain is pouring on the foreign town/The bullets cannot cut you down.'

Sparks were a unique disturbance within the UK glam scene. Ron Mael's tunes were alternately frantic and baroque, his bewilderingly smart lyrics delivered in Russell's psychotic abbess falsetto (what Morrissey himself once called 'the most beautiful female voice in pop music'). Yet their impact, and brilliance, was as much visual as musical: the ingenious contrast between the inanimate, Führer-faced Ron and his vivacious BOLAN-haired brother kicking his bare legs in sexual agitation while beckoning the viewers of TOP OF THE POPS to 'Get In The Swing'.

Just six months after Kimono My House, in November 1974 Sparks released its underrated but perhaps superior sequel, Propaganda, heralded by the single 'Never Turn Your Back On Mother Earth' which would directly influence Stephen STREET's melody for Morrissey's 'SUCH A LITTLE THING MAKES SUCH A BIG DIFFERENCE'. The following year saw the TONY VISCONTI-produced Indiscreet, though by 1975 Sparks' presence within the UK top 20 singles was already waning.

Four years and three albums later, the Maels transformed themselves into the electronic disco duo of 1979's No.1 In Heaven. Produced by Giorgio Moroder, the single 'Beat The Clock' returned Sparks to the UK top ten but would be their last major hit. The 1980s saw a succession of idiosyncratic pop albums, with 1988's Interior Design almost sharing a Smiths song title in 'Stop Me If You've Heard This Before'. Sparks retained a devoted cult audience throughout the 1990s, enjoying a critical renaissance with 2002's Lil' Beethoven and its visually innovative live staging, including Morrissey's 2004 MELTDOWN festival where it was played in its entirety in a double bill with Kimono My House.

Morrissey first met the Mael brothers in Los Angeles when touring in 1991 (a photo of a bashful, nail-biting Morrissey sandwiched between

Ron and Russell can be seen in Linder STERLING's *Morrissey Shot*) and became good friends after moving to the city years later. Glowing tributes have been mutual. Morrissey has often praised Sparks in the press and featured their earlier songs on his interval tapes. The Maels, in turn, were granted the unique honour of remixing a Morrissey song for the 2005 compilation Future Retro which included their radically restructured 'SUEDE-HEAD'. Three years later, they paid the ultimate homage with 'Lighten Up, Morrissey' from their 2008 album Exotic Creatures Of The Deep. The tune details a boyfriend's frustration with his Morrissey-obsessed girlfriend: 'If only Morrissey weren't so Morrisseyesque/She might overlook all my flaws.' As they told several interviewers, Morrissey apparently considered it 'hilarious'. [19, 190, 362]

'Speedway' (Morrissey/Boorer), From the album VAUXHALL AND I (1994). Self-martyrdom has always been a fundamental trait of Morrissey's writing, but never has he nailed himself to a proverbial cross with such sacrificial drama as on 'Speedway', Vauxhall's soul-baring, near-biblical finale which by virtue of its analytical frankness ranks as one of his most insightful and therefore most essential songs of all time.

Once again, Morrissey is the helpless victim, wounded by the slings and arrows of an ex-partner intent on destroying him but whom he strangely refuses to betray. 'I believe in my loyalty which is as developed as possible,' he explained, adding that the song set out to scrutinise 'others' loyalty towards me'. Written in the wake of the 1992 Madstock incident and the NME's ensuing accusations of racism, its most (seemingly) sensational revelation was that the many 'lies' and 'rumours' to have tarnished his career may not be 'completely unfounded'.

'I'm well aware that rumours are more important than the truth,' he coyly explained at the time. 'I've been called many names in my time, not all of them ill-fitting. Rather than defend myself I simply feel beyond it all. I get the impression that anything I say, however sensible and heart-warming, doesn't hold much water these days because of a great barrage of people still wanting to pick holes in anything I say, which is very tedious. There's no escape, I realise that. It's a very English thing. In a sick way, it's a compliment.' It was only a decade later that Morrissey ended all further debate by admitting, somewhat flippantly, that the lyrics were 'probably' just his way of winding up his detractors at the time. 'Life's a game, isn't it?'

This uncertainty over the sincerity of Morrissey's central confession – is it a genuine plea of guilt or a sly double-bluff to further muddy the truth? – is central to the song's allure. Then there's the enigma of the title itself, referring to the dirt track motor sport never once mentioned in the lyrics. Though *Speedway* is also the name of Morrissey's favourite Elvis PRESLEY film co-starring NANCY SINATRA, given the intense nature of the lyric the term evidently has more personal significance. The detail that Johnny Marr once worked at a speedway in his teens is enough to satisfy some theorists that the song is a coded address to the ex-Smiths guitarist, ignoring the fact that at the time of recording Morrissey and Marr were on cordial terms. Others have suggested it may be directed at Mike Joyce who was in the process of suing Morrissey, and Marr, at the time.

The most enlightening pointer came from Morrissey himself the year before he recorded the song. Speaking to *The Observer* newspaper in 1992, he referred to a childhood incident at a local Manchester fairground when a complete stranger head-butted him for no apparent reason. 'It was very early, about 5 p.m.,' he described, 'and I was standing by the speedway.' If nothing else, this tells us that to Morrissey the term 'Speedway' has nostalgic connotations of his own youth, albeit tinged with disturbing memories of unprovoked assault. In context of the song's more violent imagery, 'Speedway' may just be Morrissey's broad, basic metaphor for human existence in all its potential ugliness and brutality; if not a pigsty, life is a speedway.

As the soundtrack to Morrissey's strange self-crucifixion, Boorer's theme was brooding, savage and powerfully sketched, as stormy an album closer as his 'NOW MY HEART IS FULL' had been an opener. Whether by accident or design, it seemed apt that the two songs were musically related: though in different keys, the descending chord sequence accompanying the 'everyone I love' section in the latter is basically the same as the main 'Speedway' chords.

A late addition to Vauxhall, its first take was scrapped for being in an unsuitable key for Morrissey's voice. The re-recording process allowed producer Steve LILLYWHITE to infuse more blood and thunder second time around, including engineer Danton Supple supplying the opening throttle roar courtesy of a chainsaw. (Bassist Jonny BRIDGWOOD is sure it was a drill though both Supple and fellow engineer Chris Dickie swear it was a chainsaw. Either way, it was a DIY appliance, not a motorbike.) The final artillery was provided by Woodie TAYLOR's drums, recorded in the dining room at Hook End Manor for added acoustics, his last strokes booming like cannon fire.

'Speedway' would sound very different live, if just as formidable, its main variations being a more consistent, tribal drum pattern while Boorer's sweeping chords gave way to a jaggier guitar riff. The closing lines also acted as a symbolic holy communion for his audience for whom the words 'true to you' were a sacred vow of unswerving allegiance. Fittingly, his 'number one fan', Julia Riley, later used the phrase for her fanzine and Morrissey-endorsed website (see TRUE-TO-YOU.NET). An emotional bombard on record, a spiritual baptism in concert, 'Speedway' is up there bleeding beside the absolute best of Morrissey. [4, 6, 40, 154, 236]

'Spring-Heeled Jim' (Morrissey/Boorer),

From the album VAUXHALL AND I (1994). Peeling back its penny dreadful frontispiece, 'Spring-Heeled Jim' uncovers a typical Mozzerian character portrait of a charismatic bad lad prone to violence, womanising and drunken excess. Equally typical is its moral sting, that living life at 'five times the average speed' eventually takes its toll on Jim, ending his days lonely and remorseful.

As with other songs of the period which borrow their name from aspects of Victorian culture – 'BLACK-EYED SUSAN', 'BILLY BUDD' and the previous year's 'JACK THE RIPPER' – it is likely 'Spring-Heeled Jim' was inspired by the nineteenth-century urban myth of Spring-Heeled Jack, a devilish bogeyman alleged to have terrorised London and other parts of England through the mid- to late 1800s who earned his nickname from

Spring And Port Wine, 1970 British kitchen-sink drama listed among Morrissey's favourite films. Like *THE FAMILY WAY*, *Spring And Port Wine* was based on a play by Bill Naughton and shot on location in Bolton, Lancashire. The story focuses on the Cromptons, a working-class family whose lives are dominated by their outmoded, parsimonious, Bible-wielding patriarch, Rafe (James Mason in his mature, scene-stealing prime). His authority is gradually challenged by his four children, led by his teenage daughter Hilda (Susan George) who refuses to eat the 'bonnie fresh herring' prepared for supper only to have it served up cold at every subsequent mealtime until she concedes. Various subplots involving marriage, pregnancy and the pawning of a Crombie overcoat drive his selfless wife to the brink of suicide before an unconvincingly happy resolution. For all its family melodrama, the film is quite a cosy, lightweight kitchen-sink vehicle with Avril Elgar providing the best of its comedy as the Cromptons' crabby, pound-pinching, tripe-boiling next-door neighbour. The cast includes another Morrissey favourite, Marjorie RHODES, as well as Likely Lad Rodney Bewes (Tom Courtenay's best friend in *BILLY LIAR*). [227, 553]

his ability to bound over fences and walls with supernatural ease. Numerous 'victims' offered colourful descriptions of this horned, fire-breathing man-beast, though these alone tell us that all such sightings of Spring-Heeled Jack were hysterical fantasy.

One of the most striking chapters on Vauxhall, the phantom bass of 'Spring-Heeled Jim' stalked from a suitably Baskervillian fog of ominous E-bow guitar groans. Its running backing track of London teenagers discussing crime from the 1958 documentary WE ARE THE LAMBETH BOYS was, arguably, Morrissey's most creative use of a film sample yet, their excitable chat further stoking its trouble ('gonna get a team and go up and do 'em!'). Among the first tracks recorded during the Vauxhall sessions, 'Spring-Heeled Jim' would become a popular live favourite and stands as one of Boorer's fancier thrills within the Morrissey canon. [4, 6, 40, 561]

Stamp, Terence, Stunningly handsome blue-eyed English actor and original cover star of the Smiths single 'WHAT DIFFERENCE DOES IT MAKE?' As with the majority of his male icons, Morrissey's fascination with Stamp seemed less to do with the actor's craft than his physical beauty, hence his famous quip that his 'idea of happiness' was 'being Terence Stamp'.

Born and bred in east London and bearing 'the seal of shifty working-class brashness' (as Morrissey put it in EXIT SMILING), Stamp was inspired to act by James DEAN, whom he'd first heard about from his friend and fellow wannabe actor, David Baxter. A photo of the young Baxter in mock fighting pose from Stamp's second volume of autobiography, Coming Attractions, was featured in Morrissey's video for 'THE MORE YOU IGNORE ME, THE CLOSER I GET'.

As an atypical angelic blond, he made his cinema debut in the title role of Peter Ustinov's BILLY BUDD, adapted from Herman Melville's seafaring yarn about an innocent young sailor wrongly accused of conspiracy to murder his malicious master at arms. Its delayed release meant

that Stamp's second film appeared first, 1962's Term Of Trial starring Laurence Olivier as a lonely, alcoholic teacher who rebuffs the advances of besotted pupil Sarah Miles only to end up in court charged with indecent assault. Stamp played the class hooligan, Mitchell. A still from a scene where Olivier canes Stamp was considered for the sleeve of the 1985 import Smiths single 'THE HEAD-MASTER RITUAL', though Olivier failed to give his consent in time. In the film, Stamp's character also makes a joke about staying in the YWCA, which may have inspired the chorus of 'HALF A PERSON'.

In Smiths/Morrissey terms, Stamp's most important film role was his third, as the psycho-stalker Freddie Clegg in 1965's The Collector, seen on the cover of 'What Difference Does It Make?' Upon the record's release in 1984, Morrissey described the photo – a production still of Stamp smiling while brandishing a chloroform-soaked handkerchief – as 'incredibly sinister and just has immense power to it', though added that 'the film itself is quite sexist and really quite questionable. I'm not a Collector fan by any means.' It was Johnny Marr who showed the greater enthusiasm for The Collector, naming it as his favourite film in The Smiths' 1985 tour programme. Marr later made a comical comparison between the Stamp–Samantha Eggar relationship and himself and Morrissey when asked why he declined the singer's offer to play a farewell Smiths concert in 1987 after they'd split. 'I probably would have been kidnapped,' laughed Marr. 'Have you seen the film The Collector?'

Following its release in January 1984, Stamp objected to the 'What Difference' sleeve, necessitating the 'indescribably unhappy' Morrissey's hasty replacement homage; aping the same pose except with a glass of milk in place of Clegg's chloroform pad. Stamp was eventually persuaded into retracting his objection, allowing the original sleeve to be reinstated.

After 1966's kitsch pop-art romp Modesty Blaise with Dirk BOGARDE, Stamp appeared in another Morrissey favourite, Ken Loach's POOR COW, alongside John BINDON. By then, Stamp was involved with 'The Shrimp', 60s supermodel Jean

S

SHRIMPTON, whom he'd describe as '[looking] as though a fairy godmother on tour had sneaked into an Oxford Street store and blown life into a window dresser's fantasy'.

Previously, Stamp had dated Julie Christie, though by the time she began filming BILLY LIAR she'd ended their relationship. Popularly presumed to be the 'Terry and Julie' of The Kinks' 1967 hit 'Waterloo Sunset' (a myth Ray Davies has since dispelled), they'd reunite as Sgt Troy and Bathsheba in John Schlesinger's adaptation of Thomas Hardy's FAR FROM THE MADDING CROWD. Among the many 60s films Stamp either lost out on or turned down were the Tom Bell role in THE L-SHAPED ROOM, Alan Bates's part in *Georgie Girl*, David Hemmings's character in *Blow-Up* and, most notoriously, 1966's *Alfie*, which Stamp had already played in an unsuccessful Broadway version. Instead, he recommended his flatmate, Michael Caine, for the role.

When The Shrimp left him – she'd later accuse Stamp of being an over-possessive freaky eater – he sought solace in hallucinogenic drugs, turning his back on English-language cinema to work with Federico Fellini on 1968's Edgar Allan Poe portmanteau piece *Spirits Of The Dead* (co-starring Alain DELON and Brigitte BARDOT), and with Pier Paolo PASOLINI as the mysterious visitor who sexually seduces an entire bourgeois household in the same year's *Theorem*. After undertaking a spiritual pilgrimage to India, Stamp all but vanished from the big screen until the late 70s when he reappeared as Kryptonian nutcase General Zod in the blockbusters *Superman* and *Superman II*. Subsequent films have seen him play similar intergalactic villains and gangster types with the notable exception of his transsexual cabaret singer in 1994's *The Adventures Of Priscilla, Queen Of The Desert*. In between, Stamp has published three memoirs (hence Morrissey's 1989 'election promise' of a 'total ban on a fourth Terence Stamp autobiography') and launched his own range of health foods for those, like himself, intolerant to wheat and dairy products. [89, 141, 168, 175, 267, 370, 374, 378, 379, 430, 494, 542, *555*]

Starland Vocal Band, See 'AFTERNOON DELIGHT'.

stationery, In 1985 Morrissey confessed to having something of a fetish for stationery. 'As I grew up I used to love stationery and pens and booklets and binders,' he gushed. 'I can get incredibly erotic about blotting paper.' He named his favourite shop as the high street stationery chain Ryman's. 'To me it's like a sweetshop,' he explained, describing a visit to Ryman's as 'the most extreme sexual experience one could ever have'. It should be noted that Morrissey was very much celibate at the time. [573]

'Stay As You Are' (Morrissey/Whyte), Outtake from the 1993 VAUXHALL AND I sessions. A semi-mythical 'lost classic' largely due to internet hype (and at least one fake 'demo'), in truth 'Stay As You Are' was a title which Morrissey had in mind for an Alain Whyte tune prior to recording Vauxhall which was never completed. Bassist Jonny BRIDGWOOD is adamant that, although a basic backing track was recorded with producer Steve LILLYWHITE, Morrissey never got as far as even a guide vocal. Consequently we have no clues as to the lyrical content beyond the subtly romantic implications of the title. The tune itself was among the first dozen earmarked for the album, a slow waltzing ballad in keeping with the understated mood of Whyte's other Vauxhall entries such as 'THE LAZY SUNBATHERS'. As Bridgwood notes, 'It's a typical Morrissey/Alain song. In 6/8 time, fairly laidback. Morrissey might have had something great planned for the vocal melody but without one it's a bit nondescript. The way Morrissey worked, we had titles but we only got the full picture at the end when he added his vocal. "Stay As You Are" was one of those which never got that far, so there was no picture.' [4]

Sterling, Linder, Visual/performance artist, photographer, singer and writer whose influence upon Morrissey, both personal and creative, is considerable. Though her reputation as 'Morrissey's

best friend' often diverts attention away from her own distinguished legacy, theirs is quite obviously a unique and close relationship.

Born in Liverpool as Linda Mulvey, she grew up in Wigan before enrolling at Manchester Polytechnic in 1974 to study graphic design. As she describes it, she 'edited' herself down to one name in 1976, deliberately choosing 'a European spelling'. On 20 July that year she attended the second SEX PISTOLS concert at Manchester's Lesser Free Trade Hall: the 17-year-old Morrissey was there also, though they did not speak. Instead, Linder struck up a conversation with the gig's organiser, Howard DEVOTO, whose recently formed BUZZCOCKS also supported. 'I met Howard again and then again,' says Linder. 'We fell into something that was sometimes recognised as love but more often felt like soul survival for that time. We lived in a room without any form of natural light and worked in parallel. We tried to make a new language and didn't quite fail.'

Living with Devoto in Salford's Lower Broughton Road, Linder began making iconic photo montages, juxtaposing bodies from porn magazines with kitchen utensils and domestic appliances. One of her earliest of a naked woman with arms raised, an Argos catalogue steam iron for a head and smiling mouths for nipples, later graced the cover of Buzzcocks' first single for United Artists, October 1977's 'Orgasm Addict'. She was paid £75. Three years later, Morrissey was still photocopying the sleeve to send to pen pals.

In January 1978, Linder and *Sounds* journalist Jon Savage produced their innovative collage booklet, *The Secret Public*, through Richard Boon's New Hormones label. Its depiction of naked couples with television heads masturbating their vacuum cleaner penises caused problems finding a willing printer. Certain 'left-wing bookshops' also refused to stock it.

Another of her montages of 'a salad with eyes' was nearly used for the cover of Buzzcocks' debut album released that March, Another Music In A Different Kitchen, though a very different Linder creation would grace the sleeve of 1978's Real

Life, the debut album by Devoto's Magazine. 'Howard and I pored over books of Symbolist art,' recalls Linder. 'I still have my sketchbook from 1977 with a quote from Odilon Redon. "One must admire black. Nothing can debauch it." Howard then sang, "… leaving me black and so healthy" [*in 'The Light Pours Out Of Me'*]. I picked up a pencil again, rolled inks on to the glass that had been used to cut up photo montage bodies and made over a hundred monoprinted, disembodied heads. Howard selected his favourite four and I completed the [Real Life] artwork in a hotel room in Birmingham after Magazine had played at Barbarella's there.'

As is popular FACTORY Records legend, her 1978 rough sketch of a menstrual egg timer – 'a very simple abacus upon which a woman could monitor and display her position within her hormonal cycle' – was given its own Factory catalogue number: Fac 8. But by the year's end Linder had already moved 'from scalpel to microphone' with the formation of her own group, Ludus (Latin for 'play'). Their impact upon the young Morrissey was to be sensationally severe.

His friendship with Linder officially began on 9 December 1976 when the Sex Pistols returned to Manchester for their third gig in the city at the Electric Circus. He, 17, approached her, 22, at the soundcheck 'to prove to her that I had no viewpoint whatsoever about anything'. Linder was to be the maturing Morrissey's confidante, mentor and muse, introducing him to Devoto (his local 'hero' for want of a better description) and pointing him in the direction of various writers and sociologists, Janice G. Raymond, Philippe Aries and Calvin C. Hernton, as well as other texts on their 'shared fascination' for sexual politics. 'We used to read obsessively, devouring book after book after book,' said Linder. 'It was an essential ingredient in our lives and most of the books we read were by women, or about women.' In the 1981 Ludus track 'Mouthpiece', Linder sang, 'I steal your books and you steal mine', later admitting the words were 'of course, about [Morrissey]'.

After splitting from Devoto she moved into a house in Manchester's Whalley Range with Ludus guitarist Ian Devine. Morrissey briefly took 'a rented room' there. Journalist Nick Kent was the first, in 1985, to examine Morrissey's past with Linder and speculate upon its influence on his early Smiths lyrics. The 'Whalley Range' line in 'MISERABLE LIE' – which Morrissey deliberately quoted in his essay for her 2006 art retrospective – is the most obvious contender. Kent also referred to intimations from 'certain sources' that both 'JEANE' and 'WONDERFUL WOMAN' are also Linder-related; again, Morrissey's introduction of Linder, in the wings, as 'a wonderful woman' on stage at the Royal Albert Hall in September 2002 was, at the very least, playfully pointed. Whether Linder did, indeed, inspire these and other early Smiths lyrics is not something Morrissey has ever cared to clarify in public.

Both friends have described their relationship during these, Morrissey's desperate years prior to forming The Smiths, as one built upon sharing books, epic walks in depressed silence and hopeless evenings peering in the windows of strangers' houses. 'We'd go wandering in Moss Side,' Linder recalled, 'hours and days wandering, just the two of us, together but very alone at the same time. It was extremely intimate but very separate … We did quite often go out. He'd say, "Let's go out tonight." There'd be all these hairdressers in wonderful clothes and they all looked so happy. They'd be dancing, drinking and Morrissey and I would be sat there looking like we were at a funeral.' Linder's similar recollections of walks with Morrissey to Manchester's Southern Cemetery have nominated her as an obvious muse for The Smiths' 'CEMETRY GATES'.

In the meantime, as he struggled to find an outlet for his own creative brilliance, Morrissey became dedicated to Ludus, who by 1980 had an EP and one single to their name, both on New Hormones. The latter, 'My Cherry Is In Sherry', typified the sound Morrissey declared 'unlike anyone else's', Linder's chilled and precise vocals pin-pricking jagged designs atop Devine's tuneful

yet irregular jazz-punk. He'd extol its charms to pen pal Robert MACKIE, also sending him a photocopy of the single sleeve. Aiding the Ludus publicity machine any way he could, Morrissey as aspiring music journalist reviewed two of their concerts for *Record Mirror*, the second as support to Depeche Mode at Manchester's Rafters on 5 August 1981: 'Ludus, plainly wishing they were elsewhere, hammered out a passionate set to an audience possibly handpicked for their tone deafness.'

Ludus had other champions in the press – August 1981's 'Patient'/'Mother's Hour' was a 'single of the week' in *Sounds*, who likened Linder's voice to that of 'a devastatingly aloof Françoise HARDY' – but their discography was too erratic and unusual for even the UK post-punk climate to fully grasp; cassette EPs, double 12-inch packages and an album of 18 short experimental pieces 'delving into the possibilities of how many sounds a larynx can make'. In the latter respect, Linder's influence upon Morrissey's own singing also bears some deliberation, her freeform canine yelps and other improvised garglings a possible stimulus for his more histrionic vocal flourishes (e.g. 'Miserable Lie', 'BARBARISM BEGINS AT HOME').

Flying their flag to the bitter end, Morrissey wrote their official press release of 1982, 'Let's Look At Ludus', concluding 'their music is a fresh mode of self-realisation'. That summer the group recorded a cover of Brigitte BARDOT's 'Nue Au Soleil' ('Naked In The Sun'), which he'd later name his 'single of the year' in the *NME* two years after its actual release.

On bonfire night 1982, Ludus played their most infamous concert at Manchester's Haçienda where Linder walked on stage in a dress made of discarded raw meat sewn on to black netting.[1] She removed it in the final song to reveal a black dildo. Meanwhile, group managers Liz Naylor and Cath Carroll distributed 'chicken innards wrapped in pornography' among the audience. A special cocktail for the evening – the 'Bloody Linder' – was removed from sale by the edgy Haçienda management.

'For me it was the end result of one too many nights at the Haçienda with its repetitive reels of pornography presiding over the dance floor,' she explains. 'Pornography can never be casual and without consequence, at least not in my world. Afterwards, the meat, the dildo and the cabaret felt like a full stop in performance.' Ludus played their final show in London the following month and recorded a swansong single in early 1983; their 'poppiest' offering of all, 'Breaking The Rules', later featured on Morrissey's UNDER THE INFLUENCE compilation. By the time of the single's release, he and Linder had reached a fork in their life's journey. She moved to Belgium while he hurtled towards his deserved destiny with the newly formed Smiths.

In October 1985, while making THE QUEEN IS DEAD, Morrissey obligingly wrote a sleeve note for a proposed (but unreleased) Ludus retrospective on the Belgian Crepuscule label. 'People who know real genius will love this record,' he declared, though more intriguing are two phrases which he'd later adapt into his lyrics: '... our hearts damaged by too many air-raids' ('I'VE CHANGED MY PLEA TO GUILTY') and '... oh Linder. I will see you sometime, somewhere' ('I WON'T SHARE YOU'). Two years later, Morrissey considered the 'GIRLFRIEND IN A COMA' pun 'Linda found a cobra' as the run-out-groove message on the final Smiths single, but resisted.

After returning to Manchester, Linder's direct involvement in Morrissey's solo career began circa VIVA HATE when he chose 'Linder Ltd' as the name of his publishing company, up to and including 1989's 'THE LAST OF THE FAMOUS INTERNATIONAL PLAYBOYS' single. The following year she sang backing vocals on 'DRIVING YOUR GIRLFRIEND HOME', the standout track on KILL UNCLE, and spent the early 1990s photographing Morrissey on tour around the world. The best images were compiled in the 1993 book *Morrissey Shot* which, originally, he'd wanted to call *Linder Shot Morrissey*. Her photos also provided the covers of the albums YOUR ARSENAL and BEETHOVEN WAS DEAF, the singles 'WE HATE IT WHEN OUR FRIENDS BECOME SUCCESSFUL', 'YOU'RE THE ONE FOR ME, FATTY' and 'CERTAIN PEOPLE I KNOW' plus other items including the 2009 redux SOUTHPAW GRAMMAR.

Linder still continues to document Morrissey's life (filming the interviews for 2004's WHO PUT THE 'M' IN MANCHESTER? DVD) between her own work as a visual and performance artist, whether filling a disused Widnes school with salt, transforming herself into Clint Eastwood's 'Man With No Name' or organising a line dance on Saddleworth Moor inspired by the Shakers, an eighteenth-century Manchester Protestant movement. More recently she's also returned to live music performance, appearing at Morrissey's MELTDOWN and supporting the re-formed Magazine at Manchester Academy in February 2009.

The precious and private nature of their friendship is such that Morrissey and Linder maintain a fierce loyalty to one another. When Linder was misrepresented in the script for Michael Winterbottom's 2002 Factory biopic *24 Hour Party People*, she took action to have it removed. Morrissey showed solidarity by refusing to accept the offer of a cameo role and denying the producers permission to include 'THIS CHARMING MAN' on the soundtrack. While both have spoken about one another in the media – always glowingly and with considerable charm and humour – neither has abused their bond of trust in divulging the unnecessary.[2] Now, as then, Linder and Morrissey illuminate an irreplaceable alcove in one another's lives. As Morrissey once admitted, 'We're just like twins really ... we've both got long ginger hair.' [37, 56, 139, 170, 177, 178, 182, 183, 380, 381, 404, 453, 468]

---

1. Linder was vegetarian: 'I didn't want to buy a dead animal so I used throwaway meat from a restaurant kitchen instead.'
2. This author's correspondence with Sterling in early 2002 was strictly on the subject of Manchester punk and Ludus, not her relationship with Morrissey.

Steven, Morrissey's Christian name. According to Eugene Stone's popular 50s pre-natal handbook *Naming Baby*, Steven is: 'Greek; "crown". In the

S

Middle Ages this was a favourite name for European royal houses. Stephen was the name borne by the first Christian martyr whose feast day is 26th December, Boxing Day. *Dim.* STEVE, STEVIE.'

Although Morrissey would later claim that he had been named in honour of minor Hollywood actor Steve Cochran – seen in Cagney's *White Heat* and with Joan Crawford in *The Damned Don't Cry!* – this seems fanciful revisionism when looking back at Morrissey's family tree. As mentioned in THE SEVERED ALLIANCE, Morrissey's father, Peter, had two younger brothers who died in infancy, among them Patrick Steven Morrissey. It seems more likely that Morrissey was christened in honour of his dead uncle rather than a 50s film star. Morrissey never liked the name Steven for two reasons. Firstly, he hated

the common abbreviation of 'Steve' ('I was never a Steve,' he'd groan). Secondly, he loathed the frequent misspelling of his name as 'Stephen'. He'd complain about both in one of his letters to Scottish pen pal Robert MACKIE. 'Please don't call me "Steve", it reminds me of The Bionic Man [*Steve Austin played by Lee Majors in the 70s television series* The Six Million Dollar Man], to whom I bear little resemblance. It's almost worse than being called "Stephen" which reminds me of someone with a snotty nose … actually I hate the name Steven, but I won't go into THAT.'

Despite Morrissey's best efforts to distinguish himself as a Steven with a V, it is still an alarmingly common mistake to see his name listed as 'Stephen Patrick Morrissey'. It's bad enough in newspapers and magazines, but the misspelling of

'Still Ill' (Morrissey/Marr), From the album THE SMITHS (1984). Written in the gap between their first attempt at a debut album with producer Troy TATE and its hasty re-recording, 'Still Ill' was a late addition to The Smiths album reflecting Morrissey's increasing sense of purpose after their first four months of media exposure. As with his earlier songs, the words still alluded to a previous relationship in its reminiscence of stolen kisses beneath a railway bridge. Such a bridge indeed existed a short walk from Morrissey's house on Kings Road in Stretford, though it's just as plausible he borrowed the scene from *Spend, Spend, Spend*, the autobiography of future Smiths cover star Viv NICHOLSON. 'We walked for miles,' writes Nicholson, 'right over the iron bridge and down underneath it on the towpath … we were kissing away and touching and getting really sore lips from biting one another.'

Yet, lyrically, 'Still Ill' set itself apart from the rest of the album as a more abstract mission statement of the principles of SMITHDOM – illness as art, rejection of mundane employment, the struggle between biology and mentality and the anthemic demand that 'England is mine and it owes me a living'. The influence of Morrissey's favoured muse, Shelagh DELANEY, is also felt in a couple of lines seemingly adapted from *The Lion In Love*: 'I'd sooner spit in everybody's eye' and another exchange between Kit ('I'll go out and get a job tomorrow') and Jesse ('You needn't bother').

Marr wrote its melody the same evening as 'THIS CHARMING MAN' in preparation for the group's second John PEEL radio session – a tune blissfully ignorant of the surrounding gutter as it paws wildly at the stars. The Peel version was later included on HATFUL OF HOLLOW, distinguished by Marr's freeform harmonica intro and outro which was eventually replaced on the album by a vigorous rhythmic bookend of jackhammer drums and cranking guitar. Issued at the time as a double A-side radio promo single with 'YOU'VE GOT EVERYTHING NOW', it's testament to the song's rhapsodic power that 'Still Ill' survived longer in the group's concert setlists than any other from their debut. As a succinct crash course in the basics of Mozzerian philosophy, it remains one of The Smiths' most essential works. [17, 27, 299, 346]

418

Morrissey's Christian name has even appeared on press releases and, worst of all, the sleeve notes for Warners' 2001 compilation The Very Best Of The Smiths. When your own record company can't spell your name properly, what hope is there for the rest of mankind?

Morrissey jettisoned his Christian name shortly after forming The Smiths with Marr in the latter half of 1982. 'I never liked the name Steven,' said Morrissey, 'so I dropped it as soon as I could.' 'I only need one name anyway,' he reasoned, 'and it was such an unusual name that I thought I wouldn't be confused with anybody else. I mean, do you know anybody else called Morrissey? These days I only hear the name [Steven] from total strangers as a term of supposed intimacy.'

Nonetheless, he seemed unruffled by Sandie SHAW's 1986 tribute B-side 'Steven, You Don't Eat Meat' and would even autograph the dress she wore for a performance of the song on BBC2's Whistle Test where, unusually, he signed himself 'STEVEN' rather than Morrissey. The name Steven has also cropped up twice on his own records. The first, shouted by the wife of Stephen STREET in the background of 1988's 'WILL NEVER MARRY'. The second, spelt out by the singer himself in 1989's 'OUIJA BOARD, OUIJA BOARD'. [79, 334, 362, 453, 456]

Stipe, Michael, R.E.M. singer and friend of Morrissey. Stipe first contacted him by letter circa 1989. 'Not a fan letter, an *interested* letter,' Morrissey explained. 'I didn't reply, and then I decided to and we met. We walked around Hyde Park, and that was the beginning.' Morrissey and Stipe seemed a likely pairing; both intellectually intense, both prickly and sexually ambiguous interviewees (though Stipe would eventually come out, ending years of speculation about his closet homosexuality) and both highly original frontmen who shared many musical touchstones, including PATTI SMITH. Yet according to Morrissey, 'The whole joy about the friendship is that music doesn't ever come into it. We don't ever talk about R.E.M. or whatever I do. There are other things to discuss.'

Their comradeship provided great intrigue for their mutual fans in the press, many of whom had spent the 80s likening The Smiths and R.E.M. as transatlantic opposite numbers. 'For a while it was a race between [us] and R.E.M. to see who was really going to break America first,' agreed Morrissey. '[When] Michael came to see me in London, [he] told me he was tired and he wanted to finish the group. And suddenly they just exploded and became absolutely enormous.' When news of their friendship first broke, R.E.M.'s international profile was significantly bigger than Morrissey's after the multi-platinum breakthrough of 1990's Out Of Time. Being suddenly linked to the singer of the biggest alternative rock band on the planet did Morrissey no harm, even feeding his imagination of recording a duet with Stipe. 'It would be nice to do something unusual.'

Scrutiny into the exact nature of their friendship soon took a sour turn after a 1991 article in which the close proximity of two separate questions about Morrissey's connection with Stipe and the lyrics of the KILL UNCLE track 'FOUND FOUND FOUND' gave rise to a misconstrued theory that the two were related. When Morrissey later praised Stipe for sticking up for him over the 1996 COURT CASE (he called the trial judge 'a fuckhead') and was later spotted dining with Stipe in Los Angeles (once joined by Courtney Love), it further fuelled rumours of romantic involvement between the two singers. By 2006, Morrissey had finally tired of such gossip, telling an Italian journalist that they 'were never that close, physically' and losing his temper altogether when an English reporter pursued the same line of enquiry. 'That's absolute shit,' he fumed, 'absolute shit and I don't know why people ever said that, do you?' That's that settled, then. [58, 94, 133, 136, 191, 213, 247]

'Stop Me If You Think You've Heard This One Before' (Morrissey/Marr), From the album STRANGEWAYS, HERE WE COME (1987). Speaking about the group four years after their split, Morrissey nominated this track as 'the sound of The Smiths at their height'. 'Very special,

very powerful,' he added, also likening it to 'The Smiths in full battle dress'.

If its title[1] acted as a crafty dig at those critics who'd dared to accuse the group of lyrical monotony, the lyrics were a more obscure narrative of bike accidents, alcoholic excess, deceit, betrayal, broken kneecaps and weekends wasted in A&E. At its bruised and bloody core, 'Stop Me' is a love song, albeit wrapped in so many bandages it runs the risk of mummification. After all, who else but Morrissey in his singular genius could sing 'I still love you' in one breath and in the next depict 'a shy bald Buddhist' planning mass murder.

Marr's tune rolled with each and every lyrical punch, its opening Apache rhythm quickening the pulse for the shower of glossy aluminium chords to come. He'd later describe the simplistic guitar solo at the end as a conscious attempt to 'sound like a punk player who couldn't play', spurred on by Stephen STREET's suggestion to make it 'more like the BUZZCOCKS'.

Both Morrissey and Marr had expressed their wish for 'Stop Me' to be released as a single. In all likelihood it would have followed 'GIRLFRIEND IN A COMA' had it not been for the events of 19 August 1987. On that date, unemployed loner Michael Ryan murdered 16 people in the Berkshire village of Hungerford before shooting himself. When ROUGH TRADE sent white label promos of the single to Radio 1, the station replied that the 'mass murder' lyric was insensitive to the relatives of Ryan's victims. 'I *desperately, desperately* wanted that [single] to be released,' Morrissey mourned, '[but] they said people would've instantly linked it with Hungerford and it would've caused thousands of shoppers to go out and buy machine guns and murder their grandparents.' (See also 'MICHAEL'S BONES'.)

Consequently, 'I STARTED SOMETHING I COULDN'T FINISH' was issued in its place. Though denied the opportunity to become one of The Smiths' last UK hits, 'Stop Me' would, in time, become one of their most popular songs. Twenty years after the original, Amy Winehouse producer Mark Ronson achieved the impossible by taking his radical cover

with vocals by Daniel Merriweather to number two in April 2007. Ironically, the fact that it was in the charts at the time of the deadliest school shooting in US history at Virginia Tech where a student murdered 32 people failed to encumber its success. Almost as odd was Ronson's decision to medley the song with The Supremes' 'You Keep Me Hanging On', presumably unaware that Morrissey had once described Diana Ross as the polar opposite of The Smiths. Though some purist fans took exception to Ronson's twenty-first-century manhandling of a much-loved Smiths classic, Morrissey reportedly gave it his approval: manager Merck Mercuriadis met Ronson by chance in an Italian restaurant and told him 'Morrissey loves your version'. [17, 19, 38, 71, 83, 196]

---

1. Coincidentally, Charles Hawtrey says the phrase during the film CARRY ON *Cleo*. It's also been speculated whether Noël COWARD's short story *Stop Me If You've Heard It* had some influence.

Strangeways, Here We Come, The Smiths' fourth and final album, released posthumously in September 1987, highest UK chart position #2. Cover star: Richard DAVALOS. Tracks: 'A RUSH AND A PUSH AND THE LAND IS OURS', 'I STARTED SOMETHING I COULDN'T FINISH', 'DEATH OF A DISCO DANCER', 'GIRLFRIEND IN A COMA', 'STOP ME IF YOU THINK YOU'VE HEARD THIS ONE BEFORE', 'LAST NIGHT I DREAMT THAT SOMEBODY LOVED ME', 'UNHAPPY BIRTHDAY', 'PAINT A VULGAR PICTURE', 'DEATH AT ONE'S ELBOW', 'I WON'T SHARE YOU'. Produced by Johnny Marr, Morrissey and Stephen STREET.

It is, alas, almost impossible to drag The Smiths' fourth album out from under the shadows which pop history and received critical wisdom cast upon it. Because it was the last album, because they split up during the six months between its recording and its release, because everybody who has ever heard it has done so with the foreknowledge that the group who created it no longer exist, Strangeways is too often dismissed as The Smiths' funeral procession. Eclipsed by the automatic assumption that THE QUEEN IS DEAD is the group's masterpiece, Strangeways has never

Don't blow your own horn: The 'entirely doomed' James Dean (1931–55)

This page – 'Now My Heart Is Full'. **Above:** Dirk Bogarde fails to raise Patric Doonan in *The Blue Lamp*. **Left:** Dallow (William Hartnell), Pinkie (Richard Attenborough) and Cubitt (Nigel Stock) wind up nowhere in *Brighton Rock*.

Opposite – **Top left:** Diana Dors prepares to *Yield To The Night*. **Top right:** John Mills tinkles his teacup on the set of *Hobson's Choice*. **Bottom left:** 'Don't leave us in the dark!' Anthony Newley in *Oliver Twist*. **Bottom right:** The original Sheridan Whiteside, Monty Woolley in *The Man Who Came To Dinner*.

'The mafia of rock and roll': Left to right – Arthur 'Killer' Kane, Jerry Nolan, David Johansen, Sylvain Sylvain, Johnny Thunders. Morrissey had this same New York Dolls portrait framed in his living room.

This page – Eastenders.
Above: Ronnie Kray (left) and his twin brother Reggie practise some southpaw grammar. **Right:** 'No-nonsense, snot-nosed, brick-wall punks' the Cockney Rejects – bassist Vince Riordan (top) was the nephew of Krays victim Jack 'The Hat' McVitie.

Opposite – Top: *Well Of Loneliness* author Radclyffe Hall (right) and lover Una Troubridge with dachshund cousins.
Bottom: The wails of loneliness, Timi Yuro (left) and Nico (right).

Nothing to declare except his genius: Oscar Wilde (1854–1900).

been given its full due as the culmination of The Smiths' career rather than the misconstrued ruination. But as Morrissey was correct to brag at the time, it perfected 'every lyrical and musical notion The Smiths have ever had. It's far and away the best record we've ever made.' Marr, Rourke and Joyce all agree. Strangeways, not The Queen Is Dead, is The One.

The biggest myth about Strangeways follows that, surely, it must have been recorded in a state of acrimony, otherwise they wouldn't have split up so soon afterwards. 'I didn't want it to be our last record,' states Marr. 'I would have been really happy for it *not* to be our last record. Away from the music there were the same old business and management pressures, but it was a really liberating feeling making that album.' As Rourke concurs, 'It was the best time the four of us ever spent in a studio together.'

Notwithstanding its dramatic aftermath, the story of Strangeways is very different to that of its three predecessors. Unusually for Morrissey and Marr, they entered the studio with very little prepared, bar 'Girlfriend In A Coma', already recorded at an earlier session along with 'SHEILA TAKE A BOW'. Both writers had their respective lyrical and musical ideas but the finished songs had yet to be sketched and Strangeways is unique in being the only Smiths album not to have had any of its tracks tested in concert beforehand. This, its organic creative process, would be the secret of its splendour.

The chosen studio was The Wool Hall, a residential hideaway amid the Somerset countryside ten miles outside Bath where The Smiths arrived in March 1987 after promoting their current single 'SHOPLIFTERS OF THE WORLD UNITE' in the UK, Ireland and Italy's San Remo pop festival. Morrissey had already forewarned Marr of the album title, namechecking Manchester's notorious prison while paraphrasing a line from the 1963 kitchen-sink fantasy BILLY LIAR: 'Borstal, here we come!'

'I've learned to love the title,' says Marr. 'It was a bit overstating things somewhat. A little bit

obvious. But it's OK. I was always intrigued by the word Strangeways. I remember as a kid, when I first heard that the prison was really called that, I wondered had it not occurred to anybody to change the name? It's still befuddling, really.'

Upon its release, Morrissey explained the title as being less comedy than prophecy. 'If I ended up in Strangeways I wouldn't be at all surprised,' he quipped. 'Really it's me throwing both arms up to the skies and yelling, "Whatever next?" Strangeways, of course, is that hideous Victorian monstrosity of a prison operating 88 to a cell. I don't have any particular crimes in mind but it's so easy to be a criminal nowadays that I wouldn't have to look very far. Life is so odd that I'm sure I could manage it without too much difficulty.'

The Wool Hall proved an idyllic retreat, its fully stocked wine cellar habitually drained after a hard day's recording by the band and former engineer Stephen Street, who'd finally been granted co-producer status. 'That was always after Morrissey went to bed,' recalls Street. 'It wasn't really his bag. We'd carry on finishing overdubs and then the records would come out. We'd be partying till all hours.' The late-night Wool Hall playlist ranged from disco (Sister Sledge's 'Greatest Dancer') to northern soul ('GROOVIN' WITH MR BLOE'). Street also recalls fond memories of their 'Spinal Tap phase': arranging cigarette packets in mini replicas of Stonehenge in homage to Rob Reiner's 1984 *This Is Spinal Tap* mock rockumentary and reportedly jamming their way through the film's soundtrack. 'It's true that our night times were spent in revelry,' confirms Marr, who caught much of the action on his newly acquired video camcorder. 'But only after ten or twelve hours of making some really great music, *not* as a substitute,' he stresses. 'It wasn't all one big Spinal Tap mongo fest!'

Already harbouring concerns over their stereotypical 'indie' pigeonholing, for Marr the organic creative protocol employed on Strangeways was carte blanche to confound such preconceptions. Stephen Street felt the sharp end of Marr's new directive the very first night at The Wool Hall.

Rehearsing the keyboard riff of what became the piano-driven opener 'A Rush And A Push', the guitarist drunkenly goaded the producer: ''Ere, Streety. You don't like it when we do this, you like us to be all jingly-jangly, don't you?'

'When I got into the studio, I ended up getting fairly drunk and irate with Stephen Street,' Marr admits. 'I felt we had to enter a new phase, but it hadn't really been discussed and that frustrated me. Stephen Street took it in good nature, but I was adamant that we weren't going to just repeat any kind of formula, particularly because of where the British indie scene had got to. There was that whole C86 thing, a certain generic sound bordering on parody of bands with terrible-sounding guitars and girls singing about skipping through the flowers. Which was a scene which essentially we'd created, but I wanted us to shed that skin and find a different direction. I was just really bogged off with the words "jangle" and "jingle". That's possibly why you don't hear a lot of it on Strangeways. But it still sounds like us.'

Marr's determination, and that of Rourke and Joyce to follow him, revealed itself in one of the first Strangeways recordings. As its working title suggested, the sulphurous 'Heavy Track' was the antithesis of jingly-jangly indie. Sadly, Marr's enthusiasm – picked up on the studio mike beaming 'I really, really like that!' – wasn't shared by Morrissey. 'Heavy Track' fell clanging by the wayside, though there'd be plenty of better tunes to compensate for its loss.

The need for a 'new direction' propelled Marr to find some fresh influences. First and foremost was THE BEATLES' The White Album, most evident on their secret masterpiece 'Death Of A Disco Dancer' and, to a lesser extent, 'Unhappy Birthday'. 'That was a big thing for me at the time,' says Marr, 'purely because I knew there was an atmospheric aspect of The White Album that we could relate to musically.' Elsewhere he'd seek his muse in some of his and Morrissey's favourite singles from the 1970s, from David BOWIE's 'The Jean Genie' ('I Started Something I Couldn't Finish') to 'SHOES' by Reparata ('A Rush And A Push').

'Round about the time of The Queen Is Dead, I'd told Morrissey how as a kid I used to swap everything,' says Marr. 'So he put this idea to me that now I'd earned a little bit of money then maybe every seven-inch piece of vinyl that I used to own which I'd swapped, I should perhaps now go back and retrieve. It was a really good idea and it became really important to the two of us. We'd go on drives just to buy records. Things like "Amateur Hour" by SPARKS. "Shoes" by Reparata. Those singles definitely came out later in our music when making Strangeways.'

Complementing Marr's musical ambition, Morrissey adorned the album with his most intricate lyric sheet yet. Any first-person autobiography was buried within a series of symbolic melodramas; of prison sentences, life support machines, violent beatings, hatchet murders, poisoned pen letters and the ghostly voices of the hanged. Death stalked the album at every corner, claiming disco dancers, comatose girlfriends, pets and pop stars. While there was noticeably more hate than love, the closing 'I Won't Share You' remains, for many, Morrissey and Marr's finest romance. But it was on the epic orchestral ballad 'Last Night I Dreamt That Somebody Loved Me' that their writing partnership hit its creative zenith, the final jewel in The Smiths' crown, and the brightest.

As Marr is keen to reiterate, 'Myself and Morrissey were still very close at that time,' referring to their final live TV appearance on Channel 4's The Tube in April 1987 as an example of their public intimacy. The singer and guitarist performed sharing a pair of earrings; Morrissey in his right ear, Marr in his left. Yet as Morrissey would later surmise, though Strangeways was 'a very happy time amongst the four members of the group', surrounding them were 'the gnashing wolves'. The recurring management problems reached crisis point yet again with the short-lived tenure of Ken Friedman, an experienced American promoter who'd previously handled Simple Minds. 'While we were recording and concentrating on the album it was fine,' says Street, 'but once they started talking about the business with Ken –

'Street Life' (Bryan Ferry), Cover of ROXY MUSIC's Christmas 1973 top ten hit which Morrissey performed only twice at concerts in Sweden (Karlstad) and Norway (Oslo) in September 2006. The arrangement stayed faithful to Roxy's original glam roadblock while Ferry's lyrics – wishing 'everybody would leave me alone' and rejecting education ('the good life's never won by degrees') – were a perfect fit for Morrissey. Sadly, its cool Scandinavian reception dissuaded him from ever playing it again. Referring to its final outing in Oslo, Morrissey admitted 'I couldn't wait for the song to end … It's the first time I felt stranded in time, and that the audience hadn't a clue what the song was meant to be. I'd only sing it again under hypnosis – and that's a promise.' [244, 567]

outside of what we were actually doing in the studio – that's when the nightmares started.'

Strangeways was completed in late April '87. By the end of the following month, management nightmares coupled with brewing concerns over the financial infrastructure of the group's business and Morrissey and Marr's diverging opinions as to The Smiths' future direction led to the break-up (see V) THE SEPARATION OF MORRISSEY AND MARR under main Johnny MARR entry). When finally released that September, the new Smiths album had become The Smiths' memorial service. Bells tolled, flags were lowered, hats were respectfully removed, heads were bowed, candles were lit, prayers were whispered and children bawled in terror and confusion at the very mention of its name. In Smithdom, at any rate.

Never toured by the group, Strangeways was denied the chance to breathe. Every possibility it raises – how the songs would have sounded live, where they would have gone next, how or even *if* they could have gone one better – is swallowed up in a gulf of hypotheses. Despite Morrissey's many tributes to Strangeways in the years that followed, that it 'said everything' eloquently, perfectly at the right time and put the tin hat on it basically', the stigma remains.

If the album has one very obvious flaw – other than the universally acknowledged filler 'Death At One's Elbow' – then it is purely a cosmetic one. The cover, a pale beige close-up of James DEAN co-star Richard Davalos, may have sufficed for a single but is much too weak a shopfront for a store of Strangeways' mettle. A pity, then, that its intended cover star declined permission for what would have been the ideal sleeve: a young Harvey KEITEL from 1968's *Who's That Knocking At My Door*, head cricked to the heavens in a cackle of prison-bound hysteria.

Setting aside its inadequate sleeve and its cadaverous reputation as a carefully coded epitaph, judged purely on the art contained within, Strangeways is – probably, plausibly, conceivably, arguably, somewhat impossibly though, perhaps, just maybe – The Smiths' best album. 'It is,' stressed Morrissey in 1994. '[Myself and Johnny are] in absolute accordance on that. We say it quite often. At the same time. In our sleep. But in different beds.' [14, 17, 19, 29, 38, 99, 138, 144, 154, 469]

Street, Stephen (Smiths engineer and co-producer 1984–87, Morrissey co-writer and producer 1987–89),

Hailed by Johnny Marr as 'absolutely crucial' to The Smiths' recording history, Stephen Street's career progressed in tandem with the group, from assistant engineer on 1984's 'HEAVEN KNOWS I'M MISERABLE NOW' to eventual co-producer on 1987's STRANGEWAYS, HERE WE COME. As Morrissey surmised, 'Stephen's relationship with The Smiths as a group was totally harmonious and very natural.'

'He was always important,' Marr elaborates. 'There were five of us making those records. He was the other mind in it. Stephen was like us but different when it mattered. He felt that what we were doing was really important, and we were the same age. There was always an atmosphere around the studio with Stephen that we were doing it without the grown-ups around. There was no one acting like a school teacher. But he was technically as good as anyone else around twice his age. We all learned to make records together but we wouldn't have been able to be swift and do what we did so well unless he was on the case.'

Formerly a bassist with London ska band Bim, Street began his studio career with ISLAND RECORDS, working as in-house engineer at their basement studio in Chiswick known as the Fallout Shelter. It was there, in March 1984, that he first crossed paths with The Smiths for the recording of 'Heaven Knows' with John PORTER. Both Morrissey and Marr were immediately impressed with his enthusiasm and studio expertise. Though they retained Porter for their next single, 'WILLIAM, IT WAS REALLY NOTHING', in the autumn of 1984 Street was contacted by ROUGH TRADE boss Geoff Travis with the offer to engineer The Smiths' self-produced second album, MEAT IS MURDER.

As Marr has described, the 24-year-old Street approached their music with the same youthful zeal and willing experimentation, more than evident on the finished album with its playful use of sound effects and other sonic frills. One of Street's main Smiths trademarks was 'infinite reverb'. Achieved using old-fashioned analogue tape methods, it involved adding echo to sounds but then flipping the tape over so it played backwards. That way, instead of the reverb ringing out *after* the note is played, it builds up *before* in a slow, ethereal fade-in. Examples include the end section of 'THAT JOKE ISN'T FUNNY ANYMORE', 'OSCILLATE WILDLY' and Morrissey's opening 'Hello' on 'A RUSH AND A PUSH AND THE LAND IS OURS'.

Street remained The Smiths' engineer of choice for the bulk of their studio engagements thereafter bar a handful of singles ('PANIC', 'ASK', 'SHOPLIFTERS') and their 'last stand' with soundman Grant Showbiz in May 1987. His greatest bequest to the sonic texture of The Smiths was the introduction of synthetic string and woodwind sounds played on an Emulator keyboard, most notable on THE QUEEN IS DEAD and Strangeways.

(See also HATED SALFORD ENSEMBLE, ORCHESTRAZIA ARDWICK.)

As the chosen producer of the doomed Ivor PERRY session in August 1987 following Marr's exit, Street witnessed the disintegration of The Smiths at close quarters. He has always maintained that when he sent Morrissey a cassette of instrumental ideas that same month, it was on the presumption that the singer was still looking for new material as B-sides for the final Smiths singles culled from Strangeways. Instead he unwittingly passed his unbeknownst audition to become Morrissey's first co-writer of his solo career. 'At the time there were no other people presenting things,' Morrissey later said, 'and I happened to like what Stephen had done.'

Street's familiarity with Morrissey and Marr's working and writing methods gave him a considerable advantage, though it was still a steep learning curve: of the many songs written and demoed at Street's flat in Mortlake in September 1987 in preparation for VIVA HATE, several were swiftly discarded (see 'I DON'T WANT US TO FINISH', 'LIFEGUARD ON DUTY', 'SAFE WARM LANCASHIRE HOME' and 'TREAT ME LIKE A HUMAN BEING'). Contrasting the differences between Marr and Street, Morrissey noted, 'Johnny was very *hard*, as a musician. He played in a very interesting, *aggressive* way. Stephen does not. But the gentle side of Stephen is something I find totally precious.' Though nowhere near as skilled a musician as Marr, as a writer Street's tunes revealed an impressively strong ear for rich, melodic pop, albeit with very deliberate nods to other artists. As the entries in this book attest, Street often had a specific agenda in mind, whether inspired by Echo & The Bunnymen on the bass line for 'EVERYDAY IS LIKE SUNDAY', BOWIE's 'Andy Warhol' on 'LITTLE MAN, WHAT NOW?' or SPARKS on 'SUCH A LITTLE THING MAKES SUCH A BIG DIFFERENCE'.

Added to the responsibilities of co-writer, producer and bass player, Street also had the task of assembling suitable musicians, eventually settling on Durutti Column guitarist Vini REILLY and drummer Andrew PARESI; for the full story of its gestation, recording and all relevant personality clashes refer to the Viva Hate entry. Sadly, by the time of the album's release the relationship between Morrissey and Street was already straining. The latter's main concern was over the as-yet-unresolved 'production points' (royalties) on the album, instigating a long legal dispute which ultimately severed their partnership in 1989, also putting an end to Morrissey's brief tenure with new manager Gail Colson who also represented Street.

In the interim, Street continued writing with Morrissey. Much of their best work came after Viva Hate with the 'Everyday Is Like Sunday' B-sides (including 'WILL NEVER MARRY'), and their final session at the end of the year for the singles 'THE LAST OF THE FAMOUS INTERNATIONAL PLAY-BOYS' and 'INTERESTING DRUG'. Even after their fall-out, Morrissey continued recording and releasing Street material with 'OUIJA BOARD, OUIJA BOARD', 'AT AMBER' (remixed from an old outtake) and the 1991 B-side 'JOURNALISTS WHO LIE'. A dedicated diarist, interestingly Street's record of personal correspondence reveals that despite their legal stalemate he was still willing to send Morrissey new songs as late as July 1990.

Due to the nature of their estrangement, Morrissey's subsequent comments on Street haven't always been flattering, insisting that contrary to popular belief he 'wasn't entirely incapable' of launching a solo career without Street 'no matter what he might say'. Yet, unquestionably, it *was* Street who 'saved' Morrissey at a critical period in his career and, idle hypotheses aside, it's all but impossible to imagine his transition from Smith to solo star being as speedy or as successful with any other collaborator.

Street's big regret is that they never had the opportunity to make 'a proper second album' which he believes would have surpassed the admittedly flawed Viva Hate. Yet his contribution to the Morrissey canon speaks for itself: 'SUEDE-HEAD', 'Everyday Is Like Sunday', 'LATE NIGHT, MAUDLIN STREET', 'Will Never Marry', 'The Last Of The Famous International Playboys'. These, and possibly others bearing Street's name, are the

very best of Morrissey. And just as Street had to contend with the fixed shadow of Marr, so all future Morrissey co-writers have also had to tread respectfully in Street's footsteps. As Clive LANGER told this author: 'What Morrissey did with Stephen Street was brilliant. Coming in after that, it was a hard act to follow.'

'Looking back, at that time I was heavily wrapped up in The Smiths and upset by what happened,' says Street . 'I really did grow to love Morrissey like a brother. He's one of these people that you meet and you think, "Jesus! He's fantastic!" When things are going really well with a character like that it gives you a sense of immense power. I thought I was so close to him. I was very sad how that whole chapter ended. But I remain proud of the fact that I helped him through that initial dark and distressing stage after The Smiths breaking up. After Morrissey, I tried to cleanse my mind and get on with other things.'

Concentrating exclusively on production rather than writing, Street went on to become the award-winning producer of hit albums by Blur and The Cranberries. Since then he has continued to expand his estimable track record for commercially successful guitar-based indie-pop with various other young bands. [17, 19, 38, 39, 71, 138, 208]

'Stretch Out And Wait' (Morrissey/Marr),

B-side of 'SHAKESPEARE'S SISTER' (1985). Whereas many of Morrissey's earliest lyrics concerned themselves with sexual failure and his own negative adolescent experiences, 'Stretch Out And Wait' was an atypically positive endorsement of succumbing to carnal impulses: a moment of intimacy amid the drab surroundings of a council estate, his physical longing stalled only by the anxious philosophising of his partner. This deliberation on the world ending during day or night time was inspired by an identical exchange between James DEAN and Sal Mineo towards the end of 1955's *Rebel Without A Cause*. Morrissey also borrowed the phrase 'Eskimo blood in my veins' from 'Karen', the 1978 Australian debut single by former ROUGH TRADE label mates The

Go-Betweens while the song's climactic provocation to lust, 'We are here and it is now', was sourced from one of his favourite books, Jack Nichols's MEN'S LIBERATION.

Morrissey would later discuss the line 'God, how sex implores you' in relation to his own sexuality. 'I felt that I just wanted to be me, which was somewhere between this world and the next world, somewhere between this sex and the next sex,' he explained, 'but nothing really political, nothing really threatening to anybody on earth and nothing really dramatic. Just being me as an individual and not wishing to make any elaborate, strangulating statements.'

With the dappled sunlight from Marr's acoustic adding to its sensual surrender, 'Stretch Out And Wait' was The Smiths at their most enchanting, free of any customary melancholic subtext bar its final, lingering minor chord. Interviewed in late 1986, Morrissey even praised it as the best thing he and Marr had written together up until that point. An alternate mix of the song with a different opening lyric later appeared on 1987's THE WORLD WON'T LISTEN compilation: the original B-side version, more precious if only by a hair's breadth, is that heard on LOUDER THAN BOMBS. [17, 196, 345, 428, 545]

'Striptease With A Difference' (Morrissey/Langer), Studio outtake from the 1989 BONA DRAG album sessions. The title comes from a 1966 Julian and Sandy sketch from the radio series *Round The Horne*. Asked to hire acts for a BBC cabaret, Kenneth Horne visits their 'Bona Performers' talent agency and is tempted by their offer of 'Queenie' who performs 'Striptease with a difference. Normally she's the bearded lady at Blackpool. She's got a long beard right down to her ankles. Instead of stripping she just comes on and shaves.'

As Morrissey plainly described it, the song 'is about playing a game of cards wherein the loser of each game has to take off an item of clothing. And it's about secretly hoping one loses and in fact manipulating the game towards that end.' The lyrics also feature a rare usage in pop music

of the informal English expression to 'have a shufti' (have a look). As with his other Langer and Winstanley productions, the piano-driven 'Striptease With A Difference' is very much in the MADNESS mould, even more so than the similar 'PICCADILLY PALARE'. Alongside 'OH PHONEY', it was shelved when the original Bona Drag album was put on hold. Quizzed about its existence by a shrewd fan at a 1992 press conference, Morrissey confidently retorted, 'You've never heard it, surely?' High-quality leaks have since surfaced on the internet. [1, 15, 25, 138, 404]

'Subway Train' (Johnny Thunders/David Johansen), NEW YORK DOLLS cover performed, in part, by Morrissey in 2004 and included on the LIVE AT EARLS COURT album. The original, featured on the Dolls' 1973 debut, was a euphoric serenade to the New York underground via the old American folk song 'I've Been Working On The Railroad'. Writing about the track in his 1981 book on the Dolls, Morrissey praised its 'lazy vitality' and the Dolls' methodology which involved '[taking] their daily experiences and [making] them the subjects of their music'. Morrissey's version was comparable with The Smiths' blink-and-miss pelt through ELVIS PRESLEY'S '(MARIE'S THE NAME) HIS LATEST FLAME', being no more than a 50-second, one-verse snippet played on his YOU ARE THE QUARRY tour as a prologue to 'EVERYDAY IS LIKE SUNDAY' (as seen on *WHO PUT THE 'M' IN MANCHESTER?*) and later 'MUNICH AIR DISASTER 1958'. Although its opening lines about living a life 'cursed, poisoned and condemned' seemed quintessential Morrissey, the medley itself was never the slickest, nor most logical, of changeovers. The only intriguing detail was its subtly different arrangement which cleverly incorporated the Mark NEVIN guitar riff from 'MY LOVE LIFE'. [277, 343]

'Suedehead' (Morrissey/Street), Morrissey's debut solo single (taken from the album VIVA HATE), released February 1988, highest UK chart position #5.

'Such A Little Thing Makes Such A Big Difference' (Morrissey/Street), B-side of
'INTERESTING DRUG' (1989). Behind the coy sexual innuendo of its title, 'Such A Little Thing'
was an abstract reflection on love and hate, revisiting the mind vs body debate of 'STILL ILL' with
its repeated pronouncement that the majority of humankind are ruled by their nether regions. The
'little thing' is left unclear, so too the nature of Morrissey's relationship with the stubborn chain-
wielding hooligan who attacks him for 'only singing'.

Upon Morrissey's instruction, Street wrote the tune as a homage to SPARKS; indeed, its arpeggiated
keyboard riff follows a very similar pattern to their 1974 single 'Never Turn Your Back On Mother
Earth'. Unlike the bulk of Street's Morrissey songs which the singer selected from instrumental
demos, 'Such A Little Thing' was written in the studio, The Wool Hall near Bath, in early December 1988 at the end of the 'LAST OF THE FAMOUS INTERNATIONAL PLAYBOYS'/'Interesting Drug' sessions.
The previous week, Morrissey had scrapped various songs-in-progress, all possible single B-sides. In
desperate need of replacement material, Street, with his Sparks brief, composed the melody in a
single afternoon and, to his relief, met with Morrissey's approval.

Later included on the BONA DRAG compilation, 'Such A Little Thing' was introduced in concert in
1992, played only up until its odd middle eight before segueing into either the Suede cover 'MY INSA-
TIABLE ONE' or 'I KNOW IT'S GONNA HAPPEN SOMEDAY'; the latter medley can be heard on BEETHOVEN
WAS DEAF. The song was finally performed in its entirety in 2004. [29, 39]

Still for many the definitive Morrissey favourite, 'Suedehead' was the perfect vehicle for his rebirth as a solo artist. Musically, its jangling warmth was sufficiently Smiths-lite in spirit not to frighten off his core audience but innovative enough to suggest the beginnings of a prosperous new partnership with Stephen Street. Vocally, it saw him stretch vowels and syllables ('Wha-ha-hah-ha-ha-ha-hah-ha-haha-hyyy') with a supple beauty as stunning as anything he's recorded before or since. And lyrically, the words were luxuriously woeful yet tantalisingly mysterious, be it the significance of the title or his shocking sexual brag, 'it was a good lay'. 'Suedehead' was unpolluted Morrissey genius and, deservedly, the biggest hit of his career up until that point.

At the time it was assumed the title was inspired by *Suedehead*, a 1971 cult paperback by Richard Allen (pen name of author James Moffat). The sequel to Allen's previous *Skinhead*, it continued the story of bovver boy Joe Hawkins (his hair now grown out from shaved to suede length), an unapologetic racist and 'queer basher' who ends the book sentenced to four years in

prison for assaulting a black man. 'I did happen to read the book when it came out and I was quite interested in the whole Richard Allen cult,' said Morrissey. 'But really I just like the word suede-head.' Indeed, some critics have made too much of the Richard Allen connection: in truth, *Suedehead* is a relatively nasty piece of literature and has absolutely nothing to do with the song.

It may, however, be worth taking into consideration a recollection from Johnny Marr about a period during the latter half of The Smiths' career when he decided to 'get a motorbike and get a suedehead'. 'That was my mantra for a while,' he explains, '"Gotta get a suedehead! Gotta get a suedehead!" I can remember suedehead gangs wearing tonic suits and Crombies hanging around my street when I was growing up in Ardwick in the early 70s. So I think I may have brought that word into the vernacular, I might be wrong. But that's what I did, got myself a motorbike and a suedehead haircut.'

Which, of course, adds considerable weight to the romantic theory held by some that the song was written with Marr in mind, possibly as an

427

apology for everything that happened during the break-up of The Smiths ('I'm so sorry'). Morrissey would only comment that it was about 'a particular person' but, clouding any further autobiographical analysis, also stated he never kept a diary. 'I make so many records that in a peculiar way that becomes like a personal diary.'

The song's main narrative of being plagued by a former lover seems to have been inspired by 'The Weakness In Me', a 1982 track by Joan ARMATRADING which features several comparable lines. The contentious 'good lay' was deliberately left off the album's accompanying lyric sheet so as to 'not cause a stir'. 'It was the only record in England that had extremely good airplay for me,' he later explained, 'so I think, oddly enough, if they knew what the last line was they possibly wouldn't play it.' Probed further about when and where exactly Morrissey had experienced such pleasant shenanigans, he coyly declared he'd made it up. 'I just thought it might amuse someone living in Hartlepool.'

Recorded in the early stages of the Viva Hate sessions, 'Suedehead' saw the first clash between Stephen Street and guitarist Vini REILLY when the latter refused to play the guitar break in the middle eight because it was 'too easy'. Street duly recorded it himself, loosely following a similar passage in Echo & The Bunnymen's 'Seven Seas' (also inspiration for the bass line in 'EVERYDAY IS LIKE SUNDAY').

Morrissey later claimed he hadn't wanted to release it as a single but had been 'carried along on a wave of general enthusiasm'. Issued just nine weeks after The Smiths' swansong, 'LAST NIGHT I DREAMT THAT SOMEBODY LOVED ME', 'Suedehead' entered the charts at a victorious number six, rising to five the following week. The accompanying video was an unrelated tribute to James DEAN, mostly shot in the actor's hometown of Fairmount, Indiana. A short prologue filmed in London also featured a cameo by Morrissey's nephew, Sam, as well as a glimpse of a 'truly beautiful present' sent by an American fan – a bath mat embroidered with 'THERE IS A LIGHT THAT NEVER GOES OUT'.

A landmark commercial triumph for Morrissey

at the time, decades later 'Suedehead' remains his morning star, still twinkling brighter than most others to have joined it in his solo cosmos since. At the very end of the track, as Morrissey yodels over the horizon, Street overdubbed the faint sound effect of a cheering crowd. Therein lies the extent of its brilliance – a record of such ecstasy that it can't quite finish without giving itself a standing ovation. [25, 39, 69, 71, 203, 272, 276, 437]

'Suffer Little Children' (Morrissey/Marr),

From the album THE SMITHS (1984). One of Morrissey's earliest lyrics written before collaborating with Marr, 'Suffer Little Children' is his powerful personal tribute to the victims of Ian Brady and Myra Hindley, largely informed by Emlyn Williams's dramatised biography BEYOND BELIEF.

Between July 1963 and October 1965 Brady and Hindley committed five murders in and around Manchester. The victims were aged between ten and 17, four of whom were buried outside the city on Saddleworth Moor, hence their infamy as the 'Moors Murders'. Morrissey, born in May 1959, would have been between the ages of four and six at the time. 'I happened to live on the streets where, close by, some of the victims had been picked up,' he explained. 'Within that community, news of the crimes totally dominated all attempts at conversation for quite a few years … I was very, *very* aware of *everything* that occurred. Aware as a child who could have been a victim.'

In 'Suffer Little Children' he imagines just that: being buried upon the moors, his ghost beckoning to be found like that of the other victims, vowing to forever haunt the evil conscience of Brady and more particularly Hindley. The song's title, and many of its lyrics, are taken directly from *Beyond Belief* (see entry) which only dealt with the three murders the couple were convicted of, as named by Morrissey: 'Lesley Ann' (Downey, ten years old), 'John' (Kilbride, 12 years old) and 'Edward' (Evans, 17 years old). In 1986, four years after Morrissey wrote the song, Brady and Hindley confessed to two other murders, 16-year-old Pauline Reade and 12-year-old Keith Bennett.

Reade's remains were located on the moors the following year but Bennett's have never and probably may never be discovered, a detail which now weighs the 'find me' refrain of 'Suffer Little Children' with an unintentionally hideous poignancy.

The second successfully completed Morrissey/Marr original, it was composed in the summer of 1982 during the same practice session as 'THE HAND THAT ROCKS THE CRADLE'. Morrissey had typed the words out in preparation. 'I was sat on the floor, looking at them,' recalls Marr. 'I just started to play this chord progression, this figure I'd been fiddling around with for a couple of weeks. Straight away Morrissey said, "Is that it? Keep going." So as I was looking at the lyrics – I didn't know how the vocal melody went – but I was getting a feeling and just sticking with it. I thought it felt right.'

By gracing such solemn words with a contrastingly gentle air, 'Suffer Little Children' set in place the double helix at the heart of the Morrissey and Marr songbook, interweaving the separate elements of beauty and melancholy into a complementary whole. A first demo version recorded at Manchester's Decibel studios in August 1982, with Simon WOLSTENCROFT on drums and Marr overdubbing bass, featured a cameo from the mysterious Annalisa JABLONSKA providing its exaggerated Hindley laughter, also calling the victims by name: 'Lesley! Edward! John!' Equally experimental was a separate piece of music tacked on to the end which Marr had pre-recorded at home; a mournful piano coda, quite similar to the later 'ASLEEP', accompanied by the tinkling of a music box and the distant sound of children playing outside his window.

A more polished remake during the Troy TATE sessions adhered to the same arrangement with its piano epilogue. It wasn't until the third attempt with John PORTER for their eventual debut album that this superfluous piano piece, though recorded yet again, was removed from the finished mix. Marr would, rightly, cite Porter's 'Suffer Little Children' as one of the most accomplished tracks on the album, skilfully arranged, commandingly sung and vibrating with precisely

the right atmosphere of tranquil horror, abetted once again by the enigmatic Ms Jablonska.

Morrissey would later admit he anticipated the media controversy the song provoked though was nevertheless 'quite confused [and] very distressed'. Surprisingly, little fuss was made over 'Suffer Little Children' until September 1984, seven months after its release on the album. In the interim, it had appeared a second time as the B-side to their May single 'HEAVEN KNOWS I'M MISERABLE NOW'. When the grandfather of John Kilbride heard it on a pub jukebox, he complained to the local Manchester press. Because of The Smiths' unfortunate history with the 'child-sex song' tabloid smears over a year earlier (see 'HANDSOME DEVIL', 'REEL AROUND THE FOUNTAIN'), the Brady and Hindley connection offered their same detractors another opportunity to revive false allegations over sick lyrical content and gross insensitivity to the victims' families. Neither charge was true, though the *Sun* blew the story out of proportion, resulting in high street chains such as Woolworths and Boots temporarily removing the album from sale.

'I was only distressed because nobody would actually let me comment on it,' Morrissey later explained. 'It appeared in national newspapers the length and breadth of the country. "Morrissey does this" and "Morrissey says that" and "Morrissey believes …" and nobody asked me a thing. Nobody knew what I believed or why the lyrics were there. So that was the only distressing element. But I'm glad the record got attention, ultimately.'

An official press statement in response to the scandal clearly explained its intentions and in particular its much quoted line (and one of Morrissey's most original rhyming couplets) 'Manchester, so much to answer for' – written 'out of a profound emotion by Morrissey, a Mancunian who feels that the particularly horrendous crime it describes must be borne by the conscience of Manchester and that it must never happen again'.

The cloud of bad press would, however, bring a silver lining which itself negated the regrettable commotion in the first place, putting Morrissey in contact with Lesley Ann Downey's mother, Ann

S

West, whom he'd immediately befriend. 'I was very surprised that she was so burdened by her daughter's death given the lapse of time,' he confessed. 'It was obvious that the woman was completely destroyed.' Ann West and her husband Alan were later thanked on the credits of The Smiths' next album, MEAT IS MURDER. Nearly a decade after West's death in February 1999, Morrissey described her as 'a remarkable woman because she didn't ever give up her fight to keep Brady and Hindley in prison, but she was dismissed by the establishment because she was very working-class Manchester. I gave her £100 once – I can't remember why – but her eyes welled with tears.'

As for the Moors Murderers themselves, despite a pointless and deluded campaign led by legal reformer Lord Longford for Hindley to be released, her subsequent admission to the Reade and Bennett murders in 1986 put an end to whatever misled shreds of sympathy may have existed for her among the general public. Hindley made numerous unsuccessful attempts to have the life tariff on her prison sentence overruled by the House of Lords and after years of failing health died in November 2002 at the age of 60. Despite their belated confession, neither Hindley nor Brady – still imprisoned in the high-security Ashworth Hospital at the time of writing – was ever charged with the murders of Reade and Bennett. It is impossible not to concur with Morrissey's sombre comment in 2004 that, over four decades later, the details of the Moors Murders are 'still unbelievable'. [10, 13, 17, 27, 52, 129, 139, 217, 262, 275, 320, 395, 463, 568, 574]

Suggs, See MADNESS.

suicide, Morrissey has never shied away from speaking, or singing, on the subject of suicide. In his very first Smiths interview for *Sounds* in June 1983, he expressed admiration for the suicidal poets Stevie Smith and Sylvia Plath. 'Smith wanted to kill herself at nine. That's wonderful. I can relate to that. [And] Sylvia Plath, just before she killed herself, had this incredible sense of humour in *Letters Home*.' Like Smith, Morrissey claimed

he'd realised 'that suicide was quite appealing and attractive' at the age of eight. 'Sincerely, I was considering it. I always had this great fondness for people who'd led tragic lives. I was completely fascinated by failures.' Many years later he'd disclose sketchy details of a 21-year-old female friend who killed herself when he was only 15. 'She was six years older but 5,000 years wiser. I'm sure she's very happy now, on that pavement.'

As his fame increased, Morrissey grew cautious of promoting suicide if ever frank in communicating his empathy for its victims. 'I have to be very careful what I say about this,' he admitted, 'but having been quite close to it myself on a number of occasions, I can quite admire someone with the strength to do it. People who have never been close to it cannot hope to understand it, and the idea that it was illegal until recent years is of course laughable … To me, it's quite honourable in a way, because it's a person taking *total* control over their lives and their bodies. By not thinking about suicide, or considering it, or examining it, it means that we ultimately just do not have control over our destinies and our bodies and our brains. And I think people without that sense of control are quite shallow, thin individuals. But I'm not saying that simply by having control over your body, the ultimate destination is suicide.'

Perhaps contrary to the popular cliché of Morrissey as the patron saint of doom, his suicidal lyrics have been relatively few with most instances occurring during The Smiths. His first explicit allusion to suicide was the woeful 'and you want to die' in 1984's 'HOW SOON IS NOW?' while both 'RUSHOLME RUFFIANS' and 'THAT JOKE ISN'T FUNNY ANYMORE' also contain passing references. But it wasn't until 1985's 'SHAKESPEARE'S SISTER' that Morrissey wrote his first deliberate 'suicide song'. He'd return to the theme with even greater compassion on the same year's 'ASLEEP', 'I KNOW IT'S OVER' and the chorus death-wish of 'THERE IS A LIGHT THAT NEVER GOES OUT'. It was these in particular which the NME would describe as his 'aesthetic Exit manuals', raising concerns of irresponsibility when the singer admitted that between 1984 and 1986 he'd been made aware of six Smiths fans who'd taken their own lives.

'Their friends and parents wrote to me after they died,' he revealed. 'It's something that shouldn't really be as hard to speak about as it is because if people are basically unhappy and people basically want to die then they will … I can't feel responsible … totally. I know that in most instances that for the last sad period of these people's lives at least having The Smiths was useful to them.'

'I think suicide intrigues everybody,' he added. 'And yet it's one of those things that nobody can ever really talk about in an interesting way. You always have the usual, "Oh it's so negative, it's so wrong" attitude … So many of the people that I admire took their lives. Stevie Smith. Sylvia Plath. James Dean. Marilyn Monroe. Rachel Roberts. There are many …'[1]

In 1988 Morrissey still spoke of suicide as 'a noble decision' having briefly brushed with the theme again in 1987's 'UNHAPPY BIRTHDAY' and, more unambiguously on 'ANGEL, ANGEL, DOWN WE GO TOGETHER', his first solo 'suicide song'. Yet since then, most (but not all)

lyrical mentions of suicide have been third-person character sketches, from 'THE TEACHERS ARE AFRAID OF THE PUPILS' and 'THE FATHER WHO MUST BE KILLED' to 'MAMA LAY SOFTLY ON THE RIVERBED' via his cover of PATTI SMITH's suicide dream 'REDONDO BEACH'.

Only in 2006 would Morrissey contradict his early confessions by stating he'd never 'noticeably' come close to killing himself. Nevertheless, his description of suicide as 'an art form' in the same breath suggests time hasn't dimmed his acute understanding of the mental extremes which drive people to the last human resort. [58, 152, 165, 166, 206, 208, 218]

---

1. Morrissey's list of suicide heroes isn't technically accurate: though suicidal, Stevie Smith died of a brain tumour; James Dean had a death wish but died in a car accident; and Monroe's 'suicide' is still clouded in a fog of conspiracy theories. Of his list only Plath, who gassed herself in 1963, and Roberts, star of SATURDAY NIGHT AND SUNDAY MORNING who took an overdose of alcohol and barbiturates in 1980, are indisputable suicides. Of those with entries in *Mozipedia*, his only other 'suicide idols' are Jimmy CLITHEROE, Patric DOONAN, Phil OCHS, Anne SEXTON and *CARRY ON* star Kenneth Williams, not forgetting his brief friendship with tragic Associates singer Billy MACKENZIE.

'Sunny' (Morrissey/Whyte), Morrissey's 21st solo single, released December 1995, highest UK chart position #42. A simple plea for a departed loved one to return, 'Sunny' saves its sting for the final verse where Morrissey reveals his sympathy and concern for a heroin addict, offering a graphic description of shooting up using a belt as a tourniquet. Inevitably, this would invite wild theorising as to the extent of autobiography in the lyrics and, if so, the identity of the real 'Sunny' and the nature of their relationship with Morrissey. Taken from a third person perspective, 'Sunny' could also be translated as a revisited 'PICCADILLY PALARE', the emphasis now shifted to the anxious parents fretting over their runaway son.

Originally intended as part of an EP with the three tracks from the 'BOXERS' single, 'Sunny' made for a fine A-side in its own right thanks to Whyte's sweet yet sullen melody and its punchy staccato rhythm. Sadly, it fell victim to its own unusual release schedule which saw two Morrissey singles on rival labels issued within weeks of one another. Despite promoting both together on the BBC's *Later With Jools Holland* in November 1995, neither RCA's 'THE BOY RACER' from his current album SOUTHPAW GRAMMAR, nor PARLOPHONE's 'Sunny' made much impression on the charts. Morrissey's friend/director James O'Brien later made a video for the song for inclusion as a multimedia extra on 1998's MY EARLY BURGLARY YEARS, featuring a young working-class couple and their friend (in a WEST HAM United hat) larking around London's Victoria Park. What, if any, relevance this narrative had to Morrissey's original muse for 'Sunny' is unclear. [4, 40]

S

'Swallow On My Neck, A' (Morrissey/ Whyte), B-side of 'SUNNY' (1995).

Recorded in early 1994 at the same session as 'MOONRIVER' and originally planned as a B-side to 'HOLD ON TO YOUR FRIENDS', 'A Swallow On My Neck' reflected Morrissey's current tattoo fixation as demonstrated on the artwork of VAUXHALL AND I and its spin-off singles. 'It's about having a tattoo stamped on your neck,' he confirmed, 'which is a fantastic statement and always looks great … I think tattoos on necks can be very impressive.'

Against Whyte's reeling acoustic rush – fluttering in a similar direction to Marr's 'CEMETRY GATES' – Morrissey casts himself as 'a simple man' (a Klaus NOMI reference, albeit probably subconscious), wasting his days getting pie-eyed in the company of undertakers only to receive a homoerotic awakening from the man who gives him the title tattoo. The swallow itself has multiple symbolic meanings but is primarily an old sailors' tattoo, earned after travelling so many nautical miles at sea. A swallow on the hands – as seen on the back sleeve of Vauxhall – supposedly indicated 'fast fists' and an accomplished fighter while swallows on the neck are also common among prisoners. While a frivolous character sketch, 'A Swallow On My Neck' was still one of Morrissey's better songs of the mid-90s. [4, 5, 40, 422]

'Sweet And Tender Hooligan' (Morrissey/ Marr), B-side of 'SHEILA TAKE A BOW' (1987).

Developing the theme of juvenile crime previously touched upon in the earlier 'I WANT THE ONE I CAN'T HAVE' and 'THE QUEEN IS DEAD', 'Sweet And Tender Hooligan' was Morrissey's court drama of a young felon convicted of murdering the elderly, now pleading for leniency with the idle promise he'll 'never, never do it again'. The lyrics are as scornful towards liberal jurors swayed by the murderer's 'mother-me eyes' as they are appalled at the violence of the boy's crimes, ending in a twist on the standard funeral service that 'in the midst of life we are in *debt*' (a common joke, first attributed to the American author Ethel Mumford).

Its brutal imagery was intensified by Marr's bovver-booted punk riff kicking the shins of all obstructing its path. 'I was getting a little bit sick hearing that we were wimp rock,' says Marr. 'To this day people who don't know their shit say that, ignoring the rocky ones like "The Queen Is Dead". So "Sweet And Tender Hooligan" was another example of us showing people that harder side.' A first version, recorded in May 1986 and intended as a B-side for 'PANIC', was scrapped for being too slow. Seven months later, when The Smiths were invited to record what would be their final John PEEL session, they tried again. 'As I remember, we really nailed it at the BBC,' says Marr. 'It was one of those occasions when you have a bunch of chords that you know are gonna work when the glue is right, because it just totally relies on performance and flying by the seat of your pants.' Marr also threw in a 'really obscure reference' to the NEW YORK DOLLS during the end section where his high-pitched solo was intended as a homage to Johnny Thunders on 'Jet Boy'.

The Smiths never had the opportunity to play the song in concert, though Morrissey chose it as the asphyxiated encore of his solo debut WOLVERHAMPTON concert of December 1988. The latter live version was issued as a B-side to the following year's 'INTERESTING DRUG' single. [17, 19, 29]

'Sweetie-Pie' (Morrissey/Farrell), B-side of 'I JUST WANT TO SEE THE BOY HAPPY' (2006).

Sharing its title with a 1960 single by Eddie Cochran, 'Sweetie-Pie' began life as a straightforward ballad originally destined for inclusion on RINGLEADER OF THE TORMENTORS. Having fallen in love, Morrissey (naturally) decides to end his life since he's unable to bridge the chasm between the way he feels and the way he behaves. Calling upon the title 'Sweetie-Pie' to speed him on his way, he promises to be there waiting in the afterlife 'when it's your time'.

To the confusion of the tune's composer, keyboard player Michael Farrell, Morrissey scrapped the original mix and set about tampering with the backing track, processed through a fog of effects and with the added nuttiness of guest vocalist Kristeen YOUNG screeching high amid the ether. The result was one of the strangest things Morrissey has ever released, a song falling off the edge of the world into who knows what. While its deliberate melodic sabotage recalled the fate of The Smiths' 'GOLDEN LIGHTS', 'Sweetie-Pie' was a far greater success and, queer as it is, remains an amusing testimonial to Morrissey's unfathomable eccentricity. [259]

swimming, One of Morrissey's favourite leisure pursuits. 'When I say that to people their heads spin around,' he commented. 'They can't really imagine me in a life that doesn't involve very heavy books and a small stepladder. It's very nice to be underwater. It gives you a very clear perspective on life. People look much better underwater. I like diving between people's legs. And obviously coming out the other side. I don't loiter.' After moving to Los Angeles in the late 90s, swimming became Morrissey's main pastime, preferring a 'really tiny pool in the back garden' to public baths or the Pacific Ocean. 'I used to walk a lot in London,' he explained, 'but if you walk in Los Angeles people lean out of windows and point at your face … [now] I only swim.' [191, 194, 422]

Sylvain, Sylvain, See NEW YORK DOLLS.

T.Rex, See BOLAN, Marc.

'Take Me Back To Dear Old Blighty',

First World War song featured at the beginning of The Smiths' 'THE QUEEN IS DEAD' as sung by Cicely Courtneidge in the 1962 film *THE L-SHAPED ROOM*. Written in 1916 by A. J. Mills, Fred Godfrey and Bennett Scott, 'Take Me Back To Dear Old Blighty' was typical of the era's humorous music hall tunes intended to cheer up homesick troops and the loved ones they'd left behind. The full song contained four verses each dedicated to a different military caricature fighting 'over in France' but dreaming of 'Blighty' (army slang for Britain). Only half of the main chorus is heard on 'The Queen Is Dead':

> *Take me back to dear old Blighty!*
> *Put me on the train for London town!*
> *Take me over there,*
> *Drop me anywhere,*
> *Liverpool, Leeds or Birmingham, well, I don't*
> *care!*
> *I should like to see [my best girl] ...*

The chorus continues with the male narrator pining for a cuddle with his sweetheart, concluding 'Blighty is the place for me!' Its popularity spawned countless recorded versions both during and after the First World War. Among the most interesting is that by music hall star Florrie Forde in 1916 which changed the chorus destinations to include The Smiths' hometown ('Birmingham, Leeds or Manchester, well, I don't care!'). 'Take Me Back To Dear Old Blighty' can also be heard at the beginning of David Lean's 1944 directorial debut *This Happy Breed*, written by Noël COWARD and starring one of Morrissey's favourite actors, John MILLS.

For their final concert at London's Brixton Academy on 12 December 1986, The Smiths used the full clip of Courtneidge singing the first verse and two choruses as their entrance music in place of their usual PROKOFIEV theme. [519]

Tams, The, See 'BE YOUNG, BE FOOLISH, BE HAPPY'.

Taste Of Honey, A, See DELANEY, Shelagh.

Tate, Troy (Smiths producer 1983), A significant chapter in The Smiths' recording career was their first attempt at a debut album in the summer of 1983 with producer Troy Tate.

A former guitarist with The Teardrop Explodes, as a solo singer-songwriter Tate had signed with ROUGH TRADE in early 1983, releasing the self-produced single 'Love Is …' It was label boss Geoff Travis's idea to pair The Smiths with Tate when they signed soon afterwards. As Morrissey explained that June, 'Rough Trade stuck us both together, and it's been quite a magical communion.'

From mid-July to early August The Smiths spent over a month with Tate at Elephant studios in Wapping, London, recording what would have been their first album, provisionally titled The Hand That Rocks The Cradle. Bar the scrapped 'A MATTER OF OPINION' and the Cookies cover 'I WANT A BOY FOR MY BIRTHDAY', the group recorded every song they'd ever rehearsed at length or played in concert, a total of 14 Morrissey/Marr originals.

With the exception of 'JEANE', commandeered for a B-side, surviving studio masters suggest that the remaining 13 would have comprised its full running order: 'THE HAND THAT ROCKS THE CRADLE', 'YOU'VE GOT EVERYTHING NOW', 'THESE THINGS TAKE TIME', 'WHAT DIFFERENCE DOES IT MAKE?', 'REEL AROUND THE FOUNTAIN', 'HAND IN GLOVE', 'HANDSOME DEVIL', 'WONDERFUL WOMAN', 'I DON'T OWE YOU ANYTHING', 'SUFFER LITTLE CHILDREN', 'MISERABLE LIE', 'ACCEPT YOURSELF' and 'PRETTY GIRLS MAKE GRAVES'.

In contrast to the polish and occasional restraint of their re-recorded debut with John PORTER, the Tate album is raw and direct, capturing the authentic spirit of The Smiths barely twelve months after Marr first knocked on Morrissey's front door. There are noticeable differences in arrangement and other sonic trickeries distinguishing most of its tracks: on 'The Hand That Rocks The Cradle' we hear Marr's original linear guitar riff; 'These Things Take Time' is announced by a thunderous drum intro; 'What Difference

Does It Make?' adds curves of feedback and falsetto harmonies; 'Reel Around The Fountain' may well be its definitive recording, teasing with a gently effervescent guitar intro, sung with Byronic intensity; 'Hand In Glove' has a clipped intro with vocal and harmonica drenched in reverb; 'Suffer Little Children' is crisper and longer, complete with Marr's original piano epilogue; and 'Pretty Girls Make Graves' has a much folkier rhythm with cello from guest Virginia Astley.

Shortly after the album was finished, Morrissey informed *Melody Maker* that the record was perfect. 'We've done everything exactly right and it'll show.' Unfortunately, his enthusiasm waned considerably over the coming weeks as doubts over the quality of Tate's production began to fester in the corridors of Rough Trade. With hindsight, Andy Rourke philosophically suggests Tate was made a scapegoat for the band's lack of experience: 'I think Johnny and Morrissey wanted to make this big-sounding album that we just weren't capable of doing.' Others have speculated that the fate of the Tate album was part of some Machiavellian plot on Morrissey's part motivated by jealousy of Tate's close rapport with Marr. Rourke, Joyce and manager Joe MOSS all agree there's some truth in this. Just as telling is Marr's later quote to *Sounds*, that 'it meant so much to [Tate] … I felt really bad … particularly as I'd got really friendly with him. But it was a weird period for us.'

For whatever reason, Geoff Travis decided to ask John Porter for a second opinion. As he feared, Porter concurred that the Tate album was 'out of tune and out of time', instead offering to re-record it from scratch himself.

We can only hypothesise as to how The Smiths' career trajectory would have arced had the Tate debut been released instead of Porter's. But, bluntly speaking, the difference between the Tate and Porter albums is that between the (then mutually exclusive) worlds of indie and pop. As warm and exhilarating as they sound, the Tate recordings lacked the necessary carpentry the songs needed to sneak Trojan-horse-style into the 80s mainstream, even if they did capture The

Smiths with a thrilling naturalism Porter often failed to grasp.

Tate was devastated by the decision and could barely bring himself to discuss The Smiths in public again. Speaking to the NME in 1984, he would only comment, 'disappointment is not strong enough a word'. In August the same year Morrissey offered something of a belated olive branch when asked to stand in as a guest singles reviewer for *Melody Maker*, praising Tate's latest solo offering 'Thomas' as 'the best record he has ever appeared on … This should be a sizeable hit should justice prevail. However, we know that it very rarely does.' Indeed, it didn't. After working with The Smiths Tate made two solo albums, Ticket To The Dark (1984) and Liberty (1985), before dropping out of the music business.

The only consolation for Tate was 'Jeane', issued as the B-side to the group's second single as planned. His distinctively different recording of 'Pretty Girls Make Graves' was also issued posthumously on the reverse of October 1987's 'I STARTED SOMETHING I COULDN'T FINISH'. The full Tate album is widely available in umpteen bootleg versions of varying qualities and mixes, not all of which do the original justice. [12, 13, 17, 27, 102, 164, 185, 402, 406]

Taylor, Woodie (Morrissey drummer 1993–94), Another veteran of the UK rockabilly revival scene, Malcolm James 'Woodie' Taylor spent the 1980s drumming for various rockabilly/psychobilly groups, most prominently The Meteors, as well as The Escalators and The Tall Boys. A friend of Boz BOORER, he was recruited to replace Spencer COBRIN for the recording of VAUXHALL AND I in the summer of 1993; the same year Taylor joined Boorer and his wife's rockabilly group, The Shillelagh Sisters, for a tour of Japan.

In early 1994, Morrissey decided to bring back Cobrin for a B-sides session ('MOONRIVER' and 'A SWALLOW ON MY NECK') though his return was only brief. Taylor found himself back in the fold to drum on the 'BOXERS'/'SUNNY' session in the autumn of 1994, as well as the ill-fated residency at Miraval studios in France where a first draft of SOUTHPAW GRAMMAR was taped, then abandoned. The latter would be Taylor's last engagement for Morrissey.

In early 1995, Cobrin was rehired again for the singer's imminent UK tour, staying in the band for his next two albums. 'Morrissey preferred Woodie in the studio but Spencer for live work,' claims bassist Jonny BRIDGWOOD. 'But then he decided he wanted Spencer back. Woodie was perfect for Vauxhall because he was better technically and more subtle. Spencer was a much harder drummer, so it made sense to use him on Southpaw Grammar.'

Two years after his exit from the band, Taylor auctioned the kit he used on all his Morrissey recordings. No longer Woodie, as M. J. Taylor he continues to play drums and is also a respected engineer and producer, writing for and recording with his own group, Comet Gain. [4, 36, 40]

tea, Morrissey's favourite drink. 'I absolutely never get sick of drinking tea,' he explained. 'It's a psychological thing really. It's just very composing and makes me relax. I'm very avid, I have to have at least four pots a day.' Morrissey prefers properly brewed tea in a teapot as opposed to the teabag-squeezed-in-a-mug method. 'You have to heat the pot first with hot water, and then put the teabags in,' he instructs, also stipulating that milk should be added to the cup before the tea is poured, and not vice versa ('proper milk … you can't use the UHT fake stuff'). In terms of blends, Morrissey is 'a devoted Ceylon man' but likes it fairly weak. His former bassist Jonny BRIDGWOOD also recalls the singer drinking the more robust Assam though refusing to accept a cup of Darjeeling claiming 'it's not even tea'. Morrissey has even expressed his wish to patent his own blend. 'That would be nice – Morrissey Tea.' [4, 115, 148, 168, 192, 567]

'Teachers Are Afraid Of The Pupils, The'

(Morrissey/Boorer), From the album SOUTHPAW GRAMMAR (1995). The epic opening track of Morrissey's fifth solo album was The Smiths' 'THE HEADMASTER RITUAL' in reverse, a revenge tragedy in which the fear, humiliation and misery of the classroom is that of the victimised teacher.

By the 90s, the brutal corporal punishment of Morrissey's early 70s schooling had been outlawed. Stripped of such disciplinary aids, the modern teacher was now exposed to all manner of abuse ('mucus on your collar') which they were often unable to redress. Morrissey highlights the conundrum with the chilling parental threat: 'Say the wrong word to our children … we'll have you.' While a vivid portrait of white-collar nervous breakdown, its climactic chant 'to be finished would be a relief' had a more profound meaning. 'There are two levels of interpretation,' explained Morrissey. 'The line in the song context – these teachers who are afraid of their pupils and dream of escaping – and a second more intimate, more personal thought on my life and career. To leave would effectively be a relief. Not to feel all this pressure any more.'[1]

At just over 11 minutes 'The Teachers Are Afraid Of The Pupils' is the longest recording of his career to date. 'Morrissey tends to snatch these arbitrary times,' says engineer Danton Supple. 'We'd often say to him, "How long should this be?", and he'd say, off the top of his head, "11.15". Steve [LILLYWHITE] took him for his word so we'd work to that length. It was the same with the track "SOUTHPAW". There was no reason for it to be that long, but at least "Teachers" had the drama to occupy that time.' Supple also claims that 'Teachers' brought what he describes as 'a slight undercurrent of tension' between guitarists and co-writers Boorer and Alain WHYTE to the surface. 'We were winding up Alain about Boz's "Teachers", saying, "You do realise song royalties are related to song length?" He must have believed us because that's when Alain started coming up with these demos that were all about a quarter of an hour long.'

The backing track closely followed Boorer's demo, a slowly spiralling descent into hell engined by a looped sample of the opening bars of twentieth-century Russian composer Dmitri Shostakovich's Symphony No. 5 in D Minor; according to Jonny BRIDGWOOD, Boorer had experimented with various classical samples during this period, demoing another instrumental featuring a different orchestral work during the preliminary Southpaw Grammar sessions at Miraval studios in France. Buried in the mix towards its end is a sample from *Eight O'Clock Walk*, a 1954 British B-movie starring Richard Attenborough as a London cabbie falsely accused of murdering a young girl; the clip, taken from the beginning of the film, is of a schoolboy reciting a poem about springtime, 'slowed down slightly', explained Morrissey, 'in order to make him sound joyless and put upon, as all children should be'.

An open wound of acrid orchestral grunge, 'The Teachers Are Afraid Of The Pupils' remains one of Morrissey's most impressive and ambitious works. [4, 5, 40, 84, 236, 499]

———

1. In concert Morrissey would sometimes mock its solemnity, substituting the lyric, 'To be *Finnish* would be a relief.'

'Teenage Dad On His Estate' (Morrissey/

Whyte), B-side of 'FIRST OF THE GANG TO DIE' (2004). An amusing comment on the haves envying the freedom of the have-nots, 'Teenage Dad On His Estate' saw Morrissey needle the stereotypical middle-class breadwinner; those who've married out of obligation, now trapped in a soul-destroying job but tortured by the knowledge that working-class teenage dads still weaning themselves off methadone are somehow having the last laugh. The 'Teenage Dad' himself had echoes of 'THE BOY RACER' with his Jensen Interceptor 'runaround', while the song's socio-political thrust attacked the same *Daily Mail* mentality satirised in 'THE SLUM MUMS' from the same period. Whyte's tune skidded over a similar quiet/loud design to 'YOU KNOW I COULDN'T LAST', in places evoking the melodic pathos of his earlier 'THE EDGES ARE NO

LONGER PARALLEL'. Another worthy YOU ARE THE QUARRY contender to slip through the net.

'That Joke Isn't Funny Anymore'

(Morrissey/Marr), The Smiths' eighth single (taken from the album MEAT IS MURDER), released July 1985, highest UK chart position #49. In its scene-setting of a parked car and the careful description of leather passenger seats, 'That Joke Isn't Funny Anymore' immediately recalled the flirtatious liaison of the earlier 'THIS CHARMING MAN'. Though sex is clearly alluded to in its metaphor of driving 'the point home' and its ensuing bliss, the overall tone is far graver as, this time around, Morrissey unapologetically pampers life's complexities. For its closing cri de coeur, he adapted a line from the 1935 film *Alice Adams* where Fred Stone tells Katharine Hepburn, 'I've seen this happen in other people's lives and now it's happening in ours.'

As Morrissey explained, the root of the song was his relationship with the media. 'When I wrote the words,' he said, 'I was just so completely tired of all the same old journalistic questions … this contest of wit, trying to drag me down and prove that I was a complete fake.' In 1998, journalist Dave Simpson was first to infer it may have been much more specific. 'Strong rumours suggest an "intimate friendship" with a journalist around 1984–85,' wrote Simpson, 'and that this person was the subject of "That Joke Isn't Funny Anymore". Nowadays, that person steadfastly refuses to talk about Morrissey.'

The key track from their second album, Marr would later describe it as 'an important, new progression in our dark beauty'. There was, indeed, an intrepid elegance about its slow waltzing melody and a knowing grandeur in its size; just under five minutes and with a false fade-out, suggested by engineer Stephen STREET, similar to that of Elvis PRESLEY's 'Suspicious Minds'. But, as Marr says, there was also a perceptible darkness in its atmosphere, a tremor of foreboding, of imminent danger, of bad times just around the corner; a song with already too much sea water

in its lungs thrashing to the surface for its final breath. As it ends, Morrissey's impassioned groans and Marr's hollering guitar lines reverberate as one, the unmistakable clang from the belfry of human melancholy.

Though one of The Smiths' more obvious masterpieces, it fared less well when released as a single, in part due to their erratic discography. It was five months after Meat Is Murder's release before Rough Trade finally addressed the absence of a tie-in single. Morrissey's choice of 'That Joke' was a surprise to Marr. 'I wasn't expecting it,' he says, 'but I was proud he made that choice. I secretly wanted it to chart because I loved it as a song and I thought it could be our torch song single. Dusty Springfield's "All I See Is You", but with our weird approach. So I harboured that ambition for about two days and then reality struck. Like, why would they play that on daytime Radio 1?'

Why indeed, yet with hindsight the single's failure was to be expected. By July 1985, it was already old news, though more crucially it was the first Smiths single not to feature new and exclusive B-sides but instead four live tracks previously broadcast on Radio 1. This oversight wasn't lost on Marr: 'That's when I realised people weren't just going to buy everything because of the flowers routine.' The seven-inch also chopped off its vital reprise in a half-hearted attempt to make it more radio-friendly (as heard on THE WORLD WON'T LISTEN). With no promotion, plus Morrissey's notorious veto of its scheduled primetime mimed performance on the BBC's *Wogan* chat show (for reasons he never explained, he didn't turn up), 'That Joke Isn't Funny Anymore' became the only Smiths single, other than 'HAND IN GLOVE', not to chart inside the UK top 40. [17, 18, 38, 129, 221, 267, 426, 482]

'That's Entertainment'

(Paul Weller), B-side of 'SING YOUR LIFE' (1991). A surprising cover choice for Morrissey at the time, 'That's Entertainment' was originally recorded by The Jam, the biggest and most important British guitar group before The Smiths. In Morrissey's words, the Woking trio were 'part of that small genuinely British family tree that somebody should document: The Small Faces, Kinks, The Who, early David BOWIE, The Jam. Well, that's all. And me. And perhaps also MADNESS.'

First appearing on The Jam's 1980 album Sound Affects, though only released as a single in Europe it still made number 21 in the UK on the strength of import copies alone. Named after MGM's 1974 compilation of Hollywood musical highlights, Paul Weller maintains he wrote the lyrics in ten minutes sat looking around his Pimlico flat after a night in the pub, a stream of consciousness urban flicker book of random sounds and images. 'The original is a classic,' said Morrissey, 'and Paul Weller is, when he wants to be, a genius.'

Rather than copy The Jam version, Morrissey deconstructed 'That's Entertainment', softening its edges into a reflective acoustic ballad bookended by an odd creaking train noise. 'I wanted to make it different from the original,' he explained, 'but maybe I shouldn't have.' Recorded at the end of the KILL UNCLE sessions, it featured backing vocals from Madness's Cathal SMYTH. 'I don't know why Morrissey asked me to sing on it,' says Smyth. 'I suspect he wanted that laddish edge. One thing he's really good at is taking iconographic moods. He's very clever and discerning about associations.'

Upon Morrissey's request for some added woodwind, co-producer Clive LANGER called Kate St John to Hook End to provide cor anglais. 'It was a bit embarrassing,' remembers Langer, 'because I got her in but then Morrissey wouldn't let her stay for dinner or sit at the table with us.'[1] Comedian Vic REEVES was also present during the session and was thanked on the finished single sleeve under his real name of Jim Moir.

After its release, Morrissey denounced the languid end product as 'completely worthless'. In concert, he tried to make amends with a contrastingly manic punk arrangement (as seen on LIVE IN DALLAS) and continued to praise Weller in the press. 'Hopefully we, Paul and I, will record a duet,' said Morrissey, divulging his intention

to perform with Weller at the August 1992 Madstock weekend at Finsbury Park. Weller became aware of this in the run-up to the event when he and Morrissey found themselves staying in the same hotel (sadly Weller can't recall the exact location). Though they'd crossed paths several times before, Morrissey was characteristically cautious in his approach. One morning, Weller awoke to find a postcard slipped under the door of his room. The handwriting was Morrissey's: 'The thought of us on stage together is positively hallucinatory.' When Weller tried to contact him in return, he was told Morrissey had already checked out.

Though their positively hallucinatory duet never happened, it didn't taint Morrissey's love of The Jam ('one of my favourite groups of all time') or Weller. In 1995, Morrissey even credited Weller with the best piece of advice he'd ever received: 'Just watch those fuckin' flowers.' [15, 36, 90, 150, 154, 569]

---

1. Kate St John had previously been a member of The Dream Academy who in 1985 released a cover of The Smiths' 'PLEASE PLEASE PLEASE LET ME GET WHAT I WANT'.

'That's How People Grow Up' (Morrissey/Boorer),

Morrissey's 34th solo single (first included on the compilation GREATEST HITS, repeated on the album YEARS OF REFUSAL), released February 2008, highest UK chart position #14. A song which 'fell out' of Morrissey's head like 'a shower of panic', 'That's How People Grow Up' was his darkly comic résumé of the hard knocks that made him the man he is. Its catalogue of pessimism was strewn with knowing self-parody: the chin-jutting gurn of 'sunlit dreeeeam', the absurd account of breaking his spine in a 'THERE IS A LIGHT'-style car crash and the delightfully daft use of 'sweetie'.

Ushered in by the Klaus NOMI-esque siren song of Kristeen YOUNG, Boorer's accordion-powered tune had a black humour of its own, a garage band Jacques Brel sent to lift the spirits of a TB ward too weak to protest. Issued as the trailer single of his Greatest Hits collection, the absence of new studio B-sides in favour of live tracks may have accounted for its moderate chart success. A whole year later, 'That's How People Grow Up' reappeared on Years Of Refusal, instigating petty mithering in some quarters but giving due prominence to a song Morrissey has since named as his favourite solo recording. [245, 579]

Thatcher, Margaret, British Conservative prime minister (the first woman to reach the post) from 1979 to 1990 whose hardliner right-wing ideology, Thatcherism, aroused passionate hostility among the strongly politicised youth of the 1980s.

Thatcher believed in the needs of the individual over the needs of society: as she famously told that unlikely hotbed of political discussion *Woman's Own* in 1987, 'There is no such thing as Society.' Thatcherism favoured the wealthy and entrepreneurial while targeting the poor and communal, destroying trade unionism, privatising public sector industries, creating mass unemployment and introducing injurious benefit reforms. A saviour to the country's upper and aspirational middle classes, Thatcher was vilified by the left as an enemy of the underprivileged working classes. She was, therefore, a natural nemesis to Morrissey, the rest of The Smiths and the majority of their audience who similarly opposed her pro-nuclear policy and her government's controversial introduction of the anti-gay legislation known as Clause 28.

The Smiths' debut single, 'HAND IN GLOVE', was released during the 1983 General Election campaign which saw Thatcher cruise into her second term with a landslide victory. After four years in office, she'd already been attacked umpteen times on record, and in print, by various groups and singers from The Specials to Paul Weller and Elvis Costello, though it took the arrival of Morrissey to publicly call for her assassination in 1984. 'The entire history of Margaret Thatcher is one of violence and oppression and horror,' he proclaimed. 'I think that we must not lie back and cry about it. She's only one person, and she can be destroyed.' He further prayed that 'somewhere' was an equivalent of

Bobby Kennedy's assassin Sirhan Sirhan willing to do the same to Thatcher. Asked how he'd react if a Smiths fan took him at his word and killed her in his name, Morrissey retorted, 'I'd obviously marry [that] person.'

On 12 October 1984, Morrissey's wish very nearly came true when an IRA bomb ripped apart Brighton's Grand Hotel where Thatcher and most of her cabinet were staying for that week's Conservative Party Conference. The bomb killed five people: Thatcher wasn't one of them. 'The sorrow of the Brighton bombing is that she escaped unscathed,' mourned Morrissey. 'The sorrow is that she's still alive. But I feel relatively happy about it. I think that for once the IRA were accurate in selecting their targets.' When Marr read Morrissey's latter comments as printed in *Melody Maker*, he immediately rang the singer up to congratulate him.

The following year Morrissey toyed with calling The Smiths' third album MARGARET ON THE GUILLOTINE (in due course THE QUEEN IS DEAD) only to save the title for the closing track of his 1988 solo debut, VIVA HATE. In the interim, Thatcher won her third General Election in June 1987 and had given the green light to Clause 28, an amendment in the Local Government Act which forbade schools and any other local authority from 'intentionally promoting' homosexuality or its 'acceptability ... as a pretended family relationship'. By the time Morrissey got round to recording 'Margaret On The Guillotine', he'd evidently had enough.

'I find the entire Thatcher syndrome very stressful and evil and all those other words,' he explained, 'but I think there's very little that people can do about it. The most perfect example, I suppose, is Clause 28. I think that absolutely embodies Thatcher's very nature and her quite natural hatred ... But protesting, to me, is pointless because people suffer this delusion that the very issue of Clause 28 is actually anything to do with the British people. They have no say in the matter. I think that's been the story throughout Thatcher's reign, so I don't see the point of wandering around Marble Arch in a pink T-shirt,

'There I've Said It Again', 1959 single by US soul singer Sam Cooke listed among Morrissey's favourite records. Written in the 1940s by David Mann and Redd Evans, the song was the B-side to the Johnny Cash-style novelty romp 'One Hour Ahead Of The Posse', released in the UK on the HMV label. A dreamily romantic rock and roll ballad, 'There I've Said It Again' sees Cooke deliver a simple heartfelt pledge: 'I love you/No use to pretend/There! – I've said it again'. Cooke's version wasn't a hit though Bobby Vinton would later take the song to number one in the US in January 1964 prior to the onslaught of the BEATLES-led British Invasion. In December of that same year, Cooke was shot dead by a woman in alleged 'self-defence' at the age of 33 in highly suspicious circumstances. Morrissey's love for this relatively obscure Cooke single may have been the influence of Johnny Marr, who named Cooke as one of his favourite singers during the early days of The Smiths. [168, 175]

carrying books by [*radical feminist*] Andrea Dworkin.'

'Margaret On The Guillotine' would be one of the most explicit protest songs during Thatcher's 11 years in office, its malicious sentiment – 'when will you die?' – equalled only by Elvis Costello's 'Tramp The Dirt Down' released a year later.

Nonetheless, it was shocking to hear Morrissey express something dangerously close to compassionate respect for Thatcher after she was ousted from Number 10 by her own government in November 1990 and replaced as prime minister by John Major. 'I found it astonishingly un-English and very strange,' he confessed. 'Her policies, I thought, were the work of the devil. I thought she was purely, intentionally evil. But it's impossible to deny that she was a phenomenon, and you couldn't help but over-discuss her. The blunder wasn't that she was decapitated, but that she hasn't effectively been replaced. I think that John Major is in nobody's mind a prime minister. He seems to have no human presence at all.' Morrissey also admitted that he firmly agreed with Thatcher's stance against Britain adopting a single European currency. [71, 90, 122, 135, 153, 203, 204, 208]

'There Is A Light That Never Goes Out'

(**Morrissey/Marr**), From the album THE QUEEN IS DEAD (1986). The national anthem of Smithdom and, for the majority of their audience, Morrissey and Marr's greatest, and most meaningful, collaboration. In the aftermath of their split, and throughout Morrissey's solo career, 'There Is A Light That Never Goes Out' has grown in stature as a hugely symbolic hymn, be it in memoriam of the group themselves or a vow of undying faith in their former singer: an equivalent 'You'll Never Walk Alone'.

It is, first and foremost, a love song, but a love song like no other which finds sublime romance in an imminent road traffic accident. Morrissey inverts the traditional 60s 'death disc' scenario as typified by The Shangri-Las' tales of young love cut short through careless driving. As the car passenger nervously fretting whether to confess his deepest desire for his driver, death is no longer a tragic prospect but a blissful climax uniting Morrissey and his true love for all eternity. For all its surface morbidity, almost bordering on the absurd in its chorus prayers of collision with an oncoming vehicle, 'There Is A Light' is an emotionally overwhelming celebration of what it feels to be hopelessly in love.

Morrissey himself would refer to its lyrics as 'like somebody hitting me with a hammer', in particular the lines where he contemplates making his move in 'a darkened underpass', which he admitted he could 'never bear to listen to because I find them so close'.

The popular, and heavily romanticised, interpretation of this closeness is that 'There Is A Light' is a love song to Johnny Marr, who regularly ferried the singer around by car. Asked in 2005 if this was the case, Morrissey stated, 'It wasn't and it isn't.'

'I never spent much time thinking about that stuff,' adds Marr. 'It was only after the band split that these theories came out. Only Morrissey knows. When we recorded it I wasn't there thinking, "Aw, this is about me," or anything. If it is, great. If it's not, then it's still a great song. I'm sure there's worse songs written about me so it might as well be a good one. But, for the record, I wasn't the only person who used to drive Morrissey around by car, put it that way.'

Beyond its obvious autobiographical influence, 'There Is A Light' was a rare instance where Morrissey drew from the lyrics of his favourite group, the NEW YORK DOLLS. In their 'Lonely Planet Boy', David Johansen sings of 'drivin' in your car' and asks 'How could you be drivin' down by my home, when you know I ain't got one?' It's also likely that the opening lines were, in part, inspired by the film SATURDAY NIGHT AND SUNDAY MORNING, in which Shirley Anne Field nags Albert FINNEY, 'Why don't you take me where it's lively and there's plenty of people?' Early takes of the song also clarified the title with the line, 'There is a light *in your eye* and it never goes out,' bringing to mind 'the light of love is in your eyes' from The Shirelles' 'Will You Love Me Tomorrow?'

Written in the late summer of 1985, Marr vividly recalls the time he first played the tune to Morrissey during a lucrative night's writing session which also produced 'FRANKLY, MR SHANKLY' and 'I KNOW IT'S OVER'.

'Morrissey was sat on a coffee table, perched on the edge,' says Marr. 'I was sat with my guitar on a chair directly in front of him. He had a Sony Walkman recording, waiting to hear what I was gonna pull out. So I said, "Well, I've got this one," and I started playing these chords. He just looked at me as I was playing. It was as if he daren't speak, in case the spell was broken.'

Adapting its stuttering intro from The Rolling Stones' cover of Marvin Gaye's 'Hitch Hike' (also utilised by The Velvet Underground on 'There She Goes Again'), Marr's melody was in keeping with his other minor key tunes of the same period; musicologists analysing it in terms of chord groupings will discover that 'There Is A Light' shares many characteristics with 'RUBBER RING' and 'BIGMOUTH STRIKES AGAIN'.

'When we first played it, I thought it was the best song I'd ever heard,' adds Marr. A surviving rehearsal tape attests to his enthusiasm, captured at the end telling Morrissey, 'Your singing on the end of that was *brilliant*!' Progressing from his earlier experiments on the instrumental 'OSCILLATE WILDLY', Marr furnished the final recording with an exquisite orchestral arrangement, created synthetically using an Emulator and credited on the album sleeve to the fictitious HATED SALFORD ENSEMBLE.

Within ROUGH TRADE, 'There Is A Light' was the favoured candidate for The Queen Is Dead's trailer single. It was Marr alone who dug his heels in by insisting that 'Bigmouth Strikes Again' be released instead. 'I was a bit unpopular in *certain quarters* for that,' he infers. 'But to this day I think I was right. As a fan of records I had this thing that all my favourite albums nearly always have one track which should have been a single. We always had that. "WELL I WONDER" on MEAT IS MURDER is the same. "There Is A Light" is exactly that. It exists on the cusp. It's not just your regular old album track. It's a glimmery super album track. I recognised that straight away and I don't regret that decision.'

What's most interesting about the song's subsequent eminence in The Smiths' canon is the fact that, at the time, though 'There Is A Light' was a staple of their final tours of 1986, it was never granted encore status and always played mid-set. Uniquely, and very significantly, it was The Smiths' audience rather than they themselves who seized upon it as *the* song which personified the group. The first indication that this was the case was John PEEL's annual end-of-year listener poll, the Festive 50. The Smiths claimed half of the top 12 entries, with 'There Is A Light' at number one.

Five years after the split, it was issued as a posthumous single by WEA to promote 1992's Best II compilation, reaching number 25. Marr was first to revisit the song in concert in 2001 with Crowded House singer Neil Finn (as featured on the latter's 7 Worlds Collide album), though, undeniably, its anthemic reputation has been cemented by Morrissey's solo performances. Introducing it into his set in 2002, 'There Is A Light' triggered unprecedented hysteria among his audience as an encore of biblical proportions. Consequently, its most successful single placing to date remains Morrissey's version from 2005's LIVE AT EARLS COURT album, released as a double A-side with the PATTI SMITH cover 'REDONDO BEACH', reaching number 11.

While neither Morrissey nor Marr has ever nominated it as his personal favourite, the halo of audience affection surrounding 'There Is A Light That Never Goes Out' has placed it on a sacrosanct pedestal out of reach of everything else they ever recorded. For that reason, it stands, whether figuratively or literally, as the ultimate Morrissey/Marr love song. Or, perhaps, as Andy Rourke prefers to surmise, 'the indie "Candle In The Wind"'. [14, 17, 18, 28, 38, 50,93, 517, 548]

'There Speaks A True Friend' (Morrissey/Whyte), B-side of 'YOU'RE THE ONE FOR ME, FATTY' (1992). Taking its title from the script of one of his favourite films, THE KILLING OF SISTER GEORGE (as spoken by actress Coral Browne), 'There Speaks A True Friend' was Morrissey's farewell to a special acquaintance who'd gone to great pains to list his faults only to walk out before they'd had a chance to help him 'put them right'. A potentially intriguing confessional, sadly the shabby tune sorely lacked the brawn of Morrissey's other Mick RONSON productions. Despite vain efforts to enliven it with guitar solos and a weird, abrupt ending (Morrissey's idea as he didn't like its original prolonged outro), it remains an inconsequential leftover. [5, 517]

'There's A Place In Hell For Me And My Friends' (Morrissey/Nevin), From the album KILL UNCLE (1991). Over a simple, atmospheric piano – a home recording taken from Nevin's original demo – and minimal added orchestration, Morrissey signed off his second album with this short but supremely touching ode to his own eternal damnation. 'A lot of people have remarked that it's a song about AIDS,' he added, 'which it isn't, but I can see it applying in that case.' In concert, the song was played in a clunkier guitar arrangement (as heard on the live B-side of 'MY LOVE LIFE'), which, alas, destroyed the exquisitely brittle church-pew hush of the original. [22, 437]

'These Things Take Time' (Morrissey/Marr), B-side of 'WHAT DIFFERENCE DOES IT MAKE?' (1984). Described by Morrissey as a song about 'the wounds of unfulfilment', 'These Things Take Time' was characteristic of other early Smiths songs in drawing on his formative sexual experiences; memories of carnal initiation with a femme fatale on a railway embankment, succumbing to his own celibate cry (via Julie Andrews in The Sound Of Music) and mourning another failed relationship sweetened only by the dull memory of drunken bliss.

Equally typical was its collage of quotes from his main sources of the period: the title stems from Shelagh DELANEY's The Lion In Love, the opening paraphrase of 'The Battle Hymn Of The Republic' is probably inspired by Marjorie Rosen's POPCORN VENUS (as quoted from 1973's The Year Of The Woman) while another lyric is modelled on a sentence in Molly Haskell's FROM REVERENCE TO RAPE ('But even then she knew where she had come from and where she belonged'). There's even the echo of James DEAN, who in Rebel Without A Cause informs Natalie Wood, 'I know a place where we can go.'

Written in the winter of 1982 and rehearsed in the same batch as 'JEANE', the 'WONDERFUL WOMAN' prototype 'What Do You See In Him?' and the short-lived 'A MATTER OF OPINION', early drafts were slightly slower with Morrissey hollering 'I'm saved! I'm saved! You took my hand!' In its aggressive yet decorative chords and stuttering drum pauses, Marr's tune hinted at the punchier 'HAND IN GLOVE' to come and was destined to become 'a cemented favourite' of Morrissey's. Considered for their original debut album produced by Troy TATE, it was finally issued as a 12-inch B-side, as heard on LOUDER THAN BOMBS. An earlier, rougher but arguably better version recorded for a June 1983 David Jensen BBC session is included on HATFUL OF HOLLOW. [12, 17, 406, 431, 545].

Thesiger, Ernest, See OLD DARK HOUSE, THE.

'This Charming Man' (Morrissey/Marr),
The Smiths' second single, released November 1983, highest UK chart position #25. Cover star: Jean MARAIS.

Exhibit A in the case for Morrissey's recognition as the most original pop lyricist of the late twentieth-century is the first line of 'This Charming Man'. Rock and roll convention dictates that a classic pop record should begin, 'Since my baby left me' or 'Yeah! Yeah! Yeah!' or 'Well I told you once and I told you twice'. Morrissey, and only Morrissey, could dare defy tradition with the priceless opening gambit, 'Punctured bicycle'.

A deflated tyre is the catalyst for a humorous reflection on the narrator's youth and inexperience until a chance offer of a lift from a 'charming' stranger becomes their erotically charged opportunity to cross the threshold into manhood. This flirtatious opening mise en scène aside, any further narrative reading of the song was confused by its sudden juxtaposition of seemingly unrelated images and dialogue which even Marr had to agree was 'flummoxing'. 'It's just a collection of lines that were very important,' Morrissey explained, 'and they just seemed to stitch themselves perfectly under the umbrella of "This Charming Man".'

Included in its lyrical stitch-work was a quote from the 1972 film of Anthony Shaffer's play *Sleuth* starring Laurence Olivier and Michael Caine: 'A jumped-up pantry boy who doesn't know his place.' 'It [refers to] a low-life street character,' the singer elaborated. 'I'm sure there are worse things that you could be rather than a jumped-up pantry boy, but it just seemed very rhythmical at the time.' Though he'd later admit its *Sleuth* origins, the same chorus contains an uncanny similarity with the plot of Henry Green's *Loving*, a 1945 novel about life below stairs in an Irish stately home involving a scheming pantry boy and the theft of a ring.

Less obvious is its possible debt to the 1961 film version of Shelagh DELANEY's *A Taste Of Honey* where Rita Tushingham as Jo tells her classmates she can't come out dancing that night: 'I haven't got any clothes to wear for one thing.' Morrissey still insisted his similar lyric came 'from total experience', explaining how 'for years and years I never had a job, or any money. Consequently I never had any clothes whatsoever. I found that on those very rare occasions when I did get invited anywhere I would constantly sit down and say, "Good heavens, I couldn't possibly go to this place tonight because I don't have any clothes, I don't have any shoes." So I'd miss out on all those foul parties. It was really quite a blessing in disguise.'

'Third Finger, Left Hand', B-side of Martha & The Vandellas' 1967 Tamla Motown single 'Jimmy Mack', which Morrissey once casually referred to as 'my favourite record of all time'. Blessed by the Midas touch of Motown's hitmaker trio Holland/Dozier/Holland, the tune was a romantic young girl's wedding fantasy ('At last my dreams come true/Today he said "I do"'). Despite Morrissey's own negative feelings towards marriage, he claimed the song had the mystical power to 'lift me from the most doom-laden depression' and later listed it as one of his cherished 'Singles to be cremated with'. Due to its popularity on the northern soul circuit, the record was re-released in August 1970 (still with 'Jimmy Mack' as the A-side, even though most preferred 'Third Finger, Left Hand' on the reverse), reaching number 21 in the UK, exactly as it had done first time around. [175, 196]

Though recorded and released prior to their eventual debut album, in writing chronology 'This Charming Man' came *after* the majority of songs featured on 1984's The Smiths bar 'Still Ill' and marked the beginning of a new phase in the Morrissey/Marr songbook; moving away from the ominous Mancunian gloom of their early repertoire into more playful pop territory. Composed in just 20 minutes one evening in early September 1983 in preparation for their second John PEEL BBC radio session, Marr would eventually admit that its crystalline melody was stirred by a healthy sense of one-upmanship against Roddy Frame, singer/songwriter with fellow ROUGH TRADE signings Aztec Camera. Hearing Frame's irresistibly perky April 1983 single 'Walk Out To Winter', Marr was inspired to go one better. Where Frame's joyful plucking merely tapped toes, Marr's response tore ligaments with its bejewelled jangling bliss.

Its creation coincided with the *Sun*'s false allegations of the group's 'child-sex' songs which dissuaded Rough Trade from releasing 'REEL AROUND THE FOUNTAIN' as their second single. 'This Charming Man' was a heaven-sent substitute, immediately wooing label boss Geoff Travis in its original, gentler, Peel session form (as heard on HATFUL OF HOLLOW).

The task of turning the song into a hit single was handed to producer John PORTER, whose ambition and perfectionism matched that of Morrissey and Marr. A first attempt at London's Matrix studios didn't quite live up to expectations. Travis duly agreed to finance a re-recording back at Strawberry studios in Manchester where they previously made 'HAND IN GLOVE'. Both versions were eventually released on the original 12-inch single, but it was the second 'Manchester' take chosen as the definitive A-side which, rightly, earned the *NME*'s praise as 'one of those moments when a vivid, electric awareness of the power of music is born or renewed'.

Porter turned up the contrast in the tune's inherent Motown melody – a speedy Mancunian hustle through The Four Tops' 'I Can't Help Myself' driven by snapping drums and popping

bass – also introducing its crucial rhythmic pauses and encouraging Marr to add as many overdubs as it took to build his Taj Mahal: hidden among the dizzying harmonic fireworks is the sound of kitchen cutlery being dropped on to one of his gaffer-taped guitars. For Marr, the record was as much a triumph for Morrissey, naming it as the first where his partner came into his own as 'a true, wonderful vocalist'. Vocally and musically, lyrically and melodically, 'This Charming Man' personified pop in all its secret paradise, proving itself as much by being the first record to take The Smiths inside both the top 30 and the nation's living rooms via *TOP OF THE POPS*.

One month after the original single's release, Rough Trade issued a club 12-inch remixed by New York DJ François Kervorkian featuring two different 'Vocal' and 'Instrumental' edits. Both Morrissey and Marr would criticise the Kervorkian single as a piece of marketing gimmickry 'against our principles' though the record itself wasn't without merit, isolating some of Marr's weirder guitar techniques (cutlery clangs included) and turning Rourke's spine-tingling bass line into the star attraction. Strangely, in view of their comments back in the day, when the 'New York Vocal' remix was chosen by Warners for the two-disc edition of 2008's The Sound Of The Smiths compilation, neither Morrissey nor Marr vetoed its inclusion.

The timeless potency of 'This Charming Man' was demonstrated in August 1992 when re-released to promote Warners' first posthumous Smiths collection, Best I. The song reached number eight, not only the group's highest charting single to date but also tying with 'THE MORE YOU IGNORE ME' as Morrissey's biggest UK hit for the whole of the 1990s. [12, 13, 17, 18, 27, 229, 270, 315, 419, 446, 551, 554]

'This Is Not Your Country' (Morrissey/ Whyte), B-side of 'SATAN REJECTED MY SOUL' (1997). Coming five years after the 1992 racism row sparked by the *NME* Madstock debacle, the title of 'This Is Not Your Country' sounded further cause for controversy. Doubly ominous

was the fact that the line originated from the script of the Australian neo-Nazi drama, ROMPER STOMPER, Morrissey's most recently named 'favourite film' at the time.

Mercifully, 'This Is Not Your Country' wasn't a song about racism. Originally titled 'Belfast', it dealt instead with political discrimination of another kind: the then-unresolved troubles in Northern Ireland and their coverage by the mainland UK media. Morrissey paints a grim tableau of life in Belfast under British army occupation where road blocks, barbed wire and gun-toting soldiers are standard scenery, then condemning the 'BBC scum' whom he accuses of having scant regard for the local victims of sectarian violence, dismissing the situation as 'old news'.[1] At over seven minutes 'This Is Not Your Country' positioned itself as a Morrissey epic, yet in execution Whyte's maudlin tune, somewhere in the trough between 'Greensleeves' and 'Hotel California', felt somewhat overstretched.

Subsequent events in the Irish peace process after the creation of the 1998 'Good Friday Agreement' may have outdated its lyrics, though as a passionately political diatribe 'This Is Not Your Country' still has relevance to the British Army's needless occupation of other foreign territories. What's most interesting about the song is that it was the last new Morrissey track to be released for the best part of seven years. It therefore seemed apt that when he returned in 2004 he did so with a song resuming its themes of republican political anger and ancestral pride, 'IRISH BLOOD, ENGLISH HEART'. [40, 191, 547]

---

1. Asked to justify the phrase 'BBC scum', Morrissey made light of the issue, joking, 'You wouldn't ask this question if you'd ever sampled the food in the BBC canteen.'

'This Night Has Opened My Eyes'

(Morrissey/Marr), From the compilation album HATFUL OF HOLLOW (1984). Inspired by Shelagh DELANEY's *A Taste Of Honey*, Morrissey openly admitted that 'This Night Has Opened My Eyes' was his attempt to '[put] the entire play to words'.

Using Delaney's characters and dialogue as a model, Morrissey's lyrics are a chilling deliberation on an unwanted pregnancy, imagining a young mother's desperation as she contemplates dumping or even drowning the baby. The mood is intensified by Marr's majestically woeful melody, something close to Bacharach and David's 'Walk On By' after being dredged through the murky depths of the Salford canal.

Although Delaney's input is great enough to warrant a third composer credit, the song's title was actually taken from a different dramatic source, the 1962 film of Eugene O'Neill's play LONG DAY'S JOURNEY INTO NIGHT, where the line is spoken by actor Jason Robards. The lyrics also borrow from singer Janis IAN, adopting the phrase 'grown man of 25' from her 1974 song 'Stars', a favourite of Morrissey's.

Written in early September 1983 among a batch of new songs for their fourth BBC radio session, due to the current tabloid farrago over the supposed 'paedophilic' content of 'HANDSOME DEVIL' and 'REEL AROUND THE FOUNTAIN', session producer Roger Pusey expressed concern over the opening description of immersing a newborn baby's head in a river. Morrissey had to reassure the sensitive Pusey of the song's honest intent before they could finish the track.

It wasn't until July 1984 that The Smiths got round to recording the song properly with John PORTER as a proposed B-side to a single release of 'NOWHERE FAST', which never materialised. As a result, the Porter recording was shelved while the Pusey BBC version was finally made available on 1984's Hatful Of Hollow compilation. Strangely, although it had been a setlist staple for most of 1984, after its vinyl release The Smiths only ever played the song twice in concert, the last being their final gig at Brixton Academy on 12 December 1986. 'There was a sense of resolve and closure,' says Marr, 'which is why we played that song that night. I remember when we made the decision to do "This Night Has Opened My Eyes" feeling a strong sense of awareness of our own history.' [17, 19, 206, 526, 544]

Thunders, Johnny, See NEW YORK DOLLS.

'To Me You Are A Work Of Art'

(Morrissey/Whyte), From the album RINGLEADER OF THE TORMENTORS (2006). With a title suggestive of Oscar WILDE's philosophy for the use of the young that 'One should either be a work of art, or wear a work of art', this was further grist to the mill for those who interpreted the contents of the Ringleader album as evidence that Morrissey had found a 'special somebody', in this case one who can 'soothe' him. Yet, being Morrissey, things are never straightforward, the sting being his inability to fully reciprocate their love because he hasn't a heart to give. In context of his poetic peaks as a lyricist, admittedly his use of the phrase 'it makes me puke' as a reaction to the state of the planet seemed a touch crass. Nevertheless, 'To Me You Are A Work Of Art' was among the album's better songs, helped by another simple but mesmeric Alain Whyte riff sharing something of the desert heat of 'GANGLORD' written during the same period. [393]

To Sir, With Love, 1967 school/musical drama

listed among Morrissey's favourite films. The story of a black engineer turned supply teacher (Sidney Poitier) who manages to tame an unruly class of problem teenagers in an East End London school, *To Sir, With Love* shared a recurring theme in Morrissey's teenage reading matter (e.g. Esther Rothman's *THE ANGEL INSIDE WENT SOUR*), also anticipating the lyrics of his own 'THE TEACHERS ARE AFRAID OF THE PUPILS'. The film is an idealistic interpretation of E. R. Braithwaite's autobiographical novel, its serious social commentary on the education system and racial discrimination tempered by its 'swinging' pop soundtrack and the presence of LULU who sings its famous signature tune – a record Morrissey himself confessed to being 'gaga over' as a 21-year-old. Towards the end of the film, Poitier is seen stepping off a number 23 bus to go to the funeral of a pupil's mother in Wapping, turning off Tench Street down Reardon Street. Morrissey would pay homage to the film with a 1990 photo session taken on the same street corner. [227, 334, 556]

Tobias, Jesse (Morrissey guitarist and co-writer

2004–), The most significant change in Morrissey's band in the 00s was the accidental arrival of Tex-Mex guitarist Jesse Tobias, prompted by the dramatic departure of long-serving co-writer Alain WHYTE at the beginning of 2004's YOU ARE THE QUARRY tour. Whyte's initial replacement was Nottinghamshire's Barrie Cadogan who pluckily filled in for ten summer festival dates in the UK and Europe. When the tour returned to America in mid-July, the 32-year-old Tobias took over as Whyte's permanent replacement and in time would himself assume full co-writer status.

A seasoned session musician who'd previously worked with the Red Hot Chili Peppers and Alanis Morissette, when Tobias joined Morrissey he was in the process of an amicable divorce from his wife, singer/songwriter Angie Hart, also his partner in a musical duo called Splendid. Their final EP together, 2004's States Of Awake, featured multi-musician Michael FARRELL, who had since become Morrissey's touring keyboard player and would provide the bridge for Tobias's recruitment. Relatively young, handsome, well built and of Mexican ethnicity, Tobias immediately appealed to Morrissey's concert aesthetic and proved himself a competent live guitarist.

In due course, Tobias began submitting music and would play a major part in the sound and style of 2006's RINGLEADER OF THE TORMENTORS, writing five of its 12 tracks plus a handful of B-sides. 'Personally and musically, Jesse has made a big impact,' Morrissey announced, even referring to Tobias as his 'new muse'. '[Jesse] has a very strong sense of pop melody,' he elaborated, 'but his playing is very guttural and very deep. So the fusion of the deepness and the pop melody I thought was enchanting.'

Opinion on the Morrissey/Tobias composer credit is divided between those who embrace the unvaryingly aggressive edge his songs have brought to the singer's repertoire and those, like this author, for whom they often lack melodic subtlety, in the worst instances veering towards the unpleasantly viscous. Clearly Morrissey thinks and hears otherwise and his fondness for Tobias's suet-pudding punk is demonstrated by the fact that all four Ringleader singles were Tobias offerings. Perhaps pre-empting exactly this kind of comment, he made a point of refuting 'poisonous assumptions' that Tobias had 'replaced' Whyte as his main co-writer. 'I would like to say that this isn't true,' he told TRUE-TO-YOU.NET. 'There is no *replacing* and there is nothing but harmony amongst all the players.'

Regardless, while Tobias has yet to demonstrate he's capable of writing anything other than ham-fisted guitar rock, his work on 2009's YEARS OF REFUSAL was much bolder, especially 'ALL YOU NEED IS ME' and 'I'M OK BY MYSELF', his finest co-writes thus far. Upon the latter album's release, when asked about Tobias Morrissey surmised, 'I simply liked him and he fitted in very well.' Like the rest of his band, Tobias stripped off for the naked group portrait inside the seven-inch vinyl of 'I'M THROWING MY ARMS AROUND PARIS': trivia fans may like to know that the old DECCA single covering his private parts appears to be Marianne FAITHFULL's 'This Little Bird'. [93, 116, 242, 461, 480]

'**Tomorrow**' (Morrissey/Whyte), From the album YOUR ARSENAL (1992). Coming after the blind faith of 'I KNOW IT'S GONNA HAPPEN SOMEDAY', Morrissey ended his third solo album in characteristically doubtful mood, begging an unrequited love to embrace him in the hope of appeasing the physical pains ravaging his 'shiftless body'. Though it shares a title with a 1966 Sandie SHAW single, lyrically it has more in common with 'Tomorrow Never Comes', a country standard popularised by Glen Campbell and Elvis PRESLEY which shares the line 'tell me that you love me'. Yet for all its apparent anguish, Morrissey skilfully throws in a coquettish U-turn towards the finish: 'I never said I wanted to ... well, did I?'

Whyte's tune strives boldly towards brighter horizons it knows it may never find, an optimistic jangle eventually stumbling to a halt, straining to hear the faint merriment of a distant piano. The latter, though much less pronounced, was very subtly reminiscent of Marr's 'ASLEEP' and a parallel piano coda attached to early versions of 'SUFFER LITTLE CHILDREN'. Also of note is Gary DAY's power ball bass line, very similar to that of 'Click Click', a 1980 album track by Birmingham ska band The Beat.

As rousing a finale as Your Arsenal deserved, 'Tomorrow' was later released in the US as a single. Its accompanying promo video remains one of Morrissey's best, singing to camera while walking through the old town backstreets of Nice in France as his band horse around behind him. Though it was the only Your Arsenal track not to be included on the live album BEETHOVEN WAS DEAF, 'Tomorrow' has proven a concert favourite, still turning up in Morrissey's setlists as recently as 2008. [5]

'**Tony The Pony**' (Morrissey/Nevin), B-side of 'OUR FRANK' (1991). A curious Morrissey sketch about sibling jealousy and its impact on the 'gullible' and 'fucked up' Tony of the title, the song was an early contender for KILL UNCLE until Morrissey was nagged by déja vu. 'Listening back to it, he said, "I've heard that sort of thing before,"' claims drummer Andrew PARESI. 'He instantly went off it.'

'Tony The Pony' was issued instead on the 'Our Frank' 12-inch with the phrase 'drunker quicker' from its lyrics carved into the vinyl matrix. In America, Sire Records added it to the end of Kill Uncle, reportedly without Morrissey's consent. The tune's jumping bass riff would be recycled by Mark Nevin on the later 'PREGNANT FOR THE LAST TIME'. [22, 25]

Top Of The Pops, BBC television's premier weekly half-hour pop show, launched on 1 January 1964 and originally broadcast from Manchester. Moving to London, it entered its heyday in the early 70s with the advent of glam rock, bringing the pomp and glory of David BOWIE, Marc BOLAN and ROXY MUSIC to 15 million viewers, the young Morrissey and even younger Marr included. In particular, Marr cites the first time he witnessed T.Rex perform 'Metal Guru' on the show in 1972 as a pivotal moment in his childhood: aged only eight, he was so stunned that afterwards he rode his pushbike in a post-Bolan daze until it was dark, when he realised he was lost, miles from home.

The beauty of *Top Of The Pops* was that, good or bad, it acted as a barometer of public tastes and changing trends, its content entirely dictated by that week's top 40 singles chart. Punk rock made it customary to either ridicule or, in the case of The Clash, boycott the show altogether, though given the opportunity to appear everyone from Howard DEVOTO's Magazine to COCKNEY REJECTS eagerly accepted. In 1980, three years before Morrissey first appeared on the programme, he referred to *Top Of The Pops* as something of a guilty pleasure when writing to pen pal Robert MACKIE: 'Yes, I watch it, damnit.'

For The Smiths, their debut *Top Of The Pops* appearance in November 1983 represented a vital transition from a cult John PEEL indie band to national pop stars. In their first half-dozen visits to the show in less than a year, Morrissey rotated an iconic array of aesthetic props – flowers, a hearing aid and various other bits of foliage dangling from the rear of his trousers – in his words 'to bring some life into *Top Of The Pops*'.

Always severely critical of the programme, by the early 90s Morrissey decided that '[it] finished in 1985. I don't feel that it actually exists any more … now *nothing* will induce me to watch *Top Of The Pops*.' The BBC experimented with various changes in format and time slot in vain efforts to 'modernise' and 'reinvent' the programme, eventually shunting it to Sunday nights in 2005 before putting it out of its misery in July 2006 after 32 years.

The Smiths appeared on the show 11 times in total: 'THIS CHARMING MAN' (November 1983); 'WHAT DIFFERENCE DOES IT MAKE?' (January and February 1984); 'HAND IN GLOVE' with Sandie SHAW (April 1984), 'HEAVEN KNOWS I'M MISERABLE NOW' (May and June 1984); Morrissey's momentous shirt-ripping 'Marry Me' moment with 'WILLIAM, IT WAS REALLY NOTHING' (August 1984); 'HOW SOON IS NOW?' (February 1985); 'THE BOY WITH THE THORN IN HIS SIDE' (October 1985); 'SHOPLIFTERS OF THE WORLD UNITE' (February 1987) and their final television appearance, 'SHEILA TAKE A BOW' (April 1987).

Morrissey also appeared in the *Top Of The Pops* studio 11 times as a solo artist: alone in a QUEEN IS DEAD T-shirt for 'EVERYDAY IS LIKE SUNDAY' (June 1988); with Rourke, Joyce and GANNON for 'THE LAST OF THE FAMOUS INTERNATIONAL PLAYBOYS' (February 1989); alone again for 'NOVEMBER SPAWNED A MONSTER' (May 1990); with his new band of BOORER and company for 'PREGNANT FOR THE LAST TIME' (August 1991); 'MY LOVE LIFE' (October 1991); 'WE HATE IT WHEN OUR FRIENDS BECOME SUCCESSFUL' (May 1992); 'THE MORE YOU IGNORE ME, THE CLOSER I GET' (March 1994); 'ALMA MATTERS' (August 1997); a live 'ROY'S KEEN' (September 1997, not broadcast until 2003's archive sister show *Top Of The Pops 2*); with full band in JOBRIATH T-shirts for 'IRISH BLOOD, ENGLISH HEART' (May 2004); and 'FIRST OF THE GANG TO DIE' (July 2004).

Also of note are a handful of Morrissey tributes by other acts on *Top Of The Pops*.

The same 8 August 1991 programme as 'Pregnant For The Last Time' also featured Voice Of The Beehive with their new single, 'Monsters And Angels'. Singer Tracey Bryn deliberately mimed with her guitar turned backwards so the cameras could pick up Morrissey's autograph on the underside.

In November 1991, Nirvana appeared on the show playing 'Smells Like Teen Spirit'. Kurt Cobain sang his live vocal in a strange, low register, later explaining it as his attempt to 'sound like Morrissey'. A year later, a more obviously recognisable impression was delivered by Evan Dando, who brilliantly mimicked Morrissey's phrasing when The Lemonheads performed their cover of Simon & Garfunkel's 'Mrs Robinson'. [17, 94, 275, 334]

Toys, The, Among the many 60s American girl groups Morrissey and Johnny Marr bonded over when forming The Smiths. Formed in the Jamaica neighbourhood of Queens, New York, The Toys were Barbara Harris, Barbara Parritt and June Monteiro. Their biggest hit was their 1965 debut 'A Lover's Concerto', borrowing its pretty melody from Bach's Minuet in G Major to reach number five in the UK and two in the US. Morrissey once named it as one of his favourite singles, also nominating its bouncier 1966 follow-up, 'Attack', among his list of 'Singles to be cremated with'. Like its predecessor, 'Attack' also snuck in a classical homage with its opening fanfare taken from Tchaikovsky's 'March Of The Wooden Soldiers'. [17, 175, 188]

'Trash' (Sylvain Sylvain/David Johansen), NEW YORK DOLLS cover performed by Morrissey in 1991 and included on the *LIVE IN DALLAS* video. Opening the second side of the Dolls' 1973 debut album, 'Trash' was an overpowering sugar rush of rock and roll abandon intended as their first domestic single but, in the event, making no impression on the US charts. '"Trash" is about, well, trash generally,' wrote Morrissey in his 1981 book on the Dolls. 'Sylvain's immaculate backing vocals are the highlight, but David is very upfront caterwauling the rules of romance.' Over 20 years later, Morrissey would include it on his 2003 various artists compilation UNDER THE INFLUENCE, likening it in his sleeve notes to both The Crystals' 1964 single 'All Grown Up' and 'John GARFIELD's far-away gaze' in the 1940 film *Saturday's Children*.

Morrissey introduced 'Trash' on the first night of his first solo tour at Dublin's National Stadium on Saturday 27 April 1991. His decision to cover the song was motivated by the death of ex-Dolls guitarist Johnny Thunders four days earlier in New Orleans. On stage in Dublin, Morrissey would dedicate it to Thunders 'who died on Tuesday … this is for him'. Morrissey's version was an unashamedly scruffy, if faithful, homage to the original with minor lyrical amendments, most noticeably his refusal to mimic Johansen's 'How do you call your lover boy?' borrowed from Mickey & Sylvia's 1957 hit 'Love Is Strange'. 'Trash' was played regularly for the first half of the 1991 KILL UNCLE tour but never recorded. Its inclusion on the *Live In Dallas* video is its only official release to date. [277, 343]

'Treat Me Like A Human Being' (Morrissey/Street), 1987 demo recording by Morrissey and Stephen Street and an early candidate for VIVA HATE. Like the album's other 'lost' contenders, 'I DON'T WANT US TO FINISH', 'LIFEGUARD ON DUTY' and 'SAFE WARM LANCASHIRE HOME', it was abandoned as Morrissey and Street, in the words of the latter, 'came up with stronger material'. The lyrics are not known, though the title suggests a throwback to Morrissey's imploring chorus of 'HOW SOON IS NOW?' and may, to some degree, have been a conscious nod to one of his favourite NEW YORK DOLLS songs which he'd later cover. [39]

'Trouble Loves Me' (Morrissey/Whyte), From the album MALADJUSTED (1997). The standout track from his weakest record, 'Trouble Loves Me' is one of *the* great Morrissey ballads; a plea for affection shipwrecked by a lust for danger, foolishly rampaging towards the fleshpits of Soho. Whyte's piano, already struck by its own iceberg, valiantly plays on as the freezing waters lap at its feet. The majesty of the track is its perfect union of words and music – never more so than when Morrissey's temple-slapping 'can't-get-you-out-of-my-head' is accentuated by Cobrin's staccato drum crashes – and the might of his vocal delivery (the way he stretches, 'frow-ning'). With hindsight, 'Trouble Loves Me' could have been Morrissey's 'big ballad single' making a welcome change from the customary Mozrock guitar fare which had become his norm by the mid-90s. At the very least, it towered above the rest of Maladjusted and deservedly became a fan favourite in concert. Morrissey demonstrated his own fondness for the song when he brought it back into his live set in 2006. [4, 5, 40]

true-to-you.net, Morrissey's official unofficial website run by his foremost 'apostle', Boston's Julia Riley. Taking its name from a lyric in 'SPEED-WAY', *True To You* began as a fanzine in 1994 before making its transition to the internet in 2000. Although the most active Morrissey website in terms of news and user interaction remains David Tseng's MORRISSEY-SOLO, true-to-you is unique in having earned Morrissey's endorsement. Despite various official record company domains created since his comeback with 2004's YOU ARE THE QUARRY, Morrissey chooses to endorse true-to-you as his main website. Accordingly, Riley's direct access to her idol allows her to publish details of new releases, album and song titles, tour dates and other special announcements before anybody else. Morrissey also uses true-to-you as a bulletin board to address certain issues as he feels necessary and has engaged in numerous enlightening fan Q&As exclusive to the site. TONY VISCONTI would also allude to the site in his autobiography *Bowie, Bolan And The Brooklyn Boy*, describing himself as 'a new, true-to-you Morrissey fan'.

Since true-to-you lacks the objectivity of Morrissey-solo, Riley has been accused in some quarters of being nothing less than the singer's 'Minister of Propaganda'. Yet such antipathy towards Riley is to be expected given her very special relationship with the singer, which has roused a great deal of envy and hostility among other fans. A small, unassuming figure in the flesh, Riley has attended virtually every one of Morrissey's concerts since 1992.

After years of following the singer across the globe at her own expense, queuing up to be in the front row every night, buying him gifts and even, according to one former band member, baking him vegetarian-friendly cakes delivered to the

stage door, Riley was awarded for her devotion beyond the call of duty by becoming his compulsory concert mascot. Since 1999, Morrissey has regularly referred to 'Julia' on stage, often passing his microphone to her in the front row so she can answer his questions and comment on the progress of the show. Riley was finally 'immortalised' on record on the bonus Live At The Hollywood Bowl CD with the limited edition of 2008's GREATEST HITS: that's her introducing 'I JUST WANT TO SEE THE BOY HAPPY'. [4, 5, 240-245, 389]

Turn The Key Softly, 1953 British drama named by Morrissey as one of his favourite films. The plot follows 24 hours in the lives of three women discharged from London's Holloway Prison: middle-class Monica (Morrissey screen fave YVONNE MITCHELL), who'd taken the rap for her safebreaker boyfriend; the old and impoverished 'Granny' (Kathleen Harrison), a habitual shoplifter devoted to her scraggy mutt, Johnny; and the hideously fickle Stella (Joan Collins), a young prostitute who plans to go straight by marrying a bus driver. The plot sees them try and make a fresh start only to be stalked by old acquaintances and lapse into bad habits. Shot on location, it offers a fantastic snapshot of 50s London while its final frames are guaranteed to have all dog lovers melting between the settee cushions. [227, 558]

Twinkle, One of Morrissey's favourite 60s British female singers who recorded the original version of 'GOLDEN LIGHTS', covered by The Smiths. When defending his decision to tackle the track, Morrissey argued that 'the history of British music' had been neglected and that he'd deliberately chosen Twinkle to challenge those who 'wouldn't see [her] as an intelligent reference point'.

Twinkle was born Lynn Ripley into a wealthy upper-class family in Surbiton, Surrey. The youngest daughter of a Tory councillor, her classmates at Kensington's Queen's Gate girls' school included Camilla Parker Bowles. As apocryphal pop myth has it, while sat in the back of the family Rolls on a Sunday outing, the 16-year-old Twinkle watched in wonder as a biker gang of ton-up boys overtook them. Returning home, she wrote 'Terry', a hymnal pop ballad to a dead biker boyfriend which became her November 1964 debut single on DECCA. Like previous death discs such as John Leyton's 'JOHNNY REMEMBER ME', 'Terry' was banned by the BBC (as well as *Ready Steady Go!*) and attacked by the press for being 'sick' and 'dangerous drivel'. Twinkle's hollow protestations that the lyrics were intended as an advertisement for road safety failed to sway the censors, not that it mattered. By January 1965, 'Terry' had reached number four in the UK. Morrissey would later list it among his 'Singles to be cremated with', having previously adapted some of its lyrics for an early draft of 'PAINT A VULGAR PICTURE'.

American radio were more receptive to 'Terry' though Twinkle was denied a US visa to promote the song. Her response was to sigh, 'Oh well, I shall have to stay at home working on my novel about the ups and downs of adolescence.' The book never appeared but a much better follow-up single did. February 1965's 'Golden Lights' was a gorgeous melodrama about fame's destructive effect on romance, based upon her relationship with Dec Cluskey, the lead singer of Dublin group The Bachelors whom she'd begun dating when she was 14 and he was 20.

Peaking at number 21, 'Golden Lights' was her last taste of chart success. A queer little thing with a putty nose and hair the texture of loft insulation, as a pop pin-up Twinkle was certainly no rival to contemporaries such as Sandie SHAW, though her subsequent failure has less to do with her looks than her label, Decca, who badly mismanaged her follow-up singles. With the exception of 1965's 'Poor Old Johnny' (an enjoyable mish-mash of 'Terry' and 'Golden Lights' about a spectacularly glum boyfriend now behind bars), the rest were mediocre covers. Though she recorded a great English version of France Gall's 1965 EUROVISION winner, the Serge GAINSBOURG-penned 'A Lonely Singing Doll' ('Poupée De Cire, Poupée De Son'), Decca foolishly confined it to an EP, robbing her of a possible third UK hit.

Discounting her ineffectual comeback attempts of 1969, 1974 and 1982, Twinkle officially retired in 1966 at the age of 18. She later married actor Gary Myers, the original 'Milk Tray man'. [52, 175]

Tyler, Parker, American writer, poet and film critic who, in 1985, was named by Morrissey as the person he'd most like to meet: alas, Tyler had already died eleven years earlier of prostate cancer at the age of 70.

Tyler first achieved infamy as the credited co-author of the 1933 novel *The Young And Evil*, an experimental work by Charles Ford based upon his experiences with, and letters from, Tyler in the gay bohemian society of 30s New York. Too shocking for American audiences, it was published by Obelisk Press in Paris, the same house who'd recently licensed an edition of Radclyffe Hall's similarly controversial THE WELL OF LONELINESS. Tyler went on to publish numerous volumes of film criticism beginning with 1944's *The Hollywood Hallucination*, later writing extensively on underground and foreign film as well as authoring the first major study devoted to 'homosexuality in the movies', 1972's *Screening The Sexes*.

Morrissey's admiration for Tyler was in keeping with his scholarly interest in gender-related film criticism; as a case in point, Tyler is referenced on several occasions in Molly Haskell's FROM REVERENCE TO RAPE, a favourite of the singer's in the formative years of The Smiths. In terms of Tyler's direct influence upon Morrissey, his 1974 book *A Pictorial History Of Sex In Films* contains the most obvious Smiths connections: its illustrations include the Joe DALLESANDRO torso portrait featured on 1984's THE SMITHS album and the relatively rare still of Rita Tushingham in *A Taste Of Honey* as used on the sleeve of the Sandie SHAW version of 'HAND IN GLOVE'. It is also a faint possibility that Tyler's caption for another shot of Dallesandro with Sylvia Miles from 1972's *Heat* – 'it seems only a question of who is going to swallow whom' – might have had some bearing upon Morrissey's use of a similar phrase in 'HANDSOME DEVIL'. [168, 326, 387]

Under The Influence, Generic series of various artists compilation CDs, each drawing 'on the inspirations and all time loves of the world's greatest recording artists'. The series was launched by the DMC label in May 2003 with the first curated by Morrissey.

Carefully avoiding 'songs that everyone's got', he celebrated his more eminent heroes, sharing some of the more obscure records he'd been featuring on his interval music tapes ever since 1991. Obviously present and correct were his beloved NEW YORK DOLLS ('TRASH'), NICO ('All That Is My Own'), Klaus NOMI ('Death'), PATTI SMITH (rare 1974 B-side 'Hey Joe'), SPARKS (1969 demo 'Arts & Crafts Spectacular'), Marc BOLAN (Tyrannosaurus Rex's 'Great Horse'), RAMONES ('Judy Is A Punk') and best friend LINDER Sterling's former group Ludus ('Breaking The Rules'). In between leaped 50s rockabilly squawkings from Nat Couty ('Woodpecker Rock'), Charlie Feathers ('One Hand Loose') and Jaybee Wasden ('De Castrow'); downcast northern soul from Jimmy Radcliffe ('(There Goes) The Forgotten Man'); a scarce 60s pop foray from Diana DORS ('So Little Time'); Acadian French Cajun from The Sundown Playboys ('Saturday Nite Special'); and 70s youth club reggae via The Cats' ska version of Tchaikovsky's 'Swan Lake'. Morrissey had also wanted to include another Cajun track, Nathan Abshire's 'Hey Mom', but failed to get permission.

Accompanied by his own engrossing sleeve notes, despite containing no new music of his own, as Morrissey's first 'release' in the six years since 1997's Maladjusted it instigated a wealth of media coverage, adding to growing anticipation for him to sign a new record deal, which he would before the year's end. Morrissey also generously donated his proceeds from the compilation to the People for the Ethical Treatment of Animals. [115, 207, 453]

'Unhappy Birthday' (Morrissey/Marr), From the album STRANGEWAYS, HERE WE COME (1987). Morrissey's vindictive side came to the fore on this stinging birthday missive to an unknown 'evil' and lying enemy. Though the lyrics contained an element of morbid role play – threatening to 'kill my dog' and vowing to shoot himself – given the general autobiographical nature of Morrissey's writing, 'Unhappy Birthday' was almost certainly a specific attack aimed at somebody in his personal life, making the final revelation that he was 'the one you left behind' all the more mysterious.

His words are doubly chilling for his beautifully composed vocal in keeping with Marr's melancholy acoustic melody. 'It's not at all what people imagine The Smiths to be,' says Marr, 'but only we could play it and only Morrissey could sing it.' Purposely written as an acoustic track, it was one of the few tunes Marr had prepared for Strangeways before the session began. Like much of the album, the guitarist was subconsciously chasing the atmosphere of THE BEATLES' The White Album, what he himself terms 'a certain bleakness'.

Recorded in under 24 hours, Marr nominates it as one of the best examples of the musical synchronicity between himself and Rourke and has often suggested that – hypothetically speaking – it represents the musical direction he'd have liked The Smiths to continue in. 'The sound just hangs in the air,' he enthuses. 'I'd thought a lot about going a bit more acoustic because I was *bananas* about "Unhappy Birthday". That was my favourite Smiths track for a long while. And I still think that it would have been a great idea for us to go down that road.' [17, 19, 38]

'Unloveable' (Morrissey/Marr), B-side of 'BIGMOUTH STRIKES AGAIN' (1986).

As its title blatantly indicated, 'Unloveable' was among Morrissey's most self-deprecating Smiths lyrics, offering a repetitive confession from a love-starved soul taking stock of their empty life, drab wardrobe and eccentric behaviour. The end of the song reveals it to be the contents of a letter, its fantasy of reciprocated affection ('if only you could meet me') sharing the tone of desperate fan mail; Morrissey perhaps assuming the role of a Smiths apostle writing to himself. Its lyrics also contained the loose, but likely, influence of Sandie SHAW, suggesting the chorus of her 1965 hit 'Message Understood'.

The tune was among Marr's most syrupy, written at home one evening while he was 'watching a Clint Eastwood film on TV with the volume down'. He was excited enough to immediately put it on tape (along with 'SOME GIRLS ARE BIGGER THAN OTHERS'), drive round to Morrissey's house and post it through the letterbox in the early hours of the morning. Recorded during the sessions for THE QUEEN IS DEAD, 'Unloveable' was initially considered for inclusion on the album itself. Instead, it was substituted by the late entry 'VICAR IN A TUTU' and consigned to a B-side, a fair reflection of its merits as a slight, rather than indispensable, Morrissey/Marr offering. Despite being soundchecked on various occasions, 'Unloveable' was never played in concert by The Smiths. [17, 18, 38]

'Used To Be A Sweet Boy' (Morrissey/Whyte), From the album VAUXHALL AND I (1994).

A dewy lament for his own lost childhood, Morrissey places himself in the shoes of his confused parents, unable to accept responsibility for the man he became. 'I don't know very well what went wrong,' Morrissey tried to explain. 'I have difficulty understanding, it's so complex. Even my parents would be unable to explain what went wrong. In [the song], these are the parents who speak and deny all responsibility. To me, though, parents must assume blame. They bring the children up, not the other way around.'

Its sentimental imagery of shiny new school uniforms and clutching 'Daddy's hand' was made rosier still by the wispy textures of Whyte's rock-a-bye waltz. 'Used To Be A Sweet Boy' was played at the beginning of Morrissey's February 1995 UK tour though never to his complete satisfaction and was dropped after four performances. [4, 40, 236]

Vauxhall And I, Morrissey's fourth solo album, released March 1994, highest UK chart position #1. Tracks: 'NOW MY HEART IS FULL', 'SPRING-HEELED JIM', 'BILLY BUDD', 'HOLD ON TO YOUR FRIENDS', 'THE MORE YOU IGNORE ME, THE CLOSER I GET', 'WHY DON'T YOU FIND OUT FOR YOURSELF', 'I AM HATED FOR LOVING', 'LIFEGUARD SLEEPING, GIRL DROWNING', 'USED TO BE A SWEET BOY', 'THE LAZY SUNBATHERS', 'SPEEDWAY'. Produced by Steve LILLYWHITE.

Summing up the events of 1992, the year of YOUR ARSENAL, Morrissey described it as 'the most exciting year of my life and the most fruitful'. By contrast, 1993 would be one of the most emotionally taxing for the singer, overcast with the deaths of loved ones and a 'long phase' of depression during which he locked himself away in his house in Camden unable to leave or take visitors. 'It doesn't really matter how people try to uplift you,' he'd later explain, 'within me it's an immovable, strange, genetic medical condition that I have never escaped from.' Yet from out of this dismal darkness came the album which Morrissey has yet to surpass. His defining 'solo masterpiece', Vauxhall And I.

The year began with the death of his manager, Nigel Thomas, who died of a heart attack in January. Morrissey praised Thomas as 'completely instrumental' in all his recent success and was devastated by the loss of that rarest of beings, a 'very dignified' and 'very optimistic' manager whom the singer had absolute faith in. Thomas's death returned Morrissey's business affairs into their more familiar state of uncertainty as a replacement was sought. His anguish was swiftly compounded by the death of his friend and video director Tim Broad and lastly, in late April, Your Arsenal producer Mick RONSON whom Morrissey had already asked to record the follow-up. In the space of four months he'd lost a trusted manager, a close friend and a valued musical mentor. Struggling to cope with the sudden collapse of his very private world, the sense-wracking depression he'd later discuss was understandable.

Preparations for his fourth album had already begun before Morrissey's grief-stricken spring of

'93. Guitarist Alain WHYTE, a proven star collaborator after his work on Your Arsenal, hoped to better himself on the sequel though he now faced serious competition from fellow guitarist Boz BOORER, also supplying Morrissey with material. There were other personnel issues with the rhythm section. Disorderly behaviour on the Your Arsenal tour had raised concerns in some quarters close to Morrissey about the 'professionalism' of bassist Gary DAY and drummer Spencer COBRIN who would both be replaced. As the more experienced musical director, it was left to Boorer to find substitutes in two old friends from the north London rockabilly circuit, bassist Jonny BRIDGWOOD and drummer Woodie TAYLOR. Ronson's death saw the producer's job offered to Steve Lillywhite, another acquaintance of Boorer's who, more significantly, had previously worked for Morrissey in 1986 when asked to remix The Smiths' 'ASK'.

After a brief band rehearsal at Nomis studios in Shepherds Bush to ensure Bridgwood and Taylor were up to scratch, the real work began on 1 June 1993 at Hook End Manor outside Reading, Morrissey's favourite residential studio and scene of the BONA DRAG and KILL UNCLE sessions. Still reeling from his triple bereavement, the singer would later reflect upon what he termed an 'odour of retreat, of departure' from the outset. 'I was aware of this end-of-reign atmosphere,' he explained. 'It was no problem for me. I was even quite happy about it. The album wasn't as fiery or as passionate as its predecessors but it seemed a bit resigned, which quite pleased me.'

Bridgwood's working cassette of preparatory demos from Whyte and Boorer (marked simply 'NEW LP') reveals the 12 main contenders Morrissey had chosen prior to the session. Eight were to make the final running order: 'Billy Budd', 'Why Don't You Find Out For Yourself', 'The Lazy Sunbathers', 'Now My Heart Is Full', 'Spring-Heeled Jim', 'The More You Ignore Me, The Closer I Get', 'Lifeguard Sleeping, Girl Drowning' and 'Hold On To You Friends'. The remaining four were all Whyte tunes of which only one, 'BLACK-EYED SUSAN', would be salvaged

as a later B-side. Both the kitschy 'SHARP BEND, FAST CAR, GOODBYE' and the slow, waltzing 'STAY AS YOU ARE' would be scrapped before Morrissey got round to adding vocals, while a similar fate befell the up-tempo rocker 'HONEY, YOU KNOW WHERE TO FIND ME', the lyrics of which would later be revived for a different tune by Boorer circa 1995's SOUTHPAW GRAMMAR.

In its split allocation between Morrissey's two new co-writers, Vauxhall was the first album to highlight the inevitable artistic rivalry between Whyte and Boorer. 'There was definitely competition there,' notes engineer Chris Dickie. 'Like when it came to recording Alain's songs, Boz tended to stay off them a bit more. They were both more concerned about their own tracks they'd written, which is understandable. But it was very subtle. It wasn't like some big face-off. Just little things you noticed where you could sense a bit of rivalry going on.' Although Whyte ended up claiming just over half the album, arguably his tender and often Marr-esque contributions were outshone by Boorer's bigger, bolder strokes, especially the two confessional epics bookending the running order. The sweet, exhilarating 'Now My Heart Is Full' and the bitter, agonising 'Speedway' were not only the best of Boorer but the best of Morrissey. Without them, and Boorer's other thumbprints on the album, Vauxhall would have been a far pastier affair.

Recorded over the summer months from June through to August, the good climate and relaxed surroundings of Hook End offered Morrissey a peaceful, meditative environment to take his mind off the year's earlier traumas. '[Vauxhall] was a way of getting everything out there,' he'd explain. 'Everything had come to a head for me … personal life, private life … the usual.' The therapeutic effects of this psychological spring clean would inevitably show in the album's lyrics.

Away from the recording booth, Morrissey found equal comfort in various indoor and outdoor pursuits with his band and crew, from five-a-side football to his favourite dice game, Perudo. Among the more frequent visitors to the studio who'd both be thanked on the album credits were Debbie Dannell, his hairstylist with impeccable taste in retro 50s fashions, and Morrissey's new personal assistant, photographer Jake WALTERS. Engineer Danton Supple and Walters were known to stage 'diving contests' in the studio pool while Morrissey also tried to coerce them into staging a boxing match. 'He said, "Wouldn't it be great if we got some boxing gloves?"' recalls Supple. 'I thought that could be fun, taking Morrissey on. But then he said, "Oh, no, no. You fight Jake." He just wanted to watch Jake punching somebody else for his own amusement. Funnily enough, I declined.'

Originally scheduled for an autumn release, Vauxhall And I was delayed until the new year, partly so as not to clash with Warners' first CD reissues of The Smiths' back catalogue in November 1993. The title, seemingly modelled on Bruce Robinson's 1987 comedy *Withnail And I*, namechecked the area of London opposite Pimlico on the south bank of the Thames, part of the borough of Lambeth. Many eyebrows were raised over the fact that Vauxhall was one of the capital's gay hotspots (famed for popular venues such as the Royal Vauxhall Tavern) though Morrissey specified the title referred to 'a certain person I know who was *born and braised* in Vauxhall'. Jake Walters would appear the likeliest contender, hailing from south London and the recipient of Morrissey's 'very special thanks' on the record itself. Just as intriguing was Walters's ambiguous back cover of (presumably) the singer's hands, complete with fake swallow tattoo, his thumbs running beneath a 1'OZ (one ounce) pendant. Asked to explain its significance, Morrissey laughed, 'That's *my* secret.'

Not for the first (nor the last) time, Morrissey trumpeted Vauxhall And I as 'the best record I've ever made'. The strength of the material and the beauty of its execution convinced many critics to concur.

'It *is* a beautiful record and I set out that it should be so,' said Morrissey. 'I thought it was time to put lots of things away in their boxes and

their cupboards, and allow age to take its natural toll, for better or worse.'

Beyond a clutch of third-person character sketches – 'Spring-Heeled Jim', 'The Lazy Sunbathers' and 'Lifeguard Sleeping, Girl Drowning' – and the deliberately playful romances of 'Billy Budd' and 'The More You Ignore Me, The Closer I Get', it was evident that Vauxhall was an exorcism of many demons: parental disappointment ('Used To Be A Sweet Boy'); the betrayal of loved ones ('Hold On To Your Friends'); an unshakable persecution complex ('Why Don't You Find Out For Yourself', 'I Am Hated For Loving'); and the letting go of nostalgic obsessions ('Now My Heart Is Full'). Most sensational was the closing 'Speedway' in which Morrissey seemed to confess all only to emerge at the end somehow doubly inscrutable in the process.

'Before [Vauxhall And I], I'd never known this feeling of fulfilment,' he enthused. 'An album on which not a track goes out of tune, on which every title is a perfect success. It was a new and terribly exciting emotion. Even on Your Arsenal, which I loved, there were one or two weak tracks. Vauxhall And I fits my idea of perfection. I couldn't make better.'

Other than the music of Whyte and Boorer, equal credit for this 'perfection' must go to Lillywhite's production. Taking Morrissey's specific brief not to repeat the heavy guitar sound characterising Your Arsenal, Lillywhite introduced a uniform textural softness which glazed nearly every track with a poised classicism.

Six years after VIVA HATE, Vauxhall And I became the second Morrissey album to enter the UK charts at number one. Referring to the NME's character assassination after the 1992 Madstock incident 18 months earlier, Morrissey would later cite the victory of Vauxhall as his proudest moment, 'coming in at number one in the midst of all the Morrissey-is-a-nasty-racist-hoo-hah'. Perhaps to his detriment, he failed to fully capitalise on the album's success at the time by touring, instead restricting promotion to a couple of signings at HMV stores in London and

Manchester, both of which witnessed Beatle-mania-style scenes of fan hysteria. Ironically, by the time he did tour again in February 1995 the critical tide had turned and his umpteenth press backlash was already under way.

Vauxhall And I is still widely regarded as Morrissey's greatest solo album. Taken as a whole, it probably is. More so than his work with The Smiths, it has become the yardstick against which all subsequent Morrissey albums must be judged and to date, none has quite surpassed it. Yet, being objective, it is also true to say that to some extent Morrissey's musical evolution halted with Vauxhall And I. For better or worse, it set a blueprint which has since been tweaked and teased to varying degrees but which still acts as a strict stylistic bible decreeing the 'ideal' he continually strives for. Then again, the Morrissey album that does manage to outstrip the magnificent Vauxhall And I would have to be very special indeed. When he said he 'couldn't make better', maybe we should take him at his word. [4, 6, 40, 84, 114, 154, 207, 217, 236]

vegetarianism, The stringency with which Morrissey exercises his vegetarian beliefs on those around him is frequently misreported as exaggerated despotism. Tales of 'poor' road crews made to 'suffer' meat-free catering for weeks on end, or 'deprived' concert goers who find there are no hot dogs on sale at the venue, or personal staff being 'forced' to eat vegan meals on long-haul flights. Their argument being, how dare Morrissey infringe upon their 'human rights', their freedom to eat as many dead animals when and where they like?

Which is one way of looking at it, but here's another. To Morrissey, vegetarianism is more than a dietary, or even ethical, choice but a moral fight against man's barbarism towards animals, intrinsic to his core values. It is his religion, and a fundamentalist one at that. If Morrissey was a Hindu, there'd be total understanding if there was a strict ban on beef in his presence, or if he was an orthodox Jew nobody would question a catering prohibition on pork. Yet as a passionate vegetarian, the

vetoing of all meat products in his organisation is reported as tyrannical crankiness. This, in itself, says much for the poor esteem with which the media still regard vegetarianism, and offers much justification for why Morrissey feels it necessary to impose his beliefs with such force in order to raise awareness on the subject. After all, being made to lug Morrissey's lighting rig around America for three months without so much as a sniff of a hamburger is still a preferable fate to being frog-marched into an abattoir, hauled upside-down by your ankles then having your throat slit.

Indeed, it was gruesome scenes of the workings of a slaughterhouse on a 1970 television documentary which first turned Morrissey vegetarian at the age of 11. 'I saw pigs and cows still thrashing about after they'd been supposedly stunned,' he recalled in 1989. 'It was so violent, so horrendous – I've never eaten meat since then.' The horror of that documentary was so vivid that, 20 years later, Morrissey was still talking about it. 'I became shy as a teenager,' he told Radio 4, 'because I became immersed in vegetarianism and I became very depressed by the existence of the abattoir. I had a dawning when I was 11 or 12. Just the knowledge that such places existed. I saw a television documentary by accident when I was 11 and I was absolutely horrified. It had such a profound effect on me as a teenager because I was very introverted. I felt I was on an alien planet.'

Though Morrissey ate meat as a child, even admitting to having had a brief 'bacon fetish', his change in lifestyle was encouraged by his mother who'd been vegetarian her whole life. 'I wasn't raised in an environment where it was thought crucial to eat meat,' he explained. Johnny Marr had also turned vegetarian by the time he began writing with Morrissey in the summer of 1982, another small but crucial bond in their blossoming friendship.

The importance of vegetarianism to Morrissey, and the manifesto of SMITHDOM, became evident when given centre stage on the group's second album, 1985's MEAT IS MURDER. Immediately embraced as a veggie anthem, the full impact of the title track is still impossible to quantify: Morrissey himself has estimated that 'thousands' have turned to vegetarianism as a result of the lyrics and, as such, it stands as one of his proudest life achievements. 'It *is* a direct statement,' he proclaimed at the time. 'Of all the political topics to be scrutinised people are still disturbingly vague about the treatment of animals. People still seem to believe that meat is a particular substance not at all connected to animals playing in the field over there. People don't realise how gruesomely and frighteningly the animal gets to the plate … [they] eat meat for negative reasons. They just can't be bothered to think about animal cruelty, or they can't be bothered to think of another diet.'

In his vegetarian offensive, Morrissey was especially vocal against multi-national fast-food chains, vowing that if he ever met KFC's Colonel Sanders in the afterlife he'd be forced to administer 'the old physical knee in the groin' and naming McDonald's as 'the core of modern evil … I just feel rage that they will promote themselves from every possible angle but they will not show the process by which the hamburger is made, they will not show the cows' throats being slit, the bull trying to commit suicide by banging his head against the stone floor.'

The Smiths' vegetarian diet, enforced in the case of Andy Rourke, notoriously created problems when touring, especially in America. 'I was right into the veggie thing, but it took me a while,' explains Rourke. 'There was one time in the early days when we were in this service station. I got bacon and eggs and sat at the table where Morrissey was already sitting. He got up, left and sat at another table, leaving me on my own like a leper. So I got the hint after that. But America was the worst because they had no idea about being veggie. You'd be in Texas and they'd give you pea soup telling you it was vegetarian. Next thing you'd find bits of bacon in it and they'd be, "That's because it's pea and ham." Stuff like that used to drive us nuts, all the time. After a while, the crew used to tease me, because they knew I really ate meat, so a couple of times I'd sneak out

with them and get a steak. Most of the time I was good, though. You had to be around Morrissey because it wasn't a joke. He was deadly serious about it and you didn't want to upset him.'

Morrissey's strength of feeling when it comes to animal welfare and vegetarianism in particular has often stirred controversy. Among his most contentious statements are those that eating meat 'is on the same moral level as child abuse' and, just as shocking, that it's 'the same as the holocaust'. Such comments haven't exactly helped endear the carnivorous public to Morrissey's cause but, outrageous as they are, go a long way to explaining the actions of a man who's been known to order the dismissal of venue door staff for eating a salmon sandwich in his vicinity.[1] 'There has never,' he reiterated, 'been a good argument in the history of the world for eating animals.'

Yet in view of Morrissey's reputation as the most famous vegetarian in pop, it was shocking, if not absurd, that when interviewed by Russell BRAND in 2006 he should casually declare, 'I'm not vegetarian.' 'I just don't eat animals,' he elaborated. 'I don't eat anything that's lived. I don't bring a life to end simply because I'm slightly peckish. I'm not vegetarian in the sense that elaborate vegetarian dishes I don't really care for. I'm still very much chocolate and crisps.' See also ANIMAL RIGHTS, MCCARTNEY, Linda. [28, 123, 132, 133, 135, 142, 211, 273, 414, 418, 425, 444, 451, 453, 459, 470, 477, 478]

---

1. When it comes to fish, the Morrissey rule is 'seafood is sea life' and therefore also murder. 'When fish are caught, they suffocate and they scream really loudly,' he insists.

Velvet Underground, The, See NICO, REED, Lou.

Venables, Terry, Dagenham-born football player/manager and cover star of Morrissey's 'DAGENHAM DAVE' single. At the time of the single's release in August 1995, Venables, or 'El Tel', was managing the national England team whom he'd lead to defeat in the following year's European Championships. The cover of Morrissey's single

showed a young Venables clownishly sticking his tongue out during his playing career with Chelsea circa 1966. Although Morrissey would later name the sleeve among those he regretted and which 'weren't designed by me', he'd still use the image for a back projection when playing Los Angeles and Latin America in early 2000. The slide added a speech bubble to Venables with the words 'qué desmadre!' – 'what a mess!' in Mexican. [242]

'Vicar In A Tutu' (Morrissey/Marr), From the album THE QUEEN IS DEAD (1986). Using a light-hearted skit about a cross-dressing clergyman as his model, Morrissey returned to the fundamental Smiths theme of freedom of expression and rebelling against accepted social behaviour. In the process he paints a vivid farce which doubly serves to gently ridicule religion and the church hierarchy with its extended cast, from the twirling vicar himself to Rose with her collection tin, the 'monkish Monsignor' and Morrissey as the dumbstruck petty thief stealing lead from the spires of Manchester's Holy Name Church. The final verse contains one of The Queen Is Dead's many lyrical references to the film BILLY LIAR ('ignorance, dust and disease'), though in mood 'Vicar In A Tutu' is more Ealing comedy than it is kitchen-sink drama, albeit with a profound subtext reinforced by Morrissey's closing admission that he, like the tutu-clad vicar, is a 'living sign' of life's glorious abnormalities.

The tune was another rockabilly creation which came together while jamming in the studio during the latter stages of The Queen Is Dead. As the last song written for the album, it would replace 'UNLOVEABLE' on the provisional running order. 'It was a bit of a no-brainer,' says Marr, 'which is why it evolved the way it did. But it was worth having on the album because the words are good, as is Andy's bass line.' Rendered with more subtlety than The Smiths' previous rockabilly forays (e.g. 'NOWHERE FAST', 'SHAKESPEARE'S SISTER'), Marr's light, almost country and western picking was markedly reminiscent of Scotty Moore on the early Sun singles of Elvis PRESLEY. 'Vicar In A Tutu'

assumed greater muscle in live performance, as heard on RANK. [14, 18, 38, 485]

Victim, Controversial 1961 British drama starring Dirk BOGARDE listed among Morrissey's favourite films. Its now obsolete plot acted as a cause célèbre protesting against the archaic legislation which still decreed homosexual acts to be an imprisonable offence, thereby creating 'unlimited opportunities for blackmail'. Bogarde plays Melville Farr, a happily married lawyer in line to become a QC who has been having a furtive relationship with 'Boy' Barrett, a young building-site clerk. Spied upon by blackmailers, they target Barrett, who resorts to theft before killing himself in a police cell. Farr is consumed with guilt and vows to uncover the blackmailers' identity by tracking down other victims whom he hopes will aid his quest.

As in Radclyffe Hall's THE WELL OF LONELINESS, *Victim* portrays homosexuality as a piteous affliction. A blackmailed hairdresser tells Farr that, by being gay, 'nature played me a dirty trick', a line which may have had some influence on the similar lyric in The Smiths' 'PRETTY GIRLS MAKE GRAVES'. Though fairly joyless viewing, historically it was the first British film to include the word 'homosexual' in its script and excelled itself in highlighting the unjust legislation which was finally amended in 1967. [175, 227, 286, 382, 559]

Visconti, Tony (Morrissey producer 2005–), Revered by Morrissey as no less than 'a genius', Tony Visconti played a vital role in one of the singer's most successful albums, RINGLEADER OF THE TORMENTORS.

As the title of his 2007 autobiography attests, Brooklyn boy Visconti is best known for his work with David BOWIE and Marc BOLAN. If they were the architects of glam rock then Visconti, without question, was the genre's master carpenter. He met both singers within months of arriving in London in 1967 and spent the next few years sculpting a series of transitional albums for each. For Bowie, whom he'd share a flat with, he produced 1969's

Visconti, Luchino, Italian film director referenced in 'YOU HAVE KILLED ME'. Due to the coincidental name of the track's producer, some listeners assumed it was a tribute to TONY VISCONTI. Morrissey later specified the lyric was, indeed, 'about Luchino', the acclaimed director of 1960's *Rocco And His Brothers*; a three-hour epic about a peasant family's struggle to set up home in Milan starring Alain DELON. The film features a notorious rape scene, as a result of which it fell foul of Catholic authorities and was initially banned from being shown in Milan itself. Bold, brutal and beautifully shot, as Morrissey says it's 'a fantastic movie', as are other Visconti works: in particular 1963's *The Leopard* (also with Delon) and 1971's *Death In Venice*, based upon Thomas Mann's novella and starring Dirk BOGARDE as a dying composer consumed by his idealistic love for a young boy. [213, 286, 382, 546]

acoustic-driven Space Oddity (bar its famous title track which Visconti passed to Gus Dudgeon, considering it 'too gimmicky') before aiding his electric transformation on 1970's The Man Who Sold The World, Morrissey's favourite Bowie album, and the first to feature guitarist Mick RONSON. Visconti himself also played bass, piano and guitar on the record.

Bolan, likewise, reinvented himself at the hands of Visconti. After four albums as the hippy folk-rock caterpillar Tyrannosaurus Rex, the glittery electric butterfly of T.Rex emerged from Bolan's cocoon in 1970. For nearly three years, and via four number ones, in the UK singles charts Bolan and Visconti were an unassailable artist–producer dream team until Marc's notorious and destructive booze and cocaine-fuelled egomania severed their partnership. Visconti went on to produce SPARKS' 1975 album Indiscreet, reuniting with Bowie as co-producer of the same year's Young Americans. In terms of influence, his most significant work with Bowie remains the acclaimed late 70s 'Berlin trilogy' of Low, "Heroes" and Lodger. (See also Brian ENO.)

By 1980, Visconti was now the favoured producer of Thin Lizzy, though it was Bowie who, again, returned him to number one in the singles chart with that August's 'Ashes To Ashes', Visconti's first chart-topper since T.Rex's 'PANIC'-inspiring 'Metal Guru' eight years earlier.

The 1980s would be the beginning of Visconti's commercial decline, pairing him with Altered Images, Adam Ant, Haysi Fantayzee and rockabilly group The Polecats featuring a young Boz BOORER. Ironically, during this time he'd be approached by, but miss, The Smiths. Morrissey insists that Visconti had been a candidate for THE QUEEN IS DEAD. Marr's memory is that he'd been considered for 'Panic' (a logical choice given the song's debt to T.Rex). Whatever the recording, Visconti was unavailable, though The Smiths would still book his central London studio, Good Earth, for their second stab at 'SHEILA TAKE A BOW' with Stephen STREET in early 1987.

Visconti was 'almost there' again for Morrissey's YOUR ARSENAL in 1992 but lost out to his old friend Mick Ronson. The 1990s were to be another fallow decade for the producer and it wasn't until early 2001, when Bowie contacted him out of the blue to co-produce the album Heathen, that his fortunes improved. Through Visconti, Bowie hired drummer Matt CHAMBERLAIN as well as backing vocalist Kristeen YOUNG, who impressed Bowie enough for him to return the favour, duetting on her 2003 Visconti-produced album Breasticles. Released in 2002, Heathen was a resounding critical success. Bowie retained Visconti for its more mixed 2003 follow-up, Reality.

For Morrissey, it was a case of third time lucky when Visconti was approached in September 2005 to produce Ringleader Of The Tormentors, admittedly not as first choice but as an emergency 'fix-it' man when sessions ran aground after three weeks. On paper, it may have looked as if

Morrissey selected him purely as a conceited means of aligning himself beside the producer's celebrated pantheon of Bowie, Bolan and Sparks (though possibly not Haysi Fantayzee). The singer was adamant that Visconti was chosen because 'he's not at all marooned in the past ... as a producer, he is completely up to date. He knows everything about modern recording techniques. [He's] very 2006, and very apocalyptic, and, of course, all this internal steel came in very useful at the point when I started singing.' The admiration was mutual, with Visconti likening Morrissey to Bowie as 'a rare breed in pop – a true gentleman'.

Since Ringleader, both singer and producer have publicly expressed a wish to work together in the future while Morrissey also supplied the foreword to Visconti's autobiography *Bowie, Bolan & The Brooklyn Boy*. 'Musical notations are images,' he concluded, 'and the Visconti style is timeless and lionized and is therefore forevermore.'

In June 2008, Morrissey refuted allegations that Visconti had been promised the production of YEARS OF REFUSAL only to be bypassed by Jerry FINN. 'Tony wasn't ever in line for the job,' he explained. 'I'd love to do another album with Tony, and I feel blessed to have eventually found two ideal producers. They are both fantastic in equal measure. I wish I had met them earlier.' After the tragic death of Jerry Finn in 2008, at the time of writing Visconti seems the most likely candidate to produce Morrissey in the immediate future. [116, 235, 259, 266, 269, 351, 389, 441, 461, 568]

Viva Hate, Morrissey's debut solo album, released March 1988, highest UK chart position #1. Tracks: 'ALSATIAN COUSIN', 'LITTLE MAN, WHAT NOW?', 'EVERYDAY IS LIKE SUNDAY', 'BENGALI IN PLATFORMS', 'ANGEL, ANGEL, DOWN WE GO TOGETHER', 'LATE NIGHT, MAUDLIN STREET', 'SUEDE-HEAD', 'BREAK UP THE FAMILY', 'THE ORDINARY BOYS', 'I DON'T MIND IF YOU FORGET ME', 'DIAL-A-CLICHÉ', 'MARGARET ON THE GUILLOTINE'. Produced by Stephen STREET.

Morrissey never intended to be a solo artist and would freely admit as much. The Smiths were his ideal musical vehicle and he would have happily continued as their frontman until such a time as he felt it necessary to disband. In May 1987, Johnny Marr took that decision out of his hands, forcing Morrissey into a state of private panic but public denial, issuing his notorious decree in the weeks following Marr's exit that 'Whoever says The Smiths have split shall be severely spanked by me with a wet plimsoll.' The folly of trying to continue with replacement guitarist Ivor PERRY in July highlighted the futility of such idle threats. Backed into a corner by Marr's legal claims to the group name and the obligation to fulfil his new contract with EMI, Morrissey was left with no choice other than to declare The Smiths finished and announce his plans to pursue the solo career he'd never anticipated.

His one lifeline amid his depression and confusion was Smiths engineer and co-producer Stephen Street, who'd sent him a tape of demos under the impression Morrissey still needed new material for fresh Smiths B-sides for the final Rough Trade singles from STRANGEWAYS, HERE WE COME ('I STARTED SOMETHING I COULDN'T FINISH' and 'LAST NIGHT I DREAMT THAT SOMEBODY LOVED ME'). Street maintains he never anticipated the positive yet dramatic response to the tape; a letter from Morrissey, dated 18 August, which praised Street's efforts before concluding, 'I want The Smiths to be laid to rest. I want to record for EMI under my own name.'

Written and recorded in relative haste, the album that became Viva Hate was created entirely on the rebound from The Smiths' break-up. Placed in the position of sink or swim, Morrissey threw himself into the project with a mixture of defiance, fear and blithe abandon. Although he'd later criticise half the album for being 'unfortunately rushed', many of its strengths were a direct result of that same swiftness of execution, including the lyrics. 'It was a very peculiar time for me, making that record so suddenly, so unexpectedly, and I wanted to try something different,' he'd explain. 'Because of the particular status I have, where many people concentrate quite scientifically over every comma, I reached a stage where I wanted to be entirely spontaneous without physically writing the words down and memorising them. Rather, just step into the vocal booth and sing it as it comes.'

To begin with, Morrissey told Street he wanted Rourke and Joyce involved 'but haven't discussed it with them'. In 1991, he'd go on record stating, 'I asked Mike and Andy to be part of Viva Hate and they declined, so that was yet another blow,' a claim which Joyce, at least, confirms, citing the bitter experience of the Ivor Perry session as his reason for refusal. It was therefore left to Street to assemble the musicians, volunteering himself as bassist and recruiting Manchester guitar virtuoso Vini REILLY of The Durutti Column and session drummer Andrew PARESI, both of whom he'd worked with in the past year. After an ice-breaking introduction round Street's flat in Mortlake, the session commenced in early October at the familiar surroundings of The Wool Hall near Bath, where Strangeways had been completed barely six months earlier.

'Morrissey was very happy at The Wool Hall, which was vital,' recalls Street. 'He must have been incredibly nervous because this was very much untested waters for everybody. EMI had signed The Smiths but they'd split up before they knew it. Nobody knew how Morrissey was going to cope without Johnny. Nobody had any guarantee of my abilities other than as a producer. It was a very tentative atmosphere at first. A lot was at stake but the biggest pressure of all was upon Morrissey himself.'

'He was enormously vulnerable,' adds Paresi. 'Every day at The Wool Hall was a terrifying experience for all of us but especially for Morrissey because what was panning out as an interesting body of work could, in Morrissey's eyes, suddenly go tits up. There were a couple of songs that never made it because he decided they weren't working for him. What tends to happen with Morrissey is if even one song isn't working it will cloud the entire session and he'll walk out.' These early casualties included 'SAFE WARM LANCASHIRE HOME', 'LIFEGUARD ON DUTY', 'TREAT ME LIKE A HUMAN BEING', 'I DON'T WANT US TO FINISH' and 'PLEASE HELP THE CAUSE AGAINST LONELINESS', the latter featuring backing vocals by Sandie SHAW who'd later re-record her own version.

Among the first successful tracks consigned to tape were the controversial 'Bengali In Platforms' (its title and lyrics being the one surviving remnant from the Ivor Perry session) and 'Suedehead', which immediately stood out as the most promising. Conscious that a deputation from EMI had arranged an early studio visit to assess Morrissey's progress, Street prioritised a near-to-finished rough mix of 'Suedehead' in preparation. 'You can imagine how tense we were,' says Street. 'They came. We played them "Suedehead". They listened. Then they said, "Brilliant. Carry on." I can remember after they'd left myself and Morrissey went for a walk around the studio. He was so relieved. I think after that he felt a sense of freedom. From that moment on it was a case of seeing how far we could go.'

In the words of album strings arranger John Metcalfe, whom Street recruited after working together on The Durutti Column's The Guitar And Other Machines, the mood of the Viva Hate session was 'very un-rock and roll' with regular visits to the gym and sauna and a diet of healthy vegetarian cuisine bar the odd sinful flapjack and a glass of red wine. 'It wasn't like Strangeways when the others would be partying every night,' concurs Street. 'Everything was kept to decent hours. Starting at midday, a break for lunch, work some more, then a civilised meal, then maybe a game of charades. Morrissey never shut himself away, he was much more involved. It was all about the work.' According to Paresi, charades often brought out Morrissey's competitive streak, deliberately 'picking obscure films so he could win'. Conversely, Sandie Shaw would praise Morrissey for letting her cheat at games of Trivial Pursuit since he empathised with her own 'competitive need to win'.

'Sandie was around a lot,' says Street. 'Morrissey would be very excited about her coming

V

down, but then minutes after she arrived he'd be totally bored of her and couldn't wait for her to go again.' Shaw, naturally, remembers things very differently and would offer her own astute observations of the Viva Hate session in her 1991 autobiography *The World At My Feet*. 'They all seemed deeply in love with [Morrissey],' wrote Shaw. 'It was intriguing to observe each vying with the other for his attention, his laughter, his approval, or his admiration of their musical prowess. They tiptoed around in his presence as if on eggshells, not wanting to offend their maestro.'

The eggshells soon began to crack as, over time, tensions between Reilly and Street bubbled to the surface. 'With Vini, it was little things at first,' explains Street. 'Like he wouldn't play the solo on "Suedehead" because he thought it was too simple. But then he became more awkward, more critical over some of the chord sequences. He was being a bit of a musical snob which upset me and upset Morrissey too. So as the album went on I was feeling as if my judgement was continually being tested by Vini.' According to Paresi, Reilly saw the humour in his own diva-ish tantrums, pinning a self-mocking list of instructions on the studio wall: 'What to do if Vini throws a wobbler.'

After a fortnight's interval in late October, the session recommenced the following month. By the time work was completed the week before Christmas, Street was confined to bed with stomach ulcers. 'The pressure of making the album, writing it and producing it, was so much that in the end I made myself physically ill,' he admits. Beyond the underlying friction between Street and Reilly, morale was further shaken when the Viva Hate group took a break to the BBC studios in Maida Vale, London to record Morrissey's debut solo radio session for John PEEL. 'A very sad experience,' recalls Street. 'The BBC engineers had a bad attitude. They were treating me like I was just a bass player so when I was trying to explain that I was the songwriter and producer they just ignored me. Morrissey was unhappy. Vini was in another one of his moods. So it was a fucking nightmare, basically.'

The session was never finished nor broadcast, though prior to his death Peel informed this author that his producer, the late John Walters, retained a copy of the tapes. The running order remains unconfirmed though Paresi is sure that 'Suedehead' and 'Margaret On The Guillotine' were among those attempted. 'The saddest thing about the whole Peel fiasco is that it had a massive impact on Morrissey in terms of thinking whether he could play live with us as a group,' adds Paresi. 'That was a huge disappointment for me, personally, but another blow to his confidence before the album was even finished.'

Morrissey's emotional fragility was worse than even his musicians realised. Any enthusiasm he held for the material at hand was tempered by rueful anguish over the demise of The Smiths. While the singer confided in The Wool Hall's chef that Street was his 'rock to cling to', in private he'd already contacted Marr in the hope of arranging a final Smiths concert as a means of proper closure. 'He suggested we play a farewell gig at [London's] Royal Albert Hall,' confirms Marr, 'which was obviously a no-no.' Street was oblivious to any misgivings Morrissey may have had towards the album provisionally titled Education In Reverse (a message later etched into the run-out-groove of the renamed Viva Hate) until early January 1988. 'We'd finished the record, Christmas had come and gone and a few weeks had gone by with no word from Morrissey,' claims Street. 'That started to make me paranoid that maybe he didn't like the album. I could tell he had his doubts about it. In fact, much later on he confessed that he was very unsure about Viva Hate before it was released. So this was the beginning of everything starting to get a bit weird.'

As well as his reservations over the album itself, Morrissey was still deliberating whether he'd work with Reilly or Paresi again. When he finally resumed contact with Street in late January, his comments betrayed great insecurity clearly swayed by the second opinions of anonymous third parties. 'I managed to get hold of him by phone,' says Street. 'He told me he didn't want to use Vini or Andrew again. There were concerns about the running order as well. A lot of people were suggesting "HAIRDRESSER ON FIRE" should go on the record. Morrissey also said he'd played the album to some people who'd criticised Vini's playing, which I completely disagreed with. Then a few days later he said he *did* want to use Vini again. He was changing his mind from one day to the next. I didn't know what to make of it.'

Of greater concern to Street was the still unresolved financial arrangements over his Viva Hate production points (percentage of record royalties), made more complicated by Morrissey's growing distrust of manager Gail Colson, who also managed Street. 'I think I was offered one point,' recalls Street. 'I knew the work I'd done was worth a lot more than that. I thought it would be easy sorting it out because we were both managed by Gail. Then I learned he'd been telling people he didn't think she was doing a good job and wanted to get a new manager, which made it very awkward.'

Street's chagrin was increased when he read Morrissey's first interview of the year published in the NME in early February in which he confessed to being 'totally in favour of a [Smiths] reunion'. 'I'll be honest, I was very annoyed,' says Street. 'Not because I didn't agree with him. I always thought they were gonna re-form. I thought it was just a tiff, that in six weeks, six months, they'd sort it out and get back together. But what upset me about that NME piece was the fact that Viva Hate wasn't even out yet and he was telling the press he wanted to re-form The Smiths.'

It took the critical and commercial success of late February's 'Suedehead', his first top five hit, to raise Morrissey out of his self-doubting doldrums. Street was cheered to receive a letter the week following the single's rapturous reviews in which the singer stated he was 'thoroughly proud of Viva', naming 'Alsatian Cousin' and 'Late Night, Maudlin Street' as his favourite tracks. Nevertheless, a telling clue as to the real reasons for his remarkable volte-face may have been his additional piece of gossip, 'I believe Johnny has a copy of Viva and considers it to be brilliant.'

Interviewed in the troubled Smiths-split summer of 1987, Morrissey admitted that he was largely driven by 'hate … this obsessive drive against normality'. Viva Hate, he would later explain, was a title which 'simply suggested itself and *had to be*. It was absolutely how I felt post-Smiths and the way I continue to feel. That's just the way the world is. I find hate omnipresent, and love very difficult to find. Hate makes the world go round.' Significantly, Marr would also refer to the break-up of The Smiths as a time when '"hate" was a big word'.

Although, on the surface, much of the album's lyrical content alluded to Morrissey's youth growing up in the early 70s ('Late Night, Maudlin Street', 'Break Up The Family', the cultural references of 'Suedehead' and the mysterious 1969 television star of 'Little Man, What Now?'), the majority of Viva Hate, and the title itself, was very obviously his direct response to the end of The Smiths and his separation from Marr. Even if Morrissey stated that the only song written with Marr in mind was 'Angel, Angel, Down We Go Together', there's scope for similar interpretation within 'Alsatian Cousin', 'Late Night, Maudlin Street', 'Suedehead', 'Break Up The Family' and 'I Don't Mind If You Forget Me'.

The speed with which Viva Hate appeared – entering the charts at number one less than six months after Strangeways debuted at two – was crucial to its success. Reviews were generally positive, stopping short of hailing it as a masterpiece but comparing the Morrissey/Street partnership favourably with the overshadowing legacy of the Morrissey/Marr songbook. 'Stephen Street is the underrated hero of that album in many, many ways,' comments Paresi. 'He purposely wrote songs in different styles, many of which Morrissey hadn't really tried before. The marshalling of it, the way those styles were used and deployed, was very much his creation.'

Morrissey would speak of Viva Hate as a fresh start, incomparable to anything he'd recorded with The Smiths. '[It's] in no way the follow-up to Strangeways,' he insisted. 'I do feel that it is the *first* record.' Yet for all its musical novelty, lyrically Viva Hate was extremely inconsistent, in places sublime ('Late Night, Maudlin Street'), in others slightly ridiculous (the much misunderstood 'Bengali In Platforms'). It took all of three months after its release for Morrissey to admit that 'lyrically, it wasn't the best', later adding that 'there's at least six tracks on it that I'd now willingly bury in the nearest patch of soil … and place a large stone on top'.

For all its flaws, its number one success would negate any criticism, immediately establishing Morrissey as a credible solo artist, one whose loyal, ever-growing audience were clearly eager to be led out of the post-Smiths vacuum. 'I feel it was more of an event than an achievement,' concluded Morrissey. 'I think the audience was simply relieved that I was still going on with living. That in itself was the celebration of Viva Hate.'

The album is still held in high regard by the majority of fans and critics, and with good reason; in 'Suedehead', 'Everyday Is Like Sunday' and 'Late Night, Maudlin Street' it contains three of the finest songs of his entire career. Sadly, it would be Morrissey's only studio album co-written with Stephen Street. Within a year of its release, the financial dispute over the producer's royalty points would put an end to their writing partnership. It would be another three years before Morrissey followed it with the odd and inadequate KILL UNCLE.

Viva Hate was later reissued by EMI in 1997 as part of a generic series commemorating the label's centenary. This new addition featured a different cover portrait of Morrissey and eight extra random B-sides of no relevance to the original album. [25, 38, 39, 45, 71, 83, 99, 138, 171, 175, 203, 208, 265, 272, 369, 463, 479]

W

Wainwright III, Loudon, American folk singer-songwriter and a favourite of Morrissey's during his teens. He would praise Wainwright in passing in several of his letters to the NME during the mid- to late 70s and in correspondence with Scottish pen pal Robert MACKIE. In his 1981 book on the NEW YORK DOLLS Morrissey also quoted a passage from 'Uptown', a track on Wainwright's eponymous debut album of 1970 ('I'm getting sick of the slums/I'm tired of dodging the bums'). Undeniably, there's a Mozzerian quality to Wainwright's songs, often bitingly sarcastic in their outlook on life, love and human misery: 1970's 'Glad To See You've Got Religion' pre-dates 'ACCEPT YOURSELF' in its sigh of being 'sorry, sick and sad' while 1972's 'East Indian Princess' teased a Westernised Asian girl in a similar vein to Morrissey's controversial 'BENGALI IN PLATFORMS'. In 2004 Wainwright was invited to play Morriseey's MELTDOWN festival. He is also the father of singers Rufus and Martha Wainwright, his children by ex-wife/Canadian folk singer Kate McGarrigle. [190, 334, 343]

Walker, Matt and Solomon (Morrissey drummer 2006–, Morrissey bass player 2007–), Morrissey's current rhythm section, Illinois brothers Matt and Solomon Walker have already made an impact with 2009's YEARS OF REFUSAL, contributing greatly to its musical might. Drummer Matt Walker first joined Morrissey's touring band in 2006 in support of RINGLEADER OF THE TORMENTORS, having previously played with The Smashing Pumpkins. His brother, Solomon Walker, had been playing bass under the name of Solomon Snyder in various groups in Chicago and Los Angeles. He joined his brother on stage with Morrissey in Chicago on 21 November 2006, substituting for Gary DAY who was unable to attend. Day completed the rest of the Ringleader tour in Europe but as of February 2007 Solomon took over as permanent bassist, losing his 'Snyder' alias, thus enabling Morrissey to introduce them on stage as 'the Walker Brothers'.

Walters, Jake

Walters, **Jake**, Morrissey's close friend, personal assistant and bodyguard circa the mid-1990s. First and foremost an aspiring photographer, Walters was also a musician, playing drums in an early line-up of pop group Eighth Wonder, formed by Patsy Kensit and her older brother Jamie (godson of Reggie KRAY). He was later involved in the short-lived Pete Wylie project Big Hard Excellent Fish responsible for 1990's 'Imperfect List' single, Wylie's inventory of miseries from Adolf Hitler to Bonnie Langford, Myra Hindley and 'weird British judges' as read by Josie Jones. It was probably Walters's connection with the track which prompted Morrissey to employ 'Imperfect List' as his stage entrance when touring 2004's YOU ARE THE QUARRY (as heard on the WHO PUT THE 'M' IN MANCHESTER? DVD).

According to engineer Danton Supple, Morrissey met Walters through producer and former co-writer Clive LANGER and became the singer's close companion around the recording of VAUXHALL AND I in the summer of 1993. It was with that album's release that both fans and critics began speculating on their friendship. Walters's south London roots coupled with the 'very special thanks' he received on the album credits led some to interpret the title of Vauxhall And I as a code for Walters and Morrissey. Equally eyebrow-raising were Walters's intimate photographs featured on the back and inside covers of the album and its two singles, 'THE MORE YOU IGNORE ME, THE CLOSER I GET' and 'HOLD ON TO YOUR FRIENDS'; details of body parts with drawn-on tattoos and a half-naked Morrissey with 'Honey' written around his nipple. Yet these were mild when compared with an image from the same period which Morrissey only made public 14 years later on his GREATEST HITS album: his naked backside with the pun 'Your arse an'all' inked across his cheeks and the accompanying credit 'Morrissey's arse photographed by Jake Walters'.

When the singer's long-serving personal assistant Jo Slee resigned, Walters stepped in to chaperon the majority of press interviews to promote Vauxhall in early 1994. Few, if any, journalists could resist commenting on Walters – then known only as 'Jake' – and his obvious devotion to Morrissey. In *Details* magazine, William Shaw described him as a shy figure who avoided his gaze and whom Morrissey listed alongside Linder STERLING and his hairstylist Debbie Dannell as his only friends. In *Q*, Stuart Maconie introduced him as 'affable and barrer-boyish' but added 'Jake's role seems unclear: driver, gofer, mucker'. Andrew Harrison of *Select* was to have a slightly shakier experience with Walters, whom he described as 'a stocky ex-boxer at the 20s/30s crossroads with a skinhead crop'. It was unfortunate for Harrison that his interview came hot on the heels of a negative Morrissey portrait by Julie Burchill in *The Sunday Times*. Walters was so angered by Burchill's 'stitch-up' that he threatened Harrison with physical retribution if he wrote something similar. At least Harrison got to see Walters' more caring side in the form of a note left next to the record player in the sitting room of Hook End studios where Vauxhall was recorded: 'Do not play this while Moz is asleep as he is old and needs his kip.'

During this period, Walters is believed to have lodged with Morrissey at his Camden home. Asked by *Q* in 1995 who was the last person he'd slept with, Morrissey answered, 'Me lodger.' Two years later, the singer told the *Guardian* that around 1994–95 he'd fallen in love but it didn't last. Joining the dots between these facts has led to the common, if wild, assumption that Walters is the subject of 'BEST FRIEND ON THE PAYROLL' and the later 'COME BACK TO CAMDEN'. Other titles which have been put forward as Morrissey's 'Jake songs' are 'A SWALLOW ON MY NECK', 'WHATEVER HAPPENS, I LOVE YOU', 'SUNNY' and even 'THE OPERATION'. All such theories are, of course, entirely speculative. To date, the only time Walters has ever spoken to the press about Morrissey was in 1998 when he told journalist Dave Simpson that the singer was 'the most interesting and fascinating character I've met'.

Walters went on to study at West Surrey Institute of Art and Design, since making his name as a leading fashion and portrait photographer. His

We Are The Lambeth Boys, 1958 documentary film following a typical week in the life of teenagers at a south London youth club and the source of the audio samples on 1994's 'SPRING-HEELED JIM'. Morrissey had previously listed it as one of his favourite television programmes ('Cathode raves').

The Lambeth boys themselves are an endearing bunch of smart-suited, Brylcreemed geezers whose idea of a good time is hanging off the back of a lorry singing 'All coppers are 'andsome!'; such were the inner-city teenage kicks of the late 1950s. The Lambeth girls are an equally entertaining gaggle (look out for the one who bears an unfortunate resemblance to Mick Jagger). Alongside other documentaries of the short-lived 'Free Cinema' movement, the film paved the way for the social realism of the 1960s British kitchen-sink dramas. Notably, director Karel Reisz went on to make *SATURDAY NIGHT AND SUNDAY MORNING*.

'Spring-Heeled Jim' uses various clips of dialogue from the film, though the most prominent are those from an organised debate about murder. At roughly one minute 30 you can hear one boy talking about the famous Derek Bentley case ('one feller was in the copper's arms, wasn't he?') while the end clip is from a heated exchange about psychopaths in general ('They catch 'im, and they say he's mental').

Lambeth's Alford House Youth Club is still a working youth centre in the original building on Aveline Street in Kennington, neighbouring Vauxhall. [175, 561]

archive photos of Morrissey were featured on the sleeves of the 2008 singles 'THAT'S HOW PEOPLE GROW UP' and 'ALL YOU NEED IS ME'. The same year Walters took new portraits of the singer in Los Angeles including those featured on the covers of 'I'M THROWING MY ARMS AROUND PARIS' and YEARS OF REFUSAL. [6, 40, 114, 152, 154, 217, 221, 568, 569]

Walters, John, See PEEL, John.

Warwick, Dionne, See 'LONELINESS REMEMBERS WHAT HAPPINESS FORGETS'.

'We Hate It When Our Friends Become Successful' (Morrissey/Whyte), Morrissey's 12th solo single (from the album YOUR ARSENAL), released May 1992, highest UK chart position #17. 'There's the most vicious sense of competition in Manchester,' commented Morrissey shortly before Your Arsenal's release. 'So many jealous, vile creatures. That is what the song "We Hate It When Our Friends Become Successful" is about. In Manchester, you are accepted as long as you are scrambling and on your knees. But if you

have any success or are independent or a free spirit, they hate your guts.'

The title mirrored one of Oscar WILDE's more famous quotes – 'Anybody can sympathise with the sufferings of a friend, but it requires a very fine nature to sympathise with a friend's success.' Prior to the song's release, Morrissey cited the same Wilde maxim in an *NME* interview where he also discussed the current success of former Smiths support group James who'd recently reached number two in the UK with a re-release of their 1989 single 'Sit Down' (see also 'WHAT'S THE WORLD'). Morrissey insisted he was pleased for James, though added, 'when I heard they were doing *Wogan* I almost dropped the teapot appalled'.

Rumours that 'We Hate It' was, indeed, a barbed message aimed at James singer Tim Booth were finally confirmed by writer Len BROWN. In his 2008 book *Meetings With Morrissey*, Brown revealed how Morrissey agreed to play the song on ITV's *Amnesty International 30th Anniversary Special* in December 1991 on the proviso that James also be included. According to Brown,

Morrissey was upset when James's slot was dropped from the broadcast version of the show, thus spoiling the intended joke. Booth later scored an equally acid touché at the following summer's Glastonbury Festival where Morrissey was due to perform but cancelled. James took his place, opening their set with a quickly rehearsed cover of 'We Hate It'.

Beyond its specific target, it was a welcome addition to Morrissey's existing repertoire on fame and frustration, something like a crueller 'YOU JUST HAVEN'T EARNED IT YET, BABY' or 'GIRL LEAST LIKELY TO' with an extra lashing of sarcasm, even resurrecting the mocking laughter of 'BIGMOUTH STRIKES AGAIN'. Discounting 'PASHERNATE LOVE' co-written with Gary DAY, it was the first Alain Whyte song Morrissey performed live, introduced towards the end of the KILL UNCLE tour in October 1991. Whyte's easy, ascending melody and the glam power-production of Mick RONSON made it an obvious choice of A-side and a fair appetiser for the album to follow. More encouragingly, it returned Morrissey to the UK top 20 for the first time in two years.

The accompanying Tim Broad video, shot on location in Wapping, comically portrayed Morrissey and his new band as a rough-and-tumble street gang, playing football, wielding penknives or, in the case of drummer Spencer COBRIN, devouring mint choc-chip Cornetto ice creams with homoerotic delight; according to Morrissey's assistant, Jo Slee, he'd wanted Cobrin to suck a more phallic Fab ice lolly but couldn't find any on the day of the shoot. The 'such a video' lyric also coincided with a cryptic message to his friend Cathal SMYTH, pictured in a freeze-frame from the promo for MADNESS's February 1982 single 'Cardiac Arrest'. [5, 36, 94, 155, 290, 374]

'We'll Let You Know' (Morrissey/Whyte),

From the album YOUR ARSENAL (1992). The key track on Your Arsenal (the album title can be heard shouted around 2:44), structurally 'We'll Let You Know' is also its strangest: a deceptively sanguine acoustic serenade slowly torn to shreds by a baying mob before being buried altogether under a deathly bovver-boy stampede. Perhaps just as unusual is the fact that on at least three occasions Morrissey has referred to it as the favourite song he's ever recorded, explaining 'it seems to sum everything up somehow'.

The high esteem with which he regards 'We'll Let You Know' poses a serious question. From such a vast array of songs, themes and emotions, why pick out a track humanising football hooligans and justifying their xenophobic pride as the prime example of his art? 'I understand the level of patriotism, the level of frustration and the level of jubilance,' he explained. 'I understand the overall character. I understand their aggression and I understand why it must be released.'

Coming just four years after ex-Clash frontman Joe Strummer caused controversy for saying scenes of English football hooligans abroad made him feel 'national pride', Morrissey was skating on very thin ice when he too admitted feeling 'amused' by 'reports on the television about hooliganism in Sweden or Denmark or somewhere'. But placed in the wider context of Morrissey's other odes to Englishness, from the claim-staking of 'STILL ILL' to the anti-national anthems of 'THE QUEEN IS DEAD' and 'IRISH BLOOD, ENGLISH HEART', the song represents another elegy for a 'lost' nation from the soul of an indignant patriot. The brilliance of his words are that they successfully communicate the individual fear and confusion which hooligans themselves can only articulate through acts of violence as part of a mob. Morrissey is sympathetic, certainly, but there is nothing in the lyrics which could be construed as condoning football hooliganism.

His main inspiration appears to have been *Among The Thugs*, a documentary investigation into 'the eerie allure of crowd violence' by American journalist Bill Buford, first published in the UK in early 1991. Like Morrissey, Buford's book (which also offers the origin of 'THE NATIONAL FRONT DISCO') doesn't moralise but attempts to understand who football hooligans are and why they do it. Towards the end of his undercover infiltration of various organised firms across the country, Buford concludes that the answer lies in the disappearance of the British working-class, a fact which 'few people' will admit. As a consequence, argues Buford, football thugs 'have simply become more exaggerated, ornate versions of an ancient style, more extreme because now without substance … This bored, empty, decadent generation consists of nothing more than what it appears to be. It is a lad culture without mystery, so deadened that it uses violence to wake itself up.'

This is the crux of 'We'll Let You Know', not a glorification of jingoistic aggression, but Morrissey's requiem for the death of his own social class. In this respect it does, indeed, 'sum everything up somehow' about who he is and where he comes from. [5, 94, 292, 404, 405, 567]

Webb, Clifton, Hollywood actor listed among Morrissey's favourite 'symbolists' in 1983. It's likely his interest in Webb stems from his most famous role in the 1944 noir thriller *Laura*. Webb's character, the acid-tongued smartarse columnist Waldo Lydecker who boasts how he writes 'with a goose quill dipped in venom', was based on New York critic Alexander Woollcott who similarly inspired the character of Sheridan WHITESIDE in *THE MAN WHO CAME TO DINNER*. Lydecker's habit of typing while in the bath also seems to have encouraged Morrissey to try the same, if only in the 'SUEDEHEAD' video. Most biographical accounts of Webb offer the same sweeping stereotype of a sexually inactive gay man who spent most of his life devoted to his mother. His friend Noël COWARD famously mocked Webb's long depression after her death by quipping, 'It must be difficult to be orphaned at 70, Clifton.' Webb died a few years later in 1966, aged 76, and was interred in what is now Hollywood Forever Cemetery where Morrissey also wishes to be laid to rest. (See GRAVE.) [184, 523]

'Well I Wonder' (Morrissey/Marr), From the album MEAT IS MURDER (1985). 'We never played this song live,' says Marr. 'Myself and Morrissey never discussed why, but I got the impression it was because it had something magical we might not be able to recapture in concert.'

'Magical' perfectly describes 'Well I Wonder', a record which suspends Morrissey and Marr's rare chemistry in a stillness of time clearer than any other. Its desolate, yearning lyrics were inspired by, and based upon, Elizabeth SMART's *By Grand Central Station I Sat Down And Wept*, the same source for 'WHAT SHE SAID', written and rehearsed at the same time, which includes the phrases 'the fierce last stand of all I have', 'lies gasping, but still living' and 'do you hear me where you sleep?' Morrissey stitches together Smart's words with those torn from his own emotional agony, an epic aloneness made more so by Marr's morosely beautiful if not beautifully morose backcloth. Written 'from scratch' in the guitarist's Earls Court flat in the summer of 1984, Marr recorded a guitar and bass demo for Morrissey the same afternoon with Andy Rourke. It was Morrissey's idea to add the sound of light drizzle from a BBC sound effects LP (perhaps a nod to the atmospheric 60s pop downpours heard on The Ronettes' 'Walking In The Rain' and Sandie SHAW's 'Run') while his recorded vocal, complete with falsetto climax, was rendered with spellbinding fragility. As Marr speculated, the delicate nature of 'Well I Wonder' may indeed have lost something in a live setting.

Rough Trade had discussed releasing the track as a single, a move Morrissey and Marr opposed, though prior to Meat Is Murder it first appeared a fortnight earlier as the B-side to 'HOW SOON IS NOW?' Morrissey later made coy use of the title when asked in 1995 who were his best male and best female friends. 'Well,' said Morrissey. 'I wonder.' [13, 17, 18, 375, 426, 569]

Well Of Loneliness, The, 1928 novel by Radclyffe Hall, famously christened 'the Bible of lesbianism' and one of Morrissey's favourite books. Although the book never mentions the words 'lesbian' or 'homosexual', nor even any graphic description of gay sex, its original publication provoked an obscenity trial. Its primary cause for offence was its suggestion that homosexuals were victims of an uncaring society and that theirs was a natural love, not an uncommon perversion. The trial found that by condoning homosexuality the book was morally corrupt and, by law, obscene. It wasn't until after Hall's death that it was eventually republished in the UK in 1949.

The novel follows the history of Stephen Gordon, the only child of a wealthy Worcestershire family who, hoping for a son, had already chosen her masculine name before she was born. Stephen herself acts as a boy, taking an interest in fencing and hunting and developing a close relationship with her doting father. Her inexplicable crush upon a housemaid is an early warning sign that Stephen is, as she'll later describe it, a sexual 'invert'. Secretly, her father realises the same, but is killed in a freak accident before he is able to tell either her or Stephen's increasingly wary mother.

The rest of the book follows Stephen into adulthood where she learns the hard way that 'the loneliest place in this world is the no-man's-land of sex'. She falls madly in love with a married American woman who eventually betrays Stephen to her husband to prevent the discovery of a separate affair with another man. In order to avoid local scandal, Stephen is sent away. She eventually becomes a successful author in London though decides to do her bit for king and country when the First World War breaks out by joining a women's ambulance unit in France. There she meets and begins a relationship with an innocent young Welsh girl, Mary, who joins Stephen in Paris after the war. In time, Stephen becomes convinced she'll never be able to make Mary happy since, even in gay Paris, the world is prejudiced against their kind. To complicate matters, Martin, a boy who'd courted Stephen as a teenager, resumes contact only to fall in love with Mary. Taking this as a sign that she and Mary are never to be, Stephen settles on a grand act of self-sacrifice, telling Mary she's been unfaithful with a mutual lesbian friend, knowing it will drive her to Martin for comfort and, eventually, a 'normal existence'. The book's climactic final pages are a political plea, directed from the heartbroken Stephen to God but in essence from Hall to society at large, demanding homosexuals be accepted. 'Acknowledge us, oh God, before the world. Give us also the right to our existence!'

West Ham, East London football club who provided the unofficial theme to Morrissey's solo tour of 1999. Morrissey had no interest in the current sporting fortunes of the club beyond its symbolic association with his latest musical obsession, the COCKNEY REJECTS. Throughout the tour, Morrissey appeared on stage wearing a replica 'West Ham Boys Club' T-shirt as worn by Rejects singer Stinky Turner, though he'd sometimes rotate with variant designs for two other east London institutions: the fictitious 'Canning Town Sauna Club' and the 'English Martyrs', a private members club in Whitechapel. Though in different colours, all T-shirts used the same West Ham United crest of two crossed hammers over a castle motif.

Official press advertisements for the November to December UK leg featured a scantily clad Adonis with 'West Ham' crudely superimposed as a tattoo on his upper arm. Throughout the tour, Morrissey would also substitute certain lyrics for the words 'West Ham' (e.g. 'You're gonna need West Ham on your side'). Even after the tour moved on to the US and Latin America in early 2000, he was still including a photo of the gates of West Ham United's home ground, Upton Park, as a backdrop projection. It was, however, just a phase, albeit a bamboozling one which had absolutely nothing to do with football. To the disappointment of equally devout Morrissey/Hammers fan Russell BRAND, Morrissey's brief allegiance to the 'claret and blue' of West Ham was purely for aesthetic, if not eccentric, reasons. [287, 386]

It's easy to see why Morrissey referred to *The Well Of Loneliness* as stirring 'very powerful passions' within him, not merely as a masterpiece of gay polemic but because of its central themes of societal ostracism, romantic martyrdom and the rejection of rigid sexual definition (Hall's 'third sex') endemic in his own writing. The difference in spelling aside, the coincidence of the protagonist's forename adds further uncanny symbolism, as noted by the writer Michael Bracewell who quoted a passage during his introduction to Linder STERLING's photo souvenir of 1991's KILL UNCLE tour, *Morrissey Shot*. The androgynous character of Stephen Gordon, like that of Radclyffe Hall herself, also bears similarities with Morrissey's favourite painter Hannah GLUCKSTEIN, who read the book some years after its publication.

Morrissey has named Radclyffe Hall one of his favourite writers on several occasions. Though best known for *The Well Of Loneliness*, she wrote seven other novels and various volumes of poetry. Her strange forename is actually a derivation of her original double-barrelled family name, born Marguerite Radclyffe-Hall in 1880. She died in 1943, aged 63, and is buried in the west side of London's Highgate Cemetery, across the road from the grave of another of Morrissey's favourite writers, George ELIOT, buried in the east. A plaque on Hall's tomb, dedicated to her lover Una Troubridge, quotes from Elizabeth Barrett Browning: '… and, if God choose, I shall but love thee better after death'. (See also *BARRETTS OF WIMPOLE STREET*.) [141, 154, 322, 377]

Whale Nation, See WILLIAMS, Heathcoate.

'What A Nice Way To Turn Seventeen',
1962 Phil Spector production by New York girl group The Crystals listed among Morrissey's 'Singles to be cremated with'. Written by Larry Kolber and Jack Keller, the song was the B-side of The Crystals' second single for Spector's Philles label, 'Uptown'. The lyrics are a young girl's subtly euphemistic celebration of losing her virginity on the night of her 17th birthday. 'The party's through and I'm alone with you,' sings Barbara Alston, leaving the listener to fill in the blanks over a fittingly smoochy soundtrack. Morrissey's fondness for the tune is indicative of his interest in 60s girl groups and a discerning taste for the lesser known works by the genre's biggest stars. In the UK, The Crystals would achieve far greater success with their two top ten hits of 1963, 'Da Doo Ron Ron' and 'Then He Kissed Me'. [175]

'What Difference Does It Make?'
(**Morrissey/Marr**), The Smiths' third single (taken from the album THE SMITHS), released January 1984, highest UK chart position #12. Cover star: Terence STAMP.

A guilty confession of lingering love after a relationship destroyed by deceit and petty theft, 'What Difference Does It Make?' was typical of Morrissey's early Smiths lyrics in its sense of regret, hopelessness and betrayal. Written circa November 1982, as one of their oldest songs Morrissey became increasingly embarrassed by it as time dragged on, extremely ironic since it was his first top 20 hit and one of the biggest of The Smiths' career. Two years after its release he dismissed it as 'quite shameful', particularly in what he called its 'juvenile' use of the religious idiom 'the devil will find work for idle hands to do'; a common phrase which, maybe coincidentally, also occurs in Shelagh DELANEY's *Sweetly Sings The Donkey* and Emlyn Williams's *BEYOND BELIEF*, both to be found on his bookshelf back in 1982.

Marr's sleek shadowy twang demonstrated his gift for pickaxing vivid original riffs from otherwise familiar rock and roll surfaces. First recorded in primitive form as the lead track on an EMI-funded demo at Manchester's Drone studios in December 1982, it remained the most commercially obvious debut single choice until the arrival of the superior 'HAND IN GLOVE' early in the new year.

In Morrissey's view, its definitive recording was that recorded for their debut John PEEL BBC radio session in May 1983 and subsequently included on HATFUL OF HOLLOW, distinguished by Joyce's rumbling drum pattern and Rourke's strolling bass line. After two more trial versions with producer Troy TATE for their aborted debut album, by the time they recorded it again with John PORTER for The Smiths their fatigue was starting to show. Consequently Porter took control, making a significant change to the arrangement by regulating its beat to a sharp, constant hammer, also lacquering Marr's vicious riff with a shower of atmospheric guitar overdubs. Where on the original Drone demo during the 'no more apologies' section they'd overdubbed the sound of applause (a move they'd repeat years later on 'PAINT A VULGAR PICTURE'), here Morrissey added the noise of children playing from an old sound effects album.

For all Morrissey's subsequent savage criticisms of the record ('I thought it was absolutely awful the day after [it] was pressed'), on 'What Difference Does It Make?' Porter turned The Smiths' weird, dysfunctional Mancunian R&B into a gleaming, accessible and classic 80s pop single, a populist Smiths favourite to this day. At his most even-tempered, Morrissey rationalised his dislike by admitting that in his view it failed to surpass the previous 'THIS CHARMING MAN'. 'I think every record should equal if not go beyond the last one,' he mourned. Nor has time done much to change his opinion. Asked to approve Warners' posthumous 2008 compilation The Sound Of The Smiths, the original single version was removed in favour of the Peel session recording upon Morrissey's request. [17, 27, 50, 94, 275, 300, 430, 395]

'What Do You See In Him?' (Morrissey/Marr), See 'WONDERFUL WOMAN'.

'What She Said' (Morrissey/Marr), From the album MEAT IS MURDER (1985). Many of Morrissey's songs written in the latter half of 1984 were influenced by Elizabeth SMART's 1945 prose poem By Grand Central Station I Sat Down And Wept, none more explicitly than 'What She Said' and 'WELL I WONDER'. The two songs were rehearsed in tandem, with 'What She Said' being one of the rare instances where Morrissey and Marr wrote 'eyeball to eyeball'. Smart is effectively the 'She'

of 'What She Said', inasmuch as the song's central female character quotes more or less direct passages from her book: 'I wonder why no one has noticed I am dead and taken the trouble to bury me' and 'I have learned to smoke because I need something to hold on to'. Morrissey employs Smart's dialogue to paint a tragic-comic portrait of a bookish depressive, not unlike his former teenage self, who finally receives an abrupt lesson in more earthly pleasures from a 'tattooed boy from Birkenhead'.

The song's inexorable ecstasy owes less to its lyrics than it does Marr's breakneck guitar riff, a Catherine wheel of a tune encouraging similar pyrotechnics from Rourke and an especially boisterous Joyce (early rehearsals even featured something close to a drum solo). A rambunctious concert highlight, during their final tours of 1986 The Smiths incorporated 'What She Said' into a medley with 'RUBBER RING', as heard on RANK. [17, 38, 375, 426]

'What's The World' (Jim Glennie/Paul Gilbertson/Gavan Whelan/Tim Booth), B-side of 'I STARTED SOMETHING I COULDN'T finish' (1987). A cover of the 1983 FACTORY Records debut single by Manchester indie group James, 'What's The World' is little more than a footnote in The Smiths' repertoire. Intended as a whimsical setlist bonus played exclusively on all seven nights of their autumn 1985 tour of Scotland, a live recording from their 25 September Glasgow Barrowlands gig ended up being posthumously released on the cassette-single of 1987's 'I Started Something'.

'It added another slightly different dynamic to the live set,' says Marr, 'but it was never meant to be released and I was never really mad about it. It never felt like us. Morrissey had his reasons for wanting us to play that.'

James had previously supported The Smiths on the MEAT IS MURDER tour that spring after earning the accolade of Morrissey's favourite new group of 1985. His decision to cover 'What's The World' appeared a magnanimous attempt to highlight the work of an unknown, up-and-coming band, an act he'd later repeat in his solo career with Bradford's 'SKIN STORM' and Suede's 'MY INSATIABLE ONE'. The Smiths' version of the song remained faithful to James's arrangement of giggling indie minus the vague folky influence of the original. In view of his habit of tapping other writers for source material, it was also pertinent to hear Morrissey playfully sing Tim Booth's lyrics about seeking 'words to call my own' rather than 'worn-out phrases'.

Although James benefited greatly from The Smiths' patronage in terms of gaining press coverage, it took another five years of line-up and label changes before they finally achieved mainstream chart success with 1991's re-release of 'Sit Down'. (See also 'WE HATE IT WHEN OUR FRIENDS BECOME SUCCESSFUL'.) [17, 182]

'Whatever Happens, I Love You' (Morrissey/Whyte), B-side of 'BOXERS' (1995). Morrissey in love can only ever end in disaster and, sure enough, this assumedly autobiographical declaration already marks the end of the affair. There are strong indications that the romance was inevitably destined to fail and possibly controversial ('fights for rights') while the most intriguing detail is that he and his ex-love stole from one another's wardrobes. In its requiem for a doomed or finite partnership the lyrics hark back to the emotions of 'HAND IN GLOVE', its melody mired in hopelessness by the klaxons of grief provided by Boz BOORER's clarinet. First issued on the 'Boxers' single, 'Whatever Happens, I Love You' was granted greater prominence as the opening track on the ensuing WORLD OF MORRISSEY compilation, becoming a concert fixture of his February 1995 UK tour. [4, 40]

'When Last I Spoke To Carol' (Morrissey/Whyte), From the album YEARS OF REFUSAL (2009). The macabre and mysterious tale of a young woman born in 1975 with an intrinsically bleak outlook on life whose love for Morrissey goes unreciprocated, thus sending her to an early grave. Whether autobiographical or allegorical, the tragic story of pasty-faced Carol was an archetypal Morrissey sermon on life in all its misery, futility of purpose and, in Carol's case, shocking brevity. Such gloomy words assumed a strangely camp edge on the back of its galloping death disc tune, not dissimilar to one of his favourite singles, John Leyton's 'JOHNNY REMEMBER ME', albeit lacquered with Tijuana brass in another of the album's subtle homages to Herb Alpert, the Mexican trumpet maestro whom Morrissey had originally wanted to play on the record. Equally curious was its fading wind chill, a seemingly conscious throwback to the same squall of death ushering in The Smiths' 'ASLEEP'.

Whitelaw, Billie, Northern actress and replacement cover star for later pressings of The Smiths' single 'WILLIAM, IT WAS REALLY NOTHING'. The original 1984 release had featured a detail from an American press advert for ADS SPEAKERS: when the company complained, in 1987 a different version was issued featuring a tousled Whitelaw rising from her slumber in a scene from 1967's *Charlie Bubbles*, one of Morrissey's favourite films written by Shelagh DELANEY and starring/directed by Albert FINNEY. Whitelaw was 'more than happy' to appear on the sleeve and the following year took a cameo in the video for 1988's 'EVERYDAY IS LIKE SUNDAY'. Also of note are one of Whitelaw's earliest roles as a RUSHOLME housewife in 1960's Manchester crime thriller *Hell Is A City* starring Stanley BAKER, and her portrayal of the mother of *The KRAYS* in Peter Medak's 1990 biopic. [374, 491]

Whiteside, Sheridan, Morrissey's occasional writing pseudonym prior to forming The Smiths. The name was taken from the character played by Monty Woolley in one of his favourite Bette DAVIS films, *THE MAN WHO CAME TO DINNER*. The original Whiteside, as created by playwrights George S. Kaufman and Moss Hart, was based upon the opinionated New York critic Alexander Woollcott, a member of the Algonquin Round Table alongside Dorothy Parker and the alleged 'inventor' of the Brandy Alexander cocktail. Coincidentally,

Woollcott was also the inspiration for the character of Waldo Lydecker in 1944's *Laura* as played by Morrissey symbolist Clifton WEBB.

The Whiteside of *The Man Who Came To Dinner* describes himself as a 'critic, lecturer, wit, radio orator [and] intimate friend of the great and near great'. To everyone else, however, he's a thoroughly unpleasant and boorish egomaniac, best summed up by his nurse's complaint that, 'If Florence Nightingale had ever nursed you, Mr Whiteside, she would have married JACK THE RIPPER instead of founding the Red Cross.' Morrissey's decision to adopt the name of such a character was, therefore, deliberately mischievous, although interestingly he shares Whiteside's fascination with famous murders.

Although his use of the Whiteside nom-de-plume prefigured The Smiths, it was interesting that he should resurrect it on the run-out-groove messages of the group's final two singles of 1987. 'I STARTED SOMETHING I COULDN'T FINISH' bore the inscription '"Murder At The Wool Hall" (X) Starring Sheridan Whiteside' while the vinyl of 'LAST NIGHT I DREAMT THAT SOMEBODY LOVED ME' carried the similar pairing of '"The Return Of The Submissive Society" (X) Starring Sheridan Whiteside' and '"The Bizarre Oriental Vibrating Palm Death" (X) Starring Sheridan Whiteside'. [184, 362, 374, 523, 529]

'Why Don't You Find Out For Yourself'

(Morrissey/Whyte), From the album VAUXHALL AND I (1994). One of a handful of Morrissey titles possibly adapted from Buffy SAINTE-MARIE (in this case her 1969 track 'Better To Find Out For Yourself'), here he lays bare his paranoid distrust of the music industry as addressed to an unsympathetic partner who dares to remind him of his past mistakes. By 1993, when he recorded the song, Morrissey was celebrating his tenth year as a

Who Put The 'M' In Manchester?, Official DVD of Morrissey's 2004 'Manchester Homecoming show', released in the UK in April 2005. See Mozography appendix for full tracklisting.

Released in tandem with the LIVE AT EARLS COURT album, *Who Put The 'M' In Manchester?* celebrated Morrissey's highly successful 2004 comeback with YOU ARE THE QUARRY, documenting his hugely anticipated concert at Manchester's MEN Arena on Saturday 22 May – the first UK date on the Quarry tour (five days after the album's release), his first hometown show in 12 years and, to cap it all, his 45th birthday. All of which served to make it a historic gig if, in the cold light of day, an average rather than ecstatic concert film.

Though a precious souvenir for the 18,000 who attended the event, in pure performance terms it failed to capture the best of Morrissey or that of his musicians, some of whom sound only partially awake ('THE HEADMASTER RITUAL' is especially drowsy). Even so, the DVD isn't without its moments: Morrissey's entrance with an a cappella twist on FRANK SINATRA's 'My Way'; the sheer awe of the venue size and the Elvis-inspired neon stage lettering; footage of awestruck and tattooed fans before and after the show being interviewed by Linder STERLING; and a wonderfully atmospheric tour-of-Manchester prologue featuring images of Saddleworth Moor and STRANGEWAYS prison. If nothing else, the final emotional encore of 'There Is A Light' almost compensates for the sterility of the main set, Morrissey clearly moved by his home crowd's wild adoration.

The MEN show would subsequently become of less celebratory significance as the penultimate Morrissey concert featuring guitarist and longest-serving co-writer Alain WHYTE. The following month he was replaced by Barrie Cadogan, who can be seen in the DVD bonus material filmed at Morrissey's next hometown gig, the Move festival at Lancashire County Cricket Club on 11 July 2004.

recording artist, not that the lyrics presented much to celebrate. Instead, 'Why Don't You Find Out For Yourself' is a battle-scarred catalogue of his many dealings with exploitative parasites who, as in 'PAINT A VULGAR PICTURE', are entirely motivated by money. 'I find the business side [of music] very distasteful, harrowing and soul-destroying,' he'd told the press five years earlier. 'I always had a basic view that if you earned money it belongs to you. But that is obviously not the case. People have very slim rights over the money they earn.' Though the post-Smiths COURT CASE was still three years away, it would be fair to assume that the song's proverbial backstabbers would include his current litigant, Mike Joyce.

In its original form, Whyte's tune was rendered a similar industrial strength to much of YOUR ARSE-NAL before producer Steve LILLYWHITE decided to strip the instrumentation back. Rather than re-record the song from scratch, Lillywhite left Morrissey's vocal as it was but replaced its rocking anger with a pained acoustic sigh enriched by Whyte's vaporous harmonies. As bassist Jonny BRIDGWOOD points out, the finished track also includes a sampled loop of Boz BOORER rattling some tea cups in the control room as extra percussion, taken during a playback at the point where Morrissey sings 'some men here' which, if you listen carefully, you can hear repeated throughout the entire track in the right-hand speaker. [4, 6, 40, 208]

Whyte, Alain (Morrissey guitarist and co-writer, 1991–), It is impossible for any co-writer to ever eclipse the divine magic Morrissey created with Johnny Marr. But, taking Morrissey's career as a whole, his most prolific co-writer remains Alain Whyte. Though others such as Boz BOORER have left an indelible mark upon his legacy, it is Whyte, alone, who since 1992 has defined the classic solo Morrissey sound after four years of trial and error with Stephen STREET, Clive LANGER, Kevin ARMSTRONG, Andy Rourke and Mark NEVIN.

In some ways – tenuous if symbolically parallel ways – Whyte is Eliza Doolittle to Morrissey's Professor Henry Higgins: a rough diamond plucked from the streets of London (before Morrissey, Whyte's previous employment was sweeping roads for Camden Council) given a once-in-a-lifetime opportunity to radically change their life and live the dream. Some have argued that it is Whyte's naïveté and inexperience which have made him the perfect foil for Morrissey, who could control and manipulate him as a result. Others have criticised Whyte for 'writing to order', unwilling or unable to challenge or push Morrissey out of his comfort zone, instead working within failsafe criteria guaranteed to sustain their partnership indefinitely. Yet, whatever their methodology involved, the fact remains that the Morrissey/Whyte composer credit has produced many of the most powerful, and beautiful, records among his repertoire. Morrissey has described Whyte's work as possessing 'a melodious sadness' and, indeed, it's true to say that, Marr aside, no writer can surpass Whyte in his ability to match the pathos and poignancy of Morrissey's words in the language of music.

His entry into Morrissey's band, and life, couldn't have been more haphazard. In the winter of 1990, having just finished making KILL UNCLE, Morrissey became smitten with 50s rockabilly, enchanted by the regular themed nights at the Camden Workers Social Club near his new home in north London. His enthusiasm was great enough to inform Kill Uncle co-writer Mark Nevin and producer Clive Langer that he intended to record a 'rockabilly mini-album' straight away. Though he'd not dismissed his current studio band of Nevin, MADNESS bassist Mark Bedford and drummer Andrew PARESI, he despatched Langer and Nevin to find and audition some suitable rockabilly musicians to bring the project to life. Langer asked the help of his friend Cathal SMYTH, who in turn passed him on to Boz Boorer, a reputed rockabilly authority who spearheaded the 80s rockabilly revival with The Polecats. Boorer then brought in double bassist Jonny BRIDGWOOD.

The exact chronology of when, and how, the quiffed and handsome 23-year-old Whyte entered the equation is slightly hazy. Whyte was currently fronting his own rockabilly trio, The Memphis Sinners, with bassist Gary DAY and drummer Spencer COBRIN; all three had previously been in another rockabilly group, Born Bad. Whyte's version of events is that he'd heard Morrissey was looking to recruit a band from the Camden Workers Social Club rockabilly scene and went there every week armed with a cassette hoping he'd be there. The second week, says Whyte, Morrissey turned up so he made his approach.

Cobrin recalls being approached by Langer first, then introducing him to Whyte. Meanwhile, both Langer and Mark Nevin's memories are that prior to any recording they went to watch The Memphis Sinners audition at Cobrin's home in Stanmore. 'They were playing in this nouveau-riche Grecian boudoir,' says Langer. 'The idea was to see if they were fit to record. I thought they were pretty limited. They looked good, but they weren't "musicians". But they had the right clothes and the right tattoos.'

'They looked like 14-year-olds,' says Nevin. 'You couldn't deny that they looked fantastic. But Spencer had this really cheap drum kit and, in my mind, they weren't really very good. I thought there was no way they could work with Morrissey.'

Regardless of the process involved, Whyte alone would join Boorer and Bridgwood at Hook End studios in December 1990 for the recording of 'PREGNANT FOR THE LAST TIME' – not as guitarist, but harmonica player.[1] He was, by far, the most nervous of the new recruits, a tension which almost sabotaged his future with Morrissey from the off. 'Alain was *completely* nervous,' says Bridgwood. 'I felt bad for him because he was trying to cover up by motor-mouthing the whole time. You could see Morrissey stood there thinking, "Who *is* this person?" There was no real arrangement with the music either so we just jammed it. Alain made up this harmonica part for "Pregnant For The Last Time" but they decided it didn't fit. So Alain was wiped from the session.'

Langer and co-producer Alan Winstanley were also taken aback by Whyte's verbal diarrhoea. 'Alain was nice,' says Winstanley, 'but he never

shut up. We used to nickname him "Carpet" after this boring story he once told about a carpet. The truth is that it was Alain yapping drivel that sent Morrissey to his room for two days. The session fell apart and we had to chuck the band out.'

Despite their swift ejection, Whyte was still called back three months later, this time with Day and Cobrin, to 'play' Morrissey's band in the video for 'SING YOUR LIFE' alongside Mark Nevin. Within a month, the three Memphis Sinners, along with Boorer, would be playing for real on the Kill Uncle tour. Again, the exact chain of events is blurry, but Whyte maintains that, in desperation to impress Morrissey, he made the blindly ambitious and calculated move of learning the bulk of the singer's recent back catalogue, including the new Kill Uncle album, in an intense two-week rehearsal period with Boorer, Day and Cobrin. The latter concurs this was pretty much the case. 'I seem to remember an entire week, sitting on the edge of my bed, drumming along to the whole of Kill Uncle,' says Cobrin. 'Then we arranged a rehearsal, probably through Clive. Morrissey came down, heard us play and spent about half an hour singing along. He turned round to us at the end and said, "I love it." It was that simple.'

So began Whyte's long-term partnership with Morrissey. Five months into the Kill Uncle tour, he made his writing debut with 'PASHERNATE LOVE', one of a handful with Gary Day, then 'WE HATE IT WHEN OUR FRIENDS BECOME SUCCESSFUL'. By the time Morrissey was ready to record YOUR ARSENAL the following spring, Whyte had all but usurped Kill Uncle's Mark Nevin as his main co-writer, responsible for eight of its ten tracks.

The early Morrissey/Whyte songs betrayed his love of loud guitar-based rock such as The Clash (e.g. 'THE NATIONAL FRONT DISCO'), though were sometimes transparent in their desperate appeal to the singer's love of glam, whether the BOWIE 'Jean Genie'-swagger of 'GLAMOROUS GLUE' or the audacious aping of BOLAN's 'Ride A White Swan' on 'CERTAIN PEOPLE I KNOW'. While he'd maintain this musically tough approach on later material –

from 'THE BOY RACER' to 'IRISH BLOOD, ENGLISH HEART' and 'SOMETHING IS SQUEEZING MY SKULL' – the majority of Whyte's songs are distinguished by a sweetness of melody, often wistfully sentimental and with a tangible, possibly self-conscious, air of sadness. It is perhaps telling that, as Jonny Bridgwood claims, Whyte quickly became a Smiths scholar, enamoured with the workings of Johnny Marr's melodies and the lessons they contained within. 'I remember Alain once bragging, "I know what Morrissey likes,"' says Bridgwood, 'but that seems to be the case.'

Boorer's progression to co-writer on 1994's VAUXHALL AND I introduced a competitive element, if not a threat, to Whyte's relationship with Morrissey. The singer has always vehemently denied accusations of co-writer rivalry. Spencer Cobrin recalls otherwise. 'There was a tension there,' says Cobrin. 'Boz had been making records longer than the rest of us so he was very aware of song publishing and the whole money-making aspect. As things progressed you could sense the competition between Boz and Alain, definitely. It was always there in the background, a constant atmosphere.'

If there ever was any competition, then Whyte has always won. From 1992's YOUR ARSENAL, he's written the majority of tracks on every Morrissey album, consistently overshadowing those of Boorer, Cobrin (on MALADJUSTED) and latterly Michael FARRELL and Jesse TOBIAS.

A lyricist and singer himself (Whyte's high harmony vocals feature frequently on Morrissey's 90s recordings), during Morrissey's Los Angeles 'wilderness years' between 1998 and 2003 he kept his hand in fronting a succession of north London groups. Many of Whyte's later Morrissey songs first appeared with his own lyrics in Johnny Panic And The Bible Of Dreams and The Motivators,[2] among them 'Not Bitter But Bored' ('Irish Blood, English Heart'), 'Paranoia' ('DON'T MAKE FUN OF DADDY'S VOICE') and 'She Doesn't Love Me' ('THE NEVER-PLAYED SYMPHONIES'). The latter best illustrates both Whyte's failings as a lyricist and Morrissey's genius for radically altering the guitarist's original designs – a song about losing a girlfriend suddenly becomes a song about regretting an inactive sex life in the throes of death.

As an integral part of the Morrissey machinery, especially in concert, Whyte was held in great affection among his core audience. Consequently, his sudden exit from the early stages of 2004's YOU ARE THE QUARRY tour was both shocking and suspect. On 5 June, Morrissey played the Dublin Castle, his first since his victorious 45th birthday Manchester homecoming show two weeks earlier. Fan reports of the performance concur that Whyte looked pasty and emotional. Between songs, he informed the crowd, 'I'm not feeling very well so if I'm not playing well that's my excuse, sorry.' It was to be Whyte's last concert with Morrissey. Six days later, when Morrissey played the first of his three MELTDOWN concerts at London's Royal Festival Hall, emergency substitute Barrie Cadogan appeared in Whyte's place.

The official reason for Whyte's departure has yet to be given. His on-stage admission of illness in Dublin has led to various unsubstantiated rumours of physical, or even mental, ill health. Fortunately, whatever the cause of Whyte's disappearance from Morrissey's tour, his status as co-writer would be unaffected. He'd return for the autumn 2005 recording of RINGLEADER OF THE TORMENTORS in Rome, writing half its tracks. In the interim, and now living in Los Angeles, Whyte formed and fronted another group, Red Lightning, who disbanded in 2007.

As of 2009, Whyte is still Morrissey's main co-writer of choice though with YEARS OF REFUSAL his role now seems to be restricted purely to writing rather than recording – a situation which, as the strength of material on that album attests, evidently works best for both parties. [4, 5, 15, 22, 25, 242]

---

1. Whyte is still miscredited as 'Harmonica' on the sleeve of the 'SING YOUR LIFE' single. As with the names of Boorer and Bridgwood also listed, Whyte never played on the song or any of its B-sides.
2. The Motivators were a trio of Whyte, Gary Day and former Morrissey tour drummer Spike T. Smith. They recorded a debut album in 2003 for the Pop Fiction label which was never released.

'Wide To Receive' (Morrissey/Cobrin), From the album MALADJUSTED (1997). Employing computer terminology as a metaphor for unrequited love, the title of 'Wide To Receive' seemed knowingly suggestive. 'It's supposed to be an internet song,' Morrissey explained. 'You know, lying by your computer waiting for someone to tap into you and finding that nobody is, and hence being wide to receive. How *awful*, of course, to be wide to receive and finding there's no reason to be.' At the time Morrissey remained extremely coy about his own use of the internet, refusing to divulge whether he even owned a computer. As late as 2002 – by which time he was already using email in private – the singer still made unconvincing claims that he'd 'never been on-line'.

The first Morrissey song co-written with drummer Spencer Cobrin – who'd clearly been listening to and learning from the kind of placid, reflective melodies the singer favoured from Alain Whyte – 'Wide To Receive' was a superior ballad, beautifully sung (including some fine harmonising from Whyte) and boasting a wonderfully hypnotic BEATLES-esque end section. Originally considered as a B-side, Morrissey added it to Maladjusted at the eleventh hour at the expense of BOORER'S 'I CAN HAVE BOTH'. [4, 5, 36, 40, 194, 411]

Wilde, Oscar,

The ultimate Morrissey symbolist and if not his greatest influence overall then certainly his greatest influence in terms of literature. Wilde himself famously argued that he'd put his genius into his life and only his talent into his work and, indeed, it's for the life, as much as the work, that Morrissey cherishes Wilde so intensely. 'Regardless of how he wrote and how he lived in the public sense, his private life was just as astounding,' Morrissey once gushed. 'And that's the final judgement of all artists. I don't think it's enough to switch on and switch off, to be there in the daytime but to be playing hockey at night.'

Wilde's life and martyrdom – imprisoned for being homosexual, a criminal offence in Victorian England – is established legend but deserves reiterating in context of his fundamental importance to Morrissey.

Oscar Fingal O'Flahertie Wills Wilde was born in Dublin, 16 October 1854: Wilde would later declare, 'I am not English. I am Irish, which is quite different,' a difference which the second generation Irish Morrissey understands just as keenly (see 'IRISH BLOOD, ENGLISH HEART'). His father, Sir William, was a renowned ear and eye surgeon. His mother, Lady Jane Francesca, was a poet and Irish nationalist who wrote inflammatory verse under the pseudonym 'Speranza': Lady Wilde's 1848

Speranza editorial for the newspaper *The Nation* headed 'Jacta Alea Est' ('The die is cast') would provide the inspiration for the title of The Smiths' 'A RUSH AND A PUSH AND THE LAND IS OURS'. Educated at Dublin's Trinity College, Wilde won a scholarship to Oxford's Magdalen College where he'd prove his intellect by graduating with a Double First and his artistry by winning the university's Newdigate Prize Poem with an ode to the Italian town of Ravenna, his first published work.

Settling in London in 1878, Wilde declared himself 'Professor of Aesthetics' and embarked on a one-man sartorial revolution of 'dress reform', turning up at evening parties in 'a velvet coat edged with braid, knee-breeches, black silk stockings, a soft loose shirt with wide low turn-down collar, and a large flowing pale green tie'. In Victorian England, Wilde all but single-handedly created 'the fashion statement', his buttonholes sprouting with giant lilies, sunflowers and, eventually, his trademark aesthete's badge of honour, the green carnation. Morrissey's use of FLOWERS in The Smiths, as he admitted, was entirely Wilde's influence.

In 1881 he self-published the collection *Poems* containing his celebrated 'Requiescat' written in honour of his younger sister, Isola, who died of a fever at the age of nine; the 12-year-old Oscar cut a lock of her hair and placed it in an envelope which he decorated and kept for the rest of his life. His poetry was ridiculed by critics of the time, many of whom already regarded Wilde as an arrogant and offensively flamboyant celebrity who needed taking down several pegs. Even his alma mater disowned him when the copy of *Poems* he presented to the Oxford Union Debating Society was returned to its author for being not merely 'immoral' but plagiarised from the great poets of the past. As Morrissey would note in defence of his own cultural ransackings, 'I've found so many instances where [Wilde] has directly lifted from others.'

On Christmas Eve that same year, Wilde left England for a lecture tour of America. He'd been invited in response to the success of Gilbert and Sullivan's comic opera *Patience*, a spoof of the growing English aesthetic movement of which, by dint of dress and demeanour, he'd become self-appointed figurehead. Reports of Oscar's character had been so exaggerated that by the time his ship arrived in New York the gathering crowd had expected to see, in the words of biographer Hesketh Pearson, 'a man rather resembling a tropical plant'. They were initially disappointed when he disembarked looking more human than hyacinth, though he'd secure his fame when asked at customs if he had anything to declare. 'No. I have nothing to declare, except my genius.' And with that the legend of Oscar Wilde was set not so much in stone as a Corinthian pillar of the finest marble.

The bigoted and bewildered American media harangued this 'ass-thete', ridiculing him in pamphlets and cartoons; one such caricature by Chas Kendrick on the cover of 1882's *Ye Soul Agonies In Ye Life Of Oscar Wilde* showing the writer grasping a giant sunflower was engraved on the limited etched 12-inch version of Morrissey's 1989 single 'INTERESTING DRUG'. But to his critics' dismay, Wilde bedazzled the American public, even delivering a lecture to no-nonsense miners in the Rocky Mountains. Morrissey would allude to this latter incident when summarising his

hero's life for *Smash Hits* in 1984 only to greatly exaggerate Wilde's reception as being 'stoned to death', both for comic effect and to emphasise Oscar's fearlessness in his aesthetic beliefs; in truth, Wilde got on famously with the miners who later took him to a saloon where he earned their further admiration demonstrating his remarkable capacity for strong liquor.

Returning to England, at the age of 29 Wilde married QC's daughter Constance Lloyd in 1884. Shortly before the birth of their second son, Vyvyan, Wilde began what is believed to be his first homosexual affair with a 17-year-old Oxford undergraduate named Robert Ross, the start of a lifelong friendship which would end in the grave when Ross had his ashes interred in Oscar's tomb in Paris's Père Lachaise cemetery.

Fatherhood inspired Oscar to write his collection of stories for children *The Happy Prince and Other Tales*. Significantly, the eight-year-old Morrissey's first introduction to Wilde was through his children's writing. He was especially struck by the profoundly ironic *The Nightingale And The Rose*. 'It was about a nightingale who sacrificed herself for these two star-crossed lovers,' he explained. 'It ends when the nightingale presses her heart against this rose because in a strange, mystical way it means that if she dies, then the two lovers can be together.' What Morrissey failed to add was that, after the nightingale dies, the two lovers don't unite at all. The boy, a student, is snubbed by the girl who tells him the rose won't match her dress. The rose is thrown in the gutter and the rejected student decides love is foolish, vowing to study philosophy and metaphysics: the nightingale died in vain. Either way, a far more Mozzerian ending than that which the singer described.

Wilde's prose masterpiece followed in 1891, *The Picture Of Dorian Gray*. It was to be his only novel, inviting by now customary condemnation from critics disgusted by its immorality and homoeroticism; the Faustian parable of a corrupt young narcissist whose cruelty and vice are only evident on the decaying painted likeness he hides from public view while his physical beauty remains ageless and without blemish. The same year Wilde met his own real life Dorian Gray: the poet Lord Alfred Douglas, nicknamed Bosie and destined to become the 'grotesque element' whose selfishness engineered Oscar's downfall.

His relationship with Bosie began just as he was entering his creative peak as a dramatist with the four comedy plays commencing in 1892 with *Lady Windermere's Fan* and climaxing in 1895 with Wilde's defining masterpiece, *The Importance Of Being Earnest*. For over a century, biographers have struggled to portray Bosie as anything other than a self-seeking, neurotic, ungrateful, vain, reckless, disloyal, shamelessly promiscuous, smartarse, manipulative and habitual snivelling shit. Sadly, by the time Wilde awoke to the same he was already in prison, having been led there by his hopeless and symbolically suicidal infatuation for the boy 16 years his junior.

It was catastrophic for Oscar that Bosie's dad should happen to be the ninth Marquess of Queensberry, a man who would lend his name to the established rules of boxing and who took a dim view of his effete and rebellious son's choice of companions. Incensed by scandalous gossip concerning Oscar and Bosie – hardly discreet in their public displays of intimacy – on 18 February 1895 he left the poet a short, decisive and misspelt card at Wilde's gentleman's club: 'To Oscar Wilde, posing as a somdomite.'

Bosie egged on Wilde to sue his father for libel. Duly coerced, at first Wilde turned the prosecution of Queensberry into another public performance, playing to the gallery and annihilating the defence counsel with his quicksilver intellect. Then, in a momentary lapse of concentration, he hung himself. Cross-examined as to whether he'd kissed one of Bosie's servants in Oxford, Wilde replied he hadn't since 'he was, unfortunately, extremely ugly'. In a few seconds of casual wit, Wilde had accidentally admitted a physical attraction to men and neutered his own prosecution against Queensberry's slander. Wilde's case was thrown out of court and on 5 April 1895 Queensberry was acquitted. Later that day, Wilde was arrested at the Cadogan Hotel in Chelsea on the charge of committing indecent acts. He was tried twice after a first jury failed to reach a verdict on all counts. The second found him guilty. Wilde's persecution by British law would, undoubtedly, haunt Morrissey's experience of the Smiths COURT CASE 101 years later; it is certainly uncanny that the judges who respectively described Wilde as 'dead to all sense of shame' and Morrissey 'devious, truculent and unreliable' even shared the initials J.W. (Justice Wills, John Weeks).

For 'the love that dare not speak its name' – a phrase frequently misattributed to Wilde but ironically coined by Bosie in his poem 'The Two Loves' – Oscar was sentenced to two years' hard labour, a fate slightly longer than that handed to Morrissey in 'I STARTED SOMETHING I COULDN'T FINISH'. As his youngest son Vyvyan Holland would write, 'The maxim that the higher you climb the further you have to fall was seldom so true as it was in his case.' While being transported between prisons, Wilde was subject to the humiliation of standing on the platform of Clapham Junction for half an hour, shackled for all the world to see and mocked by a cruel and jeering mob. A complete stranger spat in his face, an act so hateful and vulgar it haunted Wilde to the end of his days.

As a prisoner in Reading gaol, Wilde wrote his epic letter of recrimination to Bosie, later published as *De Profundis*; it contains the phrase 'flower-like life', a simile repeated by Morrissey in 'MISERABLE LIE'. After serving his full sentence, the everfaithful Robert Ross accompanied him to Berneval in France where he wrote his epic poem 'The Ballad Of Reading Gaol', originally published under his pseudonymous prison number C.3.3. Among his few visitors in Berneval was the French writer André GIDE whom he'd first met and 'corrupted' many years earlier. Wilde later moved to Paris where he spent his final years drunk and destitute. He died on 30 November 1900, aged 46. The official cause of death was cerebral meningitis.

'It would seem almost impossible, I think, at the height of his fame that he would end a few years later in such a bitter, ruinous state,' said

Morrissey. 'Such a lonely state, and also have such a hideous death. A remarkably sad end when you consider that this man had changed English literature and English language.'

Morrissey has publicly thanked his mother for introducing him to Wilde as a child; differing quotes claim being somewhere between the ages of 'eight' and 'ten'. 'My mother was quite dedicated and she had several books,' he explained. 'I think she had said to me before, "Look, you have to read this. It's everything you need to know about life." I ignored her largely but one day I became nailed to the book and things were never quite the same since then. It was *The Complete Works Of Oscar Wilde*. [It changed] almost everything [because] he used the most basic language and said the most powerful things.'

'This sense of truly high drama zipped through everything he wrote,' he added. 'He had a life that was really tragic and it's curious that he was so witty. Here we have a creature persistently creased in pain whose life was a total travesty. He married, rashly had two children and almost immediately embarked on a love affair with a man. He was sent to prison for this. It's a total disadvantage to care about Oscar Wilde, certainly when you come from a working-class background. It's total self-destruction almost … As I blundered through my late teens, I was quite isolated and Oscar Wilde meant much more to me. In a way he became a companion. If that sounds pitiful, that was the way it was.' Blundering through his teens, it must have been extraordinarily symbolic for Morrissey when he discovered the NEW YORK DOLLS, only to learn that their career had begun in a venue at the Mercer Arts Centre named the Oscar Wilde Room.

In early Smiths interviews he'd state how he'd 'read everything [Wilde] wrote and everything written about him'. There's ample evidence that this is the case. As early as 1981, in a letter to pen pal Robert MACKIE the 22-year-old Morrissey wrote, 'Life is a terrible, terrible thing.' Mackie was probably unaware that he was quoting Wilde's letter to Robert Ross after visiting the grave of his estranged wife, Constance: 'Life is a very terrible thing.' More explicit, in an earlier letter to Mackie, he signed off 'Aesthetically, Oscar Wilde'.

Morrissey is also prone to quoting Wildeisms in interviews. For example, in a 2003 interview with *Word* magazine he described his 'purist approach' to songwriting: 'What I do is so precious and so pure that, as someone once said, touch it and the bloom is gone.' That someone was Wilde, or rather the formidable Lady Bracknell in *The Importance Of Being Earnest*: 'Ignorance is like a delicate, exotic fruit. Touch it, and the bloom is gone.'

Earnest is a particular favourite of Morrissey's. In 1984 he told *Smash Hits* 'a day rarely [passed]' when he didn't listen to the play on cassette, almost certainly the same 1953 performance featuring Sir John Gielgud as later sampled on The Smiths' 'RUBBER RING'. Asked to name his favourite Wilde saying, Morrissey quoted Oscar's letter in defence of *Dorian Gray* to the editor of the *Scots Observer*: 'The artist must educate the critic.' 'Because it's true,' he argued. 'The artist should be up above the critic. The critic should be a fan after all. As for Oscar Wilde, his dandy style was greatly ridiculed but I can't think of anything he wrote that doesn't move me.'

To list *all* his many homages to Wilde would be needlessly repetitive, though they've taken almost every conceivable form: song lyrics (named in 'CEMETRY GATES'); vinyl run-out-groove messages ('Talent borrows, genius steals' on 'BIGMOUTH STRIKES AGAIN, the KILL UNCLE pun 'Nothing to declare except my jeans'); promo videos (an 1882 Wilde portrait by Napoleon Sarony can be seen in 'I STARTED SOMETHING I COULDN'T FINISH'); stage backdrops (another Sarony portrait used in 2006 when touring RINGLEADER OF THE TORMENTORS); T-shirts (the fan-made Wilde 'Smiths Is Dead' design as photographed on the singer by Kevin Cummins in 1991); record sleeves (the 'Oscar Wilde Campus' shorts on the reverse of 'MY LOVE LIFE'); and badges (a large badge of Oscar's face could be seen on the bottom of his shirt when performing

'THE LAST OF THE FAMOUS INTERNATIONAL PLAYBOYS' on *TOP OF THE POPS* in February 1989).

The spirit of Wilde permeates every nook and cranny of Morrissey's art and life which, exactly like Oscar's, have been successfully blurred so one is indistinguishable from the other. This is his ultimate homage to Wilde: not to merely wear a work of art or create a work of art but to be, oneself, a work of art. 'As I get older, the adoration increases,' he admitted. 'I'm never without him. It's almost biblical. It's like carrying your rosary around with you.' [59, 71, 82, 122, 165, 166, 168, 175, 184, 209, 267, 275, 313, 318, 325, 327, 334, 336, 349, 393, 448, 539, 557, 567, 573]

'William, It Was Really Nothing' (Morrissey/Marr), The Smiths' fifth single, released September 1984, highest UK chart position #17. An audaciously economical pop tour de force, and one of The Smiths' very best, 'William' played like a classic 60s kitchen-sink drama in concentrated form. More specifically, Morrissey's depiction of a 'humdrum town' and a young man seemingly trapped into marrying a materialistic 'fat girl' offered a loose précis of *BILLY LIAR*. The opening line also betrayed the influence of SPARKS, whose 1974 hit 'This Town Ain't Big Enough For Both Of Us' contained the similar phrase, 'the rain is falling on the foreign town/the bullets cannot cut you down'.

'Will Never Marry' (Morrissey/Street), B-side of 'EVERYDAY IS LIKE SUNDAY' (1988). Morrissey's views on matrimony were irrevocably tainted by his parents' separation when he was 17 years old. 'I've never known a marriage that was happy,' he admitted in 1984. 'I see many, many single people and they're absolutely perfectly happy … I can't really see any need for it.'

Four years later, 'Will Never Marry' eloquently expressed his views in song, politely declining such an offer and resigning himself to a life of solitude. Similar lyrics and titles pre-date Morrissey's ballad, as early as The Carter Family's 1930s folk song 'I Never Will Marry' about a 'fair maiden' who drowns herself after being deserted by her lover; her dying words, 'I never will marry or be no man's wife/I expect to live single all the days of my life'. Along the same lines was Frank Loesser's 'Never Will I Marry' written for the 1960 Broadway show *Greenwillow* and tackled by Judy Garland on her 1962 *Judy Takes Broadway* album: 'Never, never will I marry/Born to wander till I'm dead.' Significantly, both those songs were written to be sung by women, making Morrissey's delivery of the same sentiment all the more unique, doubly so with his added and intriguing admission of fitful sleep due to 'inbuilt guilt'.

Its epic score with strings by John Metcalfe was the necessary downpour Morrissey's wedding cake required. (And no, he'll never have that recipe again.) Street also repeated one of his favourite musical tics previously employed on 'LATE NIGHT, MAUDLIN STREET' and 'THE ORDINARY BOYS', ending a song with a sudden and unexpected key change (the edited version later featured on BONA DRAG is missing this section). The tune's sweeping pathos was accentuated with additional sound effects. 'Morrissey said he wanted the noise of people cheering somebody on running in a race, and kids in a playground,' recalls Street. 'He also wanted the sound of a mother calling out to her son. My wife, Sarah, was visiting the studio that day with our baby son, William. Since she was the only woman in the studio, we asked her to do it. So that's my wife shouting "Steven!" towards the end. Afterwards Morrissey told me it put a chill down his spine every time he heard it.'

One of the best Morrissey/Street recordings, 'Will Never Marry' was used to great effect as the soundtrack for a montage of stage-invading fans at the end of the *INTRODUCING MORRISSEY* video. The song was briefly played in concert in a more basic guitar version during the early stages of 1991's KILL UNCLE tour, as seen on the *LIVE IN DALLAS* video. [25, 39, 425]

As Morrissey explained, his main aim with 'William' was to address marriage from a male standpoint as opposed to pop's traditionally female perspective (e.g. his own favourite, Martha & The Vandellas' THIRD FINGER, LEFT HAND'). 'I thought it was about time there was a male voice speaking directly to another male saying that marriage was a waste of time,' he argued. 'That in effect it was absolutely nothing.' Strong speculation that the title 'William' was actually The Associates' singer Billy MACKENZIE, whom Morrissey had recently befriended, was lent extra intrigue by the revelation that MacKenzie had visited his Kensington flat only to run off with one of his treasured James DEAN books. MacKenzie added fuel to the rumour mill with his own belated response song, 'Stephen [*sic*], You're Really Something'.

The melodically compact 'William' was also the point where the 20-year-old Marr's compositional daring and youthful precocity stepped up a gear. In its cascade of quartz guitar sparkles, Marr sounded as if he was trying to play The Hollies' Greatest Hits all at once in under two minutes, lost in a trance of six-stringed speedfreakery, his eye on the clock but his heart in his mouth. Written in his Earls Court flat in the summer of 1984 along with its B-sides 'PLEASE PLEASE PLEASE LET ME GET WHAT I WANT' and 'HOW SOON IS NOW?', Marr was by now becoming wilfully challenging. Structurally, 'William' avoids all standard pop songwriting conventions, starting with one verse (which is never repeated) followed by three disorientingly joyful choruses and fading out by two minutes and ten seconds. 'To me, the two minute, ten second single was power,' said Morrissey. 'It was blunt, to the point.' In the boldness of its brevity, 'William' set a precedent for future Smiths singles, 'SHAKESPEARE'S SISTER' (2.09), 'PANIC' (2.19) and 'GIRLFRIEND IN A COMA' (2.02).

Special mention should be made of the original 12-inch single: if ever there was one artefact attesting to Morrissey and Marr's remarkable productivity, then the coupling of 'William' with 'How Soon Is Now?' and 'Please Please Please' on to a single piece of vinyl is probably it. Commercially, 'William' marked the end of The Smiths' early honeymoon period in the UK singles charts as their last to make the top 20 until 'Panic' nearly two years later. Undoubtedly one of their greatest moments at 45 rpm, it also instigated one of their most celebrated appearances on *TOP OF THE POPS* when Morrissey tore open his shirt to reveal the words 'MARRY ME' written on his chest. 'That was a key moment,' says Marr. 'Not just the actual being on *Top Of The Pops* and performing "William", but that whole week, the feeling around the band and when I saw it afterwards. In terms of our music, our private lives and our whole psychology, I felt like The Smiths were going into unchartered territory.' [17, 18, 27, 104, 267, 304, 374, 425]

Williams, Heathcote, Poet, playwright and actor once listed among Morrissey's preferred 'bedside [reading] material'. His interest in Williams stemmed from 1988's eco-poem *Whale Nation*, later a BBC Omnibus special and one of Morrissey's favourite television programmes.

An upper-class rebel, Williams was 'asked to leave' Eton as a teenager and thereafter embraced anarchy and libertarianism; slumming it with London's homeless and the eccentrics of Hyde Park's Speakers' Corner and setting up a squatters' commune in Notting Hill which he called the 'Albion Free State'. Outspoken, confrontational and so scruffy he appeared 'held together with safety pins', he was an unlikely suitor to 'The Shrimp' (model Jean SHRIMPTON), embarking on a passionate but volatile affair in 1969. The relationship ended when he turned up on her doorstep 'pretty hyped up' with the news that he was practising fire eating. Armed with a can of petrol and some matches, he set himself alight, rolling around on her sofa trying to douse the flames while The Shrimp rang for an ambulance. 'He might have made me miserable and confused,' said The Shrimp, 'but at least he was not boring.'

Williams next tried his hand at songwriting, penning the controversial lyrics of 'Why D'Ya Do It?', the expletive-ridden finale of Marianne

FAITHFULL'S 1979 album Broken English. The same year he played Prospero in Derek JARMAN'S film version of *The Tempest*. His most popular role to date remains his cameo as Emily Lloyd's 'dirty old bugger' psychiatrist in 1987's *Wish You Were Here*.

The following year, *Whale Nation* was published in conjunction with a factual essay *On The Nature Of Whales*. A profound hymn to earth's largest, and oldest, mammal, Williams uses the simplest of language to convey both the beauty of whales as an inscrutably benign species of superior intelligence to our own, and the shameful barbarism which humankind has subjected them to in return. As a mandate for animal rights, foremost among Morrissey's passions, *Whale Nation* surpasses even 'MEAT IS MURDER' in terms of emotional power. Drummer Andrew PARESI recalls *Whale Nation* being one of Morrissey's typically obscure choices when playing charades. A copy of the original book also appears in the 'INTERESTING DRUG' video, produced from one of the schoolboys' bags along with a copy of Herman Melville's *Moby Dick*.

As somebody who believed in the maxim 'fame is the first disgrace', Williams never welcomed the celebrity *Whale Nation*'s success offered him. He followed it with the equally impassioned *Falling For A Dolphin*, *Sacred Elephant* and his diatribe against the motor industry, *Autogeddon*, but stopped writing in the early 90s to concentrate on painting and sculpture, funding his art with bit-part acting roles including an episode of the US sitcom *FRIENDS*. [25, 175, 370, 396]

Williams, Kenneth, See CARRY ON.

Winstanley, Alan (Morrissey producer 1989–91), See LANGER, Clive.

Wolstencroft, Simon, Often referred to as The Smiths' 'first drummer', Wolstencroft's only association with the group was the recording of their first two-track demo at Decibel studios in August 1982.

Previously, Wolstencroft had played in local band The Patrol, whose writing core of singer Ian Brown and guitarist John Squire went on to form The Stone Roses. He first met Marr circa 1981, joining him and Andy Rourke in their pre-Smiths instrumental trio Freak Party, who recorded one demo at Decibel, 'Crak Therapy', engineered by Dale HIBBERT. When Hibbert went on to become The Smiths' first bass player ensuring them free studio time to record a demo of their own, Marr called upon Wolstencroft to help out in the absence of a drummer. He obliged, playing on early drafts of 'THE HAND THAT ROCKS THE CRADLE' and 'SUFFER LITTLE CHILDREN', but showed no interest in joining The Smiths on a permanent basis.

Mike Joyce was discovered soon afterwards in September 1982, though alleged doubts over his capabilities which arose the following spring led to Wolstencroft being 'secretly' approached as a potential replacement – the fact Joyce spotted Wolstencroft's drum kit in their rehearsal room suggests it wasn't exactly the best-kept secret. Whatever the concerns about Joyce, Wolstencroft wasn't required. Instead, he went on to join Marr's hairdresser friend Andrew Berry in The Weeds (whose only single, 1986's 'China Doll', was backed by a song named after Smiths manager Joe MOSS's clothes shop, 'Crazy Face'), before serving over a decade with The Fall. Returning full circle, in 1999 Wolstencroft reunited with ex-Patrol singer Ian Brown for the album Golden Greats. [10, 12, 13, 17, 362]

Wolverhampton (Morrissey's debut solo concert at Wolverhampton Civic Hall, 22 December 1988), The sudden and secretive nature of The Smiths' break-up during the summer of 1987 denied them the opportunity of staging an official farewell concert. Morrissey, in particular, was aggrieved by this circumstance and tried, in vain, to coerce Marr into returning for a final Smiths show at London's Royal Albert Hall that autumn to coincide with the release of STRANGEWAYS, HERE WE COME. Marr, still stinging from the split and Morrissey's futile attempts to continue The Smiths

without him, was vehement in his refusal. 'It was obviously a no-no.'

One year later, and following the solo success of VIVA HATE, Morrissey reunited with Andy Rourke, Mike Joyce and Smiths second guitarist Craig GANNON, his new backing band for the recording of the singles 'THE LAST OF THE FAMOUS INTERNATIONAL PLAYBOYS' and 'INTERESTING DRUG'. Other than the gaping void of Marr's absence, this gathering of four-fifths was a Smiths reunion in all but name, rekindling Morrissey's hope of a 'farewell' gig.

It was while recording those singles at The Wool Hall near Bath in December 1988 that Morrissey made his decision. According to producer and co-writer Stephen STREET, after a promising start the session was beginning to fall apart. Unhappy with some of the works-in-progress, on Friday 9 December Morrissey 'snapped and walked out of the studio', says Street. After spending the weekend in Manchester, the singer returned on the Monday in noticeably higher spirits, breaking the news to Street that he intended to announce a surprise gig a few days before Christmas. The chosen location was the West Midlands town of Wolverhampton (later to be granted city status). As Morrissey later explained, 'It wasn't London and it wasn't Manchester which I thought was an important gesture … it was dear old, sweet dumpy Wolverhampton.'

As Morrissey's co-writer, Street automatically assumed that he'd be joining the group on stage in some capacity, only to be told 'in no uncertain terms' that he wouldn't. 'Morrissey took me aside and told me he wanted it to be a Smiths gig,' he recalls. 'He felt it was time to move on and exorcise The Smiths so he saw it as a farewell. He even said he wasn't sure if he'd work with Mike and Andy again after this. But I was really pissed off.'

Morrissey's caution towards Rourke and Joyce was understandable, given that both had already started legal proceedings contesting their share of income from The Smiths, as had Craig Gannon. Consequently, the imminent Wolverhampton gig created the farcical scenario of a band whose guitarist, bassist and drummer were all involved in separate legal writs against their frontman. 'It's something that just wasn't discussed,' says Joyce, 'or if the subject was brought up the conversation was quickly changed. Morrissey didn't seem bothered about it, put it that way.'

The concert was announced on Radio 1 on Monday 19 December, four days prior to the show itself on Thursday 22nd. Despite Morrissey's belief that it should be 'a Smiths gig', the event was officially promoted as his debut solo concert. Discounting his impromptu cameo reading Marcel PROUST with Howard DEVOTO's Luxuria at London's Town & Country Club earlier that year, it marked Morrissey's first live appearance since The Smiths played London's Brixton Academy in December 1986. Entry was free – 'which, for someone of my status, is unheard of', noted Morrissey – to anybody who turned up in a Smiths or Morrissey T-shirt. 'I thought above all people would see a free concert as a very welcome gesture,' he added, 'regardless of who got their sandals stolen or dropped their crisps in a puddle.'

The news instigated an immediate fan pilgrimage to Wolverhampton, with the pluckiest camping outside the venue three nights before to assure their place at the front of the queue. Come the morning of the concert, with several hundred fans now gathered, those who'd spent the past few nights shivering on the pavement suddenly found themselves trampled underfoot by eleventh-hour queue jumpers. 'They didn't have to come if they didn't want to,' argued Morrissey. 'They must have been aware of a certain element of risk. It isn't my fault if at the final minute someone came from the back with huge muscles and removed them. It's symptomatic, I think, of life in general.'

Further scenes of mass hysteria greeted that afternoon's arrival of Morrissey and the band who'd made the journey from The Wool Hall to Wolverhampton in a vintage 1940s 'St Trinian's' bus. With the venue's 7,000 capacity reduced by safety officials to 1,500, approximately 3,000 people turned up hoping to gain admittance. Chaos reigned while the Midlands police struggled to control the bitterly disappointed majority, eventually having to arrest the desperate hordes engaged in last-minute attempts to gain entry by breaking windows and smashing down fire doors. 'It wasn't window smashing as senseless aggro,' mused Morrissey. 'It was frothing admiration building to the brink and beyond … I felt in order to get in you had to make a slight effort, it wasn't going to be that easy. So I knew that the people who made the effort were the important ones. It was like *The Krypton Factor*, it was a test of endurance. But nobody seemed to mind, apart, obviously, from the ones that didn't get in. That was inevitable. The T-shirts were a simple way of getting over who could get in the venue because otherwise it would have had to be tickets.'

Choosing Smiths-influenced northern indie band Bradford as his support (see 'SKIN STORM'), Morrissey's performance on the night lasted barely half an hour, an eight-song set mixing known and yet-to-be-released solo material with three late Smiths tracks: 'STOP ME IF YOU THINK YOU'VE HEARD THIS ONE BEFORE', 'DISAPPOINTED', 'Interesting Drug', 'SUEDEHEAD' (preceded by Joyce teasing the crowd with the drum intro of 'THE QUEEN IS DEAD'), 'The Last Of The Famous International Playboys', 'SISTER I'M A POET', 'DEATH AT ONE'S ELBOW' and a final encore of 'SWEET AND TENDER HOOLIGAN'.

'One of the conditions that we agreed upon,' explains Joyce, 'was that we weren't going to do any Smiths songs that we'd played live with Johnny. We were kind of mulling it over because we didn't want to pretend "this is The Smiths" because it wasn't without Johnny. So we thought if we don't play any song we played live before, some things off Strangeways, for instance, coupled with his solo stuff, then what's wrong with that?' Morrissey was even more philosophical about the choice of songs. 'That concert at Wolverhampton was me saying goodbye,' he'd reflect. 'I felt that just because The Smiths had ended … those songs really were me also. I didn't feel like walking away saying, "Oh no, no more of that. Let's move on and be massively creative." I

still feel that all of those songs are me, I had the right to play them.'

As it turned out, the setlist took second place to the historic visual spectacle of Morrissey in the flesh, marked by the kind of fanatical stage invasions that would later come to typify Morrissey's solo performances. 'It was nice to be kissed repeatedly,' he surmised. 'In the hall that night there was a great aura of love and gentleness, and all the people who came on stage treated me in a very gentle way. I wasn't kicked or punched or dragged, although they were very emotionally charged. I came away with no bruises.'

'The amount of fans getting on stage was ridiculous,' admits Joyce. 'It had never been that bad with The Smiths. At one point all you could hear was drums and vocals because Andy had his pedals stood on and his leads had come out, Craig was mobbed so his strap had come off and Moz was cramped down with his mike feeding back next to the monitor with people diving on him. It was actually dangerous with all the electrics. OK, it was a free gig and all, but I felt bad about how it must have sounded out front.' Gannon agrees: 'It was chaos. As soon as we hit the first note it was just people constantly diving on stage, leads constantly being pulled out, amps wobbling, me quiff falling. I mean, it was a good laugh but musically it was frustrating.'

The occasion was even more frustrating for Stephen Street, not only barred from the stage but symbolically confined to an outside broadcast radio van. 'So, no, I wasn't even able to watch it,' he mourns. Ironically, Morrissey would later tell the press that Wolverhampton 'must have been a joy' for Street, 'to hear his music performed, which obviously he's never experienced before'.

The day after the gig, while Rourke and Joyce recovered in Wolverhampton, Gannon and Morrissey attempted to head back to Manchester in the same antiquated transport in which they'd arrived. 'It was just me and Morrissey in this St Trinian's bus with the driver,' laughs Gannon. 'It seemed a good idea but as soon as we got to the

Woman In A Dressing Gown, 1957 prototype British kitchen-sink drama listed as one of Morrissey's favourite films. It stars one of his favourite actresses, YVONNE MITCHELL, as a loving, scatterbrained housewife on a London council estate, slavishly dedicated to her narky husband, 'Jimbo' (Anthony Quayle) and their trad jazz-loving teenage son. Her world suddenly collapses when she discovers her beloved Jimbo is a spineless weasel who wants to divorce her and run off with his posh secretary (Sylvia Syms). Mitchell's is a superb performance of masochistic denial until finally blowing a gasket during the climactic confrontation scene between wife, mistress and love rat. Directed by *YIELD TO THE NIGHT*'s J. Lee Thompson, *Woman In A Dressing Gown* was also one of a handful of serious dramatic roles for glamour model Carole Lesley, who played Mitchell's brassy neighbour. Promoted as a Diana DORS-type blonde sexpot, by the early 60s Lesley's film career had dried up. In 1974, she took a fatal overdose of sleeping pills, aged only 38. [227, 563]

outskirts of Wolverhampton it broke down. We were stranded.'

'The bus was the wrong choice because it broke down, twice,' confirmed Morrissey. 'I had a driver, he also broke down. It was very typical of Old England to let me down.' According to Gannon, he and Morrissey had no choice but to set off on foot to telephone for help. 'We eventually found this pub in the middle of nowhere,' recalls Gannon. 'It was mid-morning, so it wasn't even open. The landlord heard us knocking so came down and opened the door. He was met with Morrissey stood there, me behind him, asking, "Have you got 10p for the phone?" We managed to get hold of the tour manager who said he'd drive over and pick us up so we just waited for ages back in this bus by ourselves. This was two days before Christmas. We were freezing!'

The drama and excitement of Wolverhampton, both inside and outside the venue, was brilliantly captured by director Tim Broad on the *HULMERIST* video, though its footage of 'Sister I'm A Poet' neatly illustrates Morrissey's subsequent verdict that it 'was not really a concert, it was an event at which I didn't really sing'. The same applies to the breathless encore of 'Sweet And Tender Hooligan', released as a live B-side of 'Interesting Drug'. In the months following Wolverhampton, Morrissey's troupe of ex-Smiths would fracture due to their separate legal grievances, negating any hope of his permanent return to the concert stage in

1989. Indeed, it would be another two years before Morrissey finally did so in April 1991, with an entirely new band to promote KILL UNCLE. [7, 13, 29, 39, 69, 138, 148, 226, 290]

'Wonderful Woman' (Morrissey/Marr), B-side of 'THIS CHARMING MAN' (1983). Morrissey's ode to an enigmatic femme fatale, he admitted the song was based on fact, if 'tongue in cheek'. 'The "Wonderful Woman" was actually a very vicious person, but still at the end of the day she had a magnetic ray to me,' he explained. 'So all the things that she wanted to do, nasty as they were, vulgar as they were, were completely forgivable.' Previous critics have suggested that its secret muse seeking laughs in tripping up dwarves is his friend Linder STERLING, alleged subject of several early Smiths lyrics written during the same period. No doubt conscious of this myth, Morrissey teasingly referred to Sterling as 'a wonderful woman' on stage at London's Royal Albert Hall in September 2002 where she was taking photographs.

The lyrics evolved over a six-month period, beginning under the title of 'What Do You See In Him?', a different narrative where Morrissey vents equal parts grief and envy that the woman he desires is with somebody else ('When will you ever learn?'). The song went through several drafts and, under the same working title, was debuted at The Smiths' second concert in January 1983. Five months later, it had mutated into

'Wonderful Woman' with only the line 'ice water for blood' rescued from the original sketch of 'What Do You See In Him?'

Its musical arrangement remained the same throughout, a rainy parade of glittering gloom with faint echoes of The PATTI SMITH Group's more dirgeful moments. Recorded for the aborted Troy TATE debut album, 'Wonderful Woman' was retackled with producer John PORTER as a B-side for The Smiths' first 12-inch single. Marr credits Porter for imbuing the finished recording with 'a certain sadness', building layers of guitar, lonesome harmonica and lending Morrissey's vocal an unnerving ghostly quality. Far from the 'tongue-in-cheek' song the singer envisaged, 'Wonderful Woman' was The Smiths at their most atmospherically solemn. Alongside 'JEANE', it would remain one of the group's rarest tracks before finally being compiled on the deluxe edition of 2008's The Sound Of The Smiths compilation. [17, 27, 419]

Wood, Victoria, Lancashire-born writer,
comedian, actor and singer whom Morrissey has praised on numerous occasions for 'completely changing the face of television comedy'. Like his other northern playwright heroes Shelagh DELANEY and Alan BENNETT, Wood's warm, observational humour often caricatured mundane working-class lives, as well as satirising popular culture, most famously with *Acorn Antiques*, an absurd spoof on cheap British soaps such as *Crossroads* which she'd eventually transform into a hit West End musical.

Wood's biggest influence upon Morrissey remains *Wood & Walters*, her 1982 Granada sketch show with Julie Walters which aired in the months prior to the formation of The Smiths. '[It] was very, very revolutionary,' he explained. 'Not just for women but for men as well. They were completely different, very intelligent [and] it seemed to be a different kind of humour that hadn't been on television before. A different way of thinking, a different way of telling a joke and a different way of being silly. She was very unique.' Morrissey was equally impressed by Wood's gifts as a lyricist, famously modelling The Smiths' 'RUSHOLME RUFFIANS' upon the words of her bittersweet fairground remembrance 'Fourteen Again' and another song, 'Funny How Things Turn Out'; the latter would also leave a smaller mark upon 'FRANKLY, MR SHANKLY'.

Throughout The Smiths, Morrissey repeatedly trumpeted Wood in the *NME*'s end-of-year polls, praising her 1984 sketch series *Victoria Wood As Seen On TV*, naming her his 'most wonderful human being' of 1985 and stating that he'd happily marry her. When asked about the latter eventuality, Wood replied with characteristic wit: 'Morrissey and I have been married for 11 months, though due to touring commitments, we have yet to meet.' [115, 182, 183, 414]

work, In 'YOU'VE GOT EVERYTHING NOW' Morrissey famously sang how he'd never had a job because he never wanted one. This isn't strictly the case, as Morrissey admitted when later referring to his 'brief spasms of employment'. Those spasms, brief as they were, included working in a hospital laundry, a very short stint in a record shop and, his lengthiest employment, a tedious clerical post with the Inland Revenue in 1979 in order to save money to visit family in America. The rest of the time he spent on the dole, a circumstance he'd famously describe as 'the worst illness' he'd ever experienced. He'd recall once being pressured by the job centre into applying for a position which required him 'to keep canal banks tidy of any discarded rubbish'. As he'd describe it, 'I looked at [the woman] and laughed. She said, "You think you're too good for this, don't you?" and I stood up and walked out.'

His anti-work ethic has been clearly expressed both in song – 'STILL ILL', 'HEAVEN KNOWS I'M MISERABLE NOW', 'FRANKLY, MR SHANKLY' – and in interviews. In 1983 he raved how 'jobs reduce people to absolute stupidity'. Over 25 years later he was still causing no small amount of moral disgruntlement after his primetime appearance on BBC1's *The One Show* in February 2009. 'I was quite happy to be unemployed because I didn't

490

want to work,' said Morrissey, at which point a nation of *Daily Mail* readers gagged on their oven chips. 'I didn't want to have a job,' he continued. 'I couldn't think of a job I wanted to do, so I thought I shouldn't do any.' Asked how he felt about white-collar workers made redundant in the current economic recession, Morrissey sat back, arms folded, and suggested they should 'paint or do something creative' instead. [166, 362, 570, 573, 580]

'Work Is A Four-Letter Word' (Guy Woolfenden/Don Black), B-side of 'GIRLFRIEND IN A COMA' (1987). First recorded by Cilla BLACK in 1968 (the B-side of her 'Where Is Tomorrow?' single), 'Work Is A Four-Letter Word' was the title theme to a bizarre psychedelic comedy about a rebellious eccentric (David Warner) trying to find the perfect conditions to grow magic mushrooms. The film also starred Black herself as his oblivious fiancée and another of Morrissey's favourite 'thespians', Elizabeth Spriggs, as a neurotic personnel officer. (See also *SHINE ON HARVEY MOON*.)

Morrissey would later explain their cover as 'a bit of a tease'. Sadly, Marr never saw it that way. Although it took more than a Cilla Black song to break up The Smiths, amid the chaos of what would be their final recording session at the Streatham studio of soundman Grant Showbiz in May 1987, the singer's insistence that they tackle 'Work Is A Four-Letter Word' certainly contributed to their inevitable end. Though Morrissey would later joke that 'Cilla Black, unbeknownst to herself, actually broke The Smiths up', in 2002 he made a much more serious accusation against Marr, suggesting he used the song as a token excuse to finish the group: 'He [says] "Morrissey was evil, he made us record the Cilla Black song" and that's how he justifies his terrible decision.'

'Well, it was bad timing to say the least,' responds Marr. 'The idea of that song was *very* badly timed. I thought it had an alien feel to it. It doesn't feel like it has any of our souls in it. So, no, I didn't want to do it, but to say that's the reason we broke up is ludicrous.'

Marr's antipathy towards the song was aggravated by the breakdown in communication between himself and Morrissey, forcing Mike Joyce to act as go-between. 'It was Mike, not Morrissey, who told me that we were gonna do the Cilla song,' explains Marr. 'That pissed me off big time. It wasn't his role to tell me what song I was gonna produce and play on. But, to be fair, I think he was maybe trying to help by putting his hands on the wheel. It was a desperate situation for everybody.'

Joyce even found himself coerced into backing vocals while Rourke kept his silence but privately feared the very worst. 'It was awful,' says Rourke. 'Musically, it just wasn't us. But we were falling apart by then, every one of us. Morrissey had taken a load of valium. God knows what I'd taken. Prescription drugs, they're the worst. Dangerous stuff, especially when you're playing a Cilla Black song.'

To describe 'Work Is A Four-Letter Word' as superior to their previous cover of TWINKLE's 'GOLDEN LIGHTS' may be damning it with faint praise, but the track itself isn't as dreadful as its reputation suggests. Marr's arrangement was an admirable attempt to 'Smithsify' the twee original, even adding his own improvised outro. Thematically, the lyrics also complemented the anti-work ethic of previous Smiths songs such as 'HEAVEN KNOWS I'M MISERABLE NOW' (Morrissey wisely omitted an opening verse about 'girls who some men will slave for'). It's also not beyond reason to wonder whether Morrissey chose it for its plea of 'If you stay/I'll stay right beside you' as some veiled appeal to Marr not to exit The Smiths.

Without being the cause of the split, 'Work Is A Four-Letter Word' definitely highlighted the diverging musical and aesthetic ideals of Morrissey and Marr after five years of working together. Though it didn't *finish* The Smiths, bar 'I KEEP MINE HIDDEN', recorded during the same session, it was the finish *of* The Smiths. [13, 17, 19, 29, 32, 33, 443, 463]

'World Is Full Of Crashing Bores, The' (Morrissey/Boorer), From the album YOU ARE THE QUARRY (2004). One of Morrissey's less attractive

sermons on the ills of modern life, 'The World Is Full Of Crashing Bores' fails to fulfil the promise of its witheringly Wildean title. Casting himself as 'the boy next door' now fully grown but raging against authority, its hatred of law and the legal establishment seems one of his more transparent lyrical knee-jerks to his bitter experience of the 1996 Smiths COURT CASE.

For its final verse he squanders his intellectual venom on the unworthy soft target of 'thicker than pig-shit' pop stars of the *Pop Idol/American Idol/X Factor* variety. 'It's the entire culture of so-called pop music and the assumption that all you have to do is stand and smile and you're a pop idol,' he fumed. 'They're worse than terrorists.' Two years later, he'd calmed down somewhat, admitting that as much as he loathed the programmes he did at least 'feel sympathy for the contestants'. (In one of his more ironic sartorial gestures, when touring in 2008 he'd frequently wear an official *American Idol* T-shirt on stage.)

Between the song's main lyrical diatribes, Morrissey questions his own capacity to induce crashing boredom, only to beg 'take me in your arms and love me', a phrase possibly inspired by Gladys Knight And The Pips' 1967 Tamla Motown hit of the same name. Among the five Quarry-era tracks first previewed in concert during 2002, though 'The World Is Full Of Crashing Bores' has remained a live favourite since, neither its crude lyrics nor Boorer's gormless tune with all its slow-motion-*Batman* larks are especially inspiring. For this author at least, among Quarry's wobbliest moments. [192, 471]

World Of Morrissey, Morrissey's second
solo compilation album, released February 1995, highest UK chart position #15. Tracks: 'WHATEVER HAPPENS, I LOVE YOU', 'BILLY BUDD', 'JACK THE RIPPER (LIVE)', 'HAVE-A-GO MERCHANT', 'THE LOOP', 'SISTER I'M A POET (LIVE)', 'YOU'RE THE ONE FOR ME, FATTY (LIVE)', 'BOXERS', 'MOONRIVER', 'MY LOVE LIFE', 'CERTAIN PEOPLE I KNOW', 'THE LAST OF THE FAMOUS INTERNATIONAL PLAYBOYS', 'WE'LL LET YOU KNOW', 'SPRING-HEELED JIM'.

During the late 60s and early 70s, the DECCA label released a series of budget compilation albums of individual and various artists under the generic 'The World Of ...' title. The series included many of Morrissey's own favourites, from two volumes of The World Of Billy FURY to the worlds of David BOWIE, Marianne FAITHFULL and the specifically Lonely World Of Anthony NEWLEY. Typically, such World Of albums mixed hit singles with lesser known album tracks and B-sides to create an inexpensive taster rather than a definitive best of. In name, in inexplicably eclectic running order and in its discount price tag, World Of Morrissey was very obviously intended as his mid-90s equivalent. Unfortunately, most critics dismissed it as self-indulgent and patchy while its relatively poor chart placing suggested that even his audience approached it with some degree of scepticism.

To its detriment, the packaging made no humorous concession to the Decca series (even missing the 'The' from 'World Of') and would be the first solo Morrissey album not to feature the singer on the cover, replaced instead by a slapdash design using a still of Cornelius CARR from the 'Boxers' video. But the main problem with World Of Morrissey was one of timing. Issued in the emergent Britpop spring of '95, it missed a golden opportunity to round up all the non-album highlights in the four years since its 1990 predecessor, BONA DRAG. Although 'My Love Life', 'The Loop', the extended 'Moonriver' and the three tracks from the current 'Boxers' single were given their due place, the remainder culled from YOUR ARSENAL, BEETHOVEN WAS DEAF and VAUXHALL AND I seemed an unnecessary repetition; the most glaring omissions were 'PREGNANT FOR THE LAST TIME', 'I'VE CHANGED MY PLEA TO GUILTY', 'I'D LOVE TO' and 'INTERLUDE'.

For all its shortcomings, the fact that nine of its 14 tracks would feature in his setlist for his UK tour the month of its release tells us that, regardless of anybody else's opinion, World Of Morrissey represented his own idiosyncratic estimation of his best solo work up until that point. Even

World, The Flesh, And The Devil, The, 1959 nuclear holocaust drama listed among Morrissey's favourite films. Harry Belafonte leads its minimal cast as an Afro-American miner trapped underground in what at first appears a typical cave-in. Only after several days struggling to make contact with the outside world does he manage to climb to the surface where he realises he's survived an atomic bomb blast and may, in theory, be the last man alive on earth. Travelling to New York City in the hope of finding fellow survivors, he quickly resigns himself to the probability that he is alone only to find a young white girl (Inger Stevens). When another white male survivor turns up, their rivalry for the girl's affections brings issues of discrimination and interracial sexual tension to the fore. Of particular note is the scene where Belafonte and Stevens first meet and discuss what day of the week it is. Stevens tells him it's Sunday. 'It felt like Sunday,' replies Belafonte. Given the film's apocalyptic premise, it's *vaguely* possible this exchange had some grain of influence upon Morrissey's own 'EVERYDAY IS LIKE SUNDAY'. [184, 564]

today, while still an inadvisable primer in terms of converting the novice, as a budget-priced hour's worth of extremely random Morrissey, it contains more to commend than to criticise. [40]

World Won't Listen, The, The Smiths'
second compilation album, released February 1987, highest UK chart position #2. Tracks: 'PANIC', 'ASK', 'LONDON', 'BIGMOUTH STRIKES AGAIN', 'SHAKESPEARE'S SISTER', 'THERE IS A LIGHT THAT NEVER GOES OUT', 'SHOPLIFTERS OF THE WORLD UNITE', 'THE BOY WITH THE THORN IN HIS SIDE', 'ASLEEP', 'UNLOVEABLE', 'HALF A PERSON', 'STRETCH OUT AND WAIT', 'THAT JOKE ISN'T FUNNY ANYMORE', 'OSCILLATE WILDLY', 'YOU JUST HAVEN'T EARNED IT YET, BABY', 'RUBBER RING'. The reissue CD version adds 'MONEY CHANGES EVERYTHING' and 'GOLDEN LIGHTS'.[1]

Issued between THE QUEEN IS DEAD and STRANGEWAYS, HERE WE COME, The World Won't Listen echoed the earlier HATFUL OF HOLLOW in rounding up a large volume of material from singles and B-sides previously unavailable on any album. Its 16 tracks covered the two-year period from early 1985 to the beginning of 1987, featuring all seven singles issued in that period, from 'Shakespeare's Sister' through to the recent 'Shoplifters Of The World Unite', along with seven B-sides (including a previously unavailable alternate mix of 'Stretch Out And Wait'), one

exclusive new track ('You Just Haven't Earned It Yet, Baby') and a repeat appearance of 'There Is A Light That Never Goes Out' which had just topped John PEEL's Festive 50 listeners' poll in December 1986.

As with Hatful, it was a proud testament to The Smiths' prodigious output, highlighting the confidence of a group who could confine some of their finest work to B-sides ('Half A Person', 'Rubber Ring') as well as a glittering array of non-album hit singles ('Panic', 'Ask', 'Shoplifters'). 'It was a pretty good record,' understates Marr. 'It was never going to have the same impact as Hatful, because we'd already done it. Like Hatful, I never considered The World Won't Listen to be a bona fide record because I hadn't gone in and written new songs for it, but I was happy it came out because our audience really loved it. And it has got my favourite Smiths sleeve, without a doubt.'

The front and back cover imagery was taken from *Rock And Roll Times: The Style And Spirit Of The Early Beatles And Their First Fans* by German photographer Jürgen Vollmer, who befriended THE BEATLES in Hamburg in 1961. Morrissey explained how the front portrait of a group of young rockers collectively gazing over to their left (as if towards the beehived girls seen on the reverse) 'best exemplified' The Smiths and their audience. '[But] I was horrified when it was mauled and chopped for the cassette and CD versions,' he

W

added, 'which cropped the image to only show the boy with the puffy cheeks. I couldn't understand why the full image wasn't reproduced.'

For Marr, it was actually the back cover which offered the most intrigue. When Morrissey first showed him the finished artwork, he noticed a deliberate in-joke. The four girls seen standing amid a fairground share facial similarities with the four members of The Smiths: left to right, the girls are Joyce, Rourke, Marr and Morrissey. 'I said, "Correct me if I'm wrong ..."' jokes Marr, '"but isn't that supposed to be thingy, thingy, thingy and thingy?" I think maybe two eyebrows were raised, which probably meant, "Affirmative, Johnny." Just in case I was carrying a tape recorder.'

Though a superb compilation, the album's place in The Smiths' legacy would be immediately eclipsed by the more expansive US import LOUDER THAN BOMBS which followed two months later. [19, 117, 242, 374]

———

1. Some purely technical footnotes on The World Won't Listen: it contains the shorter, seven-inch single edit of 'That Joke Isn't Funny Anymore' as well as the original single mix of 'The Boy With The Thorn In His Side' (slightly different to The Queen Is Dead version); the B-sides 'Rubber Ring' and 'Asleep' were separated from their original 'medley' format (as heard on the 12-inch of 'The Boy With The Thorn In His Side'); Craig GANNON plays on six tracks but is uncredited; and the listed recording dates are incorrect – it should read from October 1984 ('That Joke') to November 1986 ('Shoplifters').

writing process (Morrissey's lyrics and music), While, in recent years especially, Morrissey has become increasingly reluctant to discuss the specific meaning of songs in terms of 'pat' definitions, he has always been very open in discussing the methods he uses to create them.

Morrissey has always maintained that he's written, and sung, 'persistently' from an early age, making up his own vocal melodies as a child. 'I would sing every single night,' he reminisced, 'and the neighbours would complain because I had this insane desire to sing. I was obsessed with vocal melody – and remain so. So it's been a lifetime's preoccupation.'

It is important to reiterate that, lyrics aside, much of Morrissey's creative genius lies in this innate fixation for vocal melodies; a quality which is sometimes lost in critical appraisals preoccupied wholly with the originality of his words rather than their equally original melodic delivery. The Morrissey/Marr partnership, though divided as words/music was, in practice, words and vocal melodies/music. Long before working with Marr, Morrissey wrote songs 'with only nebulous tunes because I couldn't play an instrument'. This detail is borne out by the testimony of BUZZCOCKS manager and ROUGH TRADE associate Richard Boon who remembers hearing a solo Morrissey home demo circa 1980 featuring an unaccompanied a cappella version of 'THE HAND THAT ROCKS THE CRADLE' to his own melody. As he stated early on in The Smiths, 'I also think up vocal tunes which are often completely different from the actual musical tunes that Johnny devises. So I've always had a very musical head, if you like.'

'It's important to me that lines are always soft and have soft edges,' he explained. 'I always envisage people singing the song in their homes, in the shower, in the bath and I always like to have very lilting melodies. The vocal melody to me is very, *very* important. Because people will hear the melody without knowing the words and if the melody draws them in *then* they'll listen to the words.'

Though Morrissey and Marr began writing 'eyeball to eyeball', and would continue to do so infrequently throughout The Smiths, they quickly established a method which cast the die for Morrissey's whole career. Marr would put his music on a cassette and give to Morrissey, who would then lock himself away 'and start humming'. As he once explained their chemistry, 'it all happens at the drop of a cassette'.

'I just take the basics of a backing track and shout along to it for a few days,' Morrissey explained. 'Seeing where the syllables land, and seeing how the words balance out. Suddenly the lyrics form, and a configuration presents itself. I never "jam", and almost never rehearse. I'm just very lucky that whatever it is that I do eventually becomes music.'

One of the consequential tics of the cassette-in-solitude method is Morrissey's peculiar disregard for following conventional strong structure. Co-writers such as Stephen STREET and Mark NEVIN were often surprised, if confused, that tunes they'd written with what they considered very obvious verse/chorus changes would be ignored as Morrissey turned their original chorus melody into the bridge, or their verse section into his chorus, sometimes throwing out whole segments he deemed unnecessary. A good example is offered by Marr's 'HALF A PERSON'; if you follow Marr's backing tune, you'll notice that Morrissey continues singing a different chorus melody (the 'I like it here' part) even when Marr reverts back to his original verse section.

'I prefer a completely purist approach to everything,' Morrissey once said. 'What I do is so precious and so pure that, as someone once said, touch it and the bloom is gone. The band and I do discuss the framework and the general identity of what the music will be, but how the records are actually made is a mystery to me … It is a highly charged and precious moment. If it doesn't exist in the first three takes, it never will exist. I do three at most. It's a splurge and it's a cleansing and it's a burst. I could never lose that spontaneity.'

It is another common mistake of critics to mistake Morrissey's bookishness for lofty intellectualism. Yet, as he insisted from the outset of The Smiths, '[my] words are basic because I don't want anyone to miss what I'm saying. Lyrics that are intellectual or obscure are no use whatsoever … My lyrics are only obscure to the extent they are not taken directly from the dictionary of writing songs. They're not slavish to the lyrics rule book, so you'll never catch me singing, "Oh baby, baby, yeah!" My only priority is to use lines and words in a way that hasn't been heard before.' Morrissey is especially proud of introducing what he calls 'a new language into pop' be it 'charming', 'handsome', 'coma', 'shoplifter', 'bigmouth', 'suedehead', or even 'ouija board'.

For most of his life, Morrissey has collected his ideas and worked on his lyrics in traditional pen and paper. 'I scribble things down in hundreds of notebooks and I have large boxes full of scraps of paper which I use,' he explained. 'The title comes first and the vocal melody creates itself.'

In terms of thematic inspiration, in the early days of The Smiths he admitted virtually every song he wrote was in some way autobiographical. 'They have to be,' said Morrissey. 'I can't write about things I've never felt or experienced.' He'd describe the process as 'very natural' while simultaneously 'very detached'. 'What I set out to do is to consider the sort of things people find difficult to say in everyday life,' he explained. 'I thought you could use just a very natural voice and say this is what I feel, this is what I want, this is what I'm thinking about. People in everyday life find it very difficult to tell people they're unhappy, people can't say these things. Language consists almost entirely of fashionable slang these days, therefore when somebody says something very blunt lyrically it's the height of modern revolution. People can communicate with ants in space, but they can't say they're unhappy.'

Possibly as a result of years of intense media scrutiny over the measure of autobiography in his lyrics, latterly Morrissey has clouded such analysis, claiming that even when he uses the word 'I' in a song, he really means 'We'. He'd also describe his songs as 'virtual conversation pieces' and has repeatedly referred to 'a hell of a lot of eavesdropping' as one of his primary sources. 'It's amazing what you learn while waiting to pay for your fruit juice.' The waters of autobiography are made murkier still by his frequent appropriation from cinema, literature and even pop music itself. 'There's so much buried in the past to steal from,' he once admitted, 'one's resources are limitless.' (See also PLAGIARISM.) [17, 19, 63, 69, 98, 115, 127, 130, 142, 143, 144, 165, 171, 205, 256, 267, 403, 411, 424, 425, 436, 454, 468, 477, 480]

Wrong Boy, The,

2000 debut novel by award-winning Liverpool dramatist Willy Russell of *Educating Rita* and *Shirley Valentine* fame. Its plot unfolds in a series of long, confessional letters to Morrissey by a disturbed and confused 19-year-old fan, Raymond Marks, travelling by coach from Manchester to Grimsby where his uncle has fixed him up with a building-site job he doesn't want. Through the letters, each chapter opening 'Dear Morrissey …', we learn of Raymond's troubled adolescence after a strange boyhood game called 'flytrapping' led to him being sent to a psychiatrist and placed in a special hospital under heavy medication. In Raymond's frantic, breathless correspondence, Russell perfectly captures the hysterical devotion of a self-absorbed Morrissey obsessive.

Russell originally wrote the opening portion of the book to amuse his son, Rob, and his Smiths-obsessed mates before deciding that the character of Raymond and his Morrissey fixation had the potential for an entire novel. 'I came to Morrissey and The Smiths rather late,' Russell admitted. 'Like lots of people I first heard Morrissey drifting from my son's bedroom and thought, "What a morbid caterwauler." Then one day Rob played a tape and I heard it properly for the first time. It was "FRANKLY, MR SHANKLY", and I realised what a witty writer Morrissey was, and that his mordant stance belies a truly original wit. I do find him hysterically funny.' Morrissey himself was 'thrilled' by *The Wrong Boy* and expressed his hopes that it immediately be made into a film. 'I thought the book was extraordinary,' he told the BBC's Janice Long. 'I thought it was a fantastic accolade. [Russell] did write to me which was very nice. Even the bits in the book which were a bit critical [of me], I don't mind that kind of thing. I was used to that. It was OK.'

In terms of factual authenticity, *The Wrong Boy* does contain a handful of minor errors, most occurring in the '17 June 1991' letter towards the end of the book in which Raymond rhapsodises how he first discovered Morrissey: his description of watching him sing 'HALF A PERSON' and 'CEME-TRY GATES' on television is a fantasy since The Smiths made no such broadcast; HATFUL OF HOLLOW is listed in the wrong context of a song title; and Raymond makes frequent reference to

The Smiths' Singles compilation which wasn't released until 1995, four years after the date of the letter. Arguably the most glaring error in the book is that, since it's supposed to be set in June 1991, Raymond makes no mention whatsoever of Morrissey's current album, KILL UNCLE, and seems oblivious to the fact that Morrissey is about to embark on his first solo UK tour the following month. Excusing these blunders in the name of adequate dramatic licence, *The Wrong Boy* is a deeply touching story and an astute comment on the undue emotional attachment Morrissey elicits among certain members of his audience. [365, 411]

Wuthering Heights, Emily Brontë's 1847

Yorkshire-gothic masterpiece which Morrissey has named one of his favourite books on numerous occasions, deeming it 'a landmark piece of writing'. As adapted by film (most prominently the 1939 William Wyler version starring Laurence Olivier), television, and even pop music (Kate Bush's 1978 number one), *Wuthering Heights* has accrued the status of a classic love story, yet the novel itself is infinitely darker than this misleading reputation does credit. Brontë's narrative is more a hate story than a love story, a bitter tragedy where love is an irrational, all-consuming mental illness which destroys the lives of all who try to either consummate or prevent it.

Set in Brontë's native Yorkshire moors at the turn of the nineteenth century, the story unravels in a series of flashbacks as told to Mr Lockwood, the new tenant of Thrushcross Grange, by his housekeeper, Nelly Dean. Through Dean, Lockwood learns the history of his landlord, Heathcliff, an orphan discovered in Liverpool by the benevolent widower Mr Earnshaw and brought back to his Yorkshire home, Wuthering Heights. Earnshaw's own two children take very differently to their new foster brother. His son, Hindley, despises Heathcliff for stealing his father's affection whereas his daughter, Catherine, develops an intense friendship with the boy which sets in place the ensuing catalogue of spite and misery. The novel's central tragedy is that, whether through circumstance, fear or malice, soul mates Catherine and Heathcliff are unable to reciprocate their love in adult life.

Heathcliff's life is destroyed when Catherine is wooed by the refined Edgar Linton, whom she eventually marries. Thereafter, *Wuthering Heights* is the story of Heathcliff's obsessive revenge upon all who've wronged and robbed him of his true love. When Catherine dies of consumption at the beginning of the book's second half, the grief-stricken Heathcliff attempts to wreak havoc on the next generation of Wuthering Heights, manipulating the fates of Catherine's daughter, also named Catherine, Hindley's son, Hareton, and his own son, Linton. Yet the book ends with the ageing Heathcliff finally losing 'the faculty to enjoy their destruction', a broken man on the edge of insanity who spends his final days stalking the moors in pursuit of his beloved Catherine's ghost. Dean tells Lockwood how she finally discovered his body one morning, lying in his rain-soaked bed after a stormy night with the window open, a 'life-like gaze of exultation' upon his face. Heathcliff has joined Catherine in the afterlife where, according to local superstition, they now haunt the moors together.

The book offers a possible source for at least two Morrissey lyrics. In Volume One, Chapter Nine, Catherine confides in Nelly Dean about her feelings for Heathcliff and a dream in which she died and went to heaven but found it miserable. 'Heaven did not seem to be my home,' she tells Nelly, a phrase Morrissey incorporated into 1997's 'SATAN REJECTED MY SOUL'. In Volume Two, Chapter One, during Catherine's death scene she tells Heathcliff, 'YOU HAVE KILLED ME – and thriven on it, I think,' later adding, 'I forgive you'.

Emily Brontë herself is a model Morrissey symbolist: creatively exceptional but doomed. Barely a year after *Wuthering Heights* was first published in December 1847 (attributed to the male pseudonym Ellis Bell), Brontë died on 19 December 1848 at the age of 30. Her alcoholic older brother Branwell died three months earlier while younger sister Anne, author of *Agnes Grey* and *The Tenant Of Wildfell Hall*, died six months later aged 29. All were survived by elder sister Charlotte, author of JANE EYRE, who would later tamper with *Wuthering Heights* for a revived 1850 edition which she'd patronisingly introduce as a work fashioned 'with simple tools, out of homely materials', portraying her dead younger sister as a naïve country bumpkin in order to mask her educated upbringing and acute intellect. Brontë biographer Juliet Barker would also claim that Emily had written a second novel which Charlotte jealously destroyed. The Brontës are also the subject of *Dark Quartet*, a biography by L-SHAPED ROOM author Lynne Reid Banks. The Mike Leigh film *Career Girls* starring Katrin CARTLIDGE also makes superstitious use of a paperback copy of *Wuthering Heights* and the accompanying incantation, 'Ms Brontë! Ms Brontë!' [47, 154, 289, 436, 489, 565]

Years Of Refusal, Morrissey's ninth solo album, released February 2009, highest UK chart position #3. Tracks: 'SOMETHING IS SQUEEZING MY SKULL', 'MAMA LAY SOFTLY ON THE RIVERBED', 'BLACK CLOUD', 'I'M THROWING MY ARMS AROUND PARIS', 'ALL YOU NEED IS ME', 'WHEN LAST I SPOKE TO CAROL', 'THAT'S HOW PEOPLE GROW UP', 'ONE DAY GOODBYE WILL BE FAREWELL', 'IT'S NOT YOUR BIRTHDAY ANYMORE', 'YOU WERE GOOD IN YOUR TIME', 'SORRY DOESN'T HELP', 'I'M OK BY MYSELF'. Produced by Jerry FINN.

In timing alone, Years Of Refusal was a significant milestone: released in Morrissey's 50th year and exactly 25 years, to the month, since The Smiths' eponymous debut album of February 1984. While this symbolic sense of occasion was unintentional – it was originally scheduled for release five months earlier – its status of career landmark was reiterated as much by its lyrical content as the title itself, acknowledging a life of defiance, rebellion, independence, sufferance and ostracism. If not necessarily the culmination of Morrissey's artistic life to date, Years Of Refusal nevertheless echoed and articulated his core themes with a power and purpose far greater than its two predecessors, if not, furthermore, his most commanding work since the hallowed solo high of VAUXHALL AND I some 15 years earlier.

Much of the album's vigour can be attributed to its unusually long gestation and recording during a period of persistent touring lasting the best part of two years. After dedicating most of 2006 to promoting RINGLEADER OF THE TORMENTORS predominantly in Europe, in the spring of 2007 Morrissey resumed an epic tour of America that would last until the winter. What, ostensibly, appeared to be a belated US leg of the Ringleader tour was, in fact, the beginnings of a new chapter anticipating 2008's GREATEST HITS collection. The introduction of new songs including 'That's How People Grow Up' and 'All You Need Is Me', both destined to first appear on the latter compilation, offered an early indication that Morrissey had already begun planning his next album.

Recorded wholly at Conway studios, Los Angeles, between tours in the US and Europe from August 2007 to May 2008, Years Of Refusal reunited Morrissey with YOU ARE THE QUARRY producer Jerry Finn. In the interim, the past 18 months of touring had witnessed another reshuffle in band personnel. Bassist Gary DAY had departed at the end of 2006, replaced by Solomon WALKER, brother of Ringleader tour drummer Matt. Multi-instrumentalist and keyboard player Michael FARRELL had also gone, replaced on the album by Quarry session veteran Roger Manning Jr and in concert by Kristopher Pooley (an ex-Smashing Pumpkins associate of Matt Walker).

Morrissey's pool of co-writers – guitarists Boz BOORER, Jesse TOBIAS and Alain WHYTE – remained unchanged but with one important distinction. Despite, as ever, writing the majority of its dozen tracks, for the first time in seven albums Whyte never physically contributed to the playing of his own music. After his prominence on Ringleader, Tobias contributed just three tracks whereas Boorer made a formidable return with four.

Added to its musical palette were esteemed guests Jeff Beck (cajoled into adding guitar on 'Black Cloud' after bumping into Morrissey and Chrissie HYNDE in the bar of LA's Sunset Marquis hotel) and award-winning soundtrack composer and jazz trumpeter Mark Isham, Morrissey's second choice after one of his favourite Los Angeles icons, Tijuana Brass legend Herb Alpert, proved unavailable. Alpert would nevertheless still exert a spectral presence over Years Of Refusal in its typography, based upon that of his 1964 album South Of The Border, just as the lettering on Morrissey's 2004 single 'IRISH BLOOD, ENGLISH HEART' was a homage to Alpert's 1966 LP What Now My Love.

While still completing the album, in February 2008 Greatest Hits was released. Unbeknownst at the time, the inclusion of 'That's How People Grow Up' and 'All You Need Is Me', both issued as spin-off singles, offered a premature taster of Refusal, a chronologically odd repetition which was to prompt confused criticism. By the time of its completion, a full half of the album had been previewed in concert including the emotive 'I'm Throwing My Arms Around Paris' and the beautifully barmy 'Something Is Squeezing My Skull'.

Announced at the end of May 2008 for a proposed September release, its eventual delay was due to ongoing management and label problems. Much had changed in the two years since Ringleader after the Sanctuary Music Group, home of his ATTACK label, was bought out by Universal. With Greatest Hits, Morrissey relaunched himself on the latter's DECCA imprint though by the time of Refusal's release he'd switched again to Polydor in the UK and Lost Highway in the US. Meantime his manager since Quarry, Merck Mercuriadis, had parted company with the singer in 2007. Morrissey later cited the 'long haul' of finding a suitable replacement – three managers later – as the main reason for the record's setback.

Such administrative problems were ultimately trivial in light of the shocking death of Jerry Finn in August 2008 after the producer suffered a brain haemorrhage. Though Finn had already finished work on Refusal, his untimely death added an eerie postscript to an album which, already, was as cadaverous a collection of material as Morrissey had ever assembled.

Indeed, there was some irony in the album's cover portrait by Jake WALTERS of Morrissey holding a baby boy (Sebastien Pesel Browne, son of Morrissey's tour manager Charlie). The vivacity of its music aside, lyrically Refusal was mostly preoccupied with the grave rather than the cradle. Its dozen tracks seethed with bitterness, betrayal and pain – sometimes with tongue firmly in cheek ('Something Is Squeezing My Skull', 'That's How People Grow Up') but often with clenched teeth and eye sockets bulging. There is emotional disturbance of one form or another in every song: anti-depressant-fuelled mania ('Skull'), suicide ('Mama'), unrequited lust ('Black Cloud', 'Paris'), sexual antagonism ('All You Need Is Me'), the death of a friend ('Carol'), pessimism and spinal injury ('Grow Up'), the shadow of the reaper's scythe ('One Day'), sex by force ('Birthday'), non-forgiveness ('Sorry'), misanthropy ('I'm OK') and, bleakest of all, Morrissey's self-slaughtering coup de grâce 'You Were Good In Your Time'. Those expecting more of the 'born again' romantic discovery of Ringleader or, God forbid, the mellowing of age certainly had a shock in store.

The fire and brimstone drama of the words was more than equalled by the violence and volume of the music surrounding them. Compositionally, Refusal was hardly a radical advancement from previous albums, yet Finn's clever, cohesive production and the energy in the performances merged in a new, gloriously boisterous dynamism. Special credit must go to the new rhythm section of brothers Matt and Solomon Walker. 'The players are very physical musicians,' agreed Morrissey, 'and the music that I like the most is the music that makes me feel very physical.'

Yet if there is one factor, above all else, which elevates Years Of Refusal among the greatest albums of Morrissey's career, it is the certainty and cyclone-strength of his singing. It was significant that in most promotional interviews surrounding its release, while he gave little if nothing away about the album's themes or the meaning of specific songs, he spoke often about the power of the singing voice. Vocally, Refusal is a never-ending battery of knockout punches, confirming Morrissey's unalterable legacy as one of the most sensational, and sensationally strange, singers in the history of pop. There is more art, more life, more sex, more thought and more unadulterated drama crammed in his elastic delivery of one-syllable words such as 'skull', 'up' and 'no' than lesser singers struggle to achieve over whole albums, if not careers.

Critical reaction was largely very favourable, though commercially Refusal failed to repeat the chart-topping triumph of Ringleader. Coupled with the moderate placings of his previous few singles, while still a top three success the album signified if not the bursting of a bubble then a levelling-out in the post-Quarry Morrissey hysteria surrounding its two predecessors.

Not for the first time, whispers of imminent retirement – as prompted by his comment to one reporter, 'I don't want to go on much longer' – immediately subjected Years Of Refusal to added scrutiny as Morrissey's potential last will and testament. But, for all its stench of death, for all the outward finality of the closing 'I'm OK By Myself' or the symbolic denouement of 'You Were Good In Your Time', there still seems far too much animation in its body, too much fight in his voice. At 50, Morrissey has only a finite number of songs, indeed years, left in him, but Refusal doesn't sound like the last crash of the gong. Rather, it's the start of the preceding drum roll, the gathering of the storm, not the tempest itself. One day Morrissey's goodbye *will* be farewell but, for now, pray Years Of Refusal isn't it. [60, 245, 417, 418, 568]

'Yes, I Am Blind' (Morrissey/Rourke), B-side of 'OUIJA BOARD, OUIJA BOARD' (1989). A hymn to Morrissey's inborn pessimism, 'Yes, I Am Blind' appeared a guilty admission of love towards an innocent youth who reminds the singer too much of himself, in doing so stirring ancient fears of persecution which in turn propel him to vent his frustration towards a deaf and uncaring God.

The tune was from a batch of demos that former Smiths bassist Andy Rourke had supplied Morrissey in the spring of 1989, sharing an autumnal melody and plodding tempo with Gilbert O'Sullivan's 1970 hit 'NOTHING RHYMED'; it therefore seems more than coincidence that Morrissey should cover the latter in 2002. It was unfortunate that Rourke himself never played on the record, undoubtedly the best of his three Morrissey co-writes. Instead, session bassist Matthew Seligman and guitarist Kevin ARMSTRONG faithfully copied the arrangement of Rourke's original cassette. The song's recording was particularly significant in establishing Morrissey's relationship with new producers Clive LANGER and Alan Winstanley. Initially unhappy with their work on 'Ouija Board', the singer was considering aborting the session until he heard their foundations for 'Yes, I Am

Yield To The Night, 1956 British prison drama starring Diana DORS, listed among Morrissey's favourite films. Often referred to as a fictionalised version of the story of Ruth Ellis, the last woman to be hanged in Britain the year before its release (a myth Morrissey perpetuates in his chapter on Dors in *EXIT SMILING*), it was actually based on a book published before Ellis was arrested. There is, nonetheless, a strong parallel between Ellis, a neurotic socialite who shot her playboy lover in cold blood, and the film's Mary Hilton (Dors), an obsessive shop girl who in broad daylight shoots the woman who drove her unfaithful lover to suicide. *Yield To The Night* made a compelling case against the existent death penalty of its day, humanising Dors's murderess and the relationship with her prison guardians, among them Morrissey favourites Marjorie RHODES and YVONNE MITCHELL. The script also makes an explicit reference to Morrissey's favourite poet, A. E. HOUSMAN: during a flashback, Dors quotes aloud from a copy of *A Shropshire Lad*.

In terms of Dors's career, Morrissey deemed *Yield To The Night* 'undoubtedly the only decent [film] she ever made'. Dors herself seemed to agree, stating 'if nothing else, I can always say "This I did and here it is for you to see."' A production still of Dors clinging to her cell's iron bedstead was selected by Morrissey as a potential Smiths sleeve and was eventually used, without his involvement, for Warners' posthumous 1995 Singles compilation. Another more glamorous shot of Dors from the film's New Year's Eve flashback scene was one of several stage backdrops rotated during 1992's YOUR ARSENAL tour.

Significantly, it was Shelagh DELANEY who later wrote the film documenting the real Ellis story, 1985's *Dance With A Stranger*. According to Siouxsie SIOUX, 'footage of Ellis' – which may, possibly, have been footage of Dors in *Yield To The Night* itself – was to be used in a promo video for 'INTERLUDE' which never materialised. [25, 175, 303, 341 374, 496, 566]

Blind' and changed his mind; hearing its lyrical metaphor of 'little lamb', Langer and Winstanley would humorously refer to it thereafter as 'the one about the sheep'. An outstanding Morrissey B-side, the song was granted due prominence on the following year's BONA DRAG compilation. [1, 15, 29]

You Are The Quarry, Morrissey's seventh

solo album, released May 2004, highest UK chart position #2. Tracks: 'AMERICA IS NOT THE WORLD', 'IRISH BLOOD, ENGLISH HEART', 'I HAVE FORGIVEN JESUS', 'COME BACK TO CAMDEN', 'I'M NOT SORRY', 'THE WORLD IS FULL OF CRASHING BORES', 'HOW CAN ANYBODY POSSIBLY KNOW HOW I FEEL?', 'FIRST OF THE GANG TO DIE', 'LET ME KISS YOU', 'ALL THE LAZY DYKES', 'I LIKE YOU', 'YOU KNOW I COULDN'T LAST'. Produced by Jerry FINN.

Coinciding with his relocation to Los Angeles, in the year following 1997's MALADJUSTED Morrissey found himself in the improbable position of

being without a label. His previous contract under the umbrella of the PolyGram group – licensed to ISLAND in the UK and Mercury in the US – was annulled when both imprints collapsed as part of a company takeover. Initially, his predicament seemed an attractive one: a pop icon living in Hollywood luxury, presumably free to sign a new deal with whomever he pleased. As things turned out, Morrissey was about to find himself not just unemployed but seemingly unemployable for the best part of seven years.

Throughout that absence, during which time he embarked on two independent world tours with no promotional attachments (the first from 1999 to 2000, the second in 2002), he blamed his inability to find a new deal on the outrageous stipulations of the major labels themselves. His accusations ranged from lack of advance money, demands to hear demos before signature and dubious requests that he sack his band and instead make an album either with Radiohead or Everything But The Girl singer Tracey Thorn. By 2002, Morrissey's exclusion from the record industry had become a badge of honour in his ongoing self-mythology, moaning that nobody wanted him 'because I don't fit in'.

Yet behind this façade of the ill-treated outsider, Morrissey benefited greatly from his hiatus. The cyclical nature of the British music scene, and especially the British music press, ensured that five years after the witch trial of Maladjusted and the 1996 COURT CASE, Morrissey, and the legacy of The Smiths, came back in fashion with a vengeance. In 2002, the NME voted him and his previous band jointly the most important artist(s) in their 50-year history, just as a new generation of UK indie bands such as The Libertines, and later Franz Ferdinand, began citing him as a key influence. After his victorious UK concerts of 2002, now fully integrating The Smiths' back catalogue with old and new unrecorded solo material, it was only a matter of time before some label made him a sensible offer. Persistent rumours that he'd been courted by Sanctuary Records were finally confirmed in early summer 2003. Prior to an official press statement, on 26 May Morrissey faxed BBC Radio 2's Janice Long, who read his announcement on air. 'To all 12 people in the UK who are interested,' he began, 'I have signed to ATTACK on the Sanctuary label. Have begun recording my first album in 40 years …'

Provisionally titled Irish Blood, English Heart, Morrissey had been telling the press his next album was 'written and ready to record' since 1999 yet, in theory, the added gap offered him the opportunity to cherry pick from seven years' worth of ideas. In the event, he admitted that although 'some of [the tracks] go back maybe four years', half of it was much more recent, stating his favourites were 'the ones that happened spontaneously when we went to record it'. Retaining his touring band of 2002, he drew from his long-term co-writers WHYTE and BOORER, with a minor contribution from bassist Gary DAY, making his first Morrissey album since YOUR ARSENAL over a decade earlier. It would also be the only studio album featuring recent recruit, drummer Dean BUTTERWORTH. More surprising was his choice of producer, Jerry Finn, who'd made his name with American punk acts such as Blink 182, Bad Religion and Green Day. 'It doesn't matter to me that the music he's made is very LA, for want of a better description,' explained Morrissey. 'Often producers are desperate to break out of what they've been doing.'

Ever the creature of habit, recording commenced in the autumn of 2003 at Hook End Manor near Reading; scene of most of BONA DRAG and all of KILL UNCLE, VAUXHALL & I, SOUTHPAW GRAMMAR and, his previous, Maladjusted. The rest of the album was finished in Los Angeles at Conway studios, a short distance from Morrissey's desired burial place at Hollywood Forever Cemetery. It was his most prolific session yet, spawning approximately 21 recordings of which a dozen were selected for the final album.

In January 2004, four months prior to release, the title was announced as You Are The Quarry (possibly inspired by Alan BENNETT's 1973 play Habeas Corpus, where the character Mrs Wicksteed declares 'You are my quarry. I am stalking you with all the lithe grace of a panther'). Morrissey offered multiple interpretations of the title: that it was aimed 'at one person … but not the obvious person' (presumably by 'obvious' he meant Mike Joyce); that it was aimed 'at my audience in general, saying they are a target for me to win their affection now'; and that, as worded beside his name on the album cover ('Morrissey, you are the quarry'), it was about himself. 'I have been quarry for so many years,' he stated, 'and people have taken so many pot-shots at me. So yes, I feel heavily bruised.' Its Greg Gorman cover portrait of Morrissey as the archetypal Hollywood gangster in pinstripe suit and Tommy gun was also meant as 'a remote link to the title'.

By the time it was released in May 2004, expectations for You Are The Quarry were beyond great, fuelled by the singer's own approbations that it was 'absolutely the definitive Morrissey album' and 'my best *ever*'. Coinciding with a glut of press coverage, his 45th birthday hometown concert at Manchester MEN Arena and his imminent MELTDOWN festival, the album became the catalyst for a Morrissey media frenzy not witnessed since the halcyon days of VIVA HATE. Despite a minority of dissenting voices, the critics largely hailed it as a triumphant return, predicting it to be his first deserved number one album since Vauxhall And I. Its failure to do so, hemmed in at number two by rosy-cheeked Smiths-disciples Keane, must have been a bitter blow for so fixated a chart statistician as Morrissey.

With hindsight, the British music press were a tad over-hysterical in the praise they lavished upon You Are The Quarry. It was especially ironic to hear so many critics justify its merits by contrasting it against the perceived pallor of Morrissey's mid-90s output. The stark truth, which few were plucky enough to admit, was that on a purely musical level it carried on from exactly where Maladjusted had left off. Jerry Finn had succeeded in making the 'bright'-sounding album the singer had hoped, but only in terms of its audio gloss and mild concessions to contemporary rhythms and textures. The melodies of Alain Whyte and Boz Boorer were no more challenging or surprising than anything they'd supplied Morrissey in the previous decade. It was the music industry, and the critics, who had changed. Morrissey remained impervious.

Although Morrissey had stated 'this time around I feel that the album represents something which is actually deeper than mere revenge [and] settling all those old scores', in reality You Are The Quarry was a prolonged exercise in vengeance after seven years of repressed rancour. Maladjusted's 'SORROW WILL COME IN THE END' had only been a taster for the transparent retaliations of Quarry's multiple swipes at 'policemen', 'magistrates' and all law authorities. 'How Can Anybody Possibly Know How I Feel?', 'The World Is Full Of Crashing Bores' and 'You Know I Couldn't Last' were evidence that the wounds of the court case had yet to scab over. If anything, seven years

in the LA sun had intensified his hatred of the 'northern leeches' as well as his rigid political opinions, expressed in frank and certain terms in 'Irish Blood, English Heart' and 'America Is Not The World'. The only new lyrical colour came, inevitably, from his new surroundings in Los Angeles, scene of 'First Of The Gang To Die' and 'All The Lazy Dykes'. Elsewhere the dignified resilience of 'I'm Not Sorry', the psychological self-flagellation of 'I Have Forgiven Jesus' and the wistful 'Come Back To Camden' were its most fascinating shreds of autobiography.

For all its many imperfections, You Are The Quarry was still a meritorious return, its handful of classic Morrissey moments bright enough to divert attention away from its dim flaws. Its strongest tracks were undoubtedly its singles: even if the album never made number one, Morrissey could at least boast being the only artist in 2004 to score four consecutive top ten UK hits. The quality of the Quarry-era B-sides was also exceptional, instigating some debate as to whether he may have made an error of judgement when deciding the album's final tracklisting.

Yet, in the end, its shortcomings were immaterial. By virtue of its restoration of Morrissey to the pop frontlines, earning widespread critical acclaim, sustained chart success and sell-out crowds at UK arenas such as Earls Court – an unthinkable feat not three years earlier – You Are The Quarry may not have been a *great* album but it was, in every other aspect, a glorious comeback.
[53, 74, 108, 119, 143, 248, 281, 405, 410, 411, 436, 451]

'You Have Killed Me' (Morrissey/Tobias), Morrissey's 30th solo single (from the album RINGLEADER OF THE TORMENTORS), released March 2006, highest UK chart position #3. Heavy on sexual metaphor, from the penetrative imagery of being physically 'entered' to the symbolic deflowering of the title, 'You Have Killed Me' drew much inspiration from Morrissey's newly adopted Roman surroundings. Aside from the reference to the city's Piazza Cavour, the singer likens the relationship between himself and his lover to that of an Italian film director and star. First he is Pier Paolo PASOLINI to their lead role of the Roman street pimp, ACCATTONE. He then becomes LUCHINO VISCONTI, warning his partner they'll never be as great as Italian screen legend Anna MAGNANI. Though figuratively destroyed, Morrissey finally forgives the perpetrator, hinting he'd be ready and willing to be 'killed' again. Beyond its Italian influences, the title may have been lifted from one of Morrissey's favourite masterpieces of English literature, Emily Brontë's *WUTHERING HEIGHTS*, where the dying Catherine tells Heathcliff 'you have killed me – and thriven on it, I think'.

As the first single pre-empting the Ringleader album, 'You Have Killed Me' was a well-chosen appetiser both lyrically and musically. Co-written by Jesse Tobias, its velvety melody veiled a strangely familiar chorus; though in a different musical key, it repeated the same chord arrangement Johnny Marr had used on 'YOU JUST HAVEN'T EARNED IT YET, BABY'. During the recording, Morrissey also teased producer TONY VISCONTI about being immortalised in the lyrics – 'Have you ever heard another song with your name in it?' – though he soon realised it was a homage to his cinematic namesake. Nevertheless, in concert Morrissey would often improvise, occasionally adding 'Tony' to 'Visconti', other times namechecking another giant of Italian cinema, Federico Fellini, while substituting the names of Diana DORS or Sophia Loren for Magnani.

Debuting at number three, 'You Have Killed Me' remains Morrissey's joint biggest hit to date (along with 'IRISH BLOOD, ENGLISH HEART'), offering reassuring confirmation that his 'comeback' of 2004 was now permanent. The tongue-in-cheek single sleeve depicted the singer lying across railway tracks as if calmly waiting for the next express train to slice him in half. Equally droll, the official video was a pastiche of a 70s Italian EURO-VISION Song Contest entry, intercut with original audience footage and featuring Alain WHYTE miming drums instead of Matt CHAMBERLAIN. [159, 259, 389, 481]

'You Just Haven't Earned It Yet, Baby'

(Morrissey/Marr), From the compilation album THE WORLD WON'T LISTEN (1987). A quintessential Morrissey lyric examining the agony of frustrated ambition, the title was rumoured to have been a comment from ROUGH TRADE's Geoff Travis directed at Morrissey. 'I'm sure it was,' insists Mike Joyce. 'I think Morrissey had asked for a car or a driver to pick him up or something and that's what Geoff said in reply.'

'Obviously Geoff was staunchly against [the song] because he thought it was a personal letter addressed to him,' Morrissey later disclosed. 'I never said it was.' Marr also recalls Travis 'not thinking very highly of it' while the fact Morrissey repeated the same phrase in his subsequent critique of shady record company politics, 'PAINT A VULGAR PICTURE', also seems more than coincidence.

Written during the twilight of The Smiths' career, Marr's ultramarine guitar spangles offered a mature throwback to the jangly pop of 'WILLIAM, IT WAS REALLY NOTHING' recorded two years earlier. Given its obvious commercial appeal and anthemic chorus, 'You Just Haven't Earned It Yet, Baby' was originally scheduled as The Smiths' 13th single, following 'ASK', only to be substituted for 'SHOPLIFTERS OF THE WORLD UNITE'. 'I think we just felt it was *slight* after THE QUEEN IS DEAD,' says Marr. 'That was my personal feeling about it. There was more investigating to do and we weren't short of ideas. "Shoplifters" was a better record.'

A contributing factor may also have been Morrissey's dissatisfaction with producer John PORTER's finished mix and its excess of overdubs. In the end, 'You Just Haven't Earned It Yet, Baby' was released as the one exclusive track on 1987's The World Won't Listen compilation: a slightly different mix with fewer overdubs (presumably more to Morrissey's taste) later appeared on LOUDER THAN BOMBS. The former also appeared as the 'wrong' A-side on a limited 'mispressing' of the 'Shoplifters' 12-inch single, now a highly prized rarity among Smiths collectors. Following the group's split, Marr recorded a new version of the song with Kirsty MACCOLL, first released as the

'You Must Please Remember' (Morrissey/Whyte), B-side of 'DAGENHAM DAVE' (1995). A depressing rock dirge rattles Morrissey's memories of 'so very many stupid things', begging the song's addressee to recall a dark past 'caught in your headlights like a frightened animal'. Whyte's tune had started out as a much subtler ballad with minimal percussion, gradually building to an epic finale featuring piano. By the time it was recorded at the SOUTHPAW GRAMMAR sessions, it was shortened and 'hardened' in keeping with the rest of the album. Though not strong enough to justify a place on the final running order, 'You Must Please Remember' made a fine, if frequently forgotten, B-side. [4, 40]

B-side to her 'Free World' single and since included as a CD bonus track on her 1989 album Kite. [7, 19, 27, 71]

'You Know I Couldn't Last' (Morrissey/Whyte/Day), From the album YOU ARE THE QUARRY (2004). In the run-up to its release, some critics made wild predictions that You Are The Quarry might be Morrissey's last album: a celebratory lap of honour after seven years of absence prior to retirement. Its closing track gave such theorists much to chew over. 'You Know I Couldn't Last' was a bombastic finale that could have easily been interpreted as a final farewell; 17 years after 'PAINT A VULGAR PICTURE', it saw Morrissey dissect the music industry yet again but from a very different perspective: now it's he who's the star, cowering at the mercy of the teenagers from the ugly new houses whose changing tastes could strip him of his fame in an instant. As with 'THE PUBLIC IMAGE', he expresses wariness of 'the printed word' though finds unlikely succour through the critics who 'somehow make you'. At its hammiest extreme, we're presented with the image of Morrissey with a cash till strapped to his back ringing with the proceeds from 'CDs and T-shirts', pursued by accountants and 'evil legal eagles'. The 'leeches' analogy, a likely reference to Mike Joyce, was salvaged from an older lyric written circa the 1997 MALADJUSTED sessions ('THE LEECHES GO ON REMOVING'). The title itself was also probably borrowed from the 1974 deathbed letter of 'Warhol Superstar' Candy DARLING. 'Susan, I am

sorry,' she writes. 'Did you know I couldn't last. I always knew it.'

Few who'd followed Morrissey's trials and tribulations throughout the 1990s and during his wilderness years since 1997 could have been in any doubt about its veiled references to the Smiths royalties COURT CASE and the exact '-ists and -isms' he'd been accused of after the 1992 NME Madstock furore. Its only enlightening insight into Morrissey's psyche was the parting couplet that, despite the luxuries fame had brought him, nothing could rid him of his psychological 'squalor'.

The tune, credited to Whyte and Gary Day (the bassist's only album composer credit), leapt not altogether smoothly between crashing confusion and anaesthetised bliss, its softer interludes reminiscent of Phil Spector's 'To Know Him Is To Love Him', a 1958 hit for The Teddy Bears later tackled by Marc BOLAN. Overlong and at times overblown, as the last bow on an album fuelled by old scores and unfinished business there was something inevitable about 'You Know I Couldn't Last' – an unavoidable exorcism waiting to happen. [74, 192, 297]

'You Say You Don't Love Me' (Pete Shelley), Live BUZZCOCKS cover version, played by Morrissey during his half-dozen summer festival appearances during the summer of 2008. The original was issued as a single in September 1979 but, as Morrissey noted, was a commercial flop despite being 'very strong', thus ending the group's previous unbroken run of five consecutive top 40 hits. Shelley's lyrics were an ideal vehicle for

Morrissey; a sad but tender attempt to talk himself out of his feelings for an unrequited love which in its repeated yearning not to 'live in a dream' but have 'something real' neatly evoked the sentiment of his own 'LAST NIGHT I DREAMT THAT SOMEBODY LOVED ME', albeit to a wistful punk-pop tune instead of The Smiths' Wagnerian death knell. Beyond some subtle lyrical changes, Morrissey's version was a relatively straight copy of the original. [421]

'You Should Have Been Nice To Me'
(Morrissey/Boorer), Studio outtake from the abandoned Miraval studios sessions for the 1995 album SOUTHPAW GRAMMAR, officially released on the 2009 redux edition. As recriminating a lyric as its blunt title suggested, Morrissey softly berates a partner for deserting him in his hour of need and failing to fight his corner. The song's slow, waltz-time arrangement was reminiscent of Boorer's earlier VAUXHALL AND I ballads, gradually building in intensity and perhaps trying too self-consciously to follow the model of 'NOW MY HEART IS FULL' or 'I'D LOVE TO' only to falter in the process. More than anything, 'You Should Have Been Nice To Me' was sorely lacking in any strong vocal melody or dramatic delivery and its absence on the original Southpaw was entirely justifiable. [4, 40]

'You Were Good In Your Time' (Morrissey/ Whyte), From the album YEARS OF REFUSAL (2009). Arguably the centrepiece of his ninth album was Morrissey's cryptic serenade to a once-great, now-obsolete star – cryptic inasmuch as he appeared to be singing about himself. The faded hero he describes with a Messianic gift for appeasing loneliness, who said 'more in one day than most people say in a lifetime', could very easily be the words of a Morrissey apostle. In essence, 'You Were Good In Your Time' is the nightmare vision of 'RUBBER RING' come to pass, a chilling realisation of obsolescence and the desertion of his audience. Without their love, Morrissey ceases to exist and so the song collapses two-thirds of the way

through into a deathly abyss which, as he later admitted, was meant to represent 'slipping into the next world'.

The poignancy of his fan's farewell was amplified by its mournful Latin guitar melody. More ethereal textures were provided by its running French dialogue sample, taken from 1937's *Pépé Le Moko*.[1] The film's relevance to the song, if any, may be the symbolic downfall of Pépé, a notorious gangster avoiding capture in the labyrinthine casbah of Algiers who eventually commits suicide having lost one woman and been betrayed by another.

While often accused of conservatism and failing to experiment, in its weird disintegration from ballad to abstract sound collage – in places evoking the ambient shimmers of 1994's 'I'D LOVE TO' – 'You Were Good In Your Time' is as weird and challenging a record as Morrissey has ever made. Certainly, it's one of his most profound in recent memory and may yet prove to be his most pertinent. [480, 541]

————

1. The dialogue sampled is a love scene between Pépé (Jean Gabin) and his wealthy married mistress (Mireille Balin) and not especially meaningful. For example, roughly translated what you hear at the beginning of the song is – Him: 'You sure?', Her: 'Same time.', Him: 'Here?', Her: 'Yes.', Him: 'I really like you. You're beautiful.' And so on.

'You're Gonna Need Someone On Your Side' (Morrissey/Nevin), From the album YOUR ARSENAL (1992). With a title possibly borrowed from Buffy SAINTE-MARIE's cover of the old blues song 'You're Gonna Need Somebody On Your Bond', Morrissey makes a humorous pledge of support to a beleaguered friend only to be greeted with sickened apathy. In concert, he'd often alter the lyrics, describing its subject as a collector of 'very sharp bread knives' (as heard on BEETHOVEN WAS DEAF), though its prevailing Samaritan sentiment could just as easily be interpreted as a third person appeal to Morrissey himself.

Its drag-racing guitar riff was written by Mark Nevin in the winter of 1990 alongside 'THE LOOP' and 'PREGNANT FOR THE LAST TIME' as part of his commission from Morrissey to supply 'rockabilly-type' tracks for an abandoned mini-album. While overjoyed to hear his song given its deserved ferocity in the hands of his hero, producer Mick RONSON, its brawny execution on Your Arsenal was bittersweet for Nevin who by the time of its recording was no longer part of Morrissey's band. Instead, its torrent of 'Peter Gunn'-sneers to a thrusting psychobilly beat became the perfect vehicle for his new group of BOORER, COBRIN, DAY and WHYTE, attacking it with a savage gusto emitting distant howls of Morrissey's beloved CRAMPS. [5, 22]

'You're The One For Me, Fatty' (Morrissey/

Whyte), Morrissey's 13th solo single (from the album YOUR ARSENAL), released July 1992, highest UK chart position #19. On first listen, the comical 'You're The One For Me, Fatty' sounded like Morrissey's attempt to highlight society's discrimination against the overweight by declaring his love for someone chubby; a scenario echoed in the single's promo video in which a thin male suitor courts a plump girl with cakes and flowers.

In truth, the song is Morrissey's tongue-in-cheek message to his friend Cathal SMYTH of MADNESS. '"You're The One For Me, Fatty" was written about me,' confirms Smyth, a fact which Clive LANGER verifies. 'Morrissey let it out that it was about Cathal,' says Langer. 'It was an open secret at the time.' By the early 90s Smyth had, as he puts it, 'filled out somewhat' compared to his younger, slimmer self during Madness's chart heyday. Whatever Morrissey's motives in penning such an amorous lyric, Smyth took the song and its flirtatious nature in good humour.

The title was a likely pun on 'You're The One For Me, Bobby', a 1971 B-side by THE MARVELETTES while its 'all over Battersea' refrain may have been in reference to the London locale of Nell Dunn's 1963 novel *Up The Junction*, also the source of Morrissey's recent H-BOMB quip. With its attractive Smiths-lite guitar riff, and Buddy Holly-esque vocal melody (aping the 'a-hey' hiccups of 1957's 'Everyday'), 'You're The One For Me, Fatty' was an obvious single choice, albeit among Morrissey's more disposable pop moments. [15, 36, 306]

'You've Got Everything Now' (Morrissey/

Marr), From the album THE SMITHS (1984). 'It's a throwback to when I was at school,' explained Morrissey. 'I was quite advanced at school and when I left it seemed that all these really oafish clods were making tremendous progress and had wonderfully large cars and lots of money. I seemed to be constantly waiting for a bus that never came. It seemed as though although I had the brains, I didn't really have anything else.'

Addressing one 'oafish clod' in particular, 'You've Got Everything Now' was the first song where Morrissey mocked humdrum employment by stating he'd 'never had a job'; give or take his few 'brief spasms' of work, this was more or less true. The song contained a couple of lines probably inspired by Shelagh DELANEY – the opening Shakespeare quote, borrowed from *A Taste Of Honey*, and the modification of a passage in *The Lion In Love*, 'Shall I tell you something? I don't like your face.' It's also likely that a Bette DAVIS comment in the film *MR SKEFFINGTON* – 'Although I've never really seen you smile I always have the feeling you're laughing at me' – was the basis of Morrissey's similar lyric. Written in the spring of 1983, the song was originally slightly longer with an extra verse heightening the romantic friction between Morrissey and the song's subject: 'When you lost the will to go on, I gave you some,' he sings, adding 'You never really wanted the truth and so I never gave it you' before beseeching them to 'make your move'.

Marr's punchy arrangement was one of the best tunes on The Smiths' debut, his guitar tautly slicing towards an exhilarating chorus given some subtle organ flourishes courtesy of guest Paul Carrack; Morrissey's falsetto harmonies and Rourke's hot and bothered bass line were equally magical. It was a rightful indicator of its commercial promise when 'You've Got Everything Now' was coupled with 'STILL ILL' as a double A-side radio promo single at the time of the album's release. The song was just as popular in concert, very often a riotous final encore. [17, 299, 406, 432, 531]

'You've Had Her' (Morrissey/Boorer), B-side of 'CERTAIN PEOPLE I KNOW' (1992). Echoing the title and cutting sentiment of Phil OCHS's 'I've Had Her', Morrissey reprimands a promiscuous Jack the Lad, highlighting the already obvious that such womanisers are horribly inconsiderate to their female prey. A fairly inconsequential work, 'You've Had Her' is mainly of interest for being one of Boorer's first composer credits, his sparse lilting guitar treading cautiously amid its atmospheric blustery howl.

Young, Kristeen, Operatically bonkers (or as Morrissey termed her, 'completely original') American singer/pianist who became his tour support act and general protégée from 2006 to 2007. Young also appears as 'backing voice' on the tracks 'SWEETIE-PIE' and 'THAT'S HOW PEOPLE GROW UP'.

Morrissey discovered Young through producer TONY VISCONTI while working on RINGLEADER OF THE TORMENTORS in Rome. Visconti had produced Young's two previous albums and had also employed her as a keyboard player and backing vocalist on David BOWIE's Heathen (2002). Due to commence work on her next album after Ringleader, Visconti was in the studio checking out a video clip of Young, unaware that Morrissey was watching until his voice piped up behind him: 'Who's that? She's good.'

The adopted child of strict Christian fundamentalist parents, Young was raised in St Louis ('Which, I am told, is another way of saying Mars,' joked Morrissey). She discovered The Smiths in her teens via a boyfriend's copy of HATFUL OF HOLLOW. 'I grew up listening to [Morrissey's] music,' said Young, 'so part of what I am is formed by him ... I think he is the greatest lyricist that ever existed.' To her obvious delight, in April 2006 she was invited to support him on the Ringleader Of The Tormentors tour. 'I watch her set every night and I am dazed,' swooned Morrissey. Alas, his audiences were more often than not repelled by her screechy hubbub akin to Dame Kiri Te Kanawa being lowered feet first into a tree pulper. Oblivious to their indifference, Morrissey licensed two singles through his ATTACK label, 'Kill The Father' (which he described with no small amount of hyperbole as 'the best song

I've heard for 50 years') and 'London Cry'. 'She uses her keyboard as a highly trained Nazi might use an electronic rod for shocking the parts,' he enthused, 'the hands moving so fast that whether they actually move at all is an ongoing debate. The voice is a beautiful bayonet, and the life swills out in song.'

In March 2007, they appeared together photographed for a *Guardian* magazine feature about heroes and protégées. 'Morrissey asked me to sit on his shoulders,' recalled Young. 'At first I thought he was joking, but he really wanted me to ... So there I am, literally heaving with desire for him and suddenly his head is between my thighs.' Unfortunately it was a similar allusion to the proximity of Morrissey's head and Young's nether regions which was to see her abruptly banished from his US tour the following autumn. Opening for him at New York's Hammerstein Ballroom on 23 October 2007, Young was heckled between songs. She responded by saying the following: 'Morrissey gives good head ... I mean cunnilingus.'

Young's next Morrissey show was scheduled three days later at the same venue. Instead, on that date she posted a statement on her website: 'My band, Kristeen Young, have been asked to leave the Morrissey tour. Although I have been advised not to respond or issue a statement, my feelings are that I must. We have been asked to leave because of something I said on stage ... Unfortunately, the statement has been perceived as being profane (when, actually, one of the two words in question is a scientific term found in junior high, health class textbooks, and the other word, I feel most would agree, is lightweight slang) or defamatory ... The "offending" statement, in particular, was in no way a literal statement, and was very much in keeping with the tone of my writing in general … Maybe I misjudged … but I meant no harm. I love Morrissey with all of my heart, soul, body, spirit, to the core of my existence and always will. These will be the only words I will ever write or speak on the subject ever again.'

Though her Klaus NOMI-esque vocals on the yet-to-be-released 'That's How People Grow Up' were left intact, to date it remains Morrissey's last involvement with an artist who just ten months earlier he'd described as having 'a face made to be peered at till the end of time'. [189, 244, 351, 414]

'Youngest Was The Most Loved, The'

(Morrissey/Tobias), Morrissey's 31st solo single (from the album RINGLEADER OF THE TORMEN-TORS), released June 2006, highest UK chart position #14. The familiar Morrissey themes of romanticised crime and maternal smothering combine in this brief sketch about a shy, cherubic boy from a poor family who grows up to become a criminal in spite of his mother's best attempts to shield him 'from the world's glare'. The crux of the song is the singer's revolt against the concept of normality in everyday life, echoed by a choir of Italian children which invited inevitable comparison with the kids' chorus in The Smiths' 'PANIC'. '[It was] a perverse joy,' said Morrissey, 'when you see all these seven-year-old Italian children singing ["There is no such thing in life as normal"], and quite happy to do it, full of meaning and not needing to have anything explained to them.' He was also particularly pleased with his expanding lyrical vocabulary, bragging to producer TONY VISCONTI, 'Have you ever heard another song with the word "retroussé" in it?' This description of a 'retroussé nose' betrayed the likely influence of John BETJEMAN who used the phrase in his poem 'The Olympic Girl'.

The children's choir added to an already dramatic production, opening with the wail of an Italian ambulance before undraping its grimly grinding Tobias riff. Chosen as the second single from Ringleader, Morrissey had high hopes for

'The Youngest Was The Most Loved', though it missed the UK top ten. The following week, an irate email from the singer to manager Merck Mercuriadis was leaked on to the MORRISSEY-SOLO website. In it, Morrissey spoke of the song as being, in his eyes, an inevitable number one hit in any sane universe, blaming Sanctuary Records for their lack of promotion, particularly in terms of digital sales. What was most revealing (and damaging) about the email was the extent of Morrissey's egomaniacal persecution complex, seemingly unable to reasonably comprehend why any record of his should not be a resounding success. Though some blindly adoring fans steadfastly dismissed the memo as a fake, it was confirmed as real when the singer's lawyer contacted the website and demanded it be removed.

As it turned out, 'The Youngest Was The Most Loved' still fared better than his next two Ringleader singles, which similarly missed the top ten. It also prompted one of Morrissey's better videos; shot in widescreen black-and-white, it casts him as a handcuffed criminal being led from a courthouse by Italian police, played by his band, into a waiting car surrounded by paparazzi. [159, 283, 389]

Your Arsenal, Morrissey's third solo album,

released July 1992, highest UK chart position #4. Tracks: 'YOU'RE GONNA NEED SOMEONE ON YOUR SIDE', 'GLAMOROUS GLUE', 'WE'LL LET YOU KNOW', 'THE NATIONAL FRONT DISCO', 'CERTAIN PEOPLE I KNOW', 'WE HATE IT WHEN OUR FRIENDS BECOME SUCCESSFUL', 'YOU'RE THE ONE FOR ME, FATTY', 'SEASICK, YET STILL DOCKED', 'I KNOW IT'S GONNA HAPPEN SOMEDAY', 'TOMORROW'. Produced by Mick RONSON.

The KILL UNCLE tour of 1991 marked a major turning point in Morrissey's solo career. Though he'd admit that his second album 'frustrated' him, in its live performance he re-established himself as a group leader for the first time since The Smiths. 'I didn't have a regular band,' he explained, 'so I needed to rebuild a gang spirit, to be back permanently with the same persons.' That sense of permanence was fortified on Your Arsenal, the first album with his new band led by guitarists Boz BOORER and Alain WHYTE, which wiped the slate clean of his inaugural solo years and all their varying successes, failures and creative uncertainties. More so than 1988's VIVA HATE, Your Arsenal introduced the definitive 'solo Morrissey style', the immovable groundwork pinning the rest of his solo discography in position – his proper post-Smiths rebirth.

By the close of 1991, Morrissey had spent six months on the road with his new group of Boorer, Whyte, bassist Gary DAY and drummer Spencer COBRIN, but had yet to take them into the studio. The next logical challenge was to do so and try and capture the same spirited concert chemistry they brought to the Kill Uncle songs on its successor. In the meantime, Kill Uncle co-writer Mark NEVIN had been unable to join the tour but still considered himself Morrissey's main musical collaborator. Regular correspondence over the summer of '91 had given Nevin the impression that the next album, nicknamed 'Kill Auntie', would mainly consist of his music. Unbeknownst to Nevin, Morrissey was already accepting material from Alain Whyte, previewing their first collaborations 'We Hate It When Our Friends Become Successful' and future B-side 'PASHERNATE LOVE' in the final leg of the Kill Uncle tour. By the time recording commenced in the new year, Whyte had all but completely superseded Nevin, who would contribute only two of its ten tracks.

Adding to Nevin's nagging sense of betrayal was the fact he'd been actively involved in finding Morrissey a new producer to replace the Kill Uncle team of Clive LANGER and Alan Winstanley. Nevin had first suggested John Cale, producer of one of Morrissey's most sacred scriptures, Horses by PATTI SMITH. Morrissey had also proposed BOLAN and BOWIE producer TONY VISCONTI who proved 'unavailable'. Sticking with the same glam rock lineage, they instead opted for Mick Ronson, legendary guitarist with Bowie's Spiders From Mars with an impressive list of arranging and production credits to his name. 'I chose [Ronson] because he's a very strong musician,' said Morrissey. 'I wanted to make a record which had a real sense of physicality and body to it.' Evidence of his excitement at working with Ronson can be found in a letter to Nevin during the making of the album, signed with the humorous Ziggy-pun 'Weird and Gilly and the Spiders from Moz'.

Four years earlier, Morrissey had flippantly told the press 'I'm not going to enter a glam phase – do I look as if I am?' Yet Your Arsenal was to be exactly that. Many of Whyte's riffs were rooted in the UK pop charts of the early 70s, whether aping Bolan's 'Ride A White Swan' on 'Certain People I Know' or Bowie's 'The Jean Genie' on 'Glamorous Glue'. Nevin was just as guilty of glam-theft, absorbing the spirit of Your Arsenal's producer into the Bowie 'Rock 'N' Roll Suicide' finale of 'I Know It's Gonna Happen Someday'. Ronson himself added his own uncredited fretwork to the gentler 'Seasick, Yet Still Docked'. His efforts were all the more remarkable in view of his ailing health. Diagnosed with liver cancer, the 46-year-old produced the album on a diet of tree bark juice (a homoeopathic cancer treatment), occasionally excusing himself from the studio for necessary hospital appointments. 'Mick was so kind and patient,' says Spencer Cobrin. 'A very warm person, but he looked poorly. He'd go to his room earlier than us because he needed to rest. I'm not sure we even realised just how sick he really was.'

Work on the album began in February 1992 at Utopia studios in Primrose Hill (Morrissey lived close by) where lead single 'We Hate It When Our Friends Become Successful' and the controversial 'The National Front Disco' were recorded. The remainder was completed the following month at a longer residential session at The Wool Hall near Bath, scene of STRANGEWAYS, HERE WE COME and VIVA HATE. Ronson's illness aside, the session was far from smooth. Morrissey hadn't anticipated the unruly behaviour of his new 'gang', all of whom, bar Boorer, had never made an album before. For mischievous young twenty-somethings holed up in a countryside studio, their inexperience and excitement proved too much to contain.

'It was like being on a school outing,' says Cobrin. 'We were constantly getting up to no good. The paradox was that Morrissey wanted a gang, but if you're in a gang you're not gonna stay indoors and watch CORONATION STREET. You have to act like a gang.' Cobrin recalls a typical incident in the studio kitchen. 'Gary had this great idea of starting an egg fight. There must have been about three dozen eggs in the fridge. Suddenly, the whole kitchen is caked in egg. Myself, Gary and Alain are stood there pissing ourselves, head to toe dripping with yolk. And at that very moment, Morrissey walked in. He just looked us up and down, in complete shock. Then I think he locked himself away in his room for two days. He was seriously pissed off with us.' Such schoolboy antics would, in due course, be Cobrin and Day's undoing, both ejected from his band within the year to ensure the next album was recorded without fear of similar yolk-splattering anarchy.

Regardless of these trifling upsets, the finished album was as 'physical' a musical document as Morrissey had hoped. Sonically, Ronson set the bar for the harder, teeth-grinding indie rock which became the norm for Morrissey recordings thereafter. Musically, Whyte's tentative co-writes honed a new melodic 'house style' malleable enough to be as tough ('Glamorous Glue') or as gentle ('We'll Let You Know') as Morrissey required. Just as indispensable were Nevin's two entries, its vicious, pace-setting overture 'You're Gonna Need Someone On Your Side' and the Bowie-wooing ballad 'I Know It's Gonna Happen Someday', both of which would survive in his live set well into the late 00s.

Lyrically, its ten tracks hit highs Morrissey had rarely touched since The Smiths, both in terms of thematic controversy – solvent abuse, football hooliganism, the recruitment tactics of far-right extremists – and heartfelt emotion, especially its closing triptych from the desperate 'Seasick, Yet Still Docked' to the triumphant 'I Know It's Gonna Happen Someday' and 'Tomorrow'. At the more frivolous end of its spectrum, the album's three UK singles were disposable if pleasantly

playful pop creations; the snidely comical 'We Hate It When Our Friends Become Successful', the daft ode to friend Cathal SMYTH 'You're The One For Me, Fatty' and the T.Rex pastiche 'Certain People I Know'. Mixing the personal with the political, the comic with the confessional, songs of desperate love with others of unremitting hate, the finished album would be his most impressive and cohesively assembled since Strangeways, Here We Come five years earlier.

The chosen title, Your Arsenal (a phrase from 'We'll Let You Know'), carried various connotations, from the literal offer of 'arming' the listener to more laddish associations with the north London football club. A photo taken circa 1994 by Jake WALTERS, unpublished until 2008's GREATEST HITS collection, offered a very different interpretation: the words 'Your arse'n'all' written across Morrissey's naked buttocks. Such coy innuendo was reinforced by the album's Linder STERLING cover photo: the singer on stage in an open shirt ('stomach star courtesy Davyhulme Hospital'), making a phallic gesture with his microphone.

Its inner sleeve featured an image of East End gangster Charlie RICHARDSON with his baby daughter on Dymchurch beach, though, unusually for Morrissey, Your Arsenal had no printed lyrics. 'I didn't want to use a lyric sheet,' he explained. 'I wanted to make as physical a record as I possibly could instead of constantly being curled up in a little ball at the foot of the bed.' Unfortunately, his decision later backfired in the widespread misunderstanding over 'The National Front Disco' and the use of the phrase '"England for the English"' in quotation marks.

Released in the summer of 1992, the album's inherent glam rock aesthetic struck a chord with the new breed of retro-indie groups such as Suede, Pulp and Denim in the prelude to Britpop. Critically, the album was warmly received in the UK, faring even better in the US where it consolidated Morrissey's growing American fan base, earning him a Grammy nomination and instigating his celebrated HOLLYWOOD BOWL sales record. Just as significant, Morrissey's critical revival in the

y

media coincided with the first posthumous Smiths collection – three weeks after Your Arsenal entered the UK album charts at number four, The Smiths' Best I entered at number one. Although the Madstock Union Jack incident less than a fortnight after its release cast a temporary pall over Your Arsenal, the NME's overreaction failed to damage its reputation in the long run as one of Morrissey's strongest solo achievements. Even former co-writer Stephen STREET unreservedly confesses, 'When I first heard Your Arsenal, I had to take my hat off to Morrissey. I thought it was absolutely great.'

Every Morrissey album since Your Arsenal owes some debt to its power and dynamism, whether by reacting against it (as on its softer, superior follow-up, VAUXHALL AND I) or harking back to the same guitar-blazing intensity (SOUTH-PAW GRAMMAR, YEARS OF REFUSAL). Not merely one of the finest and fiercest albums he's ever made but, all things considered, the absolute bedrock of Morrissey's solo career. [5, 22, 45, 69, 92, 94, 236]

youth of Morrissey (childhood and adolescence), Fundamental to the mythology of Morrissey is his self-confessed 'foul teenage existence', sealing himself off from the outside world in his Stretford bedroom for weeks, sometimes months at a time.

His childhood had been relatively happy. 'We had no money,' he'd state, 'but they were naïvely pleasant times.' Everything changed when severe 'family problems' reared their head when he was eight, or thereabouts. Morrissey has never been able to specify precisely what the few psychoanalysts he's hired have tried to find – the determining event in his youth responsible for his adult depression.

His parents' slow-brewing divorce was only one factor. He experienced four family deaths between the ages of five and ten, including three grandparents and the shocking alcohol-related ruin of his 24-year-old uncle Ernie, which had a devastating impact upon the Morrissey household's hitherto devout Catholicism (see RELIGION). Although he'd

be traumatised by his secondary education from the age of 11 (see SCHOOL), he'd still insist that he received most of his emotional scars at home.

It was in adolescence that the die was cast for Morrissey's intense isolation, both emotionally and physically. 'You couldn't really call it an existence,' he described. 'When I was young, I instantly excluded the human race in favour of pop music, and you can't live a fulfilled existence like that. People are invariably there. You have to go to school. You have to try to communicate with those around you. But when you've sealed up your bedroom doors and you've blackened your windows, and all you want in the world are those tiny crackles that are about to introduce that record – and you love the crackles that you hear from the needle on the vinyl as much as you love what will follow – then I don't think you will turn out to be a very level-headed human being.'

He described his bedroom in 384 Kings Road, Stretford as 'very small'. 'I remember going through periods when I was 18 and 19 where I literally would not leave it for three to four weeks. I would be in there day after day, the sun would be blazingly hot and I'd have the curtains drawn. I'd be sitting there in near darkness alone with the typewriter and surrounded by masses of paper. The walls were totally bespattered with James DEAN, almost to the point of claustrophobia and I remember little bits of paper pinned everywhere with profound comments ... Probably the most important quote was from Goethe. "Art and Life are different, that's why one is called Art and one is called Life."'

'It sounds dramatic,' he'd continue, 'but at one point, I thought I could never possibly leave [that] room. It seemed that everything I am was conceived [there]. Everything that makes me is in there. I used to have a horrible territorial complex. I would totally despise any creature that stepped across the threshold. And when somebody did, or looked at my books, or took out a record, I would seethe with anger. I was obsessive. Everything was chronologically ordered – a place for everything, everything in its place. Total neurosis.'

Yet out of that neurosis came The Smiths. Later, Morrissey would describe these fabled 'poet-in-the-garret' years in graphic, near-Dickensian detail in the media, whether as personal catharsis, deliberate self-mythologising (though it was all entirely true) or a greater, more sensitive awareness that 'back bedroom casualties' such as himself were far from uncommon and lay out there, in hermitic droves, waiting to answer the call of Smithdom.

On a more personal level, the solitude of Morrissey's bedroom years would wrack his senses to a dangerously harsh degree. If they were the incubation of Morrissey's written genius, they were also the incubation of his irreversible paranoia, mistrust and unapologetic misanthropy. He once described his 'perfect situation' as a life 'without human beings involved whatsoever'. 'Privacy to me is like the old life support machine,' he explained. 'I really hate mounds of people, simply bounding into the room and taking over. So, when the work is finished, I just bolt the door and draw the blinds, and dive under the bed.' Perhaps, then, in the furthest recess of his mind, Morrissey has yet to escape his teenage bedroom's cosy claustrophobic prison. [63, 75, 122, 124, 128, 129, 153, 204, 205, 216, 234, 236, 237, 263, 267, 419, 436, 448, 464, 468]

Yuro, Timi,

Typhoon-tonsilled white soul and country singer whom Morrissey has named as his 'favourite singer' on several occasions. Yuro sang the original of 'INTERLUDE', his duet with Siouxsie SIOUX, while her 1963 single 'Insult To Injury' has frequently been listed among his favourite records.

Morrissey's interest in Yuro stems from his mother who was 'quite dedicated' to the singer. 'She was instilled [in] me at a very early age,' he elaborated. 'Her voice is quite immaculate and incredibly powerful. I could never understand why she didn't gain more attention than she did.'

Born Rosemary Timotea Aurro in Chicago, her Italian-American parents changed their surname to Yuro when relocating to Los Angeles. At 14, she passed up the chance to study opera singing in Italy to stay beside her mother, instead convincing her dad to transform the family's ailing Hollywood restaurant into a rock and roll eatery with live music. Timi herself became its star 'singing waitress' and by the age of 20 she'd been snapped up by a Liberty Records A&R scout. After a year being forced to demo unsuitable material, she finally took matters into her own hands by bursting into the offices of the label's vice-president and sandblasting him with an a cappella version of 'Hurt', an early 50s weepie by Roy Hamilton. Yuro successfully made her point. 'Hurt' became her 1961 debut single, and biggest hit, reaching number four in the US.

Yuro's voice was a cyclone of pain, misery and heartbreak belted out with cement-cracking intensity. Because of her depth and range, many radio listeners assumed she was black; because of her forename, some European listeners even assumed she must be Japanese. Sadly, Yuro never achieved any recognition in the UK, even though both Elvis PRESLEY and American vocal group The Manhattans scored hits in 1976 with respective versions of 'Hurt'. Their success coaxed the retired Yuro back to the stage, though a few years later she was diagnosed with the first symptoms of a recurring throat cancer. After nearly two decades of numerous biopsies, in 2002 the larynx which had transmitted vocal emotion with such rare strength and clarity was removed in a bid to save her life. It didn't, and she died on 30 March 2004, aged 63.

A few years before her death, Yuro summed up her need to sing when interviewed by the writer David Freeland for his *Ladies Of Soul* anthology. Her comments could just as easily have come from Morrissey's own lips, and since this is the final entry in *Mozipedia*, let her words be the closing symbolic toast to her biggest fan: 'My greatest pleasure on earth was to go on stage and be sad. And when people would applaud it was the greatest thing in the world for me. Just going out there and crying and singing a song. It wasn't just to blow people away. It was to give them the truth of me.' [168, 175, 184, 188, 408]

Sources & Bibliography

A vast and daunting number of sources were consulted in the research and writing of *Mozipedia*. What follows is a list of the most relevant.

The numbering system is based upon that of Morrissey's beloved *The Murderers' Who's Who* and is devised as a means of identifying specific sources cited at the end of most entries in square brackets, e.g. [5, 22, 59]

Above and beyond the sources mentioned below, there were other general reference works which proved extremely helpful: *The Oxford Dictionary Of English Literature*, *The Wordsworth Dictionary Of British History*, *The Oxford Dictionary Of Quotations*, *The Guinness Book Of Top 40 Charts*, *The Guinness Book Of British Hit Singles* and the mighty *Encyclopedia Britannica* itself.

On the specifics of Morrissey and The Smiths I'm also indebted to two extremely precious portals on the world wide web. Firstly, the American website *morrissey-solo.com* run by David Tseng. In the world of Morrissey, Tseng's service is an equivalent CNN, as unrivalled as it is invaluable. Secondly, the Canadian website *passionsjustlikemine.com* run by Stephane Daigle. If by writing this book I have nominated myself the Smiths/Morrissey encyclopedist, then Daigle is akin to the University of Smithdom's chief librarian. As a Smiths/Morrissey data bank, his site is without equal on the internet – particularly his concert history – and any author writing about Morrissey today who fails to credit Daigle's meticulous archive is being disingenuous.

I. ORIGINAL INTERVIEW SOURCES

The following interviews were conducted by the author.

1 Armstrong, Kevin, interviewed 25 October 2003
2 Bradford, Richard, interview by phone 4 August 2005
3 Bragg, Billy, interviewed 3 May 2006
4 Bridgwood, Jonny, interviewed 25 November 2003
5 Cobrin, Spencer, interview by phone 3 December 2003
6 Dickie, Chris, interview by phone 18 October 2003
7 Gannon, Craig, interview by phone 27 November 2003
8 Hallay, Amanda, interview by phone 14 May 2004
9 Head, Murray, interviewed July 2006
10 Hibbert, Dale, interview by phone 20 April 2004
11 Hynde, Chrissie, interviewed 7 February 2006
12 Joyce, Mike and Andy Rourke, interviewed 17 August 2001
13 Joyce, Mike and Andy Rourke, interviewed 16 November 2001
14 Joyce, Mike, interviewed 27 September 2005
15 Langer, Clive and Alan Winstanley, interviewed 7 October 2003
16 Maker, James, interview questionnaire by email 20 July 2002
17 Marr, Johnny, interviewed 12 May 2004
18 Marr, Johnny, interviewed 26 September 2005
19 Marr, Johnny, interviewed 4 December 2006
20 Marr, Johnny, interview by phone 23 February 2007
21 Moss, Joe, interviewed February 2008
22 Nevin, Mark, interviewed 23 September 2003
23 New York Dolls sources: separate phone interviews with David Johansen, Arthur Kane, Sylvain Sylvain, Marty Thau and Todd Rundgren conducted November 2003 to February 2004 prior to the re-formation of the group for Morrissey's Meltdown.
24 Nico sources: phone interviews with John Cale, Brian Eno and Phil Manzanera in October 2001, also Frasier Mohawk in July 2006.
25. Paresi, Andrew, interviewed 15 October 2003

Sources & Bibliography

26   Peel, John, interview by phone May 2003
27   Porter, John, interview by phone 4 April 2004
28   Rourke, Andy, interviewed 26 September 2005
29   Rourke, Andy, interviewed 22 January 2007
30   Shaw, Sandie, interview by phone September 2004
31   Shelley, Pete and Steve Diggle, interviewed November 2002 and April 2005
32   Showbiz, Grant, interviewed 22 March 2002
33   Showbiz, Grant, interviewed 10 January 2007
34   Sinatra, Nancy, interview by phone August 2004
35   Sioux, Siouxsie, interviewed 18 October 2004
36   Smyth, Cathal, interviewed 22 October 2003
37   Sterling, Linder, interview by phone and email February 2002
38   Street, Stephen, interviewed 21 August 2001
39   Street, Stephen, interviewed 20 November 2003
40   Supple, Danton, interviewed 8 October 2003
41   Travis, Geoff, interviewed July 2006

II. PRINT/ON-LINE PERIODICAL SOURCES

As a working journalist myself, I extend a heartfelt comradely thanks to those in the same profession whose encounters with Morrissey and The Smiths have unearthed valuable insights, anecdotes and revelations documented in *Mozipedia*. Some of these are available on-line via fan sites such as The Arcane Old Wardrobe (*arcaneold-wardrobe.com*) though all or most are available to view in their original form at the British Newspaper Library, a lonesome gulag in the final frontiers of north London and another vital resource during the writing of this book.

The more investigative reader may also wish to visit the website Rock's Back Pages (*rocksbackpages.com*), a unique online archive of music journalism available to view for a very reasonable subscription fee and featuring rare Smiths and Morrissey content.

The corresponding numbering system highlights the relevant articles sourced for each entry and I hope is compensatory credit where, for reasons of space and fluidity of information, it's not been possible to quote every journalist by name in the text. This index, in itself, is a roll call of this author's deep gratitude.

42   Adams, Nick, 'Johnny Too Bad', *No 1* (UK), September 1984
43   ADS press advertisement, *Stereo Review* (US), November 1980
44   Albuquerque, Carlos, 'Morrissey Solta A Voz', *O Globo* (Brazil), April 2000
45   Ali, Lorraine, 'Man You Love To Hate, The', *Alternative Press* (USA), February 1993
46   Allen, Mike, 'Morrissey Makes Six Points', *Graffiti* (Canada), October 1986
47   Ambrose, Chris, 'Morrissey', *Tokion* No 40. The World Records Issue (USA), April 2004
48   Andres, Lokko, 'Den Manskliga Paskliljan', *Pop* (Sweden), January 1998
49   Ashkenazi, Lior, Morrissey interview in *Yedioth Ahronoth*, July 2008, and Gal Uchovsky interview with Morrissey in *Time Out Tel Aviv*, July 2008. Both articles published in Hebrew and translated in the forum of Morrissey-solo.com.
50   Aston, Martin, Morrissey interview from 1986 first printed in *Q Special Edition: The Inside Story Of The Smiths & Morrissey* (UK), May 2004
51   Aston, Martin, 'Witty, Sad, Poignant, Green ...', *Q* (UK), October 1994
52   Bailie, Stuart, 'Boy In The Bubble, The', *Record Mirror* (UK), February 1987
53   Barber, Lynn 'Man With The Thorn In His Side, The', *Observer Magazine* (UK), September 2002
54   Beaumont, Mark, 'New Roman Emperor, The' and 'I'm Not Celibate ...', *NME* (UK), February 2006
55   Beaumont, Mark, 'Songs To Save Your Life' CD track-by-track with comments by Morrissey, *NME* (UK), June 2004
56   Beauvallet, Jean-Daniel, 'Morrissey Strikes Again', *Les Inrockuptibles* (France), May 2004
57   Bell, Max, 'Bigmouth Strikes Again', *No 1* (UK), June 1986
58   Billen, Andrew, 'I've Always Felt Like An Exile', *The Times* (UK), May 2006
59   Birch, Ian, 'Morrissey Collection, The', *Smash Hits* (UK), June 1984
60   Bird, Cameron, 'Morrissey Rising', *Filter* (US), February 2009
61   Black, Antonella, 'Sorrow's Native Son', *Sounds* (UK), April 1985
62   Black, Antonella, 'Shakespeare Or Bacon?', *ZigZag* (UK), May 1985
63   Black, Bill, 'Keep Young And Beautiful', *Sounds* (UK), November 1983
64   Black, Johnny, 'We Could Be Heroes' *Q Classic: Morrissey & The Story Of Manchester (UK)*, April 2006
65   Boon, Richard, 'Morrissey', *The Catalogue* (UK), September 1988
66   Boorer, Boz, Q&A at bozboorer.com, 2002
67   Boyd, Brian, 'Return Of The Lyric Laureate', *Irish Times* (Ireland), September 2002
68   Bracewell, Michael, 'Heaven Knows I'm Not Miserable Now', *The Times* (UK), November 1999
69   Brown, James, 'Morrissey Comes Clean', 'The Playboy Interview' and 'It's That Man Again', *NME* (UK), February 1989
70   Brown, Len, 'Bona Contention', *Vox* (UK), November 1990
71   Brown, Len, 'Born To Be Wilde' and 'Stop Me If You've Heard This One Before', *NME* (UK), February 1988
72   Brown, Len, 'Hand That Rocks The Cradle, The', *NME* (UK), May 1987
73   Burchill, Julie, 'Meeting My Morrissey', *Sunday Times Magazine* (UK), March 1994
74   Cameron, Keith, 'Who's The Daddy?', *Mojo* (UK), June 2004

75 Carroll, Cath, 'Crisp Tunes And Salted Lyrics', *NME* (UK), May 1983

76 Cassavetti, Hugo, 'Ugly Duck, The', *Rock Sound* (France), January 1993

77 Cavanagh, Dave, 'Good Lieutenants, The', *Select* (UK), April 1993

78 Cavanagh, Dave, 'Nothing To Declare But Their Genius', *Q* (UK), January 1994

79 Chalmers, Robert, 'Morrissey Flowers Again', *Observer* (UK), December 1992

80 Cochrane, Robert, Jobriath – Lonely Planet Boy CD sleeve notes, 2004

81 Cooper, Mark, 'Flowers Of Romance', *No 1* (UK), November 1983

82 Cooper, Mark, 'Smithspeak', *No 1* (UK), February 1984

83 Corbett, Ara, 'Inner Edge, The', *Creem* (USA), April 1991

84 Corr, Alan, 'Used To Be A Sweet Boy', *RTE Guide* (Ireland), January 1996

85 Coupland, Douglas, 'Papal Attraction', *Observer Music Monthly* (UK), March 2006

86 Court case sources: 'Joyce (respondent) v Morrissey And Others (appellant)' Court of appeal judgment November 1998, plus the following articles all published between 2 and 14 December 1996 – 'Smith Versus Smith' in the *Daily Mail* (UK), 'Devious, Truculent And Unreliable' in the *Independent* (UK), 'Morrissey Fights To Keep Smiths Millions' by Fred Hackworth and 'Anger Of Rock Star Quizzed By QC' in *Manchester Evening News* (UK), 'Former Smith Lets Court Know Why He's "Miserable Now"' by Richard Duce in *The Times* (UK)

87 Cranna, Ian, 'Friendship Made In Heaven, A', *Smash Hits* (UK), December 1985

88 Crossing, Gary, 'This Charming Life', *The Big Issue* (UK), July 1997

89 Dalton, Stephen, 'Getting Away With It', *Uncut* (UK), April 1999

90 Daly, Steven, 'Lyrical King', *Spin* (USA), April 1991

91 De Jongh, Nicholas, 'Boy With A Thorn In His Side', *Guardian* (UK), October 1985

92 Décharné, Max and Boz Boorer, 'Go West, Young Man', *Mojo* (UK), April 2001

93 Deevoy, Adrian, 'Morrissey: Solo Artist of the Year', *GQ* (UK), October 2005

94 Deevoy, Adrian, 'Ooh I Say!', *Q* (UK), September 1992

95 Dieckmann, Katherine, 'Morrissey Drops His Act', *Musician* (USA), June 1991

96 DiMartino, Dave, 'Loneliest Monk, The', *Raygun* (USA), March 1994

97 DiMartino, Dave, 'We'll Meat Again: Doing It Smiths Style', *Creem* (USA), February 1986

98 Dorrell, David, 'Smiths Hunt, The', *NME* (UK), September 1983

99 Du Noyer, Paul, 'Oh, Such Drama!', *Q* (UK), August 1987

100 Du Noyer, Paul, 'War On Goons And Philistines', *The Hit* (UK), October 1985

101 Fadele, Dele with Danny Kelly, Gavin Martin and Andrew Collins, 'Caucasian Rut', *NME* (UK), August 1992

102 Felder, Hugh, 'Scratch'N'Smiths', *Sounds* (UK), February 1984

103 Fletcher, Tony, 'Smiths, The', *Jamming!* (UK), May 1984

104 Fricke, David, 'Keeping Up With The Smiths', *Rolling Stone* (USA), October 1986

105 Garfield, Simon, 'This Charming Man', *Time Out* (UK), March 1985

106 Geary, Tim, 'Nancy Kicks Off The Boots', *The Telegraph* (UK), June 2004

107 Ginsberg, Merle, 'Through Being Cool', *Creem* (USA), June 1984

108 Goldsworthy, Tim and James Murphy, 'Morrissey', *Index* (USA), March 2004

109 Gore, Joe, 'Johnny Marr – Guitar Anti-Hero', *Guitar Player* (USA), January 1990

110 Gorman, Paul, 'Good, The Bad And The Ugly Side Of Oral Deals, The', *Music Week* Business Affairs (UK), September 1999

111 Hando, Stoney (alias for Morrissey), Press release for Maladjusted, Mercury Records, August 1997

112 Harris, John, 'Trouble At Mill', *Mojo* (UK), April 2001

113 Harrison, Andrew, 'Band That Dreams That It Never Broke Up, The', *Word* (UK), June 2004

114 Harrison, Andrew, 'Hand In Glove', *Select* (UK), May 1994

115 Harrison, Andrew, 'Home Thoughts From Abroad', *Word* (UK), May 2003

116 Harrison, Ian, 'Big Guns Fire Back – Morrissey' news story on the making of Ringleader Of The Tormentors, Mojo (UK), February 2006

117 Harrison, Ian 'World Won't Listen, The' from *Q 100 Best Record Covers* special issue (UK), 2002

118 Haslam, Dave, 'Johnny, Remember Me?', *NME* (UK), June 1989

119 Heath, Ashley, 'You And I, This Land Is Ours', *i-D* (UK), May 2004

120 Heath, Chris, 'Morrissey', *Star Hits* (USA), September 1987

121 Hedblade, Jade, 'No Middle Of The Road In Cole's Middle Age Rock', *Chicago Tribune* (US), November 2006; plus comments by Lloyd Cole at www.lloydcole.com

122 Henke, James, 'Oscar! Oscar! England Goes Wilde For The "Fourth-Gender" Smiths', *Rolling Stone* (USA), June 1984

123 Hibbert, Tom, 'Meat Is Murder!', *Smash Hits* (UK), January 1985

124 Hoskyns, Barney, 'These Disarming Men', *NME* (UK), February 1984

125 Hughes, Andy, 'Smiths' Strange Ways Have Found Us, The', *Creem* (USA), July 1987

126 Hynde, Chrissie, 'Everything You'd Rather Not Have Known About Brian Eno', *NME* (UK), February 1974

127 Jones, Allan, 'Johnny Guitar', *Melody Maker* (UK), April 1984

128 Jones, Allan, 'Smiths, The', *Melody Maker* (UK), March 1984

129 Jones, Allan and various fanzine writers, 'Trial By Jury', *Melody Maker* (UK), March 1985

130 Jones, Dylan, 'Mr Smith – All Mouth And Trousers?', *i-D* (UK), October 1987

131 K, Graham, 'Glove Story', *Record Mirror* (UK), May 1984

132 K, Graham and Dylan Jones, 'Alias Smith And …', *Record Mirror* (UK), September 1984

133 Keeps, David, 'Homme Alone', *Details* (USA), December 1992

134 Kelly, Danny, 'Exile On Mainstream', *NME* (UK), February 1987

135 Kelly, Danny, 'Further Thoughts Of Chairman Mo, The', *NME* (UK), June 1985

136 Kemp, Mark, 'Wake Me When It's Over', *Select* (UK), July 1991

137 Kent, Nick, 'Band With The Thorn In Its Side, The', *The Face* (UK), April 1987

138 Kent, Nick, 'Deep End, The', *The Face* (UK), March 1990

139 Kent, Nick, 'Dreamer In The Real World', *The Face* (UK), May 1985

140 Kent, Nick, 'Isolation', *Q Classic: Morrissey & The Story Of Manchester* (UK), April 2006

141 Kill Uncle UK tour programme, 1991

142 Kopf, Biba, 'Suitable Case For Treatment, A', *NME* (UK), December 1984

143 KROQ Radio Los Angeles (USA), Morrissey internet chat, September 1999

144 Leboff, Gary, 'Goodbye Cruel World', *Melody Maker* (UK), September 1987

145 Levy, Eleanor, 'Fake', *Record Mirror* (UK), August 1985

146 Levy, Eleanor, 'Little Bit Of Soap, A', *Record Mirror* (UK), September 1985

147 Levy, Eleanor, 'Johnny Marr', *Record Mirror* (UK), June 1986

148 Levy, Eleanor, 'Playboy Of The Western World', *Record Mirror* (UK), February 1989

149 Lewis, Angela and Stuart Bailie, 'Beautiful Morrissey Looked At Me, The', *NME* (UK), March 1994

150 Lokko, Andres, 'Fan Mail', *Slitz* (Sweden), September 1992

151 Lynskey, Dorian, 'Somebody Has To Be Me', *Guardian* (UK), April 2004

152 MacKenzie, Suzie, 'After The Affair', *Guardian* (UK), August 1997

153 Maconie, Stuart, 'Do You F*@kin' Want Some?', *Q* (UK), September 1995

154 Maconie, Stuart, 'Hello, Cruel World', *Q* (UK), April 1994

155 Maconie, Stuart, 'Morrissey Comes Out (For A Drink)', *NME* (UK), May 1991

156 Maconie, Stuart, 'Prodigal Son Or Conquering Hero', *The Word* (UK), January 2005

157 Maconie, Stuart, 'Secret History, The', *Select* (UK), December 1993

158 Male, Andrew, 'Get The Message', *Q Classic: Morrissey & The Story Of Manchester* (UK), April 2006

159 Male, Andrew, 'Happy Now?', *Mojo* (UK), April 2006, also alternate version 'The Happy Prince' from *Q Classic: Morrissey & The Story Of Manchester* (UK), April 2006

160 Marr, Johnny, 'Personal File', *Smash Hits* (UK), 1984

161 Marrinan, Kevin, 'Meeting Morrissey', *Manchester Evening News* (UK), August 1997

162 Mathur, Paul 'Manchester United', *Melody Maker* (UK), 26 July 1986

163 Mathur, Paul 'These Charming Men', *Melody Maker* (UK), January 1986

164 Mathur, Paul, 'Wiping Away The Teardrops', *NME* (UK), September 1983

165 McCormick, Neil, 'All Men Have Secrets', *Hot Press* (Ireland), May 1984

166 McCullough, Dave, 'Handsome Devils', *Sounds* (UK), June 1983

167 McIlhenny, Barry, 'Strumming For The Smiths', *Melody Maker* (UK), August 1985

168 Meat Is Murder Smiths UK tour programme, 1985

169 Mieses, Stanley 'Last Doll Comes In From The Cold, The', *Melody Maker* (UK), April 1978

170 Morley, Paul, 'Last Temptation Of Morrissey, The', unexpurgated version of *Uncut* (UK), May 2006 interview from *Morrissey In Conversation*, Edited by Paul A. Woods, Plexus, 2007

171 Morley, Paul, 'Wilde Child', *Blitz* (UK), April 1988

172 Morrissey, 'Close To The Heart – On Sandie Shaw', *Sounds* (UK), December 1983

173 Morrissey, The Cramps at Manchester Polytechnic review, *Record Mirror* (UK), March 1980

174 Morrissey, 'Glam God, The', *Observer Music Monthly* (UK), November 2006

175 Morrissey, 'Headful Of Heroes', *NME* (UK), September 1989

176 Morrissey, 'Intimate Details', *No 1* (UK), 1984

177 Morrissey, 'Let's Look At Ludus' press release 1982

178 Morrissey, Ludus sleeve notes/fax via Richard Boon, 1985

179 Morrissey, 'Melancholy Meets The Infinite Sadness', interview with Joni Mitchell, *Rolling Stone* (USA), March 1997

180 Morrissey, 'Morrissey Missed The Bus' faxed Q&A, *Q* (UK), November 2001

181 Morrissey, 'Never Turn Your Back On Mother Earth', interview with Pat Phoenix, *Blitz* (UK), May 1985

182 Morrissey, Poll-Winners' Poll for 1984, *NME* (UK), February 1985

183 Morrissey, Poll-Winners' Poll for 1985, *NME* (UK), March 1986

184 Morrissey, 'Portrait Of The Artist As A Consumer', *NME* (UK), September 1983

185 Morrissey, 'Singles', *Melody Maker* (UK), August 1984

186 Morrissey, statement in response to *Exit Smiling* on Reprise Records website, September 1998

187 Morrissey, statement in response to *NME* 'Has The World Changed Or Has He Changed?' feature at true-to-you.net , December 2007

188 Morrissey, 'Yeahs And Yeuks', *No 1* (UK), February 1985

189 Morrissey and Young, Kristeen, 'Move Over, Pedro', *Guardian Weekend*, March 2007

190 Morrissey's Meltdown Official Programme (UK), June 2004

191 Needham, Alex, 'Morrissey – The Face Q&A', *The Face* (UK), November 1999

192 Needham, Alex, 'Rock'N'Roll Has Seen Many Heroes …' and 'They Thought I Was A Threat To National Security', *NME* (UK), April 2004

193 Neville, Katie, 'The Post Cool School', *The Face* (UK), February 1984

194 Nine, Jennifer, 'The Importance Of Being Morrissey', *Melody Maker* (UK), August 1997

195 "NME" ("words"), 'Has The World Changed Or Has He Changed?', *NME* (UK), November 2007

196 Owen, Frank, 'Home Thoughts From Abroad', *Melody Maker* (UK), September 1986

197 Panek, J. C., 'Ma Prison Dorée', *L'Indic* (France), November 1997

198 Parsons, Tony, 'What Now Mozzer?', *Vox* 1993

199 Parsons, Tony, 'Whatever Happened To Davie Doll?', *NME* (UK), September 1978

200 Patterson, Sylvia, 'I Don't Really Do Reality' Pete Burns interview, *Guardian Guide* (UK), April 2003

201 Patterson, Sylvia, 'Wicked Lady, The' Marianne Faithfull interview, *The Word* (UK), March 2009

202 Perrone, Pierre, Jerry Finn obituary, *Independent* (UK), September 2008

203 Phillips, Shaun, 'Private Diary Of A Middle-Aged Man', *Sounds* (UK), June 1988

204 Pye, Ian, 'Hard Day's Misery, A', *Melody Maker* (UK), November 1984

205 Pye, Ian, 'Magnificent Obsessions', *Melody Maker* (UK), November 1983

206 Pye, Ian, 'Some Mothers Do 'Ave 'Em', *NME* (UK), June 1986

207 Reardon, Ben, 'Morrissey i-Q', *i-D* (UK), July 2003

208 Reynolds, Simon, 'Songs Of Love And Hate' Parts 1 and 2, *Melody Maker* (UK), March 1988

209 Rimmer, Dave, 'Smiths Hits And Myths, The', *Smash Hits* (UK), February 1984

210 Rogan, Johnny, 'Johnny Marr's View', *Record Collector* (UK), November and December 1992

211 Samuels, Tim and Juliet Gellatley, 'Meat Is Murder', *Greenscene* (UK), November 1989

212 Sandall, Robert, 'Bigmouth Strikes Again', *The Sunday Times* (UK), May 2004

213 Santoro, Gianni, 'Morrissey', *XL* (Italy), March 2006

214 Segal, Victoria, 'Boy With The Throng On His Side, The', *NME* (UK), November 1999

215 Self, Will, 'King Of Bedsit Angst Grows Up, The', *Observer Magazine* (UK), December 1995

216 Shaw, William, 'Glad All Over', *ZigZag* (UK), February 1984

217 Shaw, William, 'Homme Alone 2', *Details* (USA), April 1994

218 Shelley, Jim, 'Soul On Fire', *Blitz* (UK), May 1984

219 Sheppard, David, Johnny Marr interview in *Q Special Edition: The Inside Story Of The Smiths & Morrissey* (UK), May 2004

220 Simpson, Dave, Interview with Howard Devoto, *Avanti* (UK), 1988, accessed at www.shotbybothsides.com/mag_fanz.htm

221 Simpson, Dave, 'Manchester's Answer To The H-Bomb', *Uncut* (UK), August 1998

222 Sinclair, David, 'This Charming Android', *The Times* (UK), February 1995

223 Smith, Sean, 'Goodbye Oxfam, Hello Gucci', *The Big Issue* (UK), November 1999

224 Smith, Sean, 'Strange Ways Indeed', *The Big Issue* (UK), June 2003

225 Snow, Mat, 'From Manchester To Memphis', *NME* (UK), February 1987

226 Snow, Mat, 'Soft Touch, The', *Q* (UK), December 1989

227 Spencer, Lauren, 'Sound And Vision', *Movieline* (USA), March 1993

228 Spitz, Marc, 'These Things Take Time', *Spin* (USA), May 2004

229 Strikes, Andy, 'Morrissey Dancing', *Record Mirror* (UK), February 1984

230 Sturges, Fiona, 'That's Why The Lady Is A Star' Nancy Sinatra interview, *Independent* (UK), October 2004

231 Suarez-Golborne, Sebastian, 'Morrissey', *Sonic* (Sweden), April 2004

232 Sullivan, Kate, 'Moz The Cat', *LA Weekly* (USA), January 2007

233 Swayne, Karen, 'Crisp Smith, A', *No 1* (UK), August 1985

234 Swayne, Karen, 'If I Ruled The World', *No 1* (UK), January 1984

235 Swift, Jacqui, 'I Am Finally Born', *Sun* (UK), March 2006

236 Tellier, Emmanuel, 'Finir Comme Orson Welles', *Les Inrockuptibles* (France), September 1995

237 Thomas, David, 'Sorrow And The Pity, The', *Spin* (USA), November 1992

238 Thrills, Adrian, 'On To A Shaw Thing', *NME* (UK), April 1984

239 Trakin, Roy, 'Not The Jones', *Musician* (USA), June 1984

240 true-to-you.net Morrissey Q&A, November 2005

241 true-to-you.net Morrissey Q&A, December 2005

242 true-to-you.net Morrissey Q&A, January 2006

243 true-to-you.net Morrissey Q&A, February 2006

244 true-to-you.net Morrissey post-tour comments, September 2006

245 true-to-you.net Morrissey Q&A, June 2007

246 Tyrangiel, Josh, 'Not So Miserable Now', *Time* (USA), May 2004

247 Uhelsziki, Jaan, 'L.A. Confidential', *Mojo* (UK), April 2001

248 Unknown, 'And Don't Forget The Songs ...', *City Life* (UK), July 2003

249 Unknown, '"Ban Child-Sex Pop Song" Plea To Beeb', *Sun* (UK), September 1983

250 Unknown, 'Camera-Shy Mozzer Duzza Runner', *NME* (UK), April 1985

251 Unknown, 'Hand In Glove', *Melody Maker* (UK), April 1984

252 Unknown, 'I Am A Victim', *Q* (UK), January 2000

253 Unknown, 'Item 38 – The Smiths', *i-D* (UK), February 1983

254 Unknown, Johnny Marr interview, *Designer Magazine* (UK), September 2001

255 Unknown, 'Marr Speaks', *NME* (UK), August 1987

256 Unknown, 'Morrissey', *Rolling Stone* (Germany), September 1999

257 Unknown, Morrissey interviewed on Alan Bennett, *Time Out* (UK), June 2005

258 Unknown, Morrissey Q&A, *Smash Hits* (UK), 1985

259 Unknown, Ringleader Of The Tormentors preview news story, *NME* (UK), December 2005

260 Unknown, 'Sandie's Boy', *NME* (UK), May 1986

261 Unknown, 'Smithereens!', *Melody Maker* (UK), December 1986

262 Unknown, 'Smiths In "Moors" Row, The', *Melody Maker* (UK) September 1984

263 Unknown, Smiths interview, *Rorschach Testing* fanzine (UK), 1984

264 Unknown, 'This Chiming Man', *Guitar Magazine* (UK), January 1997

265 Unknown, Vini Reilly interview, *Alternative Press* (USA), September 2001

266 Van Brummelen, Peter, 'Songfestival Volgens Morrissey', *BN/De Stem* (Belgium), March 2006

267 Van Poznack, Elissa, 'Morrissey – The Face Interview', *The Face* (UK), July 1984

268 Viner, Brian, 'On The Street Where I Live', *Independent* (UK), December 2000

269 Visconti, Tony, 'When In Rome, Produce A Morrissey Album' news diary at tonyvisconti.com, November 2005

270 Webb, Iain, 'This Handsome Devil', *NME* 'Undress' supplement (UK), June 1984

271 Widner, Jonanna, 'Morrissey Moments', *Santa Fe Reporter* (USA), August 2002

272 Wilkinson, Roy, 'Single Life, The', *Mojo* (UK), November 2002

273 Winters, Andrew, 'I Was Morrissey's Roadie', *The Times* (UK), January 2008

274 Worrall, Frank, 'Cradle Snatchers, The', *Melody Maker* (UK), September 1983

275 Young, Russell, 'Morrissey's Year', *Jamming!* (UK), December 1984

III. BOOK SOURCES

276 Allen, Richard, *Complete Richard Allen Volume One: Skinhead, Suedehead, Skinhead Escapes*, S.T. Publishing, 1992

277 Antonia, Nina, *New York Dolls – Too Much Too Soon, The*, Omnibus Press, 2003

278 Balfour, Rex, *Bryan Ferry Story, The*, Michael Dempsey, 1976

279 Belloc, Hilaire, *Complete Verse*, Pimlico, 2008

280 Bennett, Alan, *Forty Years On*, Faber and Faber, 1969

281 Bennett, Alan, *Habeas Corpus*, Faber and Faber, 1973

282 Bennett, Alan, *Me, I'm Afraid Of Virginia Woolf*, Faber and Faber 2003

283 Betjeman, John, *Collected Poems*, John Murray, 2001

284 Bilbow, Tony, *Diana Dors*, Channel 4 Television, 1990

285 Bockris, Victor, *Patti Smith*, Fourth Estate 1998

286 Bogarde, Dirk, *Snakes And Ladders*, Penguin, 1988

287 Brand, Russell, *Articles Of Faith*, HarperCollins, 2008

288 Brand, Russell, *My Booky Wook*, Hodder & Stoughton, 2007

289 Brontë, Emily, *Wuthering Heights*, Penguin, 2003

290 Brown, Len, *Meetings With Morrissey*, Omnibus Press, 2008

291 Brownmiller, Susan, *Against Our Will*, Simon and Schuster (New York), 1975

292 Buford, Bill, *Among The Thugs*, Secker & Warburg, 1991

293 Capote, Truman, *Music For Chameleons*, Abacus, 1980

294 Clarkson, Wesley, *Bindon*, John Blake, 2007

295 Dalton, David, *James Dean – The Mutant King*, Plexus, 1984

296 Dalton, David and Ron Cayen, *James Dean – American Icon*, Sedgwick & Jackson, 1984

297 Darling, Candy, *My Face For The World To See: The Diaries, Letters And Drawings Of Candy Darling, Andy Warhol Superstar*, Handy Marks (Honolulu), 1997

298 Davis, Bette, *Lonely Life, The* (revised edition), Berkley Books (New York), 1990

299 Delaney, Shelagh, *Lion In Love, The*, Methuen, 1962

300 Delaney, Shelagh, *Sweetly Sings The Donkey*, Methuen, 1964

301 Delaney, Shelagh, *Taste Of Honey, A*, Methuen, 1982

302 Dickens, Charles, *Oliver Twist*, Penguin, 2002

303 Dors, Diana, *Swingin' Dors*, WDL, 1960

304 Doyle, Tom, *Glamour Chase: The Maverick Life Of Billy MacKenzie, The*, Bloomsbury, 1999

305 Dunn, Nell, *Poor Cow*, Pan, 1968
306 Dunn, Nell, *Up The Junction*, Pan, 1966
307 Eliot, George, *Adam Bede*, Penguin Classics, 1985
308 Eliot, George, *Middlemarch*, Vintage 2007
309 Eliot, George, *Mill On The Floss, The*, Penguin Classics, 1985
310 Emerson, Ken, *Always Magic In The Air – The Bomp And Brilliance Of The Brill Building Era*, Fourth Estate, 2005
311 Faithfull, Marianne with David Dalton, *Faithfull*, Penguin, 1994
312 Fisher, John, *George Formby – The Entertainers*, Woburn-Fontana, 1975
313 Fryer, Jonathan, *André & Oscar*, Constable, 1997
314 Fuller, Graham, *Loach On Loach*, Faber And Faber, 1998
315 Garner, Ken, *In Session Tonight*, BBC Books, 1993
316 Gatenby, Phill, *Morrissey's Manchester*, Empire Publications (Manchester), 2002
317 Gaute, J. H. H. and Robin Odell, *Murderers' Who's Who, The*, Harrap, 1979
318 Gide, André, *Oscar Wilde*, Philosophical Library (New York), 1949
319 Goodman, Linda, *Linda Goodman's Sun Signs*, Pan, 1970
320 Goodman, Jonathan, *Moors Murderers, The*, Magpie, 1994
321 Grant, Michael, *Twelve Caesars, The*, Weidenfeld & Nicolson, 1996
322 Hall, Radclyffe, *Well Of Loneliness, The*, Virago Modern Classics, 2004
323 Harris, John, *Last Party: Britpop, Blair And The Demise Of English Rock, The*, Harper Perennial, 2004
324 Harrison, Martin, *Young Meteors – British Photojournalism: 1957–1965*, Jonathan Cape, 1998
325 Hart-Davies, Rupert (ed.), *More Letters Of Oscar Wilde*, John Murray, 1985
326 Haskell, Molly, *From Reverence To Rape*, Penguin, 1974
327 Holland, Vyvyan, *Oscar Wilde And His World*, Thames And Hudson, 1979
328 Housman, A. E., with introduction by Michael Irwin, *Collected Poems Of A. E. Housman, The*, Wordsworth Editions, 2005
329 Kerouac, Jack, *Dharma Bums, The*, Penguin, 2000
330 Kray, Reg, *Villains We Have Known*, Arrow, 1996
331 Kray, Reggie and Ronnie, with Fred Dineage, *Our Story*, Pan, 1989
332 MacColl, Jean, *Sun On The Water – The Brilliant Life And Tragic Death Of Kirsty MacColl*, John Blake, 2008
333 MacDonald, Ian, *Revolution In The Head: The Beatles' Records And The Sixties* (revised edition), Pimlico, 1997
334 Mackie, Robert, *Words By Morrissey* (fanzine), 1992
335 Mediane Libri, *Pier Paolo Pasolini*, Mediane/Cine Cult, 2007
336 Melville, Joy, *Mother Of Oscar – The Life Of Jane Francesca Wilde*, John Murray, 1994
337 Merriman, Andy, *Hattie – The Authorised Biography Of Hattie Jacques*, Aurum, 2008
338 Middles, Mick, *Smiths, The*, Omnibus Press, 1985
339 Mitchell, Yvonne, *Family, The*, Heinemann, 1967
340 Morley, Paul, *Joy Division: Piece By Piece*, Plexus, 2008; plus sleeve notes for the 2006 Korova/Warner Music CD *North By North West* compiled by Paul Morley
341 Morrissey, *Exit Smiling*, Babylon Books (Manchester), 1998
342 Morrissey, *James Dean Is Not Dead*, Babylon Books (Manchester), 1983
343 Morrissey, *New York Dolls, The*, Babylon Books (Manchester), 1981
344 Naughton, Bill, *Late Night On Watling Street*, Longman, 1969
345 Nichols, Jack, *Men's Liberation: A New Definition of Masculinity*, Penguin (New York), 1975
346 Nicholson, Viv and Stephen Smith, *Spend, Spend, Spend*, Fontana, 1978
347 O'Neill, Eugene, *Long Day's Journey Into Night*, Yale University Press (New Haven), 1978
348 Orton, Joe, *Orton Diaries, The*, Methuen, 1986
349 Pearson, Hesketh, *Life Of Oscar Wilde, The*, Penguin, 1960
350 Peel, John, *Olivetti Chronicles – Three Decades Of Life And Music, The*, Bantam Press, 2008
351 Pegg, Nicholas, *Complete David Bowie, The*, Reynolds & Hearn, 2002
352 Pratt, Guy, *My Bass And Other Animals*, Orion, 2007
353 Pryce-Jones, Alan, *Beethoven*, Collier Books (New York), 1966
354 Raudive, Konstantin, *Breakthrough: An Amazing Experiment In Electronic Communication With The Dead*, Colin Smythe, 1971
355 Reeves, Vic, *Sun Boiled Onions*, Michael Joseph, 1999
356 Reeves, Vic and Bob Mortimer, *Vic Reeves Big Night In*, Fantail, 1991
357 Reid, Pat, *Morrissey (Outlines)*, Absolute Press (Bath), 2004
358 Repsch, John, *Legendary Joe Meek, The*, Woodford House, 1989
359 Richardson, Charlie, *My Manor*, Pan, 1992
360 Ringgold, Gene, *Films Of Bette Davis, The*, Cadillac Publishing (New York), 1966
361 Robinson, Jeffrey, *Bette Davis … Her Film And Stage Career*, Proteus, 1982
362 Rogan, Johnny, *Morrissey & Marr: The Severed Alliance* (revised edition), Omnibus Press, 1993
363 Rosen, Marjorie, *Popcorn Venus: Women, Movies & The American Dream*, Peter Owen, 1975
364 Rothman, Esther, *Angel Inside Went Sour, The*, Victor Gollancz, 1972
365 Russell, Willy, *Wrong Boy, The*, Doubleday, 2000

366 Savage, Jon, *England's Dreaming*, Faber and Faber, 2001

367 Selby Jnr, Hubert, *Last Exit To Brooklyn*, Paladin, 1987

368 Sexton, Anne, *Complete Poems, The*, Houghton Mifflin (Boston), 1982

369 Shaw, Sandie, *World At My Feet, The*, Fontana, 1992

370 Shrimpton, Jean, *An Autobiography*, Sphere, 1991

371 Sims, Joan, *High Spirits,* Corgi Books, 2001

372 Sitwell, Edith, *English Eccentrics*, Penguin, 1978

373 Slattery, Paul, *Smiths – The Early Years, The*, Vision On/Omnibus Press, 2007

374 Slee, Jo, *Peepholism: Into The Art Of Morrissey*, Sidgwick & Jackson, 1994

375 Smart, Elizabeth, *By Grand Central Station I Sat Down And Wept*, Paladin, 1991

376 Smith, Patti, *Complete: Lyrics, Reflections And Notes For The Future*, Bloomsbury, 1998

377 Souhami, Diana, *Gluck*, Pandora, 1989

378 Stamp, Terence, *Coming Attractions*, Grafton, 1989

379 Stamp, Terence, *Double Feature*, Grafton, 1990

380 Sterling, Linder, *Linder Works 1976–2006*, JRP/Ringier, 2006

381 Sterling, Linder, *Morrissey Shot*, Secker & Warburg, 1992

382 Tanitch, Robert, *Dirk Bogarde – The Complete Career Illustrated*, Ebury Press, 1988

383 Taylor, John Russell, *Anger And After: A Guide To The New British Drama*, Methuen, 1962

384 Thomas, Donald, *Villains' Paradise – Britain's Underworld From The Spivs To The Krays*, John Murray, 2005

385 Thompson, Dave, *Beyond The Velvet Underground*, Omnibus, 1989

386 Turner, Jeff with Garry Bushell (foreword by Morrissey), *Cockney Reject*, John Blake, 2005

387 Tyler, Parker, *Pictorial History Of Sex In Films, A*, Citadel Press (New Jersey), 1974

388 Uglow, Jenny, *George Eliot*, Virago, 2008

389 Visconti, Tony (foreword by Morrissey), *Bowie, Bolan And The Brooklyn Boy*, HarperCollins, 2007

390 Vonnegut, Kurt, *Slaughterhouse 5*, Jonathan Cape, 1970

391 Walters, Margaret, *Nude Male, The*, Paddington Press, 1978

392 Whiteside, Johnny, *Cry: The Johnnie Ray Story*, Barricade Books, 1997

393 Wilde, Oscar, *Complete Works Of Oscar Wilde, The*, Collins, 1983

394 Willans, John and Caron Thomas (foreword by Morrissey), *Marc Bolan: Wilderness Of The Mind*, Xanadu, 1992

395 Williams, Emlyn, *Beyond Belief*, Pan, 1968

396 Williams, Heathcoate, *Whale Nation*, Jonathan Cape, 1988

397 Williams, Kenneth, edited by Russell Davies, *Kenneth Williams Diaries, The*, HarperCollins 1993

398 Wilson, Tony, *24 Hour Party People*, Channel 4 Books, 2002

399 Woolf, Virginia, *Room Of One's Own, A*, Penguin, 1970

400 Woolrich, Cornell, with introduction by Richard Dooling, *Rendezvous In Black*, Modern Library (New York), 2004

401 Young, James, *Nico – Songs They Never Play On The Radio*, Arrow, 1994

402 Young, Rob, *Rough Trade*, Black Dog Publishing, 2006

IV: RADIO/AUDIO MEDIA SOURCES
(Listed by station, in chronological broadcast order.)

403 2FM (Ireland), Dave Fanning Morrissey interview, November 2002

404 Audience recording of Morrissey Chicago Press Conference (USA), 1992

405 BBC GLR (UK), Sean Hughes Morrissey interview, November 1999

406 BBC Radio 1 (UK), Kid Jensen Morrissey interview, May 1983

407 BBC Radio 1 (UK), Janice Long Morrissey interview, September 1984

408 BBC Radio 1 (UK), *My Top Ten* with Morrissey, October 1984

409 BBC Radio 1 (UK), *Singled Out* hosted by Janice Long featuring Morrissey and Howard Devoto, October 1987

410 BBC Radio 1 (UK), Zane Lowe Morrissey interview, May 2004

411 BBC Radio 2 (UK), Janice Long Morrissey interview, October 2002

412 BBC Radio 2 (UK), Janice Long Morrissey interview, December 2004

413 BBC Radio 2 (UK), Steve Wright Morrissey interview, December 2004

414 BBC Radio 2 (UK), Russell Brand Morrissey interview, December 2006

415 BBC Radio 2 (UK), Russell Brand Morrissey interview, April 2008

416 BBC Radio 2 (UK), Janice Long Morrissey interview, October 2008

417 BBC Radio 2 (UK), Stuart Maconie Morrissey interview, February 2009

418 BBC Radio 4 (UK), Front Row Morrissey interview, February 2009

419 CKLN Toronto (Canada), Morrissey interview, December 1983

420 Fritz (Germany), *Soundgarden* Morrissey interview, May 2004

421 KCRW Radio Santa Monica, *Morning Becomes Eclectic* with Nic Harcourt, August 2008

422 KCXX Radio San Bernadino (USA), Morrissey interview, August 1998

423 Kent, Nick, interview tapes of Morrissey and Marr for *The Face* 'Dreamer in The Real World' feature 1985

424 LBC London (UK), Morrissey interview, September 1983

425 LBC London (UK), *Night Line* Morrissey interview, August 1984

426 Meat Is Murder Sire Records interview promo 1985

427 NPR Music, *World Café*, Steve Lillywhite on Vauxhall And I, December 2008

428 Piccadilly Radio (UK), Morrissey interview, November 1986

429 Radio Sheffield (UK), Morrissey and Marr interview, November 1983

430 Radio Sheffield (UK), Morrissey interview, January 1984

431 Radio Trent (UK), Morrissey interview, January 1984

432 RTE (Ireland), Johnny Marr interview, May 1984

433 RTE (Ireland), Dave Fanning Morrissey interview, February 1987

434 Snow, Mat, interview tapes of Morrissey for *Q* 'The Soft Touch' feature 1989, streamed on-line at www.rocksbackpages.com

435 Spiral Scratch magazine free 7-inch single of Morrissey interviewed for *Melody Maker* 'Trial By Jury' feature 1985

436 Virgin Radio (UK), *Razorcuts* Morrissey interview, May 2004

437 WDRE New York (USA), Malibu Sue Morrissey interview, November 1991

438 WFNX Boston (USA) Morrissey interview 1994

439 XFM (UK), Lauren Laverne Morrissey interview, December 2006

440 XFM (UK), 02 Wireless backstage interview with Steve Harris, July 2008

V: TELEVISION SOURCES
(Listed by programme name, in chronological broadcast order.)

441 *4Music Presents*, E4 (UK), Morrissey interview with Edith Bowman, April 2006

442 *Adventures Of Sherlock Holmes, The*, episode 'The Norwood Builder', Granada Television (UK), 1984

443 *Brit Girls*, Channel 4 (UK), Series featuring Morrissey discussing Cilla Black, Marianne Faithfull, Sandie Shaw, Lulu and Twinkle, interviewed by Len Brown, November to December 1997

444 *Culture Show, The*, BBC2 (UK), Morrissey interview, December 2006

445 *Danny Baker Show, The*, BBC1 (UK), Suggs sings 'Suedehead', August 1993

446 *Datarun*, ITV (UK), Morrissey and Marr interview, April 1984

447 *Earsay*, Channel 4 (UK), Morrissey and Sandie Shaw interview, March 1984

448 *Earsay*, Channel 4 (UK), Complete unbroadcast Morrissey interview, July 1984

449 *Eight Days A Week*, BBC2 (UK), Morrissey on arts review panel with Tony Blackburn and George Michael, May 1984

450 *Elektron Pop* (Belgium), Morrissey and Marr interview, March 1984

451 *Friday Night With Jonathan Ross*, BBC1 (UK), Morrissey interview, May 2004

452 *Granada Reports*, ITV/Granada Television (UK), The Smiths interviewed by Tony Wilson, February 1985

453 *Importance Of Being Morrissey, The*, Channel 4 (UK), documentary on Morrissey, June 2003

454 *In D-TV: Morrissey En El Polyforum*, Canal52MX (Mexico), Morrissey interview, January 2007

455 *Jewel In The Crown, The*, Chrome Dreams DVD (UK), unofficial documentary on Morrissey, May 2006

456 *L'Album De La Semaine*, Canal+ (France), Morrissey interview, September 2006

457 *Later With Jools Holland*, BBC 2 (UK), Morrissey interview, November 1995

458 *Later With Jools Holland*, BBC 2 (UK), Morrissey interview, May 2004

459 *LATV Central* (USA), Morrissey interview, October 2007

460 *Les Enfants Du Rock* (France), Morrissey and Marr interview, May 1984

461 *Les Inrockuptibles* (France), Morrissey interview, 2006

462 *Lydverket* (Norway), Morrissey interview, December 2002

463 *Music Express* (USA), Morrissey interview with Dave Fanning, recorded 2002, broadcast March 2005

464 *Oxford Road Show*, BBC 2 (UK), Morrissey interview, March 1985

465 *Pebble Mill At One*, BBC1 (UK), Morrissey interview, February 1985

466 PETA Linda McCartney Memorial Award, Morrissey acceptance speech, September 2005

467 *Shadowplayers: Factory Records & Manchester Post-Punk 1978-81*, LTM Recordings, 2006

468 *South Bank Show, The*, ITV (UK), The Smiths: From Start To Finish , produced and directed by Tony Knox, October 1987

469 *Strangeways, Here We Come*, Rough Trade (UK), promotional Morrissey interview with Muriel Gray, August 1987

470 *Studio One*, ITV (UK), Morrissey interview, May 1985

471 *SXSW* (USA), video of Morrissey interview with David Fricke, March 2006

472 *Tube, The*, Channel 4 (UK), Morrissey interview, January 1984

473 *Tube, The*, Channel 4 (UK), Morrissey interview, October 1985

474 *Tube, The*, Channel 4 (UK), Morrissey interview with Shaun Duggan, January 1987

475 Unknown (UK), Morrissey interview circa 1988

476 *V Festival* (UK), Morrissey interview, August 2006

477 *Whistle Test*, BBC2 (UK), Morrissey and Marr interview, February 1985

Sources & Bibliography

478 *Wrestle With Russell*, Morrissey interviewed by Russell Brand for Years Of Refusal special edition bonus DVD, February 2009

479 *Young Guns Go For It*, BBC2 (UK), documentary on The Smiths, January 1999

480 *Zane Meets Morrissey*, MTV2 (UK), February 2009

VI: FILM SOURCES
Listed as title (year), director.

481 *Accattone* (1960), Pier Paolo Pasolini

482 *Alice Adams* (1935), George Stevens

483 *Bande À Part* (1964), Jean-Luc Godard

484 *Barretts Of Wimpole Street, The* (1934), Sidney Franklin

485 *Billy Liar* (1963), John Schlesinger

486 *Blue Lamp, The* (1950), Basil Dearden

487 *Brighton Rock* (1947), John Boulting

488 *Bringing Up Baby* (1938), Howard Hawks

489 *Career Girls* (1997), Mike Leigh

490 *Champion* (1949), Mark Robson

491 *Charlie Bubbles* (1967), Albert Finney

492 *Christmas In Connecticut* (1945), Peter Godfrey

493 *Cockleshell Heroes, The* (1955), José Ferrer

494 *Collector, The* (1965), William Wyler

495 *Dance Hall* (1950), Charles Chrichton

496 *Dance With A Stranger* (1985), Mike Newell

497 *Dunkirk* (1958), Leslie Norman

498 *East Of Eden* (1954), Elia Kazan

499 *Eight O'Clock Walk* (1954), Lance Comfort

500 *Elephant Man, The* (1980), David Lynch

501 *Entertainer, The* (1960), Tony Richardson

502 *Family Way, The* (1966), Roy Boulting

503 *Far From The Madding Crowd* (1967), John Schlesinger

504 *Flame In The Streets* (1961), Roy Baker

505 *Giant* (1956), George Stevens

506 *Good Die Young, The* (1954), Lewis Gilbert

507 *Great St Louis Bank Robbery, The* (1959), Charles Guggenheim and John Stix

508 *Happiest Days Of Your Life, The* (1950), Frank Lauder

509 *Hilary And Jackie* (1998), Anand Tucker

510 *Hobson's Choice* (1954), David Lean

511 *Humoresque* (1946), Jean Negulesco

512 *I Believe In You* (1952), Basil Dearden and Michael Relph

513 *I Want To Live!* (1958), Robert Wise

514 *Inspector Calls, An* (1954), Guy Hamilton

515 *It Always Rains On Sunday* (1947), Robert Hamer

516 *Jane Eyre* (1944), Robert Stevenson

517 *Killing Of Sister George, The* (1968), Robert Aldrich

518 *Kind Of Loving, A* (1962), John Schlesinger

519 *L-Shaped Room, The* (1962), Bryan Forbes

520 *Ladykillers, The* (1955), Alexander Mackendrick

521 *Last Picture Show, The* (1971), Peter Bogdanovich

522 *Late Marriage* (2001), Dover Kosashvili

523 *Laura* (1944), Otto Preminger

524 *Leather Boys, The* (1964), Sidney J. Furie

525 *Loneliness Of The Long Distance Runner, The* (1962), Tony Richardson

526 *Long Day's Journey Into Night* (1962), Sidney Lumet

527 *Mamma Roma* (1962), Pier Paolo Pasolini

528 *Man In The White Suit, The* (1951), Alexander Mackendrick

529 *Man Who Came To Dinner, The* (1942), William Keighley

530 *Member Of The Wedding, The* (1952), Fred Zinnemann

531 *Mr Skeffington* (1944), Vincent Sherman

532 *Naked Truth, The* (1957), Mario Zampi

533 *Nomi Song, The* (2004), Andrew Horn

534 *October Man, The* (1947), Roy Baker

535 *Old Acquaintance* (1943), Vincent Sherman

536 *Old Dark House, The* (1932), James Whale

537 *Oliver Twist* (1948), David Lean

538 *Orphée* (1950), Jean Cocteau

539 *Oscar Wilde* (1960), Gregory Ratoff

540 *Passport To Pimlico* (1949), Henry Cornelius

541 *Pépé Le Moko* (1937), Julien Duvivier

542 *Poor Cow* (1967), Ken Loach

543 *Porcile* (1969), Pier Paolo Pasolini

544 *Quatre Cents Coups, Les* (1959), François Truffaut

545 *Rebel Without A Cause* (1955), Nicholas Ray

546 *Rocco And His Brothers* (1960), Luchino Visconti

547 *Romper Stomper* (1992), Geoffrey Wright

548 *Saturday Night And Sunday Morning* (1960), Karel Reisz

549 *Saturday's Children* (1940), Vincent Sherman

550 *Servant, The* (1963), Joseph Losey

551 *Sleuth* (1972), Joseph L. Mankiewicz

552 *Smash-Up: The Story Of A Woman* (1947), Stuart Heisler

553 *Spring And Port Wine* (1970), Peter Hammond

554 *Taste Of Honey, A* (1961), Tony Richardson

555 *Term Of Trial* (1962), Peter Glenville

556 *To Sir, With Love* (1967), James Clavell

557 *Trials Of Oscar Wilde, The* (1960), Ken Hughes

558 *Turn The Key Softly* (1953), Jack Lee

559 *Victim* (1961), Basil Dearden

560 *Walk On Water* (2004), Eytan Fox

561 *We Are The Lambeth Boys* (1959), Karel Reisz

562 *Whatever Happened To Baby Jane?* (1962), Robert Aldrich

563 *Woman In A Dressing Gown* (1957), J. Lee Thompson

564 *World The Flesh And The Devil, The* (1959), Ranald MacDougall

565 *Wuthering Heights* (1939), William Wyler

566 *Yield To The Night* (1956), J. Lee Thompson

VII: MISCELLANEOUS

In the final stages of completion, various sources which had either been accidentally omitted from the above lists or which newly appeared during those final stages came

to light. These stop-press additions and forgotten strag-
glers are listed below and will be included/re-numbered
in their appropriate sub-section come future editions of
this book.

567 KROQ Radio (USA), Los Angeles, Morrissey interview, July 1997

568 Nolan, Paul, 'I've Got Something To Get Off My
Chest', *Hot Press* (Ireland), July 2008

569 Morrissey, Q&A, *Q* (UK), January 1995

570 *One Show, The*, BBC1 (UK), Morrissey interview,
February 2009

571 Words + Music, Morrissey interviews Joni Mitchell,
1996

572 Morrissey press release announcing 02 Wireless Festival headline appearance at true-to-you.net, March
2008

573 Unknown, Morrissey Q&A, *Star Hits* (USA), 1985
(alternate version of interview source 258, *Smash Hits*
1985)

574 Berens, Jessica, 'Spirit In The Dark', *Spin* (USA),
September 1986

575 Kochman, Michael, 'Happiness Is A Sad Son', *Entertainment Weekly* (USA), May 2004

576 *English Programme, The*, South, Channel 4 (UK),
March 1988

577 Modern Rock Live (USA), Morrissey radio interview,
August 1997

578 *Caretaker, The* (1963), Clive Donner

579 Unknown, 'Catching Up With Morrissey', *People*
(USA), March 2009

580 Murphy, Peter, 'The Unbearable Lightness Of Being
Morrissey', *Hot Press* (Ireland), March 2009

Mozography

A complete Smiths and Morrissey UK disc-ography. (Minor releases and compilations are listed *in italics*.)

1983

May 'Hand In Glove' b/w 'Handsome Devil (live)', 7-inch RT131. Rough Trade.

Nov 'This Charming Man' b/w 'Jeane', 7-inch RT136; 'This Charming Man (Manchester)'/'This Charming Man (London)' b/w 'Accept Yourself' and 'Wonderful Woman', 12-inch RTT136. Rough Trade.

Dec 'This Charming Man (New York Vocal)' b/w 'This Charming Man (New York Instrumental)', 12-inch RTT136NY. Rough Trade.

1984

Jan 'What Difference Does It Make?' b/w 'Back To The Old House', 7-inch RT146; 12-inch + 'These Things Take Time', RTT146. Rough Trade.

Feb The Smiths album; 'Reel Around The Fountain', 'You've Got Everything Now', 'Miserable Lie', 'Pretty Girls Make Graves', 'The Hand That Rocks The Cradle', 'Still Ill', 'Hand In Glove', 'What Difference Does It Make?', 'I Don't Owe You Anything', 'Suffer Little Children', LP ROUGH61; cassette + 'This Charming Man', ROUGHC61. Rough Trade.

Apr *Sandie Shaw single; 'Hand In Glove' b/w 'I Don't Owe You Anything', 7-inch RT 130; 12-inch + 'Jeane', RTT130. Rough Trade.*

May 'Heaven Knows I'm Miserable Now' b/w 'Suffer Little Children', 7-inch RT156; 12-inch + 'Girl Afraid', RTT156. Rough Trade.

Aug 'William, It Was Really Nothing' b/w 'Please Please Let Me Get What I Want', 7-inch RT166; 12-inch + 'How Soon Is Now?', RTT166. Rough Trade.

Nov Hatful Of Hollow compilation album; 'William, It Was Really Nothing', 'What Difference Does It Make?', 'These Things Take Time', 'This Charming Man', 'How Soon Is Now?', 'Handsome Devil', 'Hand In Glove', 'Still Ill', 'Heaven Knows I'm Miserable Now', 'This Night Has Opened My Eyes', 'You've Got Everything Now', 'Accept Yourself', 'Girl Afraid', 'Back To The Old House', 'Reel Around The Fountain', 'Please Please Please Let Me Get What I Want', LP/cassette ROUGH76/C76. Rough Trade.

1985

Feb 'How Soon Is Now?' b/w 'Well I Wonder', 7-inch RT176; 12-inch + 'Oscillate Wildly', RTT176. Rough Trade.

Meat Is Murder album; 'The Headmaster Ritual', 'Rusholme Ruffians', 'I Want The One I Can't Have', 'What She Said', 'That Joke Isn't Funny Anymore', 'Nowhere Fast', 'Well I Wonder', 'Barbarism Begins At Home', 'Meat Is Murder', LP/cassette ROUGH81/C81. Rough Trade.

March 'Shakespeare's Sister' b/w 'What She Said', 7-inch RT181; 12-inch + 'Stretch Out And Wait', RTT181. Rough Trade.

July 'That Joke Isn't Funny Anymore' b/w 'Meat Is Murder (live)', 7-inch RT186; 12-inch + 'Nowhere Fast (live)', 'Stretch Out And Wait (live)', 'Shakespeare's Sister (live)' RTT186. Rough Trade.

Oct 'The Boy With The Thorn In His Side' b/w 'Asleep', 7-inch RT191; 12-inch + 'Rubber Ring', RTT191. Rough Trade.

1986

May 'Bigmouth Strikes Again' b/w 'Money Changes Everything', 7-inch RT192; 12-inch + 'Unloveable', RTT192. Rough Trade.

June The Queen Is Dead album; 'The Queen Is Dead',

'Frankly, Mr Shankly', 'I Know It's Over', 'Never Had No One Ever', 'Cemetry Gates', 'Bigmouth Strikes Again', 'The Boy With The Thorn In His Side', 'Vicar In A Tutu', 'There Is A Light That Never Goes Out', 'Some Girls Are Bigger Than Others', LP/cassette/CD ROUGH96/C96/CD96. Rough Trade.

Aug **'Panic'** b/w 'Vicar In A Tutu', 7-inch RT193; 12-inch + 'The Draize Train', RTT193. Rough Trade.

Oct **'Ask'** b/w 'Cemetry Gates', 7-inch RT194; 12-inch + 'Golden Lights', RTT194. Rough Trade.

1987

Jan **'Shoplifters Of The World Unite'** b/w 'Half A Person', 7-inch RT195; 12-inch + 'London', RTT195. Rough Trade.

March **The World Won't Listen** compilation album; 'Panic', 'Ask', 'London', 'Bigmouth Strikes Again', 'Shakespeare's Sister', 'There Is A Light That Never Goes Out', 'Shoplifters Of The World Unite', 'The Boy With The Thorn In His Side', 'Asleep', 'Unloveable', 'Half A Person', 'Stretch Out And Wait', 'That Joke Isn't Funny Anymore', 'Oscillate Wildly', 'You Just Haven't Earned It Yet, Baby', 'Rubber Ring', LP/CD ROUGH101/CD101; cassette + 'Money Changes Everything', ROUGHC101. Rough Trade.

April **'Sheila Take A Bow'** b/w 'Is It Really So Strange?', 7-inch RT196; 12-inch + 'Sweet And Tender Hooligan', RTT196. Rough Trade.

May **Louder Than Bombs** compilation album; 'Is It Really So Strange?', 'Sheila Take A Bow', 'Shoplifters Of The World Unite', 'Sweet And Tender Hooligan', 'Half A Person', 'London', 'Panic', 'Girl Afraid', 'Shakespeare's Sister', 'William, It Was Really Nothing', 'You Just Haven't Earned It Yet, Baby', 'Heaven Knows I'm Miserable Now', 'Ask', 'Golden Lights', 'Oscillate Wildly', 'These Things Take Time', 'Rubber Ring', 'Back To The Old House', 'Hand In Glove', 'Stretch Out And Wait', 'Please Please Please Let Me Get What I Want', 'This Night Has Opened My Eyes', 'Unloveable', 'Asleep', originally a US import on Sire Records, later issued by Rough Trade on LP/cassette/CD ROUGH255/C255/CD255.

Aug **'Girlfriend In A Coma'** b/w 'Work Is A Four-Letter Word', 7-inch RT197; 12-inch + 'I Keep Mine Hidden', RTT197. Rough Trade.

Sept **Strangeways, Here We Come** album; 'A Rush And A Push And The Land Is Ours', 'I Started Something I Couldn't Finish', 'Death Of A Disco Dancer', 'Girlfriend In A Coma', 'Stop Me If You Think You've Heard This One Before', 'Last Night I Dreamt That Somebody Loved Me', 'Unhappy Birthday', 'Paint A Vulgar Picture', 'Death At One's Elbow', 'I Won't Share You', LP/cassette/CD ROUGH106/C106/CD106. Rough Trade.

Oct **'I Started Something I Couldn't Finish'** b/w 'Pretty Girls Make Graves (Troy Tate)', 7-inch RT198; 12-inch + 'Some Girls Are Bigger Than Others (live)', RTT198; cassette + 'What's The World (live)', RTT198C. Rough Trade.

Dec **'Last Night I Dreamt That Somebody Loved Me'** b/w 'Rusholme Ruffians (Peel session)', 7-inch RT200; 12-inch + 'Nowhere Fast (Peel session)', RTT200; CD + 'William, It Was Really Nothing (Peel session)', RTT200CD. Rough Trade.

1988

Feb **'Suedehead'** b/w 'I Know Very Well How I Got My Name', 7-inch POP1618; 12-inch + 'Hairdresser On Fire', 12POP1618; cassette/CD + 'Oh Well, I'll Never Learn', TC/CDPOP1618. HMV.

March **Viva Hate** album; 'Alsatian Cousin', 'Little Man, What Now?', 'Everyday Is Like Sunday', 'Bengali In Platforms', 'Angel, Angel, Down We Go Together', 'Late Night, Maudlin Street', 'Suedehead', 'Break Up The Family', 'The Ordinary Boys', 'I Don't Mind If You Forget Me', 'Dial-A-Cliché', 'Margaret On The Guillotine', LP/cassette/CD CSD/TCCSD/CDCSD3787. HMV.

June **'Everyday Is Like Sunday'** b/w 'Disappointed', 7-inch POP1619; 12-inch/cassette/CD + 'Sister I'm A Poet', 'Will Never Marry', 12/TC/CDPOP1619. HMV.

Sept **Rank** live Smiths album; 'The Queen Is Dead', 'Panic', 'Vicar In A Tutu', 'Ask', 'Rusholme Ruffians', 'The Boy With The Thorn In His Side', 'What She Said', 'Is It Really So Strange?', 'Cemetry Gates', 'London', 'I Know It's Over', 'The Draize Train', 'Still Ill', 'Bigmouth Strikes Again', LP/cassette/CD ROUGH126/C126/CD126. Rough Trade.

Oct **The Peel Sessions** Smiths EP; 'What Difference Does It Make?', 'Miserable Lie', 'Reel Around The Fountain', 'Handsome Devil', 12-inch SFPS055. Strange Fruit. (Part of a generic series of Peel session EPs. All tracks previously appeared on Hatful Of Hollow bar 'Miserable Lie', exclusive to this release.)

1989

Feb **'The Last Of The Famous International Playboys'** b/w 'Lucky Lisp', 7-inch POP1620; 12-inch/cassette/CD + 'Michael's Bones', 12/TC/CDPOP1620. HMV.

Apr **'Interesting Drug'** b/w 'Such A Little Thing Makes Such A Big Difference', 7-inch POP1621 (and one-sided etched 12-inch 12POPS1621); 12-inch/

cassette/CD + 'Sweet And Tender Hooligan (live)', 12/TC/CDPOP1621. HMV.

Nov   'Ouija Board, Ouija Board' b/w 'Yes, I Am Blind', 7-inch/cassette POP/TCPOP1622; 12-inch/CD + 'East West', 12/CDPOP1622. HMV.

1990

Apr   'November Spawned A Monster' b/w 'He Knows I'd Love To See Him', 7-inch/cassette POP/TCPOP1623; 12-inch/CD + 'Girl Least Likely To', 12/CDPOP1623. HMV.

June   *Hulmerist* video compilation; 'The Last Of The Famous International Playboys', 'Sister I'm A Poet (live)', 'Everyday Is Like Sunday', 'Interesting Drug', 'Suedehead', 'Ouija Board, Ouija Board', 'November Spawned A Monster', VHS MVP9912183. PMI.

Oct   'Piccadilly Palare' b/w 'Get Off The Stage', 7-inch/cassette POP/TCPOP1624; 12-inch/CD + 'At Amber', 12/CDPOP1624. HMV.

        Bona Drag compilation album; 'Piccadilly Palare', 'Interesting Drug', 'November Spawned A Monster', 'Will Never Marry', 'Such A Little Thing Makes Such A Big Difference', 'The Last Of The Famous International Playboys', 'Ouija Board, Ouija Board', 'Hairdresser On Fire', 'Everyday Is Like Sunday', 'He Knows I'd Love To See Him', 'Yes, I Am Blind', 'Lucky Lisp', 'Suedehead', 'Disappointed'. LP/cassette/CD CLP/TCCLP/CDCLP3788. HMV.

1991

Feb   'Our Frank' b/w 'Journalists Who Lie'; 7-inch/cassette POP/TCPOP1625; 12-inch/CD + 'Tony The Pony', 12/CDPOP1625. HMV.

March **Kill Uncle** album; 'Our Frank', 'Asian Rut', 'Sing Your Life', 'Mute Witness', 'King Leer', 'Found Found Found', 'Driving Your Girlfriend Home', 'The Harsh Truth Of The Camera Eye', '(I'm) The End Of The Family Line', 'There's A Place In Hell For Me And My Friends', LP/cassette/CD CSD/TCCSD/CDCSD3789. HMV.

April   'Sing Your Life' b/w 'That's Entertainment', 7-inch/cassette POP/TCPOP1626; 12-inch/CD + 'The Loop', 12/CDPOP1626. HMV.

July   'Pregnant For The Last Time' b/w 'Skin Storm', 7-inch/cassette POP/TCPOP1627; 12-inch/CD + 'Cosmic Dancer (live)', 'Disappointed (live)', 12/CDPOP1627. HMV.

Sept   **At KROQ** live radio session EP; 'My Love Life', 'There's A Place In Hell For Me And My Friends', 'Sing Your Life', CD 9401842. Sire/Reprise (US only).

Oct   'My Love Life' b/w 'I've Changed My Plea To Guilty', 7-inch/cassette POP/TCPOP1628; 12-inch/

CD + 'There's A Place In Hell For Me And My Friends', 12/CDPOP1628. HMV.

1992

April   'We Hate It When Our Friends Become Successful' b/w 'Suedehead (live)', 7-inch/cassette POP/TCPOP1629; 12-inch b/w 'Suedehead (live)', 'I've Changed My Plea To Guilty (live)', 'Pregnant For The Last Time (live)', 12POP1629; CD b/w 'Suedehead (live)', 'I've Changed My Plea To Guilty (live)', 'Alsatian Cousin (live)', CDPOP1629. HMV.

May   *Live In Dallas* video; 'The Last Of The Famous International Playboys', 'Interesting Drug', 'Piccadilly Palare', 'Trash', 'Sing Your Life', 'King Leer', 'Asian Rut', 'Mute Witness', 'November Spawned A Monster', 'Will Never Marry', 'Angel, Angel, Down We Go Together', 'There's A Place In Hell For Me And My Friends', 'That's Entertainment', 'Our Frank', 'Suedehead', 'Everyday Is Like Sunday', MVP 4911193. PMI.

July   'You're The One For Me, Fatty' b/w 'Pashernate Love', 7-inch/cassette POP/TCPOP1630; 12-inch/CD + 'There Speaks A True Friend', 12/CDPOP1630. HMV.

        Your Arsenal album; 'You're Gonna Need Someone On Your Side', 'Glamorous Glue', 'We'll Let You Know', 'The National Front Disco', 'Certain People I Know', 'We Hate It When Our Friends Become Successful', 'You're The One For Me, Fatty', 'Seasick, Yet Still Docked', 'I Know It's Gonna Happen Someday', 'Tomorrow', LP/cassette/CD CSD/TCCSD/ CDCSD3790. HMV.

Aug   *Best I* Smiths compilation album released on WEA.

Nov   *The Malady Lingers On* video compilation; 'Glamorous Glue', 'Certain People I Know', 'Tomorrow', 'We Hate It When Our Friends Become Successful', 'My Love Life', 'You're The One For Me, Fatty', 'Sing Your Life', 'Pregnant For The Last Time', MVR 4900063. PMI.

        Best II Smiths compilation album released on WEA.

        The Complete Picture Smiths video compilation released on Warner Music Video.

Dec   'Certain People I Know' b/w 'Jack The Ripper', 7-inch/cassette POP/TCPOP1631; 12-inch/CD + 'You've Had Her', 12/CDPOP1631. HMV.

1993

May   **Beethoven Was Deaf** live album; 'You're The One For Me, Fatty', 'Certain People I Know', 'The National Front Disco', 'November Spawned A Monster', 'Seasick, Yet Still Docked', 'The Loop', 'Sister I'm A Poet', 'Jack The Ripper', 'Such A Little Thing Makes Such A Big Difference', 'I

Know It's Gonna Happen Someday', 'We'll Let You Know', 'Suedehead', 'He Knows I'd Love To See Him', 'You're Gonna Need Someone On Your Side', 'Glamorous Glue', 'We Hate It When Our Friends Become Successful', LP/cassette/CD CSD/TCCSD/ CDCSD3791. HMV.

1994

March   **'The More You Ignore Me, The Closer I Get'** b/w 'Used To Be A Sweet Boy', 7-inch/cassette R/TCR6372; 12-inch/CD + 'I'd Love To', 12R/CDR6372. Parlophone.

Vauxhall And I album; 'Now My Heart Is Full', 'Spring-Heeled Jim', 'Billy Budd', 'Hold On To Your Friends', 'The More You Ignore Me, The Closer I Get', 'Why Don't You Find Out For Yourself', 'I Am Hated For Loving', 'Lifeguard Sleeping, Girl Drowning', 'Used To Be A Sweet Boy', 'The Lazy Sunbathers', 'Speedway', LP/cassette/CD PCSD/TCPCSD/ CDPCSD148. Parlophone.

May   **'Hold On To Your Friends'** b/w 'Moonriver', 7-inch/cassette R/TCR6383; 12-inch/CD b/w 'Moonriver (extended version)', 12R/CDR6383. Parlophone.

Aug   **Morrissey & Siouxsie: 'Interlude'** b/w 'Interlude (extended)', 7-inch/cassette R/TCR6365; 12-inch/CD + 'Interlude (instrumental)', 12R/CDR6365. Parlophone.

1995

Jan   **'Boxers'** b/w 'Have-A-Go Merchant'; 7-inch/cassette R/TCR6400; 12-inch/CD + 'Whatever Happens, I Love You', 12R/CDR6400. Parlophone.

Feb   **World Of Morrissey** compilation album; 'Whatever Happens, I Love You', 'Billy Budd', 'Jack The Ripper (live), 'Have-A-Go-Merchant', 'The Loop', 'Sister I'm A Poet (live)', 'You're The One For Me, Fatty (live)', 'Boxers', 'Moonriver', 'My Love Life', 'Certain People I Know', 'The Last Of The Famous International Playboys', 'We'll Let You Know', 'Spring-Heeled Jim', LP/cassette/CD PCSD/TCPCSD/CDPCSD163. Parlophone.

Singles Smiths compilation album released on WEA.

Aug   **'Dagenham Dave'** b/w 'Nobody Loves Us', 7-inch/cassette 299807/299804; CD + 'You Must Please Remember', 299802. RCA Victor.

Southpaw Grammar album; 'The Teachers Are Afraid Of The Pupils', 'Reader Meet Author', 'The Boy Racer', 'The Operation', 'Dagenham Dave', 'Do Your Best And Don't Worry', 'Best Friend On The Payroll', 'Southpaw', LP/cassette/CD 29953-1/4/2. RCA Victor.

Nov   **'The Boy Racer'** b/w 'London (live)', 7-inch

332947; CD1 + 'Billy Budd (live)', 332942; CD2 b/w 'Spring-Heeled Jim (live)', 'Why Don't You Find Out For Yourself (live)', 332952. RCA Victor.

Dec   **'Sunny'** b/w 'Black-Eyed Susan', 7-inch/cassette R/TCR6243; CD + 'A Swallow On My Neck', CDR6243. Parlophone.

1996

Oct   *Introducing Morrissey* live video; 'Billy Budd', 'Have-A-Go Merchant', 'Spring-Heeled Jim', 'You're The One For Me, Fatty', 'The More You Ignore Me, The Closer I Get', 'Whatever Happens I Love You', 'We'll Let You Know', 'Jack The Ripper', 'Why Don't You Find Out For Yourself', 'The National Front Disco', 'Moonriver', 'Hold On To Your Friends', 'Boxers', 'Now My Heart Is Full', 'Speedway', 334818. Warner Music Video.

1997

March   *Viva Hate EMI centenary edition CD released on Parlophone.*

July   **'Alma Matters'** b/w 'Heir Apparent', 7-inch/cassette IS/CIS667; 12-inch/CD + 'I Can Have Both', 12IS/CID667. Island.

Aug   **Maladjusted** album; 'Maladjusted', 'Alma Matters', 'Ambitious Outsiders', 'Trouble Loves Me', 'Papa Jack', 'Ammunition', 'Wide To Receive', 'Roy's Keen', 'He Cried', 'Satan Rejected My Soul', LP/cassette/CD ILPS/ICT/CID8059. Island. (+ 'Sorrow Will Come In The End', CD 3145360362, Mercury Records import version)

Sept   *Suedehead – The Best Of Morrissey* compilation album released on EMI.

Oct   **'Roy's Keen'** b/w 'Lost', 7-inch/cassette IS/CIS671; 12-inch/CD + 'The Edges Are No Longer Parallel', 12IS/CID671. Island.

Dec   **'Satan Rejected My Soul'** b/w 'Now I Am A Was', 7-inch/cassette IS/CIS686; 12-inch/CD + 'This Is Not Your Country', I2IS/CID686. Island.

1998

April   *Lost Tracks CD mini-album compiling the six Maladjusted-era B-sides released on Mercury in Japan only.*

Sept   **My Early Burglary Years** compilation album; 'Sunny', 'At Amber', 'Cosmic Dancer (live)', 'Nobody Loves Us', 'A Swallow On My Neck', 'Sister I'm A Poet', 'Black-Eyed Susan', 'Michael's Bones', 'I'd Love To', 'Reader Meet Author', 'Pashernate Love', 'Girl Least Likely To', 'Jack The Ripper (live)', 'I've Changed My Plea To Guilty', 'The Boy Racer', 'Boxers', enhanced CD 9468742. Reprise (US only).

Mozography

2000

June   *The CD Singles ''88–'91' boxset released on EMI.*
Sept   *The CD Singles ''91–'95' boxset released on EMI.*
Oct   *Oye Esteban!* DVD compilation; 'Everyday Is Like Sunday', 'Suedehead', 'Will Never Marry', 'November Spawned A Monster', 'Interesting Drug', 'The Last Of The Famous International Playboys', 'My Love Life', 'Sing Your Life', 'Seasick, Yet Still Docked', 'We Hate It When Our Friends Become Successful', 'Glamorous Glue', 'Tomorrow', 'You're The One For Me, Fatty', 'The More You Ignore Me, The Closer I Get', 'Pregnant For The Last Time', 'Boxers', 'Dagenham Dave', 'The Boy Racer', 'Sunny', DVD 385152. Reprise (US only).

2001

June   *The Very Best Of The Smiths compilation album released on WEA.*
Nov   *The Best Of Morrissey compilation album released on Rhino in the US.*

2003

May   **Under The Influence** *Morrissey-curated compilation released on DMC.*

2004

May   **'Irish Blood, English Heart'** b/w 'It's Hard To Walk Tall When You're Small', 7-inch/CD ATKSI/ATKXS002; b/w 'Munich Air Disaster 1958', 'The Never-Played Symphonies', CD ATKXD002. Attack Records.
       You Are The Quarry album; 'America Is Not The World', 'Irish Blood, English Heart', 'I Have Forgiven Jesus', 'Come Back To Camden', 'I'm Not Sorry', 'The World Is Full Of Crashing Bores', 'How Can Anybody Possibly Know How I Feel?', 'First Of The Gang To Die', 'Let Me Kiss You', 'I Like You', 'All The Lazy Dykes', 'You Know I Couldn't Last', LP/CD/CD+DVD ATKLP/ATKCD/ATKDX001. Attack Records.
July   **'First Of The Gang To Die'** b/w 'My Life Is A Succession Of People Saying Goodbye', 7-inch/CD ATKSI/ATKXS003; b/w 'Mexico', 'Teenage Dad On The Estate', DVD ATKDX003. Attack Records.
Oct   **'Let Me Kiss You'** b/w 'Don't Make Fun Of Daddy's Voice', 7-inch/CD ATKSE/ ATKXS008; b/w 'Friday Mourning', 'I Am Two People', CD ATKXD008. Attack Records.
Nov   *You Are The Quarry 2CD deluxe edition released. The second CD features the nine B-sides from the album's first three singles.*
Dec   **'I Have Forgiven Jesus'** b/w 'No One Can Hold A Candle To You', 7-inch/CD ATKSE/ATKXS011; b/w 'The Slum Mums', 'The Public Image', CD ATKXD011. Attack Records.

2005

March **'Redondo Beach (live)'/'There Is A Light That Never Goes Out (live)'**, 7-inch ATKSE015; CD + 'Noise Is The Best Revenge', ATKXD015. Attack Records.
April **Live At Earls Court** live album; 'How Soon Is Now?', 'First Of The Gang To Die', 'November Spawned A Monster', 'Don't Make Fun Of Daddy's Voice', 'Bigmouth Strikes Again', 'I Like You', 'Redondo Beach', 'Let Me Kiss You', 'Subway Train/Munich Air Disaster 1958', 'There Is A Light That Never Goes Out', 'The More You Ignore Me, The Closer I Get', 'Friday Mourning', 'I Have Forgiven Jesus', 'The World Is Full Of Crashing Bores', 'Shoplifters Of The World Unite', 'Irish Blood, English Heart', 'You Know I Couldn't Last', 'Last Night I Dreamt That Somebody Loved Me', CD ATKCD014. Attack Records.
       Who Put The 'M' In Manchester? live DVD; 'First Of The Gang To Die', 'Hairdresser On Fire', 'Irish Blood, English Heart', 'The Headmaster Ritual', 'Subway Train/Everyday Is Like Sunday', 'I Have Forgiven Jesus', 'I Know It's Gonna Happen Someday', 'How Can Anybody Possibly Know How I Feel?', 'Rubber Ring', 'Such A Little Thing Makes Such A Big Difference', 'Don't Make Fun Of Daddy's Voice', 'The World Is Full Of Crashing Bores', 'Let Me Kiss You', 'No One Can Hold A Candle To You', 'Jack The Ripper', 'A Rush And A Push And The Land Is Ours', 'I'm Not Sorry', 'Shoplifters Of The World Unite', 'There Is A Light That Never Goes Out', SVE4010. Attack Records.

2006

March **'You Have Killed Me'** b/w 'Good Looking Man About Town', 7-inch/CD ATKSE/ ATKXS017; b/w 'Human Being', 'I Knew I Was Next', CD ATKXD017. Attack Records.
April **Ringleader Of The Tormentors** album; 'I Will See You In Far-Off Places', 'Dear God Please Help Me', 'You Have Killed Me', 'The Youngest Was The Most Loved', 'In The Future When All's Well', 'The Father Who Must Be Killed', 'Life Is A Pigsty', 'I'll Never Be Anybody's Hero Now', 'On The Streets I Ran', 'To Me You Are A Work Of Art', 'I Just Want To See The Boy Happy', 'At Last I Am Born', LP/CD/CD+DVD ATKLP/ATKCD/ATKDX016. Attack Records.
June   **'The Youngest Was The Most Loved'** b/w 'If You Don't Like Me, Don't Look At Me', 7-inch/CD ATKSE/ATKXS018; b/w 'Ganglord', 'A Song From

Under The Floorboards', CD ATKXD018. Attack Records.

Aug 'In The Future When All's Well' b/w 'Christian Dior', 7-inch/CD ATKSE/ATKXS021; b/w 'I'll Never Be Anybody's Hero Now (live)', 'To Me You Are A Work Of Art (live)', CDATKXD021. Attack Records.

Dec 'I Just Want To See The Boy Happy' b/w 'Sweetie-Pie', 'I Want The One I Can't Have (live), CD ATKXD023; b/w 'Speedway (live)', 7-inch ATKSE023; b/w 'Late Night, Maudlin Street (live)', 7-inch ATKSE230X. Attack Records.

2008

Feb 'That's How People Grow Up' b/w 'The Last Of The Famous International Playboys (live)', CD F20000; b/w 'The Boy With The Thorn In His Side (live)', 7-inch F20001; b/w 'Why Don't You Find Out For Yourself (live)', 7-inch F20002. Decca.

Greatest Hits compilation album; 'First Of The Gang To Die', 'In The Future When All's Well', 'I Just Want To See The Boy Happy', 'Irish Blood, English Heart', 'You Have Killed Me', 'That's How People Grow Up', 'Everyday Is Like Sunday', 'Redondo Beach (live)', 'Suedehead', 'The Youngest Was The Most Loved', 'The Last Of The Famous International Playboys', 'The More You Ignore Me, The Closer I Get', 'All You Need Is Me', 'Let Me Kiss You', 'I Have Forgiven Jesus', CD/LP SKL6003/SKL6001. Decca.

June 'All You Need Is Me' b/w 'Drive-In Saturday (live)', 7-inch F20003; b/w 'My Dearest Love', 7-inch F20004; b/w 'Children In Pieces', CD F20005. Decca.

Nov The Sound Of The Smiths compilation album released on Warner Music UK/Rhino in single CD and deluxe 2CD formats.

2009

Feb 'I'm Throwing My Arms Around Paris' b/w 'Because Of My Poor Education', CD F20007; b/w 'Shame Is The Name', CD F20008; b/w 'Death Of A Disco Dancer (live)', 7-inch F20006. Polydor/Decca.

Years Of Refusal album; 'Something Is Squeezing My Skull', 'Mama Lay Softly On The Riverbed', 'Black Cloud', 'I'm Throwing My Arms Around Paris', 'All You Need Is Me', 'When Last I Spoke To Carol', 'That's How People Grow Up', 'One Day Goodbye Will Be Farewell', 'It's Not Your Birthday Anymore', 'You Were Good In Your Time', 'Sorry Doesn't Help', 'I'm OK By Myself', LP 4781581, CD 4781435, CD+DVD 4781580. Polydor/Decca.

April 'Something Is Squeezing My Skull' b/w 'This Charming Man (live)', CD 4781875; b/w 'Best Friend On The Payroll (live)', CD 4781876; b/w 'I Keep Mine Hidden (live)', 7-inch 4781877. Polydor/Decca.

Southpaw Grammar redux edition released on Sony, including first official release of 'Honey, You Know Where To Find Me', 'Fantastic Bird' and 'You Should Have Been Nice To Me'.

Maladjusted redux edition released on Universal.

Author's acknowledgements

I extend my sincerest *Ealings* of gratitude to the following:

For their pink string and sealing wax, thank you Nina Antonia, Kevin Armstrong, Billy Bragg, Jonny and Helen Bridgwood, Spencer Cobrin, Stephane Daigle, Craig Gannon, Amanda Hallay, Dale Hibbert, Chrissie Hynde, Mike Joyce, Clive Langer and Alan Winstanley, James Maker, Andrew McGibbon, Mark Nevin, the New York Dolls, John Porter, Sandie Shaw, Grant Showbiz, Nancy Sinatra, Siouxsie Sioux, Cathal Smyth, Linder Sterling, Stephen Street, Danton Supple, David Tseng and the silent minority who politely asked not to be named.

Special coronets to the kind hearts of Johnny Marr, Joe Moss and Andy Rourke.

For stamping my passport to Pimlico, I salute Andrew Goodfellow at Ebury.

All hue and cry was handled with care by Ali Nightingale.

The day went well thanks to Wendy Hollas.

Last, but never least, love and thanks to the Titfield Thunderbolt sometimes known as Sylvia Patterson.

Picture credits

Plate section 1: Page 1 image © Retna/portrait by Barry Marsden. Page 2 images © Getty/live shots by Kevin Cummins. Page 3 images © Redferns/portraits by Stephen Wright. Pages 4 and 5 image © Retna/portrait by Lawrence Watson. Page 6 © Kobal. Page 7 top image © Rex Features, bottom image © Kobal. Page 8 image © Retna/portrait by Paul Slattery.

Plate section 2: Page 1 image © Getty/portrait by Kevin Cummins. Page 2 all images © Retna. Page 3 top image © Retna, others author's own. Pages 4 and 5 image © Retna/portrait by Andy Earl. Page 6 top left image © LFI, top right image © Redferns, bottom images © Retna. Page 7 image © Getty/portrait by Kevin Cummins. Page 8 image © Trunk Archive/portrait by Sasha Eisenmann.

Plate section 3: Page 1 image © Redferns/portrait by Stephen Wright. Page 2 top image © Rex Features, bottom image © Redferns. Page 3 top image © Getty, bottom image © Redferns. Pages 4 and 5, image © Retna/portrait by Paul Slattery. Page 6 top and bottom left images © Getty, top right image © Kobal, bottom right image © Rex. Page 7 image © Rex Features. Page 8 image © Retna/portrait by Lawrence Watson.

Plate section 4: Page 1, image © LFI. Page 2, both images © Kobal. Page 3, top images © Getty, bottom images © Rex Features. Pages 4 and 5 image © Corbis/portrait by Toshi. Page 6 top and bottom left image © Getty, bottom right image © Kobal. Page 7 top image © Getty, bottom image © Redferns. Page 8 image © Corbis/portrait by Napoleon Sarony.

All picture research and design by Simon Goddard. Layout by Ed Pickford.

About the author

Simon Goddard was born as Britain was swinging to the number one sound of Benny Hill's 'Ernie (The Fastest Milkman In The West)'. All these years later it still says nothing to him about his life.

He lives in London where he works as a music journalist.